Mike Meyers'

A+® Guide to Managing and Troubleshooting PCs

Michael Meyers
Scott Jernigan

McGraw-Hill Technology Education

New York Chicago San Francisco
Lisbon London Madrid Mexico City Milan
New Delhi San Juan Seoul Singapore Sydney Toronto

McGraw-Hill Technology Education

Mike Meyers' A+® Guide to Managing and Troubleshooting PCs

Published by McGraw-Hill Technology Education, an imprint of The McGraw-Hill Companies, Inc. 1333 Burr Ridge Parkway, Burr Ridge, IL, 60527.

567890 QPD QPD 019876

Book p/n 0-07-223147-5 and CD p/n 0-07-223148-3
parts of
ISBN 0-07-223146-7

This book was composed with Corel VENTURA™ Publisher.

Publisher
Brandon A. Nordin

Editor in Chief
Bob Woodbury

Sponsoring Editor
Christopher Johnson

Developmental Editor
Pamela Woolf

Project Editor
Mark Karmendy

IT Skills Consultant
Laurie Stephan, NWCET

Copy Editors
Claire Splan, Mike McGee, Lisa Theobald

Proofreader
Pam Vevea

Indexer
Jack Lewis

Composition
Carie Abrew, Elizabeth Jang

Illustrators
Carie Abrew, Kathleen Edwards, Melinda Lytle, Jed Gildersleeve, Glow, Inc

Cover Series Design
Jeff Weeks

Cover Photograph
Ken Davies/Masterfile

Series Design
John Walker, Peter F. Hancik

About the Authors

Michael Meyers is the industry's leading authority on A+ Certification. He is the president and co-founder of Total Seminars, LLC, a provider of PC and network repair seminars, books, videos, and courseware for thousands of organizations throughout the world. Mike has been involved in the computer and network repair industry since 1977 as a technician, instructor, author, consultant, and speaker. Author of numerous popular PC books and A+ and Network+ courseware, Mike is also the Series Editor for both the highly successful Mike Meyers' Certification Passport series and the *Mike Meyers' Computer Skills* series, both published by McGraw-Hill/Osborne. Mike holds multiple industry certifications and considers the moniker "computer nerd" a compliment.

Scott Jernigan wields a mighty red pen as Editor in Chief for Total Seminars. With a master of arts degree in Medieval History, Scott feels as much at home in the musty archives of London as he does in the warm CRT glow of Total Seminars' Houston headquarters. After fleeing a purely academic life, Scott dove headfirst into IT, working

A number of people contributed to the development of *Mike Meyers' A+ Guide to Managing and Troubleshooting PCs*. For insightful reviews, criticisms, and helpful suggestions we would like to acknowledge the following people.

Technical Editor

Rajiv Malkan is a professor of Computer Technologies and Business at Montgomery College in Conroe, Texas. He has 20 years of experience in teaching computer-related courses at different institutions and 11 years of experience as an instructional division leader. He holds a master's degree in Computer Science from Florida Institute of Technology and an MBA from Phillips University. He is currently completing his doctorate in Higher Education Leadership from University of Nebraska–Lincoln. He also holds an equivalent master's degree in Textile Management from Bombay, India and a bachelor's degree in Chemistry and Physics from University of Bombay, India.

Peer Reviewers

Thomas Trevethan
ECPI College of Technology
Virginia Beach, VA

Keith Lyons
Cuyahoga Community College
Parma, OH

Farbod Karimi
Heald College
San Francisco, CA

Scott Sweitzer
Indiana Business College
Indianapolis, IN

Tamie Knaebel
Jefferson Community College
Louisville, KY

Donat Forrest
Broward County Community College
Pembroke Pines, FL

Brian Ives
Finger Lakes Community College
Canadaigua, NY

Winston Maddox
Mercer County Community College
West Windsor, NJ

Randall Stratton
DeVry University
Irving, TX

I dedicate this book to a lovely flower that recently bloomed in my home, my daughter Emily. Emily, I blinked and discovered you've transformed into a beautiful, intelligent, confident, witty, creative, and strong young woman—all that a father could wish of a daughter. This book is like you Emily—it's been around for a while but it never rests. It continues to grow and mature, like you, and always strives to be the best. While I'm very proud of this book, my pride in this work pales in comparison to the pride I have in you.

—Mike Meyers

Acknowledgments

First off, all kudos to our Sponsoring Editor, Chris Johnson, who deftly shepherded us through this project with his usual good humor and infinite patience, keeping his cool right to the end. You're made of tougher fiber than we are! Thanks, amigo. Now that we've wrapped this project, let's get fragging!

A special thanks goes to Jane and Chuck Holcombe who contributed time and knowledge to make the Windows NT, 2000, and XP portions of this book substantially better than they would have been otherwise. It was great having you onboard!

Mary Ellen O'Shields brought years of technical teaching experience to bear on this book, facilitating the development of much of the chapter review material. You can find her excellent work also in the Instructor's Pack companion to this volume. Great job, Mary Ellen!

Laurie Stephen, Ph.D., Curriculum Program Coordinator at the National Workforce Center for Emerging Technologies, reviewed our book, mapped it to the NWCET IT Skills Standards, and created some great activities for the instructor kit. Laurie is a brilliant instructional designer and part of a wonderful organization that is doing good work to support educators. And besides that, she's a really cool person.

Martin Acuña, our in-house MCSE guru and wireless networking wizard, added his usual wit, wisdom, and wackiness to the book. In particular, he offered freely of his knowledge to improve the operating system chapters. Remember his name—you'll be seeing more of his fine work in the future.

Our senior staff editor Cary Dier did her usual amazingly excellent work on this book, carving up our occasional flurries of purple prose into something legible. She applied a fine eye and polished hand to both editing and writing chores throughout the process, from initial drafts to copyedits to page proofs. Vivat Ansteorra!

Cindy Clayton delivered excellent editing and writing throughout the book, greatly enhancing the end product. And her alter ego DeathBunny proved a worthy fragging opponent in Half-Life!

Jeremy Conn proved once again the worth of a valuable assistant, offering cutting comments, excellent photos, and careful page proofing. Great job, Jeremy—now get back to school and finish that degree!

David Biggs offered his usual exceptional graphics work for this book, both original photographs and conceptual illustrations, and his editorial work on final images and text was invaluable.

Our newest intern, Michael Smyer, took a break from Texas Tech to work on web projects here, but his knowledge of Linux and PCs in general—and his enthusiasm for technology—definitely aided in the development of this book. Thanks, Michael!

The rest of the Total Seminars crew helped in many, many ways throughout this process. Hats off to Janelle Meyers, Roger Conrad, Brandy Taylor, David Dussé, Lloyd Jeffries, Kathy Yale, and, of course, Bambi Thibodeaux. Thanks, folks!

Finally, a special thanks goes to Dudley Lehmer, partner and friend, for keeping a strong and steady hand on the tiller during the chaos of a long, hot summer. Thanks for getting us into port with nobody overboard!

The McGraw-Hill Technology Education folks worked diligently and with good humor and faith on this book. It's a pleasure doing books with you.

With gentle but insistent ~~harassment~~ prodding, Pamela Woolf made sure that we submitted every piece of the book, from start to finish. She never lost her cool, or her sense of humor, no matter how crazy things got. A tip of the hat, Pamela—you have the patience of a saint!

I dedicate this book to Robert C. Palmer, Cullen Professor of History and Law at the University of Houston. Bob, all those days spent poring over 16th century English Plea Rolls and served me well beyond anything I could have imagined. Thank you.

—Scott Jernigan

About This Book

Important Technology Skills

Information technology (IT) offers many career paths, leading to occupations in such fields as PC repair, network administration, telecommunications, Web development, graphic design, and desktop support. To become competent in any IT field, however, you need certain basic computer skills.

Mike Meyers' A+ Guide to Managing and Troubleshooting PCs *builds a foundation for success in the IT field by introducing you to fundamental technology concepts and giving you essential computer skills.*

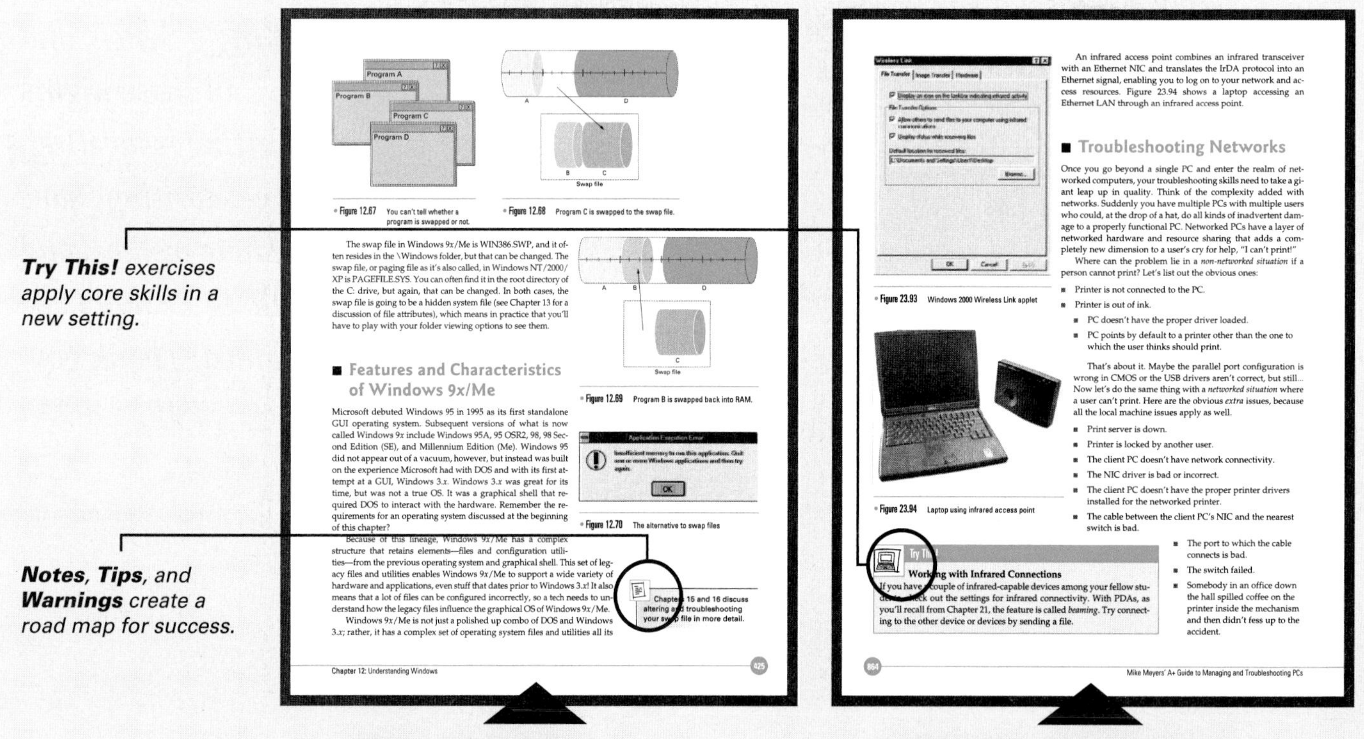

Makes Learning Fun! — *Rich, colorful text and enhanced illustrations bring technical subjects to life.*

Offers Practical Experience — *Tutorials and lab assignments develop essential hands-on skills and put concepts in real-world contexts.*

Proven Learning Method Keeps You on Track

Mike Meyers' A+ Guide to Managing and Troubleshooting PCs *is structured to give you comprehensive knowledge of computer skills and technologies. The textbook's active learning methodology guides you beyond mere recall and, through thought-provoking activities, labs, and sidebars, helps you develop critical-thinking, diagnostic, and communication skills.*

Effective Learning Tools

This pedagogically rich book is designed to make learning easy and enjoyable and to help you develop the skills and critical-thinking abilities that will enable you to adapt to different job situations and troubleshoot problems.

Mike Meyers' proven ability to explain concepts in a clear, direct, even humorous way makes these books interesting, motivational, and fun.

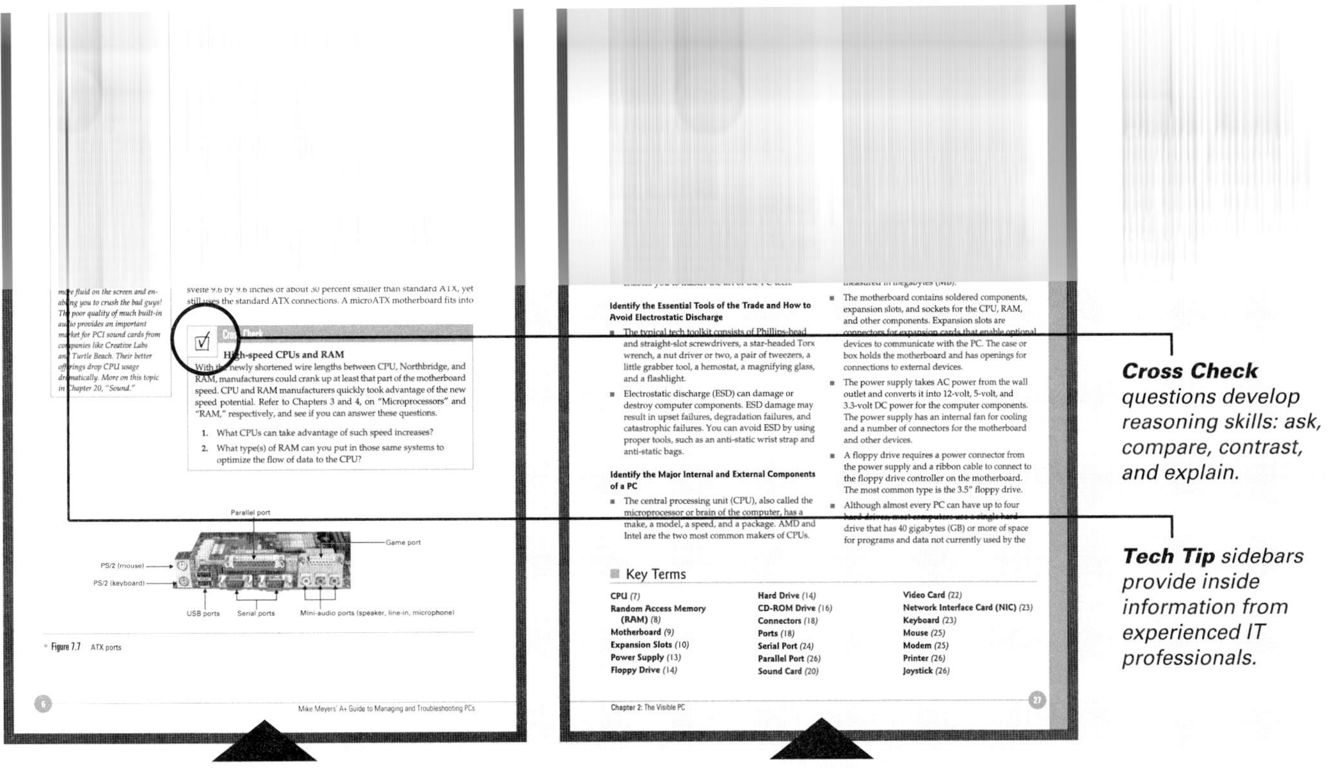

Cross Check *questions develop reasoning skills: ask, compare, contrast, and explain.*

Tech Tip *sidebars provide inside information from experienced IT professionals.*

Engaging and Motivational *— Using a conversational style and proven instructional approach, the authors explain technical concepts in a clear, interesting way using real-world examples.*

Robust Learning Tools *— Summaries, key terms lists, quizzes, essay questions, and lab projects help you practice skills and measure progress.*

Each chapter includes...

- **Learning Objectives** that set measurable goals for chapter-by-chapter progress
- **Illustrations** that give you a clear picture of the technologies
- **Tutorials** that teach you to perform essential tasks and procedures hands-on
- **Try This!**, **Cross Check**, and **Tech Tip** sidebars that encourage you to practice and apply concepts in real-world settings
- **Notes**, **Tips**, and **Warnings** that guide you through difficult areas
- **Chapter Summaries** and **Key Terms Lists** that provide you with an easy way to review important concepts and vocabulary
- **Challenging End-of-Chapter Tests** that include vocabulary-building exercises, multiple-choice questions, essay questions, and on-the-job lab projects

CONTENTS AT A GLANCE

CONTENTS

Chapter 3

■ Microprocessors 46

Chapter 4

■ RAM 108

Chapter 5

BIOS and CMOS 142

Chapter 6

Expansion Bus 176

Chapter 7

Motherboards 222

Chapter 8

Power Supplies 250

Chapter 13

Working with the Command Line Interface 463

Chapter 14

Installing and Upgrading Windows 500

Chapter 15

Maintaining, Optimizing, and Troubleshooting Windows 9x and Windows Me 536

Chapter 16

Maintaining, Optimizing, and Troubleshooting Windows NT, 2000, and XP 592

Chapter 17

CD and DVD Media 642

Chapter 21

Chapter 22

■ Printers 782

Chapter 24

The Internet 879

Glossary 917

Index 946

PREFACE

Information Technology Skill Standards and Your Curriculum

Students in today's increasingly competitive IT career market are differentiated not only by their technical skills, but by their communication, problem solving, and teaming skills. More and more, these professional skills are the

and assessed consistently and to an agreed upon set of skill and content standards. For those programs preparing students to enter the workforce, skill standards provide an excellent skeleton upon which to build courses.

Research has shown improved learning and retention of knowledge when learning takes place in a rich learning context. Students that learn in a real-world context are also better equipped to transfer their skills to the real world. IT skill standards provide the kind of real-world data that educators can use. Educators can draw from the skill standards to develop contextually rich assignments that help students to situate their learning in specific work contexts with complex and real-world problems to solve.

IT skill standards provide a common language between industry and education so that building bridges between these two groups can be more efficient. The more industry recognizes what educational programs are doing, the easier it is for education to gain industry support. Schools that use a skill standards–aligned program are better prepared to gain support from industry for technical advisory boards, student internships, job shadows, faculty internships, and a host of other support resources.

IT skill standards provide increased portability of skills because of the common language. Other institutions can clearly identify the content and skills that graduates of a skill standards–aligned curriculum have acquired. Programs that are skill standards based will effectively oil the wheels of articulation between programs that traditionally may have difficulty agreeing on what has been taught and assessed.

NWCET IT Skill Standards–Compliant Curriculum

When you use *Mike Meyers' A+ Guide to Managing and Troubleshooting PCs*, the Lab Manual designed to accompany the textbook, *and* the 24 NWCET IT skill standards–based student learning activities included on the Instructor Pack (look for "NWCET Skill Standards" in the menu on the Instructor CD), you are teaching an IT skill standards fully aligned curriculum. What does that mean? Compliant curriculum assures that your students are getting technical, foundation, and professional or soft skills that successful people have.

When you use the McGraw-Hill/NWCET–compliant materials, your students will learn current business processes and how IT skills fit into the larger business context. They will learn how to perform actual job tasks that A+ technicians perform on the job. NWCET-compliant materials achieve these goals because the NWCET engages in ongoing research of the IT industry and what it demands of its workers.

NWCET and McGraw-Hill in Partnership

McGraw-Hill Technology Education and the NWCET have partnered with the goal of helping IT educators meet these demands by making the IT skill standards more easily available and ready to use. McGraw-Hill Technology Education and the NWCET have developed four different products that will help you to address the IT skill standards in your A+ programs and courses:

- A summary crosswalk that highlights the IT skill standards addressed by the McGraw-Hill *Mike Meyers' A+ Guide to Managing and Troubleshooting PCs:*

Chapter 1	Chapter 2	Chapter 3	Chapter 4	Chapter 5
Introduction	C2—Evaluate present data and system configuration	C4—Install, configure, and test system hardware and peripherals	C4—Install, configure, and test system hardware and peripherals	C2—Evaluate present data and system configuration
Chapter 6	**Chapter 7**	**Chapter 8**	**Chapter 9**	**Chapter 10**
C4—Install, configure, and test system hardware and peripherals	C4—Install, configure, and test system hardware and peripherals	D1—Operate computer system and run system applications	C4—Install, configure, and test system hardware and peripherals	C4—Install, configure, and test system hardware and peripherals

Chapter 11	Chapter 12	Chapter 13	Chapter 14	Chapter 15
C4—Install, configure, and test system hardware and peripherals	C2—Evaluate present data and system configuration	D1—Operate computer system and run system applications	C5—Install, configure, and test new operating and application software, and software upgrades	C5—Install, configure, and test new operating and application software, and software upgrades

Chapter 16	Chapter 17	Chapter 18	Chapter 19	Chapter 20
C5—Install, [illegible]	C4—Install, [illegible]	C4—Install, [illegible]	C4—Install, [illegible]	C4—Install, [illegible]

Chapter 21	Chapter 22	Chapter 23	Chapter 24
C2—Evaluate present data and system configuration	C4—Install, configure, and test system hardware and peripherals	C2—Evaluate present data and system configuration	C5—Install, configure, and test new operating and application software, and software upgrades

- A detailed crosswalk listing Technical Knowledge, Employability Skills, and Performance Indicators addressed by the compliant curriculum (textbook, lab manual, and learning activities in the instructor pack CD):

Mike Meyers' A+ Guide to Managing and Troubleshooting PCs and support materials	Learning Outcomes	NWCET IT Skill Standards (Critical Function and Key Activity)	NWCET IT Skill Standards Technical Knowledge	NWCET IT Skill Standards Employability Skills	NWCET IT Skill Standards Performance Indicators
Exam Guide Chapter 2: "The Visible PC" Lab Manual: Chapters 1 and 2 Activity Two on the Instructor Pack CD: Memo on ESD incidents	Demonstrate techniques to avoid electrostatic discharge Identify the major internal and external components of a PC and describe their purposes and characteristics Identify the typical connectors on a PC unit and describe their purposes and characteristics Explain procedures for avoiding ESD activity	Critical Work Function C: Perform Hardware and Software Installation, Configuration, and Upgrades A: Perform Troubleshooting Key Activities C2–Evaluate present data and system configuration A7–Document hardware and software problems and resolutions	Ability to identify system components Knowledge of technical terms	Ability to understand, interpret, and recognize the accuracy of information Ability to use appropriate language and terminology Ability to accurately summarize and document information Ability to organize and present technical information in a logical and consistent manner	Information is effectively and correctly gathered, organized, and analyzed Documentation is clear and accurate Hardware and software problems are clearly identified Resolutions are documented to the appropriate level of detail

- Twenty-four skill standards–based activities with associated assessment tools
- A training document that helps instructors understand and use the features of teaching a skill standards–aligned curriculum

NWCET Background and Mission

In 1995, the National Science Foundation (NSF) designated and funded the NWCET as a National Center of Excellence in Advanced Technological Education. The Center was created to advance IT education and improve the supply, quality, and diversity of the IT workforce.

The National Workforce Center for Emerging Technologies has since become a leader in new designs for Information Technology (IT) education developing products, services, and best practices that provide timely, relevant, and lasting solutions to meet the needs of IT educators and the IT workforce. The NWCET translates the rapidly changing demands of the technology workplace into programs, curricula, courseware, and assessments that prepare students for current and future IT careers.

The NWCET is perhaps best known for its IT skill standards. Skill standards provide an agreement of what is expected to be successful in a given career area. They provide a validated, industry-derived framework upon which educators can build curricula. Using industry skill standards as the foundation for curricula will result in a closer alignment between educational programs and workplace expectations, and result in a better-skilled workforce.

To support new and innovative IT programs and degrees, the NWCET (www.nwcet.org) provides other professional development opportunities for high school teachers and community college and university faculty. The Educator-to-Educator Institute (E2E) (http://e2e.nwcet.org), the training branch of the NWCET, is dedicated to helping IT educators achieve excellence in IT instruction. CyberCareers (www.cybercareers.org) is a web site

For instructor and student resources, check out www.mikemeyersaplus.com. You'll find all sorts of stuff that will help you learn more about troubleshooting and fixing computers.

Additional Resources for Teachers

Resources for teachers are provided via an instructor's resource kit that maps to the organization of the textbook. This manual includes the following:

- Answer keys to the end-of-chapter activities in the textbook
- ExamView® Pro testbank software that generates a wide array of paper- or network-based tests, and features automatic grading
- Thousands of questions, written by experienced IT instructors
- A wide variety of question types and difficulty levels, allowing teachers to customize each test to maximize student progress
- Engaging PowerPoint slides on the lecture topics
- WebCT and Blackboard cartridges

chapter

1 Introduction

"'What is the use of a book,' thought Alice, 'without pictures or conversation?'"

—ALICE'S ADVENTURES IN WONDERLAND, BY LEWIS CARROLL, 1866

In this chapter, you will learn how to

- **Understand the importance of A+ Certification**
- **Know the structure and contents of the A+ Certification exams**
- **Plan a strategy to pass the exams**

Every profession requires specialized skills. For the most part, if you want to *get* or *keep* a job that requires those specialized skills, you need some type of certification or license. If you want a job fixing automobiles, for example, you get the *Automotive Service Excellence* (ASE) Certification. If you want to perform companies' audits, you get your *Certified Public Accountant* (CPA) certification.

Nearly every profession has some criteria that you must meet to show your competence and ability to perform at a certain level. While the way this works varies widely from one profession to another, all of them will at some point make you take a test or series of tests. Taking these tests lets you prove that you have the necessary skills to work at some level in your profession. If you successfully pass these tests, the organization that administers those tests certifies you. You receive some piece of paper or pin or membership card that you can show to potential clients or employers. This certification gives those clients or employers at least a level of confidence that you can do what you say you can do for them. Without this certification, either you will not work in that profession, or nobody will trust you to do the work. Until recently, PC technicians have been the exception to this rule.

The Importance of the A+ Certification

Since the inception of microcomputers in the late 1970s, PC technicians have had no common way to show clients or employers that they know what to do under the hood of a personal computer. Sure, there have been vendor-specific certifications, but the only way to get them was to get a job at an authorized warranty or repair facility first, and then get the certification. Not that there's anything wrong with vendor-specific training; it's just that no one manufacturer has taken enough market share to make IBM training, for example, something that works for any job. (Then there is always that little detail of getting the job first before you can get certified!)

The software/networking side of our business does not suffer from the [illegible]

But what about the person who runs around all day replacing floppy drives, repartitioning hard drives, upgrading device drivers, and building systems? What about the PC hobbyists who decide to make the jump and want to get paid for their skills? What about the folks who, because they had the audacity to show that they knew the difference between CMOS and a C: prompt, find themselves with a new title like "PC Support Technician" or "Electronic Services Specialist"? On the other hand, how about the worst title of them all: "The Person Who Doesn't Get a Nickel Extra but Who Fixes the Computers"?

For years, the *Information Technology* (IT) industry had no nationally recognized certification for PC technicians. Techs did not have a piece of paper to put on their wall to show they knew their stuff. Even more important, they didn't have the certification credentials that in other fields are an important factor in landing an interview with a prospective employer. When the industry was younger, this wasn't as critical, but in the modern computer environment, employers want proof—and now PC techs have a way to give it to them!

What Is A+ Certification?

A+ Certification is an industry-wide, vendor-neutral certification program developed and sponsored by the *Computing Technology Industry Association* (CompTIA). The A+ Certification shows that you have a basic competence in supporting microcomputers. The test covers the things it's generally assumed that a technician would know after six months of full-time PC support experience. You achieve this certification by taking two computer-based, multiple-choice examinations. A+ Certification enjoys wide recognition throughout the computer industry. To date, over 500,000 technicians have become A+ Certified, making it the most popular of all IT certifications.

Who Is CompTIA?

CompTIA is a nonprofit, industry trade association based in Lombard, Illinois. It consists of over 8,000 computer resellers, *value-added resellers* (VARs), distributors, manufacturers, and training companies from all over the world.

CompTIA provides a forum for networking (as in meeting people), represents the interests of its members to the government, and provides certifications for many different aspects of the computer industry. CompTIA sponsors the A+, Network+, i-Net+, Server+, and other certifications. CompTIA works hard to watch the IT industry and constantly looks to provide new certifications to meet the ongoing demand from its membership. Check out the CompTIA web site at http://www.comptia.org for details on the other certifications that you can obtain from CompTIA.

Virtually every company of consequence in the IT industry is a member of CompTIA. Here are a few of the biggies:

3Com	Adobe	AST	AT&T
Canon	Epson	Fujitsu	Hayes
Hewlett-Packard	IBM	Iomega	Intel
Lexmark	Lotus	Micro House	Microsoft
Minolta	NEC	NETGEAR	Netscape
Novell	Oki Data	Oracle	Panasonic
Peachtree	Rockwell	Sun Microsystems	Sybex
Symantec	Toshiba	Total Seminars, LLC (that's my company)	Plus about 8,000 more!

CompTIA began offering A+ Certification back in 1993. When it first debuted, the IT industry largely ignored A+ Certification. Over the course of the last few years, however, CompTIA has managed to position A+ Certification to the point where today it reigns as the *de facto* requirement for entrance into the PC industry. Many companies require A+ Certification for all of their PC support technicians, and the A+ Certification is becoming widely recognized both in the United States and internationally. Additionally, many other certifications recognize the A+ Certification and use it as credit toward their certifications.

Other Certifications

Most IT companies—big and small—see A+ Certification as the entry point to IT. From A+, you have a number of certification options, depending on whether you want to focus more on hardware or go toward network administration (although these aren't mutually exclusive goals). The following five certifications are worth serious consideration.

- CompTIA Network+ Certification
- CompTIA Server+ Certification
- Microsoft Certified Professional Certifications
- Novell NetWare Certifications
- Cisco Certifications

CompTIA Network+ Certification

If you haven't already taken the Network+, make it your next certification. Just as A+ shows you have solid competency as a PC technician, Network+ demonstrates your skill as a network technician, including understanding of network hardware, installation, and troubleshooting. CompTIA's Network+ is a natural fit for continuing toward your Microsoft, Novell, or Cisco certifications. Take the Network+: it's your obvious next certification!

CompTIA Server+ Certification

Like Network+, Server+ Certification fits nicely as a more in-depth testing of your knowledge of PC and server-specific hardware and operating systems. If you plan to go the path of the high-end hardware tech, Server+ is the next step. Plus, Server+ is a natural lead-in to Cisco certifications.

the Microsoft 70-210: Installing, Configuring, and Administering Microsoft Windows 2000 Professional or the 70-215: Installing, Configuring, and Administering Microsoft Windows 2000 Server exam. Either one gets you the first certification, Microsoft Certified Professional (MCP).

Once you've taken 70-210 or 70-215, take the other one, because if you've followed the path I suggested, you're well on your way to attaining the Microsoft Certified Systems Administrator (MCSA) certification. To become an MCSA, you need to pass three core exams—70-210 (or 70-270—see below), 70-215, and 70-218 (Managing a Microsoft Windows 2000 Network Environment)—and one elective exam. The cool part is that you can substitute A+/Network+ or A+/Server+ for the elective exam! Microsoft now offers a Windows XP-oriented alternative to the 70-210 exam—Exam 70–270: Installing, Configuring, and Administering Microsoft Windows XP Professional.

Finally, if you just can't get enough, Microsoft's ever-popular Microsoft Certified Systems Engineer (MCSE) certification holds a lot of clout in the job market. The MCSE consists of seven exams: five core exams covering three study areas—client operating system, networking system, and design—and two electives. You'll already have completed two of the core exams (70-210/70-270 and 70-215), and one elective (70-218). You can find more details on Microsoft's training web site at http://www.microsoft.com/traincert/.

Novell NetWare Certification

Novell's NetWare might not be the powerhouse it once was, but a huge installed base of NetWare networks is still out there! The surge of techs toward Microsoft certifications had created a bit of a shortage of good NetWare certified techs. The Certified NetWare Engineer (CNE) is the certification to go for if you want to get into NetWare networks. Check out Novell's certification web site at http://www.novell.com/education/certinfo/cne/ for more details.

Cisco Certification

Let's face it, Cisco routers pretty much run the Internet and most intranets in the world. Cisco provides three levels of certification for folks who want to show their skills at handling Cisco products. Nearly everyone interested in Cisco certification starts with the Certified Cisco Network Associate (CCNA). The CCNA can be yours for the price of only one completed exam, after which you can happily slap the word Cisco on your resume! After your CCNA, you should consider the Certified Cisco Networking Professional (CCNP) certification. See the Cisco certification web site at http://www.cisco.com/warp/public/10/wwtraining/ for more details.

The Structure and Contents of the A+ Certification Exams

How Do I Become A+ Certified?

Simple: you pass two computer-based, multiple-choice exams. No prerequisites are required for taking the A+ Certification exams. There is no required training course, and there are no training materials to buy. You *do* have to pay a testing fee for each of the two exams. You will immediately know whether you have passed or failed. By passing both exams, you become an "A+ Certified Service Technician." There are no requirements for professional experience. You do not have to go through an authorized training center. There are no annual dues. There are no continuing education requirements. You pass; you're in. That's it. Now for the details.

The Basic Exam Structure

The two exams are called *A+ Core Hardware* and *A+ Operating System Technologies*. The Core Hardware exam concentrates on the aspects of the PC that are not operating-system specific. This test is primarily a hardware identification and configuration exam. The Operating System Technologies exam concentrates on the organization, operation, function, and troubleshooting of Windows 9*x*/ME, Windows NT 4.0 Workstation, Windows 2000 Professional, and Windows XP systems, including the use of these operating systems at the command-prompt level. This exam also includes very basic network and Internet configuration questions.

The 2003 A+ Certification Exams Release

CompTIA must occasionally update the A+ exams to reflect the change in the skills expected of a technician with six months' experience. The latest version of the A+ exams is planned for the last quarter of 2003. This book covers all you need to pass the 2003 revisions of the A+ Certification exams.

How Do I Take the Tests?

Two companies, Prometric and Pearson/VUE, administer the actual A+ testing. There are thousands of Prometric and Pearson/VUE testing centers across the United States and Canada as well as in over 75 other countries around the world. You may take the exam at any testing center. You can register online, or in the United States and Canada, call Prometric at 800-776-4276 or Pearson/VUE at 877-551-PLUS (7587) to schedule the exams and to locate the nearest testing center. International customers can find a list of Prometric and Pearson/VUE international contact numbers for various regions of the world on CompTIA's web site at www.comptia.org by selecting the 'Register for Exam' link on the A+ Certification page.

You must pay for the exam when you call to schedule. Be prepared to sit on hold for a while. Have your Social Security Number (or international equivalent) and a credit card ready when you call. Both Prometric and Pearson/VUE will be glad to invoice you, but you won't be able to take the test until they receive full payment. Both Prometric and Pearson/VUE offer complete listings of all available testing centers online. They each offer you

testing locations may be a bit more limited.

How Much Does the Test Cost?

The cost of the exam depends on whether you work for a CompTIA member or not. At this writing, the cost for non-CompTIA members is $145 (U.S.) for one exam or $290 (U.S.) for two exams together. International prices vary, but you can check the CompTIA web site for international pricing. Of course, the prices are subject to change without notice, so always check the CompTIA web site for current pricing!

Very few people pay full price for the exam. Virtually every organization that provides A+ training and testing also offers discount vouchers. Total Seminars is one place to get discount vouchers. You can call Total Seminars at 800-446-6004 or 281-922-4166, or get vouchers via the web site: www.totalsem.com. If you work for a CompTIA member, you can get discount vouchers at a very steep discount. No one should ever pay full price for A+ exams!

You must pass both exams to be A+ Certified, but you may take either test first. Although you may take the exams at separate times, most people schedule both exams in one session. If you pass one exam and fail another, you only need to repay and retake the exam you failed. You must pay for every test you take, whether you pass or fail.

What Exactly Will I Encounter on the A+ Exams?

Both of the exams are extremely practical with little or no interest in theory. All questions are multiple choice or "click on the right part of the picture" questions. The following is an example of the type of questions you will see on the exam:

A dot-matrix printer is printing blank pages. Which item should you check first?

A. Printer drivers

B. Platen

C. Print head

D. Ribbon

The correct answer is D, the ribbon. You can make an argument for any of the others, but common sense (and skill as a PC technician) tells you to check the simplest possibility first.

The 2003 tests use a regular test format, where you answer a set number of questions and are scored based on how many correct answers you get, rather than the adaptive format used in recent years. These exams will have no more than 90 questions each. As of this writing, CompTIA has not announced the passing scores for either exam. The big difference between a regular exam and an adaptive exam is that on an adaptive exam, each question is assigned a difficulty level (easy, medium, or difficult). When you answer a medium question correctly, the exam adapts and asks you a harder question. If you miss one, the exam adapts and asks an easier question. There is a maximum number of questions the test will offer you, but not a set number of questions against which you are scored, like you'd find on a regular exam. To get a passing score on an adaptive exam, you need to answer enough difficult-level questions to prove your mastery of the material.

CompTIA has announced that in a departure from prior practice, it will be adding new questions to the exams continually, to keep the exam content fresh. The subject matter covered by the exams won't change, but new questions will be added periodically at random intervals. This new policy puts an even stronger emphasis on understanding concepts and having a solid PC-tech knowledge base, rather than trying to memorize specific questions and answers that may have been on the test in the past. Going forward, no book or web resource will have all the 'right answers' because those will constantly change. Lucky for you, however, this book is specifically oriented toward teaching you not just what steps to follow in a particular case, but to be a knowledgeable tech who understands *why* you're doing things, so that when you encounter a new problem (or test question), you can work out the answer. Not only will this help you pass the exams, you'll be a better PC tech!

In addition, we monitor the A+ exams for new content, and update the special Tech Files section of the Total Seminars web site (www.totalsem.com) with new articles covering subjects we believe may appear on future versions of the exams.

Core Hardware Exam

The questions on the Core Hardware exam all fit into one of the six areas or *domains*. The number of questions for each domain is based on the following percentages.

Installation, Configuration, and Upgrading	35%
Diagnosing and Troubleshooting	21%
Preventive Maintenance	5%
Motherboard/Processors/Memory	11%
Printers	9%
Basic Networking	19%

The Core Hardware exam tests you on your understanding of basic PC hardware. You should know how to recognize, clean, handle, install, diagnose, understand the function of, and know the different types of each of these components.

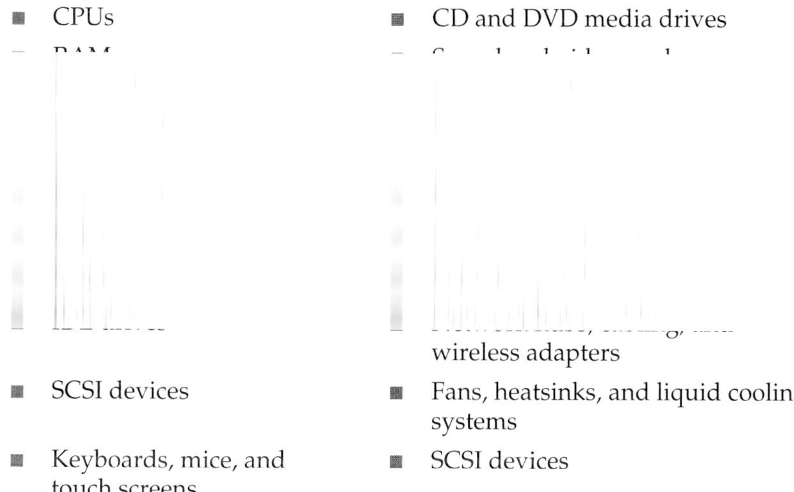

- CPUs
- SCSI devices
- Keyboards, mice, and touch screens
- CD and DVD media drives
- wireless adapters
- Fans, heatsinks, and liquid cooling systems
- SCSI devices

Basically, you should be able to install any device into a PC and completely assemble a standard PC. You should recognize every cable, every connector, and every plug used in a PC. The Core exam expects that you are comfortable with basic troubleshooting. You should be able to pick an obvious first step for a broad cross-section of symptoms linked to the previously mentioned hardware and software. You should be comfortable with the tools used for PC assembly/disassembly. You should be familiar not only with older technologies like floppy drives and keyboards, but also with new technologies like DVD-RW drives and touch screens.

The Core Hardware exam also tests your knowledge of some fundamental configuration knowledge, such as I/O addressing, IRQs, and DMA. For example, you need to know the I/O addresses and IRQs assigned to COM and LPT ports, the default functions for all IRQs and DMA, and the most common I/O addresses. You must be able to look at a diagram for jumpers or switches and properly set them for all possible I/O address, IRQ, or DMA combinations. The exam assumes a good knowledge of basic binary math, because many switches and jumpers use binary setting codes.

The network section covers a few basic issues, such as recognizing the different types of network cabling and their capacities/limits. You should know the different topologies and understand their benefits and weaknesses. The exam tests on the different network protocols, such as TCP/IP and IPX/SPX, and when to use one protocol over another. Finally, you should be able to diagnose basic network problems.

You should know how to use a *Volt-Ohm Meter* (VOM) to test power supplies. The A+ Core Hardware exam also requires you to be comfortable with the control of *electrostatic discharge* (ESD) and *electromagnetic interference* (EMI).

Operating System Technologies Exam

The Operating System Technologies exam follows on from the Core Hardware exam, assuming all of the same hardware and software knowledge that you need to pass the Core Hardware exam. However, the Operating System Technologies exam focuses exclusively on Windows 9*x*/Me, Windows NT 4.0 Workstation, Windows 2000 Professional, and Windows XP. All of the Operating System Technologies exam questions fit into one of four domains. The number of questions for each domain is based on the following percentages.

OS Fundamentals	28%
Installation, Configuration, and Upgrading	31%
Diagnosing and Troubleshooting	25%
Networks	16%

You will be expected to know how to install and configure all of the hardware devices mentioned in the Core Hardware exam on a Windows 9*x*/Me, Windows NT 4.0, Windows 2000, or Windows XP system. This includes installing and configuring non–Plug and Play (PnP) devices, and dealing with resource conflicts in a PnP environment, so you must have a strong understanding of how to configure system resources manually.

The exam tests your ability to work with older Windows 9*x*–generation system configuration files, such as CONFIG.SYS, AUTOEXEC.BAT, SYSTEM.INI, and WIN.INI. The test does not require DOS or Windows 3.x knowledge, but it does expect you to possess a working knowledge of many command prompt commands, including the proper syntax and switches, and be able to use command-line functions and utilities to manage operating systems. Both because of this exam content and because it remains such an important basic tool for a PC tech, I devote an entire chapter to using the command line.

The exam tests your knowledge of system diagnosing and troubleshooting. You need to recognize and know how to fix a large number of boot errors in Windows 9*x*/Me, Windows NT 4.0, Windows 2000, and Windows XP. Also, you should know how to defragment and scan a drive for errors using standard Windows tools, and be able to diagnose General Protection Faults (GPFs), illegal operation errors, and system lockup issues.

> CompTIA has in the past and will in the future change the content and passing grade for the A+ exams at any time. Don't assume they'll wait for a major revision—always check the CompTIA web site for new information before scheduling your exams!

Another major portion of the exam tests your ability to handle the installation and upgrading of Windows systems, including handling problems that may arise during these processes. This requires a deep knowledge of all the pertinent boot files for Windows 9*x*/Me, Windows NT 4.0, Windows 2000, and Windows XP, and the ability to make emergency repair disks/startup disks in all relevant versions of Windows.

The Operating System Technologies exam asks a number of questions regarding system optimization, on topics including virtual memory management, caching, and file management. You will be tested on your ability to configure hardware, CMOS, boot files, and TSRs to optimize a system.

How to Pass the A+ Exams

The single most important thing to remember about the A+ Certification is that CompTIA designed the exams to test the knowledge of a technician with only six months' experience—so keep it simple! The tests aren't interested in your ability to set CAS DRAM timings in CMOS manually or whether you can explain the difference between the Intel 430BX and i820 chipset. Don't bother with a lot of theory—think in terms of practical knowledge. Read the book, do whatever works for you to memorize the key con-

Obligate Yourself

The very first step you should take is to schedule yourself for the exam. Have you ever heard the old adage, "Heat and pressure make diamonds?" Well, if you don't give yourself a little "heat," you'll end up procrastinating and delay taking the exams, possibly forever! Do yourself a favor. Using the information below, determine how much time you'll need to study for the exams, then call Prometric or VUE and schedule them accordingly. Knowing the tests are coming up makes it much easier to turn off the television and crack open the book! You can schedule an exam as little as a few weeks in advance, but if you schedule an exam and can't take it at the scheduled time, you must reschedule at least a day in advance or you'll lose your money.

Set Aside the Right Amount of Study Time

After helping thousands of techs get their A+ Certification, we at Total Seminars have developed a pretty good feel for the amount of study time needed to pass the A+ Certification exams. The following table provides an estimate to help you plan how much study time you must commit to the A+ Certification exams. Keep in mind that these are averages. If you're not a great student or if you're a little on the nervous side, add 10 percent; if you're a fast learner or have a good bit of computer experience, you may want to reduce the figures.

To use Table 1.1, just circle the values that are most accurate for you, and add them up to get your estimated total hours of study time.

To that value, add hours based on the number of months of direct, professional experience you have had supporting PCs.

Months of Direct, Professional Experience…	To Your Study Time…
0	Add 50
Up to 6	Add 30
6 to 12	Add 10
Over 12	Add 0

A total neophyte usually needs around 200 hours of study time. An experienced tech shouldn't need more than 40 hours.

Total hours for you to study: ____________.

A Strategy for Study

Now that you have a feel for how long it's going to take, it's time to develop a study strategy. I'd like to suggest a strategy that has worked for others who've come before you, whether they were experienced techs or total newbies. This book is designed to accommodate the different study agendas

Table 1.1 Study Hours Guide

Tech Task	Amount of Experience			
	None	Once or Twice	Every Now and Then	Quite a Bit
Installing an expansion card	12	10	8	4
Installing hard drives	12	10	8	4
Installing SCSI devices	8	6	6	3
Installing modems and NICs	8	6	4	2
Installing printers	4	3	2	1
Installing RAM	8	6	4	2
Installing CPUs	8	7	5	3
Fixing printers	6	5	4	3
Fixing boot problems	8	7	7	5
Complete system builds	12	10	8	6
Using the command line	8	8	6	4
Installing/optimizing Windows	10	8	6	4
Using Windows 9*x*/ME	6	6	4	2
Using Windows 2000/NT	6	6	4	2
Using Windows XP	6	6	4	2
Configuring an Internet connection	6	5	3	2
Installing a sound card	2	2	1	0
Using OS diagnostic tools	8	8	6	4
Using a Volt-Ohm Meter	4	3	2	1

of these two different groups of students. The first group is experienced techs who already have a strong PC hardware and OS knowledge base, but need to be sure they're ready to be tested in the specific subjects covered by the A+ exams. The second group is those with little or no background in the computer field, who can benefit from a more detailed understanding of the history and concepts that underlie modern PC technology, to help them remember the specific subject matter information they must know for the exams. I'll use the shorthand terms Old Techs and New Techs for these two groups. If you're not sure which group you fall into, use the handy pretest at the end of this chapter to help decide which study strategy would work best for you.

I have broken down most of the chapters into three distinct parts:

- **Historical/conceptual** It's not on the A+ exams, but it's knowledge that will help you understand what is on the A+ exams more clearly.

Historical/Conceptual

Not all chapters will have all three sections!

Those of you who fall into the Old Tech group may want to skip everything but the Test Specific areas in each chapter. After reading the Test Specific section, you can jump immediately to the questions at the end of the chapter, which concentrate on information in the Test Specific section. If you run into problems, you can review the Historical/Conceptual sections in that chapter. Note that you may need to skip back to previous chapters to get the Historical/Conceptual information you need for later chapters.

After going through every chapter as described, Old Techs can move directly to testing their knowledge using the free practice exams on the CD-ROM that accompanies the ones in the book. Once you start hitting in the 750 to 800 range, you're ready to take the test!

If you're a New Tech, or if you're an Old Tech who wants the full learning experience this book can offer, start by reading the book, *the whole book*, as though you were reading a novel, from page one to the end without skipping around. Because so many computer terms and concepts build on each other, skipping around greatly increases the odds you will become confused, and end up closing the book and firing up your favorite PC game. Not that I have anything against PC games, but unfortunately, that skill is *not* useful for the A+ exams!

Your goal on this first read is to understand concepts, the *whys* behind the *hows*. It is very helpful to have a PC nearby as you read so you can stop and inspect the PC to see a piece of hardware or see how a particular concept manifests in the real world. As you read about floppy drives, for example, inspect the cables. Do they look like the ones in the book? Is there a variation? Why? It is imperative that you understand why you are doing something, not just how to do it on one particular system under one specific set of conditions. Neither the exams nor real life as a PC tech work that way!

The A+ Certification exams assume that you have basic user skills. The exams really try to trick you with questions on processes that you may do every day and not really think about. Here's a classic: "In order to move a file from the C:\WINDOWS folder to the A:\ using Windows Explorer, what key must you hold down while dragging the file?" If you can answer that without going to your keyboard and trying a few likely keys, you're better than most techs! In the real world, you can try a few wrong answers before you hit on the right one, but for the exams, you have to *know* it! Whether Old Tech or New Tech, make sure you are proficient at user-level Windows skills, including as the following:

- Recognizing all the components of the standard Windows Desktop
- Manipulating windows—resizing, moving, and so on
- Creating, deleting, renaming, moving, and copying files and folders
- Understanding file extensions and their relationship with program associations
- Using common keyboard shortcuts/hot keys

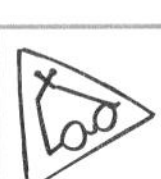

Tech Tip

Study Strategies

Perhaps it's been a while since you had to study for a test. Or perhaps it hasn't, but you've done your best since then to block the whole experience from your mind! Either way, savvy test-takers know there are certain techniques that make studying for tests more efficient and effective. Here's a trick used by students in law and medical schools who have to memorize reams of information: write it down. The act of writing something down (not typing, ***writing****) in and of itself helps you to remember it, even if you never look at what you wrote again. Try taking separate notes on the material and recreating diagrams by hand to help solidify the information in your mind. Another oldie but goodie: make yourself flash cards with questions and answers on topics you find difficult. A third trick: take your notes to bed and read them just before you go to sleep. Many people find they really do learn while they sleep!*

Any PC tech who has been around a while will tell you that one of the great secrets in the computer business is that there's almost never anything completely new in the world of computer technology. Faster, cleverer, smaller, wider—absolutely—but the underlying technology, the core of what makes your PC and its various peripheral devices operate, has changed remarkably little since PCs came into widespread use a few decades ago. When you do your initial read-through, you may be tempted to skip the Historical/Conceptual sections—don't! Understanding the history and technological developments behind today's PC hardware and operating systems can really help you understand why they work—or don't work—the way they do. Basically, I'm passing on to you the kind of knowledge you might get by apprenticing yourself to an older experienced PC tech.

After you've completed the first read-through, go through the book again, this time in textbook mode. If you're an Old Tech, this is where you start your studying. Try to cover one chapter at a sitting. Concentrate on the Test Specific sections. Get a highlighter and mark the phrases and sentences that bring out major points. Be sure you understand how the pictures and illustrations relate to the concepts being discussed.

Once you feel you have a good grasp of the material in the book, you can check your knowledge using the practice exams included on the CD-ROM in the back of the book. These can be taken in Practice mode or Final mode. In Practice mode, you can use the Assistance window to get a helpful hint for the current questions, find the chapter that covers the question using the Reference feature, check your answer for the question, and see an explanation of the correct answer. In Final mode, you answer all the questions and are given a test score at the end, just like the real thing.

In both modes you are shown a results summary gives you an overall grade, expressed as a percentage, as well as a breakdown of how well you did on each exam domain. The Review Questions feature lets you see what questions you missed and what the correct answers are. Use these results to guide further studying. Continue reviewing the topics you miss and taking additional exams until you are consistently scoring in the 85% to 95% range. When you get there, you are ready to pass that A+ exam!

If you have any problems, any questions, or if you just want to argue about something, feel free to send an e-mail to the authors—michaelm@totalsem.com and scottj@totalsem.com.

For any other information you might need, contact CompTIA directly at their web site: www.comptia.org.

chapter 2

The Visible PC

"Computers in the future may weigh no more than 1.5 tons."

—Popular Mechanics, 1949

In this chapter, you will learn how to

- **Describe how the PC works**
- **Identify the essential tools of the trade and avoid electrostatic discharge**
- **Identify the major internal and external components of a PC**
- **Identify the different connectors on a typical PC system unit**

Mastering the craft of a PC technician requires you to learn a lot of details about the many pieces of hardware in the typical PC. Even the most basic PC contains hundreds of discrete hardware components, each with its own set of characteristics, shapes, sizes, colors, connections, and so on. By the end of this book, you will be able to discuss all of these components in detail.

This chapter shows all of the major connectors, plugs, and sockets, and teaches you to recognize a particular part simply by seeing what type of connector attaches to that part. Even if you are an expert, do not skip this chapter! It introduces a large number of terms that will be used throughout the rest of the book. Many of these terms you will know, but some you will not, so take some time and read it.

It is handy, although certainly not required, to have a PC that you can take the lid off of and inspect as you progress. So get thee to a screwdriver, grab your PC, take off the cover, and see if you can recognize the various components as you read about them.

How the PC Works

You've undoubtedly seen one in action—a nice glossy monitor displaying a picture that changes according to the actions of the person sitting front of it, typing away or twisting a joystick. Sound pours out of tiny speakers that flank the screen and a bland-looking beige box whirs happily beneath the table. A computer: a machine that enables you to do work, produce documents, play games, balance your checkbook, and check up on the latest sports scores on the Internet. Magic does not power the personal computer, [illegible]

[illegible] handles the mechanical work. You can type words and commands with the keyboard and click and move things with the mouse. The monitor shows you what's going on and the printer spits out finished product. The software has two parts: operating system (OS) and programs. The OS creates the interface between human and machine. Different OSs provide different ways for you to tell the hardware to do something. Microsoft Windows provides things to click on, for example, whereas the venerable MS-DOS—for Disk Operating System—forced you to use a command line to type in commands. Programs facilitate specific tasks such as word processing, accounting, or drawing.

The A+ Certification exams focus on the first two pieces—hardware and operating systems—as you know from Chapter 1. Other certifications, such as Microsoft Office User Specialist (MOUS) and Macromedia Certified Professional, cover some, although certainly not all of the programs in common use today.

Understanding the computer at this broad conceptual level—in terms of hardware, OS, and programs—helps you troubleshoot problems to a certain level, but good techs have a much more fundamental appreciation and understanding of the complex interplay of all the software and the individual pieces of hardware. In short, techs need to know the processes going on behind the scenes.

For the A+ tech, the computer functions through four stages: input, processing, output, and storage. This is not just hardware vs. software! At each stage in the computing process, the hardware and OS interact intimately. Knowing which parts participate in a particular stage of the computing process enables you to troubleshoot on a fundamental and decisive level.

Input

To illustrate this four-step process, let's walk through the steps involved in a fairly common computer task: preparing your taxes. [Insert collective groan here.] February has rolled around and, at least in the United States, millions of people load their favorite tax software, TurboTax from Intuit, onto their computers to help them prepare their taxes. After starting TurboTax, your first job is to provide the computer with data—essential information, such as your name, where you live, how much you earned, and how many dollars you gave to federal and state governments.

Various pieces of hardware enable you to input data, the most common of which are the keyboard and mouse. Most computers won't react when you say, "Hey you!"—at least anywhere outside of a Star Trek set. Although that day will come, for now you must use something decidedly more mechanical: a keyboard to type in your data. The OS provides a fundamental service in this process as well. You can bang on a keyboard all day and accomplish nothing, after all, without the OS translating your keystrokes into code that the hardware can understand.

Processing

Next, the computer processes your data. It places information in various appropriate "boxes" in TurboTax and then it does the math for you. Processing takes place inside the system unit—the beige box—and happens almost completely at a hardware level, although that hardware functions according to rules laid out in the OS. Thus again you have complex interaction between hardware and software.

The processing portion is the magical part—you can't see it happen. The first half of this book demystifies this stage, because good techs understand all the pieces of the process. I won't go through the specific hardware involved in the processing stage here because the pieces change according to the type of process. I promise to cover all the details in overview a bit later in this chapter.

Output

What you can see quite readily is the output. Once the computer finishes processing data, it puts information up on the monitor so you can see what you've just typed. You can see the numbers added and subtracted. Eventually, you can print out copies of your tax return to mail to the Internal Revenue Service (or whatever the Tax Man is called where you live), another example of output. A hardware device does the actual printing, but the OS controls the printing process. Again, it's a fundamental interaction of hardware and software.

Storage

Once you've sent in your tax return, you most likely do not want all that work simply to disappear. What happens if the IRS comes back a couple of months later with a question about your return? Yikes! You need to keep permanent records; plus, you need to keep a copy of the tax program. Heck, the OS has to go somewhere too, right? The fourth stage in the computing process is storage. A lot of devices are used in the storage process, the most visible of which are the external storage parts, like floppy diskettes and CD-ROM discs.

The Art of the PC Technician

Using the four stages of the computing process—input, processing, output, and storage—to master how the PC works and, in turn, become a great tech, requires that you understand all the pieces of hardware and software involved **and** the interactions between them that make up the various stages. You have to know what the parts do, in other words, and how they work together.

A lot of folks take an "outside-in" approach to teaching the PC, somewhat analogous to teaching someone how the automobile works by starting with the steering wheel and working their way in. There's nothing inherently wrong with that approach, but I have always found myself in the other camp. I want to reduce the problems and complexity to the central idea, the ultimate device: start with the engine!

as great artists have mastered fundamental skills of their trade before creating a masterpiece, you'll have the fundamentals of the art of the computer tech and be on your road to mastery.

Essential Tools of the Trade and ESD Avoidance

Before we dive into the PC, you need two pieces of information: an overview of the most common tools you'll find in a tech's toolkit and how not to destroy hardware inadvertently through electrostatic discharge.

Tools of the Trade

The basic tech tool kit consists of a Phillips-head screwdriver and not much else—seriously—but a half dozen tools round out a fully-functional tool kit. Most kits have a star-headed Torx wrench, a nut driver or two, a pair of tweezers, a little grabber tool, and a hemostat to go along with Phillips-head and straight-slot screwdrivers.

A lot of techs will throw in a magnifying glass and a flashlight for those hard-to-read numbers and

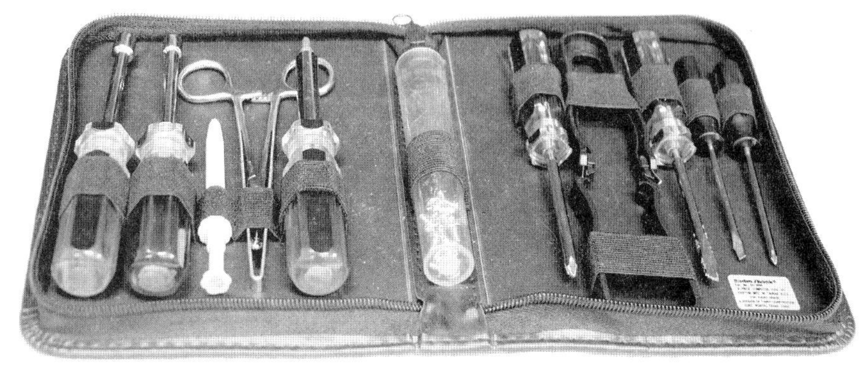

• Typical PC toolkit

text on the printed circuit boards (PCBs) that make up a large percentage of devices inside the system unit. And contrary to what you might think, techs rarely need a hammer.

• Close-up of a printed circuit board (PCB)

Test Specific

Avoiding Electrostatic Discharge

If you decide to open a PC while reading this chapter, as I encourage you to do, you must take proper steps to avoid the greatest killer of PCs—*electrostatic discharge* (ESD). ESD simply means the passage of a static electrical charge into your PC. Have you ever rubbed a balloon against your shirt, making the balloon stick to you? That's a classic example of static electricity. When that static charge discharges, you may not notice it happening—although on a cool, dry day, I've been shocked so hard by touching a doorknob that I could see a big, blue spark! I've never heard of a human being getting anything worse than a rather nasty shock from ESD, but I can't say the same thing about computers. ESD will destroy the sensitive parts of your PC, so it is essential that you take steps to avoid ESD when working on your PC.

All PCs are well protected against ESD on the outside—that is to say that unless you take a screwdriver and actually open up your PC, you really don't need to concern yourself with ESD.

Results of Electrostatic Discharge

An electrostatic discharge into a PC component can cause varying degrees of problems. We divide these problems into three types: upset failures, degradation failures, and catastrophic failures.

Upset failures cause an electrical component to fail without causing any detectable physical damage to the electronics. Upset failures are fairly common and manifest themselves as one-time errors—that time your PC just decides to reboot or lock up for no good reason. You restart the PC and everything seems perfectly fine.

Degradation failures take place when a component is physically damaged by ESD, but still works—at least some of the time. Degradation failures are one of the most common sources of the infamous intermittent failure syndrome. An *intermittent failure* is when a part of your PC fails at odd, unpredictable moments. The device in question can work perfectly well one moment, but at the next moment it suddenly stops working. Degradation failures are easily the single most challenging problems to diagnose in the PC business, but the fix is fairly simple: you replace the bad component.

An ESD can also result in a *catastrophic failure*: when the ESD damage is

Static electricity, and there-

cret to avoiding ESD is to keep you and the parts of the PC you touch at the same electrical potential. You can accomplish this by connecting yourself to the PC via a handy little device called an anti-static wrist strap. These simple devices consist of a wire that connects on one end to an alligator clip and the other end to a small metal plate that secures to your wrist with an elastic strap. You snap the alligator clip onto any handy metal part of the PC and place the wrist strap on either wrist. Figure 2.1 shows a typical anti-static wrist strap in use.

Anti-static wrist straps are standard equipment for anyone working on a PC but other tools might come in handy. One of the big issues when working with a PC stems from the fact that in many situations you find yourself pulling out parts from the PC and setting them aside. The moment you take a piece out of the PC it no longer has contact with the systems and may pick up static from other sources. We use anti-static mats to eliminate this risk. An anti-static mat acts as a point of common potential—it's very common to purchase a combination anti-static wrist strap and mat that all connect together to keep you, the PC, and any loose components at the same electrical potential (Figure 2.2).

Anti-static wrist straps and mats use tiny resistors to prevent anti-static charge from racing through the device. These resistors can fail over time so it's always a good idea to read the documentation that comes with your anti-static tools to see how to test that small resistor properly.

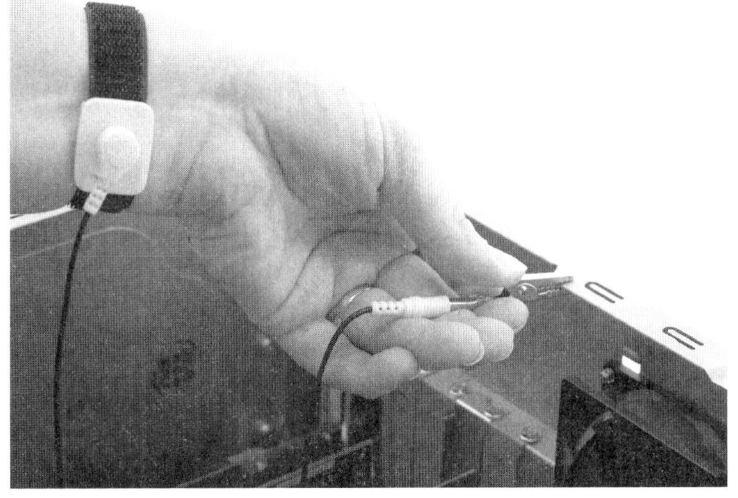

• **Figure 2.1** Proper use of an anti-static wrist strap

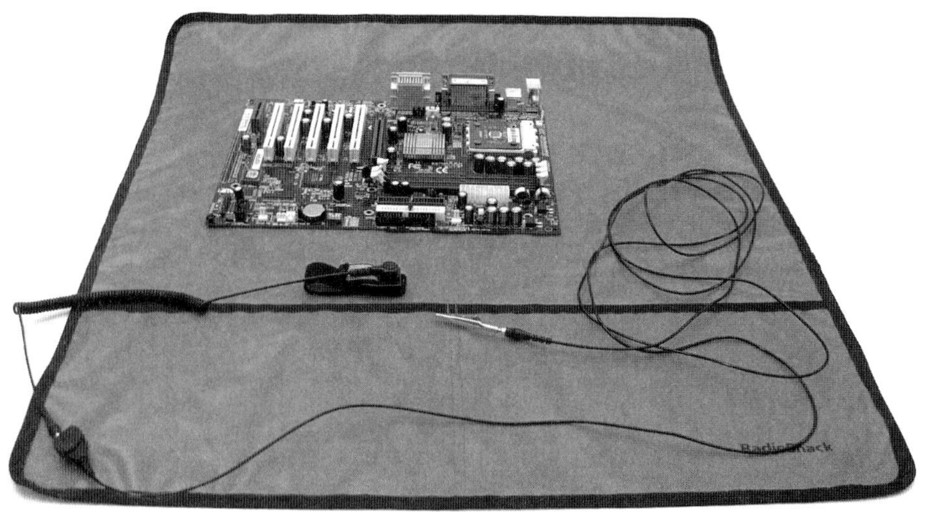

• **Figure 2.2** Anti-static wrist strap and mat

Any electrical component not in a PC needs to be stored in an anti-static bag. Almost all PC components come in an anti-static bag when purchased. Experienced techs never throw these bags away as you never know when you'll want to pull a part out and place it on a shelf for a while!

While I'd like to say that I always have a wrist strap, the reality is that from time to time you'll find yourself in situations where you lack the proper anti-static tools. This shouldn't keep you from working on the PC—if you're careful! Before working on a PC in such a situation, take a moment to touch the power supply—I'll show you where it is in this chapter—every once in a while as you work to keep you at the same electrical potential as the PC. While this isn't as good as a wrist strap, it's better than nothing at all!

The last issue when it comes to preventing ESD is that never-ending question—should you work with the PC plugged in or unplugged? The answer is simple—do you really want to be physically connected to a PC that is plugged into an electrical outlet? Granted, the chances of electrocution are slim, but why take the risk?

Have I convinced you that ESD is a problem? Good! So now it's safe to start looking at the components of the PC.

Try This!

Anti-static Protection Devices

In some circumstances, wearing an anti-static wrist strap could get in the way or otherwise stop a perfectly good tech from doing his or her job. Manufacturers have developed some alternatives to the wrist strap, so try this:

1. Take a field trip to a local computer or electronics store.
2. Check out their selection of anti-static devices. Can you find anything other than wrist straps or mats?
3. Do a web search for "static control products." Can you find anything other than wrist straps or mats?
4. Report what options you can find for protecting your equipment from ESD. Weigh the pros and cons and decide what you would use in different situations.

Recognize the Major Components of a PC

A single PC is composed of thousands of discrete components. While no one can name every tiny bit of electronics in a PC, a good PC technician should be able to name the major internal and external components that make up the typical PC. Let's take a tour of a PC to see these components and to gain at least a concept of what they do. In later chapters we'll see all of these components in much more detail.

CPU

The **central processing unit** (CPU), also called [illegible] from the processor. The fan then blows the heat out into the case. You can usually remove this cooling device, although some CPU manufacturers sell the CPU with a fan permanently attached.

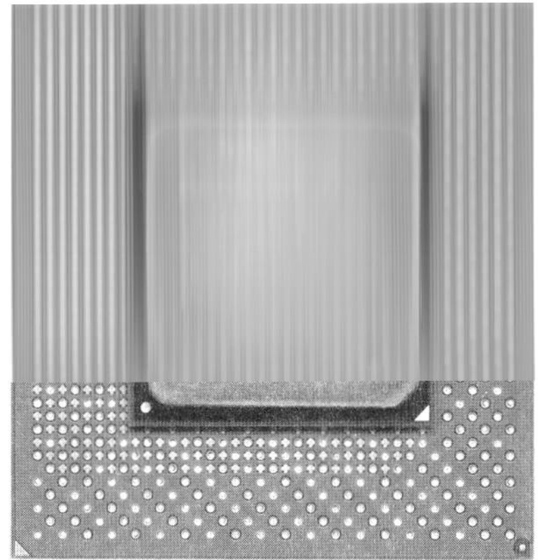

• **Figure 2.3** Typical CPUs

CPUs have a make and model, just like automobiles do. When talking about a particular car, for example, most people speak in terms of a Ford Taurus or a Toyota Camry. When they talk about CPUs, people say Intel Pentium 4 or AMD Athlon. Over the years, there have been only a few major CPU manufacturers, just as there are only a few major auto manufacturers. The two most common makes of CPUs used in PCs are AMD and Intel, although other makers with names such as Cyrix and IDT have come and gone.

Although only a few manufacturers of CPUs have existed, those manufacturers have made hundreds of models of CPUs. Some of the more common models made over the last few years have names such as Celeron, Athlon, Duron, Pentium III, and Pentium 4.

CPUs measure potential performance with a *clock speed,* much like an automobile has a (theoretical) top speed listed on the speedometer. Manufacturers determine the clock speed—measured in *megahertz* (MHz)—at the factory. The first CPU used in PCs had a clock speed of approximately 4.77 MHz. Today's latest CPUs

• **Figure 2.4** Installed CPU under a fan

• **Figure 2.5** Two nearly identical Intel Pentium 4 CPUs—1.6 MHz on the left, and 1.4 MHz on the right

have clock speeds over 3,000 MHz. One thousand MHz equals 1 *gigahertz* (GHz), so the latest CPUs are described often in terms of GHz. When talking about a CPU, people often cite the clock speed, make, and model, as in an 833-MHz Intel Pentium III or a 3-GHz AMD Athlon XP.

Manufacturers produce CPUs of the same make and model with many different clock speeds (see Figure 2.5). One particular make and model of CPU may come in five or six different speeds. The main reasons for picking one speed over another are the needs of your system and the thickness of your wallet.

Finally, CPUs come in different packages. The package defines how the CPU looks physically and how it connects to the computer. The predominant package type is called *Pin Grid Array* (PGA). The older *Single Edge Cartridge* (SEC) is no longer produced, but many existing systems still have CPUs using this distinctive package. Every package type has lots of variations. Both CPUs in Figure 2.3, for example, are PGA.

Chapter 3 goes into great detail on CPUs but for now remember that every CPU has a make, a model, a speed, and a package type.

RAM

Random Access Memory (RAM) stores programs and data currently being used by the CPU. The maximum amount of programs and data that a piece of RAM can store is measured in units called *bytes.* Modern PCs have many millions of bytes of RAM, so RAM is measured in units called *megabytes* (MB). An average PC will have from 64 MB to 256 MB of RAM, although you may see PCs with far more or far less RAM. Each piece of RAM is called a stick. RAM sticks have been packaged in many different ways over the years. The most current package is called a 184-pin *Dual Inline Memory Module* (DIMM). An older type of RAM package—basically obsolete, but included here for completeness—is called *Single Inline Memory Module* (SIMM). Figure 2.6 shows examples of a DIMM (top) and a SIMM (bottom).

Chapter 4 is devoted completely to RAM.

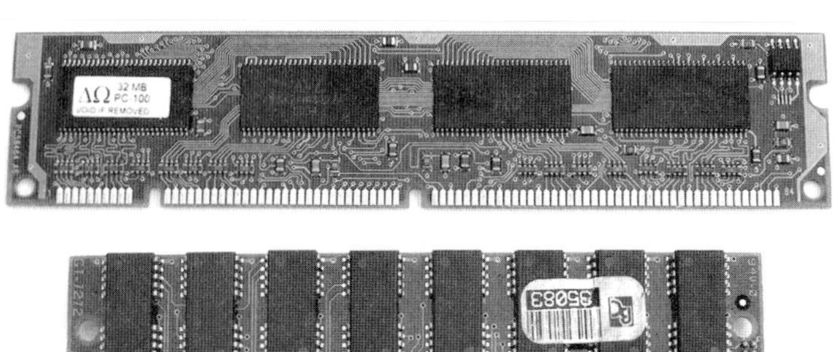

• **Figure 2.6** DIMM and SIMM RAM packages

Motherboard

You can compare a motherboard to the chassis of an automobile. In a car, everything connects to the chassis either

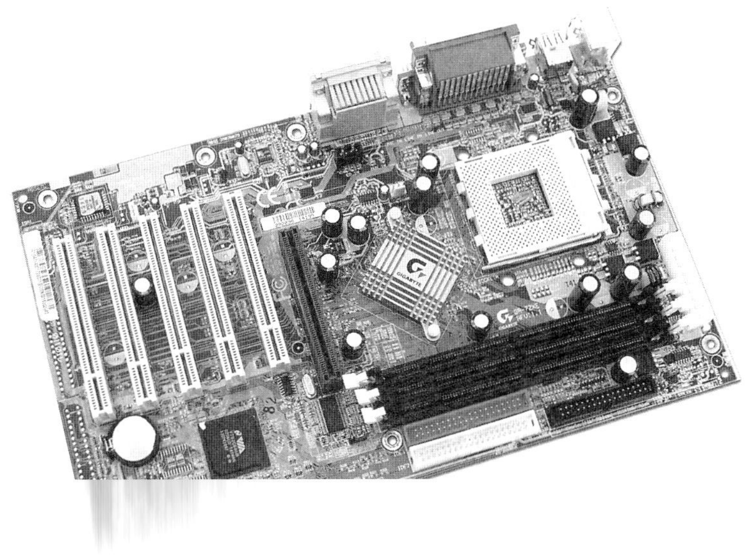

ther directly or indirectly. A **motherboard** is a thin, flat piece of circuit board, usually green or gold, and often slightly larger than a typical piece of notebook paper (see Figure 2.7).

A motherboard contains a number of special sockets that accept various PC components. Motherboards provide sockets for the microprocessor (see Figure 2.8); sockets for RAM (see Figure 2.9); sockets to provide power (see

• **Figure 2.8** Socket for CPU

• **Figure 2.9** Sockets for RAM

Figure 2.10); connectors for floppy drives and hard drives (see Figure 2.11); and connectors for external devices, such as mice, printers, joysticks, and keyboards (see Figure 2.12).

Every motherboard has a number of components soldered directly onto its surface (see Figure 2.13).

All motherboards use multipurpose **expansion slots** that enable you to add optional components. Your PC accepts thousands of different types of optional devices, including scanners, modems, network cards, sound cards, and tape backups. The expansion slots create the connection that enables optional devices to communicate with the PC. A device that connects to an expansion slot is generically called an *expansion card*, or simply a *card*. Different types of expansion slots exist for different types of cards (see Figure 2.14).

The PC industry long ago standardized the position of the expansion slots and external components. The motherboard mounts inside the *box* or *case*, which is the part of the PC that you actually see (see Figure 2.15).

• **Figure 2.10** Sockets for power plugs

• **Figure 2.11** Floppy and hard drive connectors

• **Figure 2.12** Various external connectors

• **Figure 2.13** Soldered components

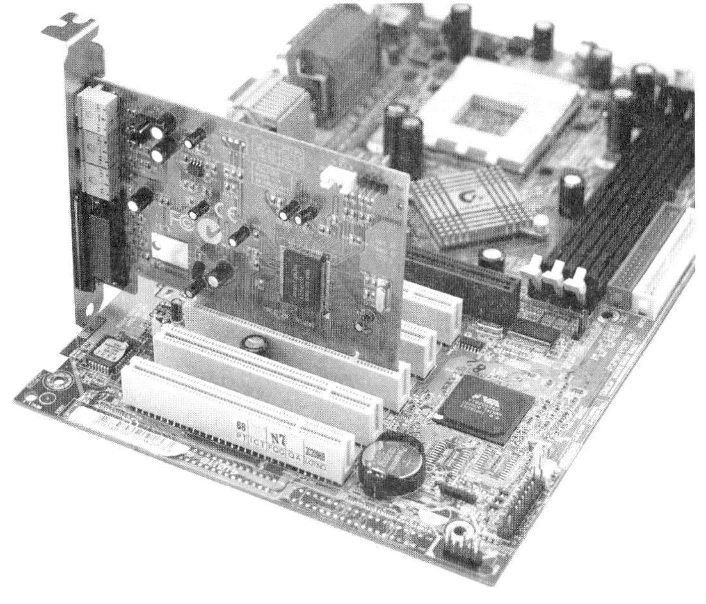

• **Figure 2.14** Expansion slots—one slot has a card inserted

• Figure 2.15 Motherboard in box

One of the fastest ways to determine whether a computer is obsolete or not is to inspect the expansion slots. Old PCs have obsolete expansion slots. Check Chapter 5 to determine which expansion slots your PC uses.

Case

The case needs to have holes that enable devices to access the external connectors. Where the motherboard has a connector for a keyboard, for example, the case must have a hole through which you insert the keyboard plug (see Figure 2.16).

Equally important, if the expansion slots enable you to add cards to the PC, then the case must also provide slots that enable external devices to connect to their cards (see Figure 2.17).

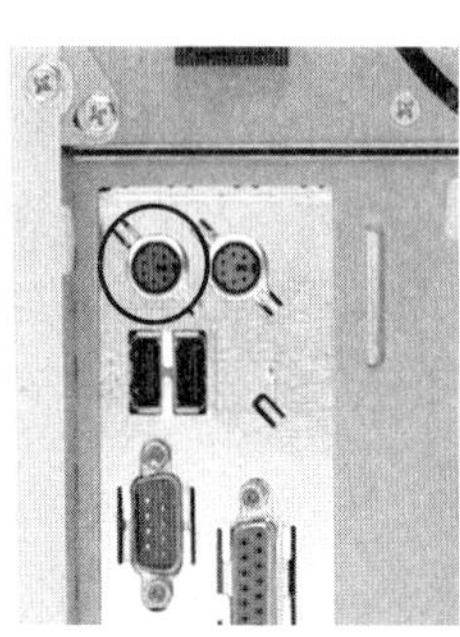

• Figure 2.16 Keyboard socket visible through a hole in the box

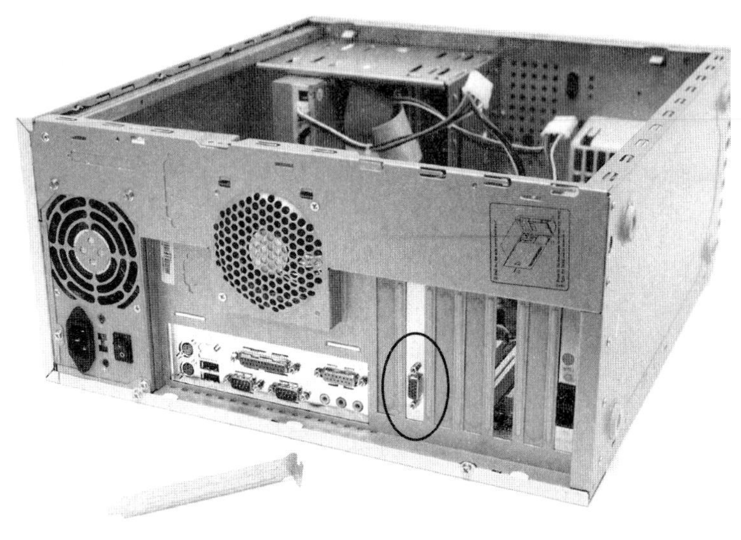

• Figure 2.17 Inserted card from the back of the PC

Certain types or layouts of motherboards require a case designed for that type. Fortunately, motherboards come in only a few layouts, requiring only a few types of cases. This is discussed in more detail in Chapter 6, which covers motherboards in detail.

You'll often hear the PC case called a *system unit* and, at the higher end of the price spectrum, an *enclosure*. All these terms are functionally interchangeable.

Power Supply

The **power supply**, as its name implies, provides the necessary electrical power to make the PC operate. The power supply takes standard (in the United States) 110-volt AC power and converts it into 12-volt, 5-volt, and 3.3-volt DC power. Most power supplies are about the size of a shoebox cut in half and are usually a gray or metallic color (see Figure 2.18).

A number of connectors lead out of the power supply. Every power supply provides special connectors for the motherboard (see Figure 2.19) and a

detailing power supplies.

Floppy Drive

The floppy drive enables you to access removable floppy disks (diskettes). The modern floppy drive used in PCs today is called a 3.5" floppy drive (Figure 2.22).

• Figure 2.18 Typical power supply

• Figure 2.19 Power connector for the motherboard

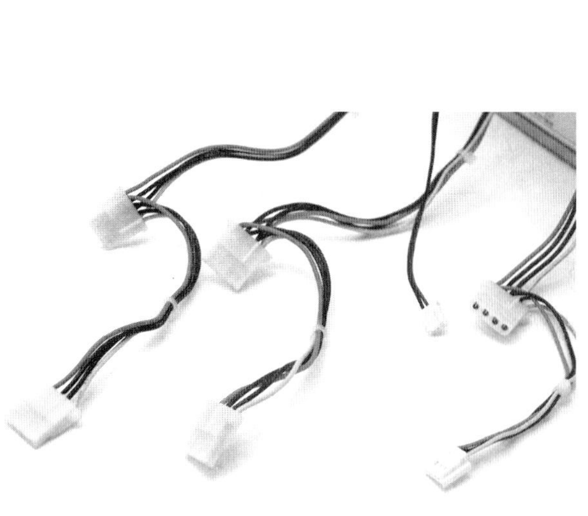

• **Figure 2.20** General-use power connectors

• **Figure 2.21** PC cooling fan

The **floppy drive** connects to the computer via a *ribbon cable,* which in turn connects to the motherboard. The connection to the motherboard is known as the *floppy controller* (see Figure 2.23).

Because floppy drives need power, a connector from the power supply must attach to the floppy drive (see Figure 2.24).

Many PCs now also come with special drives that look very similar to floppy drives, like the popular Iomega Zip drives. These special drives look like floppies, but the PC sees them very differently. In Chapter 9, we will look at the different types of floppy drives, and we'll see a few of these special drives, too.

Hard Drive

Hard drives store programs and data that are not currently being used by the CPU (see Figure 2.25). As with RAM, hard drive capacity is measured in megabytes. Even though both hard drives and RAM use the same storage unit (MB), a PC's hard drive stores much more data than a

• **Figure 2.22** Typical modern floppy drive with disk

• **Figure 2.23** Floppy drive controller

• **Figure 2.24** Floppy drive power connector

An average PC will have one hard drive, although almost every PC accepts up to four drives. Special PCs that need to store large amounts of data—such as a large corporation's main file storage computer—can contain many hard drives—8 to 16 drives in some cases. Although the PC design allows for many hard drives, most generic desktop PCs have only one hard drive.

As with so many other parts of the PC, industry standards define two common types of hard drives: *Enhanced Integrated Drive Electronics* (EIDE) and *Small Computer System Interface* (SCSI) (see Figure 2.26). EIDE drives are inexpensive and easy to install: more than 95 percent of all PCs use EIDE

• **Figure 2.26** EIDE and SCSI hard drives with cables

drives. SCSI drives are generally faster and more expensive, so they usually show up only in high-end PCs such as network servers or graphics workstations.

Both EIDE and SCSI hard drives connect to the computer via a ribbon cable. Given the predominance of EIDE, most motherboards come with built-in (or *onboard*) EIDE controllers (see Figure 2.27).

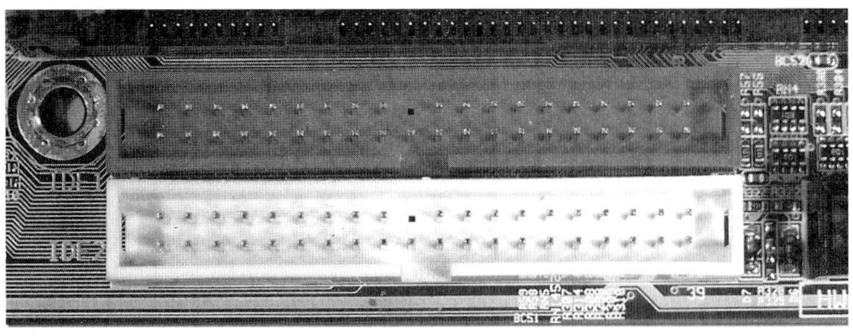

• **Figure 2.27** Onboard EIDE controllers

Note that the motherboard shown in Figure 2.27 has two connectors—the most common setup on today's PCs. A ribbon cable attaches to each connector. Each ribbon cable has two connectors for hard drives. With two controllers, each controlling two drives, a PC can support up to four EIDE drives.

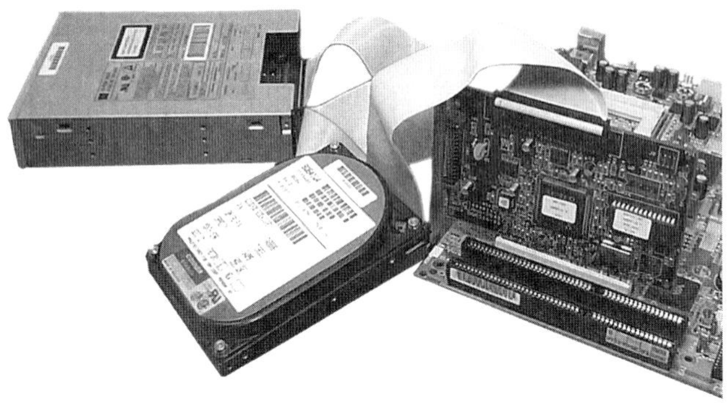

• **Figure 2.28** SCSI chain with multiple devices

SCSI drives might look like EIDE drives, but SCSI manifests in a PC very differently than EIDE does. First, very few motherboards have SCSI controllers. You usually need to buy a special SCSI controller card called a *SCSI host adapter*. Also, you can put more than two SCSI drives on the same cable. Additionally, SCSI supports many different types of devices other than hard drives. It is not at all uncommon to see CD-ROM drives, tape backups, and other devices connect to the same ribbon cable as the SCSI hard drive (see Figure 2.28).

Both EIDE and SCSI need electricity. Every drive needs a power connector (see Figure 2.29). Read Chapters 10 and 19 for all the details on hard drives.

A new type of EIDE drive technology called Serial ATA is quickly gaining popularity. Check out Chapter 10 for information on Serial ATA.

CD-ROM Drive

CD-ROM drives enable the system to access CD-ROM discs. CD-ROM drives are quite large, usually the single largest component inside the PC, aside from the power supply. With the front of the CD-ROM drive visible in the front of the PC, as well as its boxy shape and metallic appearance, you should easily recognize the CD-ROM drive (Figure 2.30).

CD-ROM drives come in EIDE and SCSI versions that run on either EIDE or SCSI controllers, just like hard drives. Many PCs have an EIDE hard drive and an EIDE CD-ROM drive on one controller (see Figure 2.31).

New PCs now come with some type of recordable CD-ROM drive. For many years, the *Compact Disc-Recordable* (CD-R) was the only available form of recordable CD. CD-R drives enabled you to record onto special CD-R discs, but once the data was "burned" onto the CD-R, it could not be erased. Most regular CD-ROM drives as well as CD-R drives could read the CD-R discs.

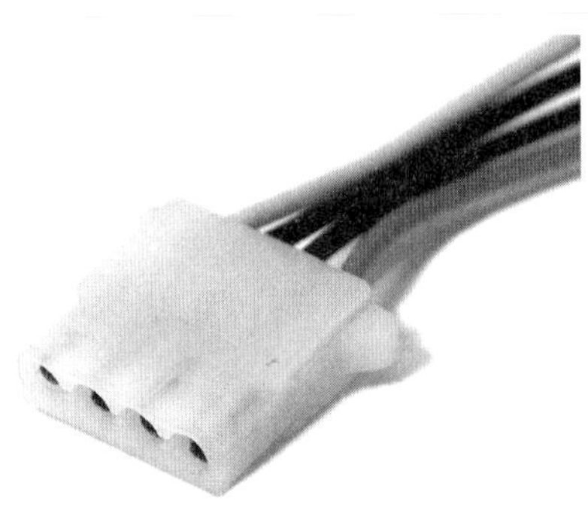

• **Figure 2.29** Hard drive power connector

Today, *Compact Disc-Rewritable* (CD-RW) drives have completely eclipsed the CD-R drives on PCs (see Figure 2.32). CD-RW drives can write to special CD-RW discs, and then delete and rewrite to those discs numerous times. CD-RW drives can also write to CD-R discs. Further, CD-RW drives can read all three media types (CD-ROM, CD-R, and CD-RW).

• **Figure 2.30** Typical CD-ROM drive

• **Figure 2.31** Hard drive and CD-ROM sharing a cable and controller

• **Figure 2.32** CD-RW drive

• **Figure 2.33** DVD drive

Initially, only CD-RW drives could read CD-RW discs, but current CD-ROM drives can read them as well. You'll usually find a CD-RW drive on a cable separate from the main hard drive.

Many PCs now come with *digital video disc* (DVD) drives. DVDs store huge amounts of information and are commonly used to store movies. Some types of DVD drives now available enable you to write data to (as well as read from) a DVD (Figure 2.33).

There are a number of writable DVD standards with names like DVD-RW or DVD+RW. The DVD industry is still fighting to see which will become dominant.

■ Connectors

Up to this point, all of the described devices reside in the PC—you can't see how these devices connect unless you open the PC's case. The rest of the components that need to be discussed have some type of visible connection on the outside of the system case. So before diving into the realm of sound cards, modems, network cards, mice, and so on, you need to understand the many types of **connectors** used by these different devices and the **ports** into which they plug. All these connectors and ports have their own naming conventions that you should know. It's not acceptable to go around saying things like "that's a printer port" or "that's a little-type keyboard connector." You need to be comfortable with the more commonly used naming conventions, so you can say "that's a female DB-25" or "that's a mini-DIN."

Although PCs use close to 50 different connectors, almost all connectors fit into one of eight major types: DB, DIN, Centronics, RJ, BNC, audio, USB , and FireWire. Let's get acquainted with each type.

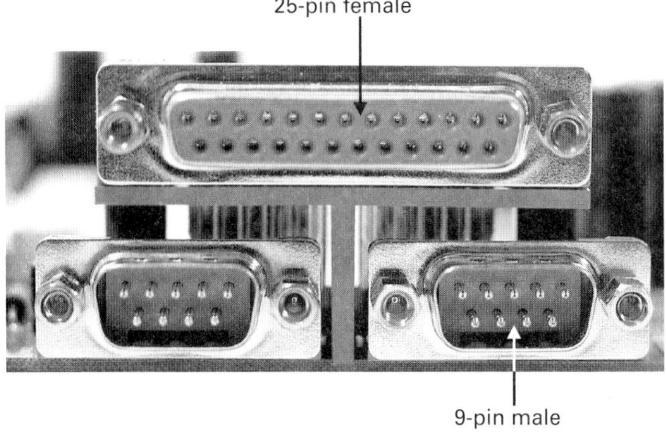

• **Figure 2.34** DB connectors

DB Connectors

DB connectors have a slight *D* shape, which allows only one proper way to insert a plug into the socket and makes it easier to remember what they're called. Technically, they're known as *DataBus* connectors, but techs always shorten that to DB. Each DB connector has groups of small pins—thus male—or sockets—female—that plug in as a group. DB connectors in the PC world can have from 9 to 37 pins or sockets, although you rarely see a DB connector with more than 25 pins or sockets. Figure 2.34 shows some examples. DB ports on the PC can be either male or female. DB-type connectors are some of the oldest and most common connectors used in the back of PCs.

DIN Connectors

Most PCs sport the European-designed DIN connectors. The round DIN connectors come in only two sizes: DIN and mini-DIN. The sockets are always female (see Figure 2.35).

• **Figure 2.35** DIN and mini-DIN ports

Centronics Connectors

Similar to DB connectors, Centronics connectors have the same *D* shape to ensure proper insertion. Unlike DBs, however, Centronics connectors use one large central tab, covered with contacts instead of pins. Even though the Centronics connectors have flat contacts instead of pins, the word *pins* is still used to describe the number of contacts. For example, a Centronics connector with 36 contacts is still called a 36-pin connector. Centronics connectors

RJ Connectors

You have more than likely seen an RJ-type connector, whether or not you knew it by that name. The little plastic plug used to connect your telephone cord to the jack is a classic example of an RJ plug. Modern PCs use only two types of RJ jacks: the RJ-11 and the RJ-45. The phone jack is an RJ-11. It is used almost exclusively for modems. The slightly wider RJ-45 jack is used for one very popular type of network cabling. Most network cards have an RJ-45 socket. Figure 2.37 shows an RJ-45 jack (top) and an RJ-11 jacks (bottom).

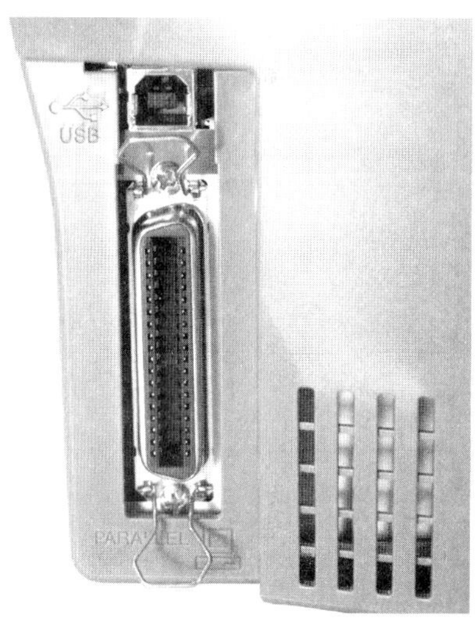

• **Figure 2.36** Centronics socket

BNC Connectors

BNC connectors, also commonly known as *coaxial* or *coax* connectors, are beginning to fade from PC use, but many PCs still have coax connectors hanging out the back (see Figure 2.38). The coax cable used with PCs looks similar to the one that runs into the back of your TV. The connectors, however, are different in that they don't screw in the way the TV coax connectors do. The connectors use a twist-type connection. You insert the cable onto the BNC connector and twist to lock the cable into place, a move that's similar to connecting a bayonet to a rifle. (This is why many techs assume BNC stands for *bayonet connector*, although no one seems to have a definitive answer on the meaning of the initials.) Only one somewhat common type of network card, called a Thinnet card, still uses coax and a BNC connector.

Most new networks use RJ-45-based cabling, rather than BNC, and many of the older coax networks are being replaced with RJ-45 networks. While BNC slowly fades from the PC scene, screw-type coax connectors may show up in the back of a PC. You can purchase cards right now, for example, that enable your PC to act as a television. They have a screw-type coax connector for your TV cable! Hmmm, Microsoft Word and TechTV on the same screen at the same time. Could life be any better?

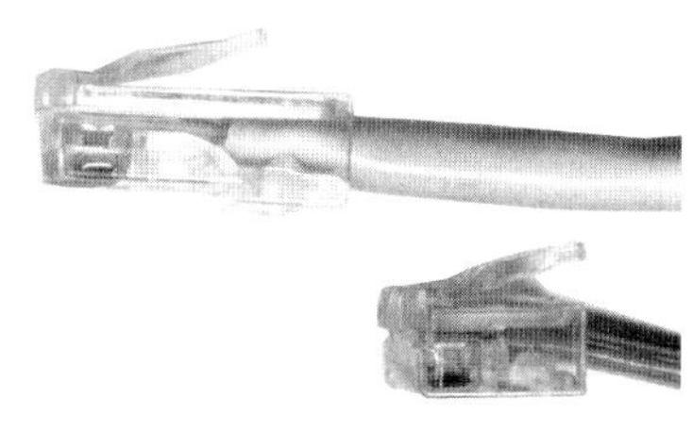

• **Figure 2.37** RJ jacks

• **Figure 2.38** BNC connector on a network card

Audio Connectors

Audio connectors are perhaps the simplest of all. Really only one type of connector sees popular use: the mini-audio connector. These small connectors have been around for years; they're just like the plug you use to insert headphones into a Sony Walkman or similar device. Audio connectors are used almost exclusively on **sound cards** (see Figure 2.39) for connecting speakers, microphones, and audio devices.

USB Connectors

The *Universal Serial Bus* (USB) provides a general-purpose connection for PCs. You can find USB versions of many different devices, such as mice,

• **Figure 2.39** Mini-audio connector and ports on a sound card

keyboards, scanners, cameras, and printers. A USB connector's distinctive rectangular shape makes it easily recognizable (see Figure 2.40).

USB has a number of features that make it particularly popular on PCs. First, USB devices are *hot-swappable,* which means you can insert or remove them without restarting your system. Almost every other type of connector requires you to turn the system off, insert/remove the connector, and then turn the system back on. Hot swapping completely eliminates this process.

USB also enables you to *daisy-chain* USB devices. A USB *hub* links together USB devices, thus the term daisy-chain (see Figure 2.41).

USB enables up to 127 USB devices to daisy-chain from one USB port. You can even put USB hubs into USB devices, en-

Figure 2.40 USB connector

Figure 2.41 USB hub

known as IEEE 1394. FireWire moves data at incredibly high speeds, from 100 to 400 Mbps, making it the perfect connection for highly specialized applications such as streaming video from a digital video camera onto a hard drive. FireWire consists of a special 6-wire cable and a unique, FireWire-only connector, as shown in Figure 2.43. Sony Corporation has also developed a smaller, 4-pin version. The 6-pin connection provides power in addition to data transfer, while devices that use the 4-pin version must use a separate power supply. You can purchase cables that convert from the Sony 4-pin to the standard 6-pin connection. Most devices use the larger standard connector, while the smaller one is found on devices such as digital video cameras; in fact, this is one of the most popular uses for FireWire. Any single FireWire cable can be no longer than 5 meters, often misquoted as 15 feet in the United States.

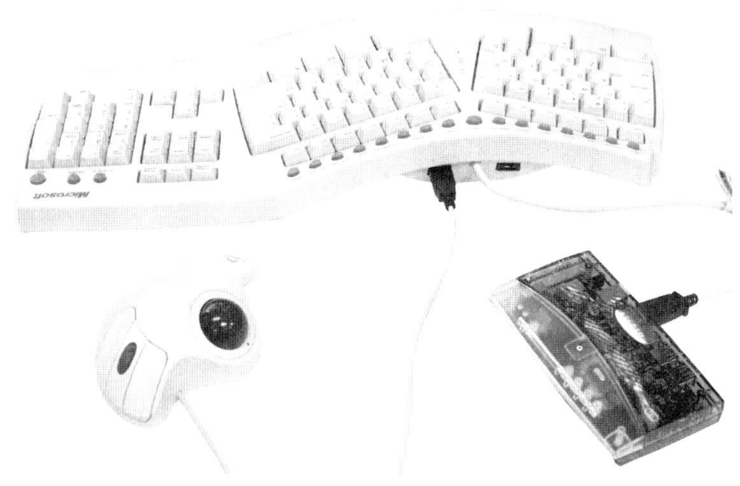

Figure 2.42 USB hub with daisy-chained devices

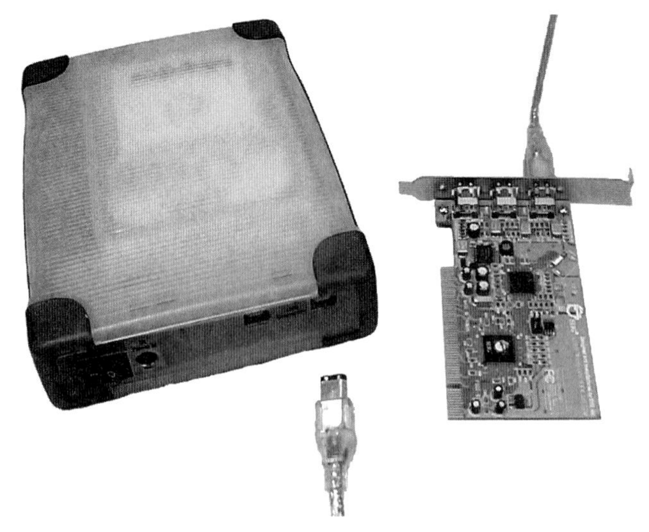

• **Figure 2.43** IEEE 1394 FireWire drive, connection, and controller

Many newer PCs have built-in FireWire ports, but you can add FireWire to any modern PC with a FireWire adapter card, as shown in Figure 2.43.

Note that the card in Figure 2.43 has three controllers. Like USB, FireWire supports daisy-chaining, allowing up to 63 devices to run from a single controller. FireWire is totally hot-swappable and fully compliant with Plug and Play, making it amazingly simple to use.

■ All Kinds of Connectors

Keep in mind that the variety of connectors is virtually endless. The preceding types of connectors cover the vast majority, but many others exist in the PC world. No law or standard requires device makers to use a particular connector, especially if they have no interest in making that device interchangeable with similar devices from other manufacturers.

Now that you have a sense of the connectors, let's turn to the devices common to almost every PC in order to learn which connectors go with which device.

Sound Cards

Sound cards perform two functions. First, they take digital information and turn it into sound, outputting the sound through speakers. Second, they take sound that is input through a microphone and turn it into digital data.

To play and record sounds, a sound card needs to connect to at least a set of speakers and a microphone. Virtually all sound cards have two miniature audio jacks for a microphone and a speaker. Many will also provide miniature audio jacks for *line in* and *line out*. Most sound cards will also provide a female 15-pin DB socket that enables you to attach an electronic musical instrument or add a joystick to your PC (see Figure 2.44).

Try This!

Feeling Your Way Around Connectors

Given that most PCs tend to sit on the floor under desks, a good PC tech learns to recognize most every PC connector by touch. This is a great exercise to do with a partner!

1. Look at all of the connectors on the back of any PC's system unit.
2. Turn the system unit around so that you can no longer see the connections.
3. Try to identify the connectors by feel.

Video Cards

Of all the cards in a PC, the **video card** is by far the easiest to identify. Unless you use a PC made before roughly 1986, the video card uses a 15-pin female DB connector or the unique, video-only *digital video interface* (DVI) connector. Many video cards have both types of connectors (see Figure 2.45).

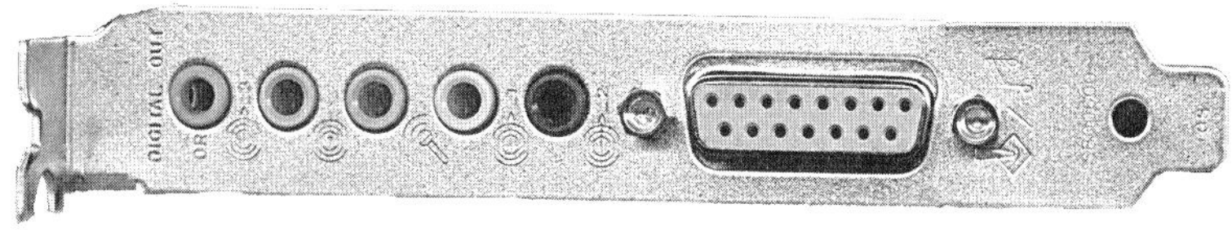

• **Figure 2.44** Typical sound card ports

Network Cards

Networks are groups of connected PCs that share informa-

Figure 2.46 shows a typical network card with multiple connector types.

It is not uncommon to see NICs with more than one type of connector. Although a NIC may have any of these connectors, the networking industry has concentrated on networks that use the RJ-45 connection. Today, the most common NIC has a single RJ-45 connection (see Figure 2.47).

> Many video cards come with multiple connectors. These are to support video input/output or for a second monitor.

Keyboard

Today's **keyboards** come in many shapes and sizes, but use only one of two keyboard-specific connectors. All PCs have a keyboard port connected directly to the motherboard. The oldest type of keyboard connector, no longer used on new systems, is a special DIN-type connector popularly known as the AT style. The original IBM PC used the AT-style DIN, but most current PCs use the mini-DIN PS/2-style keyboard connector (see Figure 2.48).

You can use an AT-style keyboard with a PS/2-style socket (or the other way around) by using a converter. Although the AT connector is unique in PCs (see Figure 2.49), the PS/2-style mini-DIN is also used in modern PCs for the mouse. Fortunately, most PCs that use the mini-DIN for both the keyboard and mouse clearly mark each mini-DIN socket as to its correct use. Some new keyboards have a USB connection, but these are fairly rare compared to the PS/2-connection keyboards.

• **Figure 2.46** Typical network card connectors

Nothing gets used and abused on your system more than your keyboard. The constant tapping of your fingers, combined with the occasional coffee spill and cookie crumbs, tend to get keyboards filthy over time. Use a general purpose cleaner to clean your keyboard—don't use alcohol as it tends to remove the printing off the letters on some keyboards!

• **Figure 2.47** Common network card with single RJ-45 connection

• **Figure 2.48** Mini-DIN keyboard connector

• **Figure 2.49** AT-style keyboard connector

After a good cleaning, grab some silicon lubricant and apply it to the undersides of the keys to keep them moving smoothly.

Mouse

Before we talk about mice in general, we need a short discussion on something called *serial ports.* A better name for this section might be, "What's a serial port, what does it look like, and what does a mouse have to do with it?"

It's hard to believe, but there was a time, long ago and far away, when PCs worked just fine without mice. When IBM created the PC, mice were not part of the picture. But IBM did something very smart that enabled mice, as well as many other devices invented after the introduction of the PC, to become part of the PC quite easily.

IBM made the PC easily customizable by providing two ways to add components: expansion slots and standardized ports. IBM added many unused slots to which anyone (at least anyone with the technical know-how) could add special cards in order to add functions. The original PC had only two cards: the video card and the floppy drive controller. Hard drive controller cards, network cards, sound cards, modems, and a few thousand other devices were all created because IBM had the foresight to add expansion slots. This book devotes all of Chapter 6 to expansion slots.

Second, IBM included standardized ports on the PC that enabled people to add devices without opening the case. The first of these standardized ports was (and still is) called a serial port. Now, please understand that IBM didn't invent serial ports. Serial ports had been around long before the PC was invented in 1980, but IBM made sure that every IBM PC came with two serial ports. Even today, every PC has at least one serial port. Isn't that fascinating? One of the oldest technologies in the computer world still soldiers on in the back of the most modern, powerful PCs!

Serial ports are one of the few connectors on modern systems that were also used in the first PCs more than 20 years ago!

A **serial port** does only one thing: it takes a stream of serial data (which runs on only one wire) and converts it into a format that the CPU can easily understand. Equally, a serial port takes data from the CPU and outputs it in serial format. Think of serial data as a telegraph wire sending Morse code, but instead of sending dots and dashes, it sends ones and zeros. Not only did IBM put serial ports in all its PCs, it told everyone how to write software that could talk to the serial port and manipulate the incoming or outgoing data. To top it all off, IBM standardized the serial connector, defining the size, shape, number, and function of all the pins. That way you knew if you invented a device that worked in one IBM PC, it would also work in all the others.

The super-standard IBM serial port is either a 25- or 9-pin male DB port. No other port in the back of a PC looks like these serial ports. The 25-pin port was the first of the two sizes, but over time it became obvious that most devices needed only about 9 pins. As a result, very few systems still use the 25-pin serial port. Today, the 9-pin serial rules. You can get an adapter that enables you to convert 9 to 25 or 25 to 9. You would be hard-pressed to find a PC without at least one 9-pin serial port. Figure 2.50 and Figure 2.51, respectively, show 25-pin and 9-pin serial ports.

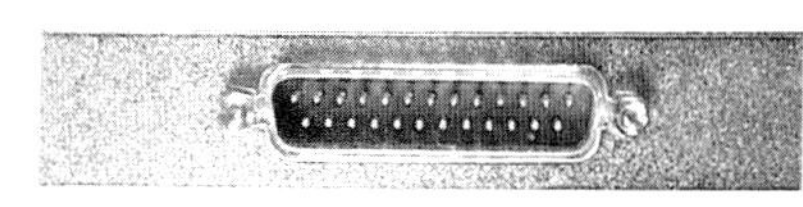

• Figure 2.50 25-pin serial port

Most people reading this book have some PC experience. Somebody out

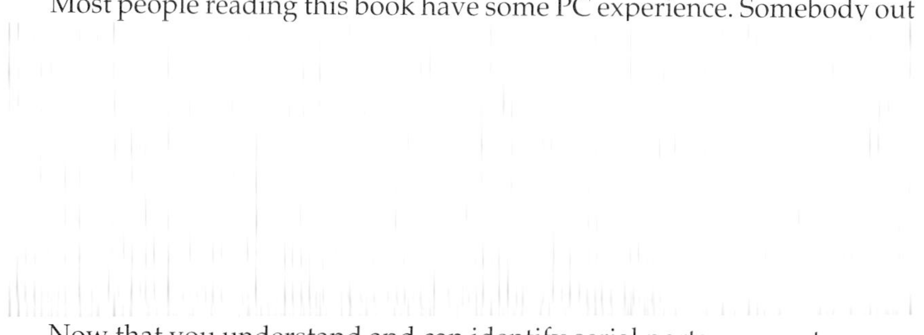

Now that you understand and can identify serial ports, we can turn our attention back to mice. Most folks are pretty comfortable with the function of a **mouse** —it allows you to select graphical items on a graphical screen. For many years, a dedicated mouse port did not even exist. Mice simply connected via either 9-pin or 25-pin serial ports. The acceptance of the mouse as an integral part of the PC, however, created a demand for the mouse to have its own connector, just as the keyboard had its own connector. In the mid-1980s, a new type of mouse connection made its debut with the introduction of the IBM PS/2 personal computer. Although still a serial port, the new PS/2-style dedicated mouse port used a mini-DIN connector (see Figure 2.52).

• Figure 2.52 PS/2 mouse port

A variation of the mouse is a *trackball*. A trackball does the same job as a mouse but instead of being pushed around like a mouse, the trackball stays in one place as you roll a ball with your fingers. Many PC systems now use a USB port for the mouse. USB's daisy-chain feature often enables you to connect a USB mouse or trackeball to the front of the system or into the keyboard, significantly reducing the amount of cable lying around your PC (see Figure 2.53).

Modem

A **modem** works with your telephone line to translate analog telephone signals into digital serial data. Modems can also translate digital serial data into analog telephone signals. There are two types of modems: internal and external. An external modem sits outside the PC and plugs into a serial port. An internal modem is a card that snaps into an expansion slot. A modem is another easily identifiable device in PCs. All modems, internal or external, have two RJ-11 sockets. One connects the modem to the telephone

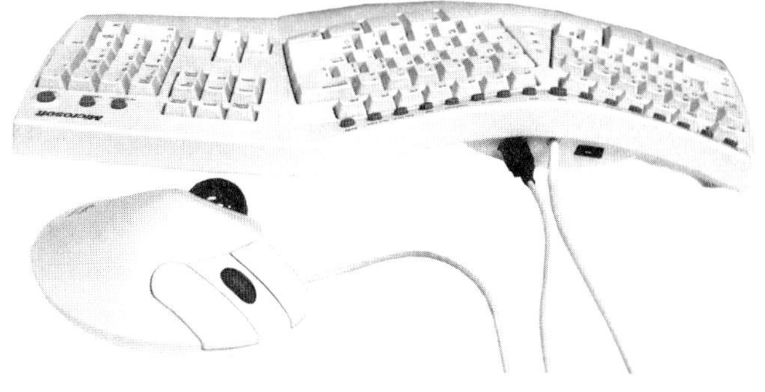

• Figure 2.53 USB trackball connected to keyboard

• **Figure 2.54** Typical modem connections

The RJ-11 connectors on a modem look very similar to the RJ-45 connectors on a network card. Compare the graphic of the RJ-45 connector you saw in Figure 2.47 with to the RJ-11 connector—could you tell the difference?

jack on the wall, and the other is for an optional telephone so that you can use the phone line when the modem is not in use (see Figure 2.54).

Printer

Most **printers** use a special connector called a **parallel port**. Parallel ports carry data on more than one wire, as opposed to the serial port, which uses only one wire. Parallel ports use a 25-pin female DB connector (see Figure 2.55).

After almost 20 years of domination by parallel ports, USB is now showing up on more and more printers as an alternative connector. Most models of printers now come with USB, parallel, or both types of connections. Some better models even offer FireWire.

Joystick

Joysticks weren't supposed to be used just for games. When the folks at IBM added the 15-pin female DB joystick connector to PCs, they envisioned joysticks as hard-working input devices, just as the mouse is today (see Figure 2.56). Except in the most rare circumstances, however, the only thing joysticks do today is enable you to turn your PC into a rather expensive game machine! But is there a more gratifying feeling than easing that joystick over, pressing the Fire button, and watching an enemy fighter jet get blasted by a well-placed Sidewinder missile? I think not.

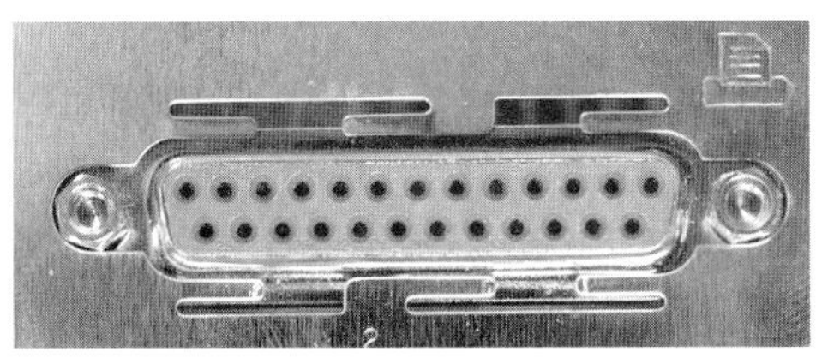

• **Figure 2.55** Parallel port

• **Figure 2.56** Joystick port

Chapter 2 Review

Chapter Summary

After reading this chapter and completing the exercises, you should understand the following about the Visible PC.

Describe How the PC Works

- The two parts of the PC—hardware and software—work intimately together to enable you to do work. The computer tech knows the four stages or [illegible]

[illegible] and straight-slot screwdrivers, a star-headed Torx wrench, a nut driver or two, a pair of tweezers, a little grabber tool, a hemostat, a magnifying glass, and a flashlight.
- Electrostatic discharge (ESD) can damage or destroy computer components. ESD damage may result in upset failures, degradation failures, and catastrophic failures. You can avoid ESD by using proper tools, such as an anti-static wrist strap and anti-static bags.

Identify the Major Internal and External Components of a PC

- The central processing unit (CPU), also called the microprocessor or brain of the computer, has a make, a model, a speed, and a package. AMD and Intel are the two most common makers of CPUs. CPU speed is measured in megahertz (MHz) or gigahertz (GHz). The Pin Grid Array (PGA) is the most common CPU package, but some older Single Edge Cartridge (SEC) packages still exist. A CPU cooling fan or heat sink is essential to dissipate the heat.
- Random Access Memory (RAM) contains the current programs and data that the CPU is using. Most PC memory is installed on sticks called either Dual Inline Memory Modules (DIMMs) or Single Inline Memory Modules. RAM capacity is measured in megabytes (MB).
- The motherboard contains soldered components, expansion slots, and sockets for the CPU, RAM, and other components. Expansion slots are connectors for expansion cards that enable optional devices to communicate with the PC. The case or box holds the motherboard and has openings for [illegible]
- A floppy drive requires a [illegible] the power supply and a ribbon cable to connect to the floppy drive controller on the motherboard. The most common type is the 3.5″ floppy drive.
- Although almost every PC can have up to four hard drives, most computers use a single hard drive that has 40 gigabytes (GB) or more of space for programs and data not currently used by the CPU. Most PCs use Enhanced Integrated Drive Electronics (EIDE) hard drives. These drives connect to one of the two EIDE controllers on the motherboard via a ribbon cable. High-end PCs may use more expensive Small Computer Systems Interface (SCSI) drives that attach to a SCSI host adapter card. This card can also support other kinds of SCSI devices, such as CD-ROM drives or tape backups.
- CD media drives, either SCSI or EIDE, enable the computer to access CD discs. Some CD media drives can record CDs, such as the Compact Disc-Recordable (CD-R) or the Compact Disc-Rewritable (CD-RW) drives. Many PCs now have digital video disc (DVD) drives that support capacities large enough for a full-length movie.

Identify the Different Connectors on a Typical PC System Unit

- PCs use many kinds of connectors, but most fit into one of eight major types: DB, DIN, Centronics, RJ,

BNC, audio, USB, and FireWire. Connectors are often identified by their shape (such as DB connectors that look like a capital D), gender (male or female), and by the number of pins.

- DB connectors look like a capital D, while DIN connectors are round. Rarely used except on printers, Centronics connectors have a D shape, but instead of pins, they have a large central tab.
- The telephone jack is an RJ connector, called an RJ-11. Most network cards have a wider RJ-45 jack. The round BNC connector, also called coaxial or coax connector, is found on one type of older network card.
- Sound cards have mini-audio connectors for speakers or microphones.
- The rectangular Universal Serial Bus (USB) connector allows up to 127 USB devices, including keyboards and cameras, to daisy-chain or link together with USB hubs. USB is hot-swappable so that devices may be inserted or removed without restarting the computer.
- Also known as the IEEE 1394, the FireWire interface is perfect for high-speed devices, such as digital video cameras. Since PCs rarely have built-in 4- or 6-wire FireWire connectors, users typically purchase a FireWire adapter card. FireWire is also hot-swappable and able to daisy-chain up to 63 devices.
- Most PCs include a number of standard devices, such as a sound card and speakers, a video card, a network card, a keyboard, and a mouse. A sound card digitizes sound and outputs it through speakers. Today's computers use a 15-pin female DB connector or a video-only DVI connector to attach the monitor to the PC. Network interface cards (NICs) connect cabling to the PC to set up a network that allows computers to share information. Today keyboards use a mini-DIN PS/2 style connector or a USB connector.
- Many kinds of standardized ports allow external devices to be added to the PC. Either a 25- or 9-pin male DB connector, a serial port uses only a single wire to send a stream of serial data. A COM port is a serial port that is assigned two values: an I/O address and an IRQ. A mouse may connect to a serial port or to a dedicated PS/2-style port using a mini-DIN connector. Newer PCs may use a USB port for the mouse.
- A parallel port carries data on more than one wire. Most printers use a parallel port, identified as a 25-pin female DB connector. Newer printers may connect via a USB port.
- A modem translates the digital serial data from your computer into analog telephone signals that can travel on regular telephone lines. A modem may be internal or external, but you can identify it easily by its two RJ-11 sockets.
- A joystick or game port is a 15-pin female DB connector.
- Take care of the documentation that comes with your computer. The motherboard book is especially important for showing how to configure the board. If you do not have documentation for your computer, you can probably find it on the Internet, but it is a time-consuming process.
- A+ Certification exams expect you to be able to recognize the main parts of a PC, identify expansion cards, name different types of connectors, and explain the kinds of devices that connect to various ports.

Key Terms

CD-ROM Drive *(30)*
Connectors (32)
CPU *(21)*
Expansion Slots *(24)*
Floppy Drive *(28)*
Hard Drive *(28)*
Joystick *(40)*
Keyboard *(37)*
Modem *(39)*
Motherboard *(23)*
Mouse *(39)*
Network Interface Card (NIC) *(37)*
Parallel Port *(40)*
Ports *(32)*
Power Supply *(27)*
Printer *(40)*
Random Access Memory (RAM) *(22)*
Serial Port *(38)*
Sound Card *(34)*
Video Card *(36)*

Key Term Quiz

Use the Key Terms list to complete the sentences that follow. Not all the terms will be used.

1. Two RJ-11 connectors identify the ________ .
2. If you install a DIMM stick, your computer will have more ____________ .
3. The ________ transmits data on a single wire.
4. The __________ takes AC voltage from the wall outlet and converts it to DC voltage for the computer components.
5. ________ are identified by their shape,

[illegible]

6. If an expansion card contains an RJ-45 jack, it is a ________________.
7. A 25-pin female DB connector with a printer attached to it is a ______________
8. The monitor attaches to the ________ with a 15-pin female connector.
9. An internal storage device that typically holds 20 GB or more is a __________.
10. The _________ has a make, a model, a speed, and a package.

[illegible]

telephone signals.

B. It attaches to the monitor.

C. It translates analog telephone signals into digital serial data.

D. It has two RJ-11 ports.

2. Serial ports ________________.

A. Use a single wire to transmit data

B. Are very fast ports designed for devices such as a digital video camera

C. Use multiple wires to transmit data

D. Are hot-swappable

3. Which of the following devices attaches with a ribbon cable?

A. CPU

B. CD-ROM drive

C. RAM

D. Sound card

4. You will usually need to buy a controller card called a host adapter to use _________.

A. A floppy drive

B. An EIDE hard drive

C. A printer

D. A SCSI hard drive

[illegible]

A. USB

B. Centronics

C. FireWire

D. USB and FireWire

6. Which of the following devices measure(s) storage capacity in megabytes or gigabytes?

A. Floppy disk and hard disk

B. NIC

C. CPU

D. Modem

7. Which of the following devices has enough storage capacity to hold a movie?

A. CD-ROM

B. CD-R

C. CD-RW

D. DVD

8. The motherboard typically contains all of the following *except* ______________.

A. A keyboard port

B. A FireWire port

C. Expansion slots

D. RAM sockets

9. The expansion slots create the connection that enables ______________________.

   A. The CPU to communicate with the RAM

   B. A keyboard to attach to the PC

   C. Optional devices to communicate with the PC

   D. The CPU to attach to the motherboard

10. Which of the following statements is true about a USB port?

   A. USB is a parallel port.

   B. A USB port can support up to 127 devices.

   C. A USB port has a 9-pin DB male connector.

   D. A USB port allows the computer to attach to a network.

11. Which kind of connector has one large central tab instead of pins and locks into the socket with wire "wings"?

   A. USB

   B. Centronics

   C. FireWire

   D. DIN

12. Which of the following best describes the function of a sound card?

   A. A sound card provides a way to attach a computer to a local area network.

   B. A sound card attaches to a digital camera to transfer pictures to the computer.

   C. A sound card takes digital information and turns it into sound that is then output through speakers.

   D. A sound card attaches to a modem to transmit sound via the telephone line.

13. Which of the following tools would you find in a typical PC tech's toolkit? (Select all that apply.)

   A. Phillips-head screwdriver

   B. Torx wrench

   C. Hammer

   D. File

14. The easiest kind of electrostatic discharge (ESD) damage to diagnose is ____________.

   A. Degradation failure

   B. Intermittent failure

   C. Upset failure

   D. Catastrophic failure

15. Which of the following best describes the function of a NIC?

   A. A NIC provides the interface between the network and the PC.

   B. A NIC provides an RJ-11 connector that goes to the telephone jack and allows the user to access the Internet.

   C. A NIC is an expansion card that adds additional memory to the computer.

   D. A NIC connects the computer to external devices, such as a printer.

Essay Quiz

1. While serial and parallel ports have been around forever, newer and faster ports such as USB and FireWire are now available. At the same time, new computers have faster CPUs, more RAM, and larger capacity hard drives. What factors do you think are driving the PC market for these improvements? Do you feel that you need to have the newest and the greatest PC? Why or why not?
2. Jason, one of your coworkers who knows nothing about computer hardware, needs to move his computer and will be responsible for reassembling it himself in his new office across town. What advice can you give him about disassembly steps that will help ensure that he can reassemble the computer successfully? List at least five things that Jason should do as he disassembles the computer, transports it, and reassembles it. Do shapes and colors help him?
3. A floppy drive has been a standard component for personal computers from their beginning. Now, some manufacturers, such as Dell, have decided to build PCs without a floppy drive. Would you want to purchase a PC without a floppy drive? Why or why not? If so, what kinds of alternative devices would you want your computer to have?

4. Hearing that you are taking a computer hardware course, Aunt Sally approaches you about helping her select a new computer. She wants to use the computer primarily for office applications, to track her budget, to receive and send e-mail, and to surf the Internet. What are you going to tell her about the kind of PC to buy? What peripherals should she purchase? Why?

5. Your worksite currently has no ESD protection. If fact, your supervisor doesn't feel that such protection is necessary. Write a proposal to purchase ESD protection equipment for the computer assembly/repair facility that will convince your supervisor that ESD protection is necessary and cost-effective in the long run. What kinds of protection will you recommend?

Lab Projects

• Lab Project 2.2

Find an advertisement for a new personal computer in a current newspaper or magazine and examine it to determine the following:

- What make, model, and speed of CPU does it have?
- How much RAM does it have?
- What is the storage capacity of the hard drive?
- Does it include a CD-ROM, CD-R, CD-RW, or DVD?
- Does it come with a network interface card?
- Is a monitor included? If so, what kind and size?

chapter 3

Microprocessors

"Asking if computers can think is like asking if submarines can swim."

—Unknown

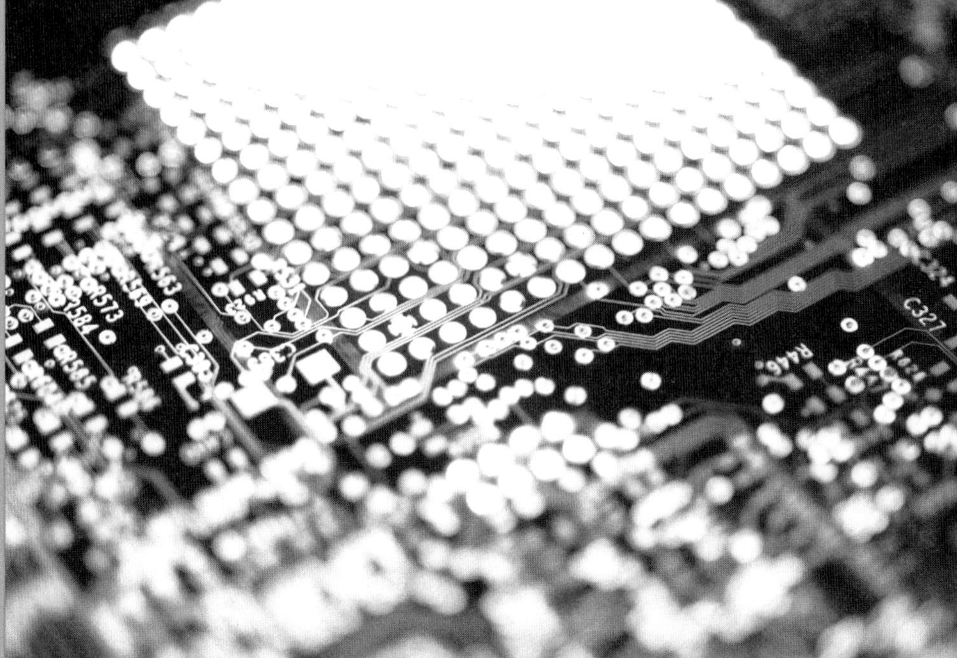

In this chapter, you will learn how to

- **Identify the core components of a CPU**
- **Explain the varieties of modern CPUs**
- **Identify specialty CPUs**
- **Install and upgrade CPUs**

For all practical purposes, the terms *microprocessor* and *central processing unit* (CPU) mean the same thing: it's that big chip inside your computer that many people often describe as the brain of the system. From the previous chapter we know that CPU makers name their microprocessors in a fashion similar to the automobile industry: CPU names get a make and a model, such as Intel Pentium 4 or AMD Athlon XP. You probably already know what a CPU looks like—invariably covered by some huge fan or heat sink, a CPU stands out inside the case. See if you can spot the CPU in Figure 3.1.

Historical/Conceptual

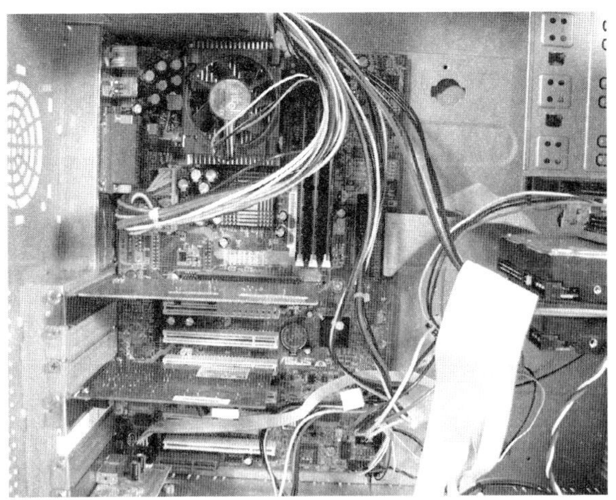

■ CPU Core Components

Although the computer might seem to act quite intelligently, comparing the CPU to a human brain hugely overstates its capabilities. A CPU functions more like a very powerful calculator than a brain—but, oh, what a calculator! Today's CPUs add, subtract, multiply, and divide billions of numbers per second. Processing that much information so quickly makes any CPU look quite intelligent. It's simply the speed

famous Intel 8088, invented in the late 1970s. Although this CPU first appeared over 20 years ago, it contains the same basic parts used in even the most advanced CPUs today. Stick with me, my friend. Prepare to enter that little bit of magic called the CPU.

The Man in the Box

Let's begin by visualizing the CPU as a man in a box (Figure 3.2). This is one clever guy in this box. He can perform virtually any mathematical function, manipulate data, and give us answers *fast*.

This guy is potentially very useful to us, but there's a catch—he lives closed up in a small beige box. Before he can work with us, we must come up with a way to exchange information with him (Figure 3.3).

External Data Bus

The Man in the Box is, of course, the CPU, and the first problem for computer engineers once they made a CPU was how to get information in and out of it. Their solution—still the solution today—was the External Data Bus (EDB). Returning to my analogy, imagine that we install a set of 16 light bulbs, 8 inside his box and 8 outside his box. Each of the 8 light bulbs inside the box connects to one of the 8 bulbs outside the box to form a pair. Each pair of light bulbs is always either On or Off. We can control the 8 pairs of bulbs using a set of 8 switches outside the box, and the Man in the Box can also control them using an

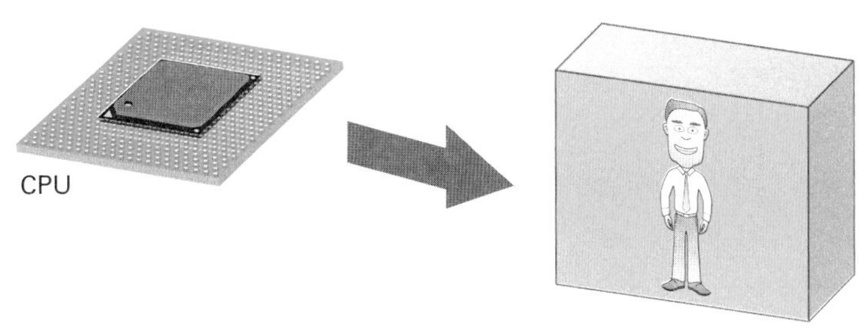

• **Figure 3.2** Imagine the CPU as a man in a box.

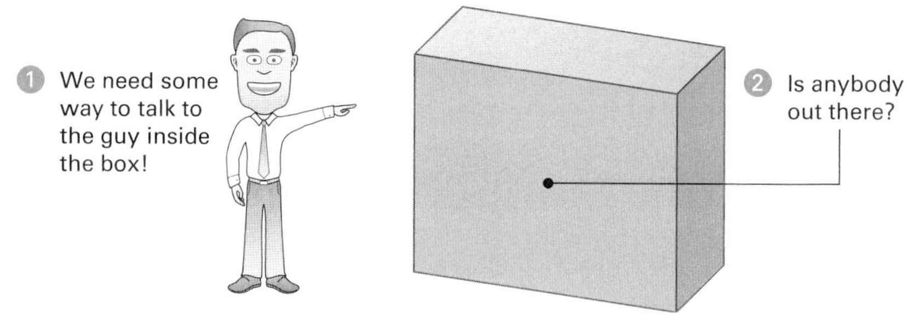

• **Figure 3.3** How can we talk to the Man in the Box?

identical set of 8 switches inside the box. We call this light bulb communication device the **external data bus** .

Figure 3.4 shows a cutaway view of the external data bus. When either we or the Man in the Box flip a switch on, *both* light bulbs go on, and the switch on the other side is also flipped to the On position. If we or the Man in the Box turn a switch off, the light bulbs on both sides are turned off, along with the other switch for that pair.

Can you see how this will work? By creating On/Off patterns with the light bulbs that represent different pieces of data or commands, we can send that information to the Man in the Box, and he can send information back to us the same way—assuming that we've agreed ahead of time on what the different patterns of lights mean. To accomplish this we create a sort of codebook that assigns meanings to the many different patterns of lights that the external data bus might display.

Before going any further, make sure you're clear on the fact that this is an analogy, not reality. There really is an external data bus, but you won't see any light bulbs or switches on the CPU (Figure 3.5). You can, however, see little wires sticking out of the CPU. If you apply voltage to one of these wires, you in essence flip the switch. Get the idea? So if that wire had voltage, and if a tiny light bulb were attached to the wire, that light bulb would glow, would it not? By the same token, if the wire had no power, then the light bulb would not glow. That is why the switch-and-light-bulb analogy is used to help you appreciate that these little wires constantly flash on and off.

Now that we have an external data bus to communicate with the Man in the Box, we need to see how it works by placing voltages on the wires. This brings up a naming problem. It's a hassle to say terms such as "on-off-off-off-on-on-off-off" when talking about which wires have voltage or not. Rather than saying that one of the external data bus wires is on or off, I'm going to use the number 1 to represent on and the number 0 to represent off (Figure 3.6). That way, instead of describing the state of the lights as "on-off-off-off-on-on-off-off," I can instead describe them by writing "10001100."

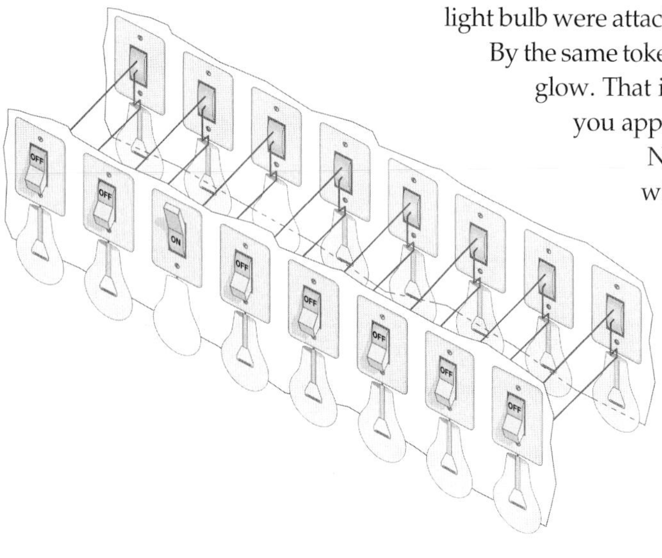

• **Figure 3.4** Cutaway of the external data bus—note one light is on.

In the world of computers, we constantly turn wires on and off. As a result, this "1 and 0" or **binary** system is used to describe the state of these wires at

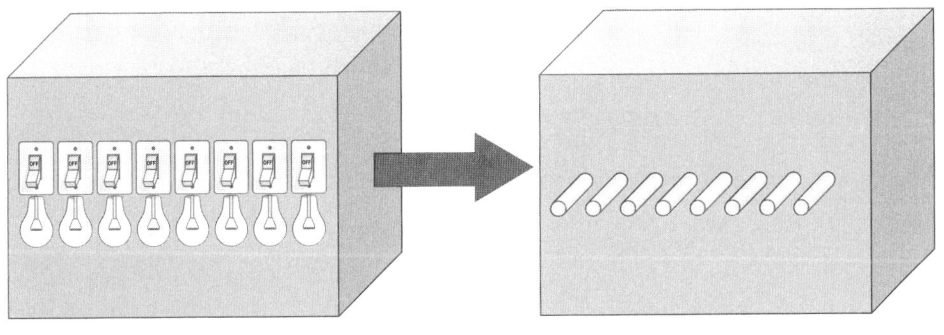

• **Figure 3.5** Analogy and reality, side by side

the workspace inside a CPU. The EDB gives us a way to communicate with the Man in the Box, and him with us, so we can give him work to do. But to do this work he needs a worktable; in fact, he needs at least four worktables. Each of these four worktables has 16 light bulbs. These light bulbs are not in pairs; they're just 16 light bulbs lined up straight across the table. Each light bulb is controlled by a single switch, operated only by the Man in the Box. By creating On/Off patterns like the ones on the EDB, the Man in the Box can work math problems using these four sets of light bulbs. In a real computer, these worktables are called **registers** (Figure 3.7).

Registers provide the Man in the Box with a workplace for the problems you give him. All CPUs contain a large number of registers, but for the moment let's concentrate on the four most commonly used ones: the *general purpose registers*. Intel gave them the names AX, BX, CX, and DX (Figure 3.8).

Great! We're just about ready to put the Man in the Box to work, but before you close the lid on the box, you must give the Man one more tool.

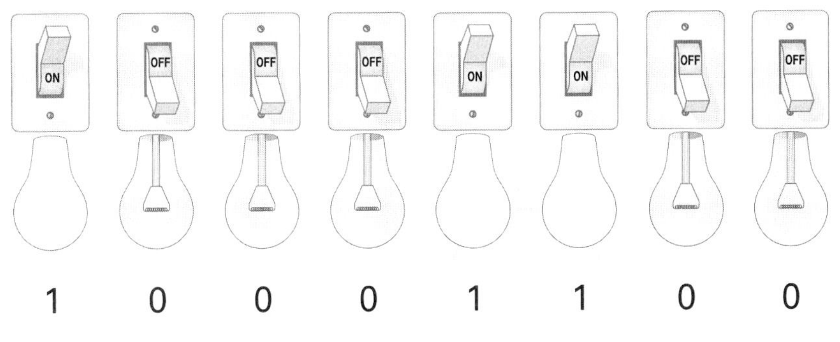

• **Figure 3.6** Here "1" means on; "0" means off.

Figure 3.7 A register

Remember the codebook we talked about earlier? Let's make one to enable us to communicate with him. Figure 3.9 is the codebook we are going to use.

In this codebook, for example, 10000111 means *MOVE the number 7 into the AX register*. In this example, light bulbs 8-3-2-1 are on, because of the rules for creating these sequences of commands. We number the bulbs from right to left, so Bulb #1 is the right-most bulb, then 2, 3, and so on up to the left-most bulb, which is #8. Another rule: commands start in light bulbs 8-7-6-5, known in tech lingo as the *high-order bits*. Data goes in light bulbs 4-3-2-1, known as the *low-order bits*. These commands are called the microprocessor's *machine language*. The commands listed the codebook above are not actual commands—as you've probably guessed, I've simplified things dramatically. However, the famous Intel 8088 CPU, invented in the late 1970s, actually used commands very similar to these, plus a few hundred others.

Here are some examples of real machine language for the Intel 8088:

10111010	The next line of code is a number. Put that number into the DX register.
01000001	Add 1 to the number already in the CX register.
00111100	Compare the value in the AX register with the next line of code.

By placing machine language commands onto the external data bus one at a time, we can instruct the Man in the Box to do specific tasks. Each time we place a command on the EDB, we call that command a *line of code* or just a *line*. We refer to the complete set of these machine language commands as the CPU's *instruction set*.

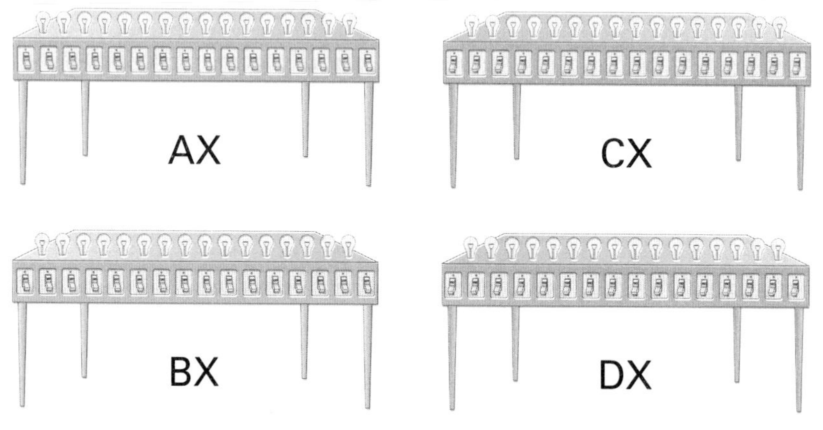

Figure 3.8 The four data registers

8088 External Data Bus Codebook

LIGHTS	MEANING
10000000	The next line is a number, put it in the AX register
10010000	The next line is a number, put it in the BX register
10110000	Add AX to BX and put the result in AX
11000000	Place the value of AX on the External Data Bus
00000000	The number 0
00000001	The number 1
00000010	The number 2
00000011	The number 3
00000100	The number 4
00000101	The number 5
00000110	The number 6
00000111	The number 7
00001000	The number 8

outside world via the external data bus, he has ...
work on the problems we give him, and he has a codebook so he can understand the different patterns (machine language commands) on the external data bus (Figure 3.10).

Clearly, the next action to perform here is to start loading some code into the CPU to watch it work, but before we do this we need to understand one more critical part of every CPU: the CPU clock.

Clock

Okay, so we're ready to put the Man in the Box to work. We start sending him data and commands over the EDB. How does he know when we're done and it's time to act?

Have you ever seen one of those old-time manual calculators with the big crank on one side? To add two numbers, you pressed a number key, the + key, and another number key, but then to make the calculator do the calculation and give you the answer, you had to pull down the crank. That was the signal that you were done entering data and instructions, and, as the accountant-types say, wanted it to crunch the numbers for you.

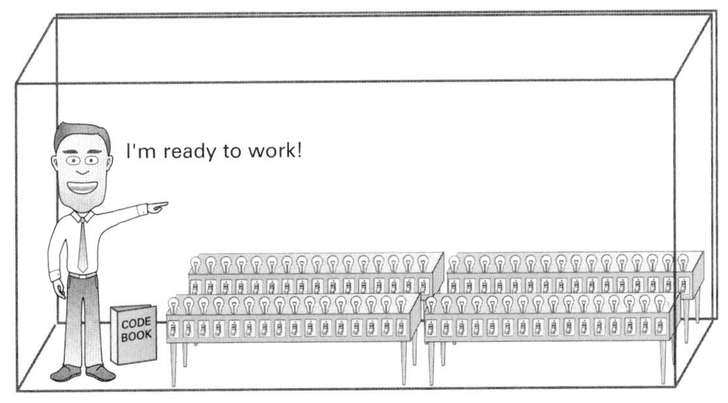

• **Figure 3.10** Our CPU so far

Well, a CPU also has a type of crank. To return to the Man in the Box, imagine there's a buzzer inside the box activated by a button on the outside of the box. Each time you press the button to sound the buzzer, the Man in the Box reads the next set of lights on the external data bus. Of course, a real computer doesn't use a buzzer. The buzzer on a real CPU is a special wire called the CLOCK wire (most diagrams label the

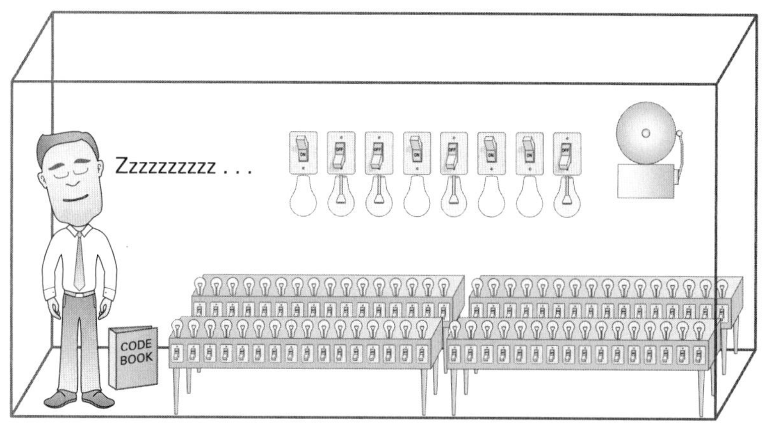

• **Figure 3.11** The CPU does nothing unless activated by the clock.

clock wire CLK). A charge on the CLK wire tells the CPU there's another piece of information waiting to be processed (Figure 3.11).

For the CPU to process a command placed on the external data bus, a certain minimum voltage must be applied to the CLK wire. A single charge to the CLK wire is called a **clock cycle** . Actually, the CPU requires at least two clock cycles to act on a command, and usually more. Using the manual calculator analogy, we need to pull the crank at least twice before anything happens. In fact, a CPU may require hundreds of clock cycles to process some commands (Figure 3.12).

The maximum number of clock cycles that a CPU can handle in a given period of time is referred to as its *clock speed*. The clock speed is the fastest speed at which a CPU can operate, determined by the CPU manufacturer. The clock speed of a particular CPU is always marked somewhere on the CPU chip itself. The Intel 8088 processor had a clock speed of 4.77 MHz (4.77 million of cycles per second), extremely slow by modern standards but still a pretty big number compared to using a pencil and paper! Today's modern CPUs run at speeds in excess of 3 GHz (3 billion cycles per second).

> CPU makers sell the exact make and model of CPU at a number of different speeds. All of these CPUs come off of the same assembly lines, so why different speeds? Every CPU comes with subtle differences—flaws, really—in the silicon that makes one CPU run faster than another. The speed difference comes from testing each CPU to see what speed it can handle.

1 Hertz (1 Hz) = 1 cycle per second

1 Megahertz (1 MHz) = 1 million cycles per second

1 Gigahertz (1 GHz) = 1 billion cycles per second

Understand that a CPU's clock speed is its *maximum* speed, not the speed at which it *must* run. A CPU can run at any speed, as long as that speed does not exceed its clock speed. Manufacturers usually print the CPU's clock speed directly onto the CPU casing (Figure 3.13).

The *system crystal* determines the speed at which a CPU and the rest of the PC operate. The system crystal is usually a quartz oscillator, very similar to the one in a wristwatch, soldered to the motherboard (Figure 3.14). As long as the PC is turned on, the quartz oscillator fires a charge on the CLK wire, in essence pushing the system along.

You can visualize the system crystal as a metronome for the CPU. While the PC is turned on, the quartz oscillator repeatedly fires a charge on the CLK wire, setting the beat, if you will, for the CPU's activities (Figure 3.15). If the system crystal sets a beat slower than the CPU's clock speed, the CPU will

• **Figure 3.12** The CPU needs more than one clock cycle to do anything.

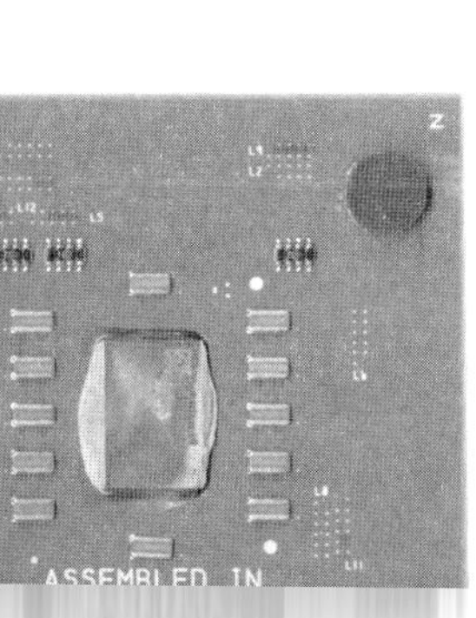

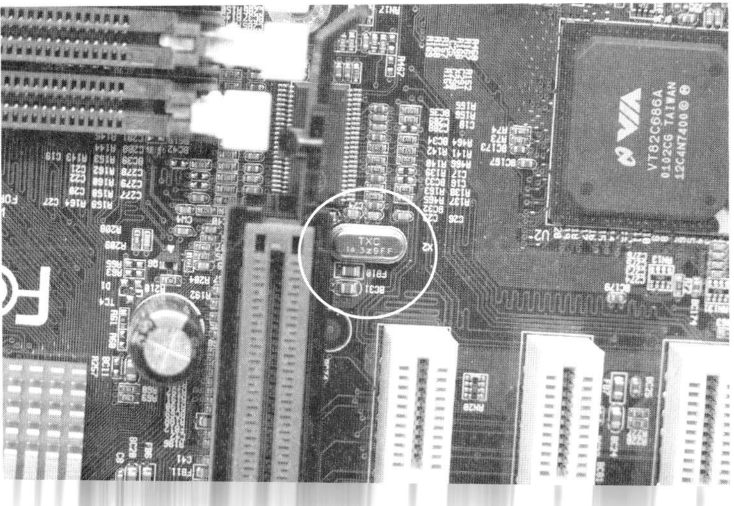

work just fine, but it will operate at the slower speed of the system crystal. If the system crystal forces the CPU to run faster than its clock speed, it can overheat and stop working.

A crystal can push a CPU with a rated clock speed higher than its own, but the CPU will operate at the slower speed of the crystal. Don't try to run a CPU faster than its clock speed, or it will overheat and then lock up. *Underclocking* means to run a CPU *slower* than its rated clock speed. Similarly, *overclocking* means to run a CPU *faster* than its maximum clock speed.

• **Figure 3.15** The crystal determines the speed of the CPU.

Aggressive users sometimes intentionally overclock CPUs. They do this to make slower (cheaper) CPUs run faster. This is a risky business that can destroy your CPU, but those willing to take that risk often do it. We go into more detail on overclocking in the section "Beyond A+," later in this chapter.

If you underclock, you are not taking advantage of all of the power of the CPU. If you overclock, you can fry the CPU.

Back to the External Data Bus

One more reality check. We've been talking about tables with racks of light bulbs, but of course real CPU registers don't use light bulbs to represent On/1 and Off/0. The four registers we discussed are tiny storage areas on the CPU, microscopic semiconductor circuits called TTL logic. When one of these circuits is holding a charge, you can think of the light bulb being on; no charge, the light bulb is off.

Figure 3.16 is a diagram of a real 8088 CPU, showing the actual wires that comprise the external data bus and the single clock wire. Because the registers are inside the CPU, they can't be shown in this figure.

Now that you have learned what components are involved in the process, try the following simple exercise to see how the process works. In this example, you tell the CPU to add 2 + 3. To do this, you must send a series of commands to the CPU—the CPU will act on each command, eventually giving you an answer. Refer to the codebook in Figure 3.9 to translate the actual instructions you're giving the Man in the Box into binary commands.

Did you try it? Here's how it works:

1. Place 10000000 on the external data bus (EDB).
2. Place 00000010 on the EDB.
3. Place 10010000 on the EDB.
4. Place 00000011 on the EDB.
5. Place 10110000 on the EDB.
6. Place 11000000 on the EDB.

When you finish Step Six, the value on the EDB will be 00000101, the decimal number 5 written in binary.

Congrats! You just added 2+3 using individual commands you saw in the codebook. This set of commands is known as a *program,* which is a series of commands sent to a CPU in a specific order for the CPU to perform work. Each discrete setting of the external data bus is a line of code. This program, therefore, has six lines of code.

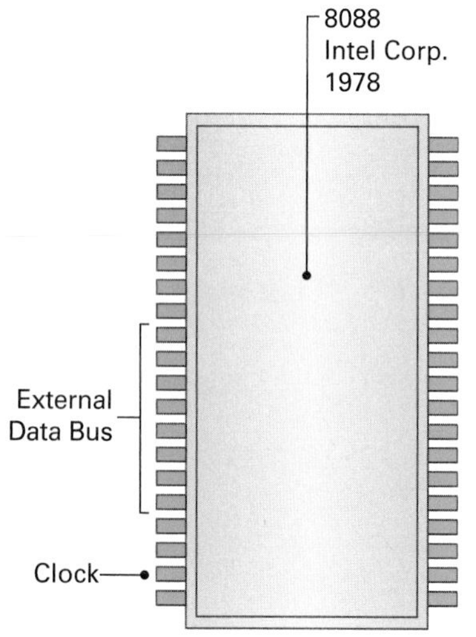

Figure 3.16 Diagram of 8088 showing clock and external data bus

Memory

Now that we've seen how the program code is executed by the CPU, let's work backward in the process for a moment, and think about how the program code gets to the EDB. The program itself is stored on the hard drive. In theory, you could build a computer that sent data from the hard drive directly to the CPU, but there's a problem: the hard drive is too slow. Even the ancient 8088, with its clock speed of 4.77 MHz, could conceivably process several million lines of code every second. Modern CPUs can crank out over a billion lines every second. Hard drives simply can't give the data to the CPU at a fast enough speed.

We need some other device that can store the lines of code at least temporarily, and pass them to the CPU fast enough to keep up with its demands. Because each line of code is nothing more than a pattern of eight 1s and 0s, any device that can store 1s and 0s eight across will do. Devices that in any way hold 1's and 0's that the CPU accesses are known generically as *memory*.

At this point, you might be using words like "RAM" and "hard drive" to understand what I'm talking about. Stop that right now! Clear your mind. Pretend that only CPUs—and no other technology—exist. We must come up with some new technology that stores the 1's and 0's for the CPU to use. Let's take these ideas one at a time.

Memory Storage Options

Why not store each line of code on a paper card? You could use one card for

Plus, a small problem exists. Programs generate data. [illegible] adds 2 + 3, it generates the answer of 5 on the external data bus. Cards store programs well, but what about data? You need some type of storage that accepts data from the CPU. When the CPU takes 1's and 0's from something, we call that *reading* data. The process of the CPU sending data to a storage place is called *writing* data. There's no way we can get a card to do this.

Okay, so paper cards cannot accept data. Some type of memory medium is needed that enables the CPU to both read from and write to in order to get work done. One early way of handling this problem was to place data on magnetic tape. Unlike paper cards, the CPU could write data on magnetic tape fairly easily. Magnetic tape, however, could not be randomly accessed (Figure 3.18). Every CPU has the ability to jump from one place in a program to another. If the CPU often has to jump to a new line of code, the tape would need to rewind and fast-forward constantly to get to the line of code the CPU needs.

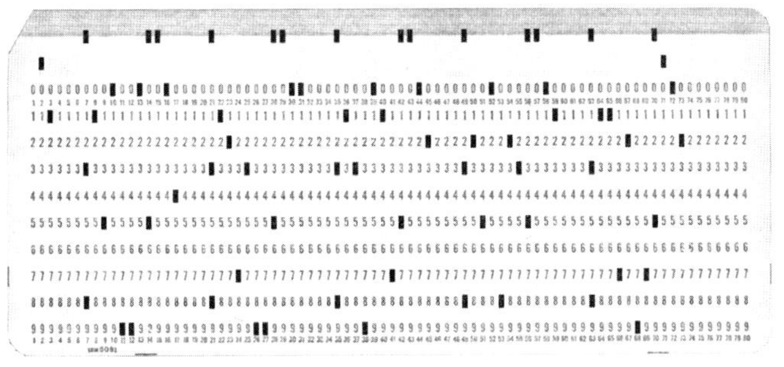

• **Figure 3.17** Paper cards can hold programs.

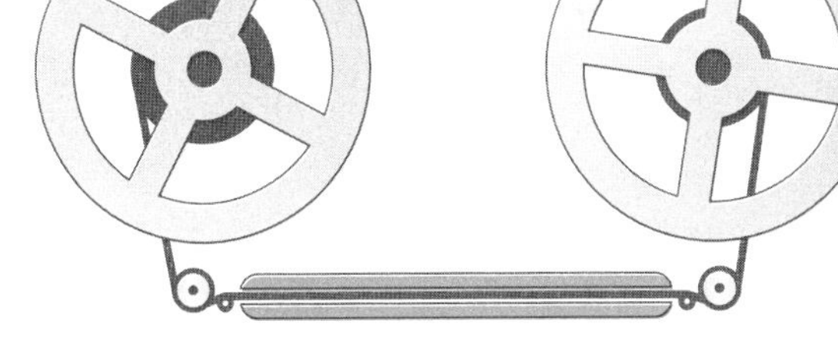

• **Figure 3.18** Streaming tape is not random access.

1	0	1	0	1	0	1	0
0	0	0	0	1	1	0	1
1	0	1	0	0	0	0	0
0	0	1	0	1	1	0	1
1	0	1	0	0	0	0	0
1	0	1	0	1	0	1	0
0	1	0	0	1	1	0	1
1	0	1	1	1	1	1	1
0	0	1	1	1	1	0	1
0	1	0	1	1	0	1	1
1	0	1	0	0	0	0	0
0	1	0	1	1	0	1	1
1	0	1	0	0	0	0	0
1	0	1	0	1	0	1	0
0	1	0	0	1	1	0	1

• **Figure 3.19** To the CPU, RAM looks like a spreadsheet.

RAM: Random Access Memory

Both paper cards and magnetic tape fail as storage media. A storage system is needed that stores not only programs, but also data. The CPU needs to be able to read and write to this storage medium. Additionally, this system must enable the CPU to jump to *any* line of code as easily as to any other line of code that it stores. All of this must be done at or at least near the clock speed of the CPU. Fortunately, this magical device has existed for many years: Random Access Memory (RAM).

In Chapter 4 the concept of RAM is developed in detail, so for now let's look at RAM as an electronic spreadsheet, like one you can generate in Microsoft Excel. Each cell in this spreadsheet can store only a one or a zero. Each cell is called a *bit*. Each row in the spreadsheet is eight bits across to match the external data bus of the 8088. Each row of eight bits is called a *byte*. In the PC world, RAM transfers and stores data to and from the CPU in byte-sized chunks. RAM is therefore arranged in byte-sized rows. Here are the terms used when talking about quantities of bits:

- Any individual 1 or 0 = a *bit*
- 4 bits = a *nibble*
- 8 bits = a *byte*
- 16 bits = a *word*
- 32 bits = a *double word*
- 64 bits = a *paragraph* or *quad word*

The number of bytes of RAM varies from PC to PC. In the earlier PCs, from around 1980 to 1990, the typical system would have only a few hundred thousand bytes of RAM. Today's systems often have hundreds of millions of bytes of RAM.

Let's stop here for a quick reality check. Electronically, RAM looks like a spreadsheet (Figure 3.19). Of course, RAM is not a spreadsheet. Physically, RAM is groups of semiconductor chips on small cards that snap into your computer (Figure 3.20).

The CPU can access any one row of RAM as easily and as fast as any other row, which explains the "random access" part of RAM. Not only is RAM randomly accessible, it's also fast. By storing programs on RAM, the CPU can access and run programs very quickly. RAM also stores any data that the CPU actively uses.

Don't confuse RAM with mass storage devices like hard drives and floppy drives. You use hard drives and floppy drives to store programs and data permanently. Later chapters discuss permanent storage in intimate detail.

• **Figure 3.20** Typical RAM

Address Bus

So far, our entire PC consists of only a CPU and RAM. We now need some connection between the CPU and the RAM so they can talk to each other. To do so, let's extend the external data bus from the CPU so that it can talk to RAM as well as other devices (Figure 3.21).

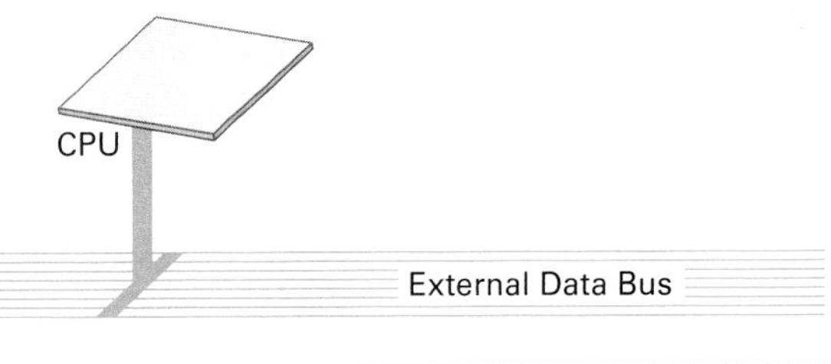

• **Figure 3.21** Extending the external data bus

Wait a minute. How can you connect the RAM to the external data bus? (See Figure 3.22.) This is not a matter of just plugging it into the external data bus wires! RAM is a spreadsheet with thousands and thousands of discrete rows, and you only need to look at the contents of one row of the spreadsheet at a time, right? So how do you connect RAM to the external data bus in such a way that the CPU can see any one given row, but still give the CPU the capability to look at *any* row in RAM?

We need some type of device to facilitate the flow of data from RAM to CPU. The CPU must be able to tell this device which row of RAM it wants, and the device should handle the mechanics of retriev-

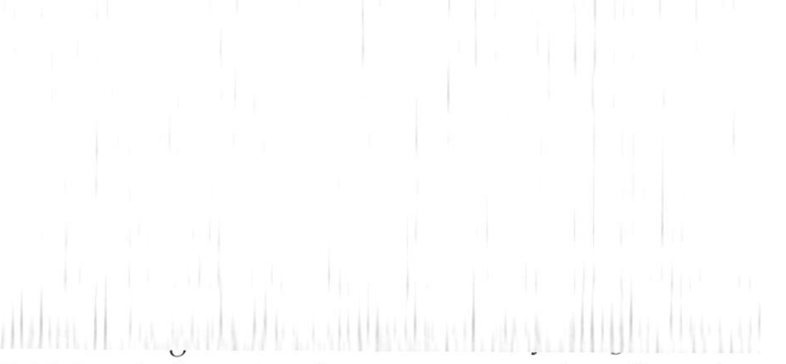

RAM and place that data or command on the external data bus. This in turn enables the CPU to act on that code (Figure 3.23).

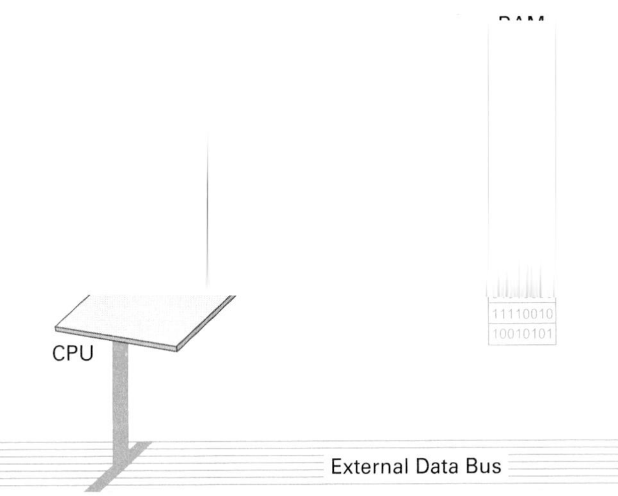

• **Figure 3.22** How can we connect RAM to the CPU?

Once the Northbridge is in place to grab any discrete byte of RAM, we need to give the CPU the capability to tell the Northbridge which line of code it needs (Figure 3.24).

The address bus enables the CPU to control the Northbridge. The address bus is another set of wires (the external data bus being the first) that runs from

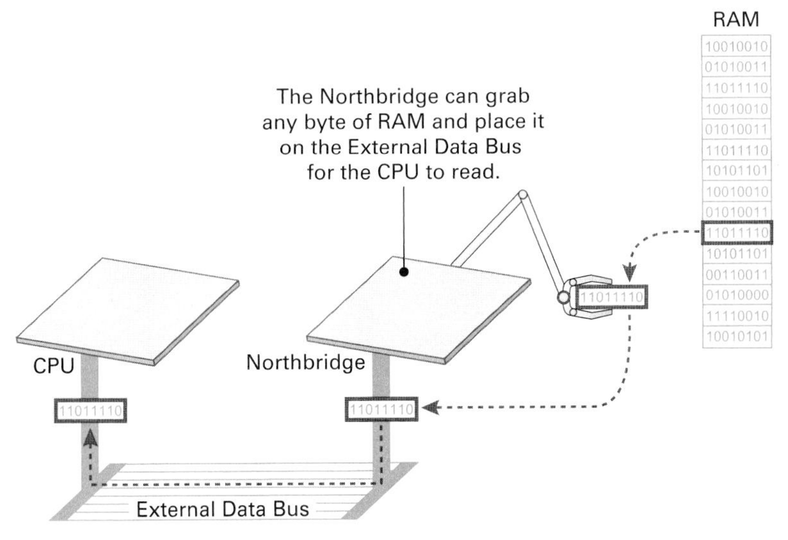

• **Figure 3.23** The Northbridge grabs a byte of RAM.

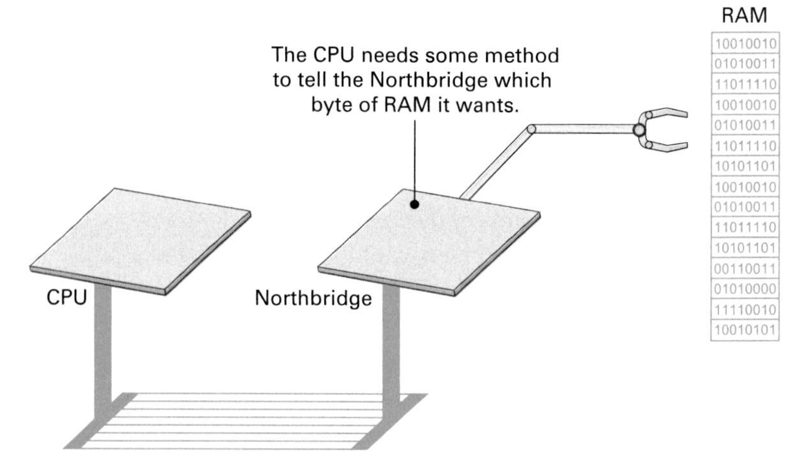

• **Figure 3.24** How can the CPU control the Northbridge?

the CPU. Different CPUs have different numbers of wires (which, you will soon see, is very significant). The 8088 had 20 wires in its address bus (Figure 3.25).

By turning wires on and off in different patterns, the CPU can tell the Northbridge which line of RAM it wants at any given moment. Let's consider these 20 wires. There are two big questions here: How many different patterns of "on" and "off" wires can exist with 20 wires? And which pattern goes to which row of RAM?

Going forward, let's put the external data bus next to the address bus, as shown in Figure 3.26. While we are at it, let's draw RAM as it really looks—just as long as you remember that to the CPU it still looks like a spreadsheet!

How Many Patterns?

The answer to the first question can be reached fairly easily by using basic math. Each wire can be only on or off, so an individual wire exists in only one of two different states: on or off. If the address bus consisted of only one

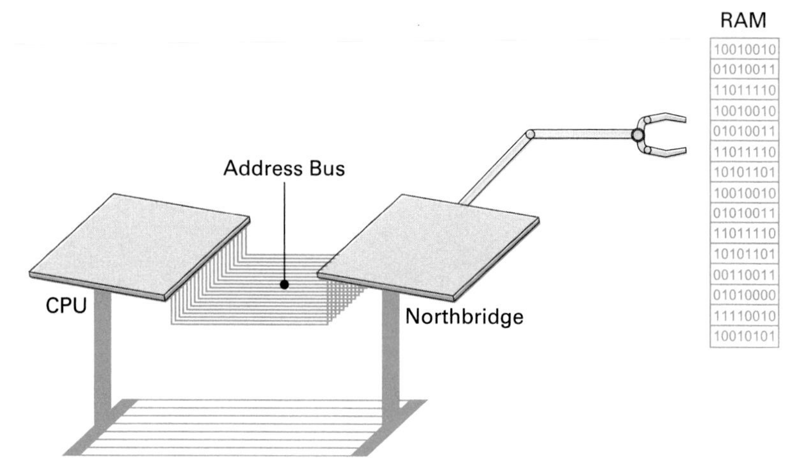

• **Figure 3.25** The address bus

wire, that wire would be at any given moment either on or off. Mathematically, that gives us (pull out your old pre-algebra books) $2^1 = 2$ different combinations. If you have two address bus wires, the address bus wires create $2^2 = 4$ different combinations. If you have 20 wires, you would have 2^{20} (or 1,048,576) combinations. Because each pattern points to one line of code and each line of RAM is one byte, *if you know the number of wires in the CPU's address bus, you know the maximum amount of RAM that a particular CPU can handle.* Because the 8088 had a 20-wire address bus, the most RAM it could handle was 2^{20} or 1,048,576 bytes. The 8088, therefore, had an *address space* of 1,048,576 bytes. This is not to say that every computer with an 8088 CPU had 1,048,576 bytes

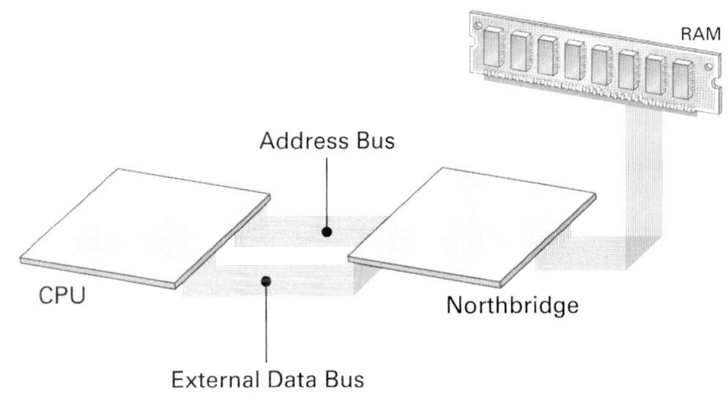

• **Figure 3.26** CPU, RAM, and Northbridge

with computers we are constantly dealing with the number of patterns a set of wires can handle. Certain powers of 2 have names that we use a lot in the computing world. The following chart explains.

1 kilo = 2^{10} = 1,024 (abbreviated as "K")
1 kilobyte = 1,024 bytes (abbreviated as "KB")
1 mega = 2^{20} = 1,048,576 (abbreviated as "M")
1 megabyte = 1,048,576 bytes (abbreviated as "MB")
1 giga = 2^{30} = 1,073,741,824 (abbreviated as "G")
1 gigabyte = 1,073,741,824 bytes (abbreviated as "GB")
1 tera = 2^{40} = 1,099,511,627,776 (abbreviated as "T")
1 terabyte = 1,099,511,627,776 bytes (abbreviated as "TB")
1 K is *not* equal to 1,000 (one thousand)
1 Mega is *not* equal to 1,000,000 (one million)
1 Giga is *not* equal to 1,000,000,000 (one billion)
1 Tera is *not* equal to 1,000,000,000,000 (one trillion)
(But they are pretty close!)

Which Pattern Goes to Which Row?

The second question is a little harder: "Which pattern goes to which row of RAM?" To understand this, let's take a moment to discuss binary counting. In binary, only two numbers exist, 0 and 1, which makes binary a handy way to work with wires that turn on and off. Let's try to count in binary: 0, 1 ... what's next? It's not 3—we can only use 0's and 1's. The next number after 1 is 10! Now let's count in binary to 1000: 0, 1, 10, 11, 100, 101, 110, 111, 1000. Try counting to 10,000. Don't worry; it hardly takes any time at all.

Super, you now count in binary as well as any math professor. Let's add to the concept. Stop thinking about binary for just a moment and think about good old base 10 (regular numbers). If you have the number 365, can you put zeros in front of the 365, like this: 000365? Sure you can—it doesn't change the value at all. Well, the same thing is true in binary. Putting zeroes in front of a value doesn't change a thing! Let's count again to 1000 in binary. In this case we will add enough zeros to make 20 places:

00000000000000000000
00000000000000000001
00000000000000000010
00000000000000000011
00000000000000000100
00000000000000000101
00000000000000000110
00000000000000000111
00000000000000001000

Hey! This would be a great way to represent each line of RAM on the address bus, wouldn't it? The CPU can identify the first byte of RAM on the address bus as 00000000000000000000. The CPU identifies the last RAM row with 11111111111111111111. When the CPU turns off all the address bus wires, it wants the first line of RAM; when it turns on all the wires, it wants the 1,048,576th line of RAM. Obviously, the address bus also addresses all the other rows of RAM in between. So, by lighting up different patterns of 1's and 0's on the address bus, the CPU can access any row of RAM it needs.

Test Specific

■ Modern CPUs

Modern CPUs retain the core structures of the Intel 8088, such as registers, instruction sets, and of course, the arithmetic logic unit—our friend, the Man in the Box. But in the decades of the personal computer, many manufacturers have risen to challenge Intel's dominance—some have even survived—and all processor makers have experimented with different processor shapes, connectors, and more. The amazing variety of modern CPUs presents unique challenges to a new tech. Which processors go on which motherboards? Can a motherboard use processors from two or more manufacturers? Aren't they all PCs and thus interchangeable?

This section maps out the modern processor scene. I'll start with a brief look at the manufacturers, so you know who the players are. The second part examines the two dominant styles of CPU package. The third and by far the largest part goes through the generations of CPU in wide use today, starting with the Intel Pentium.

All modern processors share fundamental technology first introduced by Intel in the Pentium CPU. I use the Pentium, therefore, to discuss the details of the shared technology and then add specific bonus features when discussing subsequent processors.

Manufacturers

Intel won the first round of the CPU competition wars, hitching up with IBM to oust almost every other competitor. Tandy, Commodore, Texas Instruments—no one could compete directly with Intel. Of all the early CPU competitors, only Motorola managed to survive the Intel onslaught by teaming with Apple, designing CPUs for their proprietory machines. Over time, other competitors have risen within the PC side to challenge Intel's market segment share dominance. Many fell by the wayside, such as Cyrix and IDT, but a few have survived and continue to flourish. Let's look at the two major players today, Intel and AMD, followed by a brief nod at the lesser players, VIA Technologies and Transmeta.

Intel

Pentium 4 and the Pentium M. Their lower-end CPUs use the Celeron branding; their highest-end ones are called Xeon.

AMD

You can't really talk about CPUs without mentioning Advanced Micro Devices—the "Cogswell's Cogs" to Intel's "Spacely's Sprockets." AMD makes superb CPUs for the PC market and has grabbed roughly 30–40 percent of the CPU market. Like Intel, AMD doesn't just make CPUs but their CPU business is certainly the part that the public notices. AMD has made CPUs that "clone" the function of Intel CPUs. If Intel invented the CPU used in the original IBM PC, how could AMD make clone CPUs without getting sued? Well, chipmakers have a habit of exchanging technologies through cross-license agreements. Way back in 1976 AMD and Intel signed just such an agreement, giving AMD the right to copy certain types of CPUs.

The trouble started with the Intel 8088. Intel needed AMD to produce CPUs. The PC business was young back then and providing multiple suppliers gave IBM confidence in their choice of CPUs. Life was good. But after a few years, Intel had grown tremendously and no longer wanted AMD to make CPUs. AMD said, "Too bad. See this agreement you signed?" Throughout the 1980s and into the 1990s, AMD made pin-for-pin identical CPUs that exactly matched the Intel 8088, 80286, 80386, and 80486 lines of CPUs (Figure 3.27). You could yank an Intel CPU out of a system and snap in an AMD CPU—no problem!

• **Figure 3.27** Old Intel and AMD 486s—identical

In the early-mid 1990s, after many years of legal wrangling, Intel and AMD settled and decided to end the licensing agreements. Starting with the Pentium II CPUs, AMD chips were no longer compatible—even though in some cases the chips look similar. The details of these differences fall outside the scope of this book as they matter more to programmers and high-end users than to techs, but if you're curious about the competing architecture of CPUs, check out the Tech Files at my web site, www.totalsem.com.

Today, if you want to use an AMD CPU, you must purchase a motherboard designed for AMD CPUs. If you want to use an Intel CPU, you must purchase a motherboard designed for Intel CPUs. So you now have a choice: Intel or AMD. We'll look at both brands as we learn more about modern processors in this chapter.

Lesser Players

Back in the days of the 80486 processor, a little corporation from Texas, called Cyrix, joined forces with IBM to create Intel-clone CPUs, just like AMD had done. Cyrix created a decent line of 486 clones and later, Pentium clones. Unlike AMD, however, Cyrix couldn't quite manage the heat of competition and slipped away, seemingly forever. The intellectual property of Cyrix was picked up eventually by Taiwan chip giant, VIA Technologies, who has taken full advantage of the cross-licensing agreements Cyrix had with Intel to produce clones. VIA produces a lot of Intel-compatible chipsets for motherboards and even dusted off the processor division to create low-heat versions of Intel-compatible CPUs.

Transmeta corporation produces the Crusoe, an extremely low-power Intel-compatible processor that has made inroads into the portable computer market. Lower power means less electricity needed, obviously, and thus longer battery life. The Crusoe is further distinguished because it does not completely use the same architecture as other PC CPUs, relying on a tiny software layer to emulate full Intel compatibility. Transmeta argues that the software layer enables the Crusoe to be programmed for new instructions and thus much more adaptable than other PC CPUs. It's certainly interesting technology and time will tell whether it will be adopted by other manufacturers.

Neither VIA nor Transmeta CPUs show up on the A+ Certification exams.

CPU Packages

CPUs have gone through many packages, with manufacturers changing designs like snakes shedding skins. The fragile little DIP package of the 8088 gave way to rugged slotted processors in the late 1990s, which have in turn given way to CPUs with hundreds of fragile, exposed pins. Modern CPUs have only used two types of packages: the PGA and the SEC. Let's look at both of these.

PGA

Although there are many types of PGA packages, most techs just call them all "PGA."

The **Pin Grid Array** (PGA) package has been popular since the mid-1980s. Although it did fall out of favor during the Pentium II years, it is once again the predominant CPU package. PGA CPUs are distinguished by their square shape with many—usually hundreds—of tiny pins.

The PGA package has a number of variations (Figure 3.28). There are three common variations based on material used to make the CPU. Ceramic PGA (CPGA) is the oldest type of package, followed by Plastic PGA (PPGA). The most common PGA is called Flip-Chip PGA (FC-PGA). FC-PGA means the CPU is soldered onto a small board.

There are also many different varieties of PGA CPUs based on the number of pins sticking out of the CPU. These CPUs snap into special sockets on the motherboard, with each socket designed for the number of pins the CPU needs. The first PGA sockets were difficult to use and required a special tool to remove the CPU. To make CPU insertion and removal easier, Intel designed a type of socket called **Zero Insertion Force** (ZIF) sockets (Figure 3.29). ZIF sockets are now universal and are easily identified by their squarish shape and removal arm.

Intel standardized each type of ZIF socket by the number of pins it used. At first, (back in the 486 days) Intel called their sockets "Socket 1," "Socket 2," etc. You could easily tell the socket simply by looking at the identification label on the socket itself (Figure 3.30).

Our interest in sockets starts with the Pentium. Intel de-

AMD likes to separate itself from Intel so it gives all of the AMD-specific sockets letters instead of the number of pins. So far, AMD has only one type of socket, the 462-pin *Socket A*.

AMD CPUs and sockets are totally different than Intel CPUs and sockets so we often use the name of the socket instead of the model. For example: "Hey, is that a Socket A motherboard?"

SEC

With the Pentium II, Intel made a bold move by ditching the traditional PGA package and unveiling a totally new CPU packaging called the **Single Edge Cartridge** (SEC). As the name implies, the SEC was a cartridge that snapped into a special slot on the motherboard called *Slot 1*. (See Figure 3.31.)

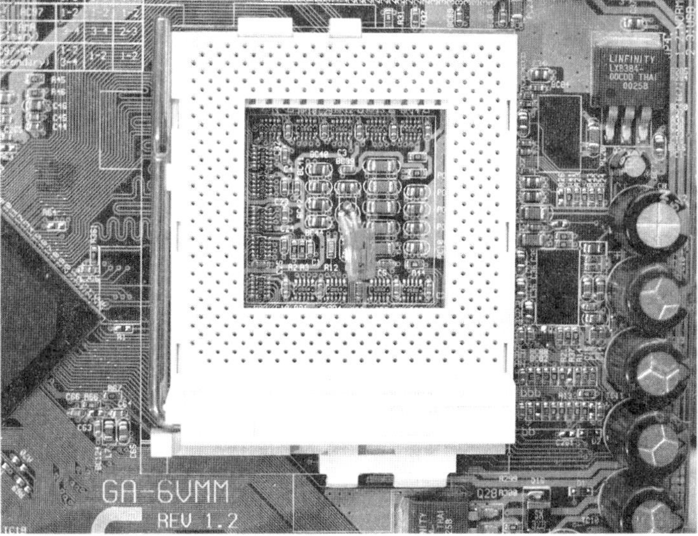

Figure 3.29 Typical ZIF socket

• **Figure 3.30** Close-up of socket showing its identifier

Intel had two variations of the SEC cartridge, both of which still snapped into the same Slot 1 connector. SEC2 cartridges only had a front cover while the short-lived Single Edge Processor (SEP) connectors had no cover at all! (See Figure 3.32.)

Not to be left out, AMD processors used the same general concept although their CPU packages were known as Slot A (Figure 3.33).

Slot A and Slot 1 were physically very similar but completely incompatible. It would be difficult to tell a Slot 1 CPU from a Slot A CPU with a quick glance.

The Pentium CPU: The Early Years

Since the advent of the 8088 way back in the late 1970s, CPU makers have added a large number of improvements. As technology has progressed from the 8088 to the most current CPUs, the sizes of the external data bus,

• **Figure 3.31** SEC cartridge CPU

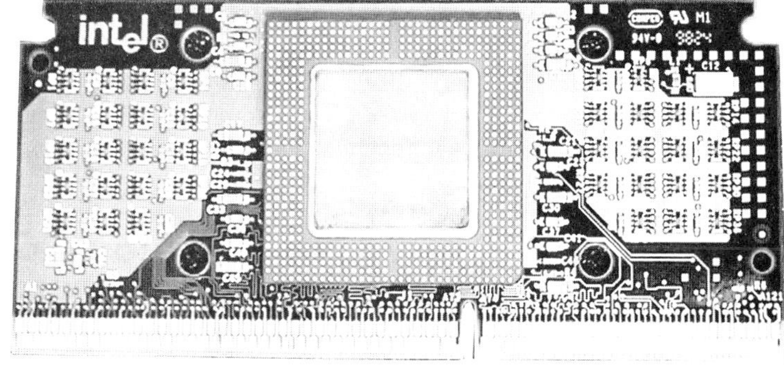

• Figure 3.32 SEP cartridge

• Figure 3.33 Slot A CPU

speeds, and other improvements.

In the early 1990s, Intel unveiled the famous Pentium CPU. Although no longer manufactured, the Pentium CPU was the first Intel CPU to contain all of the core functions that define today's modern CPUs.

Man in Box Redux

Let's take a look at these improvements by evolving our friendly Man in the Box to the standards of an Intel Pentium processor. The Pentium retained the core features of the 8088 and subsequent processors, although the clock

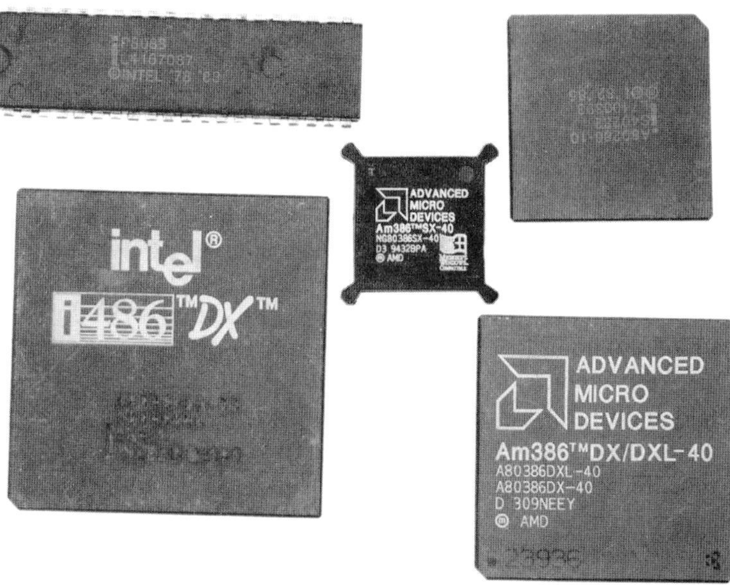

• Figure 3.34 Intel 8088, 80286, 80386, and 80486 CPUs

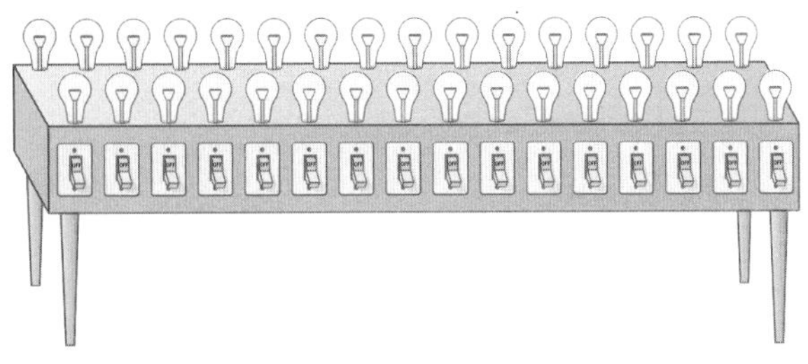

• **Figure 3.35** 32-bit register

is much faster, the address bus and external data bus are wider, and the registers have more bits. You'll also see a number of other improvements that simply didn't exist on the original 8088. For starters, all the registers in the Pentium are 32-bit, enabling the Pentium to process larger numbers at a single time. So instead of just having 16 light bulbs, each Pentium register had 32! (See Figure 3.35.)

Additionally, the Pentium CPU ran at speeds up to roughly 300 MHz, quite a bit faster than the old 8088's 4.77 MHz! So let's upgrade the Man in Box to Super Man in Box (Figure 3.36).

The Pentium has many other features that are standard on all CPUs today, such as the ability to run multiple programs at once, access super-fast cache RAM, and process two or more lines of code at the same time. Pentium and later processors run at some multiple of the system clock speed, but do so at voltages far below the rest of the PC. Let's look at each feature in detail for the Pentium processor and then turn to developments in later processors.

Modern multiprocessor support was first introduced with the Intel 80386 CPU.

Tech Tip

Multiprocessing, Multiple Processors, What Gives!

Don't confuse "multiprocessing" with "multiple processors." The nomenclature is a bit confusing here—all the term "multiprocessing" means is that the CPU can handle "multiple processes," or programs, at one time. Multiprocessing does not mean that the CPU can be used in system with other CPUs, like in large-scale servers, which sometimes have two, four, or even eight CPUs total!

Multiprocessing

Most PC users today do not think twice about running two or more applications at the same time, such as surfing the Internet in Internet Explorer, a half-finished Word document open in the background, and Media Player dishing out your favorite tunes. But when the 8088 first came out the concept of running more than one program at a time—a feature called *multiprocessing*—simply didn't exist. In those days, we started up one program, did whatever we needed to do, closed that program, and then started another. The 8088 could not process more than one program at a time. Intel designed the Pentium processor from the ground up to support multiprocessing with two critical features: a wider address bus and special registers that track all running programs.

The Pentium processor has a 32-wire address bus, giving it the ability to address 2^{32} or 4,294,967,296 bytes (four gigabytes) of memory. If a CPU is going to run more than one program at a time, it needs to support lots of RAM, as all running programs must reside in memory. A 32-bit address bus provides plenty of RAM support (Figure 3.37).

I'm going to let you in on a little secret—your CPU can't run more than one program at a time! It's true! All CPUs actually run multiple programs by quickly switching from one program to the next, running a few lines of one program, then another, then another, and back again to the first program. The Pentium has special memory management registers that track the location in memory of every running program so that when the CPU returns to a certain program, it picks up exactly where it left off! (See Figure 3.38.)

• **Figure 3.36** Super Man in Box

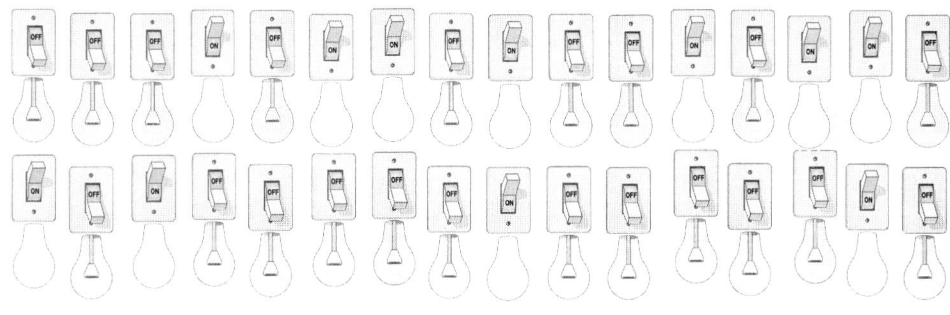

• **Figure 3.37** 32-wire address bus

With a 32-bit address bus and 32-bit registers, the Pentium CPU is con-

easily (and much more quickly) access that data.

Programs and data usually reside on some sort of mass storage device, such as a floppy disk, hard drive, or CD-ROM disc. When you access that data or application, the system must go first to the mass storage and then copy all the relevant files into RAM. Only then can the CPU work with that information. The data returns through the same process: the CPU writes to RAM, and RAM writes to mass storage (Figure 3.39).

This process runs into two major bottlenecks: mass storage is much slower than RAM, and RAM is much slower than the CPU. **Caching** enables you to speed up the system by creating special storage areas for data that is being moved from the hard drive, RAM, and CPU. Based on the diagram in Figure 3.40, you can see that there are two distinct types of caches: one for data moving between mass storage and RAM—a *disk cache*—and another for data moving from RAM to the CPU—a *RAM cache*. At this point, let's concentrate on the RAM cache.

• **Figure 3.38** Super Man in the Box with memory manager registers

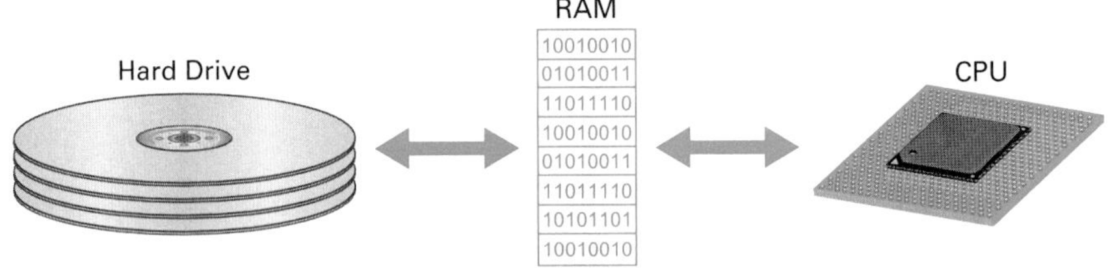

• **Figure 3.39** Mass storage, RAM, and the CPU

DRAM and Why It Is Cached Dynamic RAM (DRAM) is the RAM of choice for the PC world. DRAM is cheap, small, and relatively fast, although not as fast as today's CPUs. DRAM uses a microscopic capacitor and transistor for each storage bit. A charged capacitor is a "1" and a discharged capacitor is a "0" (Figure 3.41).

DRAM, however, has a small problem: the capacitors. A capacitor resembles a battery in that it holds a charge and then discharges it. Unlike a battery that holds a charge for months, the tiny capacitors in the DRAM hold their charges for about 16 milliseconds. Therefore, the DRAM needs an entire set of circuitry to keep the capacitors charged. The process of recharging these capacitors is called *refresh*. Without refresh, data added to RAM would disappear after 16 milliseconds, which is why DRAM is considered volatile RAM. Imagine the refresh circuitry as the Northbridge using an electronic garden hose to spray a refreshing charge of electricity on the DRAM (Figure 3.42).

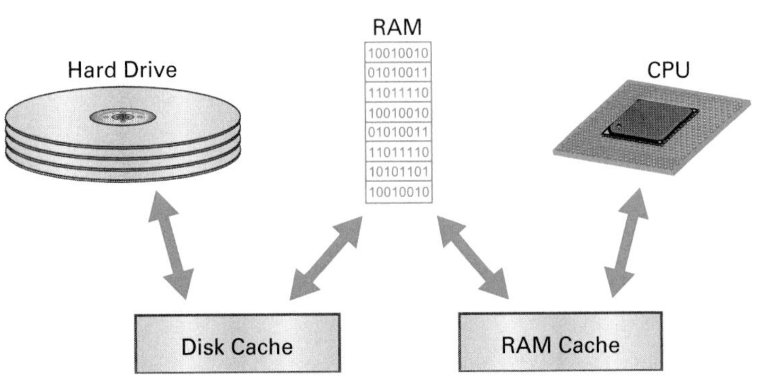

• **Figure 3.40** Disk cache and RAM cache

The Northbridge tells the refresh circuitry on the DRAM chip when to refresh. Every few milliseconds, the Northbridge sends a refresh signal to the RAM, and the RAM chips begin their refresh. Unfortunately, if the CPU decides to access the RAM at this point, the Northbridge creates a *wait state* (Figure 3.43). The other problem with DRAM is that it is not as fast as

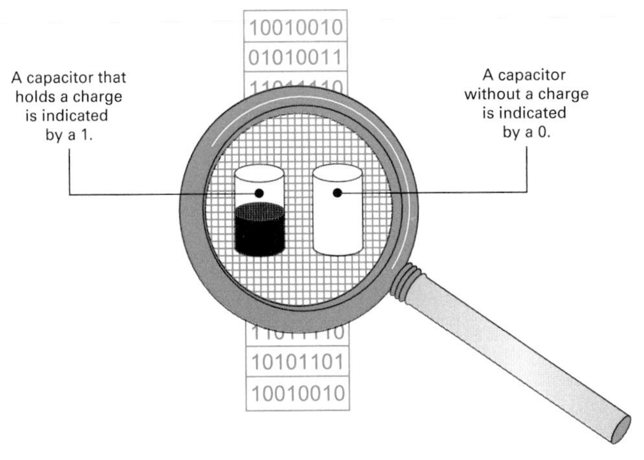

• **Figure 3.41** Each "1" or "0" is a capacitor.

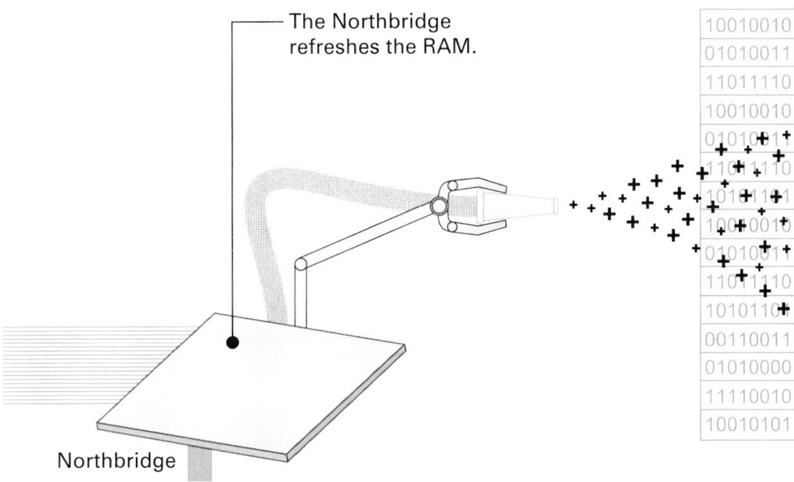

SRAM Wait states cause the computer to slow down. By getting around wait states, you could significantly increase computer speed. You can do this by adding special **Static RAM** (SRAM) chips to the computer. SRAM is a type of RAM that does not use tiny capacitors to store 1's and 0's. Instead, SRAM uses a special circuit called a *flip-flop*. Using flip-flops instead of capacitors means that SRAM does not have to be refreshed. SRAM is almost as fast as the fastest CPU. SRAM easily trumps DRAM in terms of performance, but its relatively high cost (up to ten times that of DRAM!) keeps it from replacing DRAM as the main system memory. Manufacturers instead have inserted a tiny amount of SRAM as a special RAM cache for the CPU.

DRAM is fast, cheap, and must be refreshed; SRAM is much faster, very expensive, and requires no refresh.

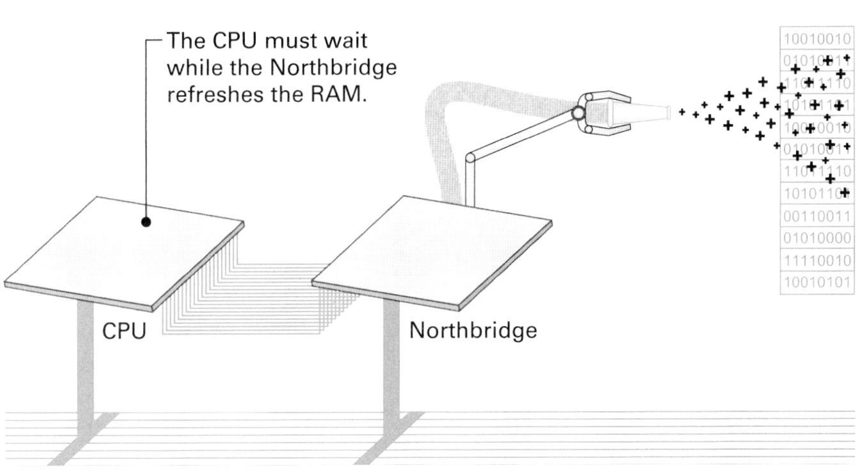

• **Figure 3.43** Northbridge forcing a wait state

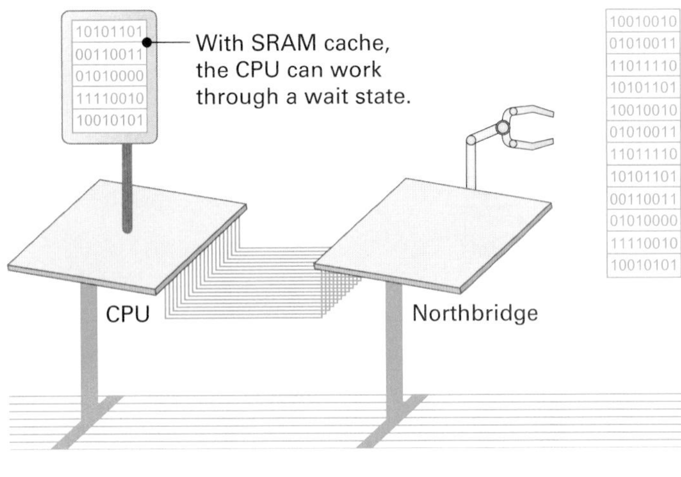

• **Figure 3.44** Northbridge using cache

RAM caching stores the upcoming code for the CPU to use when it (the CPU) is ready.

RAM Cache Inside of every Pentium CPU is a small (16 KB) SRAM cache, called the *internal cache* (Figure 3.44). The internal cache stores a backlog of commands so that when the CPU encounters a wait state, the Pentium does not have to stop; it simply keeps processing commands stored in the cache.

The Pentium cache was capable of *branch prediction,* where the program cache attempted to anticipate program branches before they got to the CPU itself. An IF statement provides a nice example of this: "If the value in the AX register = 5, stop running this code and jump to another memory location." Such a jump would make all of the data in the cache useless. The internal cache in the Pentium could recognize a branch statement and would take code from both sides of the branch (it wasn't smart enough to know which way it was going to go) so that no matter which way the code went, the cache would have good data.

Although an internal cache on the CPU is very helpful, a CPU will happily use all the cache it can get. Therefore, almost all the Pentium CPUs used an *external* cache as well. The first external caches manifested themselves with special SRAM chips that sat on the motherboard. An external cache was much larger than the Pentium's internal cache: usually around 64 KB to 1 MB, depending mainly on the size of your wallet (Figure 3.45).

Wait a minute, why didn't Intel just make a Pentium with a bigger internal cache? Why have two caches and mess things up? Well, the first reason is cost. Making a cache tiny enough to fit inside a CPU is very expensive. The other reason is that a big external second cache that works well with the internal cache is almost as good as one internal cache of the same size as the external.

The next generation of Intel CPUs after the Pentium was the Pentium Pro. The Pentium Pro has a built-in second cache, so suddenly the terms external and internal don't work very well. Instead we use the term *L1 cache* to

• **Figure 3.45** Pentium-era external cache chips

define the first cache the CPU uses. L1 caches are the smallest but they also run at close to if not the same speed as the CPU. The next cache the CPU uses is the *L2 cache;* and yes, the latest CPUs have an *L3 cache*!

It is common to combine the terms internal/external and L1/L2. For example: "The Intel Pentium CPU could use an external L2 cache."

Multiple Pipelines

All CPUs have a **pipeline**, the series of steps the CPU needs to process a command. Remember how we discussed the fact that you have to hit the clock wire a number of times before the answer appeared when we added 2 + 3? That is a perfect example of the CPU's pipeline processing the command. Each clock cycle moves the command one step along the pipeline. Different CPUs have different pipelines, but they all have the same basic steps. Figure 3.46 illustrates the pipeline for a Pentium.

Think of pipelining as doing laundry. You don't sort, wash, dry, fold, [illegible]

Well, a Pentium has a second, separate set of circuitry that enables more than one command (of certain types) to be processed at a time. This is called *dual pipelining.*

While the Pentium has two pipelines, you'll see that later CPUs have even more.

Clock Speed and Multipliers

In the earliest motherboards, the clock chip pushed every chip on the motherboard, not just the CPU. This setup worked great for a while until it became obvious that CPU makers (really Intel) could make CPUs with a much higher clock speed than the rest of the chips on the motherboard. So Intel had a choice: either stop making faster CPUs or come up with some way to make CPUs run faster than the rest of the computer (Figure 3.49).

To circumvent this problem, Intel came up with the idea of a clock multiplying CPU. A **clock multiplying CPU** takes the incoming clock signal and multiples it inside the CPU to let the internal circuitry of the CPU run faster. The secret to making clock multiplying work is caching. CPUs with caches spend the majority of the clock cycles performing internal calculations, not sending any data on the external buses.

Clock multiplying first surfaced during the reign of the 486 CPUs. All the first clock multipliers exactly doubled the clock speed, resulting in the term "clock doubling." This term is used interchangeably with "clock multiplying," even though modern CPUs multiply far more than just x2!

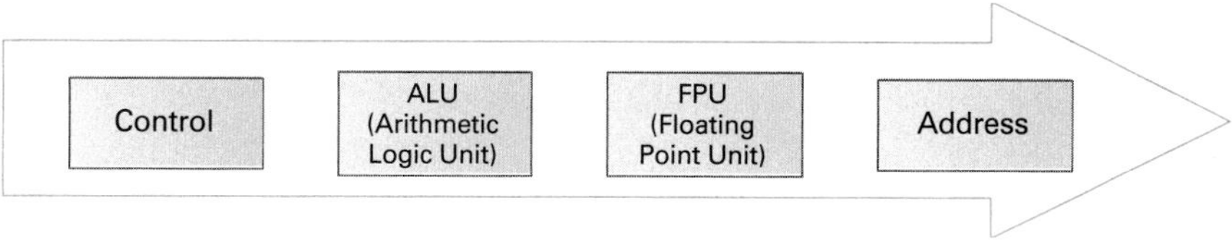

• **Figure 3.46** Simplified CPU pipeline

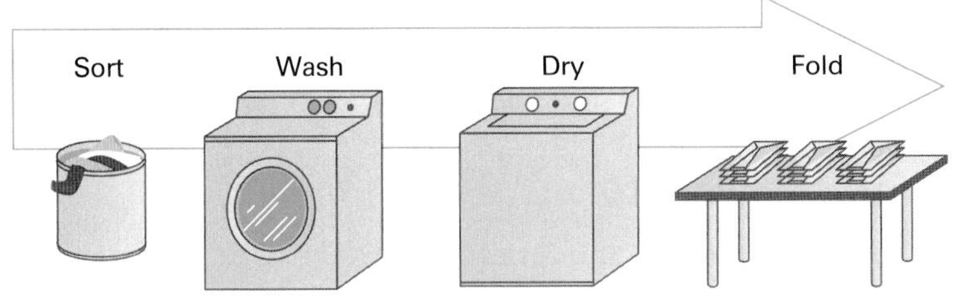

• **Figure 3.47** Pipelining is like doing laundry.

All modern CPUs are clock multipliers. So in reality, all CPUs now have two **clock speeds** : the speed that it runs internally and the speed that it runs when talking on the address bus and the external data bus. Multipliers run from x2 up to in excess of x20! Multipliers do not have to be whole numbers. You can find a CPU with a multiplier of x6.5 just as easily as you would find one with a multiplier of x7. A late-generation Pentium would have an external speed of 66 MHz multiplied by x4.5 for an internal speed of 300 MHz. The Intel Pentium 4 3.06-GHz CPU runs at an external speed of 133 MHz with a x23 multiplier to make—yes, you've got it—3.06 GHz. Without the invention of multiplying, modern CPUs would be nowhere near their current blazing speeds.

The clock speed and the multiplier on Pentium CPU systems had to be manually configured via jumpers on the motherboard (Figure 3.50). Today's modern CPUs actually report to the motherboard through a function called CPUID (CPU Identifier) and the speed and multiplier are set automatically. Given the automatic nature of multiplying, you'll rarely find a CPU that advertises its slow external speed. When you see the advertised speed of the CPU, you're seeing the much faster internal speed.

CPU Voltages

A CPU is little more than a huge conglomeration of millions of tiny transistors. All transistors create heat, and the faster you make a transistor work, the more heat it generates. Each of the tiny transistors in a CPU generate a trivial amount of heat individually, but as you add more and more transistors to faster and faster generations of CPUs, the amount of heat becomes significant. If a CPU gets too hot, it locks up and does not operate.

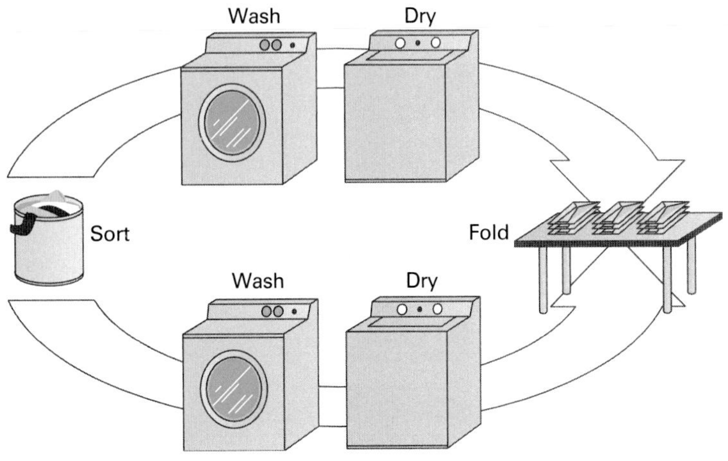

• **Figure 3.48** Dual pipelines are comparable to having extra equipment.

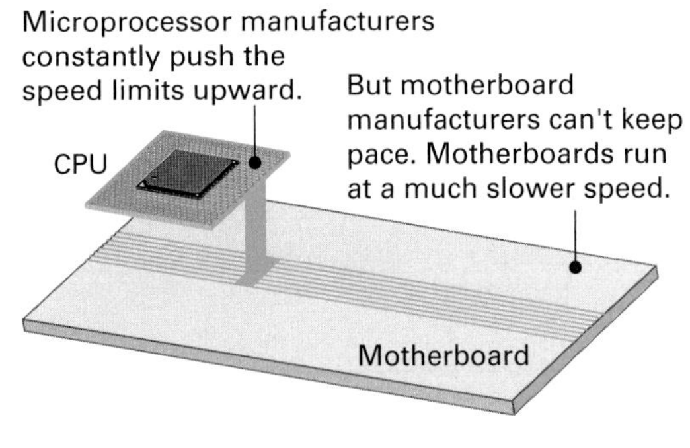

• **Figure 3.49** Simplified graphic showing clock and CPU

For the first ten years of the personal computer, every CPU ran at 5 volts. As CPUs developed the number of transistors inside a CPU grew dramatically. Lots of voltage makes lots of heat so CPU makers long ago worked to reduce the power usage from 5 volts to lower voltages with each generation of processor. While CPUs used lower voltages, however, motherboards continued to use 5V. As a result, every motherboard made today has at least one or more built-in voltage regulators (Figure 3.51).

When the Pentium was popular you had many different models of Pentium to choose from, each with different voltages. You had to set the right voltage manually using jumpers. If you installed a CPU with the wrong voltage—oh, boy!—you *did not* want to do that! Reducing voltages is great for making cooler CPUs but it is hard on the motherboard makers. During the Pentium years, the number of different voltages was staggering, often forcing one motherboard to have to support six to ten different volt-

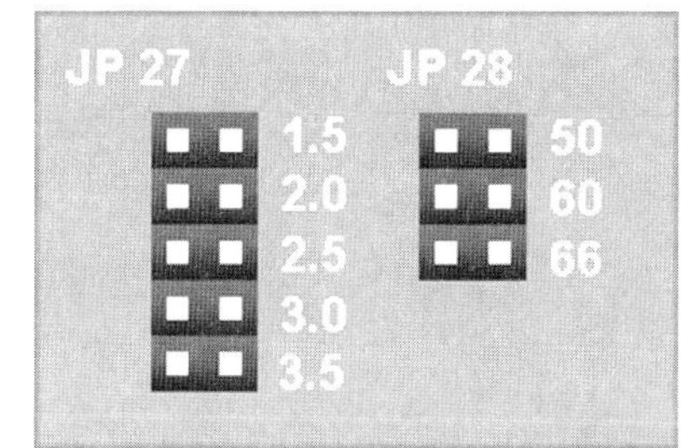

• **Figure 3.50** Manual jumper settings on a Pentium motherboard

CPU voltage unless necessary. That, combined with advancements in voltage regulators, has reduced VRMs to just a few brands of computers. Odds are good that unless you stumble into a fancy server, you'll never see a VRM.

Getting the voltage right on today's CPUs is no longer a concern. Just as for clock speed and multiplier, today's CPUs tell the motherboard the voltage they need automatically.

Intel provided a major technological leap forward when they introduced the Pentium processor in 1993 (Figure 3.53). The Pentium had a 64-bit external data bus that split internally as two dual-pipelined 32-bit data buses. These data buses enabled the CPU to process two separate lines of code simultaneously.

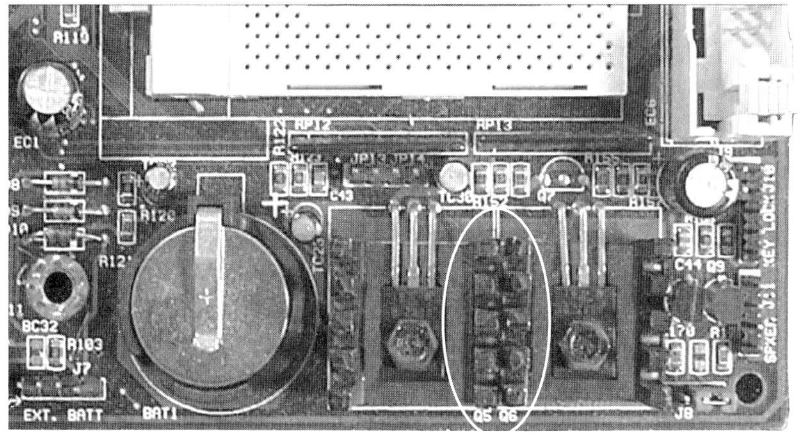

• **Figure 3.51** Modern voltage regulator

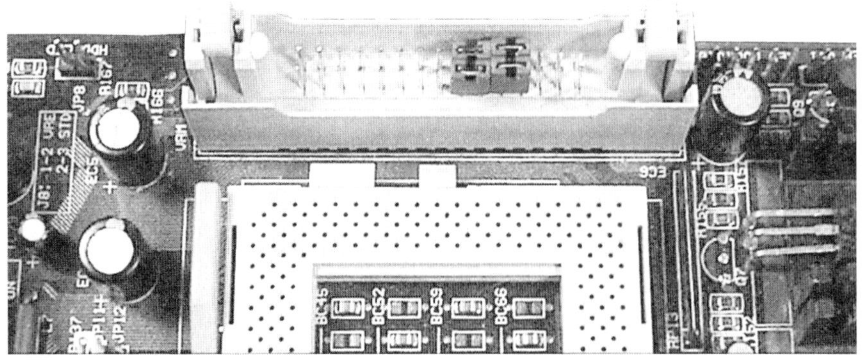

• **Figure 3.52** VRM socket

• **Figure 3.53** Early Pentium

Here's a synopsis of the early Pentium-class CPUs.

Early Intel Pentiums

- 5th Generation CPU
- External Speed Range: 50–66 MHz
- Internal Speed Range: 60–200 MHz
- Multiplier Range: x1–x3
- L1 Cache: Yes, 16 KB
- L2 Cache: No
- L3 Cache: No
- Package: PGA
- Socket(s) used: Socket 4, Socket 5

• **Figure 3.54** AMD K5

AMD made a competitor to the Pentium called the AMD K5 (Figure 3.54). The AMD K5 was pin-compatible to the Pentium, but to keep Intel from suing them AMD made the K5 very different on the inside, using a totally new (at least for Intel) method of processing. The AMD K5 had some success but was rather quickly upstaged by better AMD CPUs.

While AMD and Intel are by far the primary CPU makers for the PC market, they are not alone. One CPU that was rather popular back in the Pentium days was the Cyrix 6x86 (Figure 3.55). This Pentium-compatible CPU had support from IBM, giving it some rather hot sales, but was quickly overwhelmed by better CPUs. Cyrix stills sells CPUs under the VIA name but their sales are not significant.

AMD/Cyrix Pentium Equivalents

- 5th Generation CPUs
- External Speed Range: 50–75 MHz
- Internal Speed Range: 60–150 MHz
- Multiplier Range: x1.5–x2
- L1 Cache: Yes, 16 KB
- L2 Cache: No
- L3 Cache: No
- Package: PGA
- Socket(s) used: Socket 7

• **Figure 3.55** Cyrix 6x86

Pentium—the Basis of Today's CPUs

The Pentium is not a new chip—it's been around since 1990 and the last versions of the Pentium chip were discontinued in 1995. However, newer CPUs with names like Pentium II, Pentium III, and Pentium 4 all still use the many components that you've just seen on the original Pentium CPUs. However, almost all of these components have evolved considerably. We'll look at all the popular CPUs developed since the Pentium and see how they've built on this legacy CPU.

Pentium Pro

In 1995, Intel released the next generation of CPU, the Pentium Pro, often called the P6. The P6 had the same bus and register sizes as the Pentium. Three new items made the P6 more powerful than its predecessor: quad pipelining, dynamic processing, and an on-chip L2 cache. We'll discuss what these are next. On the other hand, Intel optimized the P6 for true 32-bit code, which made the Pentium Pro often slower than a Pentium when running 16-bit code (DOS and Windows 3.x). The Pentium Pro had a distinc-

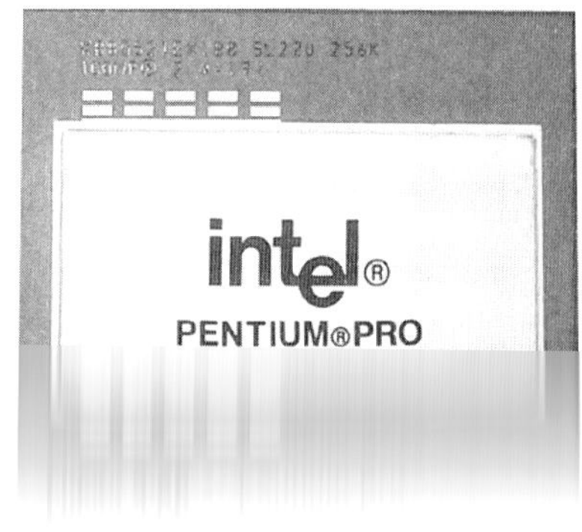

- Multiplier Range: x2.5–x3
- Socket(s) used: Socket 8
- L1 Cache: Yes, 16 KB

Quad Pipelining

The Pentium was a dual-pipelined CPU, but the P6 could handle four separate pipelines simultaneously. On average, this enabled the equivalent of three simultaneous processes.

Dynamic Processing

From time to time, a CPU must go to DRAM to access code, no matter how good its cache. When a RAM access takes place, the CPU must wait a few clock cycles before processing. Sometimes the wait can be 10 or 20 clock cycles. When the P6 was forced into wait states, it took advantage of the wait to look at the code in the pipeline to see if any commands could be run while the wait states were active. If it found commands it could process that were not dependent on the data being fetched from DRAM, it would run these commands *out of order*. After the DRAM returned with the code, it rearranged the commands and continued processing.

On-Chip L2 Cache

The P6 had both an L1 and an L2 cache on the CPU. Because the L2 cache was on the chip, it ran almost as fast as the L1 cache (Figure 3.57). Be careful with the term "on-chip"! Just because it was on the chip, that doesn't mean that the L2 cache was built into the CPU. The CPU and the L2 cache shared the same chip but electronically they were separate!

The inclusion of the L2 cache on the chip gave rise to some new terms to describe the connections between the CPU, Northbridge, RAM, and L2 cache. The address bus and external data bus are now lumped between the CPU, Northbridge, and RAM into a single term called the **frontside bus** and the connection between the CPU and the L2 cache into the term **backside bus**.

So, even though the external data bus still exists, we rarely use that term anymore. Figure 3.58 shows a more modern configuration, labeling the important buses. Note that the external data bus and address bus are there, but the chipset provides separate address buses and external data buses—one set just for the CPU and another set for the rest of the devices in the PC. No official name has been given to the interface between the RAM and the chipset. On the rare occasions when it is discussed, most techs simply call it the *RAM interface*.

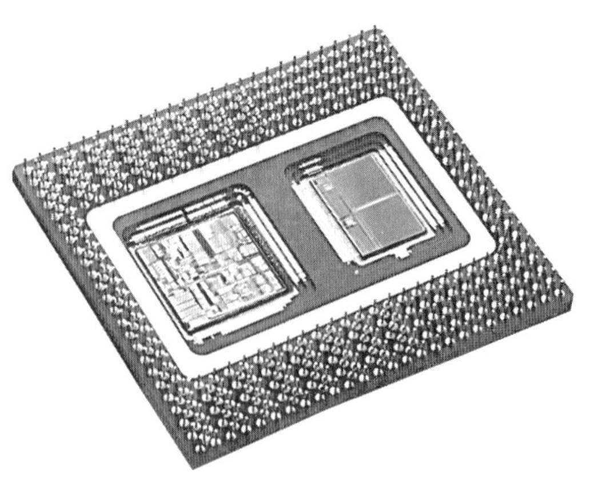

• **Figure 3.57** Open sample Pentium Pro showing CPU and L2 cache

The Pentium Pro had a unique PGA case that fit into a special socket, called Socket 8. No other CPU used this type of socket (Figure 3.59). The Pentium Pro made strong inroads in the high-end server market, but its poor performance running DOS and Windows 3.*x* programs, combined with its high cost, made it unacceptable as most people's desktop computer.

Although the Pentium Pro never saw a large volume of sales compared with the Pentium or Pentium II, many people in the industry consider it to be the most important chip ever created by Intel. The feature set of the Pentium Pro was the prototype for all CPUs designed ever since.

Later Pentium-Class CPUs

Intel's usual game plan in the rough and tumble business of chip making is to introduce a new CPU and simultaneously declare all previous CPUs obsolete. This did not happen with the Pentium Pro, however, because Intel never really developed the P6 for most users. It was to be the CPU for powerful, higher-end systems. This kept the Pentium as the CPU of choice for all but the most power-hungry systems.

While the Pentium Pro languished on the high end for several years, Intel and AMD developed new Pentium-class CPUs that incorporated a series of powerful improvements, some of which were taken from the Pentium Pro.

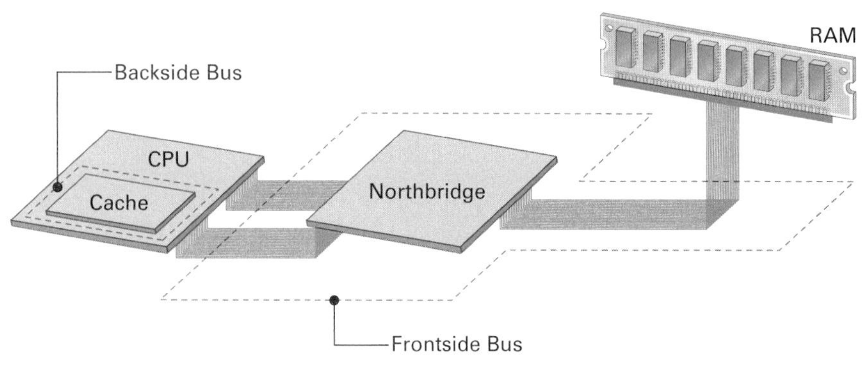

• **Figure 3.58** Frontside and backside buses

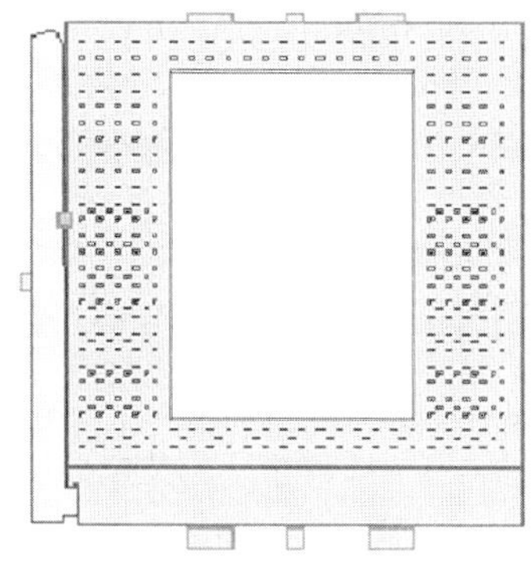

• **Figure 3.59** Socket 8, used by the Pentium Pro

These improvements required that they be regarded as a new family of CPUs, which I call the "later Pentium-class CPUs" (Figure 3.60). Although certainly some profound differences exist between these CPUs, they all have four groups of similar improvements: multimedia extensions (MMX), split voltage, increased multipliers/clocks, and improved processing.

• **Figure 3.60** Late-generation Pentium

Later Pentium CPUs

- 5th Generation CPU
- External Speed Range: 66–75 MHz
- Internal Speed Range: 166–200 MHz
- Multiplier Range: x2.5–x4.5
- L1 Cache: Yes, 32 KB
- L2 Cache: No
- L3 Cache: No
- Package: PGA
- Socket(s) used: Socket 7

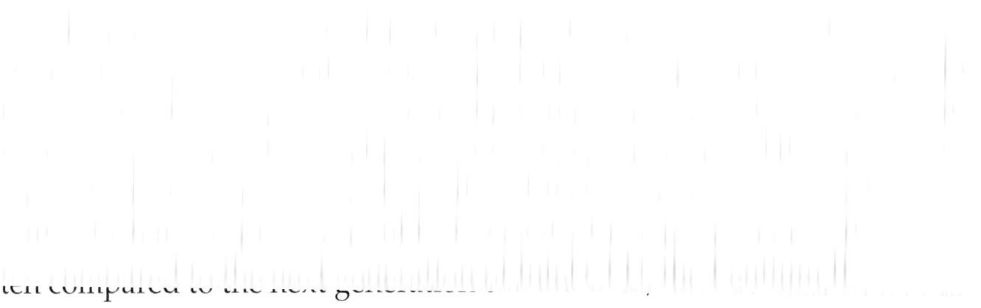

MMX

In 1996, Intel added a new enhancement to its Pentium CPU, called **multimedia extensions** (MMX). MMX manifests as four new registers and 57 new commands added to the Pentium codebook. These commands can be used to move and manipulate large chunks of data. This capability is particularly helpful (and was designed) for graphical applications such as games. Both Cyrix and AMD copied the MMX extensions in their CPUs. The downside to MMX is that applications need to be written to take advantage of MMX. Although a few such applications have been written, more advanced functions have been added to CPUs that have somewhat eclipsed MMX.

MMX is kind of like the built-in math coprocessor. You get it whether you need it or not. All new CPUs from all manufacturers are MMX enabled. You can't save money by trying to buy a non-MMX CPU.

Split Voltage

Most Pentium CPUs ran at 3.3 volts. Improvements in CPU manufacturing continued, resulting in Pentium-class CPUs that ran at voltages even lower than 3.3 volts. Yet these CPUs still needed 3.3 volts in order to communicate with other chips on the motherboard. To fulfill both needs, all later Pentium-class processors had *split voltage*. They need two different voltages to operate properly. Although later Pentium-class processors used the same Socket 7 used by earlier Pentiums, you couldn't install a later Pentium-class CPU into these earlier motherboards, as those motherboards did not provide the proper voltage.

Manufacturers produced a whole new family of motherboards to support split-voltage CPUs. This new type of motherboard, Super Socket 7,

Cross Check

Microprocessor Improvements

During the reign of the Pentium and Pentium Pro CPUs, chip makers added a number of significant improvements to their design and capabilities. Can you identify which microprocessor features date from the original Pentium CPU, which from the Pentium Pro, and which from later Pentium-class processors?

could support any Socket 7 CPU, from the early Pentiums to the last of the powerful AMD K6 series. The actual socket on a Super Socket 7 motherboard was absolutely identical to a regular Socket 7—the difference is in the broad selection of voltages, motherboard speeds, and multipliers provided by the Super Socket 7 motherboard.

Increased Clocks and Multipliers

Later Pentiums all have vastly increased multipliers, resulting in higher speeds. Most early Pentiums used x2.5 multipliers at best, but later Pentium-class processors had up to x4.5 multipliers.

Improved Processing

All later Pentium-class processors have some improvement over the earlier Pentium's original branch prediction. The Intel Pentium has made a slight improvement by making the branch prediction a little smarter, giving it a better chance of getting the correct code. The AMD K6 incorporated the Pentium Pro features of speculative execution and out-of-order execution, making it more like the Pentium Pro and Pentium II (see the next section) than the Pentium.

Pentium II

Intel's next major CPU was the Pentium II. Although highly touted as the next generation of CPU, the Pentium II was little more than a faster Pentium Pro with MMX and a refined instruction set. The Pentium II came in a distinctive SEC cartridge that gave more space for the L2 cache and made CPU cooling easier while freeing up more room on the motherboard (Figure 3.61). Aggressive advertising and pricing made the Pentium II extremely popular.

Intel Pentium II CPUs

- 6th Generation CPU
- External Speed Range: 66–100 MHz
- Internal Speed Range: 233–450 MHz
- Multiplier Range: x3.5–x4.5
- L1 Cache: Yes, 32 KB
- L2 Cache: Yes, 512 KB
- L3 Cache: No
- Package: SEC
- Socket(s) used: Slot 1

The Pentium II initially achieved the higher clock speeds by using high multiples of a 66 MHz external speed. During this time, however, AMD began to sell CPUs designed to run on 100 MHz motherboards. Although the final Pentium II models also ran on 100 MHz motherboards, Intel's slow adoption of 100 MHz external speed CPUs lost market share for Intel.

The SEC cartridge also created another problem: it was not free to copy. This prevented other CPU manufacturers from making CPUs that fit in the SEC's special Slot 1 connection. Although this might have been seen by Intel as a big opportunity to take even more market share, it virtually guaranteed that many systems would continue to use the older PGA-type Socket 7 and, as in the case of AMD, would create their own SEC and PGA packages that are incompatible with Intel's. From this point forward we live in a world where AMD CPUs must have motherboards designed for AMD while Intel CPUs must have motherboards designed for Intel.

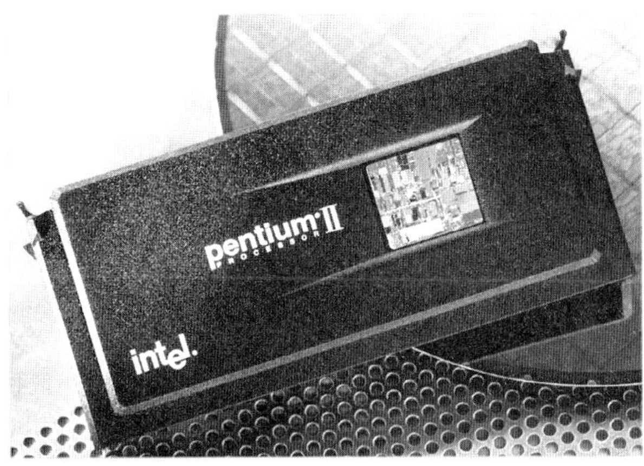

Figure 3.61 [illegible]

AMD K6 Series

[illegible]

board speeds of up to 100 MHz (on later models). The K6-2 added AMD's proprietary 3DNow!™ instruction set—a significant advancement in graphics-handling capabilities—and increased clock speeds. The K6-III included even more advancements in pipelining and added a 256 K L2 cache, all on a standard Socket 7 PGA package. All K6s required a Super Socket 7 motherboard.

• **Figure 3.62** AMD K6 (picture courtesy of AMD)

AMD K6-Family CPUs

- 6th Generation CPU
- External Speed Range: 66–100 MHz
- Internal Speed Range: 200–550 MHz
- Multiplier Range: x3–x5.5
- L1 Cache: Yes, 32 KB on K6 and K6-2; 64 KB on K6-III
- L2 Cache: No on K6 and K6-2; Yes, K6-III: 256 KB
- L3 Cache: No
- Package: PGA
- Socket(s) used: Socket 7

Intel Celeron (Pentium II)

In an attempt to capture more market share of low-end PCs, Intel developed an offshoot of the Pentium II called the Celeron (Figure 3.63). The first Celerons were SEC, but lacked any protective covering, making them distinct from a Pentium II. Intel calls this the *Single Edge Processor* (SEP) package. While the first Celerons used the SEP package and snapped into a standard Slot 1, later Celerons based on the Pentium used a socket that was designed for the Pentium III called Socket 370.

The first two versions, running at 266 and 300 MHz, also lacked any L2 cache, making them very poor performers; as a result, they were rather unpopular. Intel quickly added a 128 K cache, starting with the Celeron 300 (the improved 300s were called the 300A to distinguish them from the 300

There are Pentium II, Pentium III, and Pentium 4 versions of Celeron CPUs.

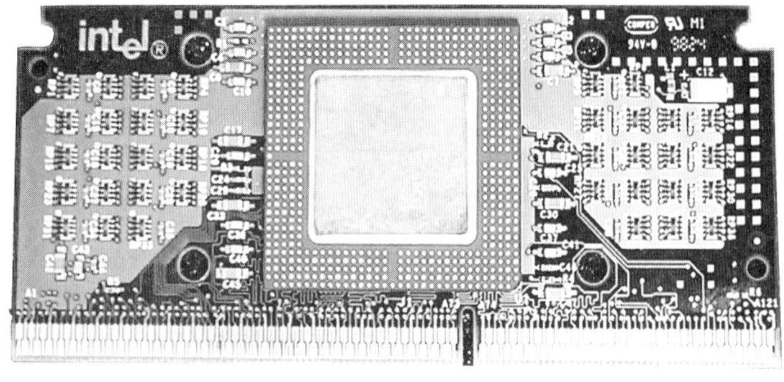

• Figure 3.63 Pentium II class Celeron in an SEP package

without the L2 cache). Although touted by Intel as a low-end solution and limited to only a 66 MHz bus speed, the Celeron CPU's cheap price made it a huge success in a broad cross-section of systems.

Intel Pentium II-Based Celeron CPUs

- 6th Generation CPU
- External Speed Range: 66 MHz
- Internal Speed Range: 266–700 MHz
- Multiplier Range: x4–x10.5
- L1 Cache: Yes, 32 KB
- L2 Cache: Not originally. Later versions had 128 KB
- L3 Cache: No
- Package: SEP, PGA
- Socket(s) used: Slot 1, Socket 370

Pentium III

The Pentium III improved on the Pentium II by incorporating *Streaming SIMD Extensions* (SSE), Intel's direct competitor to AMD's 3DNow!; a number of internal processing/pipelining improvements; full support for 100 MHz and 133 MHz motherboard speeds; and high-speed L2 caches. This combination of improvements makes the Pentium III an incredibly powerful and popular processor. The Pentium III was first produced in a derivative of the SEC package called SEC-2 (Figure 3.64), but improvements in die technology enabled the Pentium III to use the PGA package. Intel can produce these packages more cheaply than the SEC-style packages, and they take up much less real estate inside the PC.

Intel Pentium III CPUs

- 6th Generation CPU
- External Speed Range: 100–133 MHz
- Internal Speed Range: 450 MHz–1.26 GHz
- Multiplier Range: x4–x10
- L1 Cache: Yes, 32 KB
- L2 Cache: Yes, 256 KB or 512 KB
- L3 Cache: No
- Package: SEC-2, PGA
- Socket(s) used: Slot 1, Socket 370

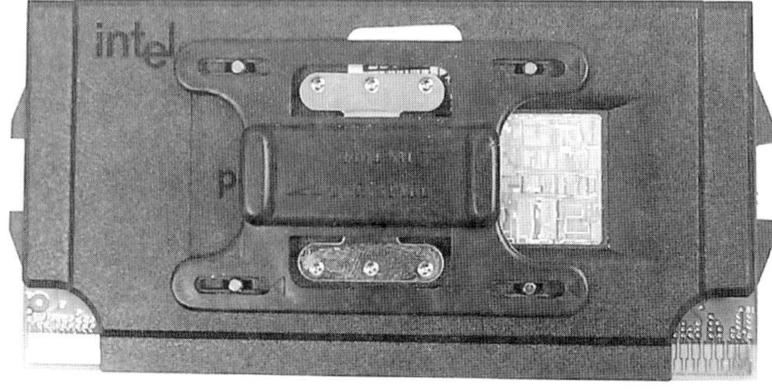

• Figure 3.64 Pentium III SEC-2 (fan mount attached)

Unfortunately, Intel makes no differentiation between classes of Celerons. The next generation of Celerons, unofficially known as the "Celeron II," was based on the Pentium III CPU (Figure 3.65).

Intel Pentium III-Based Celeron CPUs

- 6th Generation CPU
- External Speed Range: 66–100 MHz
- Internal Speed Range: 533–700 MHz
- Multiplier Range: x8–x11.5
- L1 Cache: Yes, 32 KB
- L2 Cache: Yes, 128 KB
- L3 Cache: No
- Package: PGA
- Socket(s) used: Socket 370

• Figure 3.65 Celeron II PGA

Early AMD Athlon CPUs

Often referred to as "the CPU that keeps Intel awake at night," the Athlon CPU has evolved from the name of a single class of CPUs into a broad over-

you could snap an Athlon into a Slot 1 motherboard, but it wouldn't work.

Classic AMD Athlon CPUs

- 6th Generation CPU
- External Speed Range: 100 MHz (Doubled)
- Internal Speed Range: 500 MHz–1 GHz
- Multiplier Range: x5–x10
- L1 Cache: Yes, 128 KB
- L2 Cache: Yes, 512 KB
- L3 Cache: No
- Package: SEC
- Socket(s) used: Slot A

The classic Athlon contained a number of amazing technologies, including a whopping nine pipelines and very advanced dynamic branch prediction, but the most talked about aspect of the Athlon stems from its use of either a 200 MHz or 266 MHz system bus. This gets a little confusing. What AMD calls the system bus, we would call "most of the frontside bus." These are the wires leading between the CPU and the chipset. To make it a tad more confusing, the bus still runs at just 100 MHz or 133 MHz, but the CPU and the chipset perform two calculations on every clock cycle. The data truly does move at double the motherboard speed so you can enjoy much faster processing at either 200 MHz or 266 MHz, depending on the processor you buy (Figure 3.67).

• Figure 3.66 Early Athlon

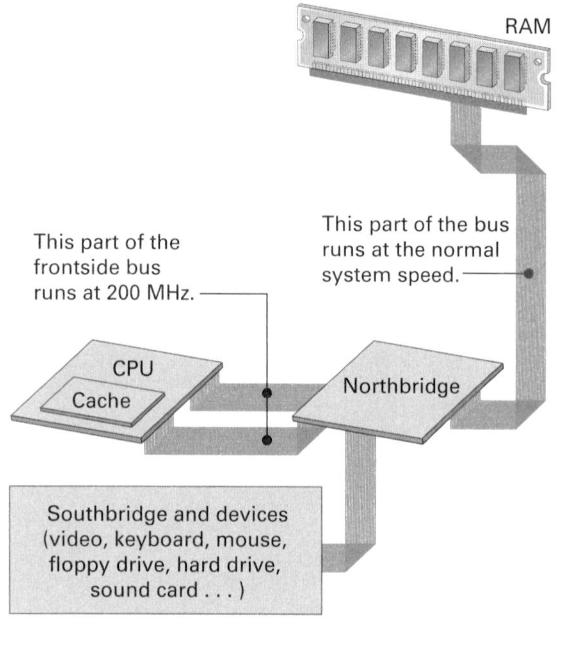

• **Figure 3.67** Athlon system bus

AMD "Thunderbird" Athlon CPUs

AMD's first major improvement to the Athlon CPU was known as the Thunderbird Athlon. The Thunderbird Athlon is most easily distinguished from the classic Athlon by returning to a PGA package with the adoption of the proprietary 462-pin socket called *Socket A* (Figure 3.68).

The change between the Classic and the Thunderbird wasn't just cosmetic. Thunderbird Athlon CPUs have smaller but far more powerful L2 caches as well as a number of other minor improvements.

AMD Thunderbird Athlon CPUs

- 6th Generation CPU
- External Speed Range: 100–133 MHz (Doubled)
- Internal Speed Range: 650 MHz–1.4 GHz
- Multiplier Range: x3.5–x14
- L1 Cache: Yes, 128 KB
- L2 Cache: Yes, 256 KB
- L3 Cache: No
- Package: PGA
- Socket(s) used: Socket A

AMD Duron

The Duron is AMD's direct competitor to the Intel Celeron. Basically an Athlon with a smaller cache, the Duron supports the same 200 MHz frontside bus as the Athlon, giving it a slight edge over the Celeron. The Duron enjoys a sizable market on lower-end PCs, although the Celeron continues to dominate. The Duron connects to the same 462-pin Socket A as the later Athlon CPUs (Figure 3.69).

• **Figure 3.68** Athlon Socket A (graphic courtesy of AMD)

AMD Duron CPUs

- 6th Generation CPU
- External Speed Range: 100 MHz (Doubled)
- Internal Speed Range: 600 MHz–1.3 GHz
- Multiplier Range: x3.5–x14
- L1 Cache: Yes, 128 KB
- L2 Cache: Yes, 64 KB
- L3 Cache: No
- Package: PGA
- Socket(s) used: Socket A

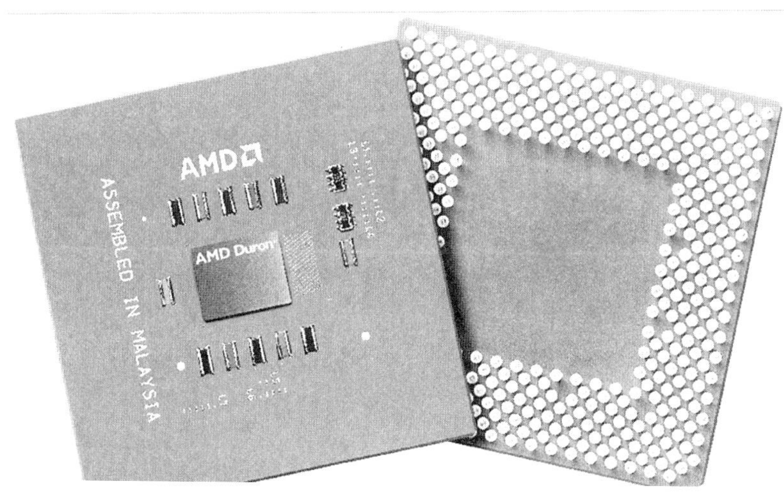

Intel Pentium 4

For all the improvements in speed and caching, [illegible] based on the powerful, but now aging, Pentium Pro technology. The Pentium 4 breaks that tradition and defines the seventh generation of CPUs with a totally new, dramatically more powerful core processing function that includes an incredible 20-step pipeline and an amazing array of new hyper-intelligent features. The Pentium 4 includes a number of enhancements for graphics, which make it very popular for the high-end workstation market.

The P4 started by achieving a 400 MHz system bus speed—twice the Athlon's 200 MHz—by utilizing four data transfers per clock cycle on a 100 MHz bus. Intel used the same "quad-pumped" frontside bus technology on a 133 MHz bus to achieve a 533 MHz frontside bus. Then in late 2002, Intel topped that as well, announcing new versions of the Pentium 4 that feature a (quad-pumped 200 MHz) 800 MHz frontside bus.

There are basically two classes of Pentium 4 CPUs. The first Pentium 4 CPUs came in a 423-pin PGA package and had a 256 KB L2 cache. These were replaced by the 512 KB L2 cache Pentium 4s with a 478 pin PGA package (Figure 3.70). Even though the new package has more pins it is considerably smaller than the earlier package.

• **Figure 3.70** Two Pentium 4 packages

Intel Pentium 4 CPUs

- 7th Generation CPU
- External Speed Range: 100 MHz (Quad Speed); 133 MHz (Quad Speed); 200 MHz (Quad Speed)

- Internal Speed Range: 1.3–3.20 GHz
- Multiplier Range: x13–x23
- L1 Cache: Yes, 128 KB
- L2 Cache: Yes, 256 KB, 512 KB
- L3 Cache: No
- Package: 423-pin PGA, 478-pin PGA
- Socket(s) used: Socket 423, Socket 478.

AMD Athlon XP

Not to be left in the dust by Intel's Pentium 4, AMD released an upgraded version of the Athlon Thunderbird called the Athlon XP. Physically, Athlon XP CPUs look virtually identical to the earlier Athlon processors with the same regular 462-pin PGA package, but Athlon XP CPUs incorporate a number of performance enhancements to the Athlon core. Pipeline improvements combined with very high clock speeds make the Athlon XP the Pentium 4's main competitor.

One interesting aspect of the Athlon XP is AMD's attempt to ignore clock speeds and instead market the CPUs using a number that matches the equivalent power of an Intel Pentium 4 processor. For example, the Athlon XP 1800+ actually runs at 1.6 GHz, but AMD claims it processes as fast or better than a Pentium 4 1.8 GHz—ergo "1800+."

AMD Athlon XP CPUs

- 7th Generation CPU
- External Speed Range: 133 MHz, 166 MHz (Dual Speed)
- Internal Speed Range: 1.3 GHz (1500+)–2.16 GHz (3000+)
- Multiplier Range: x13–x16.5
- L1 Cache: Yes, 128 KB
- L2 Cache: Yes, 256 KB, 512 KB
- L3 Cache: No
- Package: 462-pin PGA
- Socket(s) used: Socket A.

Try This!

CPU Converters

The many different types of CPUs with their many types of sockets and slots created the demand for an entire class of special devices called CPU converters. In general, these devices enable you to take a CPU of one type and snap it into a motherboard designed for a different type of CPU. They do have their limits—let's define those limits to see how useful—or not useful—a converter might be for you.

1. Use the Internet and do a search on "CPU Converters." See if you can find converters for different socket types of the same CPUs. For example, you should have little trouble finding a converter to let you snap a Pentium 4 socket 478 CPU into the older style Socket 423.
2. See if you can find any "slockets"—special converters designed to allow you install PGA-type CPUs into motherboards designed to take slotted CPUs.
3. Try finding converters for different models of the same make of CPU. Can you locate a converter that enables you to install a Pentium 4 CPU onto a Pentium III motherboard?

Specialty Processors

All the CPUs you've learned about up to this moment share one common aspect—they all were or are very common on the typical desktop PC. Yet there are other processors that don't really fit so nicely into that group—these are CPUs that for one reason or another make them much less common on the typical desktop PC. That doesn't make the CPUs rare! In fact, most if not all of these CPUs are quite common—just not on your typical desktop PC. For lack of a better term, let's call them specialty processors.

Intel Xeon Processors

Just as Celeron describes a series of lower-end processors built around the Pentium II, Pentium III, and Pentium 4, the term *Xeon* (pronounced Zee-on) defines a series of high-end processors built around the Pentium II, Pentium III, and Pentium 4. Based originally on the Pentium II and

more than one processor. Most any modern CPU has the ability to run with one other identical CPU but making two CPUs that were never designed to work together requires an incredibly complex Northbridge. Xeon processors, on the other hand, are carefully designed to work together in sets of two, four, or even eight CPUs. Although very expensive, their immense power lets them enjoy broad popularity in the high-horsepower world of server systems.

Intel Pentium II–Based Xeon CPUs

- 6th Generation CPU
- External Speed Range: 100 MHz
- Internal Speed Range: 400–450 MHz
- Multiplier Range: x4–x4.5
- L1 Cache: Yes, 32 KB
- L2 Cache: Yes, 512 KB–2 MB
- L3 Cache: No
- Package: SEC
- Socket(s) used: Slot 2

Intel Pentium III–Based Xeon CPUs

- 6th Generation CPU
- External Speed Range: 100–133 MHz
- Internal Speed Range: 500 MHz–1 GHz
- Multiplier Range: x5–x7.5
- L1 Cache: Yes, 32 KB
- L2 Cache: Yes, 256 KB, 512 KB, 1 MB, 2 MB
- L3 Cache: No
- Package: SEC
- Socket(s) used: Slot 2

The Pentium 4 Xeon is quite a different beast for the previous Xeon types. First, the Pentium 4 Xeon's caches are quite a bit smaller than other Xeons—advancements in pipelining make anything larger less valuable. Second, Intel sells two lines of Pentium 4 Xeons: one line, simply called the *Pentium 4 Xeon*, is for single or dual processor systems and the second line, called the *Pentium 4 Xeon MP*, is for four or eight multiprocessor systems. Last, Pentium 4 Xeons eschew the Slot 2 and mark the complete return of all Intel CPUs to PGA with a Pentium 4 Xeon-only 603-pin package (Figure 3.72).

Figure 3.72 Intel Pentium 4 Xeon (photo courtesy of Intel)

Intel Pentium 4–Based Xeon CPUs

- 7th Generation CPU
- External Speed Range: 100–133 MHz (Quad Speed)
- Internal Speed Range: 1.4–3.06 GHz
- Multiplier Range: x14–x28
- L1 Cache: Yes, 12 KB
- L2 Cache: Yes, 256 KB, 512 KB
- L3 Cache: No
- Package: PGA
- Socket(s) used: Socket 603

The Intel Pentium 4 Xeon MP has one very special extra—a level 3 cache! Seems that Intel thinks big caches are still good—but only if you are running four or more CPUs.

Intel Pentium 4–Based Xeon MP CPUs

- 7th Generation CPU
- External Speed Range: 100–133 MHz (Quad Speed)
- Internal Speed Range: 1.4–2 GHz
- Multiplier Range: x14–x20
- L1 Cache: Yes, 12 KB
- L2 Cache: Yes, 256 KB, 512 KB
- L3 Cache: Yes, 512 KB, 1 MB, 2 MB
- Package: PGA
- Socket(s) used: Socket 603

64-Bit Processing

Both AMD and Intel are currently shipping the newest thing in microprocessing: 64-bit CPUs. The term "64-bit" might seem a little misleading. Don't we already have CPUs with 64-bit external data buses and registers? Yes we do, but this new class of processors will expand the only item left on a CPU that is still effectively at 32-bits: the address bus. At the beginning of this chapter, you saw that the number of wires on the address bus defined the maximum amount of memory a CPU could address. With a 32-bit address bus, the maximum amount of memory the CPU can address is 2^{32} or 4,294,967,296 bytes. With a 64-bit address bus, we will see CPUs that can address 2^{64} bytes of memory, or more precisely, 18,446,744,073,709,551,616 bytes of memory—that's a lot of RAM!

Several 64-bit CPUs have been around for a few years. Companies like Sun Microsystems use their own special 64-bit CPUs in their own special computer systems, but a Sun workstation isn't a PC. Sun CPUs can't (won't?) run Microsoft Windows, for example. Only the DEC Alpha CPU made forays into the PC, running a version of Windows NT. New offerings from Intel and AMD promise to make the 64-bit plunge more mainstream soon.

Wait a minute—just because a CPU has a 64-bit addressing capability doesn't mean current operating systems like Microsoft Windows or Linux know how to use it! All current operating systems are designed to run on 32-bit processors—we call that 32-bit operating mode. For the first time [illegible] CPU only have a 44-bit address bus? Simple—the chances of anyone needing that much RAM in the next few years is slim. Later CPUs will add to their address buses as the needs increase. Do you remember the register that keeps track of where the CPU is looking in memory? On these 64-bit processors, that register stays 64-bit, even if it can't use 20 of the 64 bits!

Both AMD and Intel are racing ahead with competing 64-bit processors. Interestingly, they take very different paths. Let's look at the Intel Itanium and the AMD Opteron.

Intel Itanium

Intel made the first strike into the 64-bit world for PCs. Really more of a proof of concept product than one that was going to make Intel any money, its unveiling struck the first bell in the 64-bit PC world. The Itanium has a unique 418-pin Pin Array Cartridge (PAC) to help house its big Level 3 cache (Figure 3.73).

Intel Itanium CPUs

- 8th Generation CPU
- Physical Address: 44 bits
- Frontside Bus width: 64-bit
- External Speed Range: 133 Mhz (Quad Speed)
- Internal Speed Range: 733 MHz, 833 MHz
- Multiplier Range: x6–x8.5
- L1 Cache: Yes, 32 KB
- L2 Cache: Yes, 96 KB
- L3 Cache: Yes, 2 MB, 4 MB

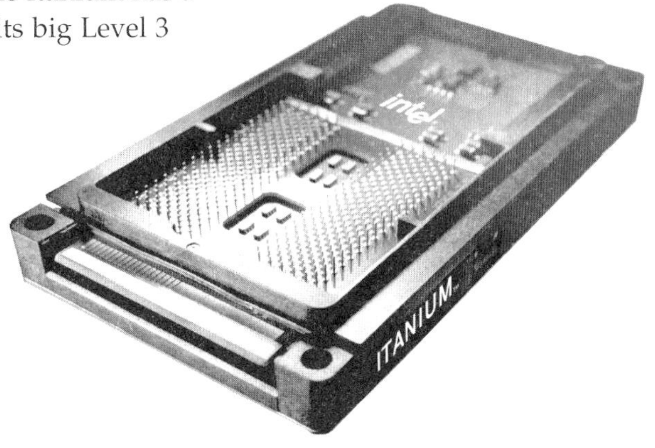

• **Figure 3.73** Intel Itanium (photo courtesy of Intel)

- Package: PAC
- Socket(s) used: Socket 418

• Figure 3.74 Itanium II (photo courtesy of Intel)

Intel Itanium II

The Intel Itanium II is Intel's first serious foray into the 64-bit world. To describe the Itanium II simply in terms of bus sizes and clock speeds is simply unfair. The power of this processor goes far deeper. Massive pipelines, high speed caching, and literally hundreds of other improvements make the Itanium II the current 64-bit leader for the PC. The Itanium II uses a unique form of PGA that Intel calls OLGA (Organic Land Grid Array—see Figure 3.74).

Intel made a bold move with the Itanium and the Itanium II by not making them backwardly compatible to 32-bit programming. In other words, every OS, every application, every driver of every device has to be rewritten in order to work on the Itanium and Itanium II. Intel's answer is simple: if you need 32-bit, use a Pentium 4. If you need 64-bit, get an Itanium.

Intel Itanium CPUs

- 8th Generation CPU
- Physical Address: 50 bits
- Frontside Bus Width: 128 bit
- External Speed Range: 100 MHz (Quad Speed)
- Internal Speed Range: 900 MHz, 1 GHz
- Multiplier Range: x9–x10
- L1 Cache: Yes, 32 KB
- L2 Cache: Yes, 256 KB
- L3 Cache: Yes, 1.5 MB, 3 MB
- Package: OLGA
- Socket(s) used: Socket 611

• Figure 3.75 AMD Opteron (photo courtesy of AMD)

AMD Opteron

Coming in after the Itanium, AMD's Opteron doesn't try to take on the Itanium head-to-head. Instead, AMD presents the Opteron as the lower-end 64-bit CPU. But don't let the moniker "lower-end" fool you. While the Opteron borrows heavily from the Athlon, it includes an amazing new I/O data path known as Hypertransport. Think of Hypertransport as built-in Northbridge, providing direct connection to other parts of the PC—and to other CPUs for multiprocessing—at a blistering speed of over 6 GB/sec! The Opteron comes in a micro PGA package, looking remarkably like a Pentium 4 (Figure 3.75).

AMD Opteron CPUs

- 8th Generation CPU
- Physical Address: 40 bits

- Frontside Bus width: 128 bit
- External Speed Range: 6.4 GHz (Hypertransport)
- Internal Speed Range: 1.4–1.8 GHz
- Multiplier Range: x14–x20
- L1 Cache: Yes, 128 KB
- L2 Cache: Yes, 1 MB
- L3 Cache: No
- Package: micro-PGA
- Socket(s) used: Socket 940

AMD has done something rather remarkable with the Opteron. Unlike the Itanium, the Opteron can run both 32-bit and 64-bit code. AMD gives [illegible]

[illegible]

specting CPU should ever need to operate. Since mid-1980s, CPU manufacturers have endeavored to make specialized versions of their processors to function in the rugged world of laptops. Over the years, a number of CPU laptop solutions have appeared.

An early solution was simply to use regular CPUs. Every desktop CPU has relatively low voltage and has some form of power management. The biggest problems are heat and lack of space. During the 486 and Pentium days, it was quite common to see regular desktop CPUs installed inside laptops. Many laptop makers demanded, and got, CPUs with thinner packages and lower MHz (and thus less heat). The CPU makers realized that they had a market for specialized "mobile" CPUs.

Virtually every CPU made by Intel or AMD comes in a mobile version. You can tell a mobile version by the word "mobile" or the letter "M" in its name. Here are a few examples:

- Mobile Intel Pentium 4-M
- AMD Athlon XP-M
- Mobile Intel Pentium III- M
- Mobile AMD Duron

So what separates these **mobile CPUs** from their desktop brethren? Well, there are three major areas that differentiate a mobile CPU. A mobile CPU needs to be smaller, use less power, and run cooler than the same type of desktop CPU.

Smaller

One of the first manifestations of making mobile CPUs smaller was the *Tape Carrier Package* (TCP). These are nothing more than the CPU without the packaging. Some notebook makers take the TCP and solder it directly to the

• **Figure 3.76** TCP

motherboard, giving the motherboard the responsibility for heat dissipation. TCPs, although still used, have lost ground to other mobile packages (Figure 3.76).

Pentium II processors presented a serious problem for Intel, as their huge size made them impractical for laptops. To make the Pentium II attractive to the laptop market, Intel unveiled the mobile module. The mobile module is virtually an entire PC on a small card. The mobile module includes the processor and primary support chips on a standardized, replaceable package. Intel's mobile modules are very popular on today's laptops and are a major contributor to Intel's dominance of the mobile market (Figure 3.77).

Most mobile Intel processors use a Micro-PGA package. These packages look like any other PGA-type CPU package except that they are quite small—a nice fit for a crowded laptop! (See Figure 3.78.)

AMD also makes a powerful series of mobile processors. Unlike Intel, AMD simply chooses to make its mobile processors using the same PGA packaging as their desktop brethren.

Uses Less Power/Cooler

A mobile processor needs to use less power than an equivalent desktop model. This provides two advantages. First, it allows the battery in the laptop to last longer. Second, it makes the CPU run cooler, and the cooler the CPU, the fewer cooling devices you need.

Almost every mobile processor today runs at a lower voltage than the desktop version of the same CPU. As a result, most mobile CPUs also run at lower speeds—it takes juice if you want the speed! Mobile CPUs usually top out at about 75 percent of the speed of the same CPU's desktop version.

Reducing voltage is a good first step but making a smart CPU that can use less power in low-demand situations will reduce power usage even more. The first manifestation of this was the classic **System Management Mode** (SMM). Introduced back in the times of the 386, SMM provided the

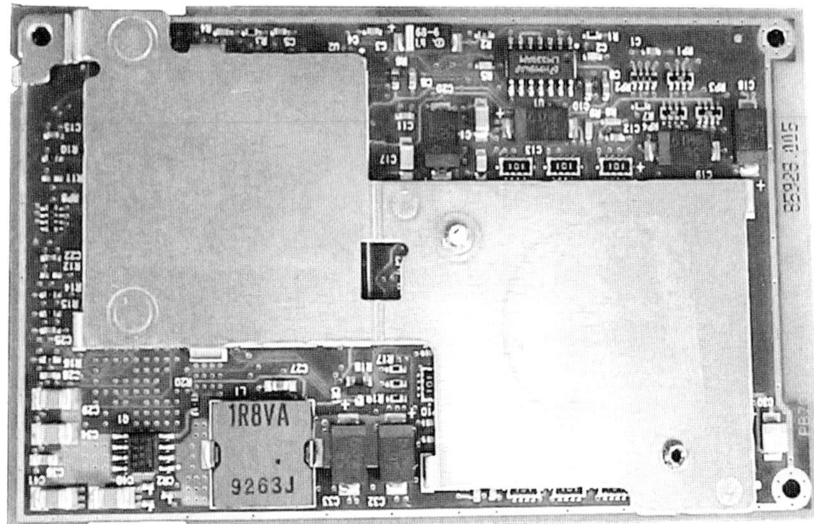

• **Figure 3.77** Intel mobile module (chips covered by heat sink)

CPU with the ability to turn off devices that use a lot of power such as the monitor or the hard drives. While originally just for laptops, SMM is now built into all AMD and Intel CPUs.

CPU makers have taken power reduction one step further by giving CPUs the ability to slow themselves down during low demand times or if the CPU detects that it is getting too hot. Intel's version of this capability is called *Speedstep* while AMD's version is known as *PowerNow!*

• **Figure 3.78** Micro-PGA CPU

Installing CPUs

Installing or replacing a CPU is a remarkably straightforward process. You take off the fan and heat sink assembly, remove the CPU, put a new CPU in,

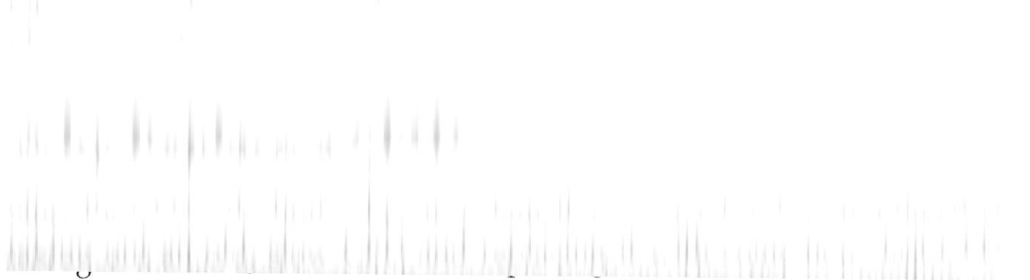

more about these in Chapter 21.

would make your computer run faster. No doubt it will, but before you do you need to consider a few issues, such as cost, cooling, and performance.

Cost

If you have an older CPU there's a better than average chance that a faster version of your CPU is no longer available for retail purchase. In that case, replacing your CPU with a new one would require you to replace the motherboard and probably the RAM too. This is doable, but does it make sense cost-wise? How much would this upgrade compare to a whole new system?

Cooling

Faster CPUs run hotter than slower ones. If you get a new CPU, you will almost certainly need a new fan to dissipate the heat generated by the more powerful processor. In addition, you may discover your case fans are not sufficient, causing the CPU to overheat and making the system

Try This!

Comparing CPUs

AMD and Intel are in a constant battle to have the fastest and cleverest CPU on the market. One result is that computer system vendors have a range of CPUs for you to choose from when customizing a system. So how do you know what you can and should choose? Try this:

1. Surf over to one of the major computer vendor's websites: dell.com, gateway.com, hp.com, and ibm.com all have customization features on their sites.
2. Select a low-end desktop from the available offerings, and pretend you're considering purchasing it. Select the customization option, and record the CPU choices you're given, and the price differentials involved. Note which CPU comes as the default choice. Is it the fastest one? The slowest?
3. Now start again, only this time select a high-end model. Again choose to customize it as if you're a potential purchaser. Record the CPU choices you get with this model, the price differentials, and which choice is the default.
4. Finally, do an internet search for benchmarking results on the fastest, slowest, and at least one other of the CPU choices you found. What differences in performance do you find? How does that compare to the differences in price?

Tech Tip

Motherboard Book Versus Instruction Manual

Don't confuse the motherboard book with the instruction manual or user's guide that comes with many OEM systems. The user's guide describes only issues like opening the system unit and inserting a keyboard—it won't help with more complex issues like motherboard-CPU compatibility. If you can't find a motherboard book for your system, odds are good that either the motherboard book is lost, or you never got one in the first place. Most OEMs (Dell, Gateway, IBM, and so on) do not provide a motherboard book with their systems.

lock up. Adding improved cooling can be done but it might require a new case.

Performance

A faster CPU will make your computer run faster but by how much? The results are often disappointing. As we go through this book, you will discover many other areas where upgrading might make a much stronger impact on your system's performance.

Determining the Right CPU

So you go through all the decision-making and decide to go for a new CPU. Perhaps you're building a brand new system or maybe you're ready to go for that CPU upgrade. Either way, the beginning is the motherboard book. Remember all that documentation we discussed in the last chapter? Well, the single most import bit of documentation is called the motherboard book. Many companies call it the "User's Manual." This book contains all the details about what CPUs you can use as well as anything special about installing a CPU (Figure 3.79).

Usually in the first few pages the motherboard book will tell you exactly which CPUs your system can handle (as shown in Figure 3.80).

If you don't have a motherboard book, call the place you got the PC from and ask for it. If they don't have it, you can always go to the motherboard maker directly—we'll talk about how to do that in Chapter 7.

Your first concern is the socket or slot. You can't install an AMD Athlon XP into a Pentium 4's Socket 478—it won't fit! There are some adapters you can purchase to allow you to install various CPU packages into motherboards. For example, you can install a socket 370-type Intel Celeron into a Slot 1 motherboard (Figure 3.81) using a special adapter called a *slocket*. In general,

• **Figure 3.79** Typical motherboard book

3. HARDWARE SETUP

Manual CPU Settings

NOTE: JumperFree mode must be disabled .

Set the DIP switches by the internal speed of your processor as follows:

CPU	Freq.	Mult.	Bus F.	1	2	3	4
				(CPU Bus Freq.)			
Athlon	1.2GHz	9.0x	133MHz	[ON]	[ON]	[ON]	[OFF]
Athlon	1GHz	7.5x	133MHz	[ON]	[ON]	[ON]	[OFF]
Athlon	1.1GHz	11.0x	100MHz	[ON]	[OFF]	[ON]	[ON]
Athlon	1GHz	10.0x	100MHz	[ON]	[OFF]	[ON]	[ON]
Athlon	950MHz	9.5x	100MHz	[ON]	[OFF]	[ON]	[ON]
Athlon	900MHz	9.0x	100MHz	[ON]	[OFF]	[ON]	[ON]
Athlon	850MHz	8.5x	100MHz	[ON]	[OFF]	[ON]	[ON]
Athlon	800MHz	8.0x	100MHz	[ON]	[OFF]	[ON]	[ON]
Athlon	750MHz	7.5x	100MHz	[ON]	[OFF]	[ON]	[ON]
Athlon	700MHz	7.0x	100MHz	[ON]	[OFF]	[ON]	[ON]

• **Figure 3.80** Showing list of CPUs

however, these adapters do not have good track records and are frowned upon. And none will enable you to install an AMD CPU in a motherboard designed for an Intel CPU, and vice versa. Usually, it's best to stick with a CPU package designed for your motherboard.

If your motherboard book lists the CPU you want to install, you're ready to start installing! If the CPU you want to use is the same package as the motherboard but not listed in the motherboard book, you still have a chance. You might be able to upgrade special onboard programming on the motherboard through a process called "flashing the BIOS." We talk about what this means in Chapter 5.

• **Figure 3.81** CPU slocket

Buying a CPU

Buying a CPU is a tricky game as most stores will not accept returns unless the CPU is bad. If you're not careful you could get stuck with a useless CPU. Here are a few tricks.

CPUs come packaged two ways, as retail-boxed CPUs or OEM CPUs. Retail-boxed CPUs have two advantages. First, they are the genuine article. There are a surprising number of illegal CPUs on the market. Second, they come with a fan that is rated to work with that CPU.

Most stores have an installation deal where they will install a new CPU for very cheap. I will take advantage of this sometimes, even though it may mean I don't have my PC for a few days. Why does your humble author, the Alpha Geek, have others do work he can do himself? Well, that way I'm not out of luck if there is a problem! Heck, I can change my own oil in my car but I let others do that too!

If you buy an OEM CPU, you will need the right fan. See "The Art of Cooling" section later in this chapter.

Preparing to Install

Many motherboards have no jumpers or switches.

Once you're comfortable that your new CPU will work with your motherboard, get back to that motherboard book and see if there are any tiny jumpers or switches that you must adjust for your CPU. Failure to do this is the primary reason for unsuccessful CPU installations. These jumpers might adjust the motherboard speed, the multiplier, or the voltage. Take your time, read the motherboard book, and set those jumpers or switches properly.

Inserting a Slot 1/Slot A CPU

Before attempting to do anything inside the system unit, make sure you have adequate ESD protection. Make sure the power is off and the system is unplugged.

Because Slot 1 and Slot A are mechanically identical, we can lump their installation process together. First, you need to install the CPU mount, which keeps the CPU secure. Many different types of mounts exist. Most mounts require the motherboard to be out of the case to install them. Figure 3.82 shows one of the more common types of mounts.

All SEC CPUs must have a fan. Like CPU mounts, fans come in a bewildering variety of shapes and sizes. Be sure to add a *small* amount of heat sink compound—also known as thermal paste or heat dope—before you mount the fan (Figure 3.83). This paste, usually white, helps transfer heat from the CPU to the heat sink/fan. Any electronics store sells heat sink compound.

To install the CPU, just slide it straight down into the slot (Figure 3.84). Special notches in the slot make it impossible to install them incorrectly.

• **Figure 3.82** Typical slot mount

plug in the CPU fan's power.

Inserting a PGA-Type CPU

Inserting and removing PGA CPUs is a relatively simple process; just *don't touch the pins,* or you might destroy the CPU. Figure 3.85 shows a technician installing a Celeron PGA into Socket 370. Note the notch and dot printed on the corners of the CPU. These *orientation markers* or *index corners* are designed to help you align the CPU correctly. It must line up with the notch(es) on the socket. Although the orientation marks make it very difficult to install a CPU improperly, incorrectly installing your CPU will almost certainly destroy the CPU or the motherboard, or both!

Installing a CPU into a ZIF socket is as simple as making sure that the orientation notches line up on the CPU and ZIF socket. Lift the ZIF arm, align the CPU, and it should drop right in (Figure 3.86). If it doesn't, verify your alignment and check for bent pins on the CPU. If I encounter a slightly bent pin, I often use a mechanical pencil that takes thick (0.9mm) lead. I take the lead out of the mechanical pencil, slide the pencil tip over the bent pin, and straighten it out. Be careful! A broken CPU pin ruins the CPU. Make sure the CPU is all the way in (no visible pins), and snap down the ZIF arm.

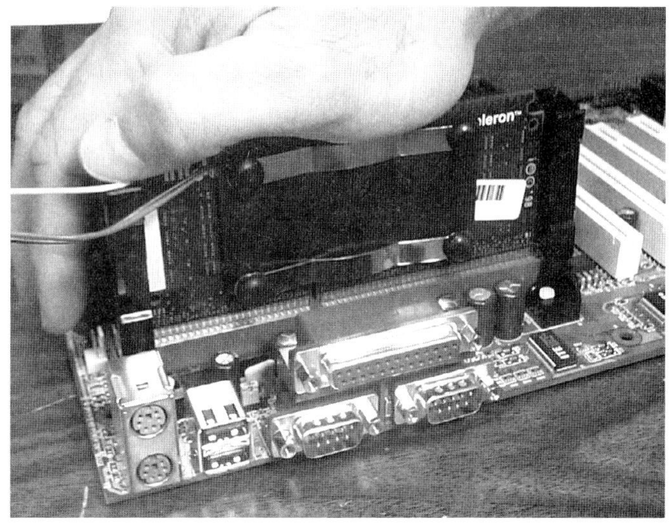

• **Figure 3.84** Snapping down the CPU

Now it's time for the fan! Before inserting the fan, you need to add a small amount of heat sink compound. Many PGA fans come with heat sink compound already on them; the heat sink compound on these pre-doped fans is covered by a small square of tape—be sure to take it off before you snap down the

• **Figure 3.85** Close-up of CPU and socket showing orientation marks and notches

fan. (See Figure 3.87.) If you're putting this on from a tube, know that it only takes a tiny amount of this compound! Spread it on as thinly as you can. Unlike so many other things in life, you can have too much heat dope!

Securing fans makes even the most jaded PC technician a little nervous. Figure 3.88 shows a more common type of fan that snaps into notches on the socket. In most cases, you must apply a fairly strong amount of force to snap the fan into place—far more than you might think. Also, make certain that the fan you install can work with your CPU package. Some Socket 370-specific fans, for example, will crack the ceramic casing on Socket A Duron CPUs, and vice versa.

Fans require power. Look for a power connection on the motherboard, and snap it into place. Most motherboards clearly mark this connector (Figure 3.89).

• **Figure 3.86** Inserting a PGA-type CPU

• **Figure 3.88** Snapping down the fan

Testing Your New CPU

The next step is to turn on the PC and see if the system boots up. If life were perfect, every CPU installation would end right here as we watched the system happily boot up. Unfortunately, the reality is that sometimes nothing happens when you press the On button. Here's what to do if this happens.

First, make sure the system has power—we'll be going through lots of power issues through the book. Second, make sure the CPU is firmly pressed down into the socket. Get your head down and look at the mounted CPU from the side—do you see any of the CPU's wires showing? Does the CPU look level in its mount? If not, reinstall the CPU. If the system still

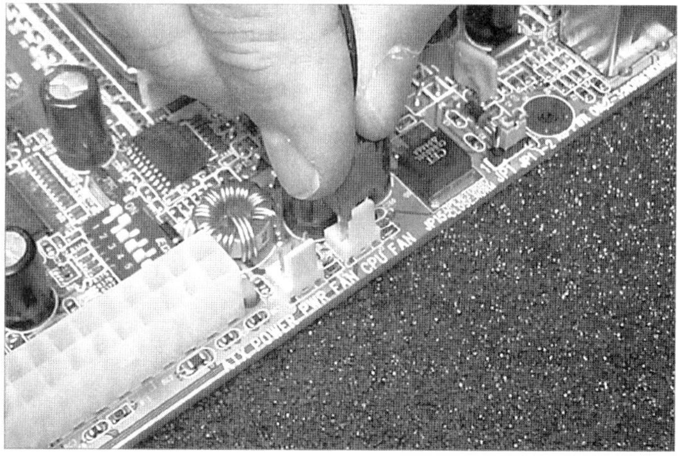

• **Figure 3.89** Inserting the CPU fan power. Note the identical connector for a secondary fan.

does not boot, double-check any jumper settings—it's very easy to mess them up.

The Art of Cooling

There once was a time long ago when CPUs didn't have to have any type of cooling device. You just snapped in the CPU and it worked. Yeah, well, those days are gone. Long gone. If you're installing a modern CPU you will have to cool it. Fortunately, you have choices.

- **OEM Fans** OEM fans are included with a retail-boxed CPU. OEM CPUs, on the other hand, don't normally come bundled with fans. Crazy, isn't it? OEM fans have one big advantage: you know absolutely they will work with your CPU.
- **Specialized Fans** Lots of companies sell third-party fans for different CPUs. These usually exceed the OEM fans in the amount of heat they dissipate. These fans invariably come with eye-catching designs—some are even lighted—to look really cool inside your system! (See Figure 3.90.)

The last choice is the most impressive of all—liquid cooling! That's right, you can put a little liquid cooling system right inside your PC case! Liquid cooling works by running some liquid—usually water—through a metal block that sits on top of your CPU, absorbing heat. The liquid gets heated by the block, runs out of the block and into something that cools the liquid off, and the liquid is then pumped through the block again. So any liquid cooling system consists of three main parts:

- A hollow metal block that sits on the CPU
- A pump to move the liquid around
- Some device to cool the liquid

And of course plenty of hosing to hook them all together! Figure 3.91 shows a typical liquid-cooled PC.

A number of companies sell these liquid-cooling systems. While they look really impressive and certainly cool your CPU, the reality is that unless you do your computing in the middle of the Sahara Desert, a good fan will more than suffice.

• **Figure 3.90** Neat looking fan!

Know Your CPUs

In this chapter, you have seen the basic components and functions of a PC's CPU. A historical view has been provided to help you better understand the amazing evolution of CPUs in the less than 20-year life span of the personal computer.

The information in this chapter will be referred to again and again throughout the book. Take the time to memorize certain facts, such as the size of the L1 and L2 caches, CPU speeds, and clock-doubling features. These are things that good technicians can spout off without having to refer to a book.

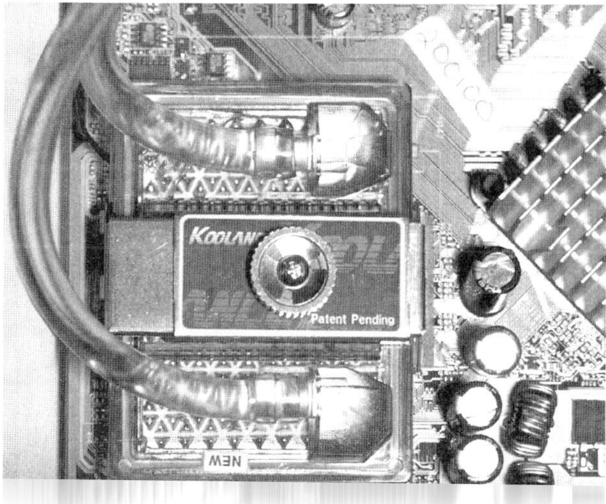

Overclocking

If you remember from the beginning of this chapter, the concept that the system clock pushes the CPU on the motherboard was discussed in detail. Jumpers or software are used to set the motherboard speed, multiplier, and voltage; or as is the case in many systems, we count on the motherboard to use CPUID functions to set this automatically.

The fact that a CPU must run at its designed speed was also discussed. For example, if I have a Celeron 566, Intel tells me that it should run at 66 MHz motherboard speed with an x8.5 multiplier. Starting way back in the days of the 486, however, people began to run their systems intentionally at clock speeds higher than the CPU was rated, and they worked. Well, *sometimes* the systems worked, and sometimes they didn't. Intel has a reason for marking a CPU at a particular clock speed—that's the highest speed that Intel will guarantee that it will work. If you intentionally run

Try This!

Comparing CPU Coolers

Knowing what size and type of CPU cooler assembly to choose for your system can be a challenge, but if you value the life of your expensive new CPU chip, it's important to be able to choose well. Try this:

1. Do a couple of online searches on the topic of CPU coolers for sale. Search on "CPU coolers" as well as "CPU fan" and "CPU heat sink" and finally, add "overclocking" to one of your searches. See if you can find one for less than $10, and one for more than $35.
2. Identify the two most common materials found in the heat sink part of the assembly. See if you can find a cooler assembly that doesn't have a cube-shaped heat sink.
3. Compare at least four different fans that are part of a CPU cooler assembly. Can you find one with a noise level under 20 dBA? Over 50 dBA? Examine the noise level in relation to the fan's other specs, in particular its fan speed (RPM) and airflow (CFM). Can you see any correlation?

a CPU at a speed higher than its rated clock speed, you are overclocking the CPU.

Before I say anything else, I must warn you that intentional overclocking of a CPU immediately voids any warranty. Overclocking has been known to destroy CPUs. Overclocking might also make your system unstable and prone to lockups and reboots. I neither applaud nor do I decry the practice of overclocking. My goal here is simply to inform you of the practice. You make your own decisions.

CPU makers dislike overclocking. Why would you pay more for a faster processor when you can take a cheaper, slower CPU and just make it run faster? To that end, CPU makers, especially Intel, have gone to great lengths to discourage the practice. For example, both AMD and Intel now make all their CPUs with locked multipliers and special overspeed electronics to deter the practice.

I don't think Intel really cares too much what end users do with their CPUs. You own it; you take the risks. A number of criminals, however, have learned to make a good business of remarking CPUs with higher than rated speeds and selling them as legitimate CPUs. These counterfeit CPUs have created a nightmare where unsuspecting retailers and end users have been given overclocked CPUs. When they run into trouble, they innocently ask for warranty support, only to discover that their CPU is counterfeit and the warranty is void.

Intel provides a handy free utility to tell you exactly what type of CPU you have, the rated clock speed and multiplier, and the clock and multiplier that the CPU is currently running. They call this tool the Intel Processor Frequency ID Utility. This tool runs under DOS, Windows *9x*, and Windows 2000/XP. You can download the utility at http://support.intel.com/support/processors/tools/frequencyid/freqid.htm.

Of course, Intel is notorious for changing their web site. If this link becomes invalid, simply go to http://support.intel.com and search for the utility. Figure 3.92 shows a detail of the utility in action, displaying a Celeron 566 that has been intentionally overclocked to 850 MHz.

• **Figure 3.92** A Celeron 566 that has been intentionally overclocked to 850 MHz

Chapter 3 Review

Chapter Summary

After reading this chapter and completing the exercises, you should understand the following about microprocessors.

Identify the Core Components of a CPU

- The external data bus allows the CPU to communicate with the rest of the computer.
- Computers use a binary system with only two [illegible] that allows the CPU to process a command. The CPU requires at least two clock cycles to act on each command. The maximum number of clock cycles that the CPU can handle is called the clock speed or the maximum rated speed for the CPU. It is measured in megahertz (1 million cycles per second) or gigahertz (1 billion cycles per second). The system crystal determines the speed at which the CPU and the rest of the PC operate. Overclocking or running a CPU faster than its maximum clock speed is risky and may damage the CPU.
- Memory holds 1's and 0's that the CPU accesses or reads and writes. Random Access Memory allows the CPU to access any line of code, programs, or data very fast. RAM consists of semiconductor chips on small cards, but electronically it looks like a spreadsheet to the CPU. The CPU's address bus communicates with the Northbridge, which acts as a "RAM-grabbing" device to access any row of RAM that the CPU wants. By turning on and off the wires in the address bus, the CPU indicates the particular byte of RAM it wants. The number of wires in the address bus determines the maximum addressable RAM. Because the original 8088 CPU had only 20 address wires, it could address only 1 MB of RAM.

Explain the Varieties of Modern CPUs

- Advanced Micro Devices (AMD) had an agreement with Intel to copy certain types of CPUs, making it possible to do a pin-for-pin replacement of an Intel or AMD CPU. Starting with the Pentium II CPU, AMD CPUs were no longer compatible, requiring an Intel motherboard for an Intel processor and an AMD motherboard for an AMD processor.
- [illegible] only one type of socket, the 462-pin Socket A. The Pentium II uses a Single Edge Cartridge (SEC) and fits into a Slot 1. AMD's variation fits into Slot A. Slot 1 and Slot A are not compatible.
- Since the original 8088 CPU, the sizes of the external data bus, address bus, and registers have grown dramatically. The clock speeds kept getting faster throughout the 80286, 80386, and 80486 generations of CPUs.
- Dynamic RAM (DRAM) consists of capacitors that must be recharged or refreshed by the Northbridge approximately every 16 milliseconds. During a refresh, DRAM is not available to the CPU. Static RAM (SRAM) uses a flip-flop circuit instead of capacitors and does not have to be refreshed. It is almost as fast as the fastest CPU, but it is expensive. A cache is a holding area to speed up a slow device. Both disk and memory caches are common. Because the CPU has developed at a faster rate than dynamic RAM, a small static RAM cache enables the CPU to access data faster.
- The Pentium includes an internal or L1 SRAM cache. Additional SRAM may be installed externally on the motherboard. The Pentium Pro and later processors also had an L2 cache built into the processor housing.

- Processors work faster internally by multiplying the clock speed. The secret to making clock multiplying work is caching. All modern CPUs are clock multipliers, using the faster speed when working internally and the slower speed when accessing the external data bus or the address bus. Earlier motherboards had jumpers that were used to configure the clock speed and the multiplier manually. Today's computers automatically set the speed and the multiplier.
- As more transistors are included in the CPU, heat becomes a greater problem. One way of reducing heat is to reduce the power that the CPU needs. While early CPUs required 5 volts, today's CPUs use lower voltages. Running a CPU at the wrong voltage can destroy it. Intel created voltage regulator modules (VRM) on a small card that was installed into a VRM socket. Each VRM was appropriate for a particular CPU. Servers are usually the only kind of computer today that still uses a VRM. Instead, now CPUs automatically tell the motherboard the voltage they need.
- Power management is another way to save power. Intel created System Management Mode (SMM), a hardware-based function that shuts down peripherals not in use. Microsoft added Advanced Power Management (APM) functions to operating systems to work with SMM-capable CPUs.
- The Pentium processor has a 64-bit external data bus split into two dual-pipelined 32-bit data buses. It uses a 16K L1 cache and can do branch prediction. The AMD K5 is a Pentium competitor and is pin-compatible to the Pentium. Cyrix also made CPUs such as the Cyrix 6x86. Now selling under the name VIA, sales of these CPUs are not significant.
- Intel's Pentium Pro offered the first on-chip L2 cache, but electronically it was separate from the CPU with its L1 cache. The connection between the CPU and the L2 cache is described as the backside bus, while the address bus and external data bus are now referred to as the frontside bus and connect the CPU with the Northbridge and RAM. The terms backside and frontside bus apply to all later CPUs. With its quad pipelining, the Pentium Pro could run commands out of order. It had a larger rectangular SPGA case, and it was the only processor to use Socket 8. Some regard the Pentium Pro as the most important chip ever created by Intel because the feature set of this processor became the prototype for all later CPUs.
- Later Pentium CPUs have four groups of improvements: MMX, split-voltage, increased multipliers/clocks, and improved processing. Multimedia extensions (MMX) provide four new registers and 57 new commands for processing graphics. MMX also supports Single Instruction Multiple Data (SIMD) for faster processing. Instead of using 5 volts like earlier CPUs, the later Pentiums use split voltage. Requiring 3.3 volts to communicate with other chips, they use a lower core voltage that allows them to run cooler. By increasing the multipliers, the processors run faster internally.
- The AMD K6 was the first to provide support for motherboards up to 100 MHz. It also used 3DNow! instruction set for multimedia. Fitting into the Super Socket 7, the K6 became very popular.
- The Pentium II introduced the SEC cartridge and fit into a proprietary Slot 1. In response to AMD's using 100 MHz motherboards, later Pentium II models also ran at 100 MHz externally. AMD designed its own SEC and PGA packages that are incompatible with Intel's. An Intel CPU must go in a motherboard designed for Intel, while an AMD CPU must have a motherboard designed for AMD.
- The Intel Celeron was targeted to the low-end PC user. It came in a Single Edge Processor (SEP) package and fit into Slot 1. Later Celerons used the PGA package and fit into Socket 370. Intel produced Celeron versions of the Pentium II, III, and 4. Although limited to a 66 MHz, the inexpensive Celerons were big sellers.
- The Pentium III introduced Streaming SIMD Extensions (SSE) and used either 100 or 133 MHz motherboards. It used a more efficient SEC-2 package and was very popular. AMD's Athlon competed with the Pentium III. Produced in a SEC package, it fit into AMD's Slot A. With 9 pipelines and dynamic branch prediction, the Athlon also introduced the first 200 or 266 MHz system bus. Actually, it was a doubled frontside bus that allowed two calculations for every clock cycle of the 100 or 133 MHz bus. AMD Thunderbird Athlon CPUs used a proprietary 462-pin socket called Socket A and featured a more powerful L2 cache. The lower-end AMD Duron is a competitor to the

Intel Celeron. It has a 200 MHz frontside bus and also used Socket A.

- The Pentium 4 uses a 20-step pipeline and quadruples a 100 MHz frontside bus to run at 400 MHz or a 133 MHz bus to run at 533 MHz. This allows four data transfers per clock cycle. The latest versions feature an 800 MHz frontside bus. Early P4s use a 423-pin PGA package with a 256 KB L2 cache while later versions use the 478-pin package with a 512 KB L2 cache. AMD's answer to the P4 is the Athlon XP. With its advanced features, these processors are identified, not by actual clock speeds, but by higher numbers that represent equivalent performance to Intel's [illegible]

[illegible] Xeons. One is built for single or dual processor systems while the other, the Pentium 4 Xeon MP, is designed to support four or eight processors and features a large level 3 cache. Pentium 4 Xeons use a 603-pin PGA package and fit into the Xeon-only Socket 603.

- While processors already exist with 64-bit external data buses and registers, the term "64-bit CPUs" refers to an expanded address bus that will eventually address 2^{64} bytes of memory. Current 32-bit operating systems will be unable to take full advantage of 64-bit processors. The Intel Itanium, although called a 64-bit CPU, actually has a 44-bit address bus, but it will likely be expanded when the need for additional memory materializes. Using a 418-pin Pin Array Cartridge (PAC), the Intel Itanium includes a big Level 3 cache. Intel's new Itanium II has massive pipelines, high-speed caching, and hundreds of other improvements. It uses a unique PGA package called OLGA (Organic Land Grid Array) and fits into Socket 611. Neither version of the Itanium is backwardly compatible to 32-bit programming. AMD's Opteron is a 64-bit CPU that can run either 32-bit or 64-bit code. It also includes Hypertransport I/O data path and provides multiprocessing at a speed of over 6 GB/sec. It has a micro-PGA package and fits into Socket 940.

- CPU makers now produce specialized "mobile" CPUs for laptops. Identified by the word "mobile" or the letter "M" in the name, these processors are smaller, use less power, and run cooler than the desktop CPUs. Because of these requirements, mobile CPUs usually top out at about 75 percent of the speed of the same CPU's desktop version. All of today's mobile CPUs include a power management feature called System Management Mode (SMM) that allows the CPU to turn off devices. They also feature the ability to slow down if the CPU detects that it is getting too hot. Intel calls this capability *Speedstep*, while AMD calls it *PowerNow*!

[illegible] performance. CPU upgrades usually produce disappointing performance results. Other kinds of upgrades have a stronger impact on system performance. Use the motherboard book to determine what kind of CPU your motherboard can support. Be sure to match socket or slot and don't mix AMD with Intel since they are incompatible. Before you upgrade your CPU, you may need to flash the BIOS. When purchasing a CPU, be sure to get an OEM-boxed CPU to assure a "genuine article." You'll also need a fan that works with the particular CPU.

- To install a CPU, first check the motherboard book to see if you need to set jumpers or switches on the motherboard for the CPU multiplier or voltage. Some motherboards are jumperless. To insert a Slot 1/Slot A CPU, after installing the mount, slide the CPU straight down into the slot until it snaps in position. Be sure to plug in the CPU fan's power. To insert a PGA CPU, lift the arm of the ZIF socket, align the orientation markers or index corners, and let the CPU drop into position. Then close the socket arm. Add some heat sink compound and the CPU fan. Be sure to attach the power for the fan. If your newly installed CPU does not work, first check the power. Then check that the CPU is inserted correctly in the socket. Make sure that the jumper settings are correct.

Key Terms

Address bus *(57)*
Backside bus *(76)*
Binary *(48)*
Caching *(67)*
Clock cycle *(52)*
Clock speed *(72)*
Clock multiplying CPU *(71)*
Dynamic RAM (DRAM) *(68)*
External data bus *(48)*
Frontside bus *(76)*
Mobile CPU *(89)*
Multimedia Extensions (MMX) *(77)*
Northbridge *(57)*
Pin Grid Array (PGA) *(62)*
Pipeline *(71)*
Registers *(49)*
Single Edge Cartridge (SEC) *(63)*
Static RAM (SRAM) *(69)*
System management mode (SMM) *(90)*
Zero Insertion Force (ZIF) *(63)*

Key Term Quiz

Use the Key Terms list to complete the sentences that follow. Not all the terms will be used.

1. The ________________ allows the CPU to communicate with the motherboard and other devices in the computer.
2. By lifting the arm on the ________ socket, you can easily install a PGA CPU.
3. The computer uses the ________________ numbering system.
4. A CPU can run at any speed, as long as that speed does not exceed its ______________.
5. ______________ are areas inside the CPU where it temporarily stores internal commands and data while it is processing them.
6. Divided into L1 and L2, a __________ consists of a small amount of __________ that serves as a holding area to provide data to the CPU faster than getting it from regular memory or when RAM is unavailable due to refreshes.
7. If you know the number of wires in the CPU's ______________, you know the maximum amount of RAM that a particular CPU can handle.
8. A ________________ runs at a faster speed internally and at a slower speed externally when using the address bus and the external data bus.
9. Especially designed for laptops, ___________ usually runs at only about 75 percent of the speed of a desktop CPU.
10. The __________ connects the CPU to the L2 cache.

Multiple-Choice Quiz

1. With its unique SPGA case, the only microprocessor that fits into Socket 8 is the ______________.
   - **A.** Pentium
   - **B.** Pentium Pro
   - **C.** Pentium II
   - **D.** Pentium III
2. All the following kinds of memory store data by using microscopic capacitors that must be refreshed *except* ________________.
   - **A.** DRAM
   - **B.** SRAM
   - **C.** RDRAM
   - **D.** SDRAM
3. Which of the following statements is true?
   - **A.** The address bus allows the CPU to communicate with the Northbridge.
   - **B.** The external data bus allows the CPU to communicate with the Northbridge.
   - **C.** The address bus allows the CPU to communicate with the hard drive.
   - **D.** The system bus allows the CPU to communicate with the memory.
4. Often regarded as the prototype for later CPUs, the ________________ was the first microprocessor to include both an L1 and an L2 cache.
   - **A.** Pentium
   - **B.** Pentium Pro

C. Pentium II

D. Pentium III

5. The new 64-bit processors will expand the ____________, the only part of the computer that is not currently 64 bits.

A. System bus

B. Frontside bus

C. Address bus

D. Registers

6. CPU speed is measured in ____________ while RAM capacity is measured in ____________.

the Pentium 4?

A. It was the first processor to use a SCA package and fit into Slot 1.

B. It was the first processor to use a 100 MHz or 133 MHz system bus.

C. It uses a unique PGA package and fits into Socket A.

D. It uses a 20-step pipeline and a quadrupled frontside bus that allows four data transfers per clock cycle.

8. The first processor to use a 200 or 233 MHz system bus (or frontside bus) was the ____________.

A. Intel Pentium

B. Intel Pentium II

C. AMD K6

D. AMD Athlon

9. Designed to support from four to eight processors, the ____________CPU also features a large Level 3 cache.

A. Pentium 4

B. Itanium

C. Xeon MP

D. Opteron

10. Which of the following statements is true?

A. If you have an AMD-compatible motherboard, you can install a Celeron processor.

B. Replacing the CPU may not be the upgrade that is most cost effective or that has the strongest impact on your system's performance.

C. As the size of the address bus increases, the amount of RAM the CPU can use decreases.

D. You can upgrade your CPU if you make sure that a new CPU will fit into the socket or slot on your motherboard.

11. The ____________ processor comes in a SEC

A. The Itanium is a 32-bit processor while the Opteron is a 64-bit processor.

B. The Itanium can run only 64-bit code while the Opteron can run both 32-bit and 64-bit code.

C. The Itanium is made by AMD while the Opteron is made by Intel.

D. The Itanium fits in Slot 1 while the Opteron fits in Slot A.

13. Intel produces the ____________ as a low-end processor and the ____________ as a high-end processor.

A. Celeron, Xeon

B. Celeron, Pentium 4

C. Xeon, Celeron

D. Duron, Itanium

14. If you have a 133 MHz system bus and your CPU runs at 2.53 GHz, what is the CPU multiplier?

A. 12

B. 14

C. 17

D. 19

15. If you change the CPU, you may also have to set jumpers or switches on the motherboard for all of the following *except* ____________.
    A. CPU voltage
    B. CPU multiplier
    C. Address bus
    D. Motherboard speed

Essay Quiz

1. It is important that the CPU stays cool. A number of different technical advances have been made in the design of CPUs along with various devices made to keep the CPU from overheating. Discuss at least two cooling features or cooling options.
2. Juan wants to buy a laptop computer, but he finds that laptops are more expensive than desktop computers. Moreover, he is complaining that he can't find a laptop that is as fast as the newest desktop PCs. Explain to Juan three special considerations that make a laptop more expensive and less powerful than desktop computers.
3. On the bulletin board outside your classroom, your friend Shelley notices two flyers advertising used computers. The first one is a 700 MHz Celeron with 100 MHz system bus, 32 KB L1 cache, 128 KB of L2 cache, and 128 MB RAM. The other one is an 800 MHz Athlon with a 200 MHz system bus, 128 KB L1 cache, a 512 KB L2 cache, and 256 MB RAM. Since Shelley does not know much about computer hardware, she asks you which one is the better computer and why. In simple terms that Shelley will understand, explain five differences that determine which of the two computers is better.
4. You're forming a study group with a few of your friends to review microprocessors. Each one of you has decided to study a particular aspect of this chapter to explain to the group. Your responsibility is buses, including the system bus, address bus, backside bus, and frontside bus. Write a few sentences that will help you explain what each bus does and the differences in the buses.
5. This chapter makes the statement that "The secret to making clock-multiplying work is caching." Write a paragraph in which you explain why that statement is true. Be sure to explain what caching does and the different kinds of caches found in today's computers.

Lab Projects

• Lab Project 3.1

Perhaps newer and faster CPUs have come out recently. Go to www.intel.com and to www.amd.com and investigate the newest CPUs for desktop computers from each manufacturer. Write a paragraph comparing the newest Intel CPU with the newest AMD CPUs. Try to include the following information:

- What is the size of the system bus?
- What is the size of the address bus?
- What is the speed of the CPU?
- What is the speed of the frontside bus?
- What are the sizes of the L1 and L2 caches?
- What kind of chip package houses each CPU?
- What kind of slot or socket does each use?
- What other new features does each site advertise for its newest CPU?

• Lab Project 3.2

Imagine that you are going to buy components to build your own computer. What processor will you use? Typically, the latest and greatest CPU is a lot more expensive than recent models. Intel processors usually cost more than comparable AMD processors. Check CPU features and prices in newspapers or magazines or on the Internet at a site like www.newegg.com. Decide what CPU you want to use for your computer. Write a paragraph explaining why you selected it and how much you will spend for the CPU.

chapter 4

RAM

"Anyone who conducts an argument by appealing to authority is not using his intelligence; he is just using his memory."

—LEONARDO DA VINCI

In this chapter, you will learn how to

- **Identify the different types of RAM packaging**
- **Explain the varieties of DRAM**
- **Install RAM properly**
- **Perform basic RAM troubleshooting**

Anytime someone comes up to me and starts professing their computer savvy, I will ask them a few questions to see how much they really know. Just in case you and I ever meet and you decide you want to "talk tech" with me, I'll tell you my first two questions just so you'll be ready.

1. "How much RAM is in your computer?"
2. "What is RAM and why is it so important that every PC has some?"

Can you answer either of these questions? Don't fret if you can't—you'll know how to answer both of them in this chapter. Let's start by reviewing what we know of RAM thus far.

Random Access Memory (RAM) stores all the running programs on your PC. What exactly is a *running* program? Your PC is full of different programs, such as a word processing program (or two or three), a web browser, and if you're anything like me, a bunch of games. Do you use all of these programs at the same time? Of course not! While we're at it, where are all of those sound files you like to play, and where are all of your documents?

When not in use, programs and data are held in mass storage, which usually means a hard drive, but could also mean floppy disks, a CD-ROM, or some other device that can hold data when the computer is turned off (Figure 4.1). When you load a program by clicking an icon in Windows, the program is copied from the mass storage device to RAM and then run (Figure 4.2).

The term "Random Access Memory" makes more sense when broken into its parts. Any device that holds programs or data that the CPU can access via the address bus is defined as *memory*. The CPU cannot access the data on your hard drive by the address bus. Instead, it must first talk to the hard drive and then the hard drive retrieves the data. *Random access* means that any one byte of that memory can be accessed as easily as any other byte. Don't limit your thinking on this topic just to electronic components. A sheet of paper with a list of names could be called random ac-

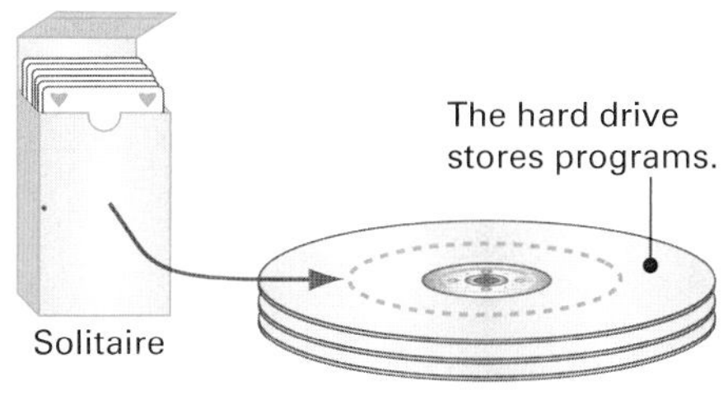

• **Figure 4.1** Mass storage holds unused programs.

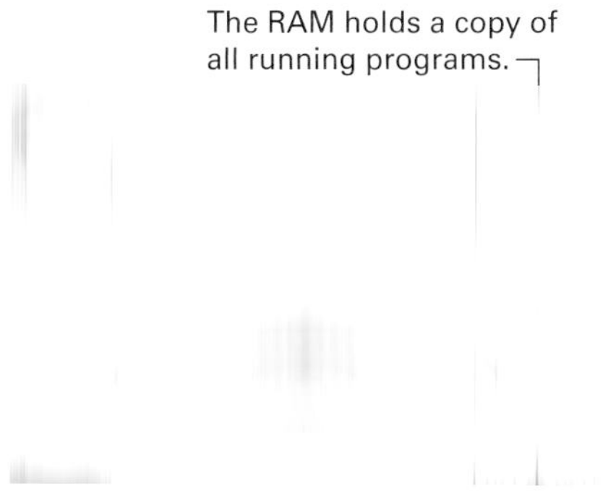

The RAM holds a copy of all running programs.

• **Figure 4.2** Programs run in RAM.

Historical/Conceptual

■ DRAM

DRAM functions like an electronic spreadsheet, with numbered rows containing cells. Each cell can hold a 1 or 0. You'll recall the concept from Chapter 3, but now let's put it into physical shape. Each spreadsheet cell is a special type of semiconductor that can hold a value—1 or 0—using microscopic capacitors and transistors (Figure 4.3). DRAM usually manifests itself as a number of chips soldered onto a card of some type. We refer to these cards as RAM *sticks*. (Figure 4.4)

DRAM stick makers need to organize individual chips into a set that the PC can use. This is made interesting because DRAM chips come in varying capacities. One chip might be able to store a million lines of code—think of each line as one of the rows on the electronic spreadsheet used as an analogy for RAM—but each line is limited to only four bits. In old tech shorthand,

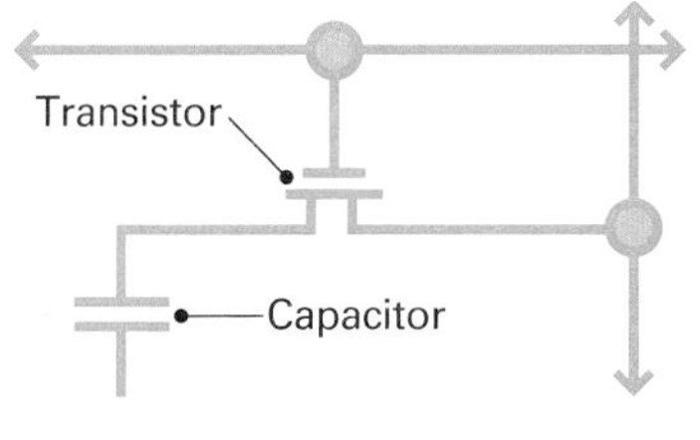

• **Figure 4.3** Schematic of a 1-bit DRAM storage chip

• **Figure 4.4** A typical RAM stick

• **Figure 4.5** What do these numbers mean?

you'd call such a chip a *1 Meg x 4*. (A *Meg* in this case means the number 1,048,576.) Another chip might have over a billion distinct rows, each able to hold 8-bit-wide data, a *512 Meg x 8* chip. It is difficult if not impossible to tell the size of a DRAM chip just by looking at it—only the DRAM makers know the meaning of the tiny number on the chips (although sometimes you can make a good guess). See Figure 4.5.

Organizing DRAM

Due to its low cost, high speed, and capability to contain a lot of data in a relatively small package, DRAM has been the standard RAM used in all computers—not just PCs—since the mid-1970s. DRAM can be found in just about everything, from automobiles to automatic bread makers.

The PC has very specific requirements for DRAM. The original 8088 processor had an 8-bit frontside bus. All the commands given to an 8088 processor were in discrete, 8-bit chunks. (Refer to Chapter 3 if this is not clear.) Therefore, you need RAM that can store data in 8-bit chunks. Even today's latest and greatest CPUs still run all of the original 8088 commands (along with all of their own more advanced commands) for backward compatibility, so the minimum RAM width is still 8 bits. When people talk about PC memory, they say things like "64 megabytes," "512 megabytes," or, if your computer is really old, "640 kilobytes." You'd never say something like "16 megawords" or "32 megabits" to describe system RAM. That's because your CPU needs memory that stores programs and data in 8-bit (1-byte) chunks. So when discussing memory in PCs, we always talk about *byte-wide* memory.

Although today's DRAM chips may have widths greater than 1 bit, back in the old days all DRAM chips were 1 bit wide. That means you only had sizes like 64 K x 1 or 256 K x 1—always 1 bit wide. So how was 1-bit-wide DRAM turned into 8-bit-wide memory? The answer was quite simple: just take eight 1-bit-wide chips and electronically organize them with the Northbridge memory controller chip to be eight wide. First, put eight 1-bit-wide chips in a row on the motherboard (Figure 4.6), and then wire up this row of DRAM chips to the Northbridge chip (which has to be designed to handle this) to make byte-wide memory (Figure 4.7). You just made eight 1-bit-wide DRAM chips look like a single 8-bit-wide DRAM chip to the CPU.

You Are a Byte Victim!

Okay, before we take even one more step we need to get a critical point extremely clear. When you first saw the 8088's machine language in the previous

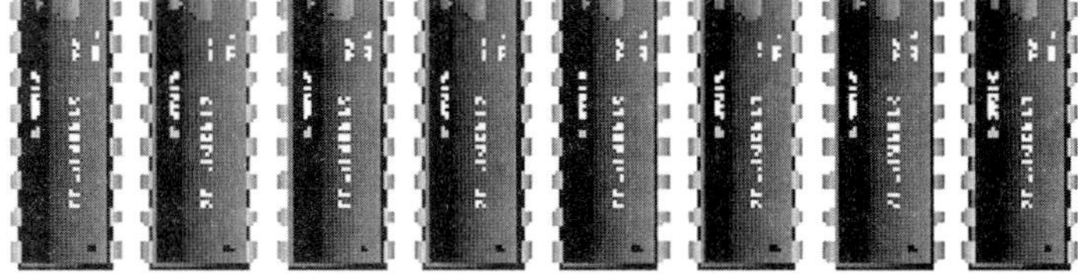

• **Figure 4.6** One row of DRAM

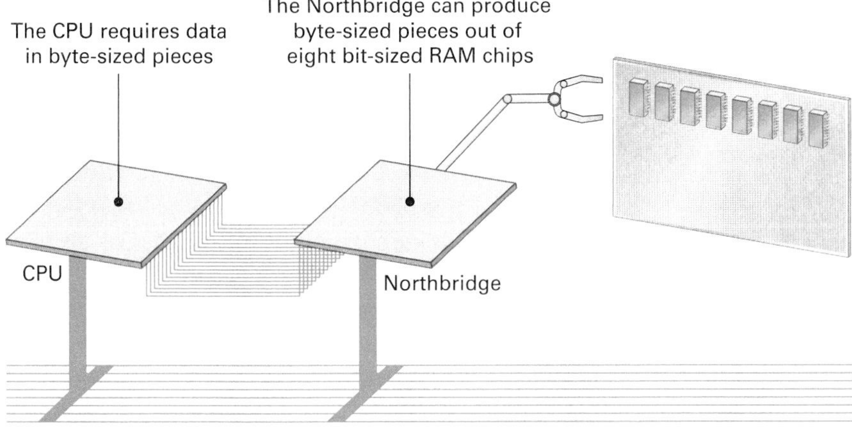

commands are 1 byte, but a few more complex commands need 2 bytes. For example, the command below tells the CPU to move 163 bytes "up the spreadsheet" and run whatever command is there. Cool, eh?

```
1110100110100011
```

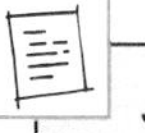

Just because you have a byte-wide frontside bus doesn't mean all your commands have to be 1 byte!

But the problem here is that the command is 2 bytes, not 1 byte wide! So how does the 8088 handle this? Simple—it just takes the command 1 byte at a time. It takes twice as long to handle the command since the Northbridge has to go to RAM twice, but it works.

Okay, so if some of the commands are more than 1 byte wide, why didn't Intel make the 8088 with a 16-bit frontside bus? Wouldn't that have been

8088 External Data Bus Codebook

LIGHTS	MEANING
10000000	The next line is a number, put it in the AX register
10010000	The next line is a number, put it in the BX register
10110000	Add AX to BX and put the result in AX
11000000	Place the value of AX on the External Data Bus
00000000	The number 0
00000001	The number 1
00000010	The number 2
00000011	The number 3
00000100	The number 4
00000101	The number 5
00000110	The number 6
00000111	The number 7
00001000	The number 8
00001001	The number 9

• **Figure 4.8** Codebook again

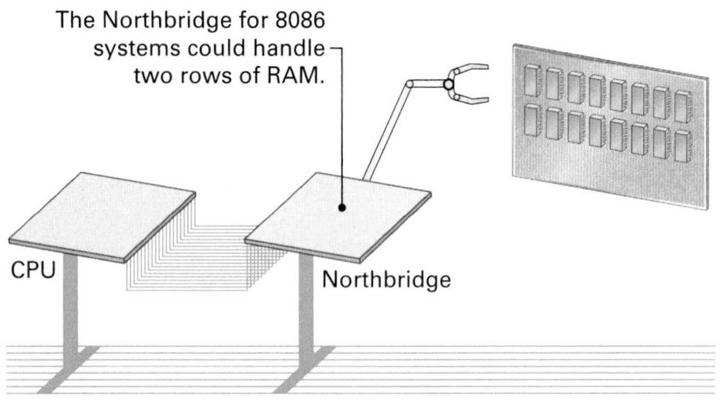

• **Figure 4.9** Pumped up 8086 Northbridge at work

better? Well, Intel did! Intel invented a CPU called the 8086. The 8086 actually predated the 8088 and was absolutely identical to the 8088 except for one small detail—it had a 16-bit frontside bus. If Intel and IBM had wanted to, they could have used the 8086 instead of the 8088, and they could have used 2-byte-wide RAM instead of 1-byte-wide RAM. Of course, they would have needed to invent a Northbridge that could handle that kind of RAM (Figure 4.9).

So what happened? Why didn't Intel sell IBM the 8086 instead of the 8088? Two reasons. First, nobody had invented a cost-affordable Northbridge or RAM that could handle 2 bytes at a time. Sure, chips were invented but they were *expensive* and IBM probably didn't think that anyone would want to pay $12,000 for a personal computer. So IBM bought the Intel 8088, not the Intel 8086, and all our RAM came in bytes. But as you might imagine, it didn't stay that way too long!

Modern CPUs are a lot smarter than the old Intel 8088. Their machine languages have some commands that are up to 64 bits (8 bytes) wide. They also have at least a 64-bit frontside bus that can handle more than just 8 bits. They don't want RAM to give them a puny 8 bits at a time! To optimize the flow of data into and out of the CPU, the modern Northbridge provides 64 bits of data every time the CPU requests information from RAM.

When the CPU needs certain bytes of data, it requests those bytes via the address bus. The CPU does not know the physical location of the RAM that stores that data, nor the physical makeup of the RAM—such as how many DRAM chips work together to provide the 64-bit-wide memory rows. The Northbridge keeps track of this and just gives the CPU whatever bytes it requests (Figure 4.10).

So if modern RAM comes in sizes much wider than a byte, why do we still use the word "byte" to describe how much RAM we have? Why do we say we have 32 megabytes of RAM when we really have 4 Meg x 8-byte wide RAM? Convention. Habit. Rather than using a label that describes the electronic structure of RAM, common usage describes the *total capacity of RAM in bytes*. You can use RAM of any width (although going wider than the frontside bus is a waste of time) just as long as the Northbridge knows how to handle the RAM. The trick is in knowing the different types of RAM sticks that are available.

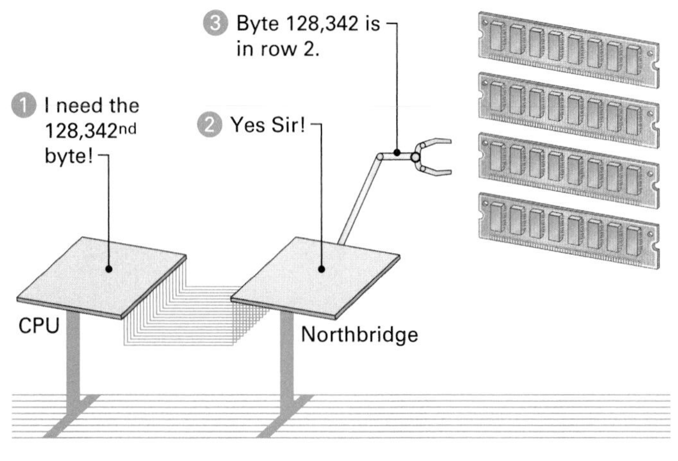

• **Figure 4.10** The Northbridge knows the real location of the DRAM.

■ RAM Sticks, Part I

Manufacturers have developed many types of RAM sticks over the years, trying to keep pace with the development of the CPUs and motherboard Northbridge chip. Newer types of sticks made RAM less vulnerable to physical damage and easier to install.

Manufacturers improved packages and technology to provide faster access times and, as the size of the data bus increased with new CPU and motherboard types, to provide a RAM stick that could deliver enough data at a single pop to optimize the flow of data into and out of the CPU. Early 8-bit RAM sticks, for example, gave way to 32-bit sticks to accommodate the 32-bit wide data bus of the 386 and 486 CPUs. Those 32-bit wide sticks in turn were replaced by 64-bit wide sticks with the development of the Pentium and later CPUs. This section takes a quick look at the more common packages used in the early part of the PC industry.

DIPPs

Very early DRAM chips connected to the motherboard directly via a **Dual Inline Pin Package (DIPP)**, two rows of pins extending from either side of the

As new and improved processors appeared and RAM prices fell, motherboard manufacturers created motherboards that had multiple rows of unpopulated RAM sockets to provide for future upgrades. The drawback to this system was space—extra rows of DIPP sockets took up too much motherboard real estate.

This demand created a new type of DRAM package. Instead of individual chips inserted into individual sockets, manufacturers soldered the RAM onto small boards—sticks—that you inserted into special connectors on the motherboard. The first popular stick was called the **Single Inline Pin Package (SIPP)**.

30-Pin SIPPs

The SIPP used a standardized set of 30 pins that mounted into the motherboard, which eliminated the need for individual mounts for each DRAM. The SIPP revolutionized the way DRAM was used in a PC. By the time SIPPs had been invented, for example, new DRAM chips were available that were more than 1 bit wide. But if you were using the old DIPPs, your old 8088 computer had eight little DIPP connectors on the motherboard. You were stuck using eight 1-bit wide DIPPs. But if you used a SIPP, you could use two 4-bit chips, or eight 1-bit wide chips—it didn't matter since the chips were soldered to the SIPP, not the motherboard! So you could take out a 30-pin SIPP with eight 256 K x 1 chips, replace it with a 30-pin SIPP with two 256 K x 4 chips, and the system wouldn't know the difference. SIPPs made installing and removing RAM much simpler (Figure 4.12).

• **Figure 4.12** 30-pin SIPP

SIPPs plugged directly into the motherboard via their own special socket. They were relatively easy to install; all you had to do was push down. Unfortunately, SIPPs also had a rather nasty Achilles' heel. The 30 pins that connected the package to the motherboard were just as delicate as the pins on the DIPP chips. Like the DIPP chips, it was just too easy to break off one of the pins accidentally—which made the whole SIPP garbage. So, although SIPPs were revolutionary, they were quickly replaced by their much more robust successor, the **30-pin SIMM** .

30-Pin SIMMs

Single Inline Memory Modules (SIMMs) were the next rung on DRAM's evolutionary ladder. Physically, they looked very similar to SIPPs, with one exception: no protruding pins. There was nothing to bend and snap off (Figure 4.13). The 30 contacts on SIMMs were flush with and thus supported by the circuit board.

• **Figure 4.13** 30-pin SIMM

SIMMs inserted into a special SIMM socket (Figure 4.14). It was virtually impossible to install SIMMs improperly due to the notch on one side of the card.

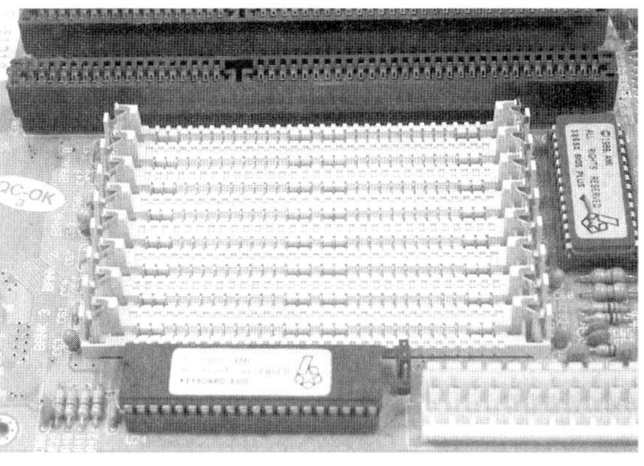

• **Figure 4.14** Eight rows for 30-pin SIMMs

Electronically, 30-pin SIMMs were identical to 30-pin SIPPs. Both were 8 bits wide, so they could provide a full byte of data onto the data bus when directed to do so by the Northbridge. You could even purchase a simple converter that enabled you to insert SIPPs into SIMM sockets, and vice versa.

RAM chip layout and number varied wildly on SIMM sticks from different manufactures. Figure 4.15 shows some examples of different chip layouts for a 30-pin SIMM.

SIMM Sticks and Parity

Early RAM technologies used a form of error checking called **parity** . Parity manifested through an extra 1-bit chip in the

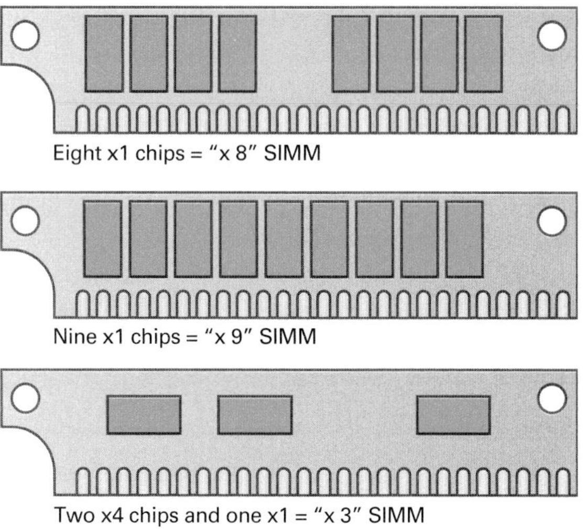

• **Figure 4.15** Different chip layouts on SIMMs

row (Figure 4.16). This ninth bit enabled the Northbridge to compare the number of 1's stored in a byte with the number of 1's found when the byte was accessed. For parity to work, you had to have a Northbridge designed to use the parity chip.

When the Northbridge chip placed new data in RAM, it set the parity bit, and then checked that bit every time it accessed that byte of RAM. If something happened [illegible] today's DRAM is so dependable that very few PCs still support parity.

Try This!

Dealing with Old RAM

Often in the PC world, old technology and ways of doing things get reimplemented with some newer technology. Learning how things worked back in the ancient days can stand a tech in good stead. Perhaps more importantly, many thousands of companies—including hospitals, auto repair places, and more—use very old, proprietary applications that keep track of medical records, inventory, and so on. If you're called to work on one of these ancient systems, you need to know how to work with old parts, so try this.

Get the use of an old computer, such as a 386 or 486. Ask your uncle or cousin or Great Aunt Edna if they have a PC collecting dust in a closet [illegible]

Manufacturers produced parity and non-parity varieties of SIMMs; when you purchased RAM, you needed to determine which variety a particular system could handle. Non-parity RAM would not work in a system that required parity RAM.

The motherboard book for a system answered the question of parity or non-parity RAM for that system. A quick visual check of a 30-pin SIMM would tell you whether it was parity or non-parity. All non-parity 30-pin SIMMs had an even number of chips. All parity 30-pin SIMMs had an odd number of chips. Some PCs enabled you to turn off the parity. Figure 4.17 shows a screen from an older PC's advanced CMOS settings. (See Chapter 5 for a discussion of the System Setup Utility.) On these machines, you could mix parity with non-parity chips, as long as the parity was turned off.

Access Speed

We know from Chapter 3 that the system clock controls the CPU speed. We know, for example, exactly how many clock cycles the CPU needs to calculate 2 + 3. The DRAM used for the first ten years of the PC industry did not

• **Figure 4.16** Here's a close-up of older-style DIPP DRAM. The three chips show it has parity.

use a clock. The Northbridge simply talked to the DRAM and then had to wait until the DRAM came up with the information it requested. This early type of RAM was called **Fast Page Mode (FPM) RAM**. It took a certain amount of time for the FPM DRAM chip to supply the Northbridge with the requested data. This was called the **access speed**, and it was typically given in nanoseconds (ns). The faster the chip, the shorter the delay and the smaller the access-speed number. Therefore, a 100-nanosecond chip was slower than a 60-nanosecond chip.

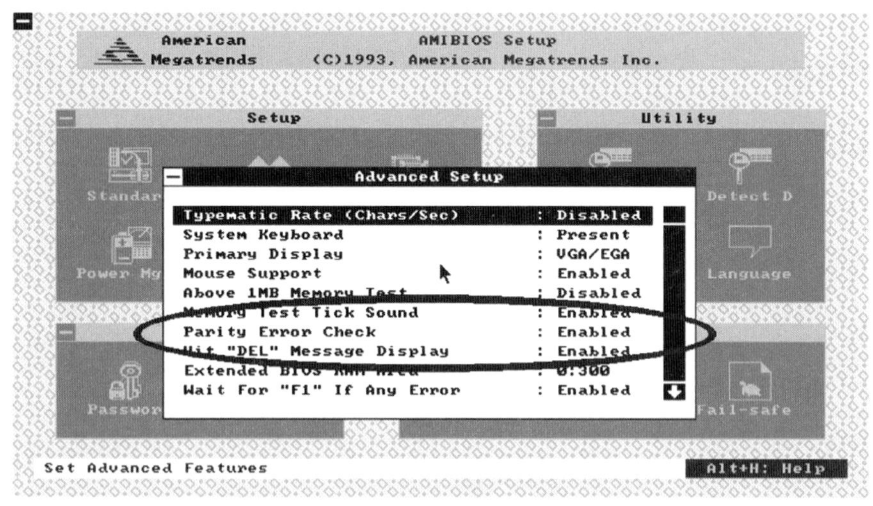

• **Figure 4.17** Parity option on older System Setup Utility

Every Northbridge was designed to send a data request to FPM DRAM and then wait a certain number of clock cycles for the answer. As a result, each motherboard required a certain speed of FPM DRAM, so it was crucial for you to be able to eyeball a DRAM chip to determine its access speed. Access speeds ranged from as slow as 200 nanoseconds on ancient 8088s, up to 50 nanoseconds for the last of the FPM DRAMs. Figure 4.18 shows some examples of chips and how to determine their access speeds.

A lower access speed number means faster access.

Although there were some exceptions, which you will visit later, the easiest guideline was to follow the motherboard book guidelines on the proper speed FPM DRAM and thus make sure that every piece of DRAM was that speed.

Even as we march along in the early twenty-first century, manufacturers continue to make small amounts of 30-pin SIMMs for system replacement, although the days of the 30-pin SIMM in a new PC have long since passed.

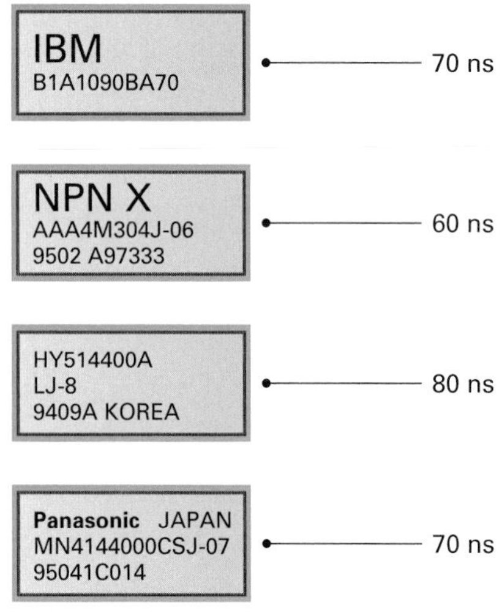

• **Figure 4.18** Determining access rates

Test Specific

■ RAM Sticks, Part II

Now that you have a basic understanding of the different types of earlier DRAM packages, you can move forward into the more modern types of DRAM with the necessary conceptual tools to appreciate why they're used in today's machines.

72-Pin SIMMs

To keep pace with CPU and motherboard developments, manufacturers created the **72-pin SIMM**. These SIMMs came in larger (for the time) capacities and faster access speeds (60-80 ns). Most importantly, 72-pin SIMMs were 32 bits wide, so each stick could deliver 32 bits of data at the

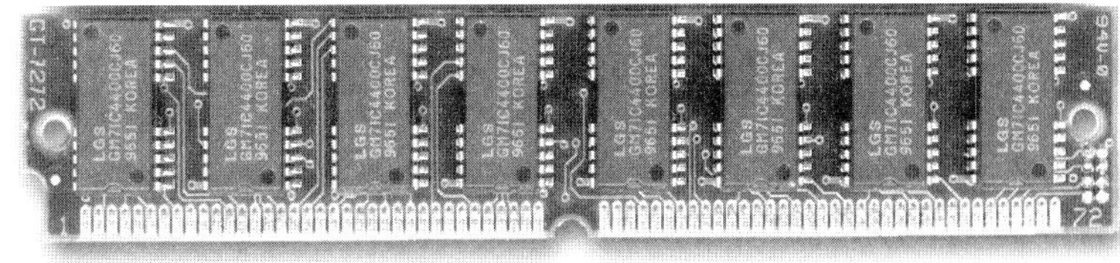

Figure 4.19 A 72-pin SIMM

Northbridge's direction, thus optimizing the flow of data into and out of the 32-bit-wide data bus of the 386 and 486 CPUs.

The 72-pin SIMM had the same number of pins on each stick as its name would imply—72, in this case. Similar in shape to the 30-pin SIMM, the 72-pin SIMM was about an inch longer and had a notch in the middle of the pins to assist in inserting the stick properly (Figure 4.19). Figure 4.20 shows some typical 72-pin SIMM slots on a motherboard.

Because 72-pin SIMMs were 32 bits wide, the term "x 32" described a non-parity SIMM and "x 36" described a parity SIMM. Don't let the num-

4 x 32 = 16 MB, no parity
4 x 36 = 16 MB, parity
8 x 32 = 32 MB, no parity
8 x 36 = 32 MB, parity
16 x 32 = 64 MB, no parity
16 x 36 = 64 MB, parity

Other than the width, 72-pin SIMMs were just like the older 30-pin SIMMs. They were FPM DRAM, they had an access speed, and you could choose parity or non-parity. Like 30-pin SIMMs, a small notch on one end made it virtually impossible to install a 72-pin SIMM incorrectly.

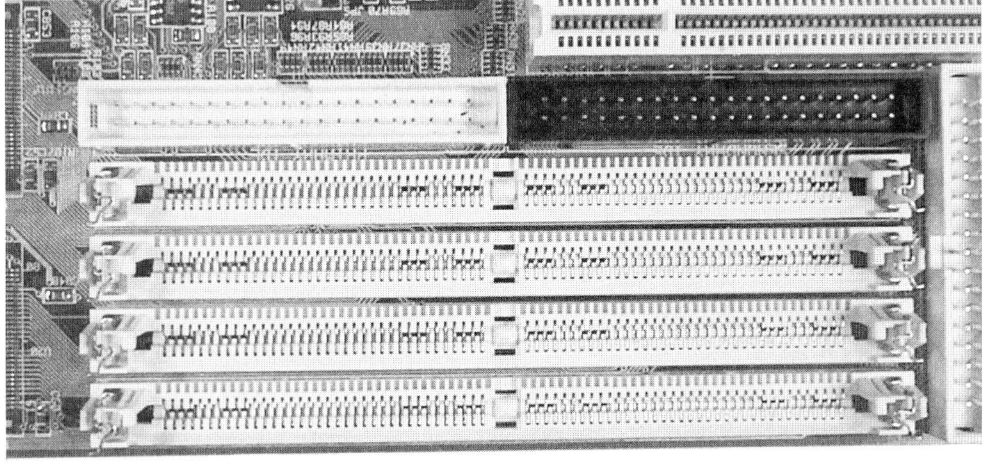

Figure 4.20 Four 72-pin SIMM slots

Cross Check

RAM Access Speeds

You learned how to decipher RAM access speed from the numbers printed on individual DRAM chips on 30-pin SIMMs.

1. Do you think it works the same way on 72-pin SIMMs?
2. If you have sticks of 72-pin SIMMs in your lab, check them out. How fast are they?

Unlike the 30-pin SIMMs, there was no definite way to tell a parity 72-pin SIMM from a non-parity 72-pin SIMM. You just made sure you wrote the type of SIMM on the back of the stick, and you never had a problem. In fact, many DRAM makers and distributors around this time began to print this information right on the SIMM (they were not being nice, necessarily; they just didn't want you to bother them with silly questions), as shown in Figure 4.21.

Banking, Part I—Filling the Bus

System developers seek to optimize the flow of data into and out of the CPU because the microprocessor does the vast majority of the work in any PC. A key part of the optimization lies in the abilities of the Northbridge and RAM. If a modern CPU with a 64-bit data bus requests a set of data and the Northbridge and RAM can only deliver that data in 32-bit chunks, is that optimal? Of course not!

Motherboard manufacturers organize RAM slots electronically into banks. Each **bank** of RAM can deliver data the full width of the data bus, so a bank on a 486 would be 32-bits wide, whereas a bank on a Pentium 2 would be 64-bits wide. To fill a bank sometimes takes more than a single stick of RAM, depending on the width of both the bus and the RAM stick. A single 72-pin SIMM, capable of holding data in 32-bit rows, for example, fills a bank on a 486 system. That same stick of RAM on a Pentium 2 system, in contrast would only handle half the duties. You'd need to add another 72-pin SIMM to make up the other 32 bits of the data bus. Just as the CPU does not care where the data it requests is physically located in RAM, it also doesn't care if the data for a single, 64-bit row actually resides on two separate RAM sticks! The Northbridge handles all the details and simply sends the requested data to the CPU on the data bus.

To keep pace with CPU and bus developments, manufacturers came out with the **Dual Inline Memory Module (DIMM)**, capable of delivering 64 bits at a pop. The DIMM is the current RAM package of choice.

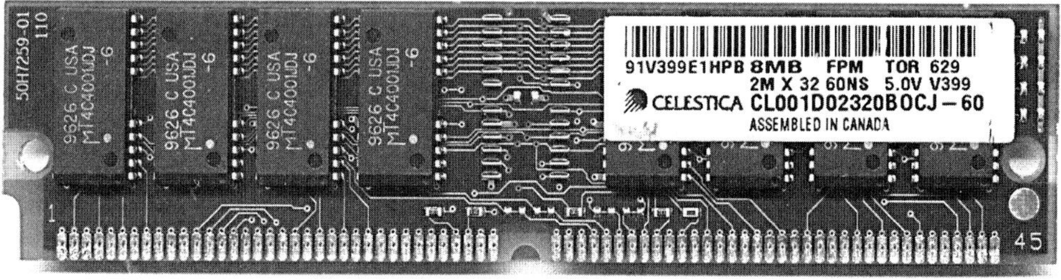

• **Figure 4.21** Labeling is the secret to identification.

DIMM

• **Figure 4.22** 144-pin micro-DIMM

DIMMs come in a wide variety of pin sizes and can use several different technologies. The most common pin sizes found on desktops are the 168-pin and 184-pin varieties. Laptop varieties come in 68-pin, 144-pin (Figure 4.22), or 172-pin *micro-DIMM*, and the 72-pin, 144-pin or 200-pin **Small Outline DIMM (SO DIMM)** (Figure 4.23). With the exception of the 72-pin SO DIMM, all these DIMM varieties deliver a full 64 bits from a single stick, which means you need but one to fill a bank in a Pentium class or later motherboard.

The Magic Banking Formula

With SIMMs, SO DIMMs, and DIMMs, it can get a little challenging to remember how many sticks of each type of DRAM are needed to make a

the SIMM or DIMM

Let's try this a couple of times:

- **How many 72-pin SIMMs are needed to make a bank on a Pentium Pro?** A Pentium Pro has a 64-bit external data bus, and 72-pin SIMMs are 32 bits wide, so 64 ÷ 32 = 2. We need two 72-pin SIMMs per bank for a Pentium Pro.
- **How many 184-pin DIMMs are needed to make a bank on an Athlon XP?** An Athlon XP has a 64-bit external data bus, and 184-pin DIMMs are 64 bits wide, so 64 ÷ 64 = 1. We need one 184-pin DIMM per bank for an Athlon XP.

Stick with this formula, no matter what they throw at you in the future. It will always tell you the number of sticks needed to make a bank.

For years, banking was a critical issue when dealing with RAM. The external data bus on all CPUs, however, has never gone beyond 64 bits since

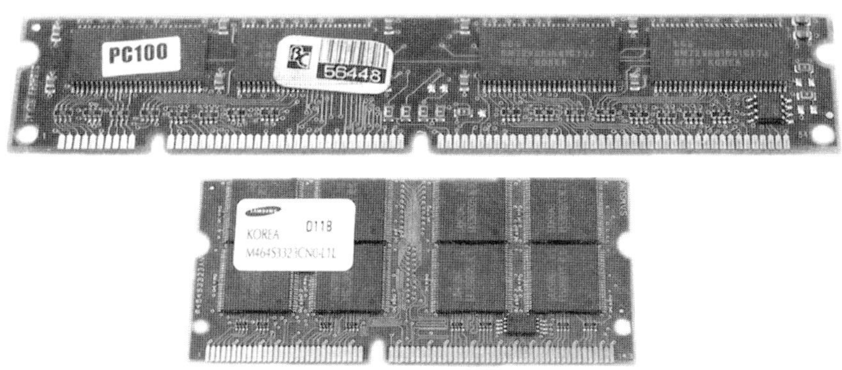

• **Figure 4.23** A 168-pin DIMM above a 144-pin SO-DIMM

the days of the original Pentium. This, combined with the overwhelming dominance of 168-pin and 184-pin DIMMs, has made banking virtually a non-issue in today's systems. Don't let this make you too complacent! Be aware that Intel and AMD are already planning new CPUs with 128-bit external data buses. These systems will need two 184-pin DIMMs per bank. Plus, both NVIDIA and VIA have Northbridge chips optimized for two banks of 64-bit RAM, as you'll read later in this chapter.

■ Improvements in DRAM Technology

As we look at RAM, you need to understand some of the improvements on the classic FPM DRAM of the original 8088 processor days. When I say improvements, I'm talking about functional technology improvements, not just widening the RAM via a new type of stick, as you saw in the previous sections. My goal here is not to go into great depth on these improvements, but rather to enable you to recognize these improvements and take advantage of them when they are available.

EDO

All DRAM needs to be refreshed to keep the data and programs it stores valid, as you'll recall from Chapter 3. The refresh process creates a big bottleneck in RAM access. Of course, things like SRAM caches certainly reduce the impact, but any way to minimize the frequency of refresh will improve the overall speed of the computer—thus, the creation of **Extended Data Out DRAM (EDO DRAM)** back in the early 1990s. EDO DRAM was nothing more than a moderate improvement on old-style FPM DRAM. EDO needed to be refreshed much less often, thereby providing an extended period where data could be taken out of RAM. EDO DRAM enabled a system to access data more quickly than a comparably equipped system with FPM DRAM. EDO RAM was on either a 72-pin SIMM or a DIMM (168-pin or SO), and looked exactly like FPM DRAM. There was no standard way to tell EDO from FPM DRAM, so again we were always careful to label our EDO DRAM as such (Figure 4.24).

To take advantage of EDO, you needed a Northbridge designed to handle EDO. Unfortunately, you couldn't just put EDO DRAM in any computer. The majority of the early Pentium systems used EDO DRAM, but that

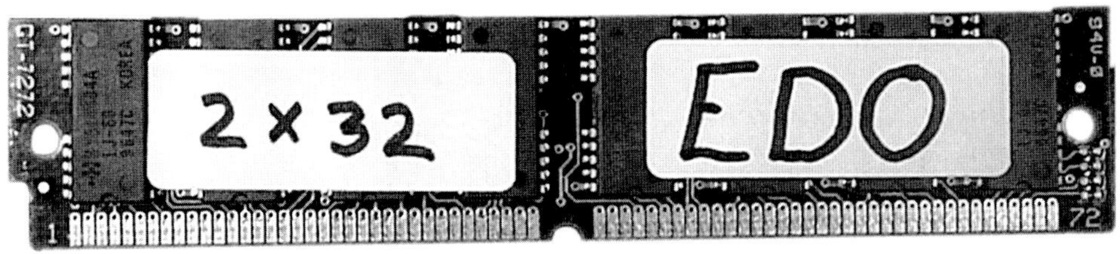

• **Figure 4.24** How to tell EDO from FPM—another label

was not true of the 486s with 72-pin SIMM slots. You had to refer to your motherboard book to see if your system could use EDO DRAM. EDO DRAM enjoyed wide acceptance through most of the 1990s until the advent of a new, extremely powerful type of DRAM called SDRAM. FPM and EDO DRAM are now obsolete.

SDRAM

Synchronous DRAM (SDRAM) supplanted FPM and EDO technologies soon after the Pentium-class CPUs and motherboards were released. SDRAM is still DRAM, but it is *synchronous*—tied to the system clock. As mentioned earlier, regular DRAM (EDO or FPM) was *asynchronous*—not tied to any clock. If the CPU wanted some data from RAM, the Northbridge sent the necessary signals to the DRAM, waited a certain number of clock ticks, and

resulting in little wasted time. Plus, SDRAM is quite a bit faster than DRAM. Further, SDRAM pipelines instructions from the Northbridge that enable commands to be ready as soon as the Northbridge takes the previous command. Collectively, these improvements make SDRAM four to six times faster than FPM or EDO DRAM.

To take advantage of SDRAM, you must have a system that is designed to use it. Chances are that if you have a system with slots for 168-pin DIMMs, your system uses SDRAM. Because SDRAM ties to the system clock, it doesn't have an access speed; it has a clock speed just like a CPU. Five clock speeds are commonly used today: 66, 75, 83, 100, and 133 MHz. Manufacturers mark these speeds on the DIMM. You need to get a stick with a clock speed that is faster than or equal to the motherboard speed. If you have a Celeron 500, for example, 66-MHz SDRAM would suffice because the Celeron talks to the motherboard at 66 MHz. A Pentium III that uses a 133-MHz frontside bus, in contrast, would obviously need SDRAM that could run at 133 MHz.

PC100/133 Standards

Athlon and Pentium III systems moved frontside bus speeds from 66 MHz to 100 MHz and even 133 MHz. If the frontside bus ran at 100 MHz or better then you need SDRAM to match that speed. The first generation of 100-MHz SDRAM DIMMs ran into some compatibility problems. Intel recognized this issue and created the famous PC100 and later the PC133 specifications that define the construction of high-speed DRAM. These standards require the use of DIMMs or SO DIMMs and a unique little chip called a *serial presence detect* (SPD) chip installed on every DIMM stick. The SPD provides the system with all of the details about the DIMM, including its size, speed, and a number of other more technical bits of information. Most motherboards

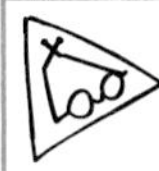

Tech Tip

Registered DRAM

Most servers and many high-end workstations sport a DRAM variant called registered DRAM that facilitates high-volume data flow in and out of RAM. Registered DRAM has logic circuits—quite logically named registers—that buffer control signals to synchronize with the system clock. This sort of RAM helps these systems keep track of the hugely complex data transfers and manage multiple sticks of RAM. Typical home and office PCs, in contrast, use unbuffered (meaning without registers) DRAM, optimizing for speed rather than perfect data transfers.

require the use of PC100 or PC133 DIMMs. People who sell DIMMs will clearly advertise which DIMMs are PC100 or PC133, and which are not.

ECC

Many higher-end systems use a special type of RAM called **Error Correction Code (ECC) DRAM**. ECC is a major advance in error checking on DRAM. As mentioned earlier, DRAM rarely goes bad anymore, but it can still have the occasional hiccup that can cause data loss. (These hiccups do not have any lasting effect on the hardware.) Parity is virtually useless for these types of occasional problems, but ECC detects problems in RAM quite well and can fix most of them on the fly. Any size RAM stick can use ECC DRAM, but it is most common as 168-pin DIMMs. To take advantage of ECC RAM, you need a motherboard that is designed to use ECC. Check your motherboard book. You rarely see ECC RAM in the standard home or office system.

Double Pumping

The introduction of the AMD Athlon and Intel Pentium 4 CPUs created a demand for a new type of RAM. Both processor families increased the speed between the CPU and the Northbridge chip: double the system bus speed for the Athlon and quadruple the speed for the Pentium 4. Double-pumping enabled the Athlon to send two bits of data with every clock cycle, effectively doubling the system bus speed. Athlons with 100 MHz and 133 MHz frontside buses ran between the CPU and the Northbridge at an effective rate of 200 MHz or 266 MHz (Figure 4.25). The frontside bus on the Pentium 4 cranked it up further, running at 400 MHz for the early models and 533 MHz for later ones.

Manufacturers scrambled for higher speed RAM solutions to optimize the other side of the Northbridge—between RAM and Northbridge—and thus increase the processing speed of the whole system. Intel initially went with the proprietary RDRAM solution, whereas AMD and the rest of the industry embraced DDR SDRAM.

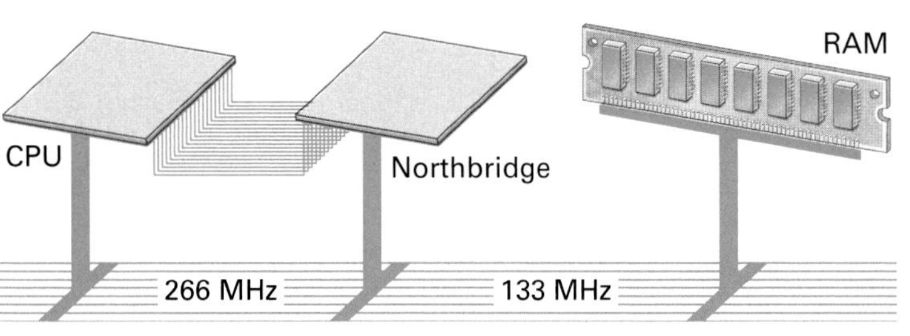

• **Figure 4.25** I want to run fast too!

RDRAM

When Intel was developing the Pentium 4, they knew that regular SDRAM just wasn't going to be fast enough to handle the quad-pumped 400 MHz FSB. Intel announced plans to replace SDRAM with a very fast new type of RAM called **Rambus DRAM**, or simply **RDRAM** (Figure 4.26). Hailed by Intel as the next great leap in DRAM technology, RDRAM can handle speeds up to 800 MHz, which gave Intel plenty of room to improve the Pentium 4.

RDRAM was greatly anticipated by the industry for years, but industry support for RDRAM proved less than enthusiastic due to

• **Figure 4.26** RDRAM

significant delays in development plus a price many times that of SDRAM. Despite this grudging support, almost all major PC makers sold systems

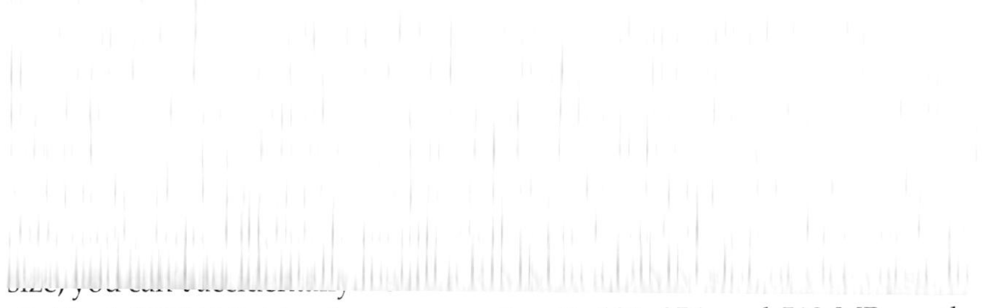

dividual RDRAM chips have a capacity: 64, 128, 256, and 512 MB are the most common. RDRAM also has a speed rating: 600 MHz, 700 MHz, 800 MHz, or 1066 MHz.

RIMMs install just like DIMMs—you push them into the proper slots until the clips snap into place—but have three quirks you need to know. First, RIMMs run hot—very hot—and need a special heat dissipation device, rather logically called a *heat spreader*, attached directly to the RIMM. Second, RDRAM motherboards require that all RIMM slots be populated. Unused pairs of slots must have a passive device called a **Continuity RIMM** (CRIMM) installed in each slot to enable the RDRAM system to terminate properly (Figure 4.27).

Finally, you have to install RIMMs in pairs because RDRAM employs a dual-channel architecture. Each RIMM is 64 bits wide, but the Northbridge can alternate between two sticks to increase the speed of data retrieval. The pair(s) of RIMMs installed must be the same speed and capacity.

RDRAM offered dramatic possibilities for high-speed PCs, but ran into three roadblocks that betamaxed it. First, the technology was owned wholly by Rambus Corporation—if you wanted to make it, you had to pay the licensing fees they charged. That leads directly to the second problem, expense. RDRAM cost substantially more than SDRAM. Third, Rambus and

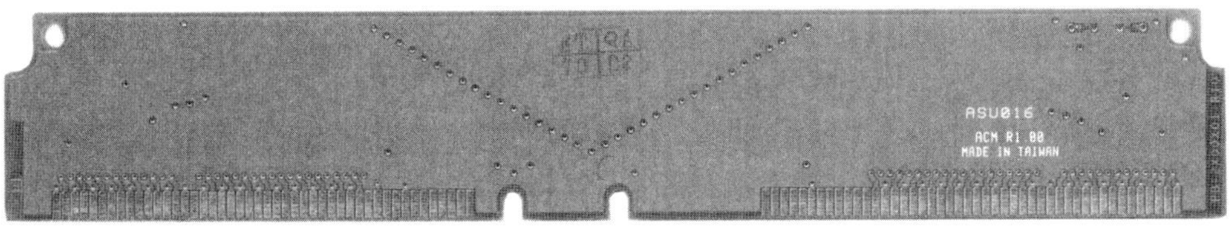

• **Figure 4.27** CRIMM

Intel made a completely closed deal for the technology. RDRAM worked only on Pentium 4 systems using Intel-made Northbridge chips. All the alternative CPU makers, such as AMD, and the other big chipset manufacturers, such as VIA and SiS, were completely out of luck. Clearly, the rest of the industry had to look for another high-speed RAM solution.

DDR SDRAM

AMD and many major system and memory makers threw their support behind **Double Data Rate SDRAM (DDR SDRAM)**. As the name implies, DDR SDRAM simply doubles the throughput of SDRAM by making two processes for every clock cycle. This synchronized (pardon the pun) nicely with the Athlon and later AMD processors' double-pumped frontside bus (Figure 4.28). DDR SDRAM could not run as fast as RDRAM—although relatively low frontside bus speeds made that a moot point—but cost only slightly more than regular SDRAM. Currently, DDR SDRAM is widely available and very cheap.

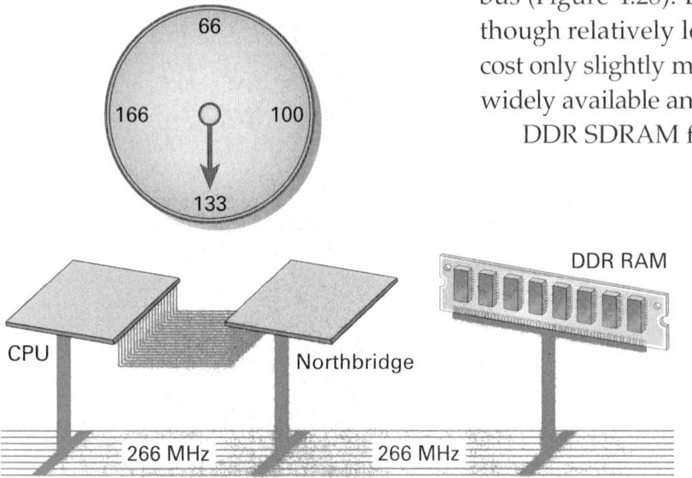

• **Figure 4.28** Schematic of Athlon FSB using DDR SDRAM

DDR SDRAM for desktops comes in 184-pin DIMMs, which match the 168-pin DIMMs of regular SDRAM in physical size, but not in pin compatibility (Figure 4.29). The slots for the two types of RAM appear similar as well, but have different guide notches, making it impossible to insert either type of RAM into the other's slot. DDR SDRAM for laptops comes in either 200-pin SO-DIMMs or 172-pin micro-DIMMs (Figure 4.30).

DDR SDRAM runs at 200, 266, 333, or 400 MHz and uses a rather interesting naming convention based on the number of bytes per second of data throughput. To determine the bytes per second, take the MHz speed times 8 bytes (the width of DDR SDRAM). So 200 MHz multiplied by 8 is 1600 bytes per second. Throw "PC" in the front to get the name: PC1600. Do this with the other three DDR SDRAM speeds to get PC2100, PC2700, and PC3200. Many techs also use a short name based on the speed of the stick, e.g., *DDR400* refers to 400 MHz DDR SDRAM.

Following the lead of AMD, VIA, and other manufacturers, the PC industry has adopted DDR SDRAM as the standard system RAM. Even Intel has relented and now supports DDR SDRAM for the Pentium 4 platform. Ironically, the first DDR SDRAM Intel-branded Northbridge appeared with

• **Figure 4.29** DDR SDRAM

Banking Part II—Dual-Channel Architecture

There's one sure thing about PC technologies—any good idea that can be copied will be copied. One of Rambus' best concepts was the dual-channel architecture—using two sticks together to increase throughput. Manufacturers have released motherboards and Northbridge chips that support dual-channel architecture using DDR SDRAM. Early implementation of this *Dual DDR* technology has a few quirks. Most notably, motherboards that use NVIDIA's nForce2 chipset have three DDR SDRAM slots, but the Dual DDR works only if you install DDR SDRAM in two of the slots (Figure 4.31). If you populate the third slot, the system will use the full capacity of RAM installed, but only in a single channel. The dual slots are blue; the third slot is black, which you could clearly see if this weren't a black-and-white photo.

While every PC uses DRAM in one of its many variations for their RAM, other forms of RAM are found in PCs with names like VRAM and SGRAM—we discuss these other types of RAM in Chapter 18.

Double-Sided SIMMs/DIMMs

Every type of RAM stick starting with the old 72-pin SIMMs and continuing through to 184-pin DDR SDRAM comes in one of two types: single-sided and double-sided. As their name implies, single-sided sticks only have chips on one side of the stick. Double-sided have chips on both sides (Figure 4.32). The vast majority of RAM sticks are single-sided but there are

Try This!

DRAM Availability

The DRAM market changes fairly rapidly at the higher end, but products tend to linger at the low end, seemingly well past their usefulness. What do your class systems need? What's available in your area today? Try this.

Check out the RAM requirements for the PCs available in your class (or home or office). You can open them up for physical examination or read the motherboard books. Then go to your friendly neighborhood computer store and see what's available. Does the store offer memory that your system cannot use, such as EDO DRAM on 72-pin SIMMs or registered DDR SDRAM? What does this tell you about the PCs available to you?

Cross Check

P4 and DDR

To optimize the flow of data into and out of the CPU, manufacturers and inventive minds have sought to increase the speed of the full frontside bus, meaning between the CPU and Northbridge, and between the Northbridge and RAM.

Why was it ironic that Intel embraced DDR SDRAM technology with the introduction of the 800 MHz FSB Pentium 4?

• **Figure 4.31** nForce2 motherboard showing the three RAM slots. The two slots bracketing the slim space can run as dual channel as long as you don't populate the third slot.

plenty of double-sided sticks out there. Double-sided sticks are basically two sticks of RAM soldered onto one board. There's nothing wrong with double-sided RAM other than the fact that some motherboards either can't use them or can only use them in certain ways—like only if you use a single stick and it goes into a certain slot.

Installing RAM

Whenever someone comes up to me and asks what single hardware upgrade they can do to improve their system performance, I always tell them the same thing—add more RAM. Adding more RAM can improve overall system performance, processing speed, and stability—if you get it right. Botching the job can cause dramatic system instability, such as frequent, random crashes and reboots. Every tech needs to know how to install and upgrade system RAM of all types.

To get the desired results from a RAM upgrade, you must first determine if insufficient RAM is the cause of system problems. Second, you need to pick the proper RAM for the system. Finally, you must use good installation practices. Always store RAM sticks in antistatic packaging whenever they're not in use, and use strict ESD handling procedures. Like many other pieces of the PC, RAM is *very* sensitive to ESD and other technician abuse!

• **Figure 4.32** Double-sided SDRAM

Do You Need RAM?

Two symptoms point to the need for more RAM in a PC: general system sluggishness and excessive hard drive accessing. If programs take forever to load and running programs seem to stall and move more slowly than you would like, the problem could stem from insufficient RAM. A friend with a new Windows XP Professional system complained that her PC seemed snappy when she first got it, but takes a long time to do the things she wants to do with it, such as photograph retouching in Adobe Photoshop and document layout for a print zine she produces. Turns out that her system had only 256 MB of RAM, sufficient for XP Pro, but woefully insufficient for her tasks—she kept maxing out the RAM and thus the system slowed to a crawl. We dropped in another 256 MB stick and suddenly she had the powerhouse workstation she desired.

The A+ Certification Core Hardware Exam wants you to know how to install older types of RAM, not just the RAM in common use today.

Excessive hard drive activity when you move between programs points to a need for more RAM. Every Windows PC has the ability to make a bit of your hard drive look like RAM in case you run out of real RAM. We call that bit of your hard drive the *swap file*. We'll have an in-depth discussion of swap files later in the book but for now appreciate the fact that if you fill your RAM up with programs, your PC will automatically start loading some programs into the swap file. You can't see this process taking place

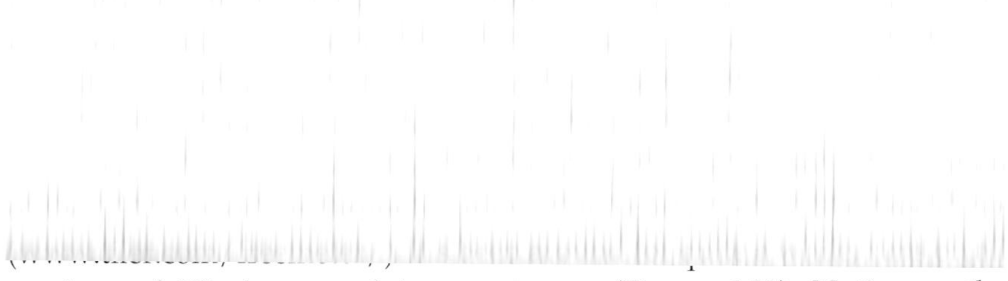

versions of Windows, and is easy to use (Figure 4.33). Notice on the FreeMeter screenshot that some amount of the Pagefile is being used. That's perfectly normal.

System RAM Recommendations

Microsoft sets the minimum RAM requirements listed for the various Windows operating systems very low to get the maximum number of users to upgrade or convert, and that's fine. A Windows XP Professional machine will run well enough on 128 MB of RAM. Just don't ask it to do any serious

Try This!

Checking the Swap File

How much of your hard drive does Windows use for a swap file? Does the level change dramatically when you open typical applications, such as Microsoft Word, Solitaire, and Paint Shop Pro? The answers to these questions can give a tech a quick estimation about RAM usage and possibly RAM needs for a particular system, so try this.

Windows 2000/XP gives you a very easy way to glance at your swap file usage through the Task Manager. To access the Task Manager, press CTRL-ALT-DEL simultaneously once. Click the Performance tab. Windows 2000/XP calls the swap file the *page file*. The second box on the left, titled PF Usage, displays the amount of hard drive the page file is currently using.

1. How big is the page file when you have no applications open?
2. How much does it change when you open applications?

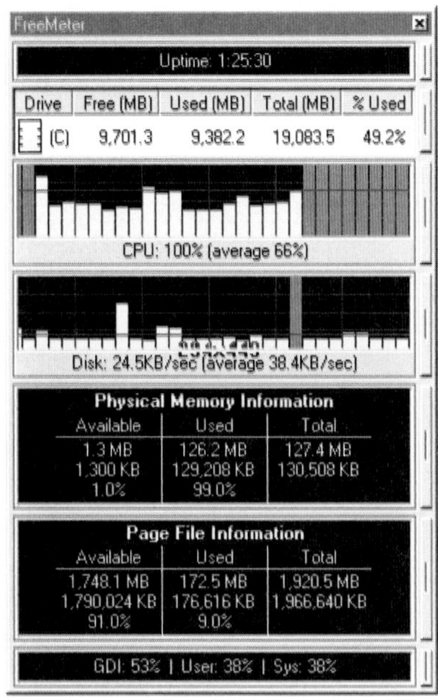

• **Figure 4.33** FreeMeter

computing, like run Doom III! Here are my recommendations for system RAM.

Operating System	Reasonable Minimum	Solid Performance	Power User
Windows 98/SE	64 MB	128 MB	192 MB
Windows ME	128 MB	256 MB	384 MB
Windows 2000	128 MB	256 MB	512 MB
Windows XP (Home or Professional)	256 MB	512 MB	1 GB

Determining Current RAM Capacity

Before you go get RAM, you obviously need to know how much RAM you currently have in your PC. Every version of Windows works the same way. Just select the Properties for My Computer to see how much RAM is in your system (Figure 4.34). If you have a newer keyboard, you can access the screen with the WINDOWS-PAUSE/BREAK keystroke combination. Windows 2000 and XP come with the handy Performance tab under the Task Manager (as shown in Figure 4.35).

Getting the Right RAM

To do the perfect RAM upgrade, determine the optimum capacity of RAM to install and then get the right RAM for the motherboard. The best solution has completely uniform RAM. Your first two stops toward these goals are the inside of the case and your motherboard manual. Open the case to see how many sticks of RAM you have installed currently and how many free

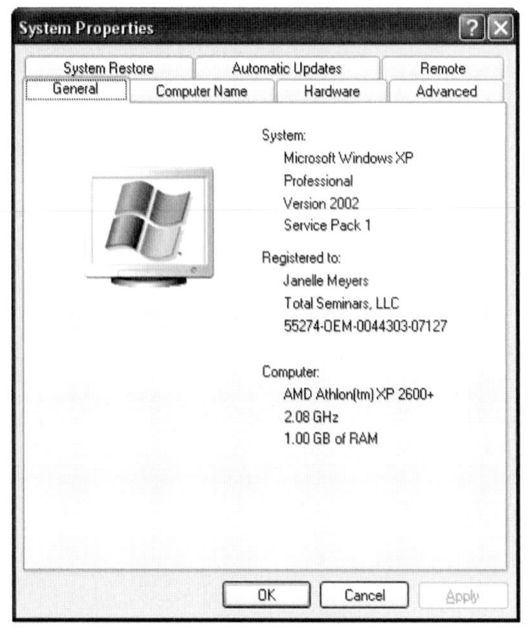

• **Figure 4.34** Janelle has a lot of RAM!

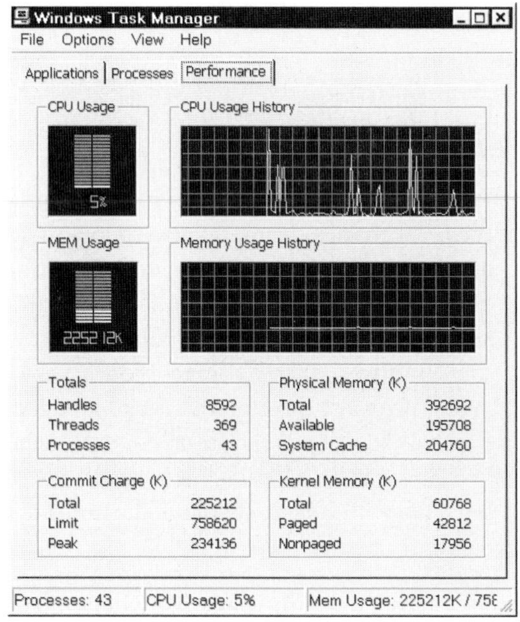

• **Figure 4.35** Windows XP Performance tab

spots you have open. Check the motherboard book to determine the total capacity of RAM the system can handle and what specific technology works with your system. You can't put DDR SDRAM into a system that can only handle *Single Data Rate* (SDR) SDRAM, after all, and it won't do you much good to install a pair of 512 MB DIMMs when your system tops out at 784 MB! Figure 4.36 shows the RAM limits for my ASUS motherboard.

2.5.2 Memory configurations

Install DIMMs in any of the following combinations.

DIMM Location	184-pin DIMM (DDR)		Total Memory
Socket 1 (Rows 0&1)	64MB, 128MB, 256MB, 512MB, 1G	x1	
Socket 2 (Rows 2&3)	64MB, 128MB, 256MB, 512MB, 1G	x1	
Socket 2 (Rows 4&5)	64MB, 128MB, 256MB, 512MB, 1G	x1	
Total system memory (Max. 3GB)		=	

To enhance system performance, utilize dual-channel feature when installing additional DIMMs. You may install the DIMMs in the following sequence: Sockets 1 and 3 or Sockets 2 and 3 or Sockets 1, 2 and 3.

Mix and Match at Your Peril

All motherboards can handle multiple types of RAM, even if the varieties are only in capacity and single or

boards with slots for more than one type of DRAM package. This adds more flexibility to motherboards and enables you to move from an older type of DRAM to a newer type without losing your investment in the older type of DRAM. Figure 4.37 shows an old 486 motherboard that can handle both 30- and 72-pin SIMMs.

Most of these transitional motherboards work great, but some have a few quirks. You might have to move a jumper or two around to get them to

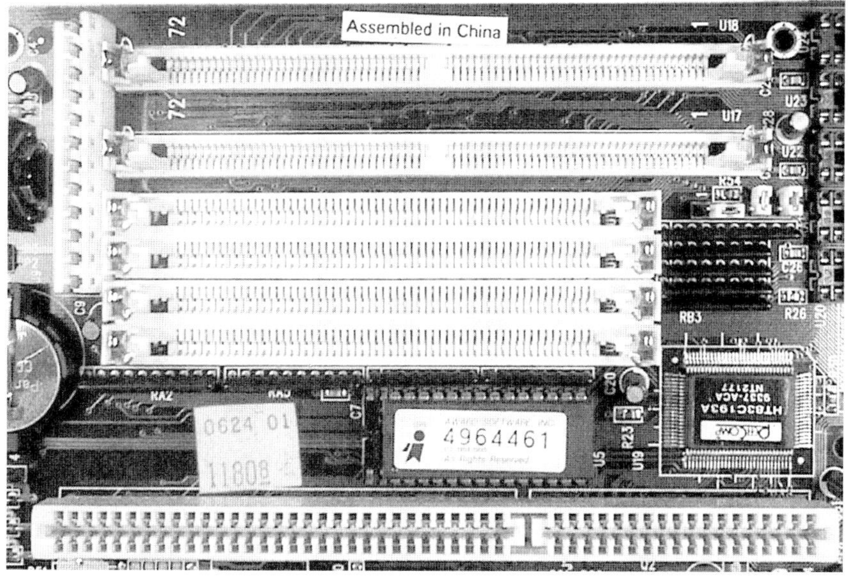

Figure 4.37 SIMM slots for 30- and 72-pin SIMMs

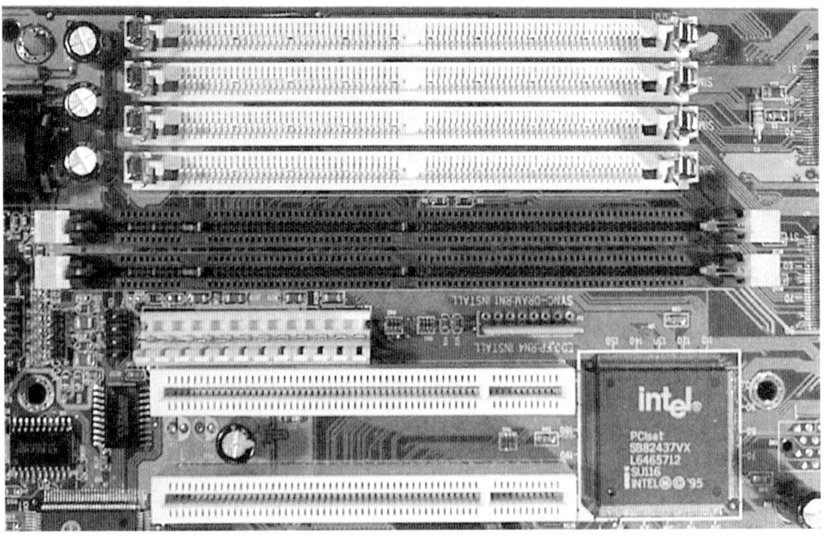

• **Figure 4.38** SIMM and DIMM slots

work, for example. Also be aware that some types of SIMMs take precedence over others. On the motherboard in Figure 4.38, for example, if you populate both of the 72-pin banks and the 30-pin bank, the system will ignore one of the 72-pin banks—I have no idea why. Figure 4.38 shows a motherboard that takes both 72-pin SIMMs and 168-pin DIMMs. In this case, you can install either SIMMs or DIMMs, but not some of each. I have another virtually identical motherboard that enables them to work together; go figure! Most current motherboards have only DIMM slots.

The transition in the industry from SDRAM to DDR SDRAM happened so quickly that few motherboard manufacturers produced or released transition motherboards. Intel's RDRAM Northbridge chips made no accommodation for SDRAM of either variety, so they made no transition boards either. For the most part, therefore, if you upgrade your motherboard today, assume you'll have to upgrade the CPU and RAM as well.

Mixing Speeds

Whether working with an old 486 with 72-pin 60-ns SIMM, or a new system sporting DDR333 (or better), you may often find yourself tempted to mix speeds of DRAM in the same system. Although in some situations you might be able to get away with mixing speeds on a system, the safest, easiest rule to follow is: always use the speed of DRAM specified in the motherboard book, and make sure that every piece of DRAM runs at that speed. In a worst-case scenario, mixing DRAM speeds can cause the system to lock up every few seconds or every few minutes. You might also get some data corruption. Mixing speeds sometimes works fine, but don't do your income tax on a machine with mixed DRAM speeds until the system has proven to be stable for a few days. The important thing to note here is that you won't break anything, other than possibly data, by experimenting.

Okay, enough disclaimers have been mentioned. Modern motherboards provide some flexibility regarding RAM speeds and mixing. First, you can use RAM that is faster than what the motherboard specifies. For example, if the system needs 200-MHz DDR SDRAM, you can put in 333-MHz DDR SDRAM and it will usually work fine. Faster DRAM is not going to make the systems run any faster, however, so don't look for any system improvement.

Second, you can sometimes get away with putting one speed of DRAM in one bank and another speed in another bank, as long as all the speeds are as fast or faster than the speed specified by the motherboard. Don't bother trying to put different-speed DRAMs in the same bank, especially with a motherboard that uses dual-channel architecture. Yes, it works once in a while, but it's too chancy. I avoid it.

Working with Multiple Banks

Although banks are generally straightforward and rarely cause problems, you need to be aware of a few situations that might cause trouble. All systems number their banks, usually starting with the number 0. Some systems require you to populate bank 0 before you populate any other bank. (Bank 0 is the one closest to the CPU.) Most systems don't care. So if you install some RAM and the system doesn't boot up, always try the RAM in another bank to be sure that your system isn't bank sensitive. Inserting RAM into an incorrect bank—with some motherboards—presents no danger. The system simply won't see the RAM when you boot up.

Not all banks take all sizes of DRAM. I have some Pentium II motherboards that take 168-pin DIMMs, for example, but that cannot handle any DIMMs bigger than 64 MB. There's no way around it.

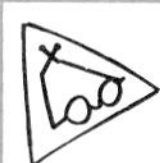

Tech Tip

Mixing PC100 and PC133

Although in theory it should work to add a PC133 stick to a system running at 100 MHz that already has a stick or two of PC100, such a move can greatly destabilize a PC. The frustrating part about this is that mixing destabilizes some systems, but not others. Worse, it doesn't seem to matter which chipset or processor

advice I can offer is don't mix at all and thus avoid all the fuss.

cause of static discharge.

All SIMMs have a notch on one side that prevents you from installing them improperly. When installing SIMMs, insert the SIMMs at a 45-degree angle, as shown in Figure 4.39. When I install SIMMs, I visualize the same motion as a chip shot in golf. If you're not a golfer, visualize scooping ice cream out of a container.

After the SIMM is securely seated in the slot, push it upright until the holding clamps on either side are secured. Make sure that the holes on either end show the small retaining pegs coming through (Figure 4.40). If the SIMM does not insert relatively easily, it's probably in backward. Also, most

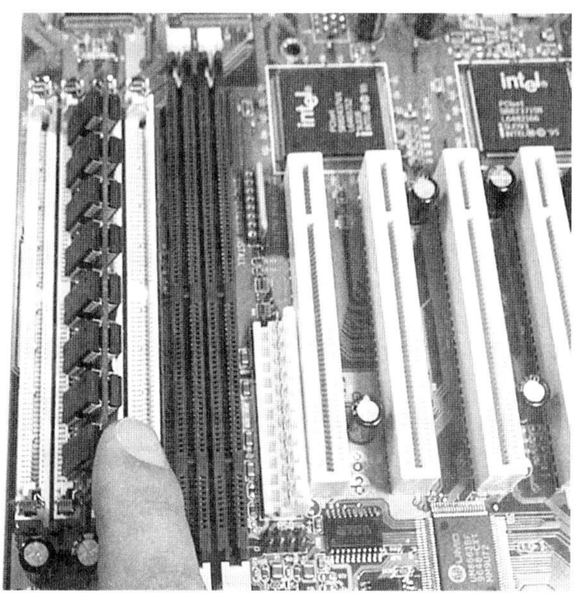

• **Figure 4.39** Inserting a SIMM

SIMMs will stand up vertically when properly installed, so if it isn't vertical, it's probably backward.

Take advantage of installing more than one SIMM to see how they line up across their tops. An improperly installed SIMM will almost always give itself away by not having a nice uniform appearance across the top, as compared with the other SIMMs (Figure 4.41).

• Figure 4.40 SIMMs need to be pushed upright and snapped into place.

Installing DIMMs and RIMMs

DIMMs and RIMMs are far easier to install than SIMMs. First, swing the side tabs on the RAM slots down from the upright position. Then a good hard push down is usually all you need to ensure a solid connection. Make sure that the DIMM snaps into position to show it is completely seated. You will also notice that the two side tabs will move in to reflect a tight connection (Figure 4.42).

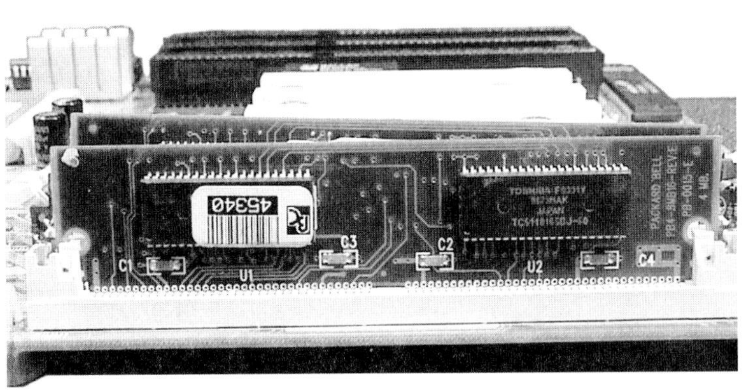

• Figure 4.41 An improperly inserted SIMM

Installing SO-DIMMs in Laptops

It wasn't that long ago that adding RAM to a laptop was either impossible or required you to send the system back to the manufacturer. For years, every laptop maker had custom-made, proprietary RAM packages that were difficult to handle and staggeringly expensive. The wide acceptance of SO-DIMMs over the last few years has virtually erased these problems. All laptops now provide relatively convenient access to their SO-DIMMs, enabling easy replacement or addition of RAM.

Access to RAM usually requires removing a panel or lifting up the keyboard—the procedure varies among laptop manufacturers. Figure 4.43 shows a typical laptop RAM access panel. You can slide the panel off to reveal the SO-DIMMs. SO-DIMMs usually insert exactly like the old SIMMs—slide the pins into position, and snap the SO-DIMM down into the retaining clips (Figure 4.44).

Remember that before doing any work on a laptop, you must make sure that the system is off, that no AC connection exists, and that all batteries are removed. Use an anti-static wrist strap, as laptops are far more susceptible to ESD than desktop PCs.

• Figure 4.42 Inserting a DIMM

The RAM Count

After installing the new RAM, turn on the PC. If you installed the DRAM correctly, the RAM count on the PC will reflect the new value. If the RAM value stays the

All RAM counts listed when your PC boots are based on units of 1,024 bytes (1 KB). So 16 MB shows up as 16384, 32 MB shows 32768, and so on.

■ Troubleshooting RAM

"Memory" errors show up in a variety of ways on modern systems, including parity errors, ECC error messages, system lockups, page faults, and other error screens in Windows. These errors can indicate bad RAM, but often point to something completely unrelated to RAM. This is especially true with intermittent problems. The challenge for techs is to determine which part of the system caused the memory error.

You can get two radically different types of parity errors: real and phantom. Real parity errors are simply errors that the Northbridge detects from the parity chips (if you have them). The operating system then reports the problem in an error message, such as "Parity error at xxxx:xxxxxxxx," where xxxx:xxxxxxxx is a hexadecimal value. If you get an error like this, write down the value. A real parity error will show up at the same place in memory each time, and almost always indicates that you have a bad RAM stick.

If Windows generates parity errors with different addresses, you most likely do *not* have a problem with RAM. These phantom errors can occur for a variety of reasons, including software problems, heat or dust, solar flares, fluctuations in the Force ... you get the idea. Seriously, if you get intermittent parity errors, check out the power supply. Often, these phantom errors show up even when you don't have parity RAM in your system.

Modern systems running the solidly dependable ECC DRAM have a completely different level of error detection. ECC DRAM can report bad RAM sections at boot and then redirect those memory addresses to good sections of RAM. This manifests as a brief message to that effect.

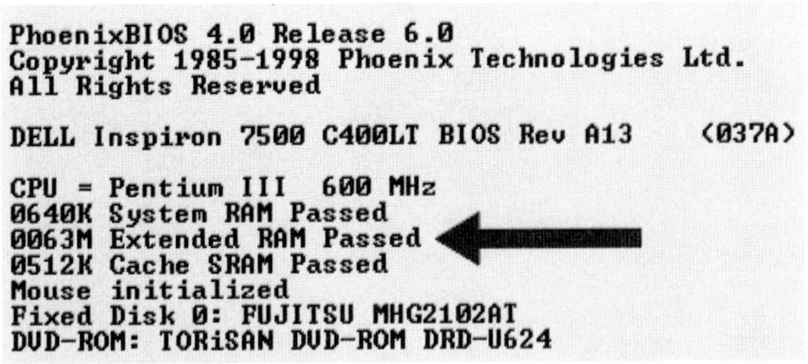

```
PhoenixBIOS 4.0 Release 6.0
Copyright 1985-1998 Phoenix Technologies Ltd.
All Rights Reserved

DELL Inspiron 7500 C400LT BIOS Rev A13     <037A>

CPU = Pentium III  600 MHz
0640K System RAM Passed
0063M Extended RAM Passed
0512K Cache SRAM Passed
Mouse initialized
Fixed Disk 0: FUJITSU MHG2102AT
DVD-ROM: TORiSAN DVD-ROM DRD-U624
```

• **Figure 4.45** Hey, where's the rest of my RAM?!

```
PhoenixBIOS 4.0 Release 6.0
Copyright 1985-1998 Phoenix Technologies Ltd.
All Rights Reserved

DELL Inspiron 7500 C400LT BIOS Rev A13     <037A>

CPU = Pentium III  600 MHz
0640K System RAM Passed
0127M Extended RAM Passed
0512K Cache SRAM Passed
Mouse initialized
Fixed Disk 0: FUJITSU MHG2102AT
DVD-ROM: TORiSAN DVD-ROM DRD-U624
```

• **Figure 4.46** RAM count after proper insertion of DIMMs

System lockups and page faults (they often go hand in hand) in Windows can indicate a problem with RAM. Certainly page faults *look* like RAM issues, because Windows generates frightening error messages filled with long strings of hexadecimal digits, such as "KRNL386 caused a page fault at 03F2:25A003BC." Just because the error message contains a memory address, however, does not mean that you have a problem with your RAM. Write down the address. If it repeats in later error messages, you probably have a bad RAM stick. If Windows displays different memory locations, you need to look elsewhere for the culprit.

Every once in a while, something potentially catastrophic happens within the PC, some little electron hits the big red panic button, and the operating system has to shut down certain functions running in order to save data. This panic button inside the PC is called a *non-maskable interrupt* (NMI), more simply defined as an interruption the CPU cannot ignore. An NMI manifests to the user as what techs lovingly call the Blue Screen of Death (BSoD)—a bright blue screen with a scary-sounding error message on it.

Bad RAM and parity errors can trigger an NMI, certainly, although often the culprit lies with buggy programming or clashing code. The BSoD varies according to the operating system, and it would require a much lengthier tome than this one to cover all the variations. Suffice it to say that RAM *could* be the problem when that delightful blue screen appears.

Finally, intermittent memory errors can come from a variety of sources, including a dying power supply, electrical interference, buggy applications, buggy hardware, and so on. These errors show up as lockups, general protection faults, page faults, and parity errors, but never have the same address or happen with the same applications. Try the power supply first with non-application-specific intermittent errors of any sort.

Testing RAM

Once you discover that you may have a RAM problem, you have a couple of options. First, several companies manufacture hardware RAM testing devices, but unless you have a lot of disposable income, they're probably priced way too high for the average tech ($1,000+). Second, you can use the method I use—"replace and pray." Open the system case and replace each stick, one at a time, with a known good replacement stick. (You have one of those lying around, don't you?) This method, although potentially time-consuming, certainly works. With PC prices as low as they are now, you could simply replace the whole system for less than the price of a dedicated RAM tester.

Beyond A+

MRAM

Current RAM solutions are all trade-offs among the ideal RAM characteristics: non-volatility, low price, fast speed, and low power consumption. The newest RAM solution, scheduled to be commercially available by mid-de- [illegible] opposite directions to create a binary 0.

MRAM has the potential to be both cheaper and faster than current RAM. Manufacturers believe they can create extremely dense, highly integrated MRAM chips, which means smaller chip size, which means a more cost-efficient product. Better yet, MRAM chips will be up to six times faster than even the current speed leader, SRAM.

The bottom line? No more long waits while your system boots up and loads your settings, or powers down and saves them, plus longer battery life for laptops. MRAM's speed, battery life and data retention benefits are being targeted for another big consumer market as well, PDAs and cell phones. Any way you look at it, MRAM is a very exciting new technology!

Chapter 4 Review

Chapter Summary

After reading this chapter and completing the exercises, you should understand the following about RAM.

Identify the Different Types of RAM Packaging

- DRAM manufacturers have been very creative over the years, adapting and changing the packaging of system RAM.
- Although originally DRAM chips were placed on the motherboard, today they are soldered on a card called a stick. Organized like a spreadsheet, RAM is 8 bits or 1 byte wide. While the original 8088 was 8 bits wide, today's CPUs can handle commands up to 64 bits or 8 bytes wide. The Northbridge links the CPU to memory and provides 64 bits of data when the CPU requests information from RAM. The address bus indicates the location of data in DRAM. Even today, the width of RAM is still quoted in byte-wide terminology.
- Manufacturers have improved RAM technology and packages to provide faster access times and to deliver data to match the faster, wider data bus of today's CPUs and motherboards.
- The first generation of DRAM was individual chips called Dual Inline Pin Package (DIPP) that fit into sockets on the motherboard. Since an entire row of DIPP chips had to be inserted or an entire row had to be populated, manufacturers invented a small board, called a stick, that had the RAM soldered onto it. At first, these sticks, called Single Inline Pin Package (SIPP), had 30 pins and were 1 bit wide. They had two 4-bit chips or eight 1-bit chips on them. They plugged into a socket, but they were difficult to insert without breaking off the pins.
- The next generation was the 30-pin Single Inline Memory Modules (SIMMs) that had a flat edge and inserted like a circuit board. A notch on the SIMM prevented it from being installed wrong. They still were 8 bits wide.
- An extra 1-bit chip, called the parity chip, provided error checking. If a 30-pin SIMM had an odd number of chips, it provided parity. If it had an even number of chips, it was non-parity. With today's more reliable DRAM, parity is rarely used.
- Fast Page Mode (FPM) DRAM, an early kind of RAM that did not use a clock, measured access speed in nanoseconds (ns), with speeds ranging from 200 ns to 50 ns. A lower access speed meant faster access as the FPM DRAM. It was important to match the speed of the FPM DRAM with the speed that the motherboard used. Today's computers use newer kinds of DRAM with different packages.
- As CPUs and motherboards advanced, 72-pin SIMMs provided larger capacities (32 bits) and faster access speeds (60–80 ns). They had a notch in the middle and were about an inch longer than 30-pin SIMMs. Available in parity and non-parity varieties, each stick could deliver 32 bits of data at the direction of the Northbridge, thus optimizing the flow of data into and out of the 32-bit wide data bus of the 386 and 486 CPUs.
- RAM slots are organized electronically into banks, with each bank equal to the full width of the CPU's data bus. A 64-bit processor such as a Pentium would need two 72-pin SIMMs to fill a bank and provide 64 bits of data. The Northbridge handles the two sticks of 72-pin SIMMs as a single bank.
- With the invention of the Dual Inline Memory Module (DIMM), capable of delivering 64 bits from a single stick, today's Pentium class or later computers need only a single DRAM stick to fill a bank. DIMMs come with different pin sizes with desktop varieties having either 168 pins or 184 pins. Two smaller packages for laptops are the micro-DIMM (with 68, 144, or 172 pins) and the Small Outline (SO) DIMM (with 72, 144, or 200 pins).

Explain the Varieties of DRAM

- RAM manufacturers have offered many types of DRAM, from the early days of FPM to the hottest dual-channel DDR today.
- Since DRAM needs to be refreshed, most of the early Pentium systems in the 1990s could use an improved kind of DRAM called Extended Data Out (EDO) DRAM that provided faster access with less frequent refreshes.

- Both FPM DRAM and EDO DRAM became obsolete with the invention of Synchronous Dynamic Random Access Memory (SDRAM). Linked to the system clock, SDRAM pipelines instructions from the Northbridge and is from four to six times faster than early kinds of RAM. Instead of having an access speed measured in nanoseconds, SDRAM speed is measured in clock speed or megahertz, with the higher the number, the faster the memory. SDRAM speed should equal or be faster than motherboard speed. By adding a small serial presence detect (SPD) chip, a DIMM stick can provide the system with details about its size, speed, and other information. PC100 identifies [illegible] 266 MHz, while the Pentium 4 quadrupled the speed of the frontside bus to 400 MHz or 533 MHz. To correspond with the higher bus speeds, Intel initially used proprietary Rambus DRAM (RDRAM), while AMD embraced DDR SDRAM. Available in either a 184-pin RIMM package for desktops or a 160-pin SO-RIMM for laptops, RDRAM has speeds ranging from 600 MHz to 1066 MHz. Because RIMMs run hot, they require a heat spreader to dissipate the heat. For proper termination, each RIMM slot must be populated, either with a RIMM or with a passive Continuity RIMM (CRIMM). Because it uses a dual-channel architecture, RDRAM must be installed in pairs of the same speed and capacity. While each RIMM is 64 bits wide, the Northbridge alternates between the two sticks for faster data retrieval. Rambus Corporation charges licensing fees for RDRAM, making it more expensive than SDRAM. It works only on Pentium 4 systems using Intel-made Northbridge chips.
- AMD and other manufacturers use Double Data Rate Synchronous Dynamic Random Access Memory (DDR SDRAM). This inexpensive memory makes two processes for every clock cycle and comes in a 184-pin DIMM package for desktops or either a 200-pin SO-DIMM or a 172-pin micro-DIMM for laptops. It runs at speeds ranging from 200 to 400 MHz. Since it has throughput of 8 bytes per second, DDR SDRAM naming conventions multiply the speed by eight. For example, PC3200 would be 400 MHz times eight bytes. Eventually, Intel also decided to support DDR SDRAM for their Pentium 4, making Rambus almost certainly history.
- The dual channel architecture introduced by Rambus is now available as Dual DDR technology. It also requires installing DDR SDRAM in pairs. While early motherboards supporting this technology, such as those using NVIDIA's nForce2 chipset, have three slots, the system will revert to a single channel if a third DIMM is installed.
- While RAM sticks from 72-pin SIMMs through [illegible] went through the essential details.
- Adding more RAM can improve overall system performance, processing speed, and stability. If your system is sluggish and you have excessive hard drive accessing, you should upgrade your RAM. Windows uses part of the hard drive as if it were memory. If the hard drive LED comes on frequently, it is disk thrashing as Windows moves programs between RAM and the hard disk swap file. Adding more RAM will help eliminate this problem.
- While Microsoft sets minimum RAM requirements for various Windows operating systems, you should install more memory for better performance. The Properties tab for My Computer will show you how much RAM is in your system.
- Before you upgrade your RAM, determine the right RAM for your motherboard. The motherboard book indicates the maximum memory your system can support. You should also open the case to determine how many slots are unpopulated. All RAM should be uniform in technology, capacity, and speed. If you mix DRAM speeds, your system may lock up frequently or data may be corrupted. Sometimes, however, you can use one speed in one bank and a different speed in another bank.
- While most of the newer motherboards have only DIMM slots, some earlier motherboards have slots

for more than one type of DRAM package. Consult the motherboard book to see if you can mix different DRAM packages. Be aware also that some motherboards are bank sensitive, requiring that you populate banks in a particular sequence. Because the technology has changed so rapidly, if you upgrade your motherboard today, you'll probably have to upgrade the CPU and RAM as well.

- Because DRAM is extremely sensitive to static electricity, use an antistatic wrist pad when installing it. Keep your fingers on the edges of the sticks, avoiding touching the chips themselves.
- To install a SIMM, place it into the slot at a 45-degree angle and push upright to secure it in the holding clamps. A SIMM has a notch on one side to prevent you from installing it wrong. If it does not insert easily, it's probably in backward.
- To install a DIMM, open the side tabs on the RAM slot, insert the stick at a 90-degree angle, being sure to align the notches on the stick, and push down firmly. When it snaps into position, the two side tabs will move in.
- Because earlier laptops used proprietary RAM packages, it was almost impossible to upgrade their memory. Today, almost all laptops use SO-DIMMs that allow you to replace or upgrade the memory by removing an easy access panel or lifting the keyboard. Be sure to turn off the system and remove all batteries before working on a laptop. The antistatic wrist strap is essential since laptops are more susceptible to ESD than desktop PCs.
- After adding additional memory, the RAM count on the PC will show the correct amount if it was installed correctly.

Perform Basic RAM Troubleshooting

- Memory errors may show up as parity errors, ECC errors, system lockups, page faults, or other screen errors in Windows. Deciphering the problem successfully requires methodical troubleshooting.
- Intermittent parity errors may be phantom errors caused by something else, such as the power supply. If you get an error message in Windows that contains a memory address, write down the address. If the same memory address repeats in later error messages, it probably is bad RAM. Different memory locations in later error messages may mean other kinds of problems.
- While RAM problems can manifest themselves as a non-maskable interrupt (NMI) and produce the Blue Screen of Death (BSoD), other sources such as buggy programs or clashing code can also produce this catastrophic problem.
- If you are getting intermittent errors unrelated to a particular application, you should suspect the power supply first.
- Some companies manufacture RAM testing devices, but they are very expensive ($1,000+). If you suspect that you may have a RAM problem, you can replace each stick, one at a time, with a known good stick.

Key Terms

30-pin SIMM *(114)*
72-pin SIMM *(116)*
Access speed *(116)*
Bank *(118)*
Continuity RIMM (CRIMM) *(123)*
Double Data Rate SDRAM (DDR SDRAM) *(124)*
Dual Inline Memory Module (DIMM) *(118)*
Dual Inline Pin Package (DIPP) *(113)*
Disk thrashing *(127)*
Dynamic Random Access Memory (DRAM) *(109)*
Error Correction Code (ECC) DRAM *(122)*
Extended Data Out DRAM (EDO DRAM) *(120)*
Fast Page Mode (FPM) RAM *(116)*
Parity *(114)*
Rambus DRAM (RDRAM) *(122)*
RIMM *(123)*
Single Inline Memory Module (SIMM) *(114)*
Single Inline Pin Package (SIPP) *(113)*
Small Outline DIMM (SO DIMM) *(119)*
Synchronous DRAM (SDRAM) *(121)*

Key Term Quiz

Use the Key Terms list to complete the sentences that follow. Not all the terms will be used.

1. If your motherboard uses RDRAM, you must fill each slot with either a ____________ or a ____________.

2. Older types of memory measure __________ in nanoseconds while newer types of memory that use clocking measure speed in megahertz.
3. If the LED for your hard drive stays on most of the time, your computer is suffering from __________, a sure sign you need to add more memory.
4. It takes two __________ to fill a __________ on a 64-bit Pentium-class computer.
5. __________ refers to a special kind of memory stick for laptops.
6. Memory that makes two data accesses during each clock tick is called __________.
7. A __________ is the earliest kind of memory that came on a stick and had a pin edge.
8. If the computer adds an extra bit to every byte, it uses __________ for error checking.
9. __________ is tied to the system clock, unlike regular DRAM.
10. Unlike regular DRAM, __________ enables error checking and correcting.

Multiple-Choice Quiz

[illegible]

C. 4 bits, 400 MHz

D. 8 bits, 200 MHz

2. Which of the following statements is true about a motherboard with a NVIDIA nForce2 chipset?
   - A. It uses Rambus or RDRAM memory.
   - B. It uses DDR DRAM memory.
   - C. If you install a third DIMM, it will revert to a single channel.
   - D. It uses EDO-DRAM.
3. A computer that can use 168-pin DIMMs needs __________ stick(s) to fill a bank.
   - A. One
   - B. Two
   - C. Four
   - D. Eight
4. If you upgrade your memory but notice that the RAM count does not reflect the additional memory, what should you do?
   - A. Remove the RAM and try to reinstall it.
   - B. Restart the computer.
   - C. Return the memory because it's probably bad.
   - D. Go to Setup and configure the memory to reflect the new amount.
5. A non-maskable interrupt causes the CPU to produce __________

[illegible]

programs or data that the CPU can access via the __________.
   - A. System bus
   - B. Frontside bus
   - C. Address bus
   - D. Expansion bus
7. Which of the following access speeds would indicate the fastest FPM DRAM?
   - A. 150 ns
   - B. 100 ns
   - C. 80 ns
   - D. 60 ns
8. All of the following statements are true about RDRAM *except* __________.
   - A. It uses dual-channel architecture.
   - B. It offers speeds ranging from 600 MHz to 1066 MHz.
   - C. Because Rambus Corporation charges a licensing fee, it is more expensive than SDRAM.
   - D. AMD and Intel use it with their newest processors.
9. Which of the following SDRAM speeds would not work with a 100 MHz motherboard?
   - A. 66 MHz
   - B. 100 MHz

C. 133 MHz

D. 200 MHz

10. The width of RAM is quoted in ___________ terminology.

A. Bit-wide

B. Byte-wide

C. Access time

D. Megabytes or gigabytes

11. If you are running Windows 2000 or Windows XP, you can use all of the following methods to find out how much RAM is installed in your computer *except* ___________.

A. From the Control Panel, select System, and then the Hardware tab.

B. Use the Performance tab under the Task Manager.

C. Select Properties from My Computer.

D. With a newer keyboard, press the WINDOWS-PAUSE/BREAK keystroke combination.

12. A 72-pin SIMM can deliver ______ bits of data at a time.

A. 8

B. 16

C. 32

D. 64

13. DDR-SDRAM uses a ___________ package for desktop PCs.

A. 30-pin

B. 72-pin

C. 168-pin

D. 184-pin

14. If a 30-pin SIMM has an even number of chips on it, it ______________.

A. Uses parity

B. Does not use parity

C. Uses a clock to synchronize with the CPU and the Northbridge

D. Performs two data accesses for each clock tick

15. What happens if you mix memory sticks of different speeds?

A. You may use different speed DRAMs in the same bank if your computer uses dual-channel architecture.

B. It may slow down your computer.

C. Your computer will work fine if all the memory sticks are slower than the speed of the motherboard.

D. It may cause your system to lock up every few seconds or to provide corrupted data.

Essay Quiz

1. Celia tells you she has an old computer, a Compaq Presario 5100 with 64 MB of RAM. Now that she's bought a new computer, she'd like to donate it to a local charity, but she knows it needs more memory. She wants to upgrade the memory to 128 MB, but, unfortunately, she does not have the motherboard book. Help her figure out what kind of memory the computer can use. Explain what kind of memory she should buy, and tell her how you discovered this information.

2. Your cousin James recently bought a new AMD computer with 128 MB of RAM and Windows XP operating system. He's complaining about how slow his new computer is, especially when he's working with his graphics applications. How can you convince him that he needs more memory?

3. Now that you've convinced your cousin James that he needs more memory for his new PC, how will you explain what kind he should buy and how he should install it? You may assume that he has the motherboard book and that his computer has a 233 MHz system bus and can support double data rate RAM.

4. Your mother just called from the local computer store. She found a special on a stick of DDR SDRAM and wants to get it if it will fit in her Pentium II computer. What will you tell her?

5. Your computer is acting funny. Sometimes you get an error message on the screen. Other times data seems to be corrupted. Sometimes the computer just locks up. You suspect that it may be bad memory. How can you find out whether a memory problem or something else is causing your trouble?

Lab Projects

• Lab Project 4.1

To learn more about memory, go to the web site www.kingston.com, select Memory Tools from the buttons at the top of the screen, and examine "The Ultimate Memory Guide." This resource contains information about all aspects of computer memory. After using this guide, answer the following questions:

1. Why do memory prices vary so frequently?
2. What are the differences in tin- and gold-edged memory sticks, and how does one know which to choose when upgrading?
3. Describe the notches on a 30-pin SIMM, a 72-pin SIMM, a 168-pin DIMM, and a 184-pin DIMM. What function do the notches serve?

one bank must be populated.

- A memory bank must supply the CPU with data equal to the width of the CPU's data bus.
- The data bus on a 486 CPU is 32 bits while the data bus is 64 bits for the Pentium through the Pentium 4 class computers.
- A 30-pin SIMM has an 8-bit data bus. A 72-pin SIMM has a 36-bit data bus. A 168-pin or 184-pin DIMM has a 64-bit data bus.
- To figure out how many sticks of memory are required for a bank with a particular CPU, divide the width of the data bus of the memory stick into the width of the CPU's data path. The result is the number of sticks required for a bank. For example, a Pentium with a 64-bit data bus requires 2 sticks of 72-pin SIMMs for a bank (64 / 32 = 2), but needs only a single DIMM stick (64 / 64 = 1).
- You can determine the capacity of a RAM stick these days by reading the label, but occasionally

Change the second number to bytes and simply multiply. So, 32 bits = 4 bytes; 64 bits = 8 bytes. What does 36 bits equal? (Look it up!)

Now, answer the following questions about memory banking and density:

1. If you have a 486 CPU with a 32-bit data bus, how many sticks of 72-pin SIMMs are necessary to fill a bank?
2. If you have a Pentium III, how many sticks of 168-pin DIMMs are necessary for a bank?
3. If you have a 72-pin SIMM that is identified as a 32M x 36 stick, how many addresses does it have and is it parity or non-parity?
4. If you have a Pentium II and you want to add 128 MB of memory to it, how many sticks will you need to buy and what will be the numeric identification if it is non-parity? You will order _______ stick(s) of ______ x _______.

chapter 5

BIOS and CMOS

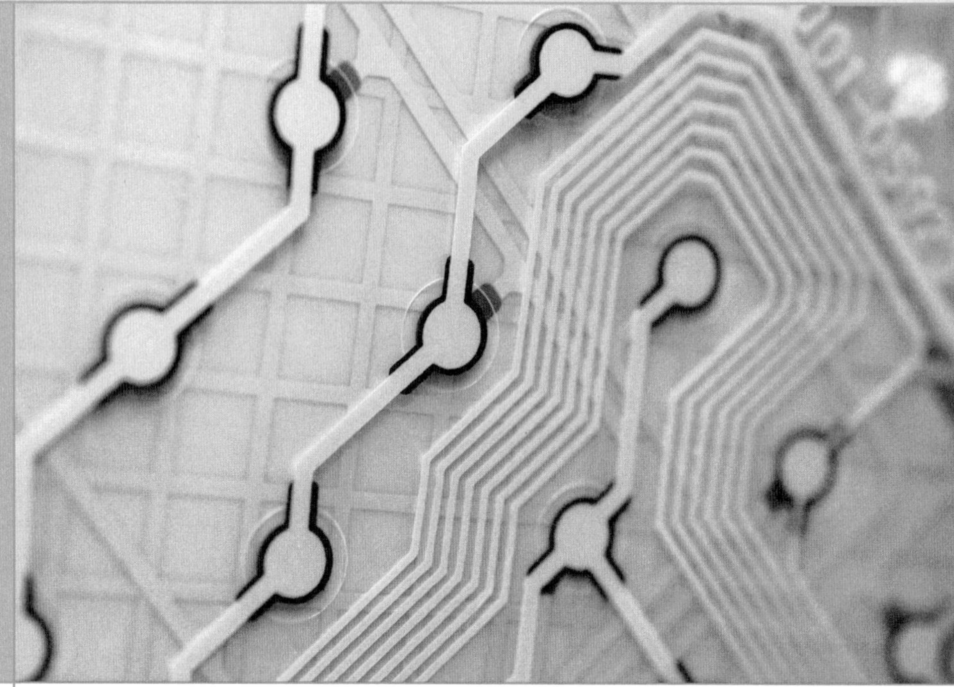

"When the apocalypse comes...beep me."

—Buffy in *Buffy the Vampire Slayer*, 1997

In this chapter, you will learn how to

- **Explain the function of BIOS**
- **Distinguish among various CMOS setup utility options**
- **Describe BIOS and device drivers**
- **Troubleshoot the Power-On Self Test (POST)**

In Chapter 3, you saw how the address bus and external data bus connect RAM to the CPU via the Northbridge in order to run programs and transfer data. Assuming you applied power and such in the right places, you don't need anything else to make a simple computer. The only problem with such a simple computer is that it would bore you to death—there's no way to do anything to it! A PC needs devices such as keyboards and mice to accept input, and output devices such as monitors and sound cards to communicate to you the current state of the running programs. A computer also needs permanent storage devices, such as hard drives and CD media, to store programs and data when you turn off the computer.

Historical/Conceptual

■ The Function of BIOS

In order for these devices to work, at least two separate functions are needed. First, the CPU needs some way to talk to the devices to tell them what it wants. Second, all the devices in the PC need some way to send data to and receive data from the CPU. To handle the interconnection between all of these devices and the CPU, your system includes a second helper chip known generically as the **Southbridge** . While the Northbridge's main job is memory, the Southbridge's job is to handle all the inputs and outputs to the [illegible]

[illegible] make the external data bus a very busy place. Data constantly flows on the external data bus among CPU, chipset, RAM, and other devices on the PC.

Not just any Northbridge will work with a given Southbridge! Specific Northbridge and Southbridge chips must be designed to work together. We call these matched pairs of chips the *chipset*. Basically, the Northbridge extends the external data bus to the Southbridge. The Southbridge in turn extends the external data bus to all of the other parts of the computer (Figure 5.1). This enables all the devices in your PC to send data to and from the CPU.

Now let's make it even more interesting! The Southbridge not only extends the data bus, it also extends the *address bus* to all the other parts of the PC (Figure 5.2).

Hey, wait a minute! Didn't I tell you in the previous chapters that the address bus was used by the CPU to tell the Northbridge the byte of RAM it

Tech Tip

Chipset Architecture

The workload of the two chips that make up the chipset in modern PCs varies according to manufacturer and model. The distinctions drawn here—Northbridge for RAM, Southbridge for devices—works for most chipsets designed for the Pentium, Pentium Pro, and Pentium II processors, and the latest and greatest Athlon XP. The North- [illegible]

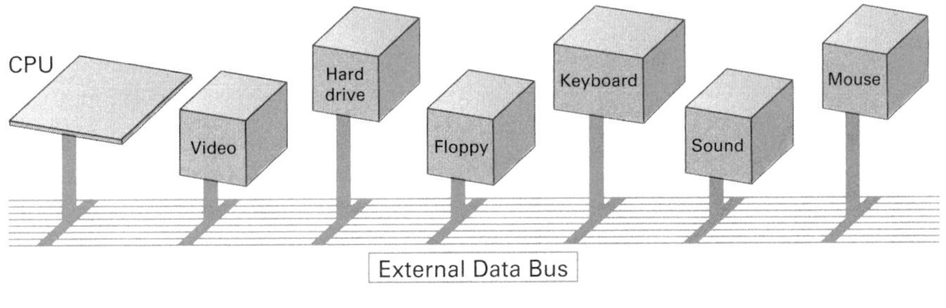

• **Figure 5.1** The Southbridge connects the rest of the computer to the CPU via the external data bus.

Chipset makers rarely use the terms "Northbridge" and "Southbridge" anymore, but because most modern chipsets consist of only two or three chips with basically the same functions, techs continue to use the terms.

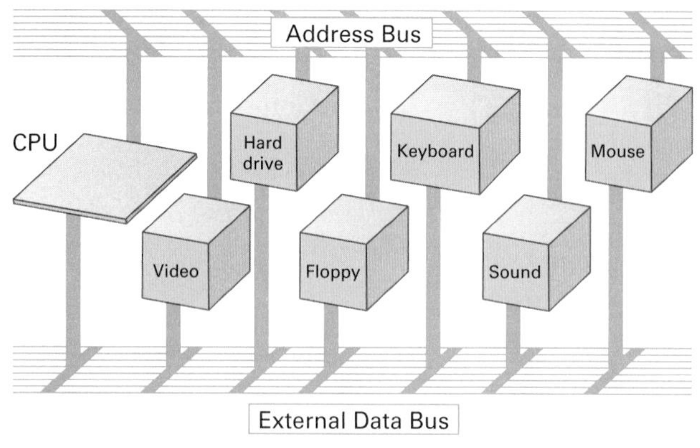

• **Figure 5.2** Everything is also connected to the address bus.

needs? What business does the address bus have with all the other devices on the PC? Good question! First of all, making the address bus accessible to any device enables any device to have RAM. While we don't see this anymore, it was very common in the early days of the PC to see RAM added to a computer by snapping a card full of RAM into an expansion slot. The main reason the address bus goes to every device in a modern PC is to enable the CPU to send commands, through the chipset, to every device in the PC.

At first this may seem confusing—doesn't the external data bus send all of the commands in RAM to the CPU? True enough, but it only handles this function between the CPU and RAM. If the CPU, for example, needs to tell the hard drive to send it a particular file, it first tells the chipset that it is going to switch the address bus from memory addressing to what is called I/O addressing, which you'll learn about in more detail in Chapter 6. The CPU then places different patterns of ones and zeros on the address bus, each of which tells a specific device to do a specific job.

It's not too hard to swallow the concept that the CPU uses the address bus to talk to the devices, but how does it know what to *say* to them? How does it know all of the different patterns of ones and zeros to place on the address bus to tell the hard drive it needs to send a file? The answer to that question comes from something called BIOS.

Talking to the Keyboard

The keyboard provides a great example of how the buses and support programming help the CPU get the job done. The keyboard connects to the external data bus via a special chip known as the *keyboard controller*. Don't bother looking for this chip on your motherboard—the keyboard controller functions are now handled by the Southbridge. The way the keyboard controller works with the CPU, however, has changed only a small amount in the last 20 years, making it a perfect tool to see how the CPU talks to a device.

The keyboard controller was one of the last single-function chips to be absorbed into the chipset. For many years—in fact, well into the Pentium III/Early Athlon era—most motherboards still had separate keyboard controller chips. Figure 5.3 shows a typical setup from those days. Electronically, it looked like Figure 5.4.

• **Figure 5.3** A keyboard chip on a Pentium motherboard

Every time you press a key on your keyboard, a scanning chip in the keyboard notices which key has been pressed. Then the scanner sends a coded pattern of ones and zeros—called the *scan code*—to the keyboard controller. Every key on your keyboard has a unique scan code. The keyboard controller stores the scan code in its own register. Does it surprise you that the lowly keyboard controller has a register? Lots of chips have registers—not just CPUs! (Figure 5.5)

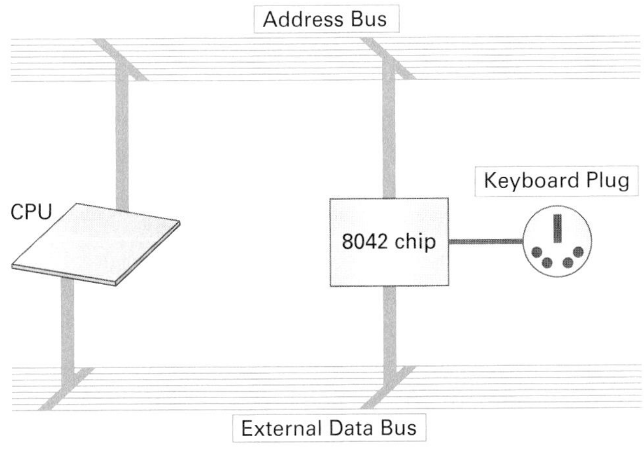

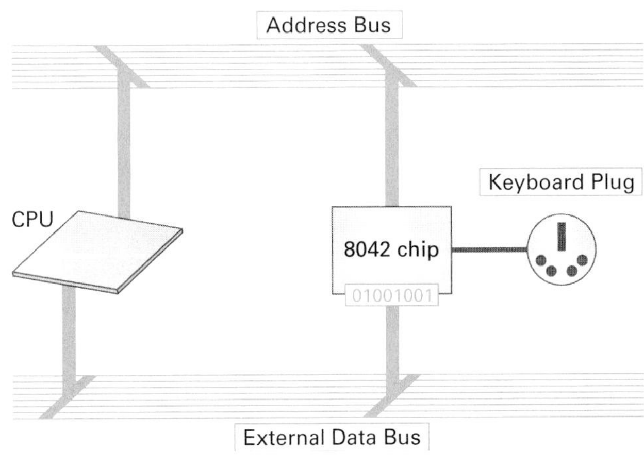

typematic buffer rate (when you hold down a key and the letter repeats) or turn the NUM LOCK led on and off, to mention just a few other jobs the keyboard needs to do for the system? The point is that the keyboard controller must be able to respond to multiple commands, not just one.

The keyboard controller accepts commands just the way you saw in Chapter 2 with the 8088 CPU. Remember when you added 2 to 3 with the 8088? You had to use specific commands from the 8088's codebook to tell the CPU to do the addition and then place the answer on the external data bus. The keyboard controller has its own codebook—much simpler than any CPU, but conceptually the same. To determine the scan code stored inside the keyboard controller, the CPU needs to know the command (or series of commands) that orders the keyboard controller to put the scan code of the letter on the external data bus so the CPU can read it.

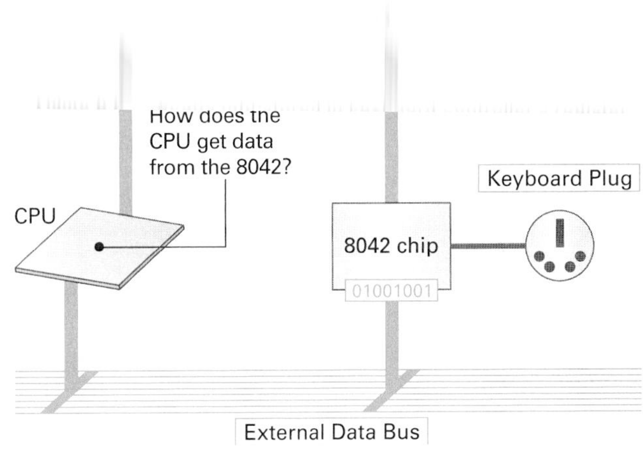

• **Figure 5.6** How does the CPU communicate with the keyboard controller?

The CPU needs a specific set of support programming to communicate with the keyboard controller. A talented programmer could readily write such a program if he or she knew the keyboard's code book, but two additional problems must also be surmounted. First, different motherboards may have different keyboard controller chips (Figure 5.7). You see, the original keyboard controller (called the 8042 chip) was designed in 1978. The keyboard controller has been redesigned and improved on many times over the years, and with each redesign the codebook of the keyboard controller changes. Motherboard manufacturers have many options for keyboard controllers, and the support programming must work

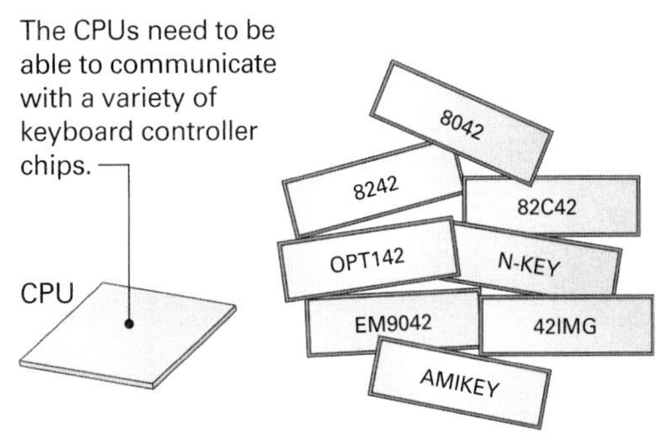

• **Figure 5.7** Many different keyboard controllers

As noted previously in this chapter, the Southbridge chip handles the keyboard interface, acting as the keyboard controller chip among its many other functions. Manufacturers today choose a specific chipset, rather than an individual keyboard controller. But you knew that!

with its motherboard's specific chip. The second problem is where to store this support programming. You can't store it on a hard drive or floppy drive—the keyboard needs to be ready at any time the CPU calls it, even before installing a mass storage device. So how do you handle these issues?

Many different keyboard controller chips are available, but your motherboard will have a specific keyboard controller chip soldered onto it, chosen by the motherboard maker. You won't change the keyboard controller, so you don't need to worry about changing the support programming. Thus the perfect place for the support programming is on the motherboard. That settles one issue, but the other looms before us: what storage medium do we use on the motherboard? DRAM? No, it would be erased every time the computer was turned off. What about on a hard drive, CD-ROM, or floppy drive? Those won't work either—as you'll soon see, you'll need the keyboard working before you can install these devices! You need some type of permanent program storage device that does not depend on other peripherals in order to work. And you need that storage device to sit on the motherboard.

• **Figure 5.8** Typical ROM chip

Motherboards store the keyboard controller support programming, among other programs, on a special type of device called a **Read Only Memory (ROM) chip**. A ROM chip stores programs exactly like RAM: that is, like an 8-bit wide spreadsheet. But ROM differs from RAM in two important ways. First, ROM chips are **non-volatile**, meaning that the information stored on ROM isn't erased, even when the computer is turned off. Second, ROM chips are read-only, meaning that once a program is stored on one, it can't be changed. Figure 5.8 shows a typical ROM chip on a motherboard. When the CPU wants to talk to the keyboard controller, it goes to the ROM chip to access the proper programming (Figure 5.9).

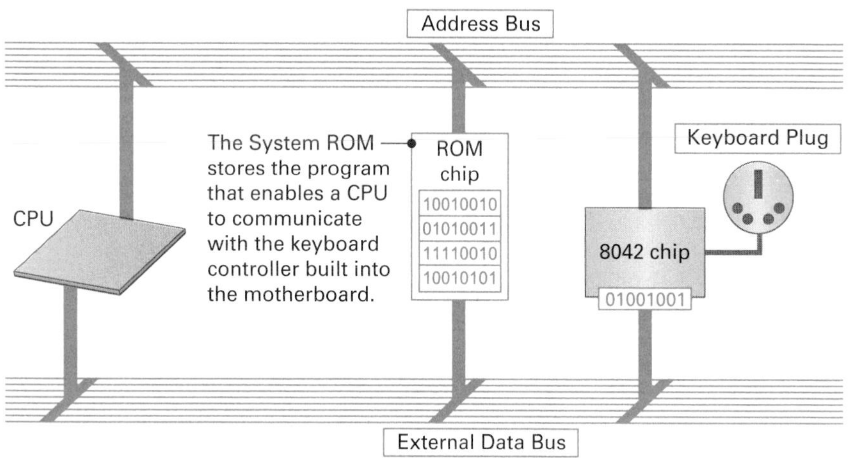

• **Figure 5.9** Function of the ROM chip

In addition to the keyboard controller support programming, the motherboard's ROM chip—called the *System ROM*—also stores programs for communicating with the floppy drive(s), hard drive(s), monitor, and a few other basic devices on your computer. Each device responds to a number of different, unique commands, and many basic devices store their communication programs on the ROM chip. To talk to all of that hardware requires hundreds of little programs (2 to 30 lines of code each). These hundreds of little programs stored on the ROM chip are called, collectively, the Basic Input/Output Services (BIOS). Each tiny program is called a *service*. (See Figure 5.10.)

The System BIOS is the collection of hundreds of little programs designed to talk to the most basic parts of your computer. Programs stored on ROM chips are known collectively as firmware, as opposed to programs stored on erasable media that are collectively called *software*.

The System ROM chips used on modern PCs store as much as 2 MB of programs, although only 65,536 bytes are used to store the System BIOS. This allows

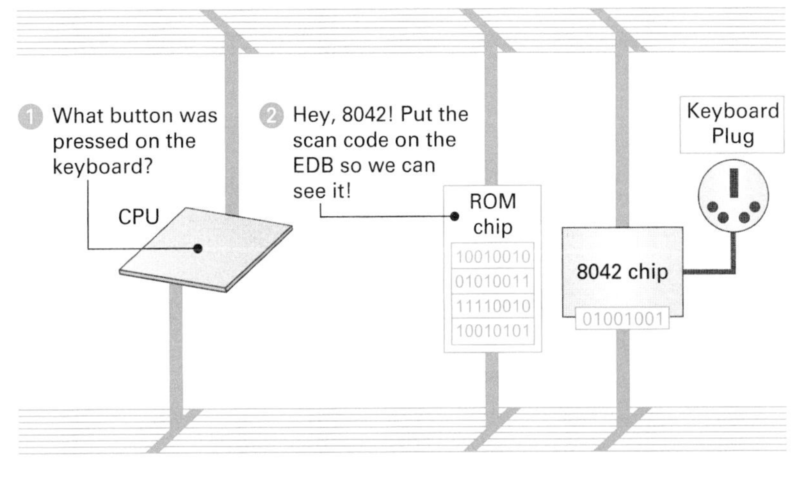

tems, but it's easier to see on a simpler model.

BIOS and Its Relation to Memory Addressing

BIOS is nothing but a set of tiny programs, correct? RAM stores all running programs and the CPU uses the address bus to specify which byte of RAM to run. On the original 8088 chip, the address bus consisted of 20 wires. These 20 wires could be turned on and off in 1,048,576 different combinations. Each individual combination of ones and zeros on the address bus is known as a *memory address*. I know the word "address" conjures up the idea of a postal address, but I prefer to think of each combination as a "memory phone number" for every byte of RAM. The CPU "dials up" a memory phone number by turning wires on and off on the address bus. The Northbridge then accesses the byte of RAM with that memory address. However, now your ROM chip is loaded with 65,536 bytes of BIOS code. How is the correct code accessed? The same way RAM is accessed—through the address bus.

The total number of memory addresses available to a CPU is its *address space*. Your local phone company provides a good analogy. In the U.S., local phone calls require a seven-digit number, such as 555-1212. In theory, I could use any number from 000-0000 to 999-9999. That's exactly 10 million telephone numbers. You could say that the address space of a local call is 10 million phone numbers. Each telephone number may not actually have a phone connected to it, but if need be, my local telephone exchange's use of seven digits enables my phone to handle 10 million telephone numbers. Since the 8088 could dial up 1,048,576 bytes, the address space for an 8088 processor is

1,048,576 bytes, or 1 megabyte (1 MB). That does not mean that every 8088 system had 1 MB of RAM, but the CPU could theoretically handle that much!

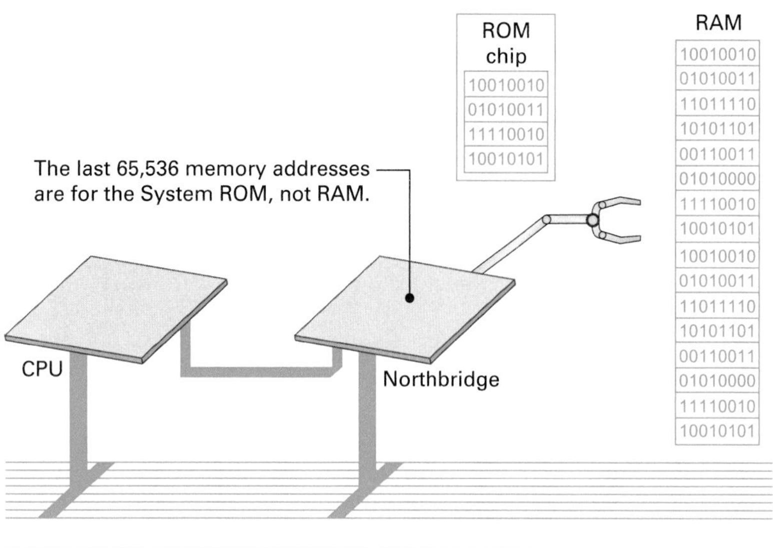

• **Figure 5.11** Reserving address space for System ROM

When IBM invented the IBM PC, they declared that the last 65,536 addresses on the address bus would be reserved for the BIOS on the ROM chip (Figure 5.11), which means that the maximum amount of RAM you could add to a computer with an 8088 chip was about 1 MB minus 65,536 bytes. Using the telephone analogy, it would be similar to the phone company keeping all the phone numbers from 888-8888 up to 999-9999 for its own use. When the chipset sees the CPU "dial up" one of these reserved addresses, the Northbridge knows to send the address directly to the ROM BIOS.

The CPU needs the capability to communicate with every piece of hardware in your computer. You have to be able to tell the sound card to play a song, or tell the video card to put graphics on the monitor. The CPU has no built-in commands of its own for talking to *any* of the hardware on your PC. It must rely on programs to tell it how to talk to any particular device, yet the ROM BIOS only contains programming for certain basic hardware.

When IBM designed the original IBM PC back in 1981, they knew that other devices would be invented that would need BIOS support. IBM did not want to get into a game where every time you added a device, you had to replace the system ROM. So, they decided the easiest way to handle the problem was to have devices with their own ROM chips. More ROMs means more address space must be taken away from RAM and reserved for ROM. Therefore, in the original 8088, IBM decided to reserve 384 K out of the 1,024 K (1 MB) of memory addresses for ROM. That left 640 K of memory addresses for RAM (Figure 5.12).

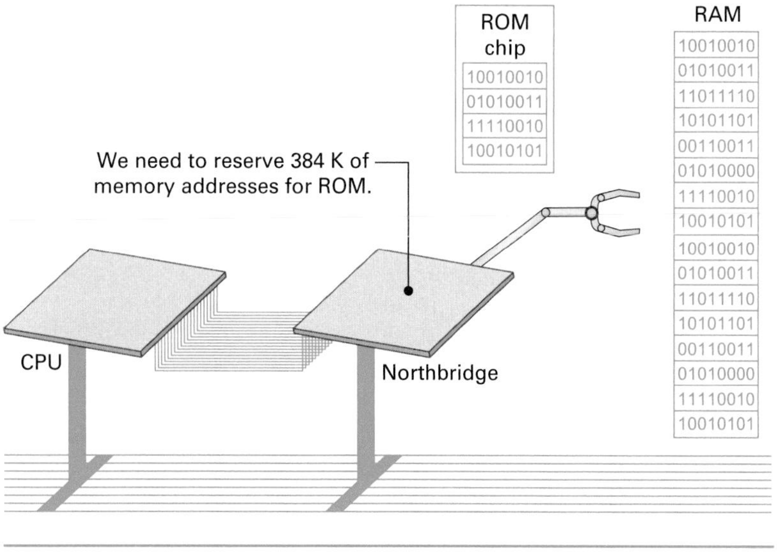

What if you have a modern CPU like a Pentium 4? A Pentium 4 has a much larger address bus—32 wires—which means it has an address space of more than 4 *billion* bytes! However, every PC must still reserve the last 384 K of the first megabyte of memory space for BIOS to provide backward compatibility with the 8088.

• **Figure 5.12** Reserving memory addresses for ROM

Test Specific

All Hardware Needs BIOS

Each piece of hardware in your computer—without exception—needs support programming for every function that piece of hardware performs. The CPU needs access to this programming to make that piece of hardware do whatever it's supposed to do. So far you've learned about the System BIOS, stored on the System ROM chip, which enables the CPU to talk to some of the core pieces of hardware in your system.

Every System BIOS has two types of hardware to deal with: the Unchangeables and the Changeables. The Unchangeable group is hardware that is common, necessary, and never changes, such as the keyboard. Its BIOS [illegible] add another floppy drive). The BIOS for these devices is also stored on the System ROM chip, but the system needs another place to store information about the specific *details* of a piece of hardware. This enables the system to differentiate between a Western Digital Caviar 80-GB hard drive and a Seagate Barracuda 60-GB drive and yet still support both drives right out of the box. A separate memory chip, often called a **Complementary Metal-Oxide Semiconductor (CMOS)** chip, stores the information that describes specific device parameters.

■ CMOS Setup Utilities

CMOS chips do not store programs; they store only data that is read by BIOS to complete the programs needed to talk to changeable hardware. The CMOS chip also acts as a clock to keep the current date and time.

At this point, don't worry about what parameters are stored on the CMOS chip; these parameters will be described in detail when the different types of hardware are discussed. For now, simply appreciate that a system ROM chip and a CMOS chip are present in your computer (Figure 5.13).

Although CMOS chips usually store around 64 KB of data, the PC usually needs only a very small amount—about 128 bytes—to store all the necessary

• **Figure 5.13** Typical CMOS chip

information on the changeable hardware. Don't let the tiny size fool you. The information stored in CMOS is absolutely necessary for the PC to function!

If the data stored on the CMOS about a particular piece of hardware (or about its fancier features) is different from the specs of the actual hardware, the computer will not be able to access that piece of hardware (or use its fancier features). It is crucial that this information be correct. If you change any of the previously mentioned hardware, you must update the CMOS to reflect those changes. You need to know, therefore, how to change the data on the CMOS chip.

Updating CMOS: The Setup Program

Almost every PC ships with a program built into the System ROM, called the *CMOS setup program*, which enables you to access and update the data on the CMOS chip. The CMOS setup program may be accessed in different ways, depending on the brand of BIOS you have on your computer. When you fire up your computer in the morning, the first thing you will likely see is the BIOS information. It might look like the example in Figure 5.14 or perhaps something like Figure 5.15.

> You'll also hear the CMOS setup program referred to by techs as simply *the CMOS* or *the System Setup Utility.* The terms are functionally interchangeable today.

Who or what is Award Software, and who or what is Phoenix Technologies? These are brand names of BIOS companies. They write BIOS programs and sell them to computer manufacturers. In the bad old days, the days of XTs and 286s, when a company made a motherboard, they usually hired a few programmers to write the BIOS. In today's world, people rarely write their own BIOS. Instead, they buy their BIOS from specialized third-party BIOS makers like Award Software and Phoenix Technologies. Although about ten different companies write BIOS, three big companies control 99 percent of the BIOS business: American Megatrends (AMI), Award Software, and Phoenix Technologies. A few years ago, Award merged with Phoenix, but the new company (Phoenix) still sells each brand name of BIOS as a separate product line.

You always access a system's CMOS setup program at boot. The real question is, how do you access the CMOS

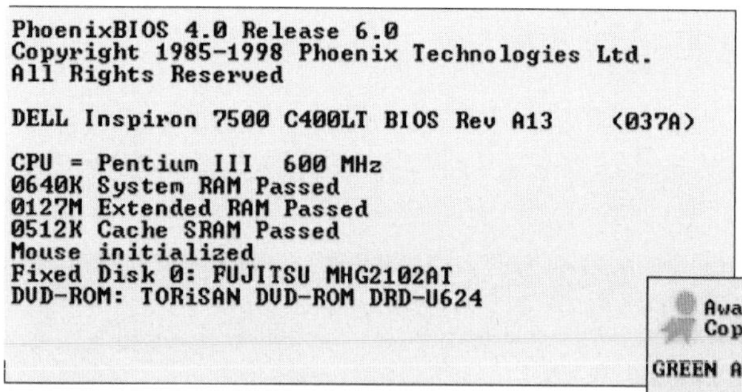

```
PhoenixBIOS 4.0 Release 6.0
Copyright 1985-1998 Phoenix Technologies Ltd.
All Rights Reserved

DELL Inspiron 7500 C400LT BIOS Rev A13     <037A>

CPU = Pentium III  600 MHz
0640K System RAM Passed
0127M Extended RAM Passed
0512K Cache SRAM Passed
Mouse initialized
Fixed Disk 0: FUJITSU MHG2102AT
DVD-ROM: TORiSAN DVD-ROM DRD-U624
```

• **Figure 5.14** Phoenix BIOS information

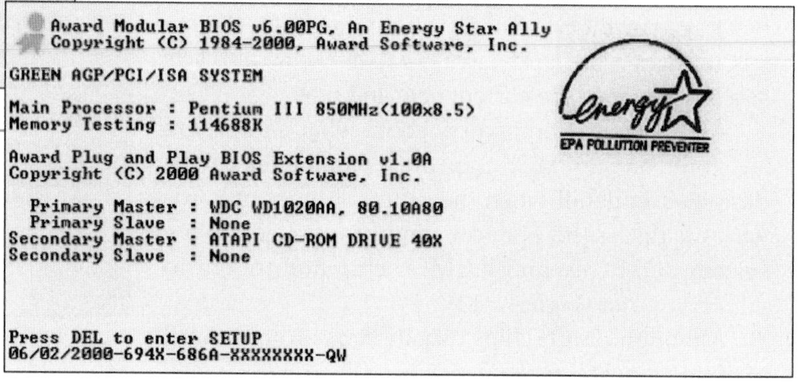

```
Award Modular BIOS v6.00PG, An Energy Star Ally
Copyright (C) 1984-2000, Award Software, Inc.

GREEN AGP/PCI/ISA SYSTEM

Main Processor : Pentium III 850MHz(100x8.5)
Memory Testing : 114688K

Award Plug and Play BIOS Extension v1.0A
Copyright (C) 2000 Award Software, Inc.

  Primary Master : WDC WD1020AA, 80.10A80
  Primary Slave  : None
Secondary Master : ATAPI CD-ROM DRIVE 40X
Secondary Slave  : None


Press DEL to enter SETUP
06/02/2000-694X-686A-XXXXXXXX-QW
```

EPA POLLUTION PREVENTER

• **Figure 5.15** Award BIOS information

setup at boot for your particular PC? AMI, Award, and Phoenix use different keys to access the CMOS setup program. Usually BIOS manufacturers will tell you how to access the CMOS setup right on the screen as your computer boots up. For example, at the bottom of the screen in Figure 5.15, you are instructed to "Press DEL to enter SETUP." Keep in mind that this is only one possible example! Motherboard manufacturers can change the key combinations for entering

combinations: DEL, ESC, F1, F2, CTRL-ALT-ESC, CTRL-ALT-INS, CTRL-ALT-ENTER, or CTRL-S. It may take a few tries, but you will eventually find the right key or key combination!

Try This!

Accessing CMOS Setup

The key or key combination required to access CMOS setup varies depending on your particular BIOS. It's important to know how to access CMOS, and how to find the BIOS information once you're in, so try this:

1. Make sure your monitor is turned on and boot your system. Watch the information that scrolls by on the screen as your computer boots. Most BIOS makers include a line indicating what key or key combination to press to access the System Setup Utility. Make a note of this useful information! You can also check your motherboard book to determine the process for accessing the System Setup program.

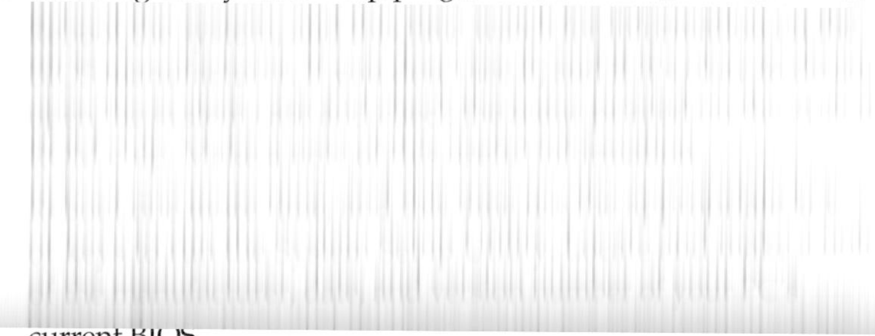

current BIOS.

4. If you can, make a note of the exact model information for your system and visit the web site of the company that manufactured your PC. Search their support files for the specs on your specific system and see if you can locate your BIOS information. Now take the detailed BIOS information and search the BIOS manufacturer's web site for the same information.

A Quick Tour Through a Typical CMOS Setup Program

Every BIOS maker's CMOS setup program looks a little different, but don't let that confuse you! They all contain basically the same settings; you just have to be comfortable poking around. To avoid doing something foolish, *do not save anything* unless you are sure you have it set correctly.

As an example, let's say your machine has Award BIOS. You boot the system and press DEL to enter CMOS setup. The screen in Figure 5.16 appears. You are now in the Main menu of the Award CMOS setup program! The setup program itself is stored on the ROM chip, but it edits only the data on the CMOS chip.

CMOS Setup Utility - Copyright (C) 1984-1999 Award Software

▸ !! CPU SOFT MENU II !!	▸ PC Health Status
▸ Standard CMOS Features	Load Fail-Safe Defaults
▸ Advanced BIOS Features	Load Optimized Defaults
▸ Advanced Chipset Features	Set Password
▸ Integrated Peripherals	Save & Exit Setup
▸ Power Management Setup	Exit Without Saving
▸ PnP/PCI Configurations	
Esc : Quit F10 : Save & Exit Setup	↑ ↓ → ← : Select Item

Change CPU's Clock & Voltage

• **Figure 5.16** CMOS Setup Main menu

```
CMOS Setup Utility - Copyright (C) 1984-1999 Award Software
                    Standard CMOS Features

Date (mm:dd:yy)            Wed, Oct 4 2000          Item Help
Time (hh:mm:ss)            10 : 40 : 45
                                                    Menu Level  ▸
▸ IDE Primary Master       Press Enter10263 MB
▸ IDE Primary Slave        Press Enter13020 MB      Change the day, month,
▸ IDE Secondary Master     Press Enter None         year and century
▸ IDE Secondary Slave      Press Enter None

Drive A                    1.44M, 3.5 in.
Drive B                    None
Floppy 3 Mode Support      Disabled

Video                      EGA/VGA
Halt On                    All,But Keyboard

Base Memory                   640K
Extended Memory            113664K
Total Memory               114688K

↑↓→←:Move  Enter:Select  +/-/PU/PD:Value  F10:Save  ESC:Exit  F1:General Help
F5:Previous Values  F6:Fail-Safe Defaults  F7:Optimized Defaults
```

Figure 5.17 Standard CMOS Features screen

If you select the Standard CMOS Features option, the Standard CMOS Features screen will appear (Figure 5.17). On this screen you can change floppy drive and hard drive settings, as well as the system's date and time. You will learn how to set up the CMOS for these devices in later chapters. At this point, your only goal is to understand CMOS and know how to access the CMOS setup on your PC, so don't try to change anything yet. If you have a system that you are allowed to reboot, try accessing the CMOS setup now. Does it look anything like these examples? If not, can you find the screen that enables you to change the floppy and hard drives? Trust me, every CMOS setup has that screen somewhere! Figure 5.18 shows the same standard CMOS screen with a Phoenix BIOS. Note that Phoenix calls this screen "Main."

The first BIOS was nothing more than this standard CMOS setup. Today, virtually all computers have many extra CMOS settings. They control

> All these screens tend to overwhelm new techs. When they first encounter the many options, some techs feel they need to understand every option on every screen in order to configure CMOS properly. Relax—every new motherboard comes with settings that befuddle even the most experienced techs! If we don't talk about a particular CMOS setting somewhere in this book, it's probably not important, either to the A+ Certification exams or to a real tech.

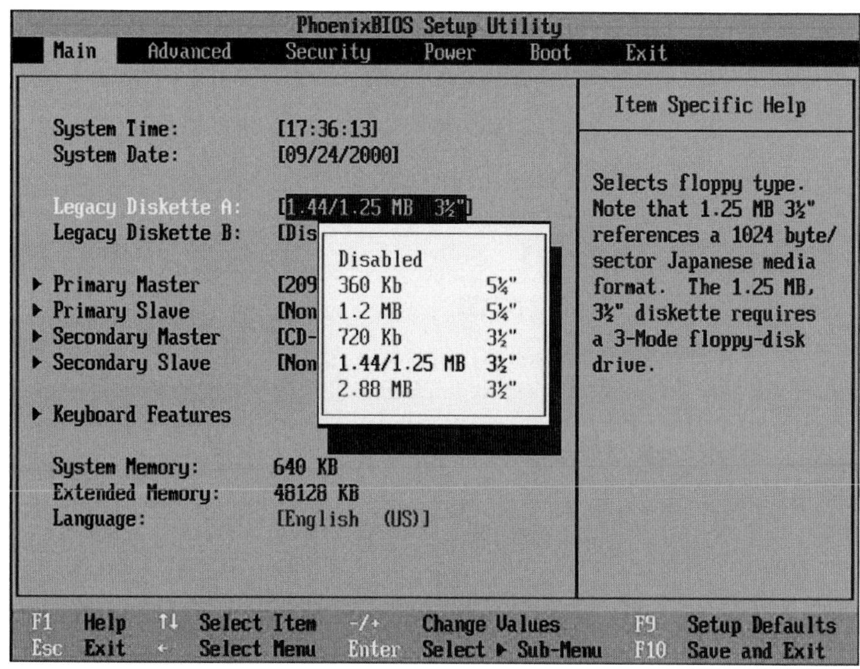

Figure 5.18 Phoenix BIOS Main screen

items such as memory management, password and booting options, diagnostic and error handling, and power management. The following section takes a quick tour of an Award CMOS setup program. Remember that your CMOS setup will almost certainly look at least a little different from mine, unless you happen to have the *same* BIOS. The chances of that happening are quite slim!

Award has virtually cornered the desktop PC BIOS market with its Award Modular BIOS. Motherboard makers buy a basic BIOS from Award and can add or remove options (Award calls them *modules*) based on the

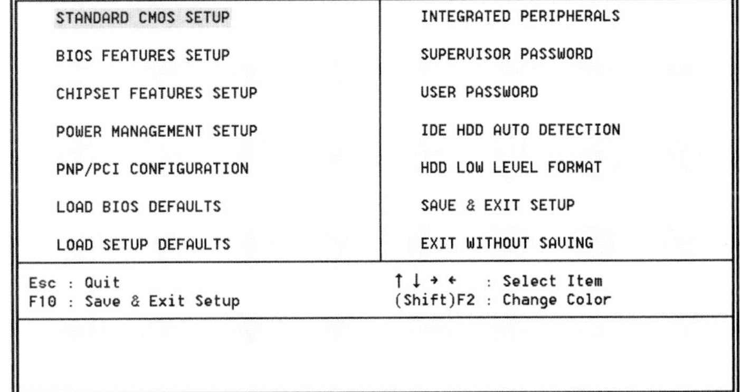

system simply doesn't need the extra options available on the newer system!

CPU Soft Menu

The CPU Soft menu enables you to set the voltage and multiplier settings on the motherboard for the CPU. Jumperless motherboards and motherboards that cater to overclockers tend to have this option. Usually you will just set this to AUTO and stay away from this screen (Figure 5.20).

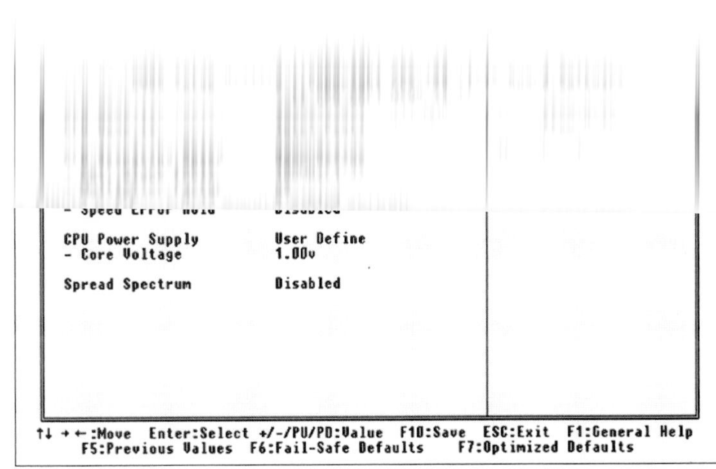

Figure 5.20 CPU Soft Menu

Advanced BIOS Features

Advanced BIOS Features is the dumping ground for all the settings that aren't covered in the Standard menu, but don't fit nicely under any other screen. This screen varies wildly from one system to the next. You will most often use this screen to select the boot options (Figure 5.21).

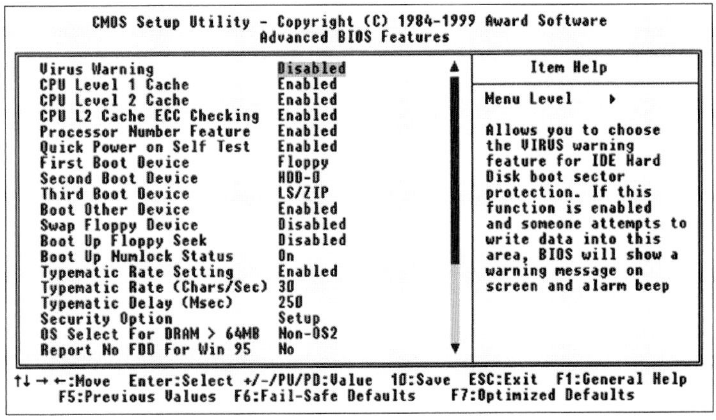

Figure 5.21 Advanced BIOS Features

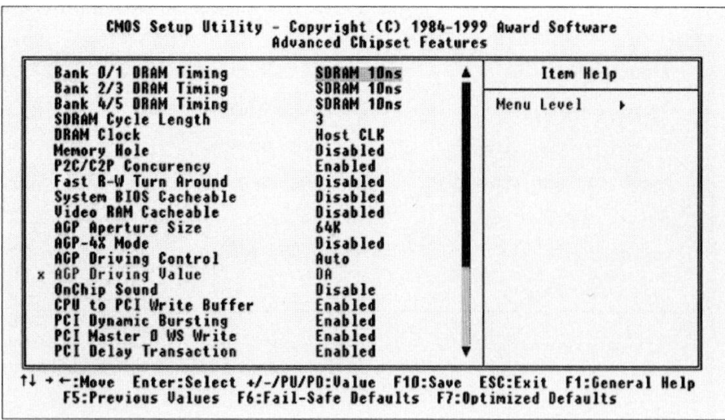

• **Figure 5.22** Advanced Chipset Features

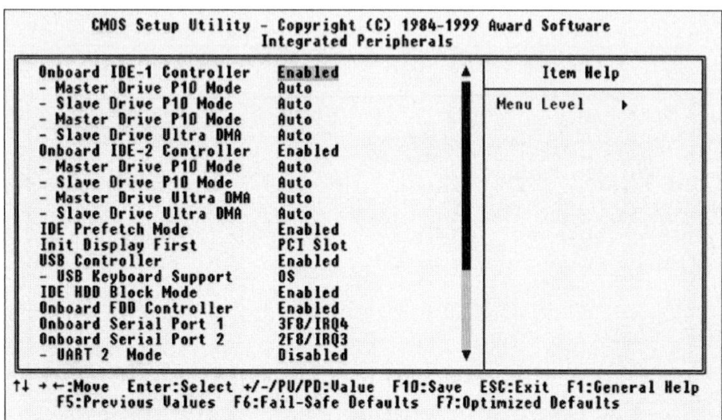

• **Figure 5.23** Integrated Peripherals

CMOS Setup Utility - Copyright (C) 1984-1999 Award Software
Power Management Setup

▸ Power Management Press Enter
ACPI Suspend Type S1(POS)
PM Control by APM Yes
Video Off Option Suspend -> Off
Video Off Method V/H SYNC+Blank
MODEM Use IRQ NA
Soft-Off by PWRBTN Instant-Off
▸ Wake Up Events Press Enter

Item Help
Menu Level ▸

↑↓→←:Move Enter:Select +/-/PU/PD:Value F10:Save ESC:Exit F1:General Help
F5:Previous Values F6:Fail-Safe Defaults F7:Optimized Defaults

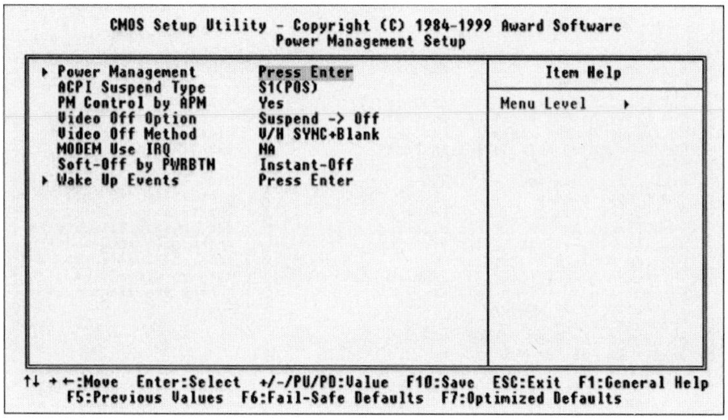

• **Figure 5.24** Power Management Setup

Advanced Chipset Features

This screen strikes fear into most everyone because it deals with extremely low-level chipset functions. Avoid this screen unless a high-level tech (like a motherboard maker's support tech) explicitly tells you to do something in here (Figure 5.22).

Integrated Peripherals

You will use this screen quite often. This screen enables you to configure, enable, or disable the onboard ports, such as the serial and parallel ports. As you'll see when we discuss these ports in more detail in later chapters, you can use this screen to get a lot of important work done (Figure 5.23).

Power Management Setup

As the name implies, we use this screen to set up the power management settings for the system. These settings work in concert (sometimes in conflict) with Windows' power management settings to control how and when devices turn off and back on to conserve power (Figure 5.24).

PnP/PCI Configurations

Anyone who deals with Plug and Play (PnP) devices will surely see this screen from time to time. We most commonly use the PnP/PCI Configurations screen to set aside certain resources called *interrupt requests* (IRQs) to prevent the system from taking that resource away from a device that needs it (Figure 5.25). We will go into gritty detail about these resources in Chapter 6.

And the Rest of the CMOS Settings...

The other options on the main menu of our Award CMOS do not have their own screens. Rather, these simply have small dialog boxes that pop up, usually with, "Are you sure?" messages. The Load Fail-Safe/Optimized defaults options keep us from having to memorize all of those weird settings we never touch. Fail-Safe sets everything to very simple settings—we occasionally use this setting when very low-level problems like freeze-ups occur, and we have checked more obvious areas first. Optimized sets the CMOS to the best possible speed/stability for our system. We often use this one when we have tampered with the CMOS too much and need to put it back like it was!

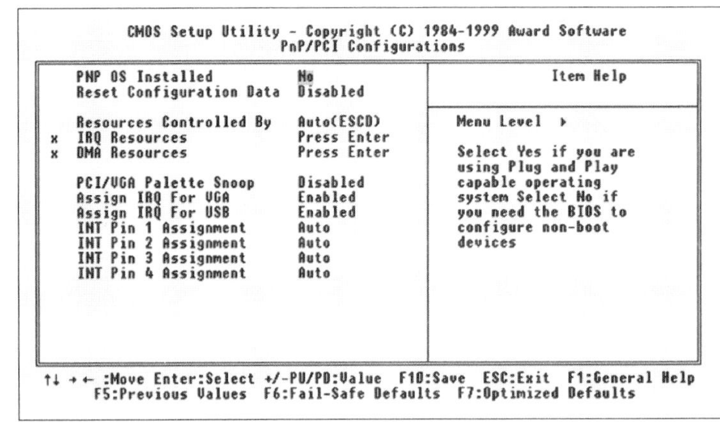

Many CMOS setup programs enable you

boot and another for accessing the CMOS setup prog password just for entering CMOS setup is a godsend for places like schools where non-techs tend to wreak havoc in areas (like CMOS) that they should not access!

Figure 5.26 CMOS password prompt

Of course, all CMOS setups provide some method to Save and Exit and to Exit *Without* Saving. Use these as needed for your situation. Exit Without Saving is particularly nice for those folks who want to poke around the CMOS but don't want to mess anything up. Use it!

Phoenix BIOS

Phoenix BIOS is the Mercedes-Benz of BIOS programs. Phoenix creates a custom BIOS for optimal use in the machine for which it is designed. As a result, Phoenix BIOS programs have fewer, more unique options. Figure 5.27 shows a Phoenix BIOS Integrated Peripherals screen. You will usually see Phoenix BIOS programs in machines with proprietary motherboards, such as laptops.

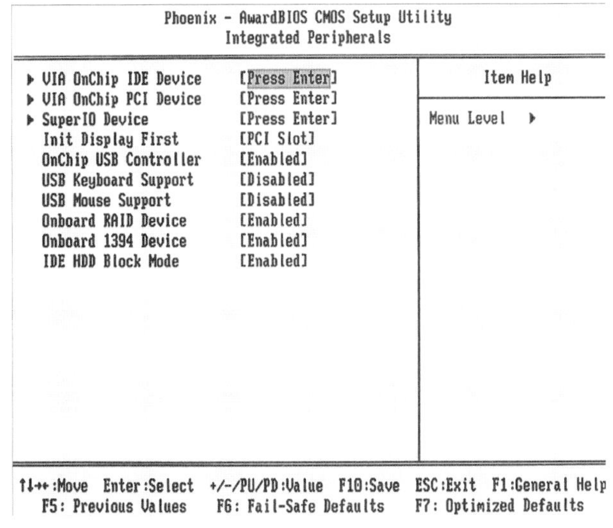

Figure 5.27 Phoenix BIOS - Integrated Peripherals

AMI

AMI competes directly with Award, providing highly flexible BIOS programs (Figure 5.28). AMI was the most-used BIOS for many years until Award gained

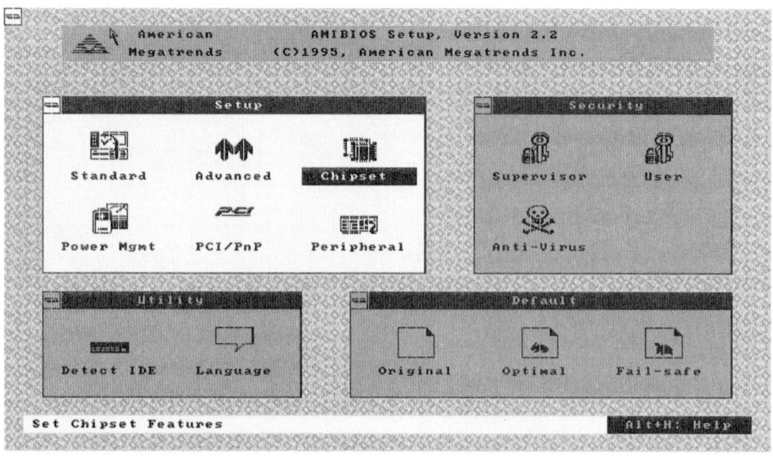

• **Figure 5.28** AMI BIOS

market share, starting around 1994/1995. Although AMI no longer holds the virtual monopoly it once had in BIOS software, it is still quite popular.

Care and Feeding of an Old CMOS

Losing CMOS information used to be a common problem on older systems. If some mishap suddenly erased the information on the CMOS chip, the computer would not boot up or you would get nasty-looking errors. Errors that pointed to lost CMOS information, like

> "CMOS configuration mismatch, CMOS date/time not set, No boot device available, and CMOS battery state low"

usually appeared while the computer was booting. Here are some of the more common reasons for losing CMOS data in the old days:

- Dead onboard battery
- Pulling and inserting cards
- Touching the motherboard
- Dropping something on the motherboard
- Dirt on the motherboard
- Faulty power supplies
- Electrical surges
- Chip creep

Most of these items should be fairly self-explanatory, but chip creep might be a new term for some of you. Let me explain. As PCs run, the components inside get warm. When a PC is turned off, the components cool off. This cycling of hot and cold causes the chips to expand and contract in their mounts. While the chip designers account for this, in some extreme cases this thermal expansion and contraction will cause a chip to work out of its mount and cause a failure. We call this failure *chip creep*. Chip creep was a common problem in the earlier days of PCs, but after 20 years of experience, the PC industry has done a pretty good job of designing mounts that will hold all your chips in place dependably.

Modern CMOS

Modern PCs store their basic system support programming in two chips: the **Flash ROM** chip (more on Flash ROM in a moment) stores the System BIOS (which normally includes the CMOS setup program), and a special SRAM chip, usually just called *the CMOS*, stores the BIOS settings you configure *using* the setup program. Figure 5.29 shows a Flash ROM chip on a motherboard. Thanks to Flash ROM and SRAM, newer motherboards are flexible and updateable (if that's a word!), and therefore able to stave off obsolescence much longer than earlier motherboards.

Before the development of Flash ROM, the only way to upgrade the System BIOS was to replace the ROM chip containing the old System BIOS with a new one containing the new System BIOS. If you're thinking, "What a pain!" you'd be right. Motherboard manufacturers had to make educated guesses about what sorts of technology might be ready for market in the next six months, year, even two years, so they could build in the support necessary to keep their products current. They often did a remarkable job at this, but they couldn't

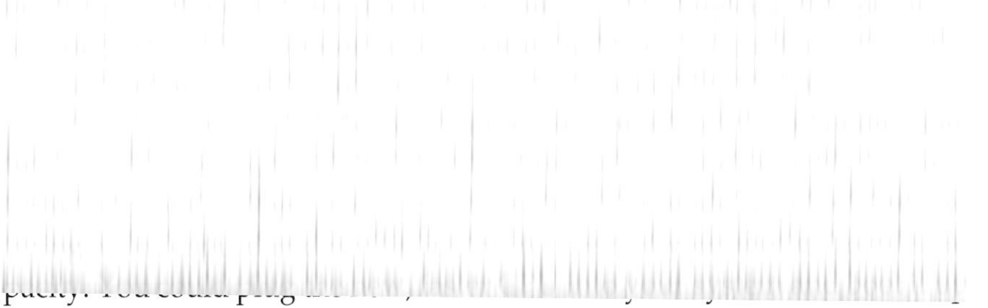

with no problem, but without a BIOS upgrade, your motherboard could not recognize its faster speeds. Your system would simply run as if it were still using the older CPU model, robbing you of any advantage from the new CPU's higher-speed processing abilities. To fix this frustrating state of affairs, manufacturers created the end-user programmable, read-only memory called Flash ROM.

Cross Check

SRAM

You first learned about SRAM in Chapter 3, "CPUs." Can you explain the role of SRAM in the PC? How does the CPU use SRAM? What features of SRAM make it desirable for this purpose? Compare this with its use for CMOS.

Figure 5.29 Flash ROM chip on motherboard

Flash ROM

The Flash ROM chips that contain the System BIOS on modern motherboards can hold data permanently, even without electricity. Unlike older ROM chips whose contents were forever fixed, however, Flash ROM chips can be reprogrammed to update their contents. With Flash ROM, when you need to update your System BIOS to add support for a new technology, you can simply run a small command-line program, combined with an update file, and voilà, you've got a new, updated BIOS! Different BIOS makers use slightly different processes for *flashing the BIOS*, but in general you must boot from a floppy diskette and then run the relevant updating command from the A:\> prompt. This example shows how simple this can be:

```
A:\> aw athxpt2.bin
```

Some motherboard makers even provide Windows-based Flash ROM update utilities that will check the Internet for updates and download them for you to install. Most of these utilities will also let you back up your current BIOS so you can return to it if the updated version causes trouble. Without a good backup, you could end up throwing away your motherboard if a Flash BIOS update goes wrong, so you should always make one! Finally, don't update your BIOS unless you have some compelling reason to do so. As the old saying goes, "If it ain't broke, don't fix it!"

Tech Tip

Programmable ROM Variants

Most techs use one of three terms—EPROM, EEPROM, or Flash ROM—as the generic catchall term for end user-programmable ROM chips, regardless of the fact that each represents a distinct technology for rewriting the System BIOS. Knowing the differences won't buy you a cup of coffee, but here goes anyway.

Erasable Programmable Read-Only Memory *(EPROM) chips were an early variant on Flash ROM. You could erase their data by exposing them to ultraviolet light using a special machine. An iridescent sticker on the top of the chip prevented accidental UV exposure. To upgrade the System BIOS on an EPROM chip, you had to send the entire motherboard to the manufacturer. Not very convenient!*

The Electrically Erasable Programmable ROM *(EEPROM) chip is a better solution. EEPROMs work basically like EPROMs, but instead of using UV, you only need electricity to rewrite their contents. To change the contents of an EEPROM chip, you simply boot to a floppy and run a simple program provided by the BIOS manufacturer.*

Flash ROM *chips are functionally equivalent to EEPROM chips, but the Flash ROM technology is faster at rewriting the chip. Most motherboards produced today use Flash ROM.*

NVRAM

Modern PCs store CMOS settings and the real-time clock on a type of SRAM chip called *Non-Volatile Random Access Memory* (NVRAM). Although you still hear techs refer to the *CMOS chip*, most modern systems actually use SRAM rather than true CMOS, relying on battery backup to ensure that the chip retains the information. You may well be thinking, how can you call this memory non-volatile if it requires power to retain its contents? I won't argue that this use of the term non-volatile is a stellar example of logical inconsistency, but that's the way the jargon has developed, so the best you can do is make sure you're clear on what's really happening.

In practice, NVRAM falls somewhere between truly non-volatile ROM and totally volatile RAM with respect to its reliability as a storage medium. Although you can definitely lose data stored in NVRAM, it's a rare occurrence, and rarely a traumatic one. If the NVRAM loses power, the CMOS will simply reset to factory defaults, which on most systems works flawlessly. If the clock in Windows resets itself to January 1st every time you reboot the system, the battery on the motherboard is probably losing its charge and needs to be replaced. Barring a defective battery, however, you'll most likely upgrade the motherboard due to obsolescence before you ever need to replace the battery.

As you can see in Figure 5.30, most motherboards use some type of coin battery like those used in wrist watches. To replace it, use a screwdriver to pry the catch gently back. The battery should pop up for easy removal. Before you install the new battery, double-check that it has the same voltage and amperage as the old battery. To retain your CMOS settings while replacing the battery, simply leave your PC plugged into an AC outlet. The 5-volt soft power on all ATX motherboards will provide enough electricity keep the NVRAM charged and the data secure. Of course, I know you're going to be *extremely* careful about ESD while prying up the battery from a live system!

• **Figure 5.30** Typical motherboard battery for the NVRAM

■ BIOS and Device Drivers

IBM could't possibly have included all the necessary BIOS routines for every conceivable piece of hardware on the system ROM chip. How could they? Most of the devices we use today didn't exist on the first PCs! When programmers wrote the first BIOS, for example, network cards, mice, and sound cards did not exist. Early PC designers at IBM understood that they could not anticipate every new type of hardware, so they gave us a few ways to *BYOB*—Bring Your Own BIOS.

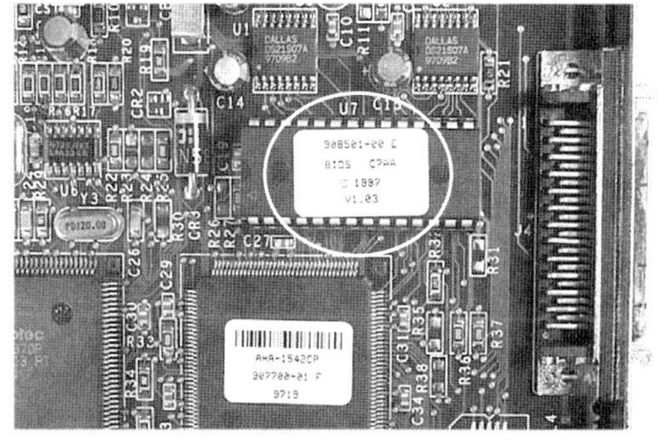

• **Figure 5.31** ROM chip on Adaptec 2940 SCSI host adapter

Option ROM

Most BIOS that come on option ROMs tell you that they exist by displaying information when you boot the system. My system has a SCSI host adapter with option ROM BIOS that makes this pretty screen at boot (Figure 5.32).

In the early days of the PC, you could find all sorts of devices with BIOS on option ROMs. Today, option ROMs have mostly been replaced by more flexible methods such as device drivers (more on that in the next section), with one major exception: video cards. Every video card made today contains its own BIOS, but it uses this BIOS only for *internal* functions. Devices using onboard BIOS do so for internal needs—the BIOS services on the device are not used to talk to the CPU as was originally planned by IBM. Instead, everything relies on device drivers for BYOB. The next section explains what device drivers are, and how they are used in modern systems.

```
Installed at IOPORT = EC00h, IRQ = 11 - Level triggered
BIOS ROM mapped at C800h
<<< Press F2 or F6 to Enter Configuration Menu >>>

ID-LUN:0-0 IOMEGA ZIP 100          E.08 Removable
       Xfer Rate=Asynchronous

No BIOS disk found ! SCSI BIOS not installed !
```

• **Figure 5.32** BIOS showing a SCSI host adapter

Device Drivers

A **device driver** is nothing more than a file stored on the PC's hard drive that contains all the commands necessary to talk to whatever device it was written to support. All operating systems employ a method of loading these device drivers into RAM every time the system boots. They know which device drivers to install by consulting some type of editable file (or files) that lists which device drivers the system needs to load at boot time. All operating systems are designed to look at this list

Device drivers have one big limitation—they don't start until the operating system starts them. Some devices still use ROM BIOS to enable them to boot the system.

early on in the boot process and employ some method of copying the listed files into RAM, thereby giving the CPU the capability to communicate with the hardware supported by the device driver.

Device drivers come with the device when you buy it. When you buy a sound card, for example, it comes with a CD-ROM that holds all the necessary device drivers (and usually a bunch of extra goodies). The generic name for these CD-ROMs is *installation discs*.

The special list of device drivers to load comes in a variety of formats. This list can be one text file, many text files, or, in the case of Windows, a special database. Without these special files, the system does not know which device drivers to load. As far as the PC is concerned, if the device driver for a particular piece of hardware hasn't been loaded, that device simply does not exist. Clearly, the files that contain the list of device drivers are extremely important—you must know all about these files, including where to find them and how to edit them, both to pass the A+ Certification exams and, equally important, to do any serious work on a PC. Let's take a look at some of these files and see how they work!

CONFIG.SYS

CONFIG.SYS is an optional text file that resides in the root directory of the C: drive on Windows 9*x* systems. CONFIG.SYS is a throwback to the first PC operating system, called DOS. Windows systems continue to support a CONIFG.SYS file if it exists. Figure 5.33 shows a typical CONFIG.SYS file from the old DOS days. The file in this example has been opened in the DOS text editor EDIT.COM. It may be old, but it still matters—the A+ Certification exam still has questions about CONFIG.SYS!

Windows NT, 2000, and XP also support CONFIG.SYS, but they do it in a very different way. Read in Chapter 16 about CONFIG.NT files.

When the computer boots up, Windows reads the CONFIG.SYS file (if it exists) and loads the device drivers from the hard drive to RAM. You will learn more about the CONFIG.SYS file in later chapters.

If you want to see your CONFIG.SYS file, try running the SYSEDIT program (Start | Run | SYSEDIT). (See Figure 5.34.) This old Windows editor is still supported by every version of Windows. It will open up CONFIG.SYS as well as a few other files you'll soon learn about. Just don't be surprised to find that your CONFIG.SYS file is blank—most systems don't use CONFIG.SYS anymore.

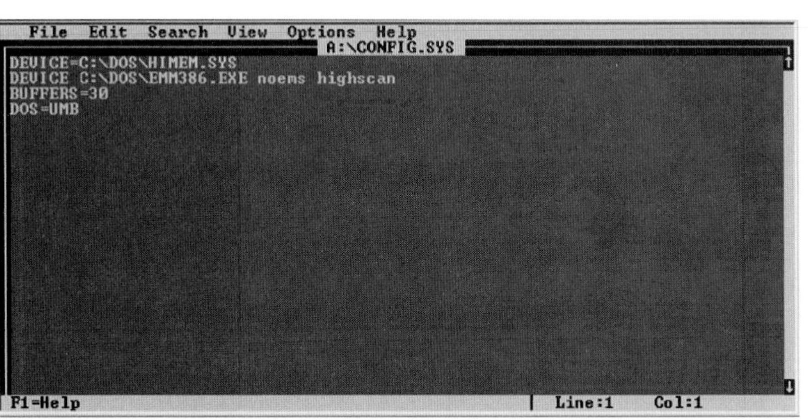

Figure 5.33 Typical CONFIG.SYS file open in EDIT program

SYSTEM.INI

SYSTEM.INI is another throwback from an earlier time. SYSTEM.INI first appeared in the precursor to Windows 9*x*/Me called Windows 3.*x*— the first truly popular version of Windows. Microsoft invented the SYSTEM.INI files to fix a serious shortcoming of CONFIG.SYS: any device driver that runs in CONFIG.SYS must be designed to run under a DOS environment. Windows 3.*x* was the first operating system to take advantage of 32-bit computing and its device drivers were redesigned to work in a 32-bit world. Windows 3.*x* used SYSTEM.INI to load those drivers when it started. Even though Windows 3.*x* is no longer with us, every version of Windows continues to support SYSTEM.INI fully. Unlike CONFIG.SYS, every Windows system still has a SYSTEM.INI file. In fact, Windows 9*x*/Me systems *must* have SYSTEM.INI or they will not boot! Windows NT, 2000, and XP don't require SYSTEM.INI, but they do include it for backward compatibility with older Windows applications.

SYSTEM.INI is a text file, broken up into sections. Each section begins with the name of that

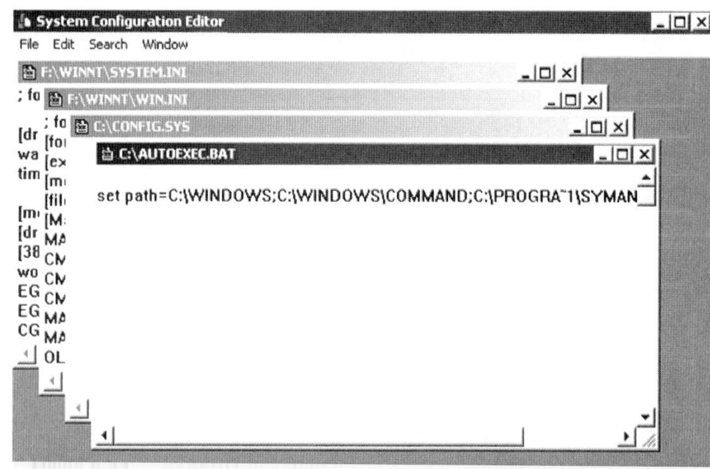

Registry

Windows 95 consolidated the functions of CONFIG.SYS, SYSTEM.INI, and a number of other files you will eventually meet in this book, into a new type of configuration file, collectively called the **Registry**. Every configuration setting in every version of Windows is stored in the Registry, including all device driver information.

Unlike CONFIG.SYS and SYSTEM.INI, the Registry is not a text file. It is an incredibly complex binary file. You will rarely edit the Registry directly. In the overwhelming majority of situations, you will use the far more intuitive interfaces of the Control Panel and the Device Manager to edit the Registry.

Windows NT 4 does not have a Device Manager. To install device drivers in Windows NT, you just use the various icons in the Control Panel.

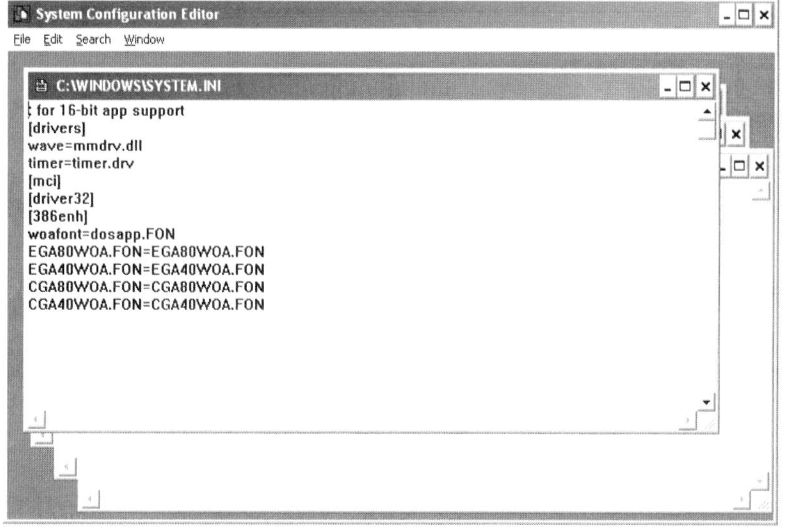

• **Figure 5.35** SYSTEM.INI file with [386Enh] section

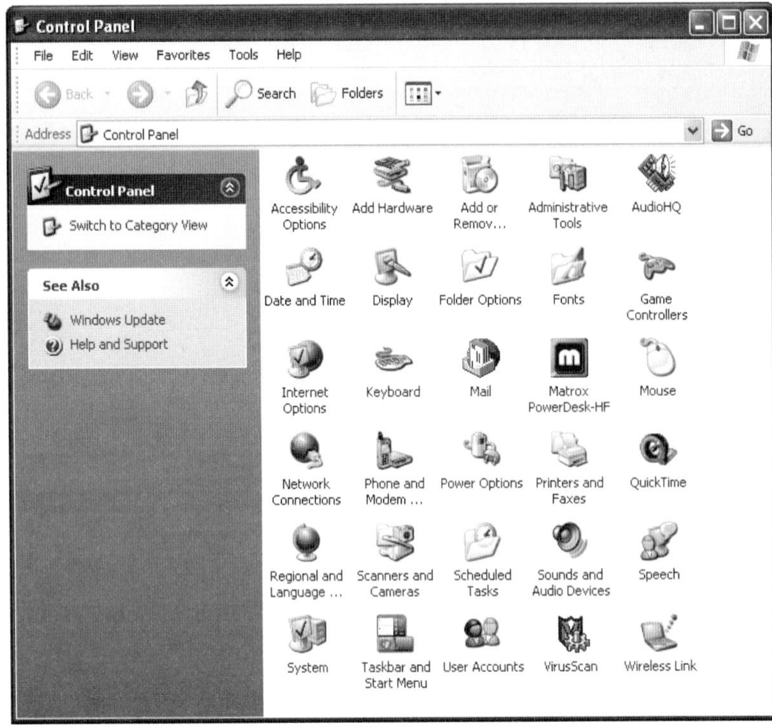

Figure 5.36 Windows XP Control Panel in Classic View

When appropriate, you can edit the Registry directly using the command line programs REGEDIT (Windows 9*x*/Me) and REGEDT32 (Windows NT, 2000, and XP).

Control Panel

You can access the Control Panel by clicking Start | Control Panel (or Start | Settings | Control Panel for pre-XP systems). The Control Panel (Figure 5.36) is really a collection of many *applets*—small programs—that enable you to configure a broad range of system settings. Each applet provides a special tool for the configuring of some aspect of the Windows system.

Not all Control Panels are the same. While all versions of Windows share many common applets, there are differences from one version to the next. Additionally, third-party applications such as Adobe QuickTime and Real Networks RealPlayer may add their own Control Panel applets. You should be comfortable seeing applets in one Control Panel that are not in another system's Control Panel. You will learn more about the important Control Panel applets as you read the relevant chapters.

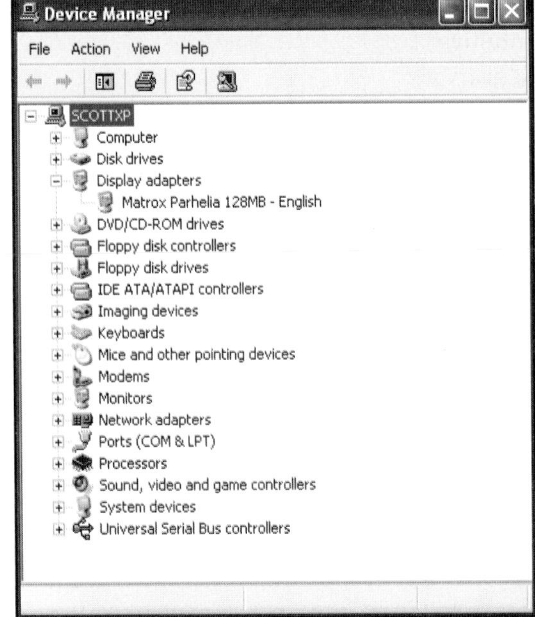

Figure 5.37 Windows XP Device Manager

Device Manager

Using the Device Manager (Figure 5.37), you can change or remove the drivers for any particular device. You access the Device Manager differently in different versions of Windows. In Windows 95, Windows 98, Windows NT, and Windows Me, you access the Device Manager by opening the System applet in the Control Panel and selecting the Device Manager tab. If you use Windows 2000 or XP, you still open the System applet, but you must then select the Hardware tab and click the Device Manager button. Although different versions of Windows have different ways to get to the Device Manager, once you open it, the appearance is basically the same (Figure 5.38).

REGEDIT and REGEDT32

Microsoft provides one or two programs that enable you to access the Registry directly. If you use Windows 9*x*/Me, you can use a program called REGEDIT.EXE to edit the Registry. Run REGEDIT by using the Start | Run menu option, and then typing **REGEDIT**. Note the two sides of the REGEDIT screen—one side looks quite similar to Windows Explorer and shows the hierarchical configuration of the Registry.

Windows NT, 2000, and XP provide a second Registry editor called **REGEDT32.EXE** (Figure 5.39). REGEDT32 has more powerful features needed by the more powerful operating systems. Interestingly, NT, 2000, and XP also provide a copy of good old REGEDIT. Microsoft never bothered to put a decent search function in REGEDT32. NT, 2000 and XP techs often run both programs simultaneously—REGEDIT to find values and REGEDT32 to do the actual editing.

Well, aren't you dangerous! Now that you know how to access the Registry, you have the ability to kill any Windows system by messing around with the Registry settings. Again, techs rarely use these tools, but the A+ Certification exams expect you to know [illegible] ware on a system must have an accompanying program that provides the CPU with the code necessary to communicate with that particular device. This code may reside on the system ROM on the motherboard, on ROM on a card, or it may be in a device driver file on the hard drive loaded into RAM at boot. BIOS is everywhere on your system, and you will need to deal with it occasionally. Make sure you know how to access the CMOS, CONFIG.SYS, SYSTEM.INI, and Registry on a given system.

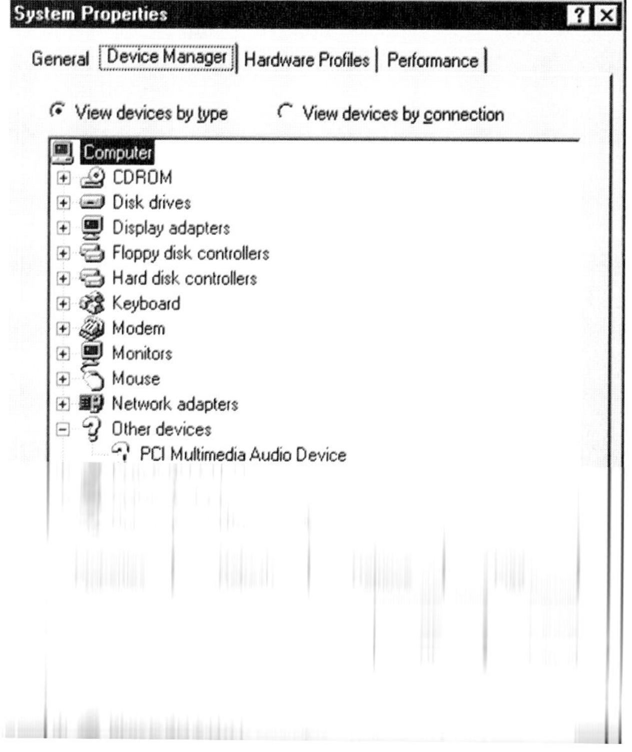

• **Figure 5.38** Windows Me Device Manager

The official name of both applications—REGEDIT and REGEDT32—is *Registry Editor.* We use the filenames to avoid confusion between the two versions.

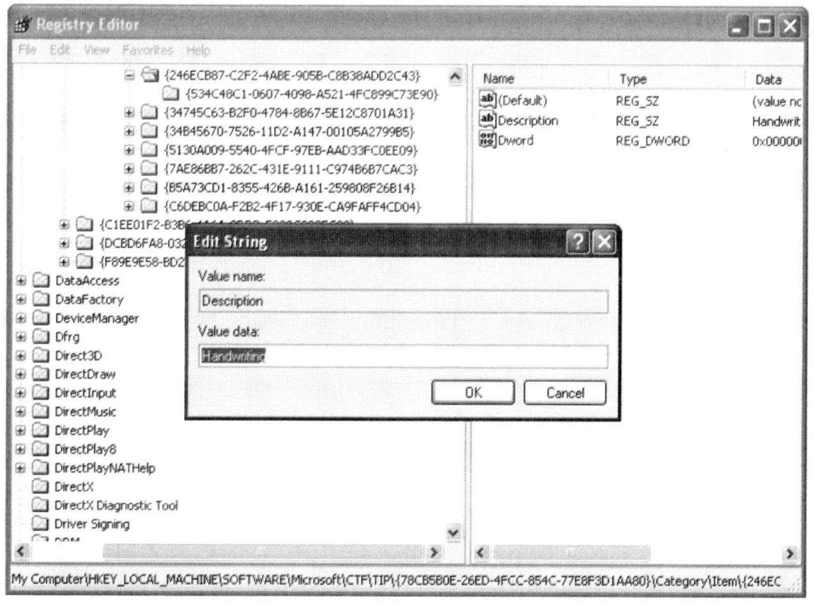

• **Figure 5.39** Making a change through the REGEDT32 screen

Here's a question for you: Is a device driver BIOS? Not really. Granted, it performs the same function—providing programming to enable the CPU to talk to hardware—but the fact that device drivers load from the hard drive like any other program makes a difference in most techs' minds.

Power-On Self Test (POST)

When the computer is turned on or reset, it initiates a special program, also stored on the system ROM chip, called the **Power-On Self Test** (POST). The POST program checks out the system every time the computer boots. To perform this check, the POST sends out a standard command that says to all the devices, "Check yourselves out!" All the assumed devices (see my Note on this) in the computer then run their own internal diagnostic—the POST doesn't specify what they must check. The quality of the diagnostic is up to the people who made that particular device.

The term *assumed devices* is not an industry standard term, but one I use to mean "all the devices supported by the System BIOS," such as the keyboard controller, floppy and hard drive controllers, RAM, basic video, and so on.

Let's consider the POST for a moment. Suppose some device—let's say it's the keyboard controller chip—runs its diagnostic and determines that it is not working properly. What can the POST do about it? Only one thing really: tell the human in front of the PC! So how does the computer tell the human? PCs convey POST information to you in two ways: beep codes and text messages.

Before and During the Video Test: The Beep Codes

The computer tests the most basic parts of the computer first. If anything goes wrong, the computer will send a series of beeps. The meaning of these beeps varies from one BIOS manufacturer to another. Additionally, BIOS makers have changed the **beep codes** over time. Tables 5.1 and 5.2 show the beep codes for the most current versions of AMI and Phoenix BIOS. Award BIOS no longer uses beep codes except when the video card fails—then it gives one long beep followed by two short beeps. Check the \SHAREWARE\SOUNDS directory on the accompanying CD for a recording of an Award BIOS reporting a failed video test.

Table 5.1 AMI Version 8 Beep Codes

Beeps	Post Routine Description
1	Refresh failure
2	Parity error
3	Main memory read/write error
4	Timer not operational
5	Processor error
6	8042—gate A20 failure
7	Processor exception interrupt error
8	Display memory read/write failure
9	ROM checksum error
10	CMOS shutdown register read/write error
11	Cache memory bad

Table 5.2 Phoenix Beep Codes	
Beeps	**Post Routine Description**
1-2-2-3	BIOS ROM checksum
1-3-1-1	Test DRAM refresh
1-3-1-3	Test 8742 keyboard controller
1-3-5-1	RAM failure on address line xxxx
1-3-5-3	RAM failure on data bits xxxx of low byte of memory bus
2-1-2-3	Check ROM copyright notice
2-2-3-1	Test for unexpected interrupts
1-2	Search for option ROMs; one long, two short beeps on checksum failure

POST is not the only time your system may beep at you. Most systems make a rather strange noise when the RAM is missing or very seriously damaged. This tone can make you think you have a beep code. Sure, the speaker beeps, but this "sound of RAM death" is not really considered a beep code. Unlike beep codes, this code repeats until you shut off the system. I've included a recording of this sound on the CD in the \SHAREWARE\SOUNDS directory.

overheating. These beeps don't take place at boot—they happen after the system has run for a few minutes. An overheated system is a serious problem, so don't confuse it with a beep error code!

Table 5.3 Common POST Beep Errors and Solutions	
Problem	**Solution**
RAM refresh failure Parity error RAM bit error Base 64 K error	(1) Reseat and clean the RAM chips. (2) Replace individual chips until the problem is corrected.
8042 error Gate A20 error	(1) Reseat and clean keyboard chip. (2) Replace keyboard. (3) Replace motherboard.
BIOS checksum error	(1) Reseat and clean ROM chip. (2) Replace ROM chip.
Video error	(1) Reseat video card. (2) Replace video card.
Cache memory error	(1) Shut off cache in CMOS. (2) Replace CPU.
Everything else	(1) Clean motherboard. (2) Replace motherboard.

• **Figure 5.40** Text error message

Text Errors

After the video has tested OK, any POST errors will display on the screen as a text error. If you get a text error, the problem is usually, but not always, self-explanatory (Figure 5.40). Text errors are far more useful because you can simply read the screen to determine the bad device. I should add here that a few PC makers (read: IBM) still use numeric error codes in some models. But in these cases, they invariably also add a text code for clarity.

POST Cards

Beep codes, numeric codes, and text error codes, although helpful, can sometimes be misleading. Worse than that, an inoperative device can sometimes disrupt the POST, forcing the machine into an endless loop. This causes the PC to act dead—no beeps and nothing on the screen. In this case, you need a device to monitor the POST and identify which piece of hardware is causing the trouble. The devices designed for this are known as **POST cards**.

POST cards are simple cards that snap into an expansion slot on your system. A small, two-character light emitting diode (LED) readout on the card indicates what device the POST is currently testing (Figure 5.41). The documentation that comes with the POST card tells you what the codes mean. BIOS makers also provide this information on their web sites. Manufacturers make POST cards for all types of PCs. They will work with any BIOS, but you need to know the type of BIOS you have in order to interpret the readout properly.

We usually only pull out a POST card when the usual POST errors fail to appear. When a computer provides a beep or text error code that doesn't make sense, or if your machine keeps locking up, some device has stalled the POST. Because the POST card will tell you which device is being tested, the frozen system will stay at that point in the POST, and the error will stay on the POST card's readout.

Many companies sell POST cards today, with prices ranging from the affordable to the outrages. Spend the absolute least amount of money you can. The more expensive cards add bells and whistles that you do not need, like diagnostic software and voltmeters. Try JDR Microdevices (800-538-5000) for a good, cheap POST card. Mention Total Seminars, and they should sell it to you for less than US$50.

Using a POST card is straightforward. Simply power down the PC, install the POST card in any unused slot, and turn the PC back on. As you watch the POST display, notice the different hexadecimal readouts and refer to them as the POST progresses. Notice how quickly they change. If you get an "FF" or "00," that means the POST is over and everything passed—time to check the operating system. If a device stalls the POST, however, the POST card will display an error code. That's the problem device! Good technicians often memorize a dozen or more different POST codes, because it's much faster than looking them up in a book.

• **Figure 5.41** POST card in action

So you got a beep code, a text error code, or a POST error. Now what do you do with that knowledge? The important thing to remember is that a POST error does not fix the computer; it only tells you where to look. You then have to know how to deal with that bad or improperly configured component. If you use a POST card, for example, and it hangs at the "Initializing Floppy Drive" test, you'd better know how to work on a floppy drive!

Sometimes the error code itself confuses us. What device do you point at when you get a "CMOS shutdown register read/write error" beep code from your system? First of all, read the error carefully. Let's say on that same system you got an "8042—gate A20 failure" beep code. What will you do? Assuming you know (and you should!) that the "8042" refers to the keyboard, a quick peek at the keyboard and its connection would be a good first step. But beyond that specific example, here is a good general rule: If you don't know what the error means or the bad part isn't replaceable, replace

[illegible]

gram. Those days are long gone. You never see a Run button on the front of the PC. Instead, when IBM first developed the PC, they decided that the user would simply flip the on/off switch and the computer would run. Once you feed power to the PC, the tight interrelation of hardware, firmware, and software enables the PC to start itself, to "pull itself up by the bootstraps" or "boot" itself. All PCs still follow the original boot process as described by IBM for the original IBM 286 AT computer.

The first electrical component to "wake up" when the computer is turned on is the CPU itself. As soon as the power supply provides the proper voltage, the CPU reads a special wire called the *power good* wire. If this wire has a certain voltage, the CPU knows the system has enough power coming in to begin the boot process. The moment the power good wire wakes it up, every CPU immediately sends a built-in memory address via its address bus. This special address is the same on every CPU, from the oldest 8086 to the most recent microprocessor. This address is the first line of the POST program on the system ROM! That's how the system starts the POST.

After the POST has finished, there must be a way for the computer to find the programs on the hard drive in order to start the operating system (usually Windows). The POST passes control to the last BIOS function: the **bootstrap loader**. The bootstrap loader is little more than a few dozen lines of BIOS code tacked to the end of the POST program. Its job is to find the operating system. The bootstrap loader will first check to see if a diskette is in the floppy drive. If a floppy diskette is inserted, the PC assumes that the operating system is on the floppy disk. If a floppy disk is not inserted, it then looks for an operating system on the hard drive. All floppy and hard disks set aside a specific location called the *boot sector*. If the disk is bootable, its boot sector will contain special programming designed to tell the system where to locate the operating system. A disk that has a functional operating system

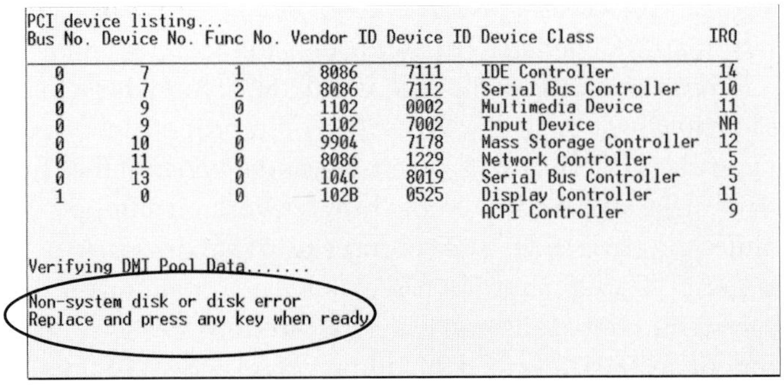

```
PCI device listing...
Bus No. Device No. Func No. Vendor ID Device ID Device Class              IRQ
  0        7         1       8086      7111    IDE Controller            14
  0        7         2       8086      7112    Serial Bus Controller     10
  0        9         0       1102      0002    Multimedia Device         11
  0        9         1       1102      7002    Input Device              NA
  0       10         0       9904      7178    Mass Storage Controller   12
  0       11         0       8086      1229    Network Controller         5
  0       13         0       104C      8019    Serial Bus Controller      5
  1        0         0       102B      0525    Display Controller        11
                                               ACPI Controller            9

Verifying DMI Pool Data......
Non-system disk or disk error
Replace and press any key when ready
```

• **Figure 5.42** The message that appears when no bootable disk is found

is called a **bootable disk** or a *system disk*. If the bootstrap loader locates a good boot sector, it passes control to the operating system and removes itself from memory. Even though BIOS has left the RAM, the little BIOS programs (the services—did you forget about them?) stand ready to assist the CPU in talking to the hard drives, floppy drives, and so on.

Boot Configuration

If the bootstrap loader cannot find a bootable disk, you will get the error shown in Figure 5.42. This error is easy to re-create. Just reboot your computer with a blank floppy disk in the floppy drive!

Many BIOS programs have CMOS settings that enable you to change the order in which the boot loader searches devices for an operating system. Figure 5.43 shows a typical CMOS search order screen. This screen enables you to choose a boot order from among a range of bootable devices: the floppy drive, hard drive, CD-ROM, LS-120/Zip drive, and network boot (booting from a special type of network card). You may put these in any order. Changing the boot order so it doesn't start with the A: drive is one way to prevent a hacker from inserting a bootable floppy and accessing a vulnerable system.

The complex world of BIOS takes up a good part of any technician's day. Unless you never change hardware and your systems never crash (in which case I want to touch you for luck!), you will spend a good deal of time accessing CMOS, installing device drivers, and editing critical files. Understanding the many features and functions of BIOS gives you the tools you need both to pass the A+ Certification exams and to become a good PC technician.

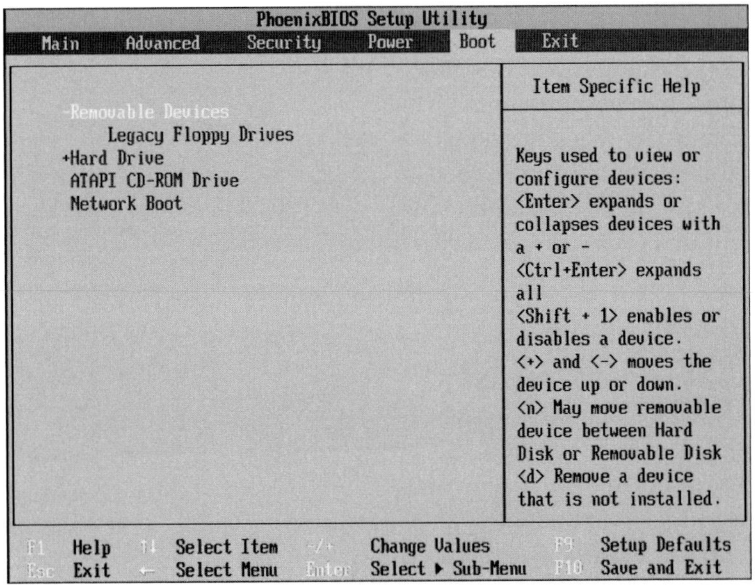

```
                    PhoenixBIOS Setup Utility
 Main   Advanced   Security   Power   Boot   Exit

                                      Item Specific Help
  -Removable Devices
     Legacy Floppy Drives
  +Hard Drive                         Keys used to view or
   ATAPI CD-ROM Drive                 configure devices:
   Network Boot                       <Enter> expands or
                                      collapses devices with
                                      a + or -
                                      <Ctrl+Enter> expands
                                      all
                                      <Shift + 1> enables or
                                      disables a device.
                                      <+> and <-> moves the
                                      device up or down.
                                      <n> May move removable
                                      device between Hard
                                      Disk or Removable Disk
                                      <d> Remove a device
                                      that is not installed.

 F1  Help  ↑↓ Select Item   -/+   Change Values       F9  Setup Defaults
 Esc Exit  ←  Select Menu   Enter Select ▸ Sub-Menu   F10 Save and Exit
```

• **Figure 5.43** CMOS changing boot sequence

Chapter 5 Review

Chapter Summary

After reading this chapter and completing the exercises, you should understand the following about BIOS.

Explain the Function of BIOS

- For computer devices to work, they need a way for the CPU to talk to them and a way to send data to and receive data from the CPU. The Northbridge [illegible]
- The Southbridge makes both the external data bus and the address bus available to other devices on the computer. The address bus, with a unique I/O address assigned to every device in the PC, enables the CPU to send commands through the chipset to the various devices.
- A ROM (Read Only Memory) chip is non-volatile, meaning it retains the information stored on it even when the power is turned off. Usually attached to the Southbridge, the ROM chip stores hundreds of little programs, collectively referred to as the Basic Input/Output Services (BIOS). Since these programs are stored on a read-only medium and can't be changed by the user, they are known as *firmware*, in contrast to programs stored on erasable media that are called *software*. The terms *System ROM* and *ROM BIOS* refer to the ROM chip on the motherboard.
- Although the ROM chip has room for as much as 2 MB of programs, only 65,536 bytes store the BIOS. Correspondingly, the last 65,536 addresses on the address bus are reserved for the BIOS on the ROM chip. When the CPU indicates one of these reserved addresses, the Northbridge sends the address directly to the ROM BIOS.
- While the ROM BIOS includes programs that enable the CPU to talk to many basic hardware devices such as the keyboard, other devices not supported by the ROM BIOS may have their own ROM chips.
- [illegible] is common and necessary but may change from time to time, such as when you install a larger hard drive or add more RAM, the BIOS for the general type of device (e.g., a hard drive) can be on the system ROM chip, but the information describing specific features unique to that particular device (e.g., a Seagate Barracuda 60-GB drive) must be stored on a changeable storage medium.

Distinguish Among CMOS Setup Utilities

- Your motherboard includes a changeable chip, capable of storing about 64 KB of data, called the Complementary Metal-Oxide Semiconductor (CMOS) chip. It stores only data needed to flesh out the details that the BIOS needs to talk to changeable hardware, not the actual BIOS programs. The CMOS chip also keeps track of the date and time.
- Within the system ROM is a CMOS setup program that lets you access and update the data on the CMOS chip. The terms *CMOS setup program, CMOS,* and *System Setup Utility* are functionally interchangeable today. Most techs just call it the

CMOS. Three major manufacturers control 99 percent of the BIOS business: American Megatrends (AMI), Award Software, and Phoenix Technology. The CMOS setup program can be started in many different ways, depending on the brand of BIOS you have on your computer. Pressing DEL when the computer boots is the most common way to access the CMOS setup program. The screen itself will usually tell you how to access setup. If it doesn't, you can check the motherboard book or the web site of your PC or BIOS manufacturer.

- All CMOS setup programs have basically the same structure. On the Standard CMOS Features screen, you can change floppy drive, hard drive, and date/time settings. Today's setup programs have extra CMOS settings that control items such as memory management, password and booting options, diagnostic and error handling, and power management. The Award Modular BIOS enables motherboard manufacturers to add or remove options from the setup program.
- Among the other things you can configure in CMOS setup are the voltage and multiplier settings for the CPU (the CPU Soft menu), boot options (check the Advanced BIOS Features menu), power management, password protection, and ports (the Integrated Peripherals menu). From the PnP/PCI Configurations setup menu, you can set resources such as interrupt requests (IRQs) for particular devices. All setup programs include options to *Save and Exit* or *Exit Without Saving*. Most techs don't understand all the fields in the setup program, and you should not change them unless you know exactly what you're doing.
- Phoenix custom designs an optimized BIOS for each specific computer. You will usually see Phoenix BIOS programs in machines with proprietary motherboards, such as laptops.
- On older systems, if the information on the CMOS chip was lost or erased, the computer would not boot. The most common cause was a dead onboard battery, but other factors such as electrical surges, chip creep or a dirty motherboard could also erase CMOS data. Lost CMOS information produced errors such as *No boot device available or CMOS data/time not set*. Making a backup copy of the CMOS data enabled you to restore the information and recover from this catastrophe.
- Unlike earlier ROM chips that you had to replace when you wanted to upgrade the BIOS programs, today's computers use Flash ROM chips that you can reprogram without removing the chip. If you install a CPU or other new hardware that the Flash ROM chip does not support, you can run a small command line program combined with an update file to change your BIOS. The exact process varies from one motherboard maker to another. If the Flash ROM utility allows you to make a backup of your BIOS, you should always do so.

Describe BIOS and Device Drivers

- Newer hardware devices that are not supported by the System BIOS have other ways to BYOB—bring your own BIOS. A hardware device, such as a SCSI host adapter, may contain its own BIOS chip or ROM chip. Every video card contains its own BIOS for internal functions. A more flexible way to BYOB is to use a file called a device driver that contains instructions to support the hardware device. Device drivers load when the system boots.
- Many devices come with device driver files on installation disks. These drivers must be loaded for the PC to recognize and use the devices. DOS loaded drivers using the CONFIG.SYS file. Today's systems rarely use CONFIG.SYS, but Windows still supports this text file, which you can create or modify using a text editor such as EDIT.COM. Windows 3.*x* used the SYSTEM.INI file to load 32-bit drivers, and Windows still supports SYSTEM.INI. In fact, Windows 9*x*/Me must have a SYSTEM.INI file to boot. SYSTEM.INI is a text file divided into sections with headers in square brackets.

- Windows 95 and newer Windows operating systems combine the CONFIG.SYS, SYSTEM.INI, and other files into the Registry. Instead of being a text file, the Registry is a complex binary file that you will usually change using the Control Panel and Device Manager. Access the Control Panel by selecting Start | Settings | Control Panel. Different versions of Windows have different Control Panel applets that you can use to configure system settings. Accessed in different ways for different versions of Windows, the Device Manager lets you change or remove drivers for any device.

- Although you can edit the Registry directly using [illegible] Techs frequently use REGEDIT to find values and REGEDT32 to do the actual editing.

Troubleshoot the Power-On Self Test (POST)

- In addition to the BIOS routines and the CMOS setup program, the system ROM also includes a special program called the Power-On Self Test (POST) that is executed every time the computer boots. POST first tests basic devices up to and including video. If it detects an error, the computer alerts you with a series of beeps. Different ROM manufacturers use different beep codes, but your motherboard book should explain them. For example, one long beep followed by two short beeps from an Award BIOS signals that the video card has failed. After the basic devices, POST tests the rest of the devices and displays a text error message on the screen if anything is wrong. Some manufacturers use numeric error codes or combine numeric and text messages.

- Two situations where the computer may beep that are not POST beep codes involve RAM and cooling. If the computer beeps constantly until you shut it off, it means that RAM is missing or damaged. If the computer beeps after it is booted, it is probably a warning that the system is overheating.

- If the computer appears dead with no beeps or screen response, you can place a POST card in an expansion slot to diagnose the problem using the LED readout on the card. The documentation that comes with the POST card will explain the LED codes for your particular BIOS.

- A beep code, text error message, or POST error [illegible]

- The last job of the BIOS is to start the boot process. The CPU is the first component that wakes up. It checks the *power good* wire of the power supply to see that it has sufficient voltage to begin the booting process. If so, the CPU issues a memory address that executes the first line of the POST program. After POST has finished, it passes control to the bootstrap loader function on the ROM BIOS. This program looks for an operating system, checking the floppy and hard drives to find the boot sector that identifies the location of the operating system. When the BIOS finds a bootable or system disk that has a functional operating system, it passes control to that disk. If it cannot find a bootable disk, you will get the error message "Non-system disk or disk error." This error usually indicates that you've left a non-bootable disk in the floppy drive. Most BIOS programs allow you to change the boot order to exclude the floppy drive or to include a CD-ROM, Zip drive, or network drive.

Key Terms

Basic Input/Output Services (BIOS) *(147)*
Beep codes *(164)*
Bootable disk *(168)*
Bootstrap loader *(167)*
Chipset *(143)*
Complementary Metal-Oxide Semiconductor (CMOS) *(149)*
CONFIG.SYS *(160)*
Device driver *(159)*
Firmware *(147)*
Flash ROM *(156)*
Non-volatile *(146)*
POST card *(166)*
Power-On Self Test (POST) *(164)*
REDEDIT.EXE *(162)*
REGEDT32.EXE *(163)*
Registry *(161)*
Read Only Memory (ROM) *(146)*
Southbridge *(143)*
SYSTEM.INI *(160)*
System BIOS *(147)*

Key Term Quiz

Use the Key Terms list to complete the sentences that follow. Not all the terms will be used.

1. Loaded when the system boots, a __________ is a file that contains instructions to support a hardware device.
2. If the computer appears dead with no beeps or screen responses, you can insert a __________ in an expansion slot to diagnose what is wrong.
3. The combination of a specific Northbridge and a specific __________ is collectively referred to as the __________.
4. If a disk contains the operating system files necessary to start the computer, it is called a __________.
5. A __________ chip can be reprogrammed without removing the chip.
6. Unlike RAM that loses all data when the computer is shut down, a ROM chip is __________, retaining the information even when the power is off.
7. The hundreds of programs in the system ROM chip are collectively called the __________.
8. The __________ is a complex binary file used with Windows that combines the CONFIG.SYS, SYSTEM.INI, and other configuration files.
9. The low-energy chip that holds configuration information and keeps track of date and time is called the __________ chip.
10. When the computer starts, it runs a program on the System BIOS called __________ that checks the hardware.

Multiple-Choice Quiz

1. When you try to boot the computer, you get the error message "Non-system disk or disk error." What is the most likely cause of this error message?
   - **A.** You left a non-bootable disk in the floppy drive.
   - **B.** The CMOS battery has gone dead.
   - **C.** Your hard drive has crashed.
   - **D.** The Registry has become corrupted.
2. Which of the following statements is true?
   - **A.** The only ROM chip in your computer is the System BIOS chip on the motherboard.
   - **B.** Every PC reserves the last 384 K of the first megabyte of memory space for BIOS.
   - **C.** The System BIOS contains the scan codes for the keyboard.
   - **D.** Data stored on the CMOS chip is called firmware.
3. The safest way to change the Registry is by using __________.
   - **A.** REGEDIT

B. REGEDT32

C. The BIOS setup program

D. The Control Panel

4. The CMOS chip stores information about all of the following *except* __________.

A. The kind of hard drive

B. The date and time

C. The scan codes for the keyboard

D. The amount of memory installed

5. When you turn on your computer, what is accessed first?

REGEDT32.EXE?

A. REGEDIT is used for Windows 9*x* while REGEDT32 came with Windows 3.*x*.

B. REGEDT32 does not include an adequate search function, but REGEDIT does.

C. REGEDIT allows you to edit any part of the Registry, while REGEDT32 only allows you to change the 32 most frequently used Registry features.

D. REGEDIT is a command line editor while REGEDT32 has a graphical user interface.

7. Although the ROM chip has room for as much as 2 MB of programs, the BIOS only takes up a maximum of __________.

A. 1 MB

B. 640 K

C. 65,536 bytes

D. 384 K

8. Which of the following statements best describes the BIOS?

A. BIOS connects the Northbridge to the Southbridge chip.

B. BIOS stores the Windows Registry.

C. BIOS contains programs that let the CPU communicate with other hardware.

D. BIOS is another name for the CPU's address bus.

9. Which of the following will result in a POST beep code message?

A. The system is overheating.

B. The video card is not seated properly.

C. The keyboard is unplugged.

D. The hard drive has crashed.

10. Which of the following statements is true

(POST) routines.

D. CMOS is the Southbridge chip that controls input and output devices.

11. You can upgrade a Flash ROM chip by __________________.

A. Removing the chip and replacing it with a different one

B. Rebooting the computer

C. Installing a different operating system

D. Running a small command line program combined with a BIOS update file

12. The major manufacturers of BIOS programs include all of the following *except*__________.

A. American Megatrends (AMI)

B. IBM

C. Award Software

D. Phoenix Technology

13. You should run the BIOS setup program when __________________.

A. The computer boots

B. You add new hardware, such as a second hard drive

C. POST displays an error message

D. You install a SCSI host adapter

14. The Southbridge chip extends the external data bus to ________________.

A. Enable all devices in the PC to send data to and from the CPU

B. Allow the CPU to get data from memory

C. Permit the CMOS chip to store configuration information

D. Define how much address space the CPU supports

15. Device drivers may be loaded ________________.

A. Only through the Registry

B. Only through the CONFIG.SYS file

C. Only through the SYSTEM.INI file

D. Through the Registry, the CONFIG.SYS, or the SYSTEM.INI

Essay Quiz

1. From this chapter you learned that every piece of hardware in the computer needs programs to make it work. Explain three different ways in which these essential programs may be provided to the CPU.

2. You've been hired as a tutor for Tom, a fellow student in your hardware class. He's having a difficult time understanding the role that the ROM BIOS plays in booting the computer. How will you explain this process to him? Be sure to explain in order the step-by-step process that the BIOS goes through from the time you turn on the computer until it relinquishes control to the operating system. Make sure Tom understands why you may get an error message if you left a diskette in the floppy drive.

3. Why do some POST error messages manifest themselves as beep codes while others display as text messages? What should you do if you get a POST error message?

4. Your instructor has asked you to give a report on the Northbridge and Southbridge chips, their functions, and how they use the address bus. Prepare a five-minute oral report to present to your class.

5. What symptoms will your computer show if the CMOS battery is dying or dead? What kinds of CMOS batteries are replaceable? What happens to the information stored in CMOS when you replace the battery? What must you do if a built-in battery goes dead?

Lab Projects

• Lab Project 5.1

Use the motherboard book (if you have one or can download one) or check the web site of your BIOS manufacturer to identify what each of the following POST error messages means:

1. A numeric message of 301
2. One long beep followed by two short beeps
3. A numeric message of 601
4. HDD controller failure

Lab Project 5.2

Watch closely as your computer boots to see if it displays a message about how to reach the setup program. If it does not, consult your motherboard book to try to locate this information. Then, using the method appropriate for your System BIOS chip, access the setup program and examine the various screens. Do not change anything! Usually, your motherboard book includes default settings for the various setup screens and perhaps includes explanations of the various choices. Compare what you see on the screen with what the book says. Are there any differences? If so, how do you account for these differences? As you examine the setup program, answer the following questions:

1. What is the boot sequence for your computer?
2. What is the core voltage of the CPU?
3. What mode does the parallel port use?
4. What IRQ does COM 1 use?

When you have finished, choose "Exit Without Saving."

chapter 6 Expansion Bus

"Increase the Flash Gordon noise and put more science stuff around!"

—Crow T. Robot, *Mystery Science Theater 3000: The Movie*, 1996

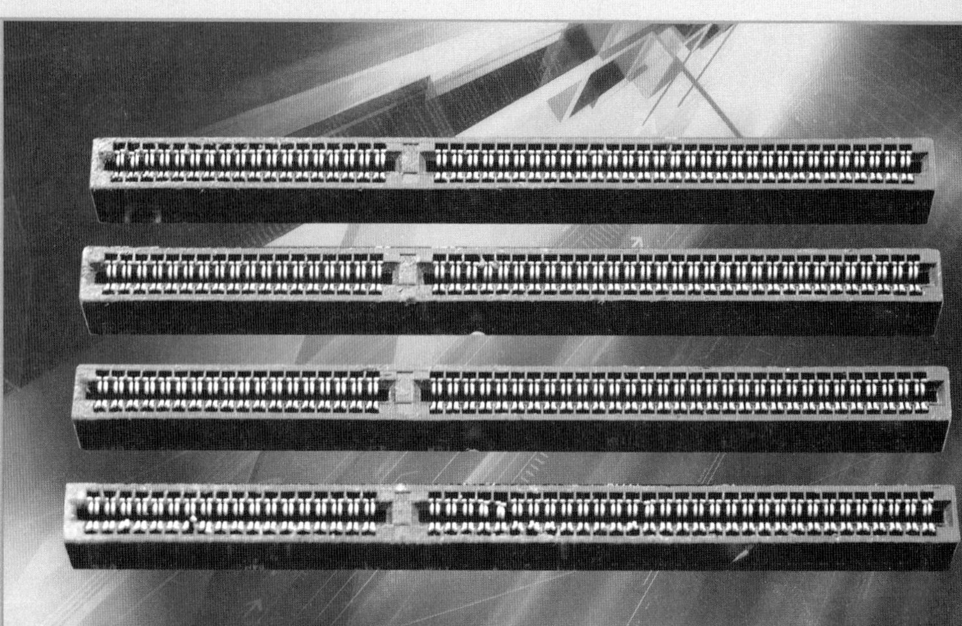

In this chapter, you will learn how to

- **Identify the structure and function of the expansion bus**
- **Explain classic system resources**
- **Identify the modern expansion bus slots**
- **Install expansion cards properly**
- **Troubleshoot expansion card problems**

IBM created the PC with an eye to the future, or at least to future expansion in capability. The original PC could not play music, for example, or connect to other PCs, although some computers of the day could already do these things. The IBM PC came with an internal **expansion bus**—slots built into the motherboard for adding expansion cards and thus new functions for the PC. This expandability might seem obvious today, but think about the three big hurdles a would-be expansion card developer would have to leap to add a card successfully. First, any expansion card would need to be built specifically for the IBM PC's slots. Second, the card would need some way to communicate with the CPU both to receive instructions and to relay information. And third, the operating system would need some means of enabling the user to control the new device and thus take advantage of its functions. Here's the short form of the three hurdles:

- Connectivity
- Communication
- Drivers

This chapter covers the expansion bus in detail, starting almost at the very beginning of the PC—not because the history of the PC is inherently thrilling, but rather because the way the old PCs worked still affects the latest systems. Installation today remains very similar to installation in 1987, in that you have to have connectivity, communication, and drivers for the operating system. Taking the time to learn the old ways first most definitely helps make current technology, terminology, and practices easier to understand and implement.

The conceptual and practical weave in and out in this chapter more than in most, so I recommend reading the full chapter rather than just skipping to the "Test Specific" section.

Historical/Conceptual

sion bus is no exception. It connects to the rest of the PC through the chipset. Exactly *where* on the chipset varies depending on the system. On some systems, the **expansion slots** connect to the Southbridge (Figure 6.1). On other systems, the expansion slots connect to the Northbridge (Figure 6.2). Finally, many systems have more than one type of expansion bus, with slots of one type connecting to the Northbridge and slots of another type connecting to the Southbridge (Figure 6.3).

The chipset provides an extension of the address bus and data bus to the expansion slots, and thus to any expansion cards in those slots. If you plug a hard drive controller card into an expansion slot, it will function just as if it were built into the motherboard, albeit with one big difference: speed.

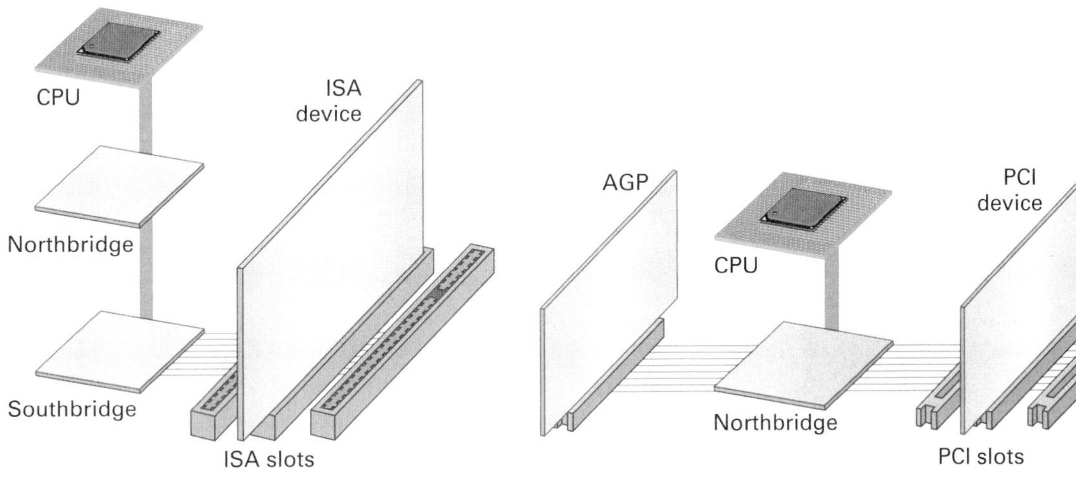

• **Figure 6.1** Expansion slots connecting to Southbridge

• **Figure 6.2** Expansion slots connecting to Northbridge

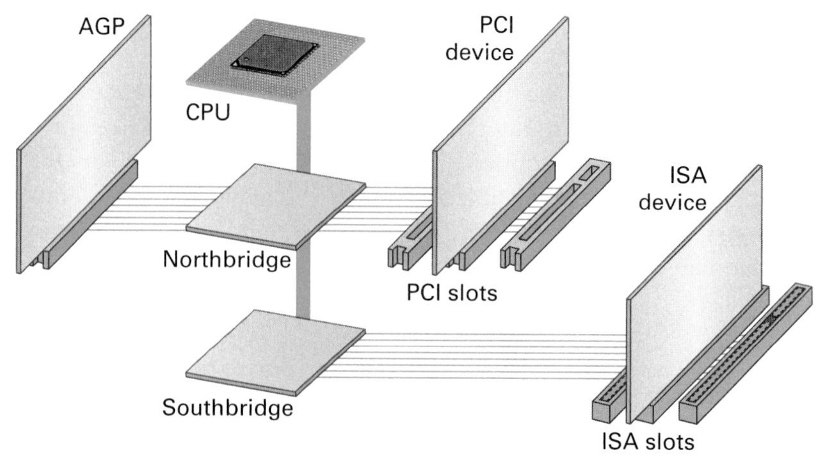

• **Figure 6.3** Expansion slots connecting to both Northbridge and Southbridge

As you'll recall from Chapter 3, the system crystal—the clock—pushes the CPU. The system crystal provides a critical function for the PC, acting like a drill sergeant calling a cadence, setting the pace of activity in the computer. Every device soldered to the motherboard is designed to run at the speed of the system crystal. A 133-MHz motherboard, for example, has at least a 133-MHz Northbridge chip and a 133-MHz Southbridge, all timed by a 133-MHz crystal (Figure 6.4).

Clock crystals aren't just for the CPU. Pretty much every chip in your computer has a CLK wire and needs to be pushed by a clock chip. Suppose you buy a device that did not come with your computer—say, a sound card. The chips on the sound card need to be pushed by a crystal. If you used the system crystal to push that sound card, you would need to have sound cards for every possible computer speed. You would have to buy a 100-MHz sound card for a 100-MHz system or a 133-MHz sound card for a 133-MHz system. That also means that if you make sound cards for a living, you would have to make them for every possible speed.

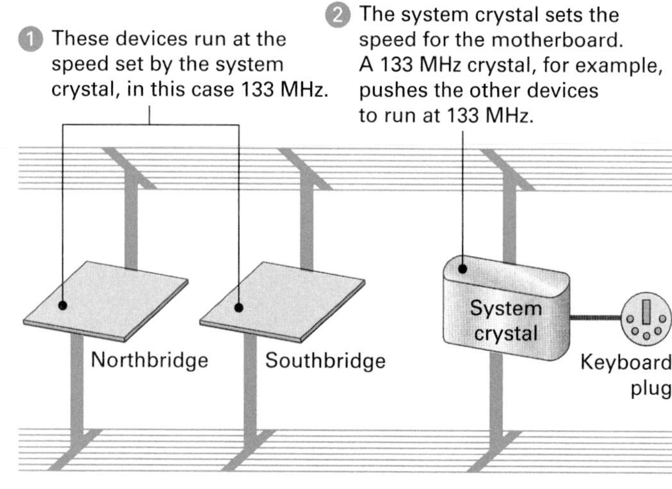

• **Figure 6.4** The system crystal sets the speed.

This is ridiculous, and IBM knew it when they designed the PC. They had to make an extension to the external data bus that *ran at its own standardized speed*. You would use this part of the external data bus to snap new devices into the PC. IBM achieved this goal by adding a different crystal, called the **expansion bus crystal**, which controlled the part of the external data bus connected to the expansion slots (Figure 6.5).

On early AMD Athlon PCs, only the frontside bus ran at the motherboard speed. The expansion slots ran at a much slower speed. The chipset acted as the divider between the two buses, compensating for the speed difference with wait states and special

1 The system crystal pushes the CPU, RAM, and chipset. It's fast!

2 The expansion crystal pushes the expansion cards at a slower, standardized speed.

System crystal

Expansion crystal

CPU

Sound card

Modem card

about 14.31818 MHz ÷ 2, or about 7.16 MHz. Figure 6.6 shows a typical expansion bus crystal.

• **Figure 6.6** Typical expansion bus crystal

PC Bus

On first-generation IBM PCs, the 8088 processor had an 8-bit external data bus and ran at a top speed of 4.77 MHz. IBM made the expansion slots on the first PCs with an 8-bit external bus connection. IBM wanted the bus to run as fast as the CPU, and even way back then 4.77 MHz was an easy speed to achieve. IBM settled on a standard expansion bus speed of about 7 MHz—faster than the CPU! This expansion bus was called the *PC bus* or *XT bus*, and the slots looked like Figure 6.7.

IBM certainly didn't invent the idea of the expansion bus—plenty of earlier computers, including many mainframes, had expansion slots—but IBM did something no one had ever done. They enabled competitors to copy the PC bus without having to pay a licensing or royalty fee. They also enabled third parties to make cards that would snap into their PC bus. Remember that IBM invented the PC bus. It was (and still is) a patented product of IBM Corporation. By enabling everyone to copy the PC expansion bus technology, however, IBM established the industry standard and created the clone market. If IBM had not allowed others to copy their patented technologies for free, companies such as Compaq, Dell, and Gateway never would have existed. Component makers like Logitech,

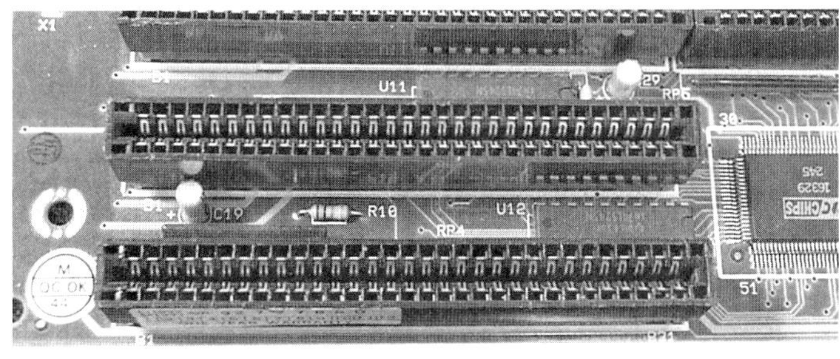

• **Figure 6.7** 8-bit PC/XT slots

Many people consider the failure of Apple to allow third parties to copy its expansion bus at no cost one of the main reasons PCs are more popular than Apple computers.

Linksys, and 3Com would never be the companies they are today without the help of IBM. Who knows, if IBM had not opened the PC bus to the world, this book and the A+ Certification exams might have been based on Apple computers!

Test Specific

16-Bit ISA

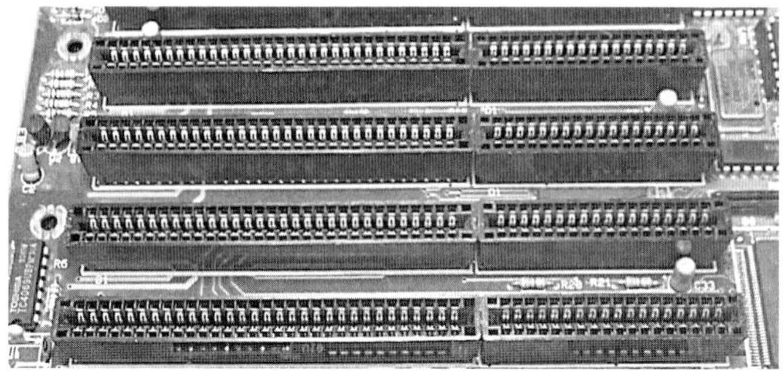

• **Figure 6.8** 16-bit ISA or AT slots

When Intel invented the 286 processor, IBM wanted to create a new expansion bus that would take advantage of the 286's 16-bit external data bus, yet still be backwardly compatible with older 8-bit cards. IBM achieved this by simply adding a set of connections to the end of the PC bus, creating a new 16-bit bus (Figure 6.8). Many techs called this bus the *AT bus* after the first system to use these slots, the 286-based IBM Advanced Technology (AT) computer. The AT bus ran at the same ~7-MHz speed as the earlier PC bus.

Even though IBM allowed third parties to copy their PC and AT expansion bus architecture, they never released the complete specifications for these two types of expansion buses. A number of clone makers got together in the early 1980s and pooled their combined knowledge of the PC/XT and AT buses to create a book of standards called the **Industry Standard Architecture (ISA)** Bus Standards. Today we call these buses *8-bit ISA* and *16-bit ISA*. Because the term ISA did not become official until 1990, many people still refer to these buses as the PC/XT and AT buses.

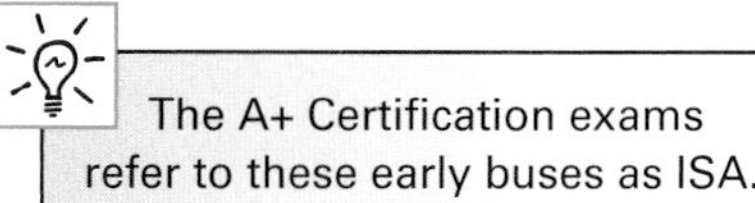

The A+ Certification exams refer to these early buses as ISA.

The ISA bus—both 8- and 16-bit—enabled manufacturers to jump the first of the three hurdles for successful expansion cards, namely connectivity. With ISA if Creative Labs wanted to build a new kind of sound card for the PC, they simply followed the specifications in the standard and built a card that would definitely fit in an expansion slot on a 386, 486, or Pentium computer. Next, they needed to make sure the card could communicate with the CPU. For that, they used what are known as system resources.

■ System Resources

Every expansion card, past and present, needs to accept commands from the CPU, and most also need some way to get the CPU's attention. To leap this second hurdle—communication—expansion cards use one or more types of **system resources**: I/O addresses, IRQs, DMA channels, and memory addresses. Although nowadays you can slap a card into an expansion slot, power on the PC, and expect it to work, the process of establishing communication between device and processor mirrors very closely the process on early PCs. It just happens more or less automatically now, not requiring you to configure the card manually for the specific PC. When the process goes wrong, though, you absolutely must know what's happening behind the scenes so you can fix it! Let's take a look.

I/O Addresses

As I mentioned earlier, the fact that the address bus and data bus connect to every device in the PC creates a bit of a communication problem. Full connectivity of the buses means that every device hears every command and sees all data! How does a hard drive, for example, distinguish between data meant for it and data sent to RAM? How does the CPU use Basic Input/Output System (BIOS) routines stored in ROM to tell peripherals to do whatever it is they are supposed to do? This boils down to two related questions: If ev- [illegible]

it has a second, very different function: communicating with devices. To understand how this works, let's go back to the old Intel 8088 CPU. The 8088 used an extra wire, called the *input/output or memory* (IO/MEM) wire, to notify devices it was using the address bus to specify an address in memory, or to communicate with a particular device (Figure 6.10).

The 8088's address bus had 20 wires, but when the IO/MEM wire had voltage, only the first 16 wires mattered. The moment the CPU placed a voltage on the IO/MEM wire, the RAM took a nap and each device in the PC started watching the address bus, waiting to see if one of its patterns of 1's and 0's came up.

> You won't find an IO/MEM wire on a modern CPU as this process is now a bit more complex, but the concept hasn't changed one bit!

This process of using the address bus to talk to devices is called **I/O addressing**, and it's still the primary way your CPU talks to the many parts of the PC. All devices, both those embedded on the motherboard and those inserted into expansion slots, respond to special, unique patterns built into them. Every device gets a set of patterns—not just one pattern. Each different

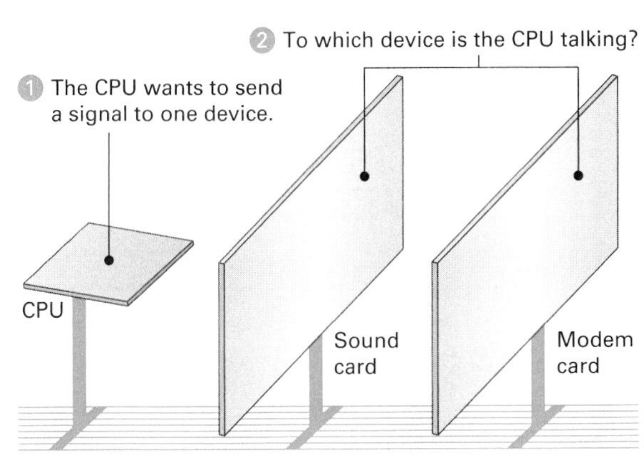

• **Figure 6.9** How can the CPU talk to only one device?

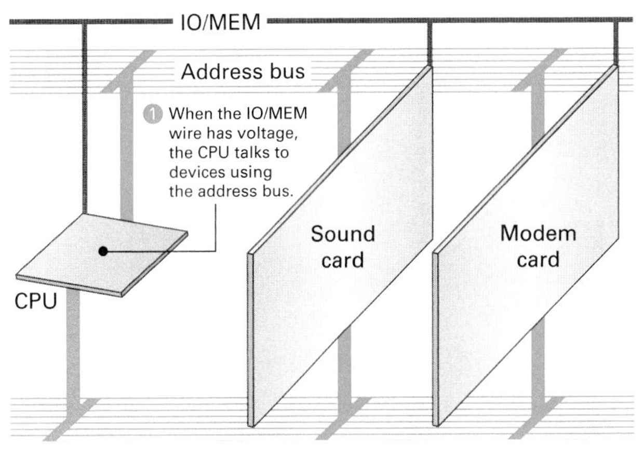

• **Figure 6.10** Function of IO/MEM wire

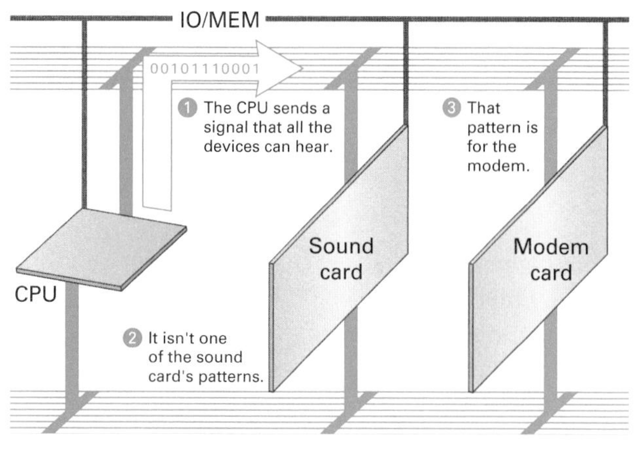

• **Figure 6.11** Sending an I/O address

pattern of 16 1's and 0's is a unique command for that device. For example, the keyboard controller has two unique patterns. The hard drive controller responds to 16 unique commands, each of which tells the hard drive to perform a specific function. For example, if the CPU lights up the IO/MEM wire and puts the pattern 0000000111110000 onto the address bus, the hard drive controller will send back a message describing its error status. These patterns used by the CPU to talk to the devices inside your computer are called *I/O addresses* (Figure 6.11).

The Device Manager in Windows 9*x* and Windows 2000/XP enables you to see all the I/O addresses in use in your PC. To open Device Manager in Windows 2000 or XP, alternate-click on My Computer and select Properties, select the Hardware tab, and click the Device Manager button (Figure 6.12). Windows 9*x* works the same way, except there's one less step, because the System Properties dialog box has a Device Manager tab. Let's say you want to see the I/O addresses for the keyboard(s) on your system. Locate the category "Keyboards" (Windows 9*x* uses "Keyboard") and click on the tiny plus sign to the left to see something similar to Figure 6.13. (For demonstration purposes, the figure shows a system with two keyboards. Most systems will have just one, probably with a different name—that's fine!) If you double-click the keyboard icon (not the

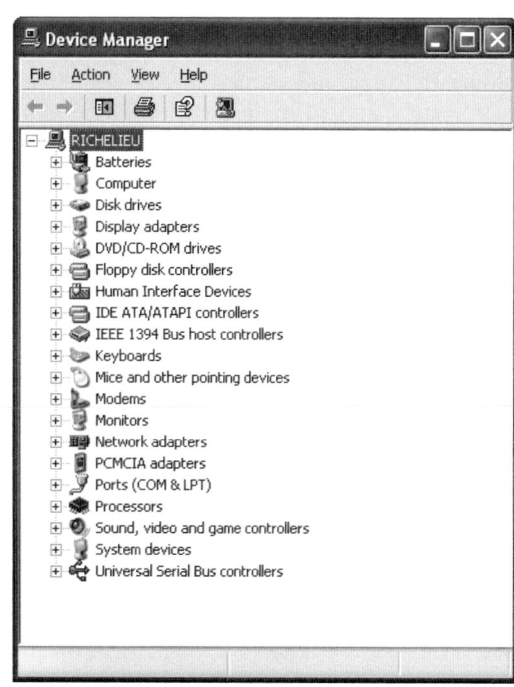

• **Figure 6.12** Device Manager in Windows XP

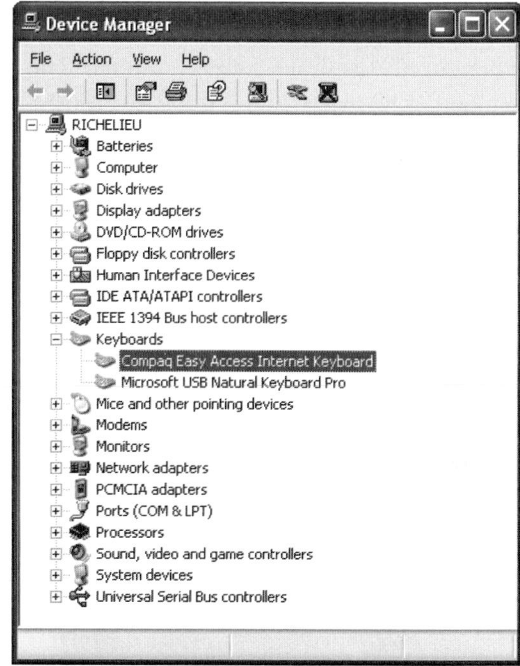

• **Figure 6.13** Keyboard in Windows XP Device Manager

Keyboards category icon you clicked on earlier!), then select the Resources tab (Figure 6.14), Device Manager will show you the system resources used by the keyboard. The keyboard's I/O addresses are listed under "I/O Range." Can you find it?

The I/O addresses used by the keyboard shown in Figure 6.14 are 0060 and 0064. How does the number 0060 relate to the 1's and 0's that make up an I/O address? This isn't some new type of I/O address—it just looks different because it's written in hexadecimal rather than binary numbers!

Hexadecimal

Sorry, but before I go any further, we have to talk about hexadecimal numbers. Some of you might be going, "Oh no!

possible to add, subtract, and even do trigonometry with hex. Fortunately, we don't have to! The only part of hex you need to know as an A+ Certified technician is how the PC world uses it.

Techs use hex to represent the patterns of 1's and 0's on the address bus. Remember that after the CPU turns on the IO/MEM wire, it sends an I/O address using the first 16 address bus wires. These wires either have voltage on them (represented by a 1) or no voltage (represented by a 0). Using 16 wires you can create 65,536 different combinations of 1's and 0's, from 0000000000000000 to 1111111111111111. Each different combination of charged and uncharged wires represents one pattern that the CPU can send down the address bus to talk to some device.

That's great, except that it is a real pain to say, "the command to tell the hard drive controller to show its error status is 0000000111110000." Imagine how difficult it would be if you had to talk about I/O addresses using long strings of 1's and 0's! For example, try telling another person to write down the following series of 1's and 0's as you dictate them:

00100100010010010010001001001001001000010011111110101010101010
000101011100

I guarantee that they will mess up somewhere as they try to write them down. Although your computer is good at talking in 1's and 0's, human beings find it very difficult. Hexadecimal provides a convenient shorthand way to describe a series of binary values.

Okay, so the "0060" address in Figure 6.14 is hex shorthand for some 16-digit binary I/O address used by that keyboard. How do you figure out what 16-digit binary address that is? It's not as hard as you might think—let me show you! Imagine that you have a computer with a four-wire address bus. How many different patterns can you create? You can create sixteen different patterns of 1's and 0's with four wires: 0000, 0001, 0010, 0011, 0100, 0101, 0110, 0111, 1000, 1001, 1010, 1011, 1100, 1101, 1110, and 1111. No computer has only a four-wire address bus, but just about every processor ever built has an address bus that's a *multiple* of four wires (16, 20, 24, 32, and even 64). In math terms, the largest common denominator of all these address bus sizes is four. The 16 unique characters of the hexadecimal (base-16) numbering system are a natural fit to substitute for the 16 4-digit combinations. The resulting hex shorthand is shown in Table 6.1.

So when you want to talk about a particular pattern being sent to a device on the address bus, you first specify the binary value—for example, 0000000111110000. Next you mentally break these 16 digits into four sets of four: 0000, 0001, 1111, and 0000. Then you translate each four-character set into the corresponding hex shorthand: 0000 (0), 0001 (1), 1111 (F), and 0000 (0). That way instead of reciting a long string of 1's and 0's, you can simply say something like "01F0."

To recap, all the possible I/O addresses can be represented by four-digit hexadecimal values, starting at 0000 and ending at FFFF. So now the I/O addresses 0060 and 0064 used by the keyboard should make more sense—they're simply two 16-bit numbers translated into hex! This explanation of hexadecimal has been heavily slanted to the concept of I/O addresses, but hex is used in many other areas of the PC. Let's get back to I/O addresses.

The Rules of I/O Addresses

Three basic rules apply to I/O addresses: all devices have I/O addresses; most devices use more than one address; and no two devices can share the same I/O address in a single system. Amazingly for the PC industry, these three rules apply universally.

All Devices Must Have an I/O Address This is how the CPU talks to everything in your computer and there is no exception. Every device in your

Table 6.1 Possible Permutations for Four Wires

Binary Number	On/Off Pattern of Wires	Hexadecimal Value
0000	All wires off	0
0001	Only 4th wire on	1
0010	Only 3rd wire on	2
0011	3rd and 4th on	3
0100	Only 2nd wire on	4
0101	2nd and 4th wire on	5
0110	2nd and 3rd wire on	6
0111	Only 1st wire off	7
1000	Only 1st wire on	8
1001	1st and 4th on	9
1010	1st and 3rd on	A
1011	Only 2nd off	B
1100	1st and 2nd on	C
1101	Only 3rd off	D
1110	Only 4th off	E
1111	All wires on	F

computer has a set of I/O addresses; some have them hard-coded into the card, whereas others give you the option of choosing one set out of several options by moving a jumper on the card. Common devices in the computer have preset I/O addresses. The hard-drive controller, for example, uses preset I/O addresses of 01F0–01FF. Sound card I/O addresses, on the other hand, differ by manufacturer and model.

Most Devices Use More Than One I/O Address As I mentioned earlier, most devices respond to more than one I/O address. The CPU uses the different I/O addresses to give various commands to each device. If the CPU sends a 01F0 pattern, for example, it asks the hard drive controller if an error occurred anywhere. The commands 01F1, 01F2, and so on tell the hard drive to do some different function. The I/O addresses for a particular device do not have to be contiguous—they can skip around, as you saw in the keyboard

The more complex the device, the more I/O addresses it uses.

sincerity to the I/O address range for a hard drive simply as "1F0h." The range of addresses is always implied by the base I/O address.

No Devices Can Share I/O Addresses in a PC! If two devices in a PC shared the same I/O address, they would both respond when the CPU sent that address, causing unpredictable problems. One or both devices would freeze up and more likely than not, bring Windows to a grinding, crashing halt. Definitely a Bad Thing! Somehow, either the system or you must make sure that no device tries to use another device's I/O addresses. This issue most often comes into play when you are installing a new device.

I/O Address Map

How does the system make sure these I/O address rules are followed? When IBM first invented the PC, they pre-defined the I/O addresses for most of the standard devices in the PC and published those I/O addresses so that everyone would use them. Table 6.2 shows a small sampling of the original IBM I/O address list.

IBM's original map was and still is completely supported by the PC industry. So for example, if some manufacturer decides to make an expansion card for a joystick, that expansion card must respond to I/O addresses 0200-0207. Manufacturers also try very hard to use unmapped portions of the I/O addresses and to avoid conflicts with devices made by others.

Take a close look at the I/O address map one more time. Notice that neither sound cards nor network cards made the list. In fact, IBM mapped out the I/O addresses for only the most common devices. So if you want to install a sound card, what I/O addresses are available? Look at I/O base address 0210, and then look at the next I/O base address—it's 0278, isn't it? All the I/O addresses between these two are open for use, so plenty of unused addresses are available! By the way, you'll notice that the last address is

Table 6.2	Sampling of Original IBM I/O addresses
I/O Address Range	**Usage**
0000 – 000F	DMA controller
0020 – 002F	Master IRQ controller
0030 – 003F	Master IRQ controller
0040 – 0043	System timer
0060 – 0060	Keyboard
0061 – 0061	System speaker
0064 – 0064	Keyboard
00C0 – 00CF	DMA controller
00E0 – 00EF	Reserved
00F0 – 00FF	Math coprocessor
0170 – 0177	Secondary hard-drive controller
01F0 – 01F7	Primary hard-drive controller
0200 – 0207	Joystick
0210 – 0217	Reserved
0278 – 027F	LPT2
02B0 – 02DF	Secondary EGA
02E8 – 02EF	COM4
02F8 – 02FF	COM2
0378 – 037F	LPT1
03B0 – 03BF	Mono video
03C0 – 03CF	Primary EGA
03D0 – 03DF	CGA video
03E8 – 03EF	COM3
03F0 – 03F7	Floppy controller
03F8 – 03FF	COM1

Don't be surprised on the A+ exams if you're asked about seemingly three-digit I/O addresses, such as 3F8. Just tack on the leading zero and you're in sync with the I/O address map.

03FF, so wouldn't all the addresses from 0400 all the way to FFFF be open for use? Yes and no. When the only expansion bus in town was the ISA bus, you could only have 1024 I/O addresses. Today's systems not only use all of the I/O addresses from 0400 up to FFFF, they actually double the number of I/O addresses wires, from 16 up to 32, allowing many more I/O addresses.

Interrupt Requests

The CPU can now communicate with all of the devices inside the computer, but a third and final hurdle remains. I/O addressing enables two-way communication, but the CPU must have some way to start all that communication. A device such as a keyboard can't send its own I/O addresses to the CPU to get the CPU's attention. So how does a device initiate a conversation with the CPU? How does the mouse tell the CPU that it has moved, for example, or how does the keyboard tell the CPU that somebody just pressed the J key? The PC needs some kind of mechanism to tell the CPU to stop doing whatever it is doing and talk to a particular device (Figure 6.15).

This mechanism is called *interruption.* Every CPU in the PC world has an INT (interrupt) wire, shown in Figure 6.16. If this wire is charged, the CPU will stop what it is doing and deal with the interrupting device. Suppose you have a PC with only one peripheral, a keyboard. The CPU is running WordPerfect, and the user presses the J key. The keyboard is connected to the CPU's INT wire and charges the wire. The CPU temporarily stops running WordPerfect and runs the necessary BIOS routine to query the keyboard.

This would be fine if the computer had only one device. As you know, however, PCs have many devices, and almost all of them need to in-

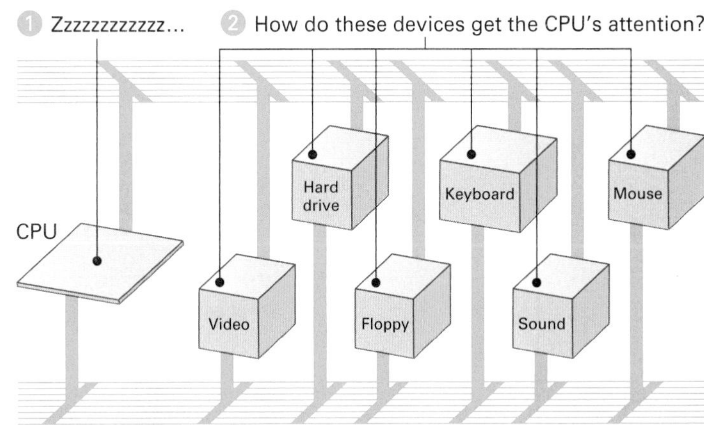

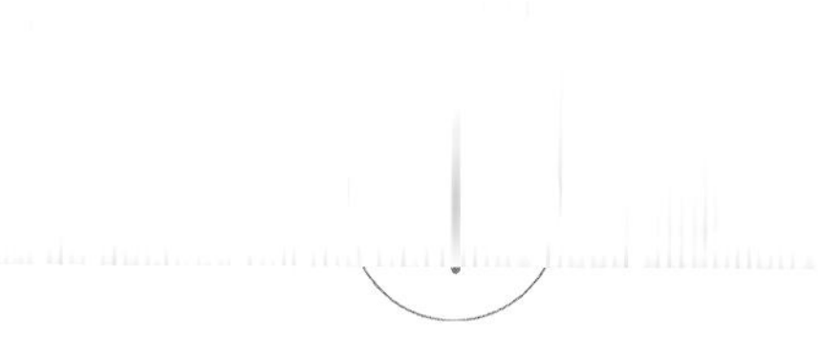

• **Figure 6.16** The INT wire

Original 8259

The 8259 hooked to the INT wire of the CPU on one side and on the other side eight **interrupt request (IRQ)** wires extended out from the chip into the motherboard (Figure 6.17). Every device that needed to interrupt the CPU got an IRQ. If a device needed to interrupt the CPU, it lit its IRQ, and the 8259 then lit the INT wire on the CPU. Whenever the INT wire lit up, the CPU talked to the 8259 using its I/O addresses to determine which device had interrupted. The 8259 told the CPU which IRQ was lit, and this enabled the CPU to know which BIOS routine to run.

Most of the IRQ wires were dedicated to certain devices. IRQ0 went to a device called the system timer that told the RAM when to refresh. IRQ1 went to the keyboard, and the other six wires ran straight to the ISA expansion bus (Figure 6.18). So, theoretically, any ISA card could use IRQs 2 through 7.

The Rules of IRQs

To set up and use IRQs in a system with an 8259 IRQ controller, you followed a clear pair of rules. First, almost every device needed an IRQ. This included

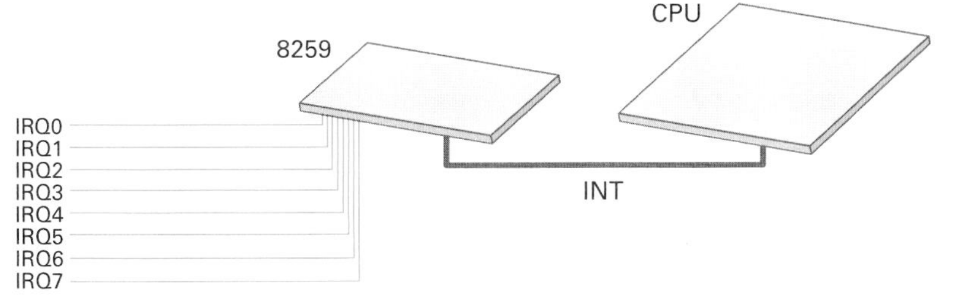

• **Figure 6.17** The eight IRQs from the 8259

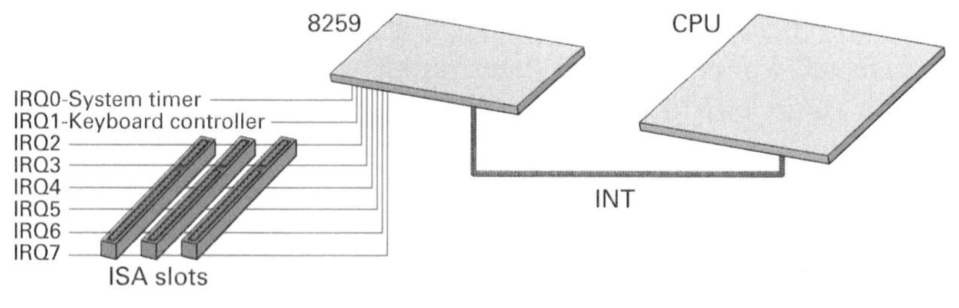

• **Figure 6.18** IRQs for the system timer, keyboard controller, and ISA slots

devices built into the motherboard as well as devices that used the expansion bus slots. Second, under most circumstances, no two devices could share an IRQ. If one device used IRQ3, for example, no other device could use that IRQ. If two devices used the same IRQ, one or both would freeze up and, more often than not, cause the PC to crash. (Sounds a lot like I/O addresses, doesn't it?)

To prevent devices from sharing IRQs, IBM gave an IRQ map to card manufacturers so they knew which IRQs to use for certain types of devices, just like IBM did for I/O addresses (Table 6.3).

The original IRQ map often creates more questions than answers for students. Where's the IRQ for the hard drive or sound cards? Unfortunately, IBM produced the original IRQ map before anyone invented either of these devices! Why is IRQ2 reserved? IBM thought that most PCs would hook up to mainframes, so they wanted to keep IRQ2 open for the 3270 PC-to-mainframe networking cards.

> Because technicians need to be able to support older devices, the A+ Certification exams expect all A+ certified techs to know the COM and LPT resource assignments. In other words, memorize the chart!

What are COM1, COM2, LPT1, LPT2, and so on? These are *preset combinations of I/O addresses and IRQs* for common devices: **COM ports** for serial devices such as mice and modems, and **LPT ports** for parallel devices such as printers. When IBM designed the PC, they wanted to simplify the installation, programming, and operation of devices. Because virtually every peripheral needs both an IRQ and I/O address, IBM created standard preset combinations of IRQs and I/O addresses. Table 6.4 lists the early preset combinations of I/O addresses and IRQs.

The lack of available IRQs in the early systems led IBM to double up the IRQs for the serial devices, creating one of the few exceptions to the rule

Table 6.3 IRQ Assignments on IBM PC and XT

IRQ	Default Function
IRQ0	System timer
IRQ1	Keyboard
IRQ2	Reserved
IRQ3	COM2, COM4
IRQ4	COM1, COM3
IRQ5	LPT2
IRQ6	Floppy drive
IRQ7	LPT1

where no two devices could share IRQs. You could share an IRQ between two devices, but only if one of the devices would never actually access the IRQ. You'd see this with a dedicated fax/modem card, for example, where you have a single phone line connected to a single card that has two different functions. The CPU needed distinct sets of I/O addresses for fax commands and modem commands, but as there was only the one modem doing both jobs, it needed only a single IRQ.

Table 6.4	COM and LPT Assignments	
Port	**I/O Base Address**	**IRQ**
COM1	03F8	4
COM2	02F8	3
COM3	03E8	4
COM4	02E8	3
LPT1	0378	7
LPT2	0278	5

8259. This created a new problem: many cards were *using* IRQ2! To enable these older cards to work, IBM ran the IRQ9 wire over to the IRQ2 position on the ISA slot. This cascading procedure added eight IRQs, but took one away in the process. The eight new wires ran to the extension on the 16-bit ISA expansion slot.

Table 6.5 lists the IRQ map as designed for the two 8259s in the original IBM AT computer. Again, notice that the cascade removed IRQ2. IRQ9 hooked to the old IRQ2 wire, so if a device was designed to run on IRQ2, it would run on IRQ9. In essence, IRQ2 and IRQ9 were the same IRQ. Three IRQs were hard-wired (0, 1, and 8). Four IRQs had assignments so common that no PC or device maker dared change them for fear that their devices would not be compatible (6, 13, 14, and 15). Four IRQs defaulted to specific types of devices, but were very changeable as long as the hardware device

shorthanded as COM ports. This can cause some confusion for techs who don't understand what's happening behind the scenes. When you assign COM1 to serial port 1 in the CMOS setup utility, you have assigned both a range of I/O addresses and an IRQ to that serial port. You know from Table 6.4 that you shouldn't turn around in the same system and assign the modem COM3, right? This would create a classic IRQ conflict and lead to system instability.

Further, many manufacturers create devices that can use nonstandard combinations of I/O addresses and IRQs, such as a modem that uses 03E8 as the base I/O (and thus is referred to as COM3), but then uses IRQ2 rather than IRQ4 to avoid a conflict with any device assigned COM1 resources. Knowing the combinations referred to by COM1, COM2, and so on—and the possible variations—helps you troubleshoot simple errors.

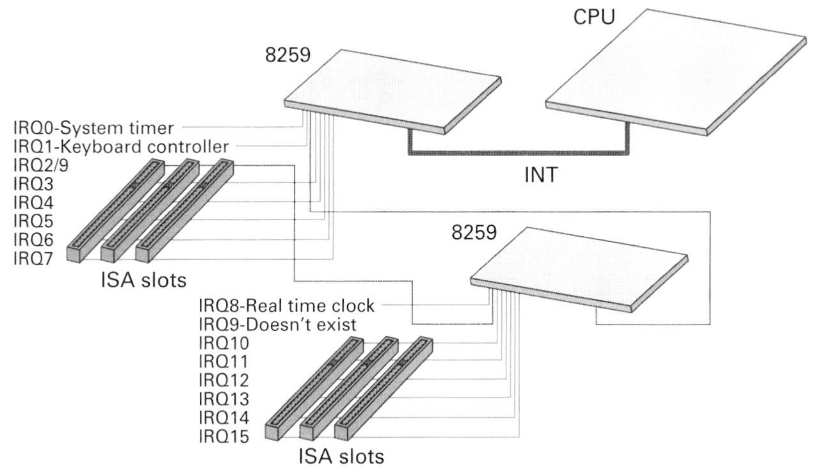

• **Figure 6.19** Dual 8259 cascade

Table 6.5	16-Bit IRQ Map
IRQ	**Default Function**
IRQ0	System timer
IRQ1	Keyboard
IRQ2/9	Open for use
IRQ3	Default COM2, COM4
IRQ4	Default COM1, COM3
IRQ5	LPT2
IRQ6	Floppy drive
IRQ7	LPT1
IRQ8	Real-time clock
IRQ10	Open for use
IRQ11	Open for use
IRQ12	Open for use
IRQ13	Math coprocessor
IRQ14	Primary hard-drive controller
IRQ15	Secondary hard-drive controller

Separate IRQ2 and IRQ9 don't exist; instead, it is called iRQ2/9.

You should know the traditional 16-bit ISA IRQ map.

enabled it (IRQ 3, 4, 5, and 7). The rest (IRQ2/9, 10, 11, and 12) IBM did not specify and thus were open for use.

Even in the early days, these settings were somewhat flexible. If a device that used a certain IRQ was not present, then another device could use that IRQ. If you didn't have a secondary hard-drive controller, for example, you could use IRQ15 for another device.

You should now understand how I/O addresses and IRQs enable devices to communicate with the CPU, both to receive commands and to request attention. Every device gets I/O addresses assigned and most use an IRQ as well. Some devices also use one or two other types of system resources—namely, DMA and memory addresses—that you need to understand if you're going to support such devices. A lot of this support happens behind the scenes, but some requires tech intervention, especially if something goes wrong. Let's look at the other two system resources and then dive into installation.

Direct Memory Access (DMA)

CPUs do a lot of work. They run the BIOS, operating system, and applications. CPUs handle interrupts and I/O addresses. CPUs also deal with one other item: data. CPUs constantly manipulate data. CPUs move data from one place in RAM to another. Peripherals such as a scanner or a laser printer send data to RAM via the CPU, and the CPU sends data from RAM to peripherals.

Moving all this data is obviously necessary, but it is a simple task—the CPU has better things to do with its power and time. Moreover, with all of the caches and such on today's CPUs, the system spends most of its time waiting while the CPU handles some internal calculation (Figure 6.20). Add these facts together

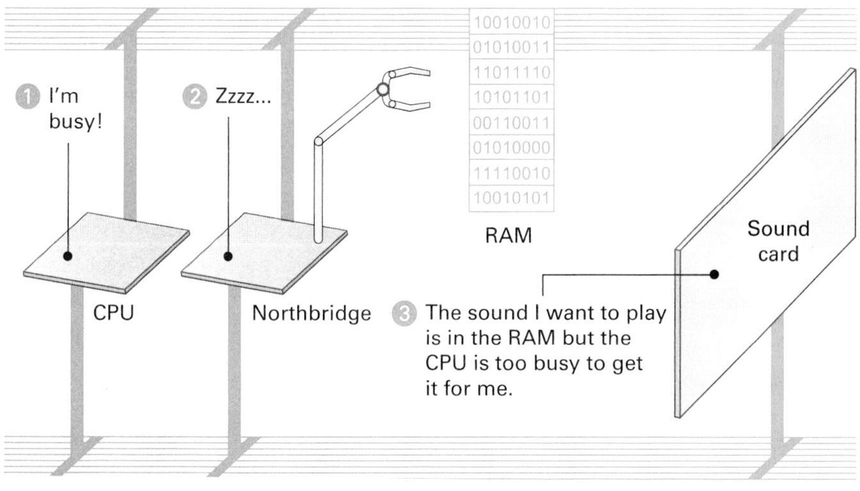

without using the CPU is called **Direct Memory Access (DMA)**.

DMA enables the system to run background applications without interfering with the CPU (Figure 6.22). This is excellent for creating background sounds in games, and for moving data from floppy and hard drives into RAM.

The concept of DMA as described here, however, has a problem. What if more than one device wants to use DMA? What keeps these devices from stomping on the external data bus all at the same time? Plus, what if the CPU suddenly needs the data bus? How can you stop the device using DMA so the CPU, which should have priority, can access the bus (Figure 6.23)? To deal with this, IBM installed another, very simple CPU called the *8237 chip* to control all DMA functions (Figure 6.24). This primitive CPU handles all

Tech Tip

Cutting-edge IRQ Handling

Modern systems assign most IRQs automatically through a mechanism called Plug and Play (discussed later in this chapter), but may use either of two interrupt controllers: the 8259 Programmable Interrupt Controller (PIC) or the Advanced Programmable Interrupt Controller (APIC). Which controller is used and how it affects device installa-

est and greatest expansion card requires an IRQ and can run into conflicts with other devices in the system. Although you can find five or more devices seemingly sharing the same IRQ and all running just fine, you can also find two devices sharing an IRQ and causing conflicts. You need to understand the old way before these new conflicts make sense. The old stuff won't die!

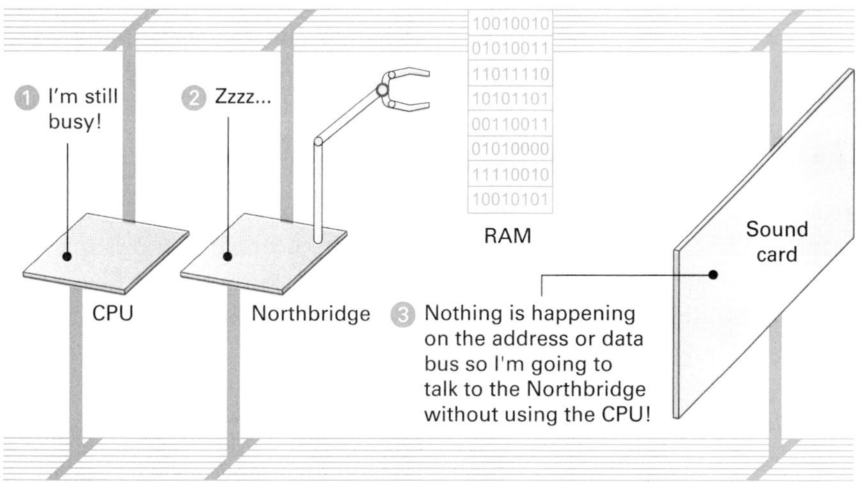

• **Figure 6.21** Why not talk to the chipset directly?

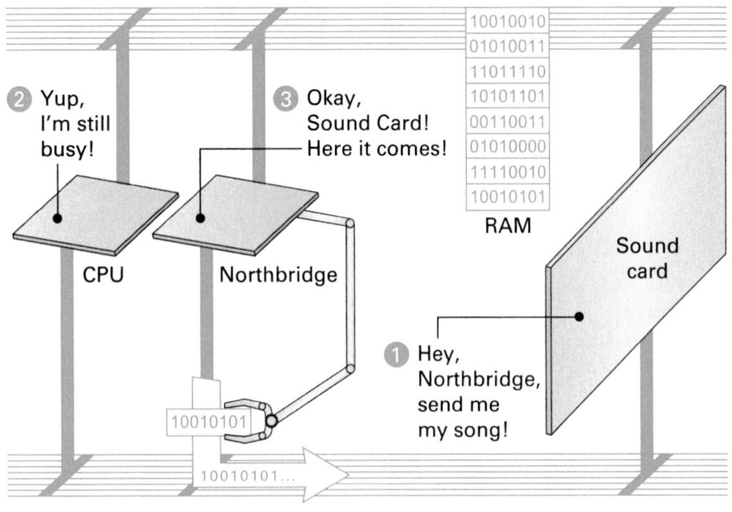

• **Figure 6.22** DMA in action

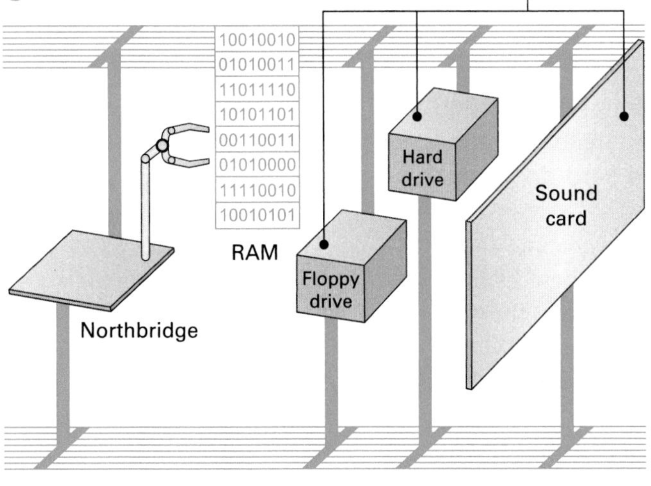

• **Figure 6.23** Dueling DMAs

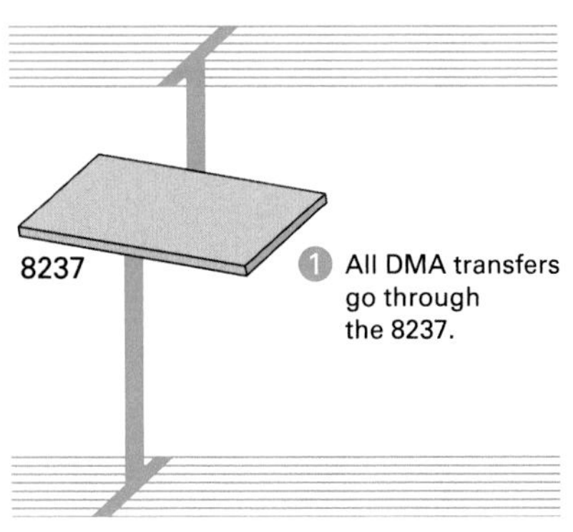

• **Figure 6.24** The 8237 controls DMA transfers.

the data passing from peripherals to RAM, and vice versa. This takes necessary but simple work away from the CPU, so the CPU can spend time doing more productive work.

The DMA chip sends data along the external data bus when the CPU is busy with internal calculations and not using the external data bus. This is perfectly acceptable because the CPU accesses the external data bus only a small percentage of the time: 20 percent of the time on a 486, and 5 percent of the time on a Pentium or later CPU.

The 8237 chip links to the CPU via the *HRQ wire*. The original 8237 used the HRQ wire to inform the CPU that the external data bus was going to be busy. The 8237 has four wires, called *DMA request (DRQ) wires*, which lead to the DRAM refresh circuitry and ISA slots. DRQs were, and still are, more commonly known as *DMA channels*. If a device wants to perform a DMA data transfer, it must activate its assigned DMA channel (Figure 6.25). DRQs work exactly like IRQs, with all the same rules, so for example, no two devices can share the same DMA channel.

From the days of the 286 to the present, all systems have two cascaded DMA controller chips, for a total of seven DRQs. DRQ0 and DRQ4 are the same, just as IRQ2 and IRQ9 are the same (Figure 6.26). However, you never say DRQ0/4, just DRQ0.

DMA Limitations

DMA, as originally designed by IBM, has some serious limitations. First, DMA is designed to run from cards installed on the ISA bus. As a result, DMA is limited to a maximum speed of roughly 8 MHz. Second, each 8237 can handle only byte-wide (8-bit) data. Although this wasn't a problem in the first IBM PC, as PCs moved from 8088s through 286s, 386s, and 486s, it was often faster to skip 8-bit DMA and just wait for the CPU to move the data.

The dual 8237s in the 286 and later systems enabled 16-bit data transfers—each 8237 controller handled one byte. But even these 16-bit data transfers ran at 8 MHz, which made them too slow for modern systems. This slowness relegated classic DMA to low-speed, background jobs like floppy drive access, sound creation, and tape backup. A process called *bus mastering*, however, created a resurgence in the use of DMA in modern systems.

Bus Mastering

Most devices today that use DMA do so without accessing the 8237s or the CPU. These devices are known as bus masters. *Bus mastering* devices skip the 8237 altogether; they have circuitry that enables them to watch for other devices accessing the external data bus and can get out of the way on their own. Bus mastering has become extremely popular in hard drives. All modern EIDE hard drives take advantage of bus mastering. Hard drive bus mastering is hidden under terms such as *Ultra DMA*, and for the most part is totally automatic and invisible. See Chapter 10 for more details on bus mastering hard drives.

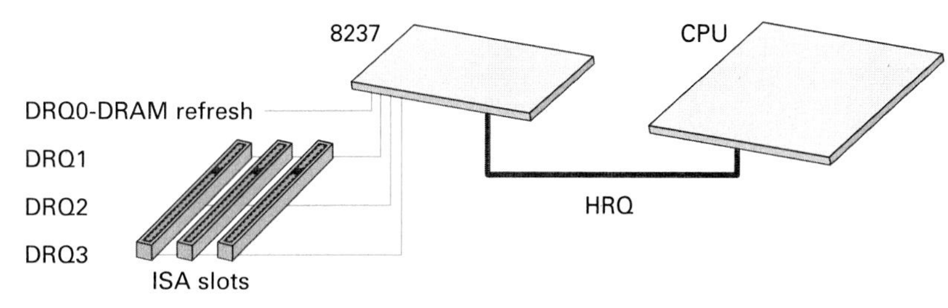

Figure 6.25 8237 in the original IBM PC

Who Uses Classic DMA?

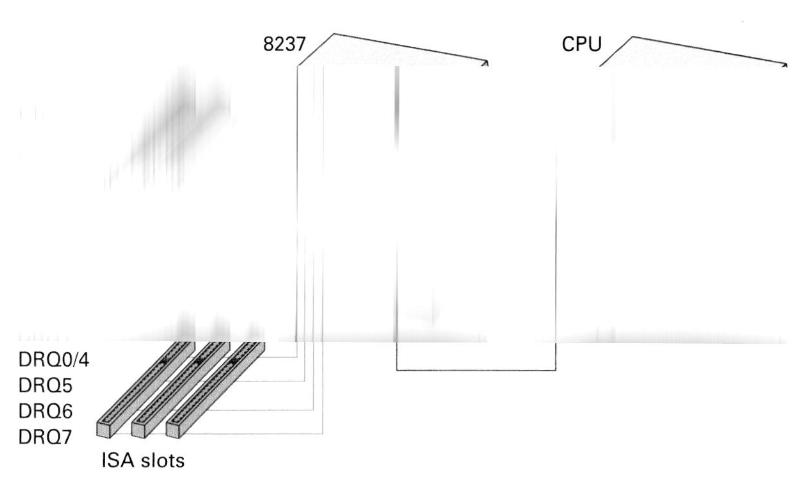

Figure 6.26 Cascaded 8237s

Memory Addresses

Some expansion cards used to come with a small bit of ROM on board, the so-called adapter or option ROM you read about in Chapter 5. This option ROM chip required addresses from the main system memory map, just like any other piece of ROM or RAM in the system. Unfortunately, there were severe limitations on the addresses these expansion cards could use. This could cause problems when you installed them in some systems. You aren't likely to run into this type of expansion card any more unless you service older machines—Pentium II and earlier—but you should be able to recognize one just in case.

You'll recall from Chapter 5 that one way for a device to BYOB was to put the BIOS on the hardware device itself, in a ROM chip. Figure 6.27

Table 6.6 DMA Assignments

DMA	Type	Function
DRQ0/4	8-bit	None
DRQ1	8-bit	Open for use
DRQ2	8-bit	Floppy drive controller
DRQ3	8-bit	Open for use
DRQ5	16-bit	Open for use
DRQ6	16-bit	Open for use
DRQ7	16-bit	Open for use

• **Figure 6.27** ROM chip on Adaptec 2940 SCSI host adapter

shows a typical ROM chip on an expansion card. The system BIOS does not have a clue about how to talk to this card, so the card has to bring its own BIOS. Most BIOS that come on option ROMs advertise that they exist by displaying information when you boot the system, but from an installation standpoint, you need to see the addresses in use.

All ISA option ROM took addresses between C8000 to EFFFF, near the top of the first 1 MB of memory addresses. Techs aware of the old technology will recognize this area as the upper memory block in the reserved area of memory, but the names don't matter much anymore. A quick scan of Device Manager displays memory addresses in use, as you can see in Figure 6.28.

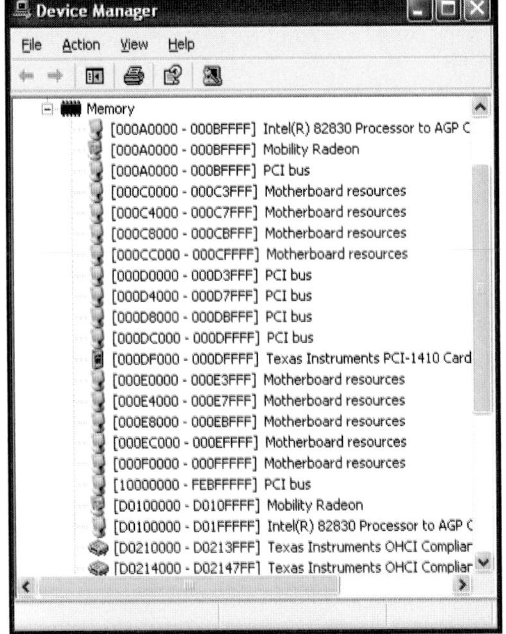

• **Figure 6.28** Windows XP Device Manager, displaying resources by type

The key fact for techs is that, just like I/O addresses, no two devices may share memory addresses, nor may their address ranges overlap. If either of these happens, one or both devices will freeze up and the system will more than likely come crashing to a halt.

Modern Expansion Bus

The first-generation expansion buses—8-bit and 16-bit ISA—were both excellent buses for their time. In fact, the 16-bit ISA bus continues to soldier on in all but the newest PCs running today. Yet the ISA bus suffered from a couple of tremendous limitations. It was slow, running at up to only 8.33 MHz. It was also narrow and unable to handle the 32-bit and 64-bit external data buses of more modern processors. Finally, because techs had to assign system resources to ISA cards manually, installation was often a nightmare.

Manufacturers clearly needed to come up with a better bus that addressed the many problems associated with ISA. They needed a bus that could take advantage of the 33-MHz motherboard speed and 32-bit-wide data bus found in 386 and 486 systems. They also

Cross Check

System Resources

As you might have noticed by this point, sharing or overlapping system resources between two devices can make the PC a very temperamental beast.

1. Of the four system resources (I/O addresses, IRQs, DMA channels, and memory addresses), which ones can two devices potentially share? Which resources can they absolutely never share?
2. If all conflicts more than likely will cause the system to crash, how can you tell one type of conflict from another?

Athlon) turned out to be false starts. MCA, EISA, and VL-Bus each addressed two of the three goals, but fizzled out in the end. Eventually, the PCI bus made the scene and met all three criteria—but first, here are the stories of the three that didn't make it.

> The A+ Certification exams do not cover MCA, EISA, and VL-Bus expansion buses. I've included them here for completeness.

MCA

When the 386 CPU appeared in 1986, IBM decided to create a new type of expansion bus called **Microchannel Architecture (MCA)**. Microchannel had a 32-bit bus to match the 386 (and later the 486) CPU's 32-bit external data bus. It was also faster than the ISA bus, running at about 12 MHz, and it was self-configuring—a tech's dream expansion bus! MCA was an excellent bus but it had two drawbacks. First, MCA slots were different than ISA slots, making MCA motherboards incompatible with ISA cards (Figure 6.29).

Figure 6.29 Microchannel slots

Second, MCA was a licensed product of IBM, meaning that IBM did not release it to the public domain, which made MCA expensive. After a short surge in the late 1980s and early 1990s, MCA was abandoned.

EISA

When MCA came out in the mid-1980s, it created quite a stir both for its technology and IBM's heavy-handedness. IBM tried not only to regain control of bus standards, but also to charge licensing fees for that standard. As you might imagine, the rest of the industry did not like that! An industry group of clone makers created a competitor to MCA called **Extended ISA** (**EISA** —pronounced "EE-suh") in 1988. EISA did almost everything that MCA did: it was a 32-bit, self-configuring expansion bus. EISA also used a unique double-slot connector that was compatible with ISA devices (Figure 6.30). Because it supported ISA devices, however, EISA was limited to the grindingly slow ~8-MHz ISA bus speed. Like MCA, EISA only solved part, but not all, of the new expansion bus needs. EISA managed to survive until the mid-1990s.

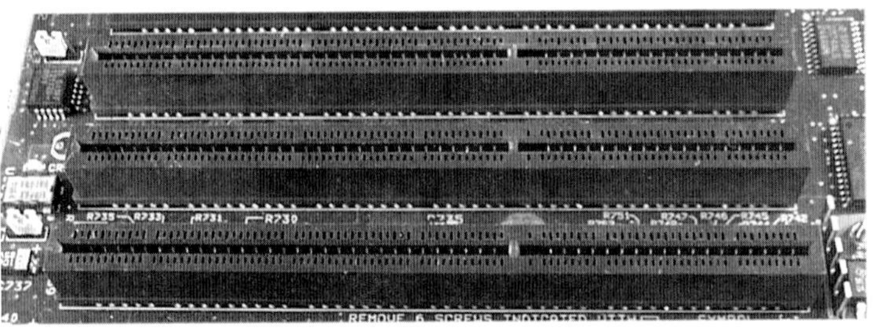

Figure 6.30 EISA slots

VL-Bus

Although MCA and EISA offered attractive 32-bit solutions, most system manufacturers (and purchasers) continued to use ISA motherboards and expansion cards. Microsoft Windows changed that—at least for video cards. The graphical user interface (GUI) of Windows put huge new demands on video. ISA video cards could not keep up with these new demands. To increase throughput, the Video Electronics Standards Association (VESA) created the **VESA local bus (VL-Bus)** . The VL-Bus solved both the speed and throughput problems by tapping into the *local* bus—what you know as the *frontside* bus today (Figure 6.31).

VL-Bus offered a 32-bit slot that could run at 33 MHz, making it the fastest of the potential ISA replacements. Plus, because it used the ISA slots on the motherboard as part of its connections, VL-Bus offered complete backward compatibility. Unfortunately, and also because it used the ISA slot, VL-Bus devices had to be manually configured. Ugh!

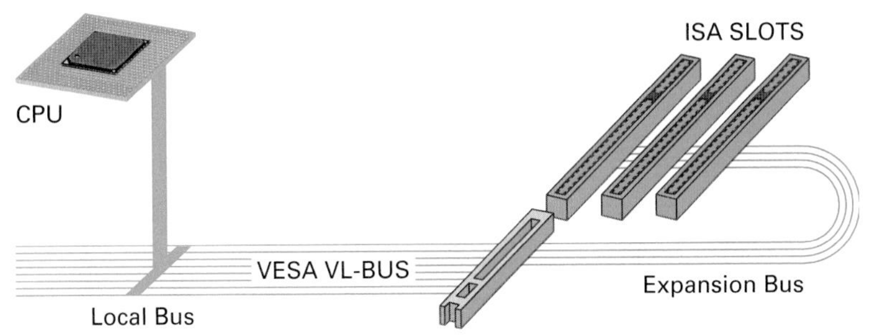

Figure 6.31 VL-Bus slots

PCI

Intel introduced the **Peripheral Component Interconnect (PCI)** bus architecture (Figure 6.32) around the same time as it debuted the Pentium processor. Intel released PCI to the public domain, which certainly made PCI very attractive to manufacturers. The exceptional technology of the new bus, combined with the lack of a price tag, made manufacturers quickly adopt PCI and turn it into the standard for every motherboard today. PCI provides a stronger, faster, more flexible alternative than any previous expansion bus.

Although the bus width and speed (32 bits, 33

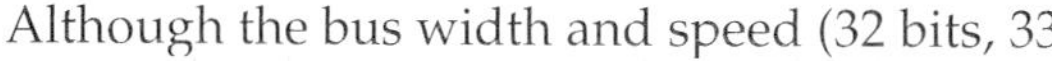

devices!

Flexible Design

Intel built tremendous flexibility into the PCI specifications. Unlike many previous expansion bus types, PCI functions independently of any type of CPU. Even Apple's Macintosh computers use PCI. We call PCI a "mezzanine" bus because it actually sits between the frontside (local) bus and any other expansion bus on the motherboard. In other words, PCI exists by itself on the motherboard, or it works with any other expansion bus. The only common combination is PCI with ISA (Figure 6.33).

• **Figure 6.33** PCI and ISA expansion bus slots

Try This!

Combo Boards

It often surprises folks how long dying technology lingers on computers. A trip to the computer store even as late as the summer of 2003 as I'm writing this reveals newly manufactured PCI/ISA combo motherboards. Certainly, you'll find such boards in millions of functioning PCs across the globe. To find out why, try this!

Visit a computer store and search for PCI/ISA combo boards. Check out sites like eBay to see if such boards are available. Then see if you can answer this question:

What purpose do they serve today?

The specifications also enable variations within PCI itself. Motherboard and expansion card manufacturers, for example, can produce 32-bit, 33-MHz components (the vast majority of PCs), or throw caution to the wind and produce 64-bit, 66-MHz components. They can even mix and match, creating 64-bit, 33-MHz components, and then put all three slots on the same motherboard!

Figure 6.34 shows a diagram of a classic PCI configuration supporting both a PCI and an ISA bus. The Northbridge performs all of the classic chipset functions and controls the PCI bus. The Southbridge acts as the intermediary between the PCI bus and ISA.

Self-Configuring

Not all PCI cards play well together! Most do, but occasional resource conflicts are inevitable given the incredible variety and number of PCI expansion cards available. You'll learn more about this in the "Installing Expansion Cards" section that follows.

Although PCI devices still need interrupts and I/O addresses, the PCI bus assigns these resources automatically. The *PCI Special Interest Group* (PCI SIG—the organization that defines the PCI standards) assumed that you would have a sound card, a network card, SCSI controller, and so on. In fact, they assumed that you might have multiple sound cards, network cards, SCSI controllers, and so on. The PCI SIG defined the I/O addresses and interrupts for multiple occurrences of virtually every device commonly in use today, as well as some not-yet-common devices. The intelligent PCI mezzanine bus interrogates PCI cards as they are installed and assigns them to preset I/O addresses and IRQs.

PCI supports I/O addresses past 3F8h—all the way up to FFFFh. PCI does not use IRQs in the classic sense; instead, it uses shareable "Interrupt Channels" labeled "INTA," "INTB," "INTC," and "INTD." The makers of the PCI devices configure these interrupt channels at manufacture, and only in the rarest of occasions will you ever need to change them.

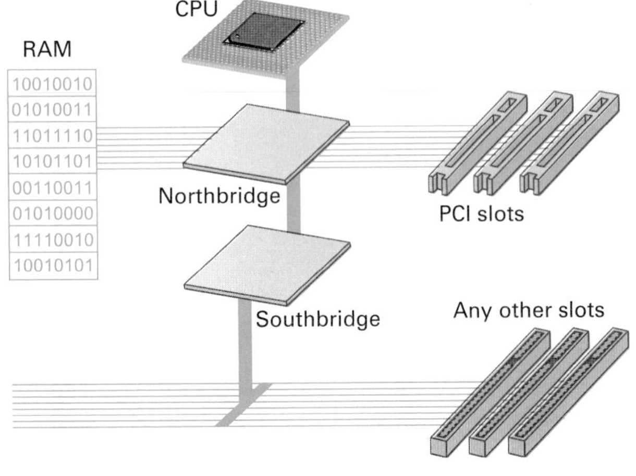

• **Figure 6.34** PCI bus configuration

AGP

Have you seen some of the amazing computer games available today? These new graphically intense games cause the same problem for PCI cards that Windows caused for the old ISA cards: PCI cards can't handle the greater requirements. To support programs that use high-end graphics, Intel invented a super PCI slot called the **Accelerated Graphics Port (AGP)**. An AGP slot is a PCI slot, but one with its own personal connection to the Northbridge. AGP slots are only for graphics—don't try to snap a sound card or modem into one. You'll learn much more about this fascinating technology in Chapter 18. Figure 6.35 shows a typical AGP slot.

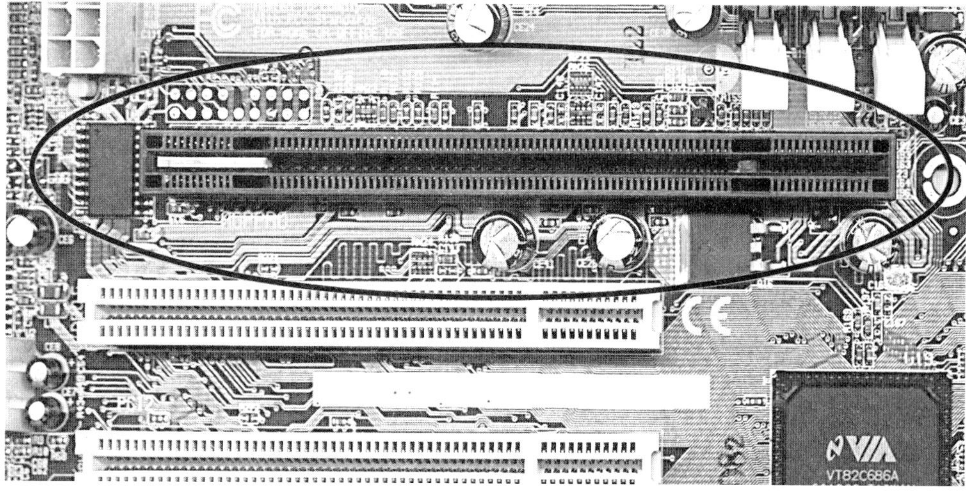

Installing an expansion card successfully—a tech's bread and butter—requires at least five steps. First, you need to know that the card works with your operating system. Second, you have to insert the card in an expansion slot properly and without damaging that card or the motherboard. Third, you have to configure the system resources required by that card, a process that's largely automated today with the magic of Plug and Play. Fourth, you need to provide drivers for the operating system—that's *proper* drivers for the *specific* OS. Fifth, you should always verify that the card functions properly before you walk away from the PC.

Step 1: Knowledge

Learn about the device you plan to install—preferably before you purchase it! Does the device work with your operating system? Does it have drivers for your operating system? If you use Windows 98 or Windows 2000, the answer to these questions is almost always "yes." If you use an old operating system like Windows 95 or an uncommon operating system such as Linux, these questions become critical. Windows XP falls somewhere in between. A lot of older, pre-XP hardware simply won't work with Windows XP at all. Check the device's documentation and check the device manufacturer's web site to verify that you have the correct drivers. While you're checking, make sure that you have the latest version of the driver. Most devices get driver updates more often than the weather changes in Texas.

Tech Tip

Installation Order

Some manufacturers insist on a different order for device installation than the traditional one listed here. The most common variation requires you to install the drivers and support software for an expansion card before you insert the card. Failure to follow the manufacturer's directions with such a card can lead to hours of frustration while you uninstall the card and reinstall the drivers, sometimes manually removing some drivers and software from the system. Bottom line? Read the instructions that come with a particular card! I'll provide more specific examples of problem devices in later chapters.

Step 2: Physical Installation

To install an expansion card successfully, you need to take steps to avoid damaging the card, the motherboard, or both. This means knowing how to handle a card and avoid electrostatic discharge (ESD) (or any other electrical

Try This!

Hardware Compatibility List

Microsoft has a master list of devices that their labs have certified to work with Windows 2000 or Windows XP. The *Hardware Compatibility List* (HCL) distinguishes somewhat between the two operating systems. Windows 2000 can handle some older devices, whereas quite a few devices have hit the market that work only with Windows XP. Microsoft has an excellent wireless keyboard and mouse combination, for example, that uses the Bluetooth networking technology—more on this in Chapter 23—but it requires Windows XP.

Microsoft includes a relatively current version of the HCL along with the Windows 2000 and Windows XP installation discs, but puts the most current version on their web site. If you build or support Windows 2000 and Windows XP machines, you should be quite familiar with the HCL. You can wait for the thorough discussion of the HCL in Chapter 14, or you can try this now, just for fun.

1. Surf over to Microsoft's web site—www.microsoft.com—and do a search for the latest HCL.
2. Open the Device Manager on your home or work computer.
3. Now compare the list of specific devices in your PC against the HCL. Are all components listed as certified to work with Windows XP? What's missing? Anything critical? If you're not running Windows XP, do you think you can successfully upgrade to XP with the current hardware? (You might have to wait for Chapter 14 for a definitive answer to that last question!)

issue). You also need to place the card firmly and completely into an available expansion slot.

Optimally, a card should always be in one of two places: in a computer or in an anti-static bag. When inserting or removing a card, be careful to hold the card only by its edges. Do not hold the card by the slot connectors or touch any components on the board (Figure 6.36).

Use an anti-static wrist strap if possible, properly attached to the PC, as noted in Chapter 2. If you don't have a wrist strap, you can use the tech way of avoiding ESD by touching the power supply after you remove the expansion card from its anti-static bag. This puts you, the card, and the PC at the same electrical potential and thus minimizes the risk of ESD.

Modern systems have a trickle of voltage on the motherboard at all times when the computer is plugged into a power outlet. Chapter 8 covers power for the PC and how to deal with it in detail, but here's the short version. *Always unplug the PC before inserting an expansion card*! Failure to do so can destroy the card, the motherboard, or both. It's not worth the risk!

Never insert or remove a card at an extreme angle. This may damage the card. A slight angle is acceptable and even necessary when removing a card. Always screw the card to the box with a connection screw. This keeps the card from slipping out and potentially shorting against other cards. Also, many cards use the screw connection to ground the card to the box (Figure 6.37).

Many technicians have been told to clean the slot connectors if a particular card is not working. This is almost never necessary after a card is installed, and if done improperly, can cause damage. You should only clean slot connectors if you have a card that's been on the shelf for a while and the contacts are obviously dull. *Never use a pencil eraser for this purpose.* Pencil erasers can leave behind bits of residue that wedge between the card and slot, preventing contact and causing the card to fail. Grab a can of contact cleaning solution and use it instead. Contact cleaning solution is designed

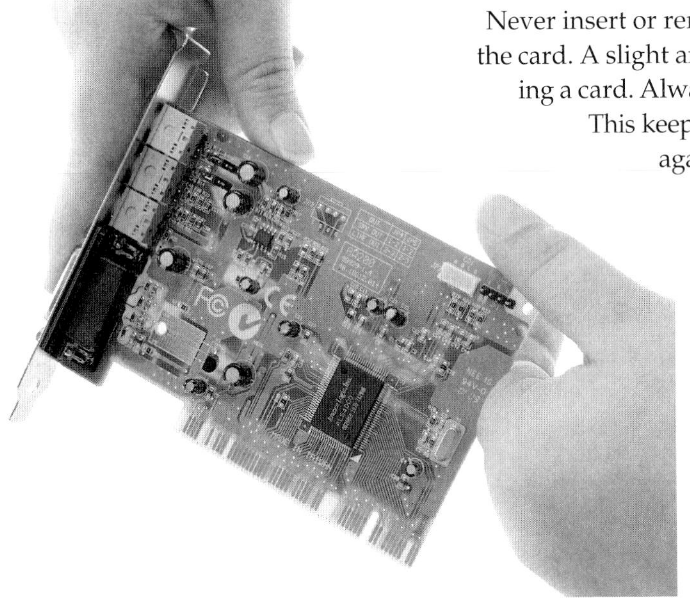

• **Figure 6.36** Where to handle a card

exactly for this purpose, will clean the contact nicely, and won't leave any residue. You can find contact cleaning solution at any electronics store.

A fully inserted expansion card will sit flush against the back of the PC case—assuming the motherboard is mounted properly, of course—with no gap between the mounting bracket on the card and the screw hole on the case. If the card is properly seated, no contacts will be exposed above the slot. Figure 6.38 shows a properly seated—meaning fitted snugly in the slot—expansion card.

• **Figure 6.38** Properly seated expansion card. Note the tight fit between case and mounting bracket and the evenness of the card in the slot.

Step 3: Assigning Resources to the Card

Every expansion card must have system resources assigned to it so that the CPU can communicate with that device, and so that the device can interrupt the CPU. Every PCI motherboard and PCI device can use a feature of mod-

[illegible]

couple of extra steps. Let's look at Plug and Play in detail.

Plug and Play

Plug and Play (PnP) consists of a series of standards designed to enable devices to self-configure. PnP is a broad standard, crossing over every type of expansion bus. PnP, in theory, makes device installation a snap. You simply install a device and it automatically configures its own I/O addresses, IRQ, and DMA with no user intervention. Unfortunately, given the amazing variety of devices currently used in PCs all over the world, PnP has yet to reach this worthy goal—but it's getting very close!

Identifying PnP For PnP to work properly, the PC needs three items. First, you need a PnP BIOS. If you have a Pentium or later processor, you have a PnP BIOS. Sometimes you can verify this by watching the boot process, but to be sure, you must go into the CMOS utility. Figure 6.39 shows a typical PnP BIOS. Figure 6.40 shows the PnP/PCI Configurations screen.

Second, PnP also requires a PnP operating system such as Windows 9*x* or Windows 2000/XP. Older operating systems, such as DOS and Windows 3.*x*, could only use PnP devices with the help of special device drivers and utility programs. Thankfully, the A+ Certification exams aren't interested in these old operating systems.

Finally, you need a PnP device. How do you identify a PnP device? It's easy! No one makes non-PnP devices anymore! Every modem, every network card, every sound card, every *everything* fully supports PnP. Non-PnP devices belong in a museum. Unfortunately, although no one makes non-PnP devices any longer, the large installed base of non-PnP devices— called **legacy devices**—motivates CompTIA to test your skills installing them.

```
CMOS Setup Utility - Copyright (C) 1984-1999 Award Software

▸ !! CPU SOFT MENU II !!           ▸ PC Health Status
▸ Standard CMOS Features             Load Fail-Safe Defaults
▸ Advanced BIOS Features             Load Optimized Defaults
▸ Advanced Chipset Features          Set Password
▸ Integrated Peripherals             Save & Exit Setup
▸ Power Management Setup             Exit Without Saving
▸ PnP/PCI Configurations

Esc : Quit                         ↑ ↓ → ←     : Select Item
F10 : Save & Exit Setup

              Change CPU's Clock & Voltage
```

• **Figure 6.39** PnP BIOS

How do you tell a PnP device from a legacy device? First of all, every PCI and AGP device is PnP. Later ISA devices clearly advertised their PnP capabilities on the box as well as in their documentation.

The word "legacy" can apply to any non-PnP aspect of a system. For example, if you have a non-PnP motherboard, it is called a "legacy motherboard." If you have a non-PnP sound card, it is called a "legacy card." If you use a non-PnP operating system, we say you use a "legacy operating system." Get the idea?

So basically, the only legacy devices are old ISA cards. If you encounter an ISA card, it's most likely old, and it's likely you don't have the box or documentation. You have a couple of installation options here. You can drop the card into a system and see if the BIOS (Figure 6.41) recognizes the device as PnP. If the BIOS fails to recognize the device, it could still be PnP. Take a close look for jumpers on the card that set the I/O addresses and IRQs (Figure 6.42).

```
CMOS Setup Utility - Copyright (C) 1984-1999 Award Software
                 PnP/PCI Configurations

   PNP OS Installed            No              Item Help
   Reset Configuration Data    Disabled
                                               Menu Level  ▸
   Resources Controlled By     Auto(ESCD)
x  IRQ Resources               Press Enter     Select Yes if you are
x  DMA Resources               Press Enter     using Plug and Play
                                               capable operating
   PCI/VGA Palette Snoop       Disabled        system Select No if
   Assign IRQ For VGA          Enabled         you need the BIOS to
   Assign IRQ For USB          Enabled         configure non-boot
   INT Pin 1 Assignment        Auto            devices
   INT Pin 2 Assignment        Auto
   INT Pin 3 Assignment        Auto
   INT Pin 4 Assignment        Auto

↑↓ →← :Move Enter:Select +/-PU/PD:Value F10:Save ESC:Exit F1:General Help
   F5:Previous Values  F6:Fail-Safe Defaults  F7:Optimized Defaults
```

• **Figure 6.40** Award BIOS PnP screen

```
CMOS Setup Utility - Copyright (C) 1984-1999 Award Software
                     IRQ Resources

IRQ-3  assigned to     PCI/ISA PnP      Item Help
IRQ-4  assigned to     PCI/ISA PnP
IRQ-5  assigned to     Legacy ISA       Menu Level ►
IRQ-7  assigned to     PCI/ISA PnP
IRQ-9  assigned to     PCI/ISA PnP      Legacy ISA for devices
IRQ-10 assigned to     PCI/ISA PnP      compliant with the
IRQ-11 assigned to     PCI/ISA PnP      original PC AT bus
IRQ-12 assigned to     PCI/ISA PnP      specification, PCI/ISA
IRQ-13 assigned to     PCI/ISA PnP      PnP for devices
IRQ-14 assigned to     PCI/ISA PnP      compliant with the
                                        Plug and Play standard
                                        whether designed for
                                        PCI or ISA bus
                                        architecture
```

How PnP Works The following scenario illustrates how PnP works. Suppose you have a machine with a PnP BIOS, a PnP operating system (Windows 2000 for this example), and a mix of PnP and legacy devices. When you install a new PnP card, such as a fax/modem, PnP goes through a fairly standard process, the majority of which takes place during the boot process. The PnP BIOS takes over immediately after the POST, first telling all PnP devices to be quiet, so the BIOS can find any legacy ISA devices (Figure 6.44).

The PnP standard lumps I/O addresses, IRQs, and DMA together under the term "system resources." For example, the system resources for the floppy drive are I/O addresses 3F0–3F7, IRQ6, and DMA channel 2.

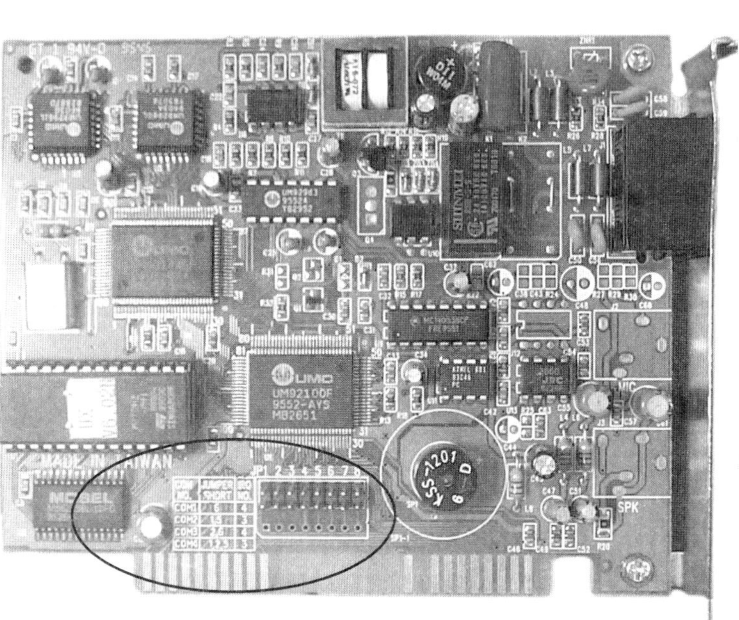

Figure 6.42 ISA device with jumper markings to set I/O addresses and IRQs manually

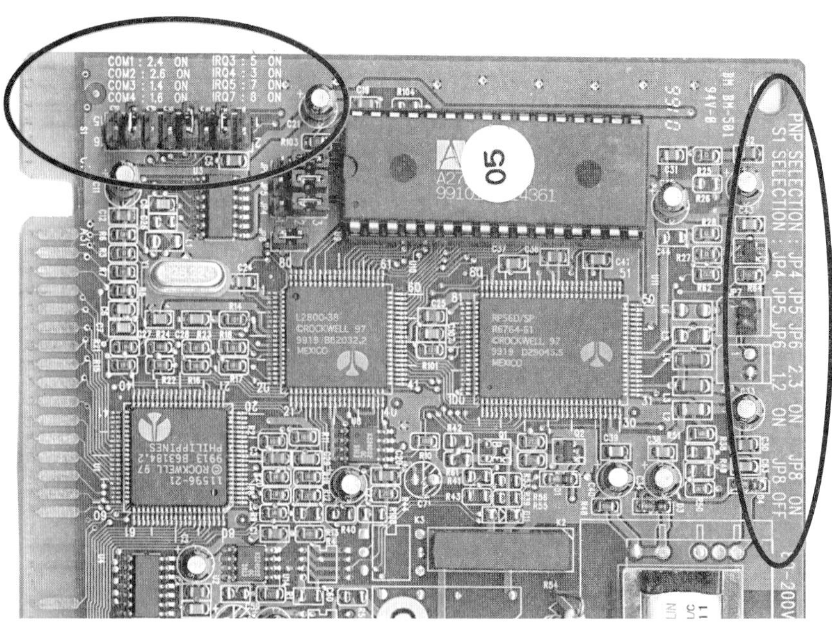

• **Figure 6.43** Modem with legacy or PnP option (jumpers open for PnP; jumpers closed for legacy)

The PnP BIOS must then determine which resources are being used by legacy devices and which are available for the PnP devices. This can happen in two possible ways: the BIOS can try to find the ISA devices by querying a special list it keeps (more on this shortly), or you can tell the BIOS what system resources the legacy devices will be using and the BIOS will set aside those resources. You can determine which method the PnP BIOS will use by changing the PnP settings in CMOS setup. Figure 6.45 shows the PnP/PCI Configurations screen from a typical Award BIOS. The left side of the screen contains the PnP settings. Two items enable you to direct how the BIOS will perform its resource search: the Resources Controlled By setting, and the Reset Configuration Data option.

The Resources Controlled By setting enables you to select between Auto and Manual. If you set this to Auto, the BIOS will defer all system resource determination to the operating system. If you set it to Manual, you must manually set all the IRQ and DMA information to either PCI/ISA PnP or Legacy ISA. Never use the manual setting unless your system contains legacy devices! If you do have legacy devices, I find the manual setting easier to use because I know what IRQs and DMAs the legacy devices use (because of jumper settings and so on).

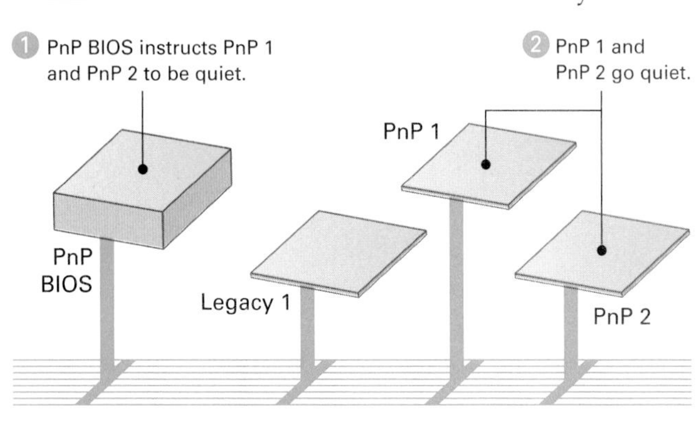

• **Figure 6.44** Initial PnP configuration—PnP devices go quiet.

This brings to light a rather interesting point. It is relatively easy to write a BIOS routine to find what I/O addresses are being used by legacy devices, but it is impossible to write one that can reliably find the IRQs and DMAs for those same devices. As a result, most PnP BIOS will automatically find I/O addresses, but give you the choice of indicating which IRQs and DMAs are used—or they will pass off the responsibility of detecting

```
          CMOS Setup Utility - Copyright (C) 1984-1999 Award Software
                           PnP/PCI Configurations

    PNP OS Installed            No                          Item Help
    Reset Configuration Data    Disabled

    Resources Controlled By     Auto(ESCD)        Menu Level  ▸
  x IRQ Resources               Press Enter
  x DMA Resources               Press Enter       Select Yes if you are
                                                  using Plug and Play
    PCI/VGA Palette Snoop       Disabled          capable operating
    Assign IRQ For VGA          Enabled           system Select No if
    Assign IRQ For USB          Enabled           you need the BIOS to
    INT Pin 1 Assignment        Auto              configure non-boot
    INT Pin 2 Assignment        Auto              devices
    INT Pin 3 Assignment        Auto
    INT Pin 4 Assignment        Auto

 ↑↓ →← :Move Enter:Select +/-PU/PD:Value  F10:Save  ESC:Exit  F1:General Help
     F5:Previous Values  F6:Fail-Safe Defaults  F7:Optimized Defaults
```

set Configuration Data option. To understand this option, you need to understand the function of what I call the "device list." Every PnP BIOS keeps a list of all system resources used, usually on the CMOS or Flash ROM. Interestingly, this storage area does not have an official name, but most folks call it the *Extended System Configuration Data (ESCD) list*. The PnP standard does not define the physical location of this data, but the standard strictly defines the PnP BIOS routines. In other words, the PnP standard doesn't care where the BIOS stores the information, just how the BIOS must respond when queried. I simply call this storage area the *device list*. For purposes of my PnP example, let's assume that the IRQ and DMA resources have been manually configured in CMOS. The PnP BIOS will refer to this list in order to determine which resources are already used (Figure 6.46).

Once the BIOS knows which resources are available, it can "wake up" each PnP device and ask it which system resources it needs (Figure 6.47).

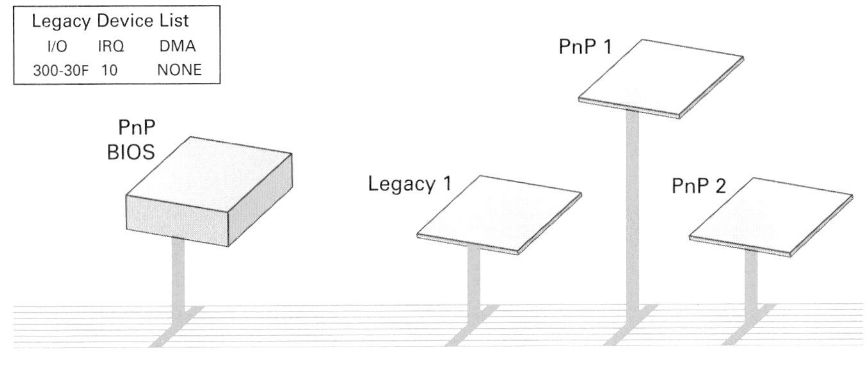

Figure 6.46 BIOS referencing device list

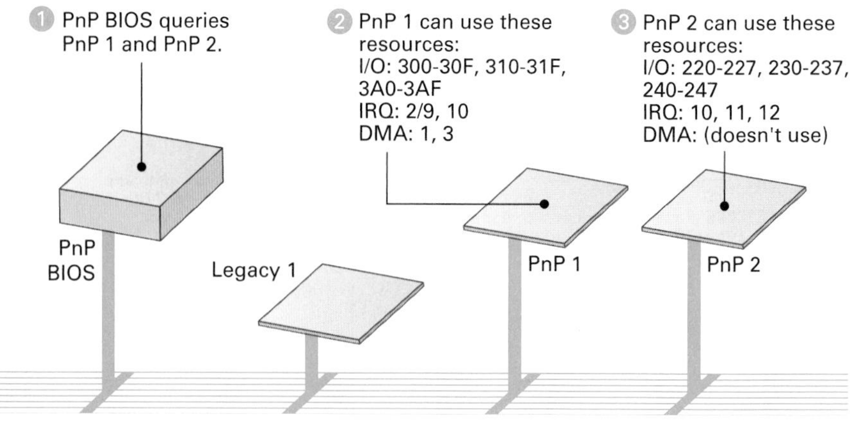

• **Figure 6.47** BIOS querying PnP for system resources

There's a catch here too, however: you can't give just any available system resource to a PnP device. Each PnP device has an internal list of acceptable system resources from which the BIOS must choose. If a device can use only IRQs 3, 5, or 7, for example, then the BIOS can't allocate IRQ10 to the device; it must choose from the device's list. As each PnP device calls for certain resources, the BIOS allocates those resources to the PnP device (Figure 6.48) and adds them to the device list (Figure 6.49).

IRQ steering As I mentioned earlier, PCI devices use dynamically assigned interrupt channels A-D rather than classic IRQs. To support older programs and legacy devices, however, the PCI bus sometimes has to make the PCI devices *appear* to support classic IRQs. Most Windows systems use a feature called **IRQ steering** to make peace between PCI and legacy expansion cards. The OS will take over an IRQ and reserve it for PCI devices, then seemingly put quite a few PCI devices on that single IRQ. You might have a sound card, USB controller, and network card all using IRQ11, for example, and all working just fine. All this stuff happens in the background and does not affect techs often, but it looks weird if you see it in Device Manager.

The PCI devices don't actually use the IRQ when communicating with other PCI devices or with the chipset, but if a program needs a classic IRQ, the chipset does a quick bit of illusion worthy of David Copperfield. The PCI network card that uses interrupt channel C magically appears to the old program to be using IRQ11. The PCI chipset handles the actual interface between the device and the old program. Thanks to this little ruse, everything works out fine—the program runs, the network card works, and the end user is happy.

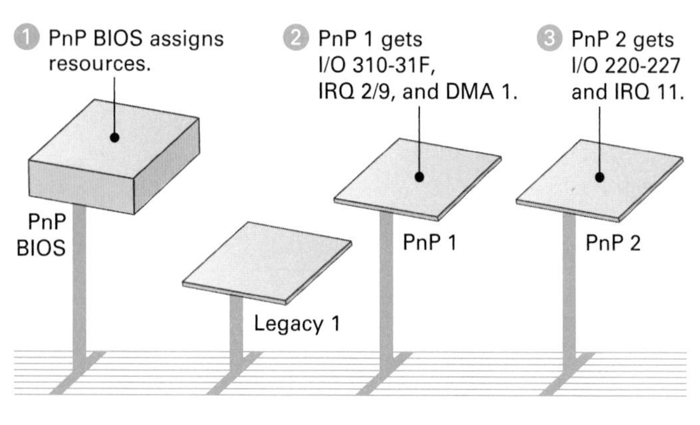

• **Figure 6.48** BIOS allocating system resources

Odds and Ends Sometimes adding another piece of equipment can confuse the PnP settings. For example, if you have a PnP device that needs a resource already taken by another device, you need to make the system reallocate the resources. You can do this using the Reset Configuration Data option, which forces the PnP BIOS to reconfigure all the devices. This happens most often when you install a device that the system doesn't seem to recognize.

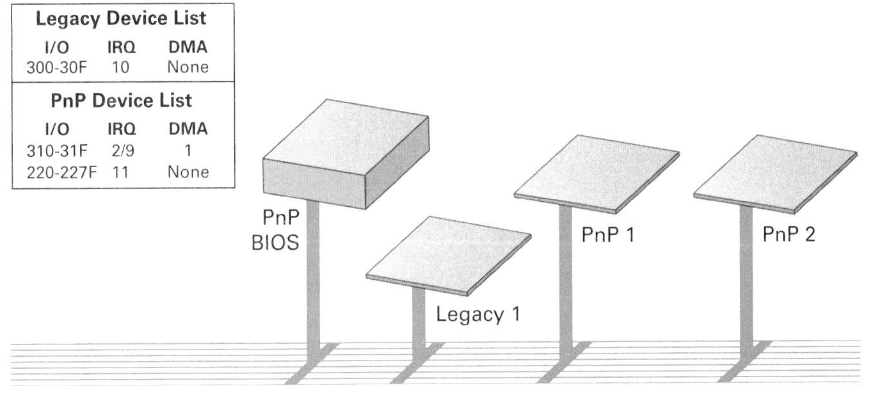

• **Figure 6.49** Updated device list

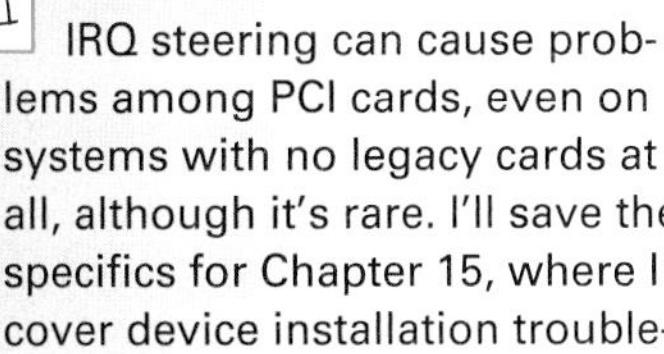

IRQ steering can cause problems among PCI cards, even on systems with no legacy cards at all, although it's rare. I'll save the specifics for Chapter 15, where I cover device installation troubleshooting in Windows 9*x*.

Windows 2000) is run from the Control Panel (Figure 6.50).

Once the operating system takes over, it queries the PnP BIOS to determine if you have installed a device. Should it discover a new device, the operating system then updates its own system resource information, makes changes to the resources if necessary, and prompts the user for the device driver (Figure 6.51).

Even with an occasional legacy device, PnP works magnificently, most of the time. On the more rare occasions when something goes wrong, a tech who lacks knowledge about system resources might find it difficult to fix the problem. Let's turn to the last two installation steps and then look at troubleshooting.

• **Figure 6.50** Windows 2000 Add/Remove Hardware Wizard

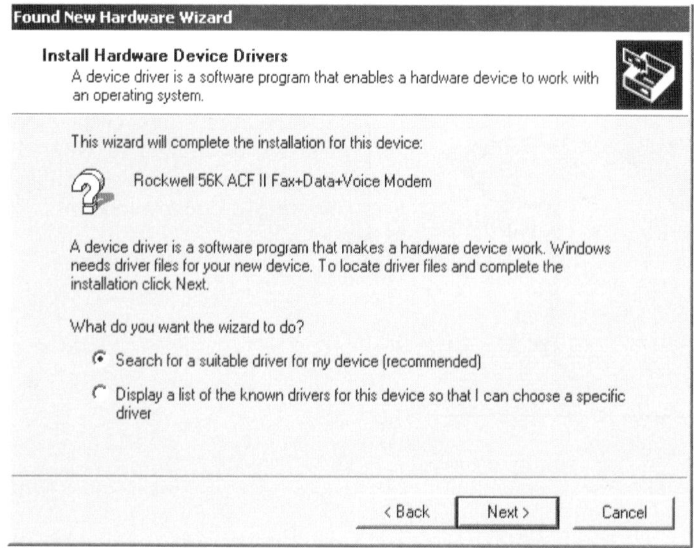

• **Figure 6.51** Windows 2000 prompts the user for new hardware device drivers.

Step 4: Device Drivers

You know from Chapter 5 that all devices, whether built into the motherboard or added along the way, require BIOS. For almost all expansion cards, that BIOS comes in the form of device drivers loaded from a CD-ROM disc provided by the card manufacturer.

Installing device drivers is fairly straightforward. You should use the correct drivers—kind of obvious, but you'd be surprised by how many techs mess this up—and, if you're upgrading, you might have to unload current drivers before loading new drivers. Finally, if you have a problem, you may need to uninstall the drivers you just loaded or, with Windows XP, roll back to earlier, more stable drivers.

Getting the Correct Drivers

To be sure you have the best possible driver you can get for your device, you should always check the manufacturer's web site. The drivers that come with a device may work well, but odds are good that you'll find a newer and better driver on the web site. How do you know that the drivers on the web site are newer? First, take the easy route: look on the CD, because sometimes the version is printed right on the CD itself. If it's not printed there, you're going to have to load the CD in your CD-ROM drive and poke around. Many driver discs have an Autorun screen that advertises the version. If there's nothing on the pop-up screen, look for a Readme file (Figure 6.52).

Removing the Old Drivers

Some cards—and this is especially true with video cards—require you to remove old drivers of the same type before you install the new device. To do

README - Notepad

File Edit Format Help

```
This driver diskette contains driver directories for Windows NT, Windows 95 & 98
Windows NT, Windows 2000 and Windows XP for the following adapters :

- UIC-315/HUV:   max 40MB/sec  16-Bit Ultra SCSI

Driver Versions:
Windows NT              Version number 1.432(NT)
Windows 95/98/Me        Version number 2.20(9x)
Windows 2000/XP         Version number 2.21(2000)

*****************************************************************************
*                                                                           *
*   In this diskette                                                        *
*                                                                           *
*   This readme file provides information for:                              *
*   1. files under the <WINNT\3_51-4_x>: Windows NT 3.51/4.x                *
*   2. files under the <WIN2000_XP>       : Windows 2000/XP                   *
*   3. files under the <WIN95_98>      : Windows 95(OSR2)/98                *
*                                                                           *
```

• **Figure 6.52** Part of a Readme file showing the driver version

this, you must first locate the driver in the Device Manager. In Windows 9*x*, simply select the device driver you want to uninstall and click the Remove button. In Windows 2000/XP, alternate-click the device driver you wish to uninstall and select Uninstall (Figure 6.53). Many devices, especially ones that come with a lot of applications, will have an uninstall option in the Add/Remove Programs (Add or Remove Programs in Windows XP) applet in the Control Panel (Figure 6.54).

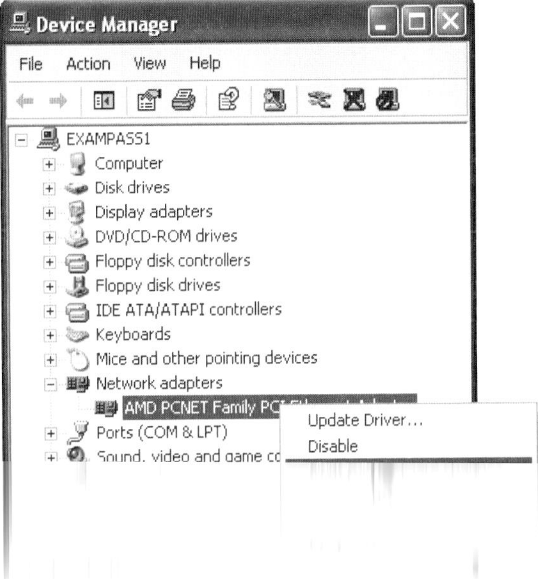

Driver Rollback

Windows XP offers the nifty feature of rolling back to previous drivers after an installation or driver upgrade. If you decide to live on the edge and install beta drivers for your video card, for

Step 5: Verify

OK, now we can talk about the last step, which is to inspect the results of the installation and verify that the device works properly. In both Windows 9*x* and Windows 2000/XP, you should immediately open the Device Manager and verify that Windows sees the device (Figure 6.56). Assuming that Device Manager shows the device working properly, your next check is to put the device to work by making it do whatever it is supposed to do. If you

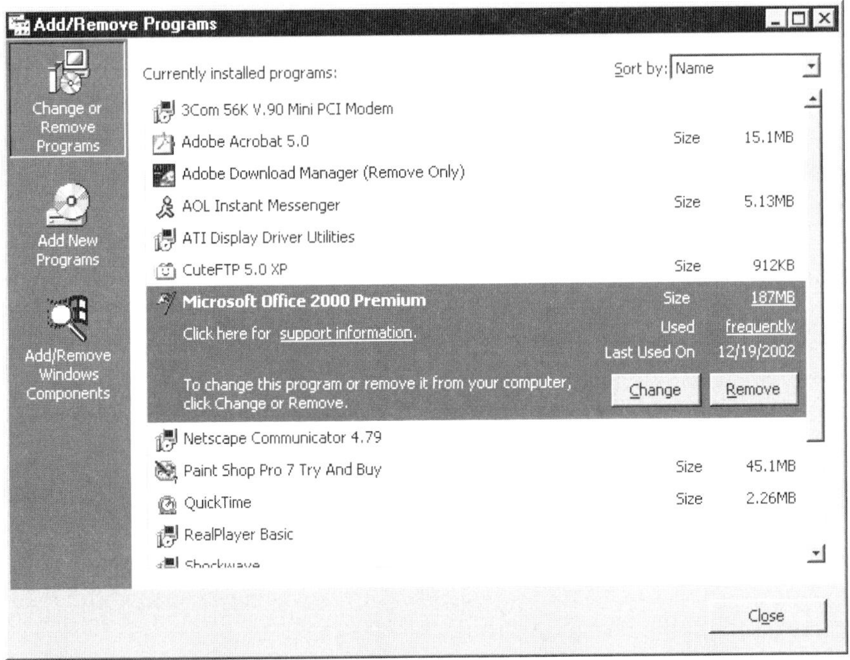

• **Figure 6.54** Uninstall option in Add/Remove Programs

Beta Drivers

Many PC enthusiasts try to coax the most possible performance out of their PC components, much like auto enthusiasts will tinker with engine tunings to get a little extra horsepower out of their engines. Expansion card manufacturers love enthusiasts, who often will act as free testers for their unpolished drivers, known as beta drivers. *Beta drivers are fine for the most part, but sometimes can cause amazing system instability—never a good thing! If you use beta drivers, make sure you know how to uninstall or roll back to previous drivers!*

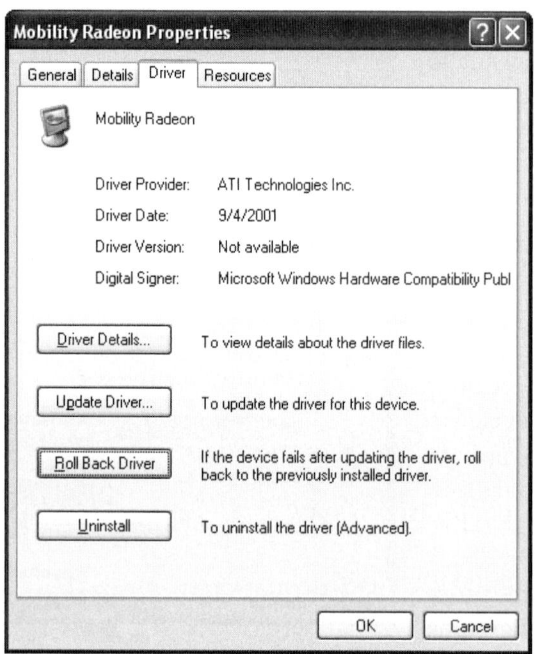

• **Figure 6.55** Driver rollback for this device?

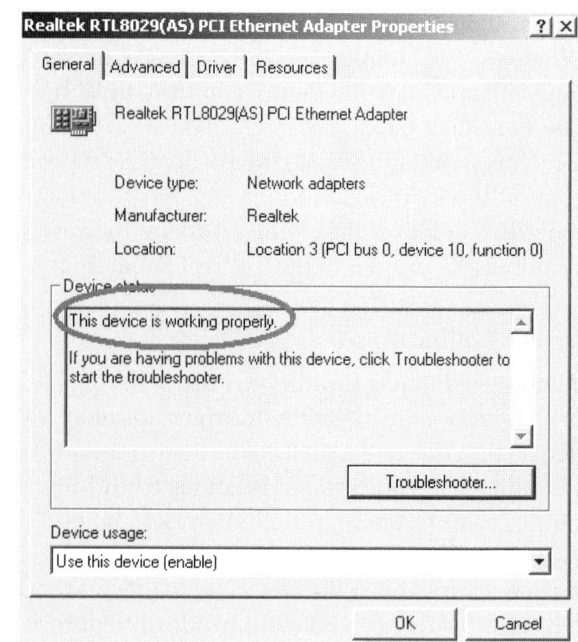

• **Figure 6.56** Device Manager shows the device working properly.

Windows NT 4.0 does not have a Device Manager. The only way to verify whether or not a device works is to give it a whirl!

installed a printer, print something; if you installed a scanner, scan something. If it works, you're done!

■ Troubleshooting Expansion Cards

Chances are high that you'll have to troubleshoot expansion card installation and conflicts at some point, especially if you mix the latest technology with earlier technology. An installation might work on paper but not in actual practice—for example, you many have two devices that both have drivers for Windows XP, but then you find that they conflict when installed in the same system.

The Device Manager is the first tool for troubleshooting expansion card problems. Other chapters in this book cover specific hardware troubleshooting—sound cards in Chapter 20, for example, and video cards in Chapter 18. Chapters 15 and 16 cover issues specifically relating to the relationship of hardware with Windows 9*x* and Windows 2000/XP, respectively. This chapter covers the use of Device Manager for troubleshooting expansion cards.

Device Manager

Device Manager provides the first diagnostic and troubleshooting tool in Windows. After you install a new device, Device Manager can give you many clues if something has gone wrong.

Occasionally, Device Manager may not even show the new device. If that happens, verify that you inserted the device properly and that the device has power, if needed. Run the Add/Remove Hardware Wizard, and see if Windows recognizes the device. If the Device Manager doesn't recognize the device at this point, you have one of two problems: (a) the device is physically damaged and you must replace it, or (b) the device is legacy and you failed to configure its system resources properly.

The Device Manager rarely fails to see a device. More commonly, device problems manifest themselves in Device Manager via error symbols—a black "!", a red "X," a blue "I," or a green "?".

- A black "!" on a yellow circle indicates that a device is missing, that Windows does not recognize a device, or that there's a device driver problem. A device may still work even while producing this error.
- A red "X" indicates a disabled device. This usually points to a system resource conflict or a damaged device. A device producing this error will not work.

Windows XP installed on a current motherboard will rarely give you manual control over a device by default. See Chapter 16 for specific details of Windows XP device troubleshooting techniques.

The "!" symbol is the most common error symbol and usually the easiest to fix. First, double-check the device's connections. Second, try reinstalling the driver with the Update Driver button. To get to the Update Driver button, alternate-click the desired device in Device Manager and select Properties. In the Properties dialog box, select the Driver tab. On the Driver tab, click the Update Driver button (Figure 6.57).

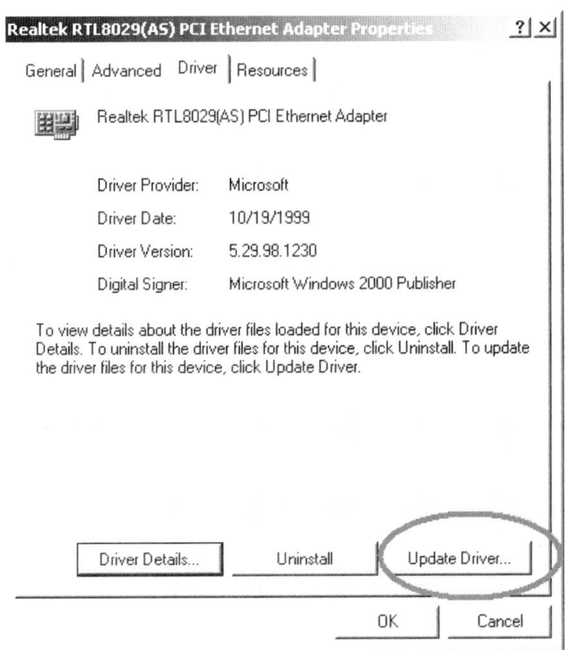

Figure 6.57 The Update Driver button on the Driver tab

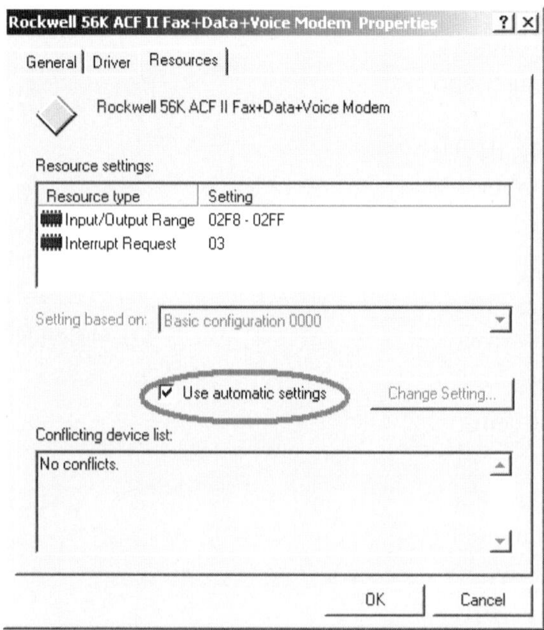

• **Figure 6.58** Use Automatic Settings option

A red "X" error strikes fear into most technicians. If you get one, check the properties for the device to see if any resource conflict exists. Once a device installs, you can accept the installation as defined by keeping the default Use Automatic Settings option (Figure 6.58). If a resource conflict takes place, you can manually change the settings by clicking the Change Setting button (Figure 6.59). Windows then "locks" that resource out of the PnP and permanently dedicates the resource to that device, effectively making that resource no longer available (Figure 6.60).

Think of PnP as you would one of your children: love it, trust it, and let it do what it wishes, but watch it carefully in case it tries to do something irrational. PnP makes installations easier, but should not make you complacent.

Installing Legacy Devices

Legacy devices add complexity to the installation process, requiring you to locate available resources, assign those resources, and then install the device! Let's go through these extra steps.

First, run Device Manager to determine the available resources for the system. All versions of Device Manager enable you to view the devices by resource. Figure 6.61 shows the Windows 2000 Device Manager sorting the devices by IRQ. Can you see any available IRQs? Once you've determined the available resources, you must configure the device to use those resources. You may have to set jumpers, flip switches, or run a special setup program to do this. Figure 6.62 shows a typical legacy setup program. After you configure the legacy device's system resources, you need to inform Windows of the legacy device by running the Add/Remove Hardware Wizard (Figure 6.63).

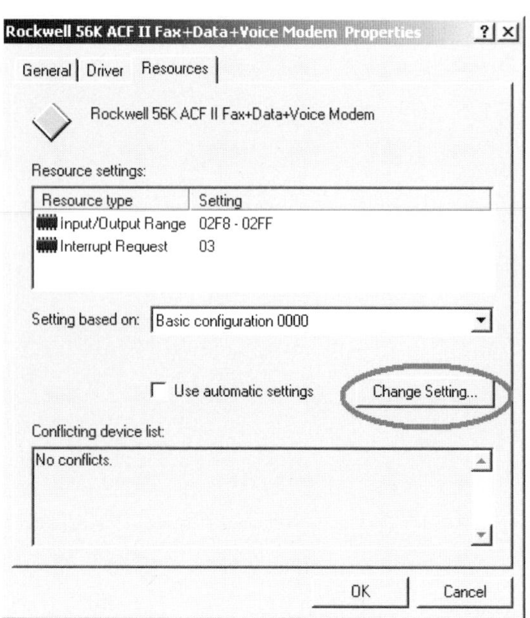

• **Figure 6.59** Change Setting button

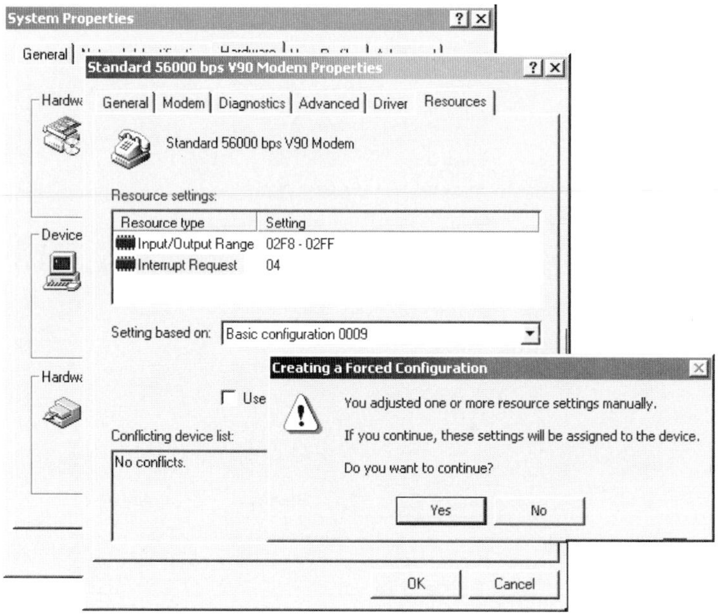

• **Figure 6.60** Manually setting a resource locks the resource out of the PnP.

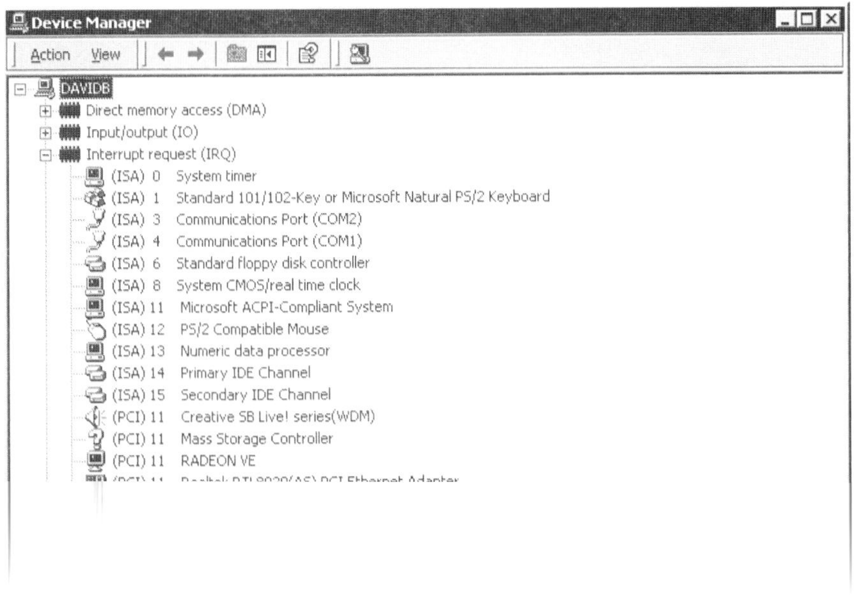

Beyond A+

PCI-X and PCI-Express

To wind up this chapter, let's look at two exciting new upgrades to the venerable PCI expansion bus you've come to know and love so well: PCI-X and PCI Express. Don't let the similar names fool you—even though they are both based on the old PCI bus, they are very different.

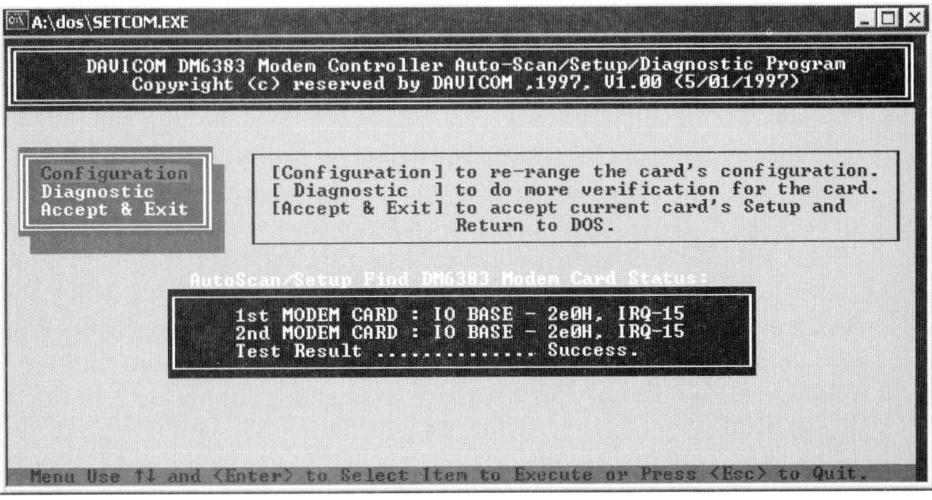

Figure 6.62 Typical legacy setup software program

Figure 6.63 Windows 2000 Add/Remove Hardware Wizard

PCI-X, already available in systems like the Macintosh G5, is a huge enhancement to current PCI that is also fully backwardly compatible, in terms of both hardware and software. It's a parallel standard, like traditional PCI, and it uses the same connectors. PCI-X slots will take regular PCI cards. Also like traditional PCI, it comes in 32-bit and 64-bit versions, but unlike current PCI, the 64-bit version is the more common.

The real bonus of PCI-X is its much enhanced speed. The PCI-X 2.0 standard features four speed grades: PCI-X 66, PCI-X 133, PCI-X 266, and PCI-X 533. The two fastest speeds are new to the 2.0 specification, and not yet in wide use as of this writing. It's worth noting that the 266-MHz and 533-MHz implementations are *not* electrically compatible with 5V PCI; they are designed to work with 3.3V and 1.5V I/O buffers only.

The obvious candidates for PCI-X are businesses using workstations and servers, because they have the "need for speed" and also the need for backward compatibility. Large vendors, especially in the high-end market, are already on board. HP, Dell, and Intel server products, for example, support PCI-X. Even a quick online shopping trip reveals tons of PCI-X stuff for sale: Gigabit NICs, Fibre Channel cards, SCSI host adapters, and more. PCI-X has clearly arrived, and seems to be growing.

PCI Express (previously known as Third Generation I/O, 3GIO, and Arapahoe) is revolutionary rather than evolutionary. Breaking away from the parallel bus architecture of traditional PCI, PCI Express is a fully *serial* interface. It is obviously *not* hardware-compatible, but it is designed to be software-compatible with current PCI, including current OSs and device driver interfaces. Besides serial bus architecture and PCI software compatibility, its key design attributes are flexibility, scalability, high speeds, multi-layered architecture, point-to-point packetized data transmission, and native hot swap/hot plug capabilities.

The really awesome aspect of PCI Express is its speed. Each pair of wires between the PCI Express controller and a device is called a *lane*. Each lane runs at an effective rate of 2.0 Gbps. Better yet, each point-to-point connection can use 1, 2, 4, 8, 12, 16, or 32 lanes to achieve a maximum bandwidth of 128 Gbps (16 GBps). Woof. I've gotta get this!

Unlike PCI-X, PCI Express still awaits actual implementation, but Intel has announced that upcoming chipsets support it. I would look for it to appear on motherboards any day now!

Chapter 6 Review

Chapter Summary

After reading this chapter and completing the exercises, you should understand the following about the expansion bus.

Identify the Structure and Function of the Expansion Bus

- By designing an expansion bus with expansion slots on the motherboard, IBM looked to the future expandability of the computer. An expansion card must have connectivity, communication with the CPU, and drivers for the operating system.
- The external data bus and the address bus connect every device in the computer, whether the device is soldered to the motherboard or snapped into a socket.
- The chipset connects expansion slots to the rest of the system, sometimes through the Northbridge and sometimes through the Southbridge. Some computers have more than one expansion bus and connect them through both the Northbridge and the Southbridge.
- The frontside bus runs at the speed of the system crystal, the same as the motherboard speed. The expansion bus runs at its own standardized speed as set by the slower expansion bus crystal that is independent of the system crystal.
- Attempting to increase speed and performance of the expansion bus, designers have offered a number of different expansion buses. Even today most motherboards provide backward support for the oldest expansion bus, the ISA bus, which requires complex configuration of system resources.
- The PC bus or XT bus appeared on the first generation of IBM PCs and featured an 8-bit external data bus and a top speed of ~7 MHz. IBM allowed this expansion bus standard to be copied free by clone makers. With the 286, IBM created the AT bus, a 16-bit bus that also ran at ~7 MHz and was backwardly compatible with older 8-bit cards. Clone makers pooled their knowledge of the PC/XT and AT buses to create the ISA Bus standards. Today, we call these buses the 8-bit ISA and 16-bit ISA.

Explain Classic System Resources

- Cards that used the ISA bus required configuration of four kinds of system resources: I/O addresses, IRQs, DMAs, and memory addresses.
- IBM assigned I/O addresses or unique patterns of 1's and 0's on the address bus for each device in the computer. Starting with the Intel 8088 CPU, an extra wire, called the input/output or memory (IO/MEM) wire informed devices that the CPU was not specifying a memory address. Instead, the CPU used I/O addresses via the address bus to communicate with a particular device. Today, while the CPU no longer has an IO/MEM wire, it still uses I/O addresses or unique combinations of 0's and 1's to communicate with a particular device. Each device gets one or more unique I/O addresses.
- In Windows 98 the Device Manager lists the I/O range for each device under the Resources tab for that device. In Windows 2000 or XP, alternate-click My Computer and select Properties. Select the Hardware tab and click the Device Manager button.
- I/O addresses are expressed in hexadecimal, a 16-digit numbering system. Like the familiar decimal system, hex uses the digits 0–9. Then, it uses A–F to represent decimal values 10–15. Each hex digit may be expressed using four wires or four binary digits, from all 0's—0000 (0)—to all ones—1111(F).
- I/O addresses follow three rules: (1) all devices have an I/O address, (2) most devices use more than one I/O address, and (3) no two devices may share an I/O address.
- IBM pre-defined I/O addresses for most standard PC devices. If a device, such as a sound card, does not have standardized I/O addresses, it can be assigned any unused addresses. While the ISA bus, with only 16 wires for I/O addresses, could use only 1024 I/O addresses, today's computers have doubled the number of wires in the address bus wires to allow many more I/O addresses.
- Techs often use only the first address or the base address in a range of I/O addresses. A leading 0 is often dropped and the letter "h" is added to the end to indicate that the address is expressed in hexadecimal.
- By charging an INT wire, a device can communicate with the CPU. The Interrupt Request (IRQ) wires from the devices are connected to an 8259 interrupt controller. When the device needs to talk to the CPU, it lights its IRQ and, by checking the 8259, the CPU knows which device has interrupted. Originally, the PC had only 8 IRQ wires, numbered 0–7 and prioritized

by number. The system timer gets the highest priority at IRQ0 with the keyboard assigned IRQ1 or the second priority IRQ.

- Realizing that the original PC did not offer enough IRQs, IBM added another 8259 controller to the 286 AT computer. It cascaded to IRQ2 on the first 8259 chip, allowing devices that were assigned IRQs 8 through 15 to get priority service from the CPU as if they were IRQ2. The exception is IRQ9 because IBM ran the IRQ9 wire over to the IRQ2 position on the ISA slot for backward compatibility. Since both IRQ2 and IRQ9 use the same wire, it is collectively referred to as IRQ2/9. IRQ8 was assigned to the real-time clock. The hard drive controller was moved from

- The third system resource is Direct Memory Access (DMA) that, as the name implies, allows devices to access memory directly without involving the CPU. Devices use DMA requests (DRQs) to move data via the external data bus, but the CPU retains priority for accessing the bus. A four-wire 8237 chip controls DMA transfers when the CPU is not using the external data bus. Only one device may be assigned to a DMA channel. When the second DMA controller chip was added to the 286 and all later computers, it was also cascaded with DRQ4 connected to DRQ0.
- DMA has serious limitations. Designed in the days of slow computers, DMA has a maximum speed of about 8 MHz and handles only 8 bits of data on DMA channels 0–3 or 16-bit transfers on DMA channels 5–7. Too slow for modern systems, DMA is limited to low-speed devices, such as floppy drives.
- Today's bus mastering devices are able to access memory without using the 8237. All EIDE hard drives use bus mastering, although this technique may be called Ultra DMA.
- Memory addresses for on-board ROM is the fourth kind of system resource. Some expansion cards, such as SCSI host adapters, have a small bit of ROM that enables the system BIOS to talk to the card. This BYOB ROM also needs to be assigned addresses from the main memory map.
- COM and LPT ports have preassigned combinations of IRQs and I/O addresses. By assigning a device to a particular COM port, you are actually assigning the IRQ and I/O address.
- Originally, IBM defined two serial ports and one parallel port. COM1 uses IRQ4 and I/O address 3F8, while COM2 uses IRQ3 and I/O address 2F8. The parallel port LPT1 uses IRQ7 and I/O address 378. When more ports were needed, IBM assigned COM3 the same IRQ as COM1, and COM4 the same IRQ as COM2. Although these ports have unique I/O addresses, you can use only one even-numbered COM port (COM2 or COM4) and one odd-numbered COM port (COM1 or COM3). If you set two devices to COM1 and COM3, the computer will lock up. Although a second line printer port was rarely used,

- With today's computers, you can change the IRQ for a COM or LPT port if the device and software can handle it. While the I/O address for COM and LPT ports remains constant even now, the ports may be assigned a nonstandard IRQ.

Identify the Modern Expansion Bus Slots

- The original ISA 8- or 16-bit bus was very slow, running no faster than 8.33 MHz. In 1986 with the first 386 computers, IBM introduced an improved bus called Microchannel Architecture (MCA). This 32-bit bus ran at about 12 MHz. Because MCA slots were different from ISA slots, only MCA cards could be used with the new bus. IBM did not release MCA to the public domain, so it remained expensive. Computers using MCA have not been produced for many years.
- Rather than paying a licensing fee to IBM to use their MCA bus, clone makers created their own 32-bit bus called Extended ISA (EISA). Like MCA, it was a faster, self-configuring bus, but it could also use ISA cards because of its double-slot connector. Manufacturers produced computers with EISA until the mid-1990s.
- In spite of the introduction of these two new buses, most companies continued to produce computers with ISA motherboards. When Windows was introduced with its graphical user interface (GUI), ISA could no longer keep up with the demands on video. By tapping into what we now call the frontside bus, the Video Electronics Standards Association

(VESA) created the 32-bit VESA local bus (VL-Bus). Mixing two or three of these slots with the standard ISA slots provided 32-bit access to devices such as video cards and hard drive controllers. The VL-Bus bus is now obsolete.

- Introduced with the Pentium processor, the Peripheral Component Interconnect (PCI) bus proved to be a stronger, faster, more flexible, and less-expensive expansion bus. Able to coexist with other buses and use bus-mastered DMA, the self-configuring PCI bus also has a burst mode feature for efficient data transfers. Found on Apple Macintosh and PCs, the PCI "mezzanine" bus sits between the frontside bus and other expansion buses. PCI can use either 32-bit, 33-MHz components or 64-bit, 66-MHz components, or a combination of these features. While the PCI bus is controlled by the Northbridge, the Southbridge serves as an intermediary between the PCI and ISA buses. With standards defined by the PCI Special Interest Group (PCI SIG), PCI interrogates PCI cards and assigns them preset system resources such as I/O addresses. Instead of using IRQs, PCI devices share interrupt channels labeled "INTA," "INTB," "INTC," and "INTD." All of today's computers use the PCI expansion bus.
- Most modern motherboards have an Accelerated Graphics Port (AGP) slot, used exclusively by the video card. This super PCI slot has its own personal connection to the Northbridge.

Install Expansion Cards Properly

- Installing an expansion card involves at least five steps: (1) select a card that works with your operating system, (2) install it correctly without damaging it or the motherboard, (3) configure system resources or allow Plug and Play to do it for you, (4) provide drivers appropriate for the operating system, and (5) verify that the card is functioning properly.
- Cards should always be either in the computer or in an anti-static bag. Hold cards only by the edges, never touching the slot connectors. When installing a card, push it straight into the slot and screw it to the case. If the slot connectors need to be cleaned, use a contact cleaning solution rather than a pencil eraser.
- With today's PnP cards, resource conflicts are rare. An understanding of the system resources will help resolve any resource problems.
- PnP allows devices to configure themselves automatically. PnP requires three things: (1) a PnP BIOS, (2) a PnP operating system such as Windows 9*x* or Windows 2000/XP, and (3) PnP devices. While all newer devices are PnP, you may occasionally encounter an older legacy device. All PCI and AGP cards are PnP, but some cards may function as legacy or PnP as determined by a jumper on the card itself. Legacy cards typically have jumpers that set the IRQ and I/O address.
- During the boot process, the PnP BIOS instructs PnP devices to "be quiet" so the BIOS can locate legacy ISA devices. If legacy devices are located, they are first assigned system resources, with the remaining resources then available for the more flexible PnP devices.
- Two CMOS setup items enable you to determine how the BIOS will search for resources. The Resources Controlled By setting switches between Auto and Manual configuration of resources. For systems with all PnP devices, leave this setting at Auto. The Reset Data Configuration setting determines whether the "device list" of all system resources, also called the Extended System Configuration Data (ESCD) list, will be updated and edited by the PnP BIOS. When the PC boots or when the Add/Remove Hardware Wizard is run, the operating systems can also update and edit the device list.

Troubleshoot Expansion Card Problems

- To ensure that the device is working properly, check the Device Manager. If the device does not show up in the Device Manager, you may not have inserted it properly or you may have forgotten to provide power to the device. You should run the Add/Remove Hardware Wizard to see if Windows sees the device. If not, you may assume that (1) the device is physically damaged and must be replaced, or (2) the device is legacy and its system resources are not configured properly.
- The Device Manager may display an error symbol next to the device. A black "!" on a yellow circle indicates that the device is missing or is not recognized by Windows. You should check the device's connections and use the Update Driver button to reinstall the driver. A red "X" indicates a disabled device, usually due to a system resource conflict or a damaged device. Check the Properties for the device to see if there is a resource conflict. If so, use the Change Settings button to manually change resources and dedicate them to this device. A blue "I" indicates manually configured resources. Used only with Windows ME, a green "?" means that a compatible driver has been installed, which may not provide full functionality for the device.

- With legacy devices, it may be necessary for you to assign the resources and then install the device. The Device Manager will show you what resources are available. Set the jumpers on the legacy card to use available resources and then run the Add/Remove Hardware Wizard to inform Windows of the legacy device.

Key Terms

Accelerated Graphics Port (AGP) *(198)*
Base I/O address *(185)*
COM port *(188)*
Direct Memory Access (DMA) *(191)*
Extended Industry Standard Architecture (EISA) *(196)*
I/O addressing *(181)*
Industry Standard Architecture (ISA) *(180)*
Interrupt request (IRQ) *(187)*
Microchannel Architecture (MCA) *(195)*
Peripheral Component Interconnect (PCI) *(197)*
Plug and Play (PnP) *(201)*
System resources *(180)*

follow. Not all the terms will be used.

1. The first address in the range of I/O addresses used by a device is called the ________________.
2. The expansion bus runs at its own standardized speed, set by the ________________.
3. Introduced by IBM with the 386 computers, the proprietary ______________ was the first 32-bit bus.
4. The _________ is usually a brown slot used only by the video card.
5. The CPU uses the ______________, a unique pattern of 1's and 0's on the address bus, to communicate with a device.

whether PC or Apple Macintosh, is the flexible ___________.

7. Used on ISA motherboards, the now obsolete _____________ provided two or three slots with 32-bit access by tapping into what is now called the frontside bus.
8. A __________ is a parallel port that has been assigned a particular IRQ and I/O address, traditionally for a printer.
9. A device uses its ___________, controlled by an 8259 chip to get the attention of the CPU.
10. An older device that does not have PnP capabilities is known as a _______________.

Multiple-Choice Quiz

1. All the following devices use an IRQ *except* the ____________.
   - **A.** Keyboard
   - **B.** Real-time clock
   - **C.** Joystick
   - **D.** Math co-processor
2. Which of the following is *not* a requirement for PnP?
   - **A.** Legacy cards
   - **B.** PnP BIOS
   - **C.** PnP device
   - **D.** PnP operating system
3. The floppy drive controller uses DMA ________.
   - **A.** 1
   - **B.** 2
   - **C.** 4
   - **D.** 8

4. Which of the following statements about the expansion bus is true?

   A. The expansion bus runs at the speed of the system clock.

   B. The CPU communicates with RAM via the expansion bus.

   C. The frontside bus is another name for the expansion bus.

   D. The expansion bus crystal sets the speed for the expansion bus.

5. Which of the following statements best describes the hexadecimal numbering system.

   A. It is a binary numbering system that uses only two digits, a 0 and a 1.

   B. It is another name for the decimal numbering system with ten digits, 0 through 9.

   C. It is an eight-digit numbering system, using letters A through H.

   D. It is a sixteen-digit numbering system that can express all its values by using four wires.

6. All the following buses are obsolete *except* __________.

   A. MCA

   B. PCI

   C. VL-BUS

   D. EISA

7. Which of the following statements is true?

   A. Because the printer and other parallel devices do not attempt to get the attention of the CPU, you can assign IRQ7 to another device without causing any difficulty.

   B. The device assigned to IRQ6 gets a higher priority than the device assigned to IRQ14.

   C. Because both COM1 and COM3 share the same IRQ, you cannot use both ports at the same time.

   D. There is no difference of meaning between the terms "parallel port" and "LPT port."

8. MCA and EISA have all of the following similar capabilities *except* __________.

   A. Both are self-configuring.

   B. Both can use ISA cards.

   C. Both are faster than the ISA bus.

   D. Both provide 32-bit data transfer.

9. The ISA bus is either a(n) ______- or ________-bit bus with a maximum speed of ________ MHz.

   A. 8, 16, 32

   B. 32, 64, 32

   C. 16, 32, 64

   D. 8, 16, 8

10. All the following are limitations of DMA *except*______________.

    A. It transfers either 8 or 16 bits of data.

    B. It has a maximum speed of 8 MHz.

    C. It offers only four DMA channels.

    D. DMA4 cascades to DMA0.

11. The standard resource assignments for LPT2 are __________.

    A. I/O address 378 and IRQ7

    B. I/O address 278 and IRQ5

    C. I/O address 3F8 and IRQ4

    D. I/O address 2F8 and IRQ5

12. To install an expansion card, you must overcome all of these hurdles *except* __________.

    A. Connectivity

    B. Plug and Play

    C. Drivers

    D. Communication

13. To determine if a device is compatible with a current operating system such as Windows XP, you should check the ________________.

    A. ROM

    B. Driver

    C. HAL

    D. HCL

14. The term "system resources" includes all of the following *except* ________.

    A. DRQs

    B. IRQs

    C. LPTs

    D. I/O addresses

15. If the Device Manager has a red "X" next to a device, it is an error symbol indicating that ________.

    A. A compatible driver has been installed that may not provide all the functions for the device.

B. The device is missing or Windows cannot recognize it.

C. The system resources have been assigned manually.

D. The device has been disabled because it is either damaged or has a system resource conflict.

Essay Quiz

1. Although today's computers use Plug and Play to assign system resources automatically, CompTIA still expects you to know about system resources. Why is this knowledge important? Briefly explain two scenarios where your knowledge of system resources may help solve

[illegible]

Manager indicates that both of these cards are working perfectly. Explain when and why two devices can share the same IRQ. What kind of expansion slot must the cards use to share an IRQ?

3. Your friend Merrill just called. He bought a new sound card for his computer and tried to install it. It's not working. What should he do now? Using the methodology for card installation that you learned in this chapter, explain the steps that he should follow to determine whether he installed the card wrong or the card itself is faulty.

4. Assume that you are tutoring a student who does not understand legacy devices or how PnP can assign resources to these older devices

[illegible]

configured correctly. Write a quick user manual to help a new technician determine how to use the Device Manager for the Windows operating system you use. Include how to access the Device Manager and which buttons/tabs to use to see if devices are installed correctly and have been assigned appropriate system resources.

Lab Projects

Lab Project 6.1

Open your computer case and determine the kind of expansion slots your motherboard has. How many of each kind are available? What cards are installed in the slots? Now examine the back and front of the computer case to see what ports are available. What devices do you have plugged into the ports?

Lab Project 6.2

As you learned in this chapter, researchers have created a number of different expansion buses to improve the capabilities of the personal computer. While some are now obsolete, research continues to attempt to improve expansion buses. As this book goes to press, an improved version of the PCI bus is starting to hit the marketplace: PCI-X. Use the Internet to research this technology. What advantages does it offer? What disadvantages, if any? What kinds of slots/connectors does it use? What future improvements to this technology are anticipated? Would PCI-X be an important consideration if you were purchasing a new computer? Why or why not?

chapter 7

Motherboards

"Form follows function."

—Louis Henri Sullivan, *Lippincott's Magazine*, March, 1896

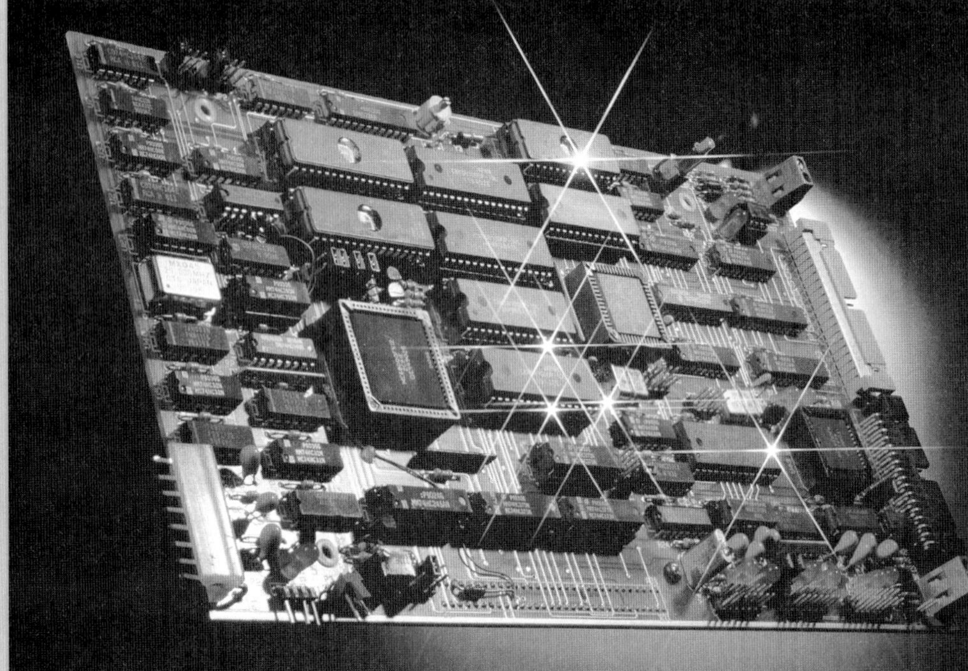

In this chapter, you will learn how to

- **Explain how motherboards work**
- **Identify the types of motherboards**
- **Explain chipset varieties**
- **Upgrade and install motherboards**
- **Troubleshoot motherboard problems**

The **motherboard** provides the foundation for the personal computer. Every piece of hardware from the CPU to the lowliest expansion card directly or indirectly plugs into the motherboard. All data and commands flow through the wires—called **traces**—embedded in the motherboard (Figure 7.1). Without the motherboard, you literally have no PC.

Historical/Conceptual

How Motherboards Work

You know from earlier chapters that all motherboards share certain characteristics, such as a socket or slot for the CPU and some way to enable the user to input data and receive data. Every motherboard has slots for RAM, although very old ones had RAM directly soldered to the board. And all have built-in support chips and the system clock that make everything work together.

Four variable and interrelated characteristics define modern mother-

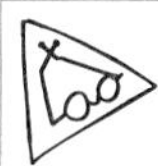

Tech Tip

Layers of the PCB

Modern motherboards—officially printed circuit boards (PCBs)—come in multiple layers and thus mask some of their complexity. You can see some of the traces on the board, but every motherboard is two or more layers thick. There's a veritable highway of wires in the layers, carrying data and commands back and forth between CPU, Northbridge,

length and width of the board. Shorter traces also allow signals to travel faster than they would if the wires were longer as would be necessary if motherboards did not use layers. The multiple layers also add strength to the board itself, helping prevent it from bending when used.

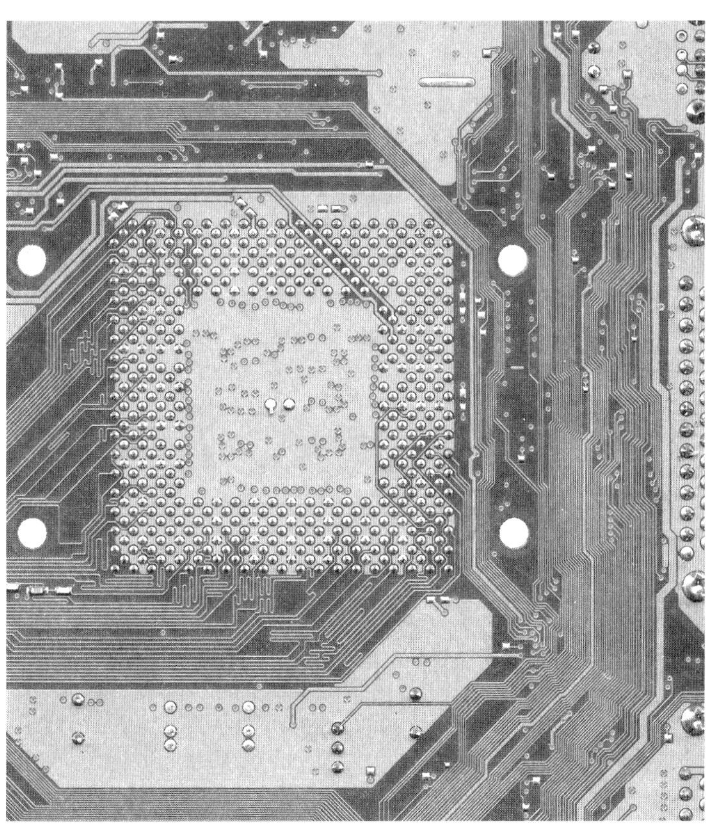

• **Figure 7.1** Traces visible beneath the CPU socket on a motherboard

Any good tech should be able to make a recommendation to a client about a particular motherboard simply by perusing the specs. Because the motherboard determines function, expansion, and stability for the whole PC, it's essential that you know your motherboards!

Test Specific

Types of Motherboards

All motherboards come in a basic rectangular or square shape, but they come in a dizzying variety of sizes. An analysis of many different motherboards will reveal that despite size differences, most share a lot of components. The expansion slots always seem to take roughly the same part of the motherboard. The particular way components are positioned on a motherboard is called the motherboard's *form factor*.

Motherboards come in variations of two standard form factors—AT and ATX—as well as in a substantial number of proprietary formats. Different form factors offer different features and sizes for a computer system, and most PC cases are designed to work with only one form factor. To perform motherboard upgrades and provide knowledgeable recommendations to clients, techs need to know their form factors.

AT Motherboards

The old-style computer motherboards followed a form factor called **AT**. The AT form factor, invented by IBM in the early 1980s, was the predominant form factor for motherboards through the mid-1990s. The AT type of motherboard has a large keyboard plug in the same relative spot on the motherboard, and it has a split **P8/P9** style of power socket (Figure 7.2).

The AT motherboard has a few size variations, ranging from large to very large. The original AT motherboard was huge, around 12 inches wide by 13 inches deep. Because the technology was new, a lot of space was necessary for the various chips needed to run the components of the PC, such as the keyboard.

Baby AT

As technology improved and the PC flourished, the demand for smaller PCs increased. After all, an old-style PC with an AT motherboard took up quite a bit of desk real estate. Need drives the PC industry, so manufacturers created a smaller motherboard, dubbed the **Baby AT**. The original AT motherboard was then called the Full AT, Regular AT, or sometimes just AT. The Baby AT became and remained the most popular AT form factor for quite a while.

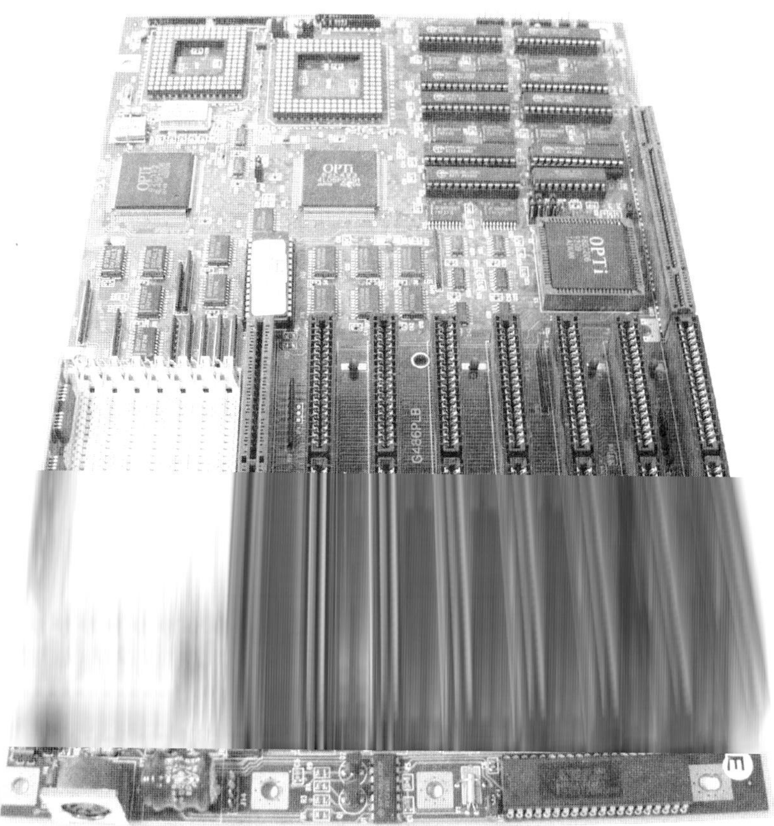

• **Figure 7.2** AT-style motherboard

Figure 7.3 shows AT and Baby AT motherboards for comparison. Note that the keyboard connector on each falls in the same spot; although it's hard to see here, the holes for connecting the boards to a system unit also line up. This standardization of permanent elements enabled people to swap one motherboard for another, as long as they stayed within the AT standard.

There is a lot of variation in size among Baby AT motherboards, but most follow a standard ~8.7-inches wide. The depth ranges from 9 inches on the short end to a full 13.25 inches for others. The standardization of the AT and Baby AT motherboards, however, demands that the keyboard and expansion slots stick to the form factor specifications.

The single greatest problem with AT and Baby AT motherboards was the lack of external ports. When PCs were first invented, the only devices plugged into the average PC were a monitor and a keyboard. That's what the AT was designed to

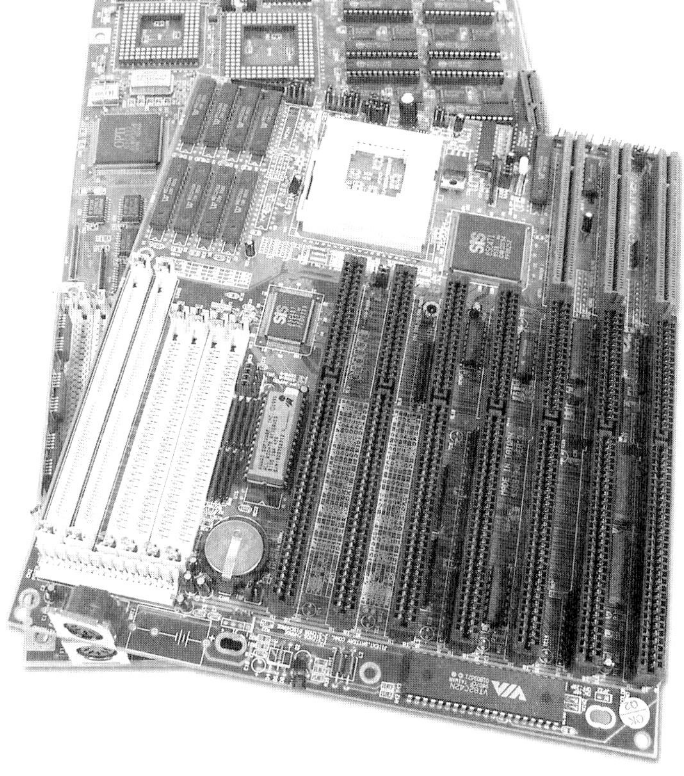

• **Figure 7.3** AT motherboard (bottom) and Baby AT motherboard (top)

Figure 7.4 AT connectors on the back of an AT motherboard

handle—the only dedicated connector on an AT motherboard is the keyboard plug (Figure 7.4). Initially, if you wanted to add connectors for anything else, you had to do so through the expansion slots. This included connections to serial and parallel ports. Later AT motherboards had the serial and parallel controllers built into the motherboard, and used a simple connector called a *dongle* to put the physical ports on the back of the case.

The Need for a New Form Factor

Over the years, the number of devices plugged into the back of the PC has grown tremendously. Your average PC today has a keyboard, a mouse, a printer, some speakers, a monitor, and a phone line connected to it. These added components created a demand for a new type of form factor, one with more dedicated connectors for more devices. Many attempts were made to create a new standard form factor. Invariably, these new form factors integrated dedicated connectors for at least the mouse and printer, and many even added connectors for video, sound, and phone lines.

One form factor that enjoyed a degree of success was the **slimline** form factor. The first slimline form factor was known as LPX (defined in some sources as *low profile extended*, although there's some disagreement). It was replaced by the NLX form factor. (NLX apparently stands for nothing, by the way. It's just a cool grouping of letters.) The LPX and NLX form factors met the demands of the slimline market by providing a central riser slot to enable the insertion of a special **riser card** (Figure 7.5). Expansion cards then fit into the riser card horizontally. Combining built-in connections with a riser card enabled manufacturers to produce PCs shorter than 4 inches. LPX and NLX motherboards were similar in size to Baby AT boards, up to 9-inches wide by 13.6-inches deep.

The main problem with form factors like LPX and NLX was their inflexibility. Certainly, no problem occurred with dedicated connections for devices like mice or printers, but the new form factors also added connectors for devices like video and sound—devices that were prone to obsolescence, making the motherboard useless the moment a new type of video or sound card came into popularity.

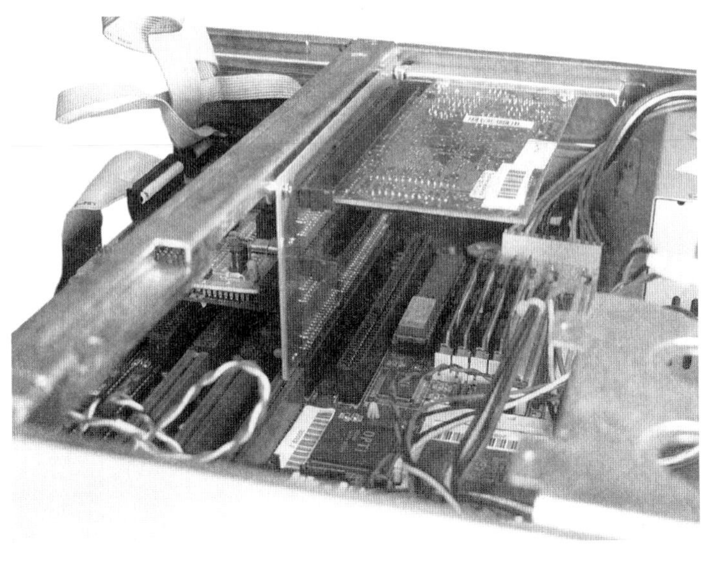

Figure 7.5 Riser card on an older motherboard

It seems ironic that I'm writing this critique of LPX, NLX, and other form factors with built-in video, sound, and other options, on a system with built-in video, sound, and more! The difference between the old all-in-one systems and the new systems—see the "Beyond A+" section of this chapter—boils down to three words: limited system resources.

You know from Chapter 6 that all devices, built-in or otherwise, require system resources. The older form factors were built around the ISA bus and thus had strict limits on I/O addresses, IRQs, DMA channels, and memory addresses available.

It was unthinkable to add a video card into a system with built-in video. They would clash horribly on almost all system resources: I/O addresses, probably IRQ, and definitely memory addresses. The system would turn into a giant paperweight!

Modern systems built on the PCI bus assume you might want more than one video card or sound card, and why not? The built-in graphics on my current system, for example, can run Microsoft Office applications perfectly and even provides a reasonably decent TV tuner (Tech TV on the PC is very geeky, but fun nonetheless!). But the motherboard manufacturer thoughtfully included a good AGP slot on the motherboard into which you can add a very high-end video card and play the latest and greatest game without dropping a frame. As an added bonus, having a built in video card and an extra AGP card means I can easily run dual monitors. More on this in Chapter 18, "Video."

PCI revolutionized the way we thought about the PC and what to expect

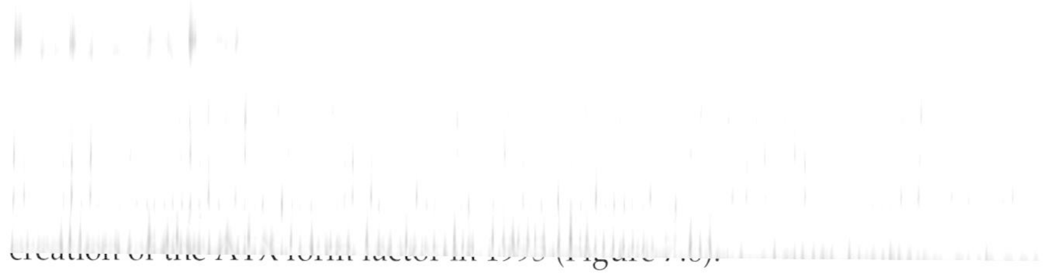

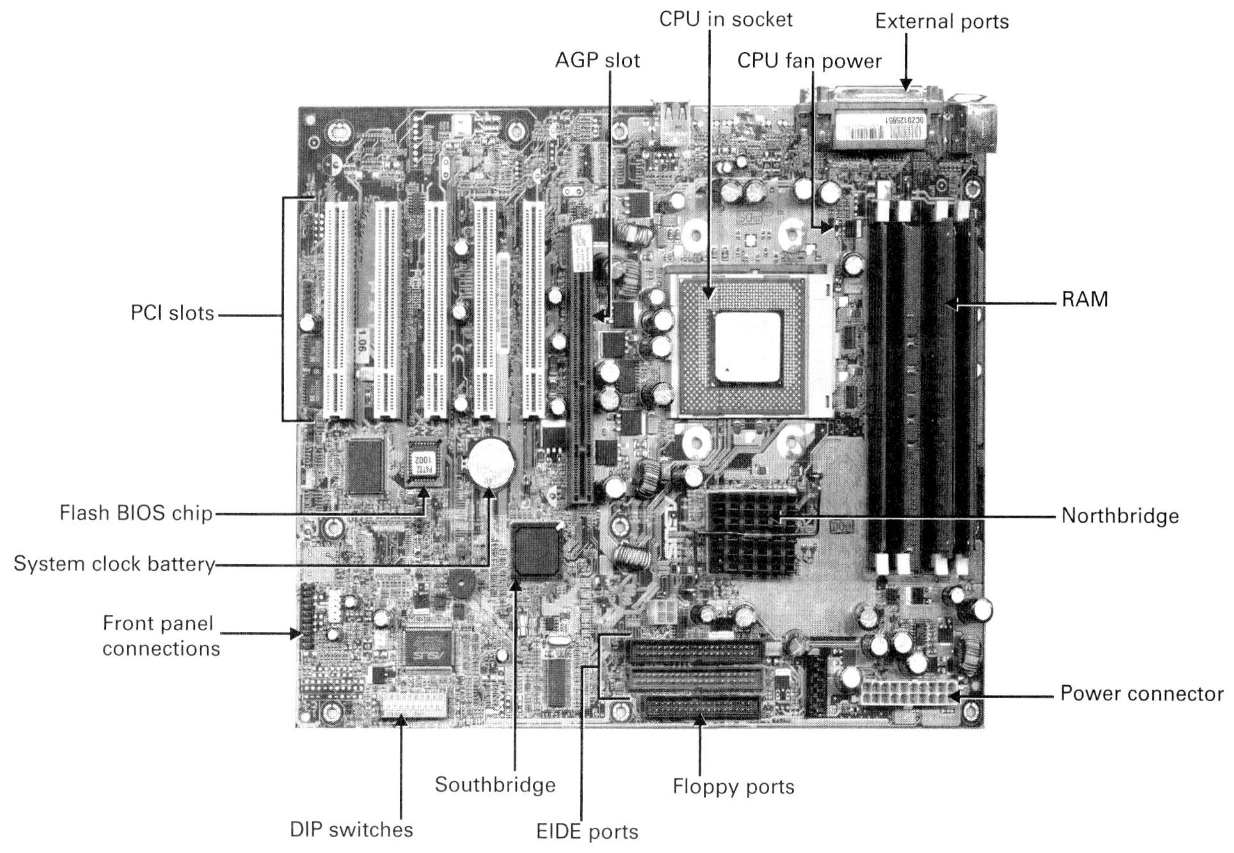

Figure 7.6 ATX motherboard

Tech Tip

Sound Cards and Resource Usage

Almost all new motherboards come with built-in sound, but most manufacturers include it as a marketing gesture rather than a desire for people to listen to high quality music or excellent game sounds. In fact, many of the built-in sound cards require heavy CPU utilization to function, upwards of 20% in sound-intensive games, for example. This represents a gigantic drain on system resources that could be better spent making the game more fluid on the screen and enabling you to crush the bad guys! The poor quality of much built-in audio provides an important market for PCI sound cards from companies like Creative Labs and Turtle Beach. Their better offerings drop CPU usage dramatically. More on this topic in Chapter 20, "Sound."

ATX got off to a slow start, but by around 1998 ATX overtook AT to become the most common form factor used today. **ATX** shares the same dimensions as a Baby AT (12 by 9.6 inches), but mounts 90 degrees relative to the computer's box. ATX is distinct from the AT in the lack of an AT keyboard port, replaced with a rear panel that has all necessary ports built in. Note the mini-DIN (PS/2) keyboard and mouse ports in Figure 7.7, standard features on almost all ATX boards.

The ATX form factor includes many improvements over AT. The position of the power supply enables better air movement. The CPU and RAM are placed to enable easier access. Other improvements, such as placement of RAM closer to the Northbridge and CPU than on AT boards, offer users enhanced performance as well. The shorter the wires, the easier to shield them and make them capable of handling double or quadruple the clock speed of the motherboard. Figure 7.8 shows an AT and an ATX motherboard—note the radical differences in placement of internal connections.

Just as the original AT generated the Baby AT, ATX has spawned smaller versions. The **microATX** motherboard (Figure 7.9) floats in at a svelte 9.6 by 9.6 inches or about 30 percent smaller than standard ATX, yet still uses the standard ATX connections. A microATX motherboard fits into

Cross Check

High-speed CPUs and RAM

With the newly shortened wire lengths between CPU, Northbridge, and RAM, manufacturers could crank up at least that part of the motherboard speed. CPU and RAM manufacturers quickly took advantage of the new speed potential. Refer to Chapters 3 and 4, on "Microprocessors" and "RAM," respectively, and see if you can answer these questions.

1. What CPUs can take advantage of such speed increases?
2. What type(s) of RAM can you put in those same systems to optimize the flow of data to the CPU?

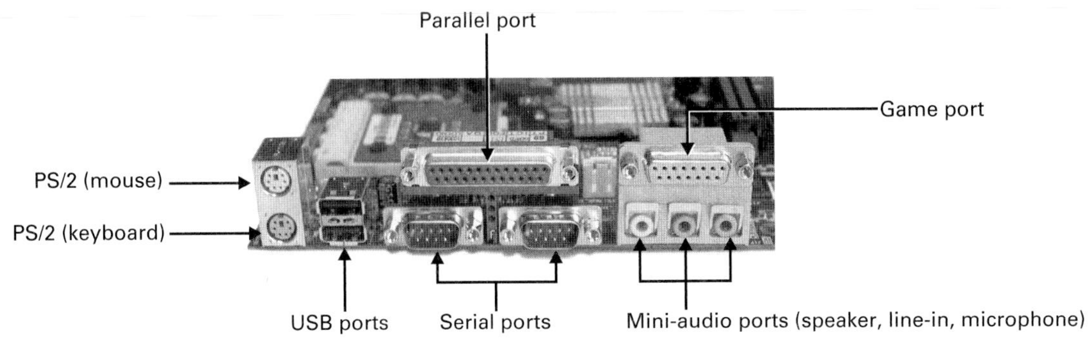

• **Figure 7.7** ATX ports

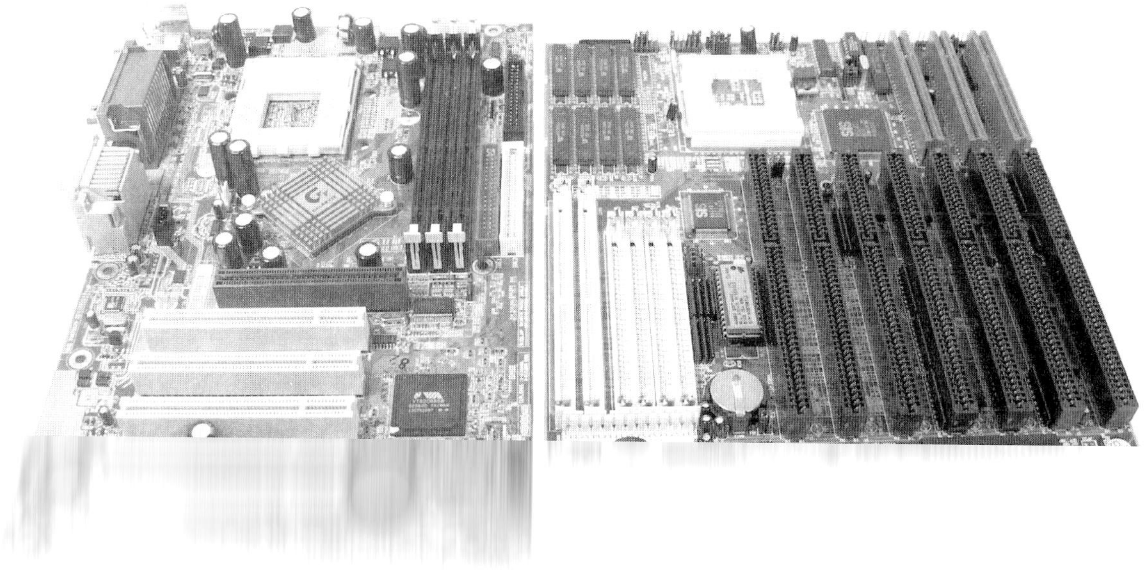

a standard ATX case or in the much smaller microATX cases (Figure 7.10). Note that not all microATX motherboards have the same physical size. You'll sometimes see microATX motherboards referred to with the Greek symbol for micro, as in μATX.

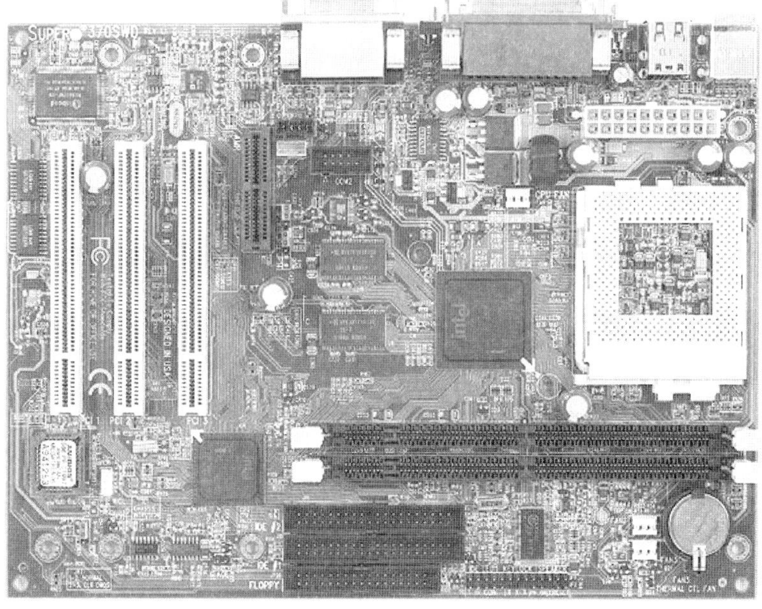

• **Figure 7.9** A microATX motherboard

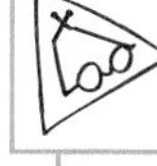

Tech Tip

Soft Power

ATX motherboards use a feature called **soft power**. *This means that they can use software to turn the PC on and off. The physical manifestation of soft power is the power switch. Instead of the thick power cord used in AT systems, an ATX power switch is little more than a pair of small wires leading to the motherboard. We will delve into this in more detail in Chapter 10.*

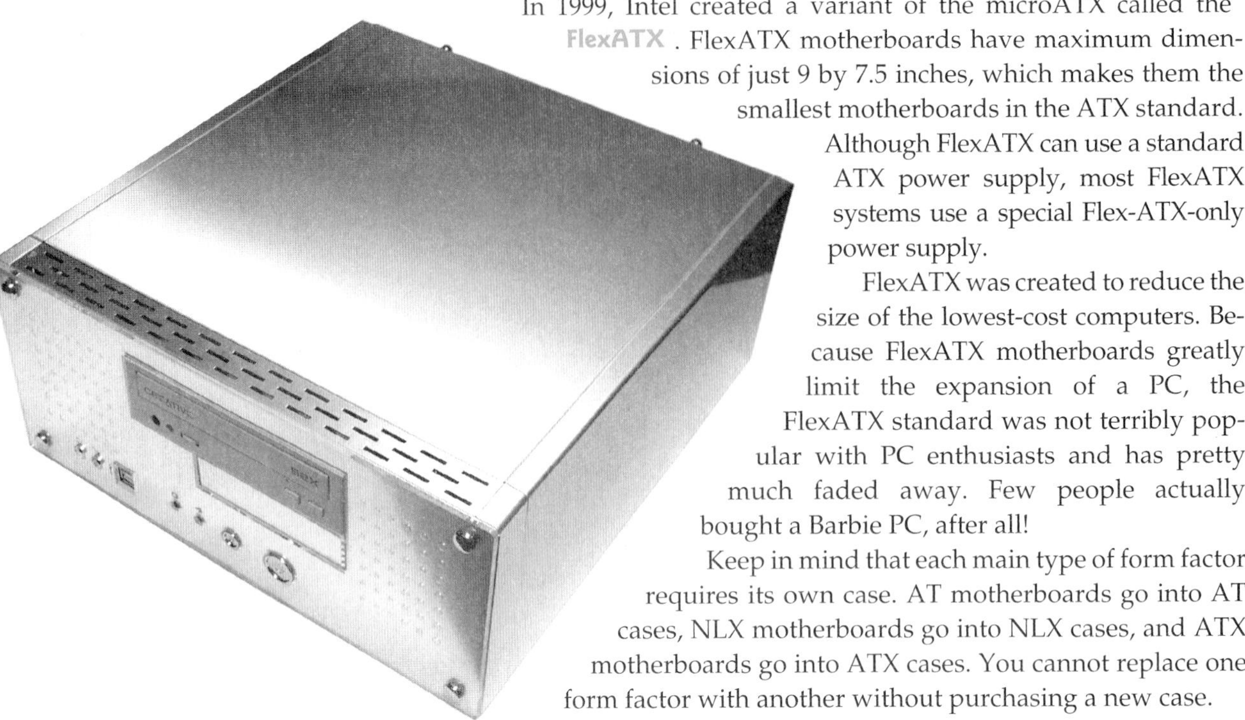

In 1999, Intel created a variant of the microATX called the **FlexATX**. FlexATX motherboards have maximum dimensions of just 9 by 7.5 inches, which makes them the smallest motherboards in the ATX standard. Although FlexATX can use a standard ATX power supply, most FlexATX systems use a special Flex-ATX-only power supply.

FlexATX was created to reduce the size of the lowest-cost computers. Because FlexATX motherboards greatly limit the expansion of a PC, the FlexATX standard was not terribly popular with PC enthusiasts and has pretty much faded away. Few people actually bought a Barbie PC, after all!

Keep in mind that each main type of form factor requires its own case. AT motherboards go into AT cases, NLX motherboards go into NLX cases, and ATX motherboards go into ATX cases. You cannot replace one form factor with another without purchasing a new case.

• **Figure 7.10** A microATX case

Proprietary Motherboards

Several major PC makers, including Hewlett-Packard and Sony, make motherboards that work only with their cases. These *proprietary* motherboards enable these companies to create systems that stand out from the generic ones and, not coincidently, push you to get service and upgrades from their authorized dealers. Some of the features you'll see in proprietary systems are riser boards like you see with the NLX form factor—part of a motherboard separate from the main one, but connected by a cable of some sort—and unique power connections. If you work on one of these systems, keep in mind that all PCs function similarly, regardless of how they look. You might not be able to figure out the specific power connection right away, for example, but you know that the proprietary system *needs* power!

You'll find many techs and web sites that use the term *mini-ATX* to refer to motherboards smaller than a full ATX board. The specifications for these small boards use the terms *microATX* and *FlexATX*.

Mattel licensed the Barbie and Hot Wheels franchises to the ill-fated PC maker, Patriot Computers. Patriot built the two systems with FlexATX motherboards, but produced few of them before going bankrupt in 2000. You **don't** need to know this for your A+ exams, but it might help in Trivial Pursuit!

Try This!

Motherboard Varieties

Motherboards come in a wide variety of form factors. Go to your local computer store and check out what is on display. Note the different features offered by ATX, microATX, and FlexATX (if any) motherboards.

1. Does the store still stock any AT motherboards?
2. What about NLX or proprietary motherboards?
3. Did the clerk use tech-boy or tech-girl slang and call the motherboards "mobos"? (It's what most of us call them outside of formal textbooks, after all!)

Chipset Varieties

The chipset defines the motherboard in many ways, determining which processor type it can use, the type and capacity of RAM, and what sort of internal and external devices the motherboard will support. As you learned in earlier chapters, the chips in a PC's chipset serve as electronic interfaces through which the CPU, RAM, and input/output devices can interact. Chipsets vary in feature, performance, and stability, so they factor hugely in the purchase or recommendation of a particular motherboard. Good techs know their chipsets!

The latest chipsets handle a ton of built-in components, but many chipsets require additional support chips on the motherboard to provide additional features for the PC. Because the chipset facilitates communication between the CPU and other devices in the system, its component chips

drives, such as hard drives and floppy disk drives. It sits between the expansion slots and the EIDE and FDD controllers on most ATX motherboards and often shows the manufacturer of the chipset, such as NVIDIA Technologies (Figure 7.13).

The **Super I/O chip** handles the plebian chores in the PC that the Southbridge now disdains, such as the exceedingly slow input and output

• **Figure 7.11** Chipset on motherboard

• **Figure 7.12** A VIA Northbridge chip beneath an MSI-branded heat sink

• **Figure 7.13** An nForce2 Southbridge chip on a motherboard

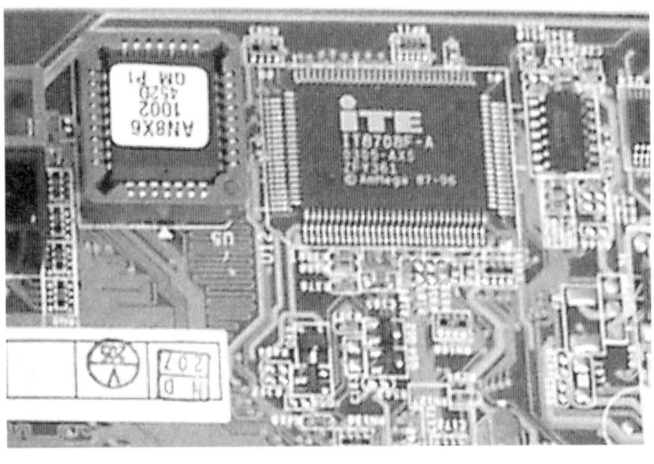

• **Figure 7.14** Super I/O chip on ASUS motherboard

of the floppy drive controller and the serial and parallel ports. You'll find some Super I/O chips handling infrared connections, some keyboard functions, and modems. Figure 7.14 shows a typical Super I/O chip.

Every device in the PC needs BIOS support so the CPU knows how to use it properly, and the chipset is no exception. The more complicated the chipset and the more devices that it supports, the more BIOS routines the CPU needs.

The System ROM chip provides part of the BIOS for the chipset, but only barebones, generic level of support. The chipset still needs support for the rest of the things it can do. So, how do expansion devices get BIOS? Software drivers, of course, and the same holds true for modern chipsets. You have to load the proper drivers for the specific OS running to support all the features of today's chipsets.

Without software drivers, you'll never create a stable, fully functional PC, so you must load the proper chipset drivers. All motherboards ship with a CD-ROM disc with drivers, support programs, and extra special goodies such as anti-virus software (Figure 7.15). I'm half expecting to see a copy of AOL in my next motherboard box!

• **Figure 7.15** Driver disc for ASUS motherboard

Six companies produce the vast majority of PC chipsets—Intel, VIA, AMD, SiS, Ali, and NVIDIA—and motherboard manufacturers incorporate the chips into motherboards that match the feature set of the chipset. Some of the companies produce chipsets designed for both Intel and AMD CPUs, while others choose one or the other company to support. Intel dominated the chipset market for many years, but VIA continues to erode Intel's market segment share, particularly because VIA produces chipsets for both Intel and AMD CPUs. Although known more for their excellent video processors, NVIDIA also makes the best chipset for AMD processors as of this writing, but VIA will undoubtedly challenge that position.

Try This!

VIA Makes What?

The giant Taiwan-based VIA Technologies produces many chips for many different markets and competes directly with Intel on several levels. Some of these might surprise you. Try this: go to VIA's web site (www.via.com.tw) and see if you can answer the following questions.

1. VIA chipsets support which CPUs?
2. What technological innovations does VIA push? What about form factors?
3. Does VIA produce processing chips of the non-chipset variety, such as for video, sound, or general computing? What are they called? Write them down!

Chipset makers don't always use the terms Northbridge and Southbridge, but tend more toward rather longer, more descriptive titles. Intel's 875P chipset for the Pentium 4 processor, for example, is composed of two chips: the 82875P **Memory Controller Hub (MCH)** —that's the Northbridge—and the **I/O Controller Hub (ICH5)** —the Southbridge. The AMD-760 chipset, in contrast calls its Northbridge the AMD-761 *system controller*; the Southbridge is the AMD-766 *peripheral bus controller*. Figure 7.16 shows a schematic with typical chipset chores for the VIA KT400A chipset.

It would be impossible to provide an inclusive chipset chart here that wouldn't be obsolete by the time you pick this book up off the shelf at your local tech pub (doesn't everybody have one of those?), but Table 7.1 gives you an idea of what to look for as you research motherboards for recommendations and purchases.

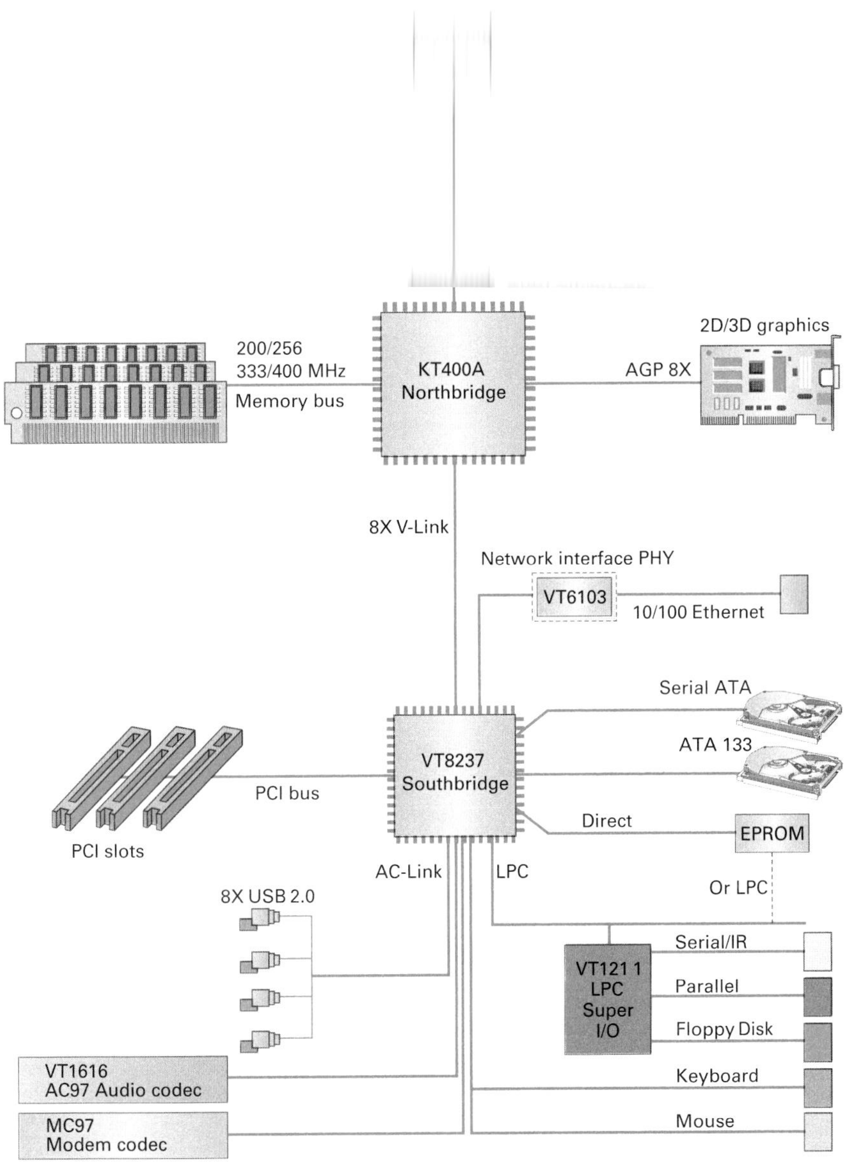

• **Figure 7.16** Schematic for VIA KT400A chipset

Table 7.1 Chipset Comparison Chart

Chipset	Northbridge	Southbridge	CPU	FSB	RAM	AGP	HDD	USB	FireWire
Intel 875P	82875P MCH	82801EB ICH5 or 82801ER ICH5R	.13 micron 478-pin Pentium 4	400, 533, 800	DDR SDRAM up to 4 GB; Dual Channel DDR266, DDR333, DDR400	v3.0 up to 8X	1 X ATA100; 2 x SATA; SATA RAID (R version)	8x USB 2.0	No
AMD 760	AMD-761	AMD-766	Athlon, Duron	200, 266	DDR SDRAM up to 4GB DDR200, DDR266	v.2.0 up to 4X	2x ATA100	USB 1.1	No
NVIDIA nForce2	SPP IGP	MCP2-T MCP2-D	Socket A	200, 266, 333, 400	DDR SDRAM Dual Channel DDR266, DDR333, DDR400	v3.0 up to 8X	2x ATA100	6x USB 2.0	Yes
VIA Apollo K8T800	VT8385	VT8237	AMD Opteron	800	DDR SDRAM 4.0 GB DDR266, DDR333	v3.0 up to 8X	2x ATA 2x SATA	8x USB 2.0	No
VIA KT400A	VT8377A	VT8237 VT8235CE	Socket A	200, 266, 333, 400	DDR SDRAM 4.0 GB DDR266, DDR333, DDR400	v3.0 up to 8X	2x ATA133	8x for VT8237 6x for VT8235CE	No
SiS648FX	SiS648FX	SiS963L	478-pin Pentium 4	400, 533, 800	DDR SDRAM 3.0 GB DDR266, DDR333, DDR400	v3.0 up to 8X	2x ATA133	6x USB 2.0	No
SiS748	SiS748	SiS963L	Socket A	200, 266, 333, 400	DDR SDRAM 3.0 GB DDR266, DDR333, DDR400	v3.0 up to 8X	2x ATA133	6x USB 2.0	No
SiSR658	SiSR658	SiS963	478-pin Pentium 4	400, 533	PC1066 RDRAM 4.0 GB (4 RIMMs)	v3.0 up to 8X	2x ATA133	6x USB 2.0	Yes
SiS755	SiS755	SiS963L	AMD Athlon 64		DDR SDRAM 4.0 GB DDR266, DDR333	v3.0 up to 8X	2x ATA133	6x USB 2.0	No
Ali MAGiK 1	M1647	M1535D+	Socket A	200, 266	DDR SDRAM 3.0 GB DDR266 SDR100 SDR133	V2.0 up to 4x	2x ATA133	USB 1.1	No
Ali	M1681	M1563	478-pin Pentium 4		DDR SDRAM DDR266, DDR333, DDR400 SDR100 SDR133	v3.0 up to 8X	2x ATA133	USB 2.0	No
Ali	M1687	M1563	AMD K8	400, 800, 1200, 1600	DDR SDRAM 4.0 GB DDR266, DDR333	v3.0 up to 8X	2x ATA133	6x USB 2.0	No
Ali ALADDi N-P4	M1671	M1535D+	478-pin Pentium 4	400	DDR SDRAM DDR266, DDR333 SDR100, SDR133	V2.0 up to 4x	2x ATA133	6x USB 1.1	No

Functions, Features, and Expandability

The chipset determines the initial built-in device support for a motherboard, and certainly the form factor dictates the maximum number and variety of connections—size does matter in some ways, after all—but manufacturers can and do add several other support chips on a motherboard to include more devices. The devices supported by the extra support chips include both the cutting edge and the fading edge of technology. Even two seemingly similar motherboards could represent opposite ends of the technology spectrum and good techs know how to tell the difference.

Intel began pushing for legacy-free motherboards in 1999—the *PC99* standard. Chipset manufacturers heeded the call and the latest chipsets from VIA, NVIDIA, and others have dropped support for ISA slots, serial and parallel ports, infrared, PS/2 ports, and floppy drives. A quick tour of a [illegible]

Both the Abit NV7-133R and the Gigabyte GA-7VAXP support AMD Athlon XP processors, DDR SDRAM, and USB 2.0, and both have five PCI slots. The former you could get in the bargain bin for $60, but the latter would set you back over twice that much. A look under the hood reveals all.

The Abit board uses an aging NVIDIA nForce chipset with an added VIA VT6202 chip for USB 2.0 support and other chips for legacy I/O. It tops out at an Athlon XP 2000+ processor and 1.5 GB of RAM. The Gigabyte board, in contrast, uses the VIA KT400 chipset with built-in USB 2.0 support. It handles all Athlon XP processors—over 2 GHz at this writing—and 3 GB of RAM. Plus it offers FireWire through a support chip—a VIA VT6306, in case you're curious—and legacy device support with a Super I/O chip. Both motherboards seem similar on the surface, but represent different ages of technology. But let's add a twist.

Compare both of the full-size ATX motherboards above with the Chaintech 7NIF2 microATX motherboard. The diminutive Chaintech board only has three PCI slots, but sports an nForce2 chipset that supports 3 GB of RAM, AGP 8.x, and FireWire. Plus the motherboard has decent gamer-class video built into the chipset and legacy devices supported by a Super I/O chip as well.

A+ technicians know chipsets and current technology so they can rate a variety of motherboards and make good recommendations to clients. All three boards offer good features and upgradeability, but represent different levels and age of technology supported.

Upgrading and Installing Motherboards

To most techs, the concept of adding or replacing a motherboard can be extremely intimidating. It really shouldn't be; motherboard installation is a common and necessary part of PC repair. It is inexpensive and easy, although it can sometimes be a little tedious and messy due to the large number of parts involved. This section covers the process of installation and replacement and will show you some of the tricks that make this necessary process easy to handle.

Choosing the Motherboard and Case

Choosing a motherboard and case can prove quite a challenge for a tech, whether new or old. You first have to figure out the type of motherboard you want, such as AMD- or Intel-based. Then you need to think about the form factor, which of course influences the type of case you'll need. Third, how rich in features is the motherboard and how tough is it to configure? You've got to read the motherboard manual to find out! Finally, you need to select the case that matches your space needs, budget, and form factor. Let's look at each step in a little more detail.

First, determine what motherboard you need. What CPU are you using? Will the motherboard work with that CPU? Because most of us buy the CPU and the motherboard at the same time, make the seller guarantee that the CPU will work with the motherboard. If you can, choose a motherboard that works with much higher speeds than the CPU you can afford, that way you can upgrade later. How much RAM do you intend to install? Are extra RAM sockets available for future upgrades?

A number of excellent motherboard manufacturers are available today. Some of the more popular brands are Tyan, Asus, Shuttle, Abit, and Gigabyte. Your supplier may also have some lesser-known but perfectly acceptable brands of motherboards. As long as the supplier has an easy return policy, it's perfectly fine to try one of these.

Second, do not worry about the size of the motherboard so much as the form factor. Virtually any motherboard will fit into any case made today. Usually, a quick visual inspection will be sufficient to see if it will fit. Keep form factor with form factor—AT motherboards for AT boxes and ATX motherboards with ATX boxes.

Third, all motherboards come with a technical manual, better known as the **motherboard book**. You must have this book! This book is your only source for all of the critical information about the motherboard. For example, if you have an onboard battery and that battery decides to die, where would you install a replacement external battery? Where do you plug in the speaker? Even if you let someone else install the motherboard, insist on the motherboard book; you will need it.

Fourth, pick your case carefully. Cases come in five basic sizes: slimline, desktop, mini-tower, mid-tower, and tower. Slimline and desktop models generally sit on the desk, beneath the monitor. The various tower cases usually occupy a bit of floor space next to the desk. The mini-tower and mid-tower cases are the most popular choices. Make sure you get a case that will fit your motherboard—many microATX and all FlexATX cases are too small for a regular ATX motherboard. A quick test fit before you buy saves a lot of return trips to the supplier. Cases come with many different options, but two more common options point to a better case. One option is a removable face (Figure 7.17)—many cheaper cases will screw the face into the metal frame using wood screws. A removable face makes disassembly much easier.

Try This!

Building a Recommendation

Family, friends, and potential clients often solicit the advice of a tech

advantage of new technology. What's the minimum system needed to run tomorrow's action games? What do you need to make multimedia sing? Does the motherboard need to have FireWire and USB 2.0 built in to accommodate digital video and better printers?

2. How much of the current system does the upgrader want to save? Upgrading a motherboard can very quickly turn into a complete system rebuild. How old is the case? If it's an AT case, you pretty much need to look at a full computer replacement, but if it's a generic ATX case, you can usually save that much. You'll most likely want to replace the CPU, so your first decision is AMD vs. Intel. The former gives you more bang for the buck, but the latter offers peace of mind for non-techs. What about RAM? Do you stick with the SDRAM currently in the PC and go for a lower-end board that supports the older technology, or buy a mainstream board that uses DDR SDRAM? Will the video card in the system work with the newer AGP slot that the motherboard sports?
3. Once you've gathered information on motivation and assessed the current PC of the upgrader, it's time to get down to business: field trip time! This is a great excuse to get to the computer store and check out the latest motherboards and gadgets to spend money on. Don't forget to jot down notes and prices while you're there! By the end of the field trip, you should have the information to give the upgrader an honest assessment of what an upgrade will entail, at least in monetary terms. Be honest and you won't get in trouble!

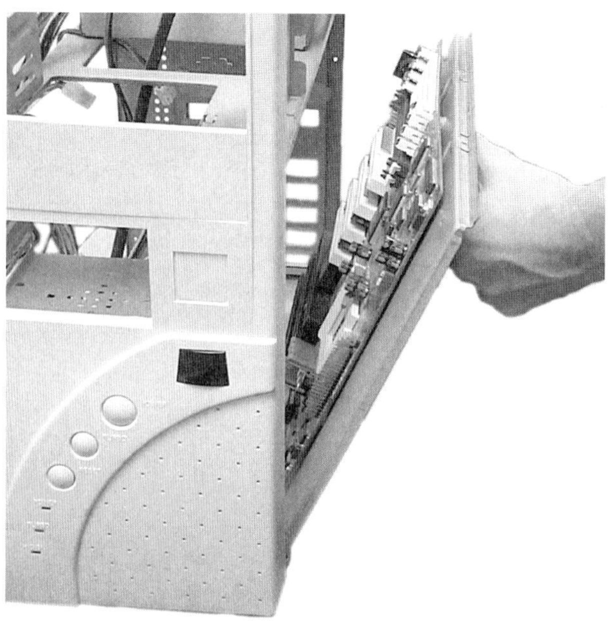

• **Figure 7.18** Motherboard tray

Watch out for ESD here! Remember that it's very easy to damage or destroy a CPU and RAM with a little electrostatic discharge. It's also fairly easy to damage the motherboard with ESD. Wear your anti-static wrist strap!

Refer to Chapter 8 for the quirks of working with AT and ATX power supplies, especially the latter's soft power feature. You can easily fry components by plugging them in with the power supply attached and supplied with electricity from the wall socket, even if the system is turned off!

Another option is a detachable motherboard mount. Clearly, the motherboard will have to be attached to the case in some fashion. In better cases, this is handled by a removable tray or plate (Figure 7.18). This enables you to attach the motherboard to the case separately, saving you from the difficult chore of sticking your arms into the case to turn screws.

Power supplies often come with the case. Watch out for "really good deal" cases because that invariably points to a cheap or missing power supply. You also need to verify that the power supply has sufficient wattage. This issue is better handled in Chapter 8.

Installing the Motherboard

If you're replacing a motherboard, first remove the old motherboard. Begin by removing all the cards. Also remove anything else that might impede removal or installation of the motherboard, such as hard or floppy drives. Keep track of your screws—the best idea is to return the screws to their mounting holes temporarily, at least until you can reinstall the parts. Sometimes even the power supply has to be removed temporarily to enable access to the motherboard. Document the position of the little wires for the speaker, power switch, and reset button in case you need to reinstall them.

Unscrew the motherboard. *It will not simply lift out.* The motherboard mounts to the case via small connectors called **standouts** that slide into keyed slots or screw into the bottom of the case. Screws then go into the standouts to hold the motherboard in place. If the CPU or RAM has been removed, be sure to replace them before installing the new motherboard.

When you insert the new motherboard, do not assume that you will put the screws and standouts in the same place as they were in your old motherboard. When it comes to the placement of screws and standouts, only one rule applies: anywhere it fits. Do not be afraid to be a little tough here! Installing motherboards can be a wiggling, twisting, knuckle-scraping process.

Once you get the motherboard mounted in the case with the CPU and RAM properly installed, it's time to insert the power connections and test it. A POST card can be helpful with the system test because you won't have to add the speaker, a video card, monitor, and keyboard to verify that the system is booting. If you have a POST card, start the system, and watch to see if the POST takes place—you should see a number of POST codes before the POST stops. If you don't have a POST card, install a keyboard, video card, and monitor. Boot the system and see if the BIOS information shows up on the screen. If it does, you're probably okay. If it doesn't, it's time to refer to the

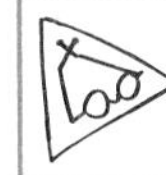

Tech Tip

Before the Case

A lot of techs install the CPU, CPU fan, and RAM into the motherboard before installing the motherboard into the case. This helps in several ways, especially with a new system. First, you want to make certain that the CPU and RAM work well with the motherboard and with each other—without that, you have no hope of setting up a stable system. Second, installing these compo-

Finally, on motherboards that require you to set jumpers or switches, it's much easier to read the tiny information stenciled on the PCB before you add the shadows from the case! Set any jumpers and switches for the specific CPU according to information from the motherboard manual.

- Soft power
- Reset button
- Speaker
- Hard drive activity LED
- Power LED

These wires have specific pin connections to the motherboard. Although you can refer to the motherboard book for their location, usually a quick inspection of the motherboard will suffice for an experienced tech (Figure 7.19).

A few rules need to be followed when installing these wires. First, the lights are LEDs not light bulbs—they have a positive and negative side. If they don't work one way, turn the connector around and try the other. Second, when in doubt, guess. Incorrect installation will not result in damage to the computer. The device that was incorrectly wired simply will not work. Refer to the motherboard book for the correct installation. The third and last rule is that with the exception of the soft power switch on an ATX system, you do not need any of these wires for the computer to run! Many techs often simply ignore these wires, although, this would not be something I'd do to any system but my own!

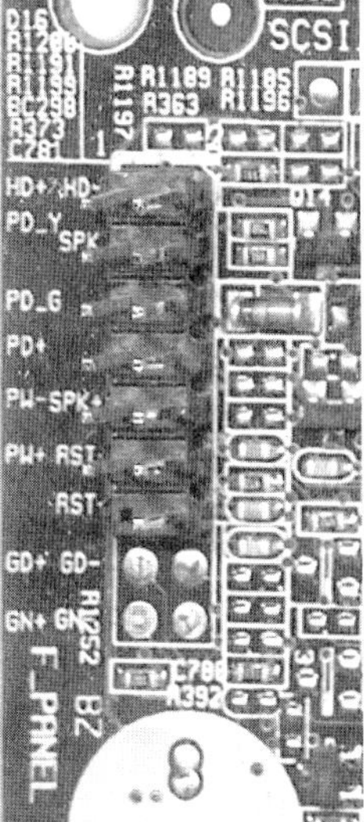

• **Figure 7.19** Motherboard wire connections labeled on the motherboard

• **Figure 7.20** Sample of case wires

No hard and fast rule exists for determining the function of each wire. Often the function of each wire is printed on the connector (Figure 7.20). If not, track each wire to the LED or switch to determine its function.

■ Troubleshooting Motherboards

Motherboards fail. Not often, but motherboards and motherboard components can die from many causes: time, dust, cat hair, or simply slight manufacturing defects made worse by the millions of amps of current sluicing through the motherboard traces. Installing cards, electrostatic discharge, flexing the motherboard one time too many when swapping out RAM or drives—any of these factors can cause a motherboard to fail. The motherboard is a hard-working, often abused component of the PC! Unfortunately for the common tech, troubleshooting a motherboard problem can be very difficult and time consuming. Let's wrap this chapter with a look at symptoms of a failing motherboard, techniques for troubleshooting, and the options you have when you discover a motherboard problem.

Symptoms

Motherboard failures commonly fall into three types: catastrophic, component, and ethereal. With a **catastrophic failure**, the PC just won't boot. This sort of problem happens with brand new systems due to manufacturing defects—often called a *burn-in failure*—and to any system that gets a shock of electrostatic discharge. Burn-in failure is uncommon, but usually happens in the first 30 days of use. Swap out the motherboard for a replacement and you should be fine. If you accidentally zap your motherboard when inserting a card or moving wires around, be chagrined. Change your daring ways and wear an anti-static wrist strap!

Component failure happens rarely, but appears as flaky connections between a device and motherboard, or as intermittent problems. A hard drive plugged into a faulty controller on the motherboard, for example, might show up in CMOS autodetect, but be inaccessible in Windows. A serial controller that worked fine for months until a big storm took out the external modem hooked to it, but doesn't work anymore, even with a replacement modem, is another example.

The most common causes of component failure are electrical surges and ESD, although sometimes you simply hit the limits of technology

USB-enabled systems running Windows 98 here at the Total Seminars' HQ yielded quite a few surprises. Some worked just fine, but others *almost* worked. The systems would recognize the devices when we plugged them in, but then stop shortly thereafter. Turns out that a simple BIOS upgrade for the motherboards brought the systems in tune with USB 1.1 and we were off for the friendly Crimson Skies (Figure 7.21).

• **Figure 7.21** A wild dog fight in Microsoft's Crimson Skies

The most difficult of the three types of symptoms to diagnose are those I call *ethereal* symptoms. Stuff just doesn't work all the time. The PC reboots itself. You get blue screens of death in the midst of heavy computing, like right before you smack the villain and rescue the damsel. What can cause such symptoms? If you answered any of the following, you win the prize:

- Faulty component
- Buggy device driver
- Buggy application software
- Slight corruption of the operating system
- Power supply problems

Err... you get the picture.

What a nightmare scenario to troubleshoot! The Way of the Tech knows paths through such perils, though, so let's turn to troubleshooting techniques now.

Techniques

To troubleshoot a potential motherboard failure requires time, patience, and organization. Some problems will certainly be quicker to solve than others. If the hard drive doesn't work as expected, as in the example above, check the settings on the drive. Try a different drive. Try the same drive with a different motherboard to verify that it's a good drive. Like every other troubleshooting technique, all you try to do with motherboard testing is to isolate the problem by eliminating potential factors.

This three-part system—check, replace, verify good component—works for the simpler and the more complicated motherboard problems. You can even apply the same technique to ethereal-type problems that might be anything, but you should add one more verb: *document*. Take notes on the individual components tested so you don't repeat efforts or waste time. Motherboard testing is time-consuming enough without adding inefficiency!

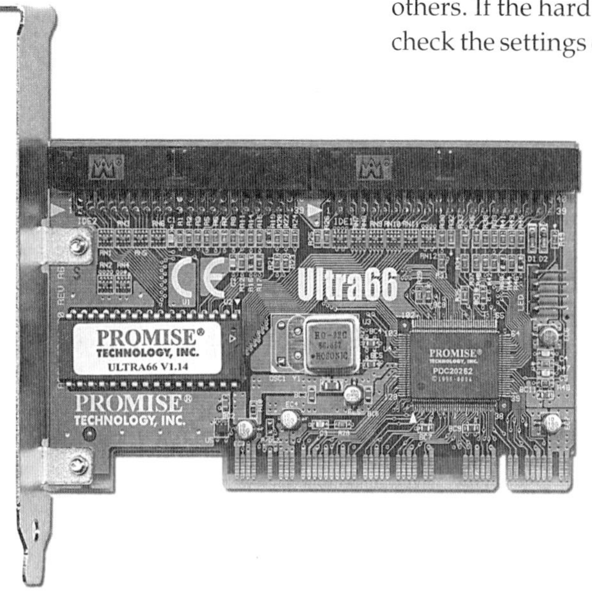

• **Figure 7.22** Promise Technologies PCI hard drive controller card

Options

Once you determine that the motherboard has problems, you have several options for fixing the three types of failures. If you have a catastrophic failure, you must replace the motherboard. Even if it works somewhat, don't mess around. The motherboard should provide bedrock stability for the system. If it's even remotely buggy or problematic, get rid of it!

If you have a component failure, you can often replace the component with an add-on card that will be as good or better than the failed device. Promise Technologies, for example, makes fine hard drive controller cards that can replace one or both hard drive controllers on the motherboard (Figure 7.22).

> If you've lost components due to ESD or a power surge, then you would most likely be better off replacing the motherboard. The damage you *can't* see can definitely sneak up to bite you and create system instability.

If your component failure is more a technology issue rather than physical damage, then you can try upgrading the BIOS on the motherboard. As you'll recall from Chapter 5 on BIOS, every motherboard comes with a small set of code that enables the CPU to communicate properly with the devices built into the motherboard. You can quite readily upgrade this programming by *flashing the BIOS*: running a small command-line program to write new BIOS in the Flash ROM chip. Figure 7.23 shows a couple of typical Flash ROMs. Refer to Chapter 5 for the details on flashing.

Finally, if you have an ethereal, ghost-in-the-machine type of problem that you have finally determined to be motherboard related, you have only a couple of options for fixing the problem. You can flash the BIOS in a desperate attempt to correct whatever it is, which sometimes does work and is less expensive than the other option. Or you can replace the motherboard.

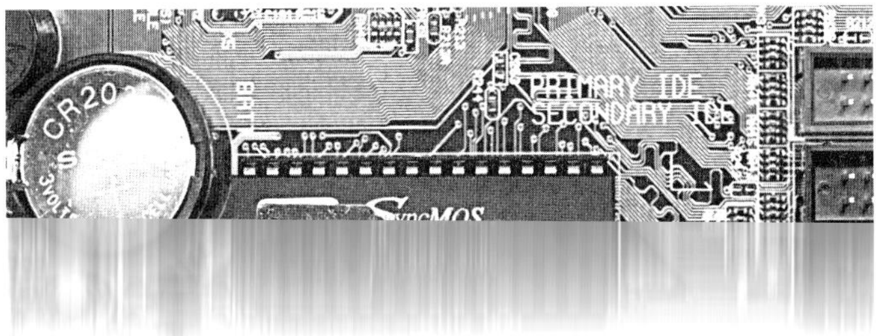

Tech Tip

Limits of BIOS Upgrades

Flashing the BIOS for a motherboard can fix a lot of problems dealing with system stability and provide better implementation of built-in technology. What it cannot do for your system is improve the hardware. If AMD comes out with a new, improved, lower-voltage Athlon XP, for example, and your motherboard cannot scale

Beyond A+

Motherboard manufacturers push the limits with new form factors, both big and small. A few years ago, for example, Intel trotted out the WTX standard for servers, a monster form factor—over twice the size of ATX—designed for multiple processor computing behemoths. On the other end of the spectrum, VIA Technologies is pushing two tiny form factors, ITX and Mini-ITX, weighing in at a whopping 215mm x 191mm and 170mm x 170mm (half the size of a FlexATX motherboard!), respectively. Finally, Shuttle practically reinvented the PC into an entertainment box with its XPC line of systems. Supporting the latest Intel and AMD processors and chipsets, the XPCs use the Shuttle Form Factor (SFF) cases and motherboards. They're so cute that everybody should have one! Figure 7.24 shows one of the very tiny boxes—about the size of a toaster. Because these tiny PCs have all the bells and whistles of their much bigger cousins, they can easily serve as the heart of a home theater or tuck into the corner of a small dorm room.

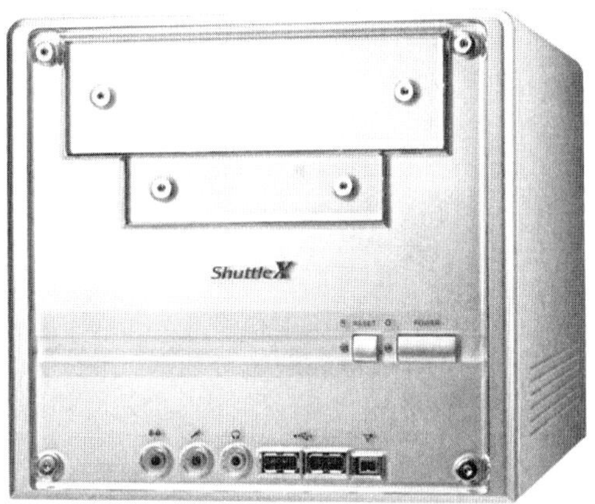

• **Figure 7.24** Shuttle XPC (photo courtesy of Shuttle Computer Group, Inc.)

Chapter 7 Review

Chapter Summary

After reading this chapter and completing the exercises, you should understand the following about the motherboards.

Explain How Motherboards Work

- Every piece of hardware directly or indirectly plugs into the motherboard. Data and commands flow through wires called traces.
- Four characteristics define motherboards: layout (form factor), chipset, expansion slots, and components.
- The layout or the form factor of the motherboard determines the maximum expansion slot limit and the kind of case. The chipset determines the kind of processor, RAM, and other built-in devices the motherboard supports. Built-in components determine the functionality and expandability of the system.

Identify the Types of Motherboards

- Although they are either rectangular or square, motherboards come in a variety of sizes.
- The layout or the way components are positioned on the motherboard is called the form factor. Two basic form factors are AT and ATX.
- The older AT form factor had a large 5-pin keyboard plug and a split P8/P9 power connector. The Baby AT is a smaller AT motherboard. The only external port provided by AT and Baby AT motherboards was a large 5-pin keyboard plug. Other ports were provided through expansion cards or dongles.
- Other form factors have been designed, including the slimline form factor, which came in the LPX and later the NLX designs. The slimline used a special riser card that contained expansion slots that allowed cards to fit horizontally.
- In 1995, the ATX form factor was introduced. Mounted 90 degrees relative to the computer's box, ATX rearranges the power supply, RAM, and other components as well as containing a rear plate that provides access to ports. Because the power flows through the motherboard itself to a pair of small wires that attach to the computer's on/off switch, ATX provides soft power that allows software to turn the PC on and off.
- microATX is a smaller version of the ATX motherboard. One variation of the microATX was the Intel's FlexATX.
- Each kind of form factor requires its own unique case.
- Many manufacturers have designed proprietary motherboards with riser cards and unique power connections.

Explain Chipset Varieties

- The chipset defines the kind of processor and RAM, as well as the internal and external devices that the motherboard will support. Most motherboard chips contain the Northbridge and the Southbridge as well as a Super I/O chip to provide legacy support. The Super I/O chip supports input and output from very slow devices such as the floppy drive and the serial and parallel ports.
- The System BIOS provides generic support for the chipset, but you must load additional chipset drivers for full functionality.
- Six companies produce most PC chipsets—Intel, VIA, AMD, SiS, Ali, and NVIDIA. Some companies design chipsets specifically for Intel processors while others support only AMD CPUs. Some produce chipsets that support both brands of processors. The Intel chipset was the dominant one for years, but VIA is now catching up.
- Many chipset manufacturers have abandoned the terms Northbridge and Southbridge. For example, the Intel 875P chipset uses the term Memory Controller Hub (MCH) for the chip that controls the memory (the Northbridge) and I/O Controller Hub (ICH5) for the chip that performs Southbridge functions. The AMD-760 chipset uses the terms system controller for its Northbridge and peripheral bus controller for its Southbridge.
- The chipset determines the built-in device support for a motherboard. Some manufacturers have dropped support for ISA slots, serial and parallel ports, infrared, PS/2 ports and floppy drives. Others include support for newer technology such as USB 2.0, FireWire, and Serial ATA hard drives.
- The chipset determines the kind of processor and the maximum RAM the motherboard can support. Even if two motherboards look similar, the chipset

is the defining factor, not only for performance, but frequently for price as well. A+ technicians need to know chipsets to be able to recommend motherboards to clients.

Upgrade and Install Motherboards

- The first job is to select a motherboard that will work with the CPU you want to use or are currently using and provide enough RAM sockets for future upgrades.
- The motherboard form factor must match the case you will use. Usually, any ATX form factor board will fit into any ATX case.
- Be sure you get the motherboard book that

[illegible]

- Since the power supply comes with the case, be sure that you will get enough wattage.
- To remove a motherboard, first remove all cards and drives that might impede access to the motherboard. Document wires and anything else necessary for you to be able to reassemble the computer. Keep track of the screws.
- The motherboard mounts to the case by connectors called standouts that slide or screw into the bottom of the case. If you install a new motherboard, you are likely to need to change the position of the standouts since the holes on the new motherboard may not align with those of the old motherboard. You should install standouts and screws anywhere they will fit.
- It is a good idea to install the CPU, the CPU fan, and the RAM into the motherboard before inserting it into the case. This prevents flexing or bending that might damage the motherboard.
- After installing the motherboard in the case, you need to insert the power connector(s) and test it. You may use a POST card if you have one available. If not, install the keyboard, video card, and monitor and check to see if the BIOS information displays on the screen. If so, the board is probably okay. If not, consult the motherboard book.
- Next, connect the wires for the LEDs and buttons on the front of the box. Be aware that these wires have specific pin connections. The motherboard book should explain where to place them. These wires have a positive and a negative side. If you plug them in incorrectly, they simply will not work, but this does not damage the computer. The only wire that has to be plugged in is the soft power switch on the ATX system. Usually, the wires have their function printed on the connector. If not, track the wire to the LED or switch to learn its function.

Troubleshoot Motherboard Problems

- Motherboards fail for a variety of reasons, including dust, manufacturing defects, electrostatic discharge, and flexing.
- There are three types of motherboard failure:

[illegible]

component failure are electrical surges and ESD.

- Ethereal symptoms are the most difficult ones to diagnose. You may get intermittent problems or the computer may reboot or you may get a blue screen of death. These problems may be caused by a faulty component, a buggy device driver or application software, a slightly corrupted operating system, or a faulty power supply.
- Troubleshooting motherboard failure requires time, patience, and organization. A three-part method works for diagnosing many problems: check, replace, verify good component. Be sure also to document or take notes about the components you have tested.
- You have several options for fixing the three types of motherboard failures. With a catastrophic problem, replace the motherboard. With a component failure, you may be able to replace the component with an add-on card. If so, be sure to disable the component on the motherboard through the CMOS setup. You may be able to solve some component problems by flashing the BIOS. Remember that flashing the BIOS may fix problems of system stability or may provide support for newer technology, but BIOS flashing does not change the hardware built into your motherboard.
- Flashing the BIOS may also solve ethereal problems, or you may have to replace the motherboard itself.

Key Terms

AT *(224)*
ATX *(228)*
Baby AT *(224)*
Catastrophic failure *(240)*
Chipset *(223)*
Component failure *(241)*
FlexATX *(230)*
Flexing *(239)*
Form factor *(223)*
I/O Controller Hub (ICH5) *(233)*
Memory Controller Hub (MCH) *(233)*
microATX *(228)*
Motherboard *(222)*
Motherboard book *(236)*
NVIDIA *(232)*
P8/P9 *(224)*
Riser card *(226)*
Slimline *(226)*
Soft power *(229)*
Standouts *(238)*
Super I/O chip *(231)*
Traces *(222)*
VIA *(232)*

Key Term Quiz

Use the Key Terms list to complete the sentences that follow. Not all the terms will be used.

1. Wires on the motherboard that carry data or information are called ___________.
2. A unique feature of the ____________ motherboard is a _______________ that contains expansion slots to allow cards to be inserted horizontally.
3. The older ________ form factor motherboard used the _________ to attach the power.
4. It is a good idea to insert the CPU, the CPU fan, and the memory before you insert the motherboard in the case to prevent ___________ or bending the board.
5. With the 82875P chipset, Intel uses the term _____________ to refer to the chip that functions as the Northbridge.
6. The layout of the motherboard is referred to as the ______________.
7. The newer _______ form factor motherboard includes ________ that allows the operating system to turn the computer on or off.
8. A _________ of the motherboard will usually occur within 30 days and necessitates replacing the motherboard.
9. Before you install a motherboard, you must insert ____________ into the bottom of the case.
10. The ________ form factor includes a rear plate that provides access to ports such as PS/2 keyboard and mouse, serial and parallel port, and USB.

Multiple-Choice Quiz

1. All the following are characteristics of ethereal motherboard failure *except* __________.
   - **A.** Intermittent failures
   - **B.** PC reboots itself
   - **C.** PC will not boot at all
   - **D.** Blue screens of death
2. Which of the following statements is true?
   - **A.** The AT form factor motherboard includes ports and connectors and offers soft power capability.
   - **B.** The ATX form factor motherboard includes only the keyboard port.
   - **C.** The ATX form factor uses a single connector from the power supply.
   - **D.** An ATX form factor motherboard will fit into an AT form factor case.
3. Which of the following statements is true about motherboard chipsets.
   - **A.** You can easily upgrade the motherboard chipset when the new technology demands it.
   - **B.** Some chipsets support only Intel processors or only AMD processors while others may support CPUs manufactured by both companies.

C. If a motherboard has the kind of expansion slots, ports, and CPU socket you need, you do not have to be concerned about the chipset.

D. The System BIOS provides all the drivers and support that a chipset needs.

4. Which of the following is *not* a consideration when buying a case to go with a particular motherboard?

A. Whether you will use an Intel or an AMD CPU

B. The form factor of the motherboard

C. Size of the motherboard and case

D. The wattage of the power supply

C. The third motherboard has two serial ports, a parallel port, a USB port, and a PS/2 mouse port.

D. The fourth motherboard includes USB 2.0, FireWire, and Serial ATA capabilities.

6. Which of the following statements is true about the wires that connect LEDs and buttons from the front of the box to the motherboard?

A. The wires have a positive and a negative side.

B. If you install the wires improperly, you may damage the computer.

C. With an ATX motherboard, you can boot the computer without plugging in any of these wires.

D. For easier installation, the connectors for the wires will always have their functions printed on them.

7. The form factor of the motherboard determines all of the following *except* __________.

A. The kind of case you can use

B. The number of expansion slots

C. The kind of processor you can use

D. The way the power supply attaches to the on/off switch

8. The most common causes of component failure are ______________.

A. Manufacturing defects

B. Corrupted operating systems

C. Electrical surges and ESD

D. Power supply problems

9. Most modern chipsets include all of the following chips *except* ____________.

A. FireWire

B. Northbridge

C. Southbridge

D. Super I/O

10. The chipset determines all of the following

11. The four characteristics that define modern motherboards are __________________.

A. Chipset, CPU socket, RAM sockets, and expansion slots

B. Expansion slots, form factor, power connector, and BIOS

C. USB, FireWire, PS/2 keyboard port, and chipset

D. Layout, chipset, expansion slots, and components

12. The ATX form factor offers all the following advantages *except* _____________.

A. Better performance by placing RAM closer to the Northbridge and CPU

B. Better airflow by repositioning the power supply connector

C. Inclusion of built-in ports and greater flexibility for technology changes

D. More flexibility by including connectors for both the 5-pin AT keyboard and the PS/2 keyboard

13. Which of the following identify Slimline AT motherboard form factors?

A. NLX and LPX

B. Flex and NLX

C. LPX and Flex

D. Micro and Flex

14. All the following may cause ethereal motherboard failure *except* ______________.

A. Buggy device driver

B. Faulty component

C. Corrupted operating system

D. ESD

15. If you have a motherboard failure, all of the following *except* ______________ may solve the problem.

A. Replacing the motherboard

B. Replacing a failed component with an add-on card

C. Upgrading the operating system

D. Flashing the BIOS

Essay Quiz

1. This chapter talks about motherboards made in layers that contain the wires or traces. If necessary, find an Internet site that talks about the motherboard manufacturing process. Why do you think motherboards are made in layers? What advantages do the layers provide?

2. Some people believe that the motherboard chipset is an even more important decision than the kind of processor. Do you agree or disagree and why?

3. Prepare a PowerPoint presentation or write a paper that would help your classmates select and replace a bad motherboard. Be sure to walk through all the necessary steps.

   - Determine what motherboard you need and make sure your CPU will work with the motherboard.
   - Make sure that the motherboard form factor matches the case and will fit inside the box.
   - Consult the motherboard book to configure any jumpers or dip switches necessary for your particular CPU.
   - Be sure you can return the motherboard if it does not match your CPU or case.
   - After unplugging the computer, remove any cards or drives that prevent you from accessing the motherboard.
   - Remove the power connector from the old motherboard.
   - Unscrew the old motherboard and lift it out.
   - Check to see if you need to move any of the standouts for the new motherboard to fit into the case. Use as many standouts as your new motherboard will support.
   - If you are going to use the same CPU or RAM, remove it from the old motherboard and place it into the new one. If you have a new CPU and new RAM, insert it into the new motherboard. Also place the CPU fan into position before you attempt to insert the motherboard into the case.
   - Plug in the wires for the LEDs and buttons on the front of the box, making sure that you align the positive and negative connections as directed in the motherboard book.
   - Test the motherboard with either a POST card or by installing a keyboard, video card, and monitor.
   - Replace the cards, drives, and other components.
   - Check the CMOS setup for anything you may need to configure.

4. Examine all the ports and connectors on the back of your computer. With the computer turned off, you may disconnect the cables from the ports. (If necessary, document where and how the cables are connected so you can replace them correctly.) Determine the kinds of ports that are built-in and those that are provided by expansion cards. From this information alone, ascertain whether your motherboard is an AT or an ATX form factor. List all the ports and connectors, their sources (either from the motherboard or from an expansion card), and the form factor of the motherboard.

5. Your neighbors Dora and Jim just learned that you're studying computer hardware. They feels that their computer is slightly out of date and they want to upgrade the processor only without replacing the motherboard. Prepare a list of at

least five questions that you should ask them before you know what CPU they can choose or whether it is feasible to upgrade their system.

- What is the manufacturer and model of your current CPU?
- What kind of CPU socket or slot does your motherboard have?
- Who is the manufacturer and what is the model of your motherboard?
- What chipset does your motherboard use?
- How much RAM does your computer currently have?
- Why do you want to upgrade your CPU?
- Are you sure you want to upgrade only the CPU or are you willing to upgrade the motherboard and the RAM as well?

Lab Projects

Consult your motherboard book or use one that your instructor provides. Then write a paragraph about your motherboard that includes answers to the following questions:

- What make and model is the motherboard?
- What chipset does it use?
- What kind of RAM slots does it contain?
- What kinds of expansion slots does your motherboard have and how many of each kind does it have?

jumpers or dip switches control?

- The motherboard book probably contains an illustration of the way that the motherboard components are laid out. By examining this illustration, determine what form factor your motherboard uses.
- Does your motherboard have any unusual or proprietary features?

• Lab Project 7.2

You know now how important the motherboard chipset is in determining the kind of CPU and RAM that can be installed in the computer. You also know that motherboards that may look similar may have very different features and prices. Imagine that you are going to build a new computer by ordering the components. Since price is not a problem, you will want to select the best and most powerful components. On the Internet, search such sites as www.intel.com or www.amd.com along with sites such as www.newegg.com to select a motherboard and a particular chipset. Then select a compatible CPU and RAM. Explain where you found the information about the components, what brands/models you selected, and how much each will cost.

Now imagine that your budget will not allow you to buy these components at this time. In fact, you've decided that you can afford only 75 percent of the cost of these components. What will you do to save money? Will you change the motherboard and the chipset or will you use a less powerful CPU with a smaller amount of RAM? Consider what you can upgrade at a later time when you have more available cash. Again, search the Internet and select components that would be satisfactory but are not the latest and the greatest. Be sure that the CPU and RAM you select are indeed compatible with your motherboard and chipset. What did you select and how much will it cost you?

chapter 8

Power Supplies

"I meant to kill a turkey, and instead, I nearly killed a goose."

—Benjamin Franklin on shocking himself unconscious while trying to kill a turkey with electricity

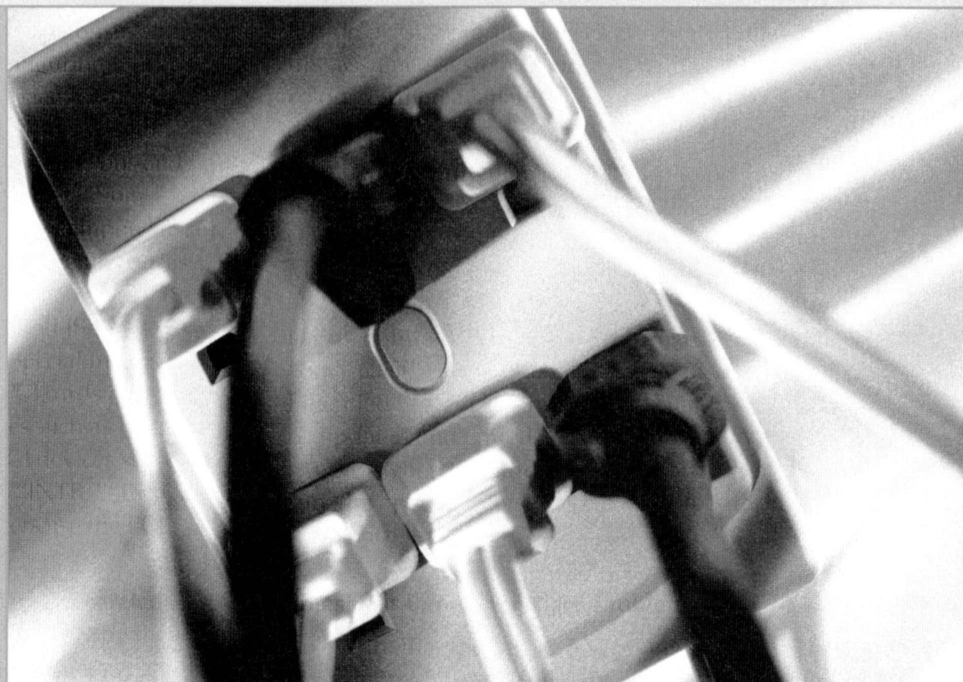

In this chapter, you will learn how to

- **Explain the basics of electricity**
- **Provide proper power and cooling to the PC**
- **Troubleshoot electrical problems**

Let me begin by stating the obvious: The PC requires electricity in order to do anything at all. It's wonderful to say to a new tech that you plug the PC into the wall socket and then push the power button on the case, but a true tech knows the ins and outs of powering the PC.

Powering the PC requires a single box—the power supply—that takes electricity from the wall socket and transforms it into electricity to run the motherboard and other internal components. Figure 8.1 shows a typical power supply inside a case. All the wires dangling out of it connect to the motherboard and peripherals.

Removal and installation of power supplies is equally simple. The typical power supply connects to the PC with four standard computer screws, mounted in the back of the case (Figure 8.2). Unscrew the four screws and the power supply lifts out easily (Figure 8.3).

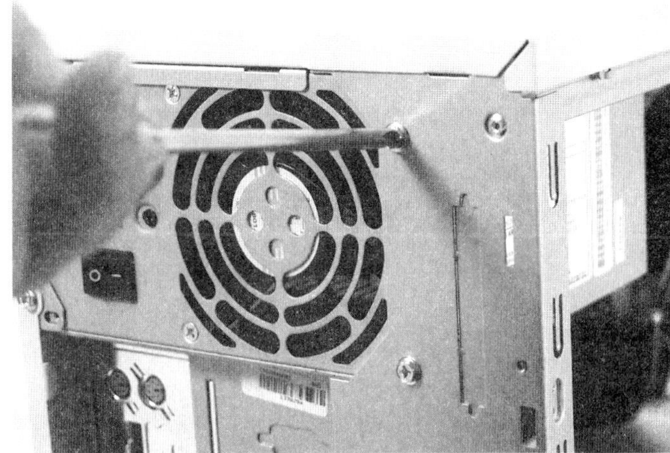

loss—all things most computer users would rather avoid! Good techs therefore know an awful lot about powering the PC, from understanding the basic principles of electricity to knowing the many variations of PC power supplies. Plus, you need to know how to recognize power problems and implement the proper solutions. Too many techs fall into the "just plug it in" camp and never learn how to deal with power, much to their clients' unhappiness.

• **Figure 8.3** Tech removing power supply from system unit

Historical/Conceptual

Understanding Electricity

Electricity is simply a flow of negatively charged particles, called electrons, through matter. All matter enables the flow of electrons to some extent. Materials in which electrons move freely are called *conductors*. As you can probably guess, metallic wire is a very good conductor. The terms electrons and conductors and all the other electrical jargon you're about to read often causes techs to tune out quickly. Most people accept electricity as something that exists and does cool stuff, but give up trying to understand how it works. But if you understand something concrete, such as how water gets to your house, you already understand the basic principles of electricity as well. Here's how it works.

Water comes from the ground, through wells, aquifers, rivers, and so forth. In a typical city, water comes to you through pipes from the water supply company that took it from the ground. What do you pay for when you pay your water bill each month? You pay for the water you use, certainly,

Some questions on the A+ Core Hardware exam could refer to a power supply as a *PSU*, for power supply unit. A power supply also falls into the category of field replaceable unit (FRU), which refers to the typical parts a tech should carry, like RAM and a floppy disk drive.

but you also pay for the surety that when you turn the spigot, water will flow at a more or less constant rate. The water sits in the pipes under pressure from the water company, waiting for you to turn the spigot. You pay for reliability, water pressure, and water used.

Electricity works essentially the same way as water. Electrons come from the ground, gathered or generated by the electricity company and then pushed to your house under pressure through wires. Just like water, the electricity sits in the wires, waiting for you to plug something into the wall socket, at which time it'll flow at a more or less constant rate. You plug a lamp into an electrical outlet and flip the switch, electricity flows, and you have light. You pay for reliability, electrical pressure, and electricity used.

The pressure of the electrons in the wire is called *voltage* and is measured in units called **volts** (V). The amount of electrons moving past a certain point on a wire is called the *current* or *amperage,* which is measured in units called **amperes** (amps or A). The amount of amps and volts needed by a particular device to function is expressed as how much **wattage** (watts or W) that device needs. The correlation between the three is very simple math: VA = W. We'll go into much more detail on wattage when we go into the PC a little later in this chapter.

An electrical outlet must have a ground wire to be suitable for PC use!

Wires of all sorts—whether copper, tin, gold, or platinum—resist the flow of electrons, just like water pipes have a certain amount of friction that resists the flow of water. Resistance to the flow of electrons is measured in **ohms** (Ω).

- Pressure = Voltage (V)
- Volume flowing = Amperes (A)
- Work = Wattage (W)
- Resistance = Ohms (Ω)

Wires can only handle so much electricity at a time. If you push too much through, the wire will break, much like an overloaded water pipe will burst. All wires have an amperage rating, such as 10 A. If you push 12 amps through a 10-amp wire, the wire will break and electrons will spill out if they have anything to touch, causing an electrical wet spot—also known as an electrical fire!—as they seek a way to return into the ground. Not a good thing!

Fuses and ground wires provide the basic protection from accidental overflow. A fuse is a glass vacuum tube with a wire inside rated at a certain amperage. If you push too much through the fuse, the wire inside will break, but it's no big deal, because the absence of oxygen in the tube prevents a fire from starting. You replace the fuse to reestablish the circuit and electricity will flow once more through the wires. A ground wire provides a path of least resistance for electrons to flow back to ground in case of an accidental overflow.

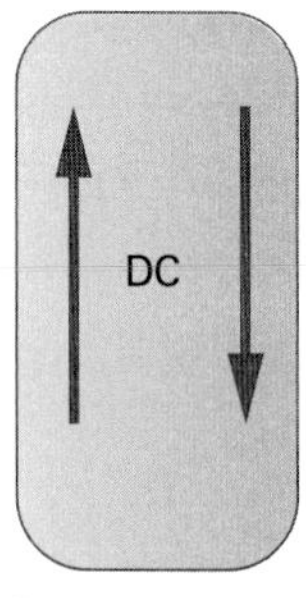

Constant voltage in one direction

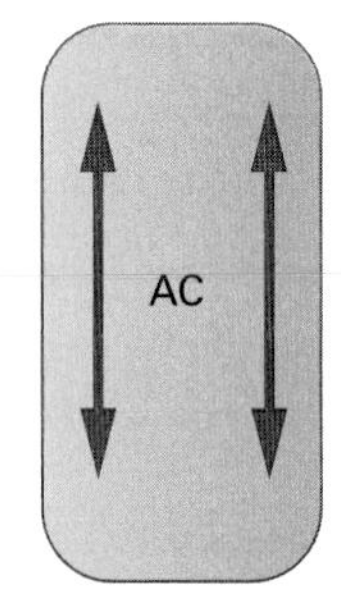

Voltage in both directions, constantly switching back and forth

• **Figure 8.4** Diagrams showing DC and AC flow of electrons

Electricity comes in two flavors: **direct current** (DC), where the electrons flow in one direction around a continuous circuit, and **alternating current** (AC), where the flow of electrons alternates direction back and forth in a circuit (see Figure 8.4).

Test Specific

Powering the PC

Flipping the AC switch on the back of a power supply can wreak all kinds of havoc on a PC. Moving the switch to ~230 V in the U.S. makes for a great practical joke (as long as the PC is off when you do it)—the PC might try to boot up, but probably won't get far. You don't risk damaging anything by running at half the AC. In countries that run ~230 standard, on the other hand, firing up the PC with the AC switch set to ~115 can cause the power supply to die a horrid,

Your PC uses DC voltage, but local power companies supply only AC voltage. Some conversion process must take place so that the PC can function. The power supply in a computer converts high-voltage AC power to low-voltage DC. The first step in powering the PC, therefore, is to get and maintain a good supply of AC power. Second, you need a power supply to convert AC to the proper voltage and amperage of DC power for the motherboard and peripherals. Finally, you need to control the byproduct of

tor. In the United States, standard AC comes in somewhere between 110 and 120 volts, often written as ~115 VAC. The rest of the world uses 220–240 VAC, so most power supplies have a little switch in the back so you can use them anywhere. Figure 8.5 shows the back of a power supply. Note the IEC-320 connector and the 115/230 switch.

• **Figure 8.5** Back of power supply showing the IEC-320 connection and 115/230 (Red) switch

Before plugging anything into an AC outlet, take a moment to test the outlet first using a **multimeter** or with a device designed exclusively to test outlets. Failure to test AC outlets properly can result in inoperable or destroyed equipment, as well as possible electrocution. The IEC-320 plug has three holes, called hot, neutral, and ground. These names describe the function of the wires that connect to them behind the wall plate. The hot wire carries electrical voltage, much like a pipe that delivers water. The neutral wire carries no voltage, but instead acts like a water drain, completing the circuit by returning electricity to the local source, normally a breaker panel. The ground wire makes it possible for excess electricity to return safely to the ground. When testing AC power, you want to check for three things: that the hot outputs approximately 115 V (or whatever the proper voltage is for your part of the world), that the neutral connects to ground (0 V output), and that the ground connects to ground (again, 0 V). Figure 8.6 shows the voltages at an outlet.

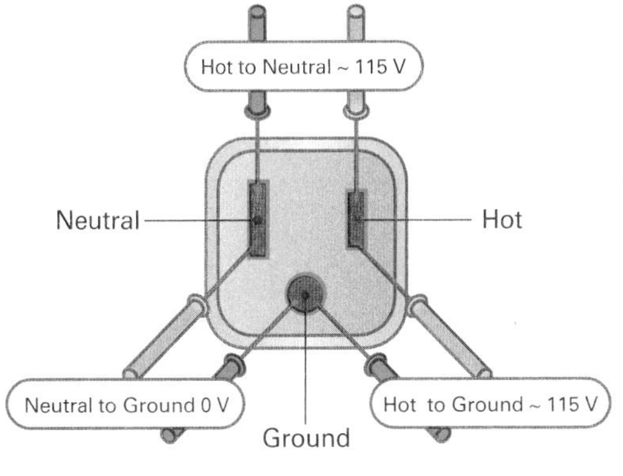

• **Figure 8.6** Outlet voltages

A multimeter—often also referred to as a *Volt-Ohm Meter* (VOM) or digital multimeter (DMM)—enables you to measure a number of different aspects of electrical current. Every multimeter provides at least four major measurements: AC voltage, DC voltage, continuity, and resistance. A multimeter consists of two probes, an analog or digital meter, and a dial to set the type of test you want to perform. Refer to Figure 8.7 to become familiar with the different components of the multimeter.

• **Figure 8.7** Digital Volt-Ohm Meter/ multimeter

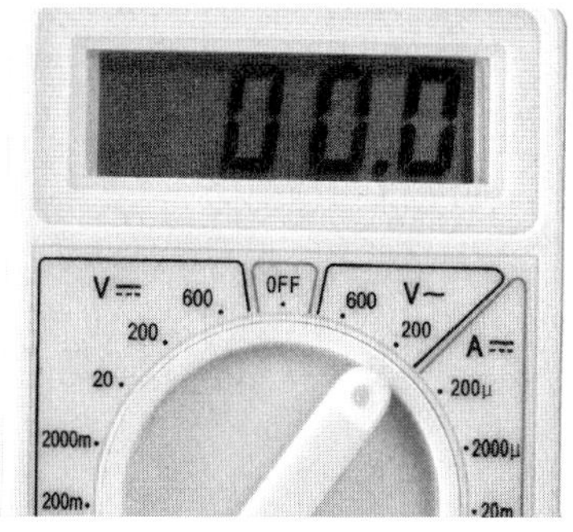

• **Figure 8.8** Multimeter featuring DC and AC symbols

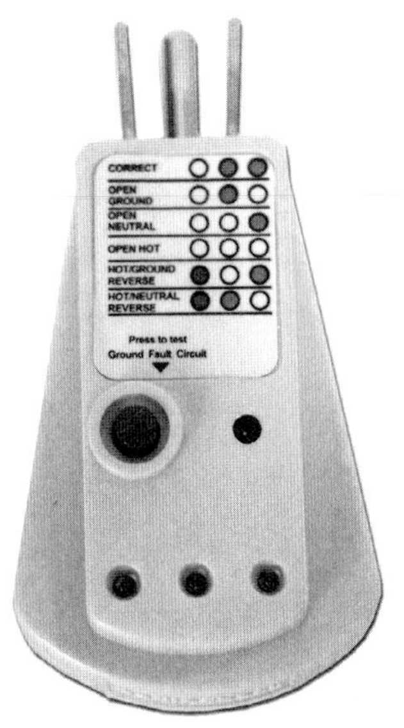

• **Figure 8.9** Circuit tester

Note that some multimeters use symbols rather than letters to describe AC and DC settings. The V with the solid line above a dashed line, for example, in Figure 8.8, refers to direct current. The V~ stands for alternating current.

Most multimeters offer four types of electrical tests: continuity, resistance, AC, and DC. Continuity tests whether electrons can flow from one end of a wire to the other end. If so, you have continuity; if not, you don't. You can use this setting to determine breaks in wires and components. You normally use the resistance test to see if a fuse is good or blown, but it can work to test for breaks too. If the multimeter shows infinite resistance between one end of a wire and the other, then there is no continuity; if the multimeter shows no resistance, then there is continuity. Testing AC and DC voltages is a matter of making sure the measured voltage is what it should be.

Using Special Equipment to Test AC Voltage

A number of good AC-only testing devices are available. With these devices, you can test all voltages for an AC outlet by simply inserting them into the outlet. Be sure to test all the outlets the computer system uses: power supply, external devices, and monitor. Although convenient, these devices aren't as accurate as a multimeter. My favorite tester is made by Radio Shack, catalog number 22-141 (see Figure 8.9). This handy device provides three light-emitting diodes (LEDs) that describe everything that can go wrong with a plug.

If all power companies could supply electricity in smooth, continuous flows with no dips or spikes in pressure, the next two sections of this chapter would be irrelevant. Unfortunately, no matter how clean the AC supply appears to be to a multimeter, the truth is that those electrons zing and zip and stumble and drip. In some cities, the lack of consistency of AC makes computing a matter of luck rather than skill. You're lucky if your PC stays on long enough to produce good work! Two essential devices handle sags and spikes in the supply of AC: uninterruptible power supplies and surge suppressors.

UPS

An **uninterruptible power supply** (UPS) protects your computer (and, more importantly, your data) in the event of a power dip (brownout) or power outage (blackout). Figure 8.10 shows a typical UPS. A UPS essentially contains a big battery that will provide AC power to your computer, regardless of the condition of the AC outlet. There are two basic types of UPS: **Online** (properly UPS) and **Standby** (SPS).

An Online UPS is a true uninterruptible power supply. A UPS converts AC power from the outlet and charges the battery. The battery in turn provides power for the computer. The UPS battery is always online, protecting your data against accidental loss from power outages. An added benefit of the UPS is *power conditioning*. The battery filters the AC power, thus giving your computer's power supply a very smooth AC current. Though not the budget choice, an Online UPS is clearly the best choice for the PC.

A *Standby UPS* (SPS) removes the battery from the AC circuit until the AC power drops below ~80–90 V. An SPS will then engage the battery and (hopefully) save your data. Although a less expensive solution than a true UPS, the SPS has two potential liabilities. Most obviously, removing the battery from the regular AC power also removes the AC conditioning. Data is not actually protected until the AC drops well below the standard 110–120 volts, and neither are the fragile electrical components of the computer. Second, if the battery dies at some point, you might

supplies are measured in watts, the amount of power they can supply in the event of a power outage. You can spend a lot of time and mental energy figuring precisely how much wattage your computer, monitor, drives, and so on require to get the proper UPS for your system. A quicker method, however, is to look on the box provided by the manufacturer. Most manufacturers will list how many minutes the UPS will last with a certain voltage. Cut the number of minutes in half, and that will give you a good conservative estimate of

Try This!

Using a Multimeter to Test AC Outlets

Every competent technician knows how to use a multimeter, so if you haven't used one in the past, get hold of one and try this!

First you need to set up the meter for measuring AC. Follow these steps:

1. Place the black lead in the common (–) hole. If the black lead is permanently attached, ignore this step.
2. Place the red lead in the V-Ohm-A (+) hole. If the red lead is permanently attached, ignore this step.
3. Move the selector switch to the AC V (usually red). If there are

1. Put either lead in hot, the other in neutral. You should read 110 to 120 V AC.
2. Put either lead in hot, the other in ground. You should read 110 to 120 V AC.
3. Put either lead in neutral, the other in ground. You should read 0 V AC.

If any of these readings are different from what was described, it's time to call an electrician.

• **Figure 8.10** Uninterruptible power supply

that UPS' abilities. Table 8.1 gives you a quick look at the low end and the very high end of UPS products.

Although a true or Online UPS provides far better protection than an SPS, almost all of the lower-priced UPSs sold today are actually SPSs. Regardless, any UPS will give protection for your data and for your equipment and should be considered a necessary part of a complete computer system today.

Try This!

Shopping for a UPS

When it comes to getting a UPS for yourself or a client, nothing quite cuts through the hype and marketing terms like a trip to the local computer store to see for yourself. You need excuses to go to the computer store, so try this!

1. Go to your local computer store—or do so online if nothing's nearby—and find out what's available.
2. Then answer this one question: How can you tell the difference between an online and a standby UPS?

Surge Suppressors

In a perfect world, power companies would supply perfect AC voltage, free of voltage spikes and sags. We do not live in a perfect world. Your PC needs protection from the fluctuations in the power coming from the electric company despite their best efforts. We need devices that, at a minimum, protect from voltage spikes that, if allowed to pass into the system, will result in massive component destruction. We call this protection **surge suppression**. The power supply itself does a good job of surge suppression. Most power supplies handle spikes up to around 600 V. But the power supply takes a lot of damage from this and will eventually fail. A surge suppressor needs to be inserted between the power supply and the outlet to protect the system from power surges (see Figure 8.11).

• **Figure 8.11** Surge suppressor

Most people tend to spend a lot of money on their PC and for some reason suddenly get real cheap on the surge suppressor. Don't do that! Make sure your surge suppressor has the UL 1449 for 330 V rating to ensure substantial protection for your system. Additionally, check the joules rating before buying a new surge suppressor. A **joule** is a unit of electrical energy. Joules are used to describe how much energy a surge suppressor can handle before it fails. Most authorities agree that your surge suppressor should rate at a minimum of 800 joules—the more joules, the better the protection! My surge suppressor rates out at 1,300 joules.

Table 8.1 Typical UPS

Brand	Model	Outlets Protected	Backup Time	Price	Type
APC	BE350U	3 @ 120V	2 min @ 200W, 21 min @ 50W	$39.99	Stand By
APC	BE725BB	4 @ 120V	4 min @ 400W, <1 hour @ 50W	$99.99	Stand By
CyberPower	CPS825AVR	3 @ 120V	25 to 60 minutes	$136.12	Line Interactive
APC	SYH2K6RMT-P1	12 @ 120V 2 @ 240V	11.9 min @ 1400W	$2,835.00	Online

While you're protecting your system, make sure to get a surge suppressor with telephone line protection if you use a modem or DSL connection. Telephone lines produce spikes just as often as your power lines! Many manufacturers make surge suppressors with telephone line protection (see Figure 8.12). Look for a UL 497A rating for the modem surge suppression.

No surge suppressor works forever. Make sure your surge suppressor has a test/reset button. Also, check the manufacturer's web site for recommended replacement schedules. Many companies provide cash guarantees against system failure due to surges, but only if you follow their guidelines.

No surge suppressor in the world can handle the ultimate surge, the ESD of a lightning strike. If your electrical system takes such a hit, you can kiss your PC good bye if it was plugged in at the time. *Always* unplug electronics during electrical storms!

Supplying DC

Once you've assured the supply of good AC electricity for the PC, the power supply takes

tronics. Manufacturers may use these voltages any way they wish, however, and may deviate from these assumptions. Power supplies come with standard connectors for the motherboard and interior devices.

Power to the Motherboard

Modern motherboards use one or two connectors for power. All have a **P1** socket into which you plug, rather logically, a P1 connector from the power supply. Figure 8.13 shows a P1 socket; Figure 8.14 shows the corresponding connector. Note the notch on the connector, only allowing you to insert it one way. Many P1 connectors have a tiny latch as well for securing the connection in the event of some jiggling or gravity storm. Figure 8.15 shows a correctly oriented P1 connection.

Many motherboards require a second, four-wire connector to push more 12-volt power into the board. This extra juice

• **Figure 8.13** P1 socket

• **Figure 8.14** P1 connector

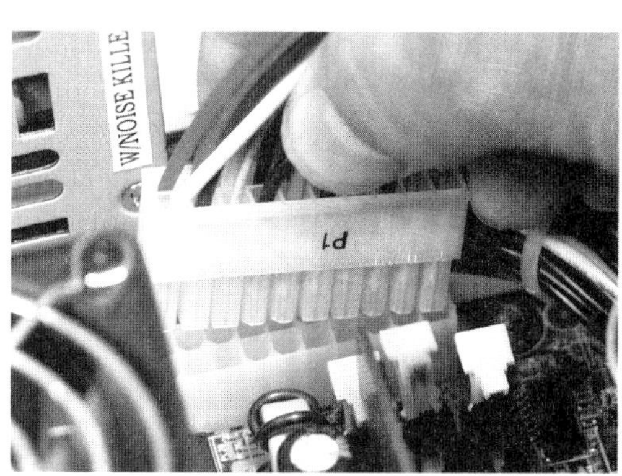

• **Figure 8.15** Correctly oriented P1 connector

Many power supplies have a 6-pin auxiliary power connector that supplies 3.3- and 5-volt DC current. Some also have a three-wire fan sensor wire.

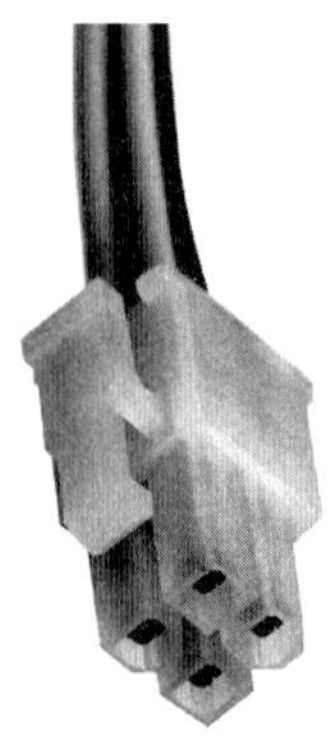

• Figure 8.16 P4 connector

helps stabilize the motherboard. The four-wire connector is commonly referred to as a **P4 12V connector**, or simply as a P4 connector (Figure 8.16), although you'll find it used on Athlon XP motherboards as well as Pentium 4 boards. It sits on the motherboard near the processor's DC-to-DC converter and voltage regulators (Figure 8.17). This position affords higher power conversion and transmission efficiencies and future platform flexibility. Figure 8.18 shows a pin-out for P1 and P4 12V with the voltages listed.

• Figure 8.17 P4 socket

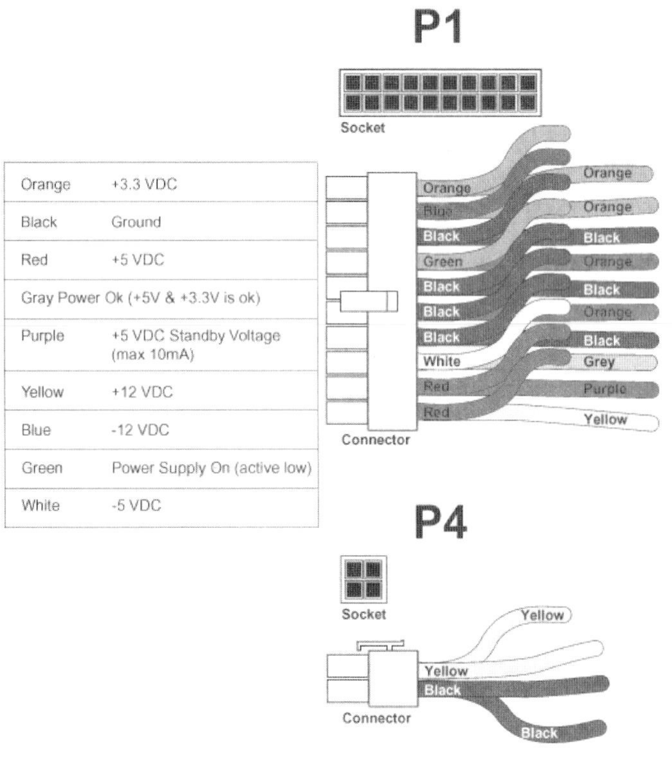

Orange	+3.3 VDC
Black	Ground
Red	+5 VDC
Gray Power Ok (+5V & +3.3V is ok)	
Purple	+5 VDC Standby Voltage (max 10mA)
Yellow	+12 VDC
Blue	-12 VDC
Green	Power Supply On (active low)
White	-5 VDC

• Figure 8.18 P1 and P4 voltages

Power to Peripherals: Molex, Mini, Sub-mini

Many different devices inside the PC require power. These include hard drives, floppy drives, CD-ROM drives, Zip drives, and fans. Your power supply has two or possibly three different types of connectors that plug into your peripherals. Let's take a look at each of these power connections.

• **Figure 8.19** Molex connector

Molex Connectors The most common type of power connection for devices that need 5 or 12 volts of power is the **Molex connector** (Figure 8.19). The Molex connector has notches, called chamfers, that guide its installation. The tricky part is that Molex connectors require a firm push to plug in properly, and a very strong person can defeat the chamfers, plugging a Molex in upside down. Not a good thing. *Always* check for proper orientation first! Figure 8.20 shows the pin-out for a Molex connector.

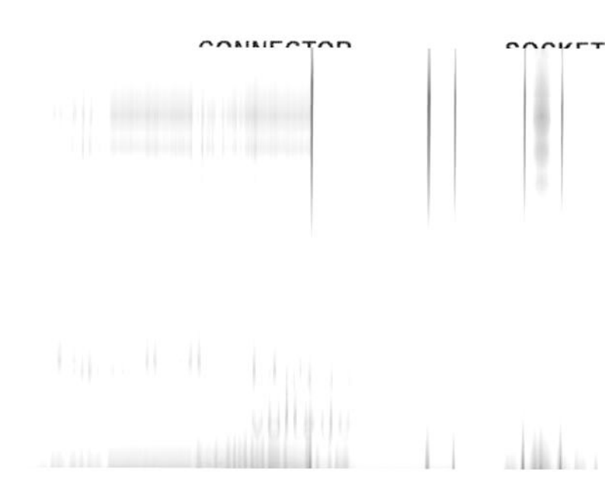

Try This!

Testing DC

It is common practice for techs troubleshooting a system to test the DC voltages coming out of the power supply. Even with good AC, a bad power supply can fail to transform AC to DC at voltages needed by the motherboard and peripherals. So grab your trusty multimeter and try this on a powered up PC with the side cover removed. Note that you must have P1 connected to the motherboard and the system must be running (you don't have to be in Windows, of course!).

1. Switch your multimeter to DC, somewhere around 20 V DC if you need to make that choice. Make sure your leads are plugged into the multimeter properly, red to hot, black to ground. The key to testing DC is that it matters which lead you touch to which wire. Red goes to hot wires of all colors; black *always* goes to ground.
2. Plug the red lead into the red wire socket of a free Molex connector and plug the black lead into one of the two black wire sockets. You should get a reading of ~5 V. What do you have?
3. Now move the red lead to the yellow socket. What voltage do you get?
4. Testing the P1 connector is a little more complicated. You push the red and black leads into the top of P1, sliding in along side the wires until you bottom out. Leave the black lead in one of the black wire ground sockets. Move the red lead through all the colored wire sockets. What voltages do you find? Do they match the schematic given in Figure 8.18?

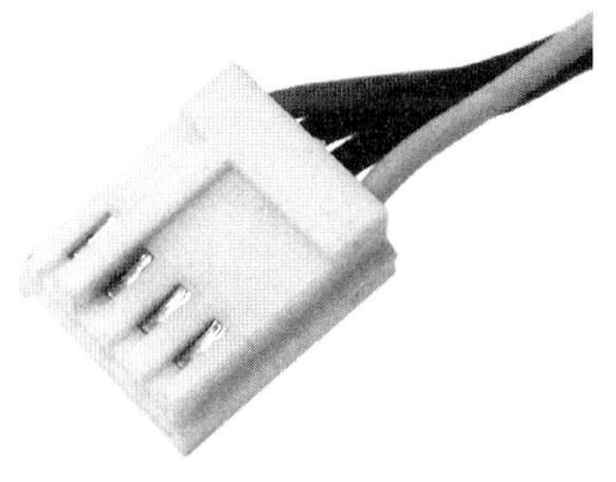

• **Figure 8.21** Mini connector

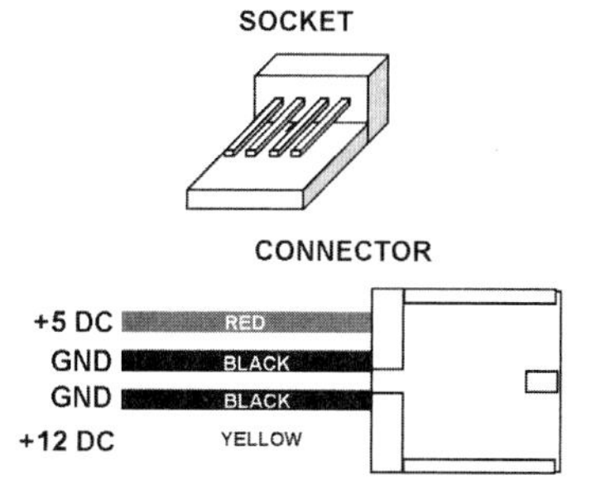

• **Figure 8.22** Mini connector voltages

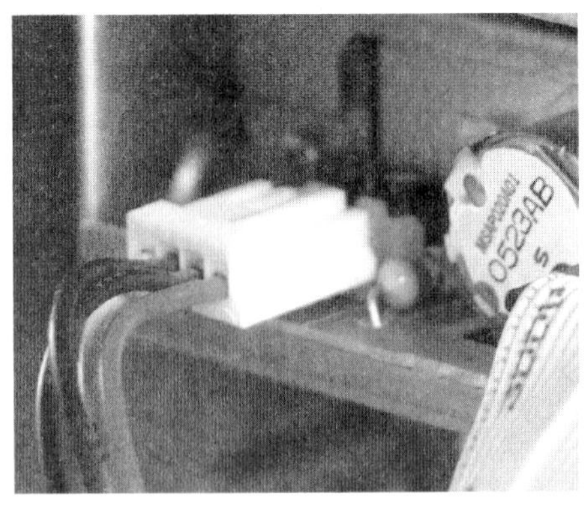

• **Figure 8.23** Correct orientation of a mini connector

As with any power connector, plugging a mini connector into a device the wrong way will almost certainly destroy the device. Check twice before you plug one in!

Be extra careful when plugging in a mini connector! Whereas Molex connectors are difficult to plug in backwards, you can insert a mini connector incorrectly with very little effort. As with a Molex connector, doing so will almost certainly destroy the floppy drive. Figure 8.23 depicts a correctly oriented mini connection.

A few power supplies have a single two-wire connector, called a sub-mini, for powering sensors or LEDs.

Splitters and Adapters You may occasionally find yourself not having enough connectors to power all of the devices inside your PC. In this case, you can purchase splitters to create more connections (see Figure 8.24). You might also run into the phenomenon of needing a mini connector but having only a spare Molex. Because the voltages on the wires are the same, a simple adapter will take care of the problem nicely.

Wattage Requirements

Every device in a PC requires a certain amount of wattage in order to function. A typical hard drive draws 15 watts of power when accessed, for example, whereas an Athlon XP 2000+ CPU draws a whopping 70 watts at peak usage—with average usage that number drops to 62 watts. The total wattage of all devices combined is the minimum you need the power supply to provide. Power supplies are rated in watts.

If the power supply cannot produce the wattage needed by a system, that PC won't work properly. Because most devices in the PC require maximum wattage when first starting, the most common result of insufficient wattage is a paper weight that looks like a PC. This can lead to some embarrassing moments. You might plug in a new hard drive for a client, for example, push the power button on the case, and nothing happens—a dead PC! Eek! You can quickly determine if insufficient wattage is the problem. Unplug the drive and power up the system. If the system comes up, you can suspect the power supply. The only fix for this problem is to replace the power supply with one that provides more wattage (or leave the new drive out—a less-than-ideal solution!).

As a general recommendation for a new system, I suggest you use at least a 400-watt power supply. This is a very common wattage and will give you plenty of extra power for booting as well as for whatever other components you might add to the system in the future.

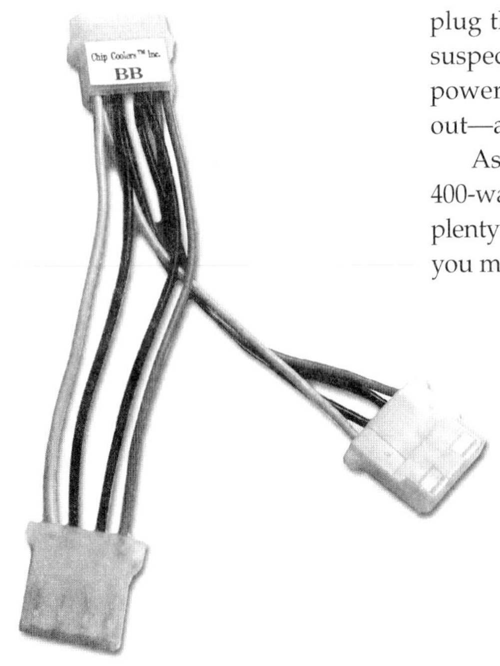

• **Figure 8.24** Molex splitter

Getting Specific with the Formulas A quick glance at the power supplies on the shelves of a computer store shows power supplies ranging from 200–600 watts. Although it's tempting to recommend that you get the most powerful power supply you can afford, such a recommendation misses crucial points. The more a power supply can produce, the more AC it draws and the more heat it produces. Thus you need a more powerful exhaust fan or fans and the noise increases. Having a PC sound like a helicopter perhaps doesn't bother the gamer in the heat of flying a fighter plane, but such a noise level is unacceptable in a box that's part of a home entertainment center. Plus, putting a monster power supply in a PC that will do nothing but surf the Internet and do e-mail is a phenomenal waste of money and electricity. In some circumstances, therefore, you need a way to determine the current and future wattage requirements of a PC so you can get the best possible power supply for the job.

Figuring out the wattage needs of a device varies according to the device. CPU manufacturers display this information freely. AMD lists the wattage for various Athlon XP processors in a product brochure that describes the Athlon XP product line, making it available for download off their web site. A 1500+ processor can take up to 60 watts at peak usage, whereas the 2000+ uses up to 70 watts, as I mentioned earlier. A typical hard drive has two measurements: how much amperage used by the motor and how much used by the logic circuits. You need to multiply both figures and add them together to get the total wattage used by the hard drive. The Seagate drive on my desk, for example, uses .37 A in the 12 V circuit, and .65 A in the 5 V (Figure 8.25). To figure the power consumption, multiply the numbers and then add the two circuits together (.37 × 12 + .65 × 5 = 4.44 +

Tech Tip

P4 Converters

If you have an older power supply that lacks a P4 12V 4-pin connector, you can try an adapter for a Molex connector—they do exist, but you're almost always better off getting a newer power supply. If you don't provide proper power to a higher-end system, you can create a very buggy machine! Check the section on wattage in this chapter for more details.

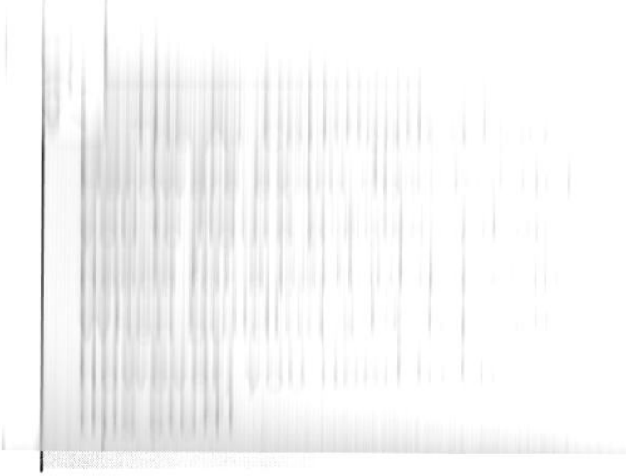

size and connectors exist. The A+ Certification Core Hardware exam expects you to know the differences between the two dominant form factor categories, **AT** and **ATX**. I've included other form factor variations at the end of this discussion because you need to know them to be a good tech! All power supplies convert AC to DC and help cool the interior of the case, no matter which form factor you look at, and all have both Molex and mini connectors. Variations come in motherboard connectors, power management, and physical size.

Wattage used by devices can vary a lot among manufacturers, by the way, so don't take the numbers above as gospel for all CPUs or all hard drives! A quick glance at a Western Digital hard drive in my system shows it draws .66 × 5 V, which puts it on par with the Seagate, but only .24 × 12 V. Total power consumption of the Western Digital drive is ~2 watts lower than the comparable Seagate.

AT The AT power supply—the earliest standard in the industry—has several defining features. The power for the motherboard is supplied on two matching connectors. The power switch is a hard on/off switch. And the AT power supply had trouble with any electricity-saving features.

The two motherboard power connectors, called **P8 and P9** (Figure 8.26), must be plugged in with the black wires next to each other. These connectors are faced and keyed, which is to say that they have different front and back faces and a small guide or key on one side so you cannot install them backward. The key also helps hold the connector in place. Sometimes you have to angle the connectors in before snapping them down all the way, to accommodate the row of small teeth on one side of the plugs.

P8 and P9 provide only 12 V and 5 V power to the PC, not 3.3 V like a standard, modern power supply. Figure 8.27 shows the pin-out for P8 and P9, including the voltages on each wire.

AT power switches simply turn the system on or off and come in only two common types: *rocker* and *plunger*. Each of these switches has four tab

• **Figure 8.25** Close up of hard drive showing voltages and amperages

Tech Tip

Build in Aging

Don't cut the specifications too tightly for the power supplies. All power supplies produce less wattage over time simply because of the wear and tear on the internal components. If you build a system that runs with only a few watts of power extra available from the power supply initially, that system will most likely start causing problems within a year or less! Do yourself or your clients a favor and get a power supply that has a little more wattage than you need.

The P8 and P9 connectors must plug in with the black ground wires in the center.

Both AT and ATX motherboard connectors provide negative voltages as well to the motherboard, such as –12 V and –5 V. Nobody messes with them and they don't show up on the exam, so most techs treat them like an appendix, a holdover of older technology no longer used.

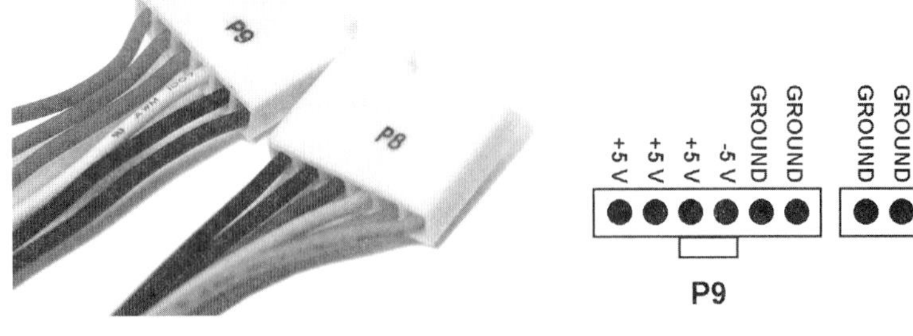

• **Figure 8.26** P8/P9 power connectors

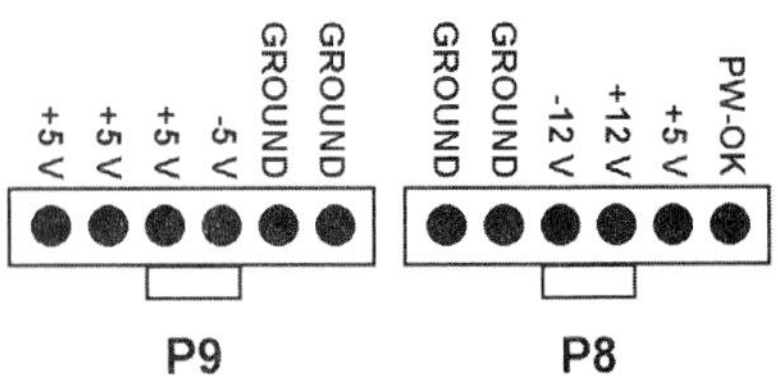

• **Figure 8.27** P8 and P9 voltages

connectors that attach to four color-coded wires leading from the power supply. These switches handle 120-volt current and are interchangeable. The type of computer box determines the type of switch used in a system (see Figure 8.28).

The AT form factor and AT power supply do not mix well with any type of power management. Let's save the big discussion of power management for Chapter 21 with the discussion of portable PCs, but for now you should appreciate that most systems have the ability to shut down hardware not currently needed by the system. Most PCs enjoy the ability to go into a "hibernate" state where every device, including the CPU, either shuts down or goes into a frozen, hibernation-like state—thus the name *hibernate* or sometimes *sleep* mode. This powered-down mode presents a difficulty because a system in hibernate mode looks exactly as though someone shut it down. But the system may still have open (and unsaved) files, and so on. So, what happens when a user walks up to a system in hibernate mode? He or she assumes the system is off and presses the on/off switch! In an AT system, if you hit that switch, the system turns off. If by any chance you don't know, turning off a Windows system without first performing a proper shutdown procedure makes several potentially bad things happen. You can lose data at the very least. At worst, you can corrupt essential operating system files, which is never a good thing! You should never turn off a Windows system without performing a proper shutdown. You know the drill: Start | Turn Off Computer | Turn Off (Figure 8.29).

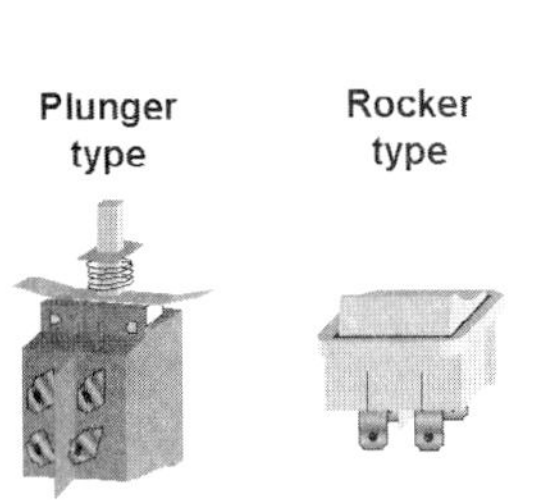

• **Figure 8.28** Types of switches

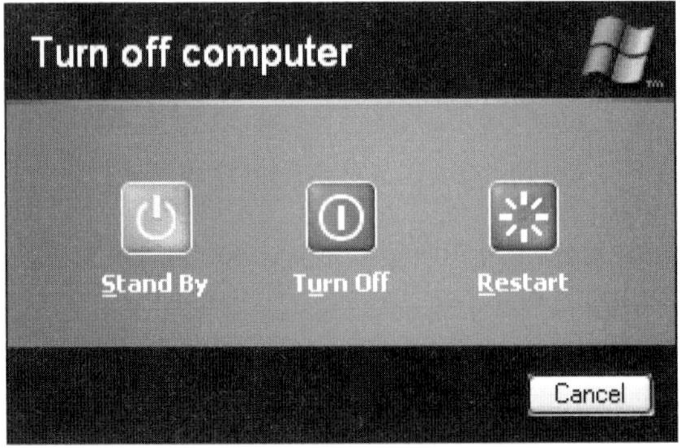

• **Figure 8.29** Shutting down Windows XP

AT's poor compatibility with power management doesn't stop with just the on/off switch. Half of the process of going into power-saving modes involves putting devices to sleep, a fairly simple process involving timers designed to wait for a certain amount of inactivity before shutting down a device. The other half of power management involves waking devices back up. What determines that the monitor should come back on? What happens to make the hard drive start spinning again? AT systems do a pretty good job of waking up a system based on pressing a keyboard button or moving a mouse. But today's PC world revolves around remote access. We need servers running the popular Windows 2000 Remote Access Server (RAS) to enable salespeople to dial in from a telephone line. Network administrators use powerful remote management tools to monitor and repair far-flung systems. What happens if the RAS server happens to kick into hibernate mode and the modem starts to receive an incoming call? How can network admin- [illegible]

power that handles all the power management issues quite nicely. ATX power supplies put a 5-volt charge on the motherboard at all times. In a way, as long as an ATX system has AC from the wall socket, an ATX system is on. This gives ATX systems amazing features. When a phone call comes in, for example, the ATX system can power up the operating system and answer the call!

All of the most important settings for ATX soft power reside in your CMOS setup. Start your CMOS and look for a Power Management section. Figure 8.30 shows a detail from a typical BIOS' Power Section. Note the Wake Up On LAN/Ring. On some older BIOS (not the one in Figure 8.30), you must also define the modem's IRQ. A quick check in Device Manager will give you that information.

Take a look at the Soft-Off by PWRBTN option in Figure 8.31. This determines the function of the on/off switch. You may set this switch to work exactly like an AT switch (instant off), or you may set it to the more common *four-second delay*. Many BIOS, most commonly laptop BIOS, give the option to kick the system into sleep mode with a quick press of the on/off button, or to go completely off if you hold down the button for a set number of seconds (usually four to six seconds).

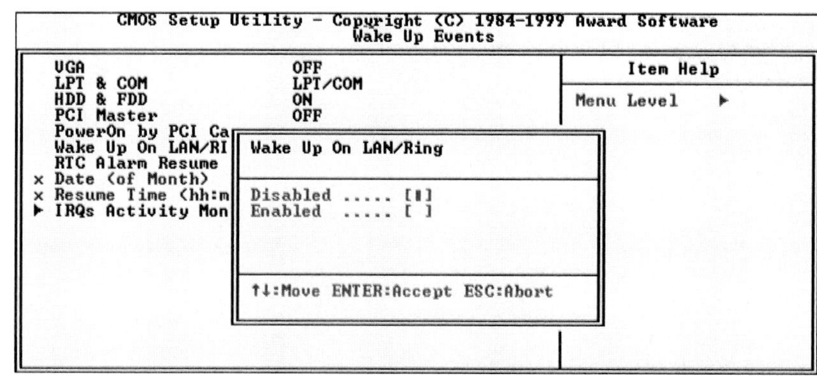

• **Figure 8.30** BIOS settings for Wake Up On LAN/Ring

Handling ATX power supplies requires special consideration. Understand that an ATX power supply *never turns off*. As long as that power supply stays connected to a power outlet, as mentioned previously, the power supply will continue to supply 5 V to the

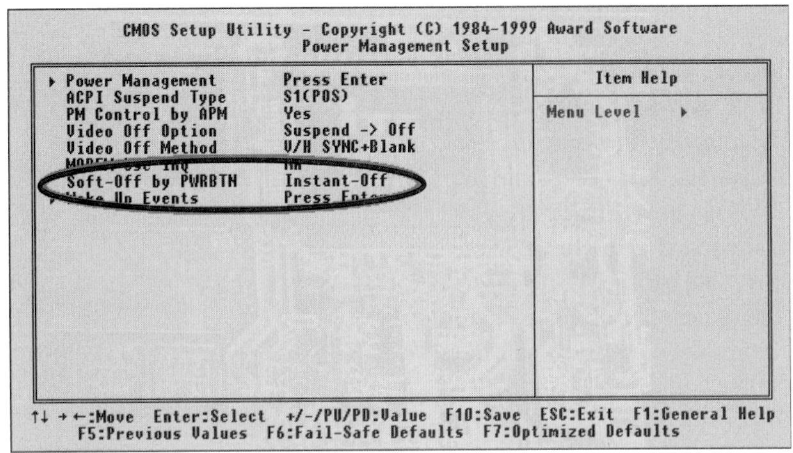

• **Figure 8.31** Soft-off options

motherboard, regardless of what power state the system is in currently. Always unplug an ATX system before you do any work! For years, techs constantly bickered about the merits of leaving a system plugged in or unplugged while you serviced a system. ATX settles this issue forever. Many ATX power supplies provide a real on/off switch on the back of the PSU (see Figure 8.32). If you really need the system shut down with no power to the motherboard, use this switch.

When working on an ATX system, I often find using the power button inconvenient because half the time I'm not using a case. That means there is no power button! One trick you can use when in that situation is to use a set of car keys or a screwdriver to contact the two wires to start and stop the system. Just make sure to short only the two power jumpers (see Figure 8.33).

• **Figure 8.32** On/off switch for an ATX system

Variations ATX power supplies come in quite a few varieties, matching the many form factors of the motherboards and cases. Original ATX power supplies are roughly cubical, 140 mm × 150 mm × 80 mm, and come with the standard P1 connection for motherboard power and Molex and mini connectors for peripheral power. Modern ATX12V power supplies add the P4 4-pin connector, as noted earlier, but match original ATX power supplies in size.

Physically smaller versions fit into microATX and FlexATX cases, and so bear names that match. You can find microATX and microATX12V power supplies, for example, distinguished by the latter having the extra P4 connector. Be careful when setting up systems with these tiny power supplies. The smaller form factor simply cannot convert as much wattage as the larger form factors. Many microATX power supplies top out at a paltry 200 watts, for example. You can quickly max one of these out when coupling them with a lot of RAM and a high end CPU!

• **Figure 8.33** Shorting the soft on/off jumpers

Cooling

Heat and computers are not the best of friends. Cooling is therefore a vital consideration when building a computer. Electricity equals heat. Computers, being electrical devices, generate heat as they operate, and too much can seriously damage a computer's internal components.

The **power supply fan** (Figure 8.34) provides the basic cooling for the PC. It not only cools the voltage regulator circuits *within* the power supply; it also provides a constant flow of outside air throughout the interior of the computer case. A dead power supply fan can rapidly cause tremendous problems, even equipment failure. If you ever turn on a computer and it boots just fine, but you notice that it seems unusually quiet, check to see if the power supply fan has died. If it has, quickly turn off the PC and replace the power supply.

Some power supplies come with a sensor built in to help regulate the air flow. This three-pin, three-wire connector plugs into the motherboard directly (Figure 8.35).

Cross Check

AT vs. ATX

The power supply form factor alone does not define a system as AT or ATX. You've got to discuss the motherboard as well. Refer to Chapter 7 on AT and ATX motherboards, and see if you can put the full pictures of these standards together. What defines a system as AT? What improvements did ATX incorporate?

Case fans (Figure 8.36) are large, square fans that snap into special brackets on the case, providing extra cooling for key components. Most cases don't come with a case fan, but no mod-

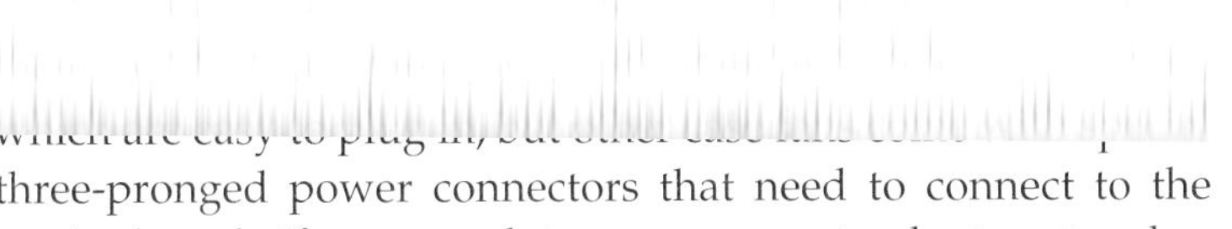

three-pronged power connectors that need to connect to the motherboard. If you need to, you can get adapters to plug three-pronged connectors into Molex connectors or Molex connectors into three-pronged connectors.

• **Figure 8.34** Power supply fan

A computer is a closed system and computer cases help the fans keep things cool: everything is inside a box. Although many tech types like to run their systems with the side panel of the case open for easy access to the components, in the end they are cheating themselves. Why? A closed case enables the fans to create airflow. This airflow substantially cools off interior components. When the side of the case is open, you ruin the airflow of the system, and you lose a lot of cooling efficiency.

An important point to remember when implementing good airflow inside your computer case is that hot air rises. Warm air always rises above cold air, and you can use this principle to your advantage in keeping your computer cool.

In the typical layout of case fans for a computer case, an intake fan is located near the bottom of the front bezel of the case. This fan draws cool air in from outside the case and blows it over the components inside the case. Near the top and rear of the case (usually where the power supply is located), an exhaust fan is located. This fan works the opposite of the intake fan: it takes the warm air from inside the case and sends it to the outside.

Another important part of maintaining proper airflow inside the case is ensuring that all empty expansion bays are covered by **slot covers** (Figure 8.37). To maintain good airflow inside your case, you shouldn't provide too many opportunities for air to escape. Slot covers not only assist in maintaining a steady airflow; they help keep dust and smoke out of your case.

• **Figure 8.35** Three-wire fan sensor connector

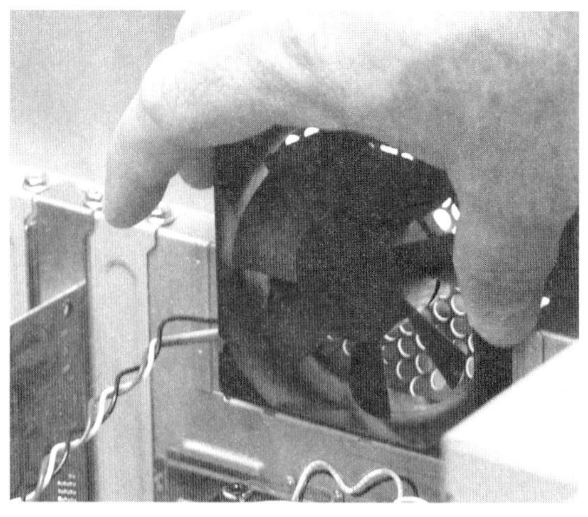

• **Figure 8.36** Case fan

• **Figure 8.37** Slot covers

■ Troubleshooting Power

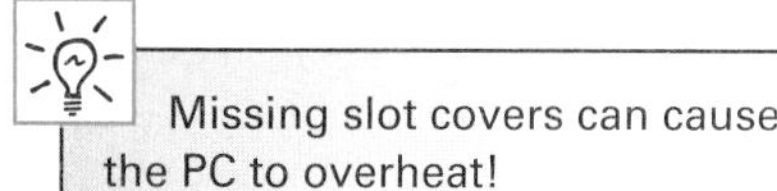

Missing slot covers can cause the PC to overheat!

Electrical problems come in many forms, from irregular AC to dying or faulty power supplies. Most of this chapter deals with how to ensure good AC and get proper DC to your motherboard and peripherals. Prevention is always easier than searching for a cure, so you should know how to deal with most power issues already. Let's wrap up the Test Specific section of this chapter with a look at a few specific troubleshooting issues that every tech should master.

When Power Supplies Die

Power supplies fail in two ways: sudden death and slowly over time. When they die suddenly, the computer will not start and the fan in the power supply will not turn. In this case, verify that electricity is getting to the power supply before you do anything! Avoid the embarrassment of trying to repair a power supply when the only problem is a bad outlet or an extension cord that is not plugged in. Assuming that the system has electricity, the best way to verify that a power supply is working or not working is to check the voltages coming out of the power supply with a multimeter (see Figure 8.38).

• **Figure 8.38** Testing one of the 12-volt DC connections

Do not panic if your power supply puts out slightly more or less voltage than its nominal value. The voltages supplied by most PC power supplies can vary by as much as –10 percent to +10 percent of its stated value. This means that the 12-volt line can vary from roughly 10.5 to 12.9 V without exceeding the tolerance of the various systems in the PC. The 5 and 3.3 volt lines offer similar tolerances.

Be sure to test every connection on the power supply—that means every connection on P1 (P8 and P9 for AT systems) as well as every Molex and mini. Because all voltages are between –20 and +20 DC, simply set the voltmeter to the 20-volt DC setting for everything. If the power supply fails to provide power, throw it away and get a new one. If you know how to use a soldering iron and can tell a capacitor from a diode, you may want to open the power supply and see if any components failed. Otherwise, don't waste your or your company's time. The price of new power supplies makes replacement the obvious way to go!

Switches

Broken power switches form a common source of problems for power supplies that fail to start. The power switch is behind the on/off button on every PC. It is usually secured to the front cover or inside front frame on your PC, making it a rather challenging part to access. On an AT system, use a [illegible]

Unfortunately, the majority of PC problems occur when power supplies die slowly over time. This means that one of the internal electronics of the power supply has begun to fail. The failures are *always* intermittent and tend to cause some of the most difficult to diagnose problems in PC repair. The secret to discovering that a power supply is dying lies in one word: intermittent. Whenever I have intermittent problems, my first guess is that the power supply is bad. Here are some other clues:

- "Whenever I start my computer in the morning, it starts to boot, and then locks up. If I press CTRL-ALT-DEL two or three times, then it will boot up fine."
- "Sometimes when I start my PC, I get an error code. If I reboot it goes away. Sometimes I get different errors."
- "My computer will run fine for an hour or so. Then it locks up, sometimes once or twice an hour."

Sometimes something bad happens and sometimes it does not. That's the clue for replacing the power supply. And don't bother with the voltmeter; the voltages will show as within tolerances, but only *once in a while* they will spike and sag (far more quickly than your voltmeter can measure) and cause these intermittent errors. When in doubt, change the power supply. Power supplies break in computers more often than any other part of the PC except the floppy drives. I keep power supplies in stock for swapping and testing.

Fuses and Fire

Inside every power supply resides a simple fuse. If you have a power supply that simply pops! and stops working, you might be tempted to go inside the power supply and check the fuse. I can't condemn the practice, having

The inside of a power supply is dangerous because of the high-voltage capacitors. Power supplies are not designed to be opened! *Do not* open a power supply!

done it in the old days myself, but I certainly don't recommend it. First off the capacitors in most power supplies carry very high voltage charges that can hurt a lot if touched. Second, fuses blow for a reason. If you have a power supply malfunctioning inside, you want that fuse to blow. The alternative is much less desirable: fire.

Failure to respect the power of electricity will eventually result in the most catastrophic of all situations: a fire. Don't think it won't happen to you! I've created about three fires in my career, and in every case it scared me to death. Fortunately, I've always had a fire extinguisher handy! Every PC workbench needs a fire extinguisher, but you need to make sure you have the right one. There are three primary classes of fires, and the fire prevention industry has divided all fire extinguishers into those three classes:

- **Class A** Ordinary free-burning combustible, such as wood or paper
- **Class B** Flammable liquids, such as gasoline, solvents, or paint
- **Class C** Live electrical equipment

As you might expect, you should only use a Class C fire extinguisher on your PC if it should catch fire. All fire extinguishers are required to have their type labeled prominently on them. Many fire extinguishers are multi-class in that they can handle more than one type of fire. The most common fire extinguisher is type ABC—it works on all common types of fires.

Beyond A+

Power supplies provide essential services for the PC, creating DC out of AC and cooling the system, but that utilitarian role does not stop the power supply from being an enthusiast's plaything. Plus, server and high-end workstations have somewhat different needs than the typical systems, so naturally they need a boost in power. Finally, technological advances in power conversion can make a fundamental difference in the quality of your workspace. Let's take a look Beyond A+ at these issues.

It Glows!

The enthusiast community has been modifying, or *modding*, their PCs for years now, cutting holes in the cases, adding fans to make overclocking feasible, and slapping in glowing strips of neon and cold cathode tubes. The power supply escaped the scene for a while, but not anymore. A quick visit to a good computer store, such as Directron.com, reveals a whole line of power supplies that light up, sport a fancy color, or have more fans than some rock stars. Figure 8.39 shows a quartet of colored, four-fan PSUs.

On the other hand, you also find super-quiet stealth power supplies, with single or double high-end fans that react to the temperature inside your PC—speeding up when necessary, but running slowly and silently when not. One of these would make a perfect power supply for a home entertainment PC, because they provide function without adding excessive decibels of noise.

Server Systems and the EPS12V Standard

Server motherboards are thirsty for power and sometimes ATX12V just doesn't cut it. An industry group called the Server System Infrastructure (SSI) came up with a non-ATX standard motherboard and power supply called EPS12V. An EPS12V power supply comes with a 24-pin main motherboard power connector that resembles a 20-pin P1 connector, but offers more voltage and thus more stability for EPS12V motherboards. It also comes with the 6-pin auxiliary power connector you find on some ATX12V power supplies and an 8-pin ATX12V as well as the 4-pin P4 connector. That's a lot of connectors! EPS12V power supplies are not interchangeable with ATX12V power supplies.

board, CPU, drives, and so on. Even adding in enthusiast-level equipment, such as multiple system fans, cathode ray tubes for interior lighting, and more, the 400-watt unit meets the demand *on paper*. But there's more to the story than simply the wattage listed on the power supply unit.

Converting from AC to DC comes at a certain cost. The average wattage lost in the conversion process is 30–50 percent! The number you really want to know when examining a power supply is the power factor (PF) number. Most power supplies have a PF number around 0.7, meaning a 30 percent power loss. In other words, the power supply only puts out 70 percent of the wattage it claims to put out! Suddenly that nice, shiny new, and oh-so-expensive 500-watt power supply looks a lot more enticing!

Some newer power supplies have added active power factor correction (Active PFC) circuits that smooth and tone the power conversion process, making it much more efficient. Active PFC power supplies have a PF upwards of 0.95, meaning only a 5 percent or less power loss in the conversion process. As an important added benefit, the Active PFC process reduces harmonics in the power supply—vibration that creates both physical noise (like a high-pitched whine) and electrical noise on the circuit. To deal with harmonics, electrical components have to work harder and thus burn out more quickly. Using Active PFC puts a lot less strain on the internal components of the power supply and quiets that background electrical hum that you don't notice until you turn out the lights.

Bottom line? An Active PFC power supply converts energy efficiently. As an added bonus, it's quieter and will last longer than a power supply without it.

Chapter 8 Review

Chapter Summary

After reading this chapter and completing the exercises, you should understand the following about power supplies.

Explain the Basics of Electricity

- The power supply takes electricity from the wall outlet and transforms it into the kind of electricity that the motherboard and other internal components use. To remove the power supply, simply unscrew the four screws in the back of the case and lift it out. Installing it is just as simple.
- Techs also need to know basic principles of electricity and how to recognize power problems. Electricity is a flow of negatively charged particles or electrons through matter. Metallic wire is a good conductor, allowing electrons to move freely. The pressure of the electrons in the wire is called voltage and is measured in volts (V). Measured in units called amperes (amps or A), current or amperage measures the amount of electrons flowing past a certain point on a wire. Wattage (watts or W) refers to the amount of amps and volts a particular device needs. The formula VA = W expresses the correlation among the three. Resistance to the flow of electrons is measured in ohms. Fuses and ground wires set limits for the flow of electrons. A ground wire provides a path of least resistance to allow the electrons to flow to ground.
- Electricity may be either direct current (DC), with electrons flowing in one direction around a continuous circuit, or alternating current (AC), with electrons flowing back and forth in a circuit. While the power company supplies high-voltage AC, the computer's power supply converts AC to low-voltage DC that is then portioned out to the internal devices. Heat is a byproduct of electricity and must be controlled in the computer.
- The power supply connects to the electrical outlet via a standard IEC-320 connector. While power in the U.S. ranges from 110 to 120 volts, the rest of the world uses 200–240 VAC. Most power supplies are able to switch between 110 and 220 voltage. The IEC-320 plug has three holes, called hot, neutral, and ground. The hot carries electrical voltage and should output approximately 115 V in the U.S. The neutral returns electricity to the breaker panel and should have 0 V output. The ground wire returns excess electricity to the ground and should also have a 0 V output. You can use a multimeter to test voltages at the outlet.
- A multimeter, also called a Volt-Ohm Meter (VOM), uses two probes to provide at least four measurements: AC voltage (V~), DC voltage (V with a solid line above a dashed line), continuity (whether electrons flow from one end of a wire to the other end), and resistance (whether a fuse is good or blown or whether a wire has breaks). Other AC-only testing devices are available that simply plug into the AC outlet and may display results via three light-emitting diodes (LEDs).
- Because the AC supply lacks consistency and actually provides power with sags and spikes, it is important to use two devices with the computer: an uninterruptible power supply and a surge suppressor. An uninterruptible power supply (UPS) continues to supply AC power to your computer during both brownouts and blackouts. An online UPS charges the battery from the AC outlet and is always online, providing power to the computer. Although it is expensive, an online UPS is the best choice to provide smooth AC current to the computer. A Standby UPS (SPS) does not provide battery power to the PC until the AC drops below ~80–90 V, kicking in just in time to save your data. It does not protect fragile electrical components against fluctuating AC. In addition, the battery may die without your being aware of it until it actually fails and you lose data. Be aware that many manufacturers of low-cost SPSs label them as UPSs. All uninterruptible power supplies measure the amount of power or watts they supply, as well as listing the number of minutes the UPS will last with a certain voltage. You should cut the number of minutes in half for a truer estimate of the abilities of the UPS.
- A surge suppressor is an inexpensive device that protects your computer from voltage spikes. Inserted between the wall outlet and the power

supply, a surge suppressor has a joule rating that measures how much electrical energy it can suppress. Be sure your surge suppressor has at least an 800 joules rating. Since telephone lines also produce spikes, your surge suppressor should bear a UL 497 A rating that indicates it has modem surge suppressor. Because surge suppressors work for only a limited time, you should check the manufacturer's recommended replacement schedules. If your surge suppressor comes with a cash guarantee, be aware that manufacturers honor it only if you follow their guidelines.

Provide Proper Power and Cooling to the PC

connector from the power supply. Some motherboards also need a four-wire P4 12V connector to provide an additional 12 volts of power.

- Peripherals use two or possibly three different kinds of connectors: the larger Molex connector and the smaller mini connector. Some power supplies also have a two-wire sub-mini. Used with hard drives and CD-ROM devices, the Molex has notches to ensure that it is connected properly. Used today only for floppy drives, the mini connector can easily be inserted incorrectly, thus destroying the floppy drive. The sub-mini, a single two-wire connector found on a few power supplies, is used for sensors or LEDs. If you do not have enough connectors for all the devices inside your PC, you can create more connections with a splitter.
- Power supplies are rated in watts. If you know the amount of wattage that every device in the PC needs, you can arrive at the total wattage required for all devices, and that is the minimum wattage your power supply should provide. If the power supply does not provide sufficient wattage for the PC, the computer will not work. For a new computer system, you should select at least a 400-watt power supply to have extra power for adding components in the future. Be aware also that power supplies produce less wattage over time, so don't cut the wattage specification too tightly. While power supplies range from 200–600 watts, you should know that the more AC it draws, the more heat it produces.
- Power supplies have been produced in two form factors: the older AT and the newer ATX. The AT form factor requires a hard on/off power switch and has trouble with electricity-saving features. Two connectors, P8 and P9, connect the AT power supply to the motherboard. Be sure to orient them with the black ground wires next to each other. The AT power supply provides only 12 V and 5 V power to the PC. Power switches for the AT feature either a rocker or plunger that turns the PC off when you touch it. That feature also makes the AT power supply unusable for today's computers that feature

interface card able to wake up the PC when there is incoming traffic. Using the soft power feature, the ATX power supply puts a 5-volt charge on the motherboard as long as there is AC from the wall socket. You can configure the ATX soft power through the Power Management section of the CMOS setup. When it is configured as "Soft-Off by PWRBTN," the on/off switch is set for a four-second delay, meaning that you must hold down the switch for four seconds before the computer cuts off. Always unplug an ATX system before you work on it. ATX power supplies use a single P1 connector for motherboard power. Available in smaller sizes, the microATX power supply fits into smaller cases, but it also provides less wattage, as little as 200 watts.

- Adequate cooling is important to prevent damage to the computer's internal components. The fan inside the power supply itself cools the voltage regulator circuits within the power supply and provides a constant flow of outside air throughout the interior of the computer case. If the fan is not working, turn the computer off before you experience equipment failure. Some power supplies regulate airflow by using a sensor, with a two-wire connector that plugs into the motherboard.
- To improve cooling, some cases come with a case fan. If the case does not have one, you should add one. Most case fans use standard Molex

connectors, but some use a special three-pronged power connector that plugs directly into the motherboard. To allow the fans to create an airflow, the case needs to be closed. If slot covers are left off empty expansion bays, it can cause the computer to overheat. Slot covers also help keep dust and smoke out of the case.

Troubleshoot Electrical Problems

- Electrical problems range from irregular AC to dying or faulty power supplies. Power supplies may fail suddenly or slowly over time. After you make sure that the wall outlet is providing electricity, checking voltages from the power supply with a voltmeter is the best way to verify that the power supply is working or has failed. A power supply is functioning properly if the output voltages are within 10 percent over or under the expected voltage. Be sure to check all the connections on the power supply. If you determine that it is bad, the most economical solution is to throw it away and replace it with a new one.
- If the power supply itself is okay, suspect that the power switch may be broken. If you can activate the switch by shorting the soft power jumpers with a key or screwdriver, you need a new switch. Although access to the switch behind the front frame of the PC may be difficult, you can replace both AT and ATX switches.
- If one of the internal electrical components in the power supply begins to fail, the result is usually intermittent problems, making it even more difficult to diagnose. If you are experiencing any intermittent problems, such as lock ups or different error codes that disappear after rebooting, suspect the power supply. Unfortunately, the voltmeter is not good for diagnosing intermittent problems. Since power supply failures rank second behind floppy drive failures, it is a good idea to keep power supplies in stock for swapping and testing.
- Never open a power supply, even to check the fuse, because they contain capacitors that carry very high voltage charges that can hurt you.
- Every PC workbench should have a Class C fire extinguisher handy in case of an electrical fire. Although some fire extinguishers are multi-class, handling all types of fire, use only a Class C fire extinguisher on your PC.
- Many new power supplies have features such as colors and multiple fans. Because servers need more power than that provided by the common power supply, the Server System Infrastructure (SSI), has created a new EPS12V power supply that uses a 24-pin connector as well as an auxiliary 6-pin connector. It provides more voltage and stability for EPS12V motherboards, but it is not interchangeable with ATX 12V power supplies.
- For most computer systems, a 300–400 watt power supply will provide adequate voltage. Because converting from AC to DC may result in a 30–50 percent loss of wattage, check the power factor (PF) number of your power supply. The PF number indicates the actual wattage that the power supply provides; for example, 0.7 means a 30 percent power loss. If a power supply has an active power factor correction (Active PFC), it has a much smaller power loss during conversion, often as small as 5 percent. Active PFC also reduces harmonics or vibration that creates physical and electrical noise on the circuit. The result is a power supply that converts energy efficiently, is quiet, and lasts longer than a power supply without Active PFC.

Key Terms

Alternating current (AC) *(252)*
Amperes (amps or A) *(252)*
AT *(261)*
ATX *(261)*
Direct current (DC) *(252)*
Joule *(256)*
Mini connector *(259)*
Molex connector *(259)*
Multimeter *(253)*
Ohms *(252)*
Online power supply *(254)*
P1 connector *(257)*
P4 12V connector *(258)*
P8 and P9 connectors *(261)*
Power supply fan *(264)*
Slot covers *(265)*
Soft-off by PWRBTN *(263)*
Standby power supply (SPS) *(254)*
Surge suppressor *(256)*
Uninterruptible power supply (UPS) *(254)*
Volts (V) *(252)*
Wattage (watts or W) *(252)*

Key Term Quiz

Use the Key Terms list to complete the sentences that follow. Not all the terms will be used.

1. Supply power to the floppy drive by using the __________ from the power supply.
2. The electric company provides __________ power that the power supply converts to __________ for use by the computer components.
3. Connect the older __________ power supply to the motherboard by placing the black wires
6. Be sure your surge suppressor has a __________ rating of at least an 800.
7. __________ is a measurement unit for the amount of electrons flowing past a certain point on a wire.
8. The __________ provides the basic cooling for the PC.
9. A __________ switches to provide battery power to the computer only when the AC drops below ~80–90 V.
10. Be sure the __________ rating for your

Multiple-Choice Quiz

1. Which UPS offers power conditioning?
   - A. Standby UPS
   - B. Online UPS
   - C. Universal UPS
   - D. Conditioning UPS
2. The ATX form factor power supply introduced all the following new features *except* __________.
   - A. It produces 5 V, 12 V, and 3.3 V.
   - B. It has a soft power feature.
   - C. It supports the Wake on Modem and Wake on LAN functions.
   - D. It has an internal power supply fan for cooling.
3. Which of the following statements best describes the differences between a UPS and a SPS?
   - A. An SPS is called an online UPS because it supplies power to the PC from a battery all the time, while a UPS provides battery power only when the AC current drops significantly.
   - B. A UPS is called an online UPS because it supplies power to the PC from a battery all the time, while a SPS provides battery power only when the AC current drops significantly.
   - C. Both a UPS and an SPS provide power to the PC from a battery all the time, but a UPS also provides power conditioning and the SPS does not.
   - D. The UPS provides protection for your data during a blackout, but it does not provide power conditioning, but the SPS both protects your data and provides power conditioning.
4. Which kind of fire extinguisher should you use for computer equipment?
   - A. Class A
   - B. Class B
   - C. Class C
   - D. Class D
5. Under what conditions should a PC technician work inside the power supply?
   - A. Only when it is unplugged
   - B. Only when the technician is wearing an anti-static wrist strap
   - C. Anytime, because the power supply only has low-energy DC electricity that will not hurt the technician
   - D. Never, because the power supply has capacitors that hold electrical charges that may harm the technician

6. The power supply dies slowly over time if one of its internal electrical components has begun to fail. All of the following statements may be indicators that the power supply is "dying slowly" *except* ________.
   - **A.** It usually produces intermittent problems that are difficult to diagnose.
   - **B.** It may result in different error codes that disappear after rebooting.
   - **C.** The computer will not start and the fan in the power supply will not turn.
   - **D.** The computer may run fine for an hour or so and then lock up, sometimes once or twice an hour.
7. When you test voltage with a multimeter, assume the outlet or connector is functioning properly if the reading is within ________ of the expected number.
   - **A.** 5 percent
   - **B.** 10 percent
   - **C.** 20 percent
   - **D.** 25 percent
8. What voltage does an ATX 12V P4 connector provide for some higher end motherboards?
   - **A.** 3.3 V
   - **B.** 3.3 V, 5 V
   - **C.** 5 V
   - **D.** 12 V
9. When inserting the motherboard power connector(s) from an ATX power supply into a motherboard, what should you keep in mind?
   - **A.** The P1 connector is keyed so it goes in easily one way. Press it in firmly.
   - **B.** The P8 and P9 connectors are keyed so they go in easily only one way. Slide them fully over the pins until they touch the motherboard.
   - **C.** The P8 and P9 connectors are keyed so they go in easily only one way, but you must orient them so that the red hot wires sit in the center. Slide them fully over the pins until they touch the motherboard.
   - **D.** The P8 and P9 connectors are keyed so they go in easily only one way, but you must orient them so that the black ground wires sit in the center. Slide them fully over the pins until they touch the motherboard.
10. When testing an AC outlet, what voltage should the multimeter show between the neutral and ground wires?
    - **A.** 120 V
    - **B.** 60 V
    - **C.** 0 V
    - **D.** –120 V
11. What sort of power connector does a hard drive typically use?
    - **A.** Molex
    - **B.** Mini
    - **C.** Sub-mini
    - **D.** Micro
12. Samwise installed a new motherboard in his case and connected the ATX power, but his system would not turn on. He sees an extra 4-wire port on the motherboard. What's he missing?
    - **A.** He needs a power supply with a P2 connector for plugging in auxiliary components.
    - **B.** He needs a power supply with a P3 connector for plugging in case fans.
    - **C.** He needs a power supply with a P4 connector for plugging into Pentium IV and some Athlon XP motherboards.
    - **D.** He needs a power supply with a Aux connector for plugging into a secondary power supply.
13. What is the effect of exceeding the wattage capabilities of a power supply by inserting too many devices?
    - **A.** The system will boot normally, but some of the devices will not function properly.
    - **B.** The system will boot normally and all of the devices will work, but only for a limited time. After an hour or so, the system will spontaneously shut down.
    - **C.** The system will not boot or turn on at all.
    - **D.** The system will try to boot, but the overloaded power supply will fail, burning up delicate internal capacitors.
14. What voltages should the two hot wires on a mini connector read?

A. Red = 3.3 V; Yellow = 5 V

B. Red = 5 V; Yellow = 12 V

C. Red = 12 V; Yellow = 5 V

D. Red = 5 V; Yellow = 3.3 V

15. Where do you put the multimeter leads when you test a Molex connector?

A. The red lead should always touch the red wire; the black lead should touch a black ground wire.

B. The red lead should always touch the black ground wire; the black lead should always touch the red hot wire.

C. The red lead should always touch the yellow hot wire; the black lead should touch the red hot wire.

D. The red lead should touch either the red or yellow hot wires; the black lead should touch a black ground wire.

Essay Quiz

How can you set a multimeter to test a fuse? What reading indicates that a fuse is good?

3. Often in the computer field, advances in one area will lead to advances in another area. Do you think that improvements in the CPU and other computer devices and functions made the ATX form factor power supply necessary?

Although she has not changed anything since then, today her computer won't even boot. You suspect that the power supply died. You know that she does not have a multimeter. What will you tell her to check to confirm this opinion? If she does need to replace the power supply, how can she be sure that new one will work with her PC?

Lab Projects

Lab Project 8.1

This chapter recommends a 400-watt power supply for a new computer. Is that the wattage that manufacturers usually offer with their computers? Check the following web sites to see what wattage comes with a new PC:

- www.dell.com
- www.gateway.com
- www.hp.com

Do any of these companies mention a power supply upgrade with a higher wattage rating? If so, what wattages and at what additional cost?

Lab Project 8.2

Every technician needs a multimeter. Visit a local electronics store and look at their line of multimeters. (If a store is not nearby, you may use the Internet instead.) What features do the different multimeters offer? What kinds of measurements do they provide? Is the output from some in digital format and others in analog? Which output do you find easier to read? Is one kind more accurate than another? What price ranges are available for multimeters? Then, select the multimeter you would like to add to your toolkit. Why did you choose that model? Now, start saving your pennies so you can buy it!

chapter

9 Floppy Drives

"Solo, I'm a soloist on a solo list. All live, never on a floppy disk."

—RAGE AGAINST THE MACHINE, "FREEDOM" FROM THE ALBUM *RAGE AGAINST THE MACHINE* (1992)

In this chapter, you will learn how to

- **Explain the basics of floppy drives**
- **Install a floppy drive correctly**
- **Perform basic floppy drive maintenance and troubleshooting**

Floppy drives enjoy the unique distinction of being the only component of a modern PC to contain basically the same technology they had in the original IBM PC. Certainly, floppy disk capacities and types have grown tremendously, from the first 160 KB, 5¼-inch, single-sided, single-density drives to the 1.44 MB, 3½-inch, dual-sided, high-density drives in the latest systems. But a modern floppy drive still uses the same cabling, configuration, and BIOS routines as the first floppy drives in the original IBM PC.

The first PCs predate hard drives. Hard to believe, but when the first PCs came out, the entire permanent storage system consisted of a single floppy drive! You booted the computer with a bootable floppy disk to get to an A: prompt. Once there, you removed your boot disk and inserted the program disk. If you wanted to save a file, you removed the program disk and inserted a data floppy. Messing with early PCs meant you were constantly swapping out floppy disks—but hey, we loved it! We were *computing*!

Some high-end systems used two floppy drives, reducing the amount of disk swapping considerably. If you had *two* floppy drives, you were the envy of the office (Figure 9.1).

Historical/Conceptual

It's important to be clear on some basic floppy terminology right at the start. The **floppy drive** reads floppy disks (once commonly called floppy *diskettes* because of their small size). **Floppy disks** are the storage media that you insert into the floppy drive. Floppy disks store the data. Many techs (myself included) unintentionally interchange these terms, and will assume that you know which one is which. Be sure you do.

Why still use such an old storage format, especially when there are newer ones like Zip disks and CD-ROMs available? Because PC makers fear incompatibility more than anything else. They must make a PC that works with any hardware or software designed for an

tems, the venerable floppy drive will disappear pretty rapidly. But until then the floppy drive, that artifact from the Dark Ages of the PC world, will continue to be a viable technology you must know.

■ Floppy Drive Basics

If you've used computers at all, you've probably used a floppy drive. When you insert a floppy disk into a floppy drive, the protective slide opens, revealing the magnetic media inside the plastic casing of the floppy disk. A motor-driven spindle snaps into the center of the drive to make it spin. A set of read/write heads then moves back and forth across the drive, reading or writing tracks on the disk as needed.

Whenever your system accesses a floppy disk in its floppy drive, a read/write LED on the outside front of the drive will flash on. You should not try to remove the floppy disk from the drive when this light is lit! That light means that the read/writes heads are accessing the floppy drive, and pulling the disk out while the light is on can damage the floppy disk. When the light is off, you can push in the small release button on the front of the drive to eject the floppy disk.

That's the basic 'User 101' version of floppy drives, but as a tech, you need to know much more. In this section, you'll learn the 'Tech 101' version of floppy drives, including disk formatting basics, disk types, and floppy drive sizes.

Formatting

Floppy drives are magnetically mapped to provide a structure for storing data on the disk. The process of mapping is called **formatting** the disk.

(You'll learn in detail how to format disks in Chapter 11.) The first step in the magnetic mapping process is the creation of a set of concentric circles called *tracks*. Then the disk is sliced up like a pie, effectively dividing each of the tracks into sections called sectors. A **sector** is the smallest data storage area on a disk. Each sector can store up to 512 bytes of data. Each track and each sector gets a number, so the system can locate any piece of data by specifying a particular sector on a particular track.

When you format a floppy disk, the system sets up four distinct areas on the disk: the boot record, the file allocation table (FAT), the root directory, and the data area. Again, you'll learn much more about these concepts in Chapter 11, but here's a brief overview. The boot record is a program that runs when you boot the computer and checks for the files required to accomplish the boot process. If it finds the required files, it transfers control to the OS to continue the boot process. The file allocation table (FAT) is a sort of spreadsheet that records the memory address locations for each file stored on the disk, and the status of each sector. The root directory is the base of the directory tree; all other directories are subsets of the root directory. The data area occupies the rest of the floppy disk; it's where the actual files are stored.

PCs aren't the only devices that use floppies. Apple Macintoshes, big IBM mainframe computers, UNIX workstations, and other devices you might not guess, like sewing machines, also use floppy drives. Each different device formats the data on the floppy disk differently; this has two consequences.

First, the usable storage capacity of physically identical disks is going to differ depending on how they are formatted, and again, that depends on what device is doing the formatting. The famous 3½-inch floppy disk provides a great example of this flexible capacity. On my PC, a 3½-inch floppy formats to hold **1.44 MB** of data. Taking that same floppy disk and formatting it in my wife's sewing machine, however, gives a different story. A sewing machine with a floppy drive? It's true! My wife's sewing machine has a floppy drive. She buys complex embroidery patterns on a floppy disk, snaps it in the machine, and *voilà*! Out comes a professional embroidery job!

Second, this is why a PC can't read a Macintosh floppy disk—it's not the data itself, or the disk itself, it's the way the data is organized on the disk that's the issue. Because of all the frustration this has caused their users, modern PC and Mac operating systems often include software enabling them to translate each other's formats. The floppy disk in my wife's sewing machine uses yet another totally different format. Don't even bother to try to put that disk into a PC—it will not know how to read the data.

Types of Disks

Floppy disk makers use a special terminology to describe how floppy disks are formatted. Because most floppy drives are intended for use in PCs, floppy disk makers usually preformat them using a PC-readable format. Because the format has been set, the makers can print the storage capacity on the disk.

Only three disk types ever saw widespread use in PCs:

- **Double-sided double density**
- **Double-sided high density**
- Double-sided extra high density

The designation "double-sided" is there because the very first floppies had only one readable side; double density refers to a jump in technology that doubled the original data capacity of those very earliest floppies. All formats except double-sided, high-density disks are now obsolete. Note also that in order to read a particular disk type, the drive has to support that type. All modern drives support both double-sided double density and double-sided high density disk types.

Floppy disks (and their drives) also come in multiple form factors, or sizes. You must know both the type and the size of a floppy disk formatted for PCs to know its capacity in bytes.

> The term "floppy" comes from the fact that these older floppy disks were actually floppy. You could easily bend one. Modern floppy disks come in much more robust rigid plastic casings, but the term has stuck—we still call them floppies!

Drive Size

The first PC floppy drives used a **5¼-inch floppy drive format**.

pay big money for these old drives.

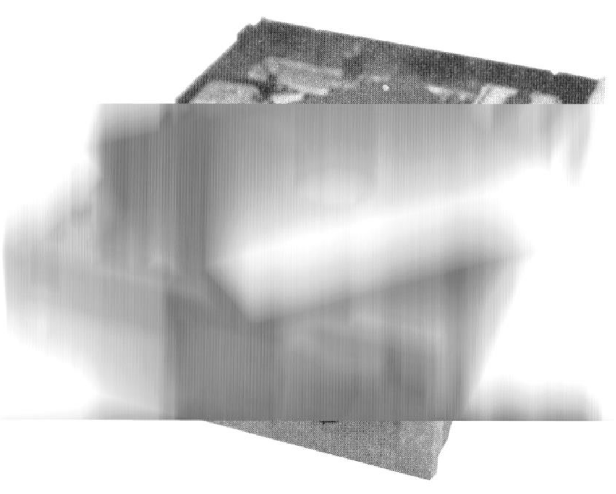

• **Figure 9.2** A 5¼-inch floppy drive

Around 1986, the **3½-inch floppy drive format** appeared, and within a few years came to dominate the floppy world completely (Figure 9.3). If you are really interested, however, pretty much every size and data format ever made is still available on the Internet!

Table 9.1 shows the data storage capacities of the three floppy disk formats listed above, in both common drive sizes.

• **Figure 9.3** A 3½-inch floppy drive

Test Specific

For all practical purposes, the only floppy drives found in PCs are the 1.44 MB, 3½-inch floppy drives. All of the other floppy drive types disappeared long ago. However, we still (barely) see enough of the 5¼-inch drives to make them interesting to us and to the A+ Certification exams. Fortunately, with the exception of a few connectors, the same procedures are used for

Table 9.1 Floppy Drive Data Capacities

Media	5¼ inch	3½ inch
Double-sided, double density	360 KB	720 KB
Double-sided, high density	1.2 MB	1.44 MB
Double-sided, extra high density	None made	2.88 MB

the installation, configuration, and troubleshooting of these two types of floppy drives.

Installing Floppy Drives

All Windows systems reserve the drive letters A: and B: for floppy drives. You cannot name them anything other than A: or B:, but you can configure a floppy to get either drive letter. In a moment, we will see how to configure a floppy for either A: or B:. However, convention dictates that if you have only one floppy drive, you should call it A:. The second floppy drive will then be called B:.

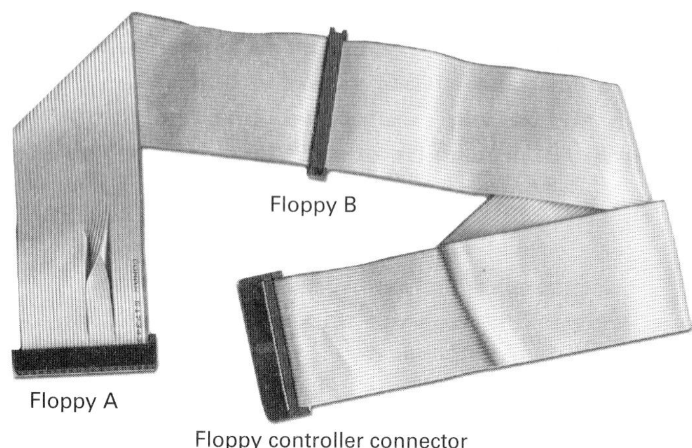

• Figure 9.4 Floppy cable that supports two drives

Floppy drives connect to the computer via a **34-pin ribbon cable** (Figure 9.4). If the cable supports two floppy drives, it will have a seven-wire twist in the middle, used to differentiate electronically between the A: and B: drives. Given that the majority of users do not want two floppy drives, many system makers have dropped the twist and saved a couple of pennies on a simpler cable (Figure 9.5).

By default, almost all PCs will first try the A: drive and then the C: drive at boot, looking for an operating system. This process enables technicians to insert a floppy disk into a sick computer to run programs when the hard drives fail. It can also enable hackers to insert bootable floppy disks into servers and do bad things. You do have a choice, however, as most systems have special CMOS settings that enable you to change this default boot order to something other than the default drive A:, then C:, and I'll show you how in a minute.

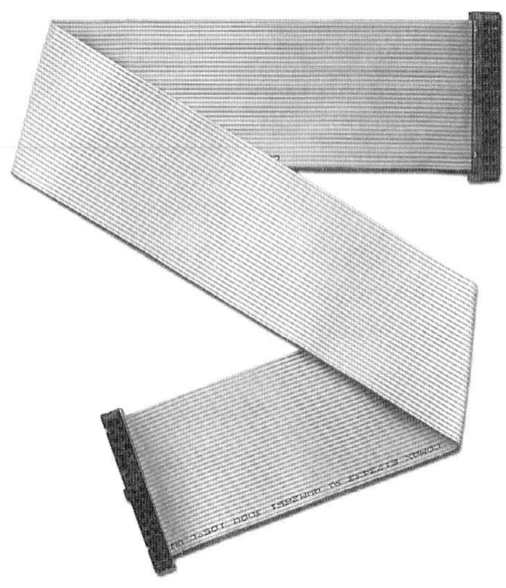

• Figure 9.5 Floppy cable for only one drive

Inserting Ribbon Cables

Look at the floppy cable in Figure 9.6. Notice the connector on the left side. This connector, identical to the other, plugs into the floppy controller on the motherboard, as shown in Figure 9.6. Notice how clearly the motherboard has **pin 1** marked in Figure 9.6. Not all motherboards are so clear. Make sure to orient the cable so that the colored stripe is aligned with pin 1.

Here are a few tips on cable orientation. By the way, these rules work for all ribbon cables, not just floppy cables! Ribbon cable connectors usually have a distinct orientation notch in the middle. If they have an orientation notch and the controller socket has a slot in which the orientation notch will fit, your job is easy (Figure 9.7).

Unfortunately, not all connectors use the orientation notch. Try looking in the motherboard book. All motherboard books provide a graphic of the motherboard, showing the proper orientation position. Look at other ribbon cables on the motherboard. In almost all mother-

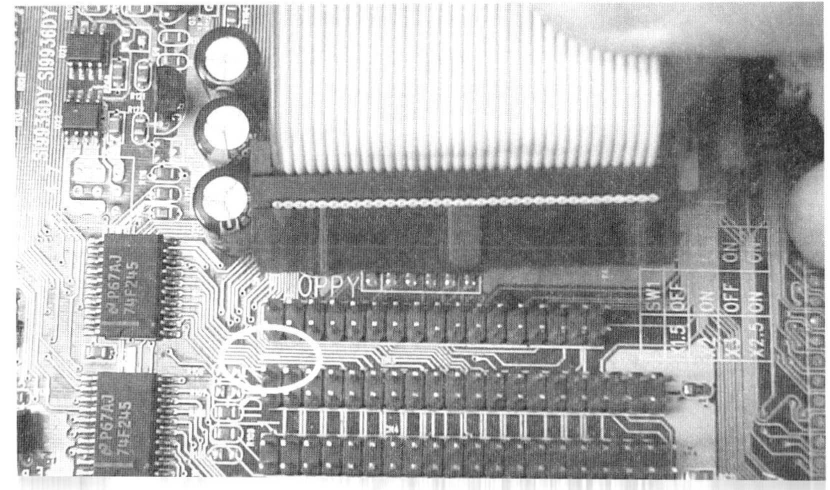

Tech Tip

Floppies and Booting

It's very common to leave a floppy disk in the computer when you shut it down. If you boot a system with a non-bootable floppy disk in the A: drive, the system will attempt to boot off that floppy and, finding no actual operating system, will respond with an error message similar to this:

```
Non-system Disk or Disk
```

message, smack yourself in the forehead (okay, that part's optional), pop out the floppy disk, and press any key to let the system start normally. Not that I have ever done this myself, of course!

stroy anything by inserting the cable backwards. But when you boot up, the floppy drive will not work! This is not a big deal; turn off the system and try again!

After you insert the floppy ribbon cable into the floppy controller, you now need to insert the ribbon cable into the floppy drive. Watch out here! You still need to orient the cable by pin 1—all the rules of ribbon cable insertion apply here, too. But before you plug in the floppy ribbon cable to the floppy drive, you need to know which connector on the cable to use; it makes a big difference. The specific connector that you insert into the floppy drive determines its drive letter!

Determining Drive Letters

If the floppy drive is installed on the end connector, it becomes the A: drive; if the drive is installed on the middle connector, it is the B: drive (Figure 9.8). If you're installing only one floppy, make sure you install it in the A: drive position or your system won't be able to boot to it! If you ever run into a situation with a two-floppy system where you want to turn the A: drive into the B: drive, or vice versa, you can accomplish this easily by swapping the connectors. (Most systems enable you to do this through CMOS, as well. More on that shortly.)

A few floppy drives come with a special set of jumpers that enable you to change the floppy drive letter. These jumpers usually say DS0, DS1, and Cable Select. (Don't count on this—floppy drive makers have wide marking variances, and no two makers do

• **Figure 9.7** Floppy controller with notch

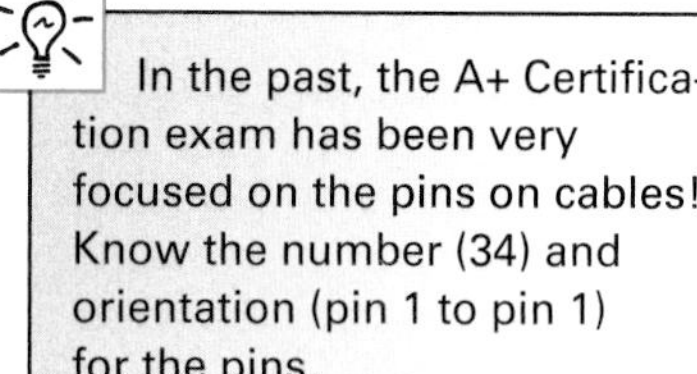

In the past, the A+ Certification exam has been very focused on the pins on cables! Know the number (34) and orientation (pin 1 to pin 1) for the pins.

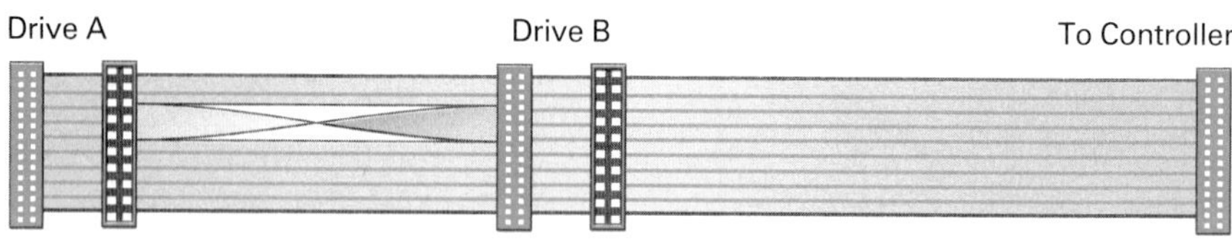

• **Figure 9.8** Cable placement determines the drive letter.

this the same way!) With this kind of drive you can set the jumper to DS0, forcing the drive to use the drive letter A:. Never do this! No one but you will remember, and the next tech who looks at that floppy will invariably want to change it to B:, won't understand why the stupid floppy drive won't switch to B:, and will throw it out. So now you know that some floppy disk drives have jumpers—you also know to leave the jumpers alone!

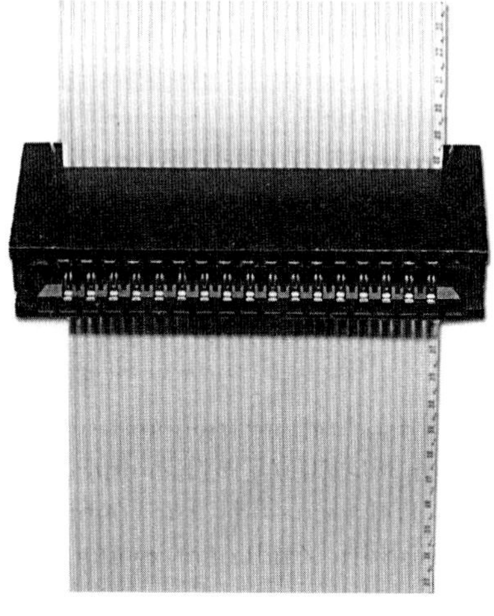

• **Figure 9.9** A 5¼-inch floppy cable connector

Connectors

All the preceding cabling examples apply only to 3½-inch drives. The 5¼-inch and 3½-inch drives use different connectors. Figure 9.9 shows a 5¼-inch drive connector, and Figure 9.10 shows a 3½-inch drive connector.

Most cables have only 3½-inch connectors. A few cables have both types of connectors, as illustrated in Figure 9.8. This may give less knowledgeable folks the idea that they can install more than two floppy drives. But look closely at Figure 9.8. Notice that one of each type of connector sits on either side of the twist. You can use either a 5¼-inch or 3½-inch drive as the A: drive, but not both. The same applies for the B: drive; you can use one or the other, but not both.

• **Figure 9.10** A 3½-inch floppy cable connector

Power

Floppy drives need electricity in order to work, just like every other device in the PC. Modern 3½-inch floppy drives use the **mini power connector**. Old 5¼-inch drives use the large Molex-type connector also used by hard drives.

Incorrectly inserting a power connector will instantly destroy the floppy drive. Inspect the power connector carefully to ensure correct orientation before you plug it into the floppy drive! Inserting a Molex connector *correctly* often takes a lot of pushing and wiggling. Inserting a Molex incorrectly, on the other hand, requires more strength than I possess, but I have watched a few brawny techs do it!

Although incorrectly inserting a Molex is difficult, inserting a mini connector incorrectly takes little effort. Look at the "from below" figure (Figure 9.11) of a properly installed mini connector—note the chamfers (beveled edges) that show correct orientation. The problem lies in the plastic used to make the connector. The plastic connector bends easily, giving even the least brawny techs the ability to put the plug in a mini backwards or to hit only three of the four pins. Be careful inserting a mini connector!

have physically installed the floppy drive, it's time to go into CMOS.

CMOS

After the floppy drive is installed, the next step is configuring the CMOS settings, which must correspond to the capacities of the drives. Look in your CMOS for something called "Standard CMOS Settings" or "Storage." Most CMOS setups configure the A: drive by default as a 3½-inch, 1.44 MB drive. Simply double-check the setting in CMOS and if it's okay, get out without changing anything. Figure 9.13 shows a typical CMOS setting for a single floppy drive.

Look in the "Beyond A+" section of this chapter for an explanation of the *Floppy 3 Mode Support* CMOS option in Figure 9.13.

On the rare occasion that you require a different setting from the typical 3½-inch, 1.44 MB A: drive, simply select the drive (A: or B:) and enter the correct capacity. Figure 9.14 shows a CMOS with another 3½-inch floppy drive on B:.

You can find three other options on a current CMOS screen that enable you to make useful, although not necessary, modifications: Swap Floppy Device, Boot Up Floppy Seek, and Boot Sequence.

The Swap Floppy Device setting enables you to change the A: and the B: drives without moving the cables (Figure 9.15). It may take some poking around to find it, and not every CMOS has the option. This is useful if you have a PC with two floppy drives that won't boot to the A: drive. You can switch the

```
CMOS Setup Utility - Copyright (C) 1984-1999 Award Software
                    Standard CMOS Features

Date  (mm:dd:yy)          Wed, Oct  4  2000        Item Help
Time  (hh:mm:ss)          10 : 40 : 45
                                                   Menu Level  ▶
▶ IDE Primary Master      Press Enter10263 MB
▶ IDE Primary Slave       Press Enter13020 MB      Change the day, month,
▶ IDE Secondary Master    Press Enter None         year and century
▶ IDE Secondary Slave     Press Enter None

Drive A                   1.44M, 3.5 in.
Drive B                   None
Floppy 3 Mode Support     Disabled

Video                     EGA/VGA
Halt On                   All,But Keyboard

Base Memory                 640K
Extended Memory           113664K
Total Memory              114688K
```

• **Figure 9.13** CMOS setting for one standard floppy drive

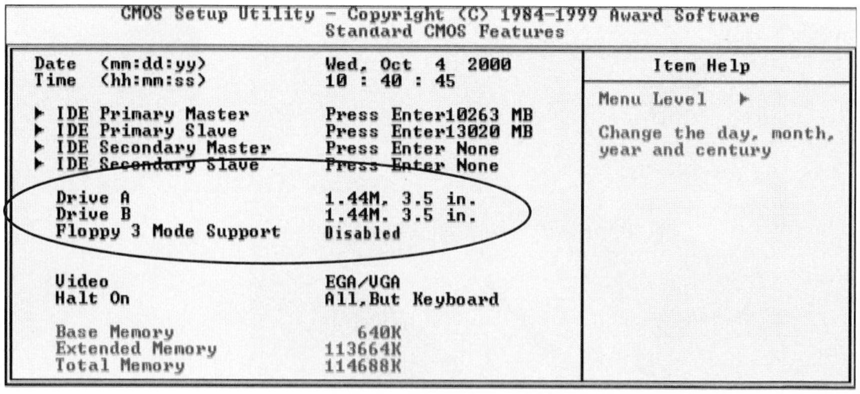

Figure 9.14 CMOS setting for two floppy drives

cable connections, of course, but this CMOS setting does the switching electronically.

Disabling the Boot Up Floppy Seek option tells the PC not to check the floppy disk during the POST, which isn't very handy except for speeding up the boot process (Figure 9.16). Please do not confuse this option with booting from the floppy! This option does not skip searching the floppy for an operating system after the POST.

The third option techs often play with in CMOS is the Boot Sequence. Earlier, I mentioned that the default boot sequence for a PC is drive A: and then drive C:. That statement is true, but in addition, almost every system provides a third choice of boot device, usually the CD-ROM. Most systems assume you may want to boot off of your CD-ROM drive, because both the Windows 2000 and Windows XP Install CD-ROMs are bootable.

Several other devices are found in boot sequences commonly enough to be worth mentioning here. High-end workstations often feature SCSI hard drives either in addition to an IDE drive, or even in place of it, so CMOS settings normally include a SCSI boot option that will look for such a drive. Two modern substitutes for the venerable floppy drive—Iomega's Zip drive, and the floppy-compatible LS-120 drive—can also be installed as bootable drives, and are now commonly included among the boot options in CMOS.

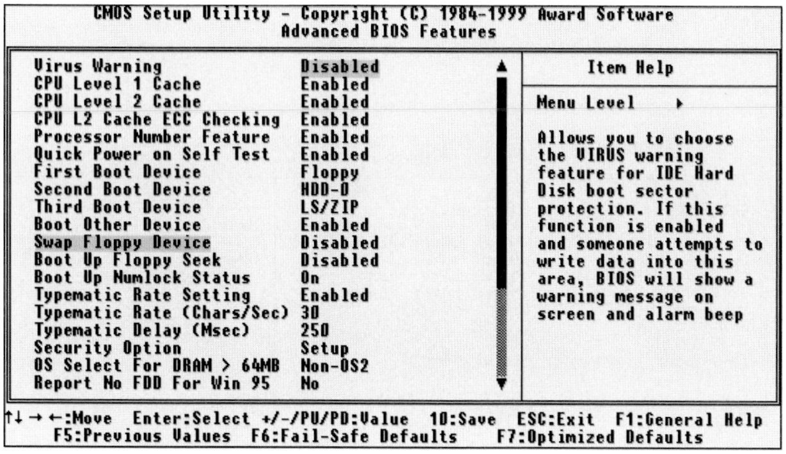

Figure 9.15 CMOS Swap Floppy Device option

The Boot Sequence CMOS option enables you to change the boot sequence. CMOS settings differ greatly between PCs, but the following list of boot options represent common options you may find:

- A, C, SCSI[1] (my usual setting)
- C, A, SCSI (when I want to boot from the hard drive, but still hit the floppy drive if the hard drive fails)

1 For more on SCSI, see Chapter 19.

- C, CDROM, A
- CDROM, C, A (when I want to boot off the CD-ROM)
- SCSI, A, C
- SCSI, C, A
- A, CDROM, C
- A, C, CDROM
- C only (Super Safety option)
- LS/ZIP[2], C

Figure 9.17 shows the Boot Sequence options in my CMOS.

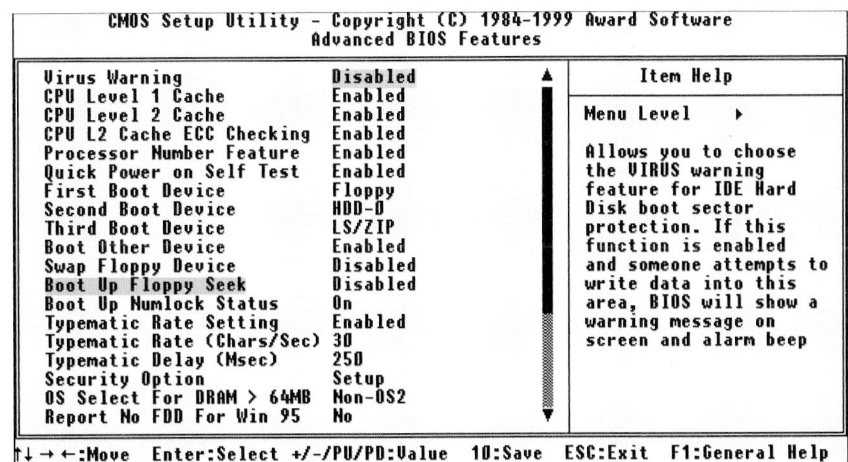

IRQ) by choosing *Report No FDD for Win 95*. You must also disable the floppy drive controller on the motherboard and give up your floppy drive. This usually isn't necessary, however, as most Plug and Play devices will not even try to use IRQ 6 even if it is available.

Floppy Drive Maintenance and Troubleshooting

No single component fails more often than the floppy drive. This is not really that surprising because floppy drives have more exposure to the outside environment than anything but the keyboard. Only a small door (or in the case of 5¼-inch drives, not even a door) divides the read/write heads from dust and grime. Floppy drives are also exposed to the threat of mechanical damage. Many folks destroy floppy drives by accidentally inserting inverted disks, paper clips, and other foreign objects. Life is tough for floppy drives!

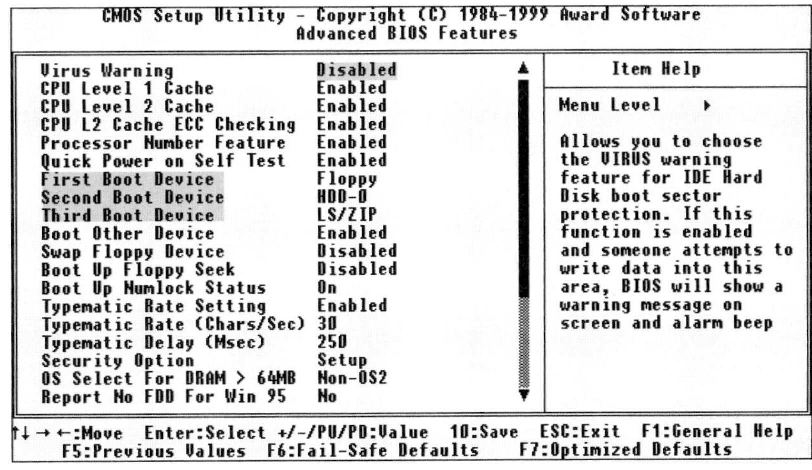

Figure 9.17 Boot Sequence options in CMOS

2 LS/ZIP is the selection for an LS-120 or Iomega Zip drive.

Cross Check

PC Installation Procedures

Review the expansion card installation procedures in Chapter 6, and compare them to the floppy drive installation procedure you just learned. In what ways are they alike? Can you deduce any generalized rules for PC installation procedures? In what ways do they differ? Why?

In the face of this abuse, the key preventative maintenance performed on floppy drives is cleaning. You can find floppy drive **cleaning kits** at some electronics stores, or you can use a cotton swab and some denatured alcohol to scour gently inside the drive for dust and other particles.

Repairing Floppy Drives

When a floppy drive stops working, follow these steps to resolve the problem:

1. Check for a bad floppy disk.
2. Check for data errors on the disk.
3. Check the CMOS settings.
4. Blame the floppy controller.
5. Check the cable.
6. Replace the floppy drive.

First, Check the Floppy Disk

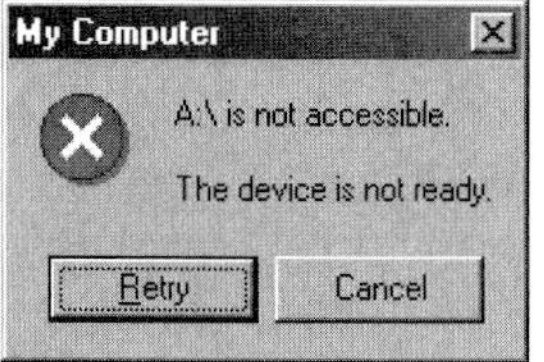

Figure 9.18 Floppy disk read error

The vast majority of the time, when the floppy drive decides it won't read a floppy disk, the bad guy is the floppy disk, not the floppy drive. When the floppy drive refuses to read a floppy disk, you usually get an error like the one shown in Figure 9.18.

If you get this error, first try inserting another floppy disk. If a new disk from a fresh box won't work, don't insert another one from the same box. Find another disk, preferably from another box or one just lying around to retest. If the floppy drive refuses to read two floppy disks, then suspect the floppy drive is the problem. Otherwise, blame the disk!

Tech Tip

Check Inside the Drive

Sometimes pieces of a floppy disk—the metal shutter, for example, or the spring—can get jammed into the drive by users who keep trying to shove a disk into the drive. The user won't notice anything different except that the disk doesn't work and sometimes sticks in the drive. If you have any trouble inserting the floppy disk, take a flashlight and peer inside the drive to check for stray bits that don't belong!

Second, Check for Data Errors on the Disk

If other floppy disks work in the drive, the floppy disk has a problem. If a floppy disk fails, you have three options. First, just throw it away. Second, reformat the floppy disk. The only downside to these two options is that you lose the data on the floppy disk, and sometimes that is not an acceptable option. Your third option is to run some sort of recovery/fixing software on the disk.

Floppy disks come preformatted from the manufacturer. We reformat floppies for one of two reasons: either as a handy way to completely erase a floppy disk or as a last-ditch effort to try to fix a bad floppy. To reformat a floppy disk in any version of Windows, go to My Computer and alternate-click (right-click) the floppy icon. Select Format to see the dialog box shown in Figure 9.19.

Note that in Windows XP, although the first three settings appear to be pull-down menus, you don't actually get any format options besides the ones showing. In Windows 2000, the Capacity pull-down menu does let you format the floppy as an ancient 720 KB as well as a modern 1.44 MB type. The Format options radio button group enables you to choose between Quick Format (just erases data), or Create an MS-DOS Startup Disk (don't format the floppy—save the data, just make it bootable). You add a Volume Label, which simply enables you to place a small amount of text on the floppy to help describe the contents. Volume labels were quite popular in the DOS days but are almost never used today.

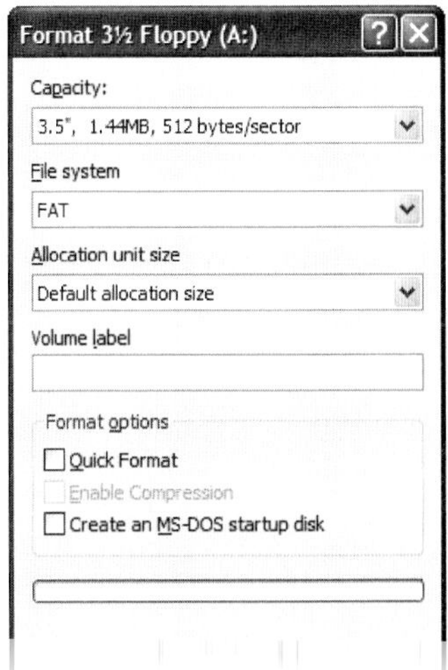

Third, Check the CMOS Settings

CMOS settings for floppies rarely cause problems. All BIOS makers default

Next, Blame the Floppy Controller

If the data cable or power plug is loose, the POST will flag with either "FDD Controller Failure" or "Drive Not Ready" errors. At this point, open the machine and verify the connections. If the connections are good, it's possible that your motherboard has a bad floppy drive controller. Checking the floppy drive controller requires two basic steps. First, turn off the onboard controller. To turn off the controller, go into CMOS and find the Onboard FDD Controller option (or something like that) and disable it as shown in Figure 9.20. Some motherboards don't give you the option to do this, in which case you need to disable the controller in Device Manager.

Second, go to the computer store (hooray!) and buy one of two things. On the off chance that the store has a PCI FDD controller card, pick it up. You can install it and plug in the floppy drive. If the drive works then, suspect the onboard controller. If the floppy drive still doesn't work, remove the card and reenable the CMOS setting for the onboard controller.

Try This!

Creating a Windows 98 Startup Disk

If you have a computer system running Windows 98, you should have a startup disk you can boot from when your computer locks up and won't boot normally. Grab a blank floppy disk and try this:

1. Open the Control Panel from the Start menu. Double-click on the Add/Remove Programs icon to start that applet. Select the Startup Disk tab and click the Create Disk button.
2. Insert a floppy disk when prompted. Windows will create a bootable floppy by formatting the disk and adding certain key files that will enable Windows to boot from it. When the process is finished, remove the floppy and label it *Windows 98 Startup Disk.*
3. Restart the system with the Startup disk inserted. You should see a Windows startup screen with several boot options. Select Start Computer with CD-ROM support, and watch the boot process progress to the A:\> prompt. Remove the startup disk and reboot into Windows.

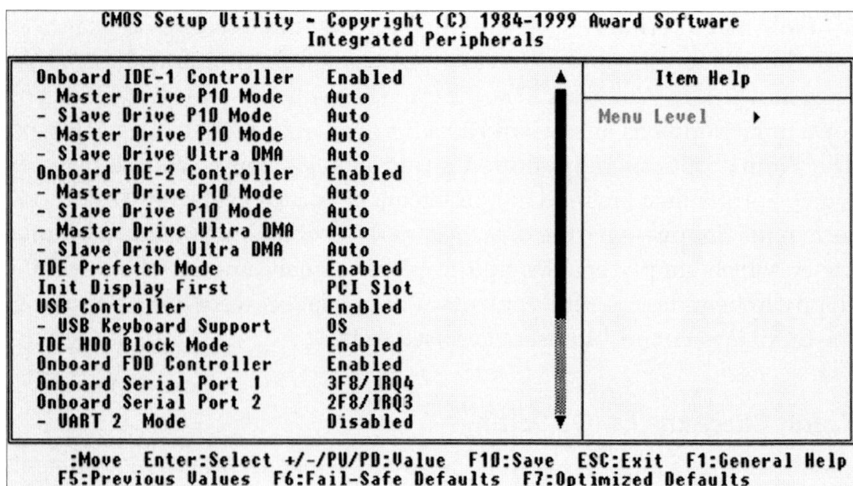

• **Figure 9.20** Onboard FDD Controller option

Alternatively, you can get an external USB floppy drive (Figure 9.21). This won't give you a bootable floppy drive, but you can bypass the internal components altogether and access it in Windows. Figure 9.22 shows My Computer in a system with only a USB FDD installed. Note that the USB device shows up as D:, but that you have the option of clicking on the A: drive as well. Clicking on either drive icon will access the same floppy disk.

Maybe It's the Cable...

Your next investigation should focus on whether the cable is the culprit. The 34th wire on the floppy-drive cable is called the **drive change signal** (or disk

• **Figure 9.21** USB floppy disk drive

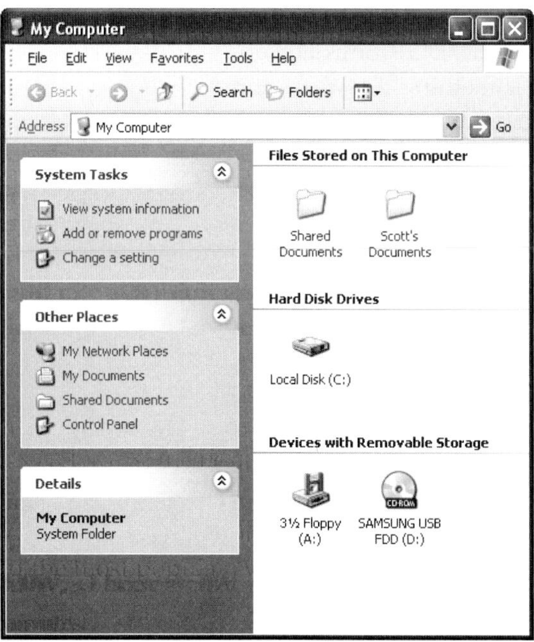

• **Figure 9.22** My Computer showing the USB FDD as both D: and A:

change signal). When a floppy drive is inserted or removed, this wire is active. When Windows first reads a floppy drive, it keeps a copy of the directory in RAM and will not update that information unless the floppy drive detects a disk removal and activates the drive change signal. This keeps the system from constantly rereading the very slow floppy drive. Windows waits until it knows it needs rereading. However, if the drive change signal disconnects because of a bent pin or bad cable, you will keep seeing the same directory, even if you change the disk! This problem almost always traces back to a bad floppy cable, so replace it and retry.

Connectivity plays a big (and sometimes embarrassing) role in floppy drive failure. One of the most common errors techs make installing floppy drives is reversing the ribbon cable on one or both ends. If you reverse it on *one end*, invariably the LED on the drive (the light) comes on the moment you turn on the system and *stays on*. Always check the light on the floppy

[illegible]

Last, Replace the Floppy Drive

At this point, if the floppy drive isn't working, the only recourse is to replace the drive. When you replace a bad drive, throw it away. Keeping a bad floppy drive is a study in frustration because almost all bad floppy drives aren't consistently bad—just "sometimes bad." Technicians are often tempted to give a bad floppy drive one more chance. They install the drive, and it works! They're convinced they made a mistake and declare the drive "good." If the drive is reinstalled somewhere else, however, it will soon die again. Throw it away.

Floppy drives fail more than any other part of a computer system. In any five PCs, at least one floppy drive will need to be replaced in a year. So keep floppy drives in stock. Purchase them in quantity, at least five at a time, so you'll receive a discount. Buying floppy drives one at a time is expensive and a waste of time.

Beyond A+

That covers the things you must know for the A+ Certification exam, but before we finish with floppy drives, I want to pass on a couple of extra nuggets of PC tech knowledge to round out your understanding. You won't be tested on these, but you may encounter them in the field. To finish up, I'll introduce you to the newest floppy drive technology, and the technology that may finally replace them!

Other CMOS Options

Many CMOS setup utilities now have an option called Floppy 3 Mode Support. Go way back to Figure 9.13 to see an example of a CMOS with this option. A Mode 3 floppy is a special 1.2 MB format used outside of the United States, primarily in Japan. Unless you use Mode 3 floppy disks, clear this option.

```
          CMOS Setup Utility - Copyright (C) 1984-1999 Award Software
                          Advanced BIOS Features

 Virus Warning               Disabled          Item Help
 CPU Level 1 Cache           Enabled
 CPU Level 2 Cache           Enabled      Menu Level    ▶
 CPU L2 Cache ECC Checking   Enabled
 Processor Number Feature    Enabled      Allows you to choose
 Quick Power on Self Test    Enabled      the VIRUS warning
 First Boot Device           Floppy       feature for IDE Hard
 Second Boot Device          HDD-0        Disk boot sector
 Third Boot Device           LS/ZIP       protection. If this
 Boot Other Device           Enabled      function is enabled
 Swap Floppy Device          Disabled     and someone attempts to
 Boot Up Floppy Seek         Disabled     write data into this
 Boot Up Numlock Status      On           area, BIOS will show a
 Typematic Rate Setting      Enabled      warning message on
 Typematic Rate (Chars/Sec)  30           screen and alarm beep
 Typematic Delay (Msec)      250
 Security Option             Setup
 OS Select For DRAM > 64MB   Non-OS2
 Report No FDD For Win 95    No

↑↓→←:Move  Enter:Select +/-/PU/PD:Value  10:Save  ESC:Exit  F1:General Help
    F5:Previous Values  F6:Fail-Safe Defaults    F7:Optimized Defaults
```

Figure 9.23 Report No FDD For Win95

Report No FDD For Win 95 shows up in many CMOS setup utilities (Figure 9.23). This option will release IRQ6 (the floppy drive's IRQ) if the system does not have a floppy drive. You must also turn off the onboard floppy drive controller. It works. The problem with this setting is that very few PCs still do not have floppy drives! If a PC does not have a floppy drive, it is probably such a simple system (a net PC or a legacy-free PC) that it doesn't need the extra IRQ. Besides, very few Plug and Play devices will ever *try* to use IRQ6, even if it is available. I guess if you were desperate for one more IRQ and were willing to give up a floppy disk, it might be useful. I would leave it alone.

Radial Misalignment

For years I have told techs to throw away bad floppy drives. But in reality, it is possible, even fairly easy, to fix floppy drives. Roughly 50 percent of all floppy drive failures are due to misaligned read/write heads—the technical term is **radial misalignment**. When you read or write data on a floppy disk, small motors in the drive move read/write heads back and forth over concentric tracks on the disk, calculating the correct distances from a predetermined zero point near the center. Because the distances involved are quite tiny, if the actual starting position of the head shifts even fractionally off this zero point, the head may have trouble reading data and may even partially overwrite data on nearby tracks when it performs a write function. Radial misalignment can be caused by normal wear and tear over time or by damage from foreign objects, including dust and grit blown in by the case fans. If your floppy drive fails to read three or four known good floppy disks, you almost certainly have a radial misalignment.

Many manufacturers make special programs, combined with special testing disks that enable you to realign the read/write heads. Some of the programs require an oscilloscope. They are all very expensive, usually around $300. Unless you intend to repair 25 floppy drives or more a year, the time it takes to fix the floppy and the cost of the product do not make sense. But if you are a *big* operation, they do save you money in the long run.

USB Floppy Drives

In the portable PC arena, the traditional internal floppy drive is fading into history. Many portable PCs either have no floppy drive at all, or it is integrated into a docking station. The other common way to add this functionality is through an external USB floppy drive (Figure 9.21). Small and light enough to tuck in a corner of your laptop case, they are a reasonable compromise if you absolutely must be able to read a floppy disk on the road, and don't fancy lugging the extra weight of a docking station/media slice.

One note of caution, though: unless your system's BIOS supports it (many laptops and newer desktop systems tout this capability), you can't boot to an external USB floppy drive, because it won't work until you boot to Windows and load its driver. In other words, for most existing systems, you can forget bringing it along so you can use your boot floppy in case of

[illegible]

about the size of your thumb! These tiny new drives (Figure 9.24) are actually just a new implementation of the Compact Flash cards now ubiquitous in the digital camera world. For a two-digit price in US$, you can get a 128 MB thumb drive that stores as much data as 80 standard 3.5-inch floppy disks.

The smallest thumb drives are slightly smaller than a regular pack of chewing gum, while others are larger and more rounded. The drives are hot Plug and Play in Windows 2000/XP, but you will need to install a driver if you're running Windows 98/SE. You can simply plug one into any USB port and it will appear as a removable storage device in My Computer. After you plug the drive into a USB port, you simply copy/move data to or from your hard disk, then unplug the unit and take it with you. You can read, write, and delete files directly from the drive. Because these are USB devices, they don't need an external power source. The non-volatile flash memory is solid state so it's shock resistant and supposed to retain data safely for a decade. One big improvement over floppies is cross-platform compatibility—you can transfer files among Mac, Windows, and Linux operating systems.

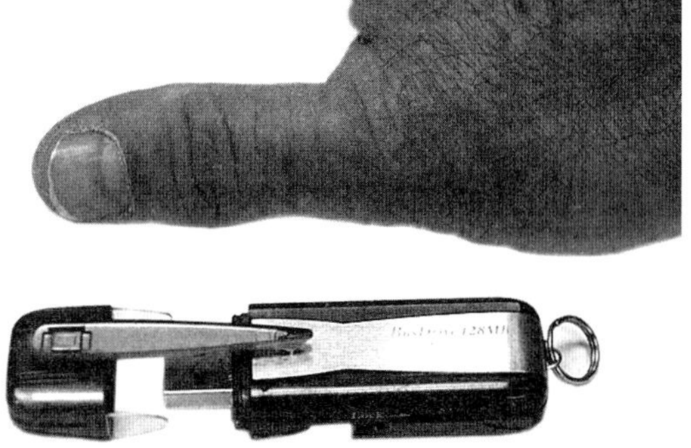

• **Figure 9.24** USB Flash memory drives

The basic USB Flash memory drive is pretty spiffy, but the various manufacturers haven't been idle. Features on newer models include capacities as big as 2 GB, USB 2.0–compliance, password protection, file encryption, built-in e-mail software, and even an upgradeable memory chip so you can make your current drive larger.

Chapter 9 Review

Chapter Summary

After reading this chapter and completing the exercises, you should understand the following facts about floppy drives.

Explain the Different Types of Floppy Drives

- The floppy drive is a hardware component inside the system box. It reads floppy disks. Floppy disks are the storage media that you insert into the floppy drive. As well as providing mobility, floppy drives also provide compatibility among different computers and different software.
- The magnetic coating on a newly made floppy disk has no charge until it is formatted. Formatting means placing organizational information on the floppy disk so that it can store data in a useful way. During the formatting process, magnetic charges are placed on the disk to create special storage areas, called sectors. Each sector can store up to 512 bytes of data.
- Over the years disks came in two different sizes and a broad array of capacities. PCs have used only three disk types, two of which are obsolete. The double-sided, double density and the double-sided, extra high density have all but disappeared, while the double-sided, high density type has survived. Both the 360 KB and the 1.2 MB capacity 5¼-inch format have also disappeared, along with the 720 KB, 3½-inch disk. The predominant format today is the 1.44 MB, 3½-inch disk.
- All PCs are designed to support up to two floppy drives, but virtually all modern PCs have only one floppy drive.

Install a Floppy Drive

- Modern 3½-inch floppy drives use a mini power connector.
- Floppy drives use a 34-pin cable. This cable may have a twist and a second connection for a second floppy drive. If there is more than one floppy drive on a system, their drive letters are determined by their positions on the cable. The drive connected on the end is A:, and the one connected in the middle is B:.
- Most recent BIOS makers default the CMOS settings for the A: drive to a 3½-inch high density floppy drive.
- The colored stripe on the 34-pin ribbon cable identifies pin 1 and should be oriented to match pin 1 on the controller socket and pin 1 on the drive itself. Many cables have an orientation notch in the middle to prevent installing them wrong. If the cable does not have an orientation notch, the motherboard book should identify pin 1 on the controller.
- The default boot sequence for a PC is drive A: and then drive C:. The Boot Sequence CMOS option enables you to change the boot sequence. On a modern system you are likely to want to include the CD-ROM drive in your boot sequence.

Perform Basic Floppy Drive Maintenance

- Use a floppy drive cleaning kit at least once a month to ensure the best possible performance from your floppy drives.
- When a floppy drive stops working, follow these steps to resolve the problem: (1) Blame the floppy disk. (2) Check for data errors on the disk. (3) Check the CMOS settings. (4) Blame the floppy controller. (5) Check the cable. (6) Replace the floppy drive.
- You may use a utility such as Scandisk or Spin Rite to try to repair a damaged disk.
- A loose data cable or power plug will result in a FDD Controller Failure or Drive Not Ready error.
- To reformat a floppy disk in any version of Windows, open My Computer, alternate-click (right-click) on the floppy icon, and select Format.
- Roughly 50 percent of all floppy drives fail due to misaligned read/write heads, a condition called radial misalignment. Radial misalignment can be caused by normal wear and tear over time or by damage from foreign objects, including dust and grit blown in by the case fans. If your floppy drive fails to read three or four known good floppy disks, you almost certainly have a radial misalignment.

- The 34th wire on the floppy-drive cable is called the drive change signal. Windows doesn't reread a floppy disk until the floppy drive detects a disk removal and activates the drive change signal. This keeps the system from constantly rereading the very slow floppy drive.
- If you reverse one end of the floppy drive ribbon cable when plugging it in, the LED on the drive (the light) will come on when you turn on the system and then stay on. If you reverse both ends, you will usually get an FDD error at POST, the LED will not come on at all, and the drive will not work.

Key Terms

1.44 MB *(278)*
34-pin ribbon cable *(280)*
3½-inch floppy drive format *(279)*
5¼-inch floppy drive format *(279)*
Double-sided high density *(278)*
Drive change signal *(288)*
Floppy disk *(277)*
Floppy drive *(277)*
Non-System Disk or Disk Error *(281)*
Pin 1 *(280)*
Radial misalignment *(290)*

1. ______________ is the most common cause of floppy drive failure.
2. You should use a ____________ at least once a month as part of your basic floppy drive maintenance.
3. Windows won't reread a floppy drive until the ___________ is activated.
4. Floppy drives use a ___________ to connect the floppy drive to the motherboard.
5. The term for the way data is organized on a floppy disk is ____________.
7. A modern floppy drive uses a _________ to connect to the power supply.
8. The red stripe on a floppy drive cable must be oriented to _________ on the controller.
9. The capacity of the most commonly used floppy disk used today is ___________.
10. The hardware is the floppy drive while the removable storage medium itself is the ______________.

Multiple-Choice Quiz

1. When you tried to boot your computer, you got the error message:
   `Non-System disk or disk error`
   `Replace and strike any key when ready`
   What caused this message and what should you do to solve the problem?
   - **A.** Your hard drive has gone bad. You'll need to replace it.
   - **B.** Your floppy drive has gone bad. You'll need to replace it.
   - **C.** Your operating system files are corrupted. You should reinstall the operating system.
   - **D.** You left a non-bootable floppy disk in drive A:. You need to remove it.
2. You installed a floppy drive that you want to function as the A: drive, but your system won't boot to it. What is the most likely cause of this problem?
   - **A.** You attached the drive to the middle connector on the cable.
   - **B.** You attached the drive to the end connector on the cable.
   - **C.** You forgot to configure the CMOS settings for drive A:.

D. You forgot to configure the CMOS settings for a single floppy drive only.

3. Floppy disks have been made in all the following types *except* ________.

   A. Single-sided low density

   B. Double-sided double density

   C. Double-sided high density

   D. Double-sided extra high density

4. What is the maximum number of floppy drives you can install?

   A. One

   B. Two

   C. Three

   D. Four

5. You just installed a floppy drive and you notice that the floppy drive LED stays on. What is most likely the problem?

   A. You attached the floppy drive to the wrong connector on the ribbon cable.

   B. You forgot to configure the floppy drive through the CMOS setup.

   C. You did not attach the colored stripe on the ribbon cable to Pin 1 at the drive or at the controller.

   D. You forgot to attach the power cable to the floppy drive.

6. After installing a 3½-inch double-sided, high density floppy drive, you should go to the CMOS setup and double-check that the drive capacity is set to ________.

   A. 360 KB

   B. 720 KB

   C. 1.2 MB

   D. 1.44 MB

7. If the floppy disk you used last week will not work today in your floppy drive, what should you do first to determine if the problem is the drive or the disk?

   A. Try another disk in the drive or try the disk in another drive.

   B. Open the computer and check the ribbon cable.

   C. Replace the floppy drive.

   D. Check the CMOS settings.

8. During the POST, your system reports a *FDD Controller Failure*. What is the most likely cause?

   A. The floppy drive controller has gone bad and needs to be replaced.

   B. Either the data cable or the power plug is loose.

   C. The CMOS settings are messed up.

   D. Pin 1 on the ribbon cable has been attached backwards.

9. How can the IT department prevent someone from booting the computer using a floppy disk?

   A. In the CMOS setup program, change the Boot Up Floppy Seek setting to disabled.

   B. In the CMOS setup program, change the Swap Floppy Device setting to disabled.

   C. In the CMOS setup program, change the Boot Sequence to C: only.

   D. There is no way to prevent someone from booting the computer with a floppy disk.

10. Which component on a typical PC fails more often than the floppy drive?

    A. None

    B. Keyboard

    C. Mouse

    D. Hard drive

11. If you have a floppy disk that contains data you want to keep, which of the following format options can you choose to make the disk bootable?

    A. Quick Format

    B. Copy System Files Only

    C. Add a Volume Label

    D. Full Format

12. A floppy drive ribbon cable has __________ pins and may have a ________-wire twist.

    A. 25, 5

    B. 34, 7

    C. 40, 9

    D. 50, 5

13. What should you do if the floppy controller built onto the motherboard goes bad?

    A. Replace the motherboard.

    B. Stop using floppy drives.

    C. Disable the floppy drive controller through CMOS setup and install an I/O card with a floppy controller.

    D. Connect the floppy drive cable to one of the IDE hard drive controllers.

14. The 5¼-inch floppy drive got its power from a __________ power connector while a 3½-inch floppy drive uses a ________ power connector.

    B. mini, Molex

    C. Molex, P1

    D. P1, mini

15. If your CMOS setup includes *Report No FDD for Win 95*, what advantage do you gain by enabling this option?

    A. It prevents anyone from booting to the floppy drive.

    B. It speeds up the boot process.

    C. It releases IRQ 6 for use by another device.

    D. It disables the floppy drive.

assuming that they first format the disks they use. John's system is an exception—his system can read floppies right out of the box. John's system can read Jane's and Dave's floppies, but not Debbie's. Jane can read John's, but not Dave's or Debbie's. Debbie cannot read anyone's floppies. Dave can read only John's floppies. What strategy would make it possible for everyone to read everyone else's floppy disks? Write a brief memo explaining your recommendation to your boss.

2. You're a contractor for a government agency that wants to replace 130 old 386 systems with modern computers. All of the 386 systems use 5¼-inch floppy drives, and you estimate that the office has close to a thousand 5¼-inch floppy disks that are actively being used to store data. Although all of the files on these floppies are around only 300 K, in many cases the users need 10 to 20 disks just to save one group of related data files. Users need to continue to pass data among themselves using some type of removable media. Create a step-by-step action plan that describes how you will upgrade these systems while preserving their existing data and still give the users a way to share data.

4. Why do most manufacturers continue to build computers with floppy drives rather than using the LS-120 or the Iomega Zip or some other higher-capacity alternative? If you bought a new computer, would you still want a floppy disk on it? Why or why not?

5. You are a PC tech for a small business with a dozen computer users. You must decide what CMOS boot options are appropriate for the different users under your care. Three of them are secretaries whose desks are just inside the door to the hallway you share with a number of other companies. They handle confidential data and are particularly concerned with security. Seven of them are writers working in a back part of the office. They are primarily concerned with always being able to boot up their systems to retrieve their documents. The remaining two are executives whose primary concern is a speedy boot process. They don't keep any data on their local systems, but you still need to be able to troubleshoot their systems if they fail to boot. Write a brief memo outlining and explaining your recommendations for each group.

Lab Projects

• Lab Project 9.1

Check all the computers in your classroom to determine whether every system can read every other system's floppy disks.

1. First go to each system with a new box of floppy disks and determine which systems can read the disks. Try copying files to and from a floppy on each system.
2. Format a floppy disk on one system and then go to every other system in the room to see if they all can read that floppy disk. Try copying a file and reading that file on each system you test.
3. Make a table outlining your results with a row for each system being tested, and columns for New Disk and Formatted Disk.

• Lab Project 9.2

Let's examine a 3½-inch floppy disk and observe the following things:

1. Does your disk have a brand name and any other identification? Does it identify the capacity or indicate if it is preformatted? If so, how can you interpret what it says?
2. The metal shutter opens when the disk is inserted in the drive. You can slide the shutter to the side and see the Mylar or plastic surface of the disk where the data is stored. Notice that the Mylar surface is available on both the top and the bottom of the disk so that the drive's read/write heads can access both sides. When you push the button to remove the disk from the drive, the shutter closes to protect the Mylar surface from dust.
3. Turn the disk over to the back side and note that the center portion is also a metal area. The drive grabs this hub to spin the disk in a circle.
4. At the lower-right side of the back is the write enable notch. When it is closed, the computer can both read and write to the disk. If you want to write protect the disk so that the data cannot be changed or erased, merely open the notch.
5. At the lower-left side of the back is a second hole that identifies to the computer that this is high-density disk. A double-density disk lacks this hole.

• Lab Project 9.3

Install two floppy drives in a test system. If possible, use both Windows 98 and Windows 2000/XP systems for comparison.

1. Review the steps involved in floppy drive installation. Consider the order in which you want to perform these steps in a two-drive installation.
2. Install and configure the first drive, keeping in mind that you will be installing a second one. In particular consider cabling issues and CMOS issues.
3. Install and configure the second drive. Did you adequately account for its needs when installing the first drive?
4. Test the drives to make sure you installed them correctly. Troubleshoot any problems you encounter.
5. Do a group 'Lessons Learned' session to compare notes on your installation experiences. What worked? What would you do differently next time? What tips would you give somebody doing their first installation?

Hard Drive Technologies

"At 0700 hours tomorrow morning my shutdown disk will be activated and all mental and

Of all the hardware on a PC, none gets more attention—or gives more anguish—than the hard drive. There's a good reason for this: if the hard drive breaks, you lose data. As we all know, when the data goes, you have to redo work or restore from backup—or worse. It's good to worry about the data, because the data runs the office, maintains the payrolls, and stores the e-mail. This level of concern is so strong that even the most neophyte PC user is exposed to terms such as backup, defragment, and scandisk—even if they don't put the terms into practice!

This chapter provides the first set of tools for the tech in dealing with hard drives, focusing on how they work and interface with the PC, and how to install them properly into a system. Chapter 11 completes the tools by adding in the operating systems, showing you how to prepare drives to receive data and how to maintain and upgrade drives in all versions of Windows. Let's get started.

In this chapter, you will learn how to

- **Explain how hard drives work**
- **Identify and explain the different hard drive interfaces**
- **Configure BIOS for hard drives and controllers**
- **Troubleshoot hard drive installation**

Historical/Conceptual

IBM did not visualize a hard drive as part of the original IBM PC. When the first PC debuted in 1980, it boasted support for up to two floppy drives and support for an external cassette tape drive. It wasn't until the IBM Advanced Technology (AT) computer in 1984 that we saw true hard-drive support in the form of system basic input/output services (BIOS) that could talk to hard drives. Since then, many improvements have been made to hard drives. They are much faster and can hold thousands of times as much data as the first 5 MB to 10 MB drives. Hard drives today are much smaller and much more dependable. They are inarguably an integral part of a modern computer.

Let's start with a trip inside a typical hard drive to see how it works. Then we'll turn to other issues, such as drive technologies in use, installation, and troubleshooting.

How Hard Drives Work

All hard drives are alike in that each is composed of individual disks, or *platters*, with read/write heads on actuator arms controlled by a servo motor—all contained in a sealed case that prevents contamination by outside air (see Figure 10.1).

The platters are made of aluminum and are coated with a magnetic medium. Two tiny read/write heads service each platter, one to read the top and the other to read the bottom of the platter (see Figure 10.2).

The coating on the platters is phenomenally smooth! It has to be, as the read/write heads actually "float" on a cushion of air above the platters, which spin at speeds between 3,500 and 10,000 rpm. The distance (flying height) between the heads and the disk surface is less than the thickness of a fingerprint. The closer the read/write heads are to the platter, the more densely the data packs onto the drive. These infinitesimal tolerances demand that the platters never be exposed to outside air. Even a tiny dust particle on a platter would act like a mountain in the way of the read/write heads and would cause catastrophic damage to the drive. To keep the air clean inside the drive, all hard drives use a tiny, heavily filtered aperture to keep the air pressure equalized between the interior and the exterior of the drive.

• **Figure 10.1** Inside the hard drive

Data Encoding

Although drives do store data in binary form on the hard drive, visualizing a magnetized spot representing a 1 and a non-magnetized spot representing a 0 grossly oversimplifies the process. Hard drives store data in tiny magnetic fields—think of them as tiny magnets that can be placed in either direction on the platter, as shown in Figure 10.3. Each tiny magnetic field is called a flux and can switch back and forth through a process called a *flux reversal* (see Figure 10.4).

The earliest hard drives used flux reversals as do the latest ones created today. Basically, as the read/write head moves over a spot, the direction of the flux reversal defines a 1 or a 0. Look at Figure 10.5. As the read/write head passes from the left to the right, it recognizes fluxes in one direction as a 0 and the other direction as a 1. Hard drives [illegible] interesting point, and the place where great leaps in technology have taken place, is in how the hard drives use the flux reversals. This is called the "encoding method." Hard drive makers have changed methods for encoding several times over the years, resulting in dramatic increases in storage capacities.

Because hard drives constantly read flux reversals at outrageously fast rates, hard drives need a way to say "where the heck am I?" on the drive. The first encoding methods reserved some percentage of the fluxes to hold *timing bits*. Every timing bit on the drive reduced the number of data fluxes, but for many years no other encoding method existed. The first method used on hard drives, called *frequency modulation* (FM), preceded every data flux with a timing bit, which took up significant (50 percent) disk space (see Figure 10.6). A substantial improvement to FM, called *modified frequency modulation* (MFM), quickly supplanted the older encoding technology in hard drives. MFM substantially reduced the number of timing bits by only placing them after two consecutive 0's (see Figure 10.7). MFM stood as the predominant encoding method on hard drives for many years.

Starting around 1991, hard drives began using a data encoding system known as *run length limited* (RLL). RLL stores data using "runs"—

• **Figure 10.2** Top and bottom read/write heads and armatures

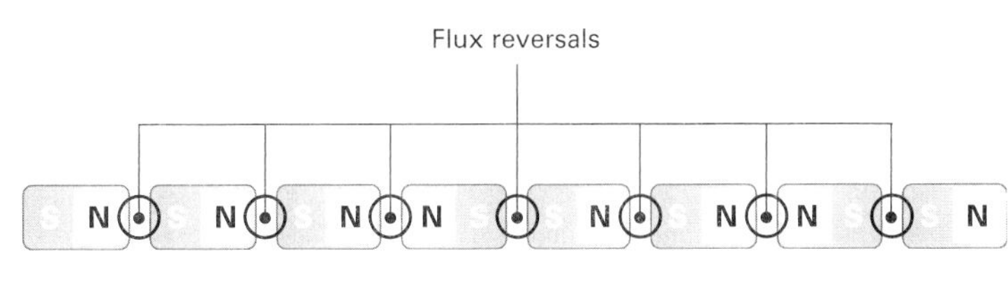

• **Figure 10.4** Flux reversals

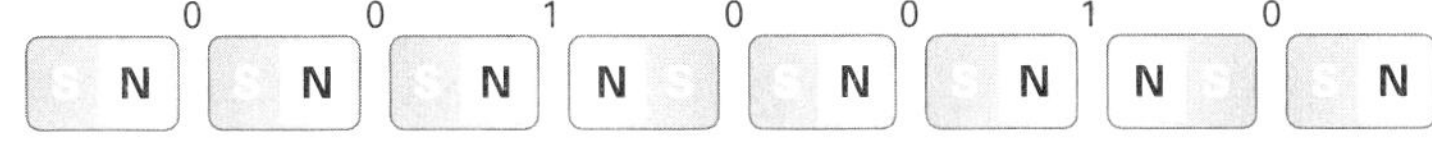

• **Figure 10.5** Fluxes in one direction are read as 0 and the other direction as 1.

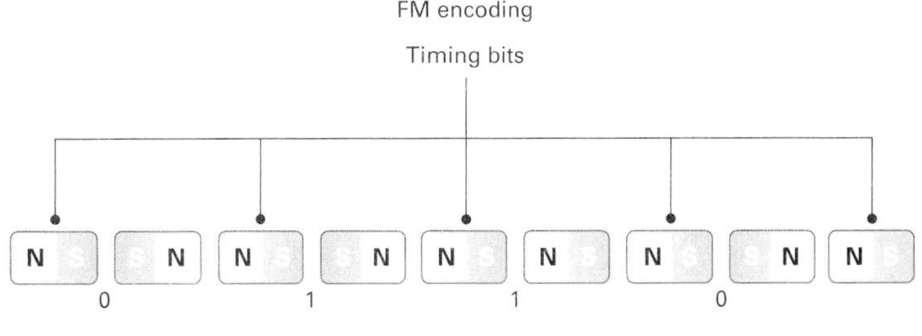

• **Figure 10.6** Frequency modulation

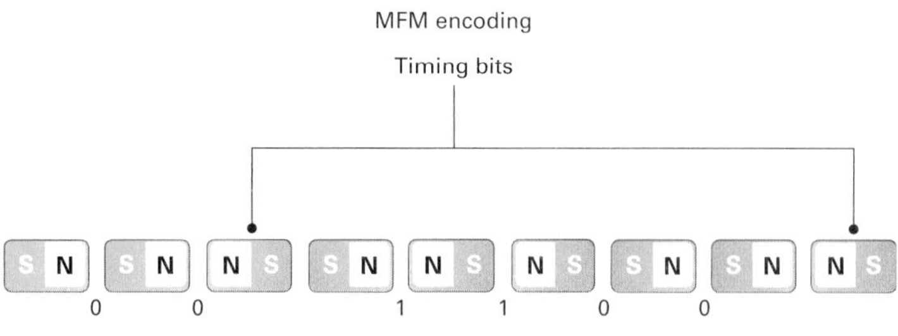

• **Figure 10.7** Modified frequency modulation

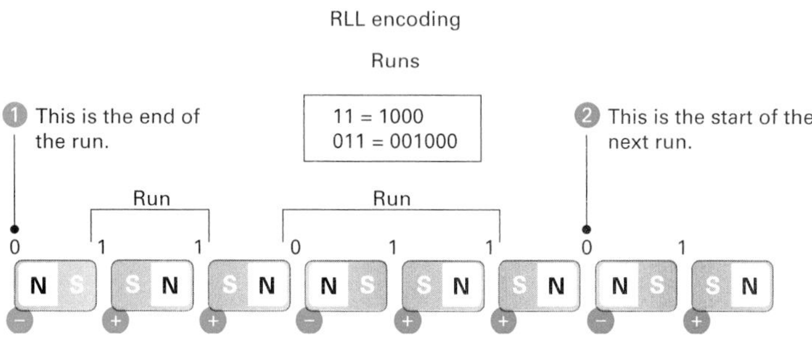

• **Figure 10.8** Sequential RLL runs

unique patterns of 1's and 0's—to represent longer patterns of 1's and 0's. For example, 110 in some versions of RLL represents 1000101. Whenever you see RLL, you also see two numbers: the minimum and the maximum run length, such as RLL 1,7 or RLL 2,7. Using distinct runs enables RLL to eliminate the need for timing bits, and small combinations of RLL patterns can represent long strings of 1's and 0's. Figure 10.8 shows two sequential RLL runs.

Today's drives use an extremely advanced method of RLL called **Partial Response Maximum Likelihood (PRML)** encoding. As hard drives pack more and more fluxes on the drive, the individual fluxes start to interact with each other, making it more and more difficult for the drive to verify where one flux stops and another starts. PRML uses powerful, intelligent circuitry to analyze each flux reversal and to make a "best guess" as to what type of flux reversal it just read. As a result, the maximum run length for PRML drives reaches up to around 16 to 20 fluxes, far more than the 7 or so we saw on RLL drives. Longer run lengths enable the hard drive to use more complicated run combinations, which gives the hard drive phenomenal data storage. For example, a hypothetical run of 1001010010101110 might equal:

1001001001001011110100100010011100100100
1010110010010101010100101010 01!

Virtually all hard drives use PRML (or a proprietary derivative) today. PRML is the unsung hero of increased drive capacities. Without PRML, hard drives could not pack the fluxes as closely as they do in today's hard drives.

For all this discussion and detail on data encoding, the day-to-day PC technician never really deals with encoding. This is important because so many questions come up on this topic and sometimes knowing what you don't need to know helps as much as knowing what you do need to know. Fortunately, data encoding is inherent to the hard drive and completely invisible to the system. You're never going to have to deal with data encoding! But you'll sure sound smart when talking to other PC techs if you know your MFM from your PRML!

Moving the Arms

The read/write heads are moved across the platter on the ends of actuator arms. In the entire history of hard drives, manufacturers have used only two technologies: stepper motor and voice coil. Hard drives first used stepper motor technology, but have long since moved to voice coil.

Stepper motor technology moved the arm in fixed increments or steps. This early technology had several limitations. Because the interface between motor and actuator arm required minimal slippage in order to ensure precise and reproducible movements, the positioning of the arms became less precise over time. This physical deterioration caused data transfer errors. Additionally, heat deformation wreaked havoc with stepper motor drives. Just as valve clearances in automobile engines change with operating temperature, the positioning accuracy changed as the PC operated and various hard drive components got warmer. Although very small, these changes caused problems. Accessing the data written on a cold hard drive, for example, became difficult after the disk warmed. In addition, the read/write heads could damage the disk surface if not "parked" (set in a non-data area) when not in use, requiring techs to use special "parking" programs before transporting a stepper motor drive.

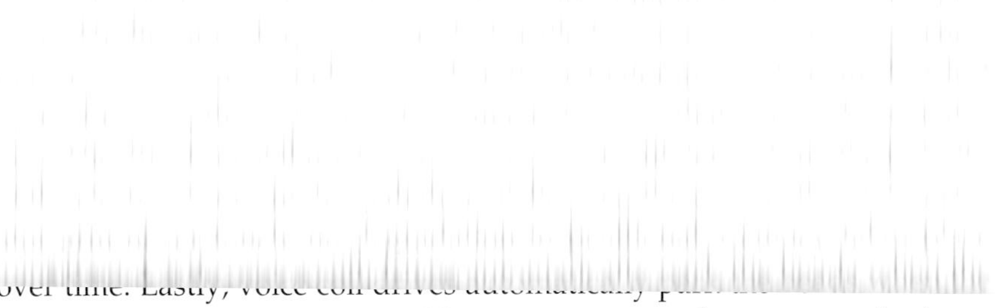

over time. Lastly, voice coil drives automatically park the drive loses power, making the old stepper motor park programs obsolete.

Lacking the discrete "steps" of the stepper motor drive, a voice coil drive cannot accurately predict the movement of the heads across the disk. To make sure voice coil drives land exactly in the correct area, the drive reserves one side of one platter for navigational purposes. In essence, this area "maps" the exact location of the data on the drive. The voice coil moves the read/write head to its best guess about the correct position on the hard drive. The read/write head then uses this map to fine-tune its true position and make any necessary adjustments.

Now that you have a basic understanding of how a drive physically stores data, let's turn to how the hard drive organizes that data so we can use that drive.

Geometry

Have you ever seen a cassette tape? If you look at the actual brown Mylar (a type of plastic) tape, you will not see anything that tells you whether sound is recorded on that tape. Assuming the tape is not blank, however, you know *something* is on that cassette tape. The music on that tape is stored in distinct magnetized lines. You could say that the physical placement of those lines of magnetism is the tape's "geometry."

Geometry determines where the drive stores data on the hard drive. As with a cassette tape, if you opened up a hard drive, you would not see the geometry. But rest assured that the drive has geometry. Every model of hard drive uses a different geometry. We describe the geometry for a particular hard drive with a set of numbers that refer to five special values: the heads, cylinders, sectors per track, write precomp, and landing zone. The following sections describe what each value means.

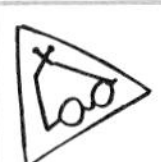

Tech Tip

Fluid Bearings

Currently, almost all hard drives use a motor located in the center spindle supporting the drive platters. Tiny ball bearings support the spindle motor, and as disk technology has advanced, these ball bearings have become the limiting factor in the three critical design criteria for hard drives: rotational speed, storage capacity, and noise levels. The higher the

platters wobble), called runout, *is now the limiting factor on how densely you can pack information together on a disk drive.*

The technological fix? Fluid bearings. A fluid bearing is basically a small amount of lubricant trapped in a carefully machined housing. The use of fluid in place of metal balls means there's no contact between metal surfaces to generate heat and wear, and no mechanical vibration, so fluid bearings can support higher rotational speeds. The runout of a fluid bearing is about one-tenth of that of the best ball bearing, increasing potential information density significantly. The absence of a mechanical connection between moving parts also dramatically reduces noise levels, and the fluid itself acts to dampen the sound further. Finally, liquid bearings provide better shock resistance than ball bearings.

"Parking" a drive is meaningless in today's PCs.

Heads

The number of heads for a specific hard drive describes, rather logically, the number of read/write heads used by the drive to store data. Every platter requires two heads. If a hard drive has four platters, for example, it would need eight heads (see Figure 10.9).

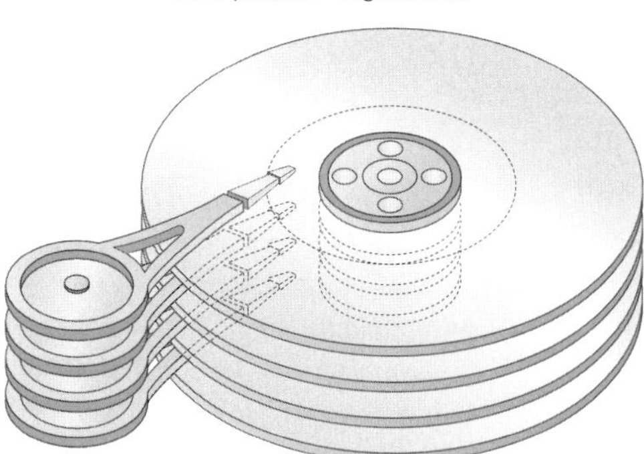

• **Figure 10.9** Two heads per platter

Based on this description of heads, you would think that hard drives would always have an even number of heads, right? Wrong! Most hard drives reserve a head or two for their own use. Therefore, a hard drive can have either an even or an odd number of heads.

Cylinders

To visualize cylinders, imagine taking a soup can and opening both ends of the can. Wash off the label and clean out the inside. Now look at the shape of the can; it is a geometric shape called a cylinder. Now imagine taking that cylinder and sharpening one end so that it easily cuts through the hardest metal. Visualize placing the ex-soup can over the hard drive and pushing it down through the drive. The can cuts into one side and out the other of each platter. Each circle transcribed by the can is where you store data on the drive, and is called a *track* (Figure 10.10).

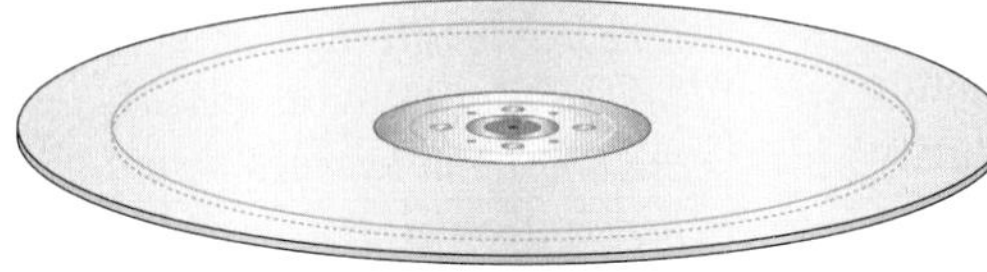

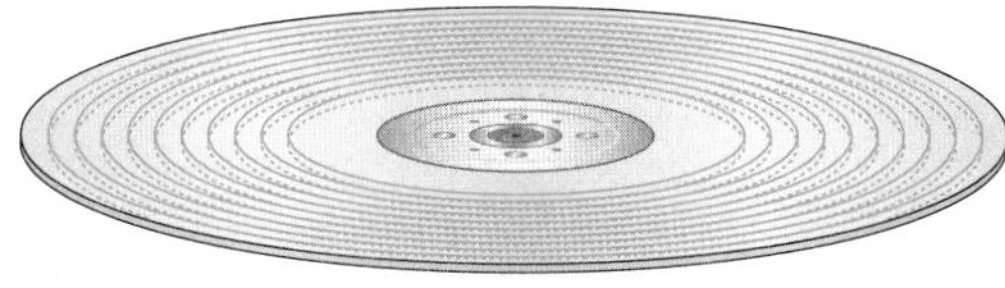

• **Figure 10.10** Tracks

Each side of each platter contains tens of thousands of tracks. Interestingly enough, the individual tracks themselves are not directly part of the drive geometry. Our interest lies only in the groups of tracks of the same diameter, going all of the way through the drive. Each group of tracks of the same diameter is a called a **cylinder** (see Figure 10.11).

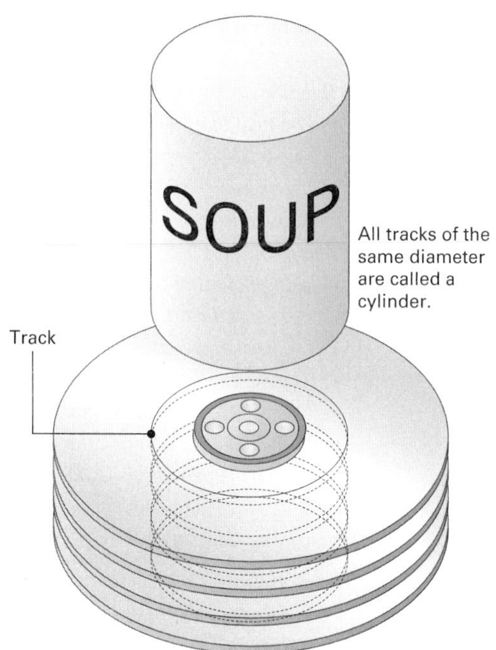

• **Figure 10.11** Cylinder

There's more than one cylinder! Go get yourself about a thousand more cans, each one a different diameter, and push them through the hard drive. A typical hard drive contains thousands of cylinders.

Sectors per Track

Now imagine cutting the hard drive like a birthday cake, slicing all the tracks into tens of thousands of small slivers. Each sliver is called a *sector*, and each sector stores 512 bytes of data (see Figure 10.12). Note that "sector" refers to the sliver when discussing geometry, but refers to the specific spot on a single track within that sliver when discussing data capacity.

The sector is the universal "atom" of all hard drives. You can't divide data into anything smaller than a sector. Although sectors are important, the number of sectors is not a geometry. The geometry value is called *sectors per track* (sectors/track). The sectors/track value describes the number of sectors in each track (see Figure 10.13).

The Big Three

Cylinders, heads, and sectors/track combine to define the hard drive's geometry. In most cases, these three critical values are referred to as *CHS*. The importance of these three values lies in the fact that the PC's BIOS needs to know the drive's geometry in order to know how to talk to the drive. Back in the old days, a technician needed to enter these values into the complementary metal-oxide semiconductor

(CMOS) manually. Today, every hard drive stores the CHS information in the drive itself in an electronic format that enables the BIOS to query the drive automatically to determine these values. More on this in the section on Autodetection.

If you recall, the geometry consists of five values, but so far only three have been introduced: cylinders, heads, and sectors/track. Unlike the CHS values, the last two values—write precomp and landing zone—no longer have relevance in today's PCs; however, most CMOS setup utilities still support them—another classic example of a technology appendix! Let's look at these two holdouts from another era so when you access CMOS, you won't say, "What the heck are these?"

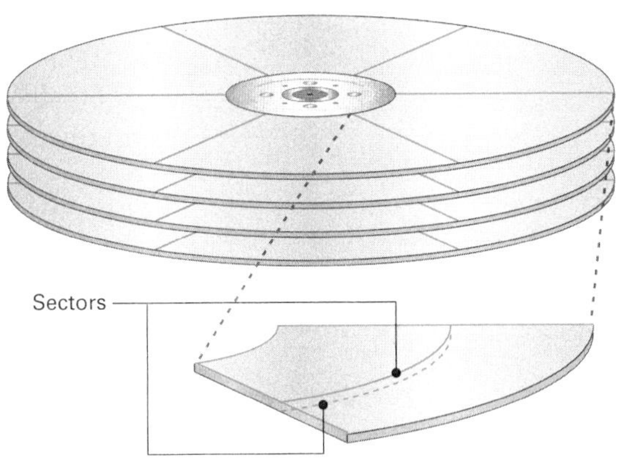

• Figure 10.12 Sectors

Write Precompensation Cylinder

this problem, making the write precomp setting obsolete.

• Figure 10.13 Sectors per track

Landing Zone

On older hard drives with stepper motors, the landing zone value designated an unused cylinder as a "parking place" for the read/write heads. As mentioned earlier, old stepper motor hard drives needed to have their read/write heads parked before being moved in order to avoid accidental damage. Today's voice coil drives park themselves whenever they're not accessing data, automatically placing the read/write heads on the landing zone. As a result, the BIOS no longer needs the landing zone geometry.

Tech Tip

External Hard Drives

A quick trip to any major computer store will reveal a thriving trade in external hard drives. You used to be able to find external drives that connected to the slow parallel port, but external drives today connect to a FireWire or Hi-Speed USB 2.0 port. Both interfaces offer very high data transfer rates and hot swap capability, making them ideal for transporting huge files such as digital video clips. Regardless of the external interface, however, inside the casing you'll find an ordinary PATA drive, just like those described in this chapter.

The A+ Certification Core Hardware exam is only concerned with internal hard drives.

Test Specific

Hard Drive Interfaces

Over the years, many interfaces existed for hard drives, with names like ST-506 and ESDI. Don't worry about what these abbreviations stood for; neither the A+ Certification exams nor the computer world at large has an interest in these "pre-historic" interfaces. Starting around 1990, a new interface called IDE appeared that virtually monopolizes the hard drive market. Only one other type of interface, the moderately popular **small computer system interface (SCSI)** interface, has any relevance for hard drives. (Chapter 19 is devoted to SCSI.) IDE drives come in two basic flavors: **parallel ATA (PATA)** and **serial ATA (SATA)**. PATA drives dominated the industry for more than a decade and have only seen competition from SATA drives since 2003.

Parallel ATA

When IBM unveiled the 80286-powered IBM PC AT in the early 1980s, it introduced the first PC to include BIOS support for hard drives. This BIOS supported up to two physical drives, and each drive could be up to 504 MB—far larger than the 5 MB and 10 MB drives of the time. Although having built-in support for hard drives certainly improved the power of the PC, at that time, installing, configuring, and troubleshooting hard drives could at best be called difficult.

The A+ Core Hardware exam uses the term IDE to refer to all PATA drives.

Earlier drive interfaces required you to perform a number of truly painful steps to get a new hard drive up and rolling. For example, back in those days, the hard drive controller was a separate card that snapped into an expansion slot. This was no big deal except that every time you installed one of these old interface drives into a hard drive controller you literally had to erase all the geometry. Not just the data; you literally wiped the drive clean and reinstalled the geometry with a new controller through a process called low-level formatting. The physical geometry didn't change on the drive; it always had the same CHS values. Subtle differences in controllers meant that once a hard drive was installed, it either stayed with the controller or you did this low-level format thing, wiping out and reinstalling all the geometry whenever you moved the drive. Not only that, but early drive interfaces also required the tech literally to type the geometry into the CMOS. If you typed in even one number incorrectly, the drive wouldn't work! Additionally, the hard drive controller only supported hard drives. This last issue didn't bother anyone back in the early 1980s, as no one had yet invented CD-ROM drives, Zip drives, or any of the other devices that today we happily snap into a hard drive controller without so much as a thought.

Don't confuse the low-level formatting discussed here with many of the "low-level format" utilities you see today; they have nothing in common but the name!

As you will learn in the section on cabling PATA drives, more recent types actually use an 80-wire cable.

To address these problems, Western Digital and Compaq developed a new hard drive interface and placed this specification before the *American National Standards Institute* (ANSI) committees, which in turn put out the *AT Attachment* (ATA) interface in March of 1989. The ATA interface required a new type of ribbon cable and a built-in controller on the drive itself, instantly and forever removing the universally hated low-level format.

Most importantly, the ATA standard used the existing AT BIOS on a PC, which meant that you didn't have to replace the old system BIOS to make the drive work—a very important consideration for compatibility but one that would later haunt ATA drives. The official name for the standard, ATA, never made it into the common vernacular until recently, and that only as PATA to distinguish it from serial ATA drives. Everyone used the technically incorrect term "IDE" when referring to ATA drives. We still do so today.

In 1990, Western Digital put forward a series of improvements to the IDE standard called **EIDE**. EIDE included powerful new features such as higher capacities; support for non-hard drive storage devices; support for two more ATA devices, for a maximum of four; and substantially improved throughput. Regular IDE drives quickly disappeared, and by 1995, EIDE drives dominated the PC world. Figure 10.14 shows a typical EIDE drive.

• **Figure 10.14** EIDE drive

The terms ATA, IDE, and EIDE are used interchangeably to describe all PATA devices that subscribe to the EIDE improvements—and all PATA devices do!

Physical Connections

IDE drives connect to the computer via a 40-pin plug and a controller. Figure 10.15 shows the "business end" of an IDE drive, with the connectors for the controller and the power cable.

The controller is the support circuitry that acts as the intermediary between the hard drive and the external data bus. Electronically, the setup looks like Figure 10.16.

In reality, the IDE drives have the controller built into the drive. What we call the IDE controller is really no more than a device that provides con- [illegible]

onboard controllers) and manifest themselves as two 40-pin male ports. Much older machines might have the controllers on a card that snaps into the motherboard. Figure 10.17 shows some examples of EIDE controllers, both on cards and the vastly more common onboard controller.

Although each of the two controllers is equal in power and capability, the traditional-style AT BIOS only looks for one of the two when the system boots up. This is the primary controller. The other controller is the secondary controller. If you're going to use only one controller, it should be the primary controller, although most newer operating systems and BIOS no longer really care. When installing ATA devices it is important that you can distinguish the primary controller from the secondary controller. First, read the motherboard book. Second, look on the motherboard to see if some printing actually identifies the ports. Figure 10.18 is a close-up of a typical motherboard, showing the primary controller marked as IDE1 and the secondary marked as IDE2.

Cabling PATA Drives PATA drives use one of two cables to connect the drive and the controller. Both have a 40-pin interface, but differ in the number of wires. Because the **40-pin ribbon cable** with 40 wires used by the Ultra ATA/33 and earlier Multiword DMA interfaces couldn't handle the shorter cycle times of Ultra DMA Modes 4 and 5, the newer Modes use a 40-pin, **80-wire cable** . This cable has 40 extra wires that act as ground conductors to shield against crosstalk, which in turn improves signal quality. (You'll learn all about Ultra DMA in the "Transferring Data" section.) The cables, although called ribbon cables, come

Tech Tip

Hard Drive Jargon

As you've undoubtedly noticed at this point, hard drives have an amazing amount of jargon attached to them. The question most new techs ask is, which term should they use in normal tech conversation and not sound ignorant? The answer depends on the context of the discussion.

For the most part, follow the lead of the A+ Certification exam and use the term IDE as an umbrella term for non-SCSI hard [illegible] *of us prefer clarity and spell them out, such as "serial A-Tee-A."*

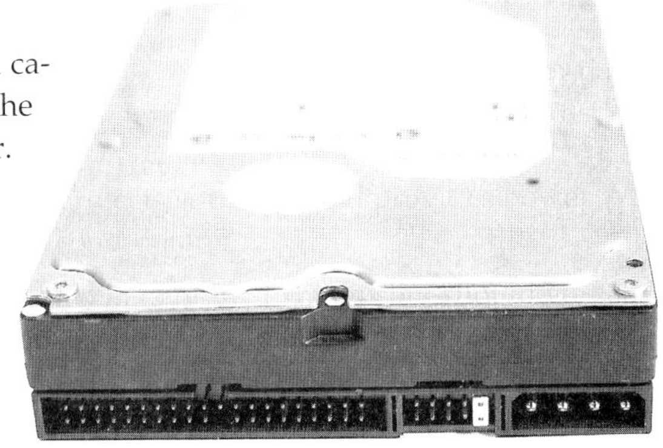

• **Figure 10.15** Back of IDE hard drives showing 40-pin connector (left), jumpers (center), and power connector (right)

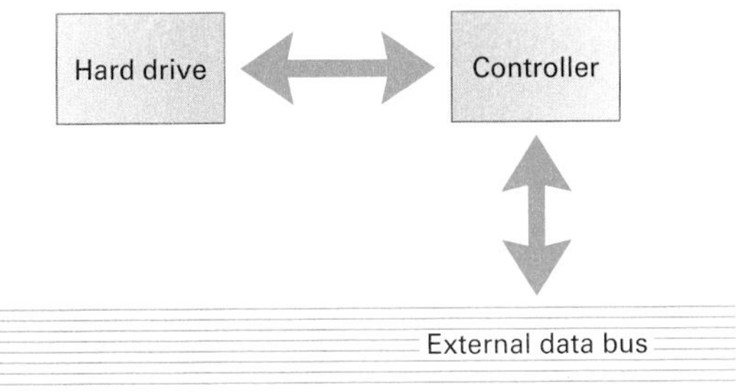

• **Figure 10.16** Relation of drive, controller, and bus

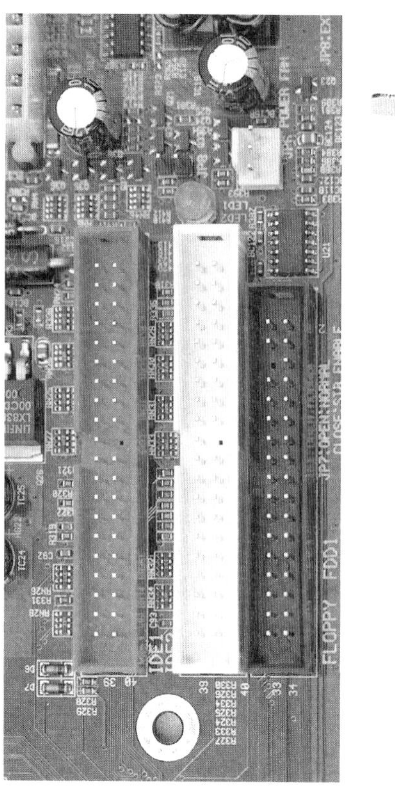

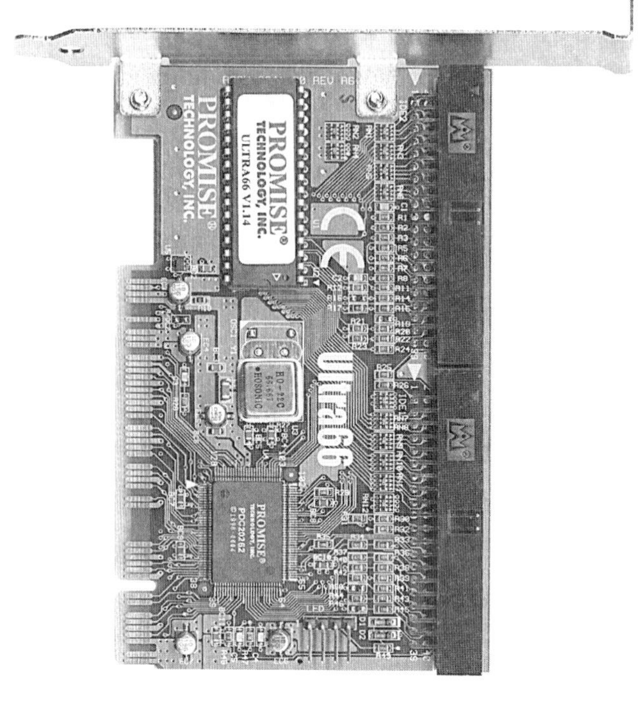

• **Figure 10.17** Onboard EIDE and EIDE controller card

flat or rounded. Rounded cables cost more, but offer better cooling and a much sexier look. There are no twists in either type of cable, although you might occasionally see a flat cable that has a split. A single cable can connect

• **Figure 10.18** Primary and secondary controllers on a motherboard

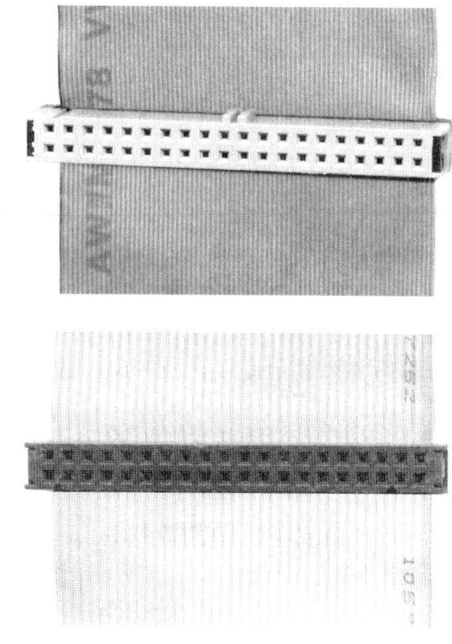

• **Figure 10.19** Two IDE cables—40-pin, 80-wire (top) and 40-pin, 40-wire (bottom)

Cross Check

Cabling

You've seen ribbon cables as recently as Chapter 9, "Floppy Drives." Refer back to that chapter and compare floppy disk drive and PATA drive cabling. What rules applied to cabling FDDs? Do those same rules apply for PATA drives? How do they differ?

The A+ Certification Core Hardware exam traditionally focuses on the numbers of pins and wires on ribbon cables of all types!

up to two hard drives. You'll occasionally see an IDE cable that has only a single connector. Manufacturers will use such cables to cut costs on new builds. Figure 10.19 shows a pair of IDE cables, 40-wire on the bottom and 80-wire on the top. Figure 10.20 shows a rounded cable.

[illegible]

beled master and slave. So how do you know how to set them properly? The easiest way is to read the front of the drive; most drives have a nice diagram on the drive housing that explains how to set the jumpers properly. Figure 10.22 shows the front of one of these drives, so you can see how to set the drive to master or slave.

• **Figure 10.20** Sleek, rounded PATA cable

Hard disk drives may have other jumpers that may or may not concern you during installation. One common set of jumpers is used for diagnostics at the manufacturing plant or for special settings in other kinds of devices that use hard drives. Ignore them. They have no bearing in the PC world. Second, many drives provide a third setting, which is used if only one drive connects to a controller. Often, master and single drive are the same setting on the hard drive, although some hard drives require separate settings. Note that the name for the single drive setting varies among manufacturers. Some use Single; others use 1 Drive or Standalone.

Many current PATA hard drives use a jumper setting called *cable select*, rather than master or slave. As the name implies, the position on the cable determines which drive will be master or slave: master on the end, slave in the middle. Most cable-select cables are color coded. The blue connector on one end goes to the controller. The gray connector in the middle goes to the slave and the black connector on the other end to the master. For cable select to work properly with two drives, both drives must be set as cable select and the cable itself must be a special cable-select cable. If you see a ribbon cable with a pinhole through one wire, watch out! That's a cable-select cable. Don't use it for a master/slave configured two-drive system!

• **Figure 10.21** Master/slave jumpers on a hard drive

If you don't have a label on the drive that tells you how to set the jumpers, you have several options. First,

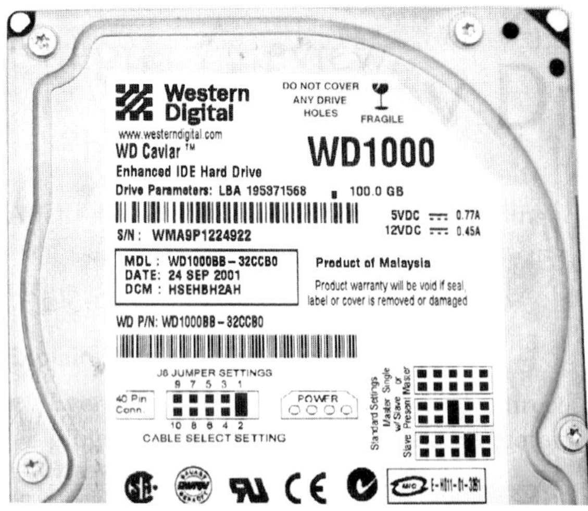

• **Figure 10.22** Drive label showing master/slave settings

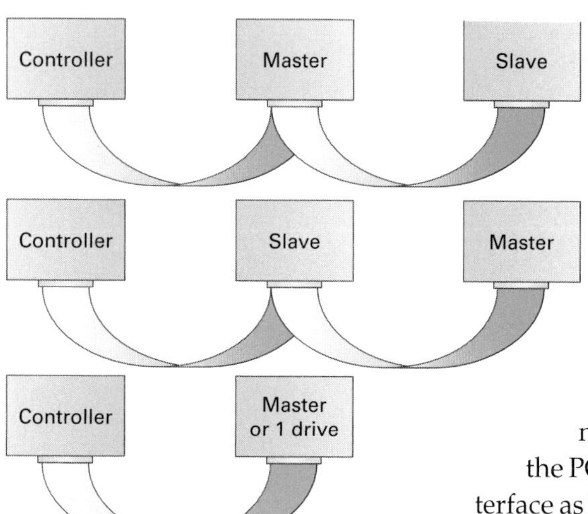

• **Figure 10.23** The three ways to connect to one controller

look for the drive maker's web site. Every drive manufacturer lists its drive jumper settings on the Web, although it can take a while to find the information you want. Second, try phoning the hard drive maker directly. Unlike many other PC parts manufacturers, hard drive producers tend to stay in business for a long period of time and have great technical support.

Plugging It In It doesn't matter where the master or slave drive is installed on the cable; just make sure you have the jumpers set properly or the computer won't be able to access the drives. It matters quite a bit where you plug a pair of cable select drives into a cable. The master should be on the end of the cable in such a case.

Hard drive cables have a colored stripe that corresponds to the number-one pin—called *Pin 1*—on the connectors, just like on floppy drives. You need to make certain that Pin 1 on the controller is on the same wire as Pin 1 on the hard drive. Failing to plug in the drive properly will also prevent the PC from recognizing the drive. If you incorrectly set the master/slave jumpers or cable to the hard drives, you won't break anything; it just won't work. There are only three ways you can install a hard drive to one controller (see Figure 10.23).

Finally, you need to plug a Molex connector from the power supply into the drive. All modern PATA drives use a Molex connector.

ATAPI—Extending the Hard Drive Interface

An extension to the ATA specification, called **Advanced Technology Attachment Packet Interface (ATAPI)**, enables non-hard drive devices—such as CD-ROM drives—to connect to the PC via the ATA controllers. ATAPI drives have the same 40-pin interface as hard drives and follow the same rules on master, slave, and cable select jumper settings. Figure 10.24 shows an ATAPI CD-RW drive attached to a motherboard. The key difference between hard drives and every other type of drive that attaches to the ATA controller is in how the drives get BIOS. Hard drives get it through the System BIOS and CMOS, whereas non-hard drives require an option ROM or a software driver. I'll get to the specifics in the section on providing BIOS.

Cross Check

Molex Connectors

Hard drives and other internal devices use Molex connectors for power. Refer back to Chapter 8, "Power Supplies," and check your memory. What voltages go through the four wires on a Molex connector? What should you note about the connector and inserting it into the corresponding socket on the drive?

Serial ATA

For all its longevity as the mass storage interface of choice for the PC, parallel ATA has problems. First, the flat ribbon cables impede airflow and can be a pain to insert properly. Second, the cables have a very limited length, only 18 inches. Third, you can't hot-swap PATA drives. You have to shut down completely before installing or replacing a drive. Finally, the technology has simply reached the limits of what it can do in terms of throughput.

Serial ATA (SATA) addresses these issues. SATA creates a point-to-point connection between the SATA device—hard disk, CD-ROM, CD-RW, DVD-ROM, DVD-RW, and so on—and the SATA controller. At a glance, SATA devices look identical to standard PATA devices. Take a closer look at the cable and power connectors, however, and you'll see significant differences (Figure 10.25). Because SATA devices send data serially instead of in parallel, the SATA interface needs far fewer physical wires— seven instead of the eighty wires that is typical of PATA—resulting in much thinner cabling. This might not seem significant, but the benefit is that thinner cabling means better cable control and [illegible]

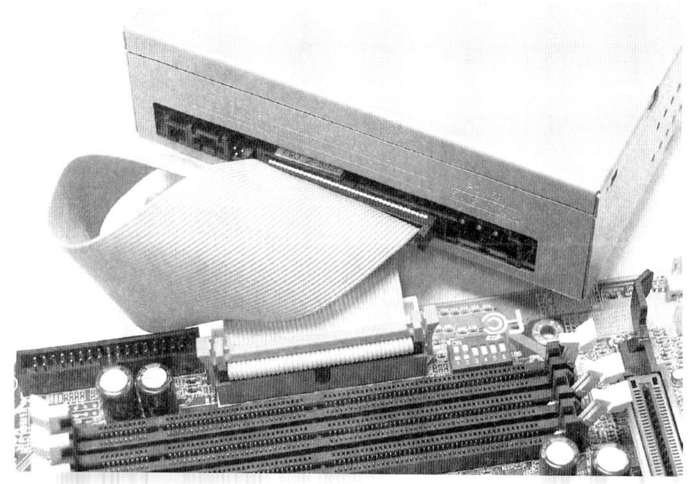

SATA devices are hot-swappable, meaning that they can be plugged into or removed from the PC without having to shut down. This makes SATA a natural fit for **Redundant Array of Independent** (or sometimes **Inexpensive**) **Disks (RAID)** technology on OSs that support it. See the section later in this chapter on "RAID" for more details.

The big news, however, is in data throughput. As the name implies, SATA devices transfer data in serial bursts instead of parallel, as PATA devices do. Typically, you don't think of serial devices as being faster than parallel, but in this case, that's exactly the case. A SATA device's single stream of data moves much faster than the multiple streams of data coming from a parallel IDE device—theoretically up to 30 times faster!

SATA devices currently have a rated maximum data burst throughput rate of 150 MBps. Granted, this isn't much of an immediate gain over current PATA speeds, but the SATA technology specification calls for eventual throughput speeds of up to 600 MBps! Obviously the potential for greatly improved performance is the biggest draw to SATA.

SATA is backward-compatible with current PATA standards, and enables you to install a parallel ATA device, including a hard drive, CD-media drive, and others, to a serial ATA controller by using a device called a **SATA bridge** . A SATA bridge manifests as a tiny card that you plug directly into the 40-pin connector on a PATA drive. As you can see in Figure 10.26, the controller chip on the bridge requires separate power; you plug a Molex connector into the PATA drive as normal.

• **Figure 10.25** SATA hard disk data (left) and power (right) connections

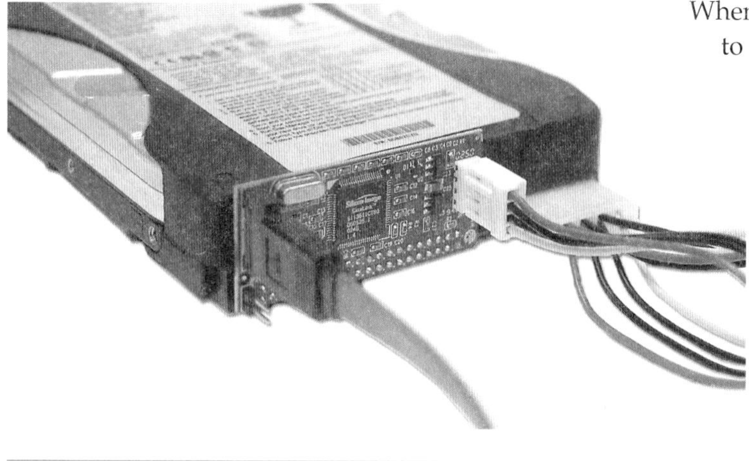

• Figure 10.26 SATA bridge

When you boot the system, the PATA drive shows up to the system as a SATA drive.

If your motherboard doesn't have SATA controller sockets (and most current ones don't), special host adapters enable you to add SATA functionality via a PCI card. Some of these offer sockets for up to eight SATA drives, and many offer both PATA and SATA sockets.

Cabling SATA Drives

Installing SATA hard disk drives is even easier than IDE devices due to the fact that there's no master, slave, or cable select configuration to mess with. In fact, there are no jumper settings to worry about at all, as SATA only supports a single device per controller channel. Simply connect the power and plug the controller cable in as shown in Figure 10.27—the OS automatically detects the drive and it's ready to go! The keying on SATA controller and power cables makes it impossible to install either incorrectly.

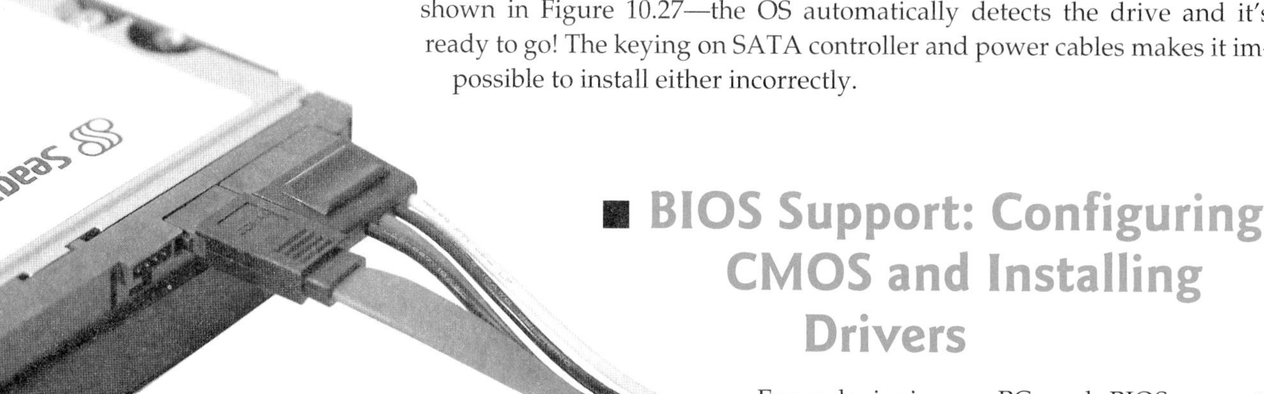

• Figure 10.27 Properly connected SATA cable

BIOS Support: Configuring CMOS and Installing Drivers

Every device in your PC needs BIOS support, and the hard drive and controller are no exception. Most motherboards provide support for the built-in PATA controllers in the system BIOS routines, but require configuration in CMOS for the specific hard drives attached. CMOS configuration entails many things, from entering drive geometry numbers to using the proper storage technology and data transfer type.

ATAPI drives get BIOS support from software drivers, even though they connect to the same controllers as PATA hard drives. Many motherboards have SATA controllers built in, but not as part of the main chipset, and they require a separate software device driver before they'll function. Other systems have the SATA controller as a separate expansion card and more obviously need a device driver. The SATA hard drives get BIOS support from the SATA controller, whether that controller is built into the motherboard or is a separate expansion bus card. The drives sometimes require configuration in a separate CMOS-like interface specific to the controller, especially in situations that employ RAID. Whew! That's quite a lot of options, so let's tackle them in order.

CMOS

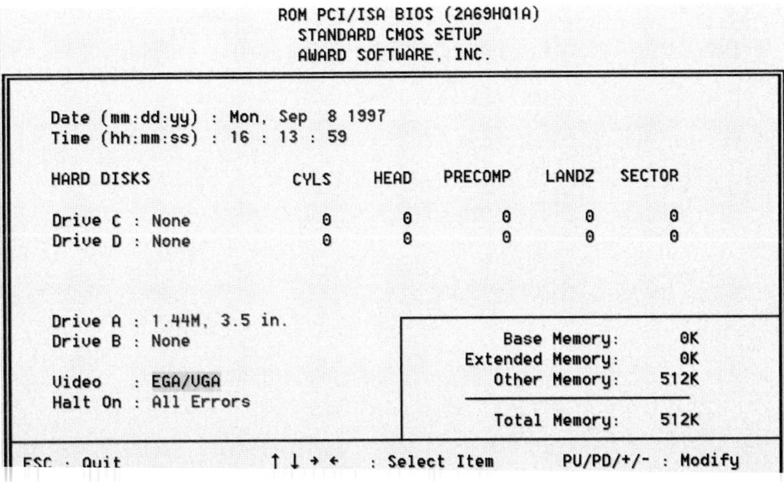

After physically installing a PATA hard drive, you must enter its geometry into the CMOS through the CMOS setup program. If the drive does not get its BIOS through CMOS—such as the case with many SATA drives and motherboards built in 2003 or earlier—then you need to configure the appropriate controller. Without this information, the hard drive will not work. Before IDE drives, you used to have to take the numbers from the drive and type in each value for the

could use only two drives. Why? The original CMOS in the first IBM 286 AT could store only 64 bytes of data. The original IBM engineers allocated just enough space for two sets of drive information, so the standard enabled only two drives. Besides, who would ever need more than two hard drives?

Today's CMOS setup utilities handle up to four ATA devices, and the days of typing in values are long gone. In fact, you can simply set the "type" to auto, and the system will set up the hard drive's CMOS settings for you. Setting up the drive in CMOS is very easy with current PCs. Nevertheless, a few concepts need to be explained, starting with hard drive types.

Hard Drive Types

The number of heads, cylinders, sectors/track, write precomp, and landing zone determine how the hard drive controller accesses the physical hard drive. Each number must be correct if the hard drive is to function properly. When IBM created the first CMOS on the 286 AT, they believed that the five different geometry numbers would be too complicated for normal users to configure. For simplicity, IBM established 15 preset combinations of hard drive geometries, called *hard drive types* (Table 10.1). So instead of worrying about five different variables, users could simply enter a hard drive type into the CMOS. The concept of types did make configuring the hard drive geometry in CMOS much easier.

Initially, this worked well, but a problem arose. Note the tiny capacities of the original hard drive types. If a manufacturer came up with a new, larger hard drive type, the list would have to be expanded. At first, IBM did exactly that, eventually expanding the list to 37 different types.

BIOS designers soon realized that adding to the list every time a manufacturer created a new hard drive geometry was not practical, so IBM simply stopped using drives that required unique geometries and stopped adding drive types. The other BIOS makers continued to add types until

Table 10.1	The Original Hard Drive Table for the IBM AT					
Drive Type	**Capacity (MB)**	**Cylinders**	**Heads**	**Sectors**	**Write Precomp**	**Landing Zone**
1	10	306	4	17	128	305
2	20	615	4	17	300	615
3	30	615	6	17	300	615
4	62	940	8	17	512	940
5	46	940	6	17	512	940
6	20	615	4	17	None	615
7	30	462	8	17	256	511
8	30	733	5	17	None	733
9	112	900	15	17	None	901
10	20	820	3	17	None	820
11	35	855	5	17	None	855
12	49	855	7	17	None	855
13	20	306	8	17	128	319
14	42	733	7	17	None	733
15		Reserved				

they got to around 45 different types. At that time, AMI created a new *User* type. With this type, instead of selecting a special type, users could enter in the five geometry values manually. This provided more flexibility for hard drive installation. Figure 10.29 shows an older Award BIOS with the CMOS set to user and the CHS values being entered manually.

EIDE drives were very forgiving if you put incorrect information into the CMOS setup. If you installed a 1,020 MB hard drive and set the CMOS to make it a 200 MB hard drive, the 1,020 MB would become a perfectly good 200 MB hard drive! However, if you then reset the CMOS back to the proper settings to enable the drive to be 1,020 MB again, you'd lose all the data on your drive! Autodetection made the concept of hard drive types obsolete, although many current CMOS setup utilities still provide drive types. On today's systems, just set the hard drive type to Auto.

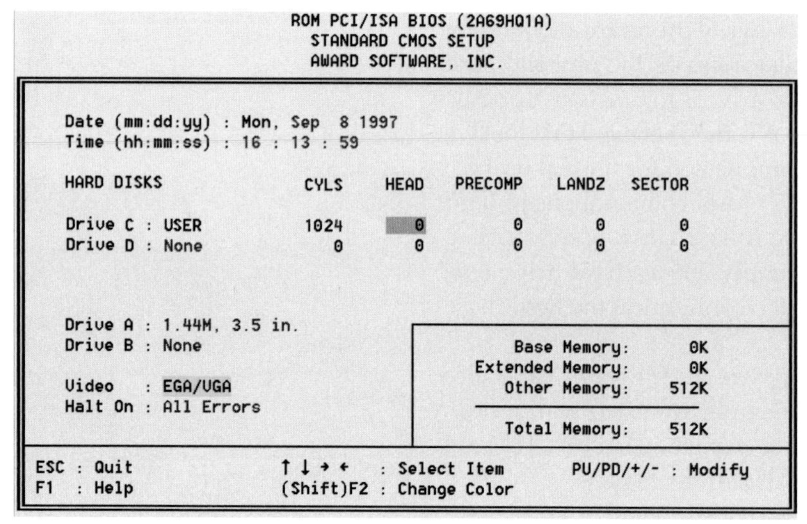

• **Figure 10.29** Award BIOS with CMOS set to User

Autodetection

Before 1994, you had to use the hard drive type to install a hard drive. This manual installation process was always a bit of a problem. You had to have the proper CHS values, you had to be sure to type them in correctly, and you had to store these values in case your CMOS was accidentally erased. Today, all PCs can set the CMOS properly by using autodetection. All PATA drives have their CHS values stored inside of them. Autodetection simply means that the

BIOS routines ask the drive for those stored values and automatically update the CMOS. There are two common ways to perform autodetection. First, most CMOS setup utilities have a hard drive type called "Auto." By setting the hard drive type to Auto, the CMOS automatically updates itself every time the computer is started. Figure 10.30 shows a typical modern CMOS with the primary master drive type set to Auto.

The second, older way to perform autodetection is to run the IDE Autodetection option manually. This is a separate option, usually accessed from the main CMOS screen,

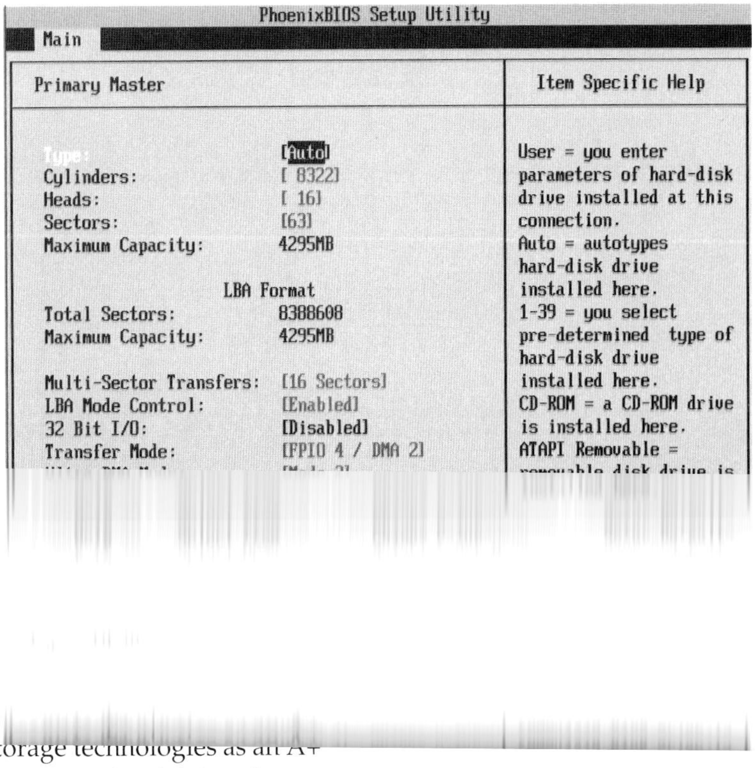

You're likely to run into an amazing array of storage technologies as an A+ Certified technician, from systems that won't recognize a hard drive of more than 8.4 GB capacity to systems that manifest four physical hard drives as a single drive volume. Let's go through the technologies, from LBA/ECHS to INT13 Extensions to ATA/ATAPI-6.

LBA/ECHS IBM created the AT BIOS to support hard drives many years before IDE drives were invented, and every system had that BIOS. The developers of IDE made certain that the new drives would run from the same AT BIOS command set. By providing this capability, you could use the same CMOS and BIOS routines to talk to a much more advanced drive.

Unfortunately, the BIOS routines for the original AT command set allowed a hard drive size of only up to 528 million bytes (504 MB). A drive could have no more than 1,024 cylinders, 16 heads, and 63 sectors/track:

> 1,024 cylinders × 16 heads × 63 sectors/track × 512 bytes/sector = 504 MB

For years, this was not a problem. But when hard drives began to approach the 504 MB barrier, it became clear—there needed to be a way of getting past 504 MB. One of the differences between an IDE and an EIDE drive is that EIDE drives can be larger than 504 MB via one of two different, competing methods: LBA and ECHS. LBA was developed by Western Digital and ECHS was developed by Seagate. They accomplish virtually the same function in almost the same way, so we'll discuss them simultaneously.

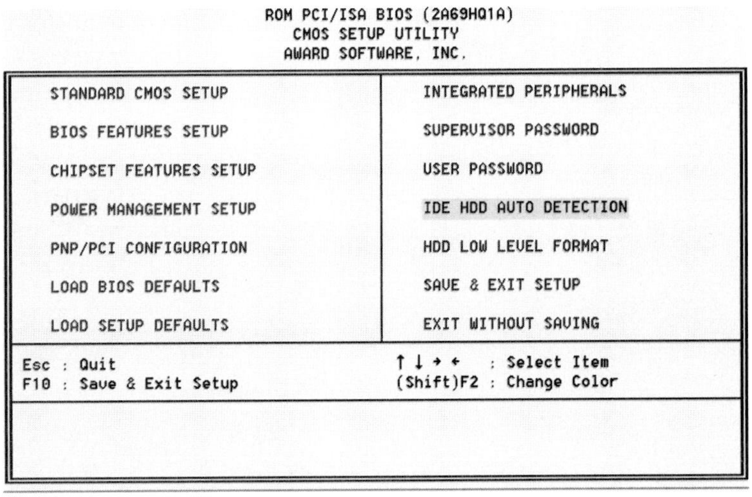

Figure 10.31 Award IDE HDD Auto Detection option

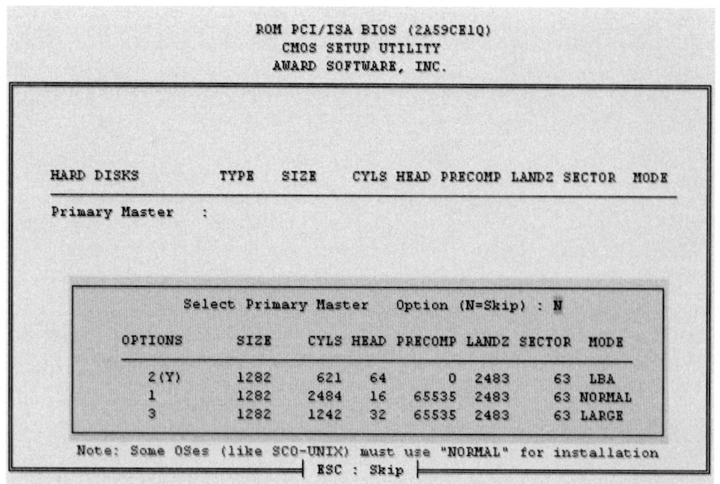

• **Figure 10.32** Hard drive detected (CMOS Setup Utility)

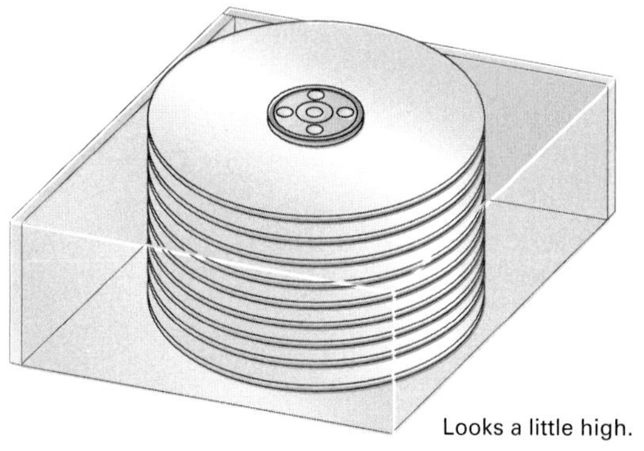

• **Figure 10.33** Too many heads

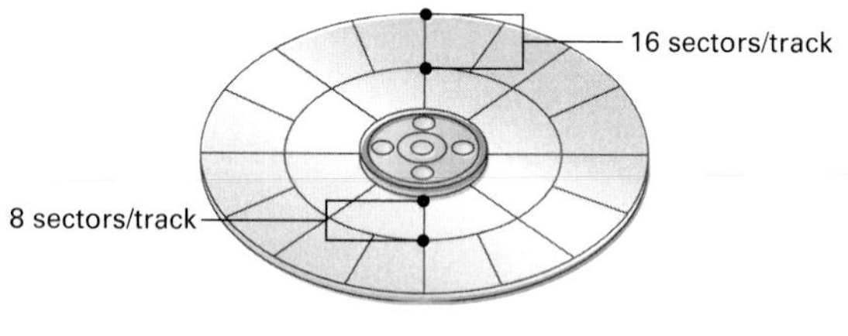

• **Figure 10.34** Multiple sectors/track

Basically, LBA/ECHS is the hard drive lying to the computer about its geometry and is really nothing more than an advanced type of sector translation. Let's take a moment to understand sector translation, and then come back to LBA/ECHS.

Sector Translation Long before hard drives approached the 504 MB limit, the limits of 1,024 cylinders, 16 heads, and 63 sectors/track caused hard drive makers fits. The big problem was the heads. Remember that every two heads means another platter, another physical disk that you have to squeeze into a hard drive. If you wanted a hard drive with the maximum number of 16 heads, you would have a hard drive with eight physical platters inside the drive! Nobody wanted that many platters: it made the drives too tall, it took more power to spin up the drive, and that many parts cost too much money (see Figure 10.33).

Manufacturers could readily produce a hard drive that had fewer heads and more cylinders, but the stupid 1,024/16/63 limit got in the way. Plus, the traditional sector arrangement wasted a lot of useful space. Sectors toward the inside of the drive, for example, are much shorter than the sectors on the outside. The sectors on the outside don't need to be that long, but with the traditional geometry setup, hard drive makers had no choice. They could make a hard drive store a lot more information, however, if hard drives could be made with more sectors/track on the outside tracks (see Figure 10.34).

The IDE specification was designed to have two geometries. The *physical geometry* defined the real layout of the CHS inside the drive. The *logical geometry* described what the drive told the CMOS. In other words, the IDE drive lied to the CMOS, thus side-stepping the artificial limits of the BIOS. When data was being transferred to and from the drive, the onboard circuitry of the drive translated the logical geometry into the physical geometry. This function was, and still is, called **sector translation**.

Let's look at a couple of hypothetical examples in action. First, pretend that Seagate came out with a new, very cheap, very fast hard drive called the ST108. To get the ST108 drive fast and cheap, however, Seagate had to use a rather strange geometry, shown in Table 10.2.

Table 10.2	**Seagate's ST108 Drive Geometry**		
ST108 Physical		**BIOS Limits**	
Cylinders	2048	Cylinders	1024
Heads	2	Heads	16
Sectors/Track	52	Sectors/Track	63
Total Capacity	108 MB		

Notice that the cylinder number is greater than 1,024. To overcome this problem, the IDE drive performs a sector translation that reports a geometry to the BIOS that is totally different from the true geometry of the drive. Table 10.3 shows the actual geometry and the "logical" geometry of our mythical ST108 drive. Notice that the logical geometry is now within the acceptable parameters of the BIOS limitations. Sector translation never changes the capacity of the drive; it only changes the geometry to stay within the BIOS limits.

Table 10.3 Physical and Logical Geometry of the ST108 Drive

Physical		**Logical**	
Cylinders	2048	Cylinders	512
Heads	2	Heads	8
Sectors/Track	52	Sectors/Track	52
Total Capacity	108 MB	Total Capacity	108 MB

work together to change the way they talk to each other. They can do this without conflicting with the original AT BIOS commands by taking advantage of unused commands to use up to 256 heads. LBA enables support for a maximum of 1,024 × 256 × 63 × 512 bytes = 8.4 GB hard drives.

ECHS is nothing more than a competitor to Western Digital's LBA. It works the same, but comes up with different values than LBA. With LBA/ECHS, you can have 1,024 cylinders, 256 heads, and 63 sectors/track for a maximum size of 8.4 GB. The ECHS option in CMOS setup utilities often shows up as Large. ECHS has been completely eclipsed by LBA.

In order to have drives larger than 504 MB, you must have a hard drive that has LBA/ECHS and a BIOS that supports LBA/ECHS. If you have an EIDE drive larger than 504 MB, you can be sure the drive supports LBA and ECHS. All current BIOS support LBA and/or ECHS. Just run the autodetection utility.

INT13 Extensions You can always count on two things going up: taxes and hard drive capacities. By the time LBA and ECHS became popular in the mid-1990s, it was painfully obvious that the 8.4 GB maximum capacity was going to become a problem. In 1994, Phoenix Technologies (the BIOS

Table 10.4 Western Digital WD2160's Physical and Logical Geometries

Physical		**Logical**	
Cylinders	16384	Cylinders	1024
Heads	4	Heads	***64***
Sectors/Track	63	Sectors/Track	63
Total Capacity	2.1 GB	Total Capacity	2.1 GB

manufacturer) came up with a new set of BIOS commands called **Interrupt 13 (INT13) extensions**. INT13 extensions break the 8.4 GB barrier by completely ignoring the CHS values and instead feeding the LBA a stream of "addressable sectors." Sure, if you run Autodetect you'll see CHS values that equal the capacity of the drive, but the hard drive reports totally different values to the BIOS, avoiding the 8.4 GB LBA limitation. A system with INT13 extensions can handle drives up to 137 GB. Most systems made since 1998 have INT13 extension support. If you install a hard drive larger than 8.4 GB and Autodetect doesn't detect more than 8.4 GB, your system does not support INT13 extensions.

Be careful with INT13 extensions! Many systems require that you set the drive to Auto only. In fact, many CMOS setup utilities have dropped all options except for Auto or None—probably not a bad idea! Many systems work perfectly by using either the User or the Auto settings.

ATA/ATAPI-6 Hard drive size exploded in the early 21st century and the seemingly impossible-to-fill 137-GB limit created by INT13 extensions became a barrier to fine computing much more quickly than most people had anticipated. When drives started hitting the 120 GB mark, the ANSI ATA committee adopted an industry proposal pushed by Maxtor (a major hard drive maker) called *Big Drives* that increased the limit to more than 144 petabytes (144,000,000 GB). The ANSI ATA committee thankfully gave the new standard a less-silly name, calling it **ATA/ATAPI-6**.

> Maxtor has an excellent, short white paper on Big Drives technology for download at its web site, http://www.maxtor.com/en/documentation/white_papers/big_drives_white_papers.pdf.

The ATA/ATAPI-6 standard features a 48-bit addressing scheme, which supplants the 24-bit addressing of LBA and INT13 extensions. Plus, the standard defines an enhanced block mode, enabling drives to transfer up to 65,536 sectors in one chunk, up from the measly 256 sectors of lesser drive technologies. This latter feature should greatly facilitate such cool activity as moving giant digital movie files around.

Transferring Data

ATA devices transfer data to and from the hard drive and memory via standardized protocols called *programmable input/output* (PIO) modes or by the far more popular **Direct Memory Access (DMA)** modes. PIO modes are older and far slower than DMA modes, but a number of slower, non-hard drive ATA devices still use PIO modes. This section looks at both of these modes and the settings available in CMOS.

PIO Modes The ATA drives could originally transfer data from the hard drive to RAM at a maximum rate of roughly 3.3 *megabytes per second* (MBps), and drive makers quickly bumped that up to 5.2 MBps, and then 8.3 MBps. The *Small Form Factor* (SFF) standards committee defined these as PIO modes 0, 1, and 2. In the ATA world, all drives, as well as most non-drive ATA devices, can use all three modes. The SFF committee released a follow-up to the ATA standard that defined some new data throughput speeds. First, there were two new PIO speeds, called PIO 3 and PIO 4 (see Table 10.5). To get the best performance out of your hard drive, you must set the proper PIO mode for the drive.

Setting the PIO mode requires you to answer the following three questions:

- What is the fastest mode the hard drive supports?
- What is the fastest mode the controller supports?
- What is the fastest mode the BIOS or device driver supports?

Table 10.5	PIO Speeds	
PIO Mode	**Cycle Time (ns)**	**Transfer Rate (MBps)**
0	600	3.3
1	383	5.2
2	240	8.3
3	180	11.1
4	120	16.6

The fastest PIO mode you can set is limited by the weakest link. For example, if you have a hard drive capable of PIO mode 4, a controller capable of mode 2, and a BIOS capable of mode 4, the best you will get is mode 2. You should never try to use a mode faster than what is recommended by the [illegible] Although a faster mode will not damage your drive, it [illegible] device generates read errors, try going back into CMOS and setting slower PIO modes until the errors disappear.

DMA Modes Newer hard drives ignore PIO modes and instead transfer data using *Direct Memory Access* (DMA) mode. DMA mode transfers bypass the CPU, sending data directly into memory, and leaving the CPU free to run programs. You first learned about DMA in Chapter 5, but that type of DMA required the device to request to use the expansion bus via the slow DMA controller (the 8237 chip). Modern drives use a bus-mastering controller that takes over the expansion bus and bypasses the built-in DMA controller. DMA data transfers can be either 16 bits (single word) or 32 bits (double word) wide. Virtually all systems have *Peripheral Component Interconnect* (PCI) and will run at one of the very popular Ultra DMA mode speeds. See Table 10.6 for the transfer rates of the various DMA modes.

> Although the official terms for the more advanced DMA modes are Ultra DMA Mode 4, Mode 5, and so on, it's more common to use the term ATA/66 for Mode 4, ATA/100 for Mode 5, and ATA/133 for Mode 6.

When DMA first became popular for hard drives in the mid-1990s, most systems did not have BIOS support for DMA, and thus required the use of third-party software drivers. Today, all BIOS have DMA, in particular Ultra DMA, support. Most CMOS setup utilities have an option to turn this on or off. This is almost always left on and forgotten, enabling users to enjoy the high speeds provided by Ultra

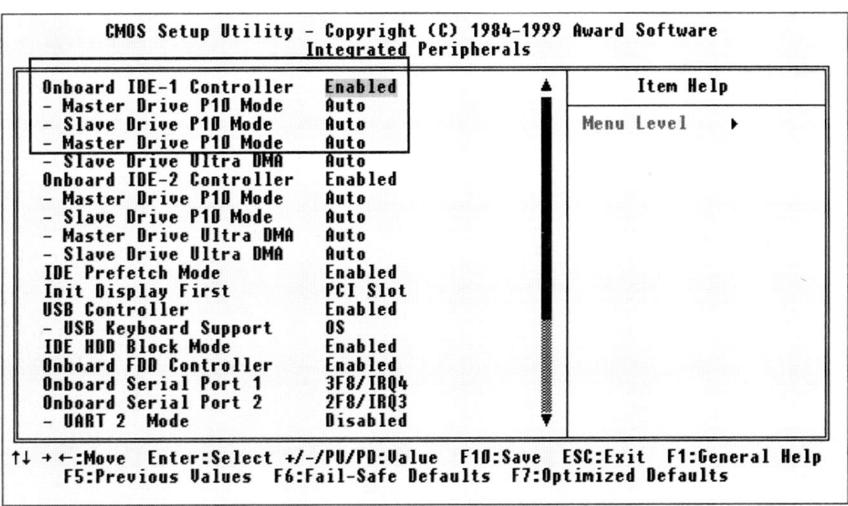

• **Figure 10.35** PIO mode settings in CMOS with onboard controller

Table 10.6	DMA Mode and Ultra DMA Mode Speeds	
DMA Mode Single Word (16 Bit)	**Cycle Time (ns)**	**Transfer Rate (MBps)**
0	960	2.1
1	480	4.2
2	240	8.3
DMA Mode Double Word (32 Bit)	**Cycle Time (ns)**	**Transfer Rate (MBps)**
0	480	4.2
1	150	13.3
2	120	16.7
Ultra DMA Mode	**Cycle Time (ns)**	**Transfer Rate (MBps)**
0	240	16.7
1	160	25
2	120	33
3	90	44.4
4	60	66.7
5	40	100
6	30	133

DMA. Ultra DMA 2 (ATA/33), Ultra DMA 4 (ATA/66), Ultra DMA 5 (ATA/100), and Ultra DMA 6 (ATA/133) now dominate the hard drive world. The alternative names indicate the data transfer speeds achievable with these drives in the optimal circumstances. An ATA/100 drive, in other words, can transfer 100 MBps of data, a phenomenally higher speed than earlier drives.

Only Ultra DMA Modes 2, 4, 5 and 6 have actually been used in hard drives.

In order to take advantage of the faster transfer rates, a drive has to connect to an appropriate controller and use the proper ribbon cable. Current motherboards have ATA/66, ATA/100, or ATA/133 controllers built into them. These controllers can do double duty, handling both old drives and new. ATA/66, ATA/100, and ATA/133 require the 80-wire cable (Figure 10.36). A number of motherboards come with one ATA/33 controller and one ATA/66, ATA/100, or ATA/133 controller. To differentiate them, motherboard makers will design the higher speed controller in some bright color. Be sure to plug the blue or red connector on the cable into the motherboard, the black connector into the master drive, and the gray connector into the slave if one is present.

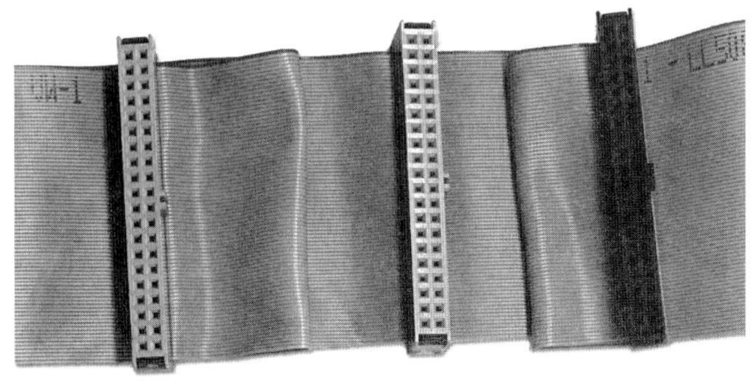

• **Figure 10.36** 80-wire ribbon cable

Figure 10.37 shows the controllers on a typical motherboard. The primary IDE controller handles the faster ATA/66 or ATA/100 drives.

All the higher-end PATA drives can run on lower-end controllers, and conversely, most controllers can handle lower-end drives. An ATA/66 controller can handle both ATA/66 and ATA/33 drives, for example, or even older PIO mode-based drives. The slower drives simply run at their slower speed. If you plug an ATA/100 drive into an ATA/33 controller, it will still work, but it will run as an ATA/33 drive, regardless of whether you use a 40-wire or 80-wire cable!

Device Drivers

Devices that do not get BIOS via the system BIOS routines naturally require some other source for BIOS. For ATAPI devices and many SATA controllers, the source of choice is software device drivers, but both technologies have a couple of quirks you should know.

ATAPI Devices and BIOS

ATAPI drives plug into an ATA controller on the motherboard and follow the same conventions on cabling and jumpers as PATA

tion to boot to a CD-media disc, such as a Windows XP disc. What it doesn't do, however, is provide true BIOS support for that drive! That has to come with a driver loaded at boot-up. I can't tell you the number of times I've had techs call me in confusion after booting to a command prompt–only environment in Windows 95 or 98 and they have no CD-ROM, even though it was working just before the system crashed. The CD-ROM most likely does still work, but its driver loaded only in the graphical portion of the Windows boot-up!

drives in detail.

Serial ATA and BIOS

Setting up most serial ATA systems requires you to load drivers for an external SATA controller and perhaps configure the controller Flash ROM settings for the specific hard drive or drives you have installed. The latter is especially true with RAID systems. (See the following section.) Although all the major chipset makers have or will have soon enough chipsets with built-in SATA controllers, many PCs have SATA controllers as either a separate chip on the motherboard or as an expansion card in a PCI slot. The non-chipset-based SATA controllers require you to load a software device driver for them to function. This is true in all versions of Windows. Chapter 14 goes into the details of installing Windows XP onto a SATA drive connected to a non-chipset-based SATA controller.

Try This!

Working with CMOS

One of the best ways to get your mind around the different drive standards and capabilities is to run benchmarking software on the hard drive to get a baseline of its capabilities. Then, change CMOS settings to alter the performance of the drive and run the diagnostics again. Try this!

1. Get a reliable hard drive benchmarking program. I recommend WinBench 99 (http://www.etestinglabs.com/benchmarks/winbench/winbench.asp) and HDTach (http://www.tcdlabs.com/hdtach.htm) as reliable and rugged.
2. Run the software and record the scores.
3. Change some or all of the following CMOS settings and then run the benchmarking utility again: PIO mode, DMA mode, Block Mode.
4. What were the effects of changing settings?

```
                Phoenix - AwardBIOS CMOS Setup Utility
                        Standard CMOS Features

  Date (mm:dd:yy)          Mon, Jan 14 2002        Item Help
  Time (hh:mm:ss)           2 : 54 : 50
                                                   Menu Level  ▶
▶ IDE Primary Master       [Maxtor 2F020J0]
▶ IDE Primary Slave        [ None]                 Change the day, month,
▶ IDE Secondary Master     [MSI      CD-RW MS-83]  year and century
▶ IDE Secondary Slave      [ None]

  Drive A                  [1.44M, 3.5 in.]
  Drive B                  [None]

  Video                    [EGA/VGA]
  Halt On                  [All , But Keyboard]

  Base Memory                 640K
  Extended Memory           261120K
  Total Memory              262144K

↑↓→←:Move  Enter:Select  +/-/PU/PD:Value  F10:Save  ESC:Exit  F1:General Help
  F5: Previous Values   F6: Fail-Safe Defaults   F7: Optimized Defaults
```

• **Figure 10.38** CMOS screen showing a CD-ROM drive detected

Protecting Data with RAID

Ask any experienced tech "What is the most expensive part of a PC?" and they'll all say the same thing: the data. You can replace any single part of your PC for a few hundred dollars at most but if you lose critical data...well let's just say I know of two small companies that went out of business just because they lost a hard drive full of data.

Data is king; data is your PC's *raison d'être*. Losing data is a bad thing. We want to come up with methods to prevent data loss. Now of course you can do backups, but if a hard drive dies, you have to shut down the computer, reinstall a new hard drive, reinstall the operating system, and then restore the backup. There's nothing wrong with this as long as you can afford the time and cost of shutting down the system.

What we need is some method to let a hard drive die without losing data. This is possible if you stop relying on a single hard drive and instead use two or more drives to store your data. Sounds good, but how do you do this? Well, first of all, you could install some fancy hard drive controller that reads and writes data to two hard drives simultaneously (Figure 10.39). The data on each drive would always be identical. One drive would be the primary drive and the other drive, called the "mirror" drive, would not be used unless the primary drive failed. This process of reading and writing data at the same time to two drives is called **disk mirroring**.

If you really want to make data safe, you can use two separate controllers for each drive. With two drives, each on a separate controller, the system will continue to operate, even if the primary drive's controller stops working. This super-drive mirroring technique is called *drive duplexing* (Figure 10.40). Drive duplexing is also much faster than drive mirroring since one controller does not write each piece of data twice.

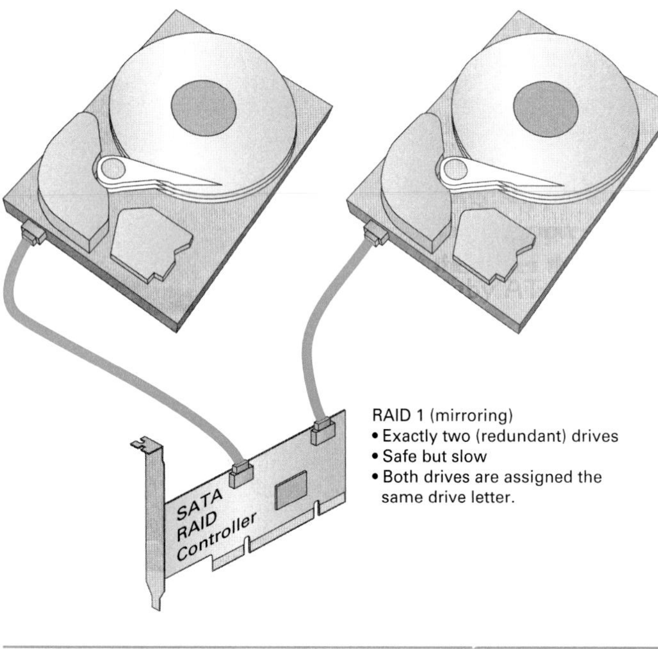

• **Figure 10.39** Mirrored drives

Even though drive duplexing is faster than drive mirroring, they both are slower than the classic one drive, one controller setup. The third and most common way to create redundant data is by a method called **disk striping with parity**. *Disk striping* (without parity) means to spread the data among multiple (at least two) drives. Disk striping by itself provides no redundancy. If you save a small Microsoft Word file, for example, the file is split into multiple pieces; half of the pieces go on one drive and half on the other (Figure 10.41).

The one and only advantage of disk striping is speed—it is a very fast way to read and write to hard drives. But if either drive fails *all* data is lost. Disk striping is not something we ever want to do—unless you're willing to increase the risk of losing data to increase the speed at which your hard drives save and restore data.

Disk striping with parity, in contrast, protects data. Disk striping with parity adds extra information, called a parity data, that can be used to rebuild data should one of the drives fail. Disk striping with parity must have at least three drives, but it is very common to use more than three. Disk striping with parity combines the best of disk mirroring and plain disk striping. It protects data and is quite fast. The majority of network servers use a type of disk striping with parity.

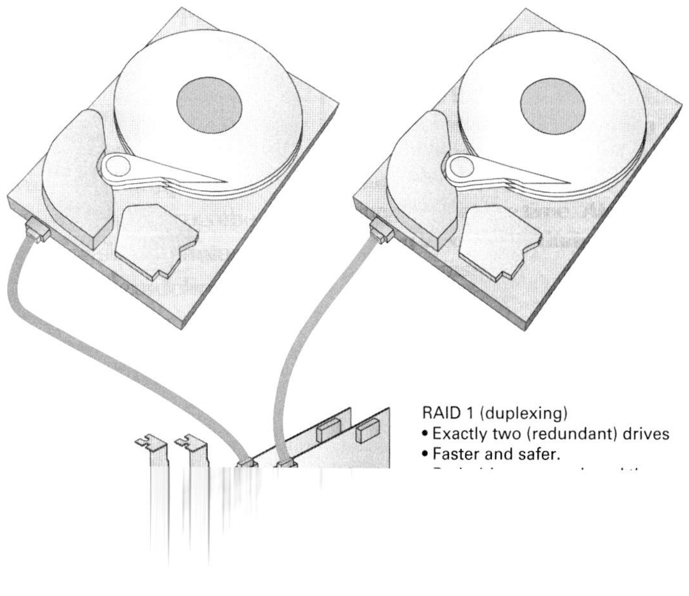

RAID

The many different techniques of using multiple

requires at least two drives. It does not provide redundancy to data. If any one drive fails, all data is lost.

- **RAID 1—Disk Mirroring/Duplexing** This requires at least two hard drives although it also works with any even number of drives. RAID 1 is the ultimate in safety, but you lose storage space since the data is duplicated—you need two 100 GB drives to store 100 GB of data.
- **RAID 2—Disk Striping with Multiple Parity Drives** A weird RAID idea that never saw practical use. Unused, ignore it.
- **RAID 3 and 4—Disk Striping with Dedicated Parity** RAID 3 and 4 combined dedicated data drives with dedicated parity drives. The differences between the two are trivial. Unlike RAID 2, these versions did see some use in the real world but were quickly replaced by RAID 5.
- **RAID 5—Disk Striping with Distributed Parity** Instead of dedicated data and parity drives, RAID 5 distributes data and parity information evenly across all drives. This is the fastest way to provide data redundancy. RAID 5 is by far the most common RAID implementation and requires at least three drives. RAID 5 storage is limited to the size of one drive. If, for example, you have three 200 GB drives, your total storage capacity is 400 GB. If you have four 200 GB drives, your total capacity is 600 GB.

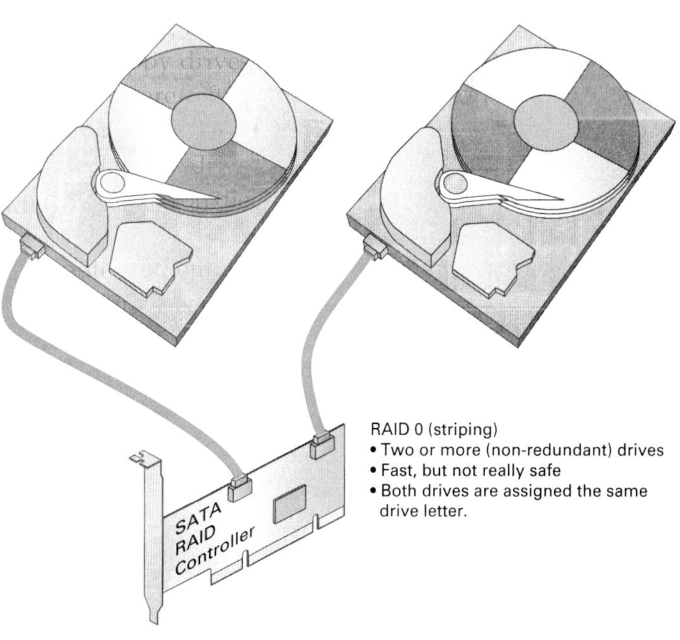

• **Figure 10.41** Disk striping

The A+ exam is only interested in your understanding RAID levels 0,1, and 5. I'm unaware of anyone actually using RAID levels 2, 3 or 4 in modern systems. Just be aware that these other levels of RAID existed.

- **RAID 6—Super Disk Striping with Distributed Parity** RAID 6 is RAID 5 with the added capability of asynchronous and cached data transmission. Think of it as a Super RAID 5.

No network tech worth her salt says things like "We're implementing disk striping with parity." Use the RAID level. Say, "We're implementing RAID 5." It's more accurate and very impressive to the folks in the Accounting Department!

After these first RAID levels were defined, some manufacturers came up with ways to combine different RAIDs. For example, what if you took two pairs of striped drives and then mirrored the pairs? You would get what is called RAID 0+1. Or what (read this carefully now) if you took two pairs of mirrored drives and striped the pairs? You then get what we call RAID 1+0 or what is often called RAID 10. Combinations of different types of single RAID are called Multiple RAID solutions. Multiple RAID solutions, while enjoying some support in the real world, are quite rare when compared to single RAID solutions RAID 0, 1, and 5.

Implementing RAID

RAID levels are a general framework: They describe different methods to provide data redundancy and/or enhance the speed of data throughput to and from groups of hard drives. They do not say *how* to implement these methods. There are literally thousands of different methods to set up RAID. The method used depends largely on the desired level of RAID, the operating system used, and the thickness of your wallet.

The obvious starting place for RAID is to hook at least three hard drives together in some fashion to create a RAID Array. For many years if you wanted to do RAID the only technology you could use was good old SCSI. SCSI's chaining of multiple devices to a single controller made it a natural for RAID. SCSI drives make superb RAID arrays, but the high cost of SCSI drives and RAID-capable host adapters kept RAID away from only the most critical systems—usually big file servers.

In the last few years, substantial leaps in ATA technology are making ATA a very viable alternative to SCSI drive technology for RAID arrays. Specialized ATA RAID controller cards support ATA RAID arrays of up to 15 drives—plenty to support even the most complex RAID needs. In addition, the inherent hot-swap capabilities of serial ATA have virtually guaranteed that serial ATA will quickly take over the lower end of the RAID business. Personally, I

Try This!

Managing Heat with Multiple Drives

Adding three or more fast hard drives into a cramped beige PC case can be a recipe for disaster to the unwary tech. All those disks spinning constantly create a phenomenal amount of heat. Heat kills PCs! You've got to manage the heat inside a RAID-enabled system or risk losing your data, drives, and basic system stability. The easiest way to do this is to add fans, so try this!

Open up your PC case and look for built-in places to mount fans. How many case fans do you have installed now? What size are they? What sizes can you use? (Most cases use 80 mm fans, but 60 and 120 mm fans are common as well.) Jot down the particulars of your system and take a trip to the local PC store to check out the fans.

Before you get all fan-happy and grab the biggest and baddest fans to throw in your case, don't forget to think about the added noise level. Try to get a compromise between keeping your case cool enough and not causing early deafness!

think the price and performance of serial ATA mean SCSI's days are numbered.

Once you have a number of hard drives the next question is whether to use hardware or software to actually control the array. Let's look at both options.

Hardware vs. Software

All RAID implementations break down into either hardware or software methods. Software is often used when price takes priority over performance. Hardware is used when you need speed along with data redundancy. Software RAID does not require special controllers—you can use the regular ATA controllers or SCSI host adapters to make a software RAID array. But you do need smart software. The most famous [illegible]

Software RAID means the operating system is in charge of all RAID functions. It works for very small RAID solutions, but tends to easily overwork your operating system, creating slowdowns. When you *really* need to keep going, when you need RAID that doesn't even let the users know there was ever a problem, hardware RAID is the only answer.

Hardware RAID centers around an intelligent controller—either a SCSI host adapter or an ATA controller that handles all of the RAID functions (Figure 10.43). Unlike a regular ATA controller or SCSI host adapter, these controllers have chips that know how to "talk RAID."

Most RAID setups in the real world are hardware-based. There are a large number of hardware RAID solutions, and almost all of these solutions provide *hot-swapping*—the ability to replace a bad drive without disturbing the operating system. Hot swapping is very common in hardware RAID.

Hardware-based RAID is invisible to the operating system. Hardware RAID is configured in several ways, depending on the specific chips involved. Most RAID systems have a special configuration utility in Flash ROM that you access after CMOS but before the OS loads. Figure 10.44 shows a typical firmware program used to configure a hardware RAID solution.

• **Figure 10.43** Serial ATA RAID controller

Personal RAID

Due to drastic reductions in the cost of ATA RAID controller chips, in the last few years we've seen an explosion of ATA-based hardware RAID solutions built into mainstream motherboards.

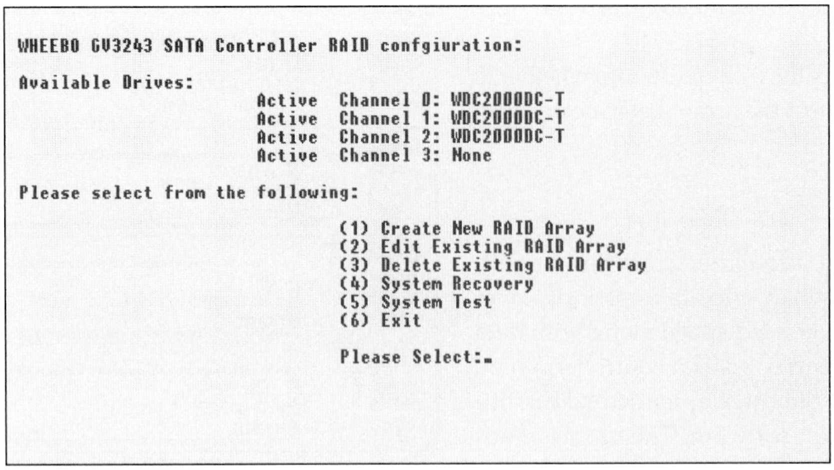

```
WHEEBO GV3243 SATA Controller RAID confgiuration:

Available Drives:
                    Active  Channel 0: WDC2000DC-T
                    Active  Channel 1: WDC2000DC-T
                    Active  Channel 2: WDC2000DC-T
                    Active  Channel 3: None

Please select from the following:

                          (1) Create New RAID Array
                          (2) Edit Existing RAID Array
                          (3) Delete Existing RAID Array
                          (4) System Recovery
                          (5) System Test
                          (6) Exit

                          Please Select:_
```

• **Figure 10.44** RAID configuration utility

While this "ATA-RAID-on-the-motherboard" began with parallel ATA, the introduction of serial ATA made motherboards with built-in RAID extremely common.

These personal RAID motherboards might be quite common, but they're not used too terribly often given that these RAID solutions usually only provide RAID 0 or RAID 1. If you want to use RAID, spend a few extra dollars and buy a RAID 5-capable controller.

The Future Is RAID

RAID has been with us for close to 20 years but only until recently it was the domain of big systems and deep pockets. However, over those 20 years a number of factors have come together to make RAID a reality for both the big servers and the common desktop system. Imagine a world where dirt cheap RAID on every computer means no one ever again losing critical data. I get goose bumps just thinking about it!

■ Troubleshooting Hard Drive Installation

The best friend a tech has when it comes to troubleshooting hard drive installation is the autodetection feature of the CMOS setup utility. When a drive doesn't work, the biggest question, especially during installation, is, "Did I plug it in correctly?" With autodetection, the answer is simple; if it doesn't see the drives, something is wrong with the hardware configuration. Either a device has physically failed or, more likely, you didn't give the hard drive power, plugged a cable in backwards, or messed up some other connectivity issue.

It takes four things to get a drive installed and recognized by the system: jumpers, data cable, power, and CMOS setup or providing BIOS. If any of these steps are missed or messed up, you have a drive that simply doesn't exist according to the PC! To troubleshoot hard drives, simply work your way through each step to figure out what went wrong.

First, set the drive to master, slave, standalone, or cable select, depending on where you decide to install the drive. If a drive is alone on the cable, set it to master or standalone. With two drives, one must be master and the other slave. Alternatively, you can set both drives to cable select and use a cable-select cable.

Second, the data cable must be connected to both the drive and controller, pin 1 to pin 1. Reversing the data cable at one end is remarkably easy to do, especially with the rounded cables. They obviously don't have a big red

Try This!

Installing a Second Hard Drive

Every tech worth his or her salt can install a PATA hard drive properly, but it takes practice to get it right. Adding a second hard drive to an existing system is one of the most common system upgrades. So get a hard drive (preferably a spare) and try this!

To complete this exercise, you will need the following:

- A computer system (with any operating system)
- A single hard drive installed in the system and configured with one primary partition (C:)
- A second hard drive compatible with the system

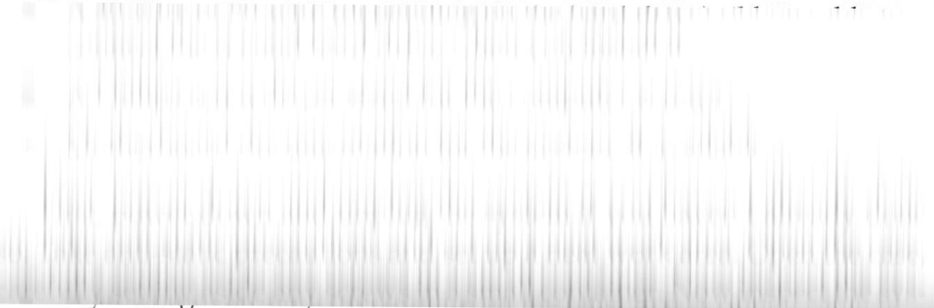

tem to see what hard drive *speed* the motherboard can handle. If you see an 80-wire cable on your system, you know that the primary controller will accept at least ATA/66, but play it safe anyway and check the motherboard documentation.

Second, determine the maximum hard drive *size* the system can handle. You can make a pretty good guess by noting the size of your existing drive. If the drive in the system is 10 GB, you can feel pretty confident that the system is running INT13 extensions, in which case it can handle a drive of up to 137 GB.

Third, once you've selected a hard drive to install, you must decide on which controller you will install it. The best place to install a second hard drive is on the primary controller, as a slave. Set the jumpers on both drives. Usually, to change the jumpers on the master drive, you will need to remove the drive from its mount so you can see the jumpers and read the jumper documentation. Remember that many hard drives have separate settings for single master and master with slave. As always, put the screws in a container so they won't fall in the case or roll under the furniture.

Fourth, reinstall the cable, making sure to orient it correctly to the number-one pin and to insert the master and slave at the correct locations on the cable. You'll probably need to install the slave drive at this point, because there won't be enough cable to let it dangle as you test. Plug in the power cables to both drives, making sure to get them all the way in.

Finally, give your installation efforts a final check and then boot the PC. Run Autodetect to verify that *both* drives are recognized by the system. If there's a problem, recheck each step, remove all the connectors and then plug them all back in, and try again. After the system recognizes the drives, *gently* attach them to the drive bays with the screws you carefully set aside for this purpose; then close the case.

stripe down the side to indicate the location of pin 1! If you can't autodetect the drive, check the cabling.

Third, be sure to give the hard drive power. Most hard drives use a standard Molex connector. If you don't hear the whirring of the drive, make certain you plugged in a Molex from the power supply, rather than from another source such as an otherwise disconnected fan. You'd be surprised how often I've seen that!

Fourth, you need to provide BIOS for the controller and the drive. This can get tricky as the typical CMOS setup program has a lot of hard drive options. Plus, you have an added level of confusion with RAID settings and non-integrated controllers that require software drivers.

Once you've checked the physical connections, run through these issues in CMOS. Is the controller enabled? Is the storage technology—LBA, Large, INT13, ATA/ATAPI- 6—properly set up? What about the data transfer settings for PIO and DMA modes? Similarly, can the motherboard support the type of drive you're installing? If not, you have a couple of options. You can flash the BIOS with an upgraded BIOS from the manufacturer or you can get a hard drive controller that goes into an expansion slot.

Finally, make certain with non-integrated hard drive controllers, such as those that come with many SATA drives, that you've installed the proper drivers for the controller. Driver issues can crop up with new, very large drives, and with changes in technology. Always check the manufacturer's web site for new drivers.

Other than the few issues listed above, troubleshooting hard drive installation is pretty straightforward. Handling issues with all the data on the drives, in contrast, can get pretty hairy. We'll tackle that in Chapter 11.

Beyond A+

Modern hard drives have many other features that are worth knowing about, but that rarely impact beginning techs. A couple of the more interesting ones are spindle speed and the S.M.A.R.T. feature. Also, if you have a burning desire to dive into hard drives in all their glory, you need not go any farther than the Storage Review, an excellent site dedicated solely to hard drives. Here's the link: www.storagereview.com.

Spindle (or Rotational) Speed

Hard drives run at a set spindle speed, measured in *revolutions per minute* (RPM). Older drives run at the long-standard speed of 3,600 RPM, but new drives are hitting 10,000 RPM! The faster the spindle speed, the faster the controller can store and retrieve data. Here are the common speeds: 4,500, 5,400, 7,200, and 10,000 RPM.

Faster drives mean better system performance, but they can also cause the computer to overheat. This is especially true in tight cases, such as minitowers, and in cases containing many drives. Two 4,500 RPM drives might run forever, snugly tucked together in your old case. But slap a hot new 10,000 RPM drive in that same case and watch your system start crashing right and left!

You can deal with these hotrod drives by adding drive bay fans between the drives or migrating to a more spacious case. Most enthusiasts end up doing both. Drive bay fans sit at the front of a bay and blow air across the drive. They range in price from $10 to $100 (U.S.) and can lower the temperature of your drives dramatically. Figure 10.45 shows a picture of a double-fan drive bay cooler.

• **Figure 10.45** Double-fan drive bay cooler

Air flow in a case can make or break your system stability, especially when you add new drives that increase the ambient temperature. Hot systems get flaky and lock up at odd moments. Many things can impede the air flow—jumbled up ribbon cables, drives squished together in a tiny case,

S.M.A.R.T.

Most modern hard drives use a function called S.M.A.R.T. (Self Monitoring Analysis and Reporting Technology). It provides a number of checks on the drive, watching for signs that it may be having problems. S.M.A.R.T. was developed to catch problems *before* the drive fails. As of this writing, no one has made a universal tool for desktop PCs using the S.M.A.R.T. technology. All hard drive makers provide free utilities that query the drive's S.M.A.R.T. functions. S.M.A.R.T. does not repair or pinpoint a problem, so these utilities just say if the drive is good or if it should be replaced.

Chapter 10 Review

Chapter Summary

After reading this chapter and completing the exercises, you should understand the following about the hard drive technologies.

Explain How Hard Drives Work

- Hard drives contain aluminum platters coated with a magnetic medium and read/write heads that float on a cushion of air. Hard drives store data as tiny magnetic fields through a process called flux reversal that defines a 0 or a 1. The incredible storage capacity of today's drives is due to Partial Response Maximum Likelihood (PRML) encoding that includes intelligent circuitry to analyze each flux reversal.
- Two different technologies have been used to move read/write heads across the platters: stepper motors and voice coil motors. Very susceptible to physical deterioration and temperature changes, the now obsolete stepper motors moved the actuator arm in fixed increments or steps, often resulting in data transfer errors or the inability to access data on a cold drive. The heads had to be parked to a non-data area when not in use to prevent possible damage to the disk surface. Today's drives use a linear or voice coil motor consisting of a permanent magnet surrounding a coil on the actuator arm. Electrical current causes the coil to generate a magnetic field that moves the actuator arm and thus the read/write heads. Containing no data, one side of one platter is used as a map to position the heads directly over the data. Voice coil technology automatically parks the heads when the drive loses power.
- Disk geometry for a particular hard drive consists of five values: heads, cylinders, sectors per track, write precomp, and landing zone. There are two read/write heads per platter. A hard drive can have either an even or an odd number of heads. A cylinder defines a group of tracks of the same diameter. Each track is sliced into tiny slivers called sectors, each of which stores 512 bytes of data. Disk geometry uses the number of sectors per track. Combining cylinders, heads, and sectors per track is referred to as CHS. Write precompensation and landing zone have no relevance in today's PCs, but most CMOS utilities still support them.

Identify and Explain the Different Hard Drive Interfaces

- Today's hard drives have either an IDE interface or a SCSI interface. IDE drives may be parallel ATA (PATA) or the newer serial ATA (SATA). A specification of the American National Standards Institute (ANSI), the AT Attachment (ATA) interface (commonly but incorrectly referred to as IDE) used a 40-pin ribbon cable, had a built-in controller, and did not require a low-level format. By 1995, EIDE was the dominant interface. Its features: higher capacities, support for non-hard drive storage devices, a four device maximum, and improved throughput. The terms ATA, IDE, and EIDE are used interchangeably to describe all PATA devices.
- IDE drives use a 40-pin plug and a controller that connects them to the external data bus. Although the real controller is built into the hard drive itself, the 40-pin connector on the motherboard is called the controller. Most modern motherboards contain two EIDE controllers, each capable of supporting up to two ATA devices. By looking at the motherboard itself or at the motherboard book, you can determine which is the primary controller and which is the secondary. If you are using only one controller, it should be the primary one.
- Older PATA drives use a 40-wire cable, while the newer Ultra DMA drives use an 80-wire cable. Either round or flat and containing no twists, each ribbon cables supports two drives. A diagram on the hard drive's housing shows how to set its jumpers to identify it as master, slave, standalone (on some drives) or cable select (cable position determines whether the drive will be master or slave. Two devices on one cable must both be set to cable select, and the cable itself must also be cable select, as indicated with a pinhole through one wire. Align the colored stripe on the cable with Pin 1 on the controller and the drive. Use a Molex connector to provide power to the drive.

- The Advanced Technology Attachment Packet Interface (ATAPI) enables non-hard drive devices to use an ATA controller. ATAPI devices, such as CD-ROM drives, use the same 40-pin interface and follow the same rules of master, slave, and cable select jumper settings. Non-hard drives must get their BIOS from option RAM or a software driver.
- Parallel ATA uses flat ribbon cables which impede airflow and have a maximum length of 18 inches. PATA is not hot-swappable, and it has reached its limits for throughput. Serial ATA (SATA) devices look identical to standard PATA devices, but their thinner seven-wire cables provide better airflow and may be up to a meter (39.4 inches) long. SATA [illegible] are keyed to prevent incorrect insertion.

Configure BIOS for Hard Drives and Controllers

- While system BIOS supports built-in PATA controllers, hard drives require configuration in CMOS. ATAPI devices require software drivers to provide BIOS support. Built-in SATA controllers on a motherboard also require software drivers, as does a SATA controller on a separate expansion card. All SATA devices get BIOS support from the SATA controller, but some drives require additional configuration; in particular, with RAID systems, you may also have to configure the controller Flash ROM settings for the specific drive(s) you install.
- When the hard drive type is set to "Auto," PATA devices can be queried directly by BIOS routines, resulting in the correct CMOS settings for up to four ATA devices. Autodetection made hard drive types obsolete. Because PATA drives have CHS values stored inside them, the BIOS routine, when set to "Auto," updates the CMOS each time the computer boots. An alternative is to run the autodetection option from the CMOS screen.
- Originally, IDE drives used the same BIOS command set introduced years earlier. Maximum values of 1,024 cylinders, 16 heads, and 63 sectors per track limited an IDE drive's capacity to 528 million bytes (504 MB). Two different sector translation methods were developed to accommodate larger EIDE drives. Western Digital developed LBA; Seagate developed the similar ECHS method. Both LBA and ECHS translation schemes supports drives with up to 256 heads, for a storage capacity limit of 8.4 GB. In the CMOS setup utility, the less-popular ECHS is often listed as "Large."
- As drive capacity neared the 8.4 GB maximum, Phoenix Technologies broke the limit by coming up with a new set of BIOS commands called Interrupt 13 extensions (INT13). Completely ignoring the CHS values, INT13 supports drives up to 137 GB by reporting a stream of "addressable sectors" [illegible]
- ATA devices transfer data through either the older programmable input/output (PIO) mode or the more popular Direct Memory Access (DMA) mode. The Small Form Factor (SFF) standards committee originally defined three different PIO modes for ATA drives: PIO mode 0 with 3.3 megabytes per second (MBps) transfer speed, PIO 1 with 5.2 MBps, and PIO 2 with 8.3 MBps. Two new PIO speeds were later defined: PIO 3 and PIO 4. It is important to set the proper PIO mode for the drive. The correct mode is the fastest among the modes supported by the hard drive, the controller, and the BIOS or device driver. If you set the mode faster than that recommended by the drive manufacturer, you will damage your data. Today's CMOS settings typically include an option to set the PIO mode automatically.
- Newer hard drives use Direct Memory Access (DMA) mode to send data directly to RAM, bypassing the CPU. Instead of using the slow DMA controller chip, today's DMA transfers use bus mastering to transfer either 16 bits or 32 bits of data. Systems with Peripheral Component Interconnect (PCI) use Ultra DMA modes. Hard drives typically use one of the following modes: Ultra DMA 2 (also called ATA/33), Ultra DMA 4 (ATA/66), Ultra DMA 5 (ATA/100), and Ultra DMA 6 (ATA/133). To use Ultra DMA, you must have a controller and an 80-wire ribbon cable.

Some motherboards combine different speeds of ATA controllers, with the higher speed controller indicated with a bright color. The 80-pin ribbon cable indicates where the master and slave drives should be connected. High-end PATA devices can use lower-end controllers, but they will operate at the slower speed.

- Even if the autodetect feature indicates that a CD-media ATAPI drive has been installed, this merely shows that the drive is connected properly and has the option to function as a boot device. This autodetection does *not* provide true BIOS support. You must still install drivers to provide the BIOS. If the driver is installed in a graphical mode, you will be unable to access the drive if you boot to a command prompt–only environment.
- Drive mirroring writes data simultaneously to two hard drives, allowing the system to continue to work if one hard drive dies. A faster and even more effective technique is drive duplexing, which performs mirroring using two separate controllers for each drive. A third way to create redundant data is disk striping with parity. This technique, requiring at least three drives, combines the redundancy of disk mirroring with the speed of disk striping. Although disk striping without parity works very fast, splitting the data across two drives means you'll lose *all* data if either drive fails.
- Numbered 0 through 6, there are seven official levels of RAID (Random Array of Inexpensive Disks or Random Array of Independent Disks), but the most commonly used ones are RAID-0 (disk striping), RAID-1 (disk mirroring or duplexing), and RAID-5 (disk striping with distributed parity).
- SCSI drives were a natural for the multiple disk RAID. Specialized ATA RAID controller cards now support ATA RAID arrays of up to 15 drives. With its hot-swap capabilities, serial ATA may soon take over lower-end RAID from SCSI.
- RAID may be implemented through hardware or software methods. While software implementation is cheaper, hardware techniques provide better performance. Windows NT Server and Windows 2000 Server include built-in RAID software for RAID-0, RAID-1, and RAID-5 for either ATA or SCSI. Windows 2000 and XP Professional include Disk Management for RAID-0 and RAID-1. RAID software solutions tend to overwork your operating system, resulting in slowdowns. Hardware RAID is invisible to users and is usually hot-swappable. A hardware ATA RAID controller usually requires CMOS configuration. Many motherboards include built-in ATA-based hardware RAID-0 and RAID-1 capabilities.

Troubleshoot Hard Drive Installation

- It takes four things to get a drive installed and recognized by the system: jumpers, data cable, power, and CMOS setup or providing BIOS. If any of these steps are missed or messed up, you have a drive that simply doesn't exist according to the PC.
- If the autodetection feature of the CMOS utility does not detect a drive, it means it is installed incorrectly or the drive itself is bad. Check the master/slave jumper settings. Make sure that the ribbon cable aligns pin 1 with pin 1, and that the Molex connector is supplying power to the drive.
- Once you've checked the physical connections, run through these issues in CMOS. Is the controller enabled? Is the storage technology—LBA, Large, INT13, ATA/ATAPI-6—properly set up? What about the data transfer settings for PIO and DMA modes? Similarly, can the motherboard support the type of drive you're installing? If not, you can flash the BIOS or get a hard drive controller that goes into an expansion slot. Make certain with non-integrated hard drive controllers, such as those that come with many SATA drives, that you've installed the proper drivers for the controller. Always check the manufacturer's web site for new drivers.

Key Terms

40-pin ribbon cable *(305)*
80-wire cable *(305)*
Advanced Technology Attachment Packet Interface (ATAPI) *(308)*
ATA/133 *(318)*
ATA/ATAPI-6 *(316)*
Cylinder *(302)*
Direct Memory Access (DMA) *(316)*
Disk mirroring *(320)*
Disk striping with distributed parity *(320)*
EIDE *(304)*

Interrupt 13 (INT13) extensions *(316)*

Parallel ATA (PATA) *(303)*

Partial Response Maximum Likelihood (PRML) *(300)*

Redundant Array of Independent (or Inexpensive) Disks (RAID) *(309)*

SATA bridge *(309)*

Sector translation *(314)*

Serial ATA (SATA) *(303)*

Small computer system interface (SCSI) *(303)*

Stepper motor *(301)*

Voice coil motor *(301)*

Key Term Quiz

Use the Key Terms list to complete the sentences that follow. Not all the terms will be used.

1. A drives that uses a(n) __________ parks its read/write heads automatically when power is

4. To install a parallel ATA device to a serial ATA controller, use a tiny card called a(n) __________.
5. LBA, developed by Western Digital, and ECHS, developed by Seagate, both use __________ to get around the limits of 1024 cylinders, 16 heads, and 63 sectors/track.
6. Also known as RAID 5, __________ uses at least three drives and combines the best features

10. Drives that use __________ bypass the CPU and send data directly to memory.

Multiple-Choice Quiz

1. CHS disk geometry computes storage capacity by using all of the following *except* ________.
   - **A.** Sectors per track
   - **B.** Tracks
   - **C.** Heads
   - **D.** Cylinders
2. Disk striping with distributed parity is also known as __________.
   - **A.** RAID 0
   - **B.** RAID 1
   - **C.** RAID 5
   - **D.** RAID 6
3. The most efficient encoding method is __________.
   - **A.** Partial Response Maximum Likelihood (PRML)
   - **B.** Frequency modulation (FM)
   - **C.** Run length limited (RLL)
   - **D.** Modified frequency modulation (MFM)
4. Counting both channels, EIDE can support a maximum of _______ drives/devices.
   - **A.** One
   - **B.** Two
   - **C.** Seven
   - **D.** Four
5. All of the following are true about cable select *except* _____________.
   - **A.** Both drives/devices should be set for cable select.
   - **B.** It requires a special cable with a pinhole through one wire.
   - **C.** The colored stripe on the ribbon cable should align with Pin 1 on the controller and drive.
   - **D.** Position of the drives on the cable does not matter.

6. If you install two IDE drives on the same cable, how will the computer differentiate them?
   A. The CMOS setup allows you to configure them.
   B. You must set jumpers to determine which drive functions as master and which functions as slave.
   C. You will set jumpers so each drive will have a unique ID number.
   D. The drives will be differentiated by whether you place them before or after the twist in the ribbon cable.
7. Using the CHS method, a drive is limited to __________.
   A. 528 megabytes
   B. 1024 megabytes
   C. 504 megabytes
   D. 1028 megabytes
8. All of the following terms describe parallel ATA devices *except* __________.
   A. IDE
   B. EIDE
   C. SCSI
   D. ATA
9. Shelby wants to add a new 100 GB hard drive to her computer. Which of the following will allow her to do so?
   A. CHS
   B. LBA
   C. ECHS
   D. INT13
10. Which of the following techniques provides redundancy by using two disks and two controllers.
   A. Drive mirroring
   B. Drive duplexing
   C. Disk striping
   D. Disk striping with parity
11. An Ultra DMA cable contains ________ wires.
   A. 24
   B. 34
   C. 40
   D. 80
12. Billy just installed a second hard drive, but the autodetection utility in CMOS does not detect it. Sara told him he probably had the jumpers set incorrectly or had forgotten to connect the Molex power connector. John told him his new hard drive is probably bad and he should return it. Is Sara or John probably correct?
   A. Sara is correct.
   B. John is correct.
   C. Neither is correct.
   D. Either John or Sara may be correct.
13. All of the following are advantages of serial ATA (SATA) *except* __________.
   A. They are hot-swappable.
   B. Thinner cables provide better airflow inside the case.
   C. SATA provides faster data throughput than PATA.
   D. SATA cable must be shorter than PATA cables.
14. Which of the following two CMOS configuration options are obsolete with today's hard drives?
   A. Cylinders and heads
   B. Heads and sectors
   C. Sectors and Write precompensation
   D. Write precompensation and landing zone
15. The ANSI ATA committee adopted ______________, a new standard that increased disk storage capacity to more than 144 petabytes.
   A. ATA/ATAPI-6
   B. LBA
   C. INT13
   D. ECHS

Essay Quiz

1. Discuss at least three advantages of serial ATA over parallel ATA.
2. Compare and contrast hardware and software RAID implementation.
3. Your friend Blaine has a Pentium III computer with a 100 MHz bus. Currently, it has only a 20 GB ATA/100 hard drive and a CD-RW drive. Since he's interested in graphics, he knows he needs more storage capacity and wants to add a second hard drive. What advice will you give him about selecting a new hard drive?

determine their features including storage capacity, interface, RPM, and cost:

- Maxtor Model # 6Y120L0 and Maxtor Model # 6Y120M0
- Western Digital Model # WD1200JB and Western Digital Model WD1200JD

5. Hard drives include other features and characteristics not included in this chapter. Choose one of the following topics and use the Internet to define and explain it to the class.

- Zone bit recording

Lab Project 10.1

Access the CMOS setup for your computer and examine the settings that apply to your hard drive(s) and EIDE interface. In particular, look at the initial screen to see if it is set to autodetect the kind of hard drive. Is the mode set to LBA or something else? Now find the screen that includes the autodetect utility and run it. Does it offer different modes with different drive capacities? Try to find a screen that includes PIO modes and examine this setting. What other screens apply to the hard drive? When you finish, be sure to choose Quit without Saving.

Lab Project 10.2

Visit your local computer store or use the Internet to discover what kinds of hard drives and hard drive interfaces are commonly offered with a new computer. Try to determine whether the motherboards offers only parallel ATA interfaces or if they offer serial ATA interfaces, either onboard or through an expansion card. If you were purchasing a new computer, would you select PATA or SATA? Why?

Lab Project 10.3

Your supervisor has decided to implement RAID on the old company server machine, where everyone stores their work-related data. Come up with two competing RAID setups, one that maximizes security of data at the lowest cost possible, and the other that maximizes speed but retains some security. Cost is not a factor on the second RAID plan.

Implementing Hard Drives

"Computer Science is the only discipline in which we view adding a new wing to a building as being maintenance."

—Jim Horning

In this chapter, you will learn how to

- **Partition a hard drive**
- **Format a hard drive**
- **Maintain and troubleshoot a hard drive**

Hard drives store the programs and files used by the CPU (and you) to get work done. To write the next great novel on your PC, for example, you need to load a word processing program from storage on the hard drive into RAM so the CPU can access that application. When you finish writing for the day, you need to store that chapter somewhere that you can access it again. This brings up a logical question. How can you store information on a hard drive so that it's safe, secure, and easily retrievable? You know about the physical components of a hard drive from Chapter 10, such things as cylinders, heads, and sectors per track; in short, the geometry. You need some mechanism or mechanisms to organize the drive and create an interface for data retrieval.

Historical/Conceptual

Once you've successfully installed a hard drive, you must perform two more steps to translate a drive's geometry and circuits into something usable to the system: partitioning and formatting. Partitioning is the process of electronically subdividing the physical hard drive into groups of cylinders called *partitions*. A hard drive must be partitioned into at least one partition, although you can create multiple partitions on a single hard drive if you wish. In Windows, each of these partitions typically is assigned a drive letter like C: or D:. After partitioning, you must format the drive. This step, sometimes still called a high-level format to differentiate it from the low-level format discussed in Chapter 10, installs a **file system** onto the drive that or- [illegible] cess of preparing a drive to hold data.

Test Specific

■ Partitioning Hard Drives

Partitions are electronic, logical divisions of a hard drive into groups of cylinders. They provide tremendous flexibility in the way we organize our hard drives. A computer might have only one physical hard drive, for example, but it can have anywhere from 1 to 24 logical drives, which are assigned the drive letters from C: to Z:.

Partitions exist for three reasons. First, when DOS was initially designed to use hard drives, the method employed by DOS to store files limited the largest hard drive size to 32 MB. Microsoft included partitioning in DOS 3.3 to enable PCs to use larger physical hard drives by creating multiple logical drives, up to 32 MB each. Modern Windows systems support individual partition sizes up to 137 GB (assuming you have INT13 extensions) and beyond (with ATA/ATAPI-6), but you still must partition the hard drive before you can use it. Second, partitions enable you to organize a drive in a way that suits your personal taste. For example, I partitioned my 30 GB hard drive into a 25 GB C: drive where I store Windows 2000 and all my programs, and a 5 GB D: drive where I store all my personal data. This is a matter of personal choice—in my case, it makes backups simpler. Finally, partitioning enables a single hard drive to store more than one **operating system (OS)** . One OS could be stored in one partition and another OS stored in a second.

Windows 9*x*/Me and NT 4.0 do not use the term "basic disk," simply because they only partition in the classic way. I use the term here because we live in a Windows XP world and good techs stay current.

The different versions of Windows in wide use today offer two radically different styles of partitioning, called basic disks and dynamic disks. All versions of Windows can create partitions with basic disks; only Windows 2000 and XP can create dynamic disks. This chapter covers basic disks first, showing you the tools in Windows 9*x*/Me and Windows NT 4.0 for partitioning. When we explore the tools for Windows 2000/XP, the chapter will plunge into dynamic disks.

Partitioning Basic Disks

Partitioning creates a couple of items on a disk, the **master boot record (MBR)** and a **partition table**. When the computer first boots to a hard drive, it looks for the very first sector of the physical drive, called the **boot sector**. The boot sector contains the MBR and the partition table. The MBR is nothing more than a tiny bit of code that takes control of the boot process from the system BIOS. The MBR has only one job: to look for a partition in the partition table with a valid operating system (Figure 11.1).

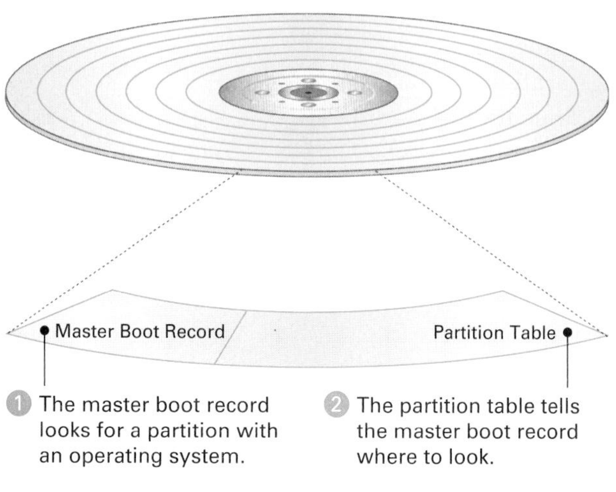

Figure 11.1 Functions of the MBR and partition table

Every partition in the partition table that contains a valid OS has a special setting called *active* that the MBR uses to determine which OS to load. All hard drive partition tables support up to four bootable partitions, but the vast majority of systems only have one bootable partition. Only one partition at a time can be made the **active partition**. I guess that makes sense since you can only run one OS at a time (see Figure 11.2).

The boot sector at the beginning of the hard drive isn't the only boot sector on a hard drive. The first sector of the first cylinder of each partition also has a boot sector called the **volume boot sector**. While the "main" boot sector defines the partitions, the volume boot sector stores information important to its partition, such as the location of the operating system boot files.

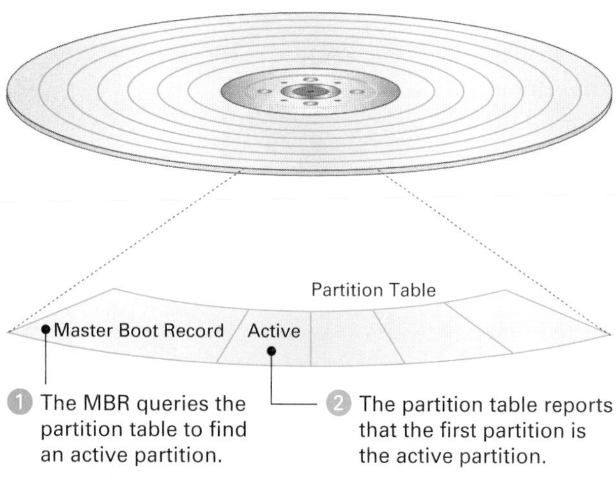

Figure 11.2 The MBR checks the partition table to find the active partition.

Partition Types

A hard drive may have up to four partitions, whether bootable or not. These partitions divide into one of two types: primary and extended. Each type of partition performs different functions. You create these partitions based on the needs of the particular system. Some of you may have seen hard drives with more than four drive letters. Be careful here—the extended partition can have more than one drive letter associated with it. No matter how many drive letters you see, there are never more than four partitions per drive.

Primary Partitions **Primary partitions** store the OS(s). If you want to boot from a hard drive, it must have a primary partition. Therefore, the MBR must check the partition table for a primary partition (see Figure 11.3). In Windows 9*x*/Me and NT/2000/XP, the primary partition is C:, and that cannot be changed.

A hard drive can have up to four primary partitions, but in the Windows 9*x* world, the built-in partitioning program, called **FDISK**, only enables you to create one primary partition on the drive (see Figure 11.4). I guess Microsoft, being a seller of OSs, didn't want you to install other OSs!

So even though hard drives support up to four primary partitions, you almost never see this in the Windows 9*x*/Me world. Other OSs, such as Windows 2000 and Linux, however, fully support multiple primary partitions on one drive. We use a number of terms for this function, but dual-boot and multiboot seem fairly common. As I constantly field questions regarding different OSs, this is a very handy option for me to use. The system [illegible] Linux come with similar tools to do this, but I [illegible] messy to use and prefer System Commander. When my computer boots, System Commander yanks control from the MBR and asks me which OS I wish to boot (see Figure 11.5). I select my OS and it appears!

Once I boot up, say, Windows 98, I don't see the other primary partitions. As far as Windows 98 is concerned, only the C: drive exists. If I boot to Linux, it only sees its own partition. If I boot to Windows 2000, it sees other primary partitions but only because it is designed to read older Windows partitions. Even Windows XP doesn't see my Linux partition.

Multiple primary partitions may sound a little confusing, so let's make it simpler. Very few systems use more than one primary partition. You may work on PCs for years and never see a system with more than one primary partition. The A+ Certification exams certainly don't expect you to show how to create a system with multiple primary partitions, but they assume that you know you *can* add more than one primary partition to a hard drive if you so desire. For the rest of this book, we will assume that you only want one primary partition.

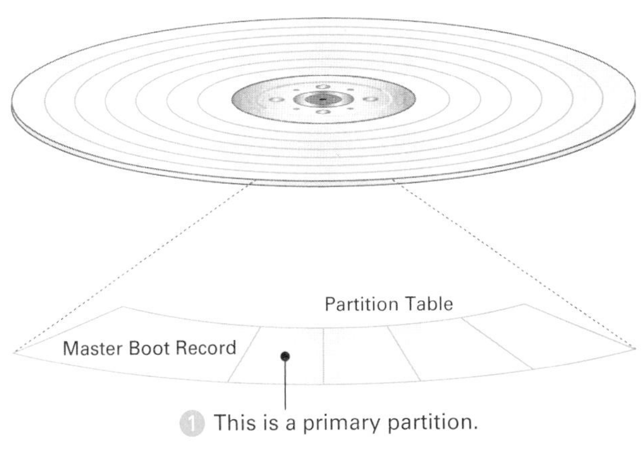

Figure 11.3 The MBR checks the partition table to find a [illegible]

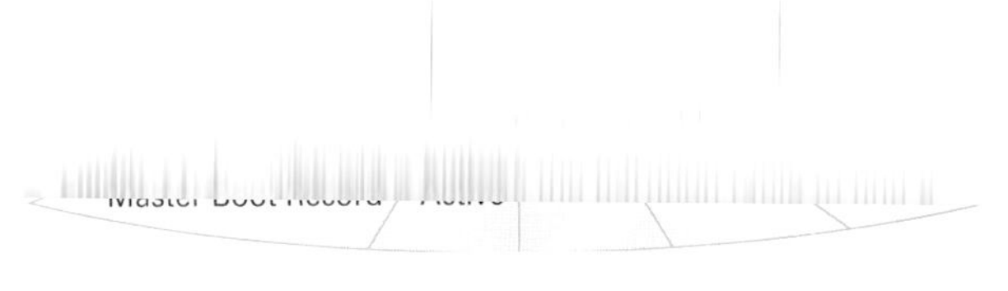

Figure 11.4 FDISK can create only one primary partition.

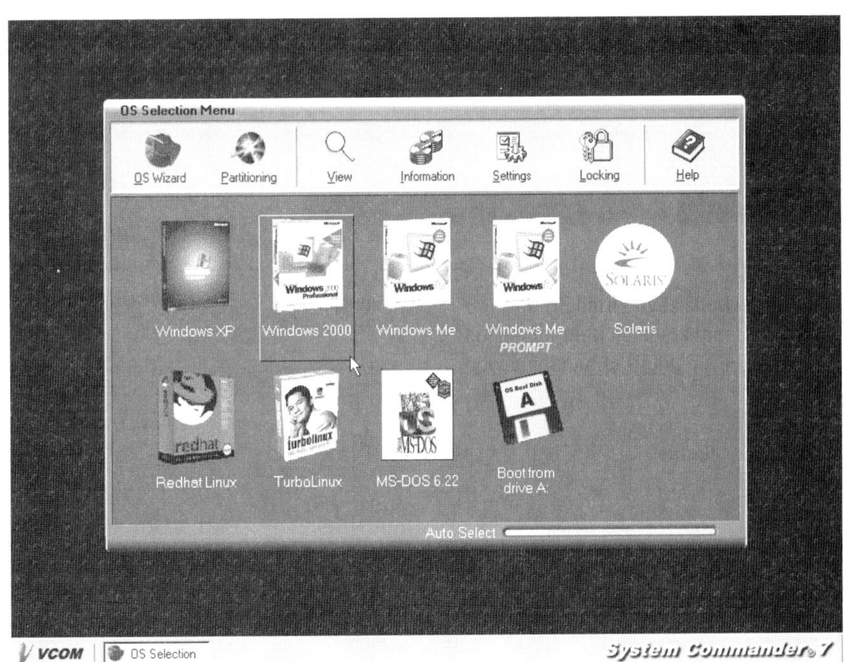

Figure 11.5 System Commander's Operating System Selection menu *(Image courtesy of VCOM)*

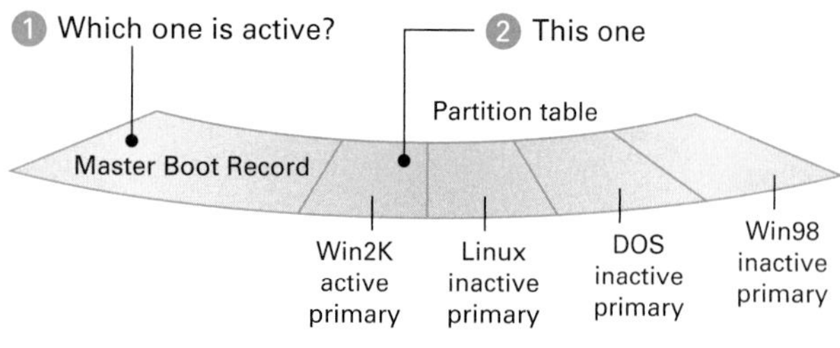

• **Figure 11.6** The MBR looks for an active, primary partition.

Active Partition When a hard drive stores multiple primary partitions, each with a valid operating system, the MBR will seek an OS to boot on the currently active primary partition (see Figure 11.6). As mentioned previously, only one primary partition may be active at a time.

When my System Commander boot screen comes up, it essentially asks me, "What primary partition do you want me to make active?" Well, that's fine for systems with many primary partitions, but what does active partitioning have to do with the system with only one primary partition? When you create your single partition, you still must set that partition as active using your partitioning software. The system requires you to do this step, even though only one primary partition exists.

Don't confuse a primary partition with the primary controller; they are totally different animals that just happen to have similar names.

Extended Partition Your hard drive may or may not have the other basic disk partition type—an **extended partition**. Extended partitions are not bootable, and a hard drive can only have one extended partition. If a hard drive has an extended partition, it takes up one of the areas in the partition map for primary partitions. You may only have up to three primary partitions on a drive with an extended partition. (Not a big deal considering the vast majority of systems never use more than one primary partition anyway!)

Extended partitions are completely optional; you do not have to create an extended partition on a hard drive. So, if you can't boot to an extended partition and your hard drive doesn't need an extended partition, why would you want to create one? First of all, many systems do not use extended partitions. Some hard drives are partitioned as one big primary partition—nothing wrong with that. You can use extended partitions in situations where you want to chop a drive into multiple drive letters.

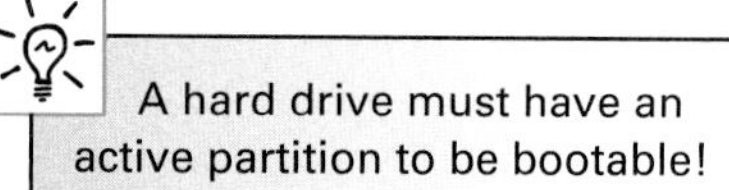
A hard drive must have an active partition to be bootable!

The beauty of an extended partition is in the way it handles drive letters. When you create a primary partition, it gets a drive letter and that's it. But when you create an extended partition, it does not automatically get a drive letter. Instead, you divide the extended partition into "logical drives." An extended partition may have as many logical drives as you wish (limited to the letters of the alphabet on Windows 9*x* systems) enabling a maximum of 24 logical drives on one system (A: and B: are reserved for floppy drives). You may turn an extended partition into one logical drive or into multiple logical drives, whatever suits you. You may set the size of each logical drive to any size you desire.

All of this flexibility can create a problem, especially for folks new to partitioning. Because a newly created extended partition doesn't yet have logical drives, working with extended partitions always requires two steps: First, you make the extended partition, and then you must create logical drives within that extended partition. This two-step process often confuses new techs; they forget to create logical drives in the extended partition and wonder why they don't see any new drive letters in My Computer when they finish partitioning (see Figure 11.7).

• **Figure 11.7** Typical new tech error

Each version of Windows offers a different tool for partitioning hard drives. In Windows 9*x*/Me, you use a program called FDISK to partition drives. Figure 11.8 shows the FDISK program. Windows NT 4.0 uses the far more powerful, graphical Disk Administrator tool. Windows 2000 and Windows XP use an enhanced version of the Disk Administrator, called Disk Management (Figure 11.9).

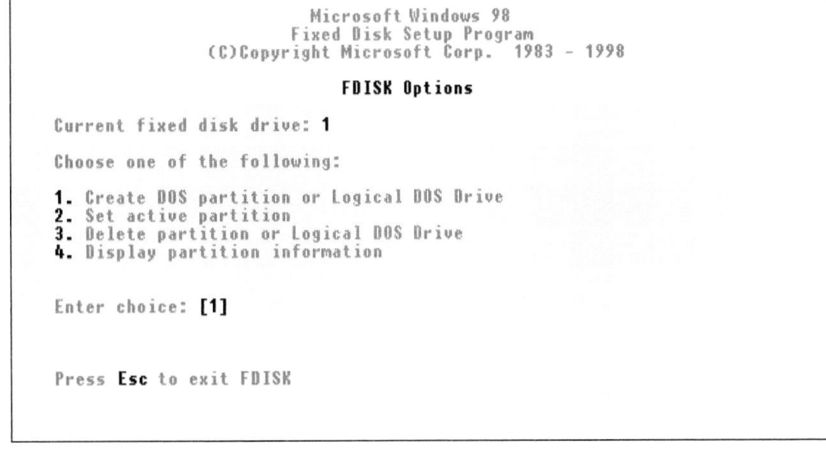

FDISK

For years, every OS associated with

hard drive to play with, you can still run FDISK and march through the screens, just don't change anything!

for the drive. Reboot, access CMOS, and try setting up the drive again.

Single Drive, One Primary Partition Let's start with the most common of all partitioning options, a single hard drive that we want to turn into one big C: drive. Clearly, we want to boot from this drive, so we need to make the entire drive a primary partition and then make it active. Assume that you have a 30 GB hard drive properly installed and configured in CMOS and that you have a Windows 98 boot disk. Boot to the floppy, selecting No CD-ROM support when asked. If you have a Windows 95 boot disk, just boot normally. Eventually, you get to an A: prompt, although Windows 98 may complain that it can't find a C: drive—just ignore it! Type **FDISK** at the command prompt to start the program. When you run FDISK, you will see one of two things on your screen: a bunch of text or the main menu. Windows 95 version B and later FDISKs place a message onscreen that starts with "Your computer has a disk larger than 512 MB" and ends by requiring you to select yes (Y) or no (N) (see Figure 11.10).

This long-winded explanation is nothing more than Windows asking you which type of file system you want to use, FAT16 or FAT32. (You'll learn all about these file systems in the next

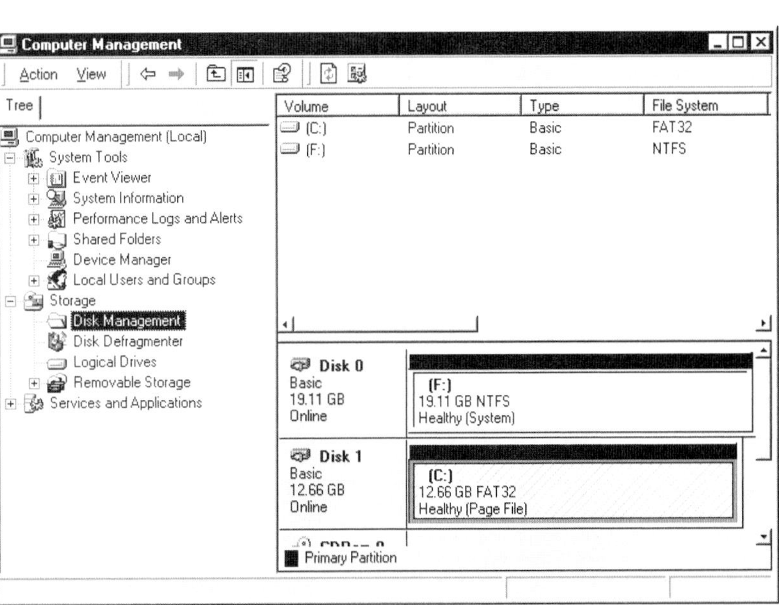

• **Figure 11.9** Windows 2000 Disk Management

```
Your computer has a disk larger than 512 MB.  This version of Windows
includes improved support for large disks, resulting in more efficient
use of disk space on large drives, and allowing disks over 2 GB to be
formatted as a single drive.

IMPORTANT: If you enable large disk support and create any new drives on this
disk, you will not be able to access the new drive(s) using other operating
systems, including some versions of Windows 95 and Windows NT, as well as
earlier versions of Windows and MS-DOS. In addition, disk utilities that
were not designed explicitly for the FAT32 file system will not be able
to work with this disk. If you need to access this disk with other operating
systems or older disk utilities, do not enable large drive support.

Do you wish to enable large disk support (Y/N) ...........? [ ]
```

• **Figure 11.10** Opening the Windows 98 FDISK screen

section; for now just understand that you have a choice.) If you press Y, everything you do will be FAT32; if you press N everything you do will be FAT16. For this example, we will select Y for yes. This brings us to the famous FDISK main menu (see Figure 11.11).

If you boot directly to the FDISK main menu without seeing the long paragraph about FAT32, you are using a Windows 95 or even a DOS FDISK. Nothing is wrong with those FDISKs, assuming that FAT16 is acceptable to you.

The FDISK main menu provides four choices. By choosing the first option, you can create a primary partition, an extended partition, or logical drives in an extended partition. The second option enables you to create an active partition. Option 3 enables you to delete partitions and logical drives. Option 4 displays current information. (Note that all versions of FDISK—from MS-DOS to Windows Me—call the partitions DOS partitions. Don't let that throw you!) Let's first select option 4 to verify that the drive is blank (see Figure 11.12).

This chapter explains how to partition a hard drive *before* it explains how to format one, because that is the order in which you as a PC tech will actually perform those tasks. You'll learn all the specifics of the various file systems—such as FAT16 and FAT32—when I explain formatting in the next section, but until then, just accept that there are several different systems for organizing the files on a hard drive, and that part of setting up a hard drive involves choosing among them.

If you see anything other than the screen shown in Figure 11.12, the drive has partitions. Jump down to the deleting partitions section to delete the partitions. (Remember, don't delete if you have *any* data on the drive that you want to keep!)

Nice, blank drive? Great! Press the ESC key to return to the main menu, just like it says at the bottom of the screen. We always use the ESC key to move back to the main menu in FDISK. Now select 1—Create DOS partition or Logical DOS Drive to open the Create Partition screen (shown in Figure 11.13).

```
                      Microsoft Windows 98
                    Fixed Disk Setup Program
             (C)Copyright Microsoft Corp.  1983 - 1998

                          FDISK Options

Current fixed disk drive: 1

Choose one of the following:

1. Create DOS partition or Logical DOS Drive
2. Set active partition
3. Delete partition or Logical DOS Drive
4. Display partition information


Enter choice: [1]


Press Esc to exit FDISK
```

• **Figure 11.11** The FDISK main menu

Display Partition Information

Current fixed disk drive: 1

No partitions defined

Press Esc to continue

Note the three options: Create Primary DOS Partition, Create Extended DOS Partition, and Create Logical DOS Drive(s) in the Extended DOS Partition. We need a primary partition, so select 1. The screen shown in Figure 11.14 displays.

If you get a "Primary partition already exists" error, you already have a primary partition. Remember, you can only make one primary partition per drive with Windows 9*x*/Me. See the section [illegible] automatically. In the vast majority of cases with clients, that's what you'll do. But A+ techs know how to play with all sorts of partitions, so press N to get the screen shown in Figure 11.15.

FDISK now wants you to choose the size of your primary partition. Notice that the prompt waits for you either to press ENTER to accept the entire drive or to type in a new value. If you only see approximately 8.4 GB (remember, our example drive is 30 GB), your BIOS does not have INT13 extensions. You will need to upgrade your BIOS or use an "overlay" program. (See the upcoming section, "Maintaining and Troubleshooting Hard Drives," for more details.) Every hard drive maker gives away special programs to enable an older, non-INT13 system to accept hard drives larger than 8.4 GB. Check the hard drive maker's web site or ask for the program where you purchased the drive.

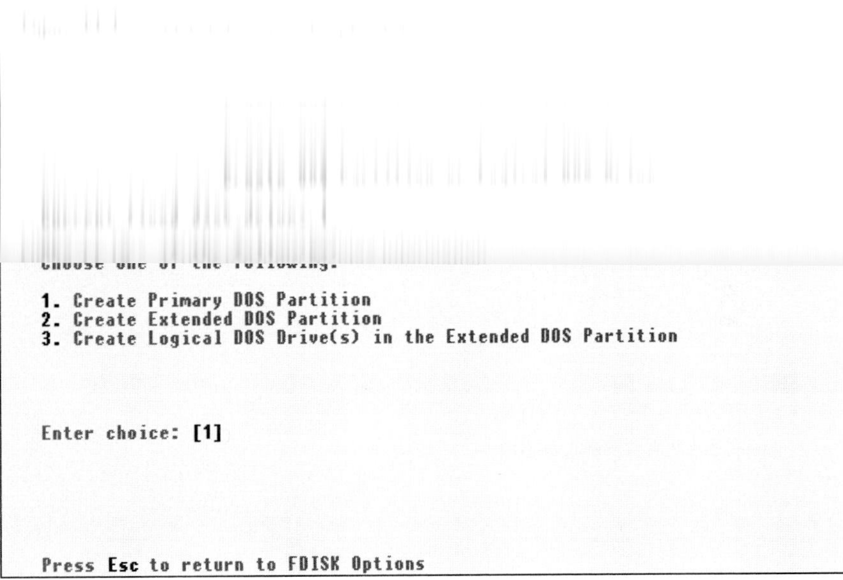

• **Figure 11.13** The FDISK Create DOS Partition screen

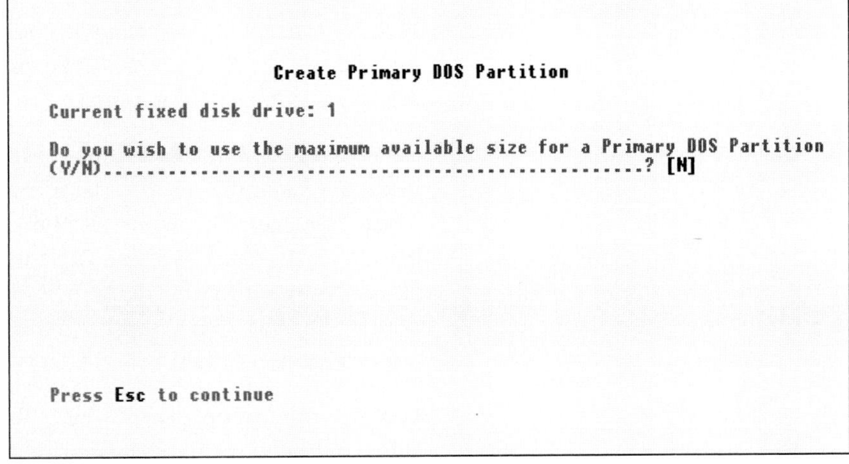

• **Figure 11.14** FDISK's "Do it all in one shot?" screen

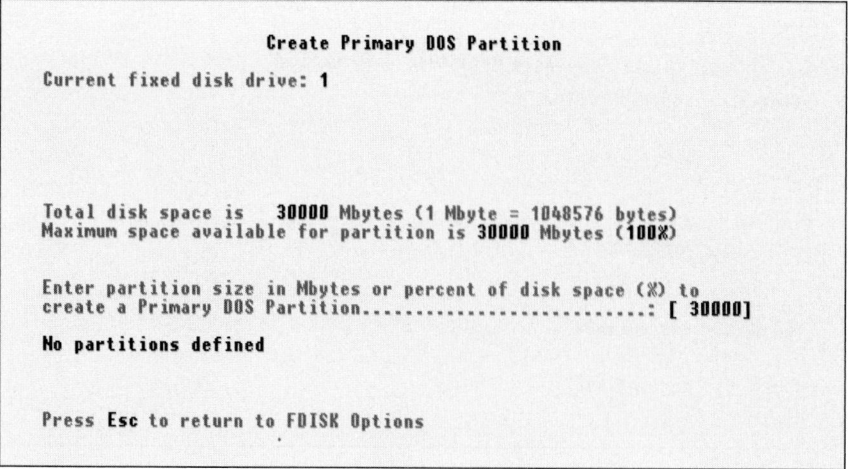

• **Figure 11.15** Setting the primary partition size

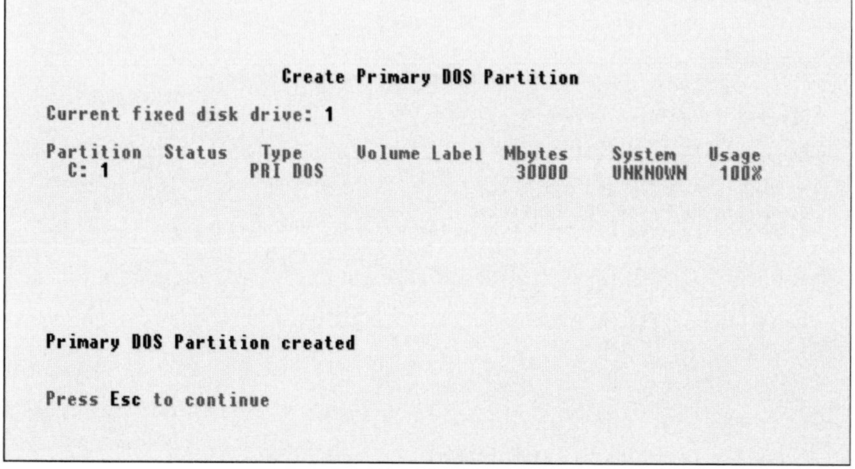

• **Figure 11.16** The entire drive is one primary partition.

If you only see approximately 2.1 GB, you are using FAT16. FAT16 only supports partitions up to 2.1 GB. Upgrade the system so that it can use FAT32 or get ready to make an extended partition with a bunch of logical drives!

If we wanted to make the drive 50 percent C: and 50 percent D:, we could type in half the total or simply type in 50 percent. (Don't forget the % sign or you will get a 50 MB primary partition!) To make the entire drive one big primary partition, just press ENTER. FDISK confirms the new primary partition with the screen shown in Figure 11.16. Press ESC to return to the main menu.

When you return to the main menu, you'll see an error message telling you there are no active partitions. What the heck? Remember, even though Windows does not do multiple primary partitions, FDISK still must have the primary partition set to active. This step is so easy I'll let you figure out how to do it yourself. Meet me back at the main screen. Do you want a clue? I'll give you two:

- Read the screen.
- The name of the drive you wish to set active is 1, not C.

That's it! You have successfully partitioned the drive. Press ESC to exit FDISK and reboot, keeping the bootable floppy in the drive. You must reboot before the changes will take effect. That's it for partitioning in FDISK. It's time to upgrade the tools.

Two Drives, Multiple Partitions Well, that was fun! So much fun that I'd like to do it again! This time, let's imagine we have two hard drives. The first drive, the primary master, is the same 30 GB drive, still containing the primary partition. For a second drive, let's install a 10 GB drive as a primary slave. We want to divide the 30 GB primary master into 50 percent C:, 25 percent D:, and 25 percent E:. We want to make the primary slave just one big extended partition called F:, as shown in Figure 11.17.

Dealing with Multiple Partitions "But wait," I hear you say. "I thought you said a hard drive must have a primary partition." No, I never said that—not exactly. I said that if you want to boot to a hard drive it must have a primary partition. I don't want to boot to the second drive; I only want to boot to the first drive. We *could* make the second drive primary. It wouldn't hurt a thing, but it would make for some strange drive letters. Here's an example. Say I had two identical 10 GB hard drives. Each drive is partitioned identically, 50 percent primary and 50 percent extended with one logical drive in each extended partition. Look at Figure 11.18 to see what I mean.

```
                      Fixed Disk Drive Status

Disk   Drv     Mbytes     Free     Usage
  1             30000       0       100%
        C:      15000
        D:       7500
        E:       7500
  2             10000       0       100%
        F:      10000

(1 MByte = 1048576 bytes)
A:/>
```

If I installed one of these drives into a PC, its primary partition would get C: and its logical drive in [illegible]

The partitions receive their drive letters at every boot. Here's the order in which hard drives receive their letters:

• **Figure 11.18** Identical drives each partitioned with 50 percent primary and 50 percent extended

1. Primary partition of the primary master drive
2. Primary partition of the primary slave drive
3. Primary partition of the secondary master drive
4. Primary partition of the secondary slave drive
5. All logical drives in the extended partition of the primary master drive
6. All logical drives in the extended partition of the primary slave drive
7. All logical drives in the extended partition of the secondary master drive
8. All logical drives in the extended partition of the secondary slave drive
9. All non-hard drives attached to an IDE controller get a drive letter

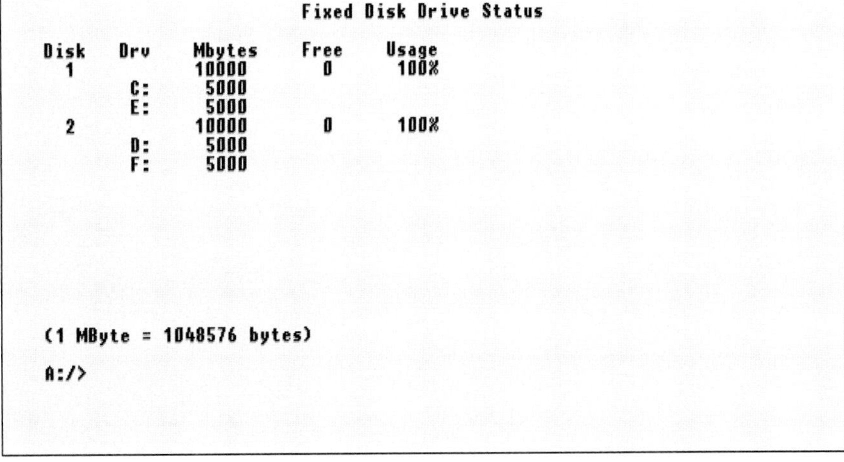

```
                      Fixed Disk Drive Status

Disk   Drv     Mbytes     Free     Usage
  1             10000       0       100%
        C:       5000
        E:       5000
  2             10000       0       100%
        D:       5000
        F:       5000

(1 MByte = 1048576 bytes)
A:/>
```

• **Figure 11.19** Messed up drive letters from two drives with primary partitions

So, let's look at our two drives again to see what's happening. At boot, the system uses this "pecking order" to assign drive letters. When these drives sit in separate systems, the primary partition becomes C: and the secondary partition becomes D:. The moment you put these two

When you load a new hard drive or add a new partition to a PC, the drive letter for any CD-media drive gets bumped down another letter. Suddenly, all those programs that insist on having the CD-ROM in the drive before they'll run—such as every modern game out there—can't see the disc because the drive letter has changed! There's no easy fix for this in Window 9*x*/Me, but Windows 2000 and Windows XP enable you to change drive letters at will, as you'll see shortly.

drives in the same system, however, this changes. The system first finds the primary partition on the primary master and assigns it the letter C:. It then continues to look for any other primary partitions, finding the primary partition on the primary slave and assigning that primary partition the letter D:. Not seeing any more primary partitions, it then goes back up to the primary master drive, now looking for logical drives in extended partitions. It finds one logical drive and assigns it the letter E:. If the system had found two logical drives on the primary master, they would receive the letters E: and F:. After giving the drive letter E: to the one logical drive in the extended partition, the system continues down the list, looking for more logical drives in more extended partitions. In this example, the system would find the other logical drive in the primary slave and assign it the letter F:.

Deleting Partitions Deleting partitions in FDISK follows a clear set of rules, but different configurations of drives and partitions require different steps. In a system where all drives have only primary partitions, the process is straightforward: boot to a floppy disk as we did previously and fire up FDISK. In a multiple-drive system, FDISK adds a fifth option to the main menu that enables you to choose the drive you wish to partition, as shown in Figure 11.20.

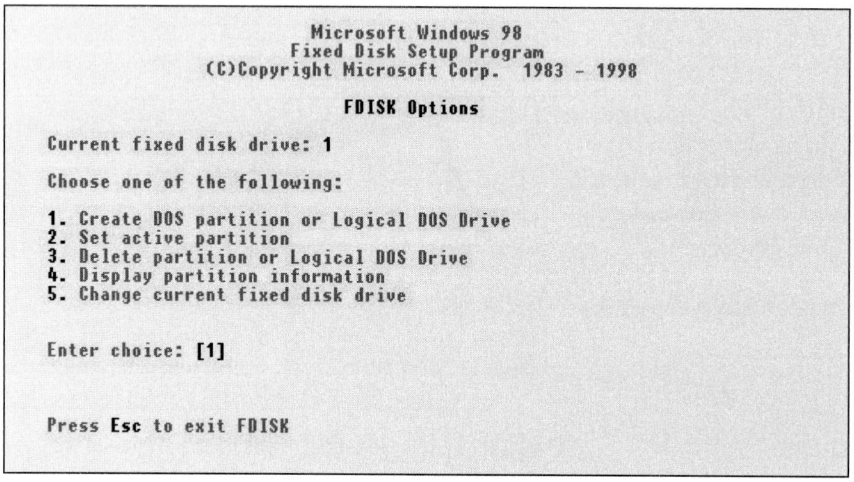

```
                    Microsoft Windows 98
                  Fixed Disk Setup Program
          (C)Copyright Microsoft Corp.  1983 - 1998

                        FDISK Options

Current fixed disk drive: 1

Choose one of the following:

1. Create DOS partition or Logical DOS Drive
2. Set active partition
3. Delete partition or Logical DOS Drive
4. Display partition information
5. Change current fixed disk drive

Enter choice: [1]


Press Esc to exit FDISK
```

• **Figure 11.20** The FDISK main menu showing five options

If you choose option 5, you see a breakdown of all the drives that FDISK sees. Select the number corresponding to the drive. Be careful here! I don't even want to tell you how many times I meant to change partitions on one drive and accidentally wiped out the partition on another drive just because I didn't look carefully! Because the first drive has the primary partition we want to delete, we select 1 and return to the main menu. Now let's delete that primary partition. Select option 3—Delete partition or Logical DOS Drive—to see the Delete Partition menu, as shown in Figure 11.21.

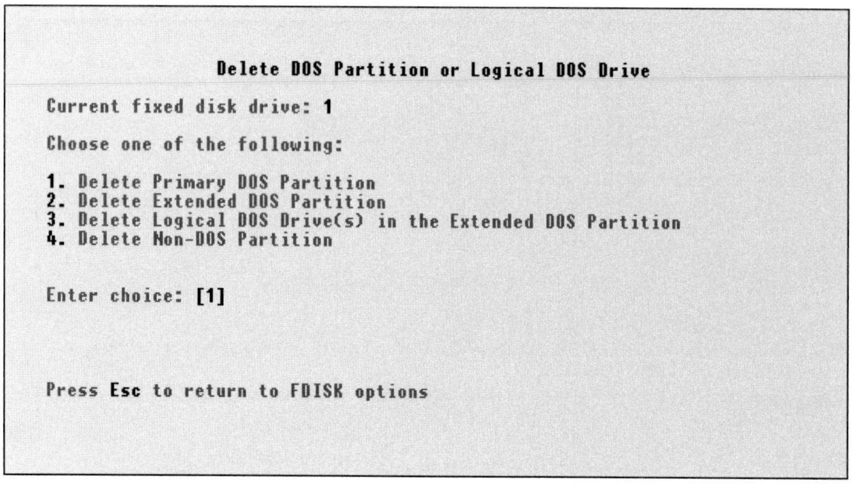

```
              Delete DOS Partition or Logical DOS Drive

Current fixed disk drive: 1

Choose one of the following:

1. Delete Primary DOS Partition
2. Delete Extended DOS Partition
3. Delete Logical DOS Drive(s) in the Extended DOS Partition
4. Delete Non-DOS Partition

Enter choice: [1]


Press Esc to return to FDISK options
```

• **Figure 11.21** FDISK's Delete Partition menu

Select 1 to delete the primary partition. You will see a big warning screen. Most of this should be obvious except for the volume label. *Volume labels* are names that you apply to partitions. They are rarely used anymore except in this one situation of deleting partitions. Note that the area under the words Volume Label is blank. (You can see this in Figure 11.22.) This volume does not have a volume label—by far the most normal case. When the Delete menu asks for a volume label, simply enter what you see under the text Volume Label in the menu. In this case, the drive has no volume label, so we just press ENTER, and then Y when prompted with "Are you sure?" FDISK then deletes the primary partition. Press ESC to return to the main menu; do not return to the Delete menu.

Deleting extended partitions requires a two-step process. You first delete any logical drives in the extended partition, and then delete the extended partition itself. If you try to delete an extended partition that still contains logical drives, you get the error shown in Figure 11.22. Note also that if you have a drive with both primary and logical drives, you must delete logical drives and the extended partition before you can delete the primary partition.

Tech Tip

Odd Volume Labels

FDISK does not give you the option to make all lowercase or mixed lowercase and uppercase labels for drives. It also does not enable you to delete any drives with that sort of name! If you run into a drive that has an odd volume label, chances are very high it has a partition already on it that FDISK doesn't know how to delete. Be careful with data and load the drive in a more sophisti-

drives.

Time to start making some partitions! Let's start with the primary master drive we just erased. No law requires you to do so, but it will make your partitioning much smoother if you partition in the pecking order described earlier.

First, make the primary partition. Follow the steps from the previous examples, except this time only partition 50 percent of the

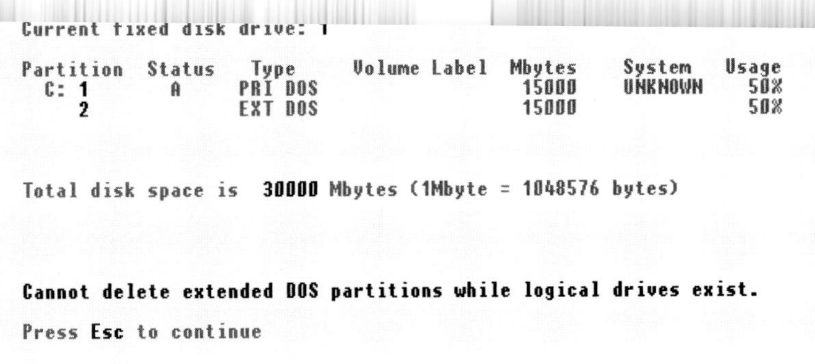

Figure 11.22 You must delete logical drives first!

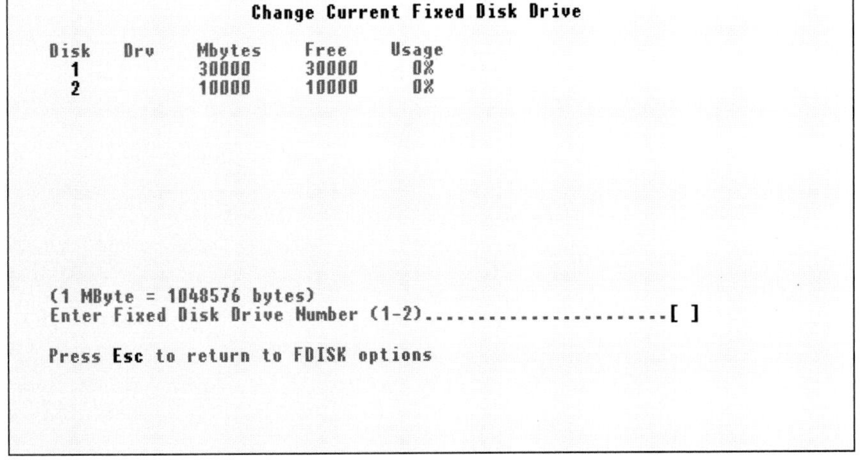

Figure 11.23 Two blank drives in FDISK

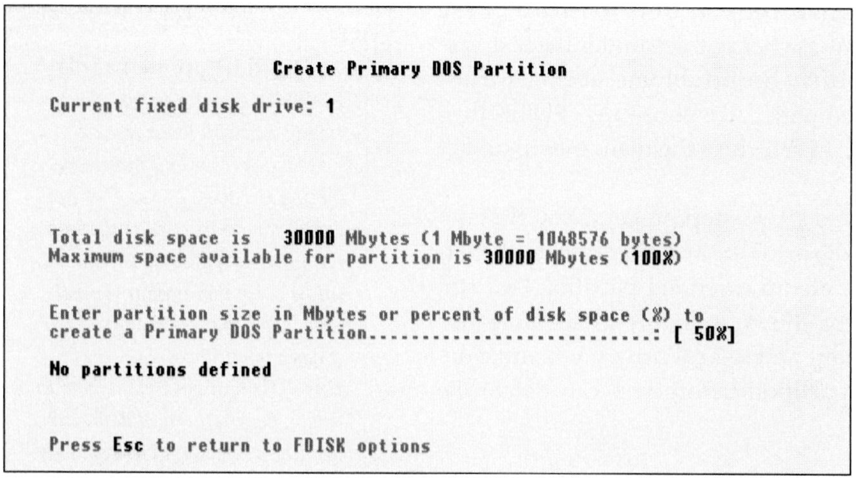

```
Create Primary DOS Partition
Current fixed disk drive: 1

Total disk space is   30000 Mbytes (1 Mbyte = 1048576 bytes)
Maximum space available for partition is 30000 Mbytes (100%)

Enter partition size in Mbytes or percent of disk space (%) to
create a Primary DOS Partition.............................: [ 50%]

No partitions defined

Press Esc to return to FDISK options
```

• **Figure 11.24** Fifty percent of the primary master will be the primary partition.

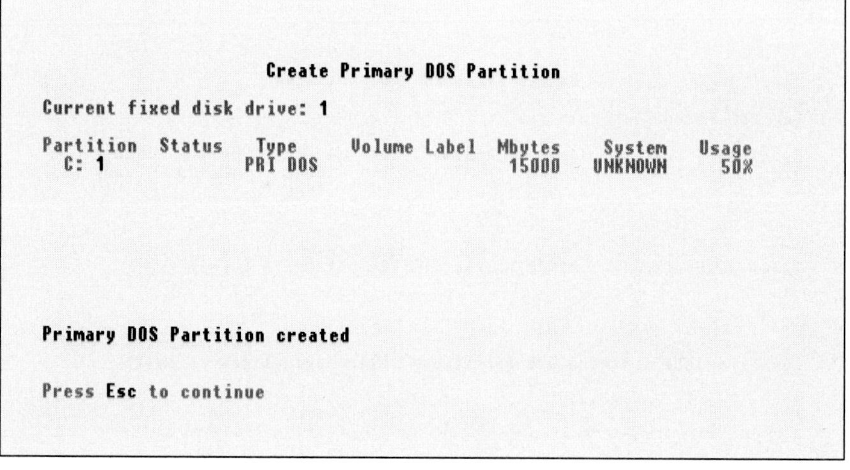

• **Figure 11.25** Creating the primary partition

drive as primary (see Figure 11.24). Enter **50%** into the partition size and press ENTER to see the screen shown in Figure 11.25. Then press ESC to return to the main menu. At this point, make the primary partition active (see Figure 11.26).

Now we need to make the extended partition. This step confuses folks unfamiliar with FDISK. Press 1—Create DOS partition—and then press 2—Create extended DOS partition—to see the screen in Figure 11.27.

You will never do anything other than press ENTER whenever you see this screen! Think about this. We've made 50 percent of the drive a primary partition. We now need to make two logical drives in an extended partition. The rest of the drive, the other 50 percent, must be the extended partition! Many people new to FDISK want to enter 25 percent here, thinking about the individual logical drives—don't do that! Make the rest of the drive the extended partition *and then* go back and chop the extended partition into two logical drives. Just press ENTER here—no situation could occur where you would not make the rest of the drive the extended partition (unless you were intending to

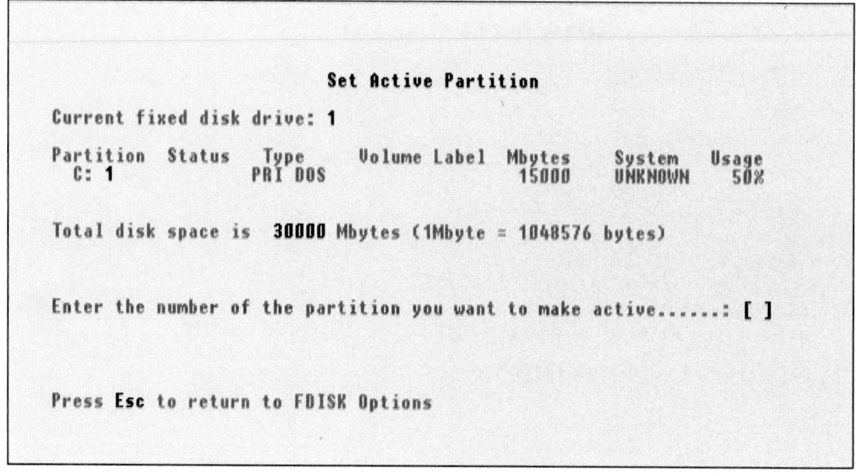

• **Figure 11.26** Making the partition active

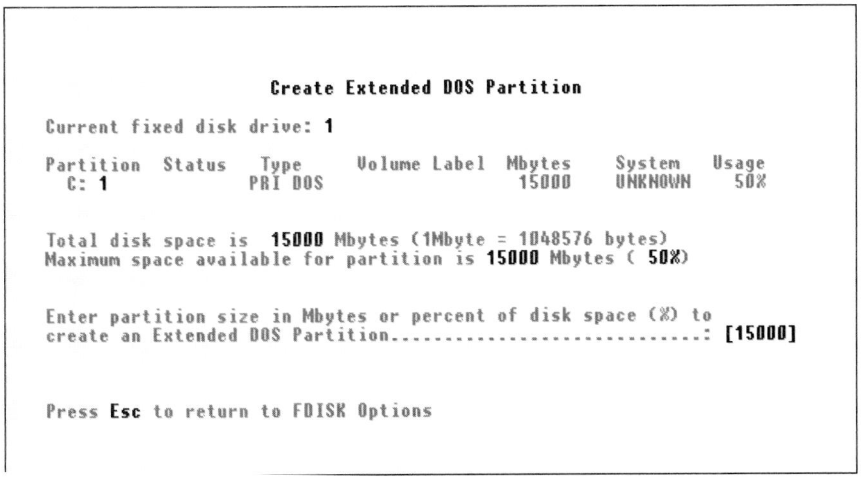

```
Create Extended DOS Partition

Current fixed disk drive: 1

Partition  Status   Type     Volume Label  Mbytes    System    Usage
  C: 1             PRI DOS                  15000    UNKNOWN     50%

Total disk space is  15000 Mbytes (1Mbyte = 1048576 bytes)
Maximum space available for partition is 15000 Mbytes ( 50%)

Enter partition size in Mbytes or percent of disk space (%) to
create an Extended DOS Partition.............................: [15000]


Press Esc to return to FDISK Options
```

instead of taking you back to the main screen, the system immediately prompts you to create the logical drives (see Figure 11.28).

We want to create two logical drives of the same size in the extended partition, each 7.5 GB. Here, type in either **7500** or **50%** (one-half of the extended partition). Try it and see what happens. It should look like Figure 11.29.

Notice that the new logical drive shows up at the top of the screen, while the bottom of the screen shows the remaining amount of unused extended partition. We want the next logical drive to use all the rest of the extended partition, so just press ENTER here to see the screen shown in Figure 11.30.

Press ESC to return to the main menu. One drive done, one to go. Use option 5 to move to the second drive. This time we just want to make the second hard drive one large extended partition. Press 1—Create DOS partition—and then press 2—Create extended DOS partition. This time the Create Extended

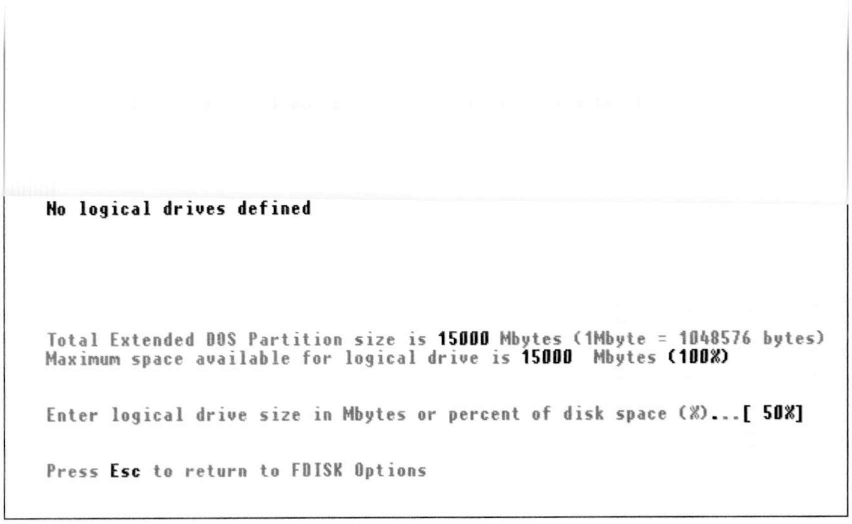

```
No logical drives defined



Total Extended DOS Partition size is 15000 Mbytes (1Mbyte = 1048576 bytes)
Maximum space available for logical drive is 15000  Mbytes (100%)

Enter logical drive size in Mbytes or percent of disk space (%)...[ 50%]

Press Esc to return to FDISK Options
```

Figure 11.28 Creating the logical drives

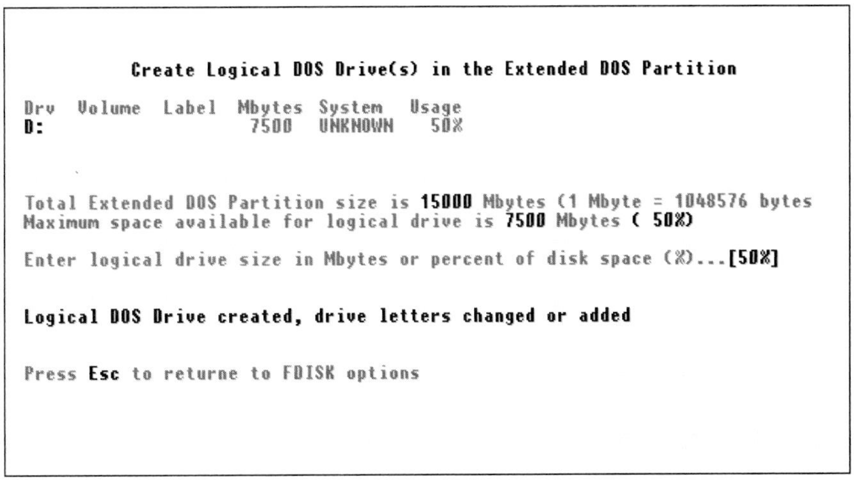

```
Create Logical DOS Drive(s) in the Extended DOS Partition

Drv  Volume  Label  Mbytes  System   Usage
D:                    7500  UNKNOWN    50%


Total Extended DOS Partition size is 15000 Mbytes (1 Mbyte = 1048576 bytes
Maximum space available for logical drive is 7500 Mbytes ( 50%)

Enter logical drive size in Mbytes or percent of disk space (%)...[50%]

Logical DOS Drive created, drive letters changed or added

Press Esc to returne to FDISK options
```

Figure 11.29 Creating the first logical drive

```
Create Logical DOS Drive(s) in the Extended DOS Partition

Drv  Volume  Label  Mbytes  System  Usage
E:                    7500  FAT32     50%




All available space in the Extended DOS Partition
is assigned to logical drives.

Press Esc to continue
```

• **Figure 11.30** Creating the second logical drive

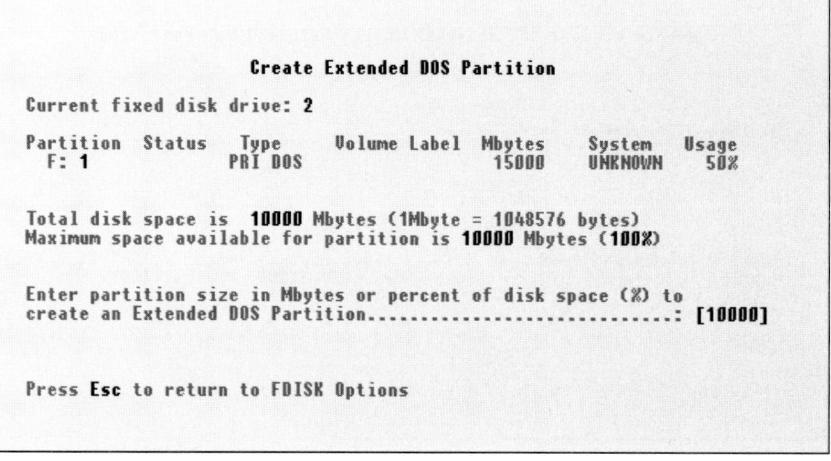

```
Create Extended DOS Partition

Current fixed disk drive: 2

Partition  Status   Type     Volume Label  Mbytes    System   Usage
  F: 1             PRI DOS                  15000    UNKNOWN    50%

Total disk space is  10000 Mbytes (1Mbyte = 1048576 bytes)
Maximum space available for partition is 10000 Mbytes (100%)

Enter partition size in Mbytes or percent of disk space (%) to
create an Extended DOS Partition.............................: [10000]

Press Esc to return to FDISK Options
```

• **Figure 11.31** Creating one large extended partition

```
Change Current Fixed Disk Drive

Disk   Drv   Mbytes   Free   Usage
  1           30000     0     100%
       C:     15000
       D:      7500
       E:      7500
  2           10000     0     100%
       F:     10000




(1 MByte = 1048576 bytes)
Enter Fixed Disk Drive Number (1-2).........................[ ]

Press Esc to return to FDISK Options
```

• **Figure 11.32** Viewing drive partitions

DOS Partition screen shows the entire drive (see Figure 11.31).

So once again, just press ENTER. At the next screen, press ESC. FDISK then will prompt you to make a logical drive. Since we only want one big logical partition, just press ENTER to make the entire extended partition one logical drive. The drive is done! Get back to the main menu and select option 5 to see your handiwork (see Figure 11.32). When you reboot, Windows will see your new drive.

Disk Administrator

Windows NT 4.0 uses a graphical tool called Disk Administrator to partition hard drives. Disk Administrator handles all the FDISK functions, such as creating primary and extended partitions and making primary partitions active, but does it all on-the-fly with a graphical interface (Figure 10.33).

Disk Administrator enables you to create simple partitions and substantially more complex setups, such as striping two drives together to enhance performance, extending volume sizes without losing data, and span a single drive letter over

Figure 11.35 Disk Administrator

multiple drives (called creating a volume set). You can't do anything special with the C: drive, but add a couple more drives to an NT machine and fire up Disk Administrator for some fun and games in Partition Land. Figure 11.34 shows two new blank drives added, both selected. (To select multiple drives or portions of drives, by the way, click one, hold the CTRL key down, and then click the other.) Alternate-click either drive and Disk Administrator gives you the option to create a stripe set or a volume set. The latter means in this case a single volume spanning two drives, although you can also create a volume on one disk that uses non-contiguous parts of the disk.

To finish any partitioning process in Disk Administrator, you must alternate-click on the drive and select the option to Commit Changes Now. This forces the tool to update Windows NT. Figure 11.35 shows a neatly configured stripe set. You probably can't tell from the black and white photo,

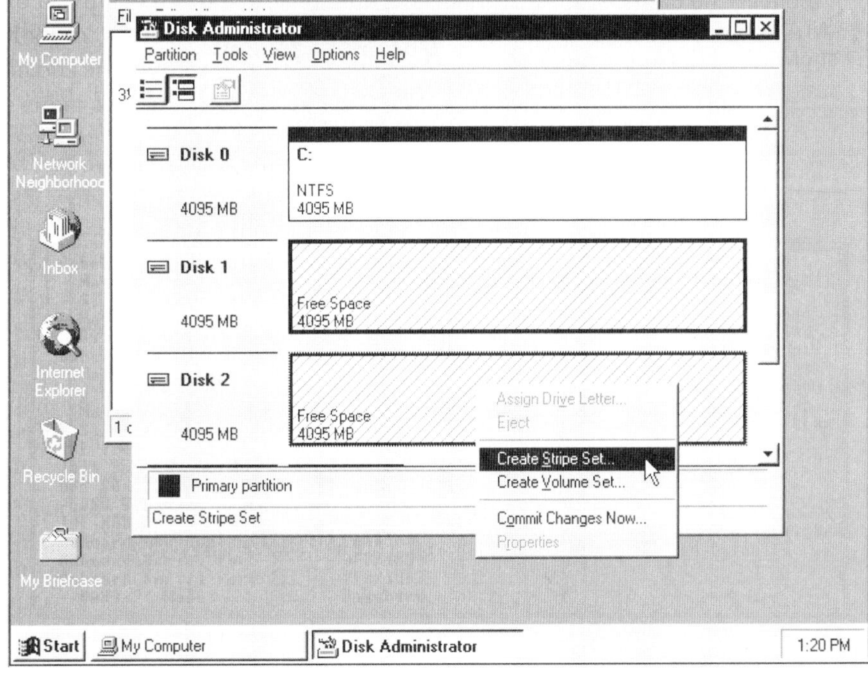

Figure 11.34 Two blank drives selected in Disk Administrator

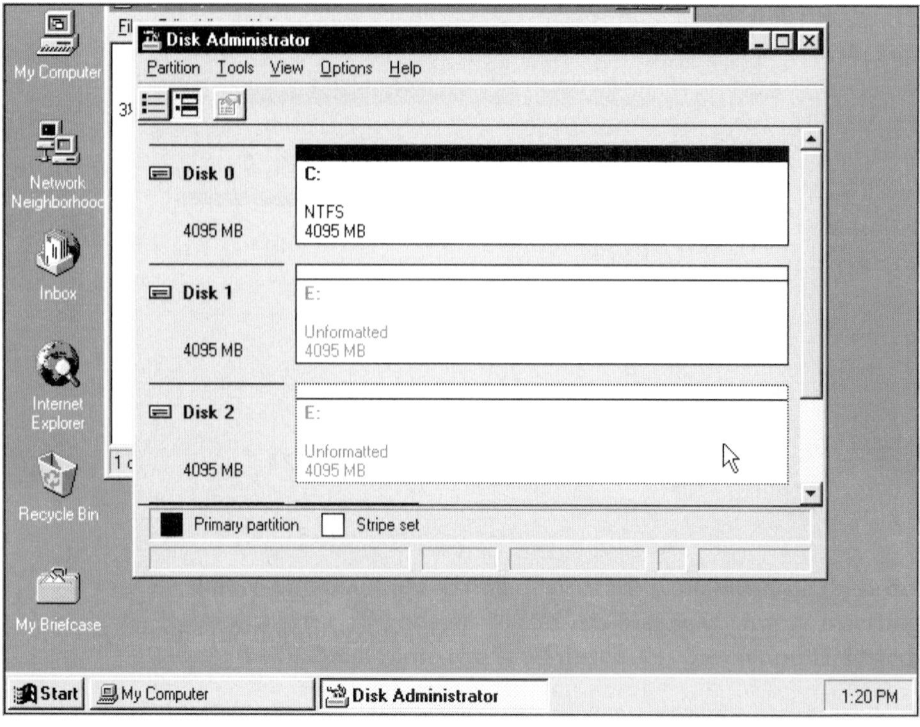

Figure 11.35 Stripe set created

but Disk Administrator nicely color coordinates the various volume types so you quickly know what you're looking at with an unfamiliar NT system.

Disk Management

The **Disk Management** console in Windows 2000 and Windows XP enables you to partition and format drives, functioning almost precisely like Disk Administrator in Windows NT 4.0. You can create multiple primary partitions and an extended partition with logical drives. Figure 11.36 shows Disk Management with four basic disks installed. The fourth disk has a 4 GB primary partition and unallocated space. To create a new partition on that fourth drive, just like with Disk Administrator, alternate-click the unallocated space and select New Partition from the options.

Disk Management will run the New Partition Wizard, enabling you to select a primary or extended partition (Figure 11.37). Afterward, you'll get a subsequent screen where you select the size partition you prefer (Figure 11.38).

After you get a confirmation screen, you'll go back to Disk Management and see a changed

Cross Check

Stripe Sets

Striping two drives enhances performance, although it doubles your chances for data loss. You've seen striping in Chapter 10, in the discussion of RAID.

1. What level of RAID is striping?
2. What sorts of RAID offer fault tolerance? For that matter, what does "fault tolerance" mean?

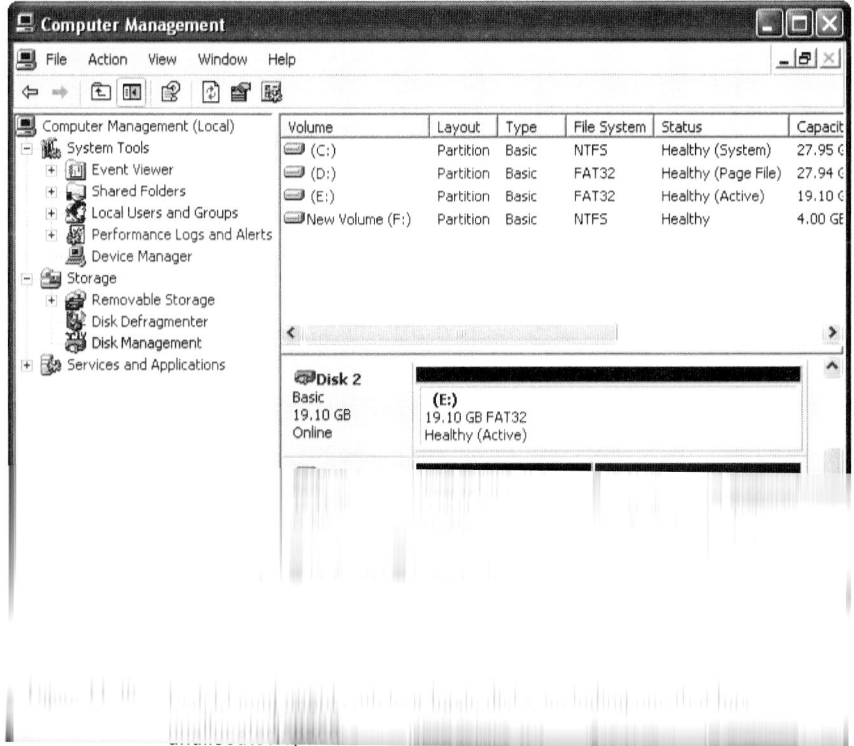

hard drive landscape. Figure 11.39 shows the extended partition as free space because it has no logical drive yet. As you can easily guess from Figure 11.39, to create a logical drive, simply alternate-click in that extended partition and select the option to create a New Logical Drive. Disk Management will fire up the New Partition Wizard again, this time with the option to create a logical drive (Figure 11.40).

When you create a primary partition or logical drive, the New Partition Wizard automatically gives you the option to format the partition using one of the three file systems available in Windows 2000/XP (see Figure 11.41).

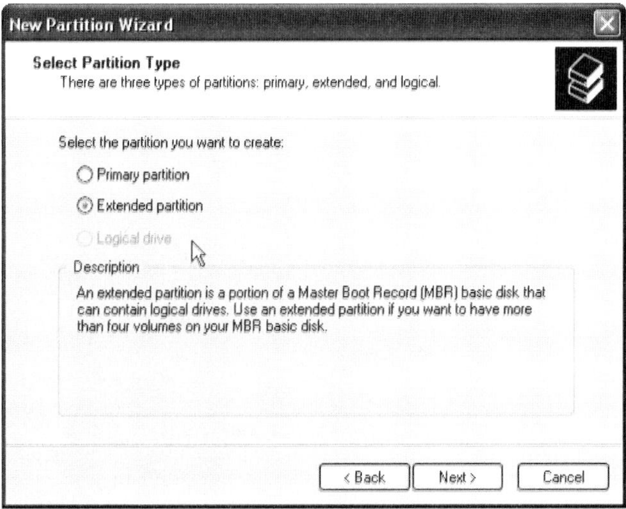

• **Figure 11.37** The New Partition Wizard

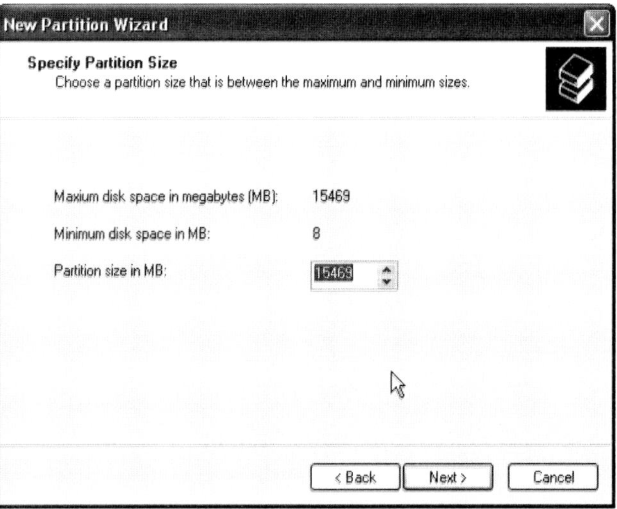

• **Figure 11.38** Selecting the partition size

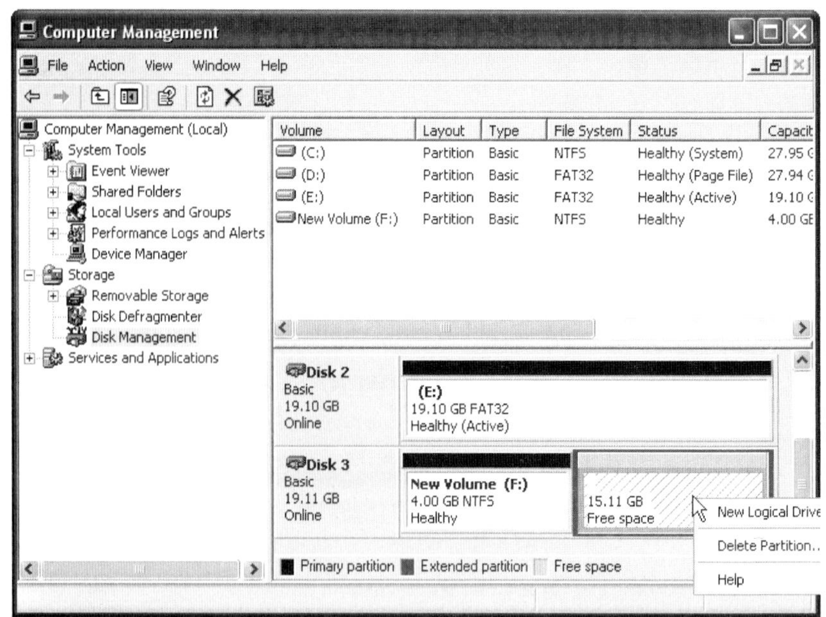

• **Figure 11.39** Selecting to create a logical drive in the extended (free space) partition

Unlike Disk Administrator, Disk Management does not require you to go through the extra step to Commit Changes Now. It just does what you tell it to do, right away.

For more insight into the various file systems, see the section titled "Formatting Hard Drives" later in this chapter. You'll get another confirmation screen, and then the Disk Management console will show you the newly created drive (see Figure 11.42).

Partitioning Dynamic Disks

When Microsoft released Windows 2000's partitioning tool, the Disk Management console, they added an improved form of disk partition called a

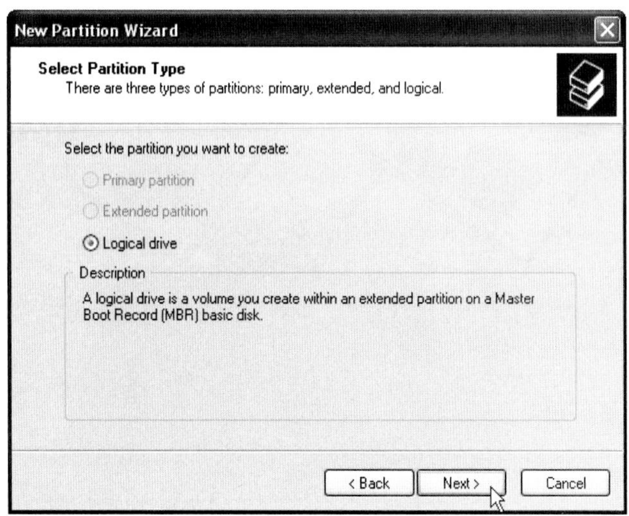

• **Figure 11.40** The New Partition Wizard offering the Logical Drive option

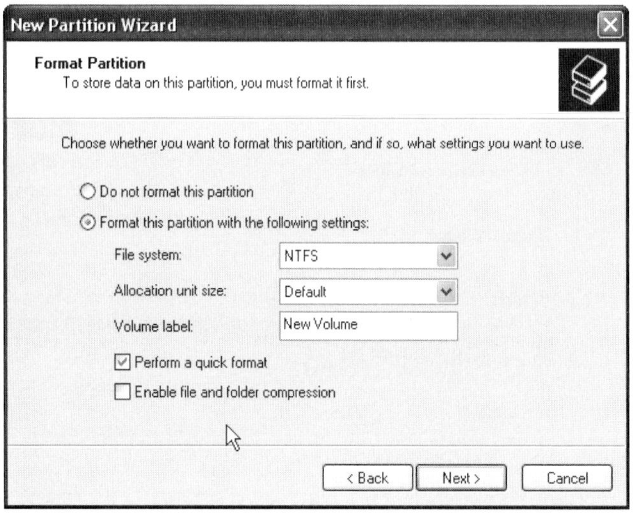

• **Figure 11.41** The New Partition Wizard offering formatting options

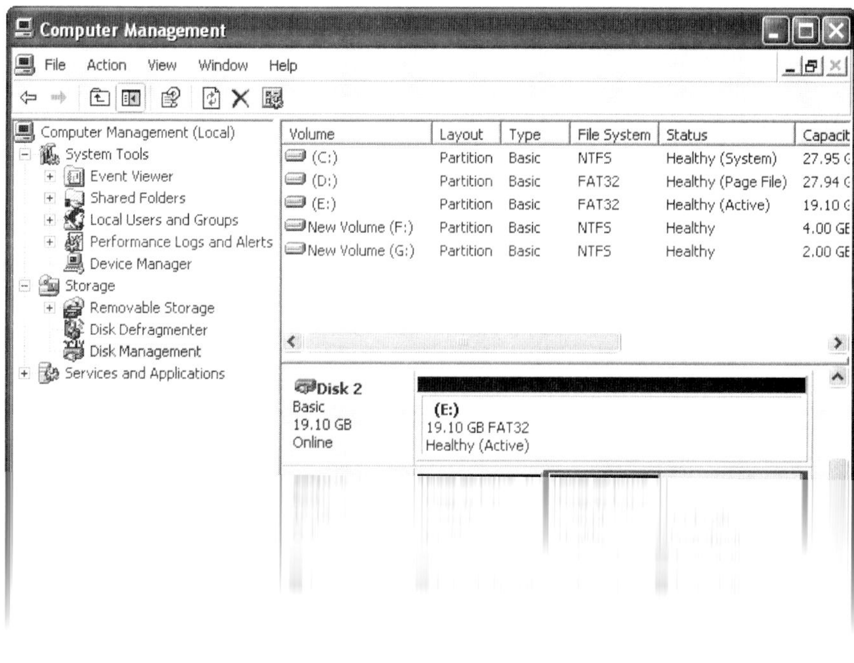

dynamic disk. Dynamic disks are a storage type unique to Windows 2000 and XP. You can do some cool things with dynamic disks, such as turn two separate hard drives into a single partition. Dynamic disk drives enable you to enlarge their partitions without first deleting the partition or losing data—something previously impossible without specialized third-party tools.

Regular drives are known as basic disks, to distinguish them from dynamic disks. Once you convert a drive from a basic to a dynamic disk, there are no longer any such things as primary and extended partitions; dynamic disks are divided into volumes instead of partitions. Dynamic disks support several different types of volumes: simple, spanned, striped, mirrored, and striped with parity.

Simple Volumes

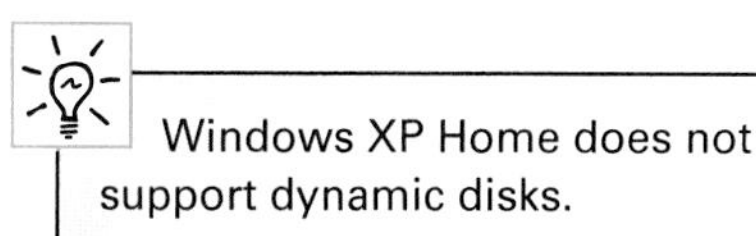

Windows XP Home does not support dynamic disks.

A simple volume acts just like a primary partition. If you have only one dynamic disk in a system, it can only have a simple volume. It's important to note here that a simple volume is not a primary partition such as you would create in Windows NT or Windows 9*x*/Me. In fact, if you installed a hard drive partitioned as a simple volume dynamic disk into any of the earlier Windows operating systems, you would see no usable partition. Oddly enough, Microsoft also disabled support for dynamic disks in Windows XP Home.

To create a simple volume requires a couple of steps. You need to convert the basic disk into a dynamic disk first, and then create the simple volume.

Alternate-click the basic disk in Disk Management and select the option Convert To Dynamic Disk (see Figure 11.43). If you have multiple basic disks in your system, you'll get prompted to select which disk to convert. If you convert a disk with primary or extended partitions already, those partitions change. In Microsoft speak, those partitions will be *dismounted* (see

The only exception is your C: drive. You can convert it to dynamic, but you don't get the full benefits of dynamic drives.

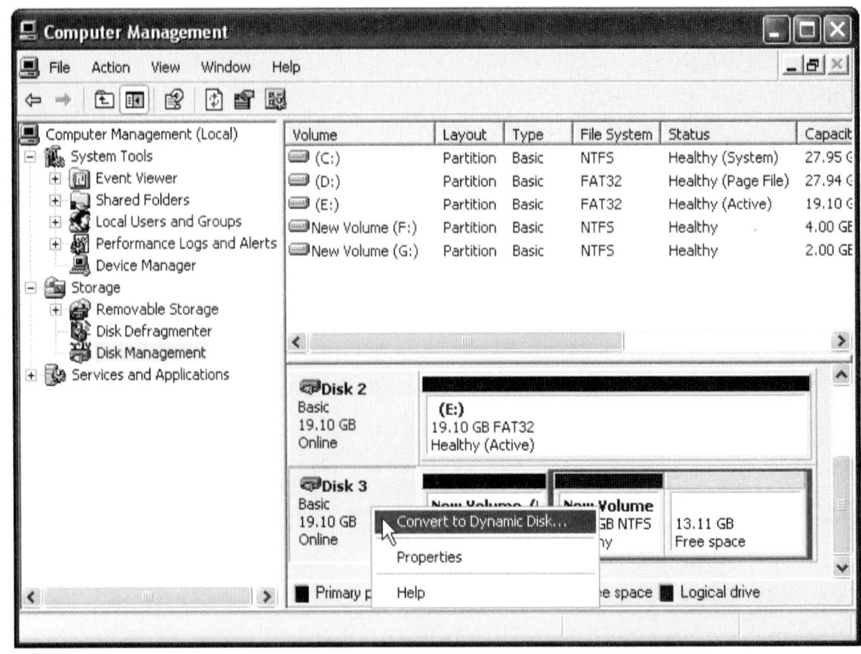

• **Figure 11.43** Converting to Dynamic Disk

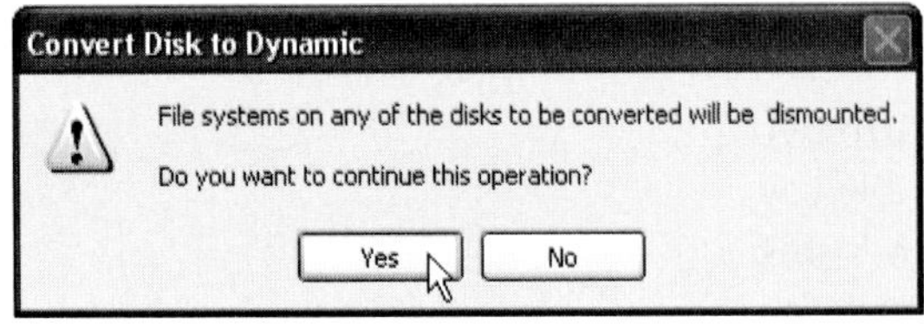

• **Figure 11.44** Lesser file systems will go away!

Figure 11.44). That sounds scary, but in effect, they become simple volumes: you don't lose the data on the drives, but you can't boot to them anymore.

Once you have the dynamic disk created, you're ready to make a simple volume. In Disk Management, alternate-click any unallocated space on the dynamic disk and select New Volume to run the New Volume Wizard (see Figure 11.45). You'll get a series of screens that prompt you on size and file system, and

• **Figure 11.45** The New Volume Wizard

then you're done. Figure 11.46 shows Disk Management with three smallish simple volumes.

Extending and Spanning

Dynamic disks enable you to extend the size of a simple volume to any unallocated space on a dynamic disk. You can also extend the volume to grab extra space on completely different dynamic disks, creating what's called a **spanned volume**. To extend or span, simply

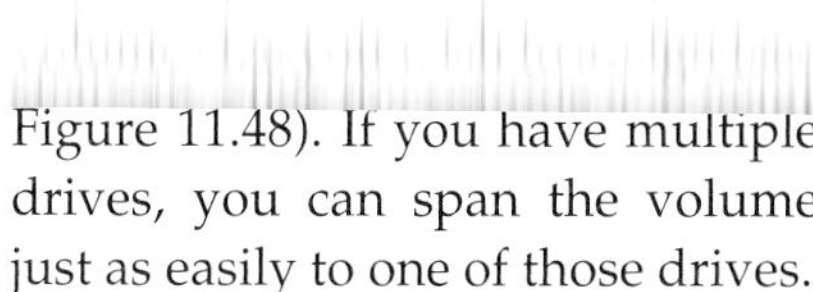

Figure 11.48). If you have multiple drives, you can span the volume just as easily to one of those drives.

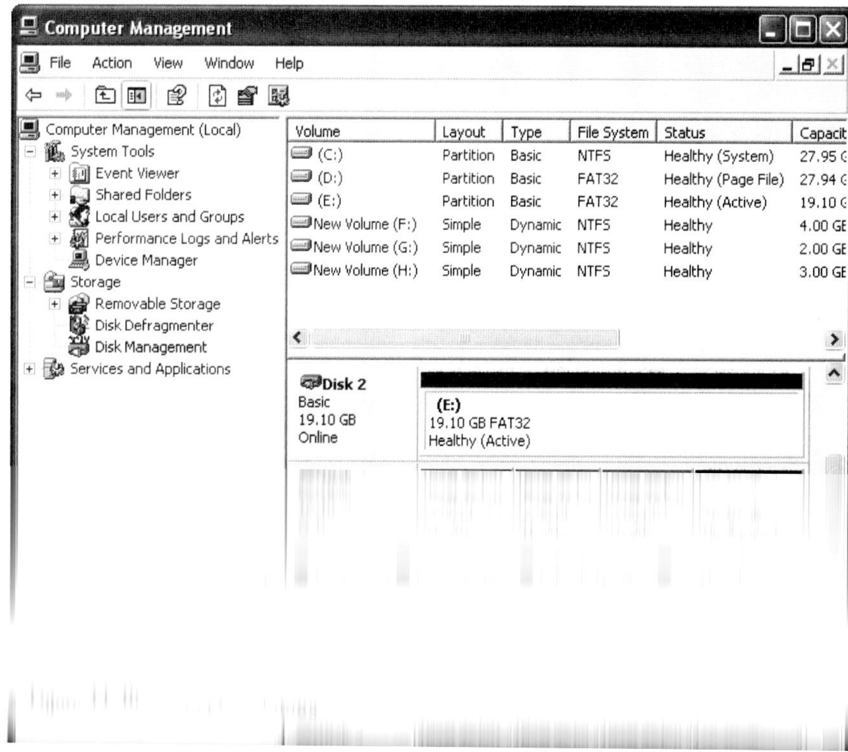

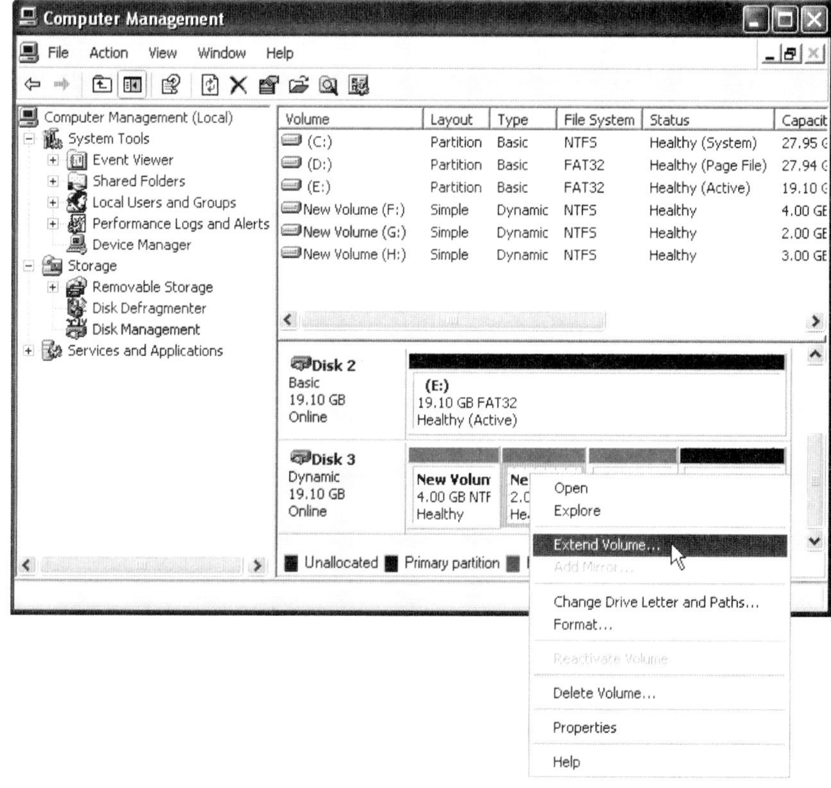

Figure 11.47 Selecting the Extend Volume option

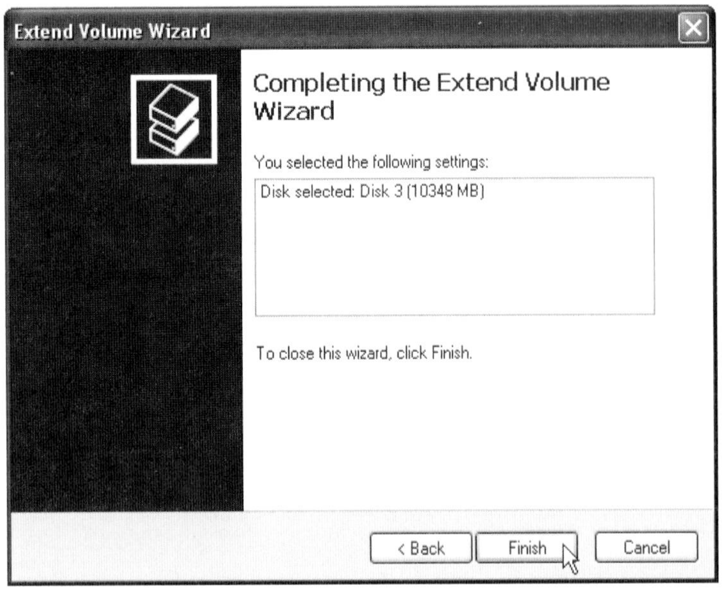

• Figure 11.48 The Extend Volume Wizard

The ability to extend and span volumes makes dynamic disks worth their weight in gold! If you start running out of space on a volume, you can simply add another physical hard drive to the system and span the volume to the new drive. This keeps your drive letters consistent and unchanging so your programs don't get confused, yet enables you to expand drive space when needed.

You can extend or span any simple volume on a dynamic disk, not just the "one on the end" in the Disk Management console. You simply select the volume to expand and the total volume increase you wish. Figure 11.49 shows a simple 4 GB volume named Extended that has been enlarged to 7.91 GB in a portion of the hard drive, skipping the 2 GB section of unallocated space contiguous to it. Windows has no problem skipping areas on a drive.

Striping, Mirroring, and Striping with Parity

If you have two or more dynamic disks in a PC, Disk Management enables you to combine them into a random array of independent disks (RAID), just as if you had a RAID controller card in your PC. Windows 2000 and XP Professional support three types of software RAID, stripes, mirrors, and stripes with parity.

A striped volume spreads out blocks of each file across multiple disks. Using two or more drives in a group called a **stripe set**, striping writes data

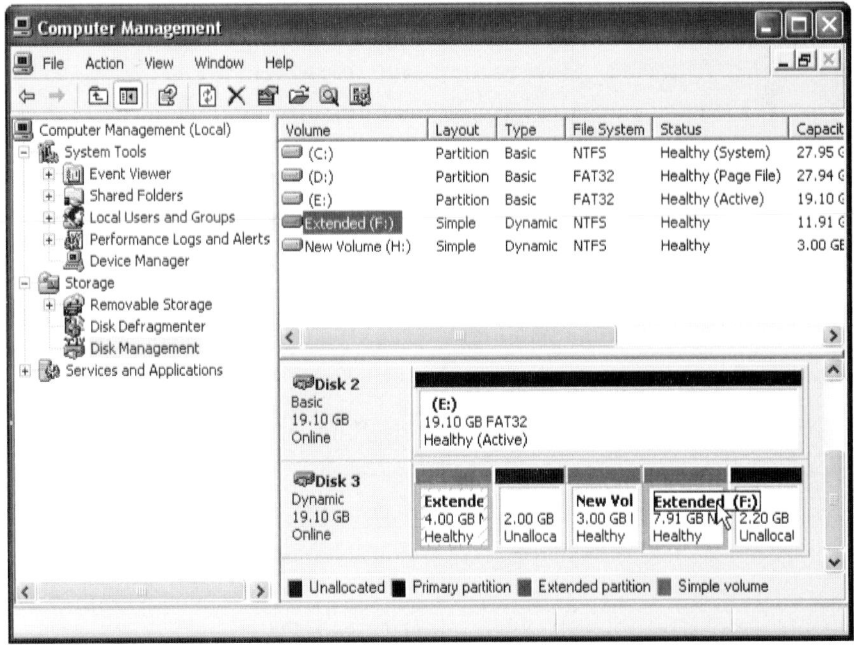

• Figure 11.49 Extended Volume

first to a certain number of clusters on one drive, then on the next, and so on. It speeds up data throughput because the system has to wait a much shorter time for a drive to read or write data. The drawback of striping is that if any single drive in the stripe set fails, all data in the stripe set is lost.

A **mirrored volume** uses two drives, where all data written on one drive is simultaneously written to the second drive. If one of the drives fails, the other remains accessible. Mirroring is a very good way to preserve data if a drive fails, but throughput is slow because two read/write operations are required every time the drives are accessed. Data on mirrored drives is duplicated on two physical disks.

A striped set with parity, also known as a **RAID-5 volume**, combines the best of striping and mirroring. RAID-5 requires at least three hard drives. Basically, RAID-5 is striping using three or more disks, with fault-tolerance added in the form of parity bits, which are also striped across the disks. If

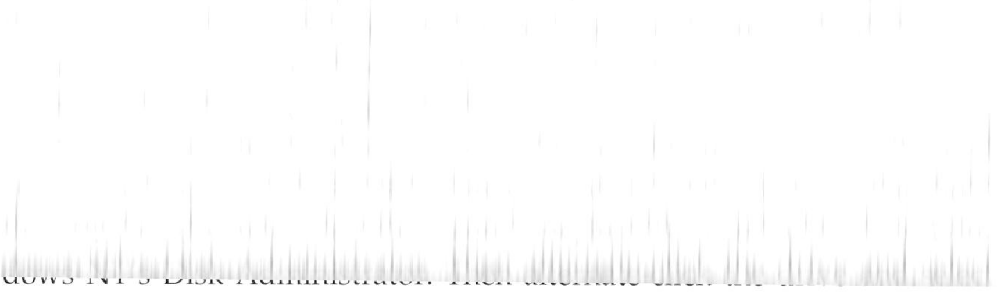

New Volume to run the New Volume Wizard. One of the options available is Striped (Figure 11.50). Select it and go through the remaining screens on sizing and formatting and you've got a striped volume.

To create a mirrored volume, you need to access a Windows 2000 or 2003 Server across the network first. You can do this directly from within Disk Management. Create a simple volume first on one drive, then alternate-click the drive and select Add Mirror from the options. Follow the screens to create a mirrored volume (Figure 11.51).

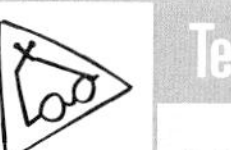

Tech Tip

Mirrored and Striped with Parity Volumes

Disk Management enables you to create mirrored and striped with parity volumes, but only on Windows 2000 or 2003 Server machines. The cool thing is that you can do this remotely across a network. You can sit at your Windows XP Professional workstation, in other words, and open Disk Management. Surf to a

than using the less-expensive Professional OS for the company server! Both mirrored and striped with parity volumes are included here for completeness and because they show up in the Windows Help Files when you search for dynamic disks. Both are cool, but definitely way beyond A+!

Mount Points

The one drive that can't take full advantage of being dynamic is the drive containing the system partition, your primary master C: drive. You can make it dynamic, but it doesn't enable you to do all the cool dynamic things, like extending and spanning. So what good is the ability to allocate more space to a volume when you start to fill up your C: drive? If you can't add to that drive, your only option is to replace it with a new, bigger drive, right?

The combination of dynamic disks and NTFS enables you to create a data structure called a mount point. A **mount point** is a drive that functions like a folder mounted into another drive. Add a second physical drive to the PC and convert it to a dynamic disk. Create a volume on it, but, rather than give it a drive letter like D:, instead *mount* the volume to a folder on the C: drive and make it nothing more than just another folder (Figure 11.52). You can load programs to that folder, just like you would to your

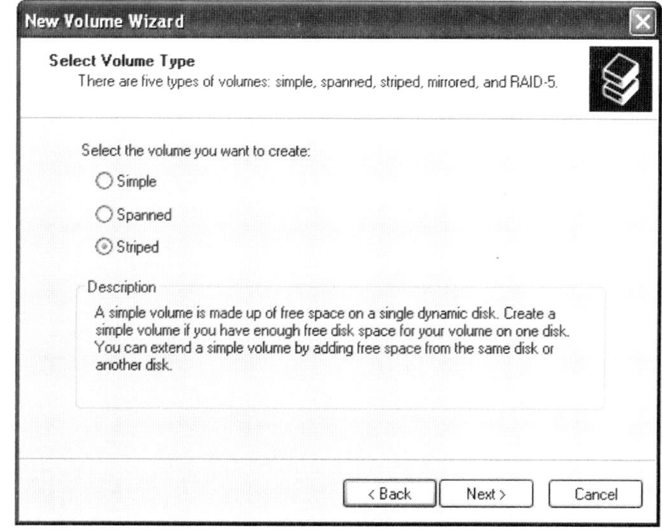

• **Figure 11.50** Creating a striped volume

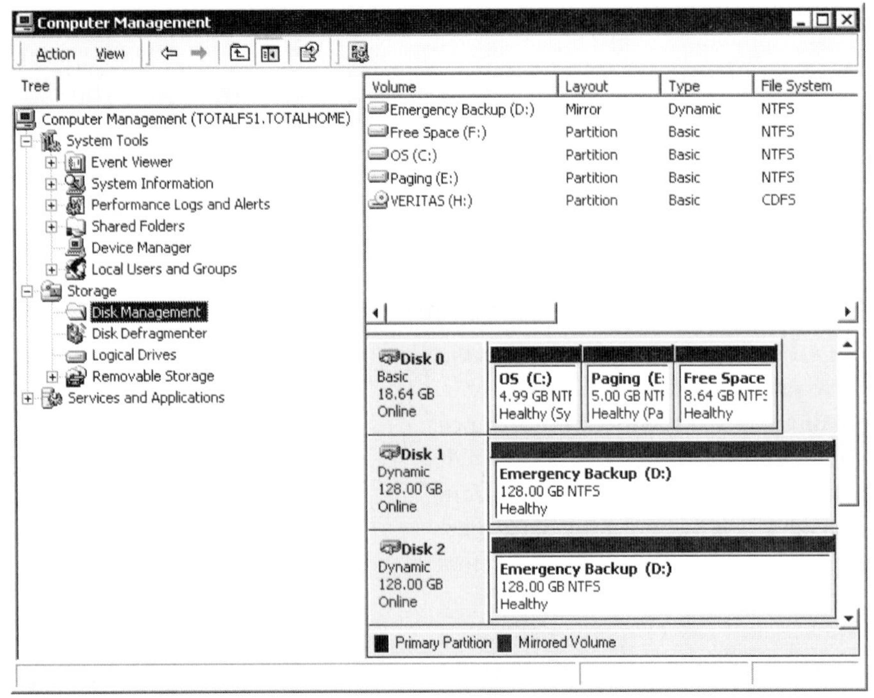

Figure 11.51 Creating a mirrored volume

Program Files folder. You can use it to store data files or backed-up system files. In *function*, therefore, the new hard drive simply extends the capacity of the C: drive, so neither you nor your client need ever trouble yourselves with dealing with multiple drive letters.

To create a mount point, alternate-click an unallocated section of a dynamic disk and select New Volume from the options. This opens the New Volume Wizard. The second screen enables you to select a mount point rather than a drive letter (Figure 11.53). Browse to a blank folder on an NTFS-formatted drive or create a new folder and you're in business!

With dynamic disks, Microsoft has dramatically changed the way techs can work with hard drives.

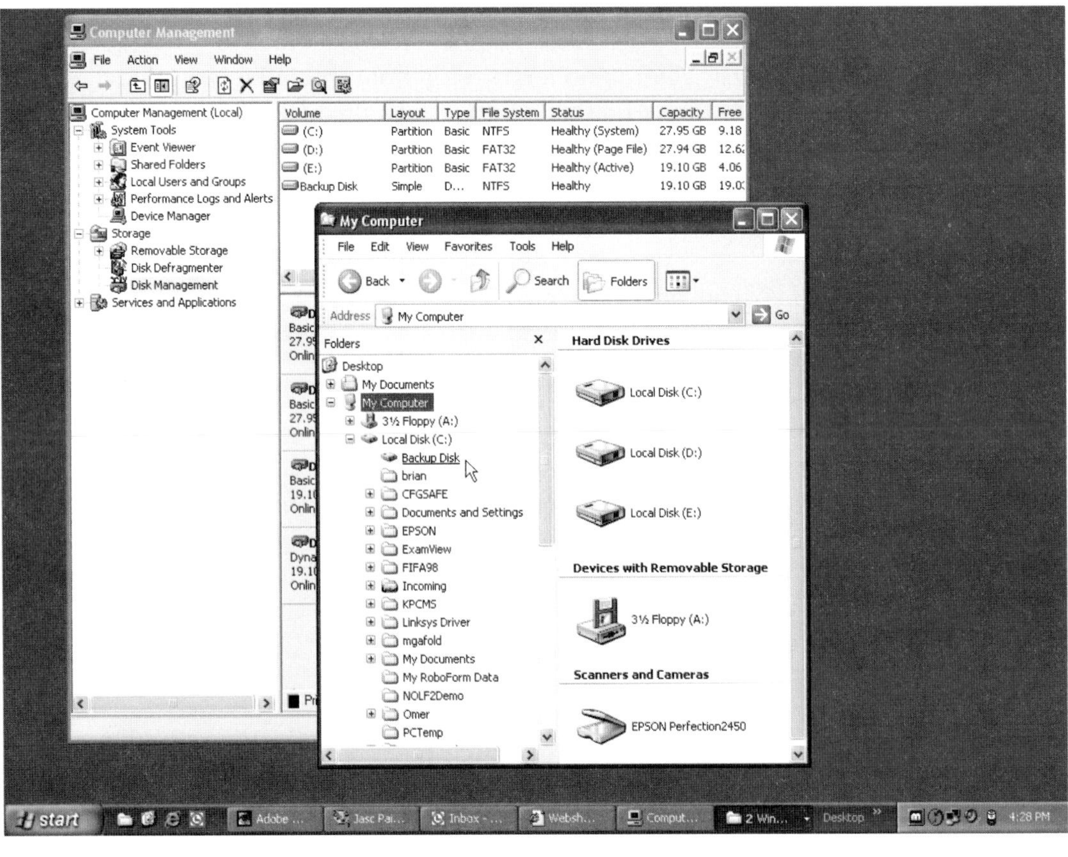

Figure 11.52 A drive volume mounted as a folder of drive C:

You're no longer stuck in the rut of adding drive letters that mess up Windows' mapping of the CD-ROM drive. You don't have to confuse clients with multiple drive letters when they just want a little more space. You can resurrect smaller hard drives, making them a functional part of today's computer. Finally, you can create nicely redundant RAID-1 mirrors without needing any special hardware, a perfect way to back up important data. With the Disk Management console in Windows 2000 and XP, Microsoft got it right!

New Volume Wizard

Assign Drive Letter or Path
For easier access, you can assign a drive letter or drive path to your volume.

Assign the following drive letter: F
Mount in the following empty NTFS folder:
Browse...
Do not assign a drive letter or drive path

tem. The various versions of Windows you're likely to encounter today can use several different file systems, so we'll look at those in detail next. The root directory provides the foundation upon which the OS builds files and folders. C:\ is the root directory of the primary master hard drive with a

You can only mount a volume to an empty folder on a drive formatted with NTFS5. In theory, the mounted volume can be formatted as FAT16, FAT32, or NTFS5, but you almost never see anything but NTFS5. See the following for a discussion of the ins and outs of the various file systems.

Try This!

Working with Dynamic Drives

You can't begin to appreciate the ease and elegant simplicity of dynamic drives until you play with them, so try this! Get a couple of spare drives and install them into a PC running Windows 2000 or Windows XP. Fire up the Disk Management console and try the following setups. Convert both spare drives to dynamic drives.

1. Make a mirror set.
2. Make a stripe set.
3. Make them into a single volume, spanned between both drives.
4. Make a single volume that takes up a portion of one drive, then extend that volume onto another portion of that drive. Finally, span that volume to the other hard drive as well.
5. Create a volume of some sort—you decide—and then mount that volume to a folder on the C: drive.

You'll need to format the volumes after you create them so you can see how they manifest in My Computer. (See the next section of this chapter for details on formatting.) Also, you'll need to delete volumes to create a new setup. To delete volumes, simply alternate-click the volume and select Delete Volume from the menu. It's almost too easy!

You can make that stack of old small-capacity disk drives collecting dust in your computer room useful again through the magic of dynamic disks. Here's the trick: install all the old drives into one system, convert them to dynamic disks, and span them all into a single drive letter. Now that you have created a decent-sized volume, you can use that system for long-term file storage, backups, and more.

Once you convert a drive to dynamic, you cannot revert it to a basic disk without losing all the data on that drive. Be prepared to back up all data before you revert.

primary partition, whereas C:\Windows is a folder (Windows) that rests in the root directory (C:\).

File Systems in Windows

Many techs use the term *data structures* to describe file systems in general. The terms are interchangeable, but the A+ OS Technologies exam uses the term *file systems*.

Every version of Windows comes with a built-in formatting utility, usually called FORMAT, which enables it to create one or more file systems on a partition or volume. The versions of Windows in current use support four separate Microsoft file systems, although no version supports more than three of the four: FAT16, FAT32, NTFS4, and NTFS5. Table 11.1 shows the list of file systems and which OSs can use them.

Understanding how file systems work helps techs maintain properly working hard drives and troubleshoot related problems. Perhaps as important for most reader's purposes, the A+ OS Technologies exam tests you on your understanding of file systems.

The simplest hard drive file system, called FAT or FAT16, provides a good explanation for how they all work, so we'll start with that one. More complex file systems fix many of the problems inherent in FAT and add extra features as well.

FAT

The base storage area for hard drives is a sector; each sector stores up to 512 bytes of data. If an OS stores a file smaller than 512 bytes in a sector, the rest of the sector goes to waste. We accept this waste because most files are far larger than 512 bytes. So what happens when an OS stores a file larger than 512 bytes? The OS needs a method to fill one sector, find another that's unused and fill it, continuing to fill sectors until the file is completely stored. Once the OS stores a file, it must remember which sectors hold that file, so that file can be retrieved later.

MS-DOS version 2.1 first supported hard drives using a special data structure to keep track of stored data on the hard drive, and Microsoft called this structure the **file allocation table (FAT)**. Think of the FAT as nothing more than a card catalog that keeps track of which sectors store the various parts of a file. The official jargon term for a FAT is **data structure**, but it is more like a two-column spreadsheet.

The left column gives each sector a number, from 0000 to FFFF (in hex, of course). This means there are 65,536 (64 K) sectors (see Figure 11.54).

Notice that the left-hand side contains 16 bits. (Four hex characters make 16 bits, remember?) We call this type of FAT a "16-bit FAT" or "FAT16." Not just hard drives have FATs. Floppy drives also use FATs, but their FATs are only 12 bits since they store much less data.

Table 11.1 File Systems in Windows Versions

Windows NT 4.0	FAT		NTFS4
Windows 95, 95A	FAT16		
Windows 95B (OSR2), 98, 98 SE, Me	FAT16	FAT32	
Windows 2000	FAT16	FAT32	NTFS5
Windows XP	FAT16	FAT32	NTFS5

The right-hand side of the FAT contains information on the status of sectors. All hard drives, even brand-new drives fresh from the factory, contain faulty sectors that cannot store data to imperfections in the construction of the drive. The OS must locate these bad sectors, mark them as unusable, and then prevent any files from being written to them. This mapping of bad sectors is one of the functions of high-level formatting. After the format program creates the FAT, it then proceeds through the entire partition, writing and attempting to read from each sector sequentially. If it finds a bad sector, it places a special status code (FFF7) in the sector's FAT location, indicating that sector is unavailable for use. Formatting also marks the good sectors as 0000.

0000
0001
0002
0003
0004
0005
0006
FFF9
FFFA
FFFB
FFFC
FFFD
FFFE

Using the FAT to track sectors, however, creates a problem. The 16-bit FAT addresses a maximum of 64 K (2^{16}) locations. Therefore, the size of a hard-drive partition should be limited to 64 K × 512 bytes per sector, or 32 MB. When Microsoft first unveiled FAT16, this 32 MB limit presented no

16-bit FAT. This need led to the development of a dramatic improvement in FAT16, called *clustering*, that enabled you to format partitions larger than 32 MB (see Figure 11.55). This new FAT16 appeared way back in the DOS 4 days.

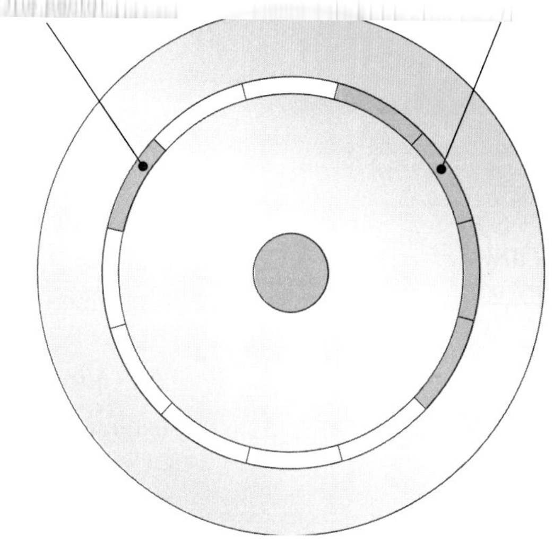

Figure 11.55 Cluster versus sector

Clustering simply means to combine a set of contiguous sectors and treat them as a single unit in the FAT. These units are called **file allocation units** or **clusters**. Each row of the FAT addressed a cluster instead of a sector. Unlike sectors, the size of a cluster is not fixed. This improved FAT16 still only supported a maximum of 64 K storage units, so the formatting program set the number of sectors in each cluster according to the size of the partition. The larger the partition, the more sectors per cluster. This kept clustering completely compatible with the 64 K locations in the old 16-bit FAT. The new FAT16 could support partitions up to 2 GB. (The old 16-bit FAT is so old it doesn't really even have a name—if someone says FAT16, they mean the newer FAT16 that supports clustering.) Table 11.2 shows the number of sectors per cluster for FAT16.

Table 11.2 FAT16 Cluster Sizes

If FDISK makes a partition this big:	You'll get this many sectors/cluster:
16–127.9 megabytes	4 sectors/cluster
128–255.9 megabytes	8 sectors/cluster
256–511.9 megabytes	16 sectors/cluster
512–1023.9 megabytes	32 sectors/cluster
1024–2048 megabytes	64 sectors/cluster

Sectors and Clusters

The introduction of clustering meant that a cluster, rather than a sector, became the basic unit of storage. Although this change enabled larger partition sizes—a good thing—it also increased the inherent wastefulness of FAT storage. With a sector-based FAT, when you saved a file of fewer than 512 bytes, the excess unused space in the sector went to waste. For example, saving a file of only 100 bytes left 412 bytes unused. We could accept this amount of waste because a typical file usually used a large number of sectors. For example, if you had a 15,000 byte file, you needed 30 sectors (15,000 bytes/512 bytes per sector) to store the entire file. The last sector was only about 30 percent full, wasting roughly 360 bytes. Big deal! Compared to the total amount of storage used by all of the sectors to store the file combined, this produced 360/15000 = .024, or less than 3 percent waste.

This changed when clusters became the smallest storage area in a hard drive. Let's say you stored that same 15,000 byte file on a 1,200 MB (1.2 GB) partition. A FAT16 partition of that size uses 64 sectors/cluster (see Table 11.2), making each cluster >32,000 bytes. In this case, the 15,000 byte file took one 32,000 byte cluster, leaving 17,000 bytes wasted. Storing files in clusters created much greater waste due to the fact that clusters were so much larger. To keep the waste as low as possible, we kept FAT16 partitions as small as possible, less than 1,023.9 MB, or smaller if possible. A 1,023.9 MB partition used 16 K clusters, keeping the level of wasted storage at an acceptable level.

For all its shortcomings, every DOS, Windows 3.*x*, and early Windows 95 systems all used FAT16. In fact, every version of Windows completely supports FAT16. You can, if you choose, install Windows 2000 on a FAT16 partition (you would lose some neat features, but that's a discussion for another chapter). One nice aspect of FAT16 is its relative simplicity. If you understand how FAT16 works, you'll better understand more modern file systems, and appreciate the need for many tools (like ScanDisk and Disk Defragmenter) that we use on today's systems. Let's watch FAT16 in action.

FAT16 in Action

Assume we have a copy of Windows using FAT16. When an application such as Microsoft Word tells the OS to save a file, Windows starts at the beginning of the FAT, looking for the first space marked "open for use" (0000), and begins to write to that cluster. If the entire file fits within that one cluster, Windows places the code FFFF (last cluster) into the cluster's status area in the FAT. Windows then goes to the folder storing the file and adds the filename and the cluster's number to the folder list. If the file requires more than one cluster, Windows searches for the next open cluster and places the number of the next cluster in the status, filling and adding clusters until the entire file is saved. The last cluster then receives the end-of-file code (FFFF).

Let's run through an example of this process, and start by selecting an arbitrary part of the FAT: from 3ABB to 3AC7. Assume you want to save a file called MOM.TXT. Before saving the file, the FAT looks like Figure 11.56.

Windows finds the first open cluster, 3ABB, and fills it. But not all of the MOM.TXT fits into that cluster. Needing more space, it goes through the FAT to find the next open cluster. It finds cluster 3ABC. Before filling 3ABC, the value 3ABC is placed in 3ABB's status (see Figure 11.57).

Even after filling two clusters, more of the MOM.TXT file remains, so Windows must find one more cluster. The 3ABD has been marked FFF7 (bad cluster), so Windows skips over 3ABD, finding 3ABE (see Figure 11.58).

Before filling 3ABE, Windows enters the value 3ABE in 3ABC's status. Windows does not completely fill 3ABE, signifying that the entire MOM.TXT file has been stored. Windows enters the value FFFF in 3ABE's status, indicating the end of file (see Figure 11.59).

After saving all the clusters, Windows now locates the file's folder (yes, folders also get stored on clusters, but they get a different set of clusters, somewhere else on the disk) and records the filename, size, date/time, and starting cluster, like this:

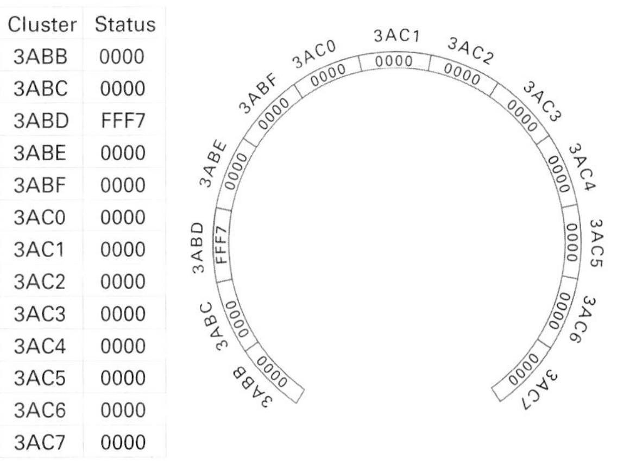

Cluster	Status
3ABB	0000
3ABC	0000
3ABD	FFF7
3ABE	0000
3ABF	0000
3AC0	0000
3AC1	0000
3AC2	0000
3AC3	0000
3AC4	0000
3AC5	0000
3AC6	0000
3AC7	0000

questing application.

Clearly, without the FAT, Windows cannot locate files. FAT16 automatically makes two copies of the FAT. One FAT backs up the other to provide special utilities a way to recover in case a FAT gets corrupted—a painfully common occurrence.

Even when FAT works perfectly, over time the files begin to separate in a process called **fragmentation** . Let me demonstrate how fragmentation happens, using our previous example.

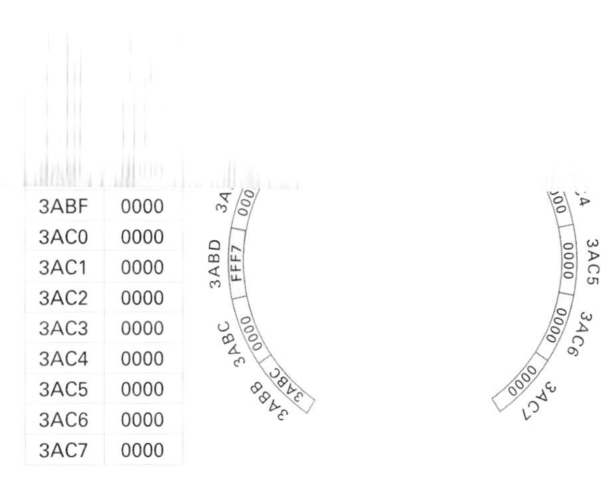

Cluster	Status
3ABF	0000
3AC0	0000
3AC1	0000
3AC2	0000
3AC3	0000
3AC4	0000
3AC5	0000
3AC6	0000
3AC7	0000

Figure 11.57 The first cluster used

Fragmentation

Continuing with our example, let's use Microsoft Word to save two more files: a letter to the IRS (IRSROB.DOC) and a letter to IBM (IBMHELP.DOC). IRSROB.DOC takes the next three clusters—3ABF, 3AC0, and 3AC1—and IBMHELP.DOC takes two clusters—3AC2 and 3AC3 (see Figure 11.60).

Now let's erase MOM.TXT. Windows does not delete the cluster entries for MOM.TXT when it erases a file. Windows only alters the information in the folder, simply changing the first letter of MOM.TXT to the Greek letter Σ (sigma). This causes the file to "disappear" as far as the OS knows. It won't show up, for example, in Windows Explorer, even though the data still resides on the hard drive for the moment (see Figure 11.61).

Because all the data for MOM.TXT is intact, you could use some program to change the Σ back into another

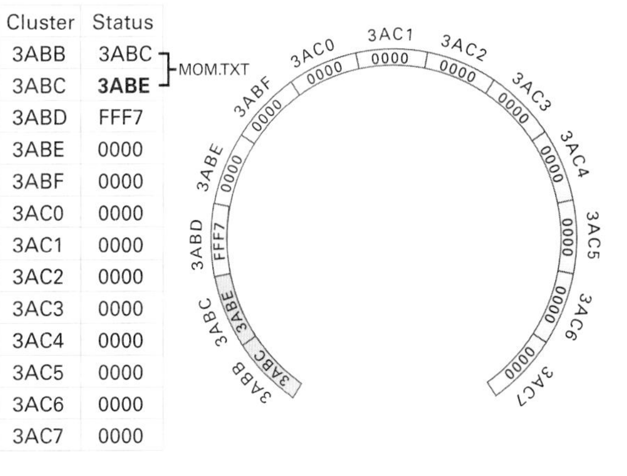

Cluster	Status
3ABB	3ABC
3ABC	**3ABE**
3ABD	FFF7
3ABE	0000
3ABF	0000
3AC0	0000
3AC1	0000
3AC2	0000
3AC3	0000
3AC4	0000
3AC5	0000
3AC6	0000
3AC7	0000

Figure 11.58 The second cluster used

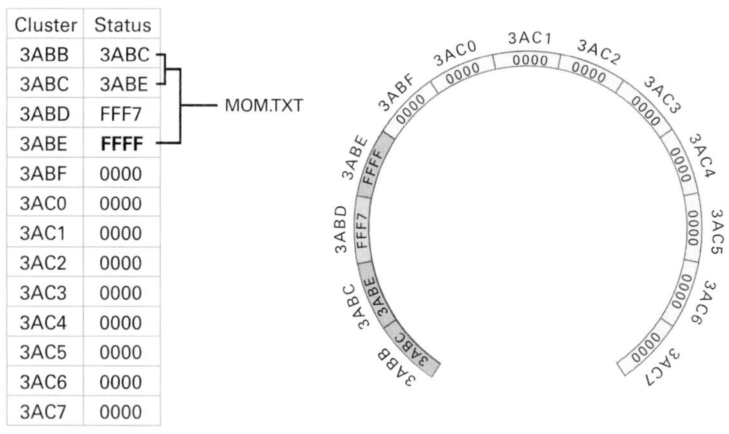

Cluster	Status
3ABB	3ABC
3ABC	3ABE
3ABD	FFF7
3ABE	**FFFF**
3ABF	0000
3AC0	0000
3AC1	0000
3AC2	0000
3AC3	0000
3AC4	0000
3AC5	0000
3AC6	0000
3AC7	0000

• **Figure 11.59** The final cluster used

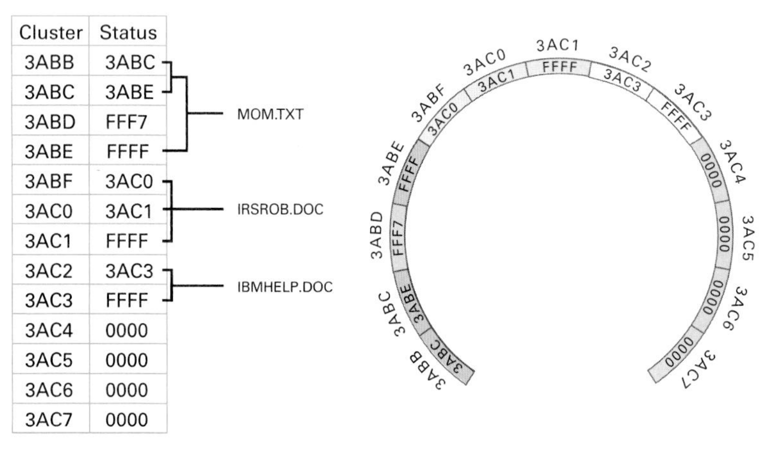

Cluster	Status
3ABB	3ABC
3ABC	3ABE
3ABD	FFF7
3ABE	FFFF
3ABF	3AC0
3AC0	3AC1
3AC1	FFFF
3AC2	3AC3
3AC3	FFFF
3AC4	0000
3AC5	0000
3AC6	0000
3AC7	0000

• **Figure 11.60** Three files saved

letter, and thus get the document back. Programs such as the Recycle Bin work by temporarily protecting these files and remembering the first letter of the file's name until you enter the Empty Recycle Bin command. In fact, good utilities such as Norton Utilities' UnErase can still recover files after you dump the Recycle Bin, as long as no other file has yet overwritten it (Figure 11.62).

Let's say you just emptied your Recycle Bin, which removes the protection from all of your deleted files. You now save one more file, TAXREC.XLS, a big spreadsheet that will take six clusters, into the same folder that once held MOM.TXT. As Windows writes the file to the drive, it overwrites the space that MOM.TXT used, but it needs three more

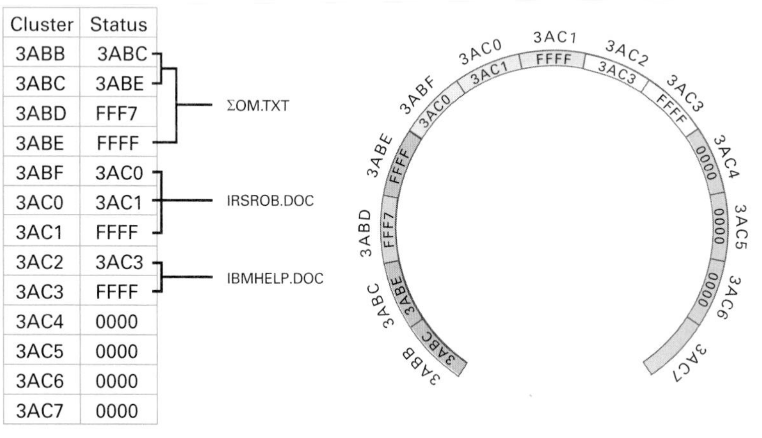

Cluster	Status
3ABB	3ABC
3ABC	3ABE
3ABD	FFF7
3ABE	FFFF
3ABF	3AC0
3AC0	3AC1
3AC1	FFFF
3AC2	3AC3
3AC3	FFFF
3AC4	0000
3AC5	0000
3AC6	0000
3AC7	0000

• **Figure 11.61** MOM.TXT erased

clusters. The next three available clusters are 3AC4, 3AC5, and 3AC6 (see Figure 11.63).

Notice that TAXREC.XLS is in two pieces; we say that the file is "fragmented." Fragmentation takes place all of the time on FAT16 systems. Although the system easily negotiates a tiny fragmented file split into only two parts, excess fragmentation slows down the system during hard drive reads and writes. This example is fragmented into two pieces; in the real world, a file might fragment into hundreds of pieces, forcing the read/write heads to travel all over the hard drive to retrieve a single file. The speed at which the hard drive reads and writes can be improved

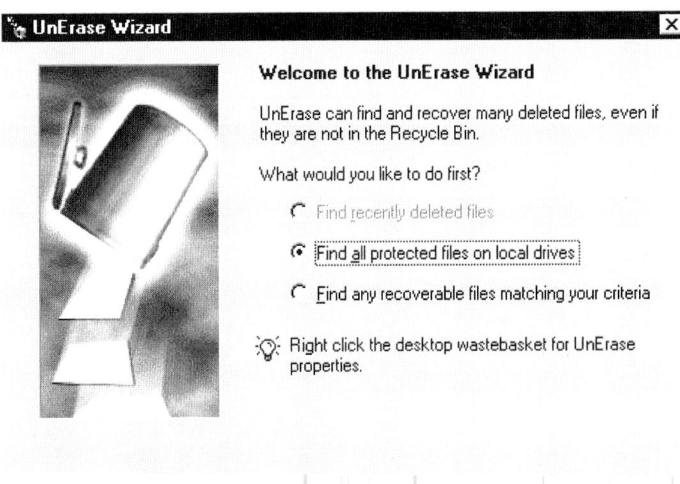

and Troubleshooting Hard Drives" section of this chapter gives the details on working with the various Disk Defragmenters in Windows.

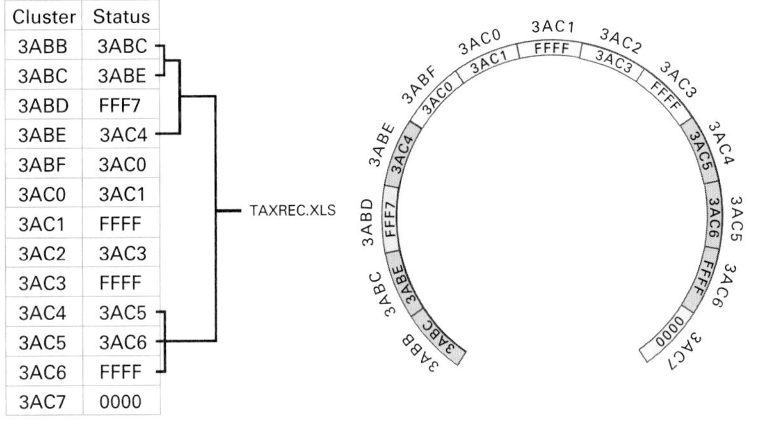

Cluster	Status
3ABB	3ABC
3ABC	3ABE
3ABD	FFF7
3ABE	3AC4
3ABF	3AC0
3AC0	3AC1
3AC1	FFFF
3AC2	3AC3
3AC3	FFFF
3AC4	3AC5
3AC5	3AC6
3AC6	FFFF
3AC7	0000

• **Figure 11.63** TAXREC.XLS fragmented

FAT32

When Microsoft introduced Windows 95 OSR2, it also unveiled a totally new file format called **FAT32** that brought a couple of dramatic improvements. First, FAT32 supports partitions up to 2 terabytes (more than 2 trillion bytes!). Second, as its name implies, FAT32 uses 32 bits to describe each cluster, which means clusters can drop to more reasonable sizes. FAT32's use of so many FAT entries gives it the power to use very small clusters, making the old "keep your partitions small" rule obsolete. FAT32 partitions still need defragmentation, however, just as often as FAT16 partitions. Always make sure that your defragmentation program on an old system supports FAT32 before you try to use it on a FAT32 partition. The results of using a FAT16 defragmenter on a FAT32 drive are not predictable! Table 11.3 shows cluster sizes for FAT32 partitions.

NTFS4

Windows NT 4.0 can format a drive with the **NT file system (NTFS)** version 4, an extremely robust and secure file system, or with FAT, its name for

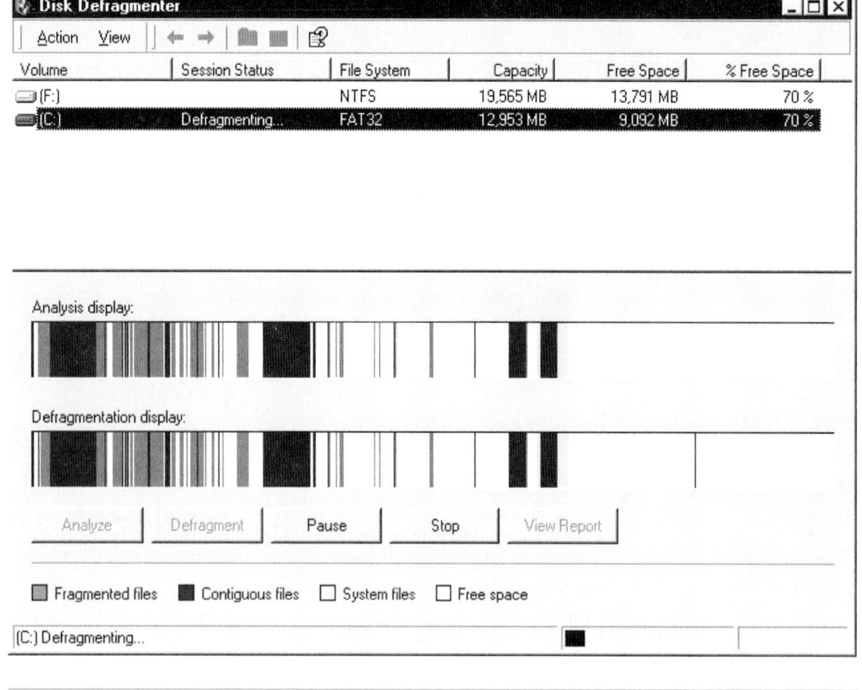

• **Figure 11.64** Windows Disk Defragmenter

FAT16. Unless you have to run a dual boot system with Windows NT and Windows 9*x*/Me, always use NTFS rather than FAT.

NTFS offers four major benefits over FAT16. First, NTFS utilizes an enhanced file allocation table called the **Master File Table (MFT)**. An NTFS partition keeps a backup copy of the most critical parts of the MFT in the middle of the disk, reducing the chance that a serious drive error can wipe out both the MFT and the MFT copy. Whenever you defragment an NTFS partition, you'll see a small, immovable chunk in the middle of the drive; that's the backup MFT.

Second, NTFS views individual files and folders as objects and provides security for those objects through a feature called the Access Control List (ACL). We'll go into this in much more detail in later chapters, but a quick example here should make the basic concept clear. Bill the network administrator sets up a Windows NT 4.0 PC as a workstation for three users, John, Wilma, and Felipe. John logs into the PC with his username and password (johns and f1f0, respectively, in case you're curious), and begins to work on his project. The project folder is stored on the C: drive as C:\Projects\John Super Secret. When John saves his work and gets ready to leave, he alters the permissions on his folder to deny access to anyone but him. When Curious Wilma logs into the PC after John leaves, she cannot access the john super secret folder contents at all, although she can see the entry in Explorer. Without NTFS, John would have no security over his files or folders at all.

Third, **NTFS4** enables you to compress individual files and folders to save space on a hard drive. Compression makes access time to the data slower, because the OS has to uncompress files every time you use them, but in a space-limited environment, sometimes that's what you have to do.

Table 11.3 FAT32 Cluster Sizes

Drive Size	Cluster Size
512 MB or 1023 MB	4 KB
1024 MB–2 GB	4 KB
2–8 GB	4 KB
8–16 GB	8 KB
16–32 GB	16 KB
>32 GB	32 KB

Finally, when you format a drive with NTFS, Disk Administrator enables you to make some very cool drive setups, like you've seen earlier in this chapter. You can extend the size of a volume to take more hard drive space. You can do this on a single drive or even across drives—a process called spanning by the rest of the world but called a Volume Set in Disk Administrator. To extend a volume, click the volume, hold down the CTRL key, and then alternate-click free hard drive space. [illegible] up as simply a larger drive in Explorer.

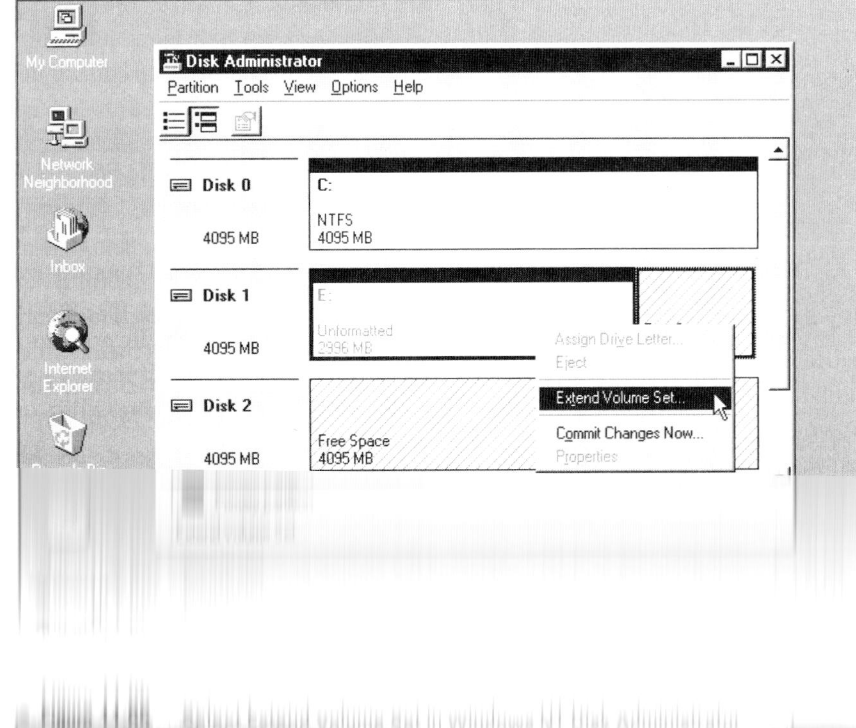

> The OS Technologies exam does not test you on EFS, but you should know about it if you work in, or service, an environment with multiple users per computer.

NTFS5

Windows 2000 and Windows XP offer **NTFS5**, an upgraded version of the NT file system that enables encryption of files, setting limits on the amount of hard drive space taken by any one user, and mounting a volume as a folder in another drive. Windows 2000/XP will automatically upgrade an NTFS4 disk to NTFS5, so be careful if you deal with dual boot NT and 2000/XP systems!

Encrypting File System

One of the biggest draws with NTFS5 is in file encryption, the black art of making files unreadable to anybody but you. You can encrypt a single file, a folder, and a folder full of files. Microsoft calls the encryption utility in NTFS5 the **encrypting file system (EFS)**, although it's simply an aspect of NTFS5 and not a standalone file system. To encrypt a file or folder, alternate-click it in My Computer and select Properties to open the Properties dialog box (Figure 11.66). Click the Advanced button to open the Advanced Properties dialog box. As you can see in Figure 11.67, encryption (and compression) is simply a selectable radio button. Click the button next to Encryption and then click the OK button and instantly your file is safe from prying eyes.

Encryption does not hide files, it simply makes them unreadable for other users. Figure 11.68 shows a couple of encrypted image files. Note that aside from the pale green color of the filenames (that you can't tell are pale green in this black and white image), the files seem readily accessible. Windows XP can't provide a thumbnail, however,

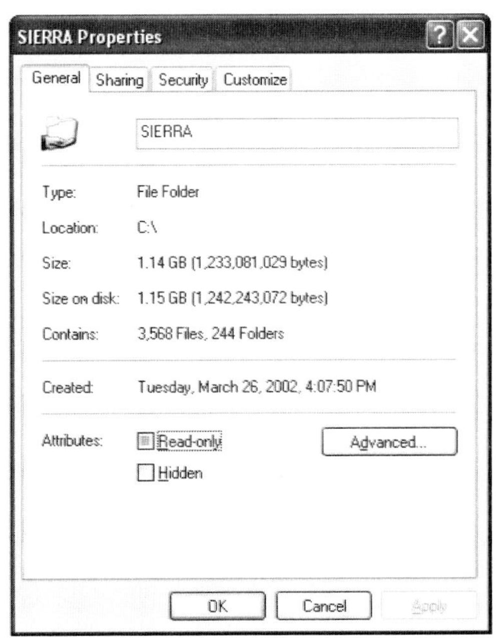

Figure 11.66 Folder Properties

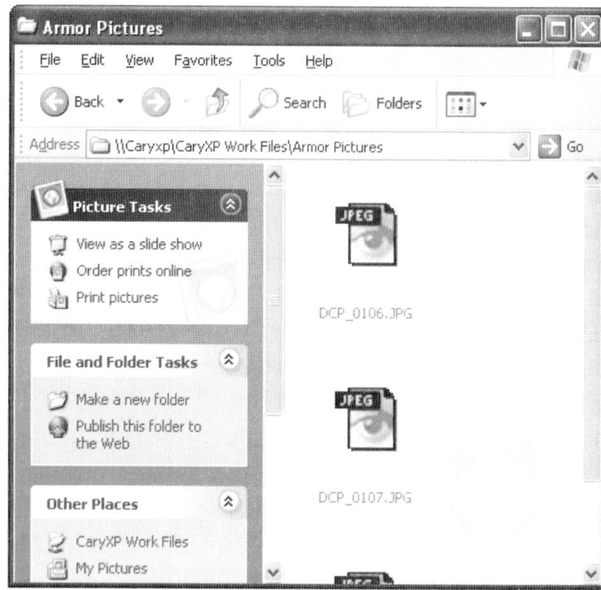

• **Figure 11.67** Options for compression and encryption

• **Figure 11.68** Encrypted files

even though it can read the type of image file (JPEG) easily. Further, double-clicking the files opens up the Windows Picture and Fax Viewer, but still won't show an image (Figure 11.69). Better still, I'm accessing the files across

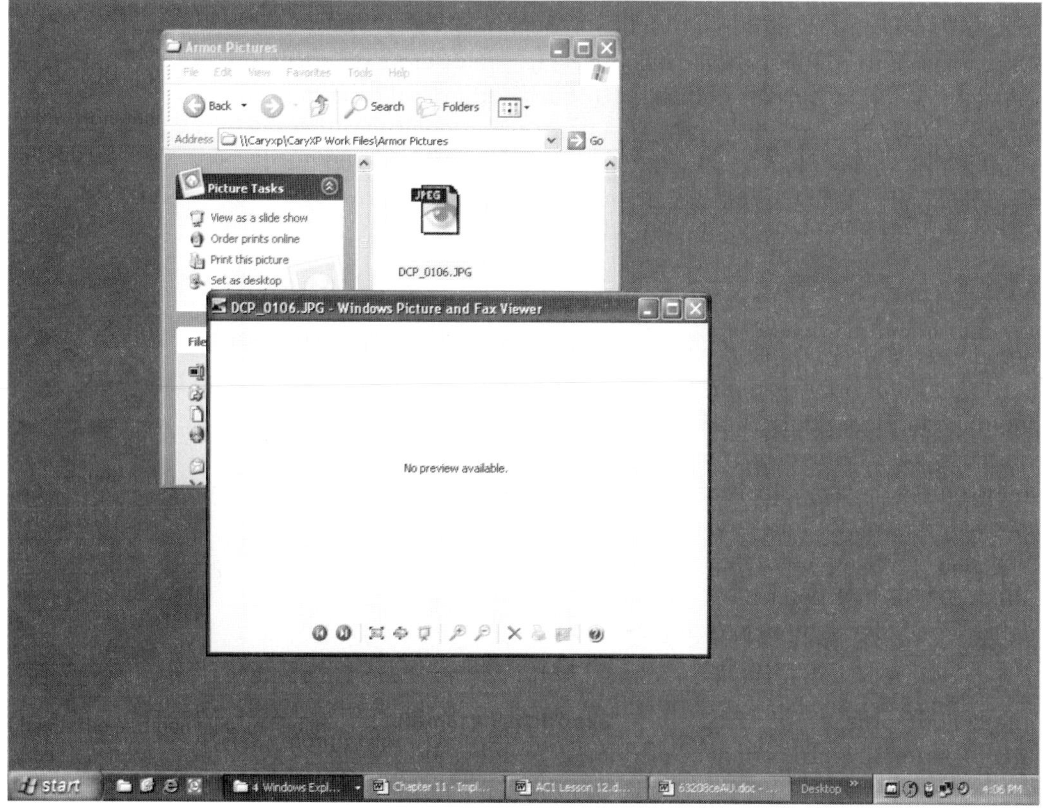

• **Figure 11.69** Windows Picture and Fax Viewer blocked by file encryption

our network and the encryption does precisely what it's supposed to do—block unwanted access to sensitive data.

Encryption protects against other users, but only if you log out. It might seem obvious, but I've had lots of users get confused by encryption, thinking that the PC *knows* who's clicking the keyboard! All protections and security are based on user accounts. If someone logs into your computer with a different account, the encrypted files will be unreadable. We'll get to user accounts, permissions, and such in later chapters in detail.

Disk Quotas

Disk quotas enable you to set limits on drive space usages for users, a feature most often implemented in PCs shared by many users. To set quotas, simply alternate-click the hard drive and select Properties. In the Drive Properties dialog box, select the Quota tab and make changes. Figure 11.70 shows configured quotas for a hard drive.

The Volume Mount Point

Mounting a volume you've seen already in this chapter, but now you know that it's a feature of NTFS that enables you to accomplish it when you

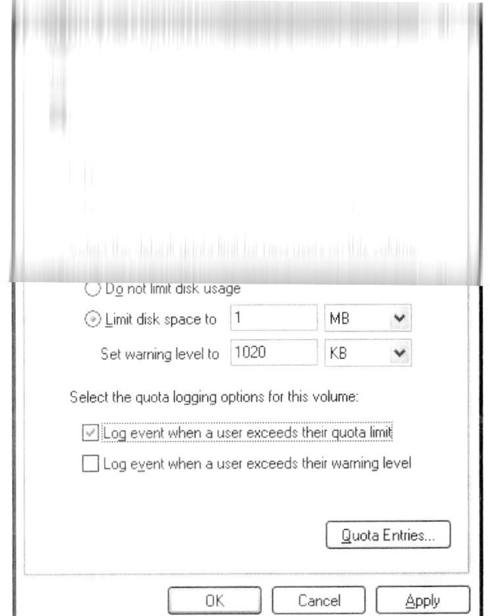

Figure 11.70 Setting quotas

Cluster Sizes

Unlike FAT16 or FAT32, NTFS enables you to adjust the cluster sizes, although we rarely do so. Table 11.4 shows the default cluster sizes for NTFS.

By default, NTFS supports partitions up to 2 terabytes (2,199,023,255,552 bytes). By tweaking the cluster sizes, you can get NTFS to support partitions up to 16 exabytes, or 18,446,744,073,709,551,616 bytes! I think that might support any and all upcoming hard drive capacities for the next hundred years or so!

With so many file systems, how do you know which one to use? In almost all cases, you want to use the best file system your OS supports. If your system supports FAT32, use it. If you have Windows NT/2000/XP, use NTFS.

Formatting a Partition

All versions of Windows offer multiple ways to format a drive and thus make the drive capable of holding data. In Windows 9*x*/Me, after you've partitioned a new drive using FDISK, the drive will show up in My Computer,

Table 11.4 NTFS Cluster Sizes

Drive Size	Cluster Size	Number of Sectors
512 MB or less	512 bytes	1
513–1024 MB (1 GB)	1024 bytes (1KB)	2
1025–2048 MB (2 GB)	2048 bytes (2KB)	4
2049 MB and larger	4096 bytes (4KB)	8

Cross Check

Comparing File Systems

The computer world is still full of Windows 9*x*/Me systems using FAT32 as well as the many Windows 2000 and Windows XP systems using NTFS, both versions 4 and 5. Can you explain the differences among them?

1. How do FAT32 and NTFS4/5 compare in the way they handle clusters?
2. How do they compare in the way they can store and keep track of files?
3. How do they differ in their security capabilities and features?

but if you try to access it by clicking it, you'll get an error. The same applies to Windows NT/2000/XP.

You can format a hard drive simply by typing **format *x*:** at a command prompt, where *x* is the letter of the drive you want to format. If the system is already running Windows 9*x*/Me, simply alternate-click the drive letter in My Computer and select Format to get the standard Windows 98 Format dialog box, as shown in Figure 11.71.

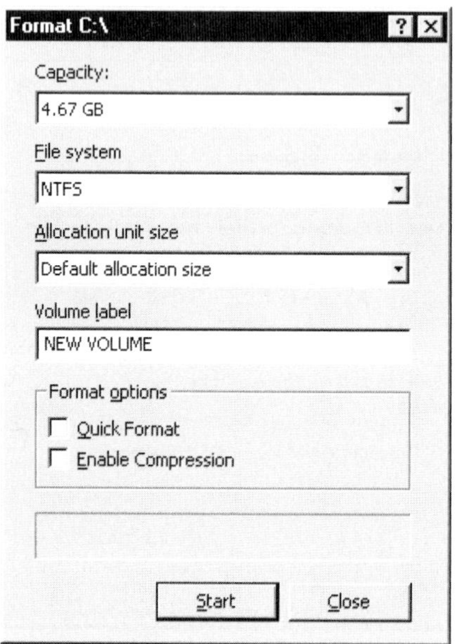

• **Figure 11.71** The Windows 98 Format dialog box

The procedure in My Computer works the same way in Windows NT/2000/XP, although the Format dialog box looks a bit different. Figure 11.72 shows the Windows XP version.

The Disk Administrator in Windows NT and the Disk Management console that comes with Windows 2000 and XP also perform disk formatting. Simply alternate-click a volume to format and select Format from the menu. The OS will prompt you for the file system to use.

Formatting on a New or Rebuilt System

To format a drive on a system without an OS installed requires you to perform one of two steps. First, more often than not you'll boot to the OS CD-ROM and partition and format as part of installing the operating system. We'll go over details of this process in Chapter 14, but it's pretty straightforward. Windows simply prompts you to partition and then format the drive. Read the screens and you'll do great. Second, you can boot to a floppy diskette in Windows 9*x* and format (and partition, for that matter)

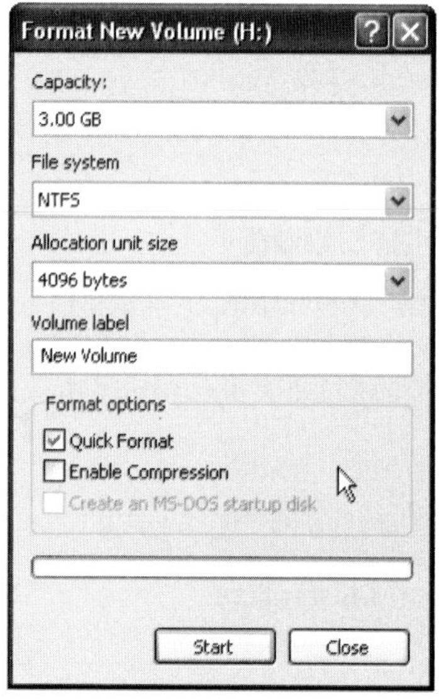

• **Figure 11.72** The Windows XP Format Local Disk dialog box

drives from the command prompt. When you see the A: prompt, type **FORMAT C:/S** and press ENTER. The warning shown in Figure 11.73 will appear.

When you format a drive, not only do you create the file system and the root directory, you wipe out all data on the drive. As a result, Windows will want to be sure that this is really what you want to do! Are you sure? Then press Y to start the formatting process.

Once the FORMAT C:/S com-

```
A:\>format C:/s

WARNING:  ALL DATA ON NON-REMOVABLE DISK
DRIVE C:  WILL BE LOST!
Proceed with Format  (Y/N)?y


Formatting  30709.65M
Format complete.
System transferred

Volume label (11 characters, ENTER for none)?

32,197,017,600 bytes total disk space
       262,144 bytes used by system
32,196,755,456 bytes available on disk

       491,520 bytes in each allocation unit.
       982,455 allocation units available on disk.


Volume Serial Number is 3166-11D9
```

A Final Warning

Please be careful using any partitioning tool and FORMAT. In the wrong hands, these powerful tools can easily wipe out everything on a partition. Many organizations delete these files from working systems to keep untrained folks from accidentally erasing their hard drives! To see your current partitions, use the System Information program. If you don't have Windows installed yet (as is often the case when building a new system), boot to a floppy disk, get to an A: prompt, and then type **FDISK/STATUS**. This handy command tells FDISK just to report the current partition information (see Figure 11.74).

```
                        Fixed Disk Drive Status

Disk   Drv    Mbytes    Free    Usage
  1            30000      0      100%
        C:     15000
        D:      7500
        E:      7500
  2            10000      0      100%
        F:     10000



(1 MByte = 1048576 bytes)

A:/>
```

• Figure 11.74 FDISK /STATUS

■ Maintaining and Troubleshooting Hard Drives

Hard drives are complex mechanical as well as electrical devices. With platters spinning at thousands of rotations per minute, they also generate heat and vibration. All of these factors make hard drives susceptible to failure. In this section, you will learn some basic maintenance tasks that will keep your hard drives healthy, and for those inevitable instances when a hard drive fails, you will also learn what you can do to repair them.

Maintenance

Hard drive maintenance can be broken down into two distinct functions: checking the disk occasionally for failed clusters, and keeping data organized on the drive so that it can be accessed quickly.

ScanDisk

Newer versions of Windows no longer call the disk-checking tool ScanDisk. Instead, Microsoft has relegated this important tool to a button called Error-checking in the Drive Properties dialog box. Even though the term ScanDisk has disappeared from the program name, however, most PC people still use it to refer to any of Windows' hard disk error-checking programs.

Individual clusters on hard drives sometimes go bad. There's nothing you can do to prevent this from happening, so it's important to check occasionally for bad clusters on drives. The tool used to perform this check is called **ScanDisk**. When it finds bad clusters, it puts the electronic equivalent of orange cones around them so that the system won't try to place data in those bad clusters. ScanDisk is one of the oldest utilities ever made for the PC market—ScanDisk was around back in the DOS days, and it continues to do its thing in the latest versions of Windows.

ScanDisk does far more than just check for bad clusters. It goes through all of the drive's filenames, looking for invalid names and attempting to fix them. It looks for clusters that have no filenames associated with them (we call these lost chains) and erases them. From time to time, the underlying links between parent and child folders are lost, so ScanDisk checks every parent and child folder. With a folder such as C:\TEST\DATA, for example, ScanDisk makes sure that the folder DATA is properly associated with its parent folder C:\TEST, and that C:\TEST is properly associated with its child folder C:\TEST\DATA.

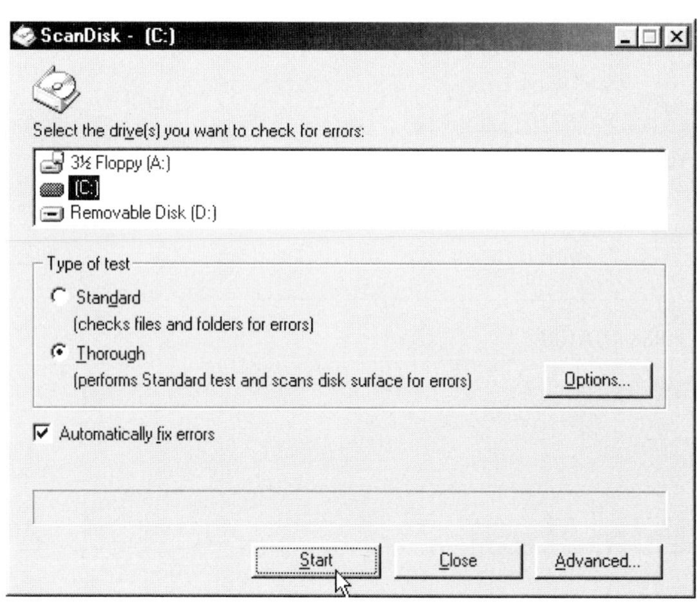

• **Figure 11.75** ScanDisk options

The best part of ScanDisk is that it works automatically. The trick is to know how to start it! In Windows 9*x*/Me, you locate ScanDisk by choosing Start | Programs | Accessories | System Tools. You can also start ScanDisk by opening My Computer, alternate-clicking the drive you want to check, and selecting Properties to open the Drive Properties dialog box. Select the Tools tab and then click the Check Now button to start ScanDisk.

The Windows 9*x*/Me version of ScanDisk gives you a choice between Standard and Thorough testing, as well as an option to have it automatically fix any errors it finds (Figure 11.75). For maintenance purposes, it's fine to use the Standard check. The Thorough check takes a long time, so you'll normally use it only when you suspect a problem. As a rule, you should also always check the Automatically fix errors check box.

To access Error-checking (a.k.a. ScanDisk) on a Windows 2000/XP system, open My Computer, alternate-click the drive you want to check, and select Properties to open the Drive Properties dialog box. Select the Tools tab and click the Check Now button (Figure 11.76) to display the Check Disk dialog box, which has two options (Figure 11.77). Check the box next to Automatically fix file system errors, but save the option to Scan for and attempt recovery of bad sectors for times when you actually suspect a problem.

Now that you know how to run ScanDisk, your next question should be, "How often do I run it?" A reasonable maintenance plan would include running ScanDisk about once a week. ScanDisk is fast (unless you use the Thorough option), and it's a great tool for keeping your system in top shape. But disk checking isn't the only thing ScanDisk can do. As you're about to see, it's a powerful tool that can help you when things go wrong on a hard drive.

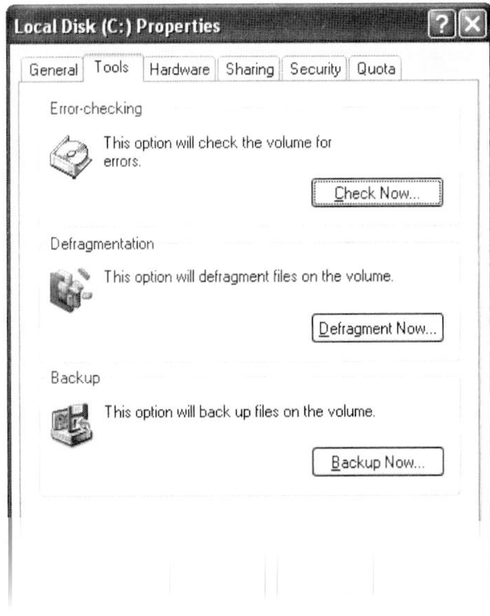

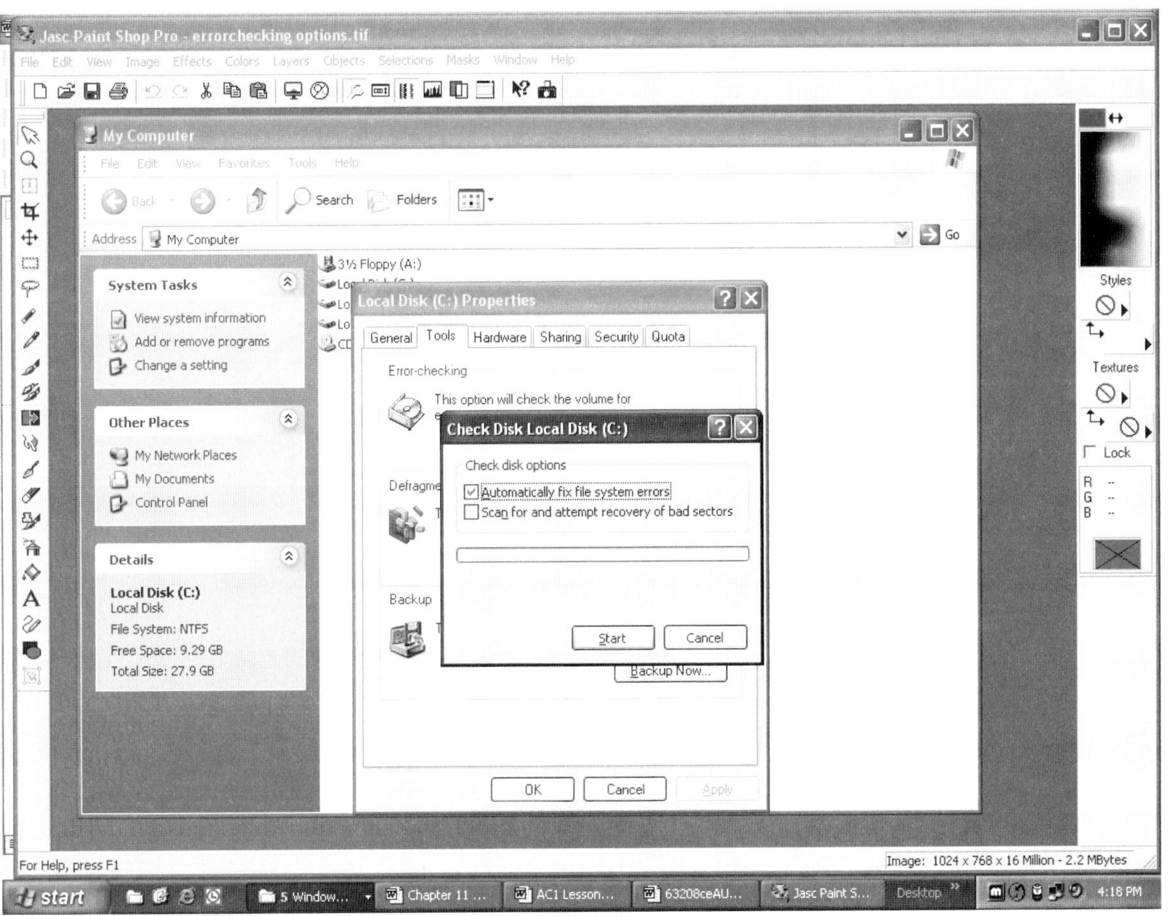

• **Figure 11.77** Error-checking options

Try This!

Comparing ScanDisk to Competing Tools

A good PC tech is an informed PC tech. A number of companies make third-party tools that they claim are better than ScanDisk. Try this:

1. Research these two competing products: SmithMicro's CheckIt utility (www.checkit.com) and Symantec's Norton Utilities (www.symantec.com). Look through these web sites and gather information on the products' features. How can these products help you maintain and repair hard drives?
2. Call or e-mail each company's sales department and ask this question, "Why should I buy your product when I already have ScanDisk?" Print the e-mail message, or if you call, write down the response.
3. Write a brief report outlining the similarities and differences among the three programs (including ScanDisk) and the advantages and disadvantages of each. Rate the programs; which seems the best buy and which the worst?

You'll be prompted to select the disk you want to defragment (Figure 11.78). Once you've selected a disk, the defragging begins. Defragmentation takes quite a while if you haven't done it before. If you want to watch the process, click the Show Details button to see the clusters get rearranged (Figure 11.79). It's fascinating to watch—kind of like watching paint dry to some, but sort of mesmerizing, too.

While simply running Disk Defragmenter with the default settings is fine in most situations, there are some specialized settings that you may want to employ. The Select Drive screen has a Settings button. Clicking this displays the settings choices you can use. The one option of interest is the Start Programs Faster option. This option tells Defrag to put all of the directory information at the beginning of the drive, which makes files load more quickly.

The defrag tool that runs with Windows 2000 and XP is accessed via the Start button exactly as described for Windows 98. Although functionally equivalent, it does look a bit different (Figure 11.80). No worry, though—it does the same job.

Defrag and ScanDisk are the two maintenance tools that everyone should run on their systems. As with ScanDisk, you should run Defrag once a week. It doesn't take long if you run it often enough.

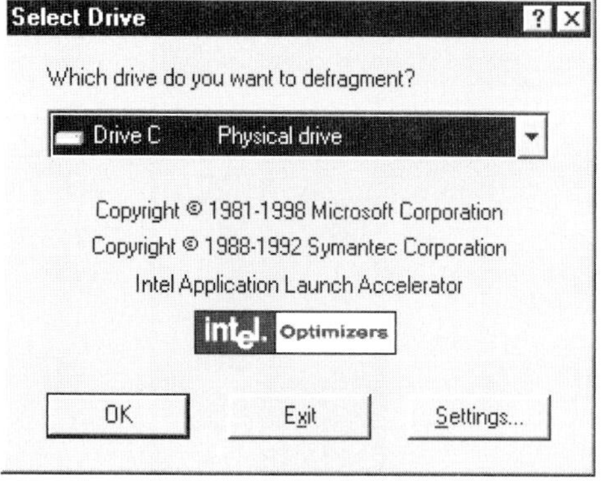

• **Figure 11.78** Selecting the drive to defragment

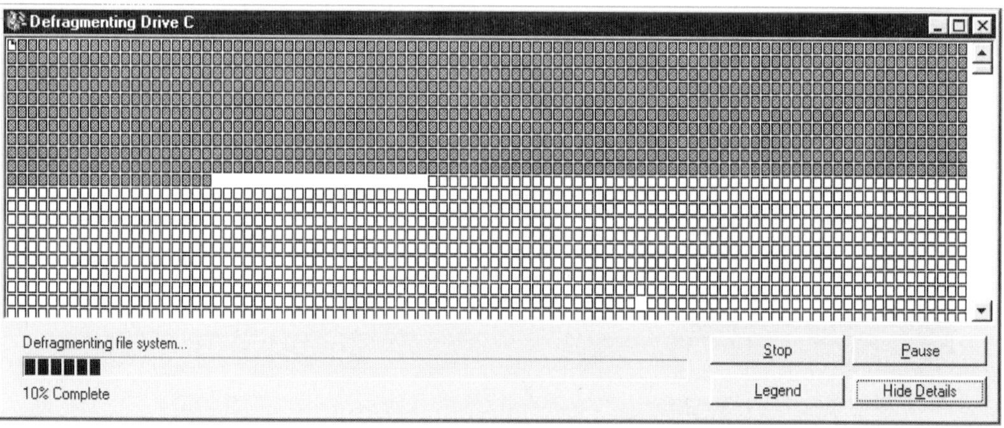

• **Figure 11.79** Disk Defragmenter running in Show Details mode

Disk Cleanup

Did you know that the average hard drive is full of trash? No, I'm not talking about the junk you intentionally put in your hard drive like the 23,000 e-mail messages that you refuse to delete from your e-mail program. I'm talking about all the files that you never see that Windows keeps for you. Here are a few examples:

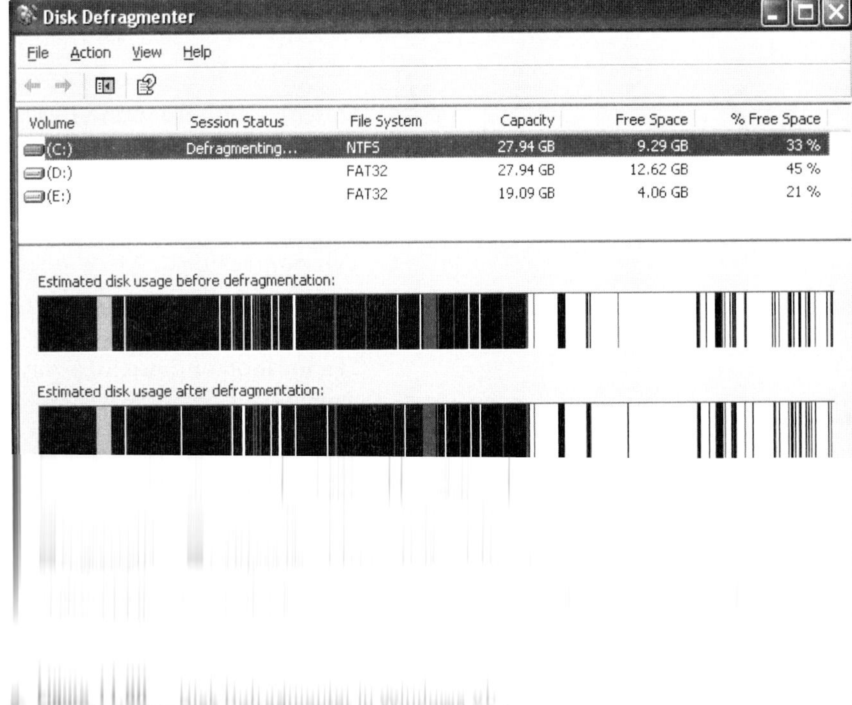

- **Files in the Recycle Bin** When you delete a file,

- **Temporary Internet Files** When you go to a web site, Windows keeps copies of the graphics and other items so that the page will load more quickly the next time you access the page. You can see these files by opening the Internet Options applet on the

Defrag can also be accessed through a drive's Properties dialog box in Windows 9x/Me, 2000, and XP.

Recycle Bin

File Edit View Favorites Tools Help

Back Search Folders History

Address Recycle Bin Go

Recycle Bin

This folder contains files and folders that you have deleted from your computer.

To permanently remove all items and reclaim disk space, click:

Empty Recycle Bin

To move all items back to their original locations, click:

Restore All

Select an item to view its description.

Name	Original Location	Date Deleted	Type	Size
1green_morph227...	D:\Documents and ...	12/19/2002 11:0...	WinZip File	8 KB
Acrobat Reader 5.1	D:\Documents and ...	12/19/2002 11:0...	Shortcut	4 KB
AcroReader51_E...	D:\Documents and ...	12/19/2002 11:0...	Application	8,632...
AOL Instant Mess...	D:\Documents and ...	12/19/2002 11:0...	Shortcut	4 KB
cc32d479.exe	D:\Documents and ...	12/19/2002 11:0...	Application	23,06...
cpu-z	D:\Documents and ...	12/19/2002 11:0...	File Folder	400 KB
cpu-z-115.zip	D:\Documents and ...	12/19/2002 11:0...	WinZip File	160 KB
flash	D:\Documents and ...	12/19/2002 11:0...	File Folder	12 KB
green_lamp.zip	D:\Documents and ...	12/19/2002 11:0...	WinZip File	580 KB
green_morph.html	D:\Documents and ...	12/19/2002 10:5...	Microsoft HTML Doc...	4 KB
green_morph.swf	D:\Documents and ...	12/19/2002 10:4...	Shockwave Flash O...	8 KB
men100tp.pdf	D:\Documents and ...	12/19/2002 11:0...	Adobe Acrobat Doc...	528 KB
psp704ev.exe	D:\Documents and ...	12/19/2002 11:0...	Application	30,90...
QuickTime Player	D:\Documents and ...	12/19/2002 11:0...	Shortcut	4 KB
Shortcut to Studio...	D:\Documents and ...	12/19/2002 11:0...	Shortcut	4 KB
shoutcast-playlist.pls	D:\Documents and ...	12/19/2002 11:0...	MP3 PlayLists (.m3u,...	4 KB
temp	D:\Documents and ...	12/19/2002 11:0...	File Folder	8,716...
temp pics	D:\Documents and ...	12/19/2002 11:0...	File Folder	1,460...
Typical computer ...	D:\Documents and ...	12/19/2002 11:0...	Microsoft HTML Doc...	32 KB
Typical computer ...	D:\Documents and ...	12/19/2002 11:0...	File Folder	36 KB
VPN Client	D:\Documents and ...	12/19/2002 11:0...	Shortcut	4 KB
vpn-5000-win-200...	D:\Documents and ...	12/19/2002 11:0...	Application	1,312...
website	D:\Documents and ...	12/19/2002 11:0...	File Folder	4 KB
WinZip	D:\Documents and ...	12/19/2002 11:0...	Shortcut	4 KB
winzip81.exe	D:\Documents and ...	12/19/2002 11:0...	Application	1,764...

25 object(s) 75.8 MB

• **Figure 11.81** Mike's Recycle Bin

Control Panel. Click the Settings button on the General tab and then click the View Files button. Figure 11.82 shows my temporary Internet files.

- **Downloaded Program Files** Your system always keeps a copy of any Java or ActiveX applets that it downloads. You can see these in the Internet Options applet by clicking the View Objects button on the General tab. You'll generally find only a few tiny files here.
- **Temporary Files** Many applications create temporary files that are supposed to be deleted when the application is closed. For one reason or another, these temporary files sometimes aren't deleted. The location of these files varies with the version of Windows, but they always reside in a folder called TEMP.

Every hard drive will eventually become filled with lots of unnecessary trash. All versions of Windows tend to act erratically when the drives run out of unused space. Fortunately, all versions of Windows starting with Windows 98 have a powerful tool called **Disk Cleanup** (Figure 11.83). You can access Disk Cleanup in all versions of Windows by choosing Start | Program | Accessories | System Tools | Disk Cleanup.

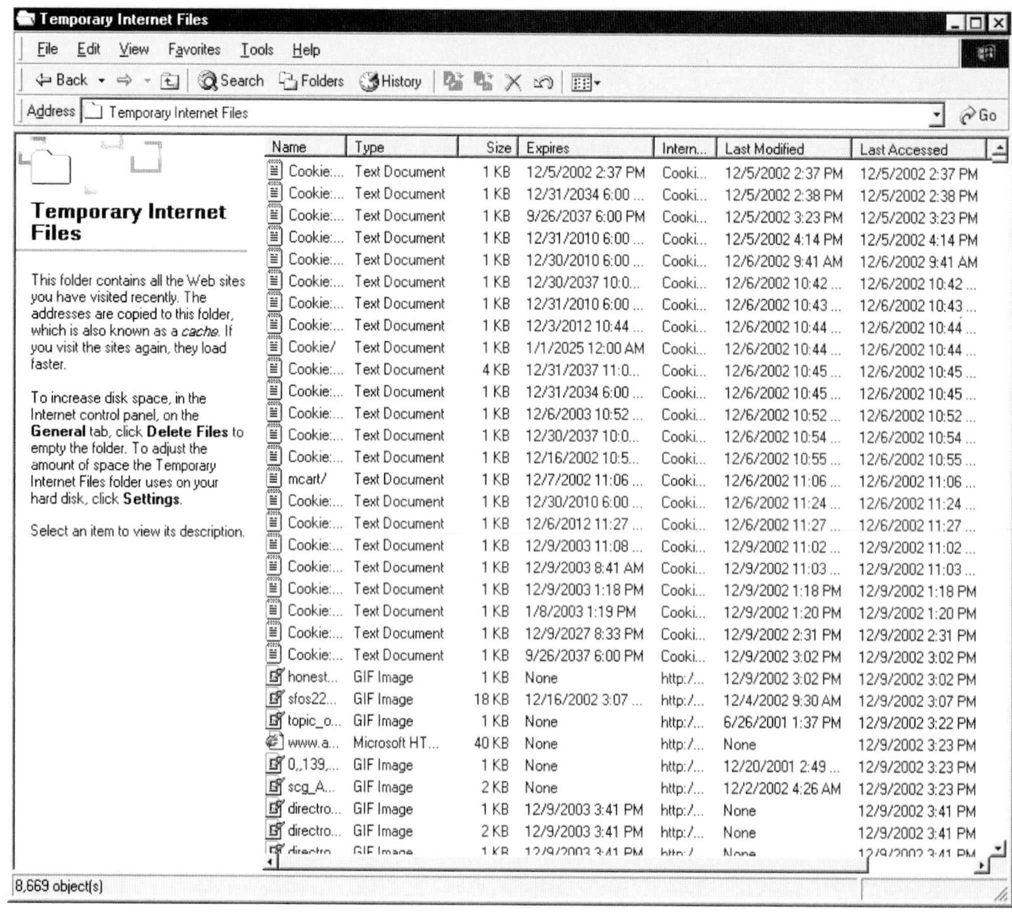

• **Figure 11.82** Temporary Internet Files in Windows 2000

Disk Cleanup gets rid of the four types of files just described. Run Disk Cleanup once a month or so to keep plenty of space available on your hard drive.

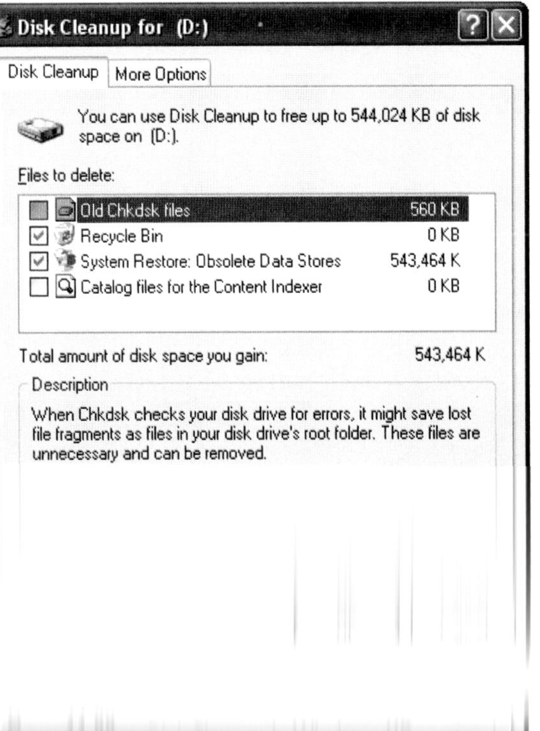

Figure 11.83 Disk Cleanup in Windows XP

Troubleshooting

There's no scarier computer problem than an error that points to trouble with a hard drive. In this section, we'll look at some of the more common problems that occur with hard drives and how to fix them. These issues fall into three broad categories: installation, data corruption, and dying hard drives.

Installation Errors

[illegible]

plugged in right or something has managed to unplug itself. These problems virtually always show themselves at boot time. Here are some classics:

- Hard drive error
- No fixed disks present
- HDD controller failure
- No boot device available
- Drive not found

If you plug the data cable in backwards for an IDE drive, the computer simply won't boot—it's a famous error and everyone who has ever installed a hard drive has done it. Just reinsert the cable properly and turn the machine back on. The power connectors aren't nearly as forgiving. If you install the power cable backward, you will destroy the drive in a dazzling display of sparks and smoke. Fortunately, the chamfers on Molex connectors make this mistake very difficult to do.

You can usually conquer connectivity errors by carefully inspecting the entire connection system (including electricity) and finding the silly mistake (welcome to the club). Always remove and reseat the controller (if it's on an expansion card) if you get an HDD controller failure, as they are prone to static build-up. It is also a good idea to keep an extra controller around to verify if the controller is good. Cables can go bad, but it is very rare unless the cable is obviously ripped or pinched. If your BIOS has an IDE **autodetection** function, use it! It will not detect a drive unless everything is installed correctly. It's a great, quick connectivity verifier.

If you've just installed the drive, also check the jumper settings. You can't have two masters or two slaves on a single controller. And don't forget the 1 Drive or Standalone setting on some drives!

Tech Tip

Dynamic Drive Overlays

Most new hard drives come with a special program called a dynamic drive overlay *(DDO), designed to enable older systems to support the new drive even if they lack native hardware BIOS support for larger hard drives (LBA). If your system doesn't support ATA/ATAPI-6 drives, for example, you could still install one of the newer 200 GB drives by running the install program that came with the drive. DDOs, also called software translation drivers, load early on in the boot process so they can be in place before any other piece of software tries to access the drive.*

This sounds like a great simple solution to a standard upgrade problem, but I can't recommend it, for a number of reasons. A DDO basically sets up logical disk volumes in its own non-standard format, which right there raises a big sign saying "future PC tech headache." In addition, the versions of this software that ship with specific hard drives are usually customized for the particular drive they ship with, so if you add another drive from a different manufacturer, you can forget the 'free' part of the deal, because you'll need to buy vendor-neutral disk management software that can handle different brands. At that point, you might as well just buy an add-on hard disk controller.

Finally, consider the implications of this being a driver that loads when you boot into Windows. What if you have to boot from a floppy? The drive overlay won't load, and like magic, your disk contents will 'disappear'! It is possible to boot to the hard disk, wait for the overlay to load, and have the DDO software generate a prompt that allows you to boot from the floppy with the overlay in place. But if you're booting to a floppy so you can remove a virus on your hard drive, this 'boot to the hard drive first' procedure won't help you. The moral to this story: if you must use a DDO, use it to make a boot floppy that contains a copy of the DDO. The further moral: don't bother with DDOs, because there are cheaper and better hardware solutions to this problem!

Installing two drives on the same controller increases the chances of errors dramatically. For example, adding a slave drive to an existing single drive requires you to check the first drive to see if its jumper needs to change from single to master. You need to make sure to install the slave drive properly or neither drive will work, causing the system to fail on boot. Additionally, some EIDE drives are simply incompatible and will not work on the same controller. I've worked on many systems where I had to add a second drive to the secondary controller since it would not work with the existing drive.

CMOS Modern systems rarely get CMOS errors, because the autodetection feature handles most drives. The errors that do occur generally fall into two groups: forgetting to run Autodetect and selecting the wrong sector translation in Autodetect. Two rules apply here: Always run Autodetect and *always* select LBA.

Older systems could lose CMOS data for a variety of reasons, including static electricity, inserting an expansion card, and blinking with too much force. It takes nothing to do a quick CMOS check to verify that the drive's geometry is correct using autodetection. Here are some of the more common errors that might point to CMOS problems:

- CMOS configuration mismatch
- No boot device available
- Drive not found
- Missing OS

If Autodetect fails to see the drive in question, it's probably a connectivity problem. Grab a screwdriver and look inside the system!

Partitions Partitioning errors generally fall into two groups: failing to partition at all, and making the wrong size/type of partition. The first error invariably shows up when you try to access the nonpartitioned drive. The OS gives you a nice "Invalid Drive Specification" error, and you can't see the drive in anything but CMOS and FDISK. Simply add your partition of choice and go on.

The most common sizing issue comes from selecting less than the full remaining space when making an extended partition. This invariably shows up as a "Hey! Why do I only have *x* megabytes of space? My drive is bigger than that!" Check the partitions in FDISK and redo them if necessary.

Format Failing to format a drive makes the drive unable to hold data. Accessing the drive in Windows will result in a drive "is not accessible" error, and from a C:\ prompt, you'll get the famous "Invalid media" type error. Format the drive unless you're certain that the drive has a format already. Corrupted files can create the Invalid media type error. Check one of the sections on corrupted data later in this chapter for the fix.

Most of the time, formatting is a slow, boring process. But sometimes the drive makes "bad sounds" and you start seeing errors like the one shown in Figure 11.84 at the bottom of the screen.

An allocation unit is FORMAT's term for a cluster. The drive has run across a bad cluster and is trying to fix it. For years, I've told techs that seeing this error a few (610) times doesn't mean anything; every drive comes with a few bad spots. This is no longer true. Modern EIDE drives actually hide a significant number of extra sectors that they use to replace bad sectors automatically. If a new drive gets a lot of "Trying to recover lost allocation unit" errors, you can bet that the drive is dying

```
A:\>format C:/s

WARNING:  ALL DATA ON NON-REMOVABLE DISK
DRIVE C:  WILL BE LOST!
Proceed with Format  (Y/N)?y


Formatting  30709.65M

Trying to recover lost allocation unit 37,925
```

"mental reinstall." Does the drive show up in the CMOS Autodetect? No? Then recheck the cables, master/slave settings, and power! If it does show up, did you remember to partition and format the drive? Did it need to be set to active? These are common-sense questions that come to mind as you march through your mental reinstall. Even though I've installed thousands of drives over the years, I'm amazed at how often I do things such as forget to plug in power to a drive, forget CMOS, or install a cable backwards. Do the mental reinstall—it really works!

Data Corruption

All hard drives occasionally get corrupted data in individual sectors. Power surges, accidental shutdowns, corrupted install media, and viruses, along with hundreds of other problems, can cause this corruption. In most cases, this type of error shows up while Windows is running. Figure 11.85 shows a classic example of this type of error.

You may also see Windows error messages saying one of the following:

- "The following file is missing or corrupt"
- "The download location information is damaged"
- "Unable to load file"

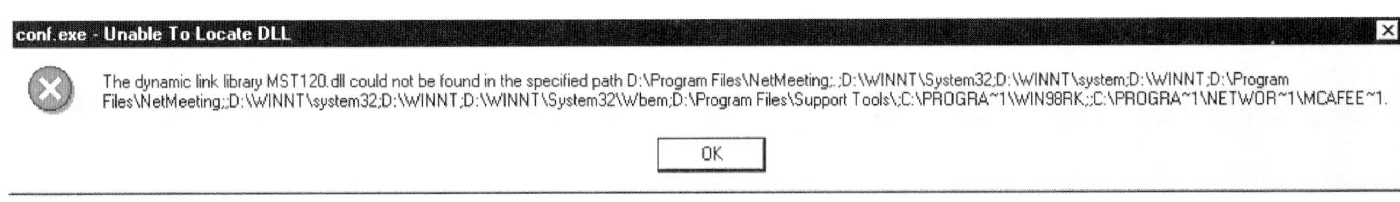

• **Figure 11.85** A corrupted data error

If core boot files become corrupted, you may see text errors at boot, such as the following:

- "Cannot find COMMAND.COM"
- "Error loading operating system"
- "Invalid BOOT.INI"

On older programs, you may see a command prompt open with errors such as this one:

```
Sector not found reading drive C: Abort, Retry, Fail?
```

The first fix for any of these problems is to run ScanDisk (or Error-checking). If you have Windows NT, remember that you need to use a third-party utility. ScanDisk will go through and mark bad clusters and hopefully move your data to a good cluster.

This section assumes some comfort with the use of a command prompt. Some folks may want to read the next three chapters to get comfortable with command prompts first.

Extract/Expand If ScanDisk fails to move a critically important file—such as a file Windows needs in order to load, you can always resort to the command line and try to extract the file from the Windows cabinet files. Most Windows programs store all files in a compressed format called CAB (which is short for "cabinet file"). One CAB file contains many files, and most install disks have lots of CAB files (see Figure 11.86).

In order to replace a single corrupt file this way, you need to know two things: the location of the CAB file that contains the file you need and how to get the file out so you can copy it back to its original spot. Microsoft supplies the EXTRACT program (Windows 95/98) or the EXPAND program (Windows 2000) to enable you to get a new copy of the missing file from the CAB files on the installation CD-ROM disk. Also notice how they are numbered—that's the secret to understanding these programs. Let's look first at EXTRACT.

In most cases, all the CAB files for a program are piled into some folder, as shown in Figure 11.86. Let's say we need a file called OLEPRO32.DLL. I have no idea what this file does. I only know that Windows can't find it and I'm going to put it back! Get to a DOS prompt within Windows (Start | Programs | MS-DOS Prompt) and tell EXTRACT to check *all* the CAB files with this command:

```
EXTRACT /Y /A WIN98_21.CAB OLEPRO32.DLL
```

EXTRACT goes through all the CAB files, starting with WIN98_21.CAB, and finds the file. If you want to see details on the EXTRACT command, use the Windows Help or type **EXTRACT /?** at a command prompt.

EXPAND works equally well, but has a slightly different command structure. Like EXTRACT, EXPAND runs at a command prompt. To get to a command prompt in Windows 2000, select Start | Run and type **CMD**. To

Cross Check

ScanDisk and Floppy Disks

ScanDisk also works perfectly well on floppy disks and other removable media. Try running ScanDisk on a floppy disk.

1. What are some of the differences in the way ScanDisk runs on a floppy as compared to a hard drive? Why do you think that you can't run FDISK on a floppy disk?
2. Reread the discussion of floppy drive maintenance and repair concepts in Chapter 9. How would you incorporate ScanDisk into your floppy disk and drive troubleshooting?

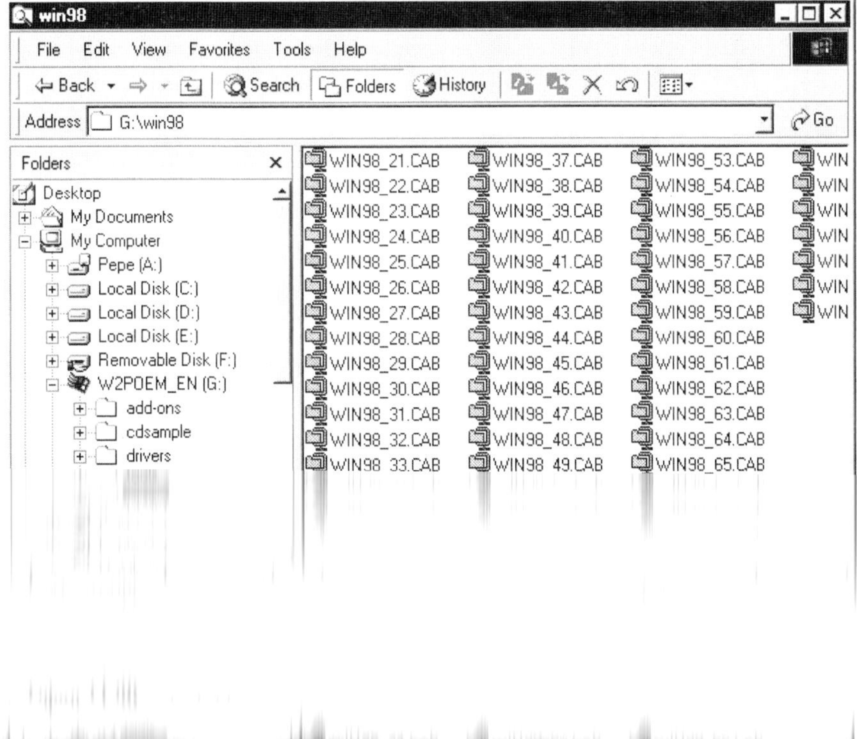

access a file, type in the proper location and name, but use a special -F: switch. For example, to search the CAB files in the I386 folder on the CD-ROM (in this case, drive letter X:\ ) for the file MWWDM.SYS, type the following at the command prompt:

```
EXPAND X:\I386\*.CAB -F:MWWDM.SYS C:\
```

EXPAND searches all CAB files in the:\I386 folder, looking for the file MWWDM.SYS. When EXPAND locates the CAB file containing the desired file, it expands the file and places it in the C:\ folder.

Bad Boot Sector Like any other part of a drive, your boot sector may occasionally get corrupted. Bad boot sectors show up as boot lockups, missing drive letters in My Computer, and errors such as the following:

- Invalid Partition
- Bad or Missing Command Interpreter

First, run an antivirus program to insure that a virus has not attacked your boot sector. See the section on viruses in Chapter 15 to learn how to deal with a boot sector virus. Assuming no virus is present, you need to replace the boot sector. Hopefully, you made a backup of the boot sector with the Ultimate Boot Disk or with another utility. You simply boot off the disk and reinstall the MBR.

Many hard drive failure situations require a copy of the boot sector. The file is tiny and easily fits on the Ultimate Boot Disk. From the Ultimate Boot Disk main screen, select More Tools and then Drive Medic to get to the screen shown in Figure 11.87.

If you don't have an MBR, you will probably be repartitioning the hard drive and doing a complete reinstall. One last-ditch effort you should make

> The Ultimate Boot Disk takes your Windows Startup disk and turns it into a real powerhouse. You can use it to make a backup of your boot sector, even on NTFS volumes! You can find the Ultimate Boot Disk at www.startdisk.com. Get it today!

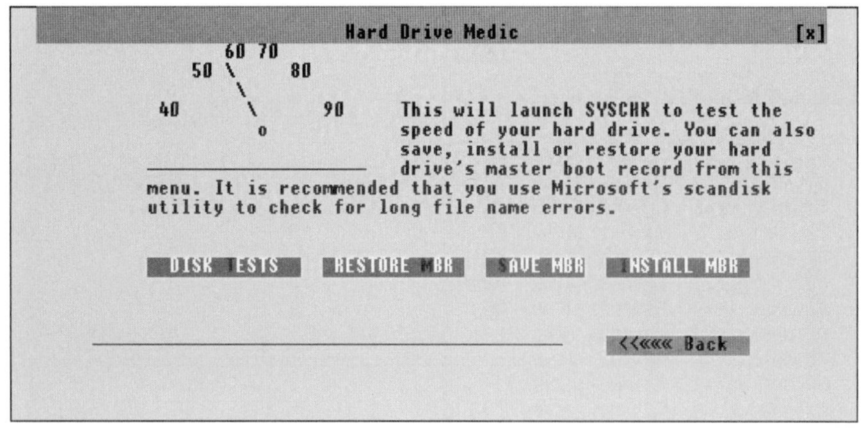

• **Figure 11.87** The boot sector backup

is to boot to an A: prompt and enter the following command to reinstall the master boot record:

```
FDISK /MBR
```

It often works!

Corrupted Data on Bad Sectors If the same errors continue to appear after running the disk-checking utility described in the previous section, there's a chance that the drive has bad sectors.

Almost all drives today take advantage of built-in **error correction code (ECC)** that constantly checks the drive for bad sectors. If the ECC detects a bad sector, it marks the sector as bad in the drive's internal error map. Don't confuse this error map with a FAT. The partitioning program creates the FAT. The drive's internal error map was created at the factory on reserved drive heads and is invisible to the system. If the ECC finds a bad sector, you will get a corrupted data error as the computer attempts to read the bad sector. Disk checkers fix this problem most of the time.

Many times the ECC thinks a bad sector is good, however, and fails to update the internal error map. In this case, you need a program that goes back into the drive and marks the sectors as bad. That's where the powerful SpinRite utility from Gibson Research comes into play. SpinRite marks sectors as bad or good more accurately than ECC and does not disturb the data, enabling you to run SpinRite without fear of losing anything. And if it finds a bad sector with data in it, SpinRite has powerful algorithms that usually recover the data on all but the most badly damaged sectors (see Figure 11.88).

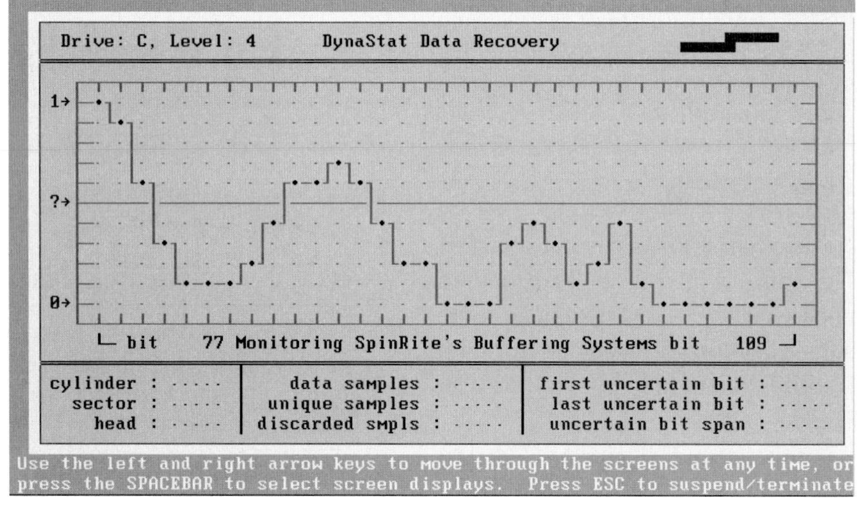

• **Figure 11.88** SpinRite

The power of SpinRite makes it required equipment in every tech's tool bag. Yet for all this power, SpinRite has an Achilles' heel—it does not work on NTFS partitions. Do me a favor—go to the Gibson Research web site and tell Steve Gibson to update SpinRite for NTFS!

Without SpinRite, you must use a low-level format program supplied by the hard-drive maker. These programs work like SpinRite in that they aggressively check the hard drive's sectors and update the internal error map. Unfortunately, all of them wipe out all data on the drive. At least the drive can be used, even if it means repartitioning, formatting, and reinstalling everything!

Dying Hard Drive

Physical problems are rare but devastating when they happen. If a hard drive is truly damaged physically, there is nothing that you or any service technician can do to fix it. Fortunately, hard drives are designed to take a phenomenal amount of punishment without failing. Physical problems manifest themselves in two ways: either the drive works properly but makes a lot of noise, or the drive seems to disappear.

All hard drives make noise—the hum as the platters spin and the occasional slight scratching noise as the read/write heads access sectors are normal. However, if your drive begins to make any of the following sounds, it is about to die:

- Continuous high-pitched squeal

Most hard drives have three-year warranties. Before you throw away a dead drive, check the hard-drive maker's web site or call them to see if the drive is still under warranty. Ask for a Return Material Authorization (RMA). You'll be amazed how many times you get a newer, usually larger, hard drive for free! It never hurts to check!

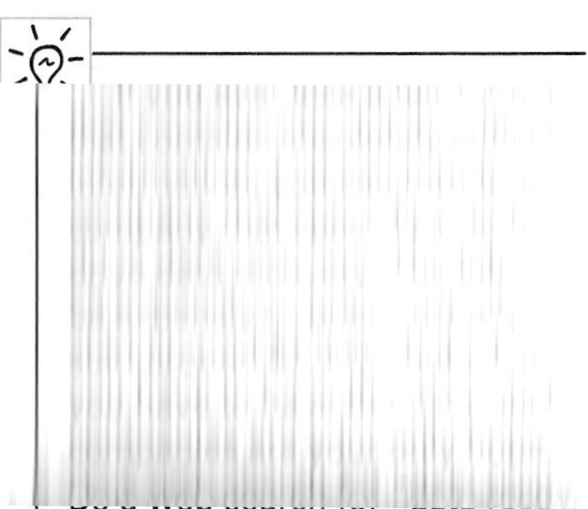

ery" or check the Yellow Pages for companies in this line of business.

the computer, you'll see this error message:

```
No Boot Device Present
```

If it's a second drive, it will simply stop showing up in My Computer. The first thing to do in this case is to fire up the System Setup program and see if Autodetect sees the drive. If it does, then you do not have a physical problem with the drive. If Autodetect fails, shut off the system and remove the ribbon cable, but leave the power cable attached. Restart the system and listen to the drive. If the drive spins up, you know that the drive is getting good power. In most cases, this is a clue that the drive is probably good. In that case, you need to look for more mundane problems such as an unplugged power cord or jumpers incorrectly set. If the drive doesn't spin up, try another power connector. If it still doesn't spin up and you've triple-checked the jumpers and ribbon cable, you have a problem with the onboard electronics, and the drive is dead.

Beyond A+

This section is always a favorite of mine, because I get to talk about new, cool, and useful hardware and software that doesn't happen to be covered by the A+ exams, but which I think you as a budding PC technician should definitely know about. In this chapter, I get to talk about some software that's both really cool and really useful—disk partition tools.

Third-Party Partition Tools

In the discussion of disk partitioning in this chapter, you learned how to use FDISK to do basic disk partitioning tasks, but as you learned, FDISK has some significant limitations. Because it destroys the data on a hard drive when partitioning it, changing the partitions on a drive requires making backup copies of the data, deleting the existing partitions, creating and formatting new ones, and then reinstalling any software (including the operating system, if it's the primary drive) on the drive and restoring the backed up data. Lots of time and trouble, so mostly you stick with what you've got.

These days, however, there are some really great third-party tools on the market that can give you incredible flexibility and power to structure and restructure your hard drive storage to meet your changing needs. The basic mission of this software is to extend the partitioning capabilities of FDISK and Windows to give you more options. Its key feature is the ability to create, change, and delete the partitions on a hard drive *without* destroying any of the programs or data stored there. Slick! This software won't be on the A+ exams, but it's a standard tool of the PC tech, so let's explore two of the most well-known examples, PowerQuest's PartitionMagic™ and VCOM's Partition Commander™.

Probably the most well-known third-party partition tool is PartitionMagic, now up to version 8. It supports every version of Windows from 95b to XP Pro. It enables you to create, resize, split, merge, delete, undelete, and convert partitions without destroying your data. Among the additional features it advertises: the ability to browse, copy, or move files and folders between supported partitions, expand an NTFS partition—even if it's a system partition—without rebooting, change NTFS cluster sizes, and add new partitions for multiple OSs using a simple Wizard.

VCOM, the same company whose System Commander software I mentioned earlier in this chapter, offers a variety of related products, one of which is the very useful Partition Commander 8. Like PartitionMagic, it supports all versions of Windows, and allows you to play with your partitions without destroying your data. Among its niftier features are the ability to convert a Windows 2000/XP/2003 dynamic disk to a basic disk (which Windows can't do), defrag the Master File Table on an NTFS partition, and move unused space from one partition to another on the same physical drive, automatically resizing the partitions based on the amount of space you tell it to move. Figure 11.89 shows the Partition Commander dialog box for moving unused space between partitions.

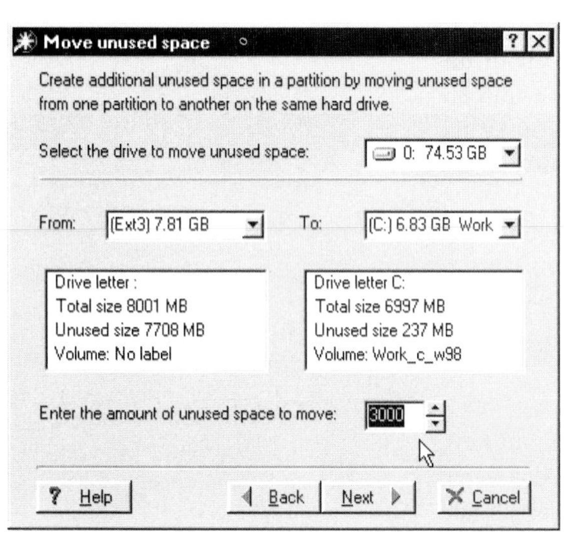

• **Figure 11.89** Partition Commander's Move Unused Space dialog box

I've just hit the highlights of what these and similar competing programs can do. If you want to find out more, you can check out Partition Commander at http://www.v-com.com/product/pc8_ind.html and PartitionMagic at http://www.powerquest.com/partitionmagic/. If you'd like to check out some of their competition, try Google's Directory listing: http://directory.google.com/Top/Computers/Software/Disk_Management/Partition/.

Chapter 11 Review

Chapter Summary

After reading this chapter and completing the exercises, you should understand the following about implementing hard drives.

Partition Hard Drives

- Partitions are electronic, logical divisions of a hard drive into groups of cylinders. Partitioning is the process of electronically subdividing the physical [illegible]
- Partitions exist for three reasons. First, to enable PCs to use larger physical hard drives than the DOS limit of 32 MB, by creating multiple logical drives of up to 32 MB each. Second, partitions enable you to organize a drive to suit your personal taste. Finally, partitioning enables a single hard drive to store more than one operating system (OS).
- Current versions of Windows offer two radically different styles of partitioning, called basic disks and dynamic disks. All versions of Windows can create partitions with basic disks, but only Windows 2000 and XP can create dynamic disks. Windows 9*x*/Me and NT 4.0 do not use the term "basic disk," simply because they only partition in the classic way.
- Partitioning creates the master boot record (MBR) and a partition table. These are stored in the very first sector of the physical drive, called the boot sector. The boot sector contains the MBR—a tiny bit of code that takes control of the boot process from the system BIOS—and the partition table. When the MBR takes control of the boot process from the system BIOS, it looks at the partition table to find a partition with a valid operating system. Every partition in the partition table that contains a valid OS has a special setting called *active* that the MBR uses to determine which OS to load. A hard drive must have an active partition to be bootable.
- Most systems have only a single bootable partition, but all hard drive partition tables support up to four. However, only one partition can be set active at a time. The first sector of the first cylinder of each partition is the volume boot sector. While the "main" boot sector defines the partitions, the volume boot sector stores information important to each partition, such as the location of the operating [illegible]

[illegible] primary partition. Windows 9*x* allows only a single primary partition, while newer versions of Windows can have up to a maximum of four primary partitions on a drive.

- If one partition is a non-bootable extended partition, the system can have only three primary partitions. An extended partition is not automatically assigned a drive letter. After you create an extended partition, you must then create logical drives within the extended partition. The logical drives may be any size you desire. You can format a second hard drive that's just for data storage as an extended partition with logical drives, but you won't be able to boot to it.
- Windows 9*x*/Me uses FDISK for partitioning hard drives. Windows NT 4.0 uses the far more powerful, graphical Disk Administrator tool. Windows 2000 and Windows XP use an enhanced version of the Disk Administrator called Disk Management.
- To start FDISK, type **FDISK** at a command prompt. Windows 95 version B and later FDISKs place a message onscreen that starts with "Your computer has a disk larger than 512 MB" and ends by requiring you to select yes (Y) or no (N). If you select no you're choosing the FAT16 file system; yes chooses FAT 32.
- The FDISK main menu provides four choices. Choose Option 1 to create a primary partition, an extended partition, or logical drives in an extended

partition. Choose Option 2 to create an active partition. Option 3 enables you to delete partitions and logical drives. Option 4 displays current information, and will be blank with a new unpartitioned hard disk.

- A submenu under FDISK option 1 lets you choose what kind of partition to create: a Primary DOS partition, an Extended DOS partition, or Logical DOS Drive(s) in the Extended DOS partition. If you create a single primary partition using all the space on the hard drive, the FDISK program will automatically set that partition to Active. If you choose more than one partition, setting a partition to Active is a separate step: option 2 from the main FDISK menu. You can define the size of each partition either in megabytes or as a percentage of the total space. If you create an extended partition, you must then create logical drives in the extended partition. With a single physical hard drive, FDISK assigns drive letters starting with D: for the logical drive(s). You must reboot the system for the changes to take effect.
- If your drive appears to have only 8.4 GB of space but you know it's larger than that, you need to upgrade your BIOS to add INT13 extensions. If you only see approximately 2.1 GB, you are using FAT16.
- Partitions receive their drive letters at every boot. If you have more than one physical hard drive, the system uses a "pecking order" to assign drive letters with the primary partition on the primary master being assigned the letter C:. Any other primary partitions get the next drive letters in this sequence: first the primary slave, then the secondary master, and finally the secondary slave. After assigning letters to primary partitions, FDISK assigns letters to logical drives in the same order of primary master, primary slave, secondary master, and secondary slave. Finally, all non-hard drives attached to an IDE controller get drive letters.
- In a multiple-drive system, FDISK adds a fifth option to the main menu: select which drive to partition or delete. Before you delete a partition, make sure you are working on the correct physical drive. Deleting partitions in FDISK follows a clear set of rules, but different configurations of drives and partitions require different steps. When you select option 3 from the main FDISK menu, a submenu will let you select which partition to delete.
- Deleting extended partitions is a two-step process: (1) delete any logical drives in the extended partition; and (2) delete the extended partition itself. Delete from the bottom of the delete submenu up: (3) logical drives, then (2) extended partition, and finally (1) the primary partition. Although not required, create from the top down on the create submenu: (1) primary partition, (2) extended partition, and then (3) logical drives.
- Windows NT 4.0 uses the graphical Disk Administrator to partition hard drives. It handles all the FDISK functions, such as creating primary and extended partitions and making primary partitions active, and it can do striping, mirroring and spanning on basic disks. To finish any partitioning process in Disk Administrator, you must alternate-click on the drive and select the option to Commit Changes Now.
- Windows 2000/XP's Disk Management console enables you to easily create and format primary and extended partitions, and switch the active partition. Disk Management uses a special type of storage unique to Windows 2000/XP called a dynamic disk to do advanced partitioning like striping, mirroring and spanning. It can convert a basic disk to a dynamic disk. Dynamic disks are divided into volumes instead of partitions. A simple volume acts just like a primary partition. If you convert a disk with primary or extended partitions, those partitions will in effect become simple volumes: you don't lose the data, but you can't boot to them anymore. You can't revert a dynamic disk to a basic disk without losing all its data. To make a simple volume using Disk Management, alternate-click any unallocated space on the dynamic disk and select New Volume to run the New Volume Wizard.
- Disk Management can mount a dynamic disk volume to a folder on the C: drive, making it unnecessary to deal with multiple drive letters or worry about the drive letters for the CD-ROM drive changing when a new physical drive is added. You cannot, however, make the system partition, your primary master C: drive, into a dynamic drive.
- Dynamic disks support five types of volumes: simple, spanned, striped, mirrored, and striped with parity. A simple volume can be extended to use unallocated space on a dynamic disk. A spanned volume uses space on completely

different dynamic disks. To extend or span, simply alternate-click the volume you want to make bigger, and select Extend Volume. The Extend Volume Wizard will prompt you for the location of free space on a dynamic disk and the increased volume size you want.

- Disk Management enables you to combine two or more dynamic disks into a random array of independent (or inexpensive) disks (RAID), just as if you had a RAID controller card in your PC. Windows 2000 and XP Professional support three types of software RAID: striped, mirrored, and striped with parity. A striped volume spreads out

[illegible]

drives. Basically, RAID-5 is striping using three or more disks, with fault-tolerance added in the form of parity bits, which are also striped across the disks. Disk Management limits implementation of RAID-5 volumes to Windows 2000 or 2003 Server machines.

- A striped volume requires two or more unallocated spaces on dynamic disks. In Disk Management, select the first one, hold the CTRL key down to select the second one, then alternate-click the drive and select New Volume. Select the Striped option in the New Volume Wizard. To create a mirrored volume, first access a Windows 2000 or 2003 Server and create a simple volume on one drive, then alternate-click the drive and select Add Mirror from the options.
- A mount point is a drive that functions like a folder mounted into another drive. You can only mount a volume to an empty folder on a drive formatted with NTFS5. You can load programs to that folder, or use it to store data files or backed-up system files. The process is: add a second physical drive to a PC, convert it to a dynamic disk, create a volume on it, and mount the volume to a folder on the C: drive. To create a mount point, alternate-click an unallocated section of a dynamic disk, select New Volume, and select a mount point rather than a drive letter on the second screen of the New Volume Wizard. Browse to a blank folder on an NTFS-formatted drive or create a new folder.

Format Hard Drives

- Every partition and volume must be formatted before it can hold data. The official term for this is high-level formatting. Formatting wipes out all data on the drive, creates a file system, and makes the root directory. C:\ is the root directory of the primary master hard drive with a primary partition. Every version of Windows comes with a built-in formatting utility, usually called FORMAT.
- Current versions of Windows support four

[illegible]

is smaller than 512 bytes, the rest of the sector goes to waste. If the file is larger than 512 byes, the OS continues the file in another unused sector, repeating this process until the file is completely stored. The last sector is rarely filled completely, leaving some wasted space, called slack.

- MS-DOS version 2.1 first supported the file allocation table (FAT). The FAT is a data structure similar to a two-column spreadsheet that tracks where data is stored on the hard drive. Floppy drives use 12-bit file allocation tables.
- Every version of Windows completely supports FAT16. FAT16 uses only 16 bits (four hex characters) on the left-hand side of the FAT "spreadsheet," for a maximum of 64 K (2^{16} or 65,536) locations and up to a 32 MB partition. As hard drives grew in size, FAT 16 added a feature called clustering that treats a set of contiguous sectors as a single FAT unit. Clusters (file allocation units) allow a maximum partition size of 2 GB. Today the term FAT16 always means FAT with clustering.
- Since FAT16, a cluster, rather than a sector, has been the basic unit of storage. Unlike sectors, the size of a cluster is not fixed; it changes with the size of the partition. Because FAT16 still only supported a maximum of 64 K storage units, the formatting program set the number of sectors in each cluster according to the size of the partition.

The larger the partition, the more sectors per cluster, and the more wasted space.

- After the format program creates the FAT, it tests each sector and places a special status code (FFF7) in the FAT for any bad sectors so they won't be used. Good sectors are marked as 0000. When an application saves a file, the OS starts writing the file to the first space marked as good. If the entire file fits within one cluster, the OS places an end-of-file marker, indicated by the code FFFF, in the cluster's status area.
- When the OS adds the filename to the folder list, it includes the number of the cluster where the file is stored. If the file requires more than one cluster, the OS searches for the next open cluster and places the number of the next cluster in the status, filling and adding clusters until the entire file is saved. The last cluster then receives the end-of-file code (FFFF). When the OS retrieves a file, it gets the number of the starting cluster from the folder list and then uses the FAT to move to the next cluster, continuing this process until it sees the end-of-file code.
- A fragmented file is one that is stored in noncontiguous clusters. Fragmentation occurs when files are revised and must continue to the next available cluster or when files are erased, freeing up clusters. Excess fragmentation slows down the system during hard drive reads and writes because the read/write heads must travel all over the hard drive to retrieve a single file. Every version of Windows, except for NT, comes with a Disk Defragmenter that can rearrange files into neat contiguous chunks.
- With Windows 95 OSR2, Microsoft unveiled the totally new and improved FAT32 file format. Using 32 bits to describe each cluster, FAT32 supports partitions up to 2 terabytes. FAT 32 creates smaller clusters for more efficient storage.
- Windows NT 4.0 formats a drive with NT file system (NTFS) version 4, an extremely robust and secure file system, or with FAT, its name for FAT16. NTFS offers four major benefits over FAT16. (1) NTFS utilizes an enhanced FAT called the Master File Table (MFT). (2) NTFS can provide security for individual files and folders through an Access Control List (ACL) and permissions. (3) NTFS4 can compress individual files and folders to save space on a hard drive, though this may slow down access time. (4) Disk Administrator can extend, mirror and span drives.
- Windows 2000 and Windows XP use NTFS5. Using the encrypting file system (EFS), NTFS can encrypt a single file, a folder, and a folder full of files. Encryption makes files unreadable, not hidden. NTFS5 Disk Quotas set limits on drive space usage, an important feature for PCs shared by many users. Using its dynamic disk capabilities, NTFS5 can mount a volume as a folder on a drive formatted with NTFS5. The mounted volume can be formatted as FAT16, FAT32, or NTFS5. NTFS5 also allows you to adjust cluster sizes, extending the maximum capacity of an NTFS volume to 16 exabytes.
- You should choose the best file system your OS supports. If your system supports FAT32, use it. If you have Windows NT/2000/XP, choose NTFS.
- The Disk Administrator in Windows NT and the Disk Management console in Windows 2000/XP both perform disk formatting. Alternate-click the volume to format and select Format from the menu. To format a drive on a system without an OS, either boot to the OS CD-ROM and partition and format as part of installation of the operating system or boot to a floppy diskette in Windows 9*x* and format from the command prompt by typing **FORMAT X:** (where **X** is the letter of the drive that you want to format).

Maintain and Troubleshoot Hard Drives

- Hard drive maintenance can be broken down into two distinct functions: checking the disk occasionally for failed clusters and keeping data organized on the drive so that it can be accessed quickly.
- ScanDisk, one of the oldest PC utilities, checks for bad clusters on drives and seals them off to prevent the system from trying to place data in them. ScanDisk also attempts to fix invalid filenames and erase lost clusters that have no file names associated with them. In newer versions of Windows you access ScanDisk by clicking the Error-checking button in the Drive Properties dialog box. ScanDisk also attempts to fix invalid filenames and erase lost clusters that have no file names associated with them.
- To run ScanDisk in Windows 9*x*/Me, select Start | Programs | Accessories | System Tools | ScanDisk, or open My Computer, alternate-click the drive

you want to check, and select Properties. Select the Tools tab in the Drive Properties dialog box and click the Check Now button. To run Error-checking (a.k.a. ScanDisk) in Windows 2000/XP, open My Computer, alternate-click the drive you want to check, and select Properties. Select the Tools tab in the Drive Properties dialog box and click the Check Now button. In the Check Disk dialog box, check the box next to *Automatically fix file system errors*, but save the option to *Scan for and attempt recovery of bad sectors* for times when you actually suspect a problem. A reasonable maintenance plan would include running ScanDisk about once a week.

- The average hard drive is filled with unneeded files, such as the contents of the Recycle Bin, temporary Internet files stored when you browse the Web, Java and ActiveX applets stored by your browser, and temporary files that aren't deleted when an application is closed. Starting with Windows 98, a powerful tool called Disk Cleanup can remove these four types of unneeded files. Access Disk Cleanup in all versions of Windows by choosing Start | Program | Accessories | System Tools | Disk Cleanup. Run Disk Cleanup once a month.
- Common hard drive troubleshooting issues fall into three broad categories: installation, data corruption, and dying hard drives. Installation errors can happen at any of the four steps: connectivity, CMOS, partitioning, or formatting. When troubleshooting, you should walk back through each step and check for problems.
- Usually showing up at boot time, a connectivity error indicates that something isn't plugged in right or something became unplugged. Some connectivity errors are harmless, such as plugging the data cable in backwards for an IDE drive, while others, such as installing the power cable backwards, will destroy a drive. The IDE Autodetect function of your BIOS will not detect a drive unless everything is installed correctly, making it a great connectivity verifier. Some EIDE drives simply will not work on the same controller.
- Because autodetection handles most drives, you rarely get CMOS errors. Those that do occur fall into two groups: forgetting to run Autodetect and selecting the wrong sector translation in Autodetect. Two rules apply here: Always run Autodetect and always select LBA. If Autodetect fails to see the drive in question, it's probably a connectivity problem.
- Partitioning errors generally fall into two groups: failing to partition at all, and making the wrong size/type of partition. If you try to access a

error, while you'll get an "Invalid media" error from a C:\ prompt. Format the drive unless you're certain that the drive has already been formatted. Corrupted files can also create the "Invalid media" error.

- A "Trying to recover lost allocation unit" error during formatting means that Format has found a bad cluster and is trying to fix it. Modern EIDE drives hide a significant number of extra sectors that they use to replace bad sectors automatically, so if a drive generates a lot of "Trying to recover lost allocation unit" errors, you can bet that it's dying and needs to be replaced.
- If a newly installed drive fails to work, do a "mental reinstall." If the drive does not show up in the CMOS Autodetect, recheck the cables, master/slave settings, and power. If it shows up, make sure you remembered to partition and format the drive. Remember also that a drive must be made active to be bootable.
- Power surges, accidental shutdowns, corrupted install media, and viruses are among the causes of corrupted data in individual sectors. These errors usually show up while Windows is running. If core boot files become corrupted, you may see text errors at boot, such as "Cannot find COMMAND.COM," "Error loading operating system," or "Invalid BOOT.INI." Older systems may generate a "sector not found" error. The first

fix for any of these problems is to run ScanDisk (or Error-checking) or a similar third-party utility.

- To replace a single corrupt file, you must know the location of the numbered Windows CAB (cabinet) file that contains the file you need and how to extract the file from the CAB file. Use the EXTRACT program (Windows 95/98) or the EXPAND program (Windows 2000) to get a new copy of the missing file from the CAB files on the installation CD-ROM disk. Both EXTRACT and EXPAND search all CAB files to find the file you specify, then expand it and place it in the C:\ folder.
- Corrupted boot sectors show up as boot lockups, missing drive letters in My Computer, and errors such as "Invalid Partition" or "Bad or Missing Command Interpreter." Always run an antivirus program first to insure that a virus has not attacked your boot sector. If no virus is present, you need to replace the boot sector. If you made a backup of the boot sector with the Ultimate Boot Disk or another utility, you can simply boot from the disk and reinstall the MBR. If you don't have an MBR, you will probably have to repartition the hard drive and do a complete reinstall. As a last ditch effort, you can boot from a floppy and try the FDISK/ MBR command.
- Almost all drives today have built-in error correction code (ECC) that constantly checks the drive for bad sectors. If it detects a bad sector, it marks the sector as bad in the drive's internal error map so that it is invisible to the system. If the ECC finds a bad sector, however, you will get a corrupted data error when the computer attempts to read the bad sector. Disk checkers fix this problem most of the time.
- The powerful SpinRite utility from Gibson Research marks sectors as bad or good more accurately than ECC and does not disturb the data. When it finds a bad sector with data in it, SpinRite uses powerful algorithms that usually recover the data on all but the most badly damaged sectors. However, SpinRite does not work on NTFS partitions. Without SpinRite, you must use a low-level format program supplied by the hard-drive maker, which will wipe out all data on the drive.
- If a hard drive is truly damaged physically, it cannot be fixed. Physical problems manifest themselves in two ways: either the drive works properly but makes a lot of noise or the drive seems to disappear. If you hear a continuous high-pitched squeal, a series of clacks, a short pause, and then another series of clacks, or a continuous grinding or rumbling, your hard drive is about to die. Back up your critical data and replace the drive. If the drive that contains your operating system disappears, the system will lock up or you'll get the error message "No Boot Device Present" when you try to reboot. If the problem is with a second drive, it will simply stop showing up in My Computer.
- If your drive makes noise or disappears, first run the System Setup program to see if Autodetect sees the drive. If it does, the drive doesn't have a physical problem. If Autodetect fails, shut down the system and remove the ribbon cable, but leave the power cable attached. Restart the system and listen to the drive. If the drive spins up, the drive is getting good power, which usually means the drive is good. Next, check for an unplugged power cord or incorrectly set jumpers. If the drive doesn't spin up, try another power connector. If it still doesn't spin up and you've triple-checked the jumpers and ribbon cable, you have a problem with the onboard electronics, and the drive is dead.

Key Terms

Active partition *(336)*
Autodetection *(377)*
Basic disks *(353)*
Boot sector *(336)*
Cluster *(361)*
Data structure *(360)*
Defragmentation *(365)*
Disk Cleanup *(376)*
Disk Management *(350)*
Dynamic disks *(353)*
Encrypting file system (EFS) *(367)*
Error correction code (ECC) *(382)*
Extended partition *(338)*
EXTRACT *(380)*
EXPAND *(380)*
FAT32 *(365)*
FDISK *(337)*
File allocation table (FAT) *(360)*
File allocation unit *(361)*
File system *(335)*
Formatting *(359)*
Fragmentation *(363)*
High-level formatting *(359)*
Master boot record (MBR) *(336)*
Master File Table (MFT) *(366)*
Mirrored volume *(357)*
Mount point *(357)*

- **NT File System (NTFS)** *(365)*
- **NTFS4** *(366)*
- **NTFS5** *(367)*
- **Operating system (OS)** *(335)*
- **Partition** *(335)*
- **Partition table** *(336)*
- **Primary partition** *(336)*
- **RAID-5 volume** *(357)*
- **ScanDisk** *(372)*
- **Simple volume** *(353)*
- **Spanned volume** *(355)*
- **Stripe set** *(356)*
- **Volume boot sector** *(336)*
- **Volume** *(353)*

Key Term Quiz

Use the Key Terms list to complete the sentences that follow. Not all the terms will be used.

1. The MBR checks the partition table to find the __________ or bootable partition.
2. If a file is not stored in contiguous clusters, you

5. You can issue the command FDISK/MBR to repair a bad _____________.
6. __________ is the tool included with Windows that attempts to fix invalid filenames, erases lost clusters, and seals off bad clusters.
7. ________ is a great way to verify that a drive is installed correctly.
8. If an operating system file has become corrupted

Multiple-Choice Quiz

1. Windows 2000 and XP can use all of the following file systems *except* __________.
   - **A.** FAT16
   - **B.** FAT32
   - **C.** NTFS4
   - **D.** NTFS5
2. The Disk Cleanup utility removes all of the following types of unneeded files *except* _______.
   - **A.** Temporary Internet files
   - **B.** Temporary files left when an application is closed
   - **C.** Backup copies of files
   - **D.** Deleted files that remain in the Recycle Bin
3. The maximum number of logical drives that a hard disk may have is _________.
   - **A.** 2
   - **B.** 4
   - **C.** 16
   - **D.** 24
4. Which of the following statements is true about hard drive connectivity problems?
   - **A.** If you plug the ribbon cable in backwards, it will destroy the drive.
   - **B.** If you plug the power cable in backwards, it will destroy the drive.
   - **C.** If you plug the ribbon cable in backwards, the drive will still work.
   - **D.** Connectivity problems are usually related to operating system problems.
5. Which of the following correctly identifies the four possible entries in a file allocation table.
   - **A.** Filename, date, time, size
   - **B.** Number of the starting cluster, number of the ending cluster, number of used clusters, number of available clusters
   - **C.** An end of file marker, a bad sector marker, code indicating the cluster is available, the number of the cluster where the next part of the file is stored

- **D.** Filename, folder location, starting cluster number, ending cluster number

6. If you get an error that indicates that the drive is not accessible or you receive an "Invalid media" error, it probably means that the drive ____________.
   - **A.** Has not been partitioned
   - **B.** Has not been set to active
   - **C.** Has not been formatted
   - **D.** Has died

7. All of the following may be advantages of partitioning a hard drive into more than one partition *except* __________.
   - **A.** It enables a single hard drive to store more than one operating system.
   - **B.** It makes backups simpler.
   - **C.** It enables PCs to use larger physical hard drives than the limit of the OS.
   - **D.** It allows two physical hard disks to function as a single volume.

8. If you have four drives, each with a single primary partition, which of the following is the correct sequence when assigning alphabetical drive letters to the drives?
   - **A.** Primary master, primary slave, secondary master, secondary slave
   - **B.** Primary master, secondary master, primary slave, secondary slave
   - **C.** Secondary master, secondary slave, primary master, primary slave
   - **D.** Secondary master, primary master, secondary slave, primary slave

9. Instead of the old FDISK program of DOS and Windows 9*x*, Windows NT uses the ________ while Windows 2000 and XP use (the) ___________ to partition and format a drive.
   - **A.** ScanDisk, Format
   - **B.** Disk Administrator, Disk Management console
   - **C.** Disk Management console, Disk Administrator
   - **D.** System Commander, SpinRite

10. Because NTFS views individual files and folders as objects, it can provide security for those objects through a(n) ____________.
    - **A.** Encryption
    - **B.** ECC
    - **C.** Access Control List
    - **D.** MFT

11. Which of these operating systems allows dynamic drives?
    - **A.** DOS and Windows 3.*x*
    - **B.** Windows 9*x* and ME
    - **C.** Windows NT and 2000
    - **D.** Windows 2000 and XP

12. Which of the following statements is true about extended partitions?
    - **A.** They are optional.
    - **B.** They are assigned drive letters when they are created.
    - **C.** They may be set to Active.
    - **D.** Each drive must have at least one extended partition.

13. The maximum number of partitions on a single hard drive is ________, but you can have only ________ extended partition(s).
    - **A.** one, one
    - **B.** two, one
    - **C.** four, one
    - **D.** eight, two

14. Which of the following correctly identifies the sequence in which partitions should be removed using FDISK?
    - **A.** Primary partition, extended partition, logical drives in the extended partition
    - **B.** Logical drives in the extended partition, extended partition, primary partition
    - **C.** Primary partition on the primary master, partition on the secondary master, extended partition on the primary master, extended partition on the secondary master
    - **D.** It does not matter; partitions may be removed in any sequence.

15. Which of the following drives cannot become part of a dynamic drive?
    - A. The primary master
    - B. The secondary master
    - C. The primary slave
    - D. The secondary slave

Essay Quiz

1. Your tech department services an office of mixed Windows 98SE and Windows XP Professional systems. Your boss just hired four new interns and has asked you to explain to them the differences between the tools used to set up hard drives. Write a few paragraphs comparing and

some of the benefits of NTFS over FAT32.

3. An employee complains to you that his hard drive has started making a high-pitched squeal that is driving him crazy. What do you tell him about the problem?

4. Sonya just installed a new hard drive, the second one on her system, but she can't access it. What advice can you give her to solve her problem?

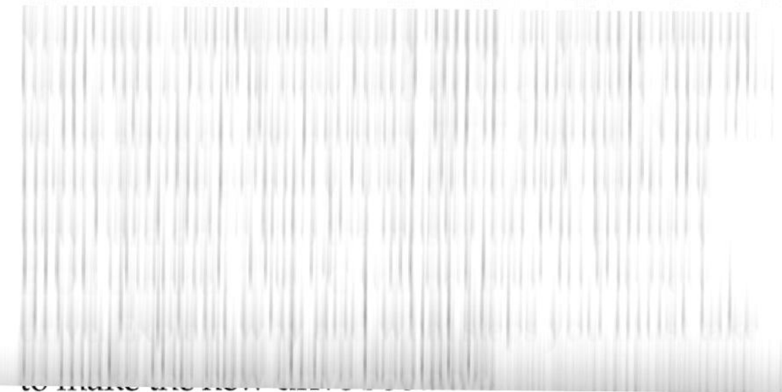

Lab Projects

• Lab Project 11.1

Grab a test system with multiple drives and experiment with the partitioning tools in Windows, both FDISK and Disk Management. If you have Windows NT in your lab, you get the added bonus of working with Disk Administrator! Create various partition combinations, such as all primary, or all extended with logical drives. Make basic disks into dynamic disks and create volumes that span multiple drives. Add to them. You get the idea—experiment and have fun!

• Lab Project 11.2

Partitioning gets all the glory and exposure in tech classes because, frankly, it's cool to be able to do some of the things possible with Windows 2000 and Windows XP Disk Management console! But the experienced tech does not forget about the other half of drive preparation: formatting. Each OS except for the early versions of Windows 95 offers you at least two different file systems. In this lab, you'll put them through their paces.

In one or more OSs, partition a drive with two equal partitions and format one as FAT32 and the other as NTFS (assuming Windows 2000/XP) or FAT16 and FAT32 (assuming Windows 9x). Then get a couple of monster files (>50 MB) and move them to those partitions. Did you notice any difference in transfer speed? Examine the drives in My Computer. Do they show the same amount of used space?

chapter 12

Understanding Windows

"Technically, Windows is an 'operating system,' which means that it supplies your computer with the basic commands that it needs to suddenly, with no warning whatsoever, stop operating."

—Dave Barry

In this chapter, you will learn how to

- **Identify and explain the basic functions of an Operating System**
- **Identify the features and characteristics common to all Windows PCs**
- **Identify and differentiate the features and characteristics of Windows 9x/Me**
- **Identify and differentiate the features and characteristics of Windows NT/2000/XP**

An operating system provides the fundamental link between the hardware that makes up the PC and the user. Without an operating system, all the greatest, slickest PC hardware in the world is but so much copper, silicon, and gold wrapped up as a big, beige paperweight. The operating system creates the interface between Human and Machine, enabling us to unleash the astonishing power locked up in the sophisticated electronics of the PC to create amazing pictures, games, documents, business tools, medical miracles, and much more.

All operating systems are not created equal. They don't look the same or, on the surface, act the same. But every OS shares essential characteristics that, once you have the concepts, help lead you to answers when troubleshooting. "I know that the OS formerly known as Y must enable me to access programs, therefore no matter how odd the interface, the option must be here!"

This chapter starts with an analysis of all operating systems, examining the functions and traits they all share. You'll see the two most common implementations of an OS, the command line and the graphical interface. At that point we'll leave the historical/conceptual issues behind and delve into the features common to every version of Microsoft Windows (or at least those covered on the A+ Operating System Technologies exam). The chapter finishes with an in-depth examination of the core structures of Windows 9x/Me and Windows NT/2000/XP systems. Let's get started.

Historical/Conceptual

■ Functions of the Operating System

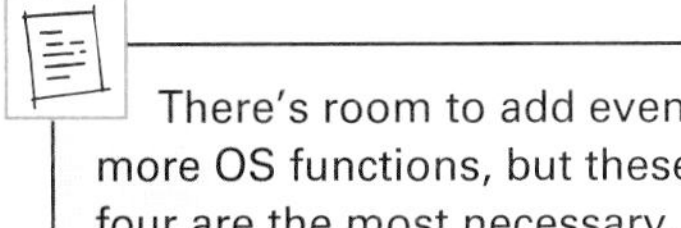

There's room to add even more OS functions, but these four are the most necessary.

An operating system (OS) is a program that performs four basic functions. First, it must communicate, or at least provide a method for other programs to communicate, with the hardware of the PC. It's up to the OS to access the hard drives, respond to the keyboard, and output data to the monitor. Second, the OS must create a **user interface** —a visual representation of the computer on the monitor that makes sense to the people using the computer. The OS must also take advantage of standard input devices, such as

- Provide a user interface
- Provide a structure for access to applications
- Enable users to manipulate programs and data

Operating System Traits

To achieve these four functions, all OSs share certain common traits. First, an OS works only with a particular type of processor. The Intel and AMD "X86" line of CPUs heavily dominates today's PCs, but other platforms use different CPUs that are completely incompatible with the Intel and AMD lines. The most obvious example of the latter is the Motorola Power PC, the CPU inside Macintosh computers. The OS must understand important aspects of the CPU, such as the amount of memory the CPU can handle, what modes of operation it is capable of performing, and the commands needed to perform any operation. Certain OSs, such as Linux, can run on more than one type of processor, but they achieve this by having versions for each type of processor they support.

Second, an OS always starts running immediately after the PC has finished its POST, taking control of the PC. The OS continues running until the PC is rebooted or turned off. The OS cannot be turned off unless the PC is also turned off.

Third, *application* programs, such as word processors, spreadsheets, and web browsers, cannot run on a PC without an OS. Therefore, programmers write application programs to function under the control of a certain OS. Table 12.1 shows a selection of OSs and applications written specifically for them. You cannot write one version of an application that works under different OSs. The creators of an OS always provide a "rule book" that tells programmers how to write programs for a particular OS. These rule books are known as *application programming interfaces* (APIs).

Tech Tip

Java

The popularity of new programming paradigms such as Java might make some folks want to challenge the idea that every application must come in different versions for different operating systems. Although a piece of Java code may run on any computer, each computer must have some programming installed that can interpret that Java code. That programming is OS specific.

Table 12.1 Operating Systems and Applications

Operating System	Application
Macintosh OS X	Microsoft Office v. X
Windows XP	Microsoft Office XP
Red Hat Linux	Sun StarOffice 6.0

Last, an OS must have flexibility and provide some facility for using new software or hardware that might be installed. It just wouldn't do, for example, to be stuck with the same game year after year! (See Figure 12.1.)

Communicating with Hardware

In earlier chapters you learned that the system BIOS, stored on some type of non-volatile memory (ROM or Flash ROM) on the motherboard, stores programs that know how to talk to the most basic and important parts of the computer. These include the hard drives, floppy drives, keyboard, and basic video. The OS must work with the system BIOS to deal with these devices. If users want to access the hard drive to retrieve a program, the OS must take the request and pass it to the appropriate hard drive BIOS instruction that tells the drive to send the program to RAM. Plus, if for some reason the BIOS lacks the ability to perform its function, the OS should bypass the system BIOS and talk to the piece of hardware directly. Most recent OSs, including Windows, skip the system BIOS and talk directly to almost every piece of hardware.

• **Figure 12.1** Progress is good: HalfLife II above Wolfenstein 3-D

For the OS to take control of a new piece of hardware, it needs to communicate with that hardware. Therefore, the OS needs a method to add the programming necessary to talk to that device, preferably in some simple and flexible way. Most OSs use device drivers to add this necessary code. An OS maker (such as Microsoft) tells hardware makers how to create these programs (and makes money selling the development tools) and also creates a method of adding the device driver to the OS code. Because makers of a particular hardware usually supply the device drivers with the hardware, and because drivers act something like BIOS, this solution can be jokingly, although accurately, thought of as BYOB (Bring Your Own BIOS).

Because the OS handles communicating with hardware, it should provide some type of error handling or at least error notification. If someone attempts to use a piece of hardware that isn't working properly, the OS should either try to fix the problem or at least attempt to communicate with the device a few more times. If the device continues to fail, the OS should provide an error screen to notify the user of the problem.

Cross Check

Working with BIOS

In Chapter 5, you learned that all hardware needs BIOS.

1. What are the two ways for a device to BYOB?
2. What are the primary tools or programs for working with BIOS?

Creating a User Interface

Most users have fairly straightforward needs. First, they want to know which applications are available; second, they want easy access to those programs; and third, they want to be able to save the data they generate with some easy-to-use label by which they can retrieve it later.

[illegible]

small door. Wonder why the salesperson looked in the shoe? To read an inventory code that shoe manufacturers print inside every shoe.

Have you ever seen the back of a shoe store? It's scary. All the shoes are organized, not by style, color, gender, or age, but by inventory code. The salesperson reads the inventory code to know where to look for that particular shoe. Without understanding the code, no one would know where to search for a pair of shoes, but it's the best way to organize an inventory of 25,000 pairs of shoes. What a customer sees in the store is not all the shoes as they really are in the back, but a "user interface" of what's available. The front display in the store—the user interface—creates a pretty, easy to use, although entirely unrealistic display of the shoes in stock (Figure 12.2).

A computer's user interface performs the same function by offering to the user a display of the programs and data on the PC. The customers (users) look at the display (the user interface) and tell the salesperson (the OS) what they want, without ever really knowing how all the shoes (programs and data) are really organized.

Finishing the analogy, the shoe store's displays are not permanent. Salespeople can easily add shoes and replace old displays. They can change a rack of men's shoes into a rack of women's shoes, for example, relatively easily. Like the shoe store, a user interface should also be flexible and scalable, depending on the system in which it is installed.

Figure 12.2 Shoe display

Accessing and Supporting Programs

An OS must enable users to start a program. This is a simple but important concept. When a program starts, the user interface must disappear and allow the application to take over the screen. If the OS is still visible, it must move away from the main part of the screen and set itself to the top, bottom, or sides. While the application runs, the OS must still provide whatever access to hardware the application needs, such as changing the screen, saving data, or printing. If a program loses control, the OS should have some way to stop it or at least to recognize what's happening and generate an error message. Finally, the OS should instantly return to the user interface when the application shuts down, so that the user may choose another application.

Organizing and Manipulating Programs and Data

A single PC might store hundreds of programs and thousands of separate pieces of data. Simply making all the programs and data visible would be like taking all the shoes in the back of the shoe store and setting them neatly on the display room floor. Yes, you could locate shoes in this fashion, but it would be an overly complicated mess. Much better to have some method of organizing the programs and data.

Okay, I hear you saying, I'll buy into that, but how? Let's break it down. First question: <holds up chunk of binary code> Is this a program or a piece of data used by a program? Read the label! The OS must provide a label or name for each program and each individual piece of data that identifies it as either a program or a piece of data. If it's data, there must also be some method by which the OS can identify what type of program uses it.

Next question: How can I distinguish between the various places I might store this chunk of data or program? Each floppy, hard, and CD-ROM drive needs some sort of identifier, again provided by the OS. It can be as simple as a letter of the alphabet or as complex as a fully descriptive phrase.

Third question: <picks up several more chunks of data> How can I make sure that related chunks of data/programs are stored in a way that permits efficient retrieval and alteration? Data and programs must be stored in distinct groups on each drive, and the OS user interface must enable users to interact with each of these groups individually. Users must be able to open and close these groups, and copy, move, or delete both programs and data. Finally, a good OS will have a user interface that enables users to perform these functions easily and accurately, especially in the case of deletions. Clearly, a good OS has a lot of work to do!

Operating System Implementations

Operating systems for the PC come in two basic varieties, **command line interface** and **graphical user interface (GUI)**. A command line interface enables you to type commands directly to the OS and, if you type them correctly, the OS responds or carries out your command. A GUI (pronounced "gooey"), in contrast, draws pictures on the monitor screen with which you interact using a mouse or similar device. In particular, GUIs use tiny pictures called **icons** to represent programs and data structures. By clicking on icons and other graphical features like menus and buttons, you can send commands to the OS. Let's look at the most famous of the Microsoft command line interfaces, DOS, and then turn to graphical interfaces.

Why look at DOS? In truth, DOS as a standalone OS has been dead for many years, but every tech needs to understand the command line interface. Not only is the command line interface still in use in all versions of Windows, it is an essential tool in the tech's arsenal. None of the discussion that follows is useless trivia. In fact, the command line is so important to a tech that I devote the entire next chapter to it!

Command Line Interface

I know that many of you will find this hard to believe, but for almost one half of the 20-plus years of the PC era, Microsoft Windows did not exist. Instead, all PCs—or at least the overwhelming majority of PCs—ran on the operating system of your forefathers, the now almost forgotten Disk Operating System (DOS).

... for us to click to get work done ...

took up the whole screen, much like a high-end game in Windows today. No windows appeared, such as those you see on modern PCs. When a DOS application was running, the only thing you could see on your screen was the application—it was as if DOS disappeared. When you closed the DOS application, however, the prompt reappeared.

Most people don't even think twice about the idea of running multiple programs in today's systems, but Microsoft designed DOS to run with CPUs that could support only one running program at a time. In the DOS days, if

I need to make a clarification about DOS and graphics. While it is correct that DOS was a character-based operating system, DOS applications themselves could be graphical. The DOS application itself had to know how to talk to the video card. Back in the old days when ...

... in Windows anymore!

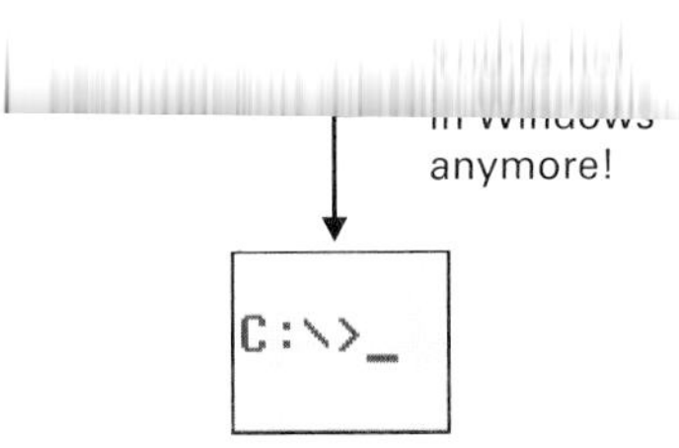

Figure 12.3 Typical DOS prompt

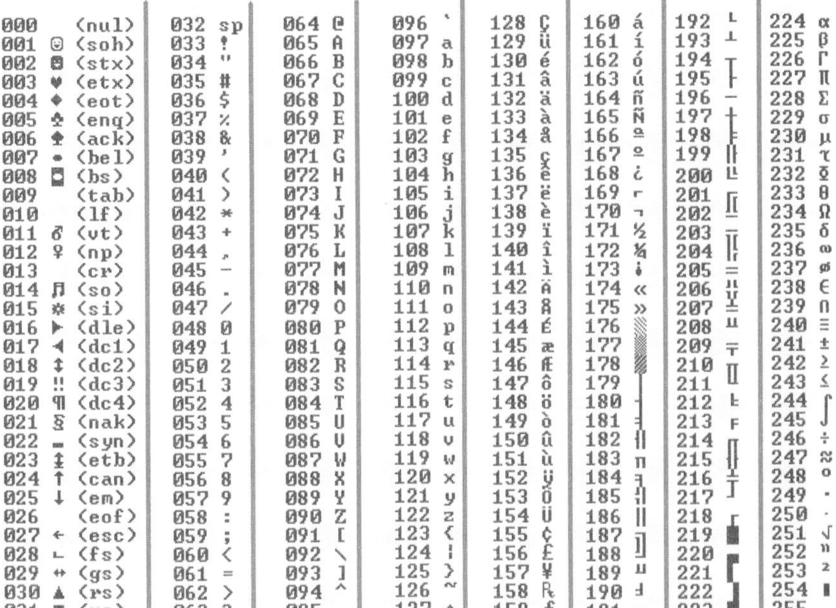

Code	Char	Code	Char	Code	Char	Code	Char	Code	Char	Code	Char	Code	Char	Code	Char
000	(nul)	032	sp	064	@	096	`	128	Ç	160	á	192	└	224	α
001	☺ (soh)	033	!	065	A	097	a	129	ü	161	í	193	┴	225	ß
002	☻ (stx)	034	"	066	B	098	b	130	é	162	ó	194	┬	226	Γ
003	♥ (etx)	035	#	067	C	099	c	131	â	163	ú	195	├	227	π
004	♦ (eot)	036	$	068	D	100	d	132	ä	164	ñ	196	─	228	Σ
005	♣ (enq)	037	%	069	E	101	e	133	à	165	Ñ	197	┼	229	σ
006	♠ (ack)	038	&	070	F	102	f	134	å	166	ª	198	╞	230	µ
007	• (bel)	039	'	071	G	103	g	135	ç	167	º	199	╟	231	τ
008	◘ (bs)	040	(	072	H	104	h	136	ê	168	¿	200	╚	232	Φ
009	(tab)	041	)	073	I	105	i	137	ë	169	⌐	201	╔	233	Θ
010	(lf)	042	*	074	J	106	j	138	è	170	¬	202	╩	234	Ω
011	♂ (vt)	043	+	075	K	107	k	139	ï	171	½	203	╦	235	δ
012	♀ (np)	044	,	076	L	108	l	140	î	172	¼	204	╠	236	∞
013	(cr)	045	-	077	M	109	m	141	ì	173	¡	205	═	237	φ
014	♫ (so)	046	.	078	N	110	n	142	Ä	174	«	206	╬	238	ε
015	☼ (si)	047	/	079	O	111	o	143	Å	175	»	207	╧	239	∩
016	► (dle)	048	0	080	P	112	p	144	É	176	░	208	╨	240	≡
017	◄ (dc1)	049	1	081	Q	113	q	145	æ	177	▒	209	╤	241	±
018	↕ (dc2)	050	2	082	R	114	r	146	Æ	178	▓	210	╥	242	≥
019	‼ (dc3)	051	3	083	S	115	s	147	ô	179	│	211	╙	243	≤
020	¶ (dc4)	052	4	084	T	116	t	148	ö	180	┤	212	╘	244	⌠
021	§ (nak)	053	5	085	U	117	u	149	ò	181	╡	213	╒	245	⌡
022	▬ (syn)	054	6	086	V	118	v	150	û	182	╢	214	╓	246	÷
023	↨ (etb)	055	7	087	W	119	w	151	ù	183	╖	215	╫	247	≈
024	↑ (can)	056	8	088	X	120	x	152	ÿ	184	╕	216	╪	248	°
025	↓ (em)	057	9	089	Y	121	y	153	Ö	185	╣	217	┘	249	∙
026	(eof)	058	:	090	Z	122	z	154	Ü	186	║	218	┌	250	·
027	← (esc)	059	;	091	[	123	{	155	¢	187	╗	219	█	251	√
028	∟ (fs)	060	<	092	\	124	¦	156	£	188	╝	220	▄	252	ⁿ
029	↔ (gs)	061	=	093	]	125	}	157	¥	189	╜	221	▌	253	²
030	▲ (rs)	062	>	094	^	126	~	158	₧	190	╛	222	▐	254	■
031	▼ (us)	063	?	095	_	127	⌂	159	ƒ	191	┐	223	▀	255	

Figure 12.4 ASCII character set

To run a program from a command line, you must know both its name and its location. Chapter 13 explains how to move around your computer from a prompt. The A+ Certification exams expect you to know how!

```
C:\>type config.sys
DEVICE=C:\DOS\SETVER.EXE
DEVICE=C:\DOS\HIMEM.SYS
DOS=HIGH
FILES=30

C:\>_
```

• **Figure 12.5** CONFIG.SYS

you wanted to run a program and another one was running, you had to stop the first program before you started up the second.

But for all of its limitations, DOS did provide the four major OS functions. It provided hardware access in two ways. First, a special file called IO.SYS acted as the intermediary to the most common hardware such as the keyboard, floppy drive, hard drive, and video. Second, you could copy special files, called *device drivers*, to the hard drive and then use a text file called CONFIG.SYS to load the drivers. Figure 12.5 shows a typical CONFIG.SYS file from the DOS days.

DOS also created a user interface—the venerable DOS prompt—via a file called COMMAND.COM. COMMAND.COM utilized a moderately complex set of commands and syntax, but once you learned how to use it, COMMAND.COM was quite powerful.

DOS consisted of only three main files: IO.SYS, MSDOS.SYS, and COMMAND.COM. You installed DOS just by booting to a DOS floppy disk and running a command called SYS.COM. This program copied the three files to the hard drive—not much to install!

DOS came with a large number of support programs. The FDISK and FORMAT utilities that you worked with in Chapter 11, for example, came with every version of DOS. These many utilities were almost always copied to a folder called C:\DOS. Figure 12.6 shows typical contents of the DOS folder. The majority of these programs are still used in every version of Windows. See Chapter 13 to learn how to use some of the more popular commands.

DOS used two configuration files: CONFIG.SYS and AUTOEXEC.BAT. As mentioned earlier, CONFIG.SYS was used to load device drivers and set various operating system environment variables. AUTOEXEC.BAT was just a text file containing a list of DOS commands that you wanted to execute every time the computer started. The .BAT extension indicates a *batch file*, which works sort of like a program, enabling you to run commands automatically that you would otherwise have to sit down at a monitor and type in yourself. Basically, you store a list of commands in the batch file, and at some predetermined time or event, the OS opens the batch file and runs the commands stored inside. While AUTOEXEC.BAT was designed to run automatically at boot, you could also make your own batch files. In the DOS days, a typical PC was stuffed with batch files. Batch files are still widely used by the people who support computer systems, for instance to run a series of backup jobs in the middle of the night.

```
 Volume in drive C is MS-DOS_6
 Volume Serial Number is 2F0C-5B0D
 Directory of C:\DOS

.            <DIR>          08-12-03  11:24a
..           <DIR>          08-12-03  11:24a
ATTRIB   EXE        11,208 05-31-94   6:22a
CHKDSK   EXE        12,241 05-31-94   6:22a
COUNTRY  SYS        26,936 05-31-94   6:22a
COUNTRY  TXT        15,920 05-31-94   6:22a
DEBUG    EXE        15,718 05-31-94   6:22a
DOSSETUP INI         3,114 05-31-94   6:22a
DRVSPACE BIN        66,294 05-31-94   6:22a
EDIT     COM           413 05-31-94   6:22a
EXPAND   EXE        16,129 05-31-94   6:22a
FDISK    EXE        29,336 05-31-94   6:22a
FORMAT   COM        22,974 05-31-94   6:22a
KEYB     COM        15,750 05-31-94   6:22a
KEYBOARD SYS        34,598 05-31-94   6:22a
MEM      EXE        32,502 05-31-94   6:22a
NLSFUNC  EXE         7,036 05-31-94   6:22a
README   TXT        60,646 05-31-94   6:22a
NETWORKS TXT        17,465 05-31-94   6:22a
Press any key to continue . . .
```

• **Figure 12.6** Typical contents of DOS folder

Graphical User Interface

Many people who use Microsoft Windows assume that *it* is the computer's OS. A GUI, however, is not necessarily also an OS. A GUI translates your interaction with graphical elements like icons into commands understandable to an OS, which actually does the work. GUIs are implemented in many different ways. Some OSs, such as Apple's OS 9, have GUIs built into them as integral parts of the OS. In other words, a C:\ prompt is not an option on any Apple computer that uses OS 9. Everything, from starting programs to installing hard drives, is done from the built-in GUI. OS 9 is a completely graphical OS.

Macintosh OS X, on the other hand, is built on top of UNIX, one of the most powerful command line interface OSs ever created. To be an OS X tech, therefore, you have to learn the command line. Windows 9*x* is a powerful GUI built on top of a command line interface OS, DOS. Windows NT, 2000 and XP, in contrast, are GUI OSs with powerful command line interfaces built in. All these variations will become clearer as you work with the various OSs. The bottom line is that a GUI isn't always an OS, and having a GUI OS does not mean you can't have a powerful command line as well!

Common Windows Features and Characteristics

You'll find it right on the home page, first on the list of Top Ten Requested Links!

get to the underlying structure of the two families of Windows (Table 12.2) in the subsequent two sections of this chapter. Let's look at the common user interface, tech-oriented utilities, and typical OS folders.

User Interface

Windows offers a set of utilities, or *interfaces,* that every user should know how and why to access. If every user should know, then certainly every A+ certified tech should know as well! Let's take a quick tour of the typical Windows GUI.

Login

Every version of Windows supports multiple users on a single machine, and thus the starting point for any tour of the Windows user interface starts with the *login screen.* Figure 12.7 shows a Windows 2000 login screen; Figure 12.8 shows a graphical Windows XP login screen. The login screen for Windows 9*x*/Me looks very similar to the Windows 2000 screen, but it offers no security for the

Figure 12.7 Windows 2000 login screen

Table 12.2 Windows Families on the A+ OS Technologies Exam

9x Family	NT Family
Windows 95, 95A, 95 OSR2	Windows NT 4.0
Windows 98, 98 SE (Second Edition)	Windows 2000
Windows Me (Millennium Edition)	Windows XP

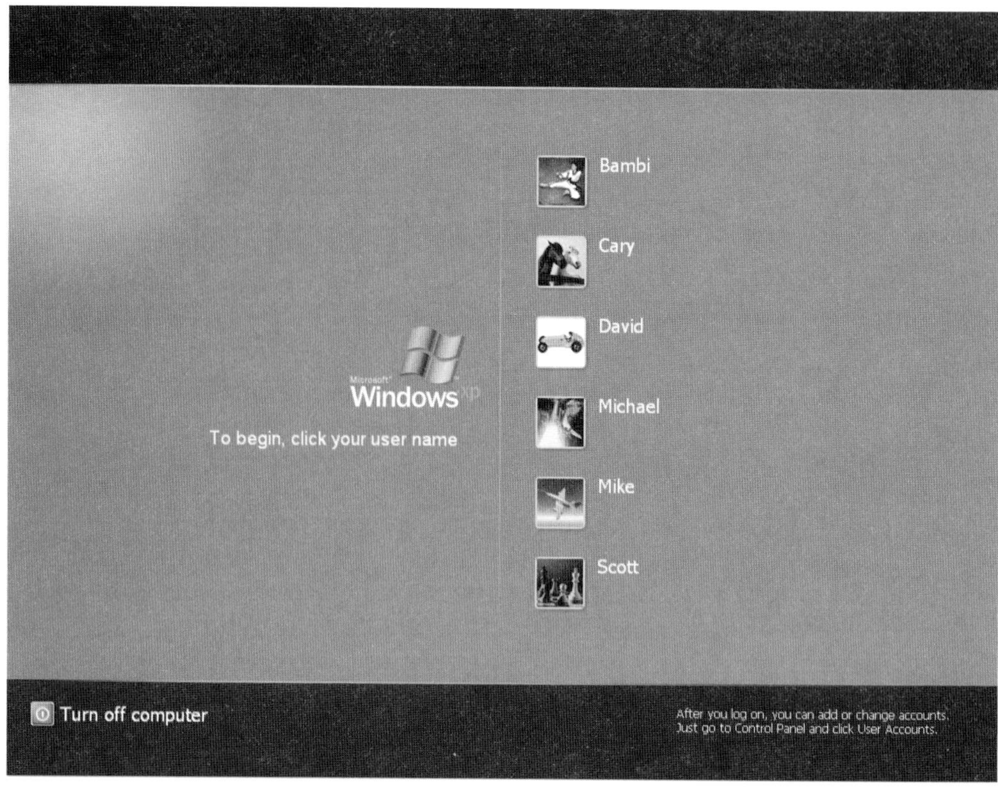

• **Figure 12.8** Windows XP login screen

system—you can simply press ESC to bypass the screen and access the OS. By requiring individual user logins, Windows NT/2000/XP, in contrast, offer a high degree of security.

Desktop

The Windows **desktop** is your primary interface to the computer. It's always there, underneath whatever else you have open to work on. The desktop analogy appeals to most people—we're used to sitting down at a desk to get work done. Figure 12.9 shows a nice, clean Windows 95 desktop. Note the icons on the left and the various graphical elements across the bottom. You can add folders and files to the desktop, and customize the background to change its color and/or add a picture. Most people like to do so—certainly, I do! As an example, here's a screen snapshot of my desktop from my home system—a Windows XP PC (Figure 12.10).

Taskbar and Start Menu

The **taskbar** runs along the bottom of all Windows desktops and includes up to four sections (depending on the version of Windows and your configuration). Starting at the left side, these are: a Start button, a Quick Launch area, a running programs area, and a system tray.

One of the main jobs of the taskbar is to show the Start button, probably the most clicked button on all Windows systems. You can find the Start button on the far left end of the taskbar (Figure 12.11). Clicking the Start button opens the **Start menu**, which enables you to see all programs loaded on the

> Although the taskbar by default sits at the bottom of the desktop, on Windows 2000/XP systems you may move it to any side: top, bottom, left, or right.

system and to start them. Click the Start button to bring up the Start menu. Now, move your mouse cursor onto All Programs. (Note that earlier versions of Windows called this menu Programs, rather than All Programs.) When the All Programs menu appears, move the cursor to the Accessories menu. Locate the Notepad program and click it, as shown in Figure 12.12. Later versions of Windows hide lesser-used menu options, so if you don't see Notepad, click the double down-ar-

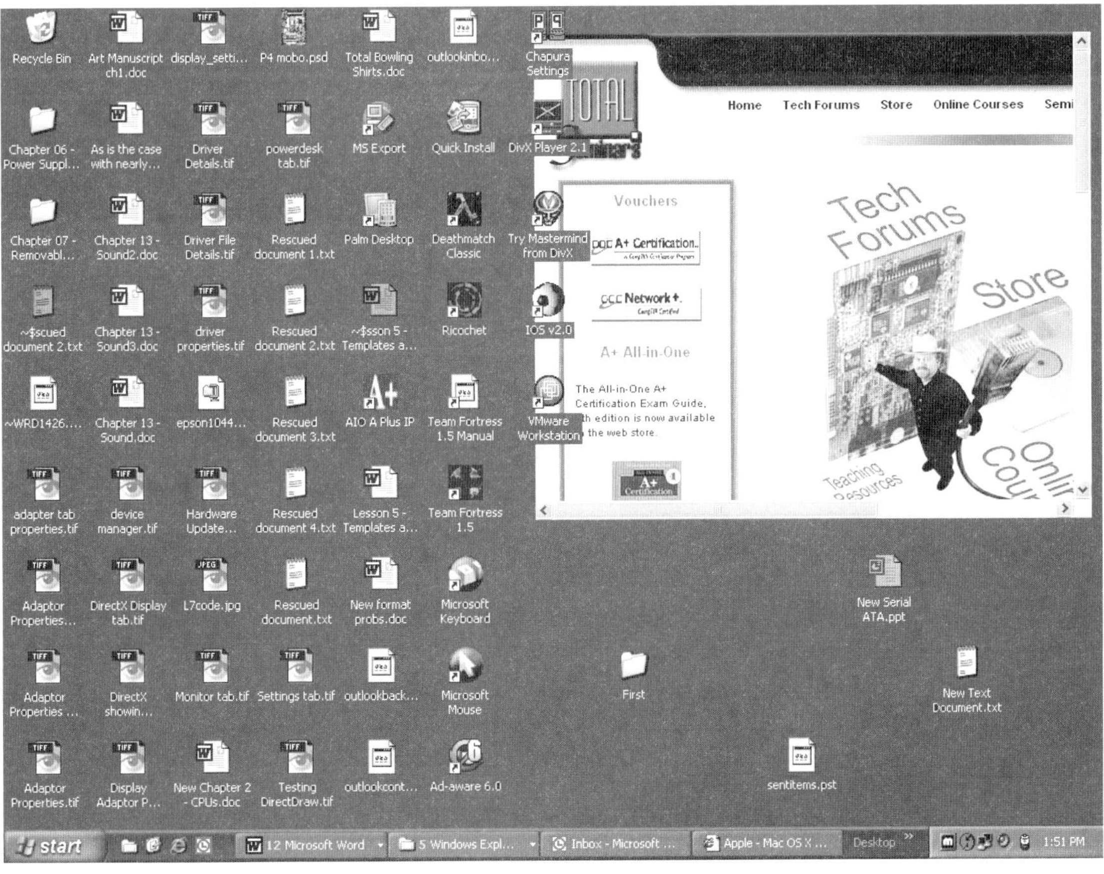

• **Figure 12.10** Mike's messy desktop

Figure 12.11 Start button

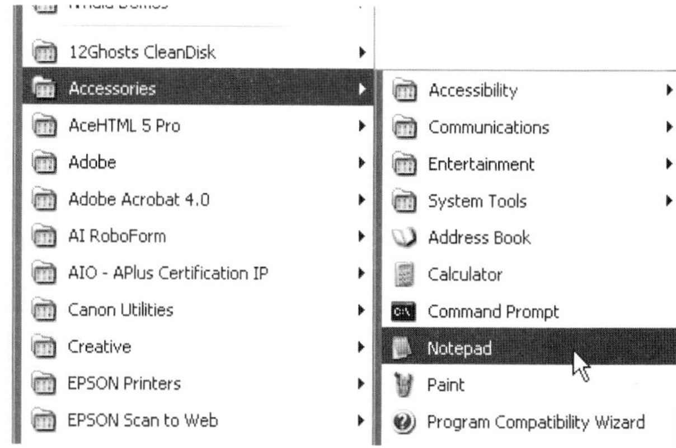

Figure 12.12 Opening Notepad in Windows XP

taskbar at the bottom of the screen. Most running programs will appear on the taskbar in this way. Close the Notepad program by clicking on the button with the "X" in the upper-right corner of the Notepad window. Look again at the taskbar to see that Notepad no longer appears there.

Now look all the way to the right end of the taskbar. We call this part of the taskbar the **system tray**. You will at a minimum see the current time displayed in the system tray, and on most Windows systems, you'll also see a number of small icons there. Figure 12.14 shows the system tray on my PC.

Tech Tip

General Rules of Clicking in Windows

Since we have so much clicking to do in this chapter, let's take a moment to reflect on what I lovingly call the "General Rules of Clicking." These rules almost always apply and really help in manipulating the Windows interface to do whatever you need done.

- *Click menu items once to use them.*
- *Click icons once to select them.*
- *Click icons twice to use them.*
- *Alternate-click anything to see its properties.*

Figure 12.13 Notepad application (note the buttons in the upper-right corner)

These icons show programs running in the background. We often see icons for network status, volume controls, battery state (on laptops), and PC Card status (also usually on laptops). What shows up on yours depends on your version of Windows, what hardware you use, and what programs you have loaded. For example, the left-most icon in Figure 12.14 is my McAfee Antivirus program, and right-most is my UPS program, both humming away in the background protecting my precious data!

If you have Windows 98/Me or Windows 2000/XP, you also get the **Quick Launch** toolbar (Figure 12.15). This handy extra enables you to select often-used programs with a single click. To change the contents of the Quick Launch toolbar, you simply drag icons onto or off of it.

• **Figure 12.14** System tray showing seven icons and the time

My Computer

My Computer provides access to all drives, folders, and files [illegible]

side provides details about that drive. If you use Windows 95 or Windows NT, or if you choose to turn off this option in Windows 98/Me or Windows 2000, you get a less sophisticated window that looks something like Figure 12.17. Windows XP offers a sophisticated My Computer, with all details and common tasks displayed on the left pane (Figure 12.18).

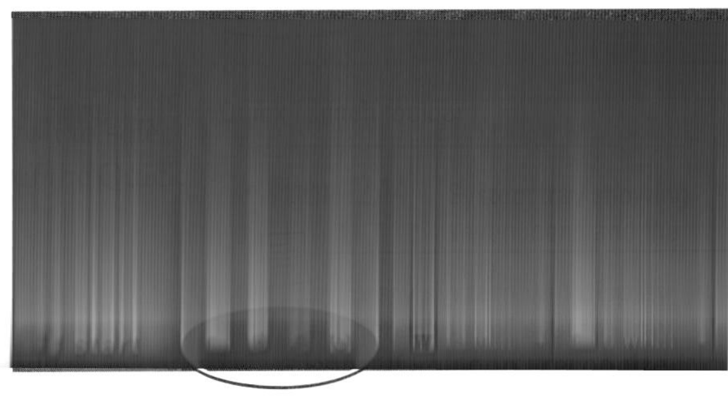

• **Figure 12.15** Quick Launch toolbar

Every system will display a different set of system tray icons. If you don't recognize one, you can double-click it to find out what it is.

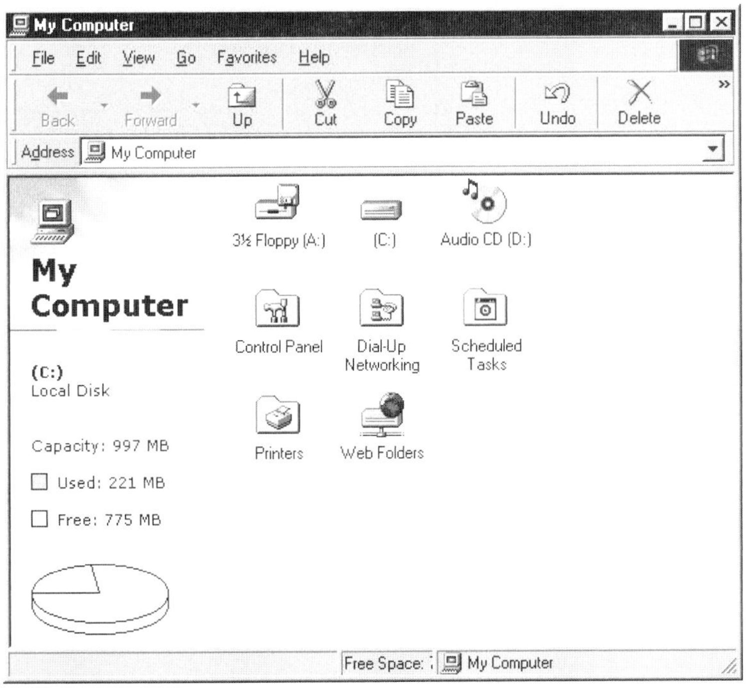

• **Figure 12.16** My Computer in Windows 98

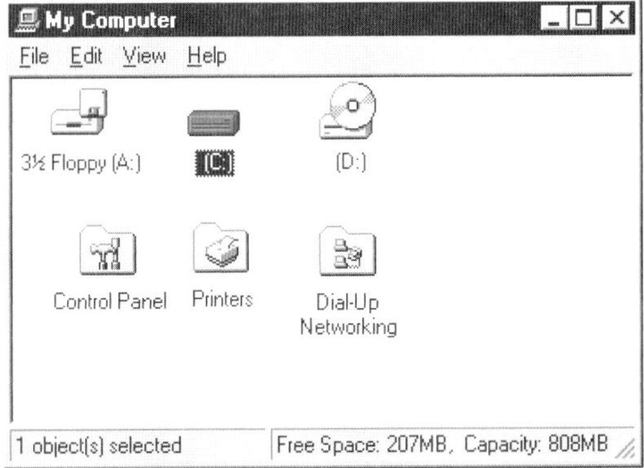

• **Figure 12.17** My Computer in Windows 95

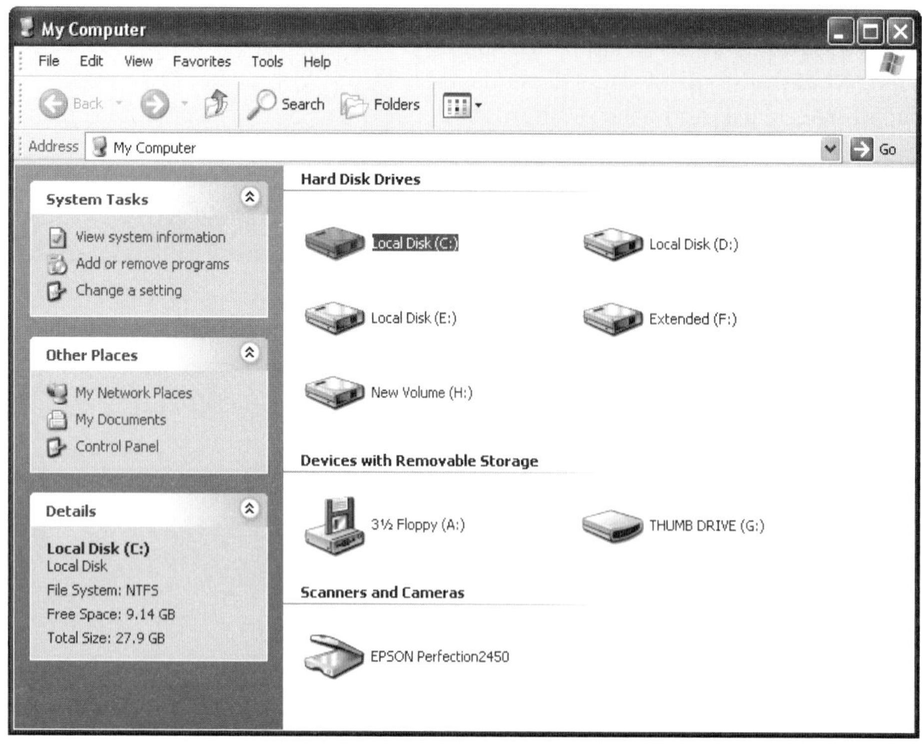

• **Figure 12.18** My Computer in Windows XP

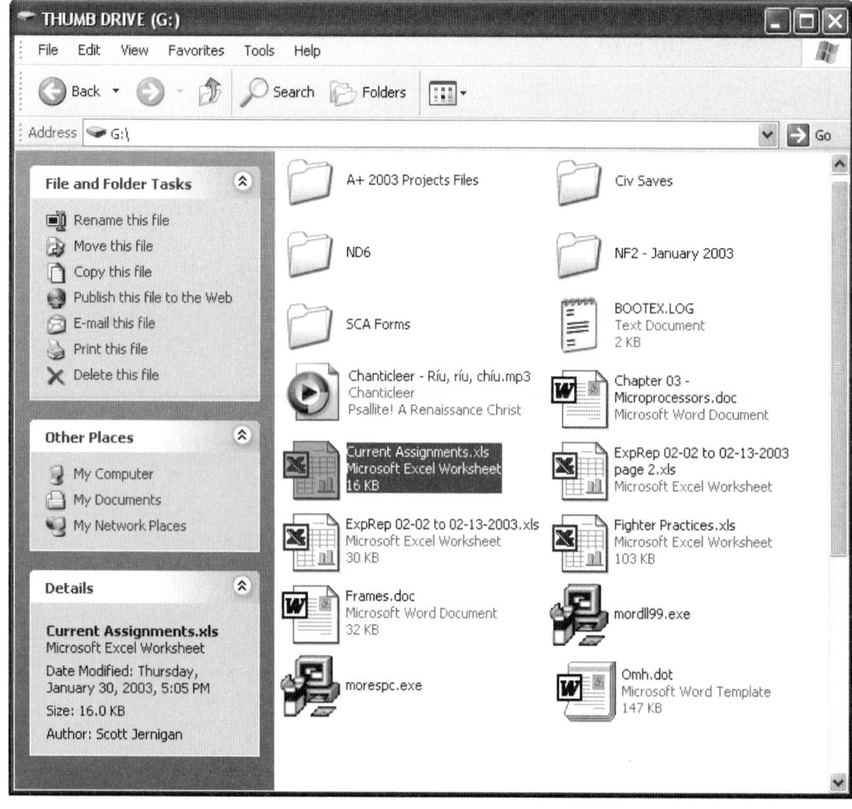

• **Figure 12.19** Displaying the contents of a thumb drive using My Computer

Most installations of Windows XP do not include My Computer on the desktop, but you can readily access it through the Start menu.

To view the contents of a drive or disk, double-click the corresponding icon in My Computer. For example, let's say you want to see the contents of a floppy disk. You insert the floppy into the floppy drive and then double-click the floppy drive icon to see what's inside. Here are the contents of a USB thumb drive I had lying around (Figure 12.19).

Notice the different icons? Windows assigns different icons to different types of files based on their *extensions*, the three-digit set at the end of a filename, such as .EXE or .JPG. As you look at these icons on your own screen, some of you might say, "But I don't see any extensions!" That's because Windows hides them by default. Revealing file extensions requires a different process in each version of Windows.

If you have Windows 95 or NT, select View | Options to open the Options dialog box (Figure 12.20). Click the View tab and uncheck Hide MS-DOS File Extensions For File Types That Are Registered (in 95) or the Hide File Extensions For Known File Types (in NT). While you're there, click the Show All Files radio button, too. Now when you return to viewing the folder in My Computer, you will see file extensions on the ends of the filenames, and in some directories you will be able to see certain critical files that Windows otherwise hides from you so you don't accidentally move, delete or change them in some unintended way.

If you have Windows 98, it's exactly the same process, except Windows 98 calls the Options dialog box the File Options dialog box. Windows Me/2000/XP, of course, also have to do things a little differently: select Tools | Folder Options, and then click the View tab. You have three tasks here: first, click the Show Hidden Files and Folders radio button; second, uncheck Hide File Extensions For Known File Types; and third, uncheck Hide Protected Operating System Files. Click the Apply To All Folders button in Windows XP, or the Apply button (bottom right) in Windows Me and 2000. The dialog box should look like Figure 12.21 (it shows the Windows 2000 version) when you are done. As before, when you return to examining the folder contents, you will see the file extensions, and possibly some previously hidden files.

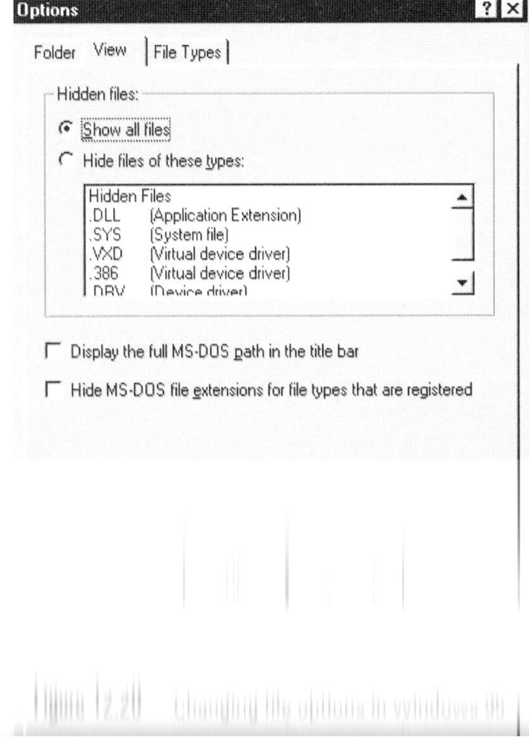

• Figure 12.20 Changing file options in Windows 98

Figure 12.23 shows My Computer exploring an important folder on my hard drive.

My Documents, My [*Whatever*]

Windows 98, Windows Me, Windows 2000, and Windows XP provide a special icon/folder called My Documents. After Windows 95's release, Microsoft discovered that users dumped their files all over the hard drive, and they often had trouble remembering where they'd put them! Microsoft

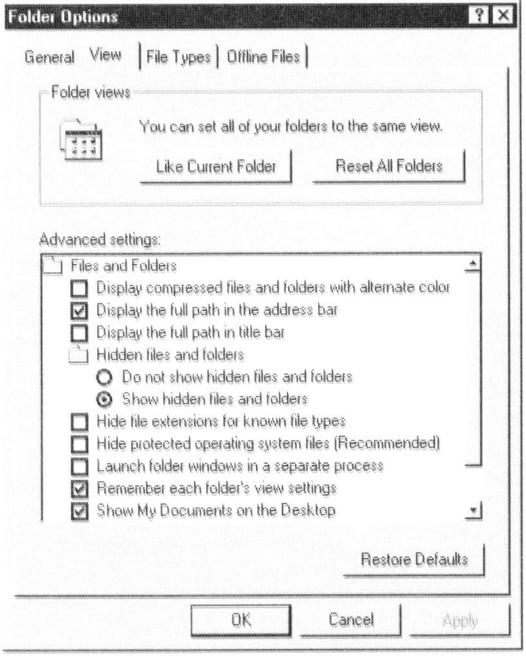

• Figure 12.21 Changing file options in Windows 2000

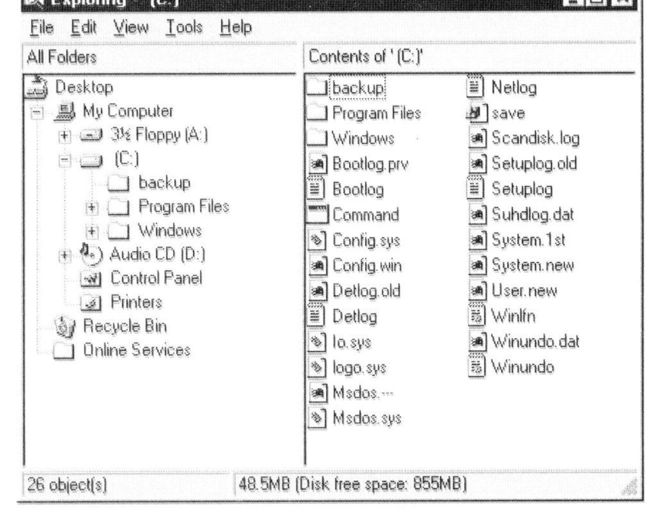

• Figure 12.22 Windows Explorer in Windows 2000

Try This!

My Computer

You should know how to navigate around your computer using the My Computer icon. Try this:

1. Open My Computer to look at the contents of your C: drive.
2. Pick any folder and open it. Does it contain folders as well as files? If not, find one that does. I suggest the Program Files folder.
3. When you find one, open a few of its subfolders. Keep drilling down through subfolders until you find one that contains only files.
4. Now that you can navigate through your hard drive using My Computer, close all the windows you opened.

recognized this issue and starting with Windows 98, created **My Documents** as a central default storage area for all files created by applications. Newer Windows programs, such as Office 2003, store their files in My Documents unless you explicitly tell them to use a different folder.

As with My Computer, most Windows XP installations do not show My Documents on the desktop. You can access it readily through the Start menu, or you can add it to your desktop. Alternate-click the desktop and select Properties to open the Display Properties dialog box. Select the Desktop tab and then click on the Customize Desktop button to open the Desktop Items dialog box (Figure 12.24). On the General tab, select the check box next to My Documents and/or My Computer and then click OK to close the box and make the icon(s) appear on the desktop.

Each version of Windows since Windows 98 seems to add more folders like My Documents, and for the most part, they're pretty cool. For example, Windows XP Professional comes with My Documents, My Pictures (it offers filmstrip and thumbnail views of pictures you store there), My Music (ready to fire up Media Player to play any file), My Videos (again, Media Player), and more. Figure 12.25 shows My Pictures, using thumbnail view. Many applications have since jumped on the bandwagon and have added their own

• **Figure 12.23** My Computer in Windows XP masquerading as Windows Explorer

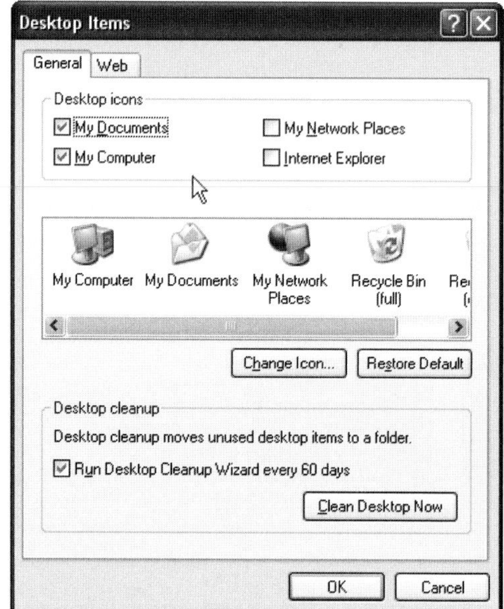

• **Figure 12.24** Desktop Items dialog box

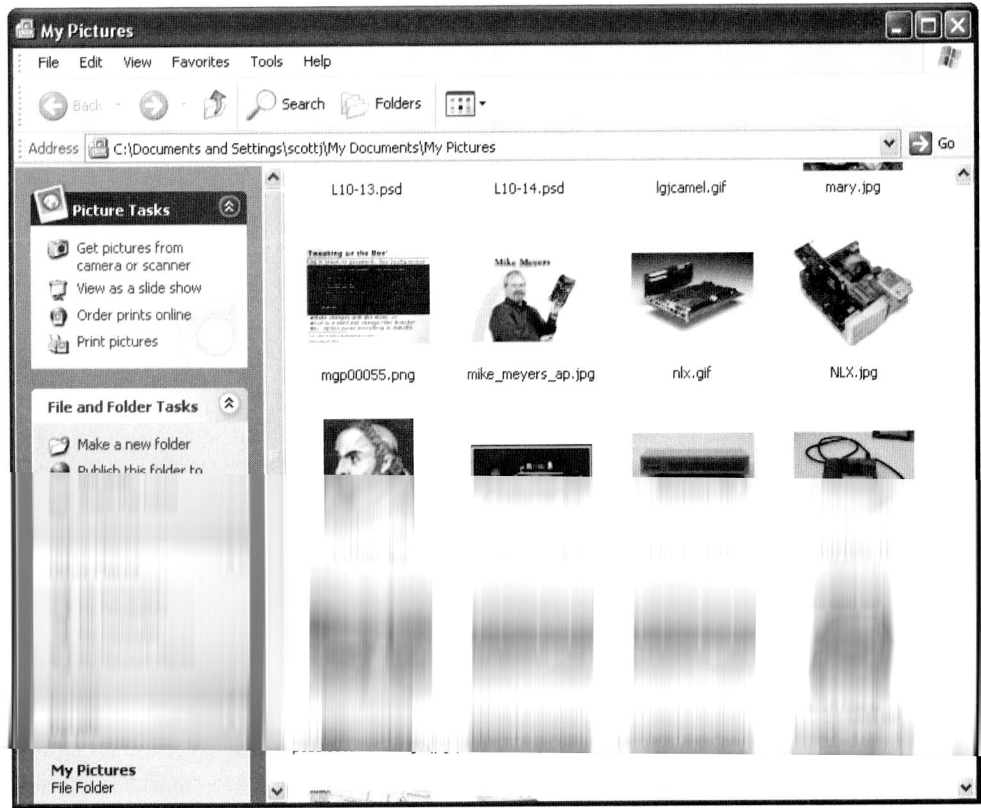

Figure 12.25 My Pictures subfolder in My Documents

My [*Whatever*] folders in My Documents. On my PC right now, I have My eBooks, My Webs, My Received Files, My Virtual Machines… My Goodness!

Recycle Bin

In Windows, a file is not erased when you delete it. Windows adds a level of protection in the form of a special folder called the Recycle Bin. When you delete a file in Windows, a copy of the file moves into the Recycle Bin. It stays there until you empty the Recycle Bin, restore the file, or until the Recycle Bin reaches a preset size and starts erasing its oldest contents. To access its properties, alternate-click the Recycle Bin and select Properties. Different versions of Windows Recycle Bin's properties look different, but they all work basically the same. Figure 12.26 shows the properties of a typical Windows 2000 Recycle Bin. Note that you set the amount of drive space to use for the Recycle Bin—10 percent being the default amount. If a hard drive starts to run low on space, this is one of the first places to check!

Everything in Windows has a Properties setting. You can access the properties by alternate-clicking and selecting Properties. From here on, when I say "access properties," you know I mean to alternate-click and then select Properties. You may also access properties by highlighting the object and pressing the ALT-ENTER key combination.

Network Neighborhood/My Network Places

Systems tied to a network, either via a network cable or by a modem, have a folder called Network Neighborhood (see Figure 12.27) or, in Windows Me/2000/XP, My Network Places. This shows all the current network connections available to you. You'll learn about Network Neighborhood in Chapter 23.

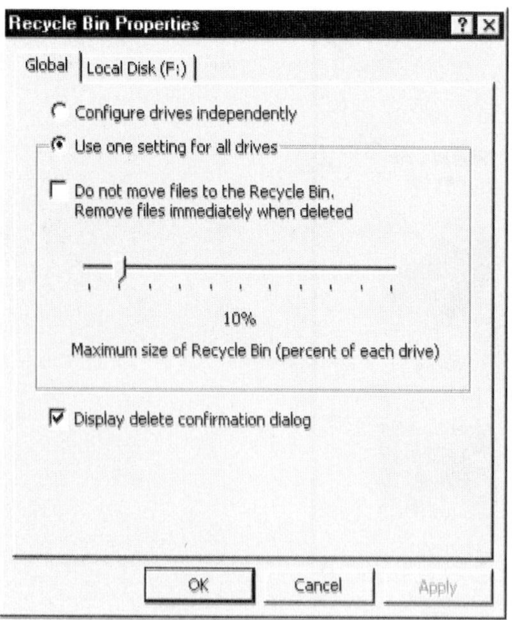

Figure 12.26 Windows 2000 Recycle Bin Properties

Tech Utilities

All Microsoft operating systems offer utilities that enable techs to configure the OS, optimize and tweak settings, install hardware, and more. All have four such utilities: Control Panel, Device Manager, System Tools, and the command line. Windows NT, 2000, and XP add two more to the mix: Administrative Tools and the Microsoft Management Console. This section discusses each utility area in general.

Control Panel

The **Control Panel** handles most of the maintenance, upgrade, and configuration aspects of Windows. As such, the Control Panel is the first set of tools for every tech. Select Start | Settings | Control Panel to open the Control Panel (Figure 12.28) except in Windows XP, where it's a Start menu item.

A large number of programs, called *applets*, populate the Control Panel. The names and selection of applets will vary depending on the version of Windows and whether any installed programs have added applets. But all versions of Windows share many of the same applets, including Display, Add/Remove Programs, and System—what I call the *Big Three* applets for techs. Display enables you to make changes to the look and feel of your Windows desktop, and tweak your

Figure 12.27 Network Neighborhood icon in Windows 98

I've covered only the most basic features of the Windows desktop in this chapter. The typical Windows desktop will include many others, but for techs and for the A+ exam, what you've learned here about the desktop is more than enough!

You'll work extensively with all these utilities in Chapters 13–16, when you play with the command line; install and upgrade the various operating systems; and learn how to maintain, optimize, and troubleshoot every modern version of Windows.

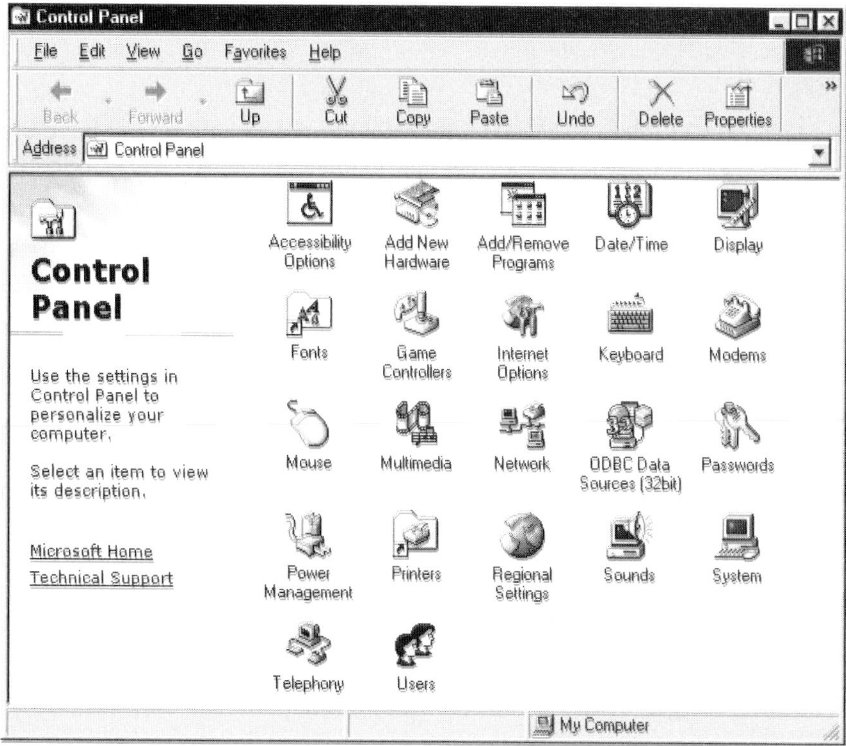

Figure 12.28 Windows 9*x* Control Panel

video settings. Add/Remove Programs does exactly what you'd think (I hope): it enables you to add or remove programs. The System applet gives you access to essential system information and tools, such as the Device Manager.

Every icon you see in the Control Panel is actually a file with the extension .CPL. Any time you get an error opening the Control Panel, you can bet you have a corrupted CPL file. These are a pain to fix. You have to rename all of your CPL files with another extension (I use .CPB), then one at a time rename them back to .CPL, each time reopening the Control Panel until you find the CPL file that's causing the lockup.

> Even these common applets vary slightly between Windows versions. The A+ Certification exams do not test you on every little variance between the same applets in different versions—just know what each applet does!

The Control Panel applets enable you to do an amazing array of things to a Windows system. Each applet displays text that helps explain its functions. The Add New Hardware applet (Figure 12.29), for example, says quite clearly, "This wizard installs the software for a new hardware device." They are all like that. Figure 12.30 shows the Users applet. Can you [illegible]

[illegible] ware and drivers in a Windows PC. As you might suspect from that description, every tech spends a lot of time with this tool! You've seen it at work in several earlier chapters, most notably in Chapter 6 with the Expansion Bus and allocation of resources via Plug and Play, and you'll work with the Device Manager many more times during the course of this book and your career as a PC tech.

How you get to the Device Manager differs among the various versions of Windows, but most often you go to the Control Panel and click the System applet. Figure 12.31 shows a Windows 98 System applet's System Properties

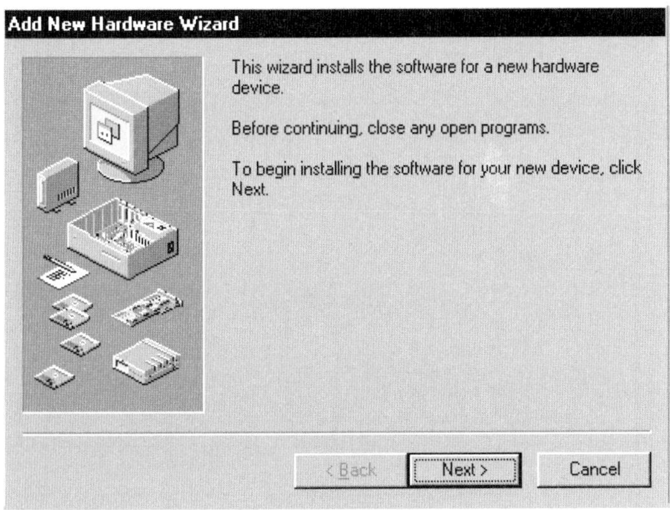

• **Figure 12.29** Add New Hardware Wizard of the Add New Hardware applet

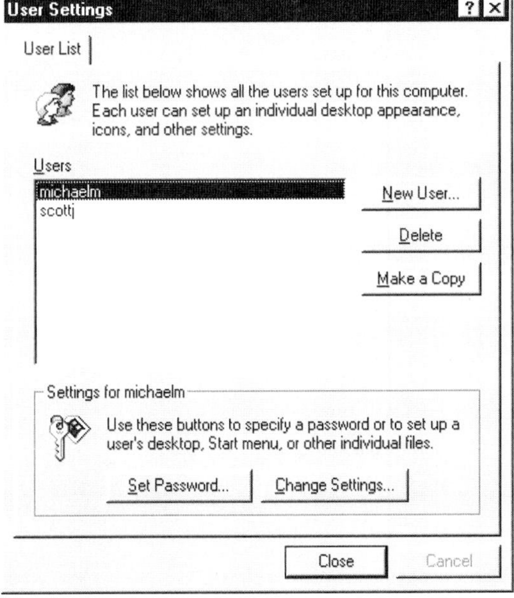

• **Figure 12.30** User Settings window of the User applet

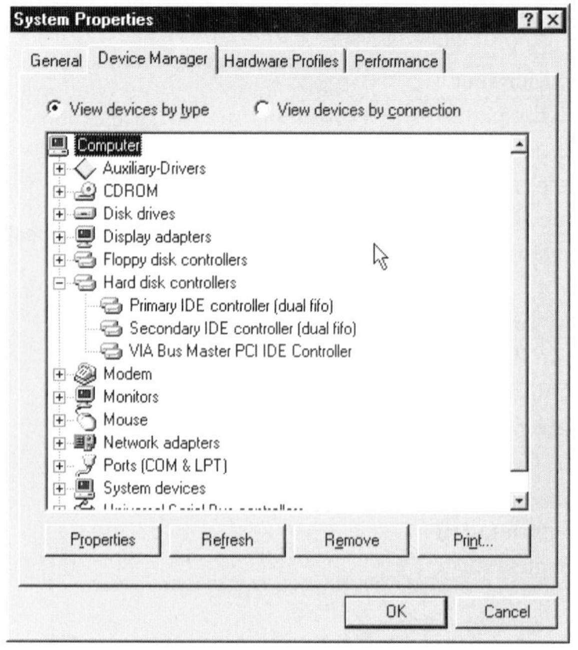

• **Figure 12.31** System applet in Windows 98 with the Device Manager tab selected

dialog box. You access the Device Manager by selecting the Device Manager tab at the top of the applet. Figure 12.32 shows the System applet's System Properties dialog box for Windows XP, which requires you to select the Hardware tab and then click the Device Manager button in the middle of that tab. (The version in Windows 2000 looks remarkably similar to the XP version.)

The Device Manager in all versions of Windows—except Windows NT 4.0—displays every device that Windows recognizes. Figure 12.33 shows a typical Windows 98 Device Manager screen with all installed devices in good order with the exception of the mouse. If Windows detects a problem, it shows the device with a red "x" or a yellow exclamation point. The Device Manager organizes devices in special groups called *types*. All devices of the same type are grouped under the same type heading. To see the devices of a particular type, you must open that type's group. Figure 12.34 shows the Ports type opened, revealing the COM and LPT ports on the system. Again, this is Windows 98.

The Device Manager enables you to update drivers with a simple click of the mouse (assuming you have a driver downloaded or on disc). Alternate-click a device—not a category—and select Update Driver from the menu to get the process started. Figure 12.35 shows the options in Windows XP. By double-clicking a device (or by selecting the device and clicking the Properties button) and then clicking the Resources tab, you can see the resources used by that device. Figure 12.36 shows the resources for a Matrox Parhelia video card.

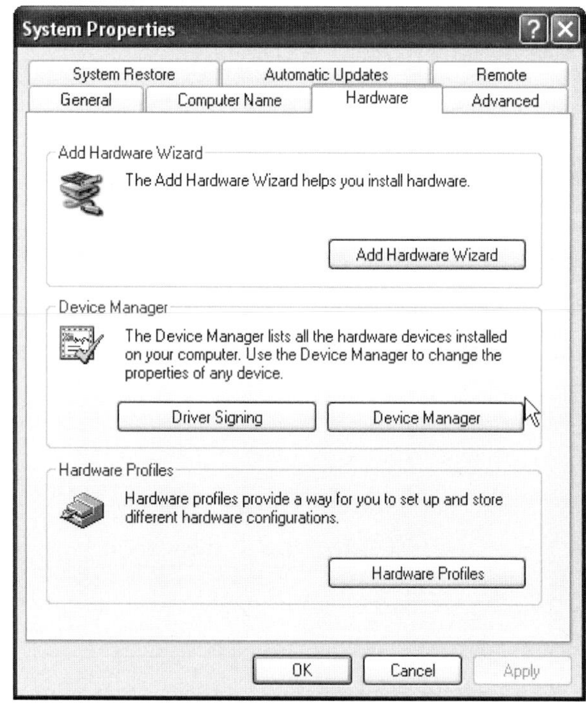

• **Figure 12.32** System applet in Windows XP with the Hardware tab selected

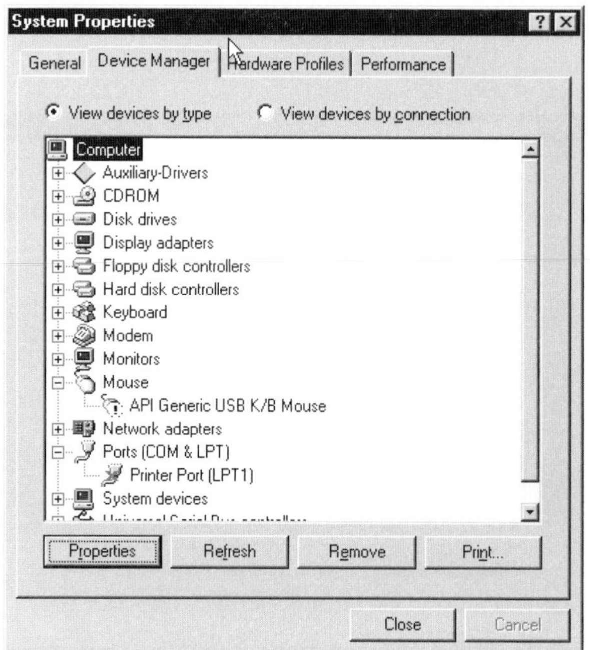

• **Figure 12.33** The Windows 98 Device Manager detects a mouse problem.

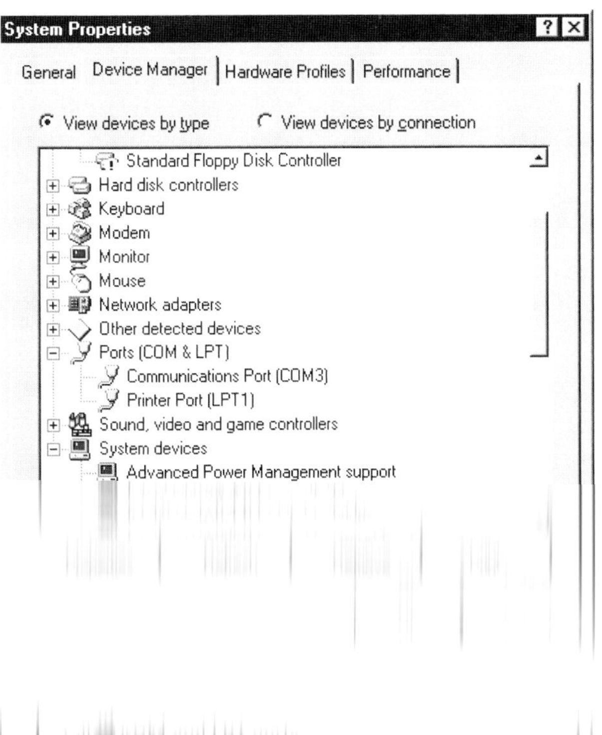

Figure 12.34 Installed COM and LPT ports

> Because Windows NT 4.0 does not support Plug and Play, it does not have a Device Manager!

You will come back to the Device Manager again and again in subsequent chapters, because it is the first tool you should access when you have a hardware problem!

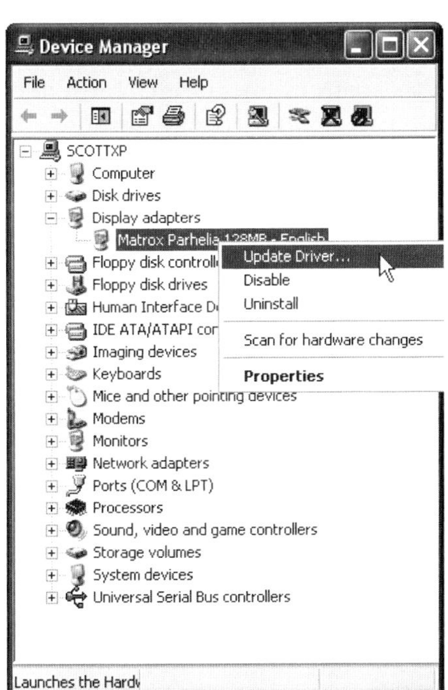

Figure 12.35 Selecting to update drivers in the Windows XP Device Manager

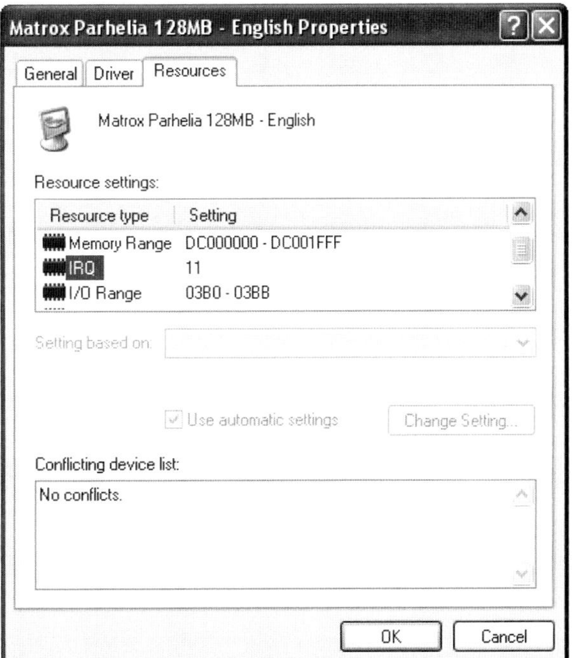

Figure 12.36 Resources revealed in the Windows XP Device Manager

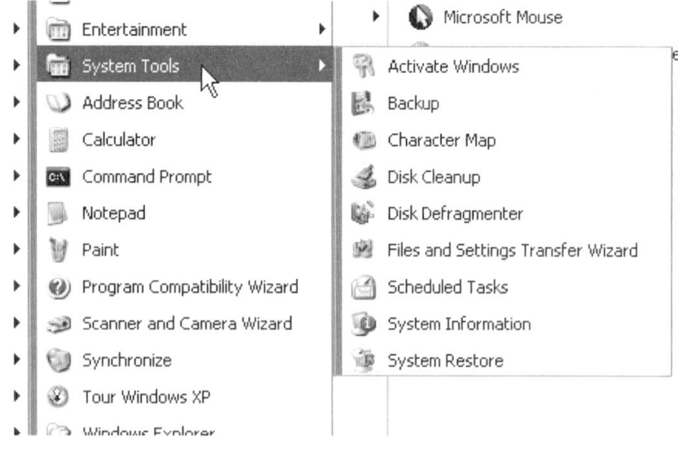

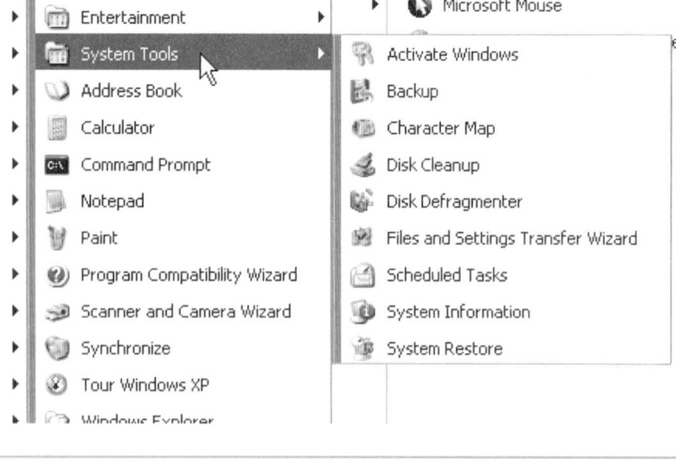

• **Figure 12.37** System Tools menu options

System Tools

The Start menu offers a variety of tech utilities collected into one place: select Start | Programs | Accessories | System Tools. In the **System Tools** menu, you'll find commonly accessed tools such as System Information and Disk Defragmenter (Figure 12.37).

One thing many techs overlook is memorizing how to find the appropriate Windows tool to diagnose problems. Nothing hurts your credibility with a client like fumbling around, clicking a variety of menus and applets, mumbling "I know it's around here somewhere." The A+ Certification exams therefore test you on a variety of paths to appropriate tools. One of those paths is Start | Accessories | System Tools!

> You need to know which tools are offered in the System Tools menu.

Command Line

The command line is alive and well in Windows, and every good tech knows how to access and use it. The entire next chapter is devoted to the command line, so I'll mention only one thing here, and that's how to access it. Select Start | Run, and type **command** in the dialog box. Click OK and you'll get to a command prompt (Figure 12.38). Windows 2000 and XP give you access to a more powerful command line interface. Same process, but you type **cmd** instead of **command** (Figure 12.39). Note that Windows NT also uses **cmd**, not **command**.

Microsoft Management Console

One of the biggest complaints about Windows NT, and to a lesser extent Windows 9*x*, was the wide dispersal of the many utilities needed for administration and troubleshooting. Despite years of research, Microsoft could never find a place to put all the utilities needed in such a way as to please even a small minority of support people. In a moment of sheer genius, Microsoft determined that the ultimate utility was one that the support person made for him or herself! This brought on the creation of the amazing Microsoft Management Console.

The **Microsoft Management Console (MMC)** is simply a shell program in Windows 2000 and XP that holds individual utilities called *snap-ins*. You can start

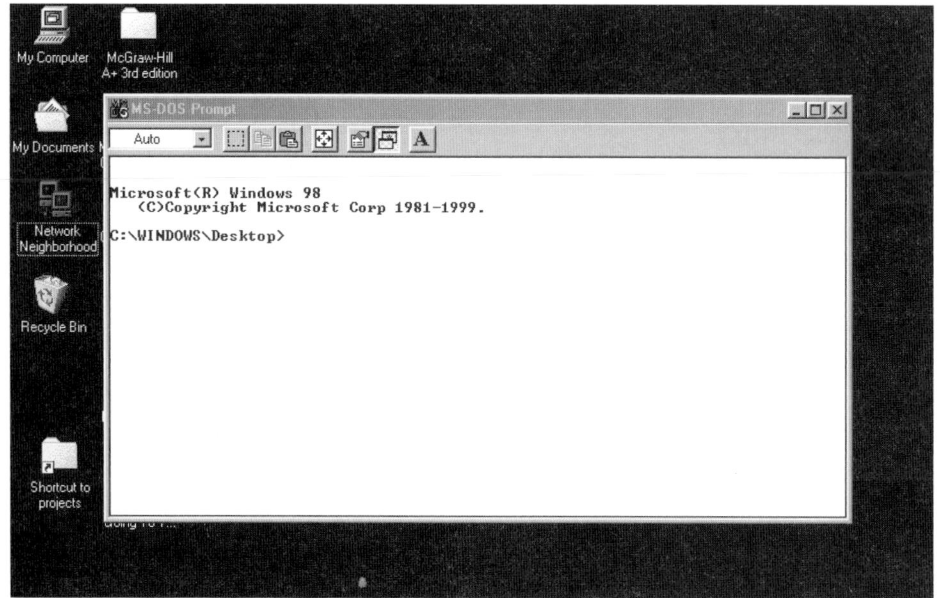

• **Figure 12.38** Command prompt in Windows 98

the MMC by selecting Start | Run and typing in **MMC** to get a blank MMC. Blank MMCs aren't much to look at (Figure 12.40).

You can make a blank console useful by adding snap-ins. Virtually every traditional tool used by either Windows NT or Windows 9*x* is available as a snap-in. Even good old Device Manager is a snap-in. For example, to add the Device Manager snap-in, open the blank MMC, select File (Console in Windows 2000) | Add/Remove Snap-in, and then click the Add button to open the Add Standalone Snap-in dialog box and see a list of available snap-ins (Figure 12.41). [illegible] dialog box. You should see Device Manager listed in the console. Click it. Hey! That looks kind of familiar, doesn't it? (See Figure 12.42.)

```
C:\WINDOWS\System32\cmd.exe
 Volume Serial Number is 94CB-9DA6

 Directory of C:\NOLF2Demo

10/23/2002  02:50 PM    <DIR>          .
10/23/2002  02:50 PM    <DIR>          ..
09/16/2002  02:05 AM         2,374,005 data1.cab
09/16/2002  02:07 AM            42,359 data1.hdr
09/16/2002  02:07 AM       160,359,386 data2.cab
09/04/2001  01:24 PM           344,923 ikernel.ex_
09/16/2002  02:07 AM               437 layout.bin
09/04/2002  05:27 AM            12,381 license.txt
09/15/2002  09:46 PM         5,283,840 NOLF2.exe
09/15/2002  09:46 PM            39,335 readme.txt
10/05/2000  04:00 PM            54,272 Setup.exe
09/16/2002  02:05 AM               110 Setup.ini
09/16/2002  02:05 AM           167,115 Setup.inx
09/12/2002  10:56 PM                28 startup.txt
01/16/2002  06:57 PM         2,041,744 WMFADist.exe
              13 File(s)    170,719,935 bytes
               2 Dir(s)   9,745,760,256 bytes free

C:\NOLF2Demo>
```

You can add as many snap-ins as you like, and there are many to choose from. Many companies sell third-party utilities as MMC snap-ins. Once you've added the snap-ins you want, just save the console under any name you want, anywhere you want. I'll save this console as DM (Device Manager) and drop it on my desktop (see Figure 12.43). I'm now just a double-click away from the Device Manager!

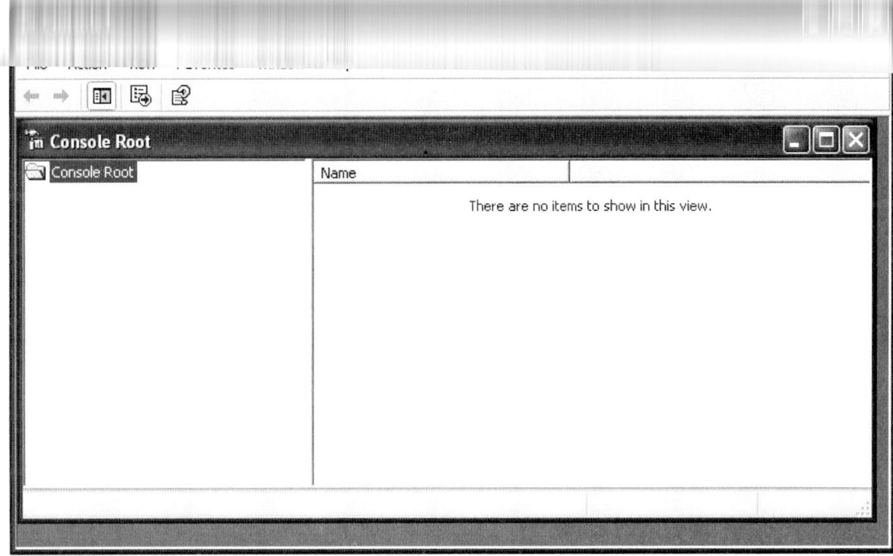

Figure 12.40 Blank MMC

Administrative Tools

Windows 2000 and XP have combined almost all of the snap-ins into a new applet in the Control Panel called Administrative Tools. Open the Control Panel and open Administrative Tools (Figure 12.44).

Administrative Tools is really just a folder that stores a number of pre-made consoles. As you poke through these, you'll notice that many of the consoles share some of the same snap-ins—nothing wrong with that. Of the consoles in a standard Administrative Tools collection, the ones you'll spend the most time with are Computer Management, Event Viewer, Performance, and Services.

Windows NT 4.0 has Administrative Tools as well, but the tools do not have the unified look and feel of the MMC. You'll find similar utilities, though.

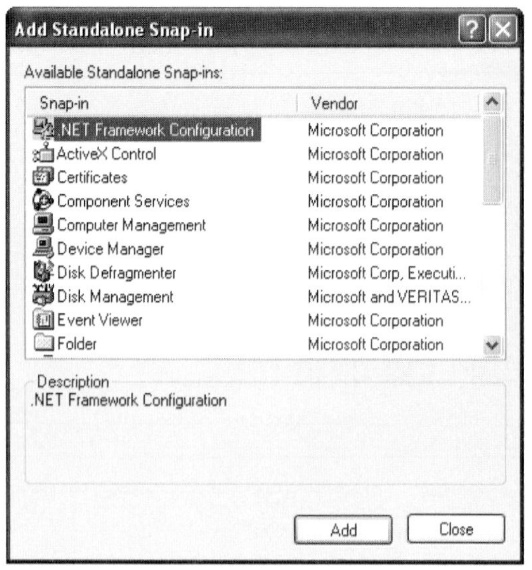

• **Figure 12.41** Available snap-ins

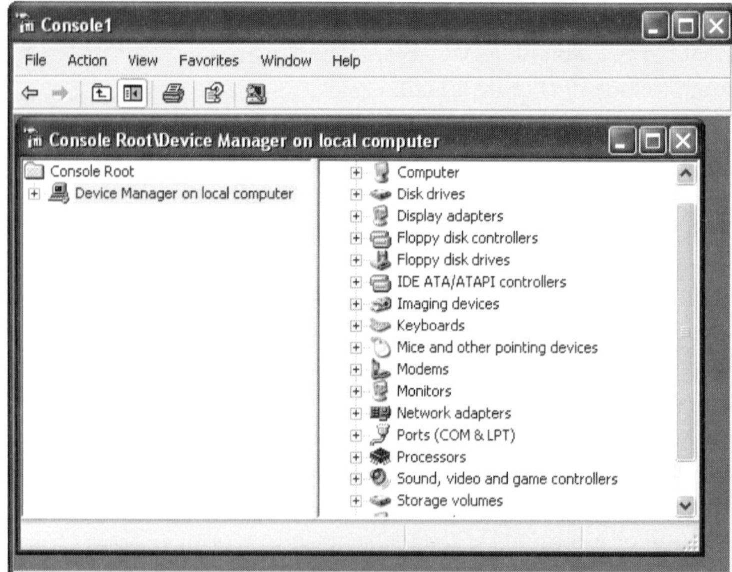

• **Figure 12.42** Device Manager as a snap-in

• **Figure 12.43** The Device Manager shortcut on the Desktop

Computer Management The Computer Management applet is a tech's best buddy, or at least a place where you'll spend a lot of time when building or maintaining a system. You've already spent considerable time with two of its components, System Tools and Storage (Figure 12.45). System Tools offers System Information, Performance Logs and Alerts, Device Manager, and more. Storage is where you'll find Disk Management. Each of these tools is of particular interest to techs, as you've seen earlier and will see again in Chapters 14 and 16.

Event Viewer Event Viewer enables you to tell at a glance what has happened in the last day, week, or more, including when people have

The A+ Certification exam has little interest in some of these snap-ins, so we won't cover them all. If we don't mention it, it's almost certainly not on the test!

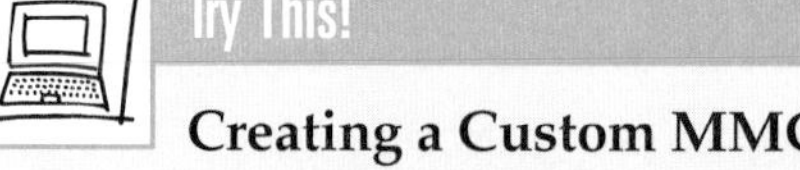

Try This!

Creating a Custom MMC

You'll work with the MMC many times in the chapters ahead, and the A+ Certification exams expect you to know the tool fairly well. Nothing beats doing it to learn how to use something, so try this!

Open a blank MMC, as discussed previously, and then add some snap-ins to create a custom MMC. Need some suggestions?

1. You've used Disk Defragmenter, so add it.
2. Since you played extensively with Disk Management, add it too.
3. Finally, add Device Manager—well, just because.
4. Now experiment with the MMC to see how useful it can be to have one custom-made!

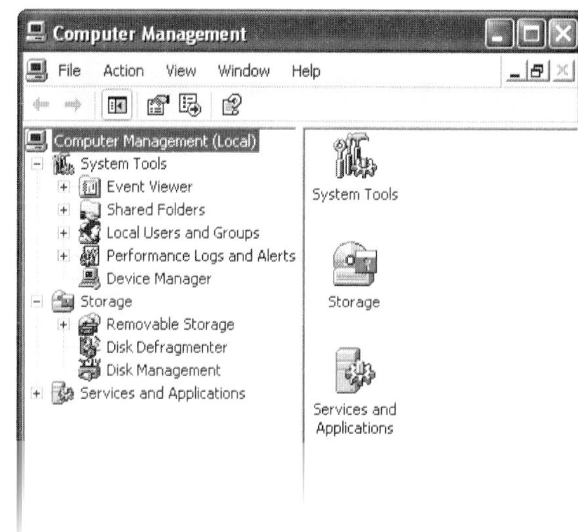

logged in and when the PC had problems (Figure 12.46). You'll use Event Viewer in some detail in Chapter 16.

Performance The Performance console consists of two snap-ins: System Monitor and Performance Logs And Alerts. You can use these for reading *logs*—files that monitor information over time. The System Monitor can also monitor real-time data (Figure 12.47).

> You'll see the Performance console at work in detail in Chapter 16.

Suppose you just got a new cable modem and you want to know just how fast you can download data. Click the plus sign (+) on the toolbar to add a counter. Click the Use Local Computer Counters radio button, and then choose Network Interface from the Performance Object pull-down menu. Make sure the Select Counters From List radio button is selected. Last, highlight Bytes Received/Sec. The dialog box should look like Figure 12.48.

Click Add, and then click Close—probably not much is happening. Go to a web site, preferably one where you can select a huge file, and then start downloading. Watch the chart jump; that's the real throughput (Figure 12.49).

Services Windows NT/2000/XP run a large number of separate programs called *services*. The best way for a Windows 9*x*/Me person to visualize a

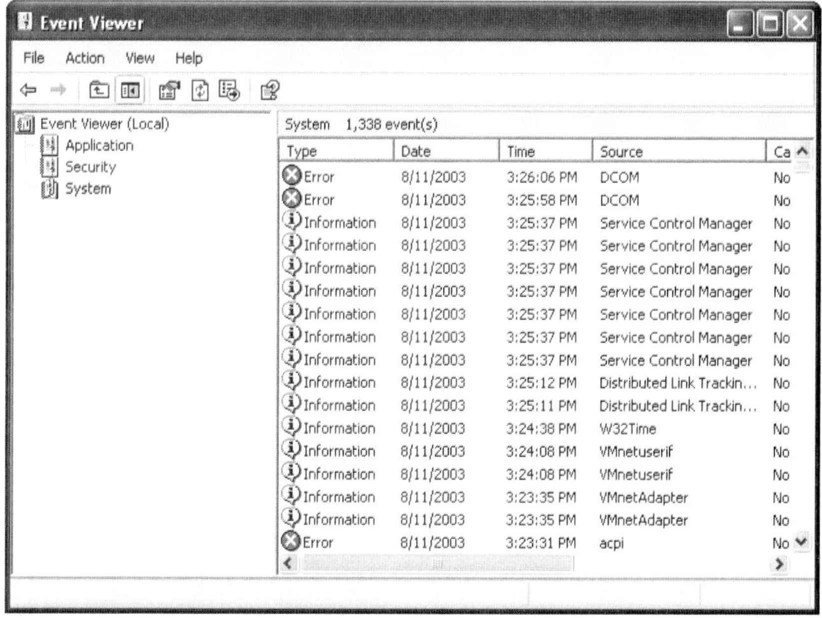

Figure 12.46 Event Viewer reporting system errors

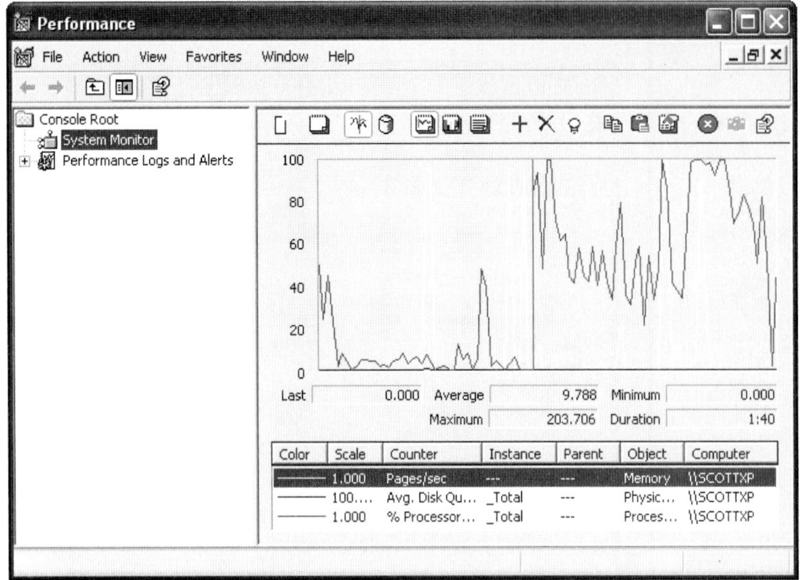

• **Figure 12.47** System Monitor in action

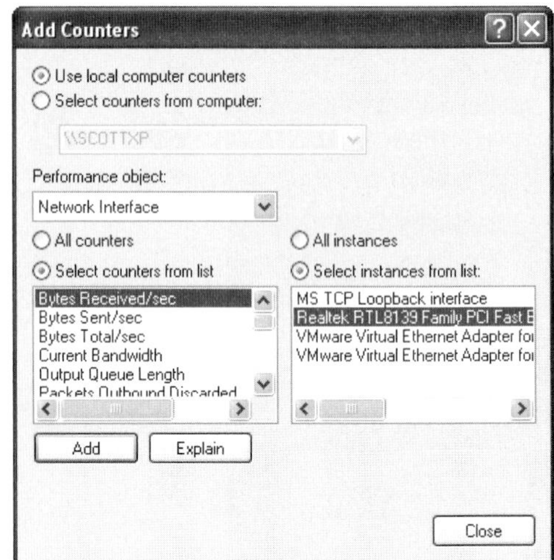

• **Figure 12.48** Setting up a throughput test

service is to think of it as something like a *terminate and stay resident* (TSR) program—it runs, yet is invisible. The Services applet enables you to see the status of all services on the system, including services that are not running (Figure 12.50).

> The A+ Certification exam is not interested in having you memorize all of these services—just make sure you can manipulate them!

Windows NT/2000/XP come with about 60 services. These services handle a huge number of functions, from application support to network functions. Alternate-click a service and select Properties to modify settings. Figure 12.51 shows the properties for the Alerter service. See the Startup Type pull-down menu? It shows three options: Automatic, Manual, and Disabled. Automatic means it starts when the system starts; Manual means you have to come to this tab to start it; and Disabled prevents anything from starting it. Make sure you know these three settings and also make sure you understand how to start, stop, pause, and resume services (note the four buttons underneath Startup Type).

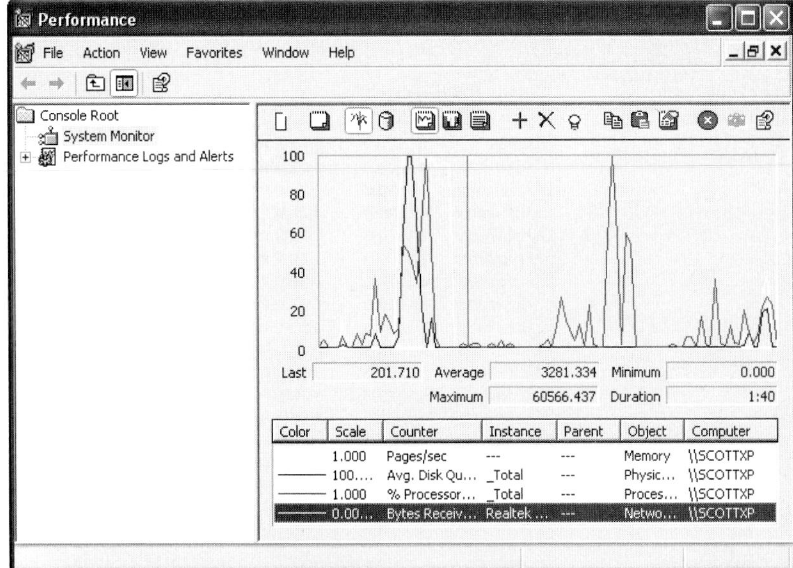

• **Figure 12.49** Downloading with blazing speed

OS Folders

Each modern version of Windows organizes essential files and folders in a similar fashion. All have a primary system folder for storing most Windows internal tools and files. All use Registry files that keep track of all the hardware loaded and the drivers that enable you to use that hardware. Finally, every version has a RAM cache file, enabling more robust access to programs and utilities.

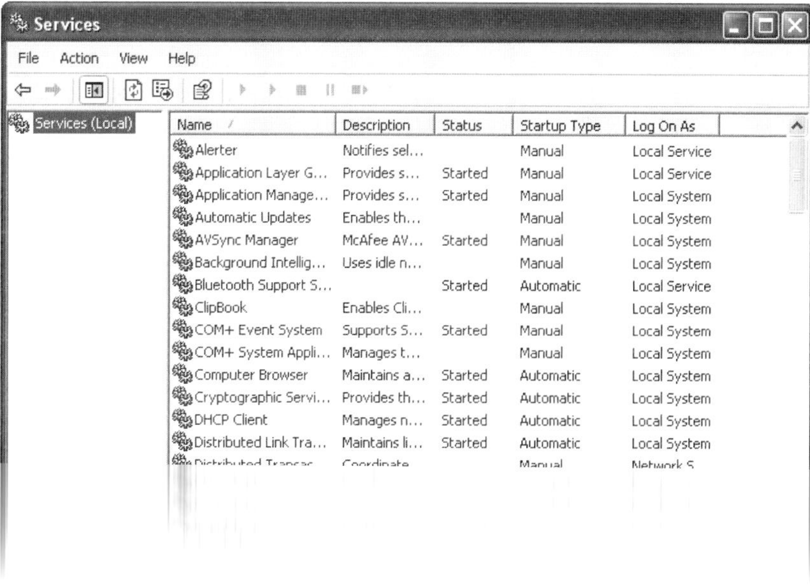

System Folder

SystemRoot is the tech name given in Windows NT/2000/XP to the folder in which Windows has been installed. In most cases, as you might expect, SystemRoot is C:\WINDOWS, but that's not always the case; during the installation process, you can change where Windows is installed, and for Windows NT, SystemRoot by default

part of a Windows configuration setting, the term is often written as %SystemRoot%.

Here's a handy trick. If you don't know where Windows was installed on a particular system, go to a command prompt, type **cd %systemroot%**, and press ENTER. The prompt will change to the directory in which the Windows OS files are stored. Slick!

WinDir is the Windows 9*x* equivalent of SystemRoot. In fact, WinDir still works in NT, 2000, and XP for backward compatibility. From a command prompt, type **cd %windir%** and press ENTER to see the name of the directory in which the OS files reside.

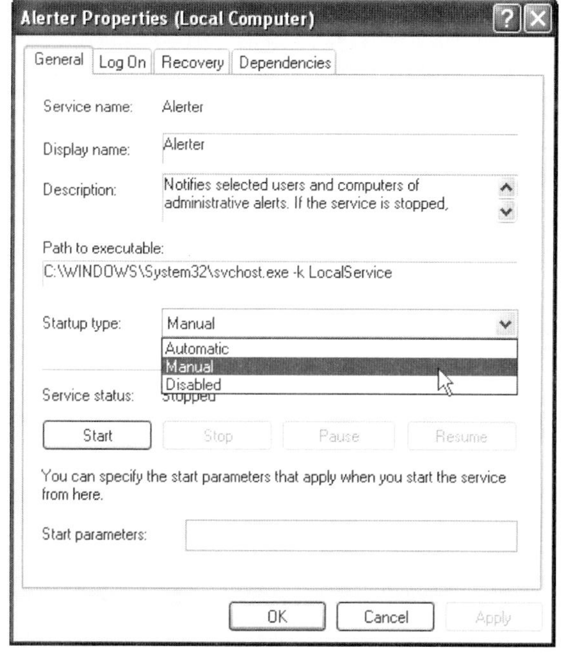

Figure 12.51 Alerter service properties

Registry

The **Registry** stores everything about your PC, including information on all the hardware in the PC, network information, user preferences, file types, and virtually anything else you might run into with Windows. Almost any form of configuration done to a Windows system involves editing the Registry. The Registry in Windows 9*x*/Me is composed of two binary files, SYSTEM.DAT and USER.DAT. These files reside in the \%WinDir% folder. In Windows NT/2000/XP, the numerous Registry files (called *hives*) are in the \%SystemRoot%\System32\config folder. Fortunately, you rarely have to access these massive files directly. Instead, you can use a set of relatively user-friendly applications to edit the Registry.

Accessing the Registry in Windows 9x/Me The main way to access the Registry is through the Control Panel (Figure 12.52). You can open the Control Panel in several ways. Double-click the My Computer icon on your

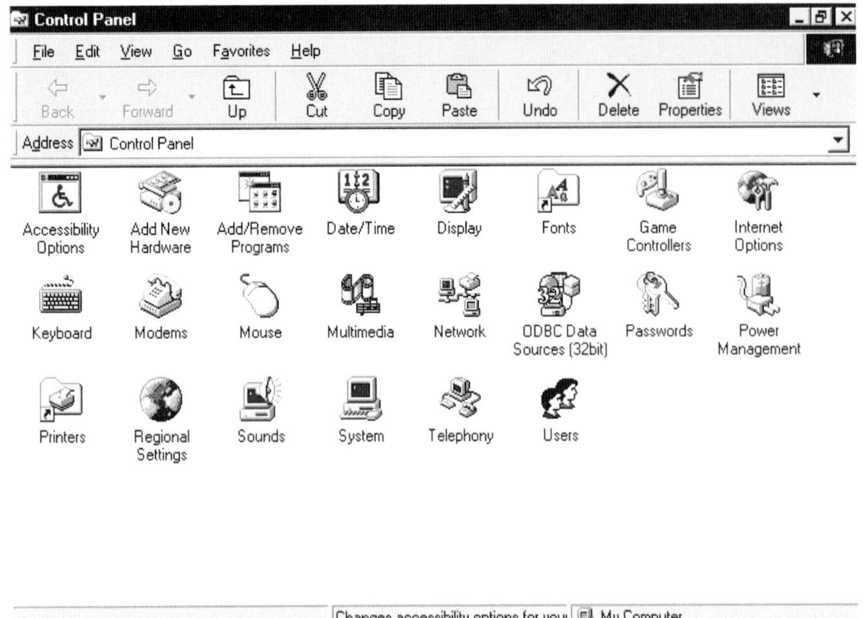

• **Figure 12.52** Windows 98 Control Panel

desktop, and double-click the Control Panel icon. Alternatively, you can select Start | Settings | Control Panel. The main function of the Control Panel applet is to update the Registry via fairly intuitive interfaces.

Everything necessary to configure the system so it works can be handled from the Control Panel, although the occasional tweak does come along that requires direct Registry access. When you want to access the Registry directly, you must use the Registry Editor. Select Start | Run, and type **regedit** (Figure 12.53). This will start the Registry Editor (Figure 12.54). Remember that the Registry files are binary. You cannot edit the registry with Edit, Notepad, or any other text editor as you could with SYSTEM.INI. You must use Regedit.

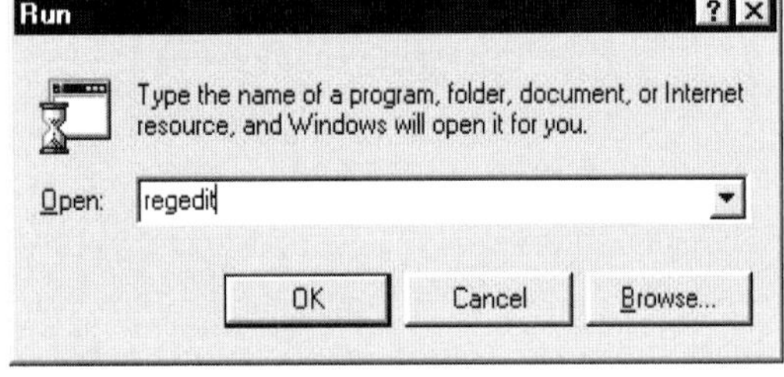

• **Figure 12.53** Opening Regedit

Registry Components The Registry is organized in a tree structure similar to the folders in the PC. Once you open the Registry Editor in Windows 9*x*/Me, you see six main subgroups, or *root keys*:

- HKEY_CLASSES_ROOT
- HKEY_CURRENT_USER
- HKEY_LOCAL_MACHINE
- HKEY_USERS
- HKEY_CURRENT_CONFIG
- HKEY_DYN_DATA

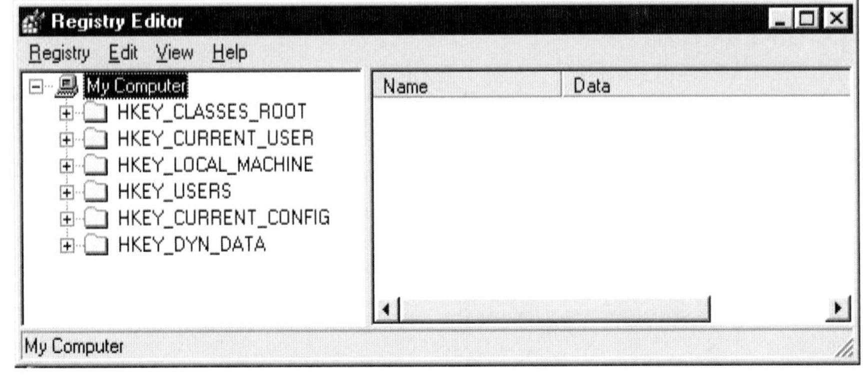

• **Figure 12.54** The Registry Editor

Try opening one of these root keys, and note that more subkeys are listed underneath them. A subkey also has other subkeys, or *values.* Figure 12.55 shows an example of a subkey with some values. Notice that Regedit shows keys on the left and values on the right, just as Windows Explorer shows directories on the left and files on the right.

When writing about keys and values, I'll use the expression *key = value.* The secret to understanding the Registry is to understand the function of the six root keys first.

Because each of these root keys has a specific function, let's take a look at them individually.

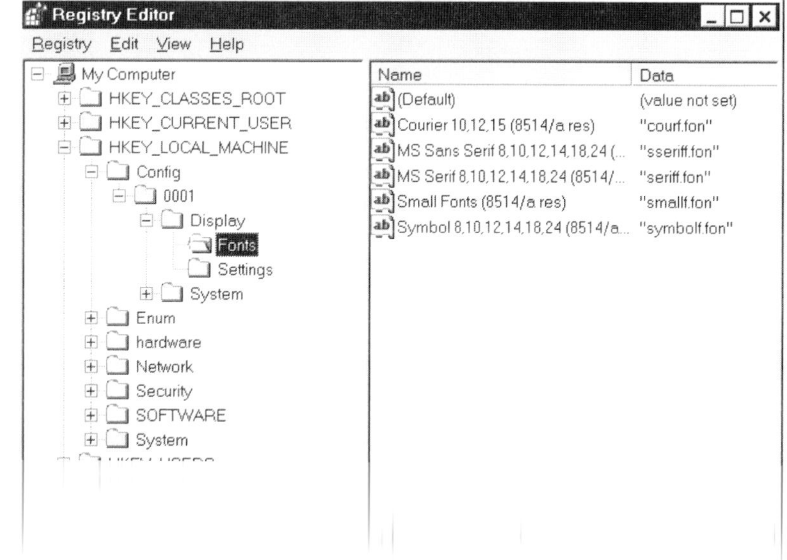

HKEY_CLASSES_ROOT This root key defines the standard *class objects* used by Windows 9*x*. A class object is a named group of functions. Pretty much everything that has to do with files on the system is defined by a class object. For example, a MIDI (Musical Instrument Digital Interface) sound file is defined using two class objects. If you search the registry for the .MID file extension, you will find the first class object, midfile.

As you can see in Figure 12.57, this subkey tells the system everything that needs to be known about a particular software item. It's here that the file associations are defined, icons are shown, and options are displayed when an item is alternate-clicked. Although it is possible to change these settings via REGEDIT, the normal way is to choose View | Options from Windows Explorer (Figure 12.58).

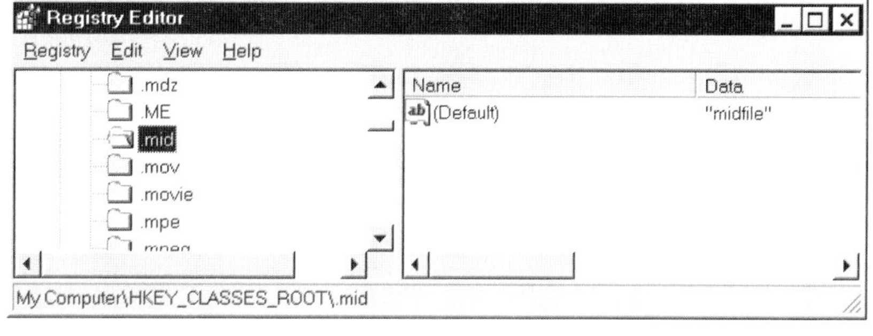

• **Figure 12.56** Association of .MID to midfile

HKEY_USERS and HKEY_CURRENT_USER Windows 9*x*/Me can be configured to support more than one user on the same PC, storing personalized information such as colors, screen savers, and the contents of the Desktop. HKEY_USERS stores all of the personalized information for all users on a PC. HKEY_CURRENT_USER stores the current user settings, which makes it a good place to fix personalizations such as fonts, icons, and colors on systems that are set up to support multiple users.

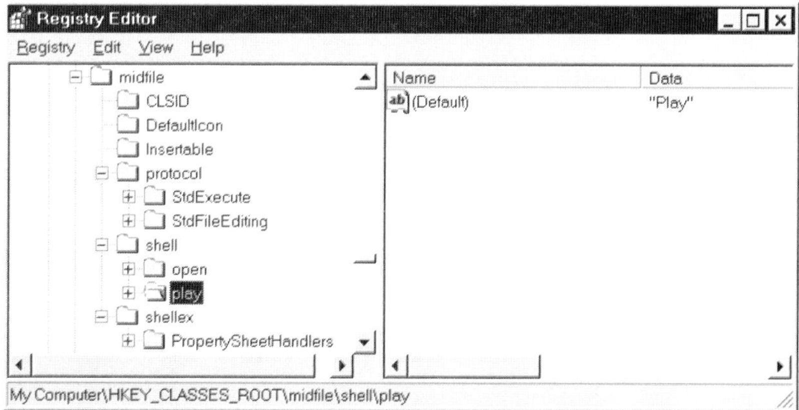

• **Figure 12.57** Midfile settings

HKEY_LOCAL_MACHINE This root key contains all the data for a system's

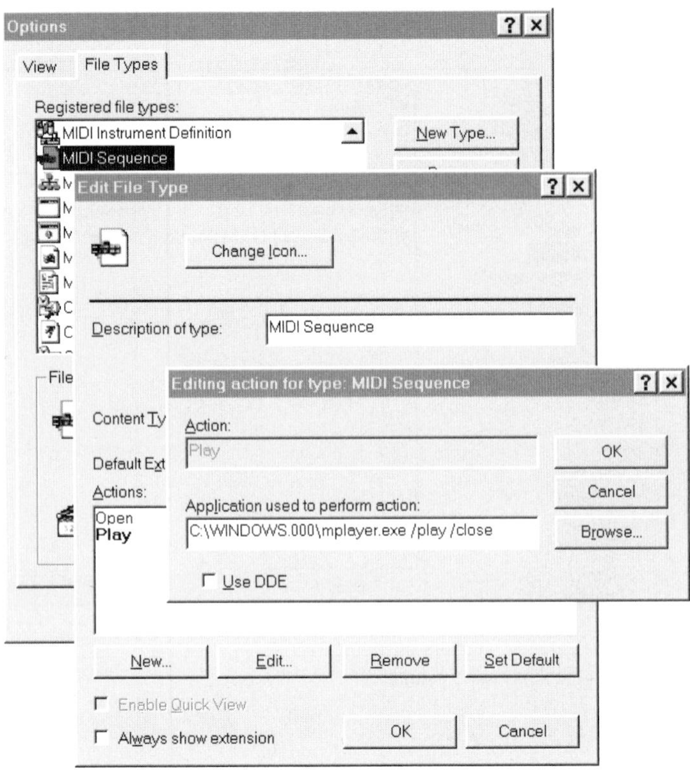

• **Figure 12.58** Changing association options

> Make sure you know the six root keys of the Windows 9*x*/Me Registry.

nonuser-specific configurations. This encompasses every device in your PC, including devices that you have removed. For example, Figure 12.59 shows the description of a SCSI Zip drive. You'll be seeing more of HKEY_LOCAL_MACHINE in Chapter 15 when we discuss configuring and repairing hardware in Windows 9*x*.

HKEY_CURRENT_CONFIG If the values in HKEY_LOCAL_MACHINE have more than one option, such as two different monitors, this root key defines which one is currently being used. Because most people have only one type of monitor and similar equipment, this area is almost never touched.

HKEY_DYN_DATA This is Registry data stored in RAM to speed up system configuration. A snapshot of all hardware in use is stored here. It is updated at boot and when any changes are made in the system configuration file.

Accessing the Registry in Windows NT/2000/XP

Windows NT/2000/XP share similar Registries, but these Registries differ from those in Windows 9*x*/Me, as you'll see in a moment. The A+ Certification exams do not expect you to memorize every aspect of the Windows NT/2000/XP Registry. You should, however, understand the basic components of the Registry, know how to edit the Registry manually, and know the best way to locate a particular setting. Microsoft included a new Registry Editor in Windows NT called REGEDT32.EXE, shown in Figure 12.60, although the company also left in the older Registry Editor (REGEDIT.EXE). Windows 2000/XP also has both REGEDT32.EXE and REGEDIT.EXE. Most techs refer to the two Registry Editor applications by their filenames, Regedt32 and Regedit.

Although Regedt32 has far more power than Regedit, we still use the older Regedit to perform searches—Regedt32's search capabilities are not very good. The best practice: search with Regedit, but make changes only with Regedt32. Figure 12.61 shows Regedit on a typical Windows 2000 system. Note that Windows 2000 lacks the HKEY_DYN_DATA folder found in Windows 9*x*, but otherwise it looks the same.

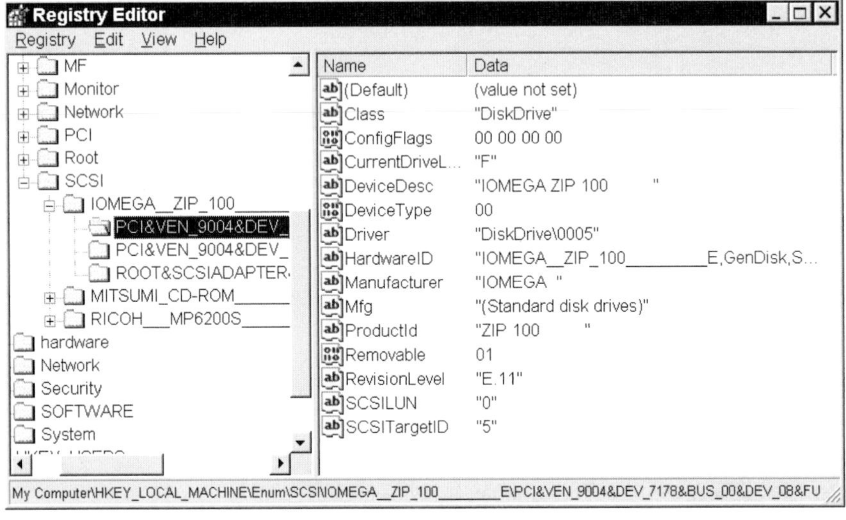

• **Figure 12.59** Registry information for a SCSI Zip drive

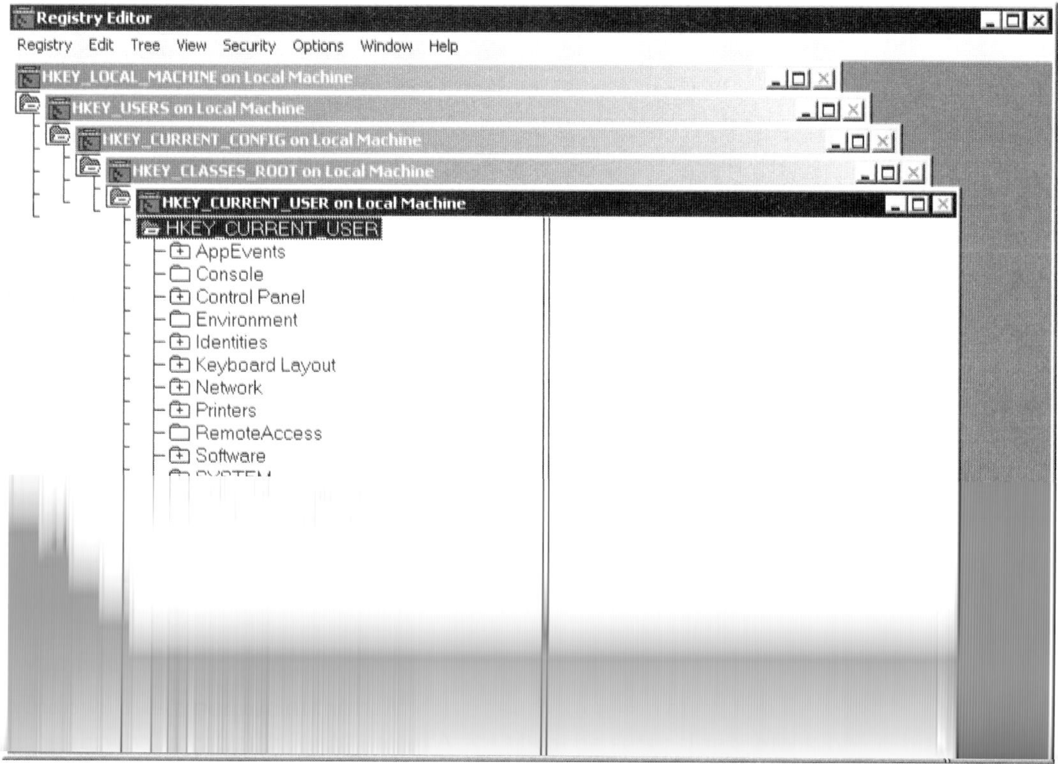

• **Figure 12.60** Regedt32

Swap File

Windows uses a portion of the hard drive as an extension of system RAM, through what's called a *RAM cache*. A RAM cache sets aside a block of cylinders on a hard drive as what's called a **swap file** or *virtual memory*. When the PC starts running out of real RAM because you've loaded too many programs, the system swaps programs from RAM to the swap file, opening more space for programs currently active. All versions of Windows use a swap file, so let's look at how one works.

Let's assume you have a PC with 256 MB of RAM. Figure 12.62 shows the system RAM as a thermometer with gradients from 0 to 256 MB. As programs load, they take up RAM, and as more and more programs are loaded (labeled A, B, and C in the figure), more RAM is used (Figure 12.63).

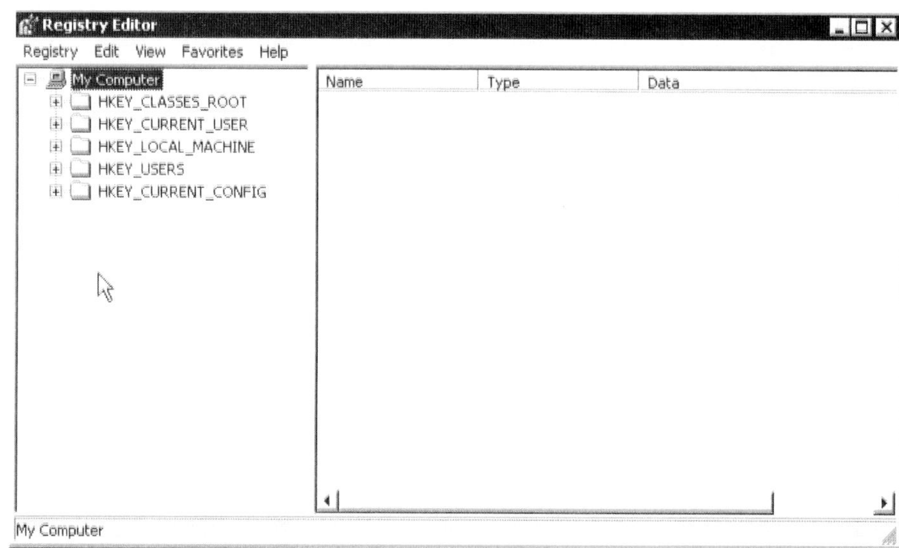

• **Figure 12.61** Regedit in Windows 2000

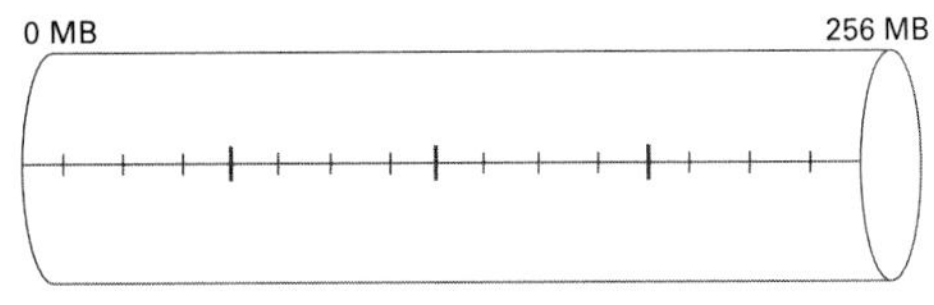

• **Figure 12.62** A RAM thermometer

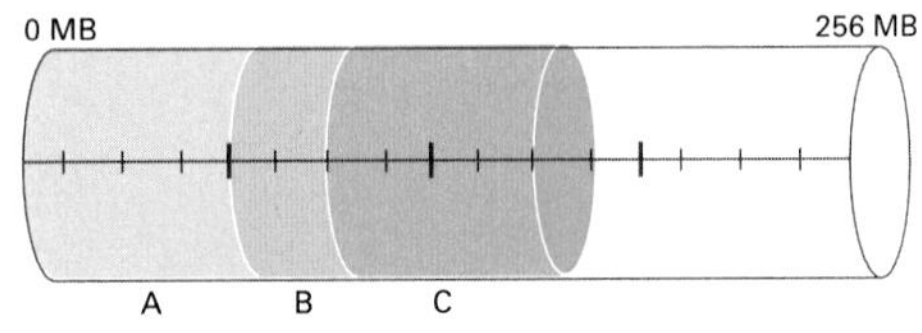

• **Figure 12.63** More programs take more RAM

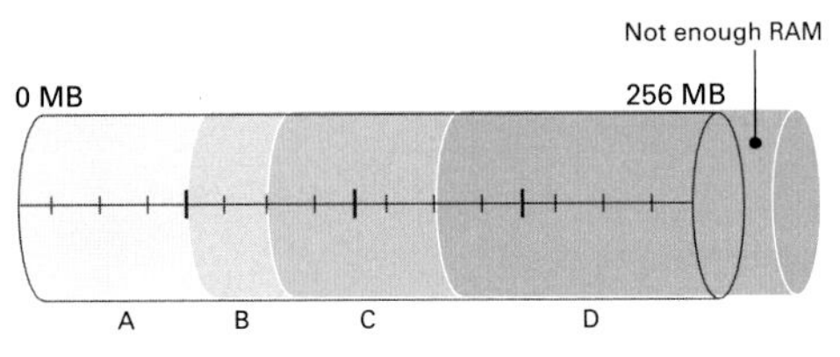

• **Figure 12.64** Not enough RAM to load program D

> Virtual memory is a fully automated process and does not require any user intervention. Tech intervention is another story!

At a certain point, you won't have enough RAM to run any more programs (Figure 12.64). Sure, you could close one or more programs to make room for yet another program, but you can't keep all the programs running simultaneously. This is where virtual memory comes into play. Windows' virtual memory starts by creating a swap file that resides somewhere on your hard drive. The swap file works like a temporary storage box. Windows uses the swap file to remove running programs temporarily from RAM so other programs can load and run. If you have enough RAM to run all your programs, Windows does not need to use the swap file. Windows brings the swap file into play only when insufficient RAM is available to run all open programs.

To load, Program D needs a certain amount of free RAM. Clearly, this requires that some other program (or programs) be unloaded from RAM without actually closing the program(s). Windows looks at all running programs, in this case A, B, and C, and decides which program is the least used. That program is then cut out of or swapped from RAM and copied into the swap file. In this case, Windows has chosen Program B (Figure 12.65). Unloading Program B from RAM provides enough RAM to load Program D (Figure 12.66).

It is important to understand that none of this activity is visible on the screen! Program B's window is still visible along with those of all the other running programs. Nothing tells the user that Program B is no longer in RAM (Figure 12.67). So what happens if you click on Program B's window to bring it to the front? The program can't actually run from the swap file; it must be reloaded back into RAM. First, Windows decides which program must be removed from RAM, and this time Windows chooses Program C (Figure 12.68). Then it loads Program B into RAM (Figure 12.69).

Swapping programs to and from the swap file and RAM takes time. Although no visual clues suggest that a swap is taking place, the machine will slow down quite noticeably as Windows performs the swaps. However, the alternative (Figure 12.70) is far less acceptable. Swap files are a crucial aspect of Windows operation. Windows handles swap files automatically, but occasionally you'll run into problems and need to change the size of the swap file or delete it and let Windows re-create it automatically.

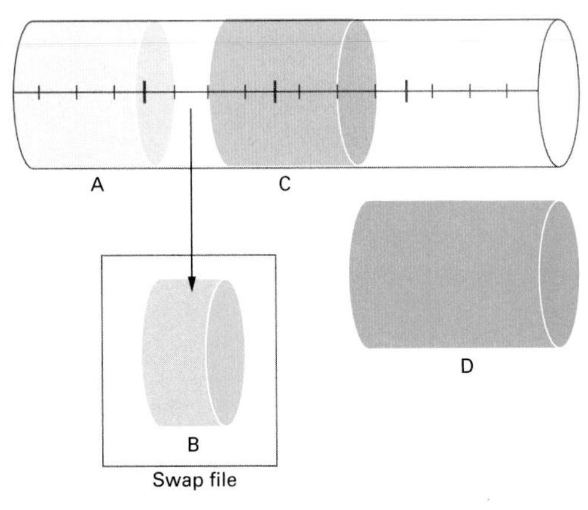

• **Figure 12.65** Program B being unloaded from memory

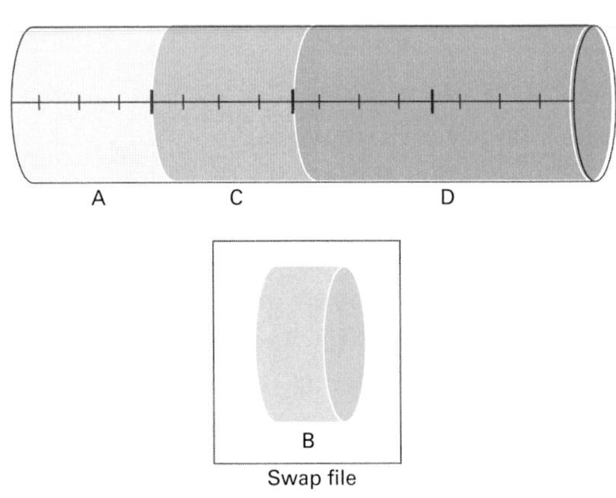

• **Figure 12.66** Program B stored in the swap file—room for Program D now!

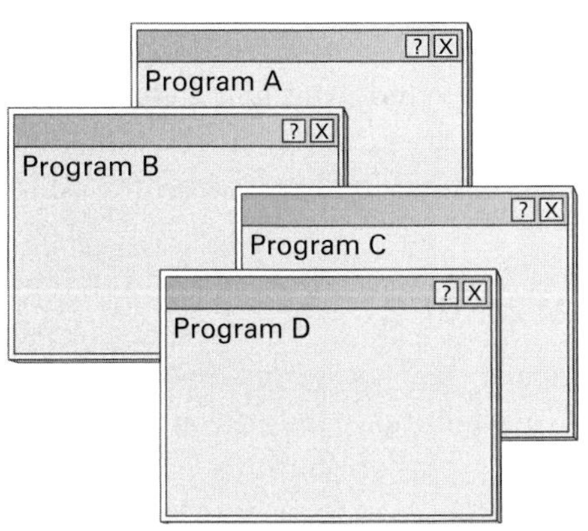

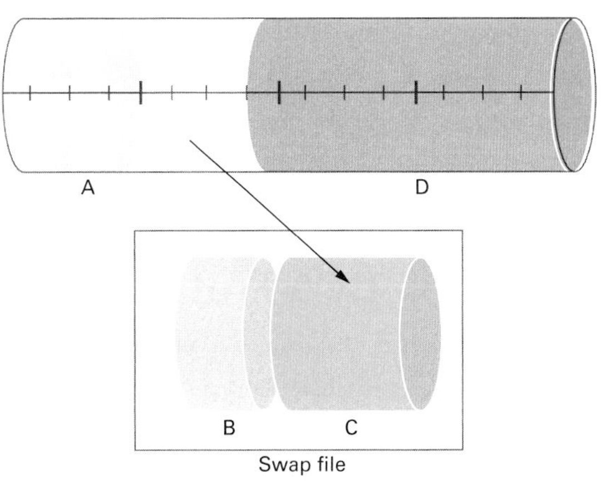

swap file is going to be a hidden system file (see Chapter 13 for a discussion of file attributes), which means in practice that you'll have to play with your folder viewing options to see them.

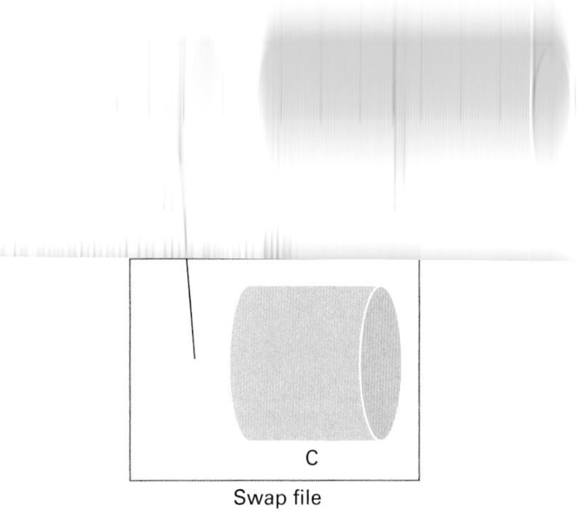

• **Figure 12.69** Program B is swapped back into RAM.

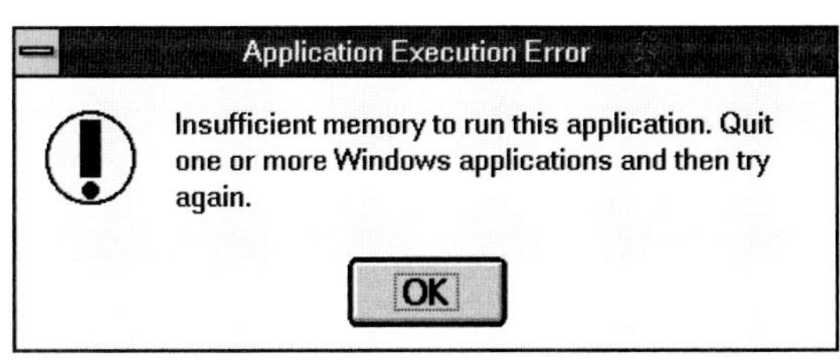

• **Figure 12.70** The alternative to swap files

Features and Characteristics of Windows 9x/Me

Microsoft debuted Windows 95 in 1995 as its first standalone GUI operating system. Subsequent versions of what is now called Windows 9*x* include Windows 95A, 95 OSR2, 98, 98 Second Edition (SE), and Millennium Edition (Me). Windows 95 did not appear out of a vacuum, however, but instead was built on the experience Microsoft had with DOS and with its first attempt at a GUI, Windows 3.*x*. Windows 3.*x* was great for its time, but was not a true OS. It was a graphical shell that required DOS to interact with the hardware. Remember the requirements for an operating system discussed at the beginning of this chapter?

Because of this lineage, Windows 9*x*/Me has a complex structure that retains elements—files and configuration utilities—from the previous operating system and graphical shell. This set of legacy files and utilities enables Windows 9*x*/Me to support a wide variety of hardware and applications, even stuff that dates prior to Windows 3.*x*! It also means that a lot of files can be configured incorrectly, so a tech needs to understand how the legacy files influence the graphical OS of Windows 9*x*/Me.

Windows 9*x*/Me is not just a polished up combo of DOS and Windows 3.*x*; rather, it has a complex set of operating system files and utilities all its

Chapters 15 and 16 discuss altering and troubleshooting your swap file in more detail.

Tech Tip

Moving the Page File in Windows 2000/XP

If you have a second hard drive installed in your PC, you can often get a nice performance boost by moving your page file from the C: drive (the default) to the second drive. To move your page file, go to the Control Panel | System applet and select the Advanced tab. In the Performance section, click the Settings button to open the Performance Options dialog box. Select the Advanced tab, and then click the Change button in the Virtual Memory section. Select a drive from the list and give it a size or range, and you're ready to go!

Just don't turn it off completely. Although Windows can run without virtual memory, you will definitely take a performance hit. You can do some more tweaking , but we'll save that for Chapters 15 and 16.

Two core differences between the original DOS and DPMI are support for the FAT32 file system and for long filenames (LFNs).

own. Windows 9*x*/Me has both 16-bit components—those that sprang from DOS and Windows 3.*x*—and 32-bit components—the native Windows 9*x*/Me code. Let's look at the legacy structures of Windows and then turn to the graphical OS. We'll finish this section with a brief discussion about the differences among the various versions of Windows 9*x*/Me.

DOS Protected Mode Interface

Windows 9*x*/Me is really two products: a **DOS protected-mode interface (DPMI)** and a protected-mode GUI. Protected-mode in this context means 32-bit, rather than 16-bit. The improved DOS part of Windows 9*x*/Me looks and acts pretty much exactly like good old DOS. Windows 9*x*/Me first starts the DOS aspect of Windows and then fires up the GUI. This means that you do not have to use the GUI to boot to Windows 9*x*.

FAT32

Later versions of Windows 95 and all versions of Windows 98, Me, and 2000/XP support the powerful FAT32 file format, enabling partitions up to 2 terabytes in size. Before FAT32, the old FAT16 format had a maximum partition size of only 2.1 GB.

Long Filenames

DOS and Windows 3.*x* both suffered from the ancient 8.3 naming convention. Windows 9*x*/Me systems allow filenames up to 255 characters while maintaining backward compatibility with the older 8.3 format. Additionally, Windows extended the old 8-bit ASCII character set and adopted a 16-bit Unicode character set. ASCII has only 2^8 (256) characters, but Unicode supports 2^{16} (65,536) characters. ASCII represents only Latin characters (a, A, b, B, c, D) and a few primitive drawing characters (↑, ↓, =, ↔), whereas Unicode supports virtually every text format known, including Cyrillic (Russian) and Kanji (Japanese) characters, as well as thousands of special drawing characters. The only trade-off with Unicode is that each character requires 2 bytes (16 bits) instead of 8 bits as in ASCII. Unicode fully supports the ASCII character set by making the first 256 characters identical to ASCII. So, for example, the Greek symbol Σ might be represented as 11100100 in ASCII, whereas Unicode just adds eight 0's to the front to make 0000000011100100. All Windows applications use Unicode. That's why you can add so many interesting symbols in Microsoft Word!

Core Files

DPMI is composed of three main files: IO.SYS, MSDOS.SYS, and COMMAND.COM, although you may not have COMMAND.COM in some circumstances. Even though the names are the same as the true DOS equivalents, the functions have changed dramatically. The functions of IO.SYS and MSDOS.SYS have been combined into IO.SYS. MSDOS.SYS has been turned into a hidden, read-only text file in the root directory of the boot drive. MSDOS.SYS is used as a startup options file. COMMAND.COM is still there and still performs the same basic function as the old COMMAND.COM, providing the prompt. COMMAND.COM is no longer required if the system will always run in the GUI mode. But if a C:\ prompt is ever needed, or if the system needs to use an AUTOEXEC.BAT file, COMMAND.COM must be present in the root directory. When the computer boots up and says "Starting Windows 95" or "Starting Windows 98," press the F8 key (on a Windows 98 system, press the leftmost CTRL key) and the Windows boot menu appears. We'll talk about this menu in a moment. For now, select Command Prompt Only. You will be at a command prompt. Type **VER** and you'll see "Windows 95" or "Windows 98," as shown in Figure 12.71.

Boot Menu

One of the many jobs of IO.SYS is to check to see whether the F8 key (leftmost CTRL key in Windows 98) has been pressed as Windows loads. If it has, the Windows boot menu loads. The Windows boot menu provides a method for technicians to perform a number of boot methods "on the fly" in different troubleshooting scenarios. Be warned that not all systems show the same

start pressing F8 at boot up. Don't hold down the key, just press it about once a second until the boot menu shows up. If you miss it, just restart the system and try again. Here's a list of the common (though not universal) boot menu options for Windows 9*x*:

- **Normal** This boots Windows normally.
- **Logged (\BOOTLOG.TXT)** This logs the boot process in a file called BOOTLOG.TXT.
- **Safe mode** This boots Windows into Safe mode. In Safe mode, only the OS and the mouse, keyboard, and VGA video drivers are loaded. A large part of the Registry isn't loaded, and neither AUTOEXEC.BAT nor CONFIG.SYS is run. Using Safe mode, you can boot to Windows without automatically loading a bad driver or other system configuration that's causing trouble. To automatically boot into Safe mode, press the F5 key at boot up.
- **Safe mode with network support** This boots Safe mode but still loads the network drivers so you can access the network. This option appears only on networked systems, which does not include Dial-up Networking!
- **Step-by-step confirmation** Similar to the old DOS F8 step-by-step, this includes a number of auto-loading features that are normally invisible.
- **Command prompt only** This processes all startup files but does not start the GUI. You can type **WIN** from the C:\ prompt to start the GUI if desired.

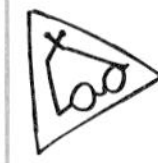

Tech Tip

The Peculiar Case of Windows Me

For reasons only known to its marketing folks, Microsoft decided to disable the ability of Windows Me to boot directly to the command line interface. Later in this chapter, I'll show you how to force Windows 9x to boot to the command line, but if you try it with Windows Me, the OS will laugh at you and load the GUI.

Your best bet when trouble-

ularly for the hard drive, are handled at a C:\ prompt. Do not confuse booting Windows 9x without the GUI with running a command prompt window inside Windows 9x/Me. The two are completely different things.

```
C:\>ver
Windows 98  [version 4.10.2222]
C:\>
```

• **Figure 12.71** The VER command

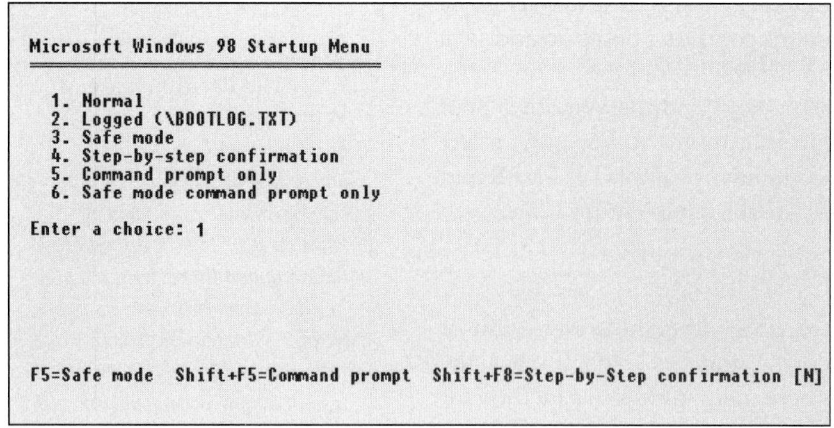

• **Figure 12.72** Windows 98 boot menu

- **Safe mode command prompt only** This skips all startup files to get to a C:\ prompt. You must reboot to start Windows.
- **Previous version of MS-DOS** If you installed Windows over a true DOS system, Windows keeps the original DOS boot files in the root directory with the extension .DOS and shows this option. You may boot to them. Do not use this option if you do not have a previous version of DOS or if the system's version of Windows uses FAT32.

Take the time to make sure you can access the boot menu. We'll use this in some of the upcoming repair scenarios. Try all the options except for Previous version of MS-DOS. I especially suggest using the step-by-step option. You can see a number of interesting options there!

Windows Me offers only a subset of the boot menu options. You do not get any of the command prompt options.

MSDOS.SYS

MSDOS.SYS is no longer part of the OS kernel in DPMI. It is now just a text file that replaces many of the AUTOEXEC.BAT and CONFIG.SYS functions that the system still needs before the GUI kicks in. A good Windows 9*x* tech should be comfortable editing an MSDOS.SYS file, so let's take a moment to see the contents of MSDOS.SYS. You may use any text editor to view or edit this file, but I prefer using the handy Notepad text editor. MSDOS.SYS has *hidden, system,* and *read-only* attributes by default, so you'll need to turn them off to see what's in this file. I don't use the ATTRIB command, although you certainly may if you want to make changing the attributes more of a challenge. (See Chapter 13 for more on the ATTRIB command.) I just boot to Windows, open the C: drive in My Computer, and make sure my Folder Options are set to show hidden and system files (as you did earlier in this chapter) and that I can see the file extensions.

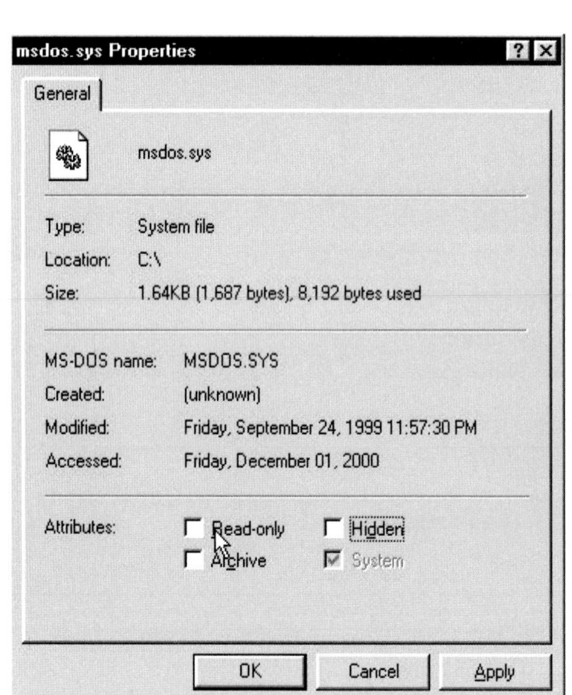

• **Figure 12.73** Changing file attributes

Click once on the MSDOS.SYS file to select it, and then alternate-click the MSDOS.SYS file to show its properties. Uncheck the attributes as shown in Figure 12.73. Now you can view the contents of MSDOS.SYS. Hold down the left SHIFT key and alternate-click on MSDOS.SYS again, but this time select the Open With option. (If you don't hold down the left SHIFT key, you won't see the Open With option.) Scroll through the list until you see Notepad, select it, and make sure the Always Use This Program To Open This Type Of File check box is unchecked. Click OK. Welcome to MSDOS.SYS. Do not make any changes! Just look! Choose File | Exit when you're done.

Notice that MSDOS.SYS is organized just like an INI file, with groups and options under each setting. The following options must be placed in the [Options] group. Each of the examples shows the default setting, but other settings are listed.

I've included all the MSDOS.SYS settings I know, but that certainly doesn't mean you'll use all of them! Most of these settings have default values that you do not want to change.

- **BootConfig=1** This enables the computer to boot up a particular hardware configuration. For example, BootConfig=2 would start configuration 2.
- **DisableLog=1** This enables the BOOTLOG.TXT file (0 = disable).
- **SystemReg=1** This loads the system Registry (0 = don't load).
- **BootSafe=0** This option does not force the machine to boot in Safe mode (1 = force Safe mode).
- **DBLSpace=1 or DRVSpace=1** This loads DoubleSpace or DriveSpace drivers (0 = don't load).
- **BootWin=1** This boots Windows (0 = DOS). This is a dangerous

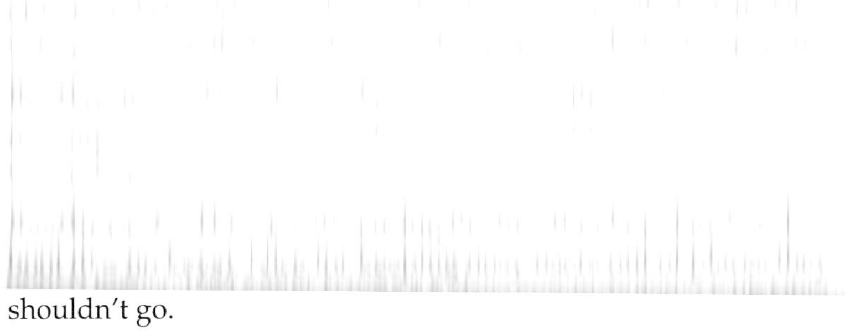

shouldn't go.
- **BootGUI=1** This specifies booting the Windows 9*x* GUI (0 = DOS prompt only). I use this when I'm working on a system that I intend to reboot to a command prompt many times.
- **Network=1** This shows boot in Safe mode, with a networking menu option available (0 = don't show). I use this option when I know I'm going to need to pull a driver off a server somewhere. Doesn't everyone keep all the drivers they use for every system on a server? You don't?
- **BootMenu=0** This does not automatically load the boot menu at boot (1 = show menu). I like to use this when I'm working on systems.
- **BootMenuDefault=1** This shows the default boot menu option if you don't pick one (I've never used this option):
  - Normal
  - 2 = Logged to Bootlog.txt
  - 3 = Safe mode
  - 4 = Safe mode with network support (if network settings are enabled)
  - 4 (if no networking) or 5 (if networking enabled) = Step-by-step
  - 5 (no networking) or 6 (networking) = Command prompt
  - 6 (no networking) or 7 (networking) = Safe mode command prompt
  - 7 (no networking) or 8 (networking) = Previous version of MS-DOS (if BootMulti=1)

Please don't kill yourself trying to memorize all these features. Do take the time to appreciate that MSDOS.SYS is now a text file. Make sure you know how to edit it if asked, and have a general idea of the types of options it provides. Take some time to appreciate what it does and does not do. Does it load device drivers or TSRs? No. Does it provide a number of boot options? Yes. Think about how some of these options might come in handy in a troubleshooting scenario.

- **DoubleBuffer=1** This loads VFAT's double buffer (0 = don't load). Obsolete command for older SCSI drives.
- **BootMulti=0** This is for dual-boot systems. If set to 0, the boot menu will not prompt for the previous version of MS-DOS. If set to 1, you will see the option "Previous version of MS-DOS." Don't mess with this option unless a) you installed on top of DOS and b) you did not use FAT32.
- **Logo=1** This shows an animated logo (0 = don't show).
- **LoadTop=1** This loads COMMAND.COM at the top of 640 K (0 = load at the bottom).
- **BootDelay=X** This specifies how long the computer waits, in seconds, after showing "Starting Windows 9*x*." Many techs set this to "0" to make booting faster.
- **AutoScan=1** This option specifies whether ScanDisk runs automatically when you reboot after a crash. If you set this to 0, ScanDisk will not run. Set to 1 means the system will prompt you before running, and set to 2 means Windows will run ScanDisk without asking your approval (although it will prompt before making changes/fixes). This is usable only in OSR2 and later versions of Windows 9*x*.

The following options must be in the [Paths] group:

- **UninstallDir=C:** This specifies where to find the Windows 9*x* uninstall file.
- **WinDir=C:\WINDOWS** This specifies the location of the Windows GUI files.
- **WinBootDir=C:\WINDOWS** This specifies the location of the Windows files needed to boot. It is normally the same as the WinDir directory.
- **HostWinBootDrv=C** This is always the C: drive.

Configuration Files

Windows 9*x*/Me can use the two DOS-era configuration files, CONFIG.SYS and AUTOEXEC.BAT, for loading legacy device drivers and terminate and stay resident (TSR) programs, such as ancient mouse drivers. You'll see both files come into play to load CD-ROM drivers in Windows 9*x*/Me Startup disks, for example, and in systems that run older applications. For the most part, though, the files sit empty in the root directory of the C: drive.

Two DOS-era memory management files can appear in CONFIG.SYS—HIMEM.SYS and EMM386.EXE—although Windows 9*x*/Me loads both files automatically in the protected mode GUI phase. HIMEM.SYS provides access to the memory beyond the first 1 MB of space, and thus is required by Windows 9*x*/Me to load the graphical portions of the operating system. EMM386.EXE was a great utility for its day, enabling us to play excellent games such as *DOOM* and *Red Baron*, and providing a tool for fine-tuning memory addresses. EMM386.EXE is obsolete in modern computers.

Legacy GUI Files

After the DPMI-level OS files, configuration files, and utilities load, WIN.COM runs and initiates the graphical portion of the operating system. During the loading process, Windows incorporates the legacy INI files to provide support for any ancient applications you might load on a Windows 9*x*/Me system. (The same holds true for Windows 2000/XP, although not for NT 4.0.)

Windows 9*x*/Me PCs require HIMEM.SYS to load the graphical portion of the OS.

Windows 3.*x* used text files with the extension .INI to initialize just about everything from device drivers to applications to Windows itself. Any Windows 3.*x* computer had at least three but usually dozens of these files stored in the \WINDOWS directory (Figure 12.74). Both Windows and Windows applications created ini- [illegible] using EDIT or any other DOS-based word proc[illegible] All versions of Windows come with a handy GUI text editor called Notepad. Figure 12.75 shows Notepad displaying the contents of SERIALNO.INI, a typical INI file of the Windows 3.*x* days. SERIALNO.INI stored the registration information of the copy of Windows 3.*x*. Don't bother looking for this INI file on a Windows 9*x*/Me or Windows 2000/XP system; it has been replaced by something else!

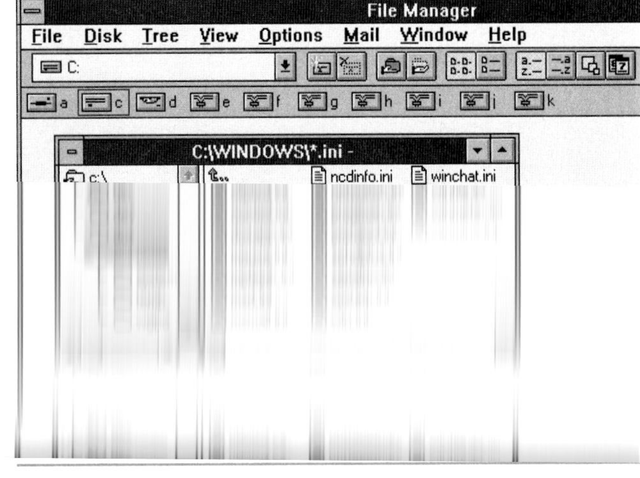

• Figure 12.74 INI files in the Windows directory

Note that all INI files are broken up into logical sections called *groups*. Each group starts with a word or words in square brackets, called a *group header*—for instance, [*mswindows*]. Following each group header are the settings for that group. They are organized with the syntax *item=settings*. Although the typical Windows 3.*x* system used many INI files, two in particular require special consideration: SYSTEM.INI and WIN.INI.

• Figure 12.75 The contents of SERIALNO.INI

SYSTEM.INI

SYSTEM.INI was the CONFIG.SYS of Windows 3.*x*. All the resources were initialized there, as well as a number of global settings that defined how resources were to be used. We often edited this file on Windows 3.*x* systems to tweak a large number of settings. The SYSTEM.INI file was absolutely required to run a Windows 3.*x* system. You still find SYSTEM.INI on all Windows systems today, including Windows 2000/XP. Keeping the SYSTEM.INI file enables backward compatibility with older Windows 3.*x* applications that still look for a SYSTEM.INI file to load or determine critical settings. All Windows 9*x*/Me systems still require SYSTEM.INI, even though the settings are no longer critical. If you don't believe me, rename

Windows 2000/XP do not require SYSTEM.INI but have one to support older programs.

the SYSTEM.INI file to YODA.INI on any version of Windows 9*x*/Me and reboot the system. You'll get this nasty error:

```
Cannot find SYSTEM.INI.

You need to run Windows Setup again to install this file

Press any key to continue...
```

Boot to Safe Mode Command Prompt Only to get to a C:\ prompt. Get into the \WINDOWS folder and type the **REN** (for *rename*) command, as follows, to put it back to normal:

```
REN YODA.INI SYSTEM.INI
```

WIN.INI

Know how to edit SYSTEM.INI and WIN.INI on Windows 9x/Me and 2000/XP systems. You can use EDIT.EXE, Notepad, or SYSEDIT to edit AUTOEXEC.BAT, CONFIG.SYS, and INI files. Also, you should know why the INI files exist on Windows 9x/Me systems and when they are needed!

WIN.INI was the AUTOEXEC.BAT of Windows 3.*x*. It defined all the personalizations of Windows, such as fonts, screen savers, and display colors, and it defined how resources interacted with applications. WIN.INI was also the dumping ground for settings that did not have a home anywhere else. This file was often manually edited. Windows 3.*x* didn't require WIN.INI to boot, but you lost a lot of functionality without it. Windows 9*x*/Me and Windows 2000/XP rarely have a WIN.INI file unless an installed application makes one.

Dealing with SYSTEM.INI and WIN.INI

Windows 9*x*/Me and Windows 2000/XP systems rarely need to bother with these two files, as all the sections in SYSTEM.INI and WIN.INI are properly created when Windows is installed and should never be changed. However, two situations warrant an occasional peek at these two files. First, we occasionally see an error in Windows 9*x*/Me systems at boot that looks like this:

```
Cannot find a device file that may be needed to run Windows or a
Windows application.

The Windows Registry or SYSTEM.INI file refers to this device file,
but the device file no longer exists.

If you deleted this file on purpose, try uninstalling the associated
application using its uninstall or setup program.

If you still want to use the application associated with this device
file, try reinstalling that application to replace the missing file.

chimchim
Press a key to continue.
```

Notice the word *chimchim*? That's a line in the SYSTEM.INI file (probably) that needs correcting. Many applications and hardware install programs dump lines into the SYSTEM.INI that are in most cases useless. To edit the SYSTEM.INI file, use the handy SYSEDIT program (Figure 12.76).

The [386Enh] section of SYSTEM.INI stores all the drivers for *386 enhanced mode*—Microsoft's term for the OS accessing the processor's 386 protected mode. Most of the problems associated with SYSTEM.INI on

Windows 9*x*/Me and 2000/XP systems can be attributed directly to drivers within this section. When I find these errors, I just add a semicolon (;) to the beginning of the offending line (turning it into a comment) and then reboot. These lines are rarely needed.

WIN.INI has two problem areas that can cause trouble on modern systems: LOAD= and RUN=. These lines automatically load programs when Windows starts, acting like a hidden Startup Group. If you find

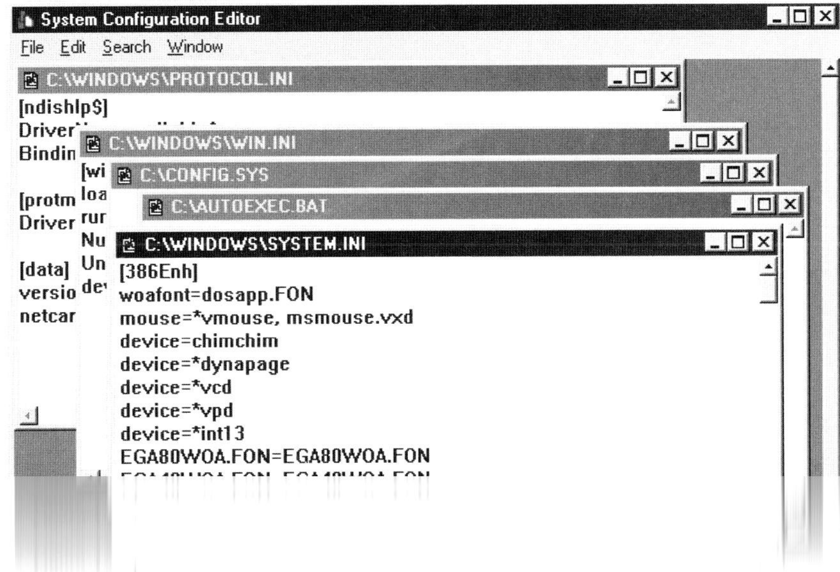

The GUI loads its own device drivers for everything. Assuming a Windows 9*x*/Me device driver is available, you don't need CONFIG.SYS to load device drivers anymore. Windows 9*x*/Me does everything CONFIG.SYS does. So again, assuming Windows 9*x*/Me drivers are available, you do not need CONFIG.SYS. In addition, the GUI provides protected-mode mouse support for Windows 95, Windows 3.*x*, and DOS applications, so you probably don't need AUTOEXEC.BAT or WIN.INI either.

Figure 12.77 shows how the GUI is organized. The lowest levels of Windows 9*x*/Me are the device drivers—either real-mode drivers loaded at CONFIG.SYS or AUTOEXEC.BAT, or protected-mode drivers loaded with the GUI. After the device drivers comes the *virtual memory manager* (VMM), which supports memory usage at both the DPMI and GUI levels. At the DPMI level, VMM does little more than load a simple command line. When the GUI is loaded, VMM takes advantage of the power of 386 protected mode to create *virtual machines*, one for Windows 9*x*/Me and one for each DOS program running in Windows 9*x*/Me. At the same level as the VMM is the *installable file system* (IFS), which provides support for hard, CD-ROM, and network drives. The IFS also provides the support for long filenames. DPMI, as well as the GUI, require the IFS.

When the GUI is running, the main functions of Windows 9*x*/Me are handled by the kernel, user, and *graphical device interface* (GDI) modules. These files—KRNL386.EXE, USER.EXE, and GDI.EXE, reside in the C:\ Windows\System folder. Most functions run in full 32-bit protected mode, although they provide support for 16-bit real mode.

At the top of the Windows 9*x*/Me architecture is the user interface—the programs you actually *see* on the screen: the icons, windows, and toolbars. Windows 9*x*/Me can use the default interface, the Windows 3.*x* interface, or even other shells.

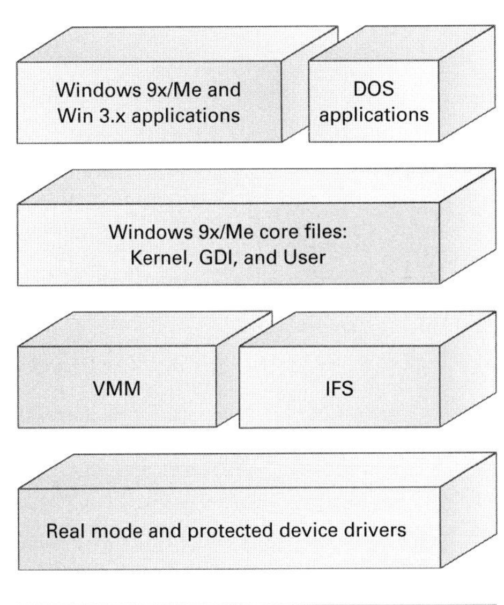

Figure 12.77 GUI architecture

Major Differences Among Windows 95, 98, 98 SE, and Me

In my opinion, Windows 98 was no more than Windows 95 with a lot of new toys added to improve usability and to prevent or address system problems. Likewise, Windows 98 SE provided a couple of extra features and incorporated all the bug fixes Microsoft wrote for Windows 98. Windows Me is the decidedly odd bird in the grouping, because it resembles Windows 2000 far more than Windows 98, even though it's built on the 9*x* rather than the NT kernel. The following list details a few of the more outstanding updates implemented with the versions of Windows 9*x*/Me.

A Great Startup Disk

Windows 9*x*/Me systems all provide a method to create a startup disk. A *startup disk* is a special bootable floppy disk that contains a number of handy utilities to help you fix a system that won't boot Windows. Startup disks enable you to boot to an A:\ prompt and then run a few basic utilities. You cannot start Windows from a startup disk, so you can't run any graphical programs—but both Windows 95 and Windows 98 enable you to make a startup disk with enough tools that can run from an A:\ prompt to fix many common problems. One huge problem with the Windows 95 startup disk is that it does not support a CD-ROM drive. In many cases, you need to access the CD-ROM to install programs, so you have to go through a rather painful process to make the Windows 95 startup disk access the CD-ROM. The Windows 98/SE/Me startup disk automatically supports almost every type of CD-ROM drive made. Why bother booting to an A:\ prompt if you can't access the CD-ROM to at least reinstall Windows? I love Windows 98/SE/Me startup disks compared to the Windows 95 startup disks.

FAT32

The first version of Windows 95 supported only FAT16 file system for hard drives. As manufacturers started cranking out bigger and bigger hard drives to meet customer needs, something had to be done. Microsoft introduced FAT32 with Windows 95 version B, also called OSR2.

Try This!

Running Windows Update

Every tech and user should know how to run Windows Update, just to patch the operating system and protect against Internet worms and other fun things, so try this!

In a Windows 9x/Me system, go to Start | Windows Update or, if for some reason your system does not have the option on the Start menu, simply go to this web site: http://windowsupdate.microsoft.com. In Windows 2000 and XP, go to Start | All Programs and select Windows Update to start the browser.

However you get it started, the outcome should be the same. The update website will prompt you to download update software and then, possibly after a reboot, you'll get a list of patches available. For this exercise, install at least one of the Critical Updates and Service Packs or Driver Update. In real life, you'd want all the critical fixes, most of the suggested Windows patches, and all the driver updates!

System Information Tool

The System Information tool provides a handy snapshot of your system in a fairly easy-to-read format. I think of the System Information tool as a "read-only Device Manager" in that you get to see all of the resource and driver information provided by Device Manager in a report format (Figure 12.78). Additionally, the System Information tool provides a launch point for

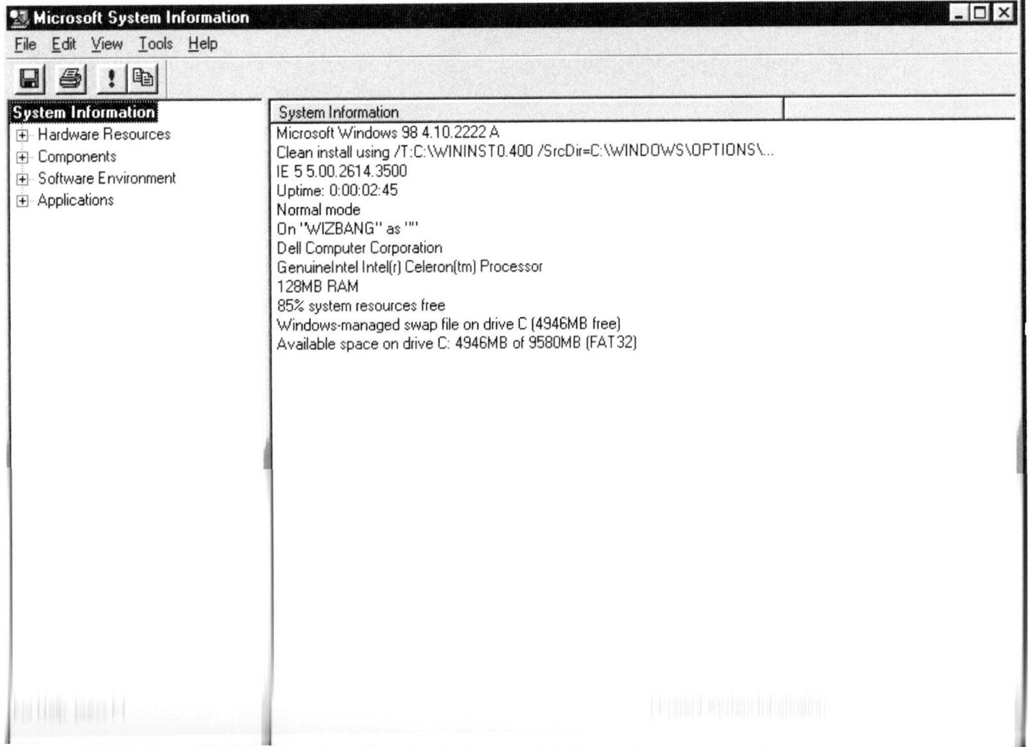

• **Figure 12.78** System Information tool

almost every utility used by Windows 98/SE/Me. If you need to run a utility but you're not sure where to find it, look under the Tools menu (Figure 12.79).

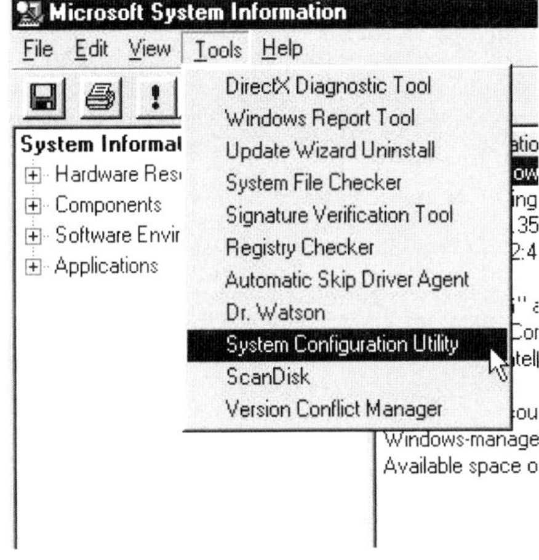

• **Figure 12.79** System Information Tools menu

Windows Update

Microsoft constantly provides free updates to its OSs. Updating Windows 95 gave the best techs a bad case of the jitters because the updating order had to be carefully monitored. (Chapter 15 goes into this in some detail.) Windows 98/SE/Me eliminates this problem completely with the Windows Update utility. This web-based utility uses a special web site to inspect your system and provides a simple method to update your system safely (Figure 12.80).

Disk Cleanup

Windows needs lots of unused disk space for swap files and temporary files generated by applications. In Windows 95, running out of disk space usually manifests itself as a "Not enough disk space" error—at best. Usually lockups and general protection faults take place. Windows 98/SE/Me has a Disk Cleanup utility that enables you to clean out unnecessary files (Figure 12.81). What makes this tool particularly handy is that it will automatically start when your drive reaches a certain minimum. Although third-party utilities such as Norton CleanSweep do a better job, Disk Cleanup works perfectly well for most systems.

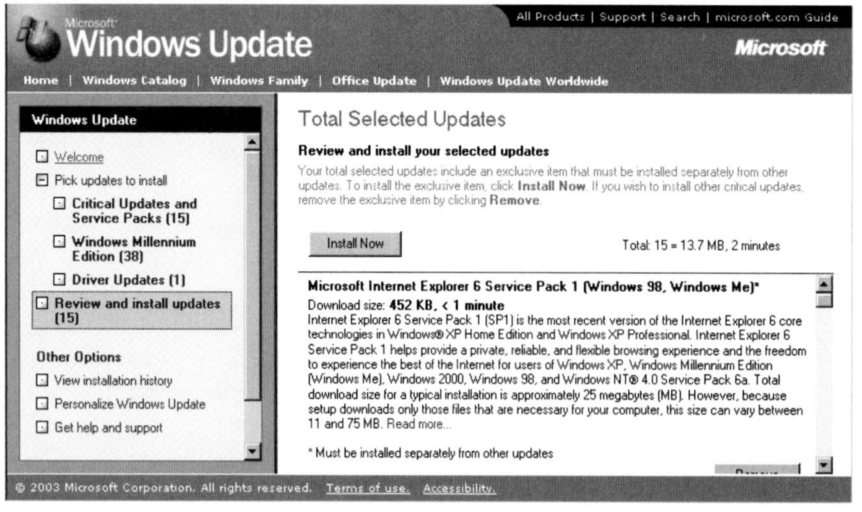

• **Figure 12.80** Windows 98 Update utility

• **Figure 12.81** Windows Disk Cleanup utility

Active Desktop

Windows 98/SE/Me come with a vastly improved version of Internet Explorer that includes the amazing Active Desktop, enabling the Desktop to load active web pages directly. Why bother opening a browser when that often-accessed web page sits on your Desktop, ready for instant viewing? New, even more powerful versions of Internet Explorer have since been released.

Internet Connection Sharing

The biggest improvement Microsoft included with Windows 98SE was Internet Connection Sharing (ICS), a way to enable multiple PCs to share a single dialup connection. Chapter 24 covers ICS in detail.

System Restore

Windows Me shares the core files and structure of Windows 9*x*, but Microsoft clearly wanted to make it more like Windows 2000 rather than 98. To that end, Microsoft changed the outward appearance to match that of 2000, including replacing the icons and changing the names of various utilities. Network Neighborhood (95/98), for example, is My Network Places in Me/2000/XP. Microsoft also included some cool multimedia tools, such as an improved Media Player and Movie Maker (both digital video editing software).

The most important enhancement that Windows Me has over its older siblings is a feature called System Restore. System Restore enables you to create Restore Points—snapshots of your system files and configurations at a particular moment—so you can restore your PC to this pristine state if you install something later that makes it unhappy. You would use this feature right before installing a big office suite, for example, or an aggressive program like Real Media. Figure 12.82 shows System Restore in action. (Chapter 15 goes into System Restore in detail.)

But Underneath…

All of the extra functions in Windows 98, 98SE, and Me do not eliminate the fact that in nearly every respect, these later OSs are identical to Windows 95. The installation process, install functions, and troubleshooting procedures vary little among the versions.

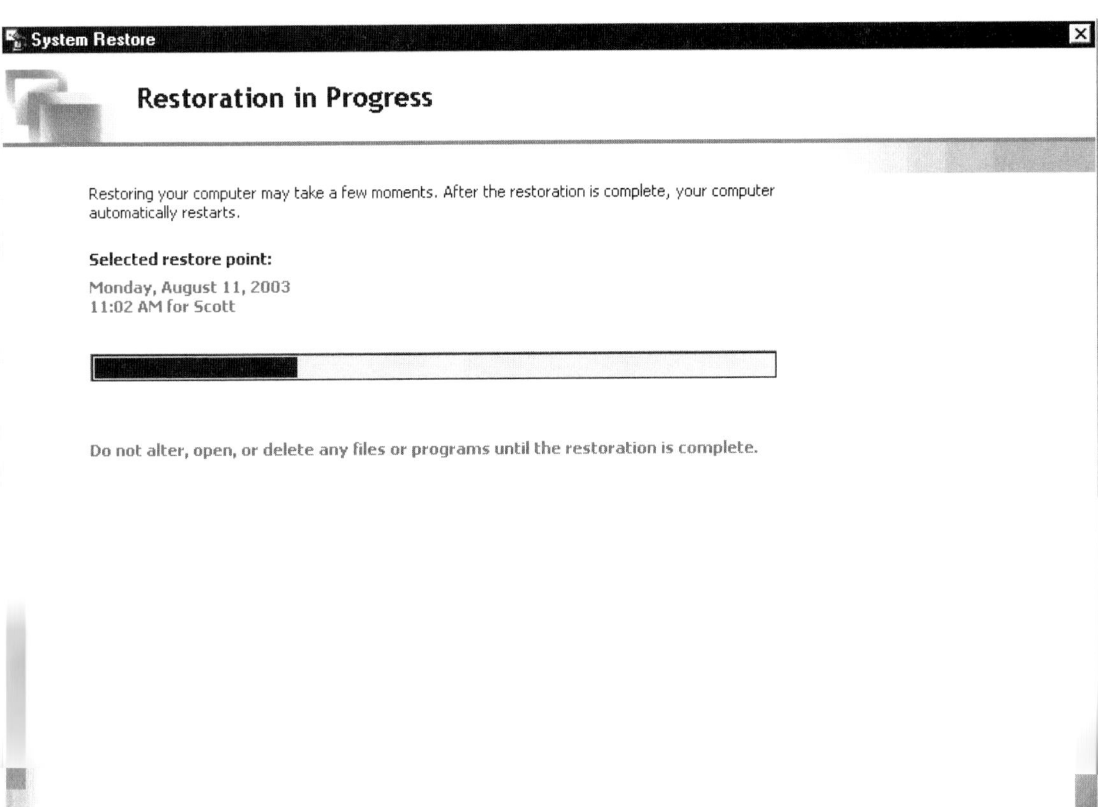

• **Figure 12.82** System Restore in action

Features and Characteristics of Windows NT/2000/XP

The mixed structure of Windows 9*x*/Me, with its support for 16-bit and 32-bit applications and drivers and the bizarre mixture of new and legacy OS and configuration files, makes that benighted OS family something of a Frankenstein monster. Even shortly after Windows 95 debuted, people were scratching their heads and wondering why they couldn't have a real 32-bit operating system! Today, it makes even less sense. Why should you need to run a program written in 1986 *natively* on a PC sporting a 3+ GHz Athlon XP, a 120 GB hard drive, and 1024 MB RAM? You can do with Windows 9*x* running at the DPMI level, but it makes no sense. Plus, such a cobbled together OS couldn't take full advantage of the 32-bit architecture available in every CPU since the 80386! Something had to change.

In 1996, Microsoft released Windows NT 4.0, a 32-bit GUI OS that provided some backward compatibility for Windows 3.*x* and Windows 95 applications, but such was not the point. With NT, Microsoft offered a rock-solid, high-performance OS that offered scalability and, above all else, security.

Windows 2000 and Windows XP share the same core structure, files, and features as Windows NT, so the discussion that follows applies to both newer operating systems. Where the later OSs differ is in ease of use and support for hardware. Let's cover NT in detail and then discuss the differences between the three OSs.

• **Figure 12.83** Windows NT and Windows 95 have a similar interface.

Windows NT

From the outside, Windows NT 4.0 looks pretty much just like Windows 95 (Figure 12.83). For the most part, that's where the similarities end. Windows NT has so many features beyond Windows 9*x* that it takes a moment to decide where to start! Let's begin with the organization of the OS.

OS Organization

Three words best describe NT's organization: robust, scalable, and cross-platform. NT takes an object-oriented approach to the OS, separating the OS into three distinct parts: the drivers, the NT Executive, and the subsystems (Figure 12.84).

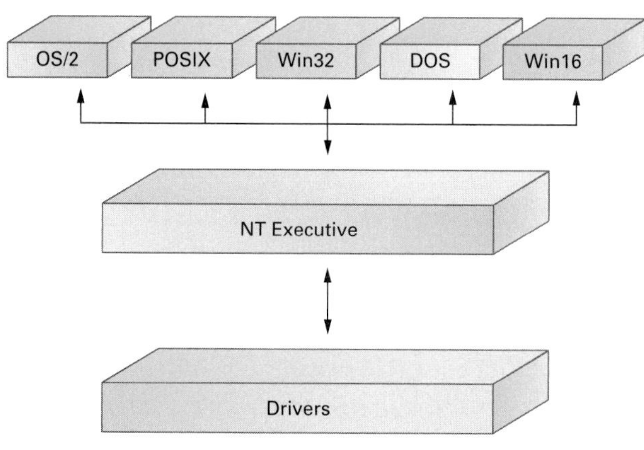

• **Figure 12.84** Windows NT organization

NT was designed to support different CPU platforms beyond the x86, such as DEC Alpha, MIPS, and PowerPC. To achieve this, the NT Executive uses a **Hardware Abstraction Layer (HAL)** to separate the system-specific device drivers from the rest of the NT system (Figure 12.85). Although Windows 2000 shares this organization, Microsoft has chosen to drop support for all but Intel x86 systems in Windows 2000.

NT and 2000's robustness comes from the separation of running processes into a myriad of subsystems. NT is fully POSIX-compliant (a UNIX thing) and has support for OS/2, DOS, and 16- and 32-bit Windows via these numerous subsystems (Figure 12.86). Windows 2000 keeps all the same supports with the exception of OS/2.

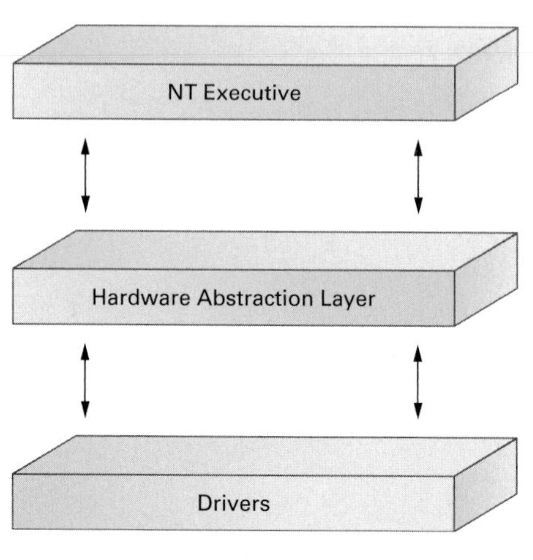

• **Figure 12.85** NT Executive and the HAL

NT's scalability makes it the only Microsoft OS to support *symmetric multiprocessing* (SMP), providing support for systems with up to 32 CPUs. Yee hah! Windows 2000 goes beyond SMP by adding the power of clustering, enabling multiple systems to share redundant data for ultimate protection. (Say that three times fast—I dare you!) If one system goes down, the other systems continue to run. (This feature is available only in high-end Server versions of Windows 2000.)

NT File System (NTFS)

From the beginning, Microsoft designed and optimized every aspect of Windows NT (and Windows 2000/XP) for multi-user, networked environments. This is most evident in the file system—how NT stores files on your hard drive(s). Whereas all previous Microsoft OSs used either FAT16 or FAT32, NT, 2000, and XP use a far more powerful and robust file system appropriately called *NT File System* (NTFS).

Chapter 11 contains a fairly good description of NTFS, but let's go into a bit more detail on this file system. NTFS offers the following excellent features:

- Long filenames
- Redundancy
- Backward compatibility
- Recoverability
- Security

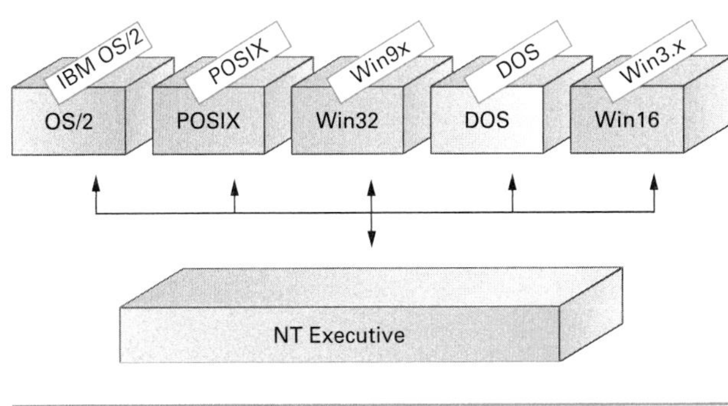

Figure 12.86 NT can handle a lot of different OSs.

Long Filenames

NTFS supported LFNs long before FAT32 even existed. Like LFNs, NTFS filenames can be up to 255 characters.

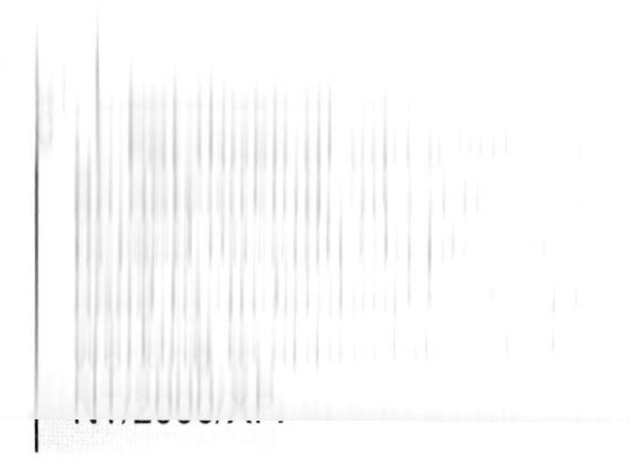

Backward Compatibility

For all its power, NTFS is amazingly backward compatible. You can copy DOS or Windows 9*x*/Me programs to an NTFS partition. Windows even keeps the LFNs.

Windows NT fully supports FAT16, NTFS, and HPFS (for OS/2). Windows 2000 and XP support FAT16, FAT32, and NTFS.

Recoverability

Accidental system shutdowns, reboots, and lockups in the midst of a file save or retrieval wreak havoc on most systems. NTFS avoids this with *transaction logging*. Transaction logging determines incomplete file transactions and restores the file to the original format automatically and invisibly.

Security

NTFS truly shines with its powerful security functions. When most people hear the term "security," they tend to think about networks. NTFS security works perfectly in a network environment, but for the moment, let's just pretend that only one Windows NT/2000 system exists in the entire world. Three different people use this computer. Each person has one personal folder that he or she doesn't want the others to access. On a Windows 9*x*/Me system, anyone who can get in front of the keyboard of a system can access any folder; the password allows only him or her on the network. This is not so with Windows NT/2000/XP! Let's look at three major features of NTFS security: accounts, groups, and permissions.

All versions of Windows can read CD-ROMs—we call the CD-ROM file system CDFS!

Accounts To use a Windows NT/2000/XP system, you must have a valid account and password. Without that account, you cannot use the system (Figure 12.87).

Don't confuse Windows 9*x*/Me login passwords with screensaver passwords! If you walk up to a Windows 9*x*/Me system that prompts for a password, it has nothing to do with the login password. Screensaver passwords for Windows 9*x* systems are set under the Screensaver tab of the system's Display Properties dialog box. Windows NT/2000/XP do not have this separate password problem. They use the login password for the screensaver, too, so you need to remember only your login password to access a Windows NT/2000/system that uses a screensaver password.

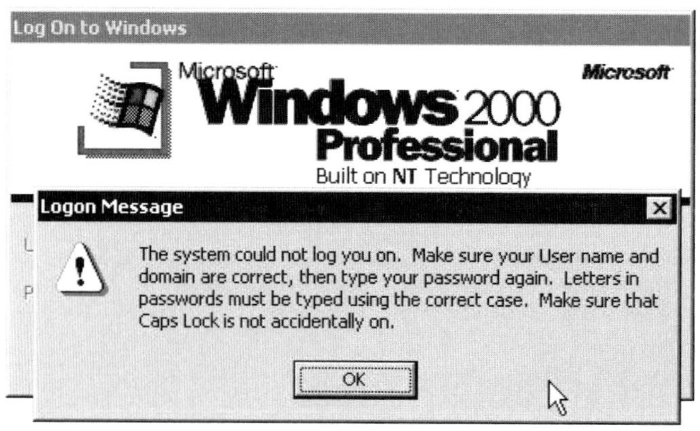

• **Figure 12.87** Login failure

Every Windows NT/2000 system has a "super" account called *administrator*. When you first install a Windows NT/2000 system, it prompts you for a password for the administrator account. As you might imagine, this account has access to everything—a dangerous thing in the wrong hands!

Groups The administrator creates user accounts with a special program called Users and Passwords in Windows 2000 (Figure 12.88) and User Accounts in Windows XP. Note the account list has three columns: User Name, Domain, and Group. To understand domains requires an extensive networking discussion, so we'll leave that for Chapter 23 and instead focus here on user names and groups. A *user name* defines an account for a person who has access to the PC. A *group* is simply a collection of accounts that share the same access capabilities. A single account can be a member of multiple groups.

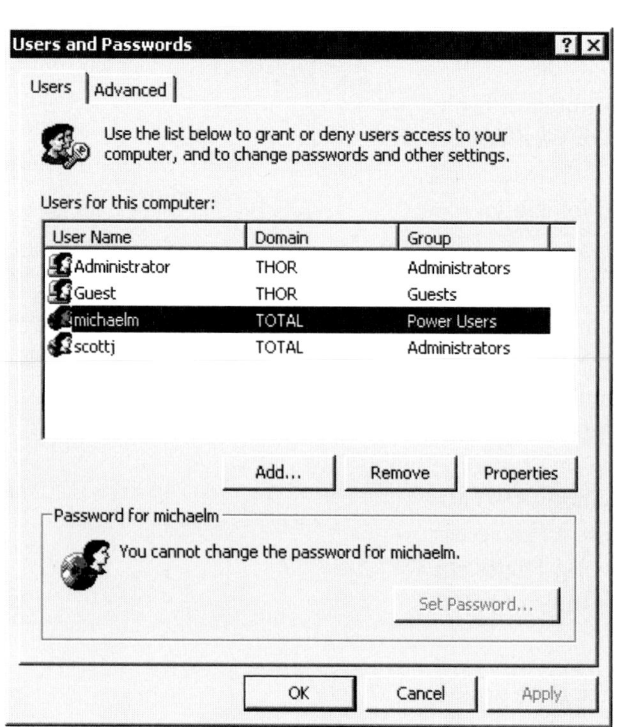

• **Figure 12.88** Users And Passwords dialog box

Groups make Windows administration much easier in two ways. First, we can assign a certain level of access for a file or folder to a group instead of to an account. We can make a group called Accounting and put all the accounting user accounts in that group. If a person quits, we don't need to worry about deleting her account and then creating a new one for her replacement, including reassigning all the proper access levels. We just make a new account and add that new person to a group!

Second, Windows provides seven built-in groups: Administrators, Power Users, Users, Backup Operators, Replicator, Everyone, and Guests. These built-in groups have a number of preset abilities. You cannot delete these groups.

- **Administrators** Any account that is a member of this group has complete administrator privileges. It is common for the primary user of a Windows 2000 system to have his or her account in the Administrators group.

- **Power Users** Power users are almost as powerful as administrators, but they cannot install new devices or access other users' files or folders unless the files or folders specifically provide them access.
- **Users** Users cannot edit the Registry or access critical system files. They can create groups but can manage only those they create.
- **Backup Operators** Backup operators have the same rights as users, but they can run backup programs that access any file or folder—for backup purposes only.
- **Replicator** Members of the Replicator group can replicate files and folders in a domain.
- **Everyone** This account applies to any user who can log onto the system. You cannot edit this group.

Computer Administrator, Limited User, and Guest. Computer Administrators can do anything, as you might suspect. Limited Users can access only certain things and have limits on where they can save files on the PC.

NTFS Permissions In the NT/2000/XP world, every folder and file on an NTFS partition has a list that contains two sets of data. First, the list details every user and group that has access to that file or folder. Second, the list specifies the level of access that each user or group has to that file and folder. The level of access is defined by a set of restrictions called **NTFS permissions**.

Permissions define exactly what a particular account can or cannot do to the file or folder and are thus quite detailed and powerful. You can make it possible, for example, for a person to edit a file but not delete it. You can create a folder and not allow other people to make subfolders. NTFS file and folder permissions are so complicated that entire books have been written on them! Fortunately for us, the A+ Certification exams test your understanding of only a few basic concepts of NTFS permissions: Ownership, Take Ownership permission, Change permissions, Folder permissions, and File permissions.

- **Ownership** When you create a new file or folder on an NTFS partition, you become the *owner* of that file or folder. A newly created file or folder by default gives full permission to everyone to access, delete, and otherwise manipulate that file or folder. Owners can do anything they want to the files or folders they own, including changing the permissions to prevent anybody, even administrators, from accessing them.
- **Take Ownership permission** This special permission enables anyone with the permission to seize control of a file or folder.

Administrator accounts have Take Ownership permission for everything. Note the difference here between owning a file and accessing a file. If you own a file, you can prevent anyone from accessing that file. An administrator who you have blocked, however, can take that ownership away from you and *then* access that file! Get it?

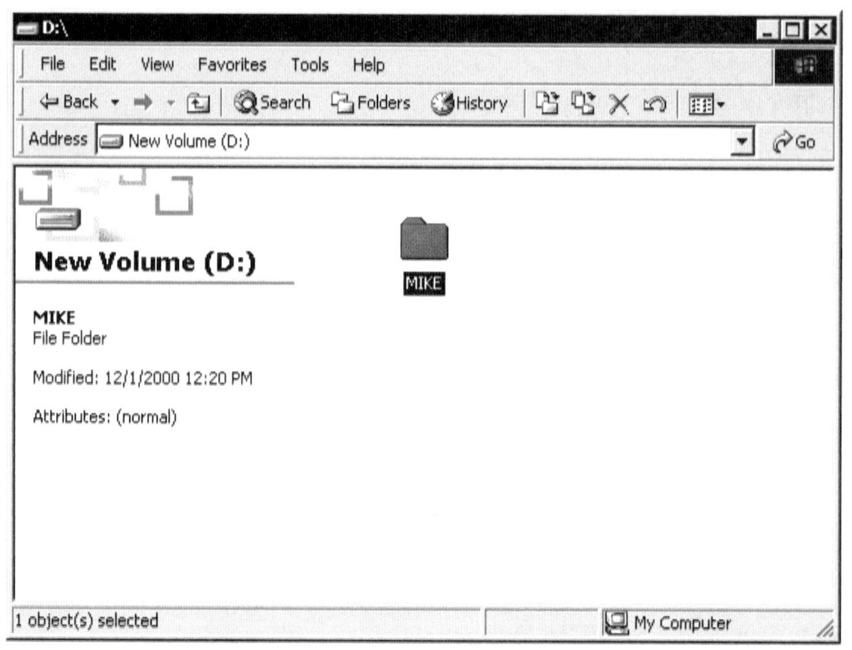

• **Figure 12.89** A typical folder—isn't it lovely?

- **Change permissions** Another important permission for all NTFS files and folders is the Change permission. An account with this permission can give or take away permissions for other accounts.
- **Folder permissions** Let's look at a typical folder in my Windows 2000 system to see how all this works. My D: drive is formatted as NTFS. On the D: drive I created a folder called D:\MIKE. In My Computer, it looks like Figure 12.89. I set the permissions for the folder by accessing the folder's properties and clicking the Security tab (see Figure 12.90).
- **File permissions** These are discussed shortly.

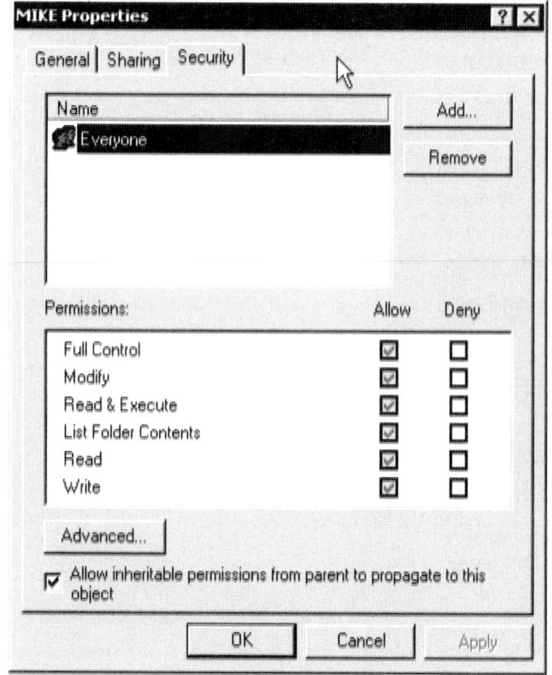

• **Figure 12.90** Security tab in folder properties dialog box

In Windows NT/2000/XP, just about everything in the computer has a Security tab in its properties. Every Security tab contains two main areas. The top area shows the list of accounts that have permissions for that resource. The lower area shows exactly what permissions have been assigned to that account.

Windows NTFS permissions are quite powerful and quite complex. The permissions shown in the permission area, for example, are not really permissions, but rather pre-set combinations of permissions that cover the most common types of access. Click the Advanced button, and then click View/Edit to see the real NTFS permissions; Microsoft calls them *special* permissions (Figure 12.91). Even the most advanced NT/2000 support people rarely need to access these.

Here are the standard permissions for a folder:

- **Full Control** Enables you to do anything you want!
- **Modify** Enables you to do anything except delete files or subfolders.
- **Read & Execute** Enables you to see the contents of the folder and any subfolders.

- **List Folder Contents** Enables you to see the contents of the folder and any subfolders. (This permission seems the same as the Read & Execute permission, but is only inherited by folders.)
- **Read** Enables you to read any files in the folder.
- **Write** Enables you to write to files and create new files and folders.

If you look at the bottom of the Security tab, you'll see a little check box that says Allow Inheritable Permissions From Parent To Propagate To This Object. In other words, any files or subfolders created in this folder get the same permissions for the same users/groups that the folder has. Unchecking this option

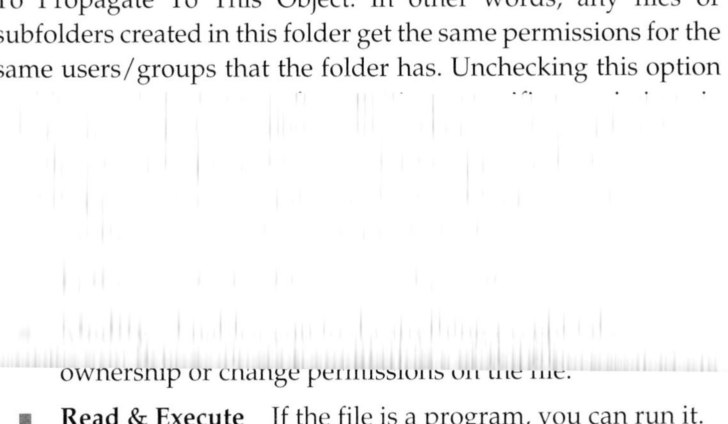

ownership or change permissions on the file.

- **Read & Execute** If the file is a program, you can run it.
- **Read** If the file is data, you can read it.
- **Write** Enables you to write to the file.

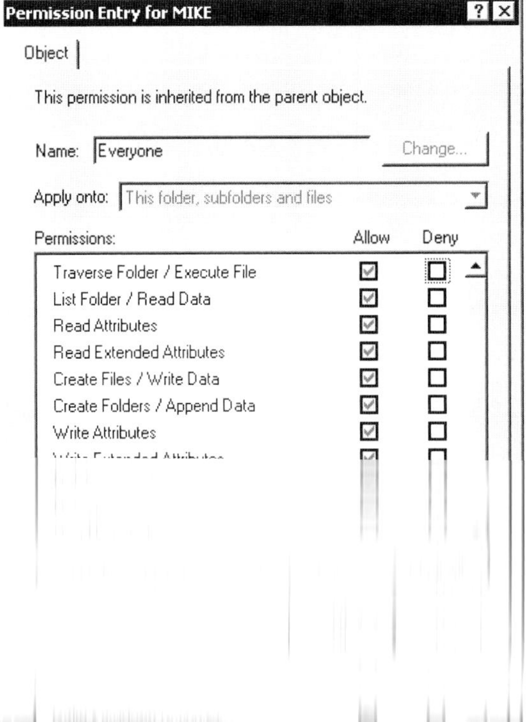

Figure 12.91 Special permissions

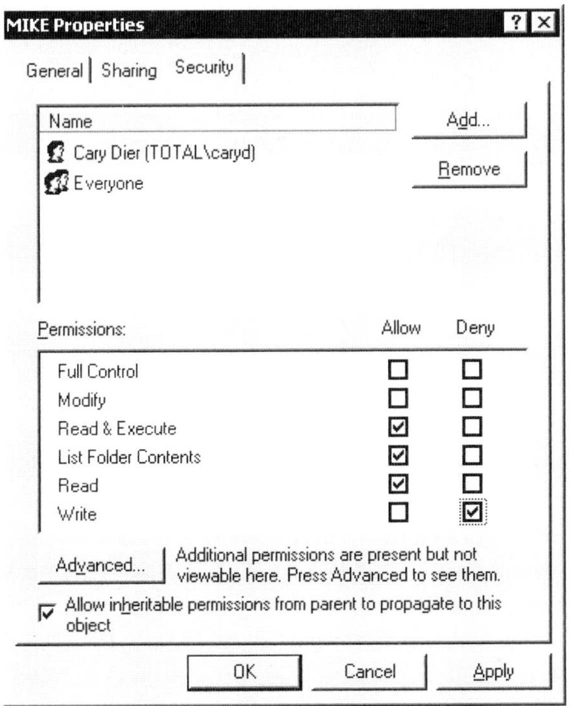

Figure 12.92 Windows 2000 folder permissions

Don't panic about memorizing special permissions; just appreciate that they exist and that the permissions we see in the Security tab cover the vast majority of our needs.

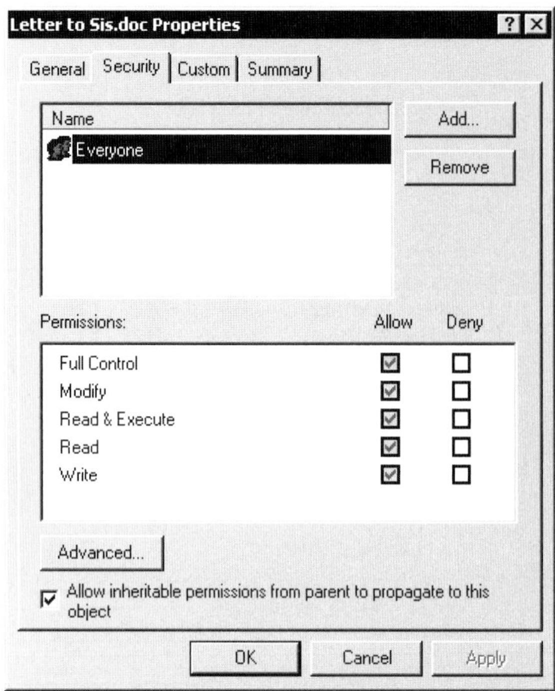

• **Figure 12.93** Security tab of file properties dialog box

Take some time to think about these permissions. Why would Microsoft create them? Think of situations where you might want to give a group Modify permission. Also, you can assign more than one permission. In many situations, we like to give users both the Read as well as the Write permission.

Permissions are cumulative. If you have Full Control on a folder and only Read permission on the file, you get Full Control on the file.

Techs and Permissions

Techs, as a rule, hate NTFS permissions. You must have administrative privileges to do almost anything on a Windows NT/2000/XP machine. Most administrators hate giving out administrative permissions (for obvious reasons). If one does give you administrative permission for a PC and something goes wrong with that system while you're working on it, you immediately become the primary suspect! If you're working on an NT/2000/XP system administered by someone else, make sure he or she understands what you are doing and how long you think it will take. Have the administrator create a new account for you with administrator privileges. Never ask for the password for a permanent administrator account! That way, you won't be blamed if anything goes wrong on that system: "Well, I told Janet the password when she installed the new hard drive ... maybe she did it!" When you have fixed the system, make sure that that the administrator deletes the account you used.

This "protect yourself from passwords" attitude transcends just Windows NT/2000/XP. PC support folks get lots of passwords, scan cards, keys, and ID tags. Most newer techs tend to get an "I can go anywhere and access anything" attitude. This is a dangerous attitude, however. I've seen many jobs lost and friendships ruined when a tape backup suddenly disappears or a critical file gets erased. Everybody points to the support tech in these situations. In physical security situations, make other people unlock doors for you. In some cases, I've literally made the administrator or system owner sit behind me reading a magazine, jumping up and punching in passwords as needed. What you don't have access to can't hurt you.

Don't bother memorizing all of these NTFS permissions! Simply appreciate that NTFS enables NT/2000/XP to provide a tremendous level of security. Windows 9*x* uses the far more primitive FAT16 or FAT32 file systems. These file systems provide almost no security. If you want powerful, flexible security, you need Windows NT/2000/XP with NTFS.

Note that you can install Windows NT on a drive with FAT (that is, FAT16) and Windows 2000/XP on a drive with FAT32 file systems. Neither file system provides any security, so forget about permissions if you use them. Only NTFS offers security.

Booting Up vs. Going Graphical

Windows 9*x*/Me and Windows NT/2000/XP share a surface resemblance; they are all graphical OSs. Inside, however, they differ significantly in the level of integration between the graphical interface and text-based functions. Both families of Windows make a strong distinction between booting the OS and "going graphical." Windows NT/2000/XP and Windows 9*x*/Me have primary boot files that start the OS. Once these files have started the system, a completely different set of files starts the GUI. The boot files are usually quite small in size and there are very few of them, compared to the size and the number of the GUI files. The distinction between text-based OS and GUI files is sharp in Windows 9*x*/Me but much muddier in Windows NT/2000/XP.

In Windows 9*x*, a clear distinction exists between the boot files and the GUI files. This can be easily shown by the many ways that you can skip the GUI completely, such as the Command Prompt Only option in the Startup Options menu. Windows Me is based on the same split of boot files and GUI files as Windows 9*x*, but it does not allow you to boot directly to the command line.

Windows NT/2000/XP do not have a pure command prompt environment. Certainly, you can access a command prompt within NT/2000/XP, but the Windows 9*x* separation of GUI from the command prompt is not valid in NT/2000/XP.

In Windows 9*x*/Me machines, the boot files must be installed onto the C: partition, but the GUI files can be installed onto any other drive letter. Of course, most installations place the GUI files in a directory called \WINDOWS on the C: drive, but this is not at all required. The boot files and

looks like Windows 9*x*'s Safe Mode Command Prompt Only mode, but in reality it is nothing more than a Windowed command prompt.

That is about where the comparisons between Windows 9*x*/Me and NT/2000/XP end. Windows NT, 2000, and XP share a vastly more complicated boot file structure and organization. Additionally, Microsoft uses some terms differently than other authorities, requiring a little bit of unlearning and accepting the "Microsoft way" of defining different aspects of the boot process. The best way to understand the NT/2000/XP boot process is to begin with an overview of the various files used in the boot process.

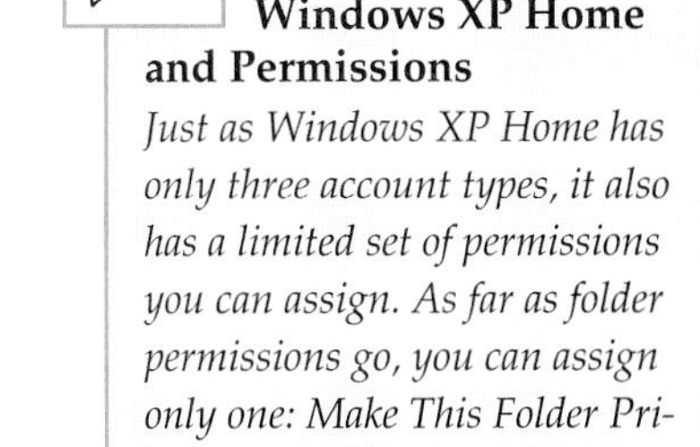

Windows XP Home and Permissions

Just as Windows XP Home has only three account types, it also has a limited set of permissions you can assign. As far as folder permissions go, you can assign only one: Make This Folder Private. To see this in action, alternate-click a file or folder and select Sharing And Security from the options. Note that you can't

The Boot Process

The Windows NT family (NT, 2000, XP) makes a clear distinction between the files that start the PC and the actual operating system files. The boot files consist of NTLDR, BOOT.INI, NTDETECT.COM, and NTBOOTDD.SYS. Of these four, **NTLDR** (pronounced *NT loader*), begins the process.

You know from earlier chapters that to make a drive bootable requires an active, primary partition, right? Let's look at the process in a PC with two NTFS hard drives, partitioned as C: and D:. Ready?

The CPU wakes up and runs the system BIOS, and then the BIOS sends out a routine looking for a valid operating system in the boot sector of the primary, master hard drive The master file table (MFT) lives in the boot sector of the C: drive. It points to the location of the NT boot files, also on the C: drive, because that's the bootable drive.

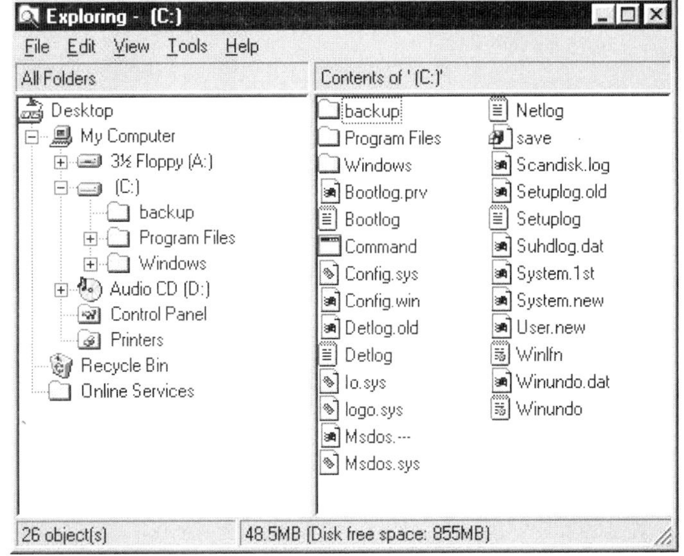

• **Figure 12.94** Boot and GUI files in Windows Explorer

Microsoft calls the area the *boot* files occupy the *system partition*.

The Windows NT OS itself consists of NTOSKRNL.EXE (the Windows NT kernel), the \WINNT\SYSTEM32\CONFIG\SYSTEM file (which controls the loading of device drivers), and the device drivers. Even though these files are the core of the Windows NT OS, they are not capable of booting, or starting, the system. For that feat, they require NTLDR, NTDETECT.COM, and BOOT.INI, the boot files.

The boot files start the PC and then, at the end of that process, point the CPU to the location of the OS files. The CPU goes over and chats with NTOSKRNL, and the GUI starts to load. By the time the CPU and NTOSKRNL finish a beer and a cigarette, the PC is up and running and you're able to do work.

Windows XP does not particularly like to share control of a PC, so it does not create a dual-boot system by default when you load it on a system with Windows 9x/Me. You need to create the dual boot manually. We'll do this in Chapter 14 .

The odd part about all this is that Microsoft decided to make the OS files mobile. *The core OS files can reside on any partition or volume in the PC.* The OS files in the system mentioned earlier, for example, could very well be on drive D:, not drive C:. More often than not, the boot files and OS files reside in the same partition or volume, so the system versus boot partition is a moot argument. NT can coexist with Windows 9*x*/Me on the same boot partition, as long as the partition is FAT16 (Windows 2000/XP also coexist with FAT32). Although you *could* do this, your inability to use NTFS makes this idea ludicrous. The best method for dual booting Windows 9*x* and Windows 2000, for example, is to make a primary partition formatted as FAT32 and install Windows 9*x* on the drive. Then install Windows 2000 on the unused portion of the drive. Both Windows NT and Windows 2000 have nice setup programs that can create a dual-boot system with ease. Many systems (including one used to write this book) have Windows 2000/Windows 9*x* dual-boot capabilities.

Windows NT/2000/XP consider the initial boot drive (usually the C: drive) to be the *system* partition. They see the area that stores the OS's GUI files as the *boot* partition.

For all these neat tricks, in the vast majority of Windows 2000 systems, the boot partition and the system partition share the same big C: partition.

You've got the process now in general, so let's look more specifically at the makeup and function of the individual files involved in the boot process.

System Partition Boot Files

Windows NT, 2000, and XP require these four files in the root directory of the system partition:

- NTLDR
- BOOT.INI
- NTDETECT.COM
- NTBOOTDD.SYS (only needed for SCSI controllers that don't have their own ROM BIOS)

Note that this list does not include IO.SYS, MSDOS.SYS, CONFIG.SYS, COMMAND.COM, or AUTOEXEC.BAT. Windows NT/2000/XP do not use these files, although you may see them in the root directory of a dual-boot system.

NTLDR

When the system boots up, the master boot record (MBR) or MFT on the hard drive starts the NTLDR program. The NTLDR program then launches either Windows NT/2000/XP or another OS. To find the available OSs, the NTLDR program must read the BOOT.INI configuration file. To accomplish this, the NTLDR program loads its own minimal file system, which enables it to read the BOOT.INI file off the system partition.

BOOT.INI File

The **BOOT.INI** file is a text file that lists the OSs available to NTLDR and tells NTLDR where to find the boot partition (where the OS is stored) for each of the OSs. The BOOT.INI file has sections defined by section headings enclosed in brackets. A basic BOOT.INI in Windows 2000 looks like this:

```
[boot loader]
timeout=10
default=multi(0)disk(0)rdisk(0)partition(2)\WINNT
```

```
multi(0)disk(0)rdisk(0)partition(2)\WINNT="Microsoft Windows 2000
 Professional" /fastdetect
C:\CMDCONS\BOOTSECT.DAT="Microsoft Windows 2000 Recovery Console"/cmdcons
C:\="Previous Operating System on C:"
```

Such a BOOT.INI would result in the boot menu that appears in Figure 12.95.

On rare occasions, you might find yourself needing to edit the BOOT.INI file. Any text editor handily edits the BOOT.INI file. However, most of us prefer to edit BOOT.INI via the System Setup dialog box. In Windows 2000, select the System applet from the Control Panel. Click the Advanced tab and then click the Startup and Recovery button. The BOOT.INI options show up at the top (Figure 12.96).

BOOTSECT.DOS

If the NTLDR detects that you chose to run another OS, such as Windows 98, it will read the BOOTSECT.DOS file to locate the IO.SYS file and then lets the other OS start.

NTDETECT.COM

If the NTLDR determines that you have chosen to start NT/2000/XP, it boots the system into

```
Please select the operating system to start:

    Microsoft Windows 2000 Professional
    Microsoft Windows 2000 Recovery Console
    Previous Operating system on C:

Use ↑ and ↓ to move the highlight to your choice.
Press Enter to choose.
Seconds until highlighted choice will be started automatically: 26

For troubleshooting and advanced startup options for Windows 2000, press F8.
```

• **Figure 12.95** Boot loader in Windows 2000 with System Recovery Console

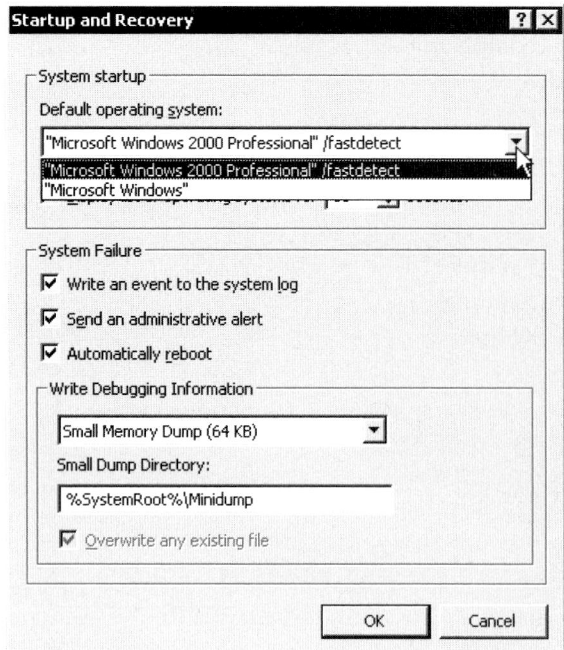

• **Figure 12.96** Choosing which OS to boot by default

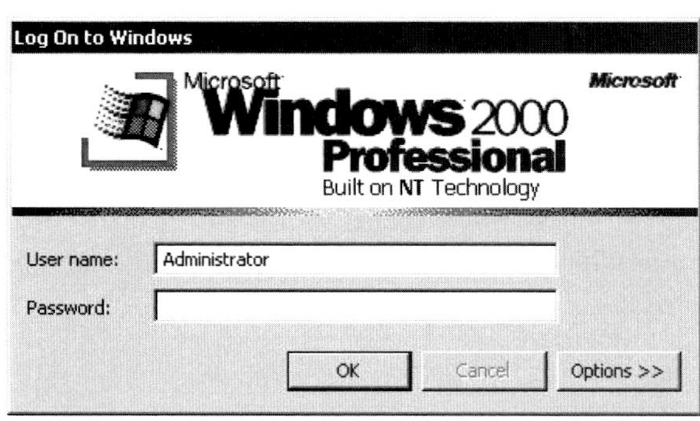

• **Figure 12.97** Where do you want to go today?

protected mode and then calls on NTDETECT.COM to detect the installed hardware on the system.

NTBOOTDD.SYS

If the NTLDR detects that the boot partition resides on a SCSI drive connected to a host adapter that lacks a ROM chip for BIOS support, it uses NTBOOTDD.SYS to provide access to the SCSI boot partition. (See Chapter 19 for more information about SCSI drives and host adapters.)

Critical Files

Naming all of the critical files for NT/2000/XP is akin to naming every muscle in the human body—completely possible, but time-consuming and without any real use. In the next section, you will see that it takes four floppy disks to boot Windows 2000 from the floppy drive! However, a few of the *most* important files certainly deserve a short notice.

Once NTLDR finishes detections, it loads NTOSKRNL.EXE, HAL.DLL, some of the Registry, and some basic device drivers, and then it passes control to the NTOSKRNL.EXE file. NTOSKRNL.EXE completes the Registry loading, initializes all device drivers, and starts the WINLOGON.EXE program, which displays the famous Windows 2000 logon screen (Figure 12.97).

Take the time to memorize the primary boot files and the boot process for Windows NT/2000. Most boot errors are easily repaired if you know which files are used for boot and in which order they load.

Service Packs

For all the power of Windows NT, the OS had bugs and a few glaring limitations in the architecture. Microsoft fixed some problems with a number of Service Packs (Microsoft sent out six service packs for Windows NT 4.0). But core limitations meant that Windows NT could not incorporate features that became increasingly in demand as technology improved, such as seamless Internet integration, true *Plug and Play* (PnP), clustering of two or more servers (where if one server failed another would pick up the load without missing a beat), and other high-end server issues. To address the obvious need for a new NT, Microsoft offered the world Windows 2000. When consumers demanded the same kind of stability business people got from Windows 2000, Microsoft responded with Windows XP, the best of both worlds.

Major Differences Among Windows NT, 2000, and XP

As mentioned earlier, Windows 2000 shares much of the same features and power of Windows NT. Many in the industry jokingly call Windows 2000

"NT 5.0." A check of the Version field in the System Information tool shows that someone at Microsoft feels the same way (Figure 12.98).

In fact, Windows 2000 combines an improved Windows NT core with many ease-of-use and tech-friendly elements from Windows 9*x*. Plus, Windows 2000 adds some excellent new features, such as the Microsoft Man- dows 2000. It then launches into the specific tasks techs will face: installing and optimizing the OS; installing new hardware; and maintaining the system, including dealing with drives. The chapter finishes with a discussion on troubleshooting Windows 2000. Let's get started!

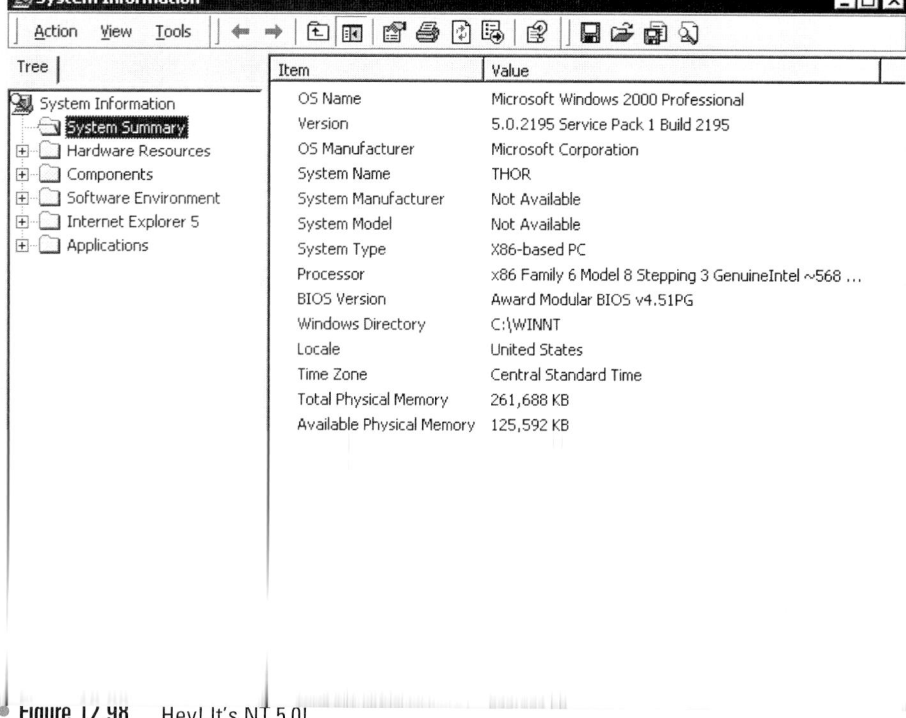

Figure 12.98 Hey! It's NT 5.0!

Unlike the step between Windows 95 and Windows 98, the jump between Windows NT and Windows 2000 was huge. Microsoft took the rock-solid foundation of Windows NT and added features to make Windows 2000 substantially more user-friendly. It'll come as a shock to some folks, but most games wouldn't even run on Windows NT! Microsoft took care of that little issue with Windows 2000. In a nutshell, Windows 2000 combined the robustness of Windows NT with the Windows 98 user interface. Windows XP extended that merger into a fully new OS that truly eclipses all three predecessors. The following list details a few of the more outstanding updates implemented with the versions of Windows 2000 and Windows XP.

Windows 9*x* Look and Feel

Windows 2000 has a look and feel that's similar to Windows 98 (and almost identical to Windows Me), as you know from the first sections of this chapter. From a user standpoint, all of the aspects of Windows 9*x*/Me are the same, with the exception of some name changes. Network Neighborhood has become My Network Places, for example, but the taskbar, Start menu, My Computer, My Documents, Run, and Find (now called Search) are still there (Figure 12.99).

For techs, most of the common tools reside in the same locations as on a Windows 9*x*/Me PC. The Control Panel, for example, contains the important Registry-changing applets, and the tools under Program | Accessories | System Tools handle other chores, such as defragmenting the hard drive.

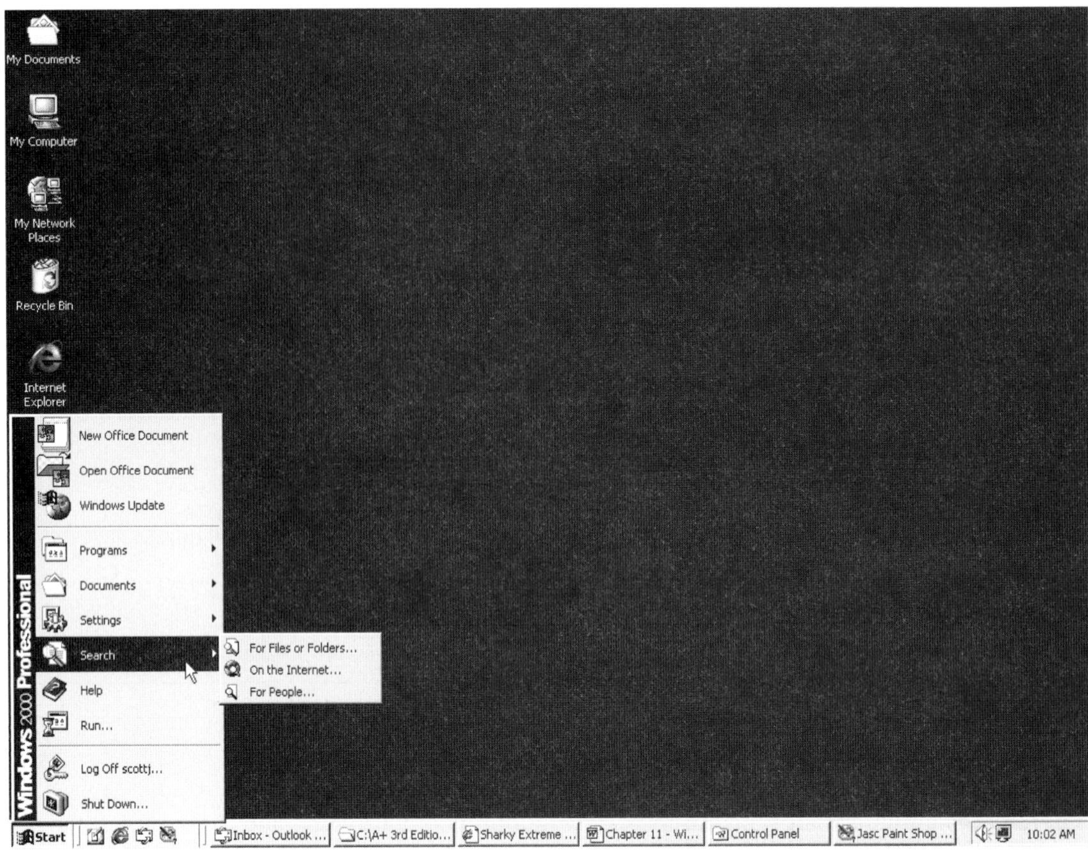

• **Figure 12.99** Windows 2000 looks a lot like Windows 98

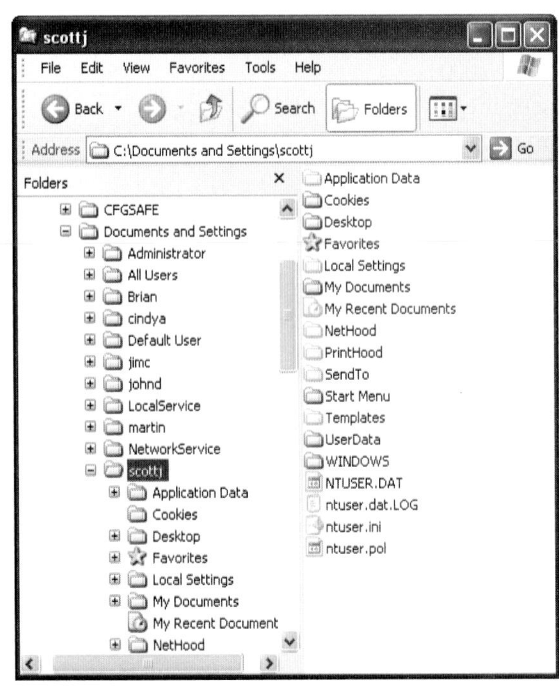

• **Figure 12.100** Documents and Settings

Improved User Organization

Windows 2000/XP offer a highly structured environment designed to enhance file and folder security on shared workstations. The biggest change from NT is the creation of the Documents and Settings folders that contain all the user accounts on a system, assigning them default data and program folders. Note the user accounts in Figure 12.100 have their own trees in the file system.

Combined with NTFS, this user organization provides a wall between users. All can access the shared folders and the programs installed for all, but one user cannot access the My Documents of another user. In the PC represented in Figure 12.100, for example, user Scottj could log into the workstation and surf the Internet and access the All Users area of the hard drive (which happens to have all the shared music files), but he could not willy-nilly mess with files in the Administrator or other user's folders.

Plug and Play (PnP)

Although later service packs of Windows NT provided rudimentary PnP support, Windows 2000/XP pack complete PnP support. Windows 2000/XP have the Device Manager and the Add New Hardware Wizard, making device installation a breeze. Plus, when you need a snapshot of all your devices, you can go to the System Information tool, just like in Windows 9*x*/Me.

NTFS5

Windows 2000/XP comes with a new type of NTFS called NTFS 5.0, as you know from Chapter 11, "Implementing Hard Drives." (The NTFS that came with NT 4.0 was called NTFS 4.0.) NTFS 5.0 adds four improvements: encryption, mount points, disk quotas, and dynamic disks.

Easier Administration

As you know from earlier in this chapter, Microsoft added the Microsoft

nology—you can burn CD-R and CD-RW discs natively, for example—to user interface tweaks that make the whole computing experience more pleasant. The Start menu *evolves*, for example, updating dynamically to display prominently those applications you access often (Figure 12.101). Windows XP incorporates the excellent Windows Update utility that emerged in later versions of Windows 9*x* to keep the operating system free from bugs and known problems. I could go on and on about various minor updates and tweaks, but let me point out three of the most important new features.

> **Tech Tip**
>
> **Windows XP Home and Folder Access**
>
> *Because Windows XP Home offers only three levels of user—Computer Administrator, Limited User, and Guest—many folks have a tendency to make all accounts Computer Administrator accounts. This is a very bad idea! Administrators can access any files in users' folders.*
>
> *Using Limited Users for the*
>
> 
>
> *folders and to their own folders in Documents and Settings. The Limited User account does not stop users from surfing the Internet or performing any other routine activity on the PC. It just helps keeps the environment tidy and secure.*

Files and Settings Transfer Wizard

It used to be that swapping out your primary hard drive for a bigger one or changing your motherboard was a huge hassle. Not only did you have to do the hardware part of the deal—the quick and easy part—but then you had to go through the laborious process of loading Windows, loading all your devices, installing all your applications, and then copying over all the thousands of files, settings, backgrounds, and so on. What a mess! And when it didn't go as planned, you simply lost a bunch of stuff.

Microsoft introduced the Files and Settings Transfer Wizard in Windows XP, and changing systems suddenly became a simpler, more efficient process. Here's how it works. Before you dismantle your current system, you run the wizard from the XP CD-ROM (Figure 12.102).

> 
>
> **Cross Check**
>
> **NTFS 5 vs. NTFS 4**
>
> You worked with NTFS in Chapter 11 extensively, and I suspect that you found it a much superior file system than either FAT available in Windows.
>
> 1. Why does encryption matter?
> 2. What's a mount point and why do we care?
> 3. What can you do with dynamic disks that you couldn't do with basic disks?

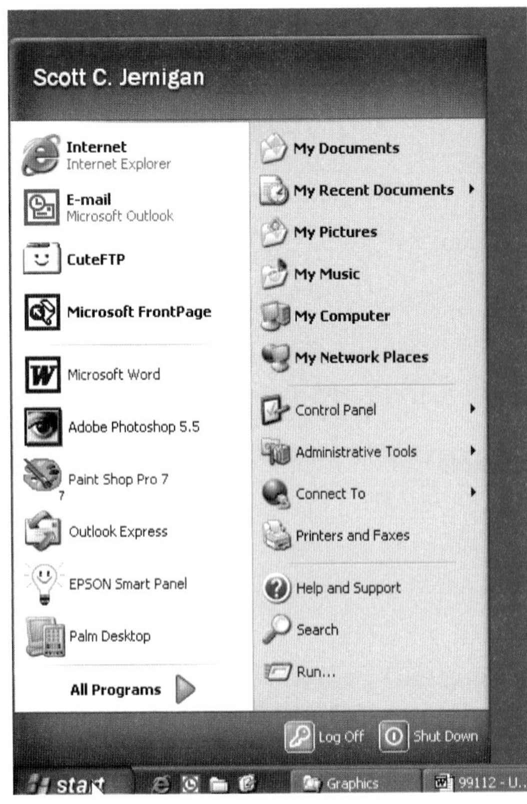

• **Figure 12.101** Scott's Windows XP Start menu (two e-mail programs? Sheesh!)

• **Figure 12.102** Files and Settings Transfer Wizard

The wizard prepares your old drive to transfer its settings. Then you install Windows XP on the new hardware and connect the old hard drive to the new drive and run the Files and Settings Transfer Wizard again. This time, choose the appropriate drive and transfer everything over (Figure 12.103).

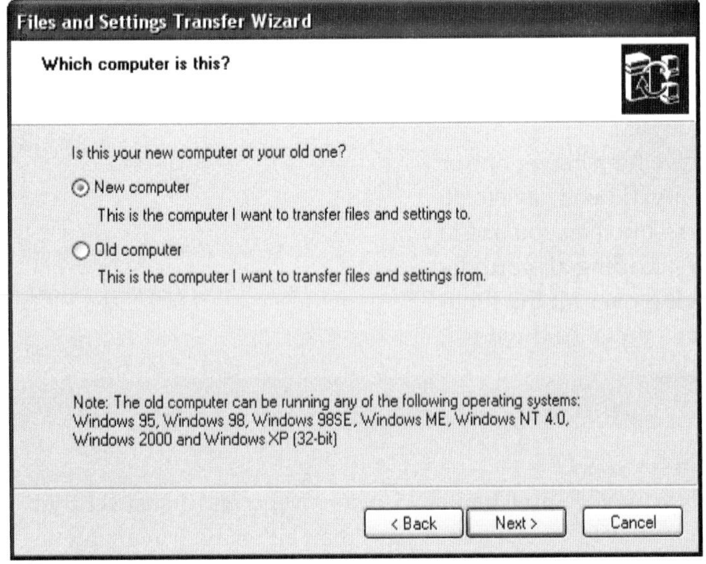

• **Figure 12.103** Selecting source or destination drive

System Restore and Driver Rollback

Windows XP comes with the same features Microsoft introduced in Windows Me, namely the ability to take a snapshot of the system state at any given time and then, if things go awry with an installation or bad download, restore the PC to a previous time when all was well.

Windows XP goes beyond Me with its Driver Rollback feature, which enables you to roll back individual device drivers for pieces of hardware. Want to try out those beta drivers for your video card but you wisely shy away from the potentially horrible outcome if they don't work? With Driver Rollback you can install what you want and then return to the old drivers if the new ones give you fits. It's a great boon to hardware enthusiasts and general users alike. It's definitely a boon to techs! You get a call from a client who "accidentally" installed a new driver for some piece of hardware, and "now it's broken!" With Driver Rollback, you can have that user back up and running in a jiffy.

Remote Assistance

Have you ever received a tech support call and you spent at least half the time trying to figure out what the problem was because the user *didn't speak tech* and therefore couldn't communicate precisely the symptoms?

"My CD doesn't work."

"What's wrong with it?"

"It doesn't work, I tell you!"

"What are you trying to do that it won't do?"

"Record a music CD."

"What software are you using...?"

You keep going with question after question until you finally realize that the user doesn't have a CD-RW drive but is trying to burn a CD-RW disc with a CD-R drive! (If this is Klingon, rather than a language you speak, turn to Chapter 17 for the details.)

[illegible]

party applications such as PCAnywhere, but by incorporating it into the OS, Microsoft has upped your chances of being able to use it by a huge factor.

> **Tech Tip**
>
> **Patch Before You Run**
>
> *The Files and Settings Transfer Wizard reportedly had a serious flaw when Microsoft first released Windows XP. Before you run the Wizard on a system that matters to you, go to Windows Update and download the appropriate patch. The data you save could be your own!*

Chapter 12 Review

Chapter Summary

After reading this chapter and completing the exercises, you should understand the following about Windows.

Identify and Explain the Basic Functions of an Operating System

- An operating system (OS) is a program that performs four basic functions. First, it must communicate with the hardware of the PC. Second, the OS must create a user interface. Third, the OS, via the user interface, must enable users to determine the available installed programs and run, use, and shut down the program of their choice. Fourth, the OS should enable users to add, move, and delete the installed programs and data.
- The OS must work with the system BIOS to deal with most basic and important parts of the computer: the hard drives, floppy drives, keyboard, and basic video.
- An OS must have some method of organizing the programs and data. First, the OS needs to give a label or name to each program and each individual piece of data. Second, the OS must provide a naming system for all the drives. Third, the user must be able to store data and programs in distinct groups on each drive, and the OS user interface must be able to interact with each of these groups individually. Fourth, the user interface must enable users to perform functions such as copying, moving, and deleting programs and data both safely and accurately.
- Operating systems for the PC come in two basic varieties: command line interface and graphical user interface (GUI).
- DOS consisted of only three main files: IO.SYS, MSDOS.SYS, and COMMAND.COM. You installed DOS just by booting to a DOS floppy disk and running a command called SYS.COM. This program copied the three files to the hard drive.
- DOS came with a large number of support programs, such as the FDISK and FORMAT utilities you learned about in the previous chapter.
- DOS used a second configuration file besides CONFIG.SYS, called AUTOEXEC.BAT. AUTOEXEC.BAT was just a text file containing a list of DOS commands that you wanted to execute every time the computer started. The .BAT extension indicates a *batch file*, which works sort of like a program, enabling you to run commands automatically that you would otherwise have to sit down at a monitor and type in yourself.
- A GUI is not necessarily also an OS. It does nothing more than translate the manipulation of icons into commands that are understandable to an OS, which actually does the work.

Identify the Features and Characteristics Common to All Windows PCs

- All versions of Windows share certain characteristics, configuration files, and look and feel. Two main "families" of Windows exist: the 9*x* family and the NT family. The 9*x* family includes all versions of Windows 95, 98, and Me. The NT family includes Windows NT 4.0, 2000, and XP.
- Every version of Windows supports multiple users on a single machine, and thus the starting point for any tour of the Windows user interface starts with the login screen. The login screen for Windows 9*x*/Me offers no security for the system—you can simply press ESC to bypass the screen and access the OS. Windows NT/2000/XP, in contrast, offer a high degree of security.
- The Windows Desktop is your primary interface to the computer. It contains icons and various graphical elements. Many people customize its look quite heavily.
- The taskbar, by default, runs along the bottom of all Windows Desktops and has up to four sections (depending on the version of Windows and your configuration): Start button, Quick Launch area, running programs area, and system tray.
- My Computer provides access to all drives, folders, and files on the system.
- In every version of Windows before XP, Windows Explorer acts like a separate and distinct tool from

My Computer, showing file and folder information in a double-paned fashion rather than all in a single pane. Windows XP merged the two into a single tool. To get the Explorer-like interface, alternate-click a folder and select Explore.

- Windows 98, Windows Me, Windows 2000, and Windows XP provide a special icon/folder called My Documents as a central default storage area for all files created by applications. Newer Windows programs store their files in My Documents unless you explicitly tell them to use a different folder.
- Systems tied to a network, either via a network cable or by a modem, have the Network [illegible] line. Windows NT, 2000, and XP add two more to the mix with Administrative Tools and the Microsoft Management Console. The Control Panel handles most of the maintenance, upgrade, and configuration aspects of Windows.
- The Device Manager enables techs to examine and configure all the hardware and drivers in a Windows PC. In all versions of Windows—except Windows NT 4.0, which doesn't support Plug and Play and so doesn't have a Device Manager—the Device Manager displays every device that Windows recognizes.
- The Microsoft Management Console (MMC) is a shell program in Windows 2000 and XP that holds individual utilities, called *snap-ins*, used for administration and troubleshooting.
- Windows 2000 and XP have combined almost all of the snap-ins into a new applet in the Control Panel called Administrative Tools. Administrative Tools is really just a folder that stores a number of pre-made consoles. The ones most used by techs are Computer Management, Event Viewer, Performance, and Services.
- All modern versions of Windows have a primary system folder for storing most Windows internal tools and files. All use Registry files that keep track of all the hardware loaded and the drivers that enable you to use that hardware. Finally, every version has a RAM cache file, enabling more robust access to programs and utilities. SystemRoot is the tech name given in Windows NT/2000/XP to the folder in which Windows has been installed.
- The Registry stores everything about your PC, including information on all the hardware in the PC, network information, user preferences, and file types. Almost any form of configuration done to a Windows system involves editing the Registry. The Registry in Windows 9*x*/Me is composed of [illegible] The Registry is organized in a tree structure similar to the folders in the PC. In Windows 9*x*/Me, the Registry has six main subgroups or root keys: HKEY_CLASSES_ROOT, HKEY_CURRENT_USER, HKEY_LOCAL_MACHINE, HKEY_USERS, HKEY_CURRENT_CONFIG, and HKEY_DYN_DATA.
- Windows NT/2000/XP share similar Registries, but these Registries differ from those in Windows 9*x*/Me. Microsoft included a new Registry Editor in Windows NT called REGEDT32.EXE, although it also left in the older Registry Editor (REGEDIT.EXE). Windows 2000/XP also has both REGEDT32.EXE and REGEDIT.EXE. The best practice: Search with Regedit, but make changes only with Regedt32.
- All versions of Windows use a swap file—a portion of the hard drive used as an extension of system RAM by using a RAM cache. A RAM cache sets aside a block of cylinders on a hard drive as what's called a swap file or virtual memory. When the PC starts running out of real RAM because you've loaded too many programs, the system swaps programs from RAM to the swap file, opening more space for programs currently active.

Identify and Differentiate the Features and Characteristics of Windows 9x/Me

- Microsoft debuted Windows 95 in 1995 as its first standalone GUI operating system. Subsequent versions of what is now called Windows 9*x* include Windows 95A, 95 OSR2, 98, 98 Second Edition (SE), and Millennium Edition (Me). Windows 3.*x* was not a true OS. It was a graphical shell that required DOS to interact with the hardware.
- Windows 9*x*/Me is really two products: a DOS protected-mode interface (DPMI) and a protected-mode GUI.
- Later versions of Windows 95 and all versions of Windows 98, Me, (and 2000/XP) support the FAT32 file format, enabling partitions up to 2 terabytes in size. Before FAT32, the old FAT16 format had a maximum partition size of only 2.1 GB.
- Windows 9*x*/Me systems allow filenames up to 255 characters while maintaining backward compatibility with the older 8.3 format. Windows extended the old 8-bit ASCII character set and adopted a 16-bit Unicode character set.
- DPMI is composed of three main files: IO.SYS, MSDOS.SYS, and COMMAND.COM, although you may not have COMMAND.COM.
- One of the many jobs of IO.SYS is to check to see whether the F8 key (left CTRL key in Windows 98) has been pressed as Windows loads. If it has, the Windows boot menu loads.
- MSDOS.SYS is no longer part of the OS kernel in DPMI. It is now just a text file that replaces many of the AUTOEXEC.BAT and CONFIG.SYS functions that the system still needs before the GUI kicks in. MSDOS.SYS has hidden, system, and read-only attributes by default. MSDOS.SYS is organized just like an INI file with groups and options under each setting. You will find many boot options in the [Options] group.
- After the DPMI-level OS files and configuration files and utilities load, WIN.COM runs and initiates the graphical portion of the operating system. During the loading process, Windows incorporates the legacy INI files to provide support for any ancient applications you might load on a Windows 9*x*/Me system. (The same holds true for Windows 2000/XP, although not for NT 4.0.)
- Windows 3.*x* used text files with the extension .INI to initialize just about everything from device drivers to applications to Windows itself. Although Windows 9*x*/Me and Windows 2000/XP rely much less on INI files, knowing how to edit an INI file is crucial to repairing all Windows PCs. All INI files are text files. You can edit them using EDIT or any other DOS-based text editor.
- All INI files are broken up into logical sections called groups. Each group starts with a word or words in square brackets, called a group header, followed by the settings for that group. The syntax is item=settings.
- SYSTEM.INI was the CONFIG.SYS of Windows 3.*x*. All the resources were initialized there, plus some global settings that defined how resources were to be used.
- WIN.INI was the AUTOEXEC.BAT of Windows 3.*x*. It defined all the personalizations of Windows, and how resources interacted with applications. WIN.INI was also the dumping ground for settings that did not have a home anywhere else. It was often edited manually.
- Windows 9*x*/Me does everything CONFIG.SYS does. Assuming Windows 9*x*/Me drivers are available, you do not need CONFIG.SYS.
- When the GUI is running, the main functions of Windows 9*x*/Me are handled by the kernel, user, and graphical device interface (GDI) modules. These files—KRNL386.EXE, USER.EXE, and GDI.EXE, reside in the C:\Windows\System folder.
- Windows 9x/Me systems can create a special bootable floppy disk called a startup disk, which enables you to boot to an A:\ prompt and run enough tools to fix many common problems.
- The System Information tool is a kind of "read-only Device Manager" in that you get to see all of the resource and driver information provided by the Device Manager in a report format. Additionally, the System Information tool provides a launch point for almost every utility used by Windows 98/SE/Me.
- When updating Windows 95, the updating order had to be carefully monitored. Windows 98/SE/Me eliminates this problem completely with the Windows Update utility, which uses a special web

site to inspect your system and provides a simple method to update your system safely.

- Windows needs lots of unused disk space for swap files and temporary files generated by applications. In Windows 95, running out of disk space results in a "Not enough disk space" error—at best; at worst, you get lockups and general protection faults. Windows 98/SE/Me has a Disk Cleanup utility that enables you to clean out unnecessary files.
- Windows Me shares the core files and structure of Windows 9*x*, but Microsoft changed the outward appearance to match that of 2000, including replacing the icons and changing the names of [illegible]

Identify and Differentiate the Features and Characteristics of Windows NT/2000/XP

- Windows 2000 and Windows XP share the same core structure, files, and features as Windows NT, but offer greater ease of use and support for hardware.
- NT is robust, scalable, and cross-platform. NT takes an object-oriented approach, separating the OS into three distinct parts: the drivers, the NT Executive, and the subsystems. To enable NT to support different CPU platforms beyond the x86, the NT Executive uses the Hardware Abstraction Layer (HAL) to separate the system-specific device drivers from the rest of the NT system. Starting with Windows 2000, only Intel x86 systems are supported. NT and 2000's robustness comes from separating running processes into subsystems.
- NT is the only Microsoft OS to support symmetric multiprocessing (SMP), providing support for systems with up to 32 CPUs. Windows 2000 (high-end server versions only) goes beyond SMP by adding the power of clustering, enabling multiple systems to share redundant data for ultimate protection.
- Microsoft designed and optimized every aspect of Windows NT (and Windows 2000/XP) for multi-user, networked environments. This is most evident in the file system—NT, 2000, and XP use a powerful and robust file system called NT File System (NTFS). Windows NT fully supports FAT16, NTFS, and HPFS (for OS/2). Windows 2000 supports FAT16, FAT32, and NTFS.
- NTFS offers the following features: long filenames, redundancy, backward compatibility, recoverability, and security. NTFS filenames can be up to 255 characters. NTFS has a very advanced FAT called the Master File Table (MFT). An NTFS partition keeps a backup copy of the most critical parts of the MFT in the middle of the disk, reducing the chance [illegible] Windows 2000 and User Accounts in Windows XP. A user name defines an account for a person who has access to the PC. A group is a collection of accounts that share the same access capabilities. A single account can be a member of multiple groups. An administrator can assign a certain level of access for a file or folder to a group instead of an account. Windows provides seven built-in non-removable groups with a number of preset abilities: Administrators, Power Users, Users, Backup Operators, Replicator, Everyone, and Guests.
- Windows XP diverges a lot from Windows NT/2000 on user accounts. XP Professional offers all the accounts listed, but it then adds four other specialized types, such as Help Services Group and Remote Desktop Users. Windows XP Home, and XP Professional installed as a standalone PC or connected to a workgroup but not a domain, have only three account types: Computer Administrator, Limited User, and Guest.
- In the NT/2000/XP world, every folder and file on an NTFS partition has a list that contains two sets of data: (1) every user and group that has access to that file or folder, and (2) the level of access that each user or group has to that file and folder. A set of detailed and powerful restrictions called permissions define exactly what a particular account can or cannot do to the file or folder.

- The A+ Certification exams test your understanding of only a few basic concepts of NTFS permissions: Ownership, Take Ownership permission, Change permissions, Folder permissions, and File permissions.
- In Windows NT/2000/XP, just about everything in the computer has a Security tab in its properties. Every Security tab contains a list of accounts that have permissions for that resource, and the permissions assigned to those accounts.
- In Windows 9*x*, a clear distinction exists between the boot files and the GUI files. This can be easily shown by the many ways that you can skip the GUI completely, such as the Command Prompt Only option in the Startup Options menu. In contrast, while you can access a command prompt within NT/2000/XP, the Windows 9*x* separation of GUI from the command prompt is not valid in NT/2000/XP.
- In Windows 9*x*/Me machines, the boot files must be installed onto the C: partition, but the GUI files can be installed onto any other drive letter. Windows NT, 2000, and XP also separate the boot from the GUI files.
- The Windows NT OS itself consists of NTOSKRNL.EXE (the Windows NT kernel), the \WINNT\SYSTEM32\CONFIG\SYSTEM file (which controls the loading of device drivers), and the device drivers themselves, all of which are stored on the boot partition. Even though these files are the core of the Windows NT OS, they are not capable of booting the system. In Microsoft's terminology, the partition that holds the actual NT/2000/XP OS is called the boot partition, while the partition that you boot from, the bootable partition, is the system partition.
- When the system boots up, the master boot record (MBR) on the hard drive starts the NTLDR program. The NTLDR program then launches either Windows NT/2000/XP or another OS. To find the available OSs, the NTLDR program must read the BOOT.INI configuration file. To accomplish this, the NTLDR program loads its own minimal file system, which enables it to read the BOOT.INI file off the system partition.
- The BOOT.INI file is a text file that lists the OSs available to NTLDR and tells NTLDR where to find the boot partition (where the OS is stored) for each of the OSs. The BOOT.INI file has sections defined by section headings enclosed in brackets. To edit BOOT.INI via the System Setup dialog box in Windows 2000, select the System applet from the Control Panel. Click the Advanced tab and then click the Startup And Recovery button.
- If the NTLDR detects that you chose to run another OS, it reads the BOOTSECT.DOS file to locate the IO.SYS file and then lets the other OS start. If the NTLDR determines that you have chosen to start NT/2000/XP, it boots the system into protected mode and then calls on NTDETECT.COM to detect the installed hardware on the system. If the NTLDR detects that the boot partition resides on a SCSI drive connected to a host adapter that lacks a ROM chip for BIOS support, it uses the NTBOOTDD.SYS to provide access to the SCSI boot partition.
- Once NTLDR finishes detections, it loads NTOSKRNL.EXE, HAL.DLL, some of the Registry, and some basic device drivers, and then it passes control to the NTOSKRNL.EXE file. NTOSKRNL.EXE completes the Registry loading, initializes all devices drivers, and starts the WINLOGON.EXE program, which displays the famous Windows 2000 logon screen.
- Core limitations meant that Windows NT could not incorporate features such as seamless Internet integration, true Plug and Play (PnP), and high-end server support. Windows 2000 has much of the features and power of Windows NT, but adds many ease-of-use and tech-friendly elements from Windows 9*x*, plus some new features like the Microsoft Management Console. Windows XP is a fully new OS.
- Windows 2000/XP offer a highly structured environment designed to enhance file and folder security on shared workstations. Documents and Settings folders contain all the user accounts on a system, assigning them default data and program folders. Combined with NTFS, this user organization allows all to access shared folders and programs, but one user cannot access the My Documents of another user.
- Although later service packs of Windows NT provided rudimentary PnP support, Windows 2000/XP have complete PnP support. Device Manager and the Add New Hardware Wizard make device installation easy.

- Windows 2000/XP come with a new type of NTFS called NTFS 5.0, which adds four improvements over Windows NT's NTFS v. 4.0: encryption, mount points, disk quotas, and dynamic disks.
- Windows XP's Files and Settings Transfer Wizard runs from the XP CD-ROM. The Wizard prepares your old drive to transfer its settings. Then you install Windows XP on the new hardware, connect the old hard drive to the new one, run the Files and Settings Transfer Wizard again, choose the appropriate drive and transfer everything over.
- Windows XP comes with the same System Restore features as Windows Me. Windows XP goes beyond Me with its Driver Rollback feature, which enables you to roll back individual device drivers for pieces of hardware.
- With Remote Access, Microsoft gives you the ability to take control of any Windows XP PC remotely, over a local area network or even over the Internet. You have to get invited to help and be granted permission to take the driver's seat remotely.

Device Manager *(411)*
DOS protected-mode interface (DPMI) *(426)*
Icon *(398)*
Graphical user interface (GUI) *(398)*
My Computer *(405)*
My Documents *(408)*
NTFS Permissions *(441)*
NTLDR *(445)*
Quick Launch *(405)*
Recycle Bin *(409)*
Taskbar *(402)*
User interface *(395)*

Key Term Quiz

Use the Key Terms list to complete the sentences that follow. Not all the terms will be used.

1. You can readily see programs loading in the background by looking at the ____________.
2. The ________________ stores information about all the hardware, drivers, and applications on a Windows NT system.
3. The first place you should look on a PC with malfunctioning hardware is ______________.
4. Most tech tools in Windows 2000 can be found in __________________.
5. The Windows 98 command line interface is not DOS, but ______________.
6. In Windows XP, __________________ starts the boot process.
7. The ___________ in Windows Me offers a great spot for accessing favorite programs without resorting to the Start menu.
8. Jill accidentally deleted a critical file. Winona the tech assures her that the file is no doubt in the ____________ and not lost forever.
9. Windows uses the __________________ for virtual memory.
10. You can edit the ________________ file in Windows 9x to change the default boot menu.

Multiple-Choice Quiz

1. Ian complains that his SYSTEM.DAT and USER.DAT files got corrupted. What is he talking about?
   - **A.** These are the Windows files that replace IO.SYS and MSDOS.SYS.
   - **B.** These are the Windows 9*x*/Me registry files.
   - **C.** These are the Windows NT/2000/XP registry files.
   - **D.** He's talking techno babble to impress the coworkers.
2. What is the best way to access the Registry Editor in Windows 9*x*/Me?
   - **A.** Start | Programs | DOS prompt icon. Type **EDIT**.
   - **B.** Start | Programs | Registry Editor.
   - **C.** Start | Run. At the prompt, type **REGEDIT** and click OK.
   - **D.** Start | Run. Type **REGEDT32** and click OK.
3. Which of the following boot menu options in Windows 9*x* enables the system to boot to the GUI for troubleshooting purposes, but without the advanced functions of Windows?
   - **A.** Safe mode
   - **B.** Safe mode Command Prompt only
   - **C.** Command Prompt only
   - **D.** Troubleshooting mode
4. Which of the following files does Windows 9*x* need to load?
   - **A.** Real mode drivers for hardware
   - **B.** CONFIG.SYS
   - **C.** AUTOEXEC.BAT
   - **D.** None of the above
5. Which of the following is *not* a Registry root key in Windows 9*x*/Me?
   - **A.** HKEY_CURRENT_MACHINE
   - **B.** HKEY_CLASSES_ROOT
   - **C.** HKEY_CURRENT_USER
   - **D.** HKEY_LOCAL_MACHINE
6. Which of the following is not an advantage of running Windows 2000 on NTFS as opposed to FAT32?
   - **A.** Security
   - **B.** Encryption
   - **C.** Long filenames
   - **D.** Compression
7. John's Windows 2000 system can also boot to Windows 98. What file does the NTFS loader read to know what OS to boot to?
   - **A.** MSDOS.SYS
   - **B.** BOOTLOG.TXT
   - **C.** NTOSKRNL.EXE
   - **D.** BOOT.INI
8. Which of the following files is not necessary for *all* Windows NT/2000 systems?
   - **A.** NTLDR
   - **B.** NTBOOTDD.SYS
   - **C.** NTDETECT.COM
   - **D.** BOOT.INI
9. Which of the following commands entered in the Start | Run dialog box will start the Windows XP 32-bit command interpreter?
   - **A.** CMD
   - **B.** COMMAND
   - **C.** WINNT32
   - **D.** CMD32
10. Windows XP provides a number of ready-made MMC snap-ins stored in the ______ applet in the Control Panel.
    - **A.** System
    - **B.** Network
    - **C.** Administrative Tools
    - **D.** MMC
11. What are the major functions of an operating system (OS)?
    - **A.** An OS provides a method for other programs to communicate.
    - **B.** An OS creates a user interface.

C. An OS enables users to add, move, and delete installed programs and data.

D. All of the above.

12. Which of the following shows a typical DOS prompt?

A. A:\\

B. D:/>

C. C:\>

D. C://

13. Which of the following *best* describes the operating system's user interface?

A. It enables the system to communicate with

displays when communicating with hardware.

14. To manipulate and organize data and programs, which of the following must the OS do? (Select all that apply.)

A. Identify all the data and programs on the system and organize them in a binary-code format.

B. Provide a method to identify data according to the type of program that uses that particular data.

C. Provide a naming system for each drive.

D. Give the user an interface to assign drive letters to drives.

15.

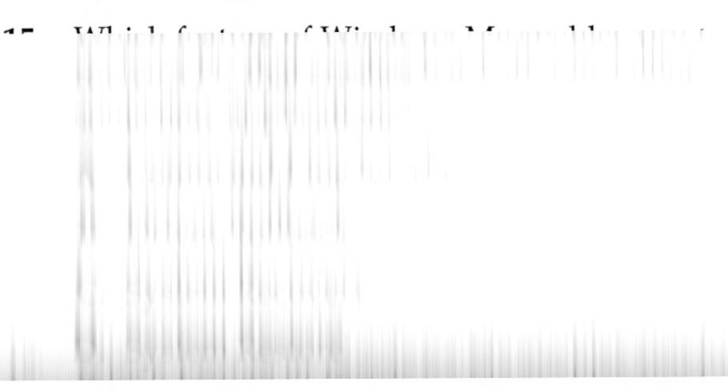

Essay Quiz

1. You've been tasked with teaching a group of new techs some of the ins and outs of working with Windows 9*x*. For the first lesson, put together a brief essay on three of the top four tools every tech should know. Include what each tool is used for and where to find it.
2. Your department just got four new interns who will share two PCs running Windows XP. Your boss has decided that you're the person who should take the newbies under your wing and teach them about Windows. Write a brief essay on some essential Windows folders and interfaces that every *user* should know.
3. Your tech firm deals with clients who use every version of Windows, often in the same offices. It's crazy! One of your colleagues has not been able to grasp the core differences between the OS files of the two families of Windows, 9*x* and NT. Write an essay discussing the files required by each OS family and how they boot.
4. Your boss just got off the phone with the corporate headquarters and is in somewhat of a panic. She doesn't know the first thing about the Microsoft Management Console, but now every tech is going to be issued a custom MMC. Write a brief essay explaining the function of the MMC to help allay her worries.
5. A colleague has approached you with a serious problem. He was on tech support for his home PC and the support person told him the only way to fix the problem he was having on his Windows XP Home PC was to edit the Registry manually. Then the tech scared him, saying that if he messed up, he could destroy his PC forever. Write a short essay discussing the Registry and the tools for editing the Registry.

Lab Projects

• Lab Project 12.1

The chapter mentions a couple of alternative operating systems, including Macintosh OS 9 and OS X. Do an Internet search or a tour of your local PC superstore and compare the OSs available. Is it only Mac vs. Windows?

• Lab Project 12.2

In a couple of places in the chapter you got a taste of working with some of the more complex tools in Windows NT/2000/XP, such as the Event Viewer and Performance console. Go back through the text and re-read those sections, and then do an Internet search for a "how-to" article. Then work with the tools.

Working with the Command Line Interface

"Real techs don't need to point and click!"

—Infamous Tech Quip

In this chapter, you will learn how to

- **Explain the operation of the command line interface**
- **Execute fundamental commands from the command line**
- **Manipulate files and folders from the command line**

Whenever I teach a class of new techs and we get to the section on working with the command line, I'm invariably met with a chorus of moans and a barrage of questions and statements. "Why do we need to learn this old stuff?" "We're running Windows XP Professional, not Windows 3.1!" "Is this ritualistic hazing appropriate in an IT class?"

For techs who master the interface, the command line provides a powerful, quick, and elegant tool for working on a PC. Learning that interface and understanding how to make it work is not only useful, but necessary for all techs who want to go beyond baby-tech status. You simply cannot work on all PCs without knowing the command line! It's not just me who thinks this way. The A+ Certification exams test you on a variety of command line commands for doing everything from renaming a file to rebuilding a system file.

This chapter gives you the interface, explaining how it works and what's happening behind the scenes. You'll learn the concepts and master essential commands, and then you'll work with files and folders throughout your drives. We'll wrap up with a brief section on encryption and file compression in the "Beyond A+" portion of the chapter.

You'll work with other aspects of the command line, such as installation and troubleshooting, in Chapters 14–16.

A good tactic for absorbing the material in this chapter is to try out each command or bit of information as it is presented. If you have some experience working on DOS-like systems, many of these commands will be familiar to you. If the command line is completely new to you, please take the red pill and join me as we step out of the Matrix.

Historical/Conceptual

Operating systems existed long before PCs were invented. Ancient, massive computers called mainframes and minicomputers employed sophisticated OSs. It wasn't until the late 1970s that IBM went looking for an OS for a new *microcomputer*—the official name for the PC—they were developing called the IBM Personal Computer, better known as the PC. After being rebuffed by a company called Digital Research, IBM went to a tiny company that had invented a popular new programming language called BASIC. They asked the president of his company if he could create an OS for the IBM PC. Although his company had never actually written an OS, he brazenly said "Sure!" That man was Bill Gates, and the tiny company was Microsoft.

After shaking hands with IBM representatives, Bill Gates hurriedly began to search for an OS based on the Intel 8086 processor. He found a primitive OS called *Quick-and-Dirty Operating System* (QDOS), which was written by a one-man shop, and he purchased it for a few thousand dollars. After several minor changes, Microsoft released it as **MS-DOS (Microsoft Disk Operating System)** version 1.1. Although primitive by today's standards, MS-DOS 1.1 could provide all the functions needed for an OS. Over the years, MS-DOS went through version after version until the last Microsoft version, MS-DOS 6.22, was released in 1994. Microsoft licensed MS-DOS to PC makers. They could add their own changes and then rename the program. IBM called their version PC-DOS.

DOS used a command line interface, as you know from earlier chapters. You typed a command at a prompt, and DOS responded to that command. When Microsoft introduced Windows 95 and Windows NT, many computer users and techs thought that the DOS interface would go away, but it turned out that techs not only continued to use the command line, they *needed it* to troubleshoot and fix problems! With Windows 2000, it seemed once again that the command line would die, but again, that just didn't turn out to be the case.

Finally recognizing the importance of the command line interface, Microsoft beefed it up in Windows XP. The command line in Windows XP offers commands and options for using various commands that go well beyond anything seen in previous Microsoft operating systems. Let's start with some essential concepts of the command line and then turn to more specific commands.

■ Deciphering the Command Line Interface

So how does a command line interface work? It's a little like having an Instant Message conversation with your computer. The computer tells you it's ready to receive commands by displaying a specific set of characters called a **prompt**.

```
Computer: Want to play a game?
```

```
Computer: A very fun game...
Mike: _
```

Once you get a new prompt, it means the computer is ready for your next instruction. You give the computer commands in the graphical user interface (GUI) of Windows as well, just in a different way, by clicking buttons and menu options with your mouse instead of typing on the keyboard. The results are basically the same: you tell the computer to do something and it responds.

When you give a command from the command line, you cause the computer to respond, and this response affects the files and folders on the PC as viewed from the GUI. As an example, suppose you want to find out the contents of a particular folder. From the command line, you'd type a command (in this case DIR, but more on that in a minute), and the computer would respond by displaying a screen like the one in Figure 13.1. In the GUI, you would open My Computer and click the C: drive icon to see the contents of that **directory**. The results might look like Figure 13.2, which at first glance isn't much like the command line screen; however, simply by choosing a different view (Figure 13.3), you can make the results look quite a bit like the command line version, albeit much prettier (Figure 13.4). The point here is that whichever interface you use, the information available to you is essentially the same.

```
D:\WINDOWS\System32\cmd.exe

C:\>dir
 Volume in drive C is LOCAL DISK
 Volume Serial Number is FC74-59D7

 Directory of C:\

02/18/2003  03:11 PM                 0 CONFIG.SYS
02/18/2003  03:11 PM                 0 AUTOEXEC.BAT
02/19/2003  11:54 AM    <DIR>          Program Files
02/20/2003  05:56 PM    <DIR>          Shared
07/25/2002  01:35 PM             5,003 pspbrwse.jbf
02/21/2003  12:46 PM    <DIR>          aioacert
02/21/2003  12:46 PM    <DIR>          Diploma
02/21/2003  12:55 PM    <DIR>          Lexfmgr
02/21/2003  12:59 PM    <DIR>          RECYCLER
02/21/2003  12:59 PM    <DIR>          W2KR128
02/21/2003  12:59 PM    <DIR>          Work Files
03/04/2003  11:59 AM    <DIR>          ExamView
03/05/2001  02:58 PM            18,963 Aplus3rdEd_sm.jpg
               4 File(s)         23,966 bytes
               9 Dir(s)     36,098,048 bytes free

C:\>
C:\>_
```

• **Figure 13.1** Contents of C:\ directory from the command line

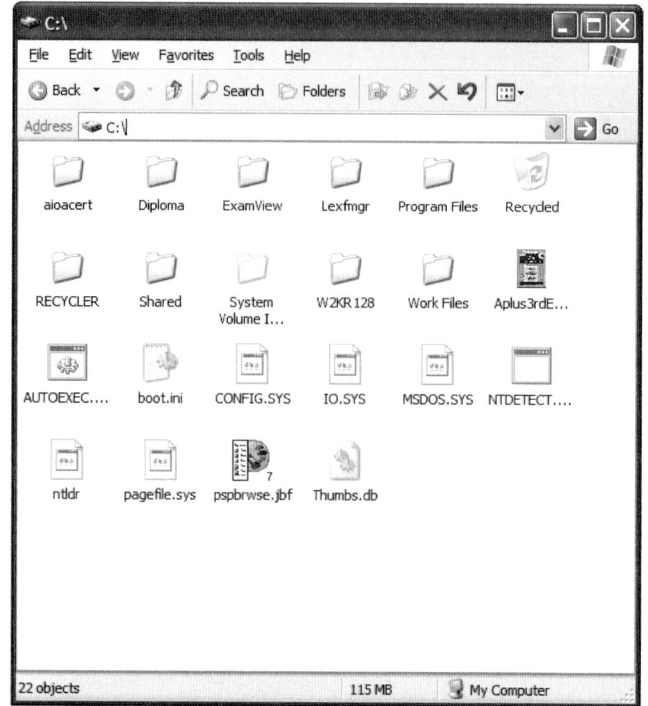

• **Figure 13.2** Contents of C:\ directory displayed in My Computer—Icon View

• **Figure 13.3** Selecting Details View in My Computer

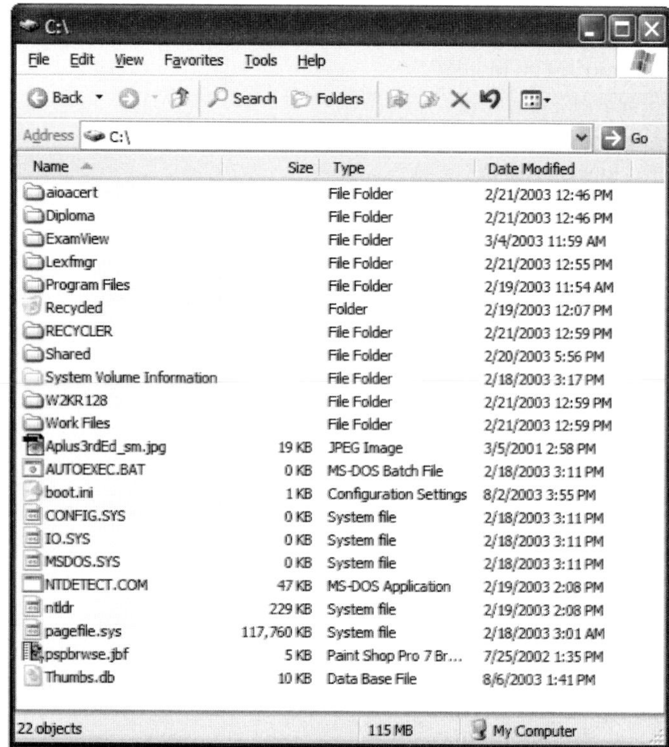

• **Figure 13.4** Contents of C:\ directory displayed in My Computer—Details View

Accessing the Command Line

Before you can use the command line interface, you've got to open it. You can use various methods to do this, depending on the flavor of Windows that you might be using. Some methods are simpler than others—just make sure that you know at least one, or you'll never get off the starting line!

One easy way to access the command line interface is by using the **Run dialog box**. Click the Start button, and then select Run. If you're using Windows NT 4.0, Windows 2000, or Windows XP, type **CMD** and press the ENTER key (Figure 13.5). A window will pop up on your screen with a black background and white text—this is the command line interface. In Windows 9*x*/Me operating systems, you must type **COMMAND** into the Run dialog box instead of CMD. Finally, buried in the Start menu of *most* computers, under Programs | Accessories, is a link to the command line interface. In Windows 9*x*/Me systems, the link is named MS-DOS Prompt; in Windows NT, 2000 and XP, it's called Command Prompt. These links, just like the Run dialog box, pull up a nice command line interface window (Figure 13.6). To close the command line interface window, you can either click the Close box, like on any other window, or you can simply type **EXIT** at any command prompt and press ENTER.

In Windows 95, 98, and 98 SE, you can boot the PC directly to the prompt, never loading the GUI at all, an essential tool for troubleshooting. To boot to the command line interface, hold down the F8 key when the screen displays "Starting Windows 9x" during the boot process. You'll get a menu that offers several selections, including Command Prompt Only. Select that option and you'll be GUI-less.

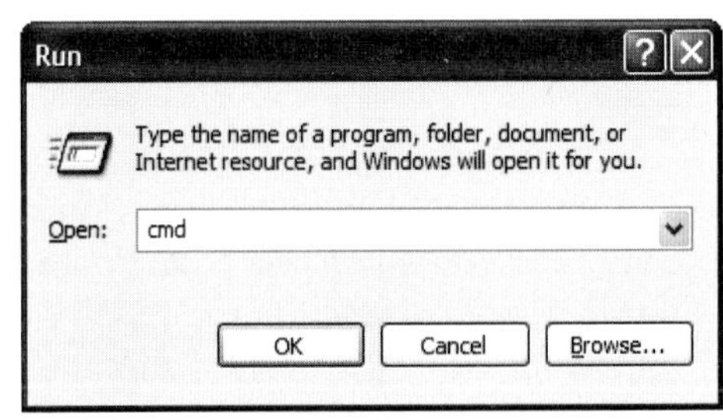

• **Figure 13.5** Type CMD in the Run dialog box to open a command line window.

The Command Prompt

The command prompt is always *focused* on a specific folder. This is important because any commands you issue are performed *on the files in the folder on which the prompt is focused*. For example, if

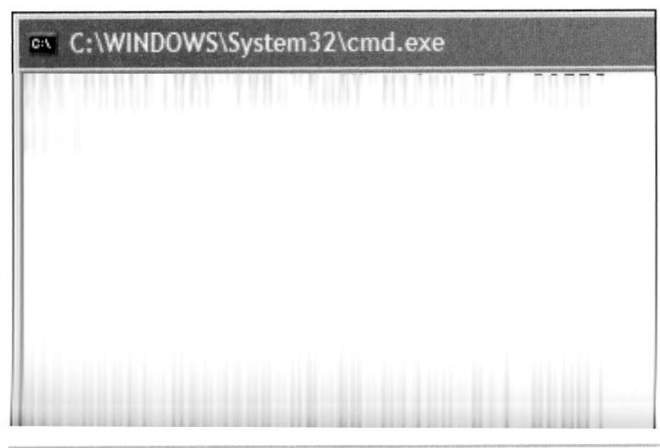

• **Figure 13.6** The command line interface window with a C:\> prompt

Filenames and File Formats

Windows manifests each program and piece of data as an individual file. This is true from the GUI and the command line. Each file has a name, which is stored with the file on the drive. Names are broken down into two parts: the **filename** and the **extension** In true DOS the filename could be no longer than eight characters, so you'll often see oddly named files on older systems. The extension, which is optional, could be up to three characters long in true DOS, and most computer programs and users continue to honor that old limit, even though it does not apply to modern PCs. No spaces or other illegal characters (/ \ [ ] I ÷ + = ; , * ?) could be used in the filename or extension. The filename and extension are separated by a period, or *dot*. This naming system was known as the **8.3** (eight-dot-three) **naming system** .

Here are some examples of acceptable true DOS filenames:

FRED.EXE	SYSTEM.INI	FILE1.DOC
DRIVER3.SYS	JANET	CODE33.H

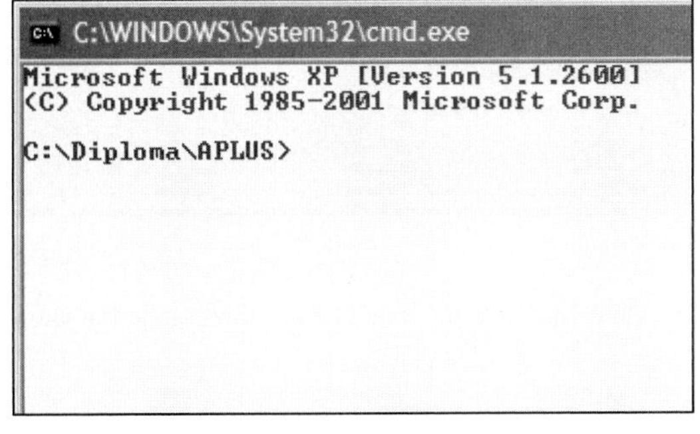

• **Figure 13.7** Command prompt indicating focus on the C:\Diploma\APLUS\ folder

Here are some unacceptable true DOS filenames:

4CHAREXT.EXEC	WAYTOOLONG.FIL	BAD÷CHAR.BAT	.NO

I mention the true DOS limitations for a simple reason: *backward compatibility*. All versions of Windows starting with 9*x* do not suffer from the 8.3 filename limitation. These OSs allow filenames of up to 255 characters. Windows 9*x*/Me retains complete backward compatibility with DOS by automatically creating two names for every file, an 8.3 filename and a long filename (if necessary).

> If brevity is your thing, you can call up the Run dialog box by pressing the WINDOWS key and the R key at the same time. This keyboard shortcut works on all versions of Windows.

Try This!

Accessing the Command Line

This chapter will be much more fun if you follow along with your own command line, so try this! Using one of the methods outlined in this section, access a command prompt in Windows. Just remember that everything you do at the prompt can affect the functioning of your PC. So don't go deleting stuff if you don't know what it's for!

Windows allows a lot of freedom in file naming, but it still has a handful of characters that you can't use for file or folder names: \ / : * ? " < > |

The extension part of the filename tells the computer the type or function of the file. Program files use the extension .EXE (for "executable") or .COM (for "command"). Anything that is not a program is some form of data to support a program. Different programs use different types of data files. The extension usually indicates which program uses that particular data file. For example, Microsoft Word uses the extension .DOC, while WordPerfect uses .WPD and PowerPoint uses .PPT. Graphics file extensions, in contrast, often reflect the graphics standard used to render the image, such as .GIF for CompuServe's Graphics Interchange Format or .JPG for the JPEG (Joint Photographic Experts Group) format.

• **Figure 13.8** What kind of file is the one on the lower right?

Changing the extension of a data file does not affect its contents, but without the proper extension, Windows won't know which program uses it. You can see this obviously in My Computer. Figure 13.8 shows a folder with two identical image files. The one on top shows the Photoshop icon, which is the program that Windows will use to open that file; the one on the bottom shows a generic icon, because I deleted the extension. Windows GUI doesn't show file extensions by default. Figure 13.9 shows the contents of that same folder from the command line.

All files are stored on the hard drive in binary format, but every program has its own way of reading and writing this binary data. Each unique method of binary organization is called a **file format**. One program cannot read another program's files unless it has the ability to convert the other program's format into its format. In the very early days of DOS, no programs were capable of performing this type of conversion, yet people wanted to exchange files. They wanted some type of common format that any program could read. The answer was a special format called **American Standard Code for Information Interchange (ASCII)**.

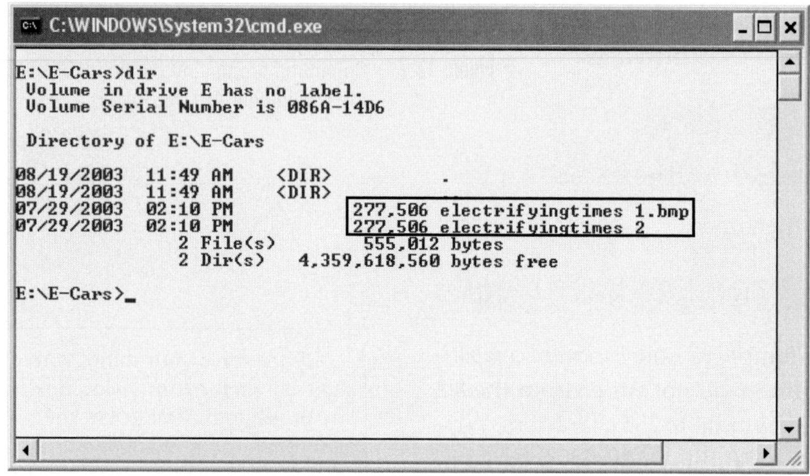

• **Figure 13.9** Hey! Who deleted my extension?

The ASCII standard defines 256 eight-bit characters. These characters include all the letters of the alphabet (uppercase and lowercase), numbers, punctuation, many foreign characters (such as accented vowels for French and Spanish—é, ì, ô—and other typical non-English characters), box-drawing characters, and a series of special characters for commands such as a carriage return, bell, and end of file (Figure 13.10). ASCII files, more commonly known as *text files,* store all data in ASCII format. The ASCII standard, however, is for more than just files. For example, the keyboard sends the letters you press, in ASCII code, to the PC. Even the monitor outputs in ASCII when you are running DOS.

ASCII was the first universal file format. Virtually every type of program—word processors, spreadsheets, databases, presentation programs—can read and write text files. However, text files have severe limitations. A text file can't store impor-

000		<nul>	032	sp	064	@	096	`	128	Ç	160	á	192	└	224	α
001	☺	<soh>	033	!	065	A	097	a	129	ü	161	í	193	┴	225	ß
002	☻	<stx>	034	"	066	B	098	b	130	é	162	ó	194	┬	226	Γ
003	♥	<etx>	035	#	067	C	099	c	131	â	163	ú	195	├	227	π
004	♦	<eot>	036	$	068	D	100	d	132	ä	164	ñ	196	─	228	Σ
005	♣	<enq>	037	%	069	E	101	e	133	à	165	Ñ	197	┼	229	σ
006	♠	<ack>	038	&	070	F	102	f	134	å	166	ª	198	╞	230	µ
007	•	<bel>	039	'	071	G	103	g	135	ç	167	º	199	╟	231	τ
008	◘	<bs>	040	(	072	H	104	h	136	ê	168	¿	200	╚	232	Φ
009		<tab>	041	)	073	I	105	i	137	ë	169	⌐	201	╔	233	Θ
010		<lf>	042	*	074	J	106	j	138	è	170	¬	202	╩	234	Ω
011	♂	<vt>	043	+	075	K	107	k	139	ï	171	½	203	╦	235	δ
012	♀	<np>	044	,	076	L	108	l	140	î	172	¼	204	╠	236	∞
013		<cr>	045	-	077	M	109	m	141	ì	173	¡	205	═	237	ø
014	♫	<so>	046	.	078	N	110	n	142	Ä	174	«	206	╬	238	∈
015	☼	<si>	047	/	079	O	111	o	143	Å	175	»	207	╧	239	∩
016	►	<dle>	048	0	080	P	112	p	144	É	176	░	208	╨	240	≡
017	◄	<dc1>	049	1	081	Q	113	q	145	æ	177	▒	209	╤	241	±
018	↕	<dc2>	050	2	082	R	114	r	146	Æ	178	▓	210	╥	242	≥
019	‼	<dc3>	051	3	083	S	115	s	147	ô	179	│	211	╙	243	≤
020	¶	<dc4>	052	4	084	T	116	t	148	ö	180	┤	212	╘	244	⌠
021	§	<nak>	053	5	085	U	117	u	149	ò	181	╡	213	╒	245	⌡
022	▬	<syn>	054	6	086	V	118	v	150	û	182	╢	214	╓	246	÷
023	↨	<etb>	055	7	087	W	119	w	151	ù	183	╖	215	╫	247	≈

beyond just printing simple characters. For example, how does the program reading the text file know when to start a new line? This is where the first 32 ASCII characters come into play. These first 32 characters are special commands (actually, some of them are both commands and characters). For example, the ASCII value 7 can be either a large dot or a command to play a note (bell) on the PC speaker. ASCII value 9 is a Tab. ASCII value 27 is an Escape.

Drives and Folders

When working from the command line, you need to be able to focus the prompt at the specific drive and folder that contains the files or program with which you want to work. This can be a little more complicated than it seems, especially in Windows 2000 and Windows XP.

At boot, Windows assigns a drive letter (or name) to each hard drive partition and to each floppy or other disk drive. The first floppy drive is called A:, and the second, if installed, is called B:. Hard drives usually start with the letter C: and can continue to Z: if necessary. CD-ROM drives by default get the next available drive

Try This!

Fun with ASCII

ASCII is alive and well on modern systems and can prove useful in many situations. A lot of e-mail programs can use ASCII characters, as can Internet message boards such as my Tech Forums. You can use ASCII characters to accent your writing or simply to spell a person's name correctly—Martin *Acuña*—when you address him. Working with ASCII is fun, so try this!

1. Open up a text editing program, such as Notepad in the Windows GUI.
2. Hold down the ALT key on your keyboard and, referring to Figure 13.10, press numbers on your keyboard's number pad. Pressing ALT-164 should display an *ñ*, whereas ALT-168 will show an *¿*.
3. If you have access to the Internet handy, surf on over to the Tech Forums (www.totalsem.com) and say howdy! Include some ASCII in your post, of course!

Cross Check

Unicode

As you'll remember from Chapter 12, Microsoft extended the old 8-bit ASCII character set and adopted a 16-bit *Unicode* character set in all versions of Windows. Refer back to Chapter 12 and see if you can answer these questions. How many characters can Unicode support? What text characters does Unicode support that ASCII does not? Is there any reason to use ASCII rather than Unicode in a modern world?

Windows calls all folders *folders* except for the root, which still gets the old term directory, as in *root directory*. In practice, though, the terms *directory* and *folder* are interchangeable. Some techs split hairs and call these data containers folders when you're in the GUI, but directories when you're at a command prompt. It's the same thing!

letter after the last hard drive. Windows NT, 2000, and XP enable you to change the default lettering for drives, so you're likely to see all sorts of lettering schemes. Windows 2000 and XP enable you to mount a hard drive as a volume in another drive.

Windows uses a **hierarchical directory tree** to organize the contents of these drives. All files are put into groups Windows calls folders, although you'll often hear techs use the term *directory* rather than *folder*, a holdover from the true DOS days. Any file not in a folder *within* the tree, which is to say, any file in the folder at the root of the directory tree, is said to be in the **root directory**. A folder inside another folder is called a subfolder. Any folder can have multiple subfolders. Two or more files with the same name can exist in different folders on a PC, but two files in the same folder cannot have the same name. In the same way, no two subfolders under the same folder can have the same name, but two subfolders under different folders can have the same name.

When describing a drive, you use its letter and a colon. For example, the hard drive would be represented by C:. To describe the root directory, put a backslash (\) after the C:, as in C:\. To describe a particular directory, add the name of the directory. For example, if a PC had a directory in the root directory called TEST, it would be C:\TEST. **Subdirectories** in a directory are displayed by adding backslashes and names. If the TEST directory had a subdirectory called SYSTEM, it would be shown like this: C:\TEST\SYSTEM. This naming convention provides for a complete description of the location and name of any file. If the C:\TEST\SYSTEM directory had a file called TEST2.TXT, it would be C:\TEST\SYSTEM\TEST2.TXT.

The exact location of a file is called its **path**. The path for the TEST2.TXT file is C:\TEST\SYSTEM. Here are some examples of possible paths:

```
C:\DOS
F:\FRUSCH3\CLEAR
A:\REPORTS
D:\
```

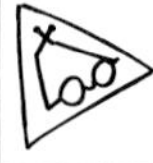

Tech Tip

Directory Trees

It helps to visualize a directory tree as upside down, because in geek speak, the trunk, or "root directory" is spoken of as if it were "above" the folders that divide it up, and those subfolders are spoken of as being "above" the folders into which they are divided. For example, "The file is in the Adobe folder under Program Files."

■ Mastering Fundamental Commands

It's time to try using the command line, but before we begin, a note of warning is in order: the command line interface is picky and unforgiving: It will do what you *say*, not what you *mean*, so it always pays to double-check that those are the same before you press ENTER. One careless keystroke can result in the loss of crucial data, with no warning and no going back. In this section, you'll explore the structure of commands and then play with four commands built into all versions of Microsoft's command line interface: DIR, CD, MD, and RD.

Structure: Syntax and Switches

All commands in the Windows command line interface use a similar structure and execute in the same way. You type the name of the command followed by the target of that command and any modifications of that command that you want to apply. The modifications are called up by using extra letters and numbers at the end, called **switches**. The key with commands is that you can't spell anything incorrectly or use a \ when the syntax calls for a /. The command line is completely inflexible!

```
[command] [target (if any)] [switches]
```

If you want to find out the syntax and switches used by a particular command, always type the command followed by a **/?** to get help.

When you open a command line window in Windows XP, it opens focused on your user folder. You will know this because the prompt will look like this: `C:\Documents and Settings\username>`. By typing in **DIR** and then pressing the ENTER key (remember that you must always press ENTER to execute a command from the command line), you will see something like Figure 13.11.

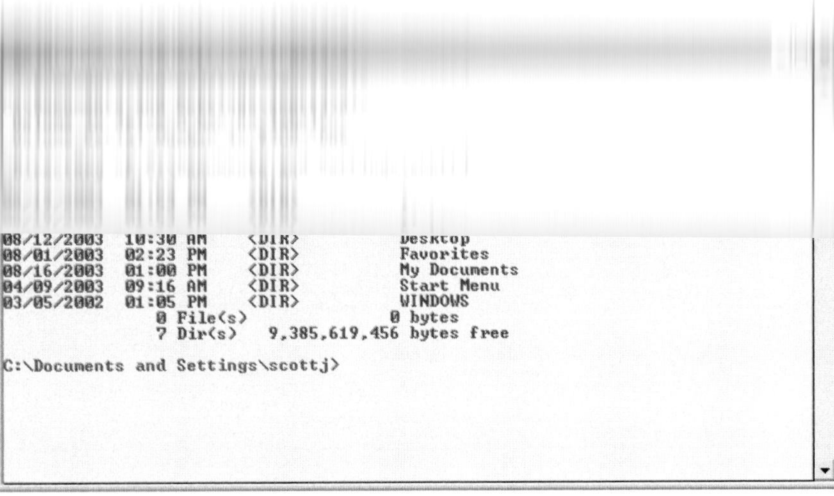

• **Figure 13.11** DIR in user folder

If you are following along on a PC, remember that different computers contain different files and programs, so you will absolutely see something different from what's shown in Figure 13.11! If a lot of text scrolls quickly down the screen, try typing **DIR/P** (pause) or **DIR/W** (wide). Don't forget to press ENTER. The DIR/P command is a lifesaver when you're looking for something in a large directory.

When you type a simple DIR command, you will see that some of the entries look like this,

```
CONFIG   SYS     34      09-03-96      4:36p
```

or this in Windows XP:

```
09/04/2003   05:51 PM           63,664 bambi.jpg
```

All of these entries are files. The DIR command lists the filename, extension, file size in bytes, and creation date/time. The DIR/W command shows you only the filenames, but they are arranged in five columns across your screen.

Extra text typed after a command to modify its operation, such as the /W or /P after DIR, is called a switch. Almost all switches can be used simultaneously to modify a command. For example, try typing **DIR/W/P**.

Those of you using the DIR command at a command prompt in Windows 9*x* should see something similar to this (I removed the beginning of the listing to concentrate on the filenames):

```
WEBSHOTS  INI          748  11-12-00  1:08p webshots.ini
WEBSHO~1  EXE       28,672  03-09-02  3:56p WebshotsUninstall.exe
SYSTEM    SYD        1,958  09-21-01  5:24p SYSTEM.SYD
EMILY000  PWL          688  09-21-00  5:23p EMILY000.PWL
EMILY001  PWL          688  09-21-01  5:52p EMILY001.PWL
EXITTO~1  PIF          967  09-24-01  3:19p Exit To DOS.pif
          LOG       29,337  10-17-00  8:09p Directx.log
EREG      DAT          501  10-17-00  8:09p eReg.dat
NPSEXEC   EXE       33,792  04-02-99  4:37p NPSExec.exe
       280 file(s)     89,898,614 bytes
        25 dir(s)   1,562,959,872 bytes free

C:\WINDOWS>
```

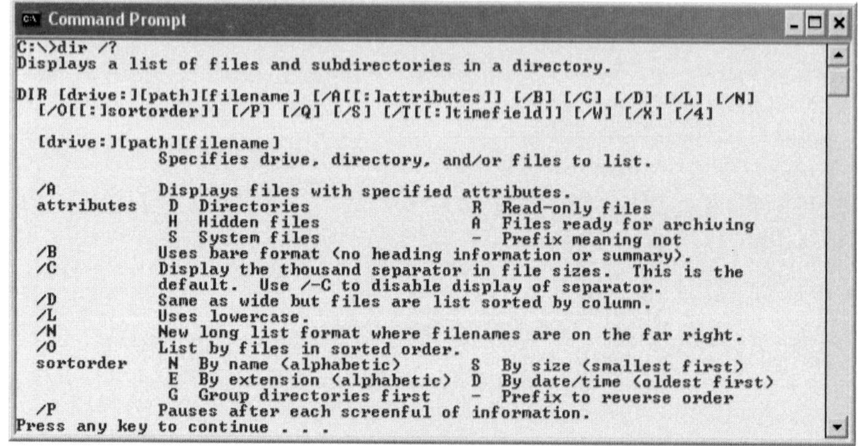

Figure 13.12 Typing DIR /? lists switches for DIR command.

Look at the second file in the list. Windows shows both its DOS-compatible 8.3 name and its full Windows name, using a tilde (~) character and a number (in this case a 1) in the 8.3 name to replace the extra characters.

Finally, type **DIR /?** to see the screen shown in Figure 13.12.

Typing any command followed by a **/?** brings up a help screen for that particular command. Although these help screens can sometimes seem a little cryptic, they're helpful when you're not too familiar with a command or you can't figure out how to get a command to do something. Even though I have almost every command memorized, I still refer to these help screens—use them!

Directories: The CD Command

Type **DIR** once again. This time ignore the file listings. See if you can find any entries that are followed by a <DIR>. They may look like these samples from a Windows 2000 system:

```
02/30/2002  08:04p     <DIR>        system
08/10/2001  07:23p     <DIR>        ts4.3
08/19/2001  10:47a     <DIR>        Office52
08/26/2001  12:23a     <DIR>        mgafold
11/10/2001  07:13a     <DIR>        BTMAGIC.PQ
01/10/2002  07:13a     <DIR>        WINNT
```

If you type **DIR/W**, these listings display differently. Instead of a <DIR> after the directory name, the directory name is enclosed in brackets. Do you see any listings that look like these when you type **DIR/W**?

```
[DOS]      [WINDOWS]      [QUAKE3]      [OBIWAN]
```

The CD (or CHDIR) command enables you to change the focus of the command prompt to a different directory. To use the CD command, type **CD** followed by the name of the directory on which you want the prompt to focus. To go to the C:\OBIWAN directory, type **CD\OBIWAN**, and then press ENTER. If the system has an OBIWAN directory, the prompt will change focus to that directory, and be C:\OBIWAN>. If no OBIWAN directory exists or if you accidentally typed something like **OBIWAM**, a Windows 9*x*/Me system will report: *Invalid directory*. If you use Windows NT/2000/XP, you get the error: *The system cannot find the path specified.* If only I had a dollar for every time I've seen those errors! I usually get them due to typing too fast. If you get this error, check what you typed and try again.

To return to the root directory, just type **CD** and press ENTER. You can use the CD command to point DOS to any directory. For example, you could type **CD\FRED\BACKUP\TEST** from a C:\ prompt, and the prompt

tory from the root directory simply by typing **CD WINDOWS** at the C:\ prompt. You can use the **CD [space]** command to move one level at a time, like this:

```
C:\>CD FRED
C:\FRED\>CD BACKUP
C:\FRED\BACKUP>CD TEST
```

Or, you can jump multiple directory levels in one step, like this:

```
C:\>CD FRED\BACKUP\TEST
C:\FRED\BACKUP\TEST>
```

A final trick: if you want to go *up* a single directory level you can type **CD** followed immediately by two periods. So, for example, if you're in the C:\FRED\BACKUP directory and you want to move up to the C:\FRED directory, you can simply type **CD..** and you'll be there:

```
C:\FRED\BACKUP>CD..
C:\FRED>
```

Take some time to move the DOS focus around the directories of your PC using the CD and DIR commands. Use DIR to find a directory, and then use CD to move the focus to that directory. Remember, CD\ will always get you back to the root directory.

Tech Tip

Errors Are Good!

Let's talk about errors in general for a moment, not just command prompt errors like "Invalid directory," but any error, including Windows errors. Many new computer users freeze in horror when they see an error message. Do not fear error messages. Error messages are good! Love them. Worship them. They will save you.

Seriously, think how confusing it would be if the computer didn't

make mistakes to familiarize yourself with the error messages. Have fun! Learn from errors!

Moving Between Drives

The CD command is *not* used to move between drives. To get the prompt to point to another drive ("point" is command line geek-speak for "switch its focus"), just type the drive letter and a colon. If the prompt points at the

C:\Sierra directory and you want to see what is on the floppy (A:) drive, just type **A:** and DOS will point to the floppy drive. You'll see the following on the screen:

```
C:\Sierra>A:
A:\>
```

To return to the C: drive, just type **C:** and you'll see the following:

```
A:\>C:
C:\Sierra>
```

Note that you return to the same directory you left. Just for fun, try typing in a drive letter that you know doesn't exist. I know that my system does not have a W: drive. If I type in a nonexistent drive on a Windows 9*x*/Me system, I get the following error:

```
Invalid drive specification
```

In Windows NT/2000/XP, I get the following error:

```
The system cannot find the drive specified.
```

Try inserting a floppy disk and using the CD command to point at its drive. Do the same with a CD-ROM disc. Type **DIR** to see the contents of the floppy or CD-ROM. Type **CD** to move the focus to any folders on the floppy or CD-ROM. Now return focus to the C: drive.

Using the DIR, CD, and drive letter commands, you can access any folder on any storage device on your system. Make sure you can use these commands comfortably to navigate inside your computer.

Making Directories

Now that you have learned how to navigate in a command-prompt world, it's time to start making stuff, beginning with a new directory.

To make a directory, use the MD (or MKDIR) command. To create a directory called QUAKE3 under the root directory C:, for example, first ensure that you are in the root directory by typing **CD**. You should see the prompt

```
C:\>
```

Now that the prompt points to the root directory, type the following:

```
C:\>MD QUAKE3
```

Once you press ENTER, Windows will execute the command, but it won't volunteer any information about what it did. You must use the DIR command to see that you have, in fact, created a new directory. Note that the QUAKE3 directory in this example is not listed last, as you might expect.

```
C:\>DIR
 Volume in Drive C is
 Volume Serial Number is 1734-3234
 Directory of C:\
DOS                <DIR>          09-03-96     9:34a
```

```
COMMAND   COM           34222  04-01-94    4:33p
AUTOEXEC  BAT              14  03-03-02   11:55a
WINDOWS          <DIR>         11-07-99    1:34a
CONFIG    SYS              34  03-03-02    4:36p
MIKE             <DIR>         09-03-99    8:15a
QUAKE3           <DIR>         09-22-01    8:15a
JUNK      DOC           55677  05-13-99   10:03a

          8 file(s)         72233    bytes
                         18288834    bytes free
```

The Windows command line interface almost never tells you that a command has been performed successfully. But be assured it will complain when you do something wrong! The old adage is: "DOS never pats you on the back, but it will slap you in the head!"

To create a FILES subdirectory in the QUAKE3 directory, first use the CD\ command to point the prompt at the QUAKE3 directory:

```
CD\QUAKE3
```

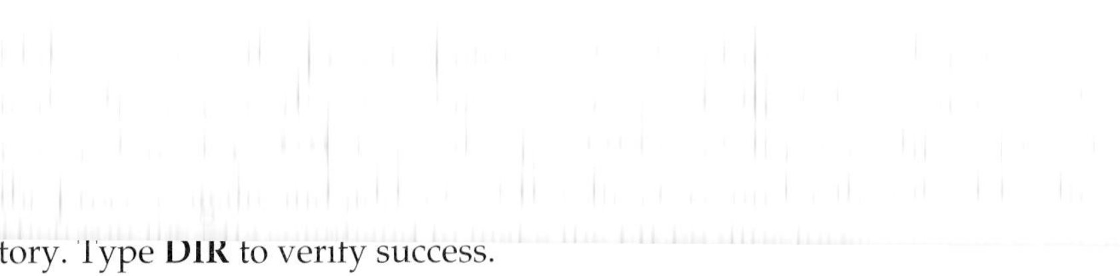

tory. Type **DIR** to verify success.

Removing Directories

Removing subdirectories works exactly like making them. First, get to the directory that contains the subdirectory you want to delete, and then execute the RD (or RMDIR) command. In this example, let's delete the FILES subdirectory in the C:\QUAKE3 directory. First, get to where the FILES directory is located—C:\QUAKE3—by typing **CD\QUAKE3**. Then type **RD FILES**. If no response was received from DOS, you probably did it right! Type **DIR** to check that the FILES subdirectory is gone.

The RD command will not delete a directory in Windows 9*x*/Me if the directory contains files or subdirectories. If you want to delete a directory that contains files or subdirectories, you must first empty that directory using the DEL (for files) or RD (for subdirectories) command. You can also use the DELTREE command. DELTREE will delete the directory as well as all files and subdirectories. DELTREE is handy but dangerous, because it's easy to delete more than you want. When deleting, always follow the maxim "check twice and delete once."

The RD command in Windows NT, 2000, and XP will delete populated directories, that is, directories containing files or subdirectories. Use the /S switch: Type **RD /S** and the directory name.

Let's delete the QUAKE3 and GAMES directories with DELTREE. Because the QUAKE3 directory is in the root directory, point DOS to the root directory with CD\. Now execute the DELTREE command: **DELTREE C:\QUAKE3**. In a rare display of mercy, DOS will respond with the following:

```
Delete directory C:\QUAKE3 and all its subdirectories? [y/n]
```

Press the **Y** key and both C:\QUAKE3 and C:\QUAKE3\GAMES will be eliminated.

Try This!

Working with Directories

It's important for a PC tech to be comfortable creating and deleting directories. To get some practice, try this:

1. Create a new directory in the root directory using the make directory command (MD). Type **CD** to return to the root directory. At the command prompt, type the following:

   ```
   C:\>MD JEDI
   ```

2. As usual, the prompt tells you nothing—it just presents a fresh prompt. Do a DIR (that is, type the **DIR** command) to see your new directory. Windows will create the new directory wherever it is pointing when you issue the command, whether or not that's where you meant to put it. To demonstrate, point the prompt to your new directory using the CD command:

   ```
   C:\>CD JEDI
   ```

3. Now use the Make Directory command again to create a directory called YODA:

   ```
   C:\JEDI>MD YODA
   ```

   Do a DIR again, and you should see that your JEDI directory now contains a YODA directory.

4. Type **CD** to return to the root directory so you can delete your new directories using the remove directory command (RD) in Windows NT/2000/XP (or DELTREE in Windows 9x/Me):

   ```
   C:\>RD /S JEDI
   ```

   In another rare display of mercy, Windows responds with the following:

   ```
   jedi, Are you sure <Y/N>?
   ```

5. Type **Y** to eliminate both C:\JEDI and C:\JEDI\YODA.

Running a Program

To run a program from the command line, simply change the prompt focus to the folder where the program is located, type the name of the program, and then press the ENTER key on your keyboard. Try this safe example. If you're using Windows 9*x*/Me, go to the C:\WINDOWS\COMMAND directory by using the CD command. If you're using Windows NT or 2000, go to the C:\WINNT\System32 directory. If you're using Windows XP, go to C:\WINDOWS\System32. Type **DIR/P** to see the files one page at a time. You should see a file called MEM.EXE (Figure 13.13).

As mentioned earlier, all files with extensions .EXE and .COM are programs, so MEM.EXE is a program. To run the MEM.EXE program, just type the filename, in this case **MEM**, and press ENTER (Figure 13.14). Note that you do not have to type the .EXE extension, although you can. Congratulations, you have just run your first program from the command line!

By and large, you can't run Windows GUI-based applications within a command line environment. Most will simply pop open in their own window, just as if you opened them from the Start menu. Try typing **SYSEDIT** at the command prompt within Windows and see what happens!

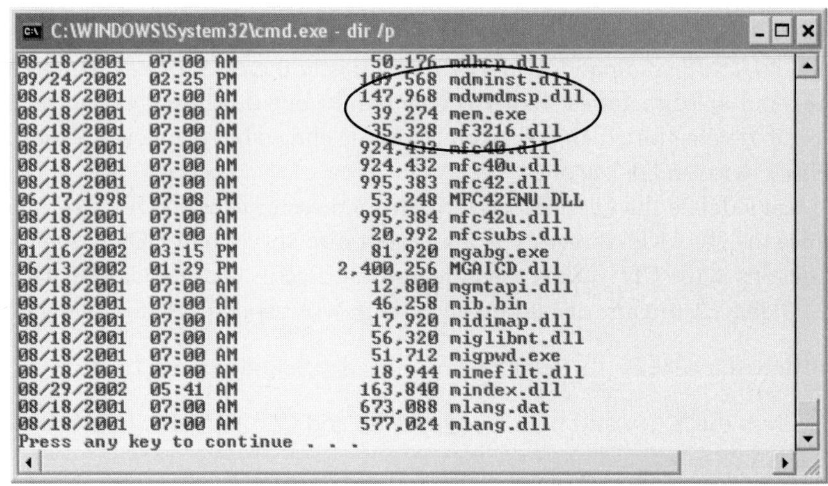

• **Figure 13.13** MEM.EXE displayed in the System32 folder

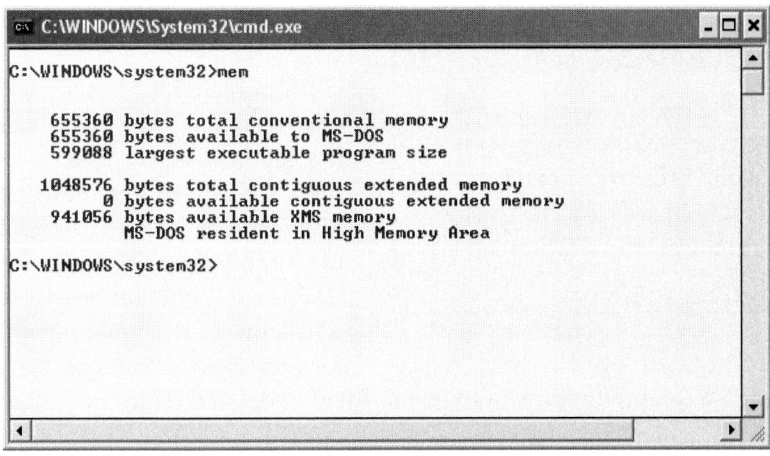

batch files. The examples in this section are based on a C: root directory with the following files and directories:

```
C:\>DIR
 Volume in Drive C is
 Volume Serial Number is 1734-3234
 Directory of C:\
DOS                <DIR>          09-03-96     9:34a
COMMAND  COM              34222  04-01-94      4:33p
AUTOEXEC BAT                 44  09-03-97     11:55a
WINDOWS            <DIR>          11-07-97      1:34a
OLD_DOS            <DIR>          09-03-97     11:55a
BACKUP             <DIR>          09-04-96      6:42p
SPINRITE COM             144654  11-02-96      8:00a
CONFIG   BAK                 34  02-03-98      4:36a
CONFIG   NU                  32  11-07-97      3:30p
AUTOEXEC OLD                 31  09-02-97     12:04a
VIRUS    COM              81222  04-01-97      5:29p
AUTOEXEC 1ST                 21  09-03-96     11:14a
CONFIG   SYS                 34  02-03-98      4:36p
QUAKE3              <DIR>         09-03-01      8:15a
JUNK     DOC              15677  04-03-98     10:03a
AUTOEXEC NU                  32  11-07-97      3:30p
       16 file(s)           3542233    bytes
                          182888343    bytes free
```

Because you probably don't have a PC with these files and directories, follow the examples but use what's on your drive. In other words, create your own folders and copy files to them from various folders currently on your system.

Cross Check

Command Line Programs

You've actually worked with at least two command line programs already in this book, right? Go to Chapter 11 and refresh your memory on FDISK and FORMAT. What do they do? How do you run them? Does either program have extra switches that might be useful? How do you determine whether they have switches?

Attributes

All files have four special values, or *attributes*, which determine how the file will act in special situations. These attributes can be set through software. The first attribute is the **hidden attribute**. If a file is hidden, it will not be displayed when the DIR command is performed. Next is the **read-only attribute**. A read-only file cannot be modified or deleted. Third is the **system attribute**, which is used only for system files such as IO.SYS and MSDOS.SYS. In reality, it does nothing more than provide an easy identifier for these files. Fourth is the **archive attribute**, which is used by backup software to identify files that have been changed since their last backup.

ATTRIB.EXE is an external command line program that enables you to inspect and change file attributes. To inspect a file's attributes, type the **ATTRIB** command followed by the name of the file. To see the attributes of the file COMMAND.COM, type **ATTRIB COMMAND.COM**. The result is

```
A       COMMAND.COM
```

The letter *A* stands for archive, the only attribute of COMMAND.COM. The letter *R* means read-only, *H* is hidden, and *S* is system.

Go to the C:\ directory and type **ATTRIB** by itself. If you're using Windows 9*x*/Me, you'll see a result similar to the following:

```
A    H       C:\AUTOEXEC.BAT
A    H       C:\CONFIG.SYS
A   SHR      C:\IO.SYS
A   SHR      C:\MSDOS.SYS
A            C:\COMMAND.COM
```

Don't panic if you see a number of different files than the ones just listed. No two C:\ directories are ever the same. In most cases, you'll see many more files than just these five. Notice that IO.SYS and MSDOS.SYS both have the System, Hidden, and Read-Only attributes set. Microsoft does this to protect these important files.

The ATTRIB command is also used to change a file's attributes. To add an attribute to a file, type the attribute letter preceded by a plus sign (+), and

Cross Check

IO.SYS and MSDOS.SYS

You've seen these two files recently! Check out Chapter 12 and get the scoop on IO.SYS and MSDOS.SYS.

1. Why are these files important?
2. Which OS(s) uses them?

then the filename. To delete an attribute, use a minus sign (–). For example, to add the read-only attribute to the file COMMAND.COM, type this:

```
ATTRIB +R COMMAND.COM
```

To remove the archive attribute, type this:

```
ATTRIB -A COMMAND.COM
```

Multiple attributes can be added or removed in one command. Here's an example of removing three attributes from the IO.SYS file:

```
ATTRIB -R -S -H MSDOS.SYS
```

Wildcards

files come up? You can! The answer is using wildcards.

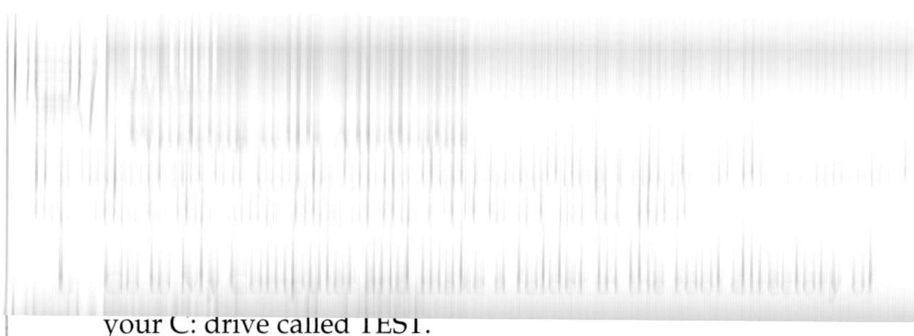

your C: drive called TEST.

2. Copy a couple of files into that folder and then alternate-click one to see its properties.
3. Open a command line window and navigate to the C:\TEST folder. Type **DIR** to see that the contents match what you see in My Computer.
4. From the command line, change the attributes of one or both files. Make one a hidden file, for example, and the other read only.
5. Now go back to My Computer and access the properties of each file. Any changes?

A **wildcard** is one of two special characters, asterisk (*) and question mark (?), that can be used in place of all or part of a filename, often to enable a command line command to act on more than one file at a time. Wildcards work with all command line commands that take filenames. A great example is the DIR command. When you execute a plain DIR command, it finds and displays all the files and folders in the specified directory; however, you can also narrow its search by adding a filename. For example, if you type the command, **DIR COMMAND.COM**, while in your root (C:\) directory, you get the following result:

```
 Volume in Drive C is
 Volume Serial Number is 1734-3234
 Directory of C:\
COMMAND   COM      34222      04-01-94   4:33p

            1 file(s)          34222 bytes
                           182888343 bytes free
```

If you just want to confirm the presence of a particular file in a particular place, this is very convenient. But suppose you wanted to see all files with the extension .COM. In that case, you'd use the * wildcard, like this: **DIR *.COM**. A good way to think of the * wildcard is *"I don't care."* Replace the part of the filename that you don't care about with an asterisk (*). The result of DIR *.COM would look like this:

```
 Volume in Drive C is
 Volume Serial Number is 1734-3234
 Directory of C:\
COMMAND     COM      34222         04-01-94       4:33p
NDOS        COM      76248         04-01-95       6:13p
SPINRITE    COM      144654        11-02-96       8:00a
VIRUS       COM      81222         04-01-97       5:29p
                4 file(s)          206338    bytes
                                182888343    bytes free
```

Wildcards also substitute for extensions:

```
C:\>DIR CONFIG.*
 Volume in Drive C is
 Volume Serial Number is 1734-3234
 Directory of C:\
CONFIG   BAK     34      02-03-98       4:36a
CONFIG   NU      32      11-07-97       3:30p
CONFIG   SYS     34      02-03-98       4:36p
      3 file(s)             100    bytes
                     182888343    bytes free
```

Even better, they can substitute for parts of filenames. This DIR command will find every file that starts with the letter *C:*

```
C:\>DIR C*.*
 Volume in Drive C is
 Volume Serial Number is 1734-3234
 Directory of C:\
COMMAND    COM      34222      04-01-94     4:33p
CONFIG     BAK      34         02-03-98     4:36a
CONFIG     NU       32         11-07-97     4:30p
CONFIG     SYS      34         02-03-98     4:36p
            4 file(s)       34322    bytes
                        182888343    bytes free
```

The ? wildcard replaces any single character. This can be handy when you're looking for filenames with a specific number of characters. To find all files having four-character filenames and the extension COM, you would type this:

```
C:\>DIR ????.COM
 Volume in Drive C is
 Volume Serial Number is 1734-3234
 Directory of C:\
NDOS     COM        76248      04-01-95     6:13p
           1 file(s)       76240     bytes
                       182888343     bytes free
```

So far, we've used wildcards only with the DIR command, but virtually every command that deals with files will take wildcards. Let's examine the REN and DEL commands and see how they use wildcards.

Renaming Files

To rename files, you use the REN or RENAME command, which seems pretty straightforward. To rename the file IMG033.jpg to park.jpg, type this and press the ENTER key:

```
ren img033.jpg park.jpg
```

That's great, you might be thinking, but what about using a more complex and descriptive filename, like Sunny day in the park.jpg? Type what should work, like this:

```
Ren img033.jpg Sunny day in the park.jpg
```

But you'll get an error message (Fig-

succeeds because of the quotation marks.

```
E:\E-Cars>ren /?
Renames a file or files.

RENAME [drive:][path]filename1 filename2.
REN [drive:][path]filename1 filename2.

Note that you cannot specify a new drive or path for your destination file.
```

Figure 13.15 Rename failed me!

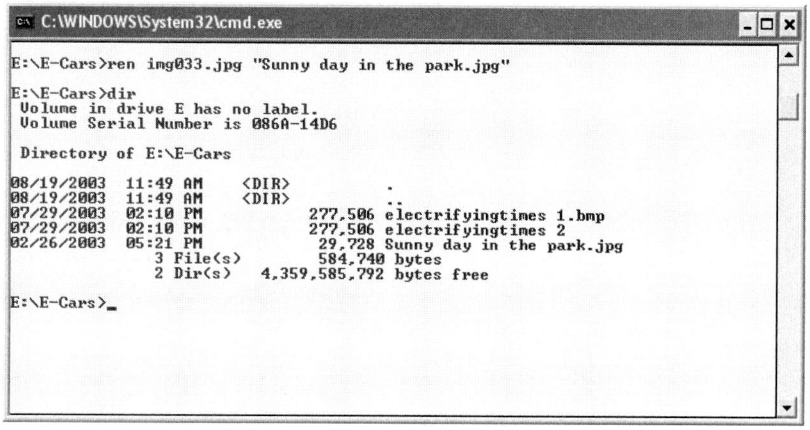

```
C:\WINDOWS\System32\cmd.exe

E:\E-Cars>ren img033.jpg "Sunny day in the park.jpg"

E:\E-Cars>dir
 Volume in drive E has no label.
 Volume Serial Number is 086A-14D6

 Directory of E:\E-Cars

08/19/2003  11:49 AM    <DIR>          .
08/19/2003  11:49 AM    <DIR>          ..
07/29/2003  02:10 PM           277,506 electrifyingtimes 1.bmp
07/29/2003  02:10 PM           277,506 electrifyingtimes 2
02/26/2003  05:21 PM            29,728 Sunny day in the park.jpg
               3 File(s)        584,740 bytes
               2 Dir(s)   4,359,585,792 bytes free

E:\E-Cars>_
```

Figure 13.16 Success at last!

Deleting Files

To delete files, you use the DEL or ERASE command. DEL and ERASE are identical commands and can be used interchangeably. Deleting files is simple—maybe too simple. Windows' users enjoy the luxury of retrieving deleted files from the Recycle Bin on those "Oops, I didn't mean to delete that" occasions everyone encounters at one time or another. The command line, however, shows no such mercy to the careless user. It has no function equivalent to the Windows Recycle Bin. Once a file has been erased, it can be recovered only by using a special recovery utility such as Norton's UNERASE. Again, the rule here is to *check twice and delete once.*

To delete a single file, type the DEL command followed by the name of the file to delete. To delete the file AUTOEXEC.BAK, for example, type this:

```
DEL AUTOEXEC.BAK
```

Although nothing will appear on the screen to confirm it, the file is now gone. To confirm that the AUTOEXEC.BAK file is no longer listed, use the DIR command.

As with the DIR command, you can use wildcards with the DEL and ERASE commands to delete multiple files. For example, to delete all files with the extension .COM in a directory, you would type this:

```
DEL *.COM
```

To delete all files with the filename CONFIG in a directory, type **DEL CONFIG.***. To delete all the files in a directory, you can use the popular *.* wildcard (often pronounced "star-dot-star"), like this:

```
DEL *.*
```

This is one of the few command line commands that will elicit a response. Upon receiving the DEL *.* command, Windows will respond with "Are you sure? (Y/N)," to which you respond with a *Y* or *N*. Pressing **Y** will erase every file in the directory, so be careful with *.*!

Don't confuse deleting *files* with deleting *directories*. DEL deletes files, but it will not remove directories. Use RD or DELTREE to delete directories.

Copying and Moving Files

The ability to copy and move files in a command line is crucial to all technicians. Due to its finicky nature and many options, the COPY command is also rather painful to learn, especially if you're used to simply dragging icons in Windows. The following tried-and-true, five-step process will make it easier, but the real secret is to get in front of a C:\ prompt and just copy and move files around until you're comfortable. Keep in mind that the only difference between copying and moving is whether the original is left behind (COPY) or not (MOVE). Once you've learned the COPY command, you've learned the MOVE command!

Mike's Five-Step COPY/MOVE Process

I've been teaching folks how to copy and move files for years using this handy process. Keep in mind that hundreds of variations on this process exist. As you become more confident with these commands, try doing a COPY /? or MOVE /? at any handy prompt to see the real power of these commands. But at first, follow this process step-by-step.

1. Point the command prompt to the directory containing the files to be copied or moved.
2. Type **COPY** or **MOVE** and a space.
3. Type the *name(s)* of the file(s) to be copied/moved (with or without wildcards) and a space.
4. Type the *path* of the new location for the files.
5. Press ENTER.

Let's try an example. The directory C:\QUAKE3 contains the file README.TXT. We'll copy this file to the floppy drive (A:).

1. Type **CD\QUAKE3** to point command prompt to the QUAKE3 directory.

   ```
   C:\>CD\QUAKE3
   ```

2. Type **COPY** and a space.

   ```
   C:\QUAKE3>COPY _
   ```

3. Type **README.TXT** and a space.

   ```
   C:\QUAKE3>COPY README.TXT _
   ```

4. Type **A:**.

   ```
   C:\QUAKE3>COPY README.TXT A:\
   ```

5. Press ENTER.

suppose you want to move those files to the C:\QUAKE3 directory. Follow these steps:

1. Type **CD\DOCS** to point the command prompt to the DOCS directory.

   ```
   C:\>CD\DOCS
   ```

2. Type **MOVE** and a space.

   ```
   C:\DOCS>MOVE _
   ```

3. Type ***.DOC** and a space.

   ```
   C:\DOCS>MOVE *.DOC _
   ```

4. Type **C:\ QUAKE3**.

   ```
   C:\DOCS>MOVE *.DOC C:\QUAKE3
   ```

5. Press ENTER.

   ```
   C:\DOCS>MOVE *.DOC C:\QUAKE3
   30 file(s) copied
   ```

The power of the COPY/MOVE command makes it rather dangerous. The COPY/MOVE command not only lets you put a file in a new location, but it also lets you change the name of the file at the same time. Suppose you want to copy a file called AUTOEXEC.BAT from my C:\ folder to my floppy disk, for example, but you want the name of the copy on the floppy disk to be AUTO1.BAT. You can do both things with one COPY command, like this:

```
COPY C:\AUTOEXEC.BAT A:\AUTO1.BAT
```

Not only does the AUTOEXEC.BAT file get copied to my floppy disk, but the copy also gets the new name AUTO1.BAT.

As another example, let's move all of the files with the extension .DOC from the C:\DOCS directory to the C:\BACK directory and simultaneously change the DOC extension to .SAV. Here is the command:

```
MOVE C:\DOCS\*.DOC C:\BACK\*.SAV
```

This says, "Move all files that have the extension .DOC from the directory C:\DOCS into the directory C:\BACK, and while you're at it, change their file extensions to .SAV." This is very handy, but very dangerous!

Let's say for example that I made one tiny typo. Here I typed a semicolon instead of a colon after the second C.

```
MOVE C:\DOCS\*.DOC C;\BACK\*.SAV
```

The command line understands the semicolon to mean "end of command" and therefore ignores both the semicolon and anything you type after it. As far as the command line is concerned, you typed this:

```
MOVE C:\DOCS\*.DOC C
```

This, unfortunately for you, means "take all the files with the extension .DOC in the directory C:\DOCS and copy them back into that same directory, but squish them all together into a single file called C." If you run this command, Windows gives you only one clue that something went wrong:

```
MOVE C:\DOCS\*.DOC C
1 file(s) copied
```

See "1 file(s) copied"? Feeling the chilly hand of fate slide down your spine, you do a DIR of the directory, and you now see a single file called C where there used to be 30 files with the extension .DOC. All of your DOC files are now gone, completely non-recoverable.

XCOPY

The standard COPY and MOVE commands can work only on one directory at a time, making them a poor choice for copying or moving files in multiple directories. To help with these multi-directory jobs, Microsoft added the XCOPY command. (Note that there is no XMOVE, just XCOPY.)

XCOPY works similar to COPY, but it has extra switches that give XCOPY the power to work with multiple directories. Here's how it works. Let's say I have a directory on my C: drive called \DATA. The \DATA directory has three subdirectories: \JAN, \FEB, and \MAR. All of these directories, including the \DATA directory, contain about 50 files. If I wanted to copy all of these files to my D: drive in one command, I would use XCOPY in the following manner:

```
XCOPY C:\DATA D:\DATA /S
```

Because XCOPY works on directories, you don't have to use filenames as you would in COPY, although XCOPY certainly accepts filenames and wildcards. The /S switch, the most commonly used of all the many switches that come with XCOPY, tells XCOPY to copy all subdirectories except for empty ones. The /E switch tells XCOPY to copy empty subdirectories.

When you have a lot of copying to do over many directories, XCOPY is the tool to use.

The power of XCOPY varies depending on the version of Windows you use. The XCOPY that comes with true DOS is fairly weak. Windows 9*x* comes with a second type of XCOPY called XCOPY32 that enables you to copy hidden, read-only, and system files. Windows 2000 no longer has XCOPY32 but has instead incorporated all the power of XCOPY and XCOPY32 into its version of XCOPY.

Their power and utility make the DEL, COPY/MOVE, and XCOPY commands indispensable for a PC technician, but that same power and utility can cause disaster. Only a trained Jedi, with the Force as his ally... well, wrong book, but the principle remains: Beware of the quick and easy keystroke, for it may spell your doom. Think twice and execute the command once. The data you save may be yours!

[illegible]

mands, one command per line. The only thing that differentiates a batch file from any other text file is the .BAT extension. Take a look at Figure 13.17. Note the unique icon given to batch files as compared to a regular text file with the extension .TXT.

Figure 13.17 Text file and batch file icons

You can create and edit batch files using any text editor program—good old Notepad is often the tool of choice. This is the command line chapter, though, so let's dust off the ancient but still important EDIT program—it comes with every version of Windows—and use it to create and edit batch files.

Batch filenames are not case sensitive.

EDIT

Get to a command prompt on any Windows system and use the CD\ command to get to the root directory (use C: to get to the C: drive if you're not on the C: drive by default). From there, type **EDIT** at the command prompt to see the EDIT program's interface (Figure 13.18).

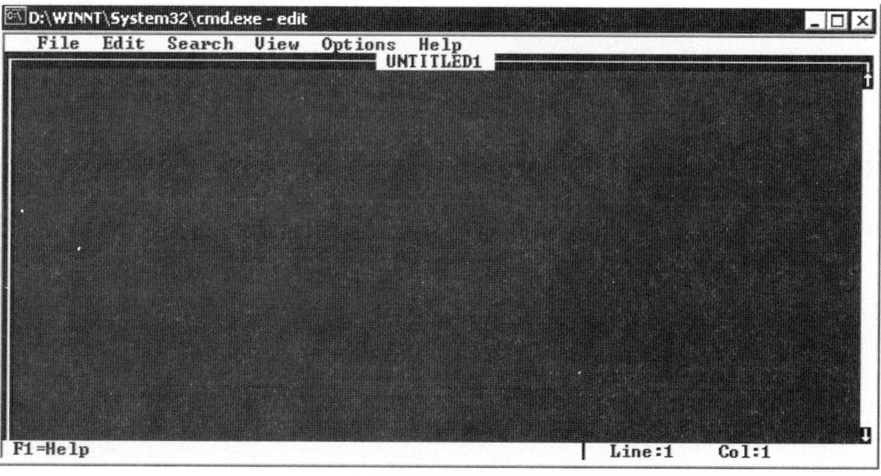

Figure 13.18 EDIT

Now that you've started EDIT, type in the two commands as shown in Figure 13.19. Make sure they look exactly the same as the lines in Figure 13.19.

Great! You have just made your first batch file! All you need to do now is save it with some name—the name doesn't matter, but this example uses FIRST as the filename. It is imperative, however, that you make the extension .BAT. Even

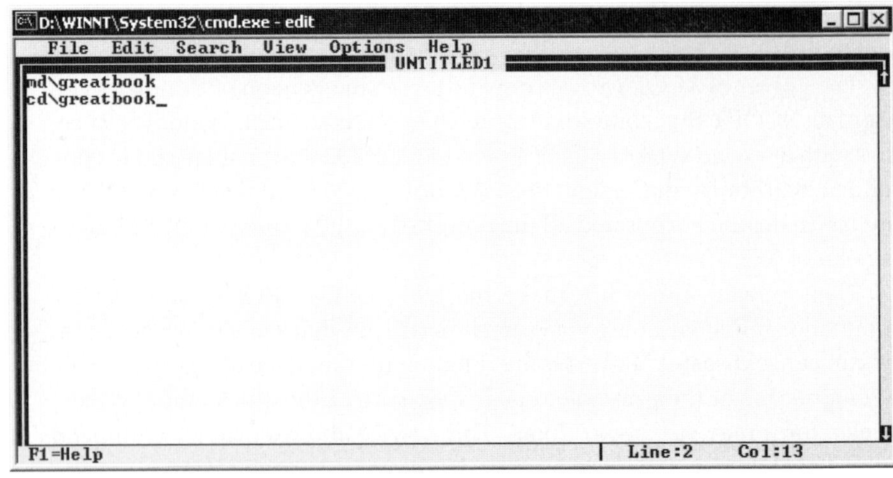

• **Figure 13.19** Edit with two command

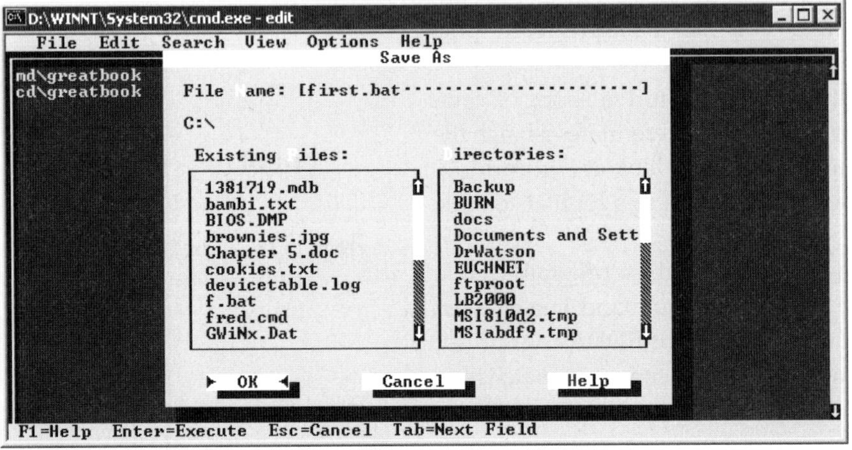

• **Figure 13.20** Saving the batch file

though you could probably figure this out on your own, let's do it together. Hold down the ALT key to activate the menu. Press the F (File) key. Then press S (Save). Type in the name **first.bat** as shown in Figure 13.20. Press ENTER and the file is now saved.

Now that you've saved the file, exit out of the EDIT program by pressing ALT-F and then X (Exit). You're back at the command prompt. Go ahead and run the program by typing **FIRST** and pressing ENTER. Your results should look something like Figure 13.21.

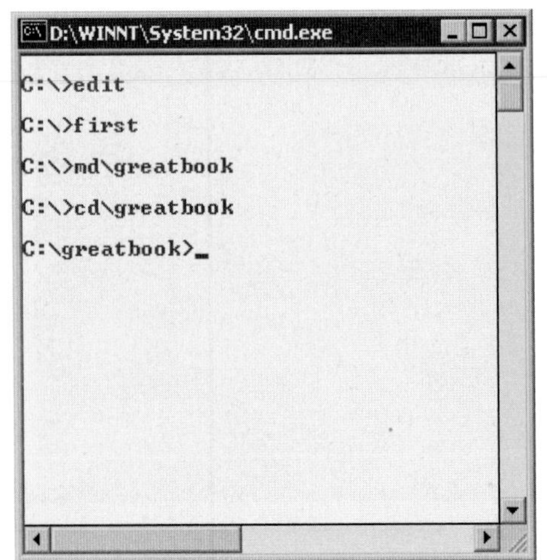

• **Figure 13.21** Running the batch file

Super! The batch file created a folder and moved the prompt to focus on that folder. Don't run the first batch file again or you'll make another folder inside the first one!

Let's now get back to the root directory of C: and edit the FIRST.BAT file again. This time type **EDIT FIRST.BAT** and press ENTER. The batch file will come up, ready to edit. Now change the batch file to look like Figure 13.22. Use the arrow keys to move your cursor and the DELETE key to delete.

The VER command shows the current version of Windows. The echo command tells the batch file to put text on the screen. Run the batch file, and it should look like Figure 13.23.

Gee, that's kind of ugly. Try editing the FIRST.BAT file one more time and add the line

```
@echo off
```

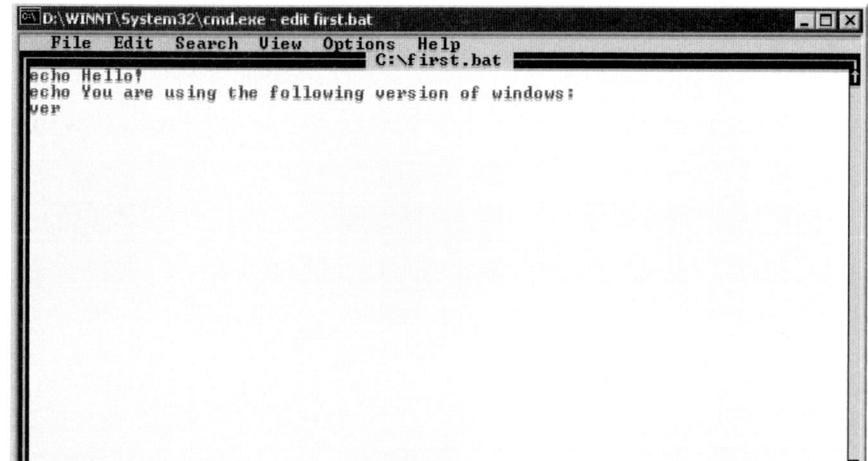

Most of the keyboard shortcuts used in WordPad, Word, and so on, were first used in the EDIT program. If you know keyboard shortcuts for WordPad or Word, many will work in EDIT.

Don't try using the TYPE command on anything other than a text files—the results will be unpredictable.

tells the system not to show the command, just the result.

Sometimes you just want to look at a batch file. The TYPE command displays the contents of a text file on the screen, as shown in Figure 13.24.

One of the more irritating aspects to batch files is that sometimes they don't work unless you try to run them in the folder in which they are stored. This is due to something called the PATH. Every time you open a command prompt, Windows loads a number of settings by default. You can see all of these settings by running the SET command. Figure 13.25 shows the results of running the SET command.

Don't worry about understanding everything the SET command shows you, but do notice a line that starts with `Path=`. This line tells Windows where to look for a program (or batch file) if you run a program that's not in your current folder. For example, let's say I make a folder called C:\batch to store all my batch files. I can run the PATH command from the command prompt to see my current path (Figure 13.26).

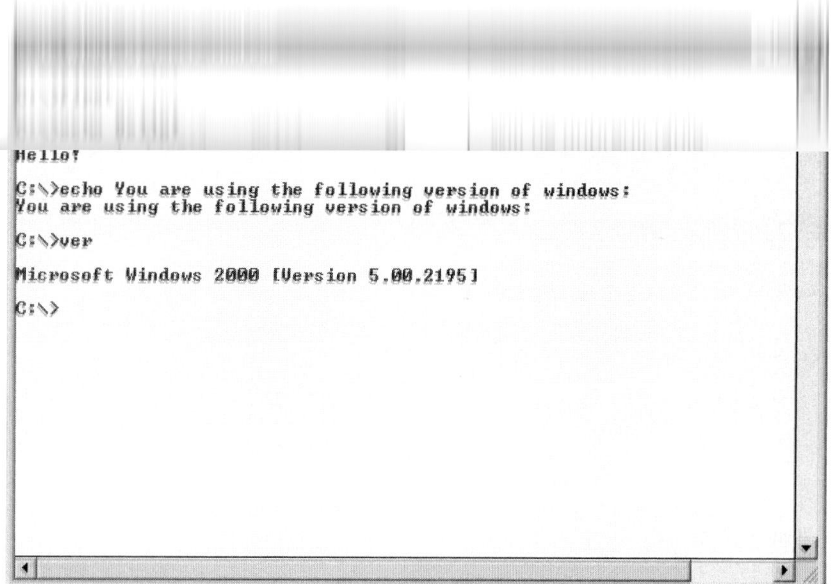

• **Figure 13.23** Running VER to show the current version of Windows

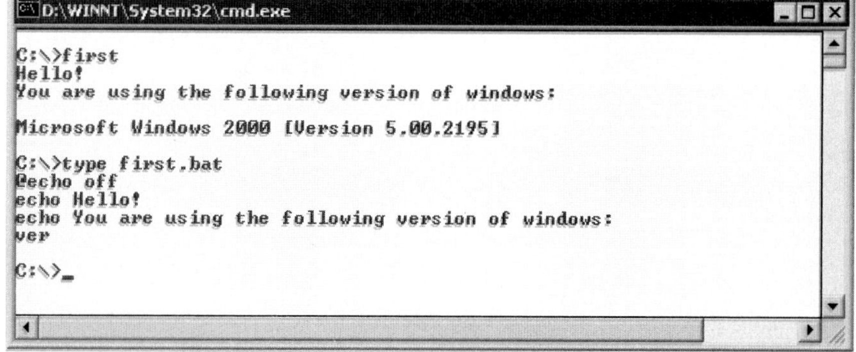

• **Figure 13.24** Using the TYPE command to see file contents

```
D:\WINNT\System32\cmd.exe

C:\>set
ALLUSERSPROFILE=D:\Documents and Settings\All Users.WINNT
APPDATA=D:\Documents and Settings\michaelm\Application Data
CommonProgramFiles=D:\Program Files\Common Files
COMPUTERNAME=MIKEOFFICE
ComSpec=D:\WINNT\system32\cmd.exe
HOMEDRIVE=D:
HOMEPATH=\
LOGONSERVER=\\TOTALHOMEDC2
NUMBER_OF_PROCESSORS=1
OS=Windows_NT
Os2LibPath=D:\WINNT\system32\os2\dll;
Path=D:\WINNT\system32;D:\WINNT;D:\WINNT\System32\Wbem
PATHEXT=.COM;.EXE;.BAT;.CMD;.VBS;.VBE;.JS;.JSE;.WSF;.WSH
PROCESSOR_ARCHITECTURE=x86
PROCESSOR_IDENTIFIER=x86 Family 15 Model 0 Stepping 7, GenuineIntel
PROCESSOR_LEVEL=15
PROCESSOR_REVISION=0007
ProgramFiles=D:\Program Files
PROMPT=$P$G
SystemDrive=D:
SystemRoot=D:\WINNT
TEMP=D:\DOCUME~1\michaelm\LOCALS~1\Temp
TMP=D:\DOCUME~1\michaelm\LOCALS~1\Temp
USERDNSDOMAIN=totalhome
USERDOMAIN=TOTALHOME
USERNAME=michaelm
USERPROFILE=D:\Documents and Settings\michaelm
windir=D:\WINNT

C:\>_
```

• **Figure 13.25** Using the SET command to see settings

• **Figure 13.26** Using the PATH command to see the current path

I can then run the PATH command again, this time adding the C:\batch folder (Figure 13.27). I can now place all my batch files in this folder, and they will always work, no matter where I am in the system.

SETVER

Back in the last days of DOS, Microsoft began to run into problems with certain DOS programs expecting a certain version of DOS or they wouldn't run. They would essentially run their own VER command, and if they saw a version of DOS they didn't like, they would not start. To counter this, Microsoft invented a program called SETVER.

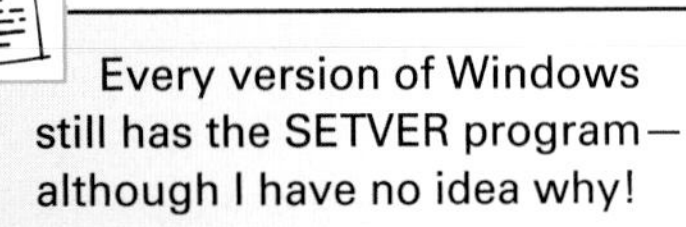

Every version of Windows still has the SETVER program—although I have no idea why!

SETVER was run in the CONFIG.SYS file so that it started every time the computer booted. You just added a line that looked like this:

```
DEVICE=C:\DOS\SERVER.EXE
```

You could also run SETVER at a command prompt to configure it. Let's say you had a program called TIMMY.EXE that required DOS 3.3 to run. From a command prompt, you would type what's shown in Figure 13.28. You could then run

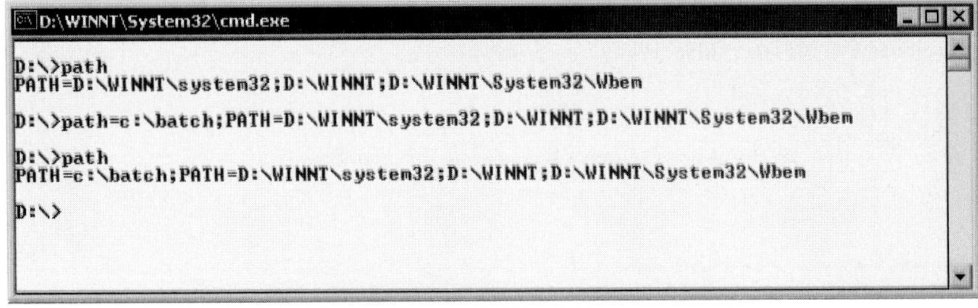

• **Figure 13.27** Using PATH to add a folder

```
D:\WINNT\System32\cmd.exe

C:\>setver timmy.exe 3.3

Version table successfully updated

NOTE: SETVER device not loaded. To activate SETVER version reporting
      you must load the SETVER.EXE device in your CONFIG.SYS.

C:\>setver

WINWORD.EXE      4.10
EXCEL.EXE        4.10
METRO.EXE        3.31
DD.EXE           4.01
DD.BIN           4.01
LL3.EXE          4.01
TIMMY.EXE        3.30

NOTE: SETVER device not loaded. To activate SETVER version reporting
      you must load the SETVER.EXE device in your CONFIG.SYS.

C:\>
```

Beyond A+

Using Function Keys

You might find yourself repeatedly typing the same commands, or at least very similar commands, when working at a prompt. Microsoft has provided a number of ways to access previously typed commands in DOS. Type the **DIR** command at a command prompt. When you get back to a prompt, press F1, and the letter *D* will appear. Press F1 again. Now the letter *I* appears after the *D*. Do you see what is happening? The F1 key brings back the previous command one letter at a time. Pressing F3 brings back the entire command at once.

With Windows 2000/XP, you can use the up and down arrow keys on the keyboard to scroll through previously typed commands.

Compact and Cipher

Windows XP offers two cool commands at the command line interface that you can't get in Windows 9*x*/Me: COMPACT and CIPHER. COMPACT displays or alters the compression of files on NTFS partitions. CIPHER displays or alters the encryption of directories [files] on NTFS partitions. If you type just the command with no added parameters, COMPACT and CIPHER display the compression

Cross Check

Command Line vs. GUI

Now that you've become familiar with the command line interface, you should be able to switch between the Windows GUI and the command line with relative ease.

Check to make sure you can explain how to do the basic tasks covered in this chapter in both Windows GUI and command line.

1 How do you delete a folder in Windows?
2 How do you delete a directory from the command line?
3 Which interface is faster for which tasks?
4 What advantage do wildcards give the command line over the GUI when you're working with files?

state and the encryption state, respectively, of the current directory and any files it contains. You may specify multiple directory names, and you may use wildcards, just like you learned earlier in the chapter. You must add parameters to make the commands change things. For example, you add /C to compress and /U to uncompress directories and/or files with the COMPACT command, and you add /E to encrypt and /D to decrypt directories and/or files with the CIPHER command. When you do these operations, you also mark the directories involved so that any files you add to them in the future will take on their encryption or compression characteristics. In other words, if you encrypt a directory and all its files, any files you add later will also be encrypted. Same thing if you compress a directory. I'll run through a quick example of each.

COMPACT

First let's try the COMPACT command. Figure 13.29 shows the result of entering the COMPACT command with no switches. It displays the compression status of the contents of a directory called "compact" on a system's D: drive. Notice that after the file listing, COMPACT helpfully tells you that 0 files are compressed, and 6 files (all of them) are not compressed, for a total compression ratio of 1.0 to 1.

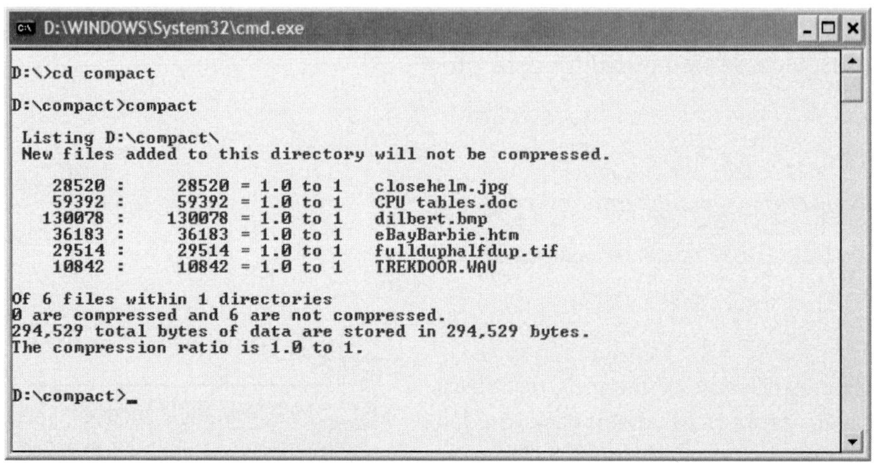

```
D:\WINDOWS\System32\cmd.exe

D:\>cd compact

D:\compact>compact

 Listing D:\compact\
 New files added to this directory will not be compressed.

    28520 :      28520 = 1.0 to 1    closehelm.jpg
    59392 :      59392 = 1.0 to 1    CPU tables.doc
   130078 :     130078 = 1.0 to 1    dilbert.bmp
    36183 :      36183 = 1.0 to 1    eBayBarbie.htm
    29514 :      29514 = 1.0 to 1    fullduphalfdup.tif
    10842 :      10842 = 1.0 to 1    TREKDOOR.WAV

Of 6 files within 1 directories
0 are compressed and 6 are not compressed.
294,529 total bytes of data are stored in 294,529 bytes.
The compression ratio is 1.0 to 1.

D:\compact>_
```

• **Figure 13.29** The COMPACT command with no switches

If you enter the **COMPACT** command with the /C switch, it will compress all the files in the directory, as shown in Figure 13.30. Look closely at the listing. Notice that it includes the original and compressed file sizes and calculates the compression ratio for you. Notice also that the JPG (a compressed graphics format) and WAV files didn't compress at all, while the Word file and the BMP file (an uncompressed graphics format) compressed down to less than a third of their original sizes. Also, can you spot what's different in the text at the bottom of the screen? COMPACT claims to have compressed *seven* files in *two* directories! How can this be? The secret is that when it compresses all the files in a directory, it must also compress the directory file itself, which is "in" the D: directory above it. Thus it correctly reports that it compressed seven files: six in the

```
D:\WINDOWS\System32\cmd.exe

Of 6 files within 1 directories
0 are compressed and 6 are not compressed.
294,529 total bytes of data are stored in 294,529 bytes.
The compression ratio is 1.0 to 1.

D:\compact>compact /c

 Setting the directory D:\compact\ to compress new files [OK]

 Compressing files in D:\compact\

closehelm.jpg           28520 :     28520 = 1.0 to 1 [OK]
CPU tables.doc          59392 :     16384 = 3.6 to 1 [OK]
dilbert.bmp            130078 :     36864 = 3.5 to 1 [OK]
eBayBarbie.htm          36183 :     16384 = 2.2 to 1 [OK]
fullduphalfdup.tif      29514 :     24576 = 1.2 to 1 [OK]
TREKDOOR.WAV            10842 :     10842 = 1.0 to 1 [OK]

7 files within 2 directories were compressed.
294,529 total bytes of data are stored in 133,570 bytes.
The compression ratio is 2.2 to 1.

D:\compact>
```

• **Figure 13.30** Typing COMPACT /C compresses the contents of the directory.

Compact directory, and one in the D: directory. Typing just **COMPACT** again shows you the directory listing again, and now there's a *C* next to each filename, indicating that the file is compressed (Figure 13.31).

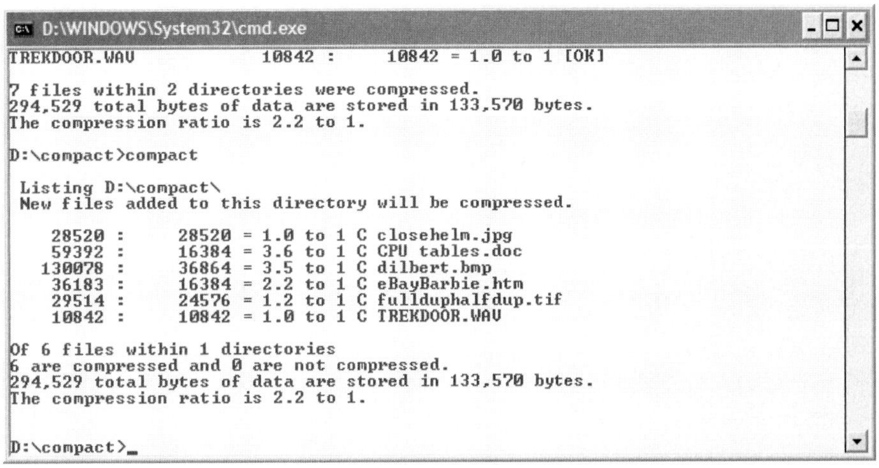

```
D:\WINDOWS\System32\cmd.exe
TREKDOOR.WAV              10842 :      10842 = 1.0 to 1 [OK]

7 files within 2 directories were compressed.
294,529 total bytes of data are stored in 133,570 bytes.
The compression ratio is 2.2 to 1.

D:\compact>compact

 Listing D:\compact\
 New files added to this directory will be compressed.

    28520 :       28520 = 1.0 to 1 C closehelm.jpg
    59392 :       16384 = 3.6 to 1 C CPU tables.doc
   130078 :       36864 = 3.5 to 1 C dilbert.bmp
    36183 :       16384 = 2.2 to 1 C eBayBarbie.htm
    29514 :       24576 = 1.2 to 1 C fullduphalfdup.tif
    10842 :       10842 = 1.0 to 1 C TREKDOOR.WAV

Of 6 files within 1 directories
6 are compressed and 0 are not compressed.
294,529 total bytes of data are stored in 133,570 bytes.
The compression ratio is 2.2 to 1.

D:\compact>_
```

Okay, now suppose you want to uncompress a file, let's say the Dilbert image, dilbert.bmp. To do this, you must specify the decompression operation, using the /U switch and the name of the file you want decompressed, as

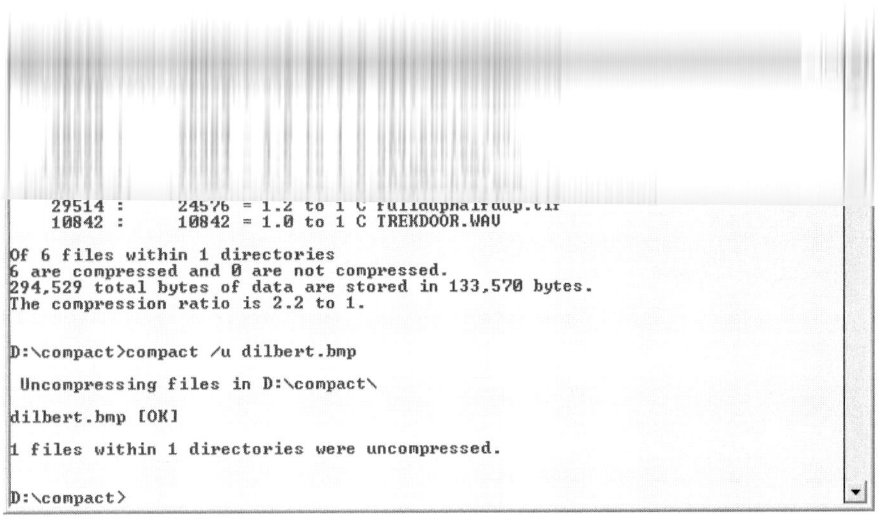

```
    10842 :       10842 = 1.0 to 1 C TREKDOOR.WAV

Of 6 files within 1 directories
6 are compressed and 0 are not compressed.
294,529 total bytes of data are stored in 133,570 bytes.
The compression ratio is 2.2 to 1.

D:\compact>compact /u dilbert.bmp

 Uncompressing files in D:\compact\

dilbert.bmp [OK]

1 files within 1 directories were uncompressed.

D:\compact>
```

Figure 13.32 Typing COMPACT /U DILBERT.BMP decompresses that file only.

CIPHER

The CIPHER command is a bit more complex, but in its most basic implementation, it's pretty straightforward. Figure 13.33 shows two steps in the process. Like the COMPACT command, the CIPHER command simply displays the current state of affairs when entered with no switches. In this case, it displays the encryption state of the files in the D:\Work Files\Armor Pictures directory. Notice the letter *U* to the left of the filenames, which tells you they are unencrypted. The second command you can see on the screen in Figure 13.33 is this:

```
D:\Work Files\Armor Pictures>cipher /E /A
```

This time the CIPHER command carries two switches: /E specifies the encryption operation, and /A says to apply it to the *files* in the directory, not just the directory itself. As you can see, the command line interface is actually pretty chatty in this case. It reports that it's doing the encryption and then tells you what it's done, and it even warns you that you should clean up any stray unencrypted bits that may have been left in the directory.

To confirm the results of the cipher operation, enter the **CIPHER** command again, as shown in Figure 13.34. Note that the *U* to the left of each filename has been replaced with an *E*, indicating an encrypted file. The other indication that this directory has been encrypted is the statement above the file listing:

```
New files added to this directory will be encrypted.
```

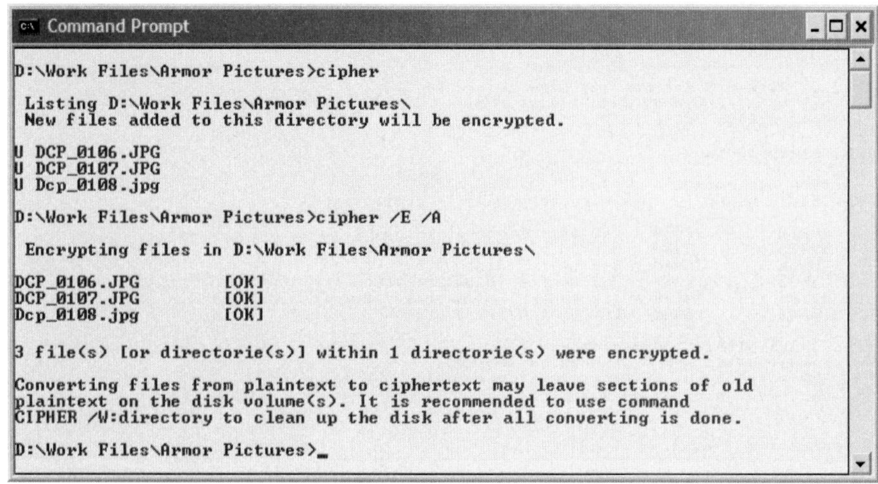

• **Figure 13.33** Typing CIPHER /E /A encrypts the contents of the directory.

Remember that the CIPHER command works on directories first and foremost, and it works on individual files only when you specifically tell it to.

That's great, but suppose you want to decrypt just *one* of the files in the Armor Pictures directory. Can you guess how you need to alter the command? Simply add the filename of the file you want to decrypt after the command and the relevant switches. Figure 13.35 shows the CIPHER command being used to decipher DCP_0106.JPG, a single file.

When using the COMPACT and CIPHER commands, you must type in *spaces* between multiple parameters (for example, switches and filenames).

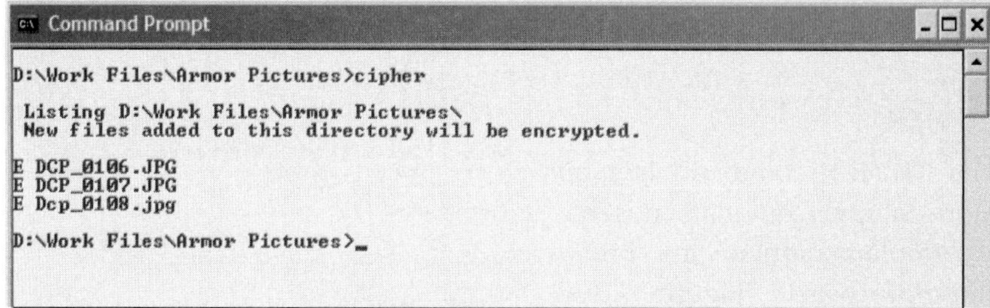

• **Figure 13.34** CIPHER command confirms files were encrypted.

```
Command Prompt
D:\Work Files\Armor Pictures>cipher

 Listing D:\Work Files\Armor Pictures\
 New files added to this directory will be encrypted.

E DCP_0106.JPG
E DCP_0107.JPG
E Dcp_0108.jpg

D:\Work Files\Armor Pictures>cipher /D /A DCP_0106.JPG

 Decrypting files in D:\Work Files\Armor Pictures\

DCP_0106.JPG [OK]

1 file(s) [or directorie(s)] within 1 directorie(s) were decrypted.

D:\Work Files\Armor Pictures>cipher

 Listing D:\Work Files\Armor Pictures\
 New files added to this directory will be encrypted.

U DCP_0106.JPG
E DCP_0107.JPG
E Dcp_0108.jpg

D:\Work Files\Armor Pictures>_
```

• **Figure 13.35** Typing CIPHER /D /A DCP_0106.JPG decrypts just that file.

Chapter 13 Review

Chapter Summary

Explain the Operation of the Command Line Interface

- The text-based DOS user interface, now known as the command line interface, still functions as a basic installation and troubleshooting tool for techs in Windows 9*x*/Me, NT, 2000, and XP. DOS comes with a text editor called EDIT that enables technicians to manipulate text files.
- When you use a command line interface, the

- You can access the command line interface by clicking Start | Run to open the Run dialog box. In Windows NT 4.0/2000/XP, type **CMD** and press the ENTER key. In Windows 9*x*/Me, type **COMMAND** and press **ENTER**. You can also select Start | Programs | Accessories | MS-DOS Prompt in Windows 9*x*/Me systems, or Start | Programs | Accessories | Command Prompt in Windows NT, 2000, and XP. To close the command line interface window, either click the Close box in the upper right-hand corner of the window, or type **EXIT** at the prompt and press ENTER.
- The command prompt is always focused on some directory, and any commands you issue are performed *on the files in the directory* on which the prompt is focused. Make sure you focus the prompt's attention on the drive and directory where you want to work.
- Windows manifests each program and piece of data as an individual *file*. Each file has a name, which is stored with the file on the drive. Names are broken down into two parts: the filename and the extension. In true DOS, the filename could be no longer than eight characters. The extension, which is optional, could be up to three characters long. No spaces or other illegal characters (/ \ [ ] | ÷ + = ; , * ?) could be used in the filename or extension. The filename and extension are separated by a period, or "dot." This naming system is known as the "eight-dot-three" (8.3) naming system. All versions of Windows starting with 9*x* allow filenames of up to 255 characters. Windows 9*x*/Me retains complete backward compatibility with DOS by automatically creating two names for every file, an 8.3 filename and a long filename.

- All files are stored on the hard drive in binary format, but every program has its own unique method of binary organization, called a file format. One program cannot read another program's files unless it has the ability to convert the other program's file format into its file format.
- ASCII (American Standard Code for Information Interchange) was the first universal file format. The ASCII standard defines 256 eight-bit characters, including all the letters of the alphabet (uppercase and lowercase), numbers, punctuation, many foreign characters, box-drawing characters, and a series of special characters for commands such as a carriage return, bell, and end of file. ASCII files, often called text files, store all data in ASCII format. The keyboard sends the letters you press in ASCII code to the PC. Even the monitor outputs in ASCII when you are running a command line.
- As a rule, the OS treats the first 32 ASCII values as commands. Some of them are both commands and characters. How these first 32 values are treated depends on the program that reads them.
- At boot, the OS assigns a drive letter to each hard drive partition and to each floppy or other disk drive. The first floppy drive is called A:, and the second, if installed, is called B:. DOS cannot support more than two floppy drives, because it

supports the original IBM PC, which was designed for only two drives. Hard drives start with the letter C: and can continue to Z: if necessary. CD-ROM drives usually get the next available drive letter after the last hard drive.

- Windows uses a hierarchical directory tree to organize the contents of these drives. All files are put into groups called directories. Windows also uses directories, but it calls them folders. Any file not in a directory *within* the tree, which is to say, any file in the directory at the root of the directory tree, is said to be in the root directory. Directories inside directoriesare called subdirectories. Any directory can have multiple subdirectories. Two or more files or subdirectories with the same name can exist in different directories on a PC, but two files or subdirectories in the same directory cannot have the same name.
- When describing a drive, you use its assigned letter, such as C: for the hard drive. To describe the root directory, add a backslash (\), as in C:\. To describe a particular directory, add the name of the directory after the backslash. To add a subdirectory after the directory, add another backslash and its name onto the end. This naming convention provides for a complete description of the location and name of any file. The exact location of a file is called its path.

Execute Fundamental Commands from the Command Line

- The command line interface will do what you *say*, not what you mean, so it always pays to double-check that those are the same before you press ENTER. One careless keystroke can result in the loss of crucial data, with no warning and no going back.
- The DIR command shows you the contents of the directory on which the prompt is focused. The DIR command lists the filename, extension, file size in bytes, and creation date/time. The DIR/P command pauses after displaying a screen's worth of the directory contents; press the SPACEBAR to display the next screen. The DIR/W command shows you filenames only, arranged in five columns, with directory names in square brackets.
- Windows shows both the DOS 8.3 name and the full Windows name for each file, using a tilde (~) character and a number in the 8.3 name to replace the extra characters.
- Extra text typed after a command to modify its operation, such as the /W or /P after DIR, is called a switch. Almost all switches can be used simultaneously to modify a command. Typing any command followed by a /? brings up a help screen for that particular command.
- The CD (or CHDIR) command enables you to change the focus of DOS to a different directory. Type **CD** followed by the name of the directory on which you want to focus the prompt, and press ENTER. If no such directory exists or if you mistyped the name, a Windows 9*x*/Me system will report: Invalid directory. Windows NT/2000/XP report: The system cannot find the path specified. To return to the root directory, type **CD** and press ENTER. The CD command also allows you to use a space instead of a backslash. The CD command is not used to move between drives; to point the prompt to another drive, type the drive letter and a colon.
- To make a directory, use the MD (or MKDIR) command. Once you press ENTER, the OS will execute the command, but it won't volunteer any information about what it did. You must use the DIR command to see that you have, in fact, created a new directory. Make sure that the prompt points to the directory in which you want to make the new subdirectory before you execute the MD command.
- To remove a directory, first point the prompt at the directory that contains the subdirectory you want to delete, and then execute the RD (or RMDIR) command. If you get no response, you probably did it right, but use the DIR command to be sure. The RD command will not delete a directory in Windows 9*x*/Me if the directory contains files or subdirectories; you must first empty that directory using the DEL (for files) or RD (for subdirectories) command. The DELTREE command will delete the directory as well as all files and subdirectories.

Manipulate Files and Folders from the Command Line

- To run a program from the command line, focus the prompt on the directory where the program is located, then type the name of the program. Typing the .COM or .EXE extension is optional.

- All files have four special values, or attributes, that determine how they will act in special situations: hidden, read-only, system, and archive. These attributes can be set through software. If a file is hidden, it will not be displayed when the DIR command is performed. A read-only file cannot be modified or deleted. The system attribute, which is used only for system files such as IO.SYS and MSDOS.SYS, just provides an easy identifier for these files. The archive attribute is used by backup software to identify files that have been changed since their last backup.
- ATTRIB.EXE is an external program that enables [illegible] sign (+), and then the filename. To delete an attribute, use a minus sign (–). Multiple attributes can be added or removed in one command.
- Wildcards are two special characters, asterisk (*) and question mark (?), that can be used in place of all or part of a filename to make a DOS command act on more than one file at a time. Wildcards work with all command line commands that take filenames. The asterisk (*) wildcard replaces any part of a filename, before and/or after the period. The ? wildcard replaces any single character. Virtually every command that deals with files will take wildcards.
- To delete files, you use the DEL or ERASE command. DEL and ERASE are identical commands and can be used interchangeably. DEL will not erase directories. To delete a single file, type the **DEL** command followed by the name of the file. No confirmation will appear on the screen. To delete all the files in a directory, you can use the *.* (star-dot-star) wildcard. Upon receiving the DEL *.* command, Windows will respond with "Are you sure? (Y/N)," to which you respond with a *Y* or *N*. Pressing Y will erase every file in the directory. It pays to check twice before you delete, because the command line has no function equivalent to the Windows Recycle Bin that allows you to retrieve an accidentally deleted file; once a file has been erased, it can be recovered only by using a special recovery utility.
- The COPY and MOVE commands are used to copy and move files. The only difference between them is whether the original is left behind (COPY) or not [illegible] same time.
- Check for the common typo of substituting a semicolon for a colon, because the semicolon means "end of command" and therefore ignores both the semicolon and anything you type after it.
- XCOPY works similarly to COPY, but has extra switches that give XCOPY the power to work with multiple directories. Because XCOPY works on directories, you don't have to use filenames as you would in COPY, although you can use filenames and wildcards. The /S switch tells XCOPY to copy all subdirectories except for empty ones. The /E switch tells it to copy empty subdirectories. The XCOPY that comes with true DOS is fairly weak. Windows 9*x*/Me comes with a second type of XCOPY called XCOPY32 that enables you to copy Hidden, Read-Only, and System files. The Windows 2000/XP version of XCOPY incorporates the improvements of XCOPY32.

Key Terms

8.3 naming system *(467)*
ASCII (American Standard Code for Information Interchange) *(468)*
Archive attribute *(478)*
ATTRIB.EXE *(478)*
DIR command *(471)*
directory *(465)*
extension *(467)*
file format *(468)*
filename *(467)*
Hidden attribute *(478)*
hierarchical directory tree *(470)*
MS-DOS (Microsoft Disk Operating System) *(464)*
path *(470)*

prompt *(465)*
read-only attribute *(478)*
root directory *(470)*
Run dialog box *(466)*
subdirectories *(470)*
switch *(471)*
system attribute *(478)*
wildcard *(479)*

Key Term Quiz

1. The command line interface tells you it's ready to receive commands by displaying a specific set of characters called a __________.
2. The ________ and the ________ are the two parts of the name of a DOS file.
3. Extra text typed after a command to modify its operation is called a ________.
4. _________ was the first universal file format.
5. The __________ shows you the contents of the directory that currently has DOS's focus.
6. The _____________ is used by backup software to identify files that have been changed since their last backup.
7. The exact location of a file is called its _______.
8. _____________ is an external DOS program that enables you to inspect and change file attributes.
9. The asterisk is a special character called a _________ that can be used in place of part of a filename when executing a DOS command.
10. You can access the command line interface by clicking the Start button and selecting the __________.

Multiple-Choice Quiz

1. Which of the following is *not* an acceptable DOS filename?
   - **A.** JACKIE.DOC
   - **B.** JAMESDEAN.BMP
   - **C.** JOE
   - **D.** JASMINE.EX
2. The ASCII standard defines how many 8-bit characters?
   - **A.** 64
   - **B.** 256
   - **C.** 512
   - **D.** 64,000
3. Which of the following is the correct path for a file named YODA.TXT on the C: drive in a directory called JEDI that's in a directory called REBELS that's in the root directory?
   - **A.** C:\ROOT\JEDI\YODA.TXT
   - **B.** C:\JEDI\REBELS\YODA.TXT
   - **C.** C:\REBELS\JEDI\YODA.TXT
   - **D.** C:\ROOT\REBELS\JEDI\YODA.TXT
4. Which of the following shows a typical command prompt?
   - **A.** C:\\
   - **B.** C:/>
   - **C.** C:\>
   - **D.** C://
5. Which command(s) can Windows use to remove files from a drive? (Select all that apply.)
   - **A.** REMOVE
   - **B.** DEL
   - **C.** RD
   - **D.** ERASE
6. Which of the following is *not* an illegal character in a Windows filename?
   - **A.** ?
   - **B.** /
   - **C.** *
   - **D.** _

7. Which command pauses after displaying a screen's worth of directory contents?

   A. DIR P

   B. PDIR

   C. PD

   D. DIR/P

8. Which of the following commands will delete all the files in a directory?

   A. DEL *.*

   B. DEL ALL

   C. DEL ?.?

10. Which command will delete a directory as well as all its files and subdirectories in Windows Me?

    A. DEL/F/S

    B. DEL/ALL

    C. DELTREE

    D. RD

11. Which attribute keeps a file from being displayed when the DIR command is performed?

    A. Hidden

    B. System

    C. Read-only

    D. Protected

12. What command enables you to make a new directory in a Windows XP Professional system?

    A. MF

    B. MKFOL

    C. MD

    D. MAKEDIR

13. What is the name of the command line text editor that comes with Windows?

    A. TEXT

    B. COM

    C. MSDOS

    D. PROMPT

15. Joey wants to change the name of a file from START.BAT to HAMMER.BAT. Which of the follow commands would accomplish this feat?

    A. REN HAMMER.BAT START.BAT

    B. REN START.BAT HAMMER.BAT

    C. RENAME /S START.BAT HAMMER.BAT

    D. RENAME /S HAMMER.BAT START.BAT

Essay Quiz

1. You've been tasked to teach some newbie techs, whose only computer experience involves Windows, about the beauty and power of the command line. For their first lesson, write a short essay explaining how the command line interface works, including the directory structure, filename limitations, and interaction with the command prompt.

2. You work the Help Desk at a college Computing Center. Some applications that the students must use are run from a command line. Write a memo for the Help Desk personnel explaining how to use the DIR, CD, MD, RD, and DELTREE commands, including any appropriate cautions.

3. Your coworker needs to remove the Hidden attribute from a file called PAYROLL.XLS that is stored in the EMPLOYEE directory on the D: drive. Write an e-mail explaining how to open a command line window, navigate to the file, verify its presence, and remove the Hidden attribute.

4. You've been tasked to teach some newbie techs, whose only computer experience involves Windows, about the beauty and power of the command line. For their second lesson, write a short essay explaining how wildcards work.

5. Write a brief essay explaining in your own words how to use Mike's Five-Step COPY/MOVE procedure. Give an example.

Lab Projects

• Lab Project 13.1

Look at the following list of files. Circle those that *do not* follow the rules for 8.3 filenames:

MYST.EXE	WHY?WHYNOT.TXT	JACK/SAM.DOC
THE.FORCE.MOV	OBI_WAN.COM	YES,PLEASE.EXE
[HALFLIFE].INI	LED ZEP.WAV	NY*GIANTS.BMP
CHAPTER13.DOC	SYSTEM.INI	hansolo.gif
X-FILES.WP1	INDEX.HTML	OLIVER|CAT.JPG

• Lab Project 13.2

For each of the following files, translate the location into a path you can type at a command prompt.

1. A file named BEACH.JPG in the subdirectory PICTURES in the directory EZIBA on the primary floppy drive:

   ____

2. A file named BLACKDOG.WAV in the subdirectory LEDZEP in the subdirectory ROCK in the directory MUSIC on the C: drive:

   ____

3. A file named WEAPON.PCX in the subdirectory BOBAFETT in the subdirectory PLAYERS in the subdirectory BASEQ2 in the directory QUAKE2 on the D: drive:

   ____

4. A file named AUTOEXEC.BAT in the root directory on a standard PC with a single hard drive:

   ____

5. A file named MEYERS.DOC in the subdirectory CONTRACTS in the subdirectory LEGAL in the directory ACCOUNTS on a CD-ROM on a system with one hard drive, one CD-ROM drive, and one floppy drive:

   ____

• Lab Project 13.3

To practice making/removing directories and copying/moving files, do the following:

1. Open a command line window and point to the root directory C:.
2. Use the MKDIR command to create a directory called WHALES. Use the CD command to point to the new directory. Use the MKDIR command again to create subdirectory of WHALES called MOBYDICK. Use the CD command to point to the new subdirectory.
3. Populate the MOBYDICK subdirectory with files by opening Notepad and creating a "dummy" file called AHAB.TXT. Save it in the MOBYDICK subdirectory.

4. Use the MOVE command to move the file AHAB.TXT to the WHALES directory. Use the DIR command to confirm that the move was successful. Use the COPY command to put a copy of AHAB.TXT back into the MOBYDICK subdirectory while leaving a copy in WHALES. Again use DIR to confirm the operation.

5. Use the RD command to delete the MOBYDICK subdirectory. Did it work? Why not? Use the DEL command to solve the problem, and then try the RD command again. Finally, use the RD command to delete the WHALES directory.

Installing and Upgrading Windows

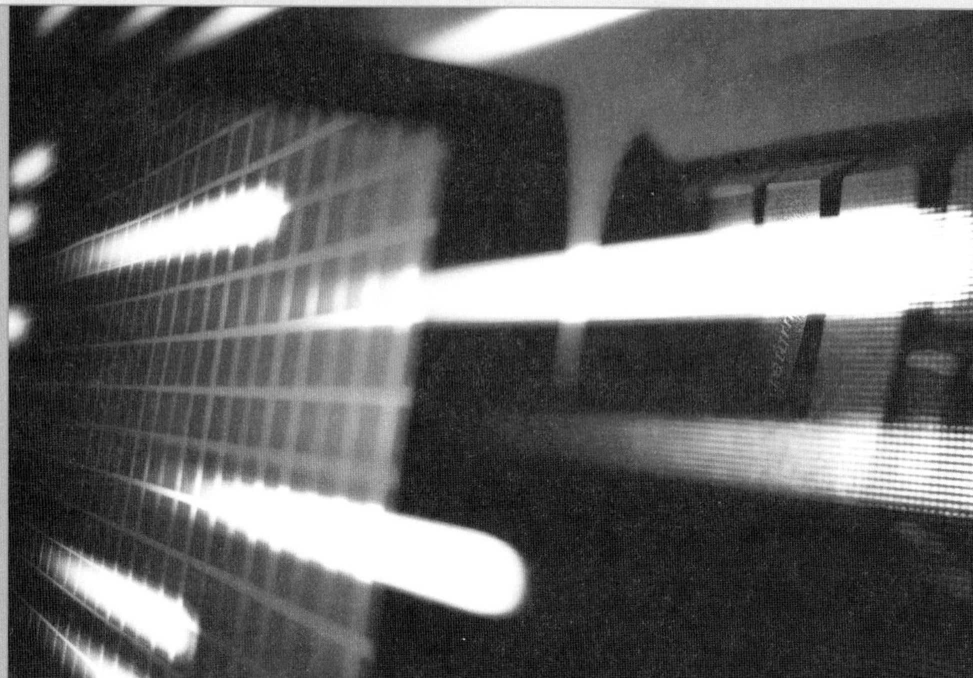

"You make a grown man cry."

—The Rolling Stones, "Start Me Up," from their album, *Forty Licks*

In this chapter, you will learn how to

- **Explain the installation and upgrade process of Windows**
- **Install and upgrade Windows 9x/Me**
- **Install and upgrade Windows 2000 Professional**
- **Install and upgrade Windows XP Professional**
- **Troubleshoot common installation problems**

If only the life of a computer technician was about nothing but hardware it would be a perfect life. Or not! A technician's work involves understanding hardware, software, and people. Yep, you can't hide from those users—at least not all of the time. One of the many tasks you may be called on to do for users is to install or update their computer to a new version of Windows.

Technicians often install new operating systems into computers. The version of Windows you are most likely to install (until a newer one appears) is Windows XP. But there is still a very real chance that you will be called upon to install Windows 9x/Me or Windows 2000. Therefore, I'll tell you about installing all three.

But wait! Before you can install you've got to prepare—so I'll talk about that first, then I'll show you what happens in most all Windows installations and the things you should do immediately after.

After you have all this basic info, I'll tell you a few things about installing each of these three OSs, and finally you'll learn about troubleshooting the most common installation problems.

Windows Installation/ Upgrade Overview

Installing or upgrading an OS is like any good story: it has a beginning, a middle, and an end. In this case the beginning is the several tasks you need to do before you actually do the installation/upgrade. If you do your homework here, the installation process is a breeze, and the post-installation tasks are minimal. In the next section, I'll give you my "short list" of preparation tasks, the generic description of a Windows installation, and the tasks you need to do after the installation.

Preparing for Installation or Upgrade

[illegible]

Don't get discouraged at all the preparation tasks. They usually go pretty fast, and skipping them can cause you gobs of grief later when you're in the middle of installing and things blow up. Well, maybe there isn't a real explosion, but the computer might lock up and refuse to boot into anything usable. With that in mind, let's look at the nine tasks you need to complete *before* you insert that CD-ROM. Here's the list; discussion follows:

1. Identify hardware requirements.
2. Verify hardware and software compatibility.
3. Decide whether to perform a clean installation or an upgrade.
4. Determine how to back up and restore existing data, if necessary.
5. Select an installation method.
6. Determine how to partition the hard disk and what file system to use.
7. Determine your computer's network role.
8. Decide on your computer's language and locale settings.
9. Plan for post-installation tasks.

Identify Hardware Requirements

Hardware requirements help you to decide whether a computer system is a reasonable host for a particular operating system. Requirements include the CPU model, the amount of RAM memory, the amount of free hard disk space, and the video adapter, display, and other storage devices that may be required to install and run the operating system. They are stated as minimums or, more recently, as recommended minimums. Although you could install an operating system on a computer with the old minimums that Microsoft published, they were not realistic if you wanted to actually accomplish work. With the last few versions of Windows, Microsoft has published recommended minimums that are much more realistic. You will find the published minimums on the packaging and at Microsoft's web site (www.microsoft.com). Later in this chapter I'll also tell you what I recommend as minimums for Windows 9*x*/Me, Windows 2000, and Windows XP.

Verify Hardware and Software Compatibility

Assuming your system meets the requirements, you next need to find out how well Windows supports the brand and model of hardware and the application software you intend to use under Windows. You have two basic sources for this information: Microsoft and the manufacturer of the device or software. How do you actually access this information? Use the Web!

If you're installing Windows XP the Setup Wizard automatically checks your hardware and software and reports any potential conflicts. But please don't wait until you are all ready to install to check this out. With any flavor of Windows, and even with Windows XP, *do your homework!*

For compatible hardware, go to Microsoft Windows Hardware and Drivers Central for the definitive **Hardware Compatibility List** (HCL) (with disclaimer) at www.microsoft.com/whdc/hcl/search.mspx. See Figure 14.1.

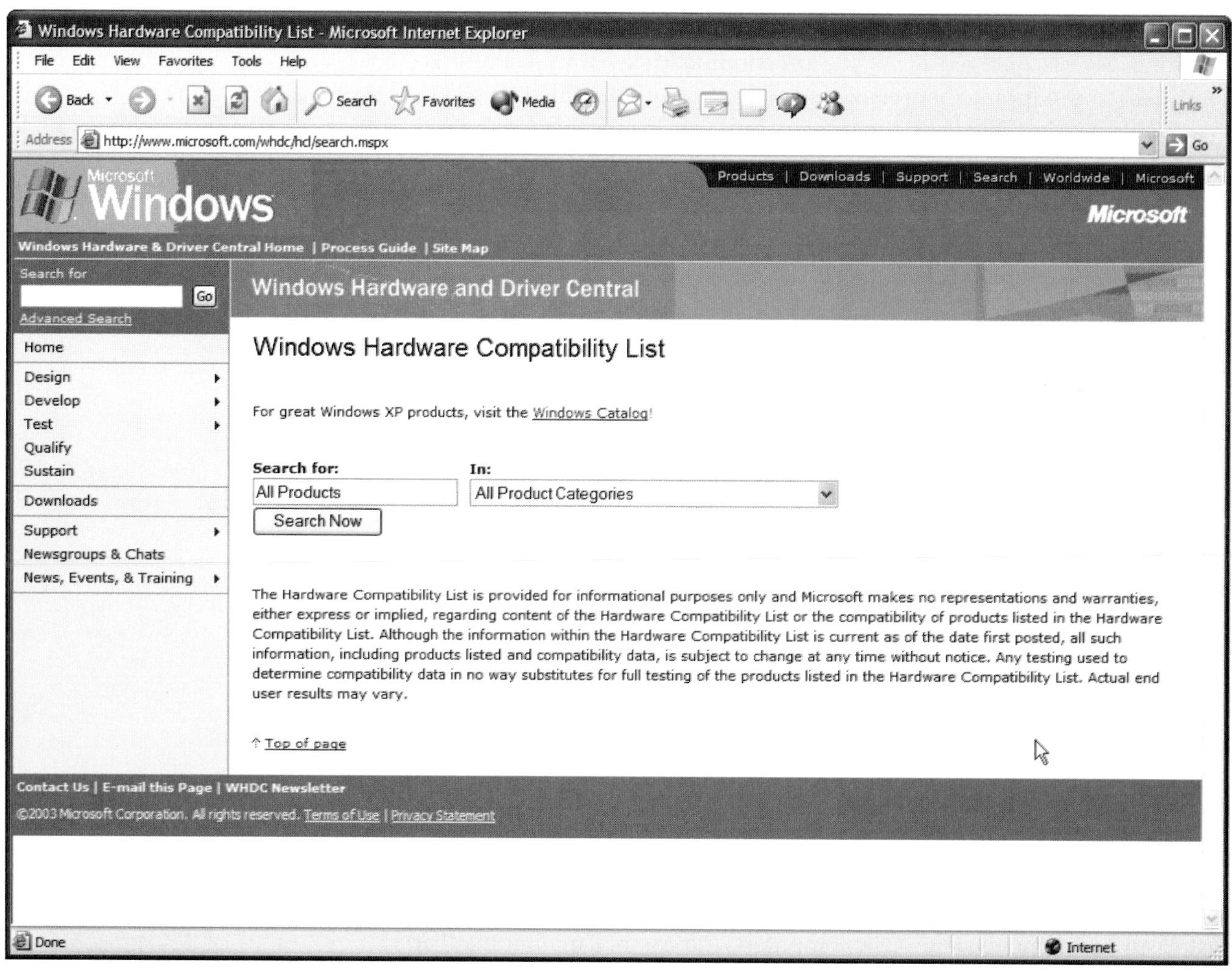

• **Figure 14.1** Windows Hardware and Driver Central

Don't panic if you don't see your device; many supported devices do not appear on that list. Check the floppies or CD-ROMs that come with your hardware for proper drivers. Better yet, check the manufacturer's web site for compatible drivers. Even when the HCL lists a piece of hardware, I still make a point to check the manufacturer's web site for newer drivers.

When preparing to upgrade, check with the manufacturers of the applications already installed in the previous OS. If there are software compatibility problems with the versions you have, the manufacturer should provide upgrade packs that can be installed during the Windows XP Setup process.

When you are upgrading, research to be sure that existing software is compatible with your new OS. For software that is not compatible, upgrade packs are available from the appropriate software manufacturer.

[illegible] with an empty hard drive and you do an upgrade of a preexisting installation. It isn't necessarily so! I'll tell you why as we look at this issue more closely.

Clean Installation A clean installation begins with a completely empty hard disk. I even prefer starting from the very beginning by repartitioning and formatting the hard drive. The advantage to doing a clean installation is that you don't carry problems from the old OS over to the new one, but the disadvantage is that all applications have to be installed and the desktop and each application reconfigured to the user's preferences.

A variation of a clean installation (but not very clean) is a **multi-boot installation** . That is, you can install the new OS into a different subdirectory or on to a different disk volume on a computer, leaving the old OS intact and usable. When this works, you can use the boot menu to select which OS to start up. However, I don't recommend multi-boot configurations unless there is a very, very compelling reason. For instance, a multi-boot configuration can work well on the computer of a help desk person who supports users working in several operating systems. Another scenario is a programmer who is writing and testing programs that must run in different operating systems. Otherwise, multi-boot configurations are a very, very bad idea for normal mortals!

Tech Tip

Multi-boot Configuration

When configuring a computer for multi-booting there are two basic rules: 1) The system partition must be formatted in a file system that is common to all installed OSs, and 2) You must install in order of vintage, that is from oldest to newest. You can't install Windows 98, for example, after you install Windows XP. The only exception to this is Windows NT—you can install NT after any version of Windows 9x/Me.

Upgrade In an upgrade, the new OS installs into the same folders as the old OS, or in tech speak, the new installs *on top of* the old. The new OS replaces the old OS but retains all saved data and inherits all the previous settings (such as font styles, desktop colors, and background, and so on), hardware, and applications. You don't have to reinstall your favorite programs!

Before starting an OS upgrade, make sure you have shut down all other open applications, including anti-virus software!

To begin the upgrade of Windows, you must run the appropriate program from the CD. The upgrade program for Windows 9*x*/Me is the same as the installation program—it is the program named Setup.exe.

WINNT32.EXE is the program to start an upgrade to Windows NT, 2000, or XP, while in the Windows GUI. From the command line interface, you use WINNT.EXE. Either of these programs can also be used to start a scripted installation, which is usually initiated by accessing a shared network directory (See "Select an Installation Method" below).

You can also start an upgrade to Windows 2000 or XP by booting from the CD, as you would do with a clean installation. Then, to do an upgrade, you indicate that Windows 2000 or XP should install into a directory that already contains an installation of Windows. You will be asked whether it is an upgrade or a new installation. If you select new installation it will remove the existing OS before installing.

Determine How to Backup and Restore Existing Data, if Necessary

You cannot upgrade from Windows 9*x*/Me to Windows NT. You can only do a clean install or dual boot.

Whether you are installing or upgrading, you may need to back up existing user data before installing or upgrading because either way things can go very wrong, and the data on the hard drive might be damaged. If this is on a user's existing computer, or on a computer that will replace an existing computer, you'll need to find out where the user is currently saving data files. If they are being saved onto the local hard drive, it must be backed up before the installation or replacement takes place in order to preserve the data. However, if all data has been saved to a network location, then you are in luck because the data doesn't reside on the local disk and is safe from damage during installation.

If the user saves data locally, and is not connected to a network, your options for backup may be limited. If the computer is connected to a network, save the data, at least temporarily, to a network location until after the upgrade or installation has taken place. If this is not an option, but the computer has a CD-R (as many do today), copy the data to one or more CDs. For older systems without CD burners, Zip disks are a good option for backing up larger data sets. Wherever you save the data, after the installation, copy or restore the data back to the local hard disk.

Select an Installation Method

Now you must select an installation method. An installation method involves how you start the installation program, the location of the source files for the installation, and whether the installation is manual (attended) or automated (unattended). I want to try to keep this simple, because, like many topics, this could really get out of hand fast.

Tech Tip

Windows NT Boot Disks

Windows NT 4.0 comes with a set of three setup floppy disks. If these are not available, you can generate them by opening a command prompt and entering ***d:\i386\winnt/ox****, where d: is the CD-ROM drive.*

Bootable CD or Boot Floppy If you are upgrading, you can run the setup program (Setup.exe or Winnt32.exe) from within the old OS.

In the case of a clean installation, there is no existing OS from which to run the Setup program. Therefore, you must be able to boot into the setup program. Windows 98 provides a special floppy boot disk for this purpose. It boots into DOS, and then runs the setup program from the CD-ROM via a line in AUTOEXEC.BAT.

Windows 2000 and Windows XP do not come with bootable floppy disks. You are expected to boot to the CD-ROM. In the unlikely event that a computer can't be made to boot from CD, however, you can create a set of setup boot diskettes. The Windows 2000 utility to create these diskettes is makebt32.exe, and you can find it in the BOOTDISK directory on the CD-ROM.

If you need to make bootable diskettes for Windows XP, you must go online, to a really wonderful part of Microsoft's web site called the **Knowledge Base**, which is a huge collection of articles on every conceivable aspect of every piece of software Microsoft has ever made, including all types of installation, troubleshooting, and compatibility problems. Its URL is support .microsoft.com (note there's no 'www'). To see the Knowledge Base article on creating the disks, search on its article number: 310994. This article provides links for several versions of the program needed to create the diskettes.

Other Installation Methods In medium to large organizations more

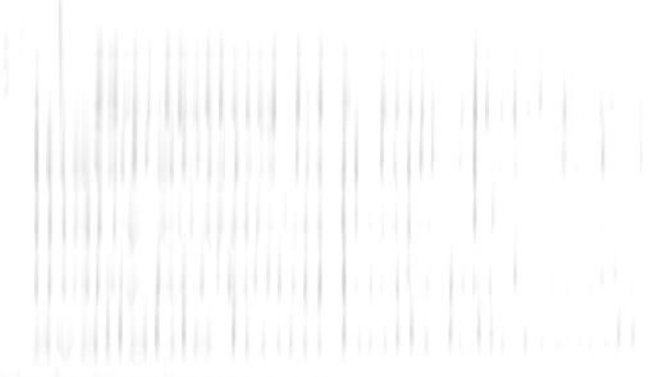

and third-party sources.

at the end of the installation—all without user intervention once the installation has been started.

Another type of installation that is very popular for re-creating standard configurations is an **image installation**. An image is a complete copy of a hard disk volume on which an operating system and, usually, all required application software has been preinstalled. Images can be on CD, in which case the tech runs special software on the computer that copies the image onto the local hard drive. Images can also be stored on special network servers, in which case the tech connects to the image server using special software and copies the image from the server to the local hard drive. A leader in this technology has been Norton's Ghost, which is available from Symantec. Other similar programs are PowerQuest's Drive Image 2002 and Acronis' True Image.

Beginning with Windows 2000 Server, Microsoft added **Remote Installation Services** (RIS), which can be used to initiate either a scripted installation or an installation of an image.

Determine How to Partition the Hard Disk and What File System to Use

On a clean installation, you need to decide ahead of time how to partition the disk space on your hard disk drive, including the number and size of partitions and the file system you will use. Actually, in the decision process, the file system comes first, and then the space issue follows, as you will see.

Cross Check

Supported File Systems

File systems used by the various versions of Windows should be old hat to you by now. Refer back to Chapter 11 and cross check your memory. What file systems does Windows NT support? What about Me? What advantages does Windows XP have over Windows NT as far as file system support goes?

If you are not planning a multi-boot installation, use the most advanced file system your version of Windows supports. If you are planning a multi-boot configuration, then the lowest common denominator rule applies, at least for the system volume, and for any volumes you want usable by the oldest OS. Once you know which file system you are using, deciding the size and number of partitions will follow, because if you decide to use FAT16 you will have the size limitations of FAT16 to deal with.

Determine Your Computer's Network Role

This question comes up in one form or another during Windows installation. A Windows computer can have one of several roles relative to a network (in Microsoft terms). One role, called standalone, is actually a non-network role and it simply means that the computer does not participate on a network. Any version of Windows can be installed on a standalone computer. This is the only role that a Windows XP home computer can play on a network. Every other modern version of Windows can be a member of either a workgroup or domain. You will learn more about the workgroup and domain member roles in Chapter 23.

Decide on Your Computer's Language and Locale Settings

These settings are especially important for Windows 2000 and Windows XP because these versions have greatly increased support for various spoken languages and locale conventions. The locale settings include properly displaying date and time information, and using the proper math separators and currency symbols for various locales.

Plan for Post-installation Tasks

After installing Windows you will need to install the latest service pack or update. You may also need to install updated drivers and reconfigure any settings, such as network settings, that were found not to work. You will also need to install any applications (word processing, spreadsheet, database, etc.) required for the work the user of the computer needs to do. Finally, don't forget to restore any data backed up before installation/upgrade.

• **Figure 14.2** Product key written on the CD-ROM disc

Performing the Installation/Upgrade

When doing a Windows installation (also called setup) you'll notice that the screen progresses from simple textual information on a plain background to full graphical screens. During **text mode** the computer is inspecting the hardware, and it will then display the **End User License Agreement** (EULA), which must be accepted for setup to continue. It is during the text display portion of an installation that you can partition your hard disk. Also during this time the computer copies files to the local hard disk, including a base set of files for running the graphical portion.

When finished with this task the computer reboots, which starts the graphical portion of the installation. You are prompted to enter the product key, which is invariably located on the CD-ROM container. Most techs learn the hard way that these covers tend to disappear when you need them most, and they write the product code directly on the CD-ROM disc itself. (Just don't use a ball-point pen; it'll scratch the surface of the disc.) See Figure 14.2.

Most of the installation process takes place in the graphical portion. This is where you select configuration options and optional Windows components.

No matter your version of Windows, the installation process always gets to the point where Windows begins to install itself on the system. I call this "The Big Copy" and use this time to catch up on my reading, eat a sandwich, or count ceiling tiles.

Windows comes in both Upgrade and Full versions. Make sure you use the correct CD-ROM! Some systems, particularly laptops, require a special OEM version made just for that system. Don't bother trying to use an upgrade version to install on a blank drive unless you also possess a CD with a full earlier version of Windows.

Post-Installation Tasks

You might think that's enough work for one day, but there are a few more things on your task list. They include updating the OS with patches and service packs, upgrading drivers, restoring user data files, and identifying installation problems (if they occur).

[illegible] about common installation problems.

Patches, Service Packs, and Updates

Someone once described an airliner as consisting of millions of parts flying in close formation. I think that's also a good description for an operating system. And we can even carry that analogy farther by thinking about all the maintenance required to keep an airliner safely flying. Like an airliner, the parts (programming code) of your OS were created by different people—and some parts may even have been contracted out. Although each component is tested as much as possible, and the assembled OS is also tested, it's not possible to test for every possible combination of events. Sometimes too a piece is simply found to be defective. The fix for such a problem is a corrective program called a **patch**. In the past, Microsoft would provide a patch for individual problems. They would also accumulate patches until they reached some sort of "critical mass" and then bundle them together as a **service pack**. They still do this. But they also make it easier for us to find and install the appropriate patches and service packs which, when combined together are called updates. They make these updates available at their web site or on CD-ROM. Many organizations make the updates available for distribution from network servers. Immediately after installing Windows, install the latest updates on the computer. I tell you more about how this is done in Chapters 15 and 16.

Upgrading Drivers

Even if you did all your pre-installation tasks, you may decide to go with the default drivers that come with Windows, and then upgrade them to the latest drivers after the fact. In fact, this is a good strategy, because installation is a complicated task, and you can simplify it by installing old but adequate drivers. Maybe those newest drivers are just a week old. Waiting until after install will give you a usable driver to go back to if the new driver turns out to be a lemon. In Chapters 15 and 16 you'll learn more about working with drivers, including a little driver magic called driver rollback.

Restoring User Data Files (If Applicable)

Remember when you backed up the user data files before installation? You don't? Well, check again, because now is the time to restore that data. Your method of restoring will depend on how you backed up the files in the first place. If you used a third-party backup program, you will need to install it before you can restore those files, but if you used Windows Backup, you are in luck, because it is installed by default. If you did something simpler, like copying to a CD-R or network location, all you have to do is copy the files back to the local hard disk. Good luck!

■ Installing and Upgrading Windows 9x/Me

Installing or upgrading Windows 9*x*/Me is usually a surprisingly painless, roughly hour-long process. The combination of PnP with an amazingly intelligent installation program makes most installations a matter of typing in commands and trying to stay awake as files are copied and the system goes through a number of reboots. The A+ exam is very interested in your ability to install Windows 9*x*/Me on a blank (unpartitioned) drive and to upgrade a Windows 95 to a Windows 98 system. This section covers both of these situations and assumes a standalone system without networking. We cover the networking installation steps and issues in Chapter 23.

Preparing to Upgrade/Install

Most Windows upgrades and installations fail for the simple reason that the tech fails to perform a few basic checks before installing/upgrading Windows 9*x*. In the first section of this chapter I defined in some depth the nine key steps for a successful upgrade/installation. Follow these few steps—they work! I went into each step in detail so we'll just focus here on specific things you need to know for successfully installing Windows 9*x*/Me.

Minimum Requirements

Microsoft defines some fairly low hardware requirements for Windows 9*x* and Windows Me. To make things more confusing, different types of Microsoft documentation give different values. The minimums listed in the left column of the table are those I found to be more or less official, but I find these requirements laughably low. Even Microsoft admits this, but it is possible to run (maybe a better term would be "walk") Windows 9*x*/Me with this minimum hardware configuration. In the right column I list the minimums that I feel are more appropriate when you plan to get real work done with a bunch of office applications:

Component	Minimum for a Windows 9x/Me Computer	Recommended for a Windows 9x/Me Computer
CPU	Pentium	Intel Pentium II CPU
Memory	32 MB of RAM	64 to 128 (128 to 256 for Windows Me) MB of RAM
Hard disk	455 to 635 MB	4 GB of available hard disk space
Display	Video capable of 640 x 480 @ 16 colors	SVGA or higher-resolution video adapter
Other	A mouse, CD-ROM, and sound card	A mouse, CD-ROM, and sound card

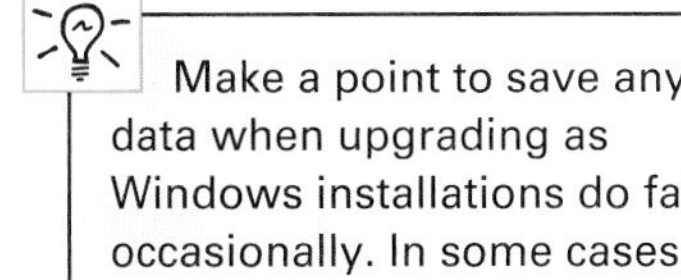

Make a point to save any data when upgrading as Windows installations do fail occasionally. In some cases, a failed installation destroys everything on the drive!

Setup Disk

Even when I have one of those setup disks, I'm more comfortable doing it myself from a regular Windows startup disk. I like the flexibility of deciding how the drive will be partitioned. If you're not a control freak like me, those setup disks work just fine. If you decide to use your own disk, make sure you have a startup disk that can access the CD-ROM!

The other option is to boot directly from the CD-ROM. This assumes that your PC enables you to boot to a CD-ROM (check your CMOS) and that the Windows installation CD-ROM is bootable. Windows 98 and Windows Me installation CD-ROMs are bootable, but Windows 95 installation CD-ROMs are not, requiring you to use some form of bootable floppy disk.

FAT16 or FAT32?

You need to decide ahead of time what type of partition you will want to use. Although you should almost always pick FAT32 for both clean installs and upgrades, three situations exist that might make you want to keep at least one FAT16 partition. First, consider whether you might want to boot to the previous version of MS-DOS to support a DOS program that will not run in Windows, even in a DOS box. Second, you might have a version of Windows 95 that simply doesn't support FAT32. Third, you

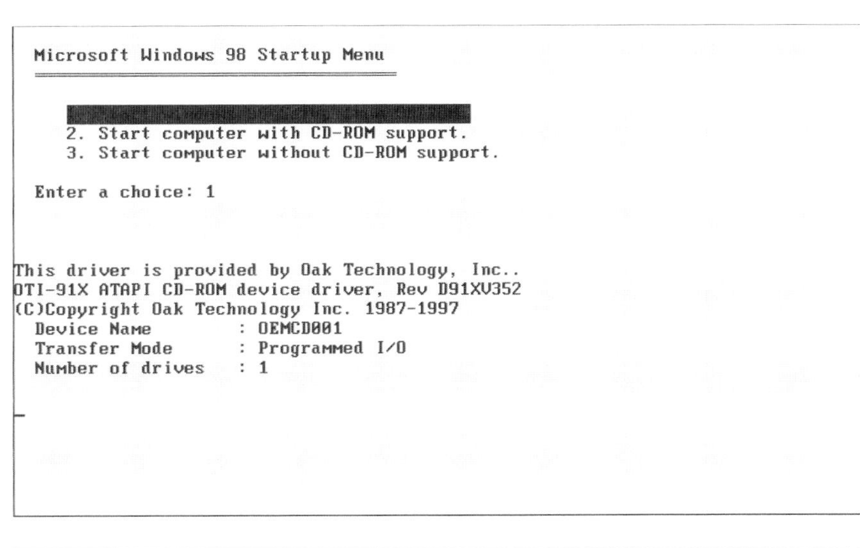

• **Figure 14.3** The Windows 98 setup boot disk Startup menu

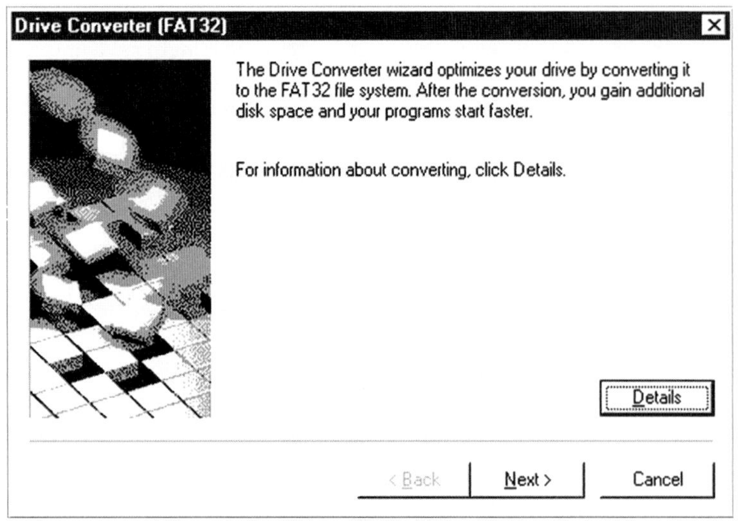

• **Figure 14.4** Drive conversion tools

might want to set up some wild multi-boot functions. Except in those rare cases, you should choose to use FAT32.

Many techs are aware of CVT.EXE (used at a command prompt) or the CVT1.EXE (Windows-based—select Programs | Accessories | System Tools | Drive Converter) utility that comes with Windows 98. These tools enable you to convert a FAT16 drive to FAT32 without losing data (Figure 14.4).

With such handy conversion tools, why bother worrying about using FAT16 or FAT32? Don't forget the 2 GB partition size limitation of FAT16. A brand-new 60 GB drive will need a lot of drive letters. Also, the convert tools have been known to fail disastrously, albeit rarely. Better to play it safe and decide ahead of time!

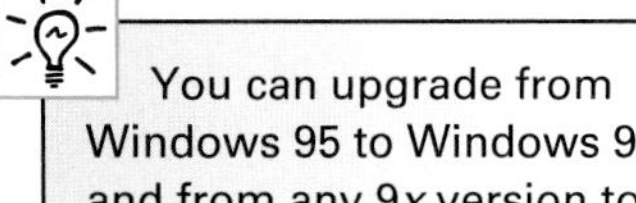

You can upgrade from Windows 95 to Windows 98 and from any 9*x* version to Windows Me .

The Windows 98/Me Installation/UpgradeProcess

Your clean installation of Windows will begin with the text mode (described earlier) and after at least one reboot, continue into graphics mode. Since I've already given you the skinny on the general steps, I'll limit the following to what is unique about the Windows 98/Me installation/upgrade process.

Text Mode

If you start Setup by booting from the Windows 98 setup boot disk, and if the hard disk drive is unformatted and unpartitioned, you will be prompted to partition the drive, as shown in Figure 14.5.

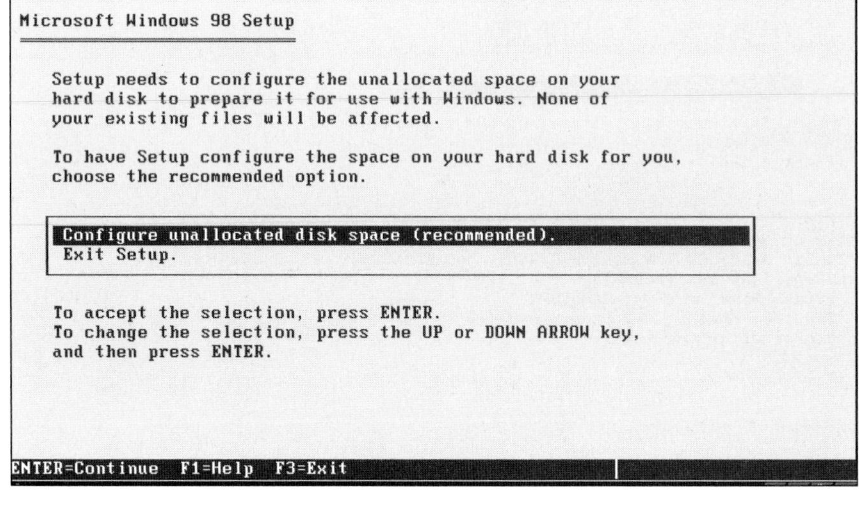

• **Figure 14.5** Windows 98 Setup detects an unpartitioned drive.

Follow the instructions on this screen and work your way through the partitioning and installation process, using the up and down arrow key to move from choice to choice and the ENTER key to make selections.

Once the blank drive is formatted, the Install and the Upgrade processes become virtually identical. If you're upgrading, just boot normally into Windows 95 and toss in the upgrade disk to see the upgrade prompt (Figure 14.6).

A common installation trick is to copy the contents of the \WIN9*x* folder from the CD-ROM to a folder

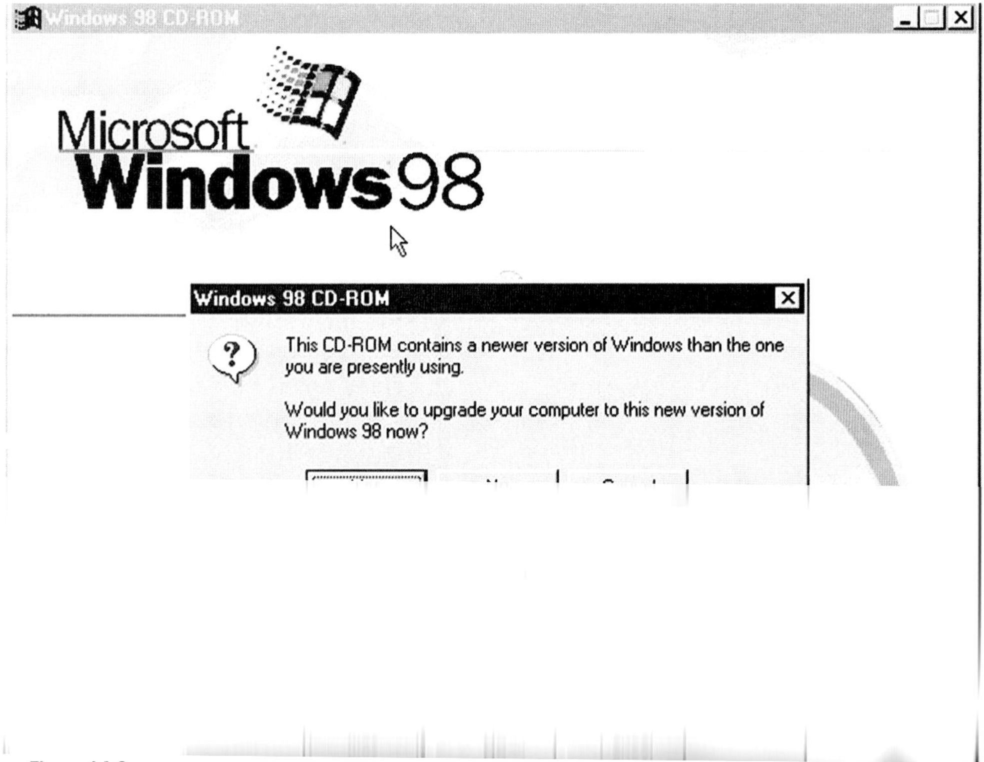

Figure 14.6 Windows 95 to Windows 98 upgrade prompt

on your hard drive. Copying the installation files to your hard drive does two things. First, it makes the installation of Windows faster, as CD-ROMs are very slow. Second, Windows is notorious for needing the original CD-ROM virtually every time you make a change to the system's configuration. Windows will remember where it was installed from and will prompt for you to "Insert the Windows Installation CD-ROM." If you put the files in a folder on a local drive and then install from there, Windows will remember that and will immediately go straight to those files, saving you the hassle of trying to find the Installation CD-ROM.

If you are not using the Windows 98 startup boot disk, your startup disk must support the CD-ROM or you won't get a CD-ROM drive letter!

At the end of the text mode portion, the setup program performs a quick ScanDisk and checks for video and mouse. Then the program loads a few critical files needed for installation, and initiates the first of many reboots.

Graphical Mode

After the initial command prompt installation process, Windows shifts into a graphical mode with the Install Setup Wizard. This wizard begins by installing a second set of critical installation files. It then uses these files first to verify that you have sufficient hard drive space, and then to prompt you for input on various Windows options. Let's look at the typical prompt screens.

Prompt for Component Options Windows Setup prompts you to install with options that look like Figure 14.7. For most users, a Typical installation is the safest bet. Once they become familiar with the many options of the Windows installation, however, most folks prefer to use the Custom option. The Compact option is rarely used; it simply skips too many features that

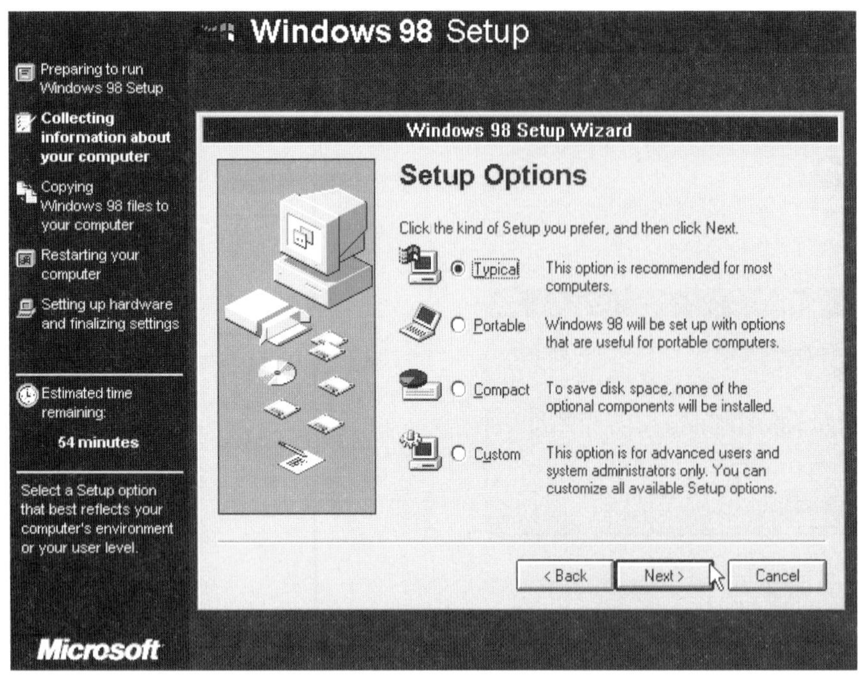

Figure 14.7 Component options: Windows 98 Setup Options: Typical, Portable, Compact, and Custom

most users want. Never worry about this screen; you can always add or remove components after Windows installs by using the Add/Remove Programs applet in the Control Panel.

Prompt for Product Key Windows 95 used to wait until near the end of the installation process to ask for the product key, driving techs crazy when they realized they had spent 20 minutes installing just to discover that their key was missing. Beginning with Windows 98 the Setup program is kind enough to ask for the key early in the process, saving considerable inconvenience when you're juggling 23 different CD-ROMs all in the wrong cases, and trying to punch in the correct product key.

Prompt for Installation Directory Clean installations will always prompt for an installation directory, recommending C:\WINDOWS (Figure 14.8). Use this default unless compelled not to. When upgrading from Windows 95 to Windows 98, you must use the same folder that contains the Windows 95 files, or Windows 98 will simply perform a clean installation, leaving you with a useless copy of Windows 95 on your system, and requiring you to reinstall all your applications.

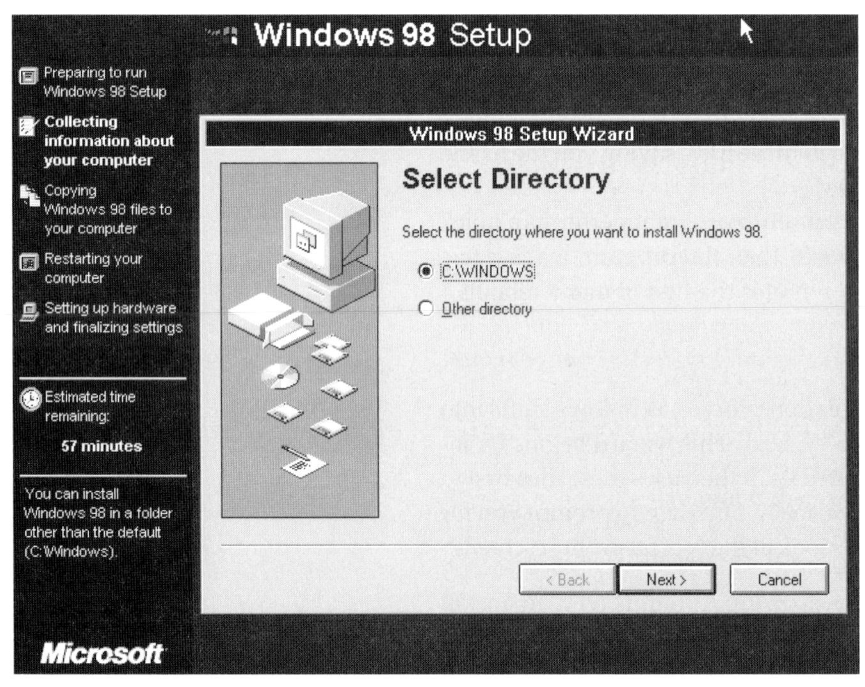

Figure 14.8 Prompt for installation directory

Prompt for Startup Disk The startup disk created here differs in two ways from the Windows 9*x* setup boot disk. First, it does not include the option to run Setup from the Startup menu. The second difference is that this startup disk creates a RAM disk to which it copies a bunch of handy utilities. So, even if you have the setup boot disk, you will still want a startup disk. If you don't already have a startup disk, you can make one now if you would like. All startup disks for the same version of Windows are identical. If you choose not to make a startup disk, simply click Cancel when given the opportunity.

Network Options The Windows 95 Installation Wizard is kind of dumb here; it always prompts for networking information even if it does not detect a network card. As our current installation example assumes a standalone system, I save this discussion for Chapter 23.

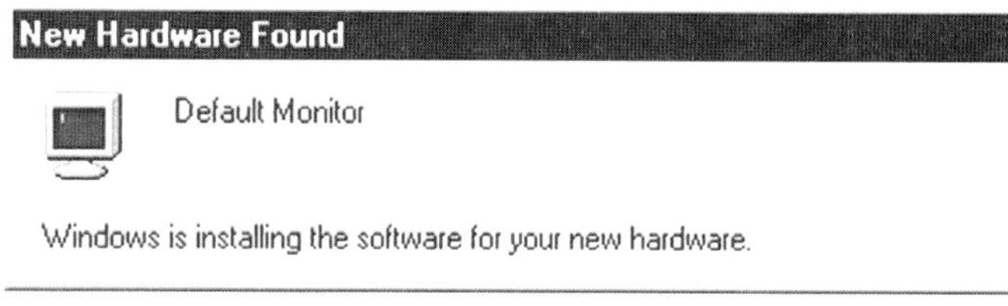

Figure 14.9 Hardware detection and configuration

Save System Files When upgrading from an earlier version of Windows, you are given the opportunity to save the Windows system files. If you save these files, you may uninstall Windows 98 or Windows Me from the Add/

the PnP hardware detection functions, searching for and configuring the detectable hardware on the system (see Figure 14.9).

In a completely PnP environment, this is usually a matter of watching the installation process. As Windows detects devices, it will load the appropriate device drivers if it has them. If not, it will prompt you for a driver disk.

Installing Windows NT 4.0 Workstation

When all is right with the world, installing Windows NT 4.0 Workstation takes only a little more effort than installing Windows 95 and follows almost all the same steps. Although it's unlikely that you'll ever experience the thrill of spending a day installing Windows NT, the OS has a very large installed base and thus a need for techs to service it, so you need to know a few of the quirks.

First off, you'll most likely install Windows NT on an older machine, not anything new, so hardware compatibility shouldn't be too much of a problem. This is good, because one of the major hassles with NT is that it is *not plug and play*! To deal with hardware issues, you should use hardware that is on the NT Hardware Compatibility list (HCL), a list you can find on the installation CD—a file called HCL.HLP in the SUPPORT folder—or at www.microsoft.com.

You can test for specific hardware incompatibility by using the NT Hardware Qualifier (NTHQ) program that comes on the installation CD, in the \SUPPORT\HQTOOL folder. The folder contains a batch file called MAKEDISK.BAT that will create a bootable floppy disk with the NTHQ tool. Create the floppy, boot to it, and then run the program to test the system.

Second, do yourself a huge favor and don't bother trying to install NT on a system that meets anywhere near the listed system requirements. Throw as much RAM into the system as the motherboard will support and go with at least a mid-range Pentium CPU. The following table shows the minimum and my recommended minimums for an NT Workstation.

Component	Minimum for a Windows NT Workstation Computer	Recommended for a Windows NT Workstation Computer
CPU	Intel 80486 25 MHz	Intel Pentium 150 MHz
Memory	12 MB	64 MB
Hard disk	128 MB	2 GB hard disk with 1 GB of free space
Network	None	Modern PCI network card
Display	Video adapter and monitor with VGA resolution	Video adapter and monitor with SVGA resolution, capable of high-color (16-bit) display
CD-ROM		12x (not required if installing over a network)
Floppy disk drive		High density

Third, NT supports FAT (a.k.a., FAT16) and NTFS 4 file systems, as you'll recall from Chapter 11. Unless you have a compelling need, go with NTFS. You'll get all the security and stability the file system offers, plus you can use partitions larger than two gigabytes.

Fourth, Windows NT assumes you will connect to a network, but offers you a chance to set up the PC as a standalone system. The second step in the installation process gives you the option to skip the network setup.

Finally, NT is very old, which means that you desperately need to patch it immediately after installation. Microsoft released six Service Packs for NT and a host of patches between packs. Luckily, you only need to install Service Pack 6a, as it contains all the fixes in the previous ones.

Installing Windows NT is not something that most techs will ever do in the 21st century, but if you run into a situation where you need to have in-depth knowledge of the subject, surf on over to www.totalsem.com for Brian Schwarz' lengthy but tasty Installing Windows NT Tech File.

■ Installing and Upgrading to Windows 2000 Professional

On the face of it, installing Windows 2000 Professional seems essentially the same as installing Windows 9*x*. You insert the CD-ROM, access the setup routine, and go! But that conceptualization does not hold up in practice.

Preinstallation Tasks

Installing Windows 2000 requires you to do many tasks *before* you install, such as making sure that your hardware and applications can handle the new OS.

Hardware Requirements

The minimum specs represent what Microsoft says you need to install the Windows 2000 Professional OS. Windows 2000 Professional will install and run on a system with the minimum specifications, but you need to take these numbers and at least double them if you want to be happy with your system's performance!

Here is a more realistic recommendation for a useful Windows 2000 Professional computer system:

Component	Minimum for a Windows 2000 Professional Computer	Recommended for a Windows 2000 Professional Computer
CPU	Intel Pentium 133 MHz	Intel Pentium II 350 MHz
[illegible]	[illegible]	[illegible]
CD-ROM		12x (not required if installing over a network)
Floppy disk drive		High density

If your test system(s) exceeds the recommended configuration, all the better! You can never have too fast a processor or too much hard disk space.

Hardware Compatibility List (HCL)

In addition to meeting the minimal specifications, your hardware also needs to be supported by the Windows 2000 OS. The **Hardware Compatibility List** (HCL) is the definitive authority as to whether your component is compatible with the OS. Items on the HCL have been extensively tested with Windows 2000 and are guaranteed by Microsoft to work with your installation.

If you contact Microsoft's technical support staff, one of the first things they ask is if all of your systems' components are on the HCL.

The HCL is located in the SUPPORT folder on the Windows 2000 CD-ROM (HCL.TXT), but for the most current list, visit the Windows 2000 page at the Microsoft web site (www.microsoft.com/windows2000/professional). From here, select Compatibility. On the resulting page (see Figure 14.10) you can search for a particular computer, hardware device, or software. But be warned, Windows 2000 Professional is now a generation behind, and it will become more difficult to find this information as Microsoft updates their web site.

Upgrading Issues

Upgrading your computer system from an earlier version of Windows can be a tricky affair, with its own set of pitfalls. It is important to note that you have a somewhat higher risk of running into errors during an upgrade than you would when performing a "clean" installation.

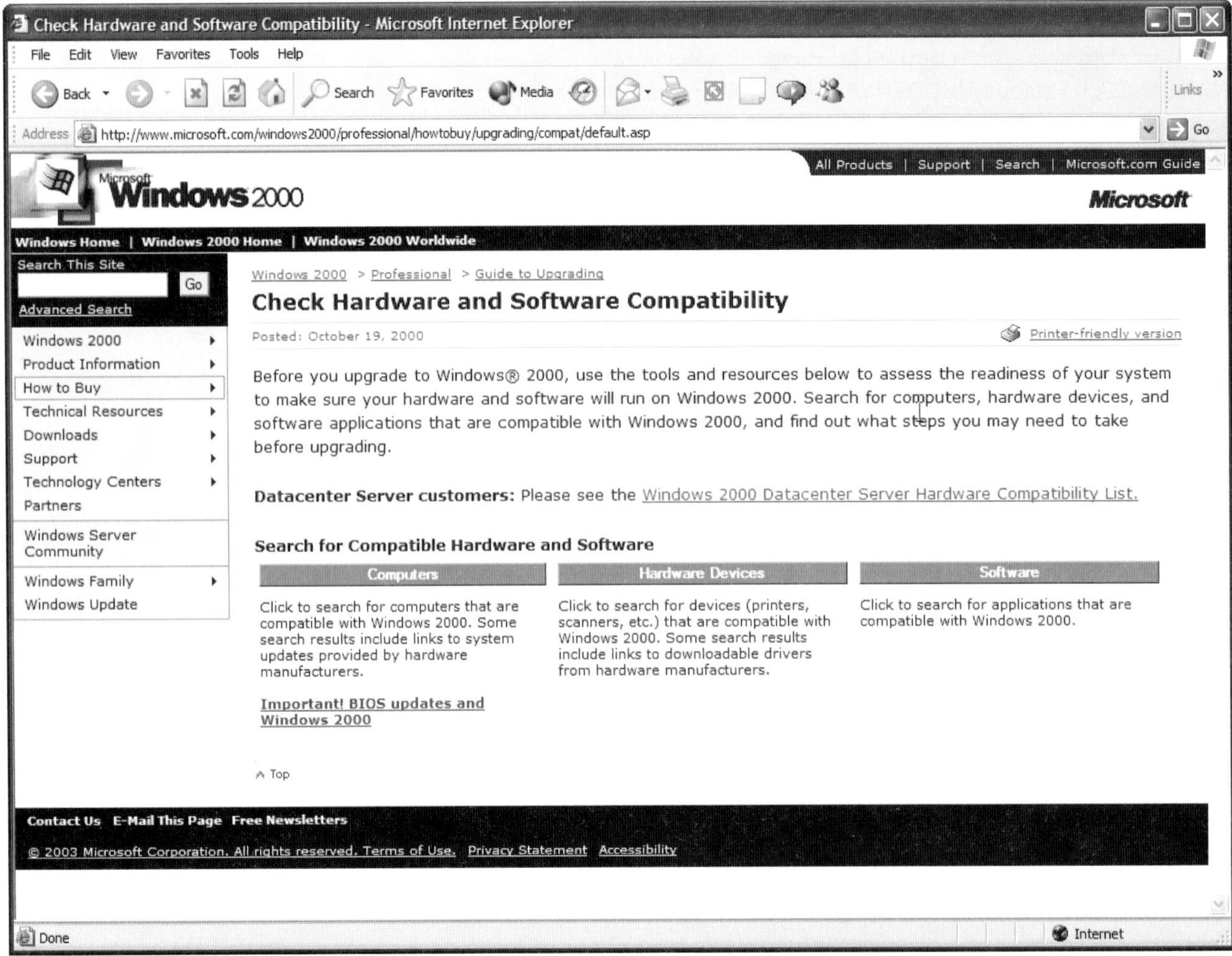

• **Figure 14.10** Check Hardware and Software Compatibility

Here are some of the issues that you should be aware of before performing an upgrade:

- You can upgrade directly to Windows 2000 Professional from Windows 9*x* (all versions) and Windows NT Workstation (versions 3.51 and 4.0). To upgrade to Windows 2000 Professional from Windows NT 3.1 or 3.5, you must first upgrade to NT 3.51 or 4.0, and then to Windows 2000 Professional.
- Because of Registry and program differences between Windows 9*x*/Me and Windows 2000, you might need upgrade packs (or migration DLLs) for your Windows 9*x*/Me applications. Not only does Windows 2000 have hardware issues, it also does not like a lot of Windows 9*x*/Me software!
- Windows 2000 does not support applications that make use of **Virtual Device Drivers** (VxDs). VxDs enable applications to access hardware directly, bypassing the OS altogether. Many older games and multimedia applications use VxDs, which makes this a potentially serious issue.

- Third-party disk compression applications are not supported by Windows 2000.
- Third-party power management applications are also likely to cause problems with a Windows 2000 installation.

Obviously, it's worth your time to take a few extra steps before you pop in that CD-ROM! If you plan to upgrade rather than run a clean installation, follow these steps first:

1. Check out the Hardware and Software Compatibility web site or run a compatibility report using the Check Upgrade utility provided with Windows 2000 Professional. The utility generates a detailed list of potentially problematic devices and applications. You can run the utility as follows: Insert the Windows 2000 Professional CD-ROM [illegible]

[illegible] or unnecessary applications and deleting old files.

4. Perform a disk scan and a disk defragmentation.
5. Uncompress all files, folders, and partitions.
6. Perform a current virus scan, and then remove or disable all virus-checking software.
7. Disable virus checking in your system CMOS.
8. Lastly, keep in mind that if worse comes to worst, you may have to start over and do a clean installation anyway. This makes step 2 exceedingly important! Back up your data!

The Windows 2000 Installation/ Upgrade Process

Like your clean installation of Windows 98/Me , your clean installation of Windows 2000 will begin with the text mode and after at least one reboot, continue into graphics mode. I'll again limit this discussion to what is unique about the Windows 2000 installation/upgrade process.

Disk Partition Options

The first thing that the Setup program does is to examine your hard disk to determine its existing partition and file system configuration. You then get the option of either installing onto an existing partition (if any) or creating a new partition for installation.

You can manage your disk partitions from within Windows 2000 using the Disk Management utility, which is covered in Chapter 11.

By default, the active partition (typically the C: drive) is where the Windows 2000 system files are copied. The boot partition is where your OS files are located. Typically, this will be C:\WINNT for a clean installation. An upgrade installation will overwrite your current OS files in their current location (that is, \WINNT if upgrading from Windows NT, and \WINDOWS if upgrading from Windows 9x). Microsoft recommends that your boot partition be at least 1 GB in size.

Be aware that if you format one partition with FAT32 and another with NTFS, the FAT partition *will not see* and therefore won't be able to access the NTFS partition!

File System Options

At the heart of any OS is the system by which you create and organize your files. Windows 2000 supports FAT16 and FAT32, just like Windows 9x, but also supports its own native NTFS.

Existing NTFS 4 partitions will be upgraded to Windows 2000 NTFS 5 automatically during the installation. If you want to dual-boot between NT 4.0 and 2000, you must first install Windows NT Service Pack 4 or later, which contains an updated Ntfs.sys driver that enables Windows NT 4.0 to read from and write to NTFS volumes in Windows 2000. However, the new features of NTFS 5 will be disabled when you boot from Windows NT 4.0.

FAT If you choose to format your disk with either version of FAT, the Windows 2000 Setup Wizard will automatically format it with FAT16 if the partition is less than 2 GB, and FAT32 if the partition is greater than 2 GB.

NTFS The NTFS that comes with Windows 2000 (NTFS 5) has a few advancements over the older NTFS from Windows NT (NTFS 4). Windows 2000 can only create NTFS 5 volumes; it cannot make the older NTFS 4 volumes. NTFS 5 offers the most options for your Windows 2000 OS installation. Using NTFS 5, you can do the following new functions that NTFS 4 could not do (or did not do as well):

- Assign disk quotas to users to limit the amount of hard disk space they can use
- Encrypt files and folders on the hard disk
- Support Windows 2000 Dynamic Disk configurations

Unless you are configuring your system for multiple-boot options, NTFS is the best way to go.

Chapter 23 covers networking terminology and concepts in detail.

Networking Options

As with previous versions of Windows NT, the Windows 2000 line is optimized for networking with other computer systems. By default, Windows 2000 installs the client for Microsoft Networks, file and printer sharing for Microsoft Networks, and Internet Protocol (TCP/IP). You are also given the option of joining either a workgroup or a domain.

Your network administrator will supply details for those folks working in a networking environment. For the rest, simply install into a workgroup and go on with the installation.

Language and Locale Settings

Windows 2000 can easily be configured to support multiple languages and regional input settings for such things as keyboard layout, currency, time/date display, and numbering.

■ Installing and Upgrading to Windows XP Professional

You'll prepare for a Windows XP installation just as you did for previous installations of Windows in this book. You'll need to check out hardware requirements and hardware and software compatibility.

Upgrade Paths

You can upgrade to Windows XP Professional from all the following versions of Windows:

- Windows 98 (all versions)
- Windows Millennium Edition
- Windows NT 4.0 Workstation (Service Pack 5 and later)
- Windows 2000 Professional (including service packs)
- Windows XP Home Edition

XP Hardware Requirements

[illegible]

Component	Windows XP Computer	Windows XP Computer
CPU	Any Intel or AMD 233 MHz or higher processor	Any Intel or AMD 300 MHz or higher processor
Memory	64 MB of RAM (though Microsoft admits XP will be somewhat crippled with only this amount)	256 MB of RAM or higher
Hard disk	1.5 GB of available hard drive space	4 GB of available hard drive space
Network	Video card that supports DirectX 8 with at least 800 × 600 resolution	Video card that supports DirectX 8 with at least 800 × 600 resolution
CD-ROM	Any CD-ROM or DVD-ROM drive	Any CD-ROM or DVD-ROM drive
Keyboard and Mouse	Keyboard and Microsoft Mouse or compatible pointing device	Keyboard and Microsoft Mouse or compatible pointing device

Hardware and Software Compatibility

You'll need to check hardware and software compatibility before installing Windows XP Professional—either as an upgrade or a new installation. Of course, if you purchase a computer with Windows XP preinstalled, you're spared this task, but you'll still need to verify that the application software you plan to add to the computer will be compatible.

Luckily, you have two tools for determining whether your hardware is compatible: the Windows Catalog and the Upgrade Advisor on the XP CD.

Windows Catalog

The **Windows Catalog** is a searchable list of hardware and software that is known to work with Windows XP. The URL for this exact page is so

Try This!

Running the Upgrade Advisor

If you have PC with Windows XP or older version of Windows, you should know how to run the Upgrade Advisor on your system, so try this.

1. Insert the Windows XP CD. If Autorun is enabled, the Welcome to Microsoft Windows XP screen will appear. If this does not appear, select Start | Run, enter the following, and then click OK:

```
d:\SETUP.EXE
[Where d is the drive letter for the CD-ROM drive.]
```

2. At the Welcome to Microsoft Windows XP screen, select Check System Compatibility to start the Upgrade Advisor. On the following page select Check My System Automatically.
3. In the Upgrade Advisor dialog select the first choice if you have an Internet connection. If you don't have an Internet connection, select No, Skip This Step and Continue Installing Windows. (Don't worry, you aren't really going to install yet.)
4. Click Next. The Upgrade Advisor will show the tasks that Dynamic Update is performing, and then it will restart Setup.
5. After Setup restarts, you'll be back at the same page in the Upgrade Advisor. This time, select No, Skip This Step and Continue Installing Windows, and click Next. The Report System Compatibility page appears next (see Figure 14.11). You can save the information in a file by clicking Save As, and selecting a location.
6. Read the findings that the Upgrade Advisor presents. If a problem was found, click the Details button for instructions, and be sure to follow them. When you have recorded any necessary instructions, click Finish.

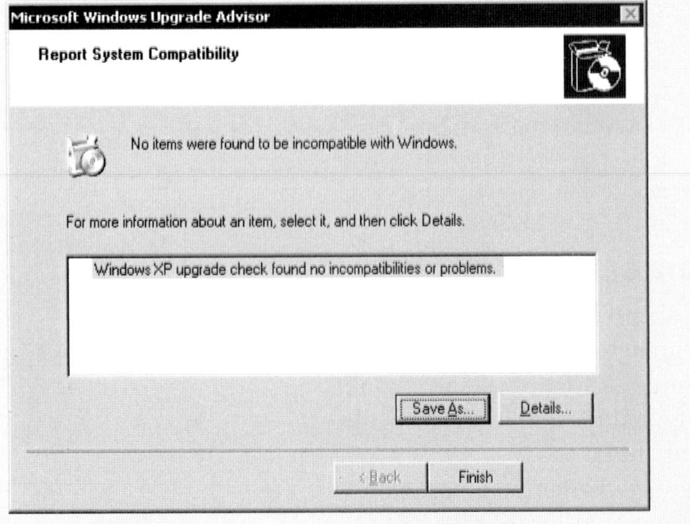

• **Figure 14.11** Report System Compatibility

long, it looks like a typing test. Here is another way to get to it through a shorter URL. First, connect to www.microsoft.com/windowsxp/compatibility/. On the Compatibility page, select the link labeled Discover the Windows Catalog.

Once at the Windows Catalog page, you can search on specific hardware or software products, or browse through the catalog of hardware and software products that will work with Windows XP.

Upgrade Advisor

In my experience, Windows XP has supported a wide range of hardware and software, even some rather old "no name" computers, but I like to be proactive when planning an installation, especially an upgrade. You may not have the luxury of time in upgrading a computer. You may be asked by your boss or client to perform an upgrade *now*. Fortunately, the **Upgrade Advisor** is the first process that runs on the XP installation CD. It examines your hardware and installed software (in the case of an upgrade) and provides a list of devices and software that are known to have issues with XP. Be sure to follow the suggestions on this list!

The Upgrade Advisor can also be run separately from the Windows XP installation. You can run it from the Windows XP CD, or, if you want to find out about compatibility for an upgrade before purchasing Windows XP, connect to the Windows XP Compatibility page, from www.microsoft.com/windowsxp/compatibility, and select Upgrade Advisor. Follow the instructions in the sidebar to use the online Upgrade Advisor.

I ran the advisor on a test computer at the office that was running Windows 98. It produced a report that found only one incompatibility—an antivirus program. The details stated that the program was compatible only if installed after Windows XP was installed. Therefore, it suggested removing the program before installing the OS, and then reinstalling it after the OS was installed. Don't ignore the instructions provided by the Upgrade Advisor!

Booting into Windows XP Setup

The Windows XP CDs are bootable and Microsoft no longer includes a program to create a set of setup boot disks. This should not be an issue, because PCs manufactured in the last several years have the ability to boot from CD-ROM. This system BIOS setting, usually described as "boot order," is [illegible]

it. Many people confuse activation with registration. These are two separate operations. Registration is informing Microsoft of the official owner or user of the product, providing contact information such as name, address, company, phone number, e-mail address, and so on. Registration is still entirely optional. Activation is a way to combat software piracy, meaning that Microsoft wishes to ensure that each license for Windows XP is used solely on a single computer. It's also more formally called **Microsoft Product Activation** (MPA).

Mandatory Activation Within 30 Days of Installation

Activation is mandatory, but you may skip this step during installation. You will have 30 days in which to activate the product, during which time it will work normally. If you don't activate it within that time frame, it will be disabled. Don't worry about forgetting, because once it's installed, Windows XP frequently reminds you to activate it with a balloon message over the tray area of the taskbar. The messages even tell you how many days you have left.

Activation Mechanics

Here is how product activation works. When you choose to activate, either during setup or later when XP reminds you to do it, the product ID code that you entered during installation is combined with a 50-digit value that identifies your key hardware components to create an installation ID code. You must send this code to Microsoft, either automatically if you have an Internet connection, or verbally via a phone call to Microsoft. Microsoft then returns a 42-digit product activation code. If you are activating online, you don't have to enter the activation code; it will happen automatically. If you are activating over the phone, you must read the installation ID to a representative and enter the resulting 42-digit activation code into the Activate Windows by Phone dialog box.

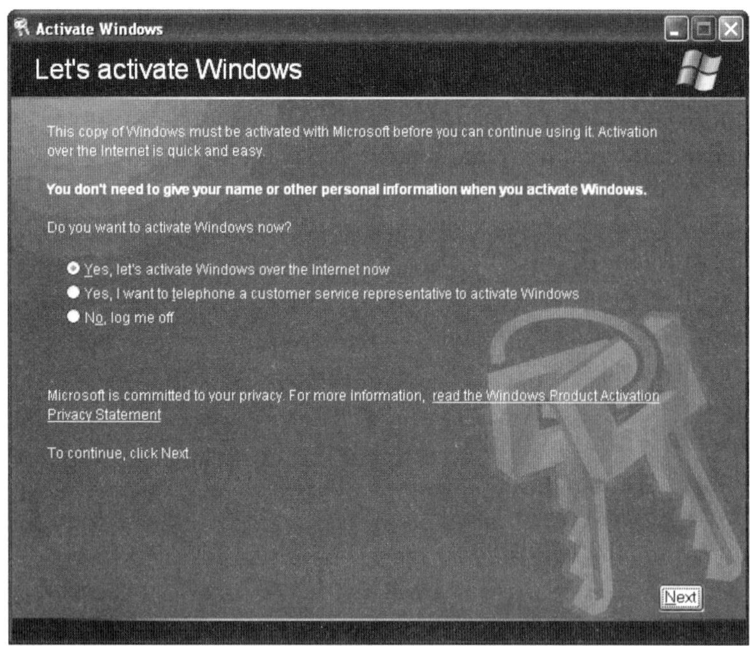

• **Figure 14.12** Activation will take just seconds with an internet connection.

No personal information about you is sent as part of the activation process. Figure 14.12 shows the dialog box that will open when you start activation by clicking on the reminder message balloon.

The Windows XP Installation Process

So you've convinced yourself that it's time to install Windows XP. Any apprehension you may have about the process should be thrown out the window. Installing XP is simple. The wizard will guide you through every step of the process. The onscreen directions are correct and clear. Very few decisions will need to be made. If you are in doubt about a setting, pressing ENTER will likely perform the correct action.

Overall, the installation process takes about an hour. Most of that time will be spent watching the screen. Feel free to walk away as the installation is taking place. If input is needed, the installation program will stop and wait until you click the correct buttons. The following steps describe a clean installation of Windows XP.

Text Mode

Insert the Windows XP CD and boot the computer. After inspecting your hardware configuration, XP setup will show the blue character mode setup screen and copy files to your computer. After the files are copied, you will be prompted to remove the CD and reboot the system. Windows setup will start, load system devices, and display the Welcome to Setup screen (Figure 14.13). Press ENTER to start the installation of XP.

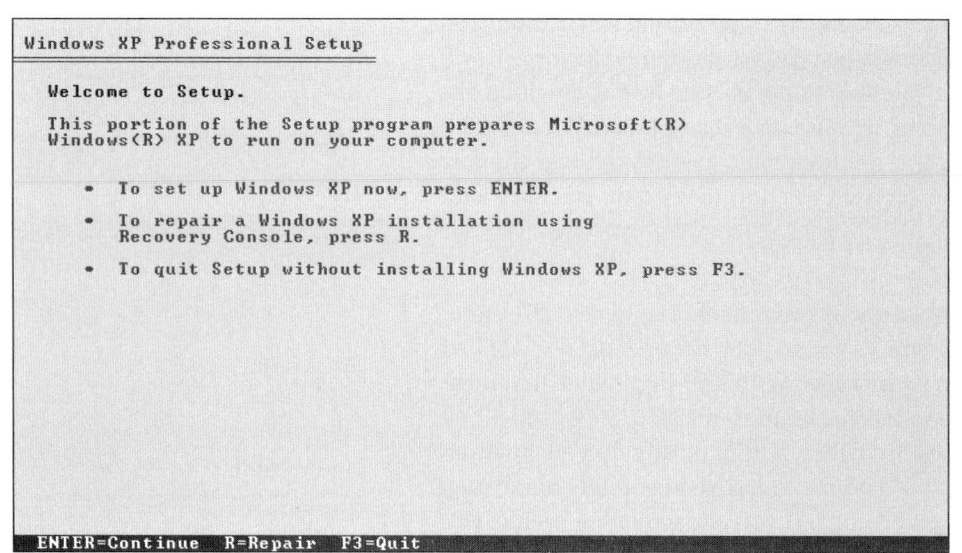

• **Figure 14.13** Welcome to Setup.

Read and accept the End User License Agreement (EULA). If your hard disk is unpartitioned, you will need to create a new partition when prompted. Follow the instructions. One tricky place here is the screen shown in Figure 14.14 that allows you to select the size of your partition. You can either accept the default size for the partition, or enter a smaller value in the highlighted box. In our example, we wanted a 2,048 MB partition, and had to first use the BACKSPACE key to overwrite the default value and enter **2048**.

Next, you will select the partition on which to install XP, and then you need to decide which file system format to use for the new partition. If you have been reading this book carefully, you will choose to format the parti-

```
Windows XP Professional Setup

  You asked Setup to create a new partition on
  4095 MB Disk 0 at Id 0 on bus 0 on atapi [MBR].

      •  To create the new partition, enter a size below and
         press ENTER.

      •  To go back to the previous screen without creating
         the partition, press ESC.

  The minimum size for the new partition is       8 megabytes (MB).
  The maximum size for the new partition is    4087 megabytes (MB).
  Create partition of size (in MB):  2048
```

• **Figure 14.14** Enter the partition size.

After it completes copying the base set of files to this location, your computer reboots, and the graphical mode of Windows XP Setup begins. On the left of the screen shown in Figure 14.15 uncompleted tasks have a white button, completed tasks have a green button, and the current task has a red button.

The following screens ask questions about a number of things the computer needs to know. Just answer them appropriately. They include the desired region and language the computer will operate in, your name and organization for personalizing your computer, and a valid product key for Windows XP. Be sure to enter the product key exactly, or you will be unable to continue.

Next, you need to give your computer a name that identifies it on a network. Check with your system administrator for an appropriate name. In addition to a valid name for your computer, you need to create a password for the Administrator user account. This will be the password that allows you to modify and fix the computer. Next, set the date, time, and time zone.

If a network card was detected, the network components will be installed and you'll have an opportunity to configure the

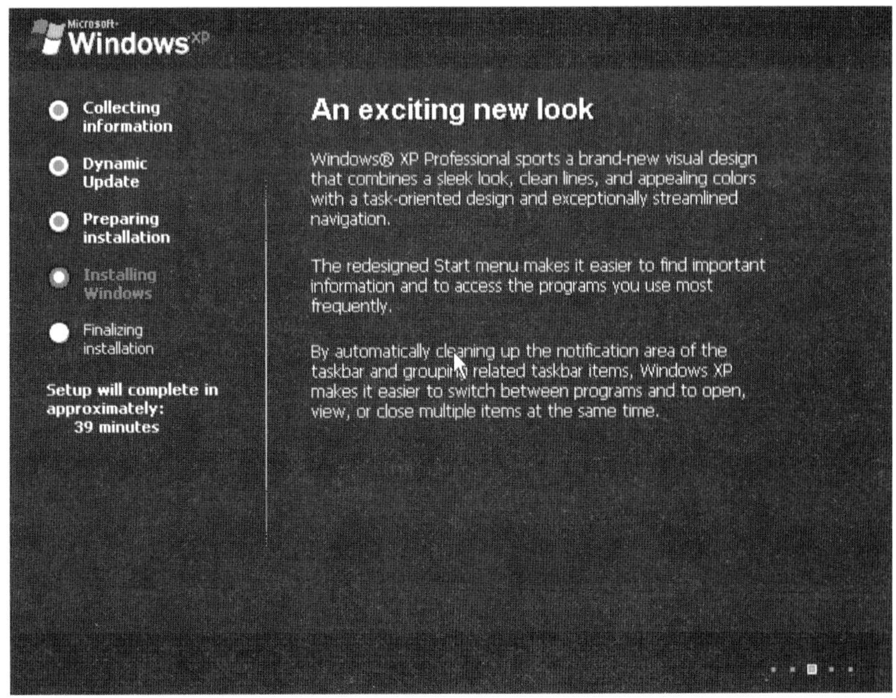

• **Figure 14.15** Beginning of graphical mode

network settings. On the Network Settings page select Typical settings. Once the networking elements are installed, you need to configure the network. Relax; XP will do most of the work for you. Unless you have specific instructions from your network administrator, the default settings are the preferred choices.

After the files required for the final configuration are copied, XP will reboot again. During this reboot, XP determines your screen size and applies the appropriate resolution. This reboot can take several minutes to complete, so be patient. Once the reboot is complete, you must log on as the Administrator. Balloon messages may appear over the tray area of the taskbar. A common message concerns the display resolution. Click the balloon and allow Windows XP to automatically adjust the display settings.

The final message in the installation process reminds you that you have 30 days left for activation. Go ahead and activate now over the Internet or by telephone. It's painless and quick. If you choose not to activate, simply click the Close button on the message balloon. That's it! You have successfully installed Windows XP and should have a desktop with the default Bliss background, as shown in Figure 14.16.

• **Figure 14.16** Windows XP Desktop with Bliss background

Cross Check

Compare and Contrast…

In this chapter you've learned the different installation procedures for Windows 9*x*/Me, Windows 2000, and Windows XP, and even a quick nod at Windows NT 4.0. It can be hard to keep them straight, but if you want to avoid being tricked on the A+ exams, you must be able to! Review the procedures and then make sure you can identify the points of similarity and even more importantly, the differences among the four.

Troubleshooting Installation

Text Mode Errors

If I'm going to have an install problem, this is the place to get one. It's always better to have the error right off the bat, as opposed to when the installation is nearly complete. Text mode errors most often take place during clean installs and usually point to one of the following:

No Boot Device Present When Booting Off the Startup Disk

Either the startup disk is bad or the CMOS is not set to look at the floppy disk first.

Windows Has Detected That Drive C: Does Not Contain a Valid FAT Partition

This applies to Windows 9*x*/Me, and means you forgot to partition the hard drive, or you're trying to install on a partition type that Windows doesn't understand.

Windows Setup Requires XXXX Amount of Available Drive Space

You forgot to format the C: drive, or there's a bunch of stuff on the drive already.

MSCDEX Error "No CD-ROM Detected"

This is usually associated with a Windows 9*x*/Me installation, but if you are a diehard DOS boot techie and like to begin any installation by booting with your trusty DOS floppy, this error could occur when you are preparing for a Windows 2000/XP installation, also. It simply means the CD-ROM driver settings are messed up. Check the CONFIG.SYS and AUTOEXEC.BAT settings.

Not Ready Error on CD-ROM

You probably just need to give the CD-ROM a moment to catch up. Press R for retry a few times. You may also have a damaged install disc, or the CD-ROM drive may be too slow for the system.

A Stop Error (Blue Screen of Death) After the Reboot at the End of Text Mode

Many Knowledge Base articles written for Windows NT and/or Windows 2000 are still helpful when troubleshooting Windows XP.

This is most common during a Windows 2000/XP installation and may mean that you didn't do your homework in checking hardware compatibility, especially the BIOS. I'll tell you more about stop errors in Chapter 16, but if you encounter one of these errors during installation, check out the Microsoft Knowledge Base, especially article 165863, "Troubleshooting 'Stop 0x0A' Messages in Windows 2000 and Windows NT."

Graphical Mode Errors

Once the install passes the text mode and moves into graphical mode, a whole new crop of problems may arise.

Hardware Detection Errors

Failure to properly detect hardware by any version of Setup can be avoided by simply researching compatibility beforehand. Or, if you decided to skip that step, you might be lucky and only have a hardware detection error involving a non-critical hardware device. You can troubleshoot this problem at your leisure. In a sense, you are handing in your homework late, checking out compatibility and finding a proper driver after Windows is installed. Windows 2000 and Windows XP inherited the underpinnings of Windows NT. In particular they all depend on the Setup program properly detecting the computer type (motherboard and BIOS stuff, in particular) and installing the correct Hardware Abstraction Layer (HAL). The HAL was explained in Chapter 12.

If you have to troubleshoot a problem with the HAL, search the Knowledge Base. My last search found 25 separate articles!

Can't Read CAB Files

This is probably the most common of all installation errors. **CAB** (as in cabinet) files are special compressed files, recognizable by their **.cab** file extension, that Microsoft uses to distribute copies of Windows. If your system can't read them, first check the CD-ROM for scratches. Then try copying all the files from the source directory on the CD (\Win9x or \i386) into a directory on your local hard drive. Then run Setup from there, remembering to use the correct program. Setup.exe starts Windows 9*x*/Me Setup and WINNT32 starts Windows 2000/XP Setup. If you can't read any of the files on the CD-ROM disc, you may have a defective drive.

This System Already Has an OS

This is a common error when upgrading from 95 to 98, but this does not stop Windows 2000 or XP in their tracks. You're probably trying to use a full

Windows 9*x* install CD-ROM for an upgrade. There's a perfectly legal way around this:

1. Exit Setup.
2. Type **C:**.
3. Type **CD\SYSTEM**.
4. Type **ren setupx.dll setupx.ol1**.
5. Type **ren setupx.w95 setupx.ol2**.
6. Start Setup again.

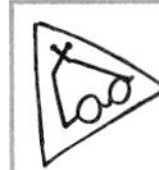

Tech Tip

The Command Prompt Shows No Mercy!

Be careful using any command prompt commands in Windows as they may do things you don't want them to do! In particular, know that using DEL, ERASE, or DELTREE at a Windows' command prompt will not put those deleted files into the Recycle Bin. Instead, those files are permanently deleted (although a

Lockups During Install

Lockups during install vary considerably depending on the version of Win-

click Reset. Unplug it! Then turn the system back on, boot into Setup, and rerun the Setup program. Windows will see the partial installation and prompt you for a "Safe Recovery" mode. This mode ignores all but the most critical hardware to complete the installation. Hopefully, once you have installed Windows, you can then use the techniques we learned earlier to focus on the problem component.

CD-ROM/Hard Drive Bad CD-ROM discs, CD-ROM drives, or hard drives may cause lockups. Check the disc for scratches or dirt and clean it up or replace it. Try a known good disc in the drive. If you get the same error, you may need to replace the drive.

Log Files Windows generates a number of special text files called log files that track the progress of certain processes. While Windows creates a number of different log files for different purposes, three files most interest us:

- **SETUPLOG.TXT** tracks the complete installation process, logging the success or failure of file copying, Registry updates, reboots, and so on.
- **DETLOG.TXT** is created during the hardware detection process. It tracks the detection, query, and installation of all devices.
- **BOOTLOG.TXT** tracks the boot process, logging as each device driver and program loads.

Windows 2000 and Windows XP also have the Setuplog.txt, but it is in the WINNT or Windows directory (the location in which the OS is installed). These OSs also have more powerful recovery options, so, honestly, the chances of your ever actually having to read a log file, understand it, and then getting something fixed as a result of that understanding are pretty small. What makes log files handy is when you call Microsoft or a hardware manufacturer. They *love* to read these files and actually have people who understand them. Don't worry about trying to understand log files for either the A+ exam or for real life; just make sure you know the names of the log files and their location. Leave the details to the Ubergeeks.

No Installation Is Perfect

Even when the installation seems smooth, issues may slowly surface, especially in the case of upgrades. Be prepared to reinstall applications or deal with new functions absent in the previous OS. If things really fall apart, you can always go back to the previous OS.

The procedures I've laid out in this chapter may seem like a lot of work—how bad could it really be to simply grab an installation CD, fling a copy of Windows onto a system, and as the saying goes, let the chips fall where they may? Plenty bad, is how bad. Not only is it important that you understand these procedures for the A+ Certification exams, they can save your, ah, hide, once you're a working PC tech and you're tasked to install the latest version of Windows on the boss's new computer!

Chapter 14 Review

Chapter Summary

After reading this chapter and completing the exercises, you should understand the following about installing and upgrading Windows.

Explain the Windows Installation/Upgrade Process

- Identify hardware requirements (listed on the packaging and at the Microsoft web site), making sure that your computer meets the recommended [illegible]

[illegible]

- A clean OS installation takes place on a new hard drive or one that has been reformatted and repartitioned. You must reinstall all applications and reconfigure preferences. In an upgrade installation, the new OS is installed in the same directory where the old OS was located. The new OS retains the hardware and software settings of the old OS, including user preferences.
- A multi-boot installation is a variation of a clean installation. With the older operating system installed first and the system partition containing a file system common to all OSs, you install the new OS in a different subdirectory or on a different disk volume.
- Before you upgrade, preserve any data that the user has saved on the local hard drive.
- With an upgrade, you can run the Setup program from within the old OS. For a clean installation, you must boot to the Setup program. While Windows 9*x*/Me provides a floppy disk for this purpose, Windows NT, 2000 and XP expect you to boot to the CD-ROM.
- An *image* is a complete copy of a hard disk volume with preinstalled OS and applications. To perform an image installation, copy the image from a CD or a special network server to the local hard drive, using an application such as Norton's Ghost.
- Use the most advanced file system your Windows supports unless you are planning a multi-boot configuration. In that case, you use the lowest common denominator for the system volume and any others that the oldest OS will use. If you use FAT16, your partition size will be limited.
- A standalone computer is not connected to a network. Windows XP Home can only be configured [illegible]

[illegible] drive, it reboots into the graphical part of the installation and asks you to enter the product key.

- Post-installation tasks include updating the OS with patches and Service Packs, upgrading drivers, and restoring data files. Patches fix individual problems with the operating system. A Service Pack is a group of patches bundled together. Updates are a combination of patches and Service Packs. You can get these corrective programs at the Microsoft web site. If the new driver you've installed has a problem, you can do a rollback to the driver installed with the OS. If you used a third-party program to back up user data files, you must install it before you can restore the files. Files copied to a CD-R, Zip disk, or network location can simply be copied to the local hard drive.

Install and Upgrade Windows 9x/Me

- Windows 9*x* and Me require a partitioned and formatted drive before Setup will run. You can boot to the setup floppy and follow the prompts to partition and format a blank drive, or can partition and format it yourself with a Windows Startup disk before you start the Windows installation. If you have a pre-existing FAT partition, you can install Windows 9*x*/Me without reformatting the drive: simply boot to the CD-ROM drive if you are installing Windows 98 or Me, or to a bootable floppy disk for Windows 95, because its installation CD is not bootable.

- You should use the FAT32 file system except for the following three situations: (1) if you want to boot to a previous version of MS-DOS, (2) if you have an early version of Windows 95 that does not support FAT32, or (3) if you want to set up a multi-boot system. Windows comes with conversion tools that will convert FAT16 to FAT32 without losing data, but these tools may fail.
- A clean installation begins with a text mode during which you can partition and format the drive. Then it enters a graphics mode where it loads files necessary for the installation. During this portion, you will select the kind of installation you want: Typical, Compact, Portable, or Custom. If you need to add or remove components after you have completed an installation, use the Add/Remove Programs applet.
- When prompted, enter the product key and then select the installation directory (C:\Windows is recommended). If you're upgrading, use the same folder that contains Windows 95 or you'll have to reinstall all your applications.
- Create the startup disk when prompted. Different from the setup boot disk, the startup disk creates a RAM disk with several handy utilities.
- If you are upgrading, you may save the current Windows systems files and later return to the previous version by uninstalling Windows 98 or Me.
- During the hardware detection phase, Windows first looks for legacy devices and then PnP devices. When it detects a device, it loads the appropriate device driver or prompts for a driver disk.

Install and Upgrade Windows 2000

- Before you perform a Windows 2000 installation or upgrade, verify that your applications will run under the new OS, and use the HCL to verify hardware compatibility. For adequate performance, your system should more than meet Microsoft's minimum system requirements.
- You can upgrade from Windows 9*x*/Me or Windows NT versions 3.51 and 4.0. If you have an earlier version of NT, you must first upgrade to NT 3.51 or 4.0. Because the Registry differs between 9*x* and 2000, you may need upgrade packs or migration DLLs for Windows 9*x* applications.
- Upgrades are more likely to be problematic than clean installs. Windows 2000 will not support applications that use Virtual Device Drivers (VxDs) because it doesn't permit applications to access the hardware directly. In addition, Windows 2000 does not support third-party disk compression and has problems with third-party power management applications.
- Before you upgrade, back up your data and configuration files, uninstall any unnecessary applications and delete old files, uncompress any compressed files, folders, or partitions; then run Scandisk and Defrag. Perform a virus scan and then disable all virus checking, including that in the system CMOS.
- You may install Windows 2000 into an existing partition, or create a new partition using the Disk Management utility. By default, the Windows 2000 system files will be copied to the active partition, usually C:, and the OS files will be copied to the boot partition—usually C:\WINNT for a new install, and the folder where the old Windows OS was located for an upgrade.
- Windows 2000 supports FAT16 and FAT32 files systems, but its native file system is NTFS. The Setup Wizard will automatically format a disk smaller than 2 GB as FAT16, and one larger than 2 GB as FAT32. The version of NT that came with Windows NT is now called NTFS 4. The improved version used by Windows 2000/XP, called NTFS 5, offers improvements including disk quotas, encryption of files and folders, and support for Windows 2000 Dynamic Disk configurations. Always select NTFS for Windows 2000 unless you are using a multi-boot configuration.
- Some network support is installed automatically with Windows 2000, including Client for Microsoft Networks, File and Print Sharing for Microsoft Networks, and TCP/IP.

Install and Upgrade Windows XP

- If you have Windows 98, Me, NT 4.0 Workstation with Service Pack 5 or later, Windows 2000 Professional, or Windows XP Home Edition, you may upgrade to Windows XP Professional.
- The Windows XP CD includes two tools for checking hardware and software compatibility. The Windows Catalog is a searchable list of hardware and software products that work with

XP. The Upgrade Advisor is the first process that runs on the XP installation CD. It provides a list of devices and software that have issues with XP. You can run the Upgrade Advisor separately from an XP installation using the XP CD or online from the Windows XP Compatibility web page.

- Windows XP does not create a set of setup boot disks and does not use a floppy diskette. Instead, you must add the CD-ROM drive to your PC's boot sequence, and boot directly to the XP CD. If this isn't possible, you can download a set of six setup book disks from the Microsoft web site.
- During installation, you will be prompted for

installation code—a 50-digit value that identifies your key hardware components—and Microsoft gives you a 42-digit product activation code.

- The XP installation process uses a wizard to guide you through each step. If you're uncertain what to select, choose the default by pressing ENTER—it's usually the correct action.
- To do a clean install of Windows XP, boot the computer to the Windows XP CD, which will copy files to your hard drive. You then remove the CD, the system reboots, and Windows loads system devices and displays the Welcome to Setup screen. When prompted, accept the End User License Agreement (EULA). If necessary, create a new partition (default size or smaller). After you select the partition where XP should be installed and the file system to use (NTFS is recommended), Setup copies files to the Windows folder and appropriate subfolders.
- When the graphical mode starts after another reboot, you can track progress of the installation. An uncompleted task has a white button, a completed task has a green button, and the current task has a red button. You will be prompted for Region and Language, your name and organization, and the product key. Windows XP requires you to give your computer a name that will identify it on a network. The Administrator user account will be created, and you will need to create a password, set date, time, and time zone. If your computer has a network card, Setup will install network components and let you configure network settings. The final reboot may take several minutes, during which screen size and appropriate resolution are set. After this reboot, you may log on as Administrator.
- The final message in the installation process reminds you that you have 30 days left for activation. If you choose not to activate, simply click the Close button on the message balloon. Because activation is based on a particular hardware configuration, it's a good idea to test the installation for a few days before activating it, so you can change hardware

something else. Text mode errors during a clean install may range from "No Boot Device Present" (the startup disk is bad or CMOS is not set to look at the appropriate drive first), to "Drive C: does not contain a Valid FAT Partition" (no partition or a partition Windows cannot use), to insufficient space on the drive, to an MSCDEX error that prevents Windows from accessing the CD ROM drive. If you get a "Not Ready Error on CD-ROM," it could be a damaged install disk or a slow CD-ROM drive that needs to catch up. A stop error (Blue Screen of Death) after the reboot at the end of the text mode points to a hardware incompatibility problem.

- Graphical mode errors indicate a different set of problems than text mode errors. Setup must be able to detect the computer type (especially the motherboard and BIOS) and install the correct Hardware Abstraction Layer (HAL). You may get a hardware detection error if Setup fails to detect a device. If it is a non-critical piece of hardware, you can work on this problem later. This error may be solved by finding the proper driver.
- Probably the most common installation problem is failure to read the compressed Windows OS distribution files called CAB files. Try copying these files to your local hard drive and running the Setup program from there.

- If you get an error that the system already has an OS, particularly when upgrading from 95 to 98, you can rename setupx.dll and setupx.w95 in the SYSTEM folder on the hard drive and restart Setup.
- If the system locks up during installation (a more common problem with Windows 95 than later versions), do *not* press CTRL-ALT-DEL or the Reset button to restart the installation. Instead, unplug the system and then turn it back on, so Windows will recognize a partial installation and go to the "Safe Recovery" mode where it can often complete the installation. A bad CD-ROM disc, CD drive or hard drive may also cause a lockup.
- During installation, Windows creates three log files: (1) SETUPLOG.TXT tracks the installation process, logging success and failures; (2) DETLOG.TXT, created during the hardware detection process, tracks detection and installation of all devices; and (3) BOOTLOG.TXT tracks the boot process, logging each device driver and program as it loads. Windows 2000 and XP store SETUPLOG.TXT with the OS.

Key Terms

Bootlog.txt *(527)*
CAB files *(526)*
Clean installation *(503)*
Detlog.txt *(527)*
End User License Agreement (EULA) *(506)*
Hardware Compatibility List (HCL) *(515)*
Image installation *(505)*
Knowledge Base *(505)*
Microsoft Product Activation (MPA) *(521)*
Multi-boot installation *(503)*
Patch *(507)*
Remote Installation Services (RIS) *(505)*
Service pack *(507)*
Setuplog.txt *(527)*
Text mode *(506)*
Upgrade Advisor *(520)*
Upgrade installation *(503)*
Virtual Device Driver (VxD) *(516)*
Windows Catalog *(519)*

Key Term Quiz

Use the Key Terms list to complete the sentences that follow. Not all the terms will be used.

1. One of the most important pre-installation tasks is to check the ________ to make sure that all your devices will work with the new OS.
2. If you do not complete the ________ within 30 days, Windows XP stops working.
3. If you have a new hard drive with nothing on it, you will likely choose to do a(n) ________.
4. If you are installing the OS and applications on a number of identical computers, you can prepare one and perform a(n) ________ using Norton Ghost or a similar program during which everything is copied from that computer to another.
5. Windows XP does not support programs that use a(n) ________ that attempts to address hardware directly.
6. If you want to boot to either Windows 9*x* or Windows 2000, you may choose a(n) ________.
7. A(n) ________ is a fix for a single problem with the OS while a(n) ________ is a combination of fixes.
8. If you wish to have only one OS and keep the applications and configuration of the current system, you should choose to do a(n) ___________ of the new OS.
9. At the Microsoft web site, you may consult the ___________ that contains articles about problems and solutions.
10. A Windows installation starts in the __________ and then switches to the ______.

Multiple-Choice Quiz

1. During installation, Windows creates all the following log files *except* ________.
   - **A.** DETLOG.TXT
   - **B.** DEVICELOG.TXT
   - **C.** SETUPLOG.TXT
   - **D.** BOOTLOG.TXT

2. The set of startup disks for Windows XP ______________.
   - **A.** Contains four disks and may be created from the Windows XP CD during the installation [illegible]
   - [illegible] cannot boot from a floppy disk

3. With Windows 9*x*, if you want to create a multi-boot configuration, ___________.
   - **A.** Choose the upgrade install option
   - **B.** Choose the clean install option
   - **C.** Choose the multi-boot install option
   - **D.** Windows 9*x* does not include the multi-boot function

4. If you do not complete the activation process for Windows XP, what will happen to your computer?
   - **A.** Nothing. Activation is optional.
   - **B.** The computer will work fine for 30 days and then Windows XP will be disabled.
   - **C.** Microsoft will not know how to contact you to provide upgrade information.
   - **D.** You will have to use a floppy disk set to boot to XP.

5. During a Windows 2000 installation, the system files are copied to the active partition while the rest of the OS files are placed in the __________ partition.
   - **A.** System
   - **B.** Boot
   - **C.** Extended
   - **D.** Secondary

6. After you have completed a Windows installation and verified that the system starts and runs okay, the next thing you should do is ___________.
   - **A.** Do nothing. You're through.
   - **B.** Configure the computer for the network.
   - **C.** Install applications and restore data.
   - **D.** Install the latest service pack or update along with any updated drivers.

[illegible]

process.
   - **D.** Unplug the computer and restart the installation process.

8. If you wish to choose the Windows 9*x* features that you want to install, you should select the _________ installation.
   - **A.** Typical
   - **B.** Compact
   - **C.** Custom
   - **D.** Portable

9. You can upgrade directly to Windows XP from all of the following operating systems *except* __________.
   - **A.** Windows NT 3.51
   - **B.** Windows Me
   - **C.** Windows 98
   - **D.** Windows 2000 Professional

10. If you are installing Windows 2000 on a 30 GB hard disk, the Setup program will automatically select which file system?
    - **A.** FAT16
    - **B.** FAT32
    - **C.** NTFS4
    - **D.** NTFS5

11. The Windows XP CD contains which two tools for checking hardware and software compatibility?

   A. The HCL and the HAL

   B. The HCL and the Windows Catalog

   C. The Windows Catalog and the Upgrade Advisor

   D. The Upgrade Advisor and the HCL

12. All of the following are considerations when selecting a Windows 2000 upgrade installation *except* __________.

   A. Windows 2000 does not support third-party disk compression applications.

   B. Windows 2000 does not support applications that use Virtual Device Drivers (VxDs).

   C. Third-party power management applications may cause problems.

   D. You will have to reinstall all applications and reconfigure settings after the OS upgrade is complete.

13. If you get an error message that the Setup program cannot read the CAB files, you should __________.

   A. Copy the CAB files from the Windows installation CD to your local hard drive and run the Setup program from there.

   B. Skip this step since the CAB files are not necessary to install Windows successfully.

   C. Go to the Microsoft web site and download the latest version of the CAB file wizard.

   D. Cancel the installation process and keep your old operating system since your hardware does not meet the minimum requirements.

14. NTFS5 offers all the following new functions *except* __________.

   A. User profiles

   B. Disk quotas

   C. Support for Dynamic Disk configurations

   D. Encryption of files and folders

15. If you receive a graphical mode error that Windows failed to detect a non-critical piece of hardware, __________.

   A. You will need to remove the hardware device or replace it with one that is compatible with the OS.

   B. You can probably solve the problem after the installation is complete by finding the proper driver.

   C. You will get a "stop error" and be unable to complete the installation process.

   D. You should reboot the computer and restart the installation.

Essay Quiz

1. You know that Windows 2000 and XP use a Hardware Compatibility List (HCL) to verify that certain hardware and software will work successfully with these operating systems. What should you do if you discover that a hardware device in your computer is not on the HCL?

2. You learned that Windows 2000 and XP include Remote Installation Services (RIS) that allows a scripted installation or an image installation. Explain the advantages and disadvantages of each of these options and when and why one would choose them.

3. Jamal, one of your classmates, has decided to help his neighbor Cindy install Windows 2000 on a system that currently uses Windows 98 Second Edition with FAT32. He tells you that Cindy has been very faithful in installing service packs for Windows 98. Since Cindy has lots of applications installed that she does not want to have to reinstall and lots of data files that she doesn't want to lose, Jamal needs to make sure that the Windows 2000 installation keeps all of Cindy's programs and files intact. He's asked you what steps he should take before he starts the Windows 2000 installation. He also wants to make sure that he is using the correct kind of installation. What will you tell him?

4. Andre has a new computer with Windows XP. His wife Ellen is more familiar with Windows 2000 and would prefer to use it. He has consulted you because he thinks that a multi-boot configuration would accommodate

both of them. Tell him what to do to be able to multi-boot between 2000 and XP.

5. Phillip just upgraded to Windows 2000 and now discovers that his favorite game will not run. Explain the likely cause of the game no longer running and the possible solutions Phillip may choose to solve this problem.

Lab Projects

• Lab Project 14.1

[illegible] prepare a five-minute report for the class about the [illegible]

[illegible] Catalog to determine if the following printers are compatible with Windows XP:

- HP LaserJet 4100
- HP PhotoSmart 2000
- Epson Stylus Colour [illegible]
- Canon LBP 660

If you have a different printer, check it also while you're looking at the Windows Catalog.

Maintaining, Optimizing, and Troubleshooting Windows 9x and Windows Me

Tout passe, tout lasse, tout casse. (Everything passes away, everything wears out, everything breaks.)

—French Proverb

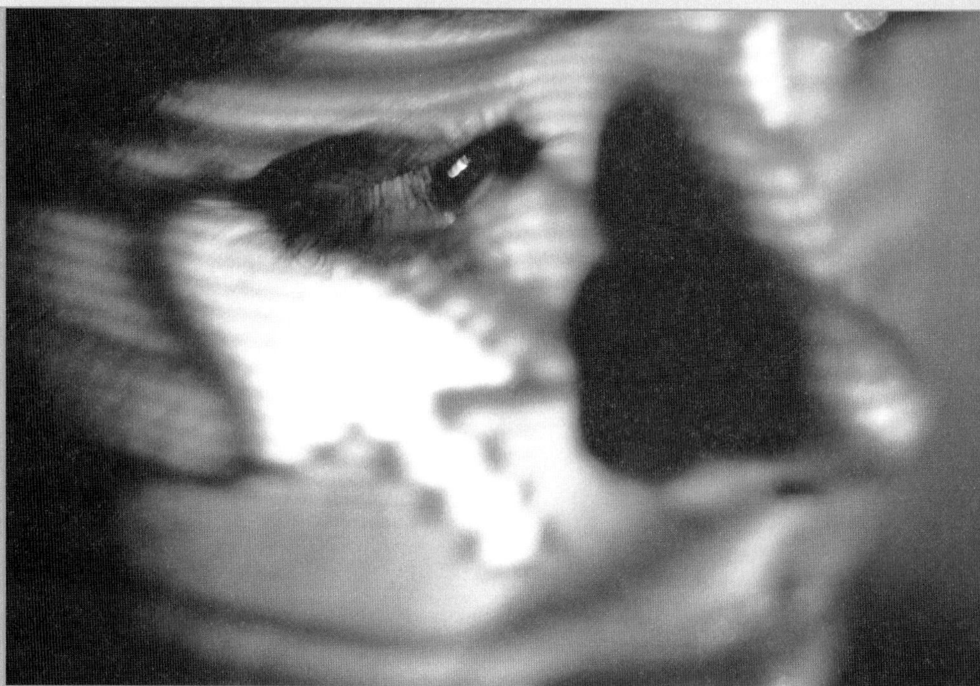

In this chapter, you will learn how to

- **Maintain and optimize a healthy Windows 9x/Me system**
- **Install and configure devices on Windows 9x/Me systems**
- **Troubleshoot Windows 9x/Me problems using key tools and procedures**

Windows 9x/Me systems may be no match for the wonders of Windows XP, but they continue to soldier on in many PCs, and CompTIA expects you to know how to maintain, optimize, and troubleshoot them, and how to install and configure both Plug and Play and legacy devices on Windows 9x/Me systems. This chapter begins with the basic "housekeeping" tasks you must know in order to keep a Windows 9x/Me system running smoothly and efficiently, including drive maintenance and OS updates. The second part of the chapter covers the sometimes frustrating process of installing devices. Plug and Play and legacy devices each have their own installation procedures and pitfalls, and you'll learn how installation works when all goes well, and what to do when it doesn't. The last section of the chapter tackles system troubleshooting issues, including boot problems, lockups, viruses, and system restore. By the time we're through, you'll be able to approach any Windows 9x/Me system confident that you can handle whatever you find. Sound good? Great, let's get started!

■ Maintaining and Optimizing Windows 9x/Me

If you were looking forward to seeing the "Hot-Rodder's Guide to Windows 9*x*/Me" in this section, you're in for a big disappointment. All versions of Windows 9*x*/Me come pretty well optimized out of the box. There is very little you can do to make a Windows system run faster or better by "tweaking the system." Sure, I read the same web sites and magazines you do that tout some bizarre Registry setting that makes a Windows system better, but on the whole I've found them to be hardly worth the effort and certainly way outside the scope of the A+ exams! Instead, optimization of Windows 9*x*/Me means little more than checking the status of a few settings, which in all probability are already set properly by Windows, and

Service Packs/Patches/Windows Update

Windows has gone through a number of evolutionary changes over the years. Since its inception, Windows 9*x*/Me has received a number of patches and upgrades to correct or improve a broad cross-section of problems. There are three different ways to update Windows: patches, service packs, and new versions.

Patches are EXE files that you get from Microsoft to fix a specific problem. You run these programs, and they do whatever they're supposed to do—update DLLs, reconfigure Registry settings, or whatever else they need to do to fix a particular problem. For example, Figure 15.1 is a patch to fix a problem Windows had with extended partitions on LBA drives.

The order in which you install patches in Windows 95 can be crucial!

What is a "TSD Virtual Device?" Who cares? What matters is that these patches are required to keep Windows running properly. This does not mean that Windows 9*x*/Me requires every patch produced. Ignore the patches that have nothing to do with what you do or that fix a problem that you don't have. Microsoft has released literally hundreds of patches for Windows 9*x*/Me, but the majority of them are important. I'll show you how to determine what you need in a moment.

Sometimes a patch might not totally fix a particular problem or might even cause other problems. In that case, you'll need a patch for the patch. Also, some patches need to be installed before another patch can be used. This creates a unique situation where the patch order is quite important.

The first Windows 95 release was followed by a long series of patches over the next few months, fixing everything from password problems to memory leaks. Microsoft packaged these together into a single EXE file that would perform the patches simultaneously.

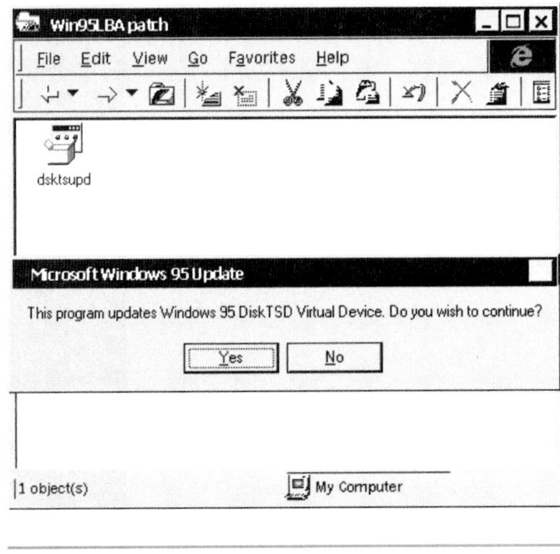

• **Figure 15.1** Patch to fix partition problem.

This grouping of patches is called a **service pack**. Currently, two Windows 95 service packs exist, predictably called Service Pack 1 and Service Pack 2 (assuming you have an original version of Windows 95).

Microsoft eventually sold Windows 95 with Service Pack 1 already installed. This version was called *OEM service release 1* (OSR 1). After OSR 1, more patches were created, and so roughly a year later, another set of patches was combined into OSR 2. A number of patches have been created since OSR 2.

As time goes by, Microsoft continues to redefine the names for patches. For example, a patch that fixes a security problem is now called a "security update." Don't let terminology prevent you from getting what you need!

Windows 98 only had one major update, which they called the Customer Service Pack. Windows 98 SE included the Customer Service Pack, plus a number of other enhancements like new versions of Internet Explorer, Outlook Express, and other applications. A number of minor patches have also been released.

Windows Me incorporates most changes and patches from Windows 98 and 98 SE, but truly is much more than an update. Microsoft added a lot of features to Me, including new consumer-oriented applications (like the very cool Movie Maker software for editing digital movies) and new utilities (such as the excellent System Restore). As you might suspect, though, Microsoft has produced fixes for Me that you need to incorporate as well.

Okay, you're convinced of the need to update Windows. You now need to be able to answer the questions "What service packs/patches are on my system now, and what should I install?" This is one area where the power of Windows 98/Me shines through. Just go to the Windows Update utility (it's usually right on the Start menu) and let Microsoft tell you (Figure 15.2). The

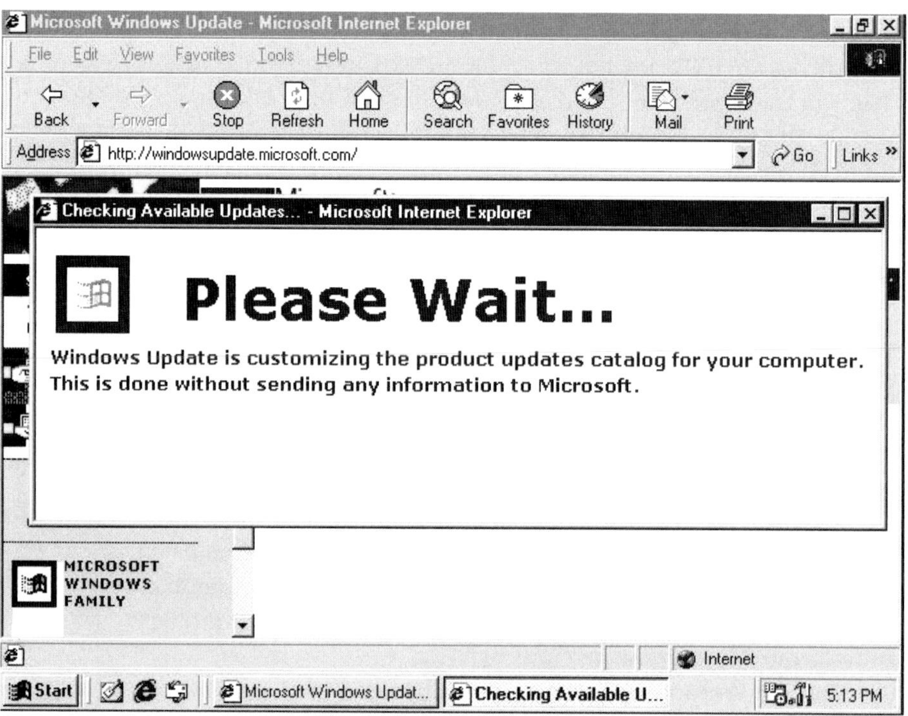

• **Figure 15.2** Windows Update utility

Windows Update utility queries your system and provides a list of the updates you require. Simply read about them and select the ones you want. Just know ahead of time that most of these updates are huge—a little tough to download on a 56 K modem. Microsoft will gladly provide them on CD-ROM for a nominal fee.

Identifying patches in Windows 95 is tougher. The best way to determine the patches currently loaded on your Windows 95 system is to use Microsoft's QFECHECK (Figure 15.3). QFECHECK can be downloaded from the Microsoft web site and generates a detailed list of all patches performed on your machine. Note that the listed patches can be expanded to show [illegible] service packs and a few other patches have been installed, but QFECHECK breaks down the service packs to show separate patches.

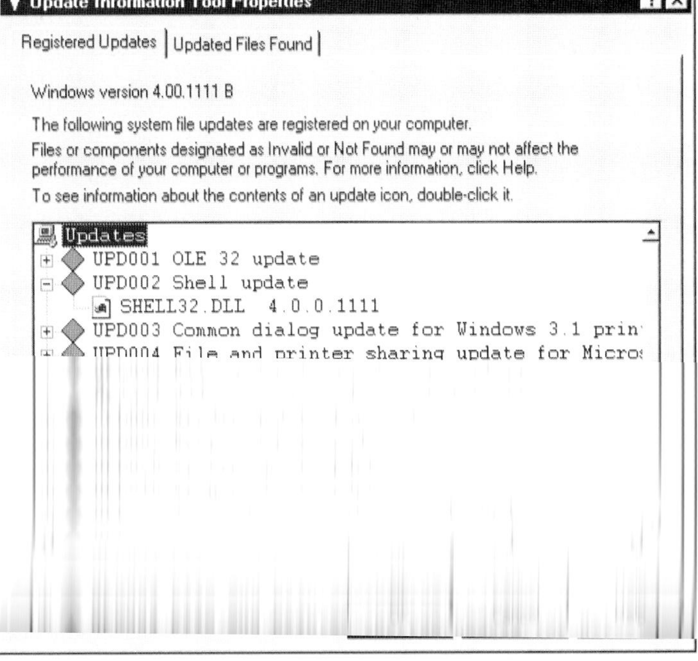

Figure 15.3 QFECHECK

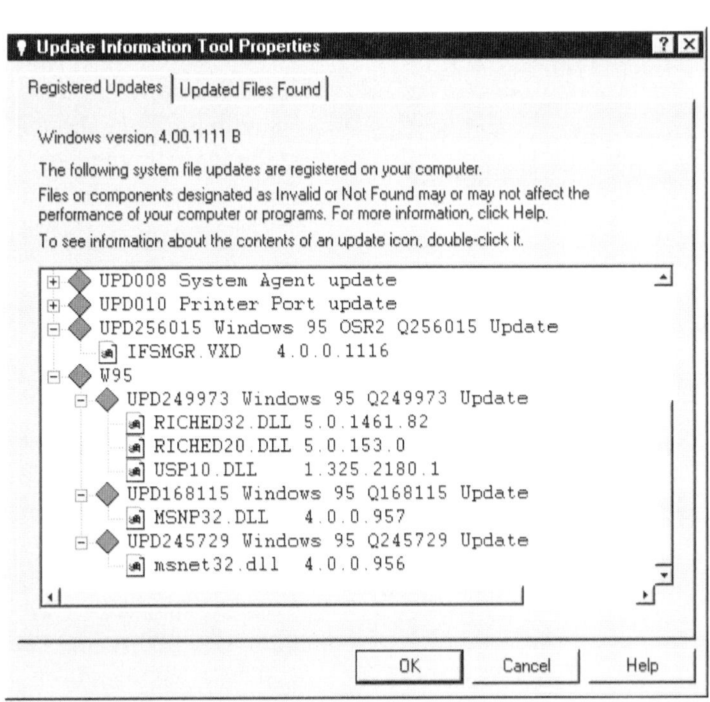

Figure 15.4 Service packs contain many patches.

> Remember, you don't need every update Microsoft offers. Make sure you understand the needs of the system before you download the latest security update or service pack. When a new one comes out, let other folks test it for a few weeks, and then do a search on the Internet to see if any problems occur with that update. There's no worse feeling than installing a patch to improve a system, only to find you've made it worse!

Try This!

Checking and Patching

You should stay current with the patches Microsoft writes for your OS. This helps maintain a healthy, stable system. Reading a thick, heavy tome like this book provides an excellent time to download a bunch of patches for your OS, so try this!

1. Go to Windows Update and run the utility on your system.
2. When the Update utility shows you updates and service packs, start the patching process.
3. Download the critical updates and service packs first.
4. Then get any OS patches that seem relevant.
5. Finish by getting driver updates.

Drive Maintenance

Drive maintenance is one of the most boring, tedious, mind-numbing jobs that a PC support person must perform. It is also the single most important way to ensure the long-term health of a PC system. As you know from other chapters, the two most important functions are disk scanning and defragmentation. Windows adds one more important function: the occasional disk cleanup. Let's look at all three.

- **Defragmentation** All versions of Windows come with a disk defragmentation utility called Disk Defragmenter. Many techs still just refer to it as *Defrag*—the name of the old DOS disk defragmentation utility. You access Defrag from the Programs | Accessories | System Tools menu (Figure 15.5). Although the look of Defrag has changed over the Windows versions, it still does the same job. Use as directed in Chapter 11.
- **Disk Scanning** Just as all versions of Windows come with a disk defragmentation utility, all versions also include a disk scanning program that checks for errors, just like the old ScanDisk utility used to do. As with the term *Defrag*, we still refer to any tool of this type as *ScanDisk*. In Windows 9*x*/Me, you access ScanDisk from the Programs | Accessories | System Tools menu. The ScanDisk section of the Tools tab is now called "Error-checking" (Figure 15.6). All versions of Windows provide access to both Defrag and ScanDisk this way—another example of Windows giving you a number of ways to do the same job. Even though ScanDisk and Defrag make a great team for fixing

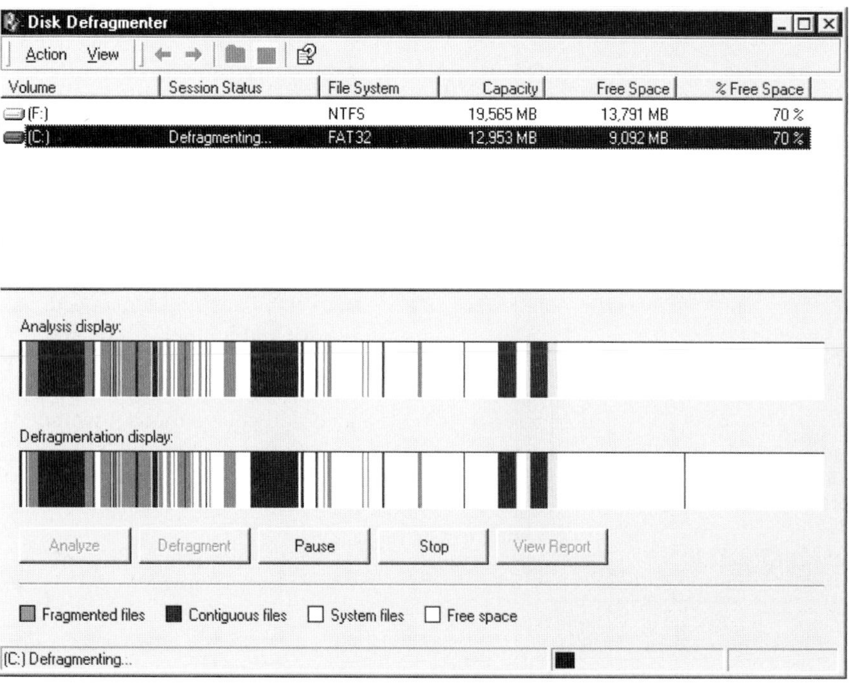

Figure 15.5 Disk defragmentation utility

file problems in Windows, do be aware that in some cases a seriously corrupted file can slip by ScanDisk and cause Defrag to lockup!

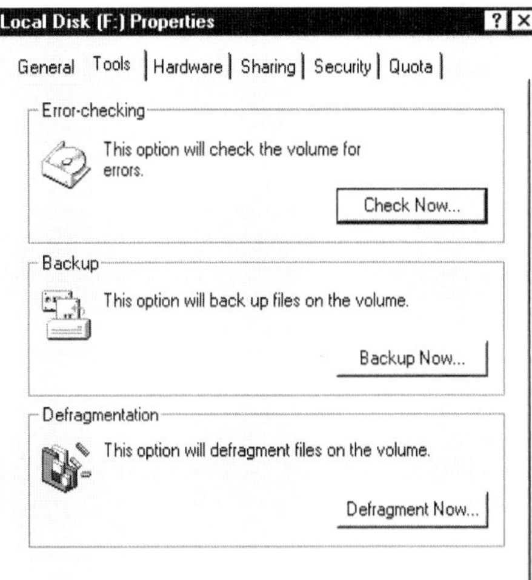

- **Drive Cleanup Utilities** Windows really puts a lot of junk files on the system. These junk files fall into one of six categories:
  - Application temporary files that failed to delete
  - Installation temporary files that failed to delete
  - Internet Browser cache files
  - Files in the Recycle Bin
  - Internet cookie files
  - Identical files in separate locations

lete fewer, and a couple of programs far more. Either way, disk cleanup has become a critical part of drive maintenance.

ScanDisk

We use term *ScanDisk* generically to cover the disk scanning function in all versions of Windows.

1. Can you identify and locate this tool in Windows 2000 and Windows XP?
2. Can you identify and locate this tool in Windows 9*x*/Me?

Starting with Windows 98, Microsoft introduced a built-in disk cleanup program called, cleverly enough, Disk Cleanup. Most third-party disk cleanup tools do a far better job than Disk Cleanup, but it's not a bad little program (Figure 15.7). I find that some of the better third-party utilities are more flexible. I want a tool, for example, that only deletes Internet cookies that haven't been accessed in the last 60 days. I hate typing in all my Amazon.com data over again!

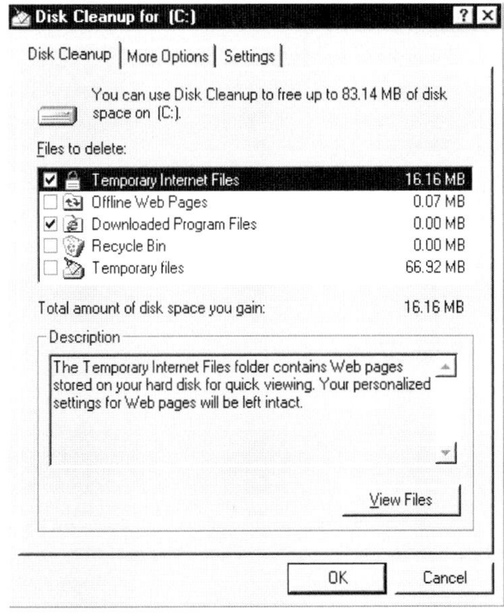

Figure 15.7 Disk Cleanup utility

Task Scheduling

Why bother running these programs manually when you can just tell the Windows Task Scheduler to run them at a certain time? Born from the same third-party utilities, handy task scheduling utilities now come with Windows 98 and Windows Me (Figure 15.8). You can simply choose the program you wish to run, when and how often you want it to run, and disk maintenance no longer becomes a part of your job description.

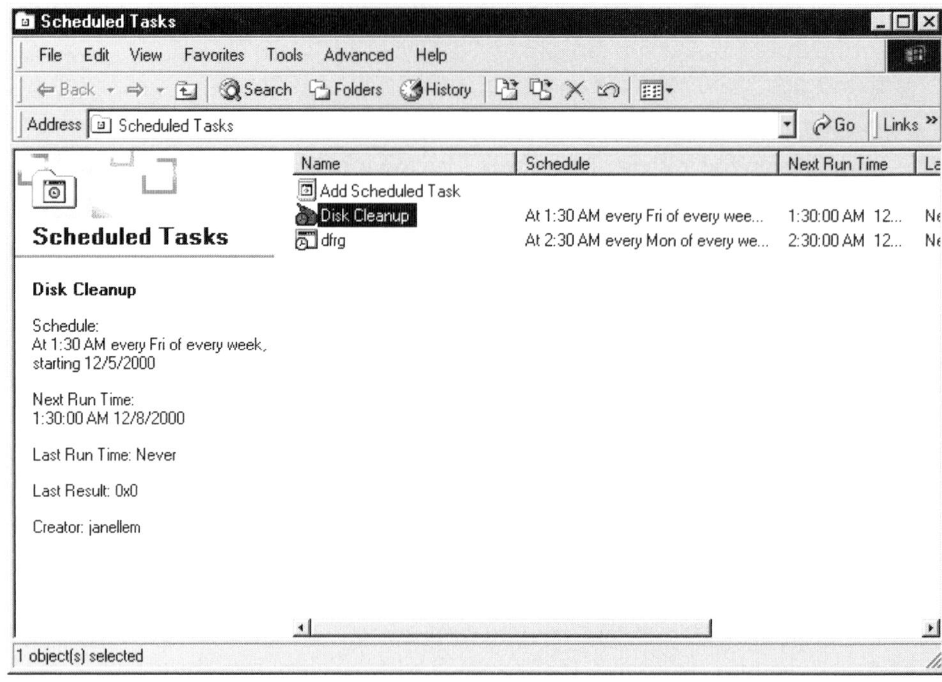

• **Figure 15.8** Windows Me task scheduling utility

Virtual Memory

All versions of Windows use **virtual memory** —mapping a portion of the hard drive with memory addresses to mimic RAM—as you'll recall from the discussion of swap files in Chapter 12. Windows creates a swap file that enables it to have more programs open on the screen than it could normally hold in real RAM. The swap file in Windows 9*x*/Me is called WIN386.SWP, while the Windows NT/2000/XP swap file is called PAGEFILE.SYS. Windows sets the initial size of the swap file automatically according to the amount of free space available on the C: drive. Although this automatic setting works fairly well, you can easily optimize Windows' use of that swap file with a few judicious alterations. The Windows 9*x*/Me swap file is configured in the System applet in the Control Panel or by alternate-clicking My Computer and selecting Properties. Click the Virtual Memory button on the Performance tab (Figure 15.9).

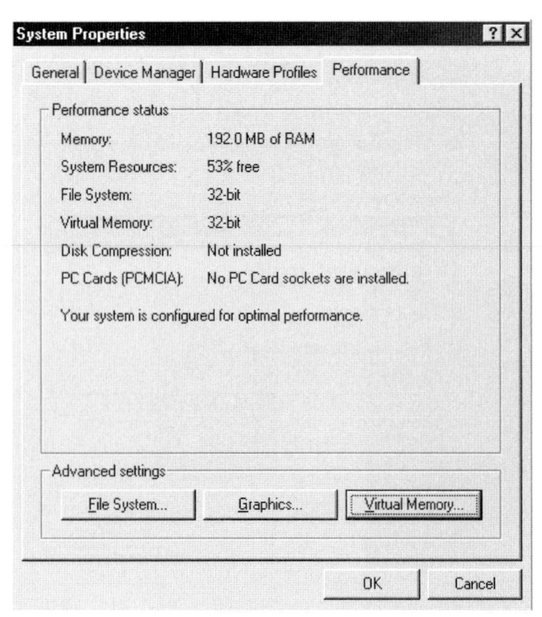

• **Figure 15.9** Configure Windows 9x/Me swap file

The Windows NT/2000/XP swap file settings can be found by alternate-clicking the My Computer icon on your desktop, selecting the Advanced tab, and then clicking the Performance Options button. The Performance Options window shows several radio buttons (we discuss those in Chapter 16); clicking the Change button opens the Virtual Memory dialog box (Figure 15.10).

The most common reason for relocating the default swap file is to move it to some drive other than C:. Many systems tend to fill up the C: drive, so little or no room is left for the swap file. The

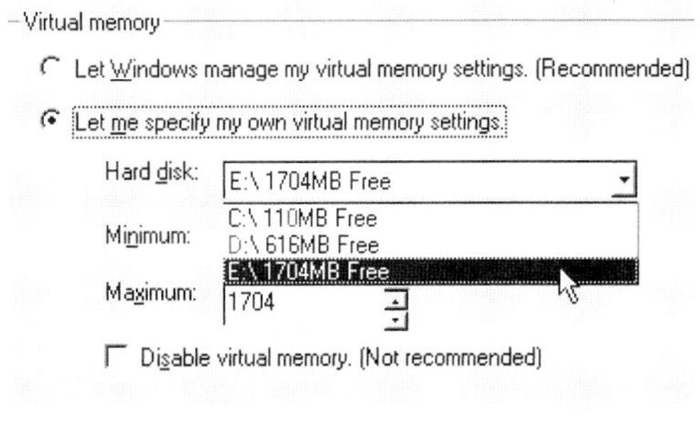

• **Figure 15.11** Selecting a new drive for the Windows 9x/Me swap file

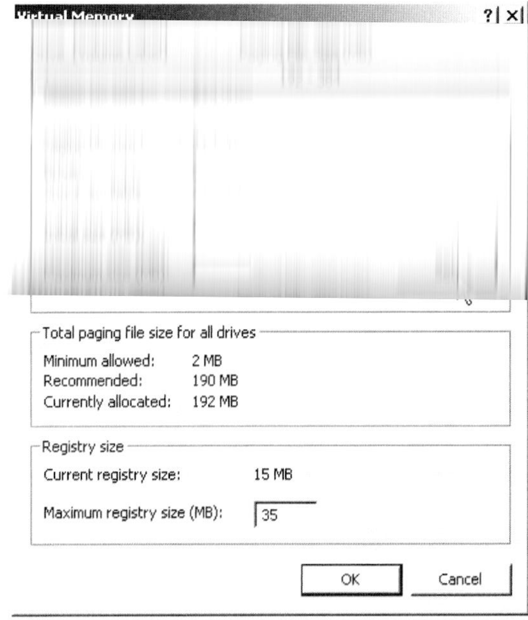

• **Figure 15.12** Setting a new drive for the Windows 2000 swap file

swap file can use only the free space on a drive. When the space is filled, the swap file can't get any larger, resulting in the nasty "Not Enough Memory" error. The solution is to move the swap file to another drive.

To move the file in Windows 9*x*/Me, click the Let Me Specify My Own Virtual Memory Settings radio button and select another drive (Figure 15.11). In Windows NT/2000/XP, click the drive letter to which you wish to move the swap file, then click the Set button (Figure 15.12), and close back out of the various windows.

Notice the minimum and maximum swap file sizes. Windows 9*x*/Me sets the minimum to zero and the maximum to the size of the free space on the drive, whereas Windows 2000 sets a minimum and maximum by a fairly complex set of rules. Experimentation has shown that leaving these settings at their defaults creates enormous swap files, far larger than you really need. The current consensus is to reduce the swap file size down to around two or three times the amount of RAM (Figure 15.13), meaning a system with 64 MB of RAM is going to have its swap file set somewhere around 128 to 192 MB. Set both the minimum and maximum to the same number.

Certain programs demand large swap files. If you use programs like CorelDRAW, you will find that the "two to three times" rule won't work. Gradually increase these settings until the "Not Enough Memory" errors go away.

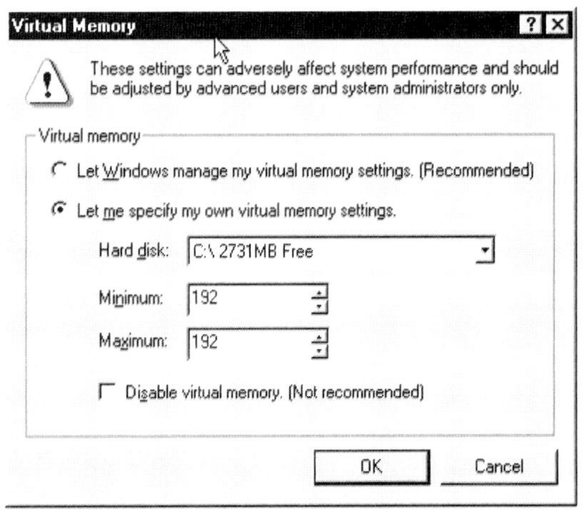

• **Figure 15.13** Set swap file size according to RAM.

Disk Cache

Running applications is an inherently messy job. The CPU asks for files, uses them, and drops them out of RAM only to turn around a split second later and request the same files. As you can imagine, this process is not necessarily efficient, but it works.

A disk-caching program such as *Vcache* that comes standard in Windows grabs a small section of RAM and monitors the files requested by the CPU. If the CPU starts asking for the same files over and over from the hard drive, the disk cache grabs a copy of those files. The next time the CPU requests those files, the disk caching program steps up and presents the files, much faster than the hard drive could ever respond and send.

Every version of Windows sets aside a small bit of RAM for a **disk cache**. Disk caches increase the efficiency of Windows. Vcache does a great job, but that doesn't mean you can't tweak the disk cache settings to optimize performance!

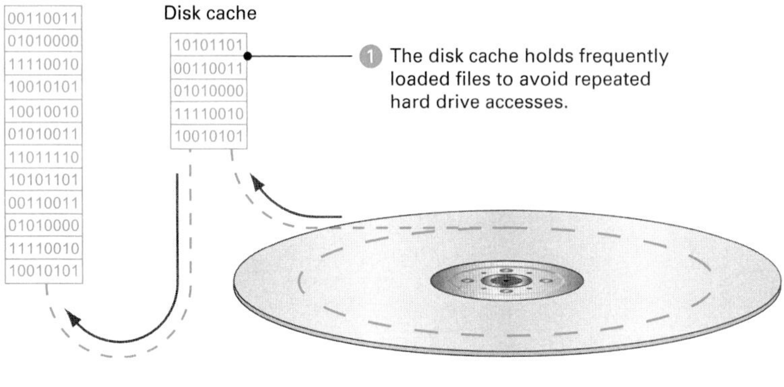

• **Figure 15.14** Read-ahead optimization

The disk caching that comes with Windows installs automatically and is virtually maintenance-free. The size of the disk cache is roughly one-fourth the total size of the RAM. Windows automatically sets the size of the disk-cache holding pen based on settings that are given at setup. You can change these settings by accessing System Properties | Performance tab | File System button, which opens the File System Properties dialog box.

There are two settings for changing the disk cache, both found on the Hard Disk tab: Typical role of this computer and Read-ahead optimization. The Typical role setting determines how much RAM to set aside for the disk cache holding pen. Setting this to Network server can produce a moderate performance boost.

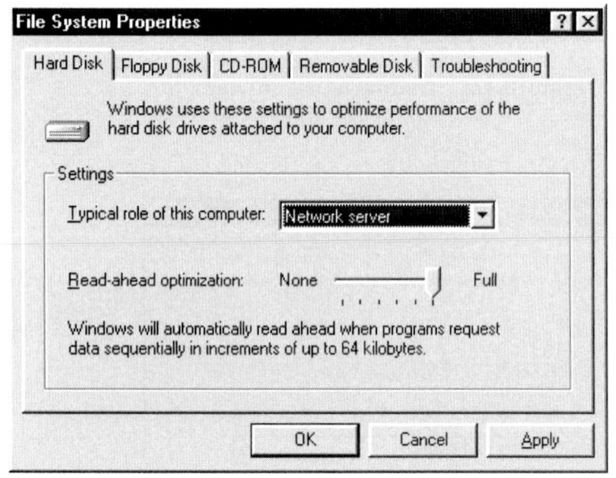

• **Figure 15.15** Sliding bar adjusts read-ahead

Read-ahead optimization determines how much to read ahead when the system goes to the hard drive. Think about this for a minute. The disk cache doesn't think in terms of files; it thinks in terms of clusters. When the hard drive asks for data, it's actually asking for a number of clusters, because files tend to span many clusters. So if the system asks for one cluster, what are the chances that it will come back in a few milliseconds and ask for the next cluster? Pretty good, it seems. So, why not have the disk cache grab a few more clusters, on the assumption that the program will ask for them? This is called the read-ahead (Figure 15.14). You can adjust the read-ahead using a sliding bar (Figure 15.15). It should always be set to Full. This enables the disk cache to read ahead 64 K worth of clusters, or two to four clusters ahead on most systems.

Resource Tracking Tools

Even though default Windows installations come well optimized, many Windows systems experience substantial system degradation over time. Good disk maintenance and basic optimization take you only so far on systems before they begin to suffer slowdowns. Most of the trouble stems from software bloat—too many programs trying to run at the same time. Sure, we know that opening a number of applications at once eats memory, but the average system is stuffed with background programs that also consume memory. Before we begin to inspect the culprits, you need to know how to use the necessary tools to watch for these problems. These tools will also come into play for other problems.

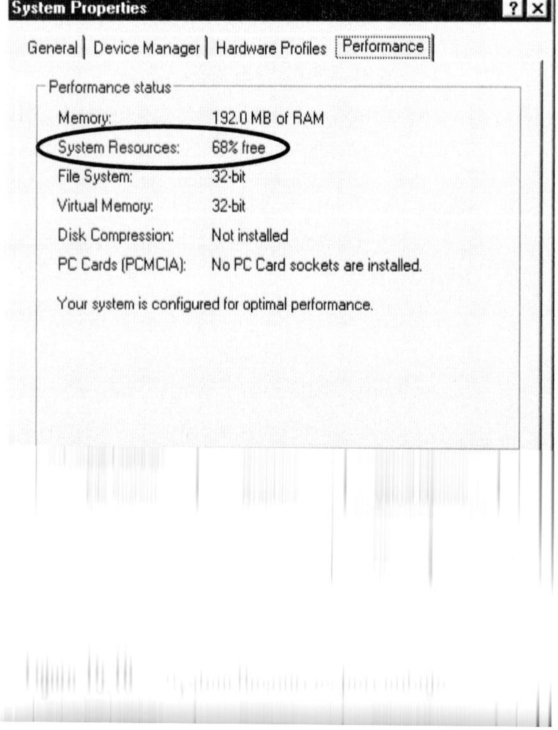

System Resources

One area that many techs look to for system resource information on a Windows 9*x*/Me system is the System Resources percentage on the Performance tab of System

lowest value for the System Resources usage. Many systems can run down into the low 20s with absolutely no ill effect.

System Monitor

My favorite tool for checking system problems is the **System Monitor**. The System Monitor provides a graphic snapshot of a broad number of system processes. You can track free physical memory, CPU usage, network throughput—in fact, almost any process where you need to see what's happening on your PC (Figure 15.17). To open the System Monitor, click Start | Programs | Accessories | System Tools | System Monitor.

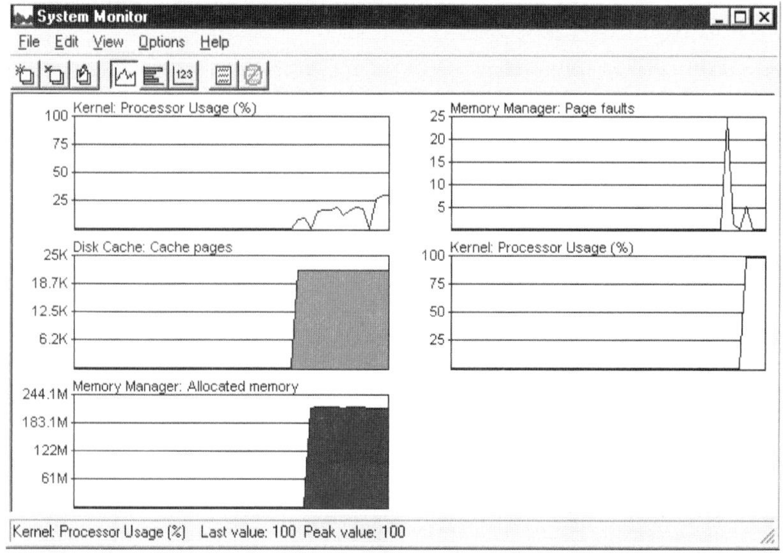

• **Figure 15.17** System Monitor

Try This!

Using the System Monitor

The system monitor contains many useful utilities. To become familiar with this tool, and find out which parts are useful for you, try this!

1. Open the System Monitor. Select Edit | Add Item… to open a dialog box with a selection of system activities you can choose to monitor.
2. Try monitoring a variety of system activities. In particular, select Cache Hits under Disk Cache, Processor Usage (%) under Kernel, and Allocated Memory under Memory Management. Can you see how these would be useful? Which ones seem less useful to you?
3. From the main System monitor screen, select Options | Chart to open the Options dialog box. Use the slide bar to increase and decrease the update interval. What do you think is the most useful setting?

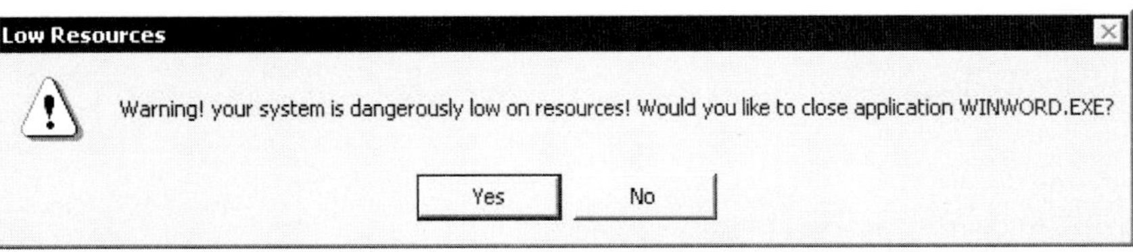

• **Figure 15.18** Overfilled heap error

System Resource Meter

Heaps are limited in size and are prone to filling up on some systems. While sometimes an overfilled heap will provide an error, as shown in Figure 15.18, other heap overflows may lock up the system. One clear result of heap filling is substantial system slowdown. To keep an eye on your heaps, use the System Resource Meter (Figure 15.19). To open the System Resource Meter, click Start | Programs | Accessories | System Tools | System Resource Meter.

This handy tool does a much better job of showing you where problems lie. I always load this when I notice a system slowdown—it runs quite nicely from the system tray. As I load applications, I see which ones are eating heap space. If I don't see any substantial heap space usage, I usually head for the System Monitor to look for other problems.

Task Manager

You access the Task Manager by pressing CTRL-ALT-DEL. The Task Manager shows all running programs, including hidden ones (Figure 15.20). I often use the Task Manager in concert with the System Resource Meter to close background programs that seem to defy all other attempts to close them. It's also a good tool to close an unresponsive program without having to crash the entire system. Just

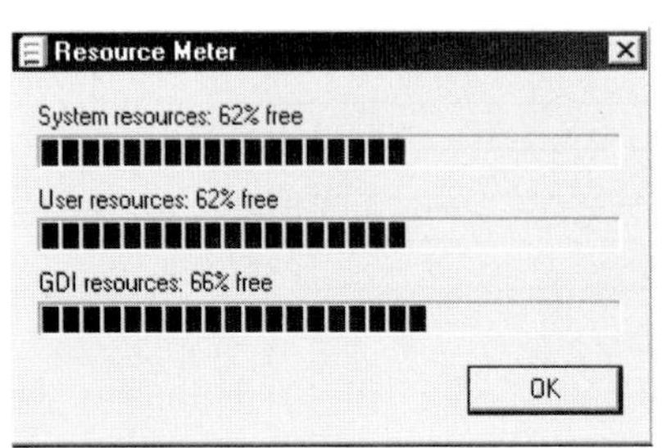

• **Figure 15.19** System Resource Meter watches heaps.

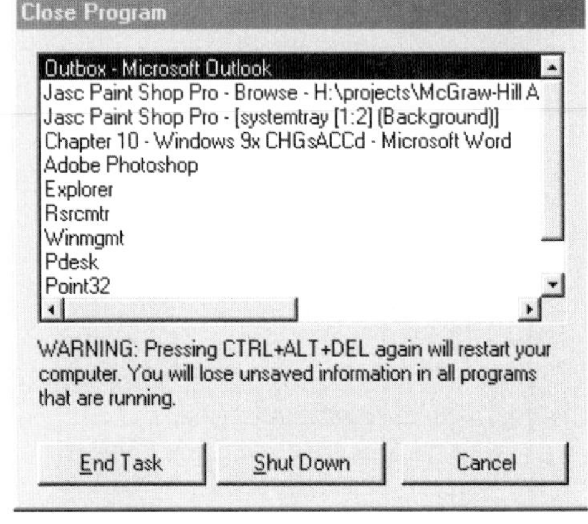

• **Figure 15.20** The Task Manager shows all programs.

remember not to close Explorer or Systray, as these two programs must run in order to keep Windows running.

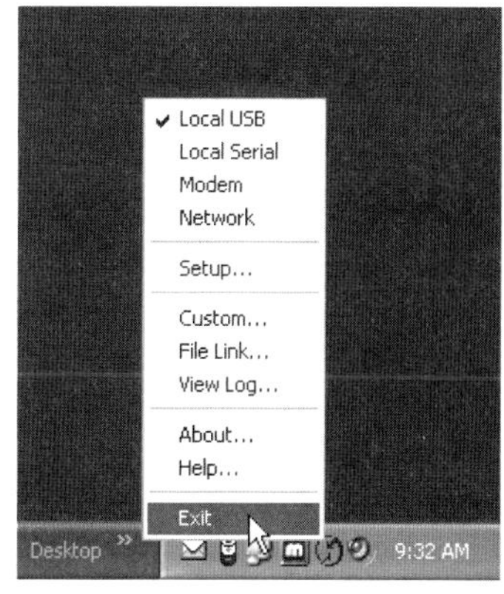

• **Figure 15.21** Remove unneeded [illegible]

Auto-Starting Programs

It seems that every third application installed on a PC today uses some form of background program. In most cases, this is perfectly acceptable—I want my antivirus program to run constantly, invisibly inspecting the system for problems. Yet when someone brings me a sluggish system, my first step is to boot normally and check the processor usage, the available physical memory, and the amount of the swap file in use by using the System Monitor. If the CPU constantly runs at nearly 100 percent, or if most of the physical memory is in use, I know that I've got way too many auto-starting [illegible] you don't (Figure 15.21).

If you have Windows 98 or Me, fire up the System Information program, and then open the System Configuration Utility from the Tools menu. Go to the Startup tab and uncheck suspicious programs. Don't turn off the System Tray. While you're here, click the WIN.INI tab and open the Windows folder to make sure that no programs are starting under Run= or Load= (Figure 15.22).

Finally, see what's running under AUTOEXEC.BAT. The TSRs rarely have much effect on Windows memory, but it never hurts to check.

If you use Windows 95, locate the \WINDOWS\START MENU\PROGRAMS\ STARTUP folder to locate auto-starting programs. Then run SYSEDIT to check the SYSTEM.INI and WIN.INI files.

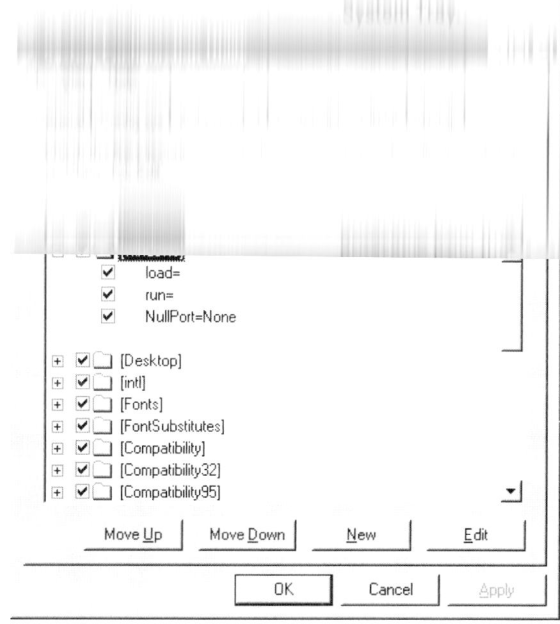

• **Figure 15.22** Check for programs loading in WIN.INI.

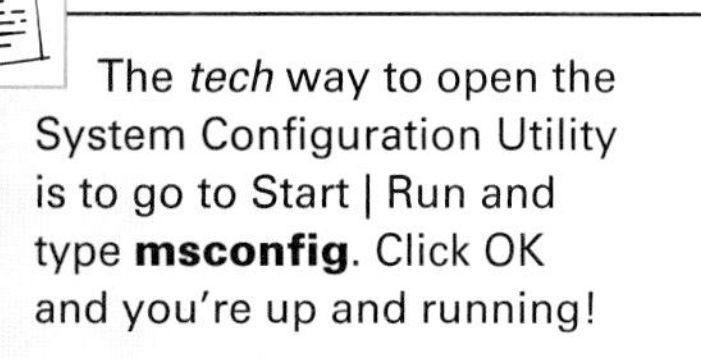

The *tech* way to open the System Configuration Utility is to go to Start | Run and type **msconfig**. Click OK and you're up and running!

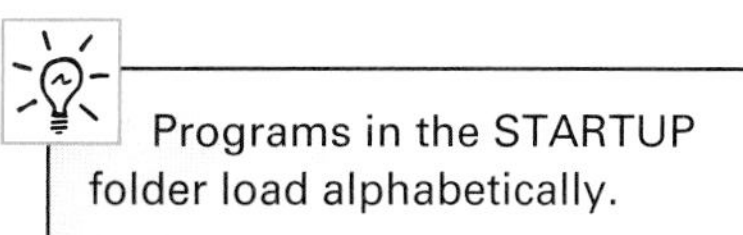

Programs in the STARTUP folder load alphabetically.

Installing Software

Once you have a Windows 9*x*/Me system up and running with the Task Scheduler set up to run maintenance programs such as ScanDisk and Defrag, you will invariably install application software. No matter how perfectly you have installed and optimized Windows, however, installing one poorly written application can completely trash the system. Part of proper system maintenance, therefore, requires you to get your system back to the way it was *before* you installed nasty Program X. There's really only one trick here: Get some kind of program that enables you to return

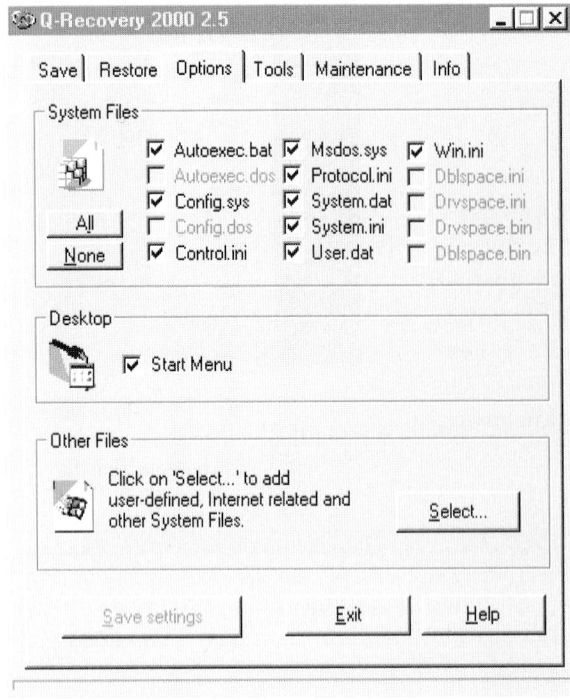

• **Figure 15.23** Q-Recovery

the system to its previous state in case the installation has problems. My favorite for Windows 9*x* is Q-Recovery from Hyper-Q (Figure 15.23).

Windows Me has a very good utility for taking a snapshot of your system and restoring it if you have a bad installation, called, appropriately, System Restore. Check the "Troubleshooting Windows 9*x*/Me" section of this chapter for a walk-through of System Restore.

■ Device Installation

Device installation, once the private domain of only the nerdiest of computer techs, has been completely transformed by the advent of *Plug and Play (PnP)*. Today almost anyone with the "do-it-yourself" spirit and enough sense to read instructions can easily succeed in installing most devices. Hard drives, CD-ROMs, motherboards, CPUs, and power supplies are, or at least should be, the few components that still require our skills. As long as the user does basic anti-ESD procedures, everything else is, honestly, a snap to install. But for all the promise of PnP, we still see a number of problems arise that require us to support device installation.

Let's look at device installation first from the perfect scenario: a truly PnP device with full PnP support from both the OS—in this example, Windows 98–and a PnP BIOS.

Most PnP install problems start due to lack of basic procedure knowledge as to how to install a PnP device. Let me show you my process for purchasing and installing PnP devices.

Before You Buy

Most hardware installation failures take place long before you put a screwdriver in your hand. They take place at the store or the web site where you purchased the device. When purchasing a device, follow these basic rules:

Know What You Need

Too many people buy the wrong hardware for their needs. Never walk into a store saying, "I need a sound card." Instead first ask yourself, "What do I want the sound card to do for me?" Make sure, whether you purchase the device for yourself or for a customer, that you have a solid understanding of the expectations. Will this sound card be for games? Do you just want to hear basic system sounds? Would you like to play CD-ROMs? How about DVD? What kind of speakers will you want? As you might anticipate, this often reduces itself to you making your best guess and spending a good amount of time educating yourself or the customer. When purchasing a device, you must juggle with four variables:

- What do I need this device to do?
- What are the expectations of the device?

- Can I or the customer afford it?
- How much do we care about this device?

Answering these questions takes time. I spend far more time researching my needs than I do actually getting the device. Every piece of PC technology changes so fast that I daily find myself confronted with a new term that I've never heard before. Never be afraid to ask questions. Remember, the most telling statement as to the quality and skill of a PC tech is his or her ability to say, "I don't know!" You need a lot of confidence to look a customer, boss, or spouse in the eye and say, "I don't know" on the one topic where everyone says you are the ultimate expert. I never trust techs with all the answers. No tech knows everything about PCs!

Physical Compatibility

[illegible] input, and you're out of power connections.

System Compatibility

Once you know, or at least feel comfortable, that the device will install into your system, you must then consider the possibility of system incompatibility. Suppose you bought a Zip drive that plugs into your parallel port. You already have a printer on the parallel port, but the Zip drive has a pass-through connector that lets you plug the printer into the Zip drive. Will that work? Once I wanted to install a second video card into my Windows Me system so I could enjoy two monitors. Will this card support a two-monitor system?

The problem with these questions is that by this point you already know the device you want, and your mouse pointer is hovering over the Add To Cart button. System incompatibilities make for real frustration due to the fact that you probably must install the device to discover them. Watch out for restocking charges or expensive return shipping costs. Never buy from a vendor who doesn't provide at least a seven-day return policy, ever. After 15 years of PC support, I still find myself returning equipment roughly one out of every five purchases, and I buy some type of equipment twice a week!

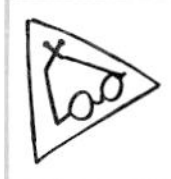

Tech Tip

Online Answers to Compatibility Questions

If you have system compatibility questions, start by surfing to the device maker's web site. Find the support area and check the frequently asked questions (FAQ) lists. If that doesn't give you an answer, or even if it does, send an e-mail to tech support. Between your fellow users/techs and the support guys, you're bound to find an answer your questions, and frequently find out a thing or two you never considered!

Driver Check

Always check the version of drivers that come with a device. Does the device you want have a driver for your OS? Most hardware comes with drivers for more mature OSs, like Windows XP, but may not for older (like Windows 95/98) or more offbeat OSs. I always check before I walk out of the store. Second, do you have the latest drivers? A large percentage of devices do not ship with the latest drivers. A quick check at the manufacturer's web site always settles this issue quickly.

Procedure Check

Okay, so now you are the proud owner of a new PnP device. Let's install that thing! Here are a few things to remember.

Create a Startup Disk

All versions of Windows 9*x*/Me provide the capability to create a startup disk. A **startup disk** is a bootable floppy disk that, in case of an emergency, enables you to boot to an A: prompt. We'll get into more detail later, but for now follow these steps:

1. Click Start | Settings | Control Panel to open the Control Panel.
2. Locate the Add/Remove Programs icon and click it.
3. Click the Startup Disk tab.
4. Get a blank floppy disk, and insert it into the floppy drive.
5. Click Create Disk.

Windows will then create a startup disk. This disk contains just enough files to perform basic troubleshooting. On some systems, Windows prompts for the Windows installation CD-ROM; on others it will not. After Windows has created the startup disk, take it out of the floppy drive and set it aside for later. Hopefully, you won't need it.

Many techs, myself included, use Windows 98 startup disks when working on Windows 95 systems—they work just fine!

One of the most important jobs for a startup disk is to enable you to gain access to your CD-ROM. Windows 95 startup disks lack the ability to provide access to the CD-ROM drive. You need to copy two files and edit two others so that a Windows 95 startup disk can access CD-ROMs. Windows 98 startup disks *do* provide CD-ROM access, so don't do this unless you still run Windows 95!

To make a Windows 95 startup disk that supports a CD-ROM drive, follow these steps:

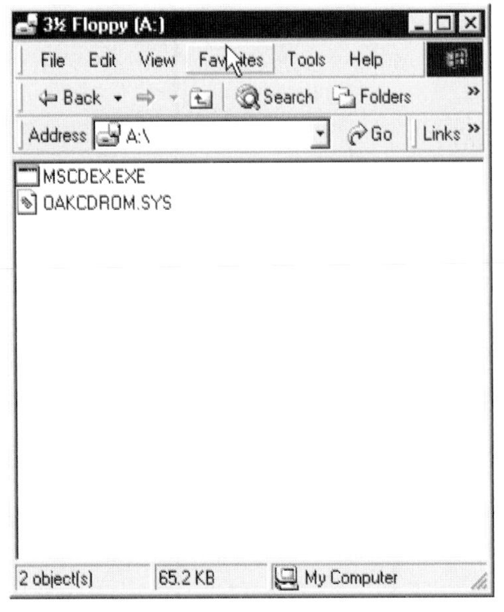

• **Figure 15.24** OAKCDROM.SYS and MSCDEX.EXE

1. Download a special device driver called OAKCDROM.SYS. Over 100 web sites provide this driver, but here's one: www.computerhope.com/drivers/cdrom.htm. Download the "Generic Driver." Remember, web sites change, so if this link stops working, just do a little searching—you'll find it! Copy the OAKCDROM.SYS file to the Windows 95 Startup disk.
2. Locate a file called MSCDEX.EXE on your system. Most systems store this file in the \WINDOWS\COMMAND folder. Copy the MSCDEX file to the floppy disk. Once you've done this, you should see both files on the floppy disk, as shown in Figure 15.24.
3. Go to the Run menu option in the Start menu, and type this command: **notepad a:\config.sys** to open the CONFIG.SYS file on the floppy disk for editing. Ignore any other text in the file; just add this line: **DEVICE=A:\CDROM.SYS /D:CDROM** to the end so it looks like Figure 15.25. Save and exit Notepad.

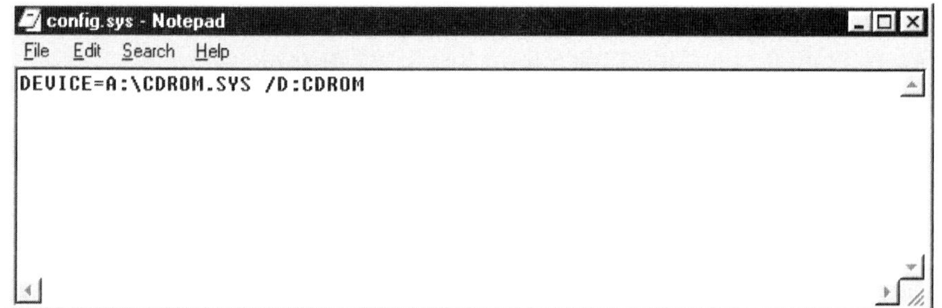

• **Figure 15.25** CONFIG.SYS

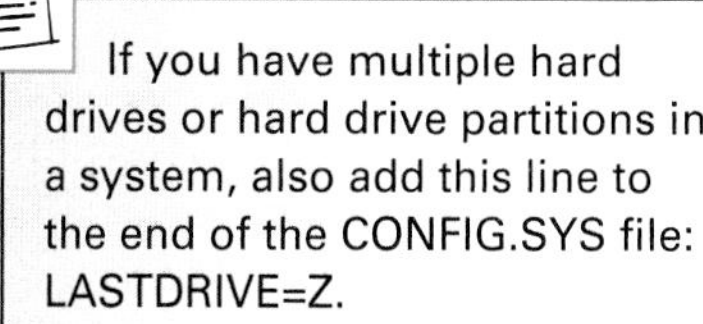

If you have multiple hard drives or hard drive partitions in a system, also add this line to the end of the CONFIG.SYS file: LASTDRIVE=Z.

4. Go to the Run menu option

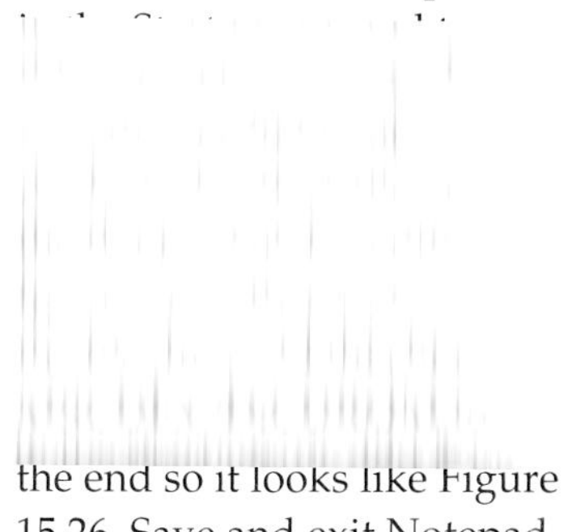

the end so it looks like Figure 15.26. Save and exit Notepad.

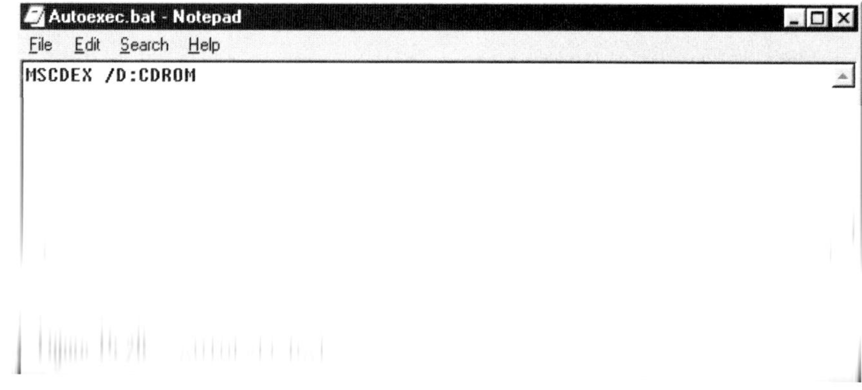

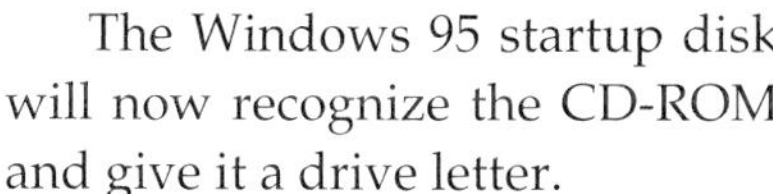

The Windows 95 startup disk will now recognize the CD-ROM and give it a drive letter.

Backup

The five most important backup steps before you install are listed here:

1. Back up the Registry.
2. Back up the Registry.
3. Back up the Registry.
4. Back up the Registry.
5. And ... back up the Registry.

When you install a new device, Windows changes the Registry to reflect that new device. If you back up the Registry and something goes wrong, you just restore the Registry and try again. Failure to back up the Registry means pain and heartache and an occasional complete system rebuild.

Try This!

Backing Up the Registry

There are so many ways to back up the Registry that listing them all would take forever. Depending on the version, Windows 9*x*/Me provides a number of methods to back up the Registry, and many third-party vendors provide excellent backup tools. Both Windows and third-party programs contain many powerful extras and conveniences that make them very worthwhile. But you don't need them just to back up the Registry. Just try this!

(Use My Computer or Windows Explorer to perform these backup steps. If you really want to, you can do it from a command prompt in Windows 95/98, but why make life hard?)

1. Create a folder called C:\BACK.
2. Open the C:\WINDOWS\SYSTEM folder.
3. Make sure to set the View option to Show All Files.
4. Turn off all the file attributes on the Windows Registry files: SYSTEM.DAT and USER.DAT. (Forgot how? Here's your clue: Properties!)
5. Copy SYSTEM.DAT and USER.DAT to the C:\BACK folder.

Congratulations. You just backed up the Registry.

Tech Tip

"I Am Not Responsible for Your Data"

Although the A+ Certification exams always say to do a full system backup (completely back up everything) before you even look at a computer, I rarely do a full system backup for basic device installs. The chances of messing up a drive by snapping in a card or plugging something into a port are very low. If I'm installing for someone else, however, I always give the same speech before I touch anything. I won't quote the whole routine, but it boils down to: "I am not responsible for your data." If they want me to back up their system, fine, but they get charged for my time. Have you ever taken a system into a shop for repair? That little piece of paper you sign invariably includes a "we're not responsible for your data" clause. Follow their lead and cover yourself, or at least have a boss you can hide behind if you wipe out all their data. Believe me, it can happen!

You can use the REGEDIT program to make a backup of the Registry. Start REGEDIT and select the Export Registry File option from the Registry menu. Select the All radio button and give the location where you wish to save the backup copy of the Registry. Your entire Registry will be stored as a REG file. Be careful—a complete backup copy of the Registry can easily surpass multiple megabytes! You can restore the Registry by using the Import Registry File from the Registry menu in REGEDIT.

REGEDIT also works from a command prompt. If you can't even get Windows to boot and you have a backup copy you would like to restore, try booting to Safe Mode Command Prompt Only and running a Registry restore. Here's the same backup creation operation, only using the command line:

```
regedit /l:c:\windows\system.dat /c c:\back\backup.dat
```

where "/l:c\windows\system.dat" is the location of the SYSTEM.DAT file and "/c c:\back\backup.dat" is the location and name of the backup file you made.

If anything doesn't go the way you want and you want to return the system to exactly the way it was before you tried installing that #^%$ device, just restore the Registry. To restore the Registry, boot from a startup floppy disk to an A: prompt, and copy the backup version into the system directory to overwrite the 'bad' version using the following command:

```
copy c:\back\*.dat c:\windows\system
```

Packaging

Remove the device carefully and try not to trash the packaging in case you ever need to return the device. Use proper anti-ESD procedures. Keep the packaging or tell the customer to keep the packaging. If possible, keep it until the warranty runs out.

Read Me!

Read every scrap of documentation. Which disk holds the drivers? What procedure do I need to follow? I know you want to pop in your new toy, but first you need to sit down and read. Check for a file on the install CD-ROM or floppy disk called README.DOC or READ.ME or README.TXT. These files always provide critical information and notice of late-breaking issues.

Make sure you understand the setup process. I once bought a USB video camera that I couldn't get to work. The install instructions clearly said: "Do not insert the camera until after the drivers are installed!" Did I read that? No. Was I sorry? Yes! Replacing one device with another invariably requires you to delete the old device from your Device Manager before you install a new one. Video cards almost always demand this procedure. If the documentation tells you to delete a driver, jump down to the "Device Manager" section to see how to delete old drivers.

Physical Installation

Now, finally, we get to have some fun! Plug in that new device where it needs to go. Don't forget your anti-static procedures. Check, double-check, and then triple-check connections, power, and any switches or jumpers that the device needs. Fortunately, you read all the documentation and know all about any special issues—deal with those now. Boot the system and go to CMOS.

CMOS Issues

Watch out for the many little gotchas that may come into play here. If you're using a serial or parallel port, make sure to activate it and set it to any special COM or LPT settings your device needs. USB devices usually need an IRQ, so check to see that Assign IRQ to USB is active if you're dealing with USB. Most PnP CMOS options are fine by default. Only make changes in here if something goes wrong or if you install legacy devices. Because this is the perfect PnP scenario, you shouldn't have to mess with the PnP settings unless you run into problems. Reboot the system.

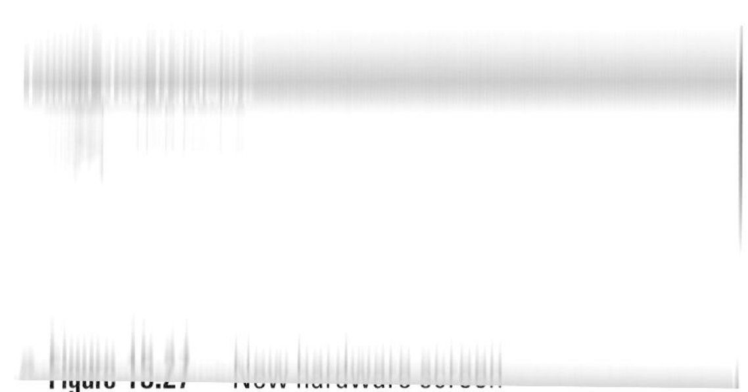

ally also come with any other files the hardware device needs, but the INF file is what Windows will look for when it prompts for a device driver. This often gets techs in trouble as many devices will come with many different device drivers for different operating systems with each driver getting its own directory on the installation CD-ROM or floppy diskette. If you're installing a new device and Windows can't find the device driver on the installation disk, check to make sure the INF file isn't tucked away in some subdirectory on the install disk. If it is, just point Windows to the right folder.

Many systems give the "Windows has found unknown hardware and is installing software..." message. This usually comes from installing two devices at once, one depending on the other for connection to the system, like a new video card and monitor. This is fine; Windows will eventually find the unknown device, although it may take a few reboots, especially with Windows 95.

Figure 15.28 Windows Me responding to a new device installed

Checking

Once the device installs, it's time to check it out. The first place we look to verify a good install is the Device Manager.

Device Manager

The Device Manager is the primary tool for dealing with devices and device drivers in Windows, a fact you'll recall from Chapter 12. The Device Manager

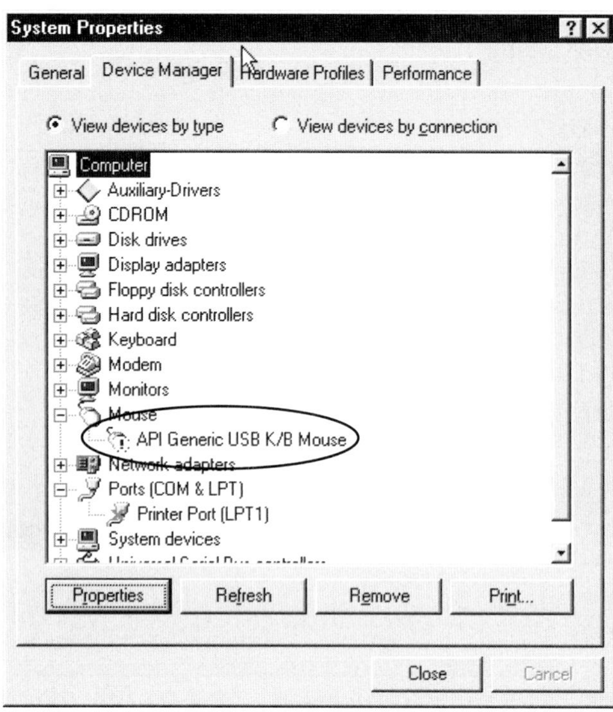

• **Figure 15.29** The Device Manager detects a problem.

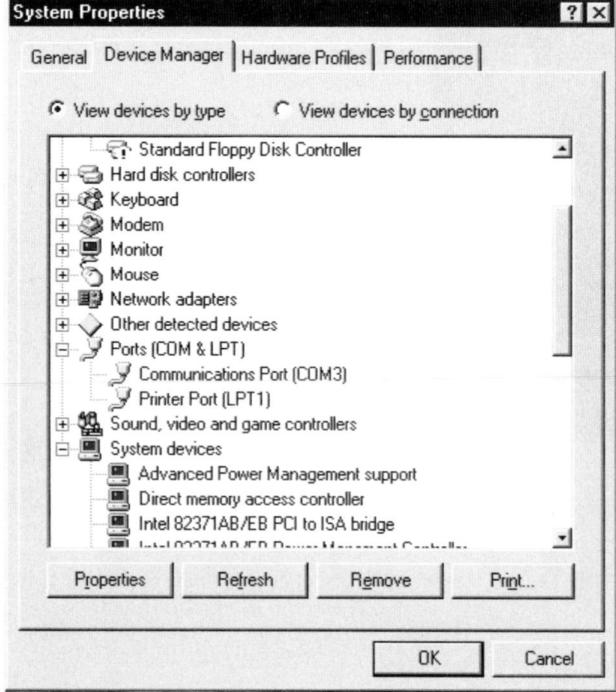

• **Figure 15.30** Installed COM and LPT ports

displays every device that Windows recognizes. Figure 15.29 shows a typical Device Manager screen with all installed devices in good order with the exception of the mouse. If Windows detects a problem, it shows the device with a red "X" or a yellow exclamation point, as you'll see in the next section.

The Device Manager organizes devices in special groups called *types*. All devices of the same type are grouped under the same type heading. To see the devices of a particular type, you must open that type's group. Figure 15.30 shows the Ports type opened, revealing the COM and LPT ports on the system.

By double-clicking a device (or by selecting the device and clicking the Properties button) and then clicking the Resources tab, you can see the resources used by that device.

Applications

A new piece of hardware is useless without some application that uses it. Where the application comes from really depends on the device and the version of Windows. But we can break down applications into five groups: Built-in, Enhanced, Supplied Critical, Supplied Helpful, and Supplied Optional.

Built-in

Windows comes with applications for many devices. Windows has complete support for a network card via the Network Neighborhood, for example, or for a CD-ROM via My Computer or Windows Explorer.

Enhanced

Many new devices supported by Windows come with greatly enhanced applications. The best example of this is Zip drives. While most versions of Windows provide basic support for Zip drives, Iomega adds extra applications that provide password protection, better formatting, and other options that Windows alone cannot provide.

Supplied Critical

Supplied critical applications come with the install CD-ROM, and you must install them to make the hardware work. That new USB docking station for your Palm Pilot won't do a thing without the synchronization software. You must install these applications.

Supplied Helpful

Supplied helpful applications come with the CD-ROM and may help but are not really required. My new USB camera came with this little utility that lets me do video captures. I don't plan to do video captures, but I may decide to install it just in case.

Supplied Optional

Supplied optional really means "supplied but I doubt you'll want it." Your new modem might come with an America Online CD-ROM, but you already have an Internet service provider. Or your new sound card comes with a "Historical Tour of Musical Instruments," but you bought the sound card to play online games. Don't fill your drive with applications you will never use.

Dealing with Plug and Play Problems

Time to jump out of fantasyland and move into the more unpleasant aspect of device installation: installation problems. Even in a perfect PnP world, I'd estimate that about one in every five installations creates unanticipated errors. Let's break these errors down and see how to deal with them.

Windows Plug and Play Can't Find a Driver

Most techs feel that failure to find a correct device driver stands as the most common PnP install issue. Although we see some variance between Windows versions, basically every version of Windows always brings up the Add New Hardware Wizard and immediately moves to the "please tell me the location of the driver" screen, as shown in Figure 15.31.

The issue boils down to the fact that Windows PnP queried the new device and knows that the device exists but cannot find the correct INF for that device. In most cases, just click the Have Disk button and point the installer to the proper directory location. You know the correct directory location because you looked this up in the documentation. If you didn't look (like that would ever happen!), use the Browse feature to navigate around the install CD-ROM/floppy until the Add New Hardware Wizard finds an INF file (Figure 15.32).

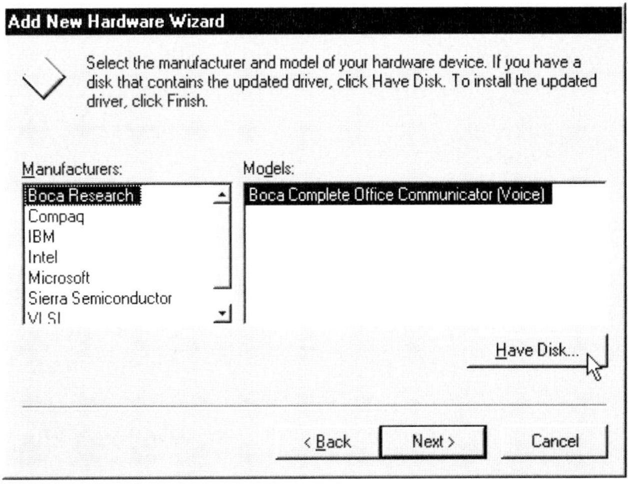

• **Figure 15.31** Windows prompts the user for the device driver.

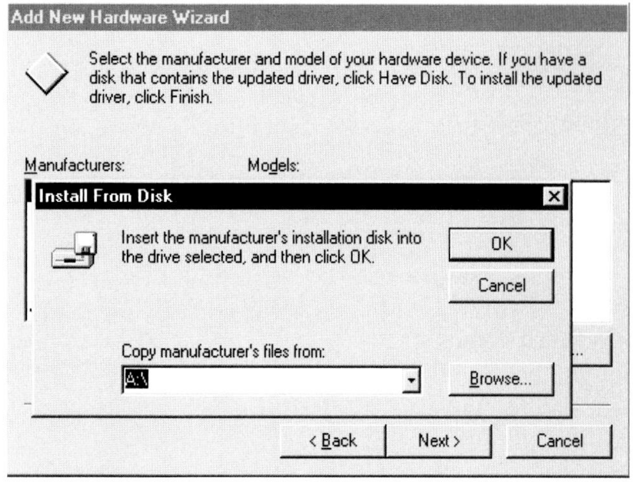

• **Figure 15.32** Browsing to find the INF file

Use a little common sense here! If you have a Windows 98 system and the install floppy shows the following folders, guess where to look first:

A:\LINUX	A:\NETWARE4	A:\NETWARE5	A:\NT4
A:\WIN2K	A:\WIN95	A:\WIN98	

Please tell me you picked the A:\WIN98 folder!

Make sure you insert the correct install disk, especially with Windows 9*x*/Me, or you might install the wrong driver, requiring you to delete the device from the Device Manager and try again. In some cases, installing the wrong driver wreaks havoc: Windows copies the INF file to the \INF folder, so even if you delete the device from the Device Manager, Windows keeps reinstalling the wrong driver! To stop this action, you must first watch Windows as it installs. This happened to me recently (Yes, I screw up every day!), and I documented it.

I purchased the Compaq iPAQ *Personal Digital Assistant* (PDA). It comes with a little USB cradle that enables you to "synch" your e-mail, web sites, contacts, and so on, between a desktop system and the PDA. When I installed the cradle, I didn't bother reading the instructions, which clearly said to install the synch program before plugging in the device. I just plugged in the device and quickly installed the wrong driver. When I dropped the PDA into the cradle, the system locked up. After a quick scan of the documentation, I said, "Oops!" and promptly deleted the "Compaq Aero USBSync" device from the Device Manager (Figure 15.33).

I rebooted, and it immediately reinstalled itself. Ouch. The fix to this problem required using the Search/Find menu to locate the INF file that contained the offending device. I knew that I needed to find the INF containing the text "Compaq Aero," so I just searched for it in the \INF folder, and it appeared! See Figure 15.34.

Once I found it, I simply deleted it and did a complete uninstall/reinstall, this time according to the directions provided (and a phone call to Compaq tech support). I'll never neglect reading the documentation again—well, at least for another two weeks.

Many times hardware makers hide device drivers and INF files in a setup program. You must run the program to get all the files you need. In many cases, these setup programs don't really set up anything; they just uncompress themselves into a folder on the hard drive. Watch them as they unpack themselves; they always clearly show the destination folder. You can then rerun the Install Wizard and point it to the folder the setup program created.

Windows Plug and Play Doesn't See Device

The second most common install error occurs when PnP doesn't see the device you just installed. You know this happens when you install the device and nothing happens. Always check the Device Manager to see if the device installed! A fast Windows 9*x* system may display the install screens so quickly you miss them, and Windows Me is even quicker! Let's assume you checked the Device Manager, and you're positive the device is not there.

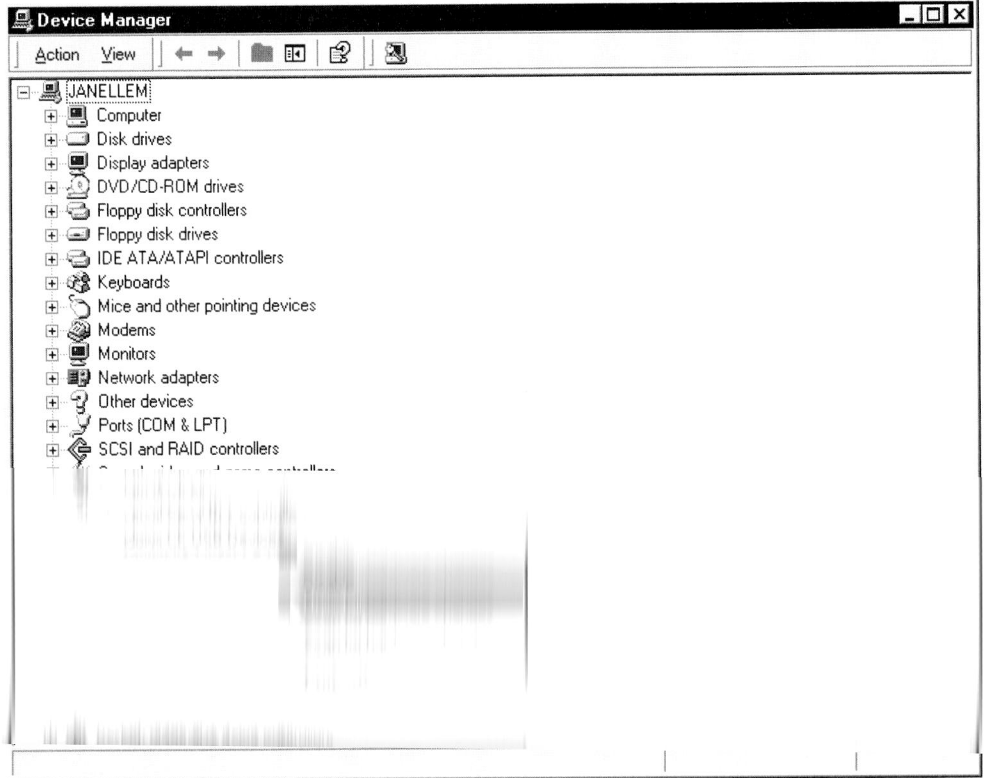

• **Figure 15.33** Removing a device in Device Manager

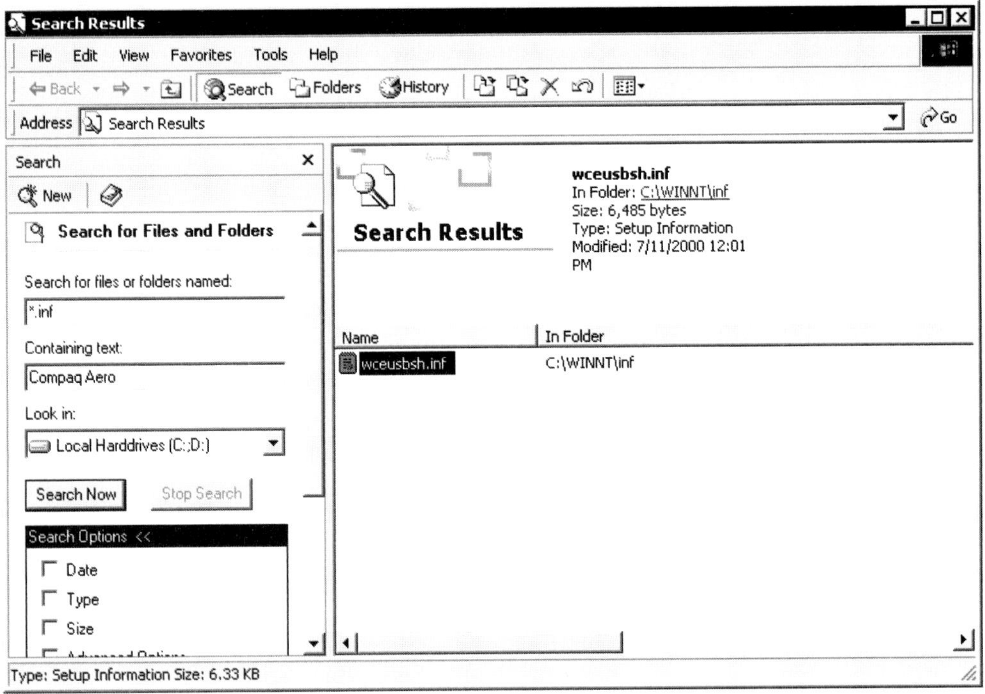

• **Figure 15.34** INF file for Compaq Aero PDA

Not Plug and Play

Make sure the device truly is PnP! No one makes legacy hardware anymore, but plenty of legacy devices still lurk at hardware swap meets, eBay, and other places. Look at the device to see if it uses any I/O addresses or IRQ jumpers, and check for jumpers or switches saying "PnP/jumperless." Many late-generation legacy devices used software installation (jumperless) configuration. If you don't have the software you need, check the device maker's web site to see if they still support the legacy device. If they don't, throw the device in the trash!

Try Again

Assuming you know you have a PnP device, shut off the system after a proper shutdown and remove the device. Reseat the device in the slot or connector and try again. PCI and AGP cards really need tight seating or they won't work. Verify all connections and make sure the device has power if it needs it. Reboot to see if Windows detects the device. Recheck the Device Manager.

Resources

Windows may fail to see a PnP device if other devices are using all its available resources. This rarely happens in PnP systems; in most cases, the Windows PnP sees the device and lists it in the Device Manager but cannot configure it. Find the fix for resource conflict resolution later in the "Legacy Devices in a Plug and Play World" section of this chapter.

Bad BIOS

Always verify that your system has the latest BIOS. Name-brand PC makers list BIOS updates by system model. Check the motherboard maker's web site for BIOS updates for your motherboard. If your system is more than two years old, a BIOS update almost certainly exists.

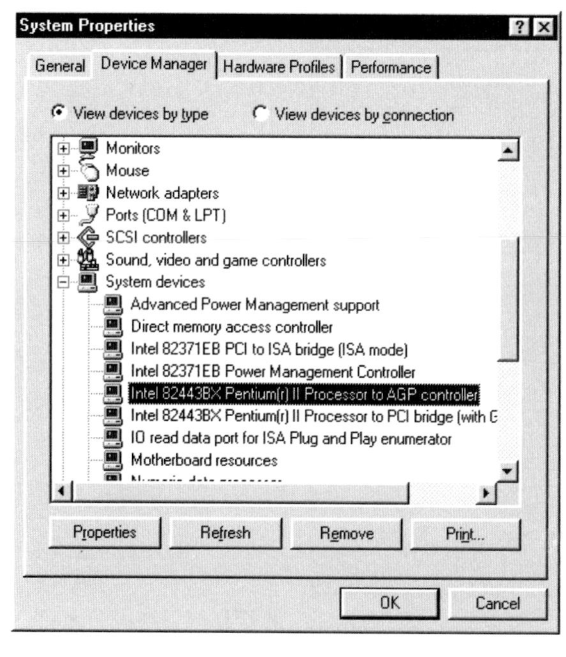

• **Figure 15.35** Proper chipset driver

Chipset Anyone?

Chipsets need drivers just like any other device on the PC. Operating systems only contain drivers for chipsets as old as they are. If a new chipset comes out, they invariably fail to see it, causing other problems such as PnP failures. That's why so many motherboards come with a driver CD-ROM—to support newer chipsets on older operating systems. Take a look in the Device Manager under System devices to see if the system installed the proper chipsets for your system, as shown in Figure 15.35. If not, you need to get them!

Blame the Hardware?

When all else fails, blame the device. You may want to try inserting the device into another slot or port (if another one exists), but otherwise you need to point your finger at the device, return it from whence it came, and move on!

Device Manager Errors

Windows often sees a PnP device and tries to install it, but for one reason or another fails to install the device properly. Unlike errors where the PnP simply fails to see the device, these devices show in the Device Manager, but they show one of two possible errors. If a device has a problem, it will show up with an exclamation point surrounded by a small yellow dot. A small red "X" on a device means the device has been disabled by Windows. Figure 15.36 shows an example of both problem icons.

There's really no difference between the two errors in terms of how I deal with them. The bottom line is that the device "ain't working," and I need to fix it. Anyone reading the

- Outdated BIOS
- Resource conflict
- Corrupted Registry
- Bad device

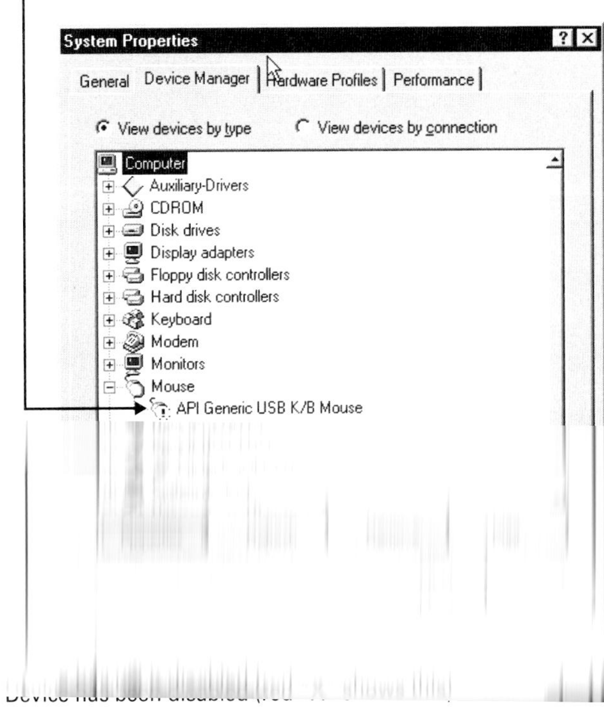

• **Figure 15.36** Improperly installed device errors

Failure to Follow Install Procedures

Failure to follow proper install procedures isn't really a Windows error; it's a human error that causes most of the Windows errors you're about to learn! All PnP devices require a very careful series of steps to ensure proper installation, particularly when you're replacing one device with a different one. You must read all documentation *carefully* before installing—have I harped on this enough yet?

Some of the more common install procedures include the following:

- Deleting the old driver first
- Running some SETUP program
- Checking for hardware incompatibilities
- Verifying the version number of some Windows EXE, DLL, or driver

Every device maker provides this information through documentation, but the last item, version numbers, deserves a little extra attention. Every device driver, Windows EXE, and Windows DLL comes with a version number. You can verify the driver version of an installed device by checking the device's properties in Device Manager. Open the Driver tab (Figure 15.37). You can check the version by clicking the Driver File Details button and then use the Update Driver button if needed. We discuss *when* to do this next. For now,

> There are situations where disabling a device comes in handy, such as disabling an unused network card. Any device can be intentionally disabled in Device Manager in all versions of Windows (except NT, which doesn't have Device Manager).

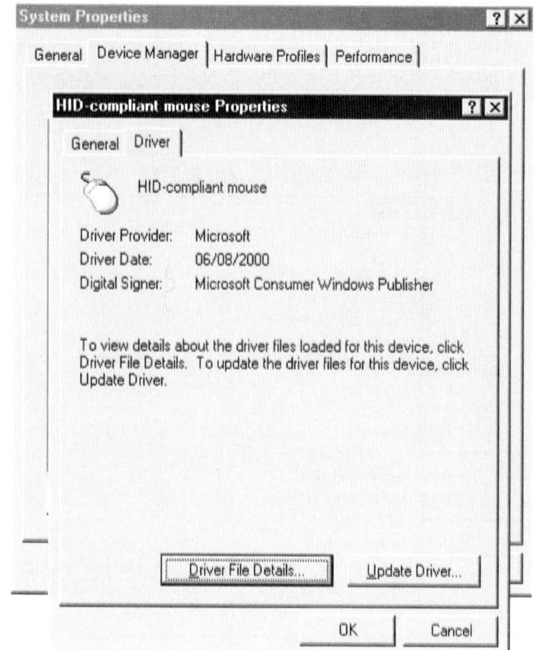

• **Figure 15.37** Driver tab for a device driver

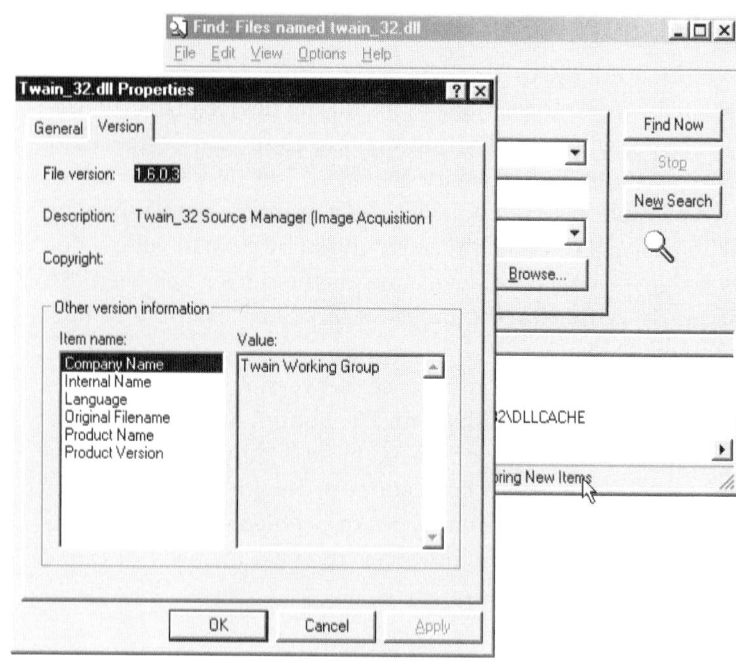

• **Figure 15.38** Verifying the file's version

just make sure you know *where* to find these options. Many times some documentation asks you to verify the version of a certain Windows EXE or DLL before you install. Just use the Search/Find utility to locate the file and click the Version tab in the file's properties to find that information (Figure 15.38).

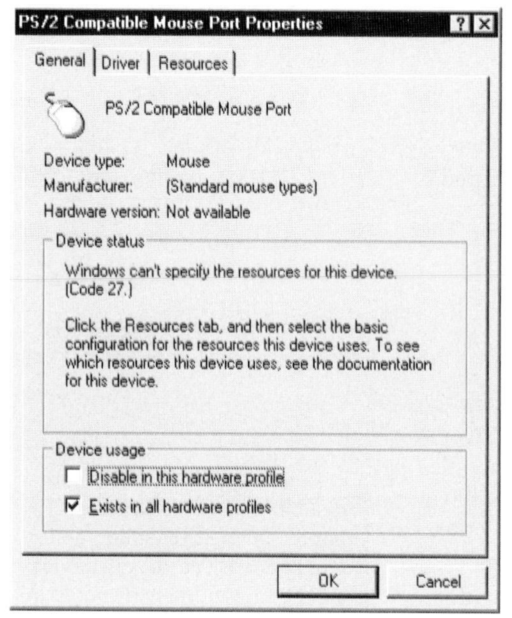

• **Figure 15.39** Error code example

A Word on Error Codes

One more item before we hit the fixes for device errors: error codes. When a device shows an error, you can use the General tab under the device's properties in Device Manager to get a clue as to where the problem lies. You will see some text with a code number (Figure 15.39). The Microsoft Knowledge Base lists all the code numbers under article number Q125174, if you want to look it up. The A+ Certification exams do not expect you to memorize them; just read the text and you'll know which of the following fixes to try first. Okay, armed with this information, let's look at how I group Device Manager errors.

Corruption/Incompatibility with Drivers or INF File

Let's start with the first part: corruption. Files get corrupted all the time. An install CD-ROM may get a scratch at the location of a critical driver; Windows may decide to lock up for some reason halfway through copying an INF file; or maybe Windows will decide to copy files onto a hard drive sector that dies half a second after they get copied. Whenever I see any error text complain about "not reading a driver," "couldn't find a driver," or "failing to load a driver," I immediately delete the driver, reboot, and try again. If that doesn't work, I download a driver from the device manufacturer's web site. Still no good? I check the hard drive. That usually fixes it.

Incompatibilities tend to be more of a challenge. The Windows platform and hardware technologies evolve so quickly that incompatibilities show up constantly. The newer the technology, the more you see it. That's why I never like to be the "first kid on the block" with the newest, coolest device or latest OS—at least when it's a system I need to rely upon. That attitude of "gotta have the newest" invariably puts you on the "bleeding edge" of technology.

One of the most famous incompatibilities shows up as the always-amusing "Unknown Device" and "Unsupported Device" errors (Figure 15.40). These errors crack me up! Basically, Windows knows that something is taking resources but has no idea *what*. If you see several device errors or unknown devices, incompatibility may be the culprit. After

nickel), and they talked and yelled and made me do all kinds of evil things to my system until they eventually discovered that my chipset was too old to support USB! The bottom line was that I couldn't upgrade the BIOS, so I needed a new motherboard. The fix was easy, but finding the incompatibility took time.

Remember, no matter how far out into "bleeding-edge technology" you go, you're never alone. Five thousand other techs are staring at the same problem, all scratching their heads and trying to fix it. Wouldn't it be great if you could all work together? That's one of the main functions of Internet newsgroups! Every type of hardware and software has newsgroups. If you don't know where to start, go to alt.certification.a-plus first. A bunch of smart techs hang out there, and although our main focus is on the A+ Certification, we handle lots of tech support issues. Heck, if you hang around, you and I will get a chance to post to each other. Be sure to say hi!

Outdated Support Drivers

Good techs know when to try to fix something and when to call tech support! The better the techs, the faster they are at determining this.

If you visualize the CPU as the center of the computer, you'll notice that almost no devices connect directly to the CPU. There's always a chipset, a controller, or some other device between the CPU and the device you install. All these "middleman" devices also need device drivers. In many cases, that exclamation point or red "x" on the device you just installed in Device Manager points to a problem with another device that your new device plugs into. Most of the time these errors show up clearly because the support device *itself* shows an error, but sometimes it's not that easy.

Windows can provide rudimentary support for most chipsets, for example, but that doesn't always mean that the device support contains everything you need. Windows Me handles this nicely by putting a green question mark on devices that do not have optimal drivers, but that doesn't help us on

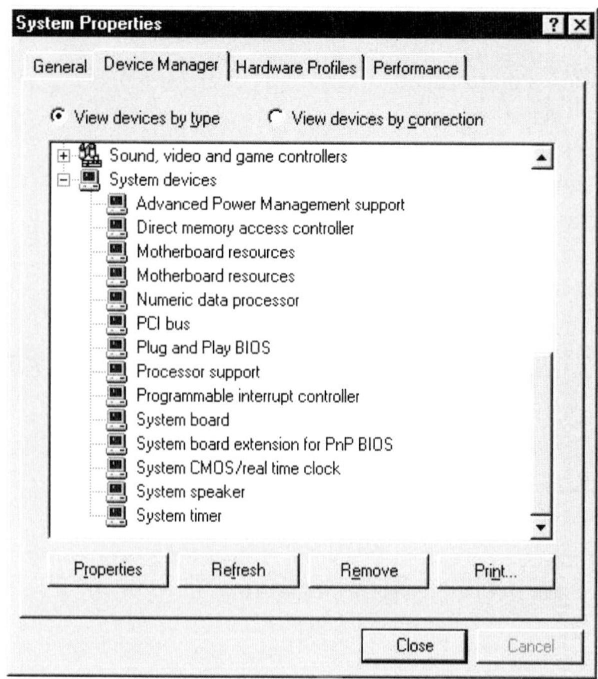

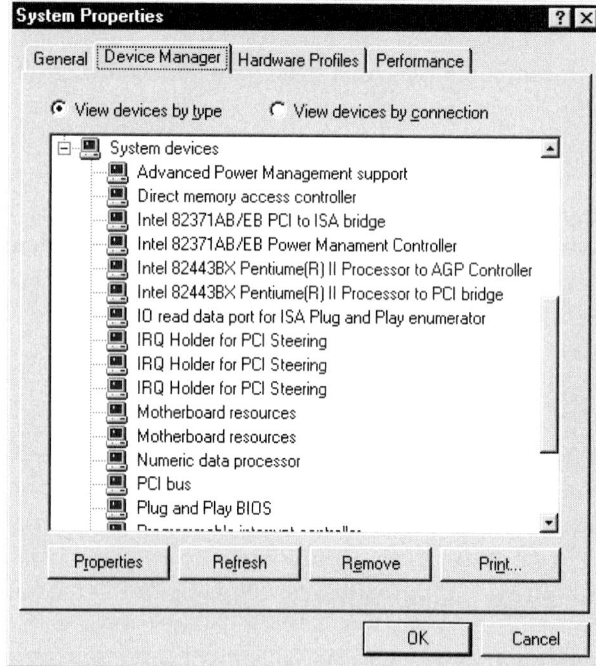

• **Figure 15.41** Default device drivers versus proper device drivers

95 or 98. Windows 98 has a device error that says, "I'm not working because device X isn't working," but it's not foolproof. A clue that a support device isn't fully supported can be found in the description of the support devices under the System heading in the Device Manager. Well-supported devices always have very detailed names, whereas less-supported devices tend to get less-detailed names. Compare these two close-ups of the same Windows 95 system's System devices heading: first with Windows default support drivers, then after I used the CD-ROM that came with the motherboard to upgrade all the support devices—quite a difference! (See Figure 15.41.)

Outdated BIOS

Hey, your BIOS can become dated just like everything else in your system. If you know you have all the latest drivers but you still get errors in Device Manager, see if the motherboard or system makers provide any BIOS updates. An outdated BIOS isn't too common, but certainly common enough to check!

Resource Conflict

Resource conflicts are not as rare as you might think, even in a system with only PnP devices. An ISA PnP device does not have access to every resource; the manufacturer specifies a range of resources in the INF file. Open the INF file for an ISA PnP device and see for yourself (Figure 15.42).

Even if your system has only PCI and AGP devices, as long as your system uses ISA slots, resource conflicts might arise. Windows clearly reports resource conflicts in the error message, so you always know when they occur. Resource conflicts cover a lot of ground, so I've devoted the "Legacy Devices in a Plug and Play World" section to this topic.

Corrupted Registry

In most cases, the device error will report this one very clearly: "Registry corrupted." No problem since you kept that backup copy, right? Right!

Bad Device

After trying everything, you need to blame the device. Techs hate blaming hardware, primarily due to the fact that no tool exists that truly tests any single type of hardware (with a few exceptions), despite the fantastic claims by a number of vendors that I choose

SND929P.INF - Notepad

File Edit Format Help

```
system.ini,drivers,"midi*=rdmpu401.drv",,1

;--------------------------------------------------------------;

[OPTi9290.LC]
ConfigPriority=NORMAL
IOConfig=220-22F, 240-24F
IOConfig=530-537, 604-60B, E80-E87, F40-F47
IOConfig=388-38B
IOConfig = F8E-F8F
IRQConfig=5, 11, 7, 9, 10

DMAConfig=0, 1, 3
DMAConfig=0, 1, 3


[OPTi9291.LC]
ConfigPriority=NORMAL
IOConfig=300-301 , 310-311 , 320-321 , 330-331
IRQConfig=5 , 7 , 9 , 10

[CUSTOM.AddReg]
; These are Manufacturer specific.
HKR,Config,,
```

the few exceptions I mention in this book, don't waste your time trying to diagnose hardware, especially in the Windows GUI.

So how do you know a piece of hardware is bad? You can try installing the device in another system, assuming your job description allows for such luxuries, or you can just guess. I use the 75 percent rule: If I think there's a 75 percent chance that the hardware has failed, I replace it. The most expensive part of computer repair is labor, that is, *you*! It kills me to watch a well-paid PC support person spend half a day trying to figure out if a $30 network card is bad! It's as though he or she is driven by some unknown force to have to figure out definitively if a device is good or bad. Well, my little chickadees, don't let the academic fascination get between you and a good paycheck. If you think there is a 75 percent probability that a part is bad, toss it (return it, whatever). Most of the time you're right—once in a while you're wrong. But unlike the other techs, you'll still have a job.

Did I start ranting again? Back to device errors! I want to talk about dealing with legacy devices in a PnP world, but we need to cover two preliminary issues that cause techs to stumble or scratch their heads in confusion: IRQ steering and Windows memory. Let's tackle IRQ steering first.

IRQ Steering

As we learned in previous chapters, PCI and AGP devices don't need IRQs. Instead, they use IRQ channels (really just advanced, sharable IRQs) that eliminate the entire issue of IRQ conflicts in these devices. The problem here stems from the fact that ISA devices still need IRQs. How can the PC control interrupts if the PCI devices ignore the ISA IRQ controller? The most modern Pentium 4 still only has one INT wire. What keeps the ISA interrupt controller from trying to interrupt the CPU when a PCI device is already sending an interrupt (Figure 15.43)?

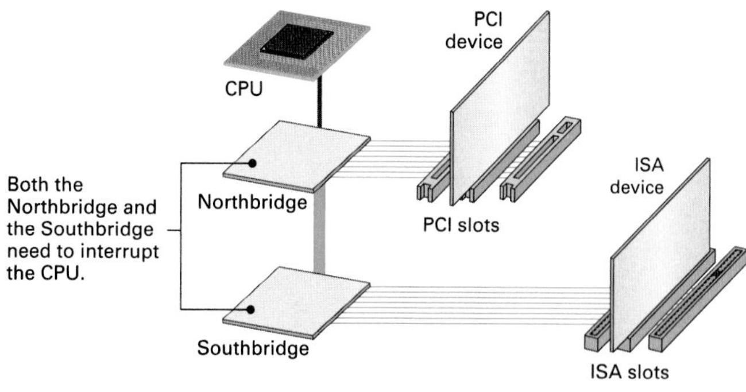

• **Figure 15.43** ISA IRQ controller (in the Southbridge chip) and the PCI controller (Northbridge) trying to interrupt the CPU at the same time

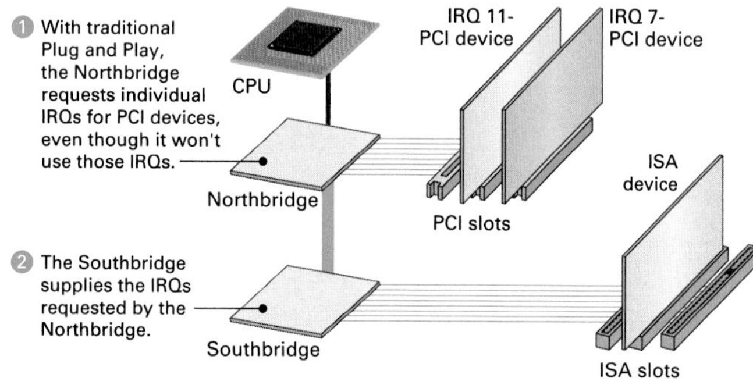

• **Figure 15.44** PnP BIOS sends false information to the IRQ controller.

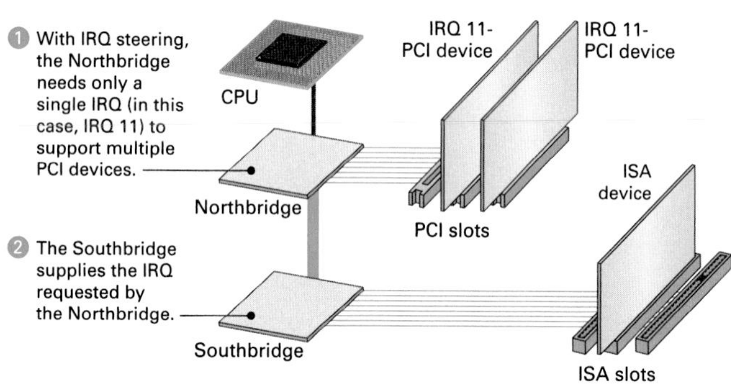

• **Figure 15.45** IRQ steering at work

The first PnP standards handled this problem by assigning an IRQ to every PCI device at boot up. This data was stored in an area called the *IRQ Routing Table*. Not that the PCI device needed the IRQ, mind you, but it kept all the devices from trying to interrupt the CPU. If a PCI device did a normal interrupt, the PnP BIOS read the interrupt routing table to determine what IRQ was assigned to the PCI device and then sent that fake IRQ to the IRQ controller in the chipset. The IRQ controller thought it was receiving a normal ISA IRQ. With a little bit of simplification for clarity, it looked like Figure 15.44.

Although this system worked well, it wasted a ton of IRQs on devices that didn't need them. So, Microsoft and Intel worked together to come up with a clever little function called IRQ steering. The basic idea of IRQ steering is based on the premise, "Who cares what IRQ we give the IRQ controller, just as long as we give it one!" And thus, IRQ steering was born. With **IRQ steering**, PCI devices share one or more IRQs, depending on the chipset and on the function of the PCI device. When any PCI device fires an interrupt channel, the same IRQ gets sent to the ISA IRQ controller (Figure 15.45).

Because IRQ sharing depends so heavily on the chipset used, you cannot predict ahead of time what PCI device will share what IRQs. That's fine with us! As long as the PnP BIOS knows how to report this information, IRQ steering works perfectly and is completely transparent.

IRQ steering has one potentially nasty downside: Systems must have IRQ9 or IRQ11 available for IRQ steering. When I'm building a new system, I never install ISA cards until *after* I've installed Windows. This enables me to see what IRQ the system wants to use for IRQ steering. I then make a point of leaving that IRQ alone when I'm installing ISA devices!

Windows Memory

In the next section, you'll learn about the processes needed to configure system resources for a legacy device manually in the automatic world of PnP. Many people think that learning how to configure legacy devices manually may seem like a waste of time in our PnP world. Not so! Even though PnP makes device installation much easier, it comes with a price. The automation of PnP hides the reality of system resources. The gritty details of IRQs, I/O addresses, and DMA channels disappear from the normal PC support person's view. So, when things go wrong (and they do), most PC techs lack the detailed skills necessary to get out of trouble. Hardly a waste of time!

The CompTIA members who define the skill sets for the A+ Certification exams respond to a very tough audience: themselves. CompTIA's membership list is comprised of the companies and the people who provide every level of the PC support structure. They know what you need to know to prove yourself as a successful tech in today's world. A good tech needs to understand resources—not so much because you'll use that knowledge every day (thankfully, you won't), but more for those rare times when the beauty of PnP fails and you're faced with the daunting task of manual system resource configuration.

Earlier chapters already covered three system resources: I/O addresses, IRQs, and DMA; yet one more critical system resource exists: memory. Devices that need memory use a range of memory addresses. These addresses are displayed using the format

dresses, IRQs, or DMAs.

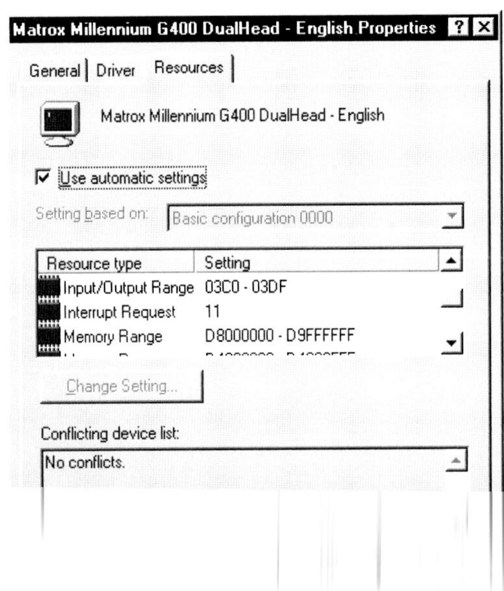

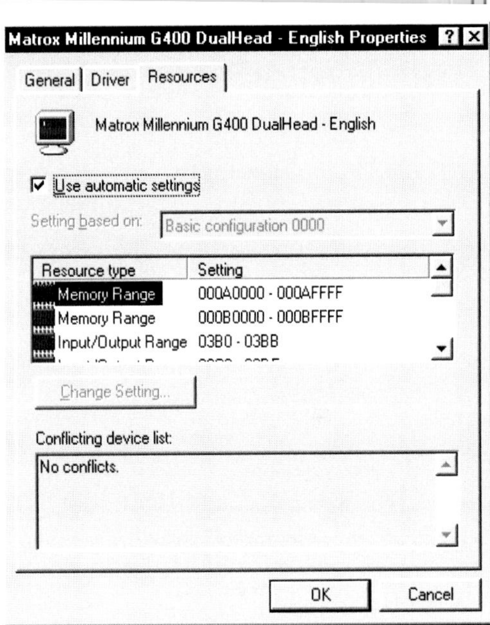

Figure 15.47 Multiple memory addresses

Legacy Devices in a Plug and Play World

Now that we know all of the resources that a device may potentially use, I think it's time to start getting messy! Installing **legacy devices** —those made before the advent of PnP—required us to perform a number of careful steps to avoid resource conflicts.

1. We kept a paper inventory of used resources, in particular IRQs, because compared with DMA or I/O addresses, relatively few IRQs were available on a typical system.
2. Lacking a precise inventory, we ran system information tools that tried to discover all the devices on the system. These DOS-based tools varied considerably in accuracy, but the better ones could find most devices.
3. We then configured the device to use available system resources. This required setting jumpers or switches on the device, or in the case of later legacy devices, running a special configuration program to set the resources.
4. We then installed the device and started the system. In the DOS and Windows 3.*x* days, the OS did not handle resource configuration. Instead, the device drivers we installed into CONFIG.SYS or SYSTEM.INI required special resource settings so that the driver knew which resources to call on to locate the device.
5. We then installed the device's application and tested. If we had lockups, we assumed (usually correctly) that we had inadvertently created an IRQ or DMA conflict. If the device did not respond, we assumed we had an I/O address or memory address conflict.

Installing a legacy device in a PnP environment creates a unique challenge. PnP does not eliminate the need to assess open resources, configure the device, or configure the device driver, although the Device Manager does make the task of determining available resources trivial. We must create an environment that enables PnP devices to avoid the fixed resources of the legacy device, and then set the resources and install and configure the driver for the legacy device.

Preparing to Install a Legacy Device

Long before you grab a screwdriver to install a legacy device, you need to answer some critical questions:

- What resources are available on the system?
- What resources can the legacy device use?
- Do you have driver support for this device?

Let's say we have a legacy sound card that must have I/O addresses 0220-022F, IRQ5 or 9, and DMA channel 1. The sound card has no jumpers and instead uses a special DOS program called UTILITY.EXE to set its resources (Figure 15.48). Before installing the card, you need to answer all three questions.

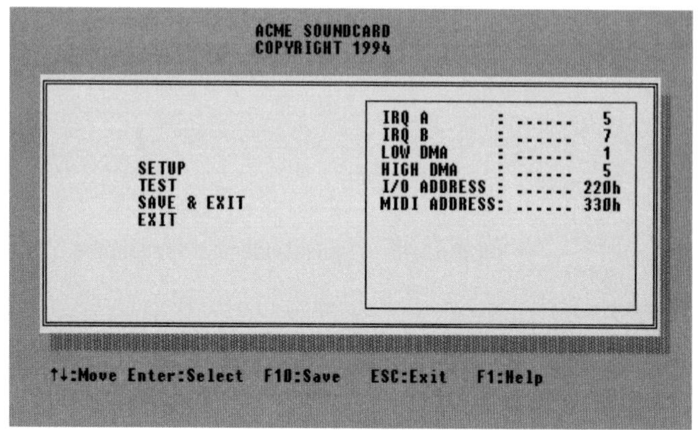

• **Figure 15.48** DOS install utility

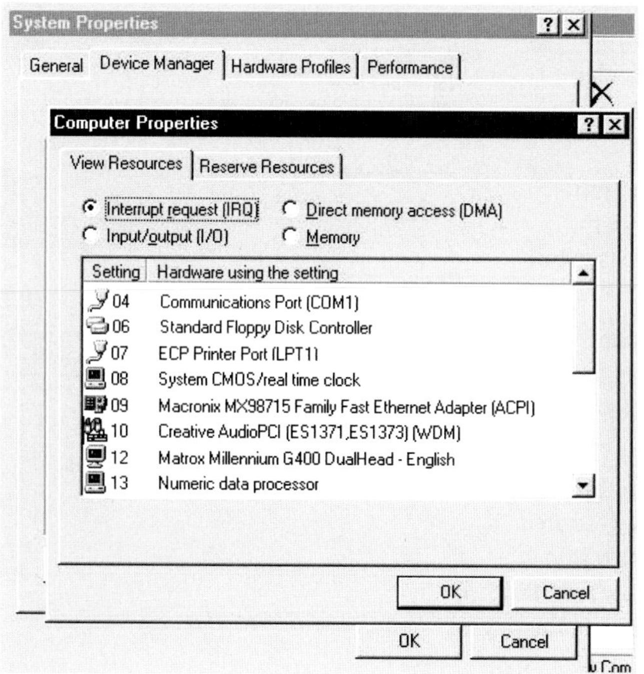

• **Figure 15.49** Resources sorted by IRQ

Determining Available Resources

The first step is by far the easiest. A quick trip to the Device Manager shows all available resources. In Windows 9*x*/Me, double-click the Computer icon at the top of the Device Manager tree to see all resources used by devices. This special screen enables you to sort by any of the four resource types, making open resources obvious. Figure 15.49 shows the resources sorted by IRQ. I scrolled past some of the lower IRQs to reveal more available IRQs. From here you can see that IRQs 5 and 11 are open for use.

Reserving Resources

Now we know what resources are available for the legacy device. That's great, but we have no assurance that the legacy device can use any of these open resources. The makers of the legacy device and ISA PnP devices only provide so many resource options. IRQs are the only serious problem here because all other resources enjoy lots of unused areas. Referring to the previous figure, what happens when some old sound card cannot use IRQ5 or 11? In that case, you have to kick a PnP device off an IRQ that the sound card will use and onto some other resource. You can accomplish this by telling the PnP to reserve a particular IRQ for that device. We perform this operation in two areas: the CMOS and the Reserve Resources tab in the Computer properties.

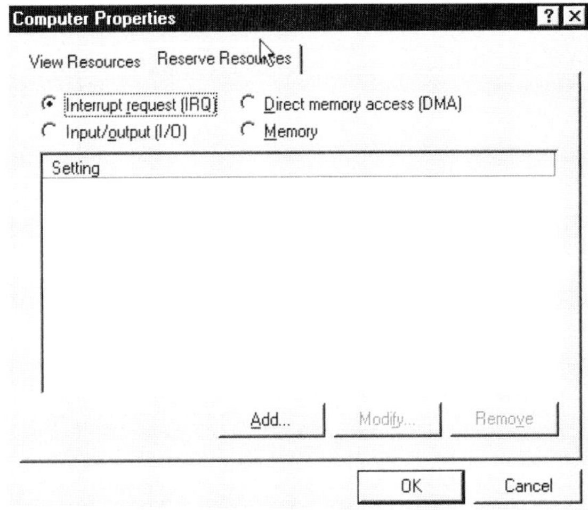

Reserving in Device Manager

Take one more peek at the previous figure—see that other tab? Click it to see Figure 15.50.

This screen enables us to tell Windows PnP to stay away from a particular resource(s). Don't do anything in here now; just know how to get to this screen when needed. Before we do this, shut down the computer, get into CMOS, and locate the PnP/PCI option menu if available (Figure 15.51).

The options available for PnP in CMOS vary so wildly that brevity requires me to limit myself to a typical Award BIOS ... Every CMOS will show at least one of the three main

A PnP BIOS normally tries to initiate all PnP devices, including ISA PnP cards. If you set the PNP OS Installed option to Yes, the PnP BIOS only initializes ISA PnP devices required for boot, such as an ISA video card. Make sure to set this option to Yes. Some newer systems that use *Advanced Configuration and Power Interface* (ACPI) require you to change this setting to "off." See Chapter 18 for details.

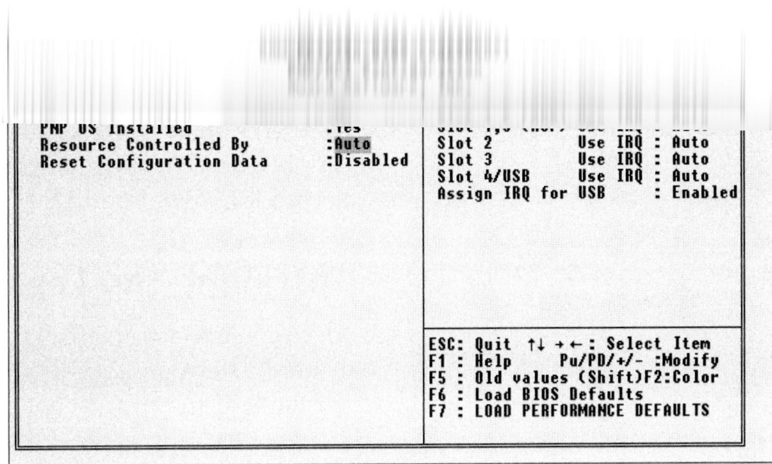

• **Figure 15.51** Award BIOS PnP/PCI Configuration menu

Reset Configuration Data

This option makes the PnP reassign all resources for all devices. Set this option to Enabled after you install any ISA device, especially a legacy ISA device, to make the PnP avoid that device's resources. This option will always set itself back to Disabled at the next reboot.

Resources Controlled By

This is the traditional place to reserve IRQs and, in some systems, DMA channels for legacy ISA devices. Set this option to manual to see the following (Figure 15.52).

Hey, wait a minute! Didn't we just see that the Device Manager enables us to reserve resources? Why do it here? Officially, you don't have to deal with this. If you just

```
                    PNP/PCI Configuration
                    Award Software, Inc.

PNP OS Installed             :Yes        Slot 1,5 (AGP) Use IRQ : Auto
Resource Controlled By       :Manual     Slot 2         Use IRQ : Auto
Reset Configuration Data     :Disabled   Slot 3         Use IRQ : Auto
IRQ - 3 assigned to : Legacy ISA         Slot 4/USB     Use IRQ : Auto
IRQ - 4 assigned to : Legacy ISA         Assign IRQ for USB     : Enabled
IRQ - 5 assigned to : PCI/ISA PnP
IRQ - 7 assigned to : PCI/ISA PnP
IRQ - 9 assigned to : PCI/ISA PnP
IRQ -10 assigned to : PCI/ISA PnP
IRQ -11 assigned to : PCI/ISA PnP
IRQ -12 assigned to : PCI/ISA PnP
IRQ -14 assigned to : PCI/ISA PnP
IRQ -15 assigned to : PCI/ISA PnP
DMA - 0 assigned to : PCI/ISA PnP        ESC: Quit ↑↓→← : Select Item
DMA - 1 assigned to : PCI/ISA PnP        F1 : Help     Pu/PD/+/- :Modify
DMA - 3 assigned to : PCI/ISA PnP        F5 : Old values (Shift)F2:Color
DMA - 5 assigned to : PCI/ISA PnP        F6 : Load BIOS Defaults
DMA - 6 assigned to : PCI/ISA PnP        F7 : LOAD PERFORMANCE DEFAULTS
DMA - 7 assigned to : PCI/ISA PnP
```

• **Figure 15.52** Manual settings

```
ROM PCI/ISA BIOS (2A69K5D9)
Integrated Peripherals
Award Software, Inc.

IDE HDD Block Mode           : Disable   Onboard Parallel Port :378/IRQ7
IDE Primary Master PIO       : Auto      Parallel Port Mode    : EPP
IDE Primary Slave PIO        : Auto
IDE Secondary Master PIO     : Auto
IDE Secondary Slave PIO      : Auto
IDE Primary Master UDMA      : Disable
IDE Primary Slave UDMA       : Disable
IDE Secondary Master UDMA    : Disable
IDE Secondary Slave UDMA     : Disable
On-Chip Primary PCI IDE      : Enable
On-Chip Secondary PCI IDE    : Enable
USB Keyuboard Support        : Disable
Init Display First           : Disable
                                         ESC: Quit ↑↓ →← : Select Item
                                         F1 : Help     Pu/PD/+/- :Modify
Onboard FDC Controller       : Enable    F5 : Old values (Shift)F2:Color
Onboard Serial Port 1        : Disable   F6 : Load BIOS Defaults
Onboard Serial Port 2        : Disable   F7 : LOAD PERFORMANCE DEFAULTS
```

• **Figure 15.53** CMOS' Integrated Peripherals

set it to Auto, the reserve settings in Windows will do all the reserving you need. I occasionally run across some systems where you reserve IRQs here, however, even though you have reserved the option in Device Manager. Many CMOS setup utilities have dropped this option and just count on you to handle reserving resources in Device Manager.

While you're still in CMOS, locate the Integrated Peripherals menu. Always turn off any unused serial ports, parallel ports, or USB ports, to open up those IRQs (Figure 15.53). You can free up a number of otherwise unavailable IRQs this way. Just remember to turn them back on if you decide to use them later!

Device Manager

After reserving resources in CMOS (or just making sure that PNP OS Installed is set to Yes and Resources Controlled By to Auto), we need to return to the Reserve Resources tab under Computer Properties in Device Manager to reserve the resources. Although Reserve Resources enables us to reserve any resource, in my many years of using Windows 9*x*/Me I've only reserved IRQs (Figure 15.54).

Installing the Legacy Device

Once you have reserved all necessary resources, install the sound card and boot to a startup disk. Run the UTILITY.EXE program to set the resources for the card and then reboot the system normally into Windows. Windows does not look for legacy devices at boot, so nothing "interesting" happens. We now need to run the Add New Hardware Wizard in the Control Panel to tell Windows to install the sound card (Figure 15.55).

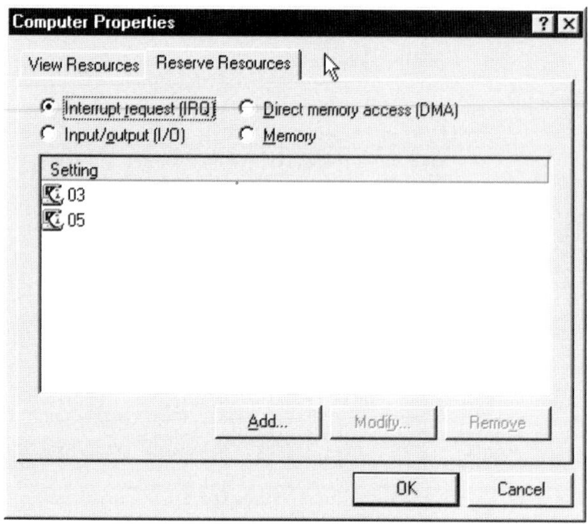

• **Figure 15.54** Reserved IRQs

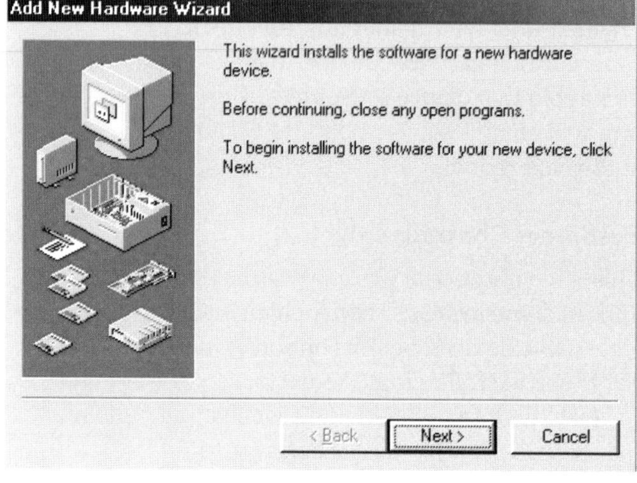

• **Figure 15.55** Add New Hardware Wizard opening screen

Windows comes with a powerful search function that finds most legacy devices. This confuses many techs into thinking their legacy card is PnP. Don't be fooled—it's just a neat aspect of Windows. In most cases, Windows will discover your card and will either install drivers if it recognizes the device (as shown in Figure 15.56), or in most cases, prompt you for a driver.

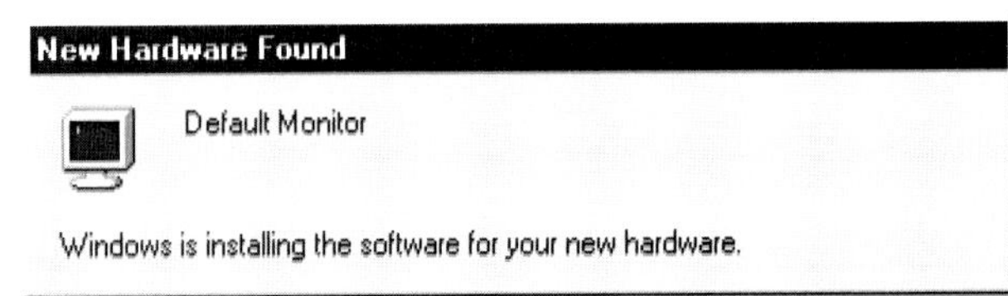

• **Figure 15.56** Windows installs drivers for the recognized device.

If Windows prompts for a driver, you must hope that the disk holding the UTILITY program also contains the proper drivers for your version of Windows. Click the Have Disk button, and let Windows install the drivers. After the installation finishes, make a point to go to the Device Manager to verify that the device works properly. All of the problems discussed earlier may come into play, but as you may recall, we saved one problem for this section: resource conflicts.

[illegible]

[illegible] vice conflicts. If you follow the preparation steps shown earlier, this error will not appear. I usually see this error when I dump in the legacy card without first reserving resources. If you failed to set the resources on the card, start over. But if you know the resources on the legacy device, you can manually configure them. Open the device's properties and go to the Resources tab (Figure 15.58).

The Resources tab differs wildly between different versions of Windows and various pieces of hardware, but almost all of them enable you to configure a device manually. To configure the device displayed in Figure 15.58, for

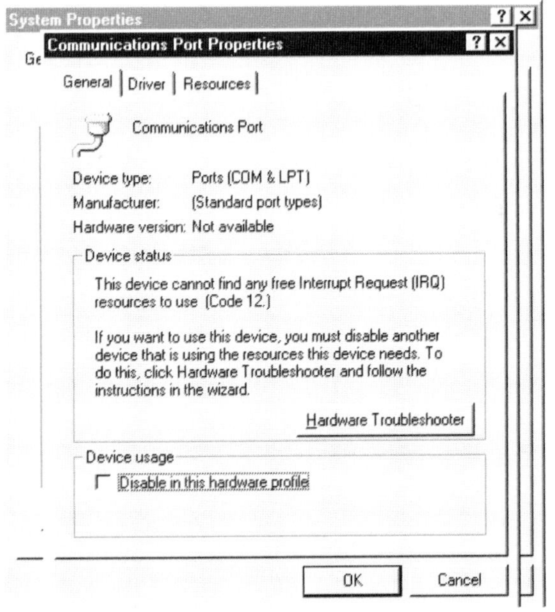

• **Figure 15.57** Resource conflict error

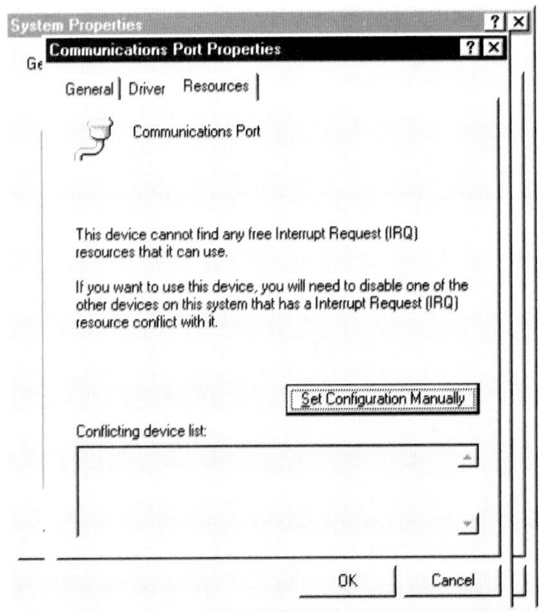

• **Figure 15.58** Resources tab

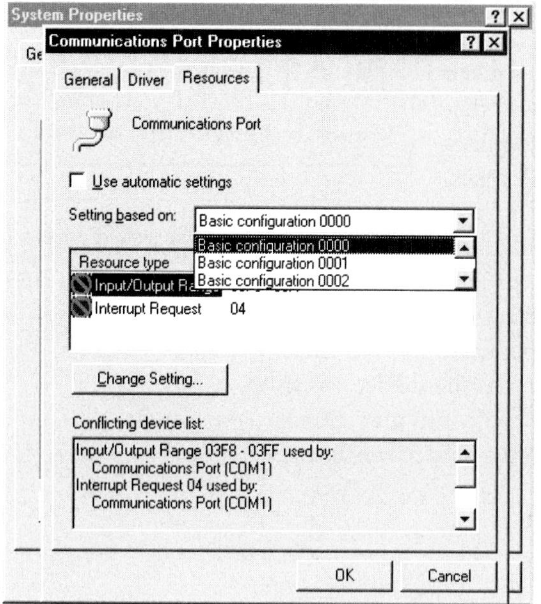

• **Figure 15.59** Resource settings pull-down menu

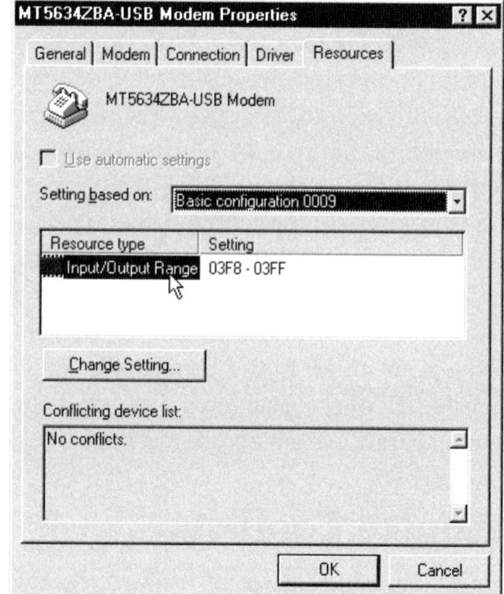

• **Figure 15.60** Changing individual resource settings

example, you must click the Set Configuration Manually button and then on the subsequent dialog box (shown in Figure 15.59), uncheck the Use Automatic Settings check box. Always leave this checked—thus leaving the PnP manager in charge of resource allocation—unless you need to repair a resource conflict manually. Uncheck the box to activate the Setting Based On pull-down menu. Click the pull-down menu to see the options (Figure 15.59).

The Basic configurations are simply preset resource combinations used to set the device. If by some lucky chance one of these fits your resource needs, you may use it, but most of the time, just scroll down and select the last Basic configuration option, which enables you to change individual resource settings (Figure 15.60). Windows doesn't like it when you set resources manually and a big "Are you sure?" screen appears when complete. Just click OK and restart the system. The device now uses the manually configured resource.

■ Troubleshooting Windows 9x/Me

We've spent quite a bit of this chapter discussing troubleshooting problems in Windows 9*x*/Me systems for particular situations such as device installation. In this section, I want to focus on some of the more common problems that seem to arise magically "out of nowhere" on a system. All these problems share one thing in common: Fixing them usually requires you to restore a previously working system. Let's look at the fix first and then address the common problems.

Be Prepared

In almost every case, you fix a broken or unstable Windows by restoring some kind of backup of some kind of data. You already know how to back up the Registry, and you know about a class of programs that enable you to go back to a previous configuration as needed, but we need to discuss the concept of backup in a more generic sense.

Backup

People get terribly confused by the word "backup." Simply put, backup means to take a copy of a file and place it somewhere else so it can be retrieved in the event of a problem with the original. To me, there are four different groups of files it may be advisable to back up (some of these overlap):

- Personal data files (usually all the stuff in My Documents)
- Personal data used by applications (for example, address book entries, favorites,

all do any of the preceding jobs. If I owned the world, I'd make sure every computer had an Iomega Zip drive onto which users would carefully copy all of their personal files every day. Every memo made by a secretary, every spreadsheet made by an accountant, and every graphic made by an artist would carefully make its way to the Zip disk. Then every user would use the export features of their contact software, account programs, e-mail, and web browsers to make a daily backup of all this data onto those same Zip disks. But that's not going to happen except in the best of circumstances. Instead, Windows provides us with the handy Backup program which, when combined with a good tape backup system, will save you from data disasters and application installation nightmares time and time again (Figure 15.61).

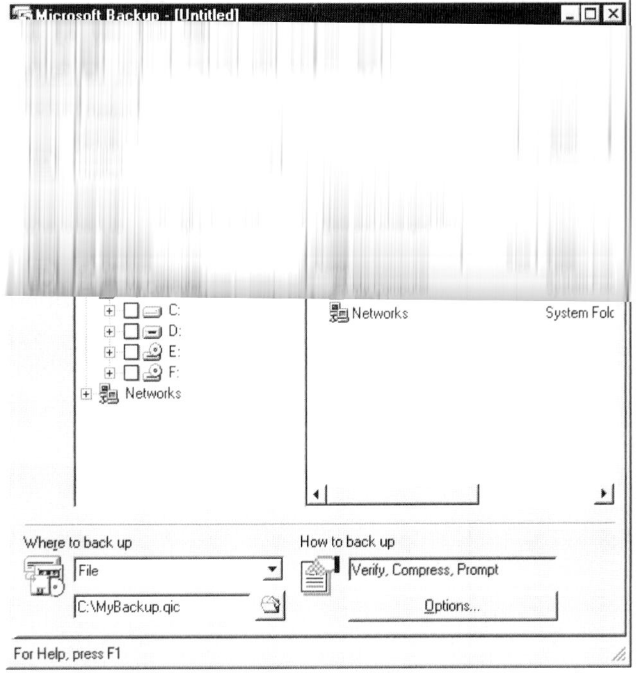

Figure 15.61 Windows Backup program

Get a tape backup that can hold all your data—the popular DAT format disks are inexpensive and reliable. Schedule the backup to run at night since backups take a lot of time. You can speed up the backup process by using a good backup program that enables you to perform different types of backups. Remember in the last chapter when we discussed the archive attribute? Now I can finally explain what it does. Backup programs use the archive bit to determine if a file has been changed since the last time it was backed up. Every time a file is accessed, Windows turns on the archive bit. Backup programs use this fact to reduce the amount of backup time. Why back up a file that's already been backed up and hasn't changed? Knowing this, we divide backups into four types: copy, full, incremental, and differential.

- **Copy** Copies selected files and folders to the backup device without turning off the archive bit

- **Full** Backs up every file and folder and turns off the archive bit
- **Incremental** Backs up only files and folders with the archive bit turned on, and turns off the archive bit
- **Differential** Backs up only files and folders with the archive bit turned on, but does not turn off the archive bit

Whoa! Copy and full make sense, but what's the deal with incremental and differential? You need to appreciate that most people do a full backup about once a week and then do only partial backups during the week. Let's assume that you set up your backup program to do a full backup automatically every Monday night at 10:00 PM. If the system performs a **differential backup** every other weeknight at 10:00 PM, here's what will happen:

- Monday night—Full backup
- Tuesday night—Back up of all files changed since last full backup
- Wednesday night—Back up of all files changed since last full backup
- Thursday night—Back up of all files changed since last full backup
- Friday night—Back up of all files changed since last full backup

A differential backup really just makes you use two tapes: one for the full backup on Monday and another tape for all the other daily backups. This works well, but each differential backup can take longer and longer each evening because every file changed since Monday night keeps getting backed up.

An **incremental backup**, in contrast, gets only the files changed since the last backup, whether full or partial. Here's the same five-day setup with an incremental backup:

- Monday night—Full backup
- Tuesday night—Back up of all files changed since Monday
- Wednesday night—Back up of all files changed since Tuesday
- Thursday night—Back up of all files changed since Wednesday
- Friday night—Back up of all files changed since Thursday

In this case you need a different tape each night because each backup stores only that day's changes. This makes for a fast backup. If you need to restore, however, you end up having to juggle a bunch of tapes. Which one should you use? It doesn't really matter—just make sure you understand how each one works and the benefits of each method. Now that you know the fix for many Windows problems, let's dive into some specific common problems.

System Restore

The **System Restore** utility in Windows Me enables you to return your PC to a recent working configuration when something goes wrong. System Restore returns your computer's system settings to the way they were the last time you remember your system working correctly—all without affecting your personal files or e-mail.

Windows Me automatically creates **restore points** each day, as well as any time you install an application, update a driver, or add a piece of hardware. You also have the option to create your own restore points whenever you want, and give them unique names that are meaningful to you. You might decide to create a restore point before tweaking a bunch of settings in the Control Panel, for example, and name the restore point *Tweak system settings*. Or, you could name it something a bit more creative, like *I hope I don't regret what I'm about to do!* All that matters is that you'll be able to remember later—while you're in a slightly panicked state—what was going on with your system when you created that restore point. If something does go wrong, you can run the System Restore Wizard, which presents you with a calendar listing of available restore points. Let's look at the process.

Creating a Restore Point

To create a restore point, go to Start | Programs | Accessories | System Restore to open the System Restore utility (Figure 15.62) At the welcome screen, you choose from the radio buttons on the right side of the screen, in [illegible]

[illegible]

To use a system restore point, return to the System Restore utility, and this time select Restore My Computer to an Earlier Time. When you click the Next button, the Select a Restore Point screen displays, with a calendar and a listing of the most recent restore points (Figure 15.64). Based on your

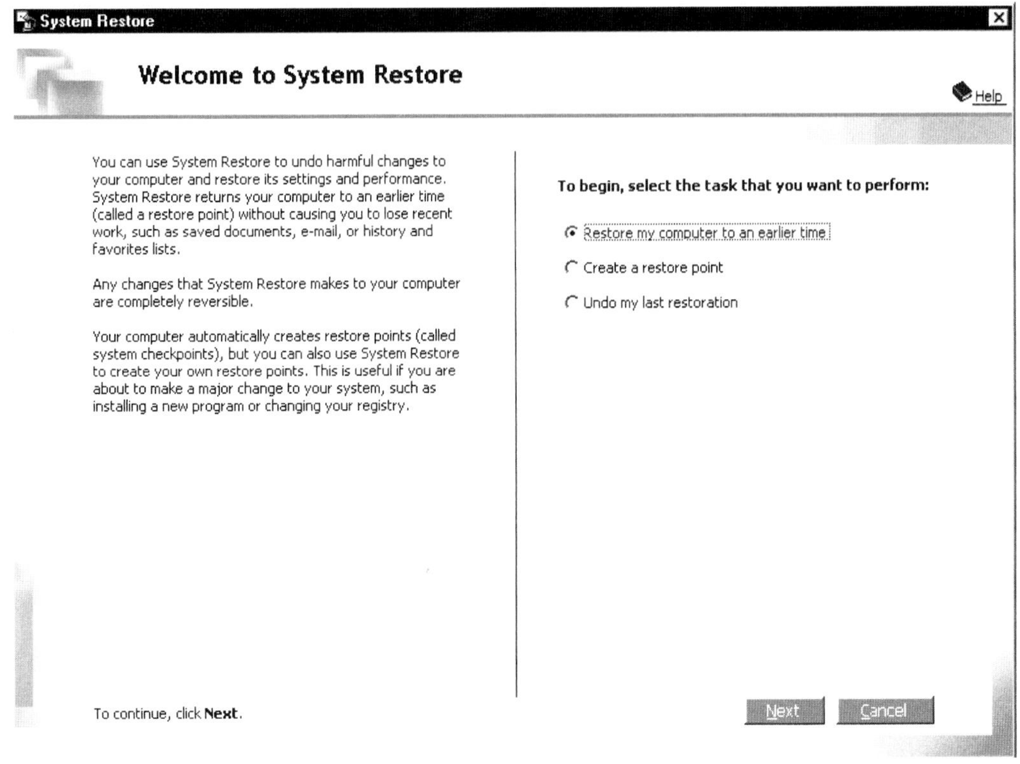

• **Figure 15.62** Welcome to System Restore

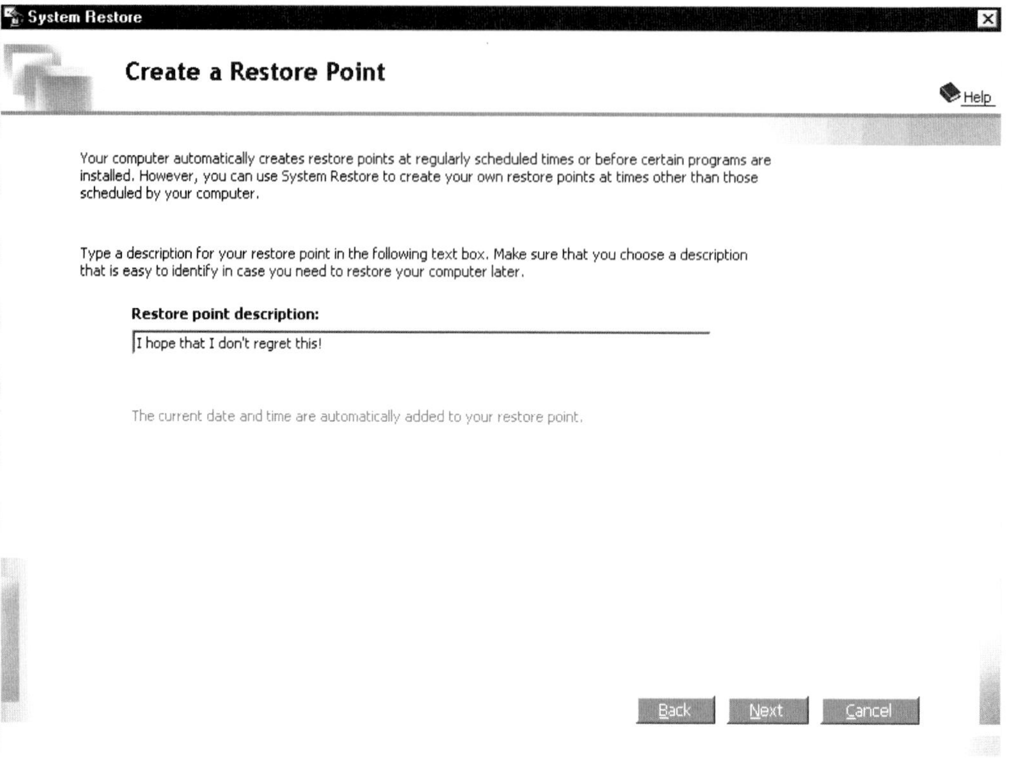

• **Figure 15.63** Filling in a description

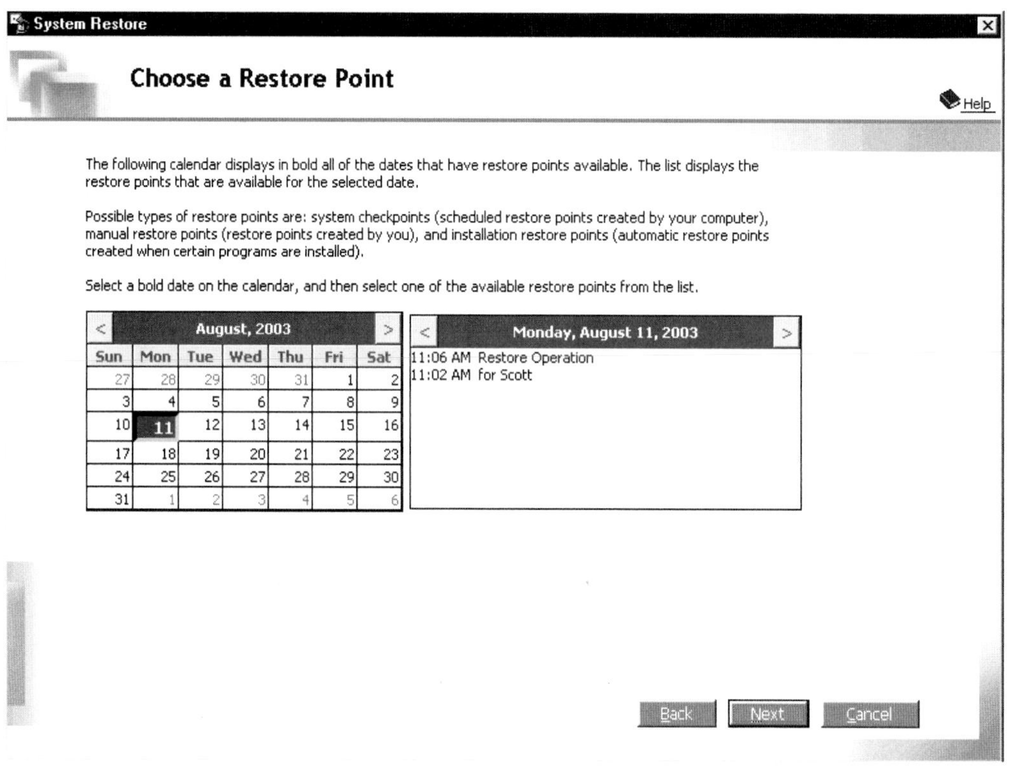

• **Figure 15.64** Selecting a restore point to load

knowledge of when your system started having problems, select a restore point and follow the prompts to complete the restore operation. System Restore is pretty powerful. Even if you crash hard and can only boot to Safe Mode, you can still run the System Restore utility to recover your system. It sure beats the alternative!

ConfigSafe

Well, that's just wonderful—*if* you have Windows Me. But what if you have Windows 98? Are you just out of luck? Don't despair—it wasn't your last hope, there is another! Solution, that is. There are a number of third party tools available that can [illegible] tions. ConfigSafe can take a "snapshot" of your system (Figure 15.66), like the System Restore utility, and then restore your system from any snapshot you've previously made (Figure 15.67). Its Advanced options enable you to see the details of any changes to your key system files in between any set of snapshots (Figure 15.68), and generate reports on any aspect of what the program has done (Figure 15.69). ConfigSafe also supports ongoing maintenance activities, allowing you to schedule snapshots at daily, weekly, or monthly intervals, or even at each startup (Figure 15.70). The ConfigSafe Install Guard feature will monitor changes to your system to help you keep your snapshot information up to date, either automatically or after prompting you (Figure 15.71).

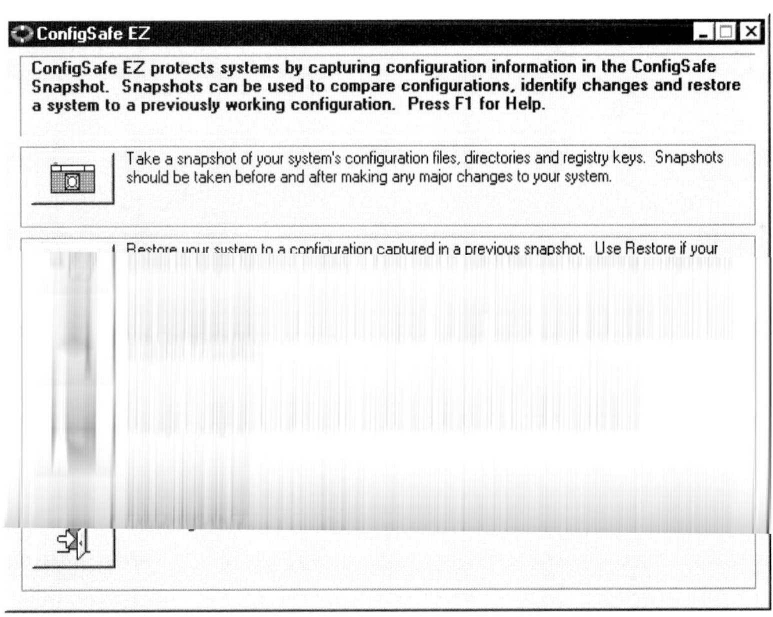

• **Figure 15.65** ConfigSafe opening screen

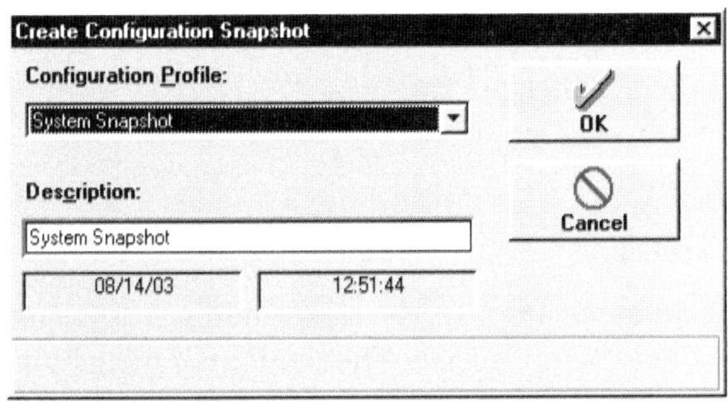

• **Figure 15.66** Take a snapshot of your system.

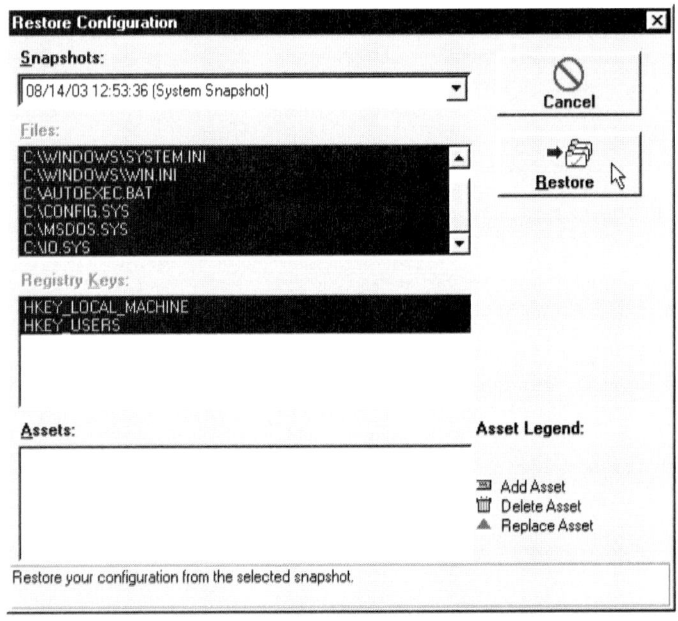

• **Figure 15.67** Restore your system from a snapshot.

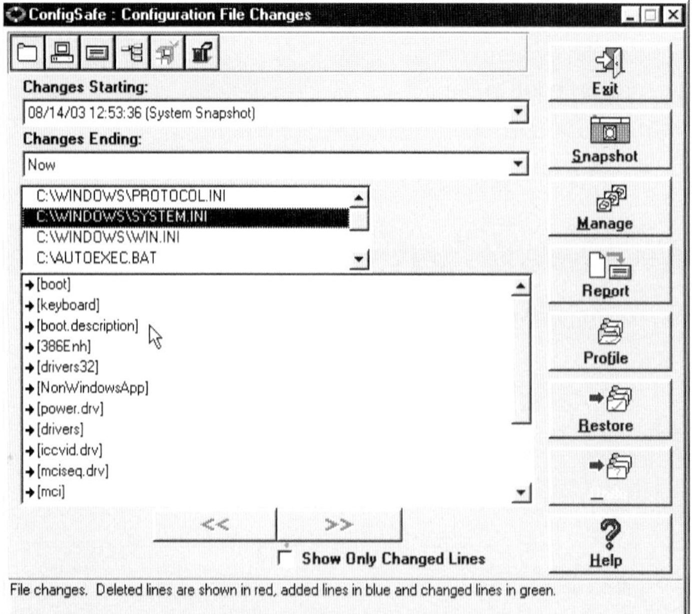

• **Figure 15.68** See details of changes between snapshots.

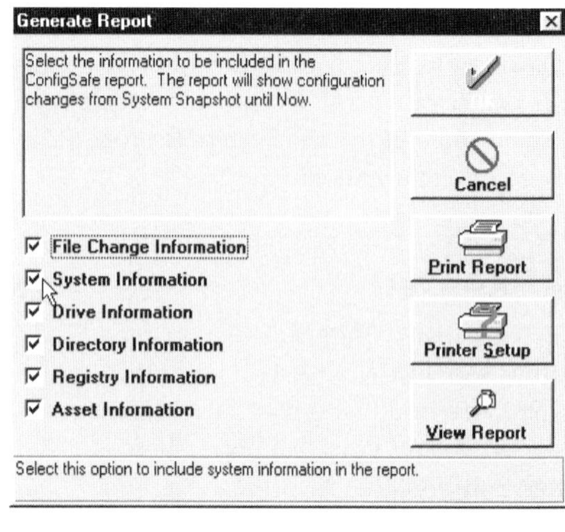

• **Figure 15.69** Generate reports in ConfigSafe.

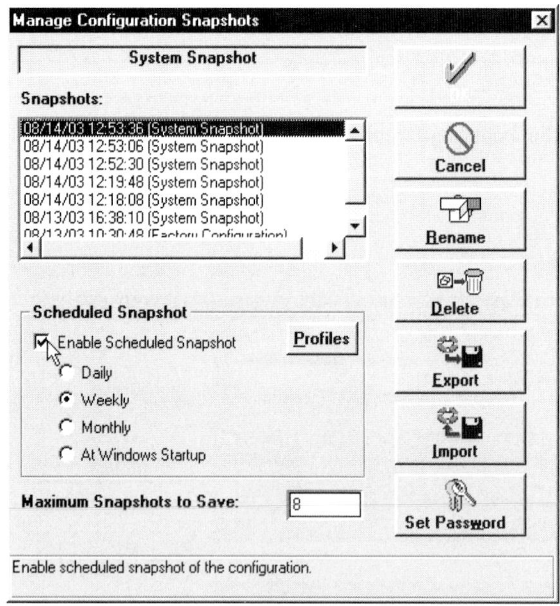

• **Figure 15.70** Schedule ConfigSafe snapshots.

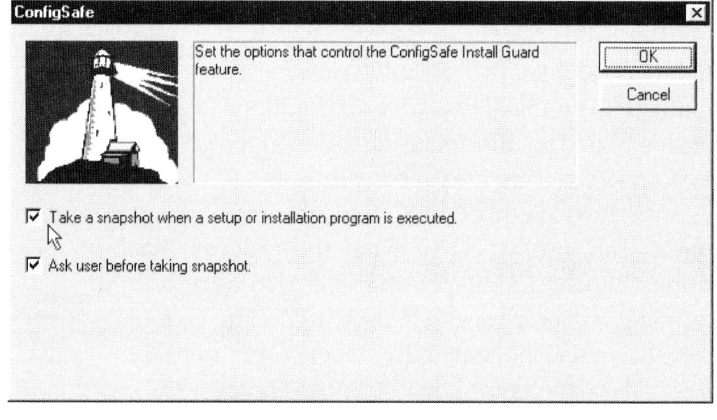

• **Figure 15.71** ConfigSafe Install Guard

Not all Windows 9*x* systems will have this software, although many will. If you want to add it to your system, or to a system you support, you can buy it online from the manufacturer, imagineLAN, Inc.

Antivirus Protection

The words, "I think your machine has a virus," can send shudders down the back of even the most competent PC technician. The thought of megabytes of critical data being wiped away by the work of some evil programmer is at best annoying and, at worst, a serious financial disaster.

So, where do viruses come from? Just like many human viruses, they live in host bodies, in this case computers. Your computer can only catch one if it interacts with other computers, or with programs or data from an infected computer. The problem is that these days almost everyone's computer (aside from folks like the CIA) is connected to the Internet, and thereby to many, many other computers. Also, many viruses are spread through the sharing of programs or information on floppy disks or CD-ROMs.

How do you know if you've caught a virus? You feel sluggish, start sneezing and coughing, want to sleep—or in this case, the computer equivalents of those symptoms: Your computer may seem unusually sluggish, generate strange error messages or other odd emissions, or possibly even lock up and refuse to function entirely. All these are classic symptoms, but you cannot assume your computer is virus-free just because it seems fine. [illegible]

[illegible] right amusing. Without going into too much gritty detail, basically only four types of viruses exist: boot sector, executable, macro, Trojan, and worm. A sixth type also exists that is really a combination of two others: bimodal/bipartite.

Tech Tip

Recovery CDs

Many pre-assembled PCs from the larger computer makers like Hewlett/Packard, Sony, IBM, Gateway, and Dell, ship with a CD-ROM innocuously labeled Recovery Disc. *These CD-ROMs contain a snapshot of the system* as it was when delivered. *Every program and file is stored on the disc, so you can restore your system to its original specifica-* [illegible] *backup, so that with luck, your system ends up the way it was at your last backup.*

The problem with the Recovery CDs is that most users never make a backup of their system. If you go in to service a client's PC that's crashed hard and, upon discovering the Recovery CD, proceed to restore the client's system to its original state, you will erase all the client's data off that PC! *Such an action is, in technical terms, a Bad Thing. If your client does not have a good backup of his or her personal data files, stay away from any Recovery CD and instead work on getting the PC up and running with more conventional tools.*

Boot Sector Boot sector viruses change the code in the *master boot record* (MBR) of the hard drive. Once the machine is booted, the viruses reside in memory, attempting to infect the MBRs of other drives such as floppy drives, connected network machines, or removable media, and creating whatever havoc they are designed to do by the programmer.

A popular method for removing a boot sector virus is to use the FDISK /MBR command to rewrite the master boot record. While this does work, keep in mind that some systems use special disk overlay programs that reside in the boot sector. As long as you can raise your right hand and promise you don't have an overlay, feel free to use FDISK /MBR.

Executable Executable viruses reside in executable files. They are literally extensions of executables and are unable to exist by themselves. Once the infected executable file is run, the virus loads into memory, adding copies of itself to other EXEs that are subsequently run, and again doing whatever evil that the virus was designed to do.

Macro Macro viruses are specially written application macros. Although they are not truly programs, they perform the same functions as regular viruses. These viruses will auto-start when the particular application is run and will then attempt to make more copies of themselves. Some will even try to find other copies of the same application across a network to propagate.

Trojan Trojans are true, freestanding programs that do something other than what the person who runs the program thinks they will do. An example of a Trojan would be a program that a person thinks is a game but that is actually a CMOS eraser. Some Trojans are quite sophisticated. It might be a game that works perfectly well, but when the user quits the game, it causes some type of damage.

Worm A worm is a very special form of virus. Unlike all of the other viruses described, a worm does not infect other files on the computer. Instead, a **worm** replicates by making copies of itself on other systems on a network by taking advantage of security weaknesses in networking protocols.

Bimodal/Bipartite A bimodal or bipartite virus uses both boot-sector and executable functions.

Antivirus Tools

The only way to protect your PC permanently from getting a virus is to disconnect from the Internet and never permit any potentially infected software to touch your precious computer. Because neither scenario is likely these days, you need to use a specialized antivirus program to help stave off the inevitable virus assaults.

An antivirus program protects your PC in two ways. It can be both sword and shield, working in an active "seek and destroy" mode and in a passive "sentry" mode. When ordered to seek and destroy, the program will scan the computer's boot sector and files for viruses, and if it finds any, presents you with the available options for removing or disabling them. Antivirus programs can also operate as virus shields that passively monitor your computer's activity, checking for viruses only when certain events occur, such as a program executing or a file being downloaded.

Antivirus programs use different techniques to combat different types of viruses. They detect boot sector viruses simply by comparing the drive's boot sector to a standard boot sector. This works because most boot sectors are basically the same. Some antivirus programs make a backup copy of the boot sector. If they detect a virus, the programs will use that backup copy to replace the infected boot sector. Executable viruses are a little more difficult to find because they can be on any file in the drive. To detect executable viruses, the antivirus program uses a library of *signatures.* A signature is a code pattern of a known virus. The antivirus program compares an executable file to its library of signatures. Instances have occurred where a perfectly clean program coincidentally held a virus signature. Usually, the antivirus program's creator will provide a patch to prevent further alarms. Antivirus programs detect macro viruses through the presence of virus signatures or of certain macro commands that indicate a known macro virus. Now that we understand the types of viruses and how antivirus programs try to protect against them, let's review a few terms that are often used when describing certain traits of viruses.

Polymorphics/Polymorphs A polymorph virus attempts to change its signature to prevent detection by antivirus programs, usually by continually scrambling a bit of useless code. Fortunately, the scrambling code itself can be identified and used as the signature once the antivirus makers become aware of the virus. One technique that is sometimes used to combat unknown polymorphs is to have the antivirus program create a checksum on every file in the drive. A *checksum* in this context is a number generated by the software based on the contents of the file rather than the name, date, or size of that file. The algorithms for creating these checksums vary among different antivirus programs (they are also usually kept secret to help prevent virus makers from coming up with ways to beat them). Every time a program is run, the antivirus program calculates a new checksum and compares it with the earlier calculation. If the checksums are different, it is a sure sign of a virus.

Stealth The term "stealth" is more of a concept than an actual virus function. Most stealth virus programs are boot sector viruses that use various methods to hide from antivirus software. One popular stealth virus will hook on to a somewhat unknown, but often used, software interrupt, running only when that interrupt runs. Others make copies of innocent-looking files.

you load it. Although the chance of commercial, shrink-wrapped software having a virus is virtually nil (a couple of well-publicized exceptions have occurred), that illegal copy of "Unreal Tournament" you borrowed from a local hacker should definitely be inspected with care.

Get into the habit of having an antivirus floppy disk—a bootable, copy-protected floppy with a copy of an antivirus program. If you suspect a virus, use the diskette, even if your antivirus program claims to have eliminated it. Turn off the PC and reboot it from the antivirus diskette. Run your antivirus program's most comprehensive virus scan. Then check all removable media that were exposed to the system and any other machine that may have received data from or is networked to the cleaned machine. A virus can often go for months before anyone knows of its presence.

General System Sluggishness

Every PC gets slower and stodgier over time. You load and unload programs, you download stuff off the Internet, the system crashes and scatters temp files all over the place—all of these factors contribute to the decline of snappiness. Sometimes the decline comes in a more dramatic fashion, though. A client of mine recently bought a new Pentium 4 system with all the bells and whistles. He raved for days about how much faster this PC was than his old Windows 95 beast running on a Pentium II. And then, silence. A week later I got a distress call from him. His PC took two minutes to start up; opening Internet Explorer to surf the Net took forever, and simple tasks like saving a document in Word would crash his PC.

When I inspected his PC, I found that at boot, more than 50 percent of his 256 MB of RAM was filled with autoloading programs (like those we talked

A lot of the applications hogging my client's system were potentially malicious programs called *spyware*. Companies use spyware applications to track where you and others go on the Internet so that they can sell the research information to other marketers. We cover these and other Internet pitfalls in Chapter 24.

about earlier in this chapter). Worse, he had a dozen programs that were set up to check the Internet periodically for updates and who knows what else. He had so much software, services, and other paraphernalia loaded on his PC that it was a wonder it would boot at all. He speedster PC had become a jalopy in less than two weeks!

The fix for this kind of a situation is to run the System Configuration Utility, which is actually a program called **MSCONFIG**. Scan for viruses, and shut down all those unwanted programs. Don't forget to wag your finger at your client for practicing unsafe computing!

Windows Boot Problems

Many Windows troubleshooting issues deal with boot problems. In most cases, these are fairly simple fixes. Here are a few of the classics.

No OS Found

This points to a corrupted or missing IO.SYS or MSDOS.SYS. Just pop in your startup disk and use the SYS program to put back the missing file. From the A: prompt, type the following command:

```
SYS C:
```

This automatically restores the IO.SYS, MSDOS.SYS, and COMMAND.COM files. If you edited the MSDOS.SYS file, you will have to restore any edits manually.

Bad or Missing COMMAND.COM

This problem is an easy one to fix. Just use your startup disk to copy the COMMAND.COM file back onto the C: drive.

Error in CONFIG.SYS (Line XX)

This one rarely happens unless you've been working in the CONFIG.SYS file or installing some older device that tossed something into CONFIG.SYS. Edit the CONFIG.SYS file and count the line numbers until you get to the one in question. Look for typos. Because most Windows systems pretty much ignore the CONFIG.SYS file anyway, just put a semicolon (;) at the very beginning of the line. If everything runs fine for a few days, go back in and remove the line completely.

Device Referenced in SYSTEM.INI Not Found

This is exactly the same scenario as described before for CONFIG.SYS, except this usually shows the device name in question.

HIMEM.SYS Not Loaded or MISSING or Corrupt HIMEM.SYS

Windows must load the HIMEM.SYS file at each boot. Because Windows does this automatically, this is rarely an issue. This error tends to result from a hard drive that needs some serious ScanDisking! As a quick fix, boot off the startup disk and add this line to the CONFIG.SYS file using EDIT:

```
DEVICE=C:\HIMEM.SYS
```

Then, copy the HIMEM.SYS file from the startup disk to the C: drive. Now boot normally and check that hard drive!

Won't Boot to GUI

Have you ever booted a copy of Windows just to get stuck at the pretty Windows startup screen? Failure to boot into the GUI can have many causes. Let's look at these in order of most to least common.

1. *The first thing to blame is a corrupted swap file.* Boot into Safe mode

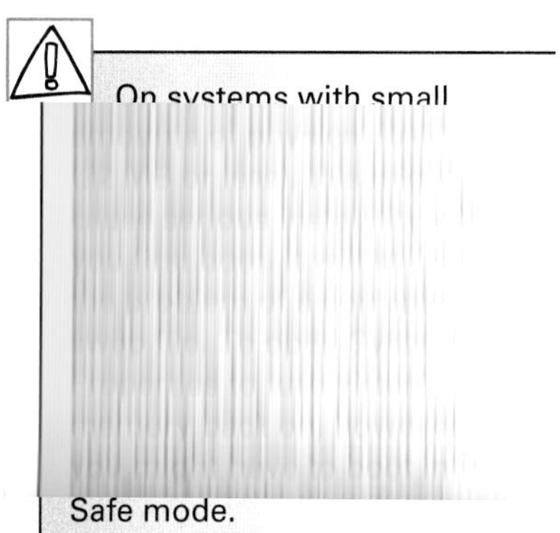

3. you have to restore a known good copy of the Registry. If you don't have one, try replacing SYSTEM.DAT and USER.DAT with SYSTEM.DA0 and the USER.DA0. All of these files are hidden and read-only, so use the ATTRIB command from the startup disk to turn off the attributes. It would look something like this:

   ```
   ATTRIB -r -s -h c:\WINDOWS\SYSTEM\*.dat
   COPY c:\WINDOWS\SYSTEM\*.da0 C:\WINDOWS\SYSTEM\*.dat
   ```

   If you have Windows 98, boot to the startup disk and run the Windows Registry Checker tool. From the A: prompt, type the following command:

   ```
   C:\WINDOWS\COMMAND\SCANREG /fix
   ```

   Try booting again. If the Registry was the problem, you should now boot normally.

4. *Resource conflicts can sometimes prevent the GUI from booting.* A quick boot to Safe mode and a check of the Device Manager should confirm this. Fix resource conflicts as described previously.
5. *A bad driver may cause problems.* For this, use the **Automatic Skip Driver** (ASD) tool in Safe mode. You can find it under the Tools menu in the System Information tool, although I usually go to Start | Run and type in **ASD**. The ASD looks over your log files and prevents any drivers that failed previously from loading at the next boot. If this works, check for a driver update or remove the offending device.

6. *Sometimes some of the core Windows files get corrupted.* If you have Windows 98/Me, you can run the System File Checker from a command prompt as follows:

```
SFC /SCANBOOT /QUIET
```

SFC doesn't show much on the screen, but it will restore any corrupted core file from its own backups automatically. You must reboot after running SFC so that Windows can reload the core files.

Lockups/Reboots

All system lockups fit into one of two groups. The first group is the lockups that take place immediately after you add a new program or device. These almost always point to resource conflicts or software version incompatibilities. Use the techniques described earlier to fix these problems. The second group is the "lockups from nowhere." These invariably point either to a virus attack, or to a hardware problem, usually the power supply, RAM, or hard drive. Test/replace until the problem goes away.

Spontaneous reboots always point to bad hardware or a virus. The power supply is the first item to check, followed closely by the CPU. Overheated CPUs love to reboot spontaneously. Make sure the fan works. Most CMOS setup utilities have a screen that enables you to set overheat alarms to monitor the CPU (Figure 15.72).

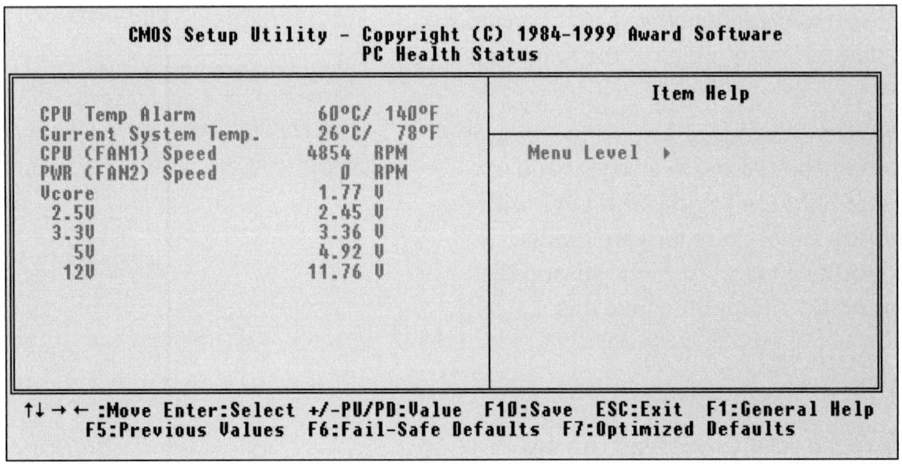

```
CMOS Setup Utility - Copyright (C) 1984-1999 Award Software
                     PC Health Status

CPU Temp Alarm              60°C/ 140°F        Item Help
Current System Temp.        26°C/  78°F
CPU (FAN1) Speed           4854  RPM           Menu Level  ▸
PWR (FAN2) Speed              0  RPM
Vcore                       1.77 V
 2.5V                       2.45 V
 3.3V                       3.36 V
   5V                       4.92 V
  12V                      11.76 V

↑↓→← :Move Enter:Select +/-PU/PD:Value F10:Save  ESC:Exit  F1:General Help
     F5:Previous Values  F6:Fail-Safe Defaults  F7:Optimized Defaults
```

• **Figure 15.72** Set CPU overheat alarms in CMOS setup.

General Protection Faults

A **General Protection Fault (GPF)** occurs when one program tries to stomp on another program's memory area. If I get an occasional GPF (say, once every two weeks), I usually just ignore it; static and subtle incompatibilities just make GPFs something we live with in Windows. GPFs that always point to the same file as the culprit, however, require attention. If the system has not been changed, the named file may be corrupt. Try reloading the file from the installation CD-ROM. Use the EXTRACT command to locate the file on the CD-ROM, and copy it to the same location as the potentially bad one. Use the search function to locate the bad file.

Windows Protection Errors

Windows protection errors take place when a special type of driver file, called a **virtual device driver (VxD)** fails to load or unload. VxDs are used to support older Windows programs, and this error usually occurs when a device somehow gets a device driver in both CONFIG.SYS and SYSTEM.INI or the Registry. Running SYSEDIT will show us any drivers in CONFIG.SYS. Put semicolons in front of DEVICE= lines until the problem goes away. If that doesn't fix it, check for resource conflicts in the Device Manager and then restore the Registry.

Fatal Exception Errors

Fatal exception errors are caused by software or hardware that sends a par- [illegible]

At this point you'll probably need to call tech support. But before you call, run the Dr. Watson utility and re-create the error. Dr. Watson generates a detailed report on the status of the system at the time of the error, and although the information in that report goes way outside of the knowledge of most techs, it provides critical insight to very high-level techs.

Shutdown Problems

I find it interesting that most shutdown problems are identical to startup issues. Bad drivers, a corrupted Registry, and faulty page files all cause shutdown problems. Let's add a few other fixes that are unique to shutdown problems.

Disable Fast Shutdown (Windows 98 Only)

Windows 98 normally "turns off" every device driver at shutdown. You can choose not to turn off device drivers, however, by using a tool called Fast Shutdown. Fast Shutdown works well on most systems but gives others fits. Make sure to disable Fast Shutdown. It's in the System Configuration Utility—click the Advanced button on the General tab. The Disable Fast Save check box is third from the bottom.

Application Not Closing

Some applications refuse to close. Windows 98 does a good job of closing them anyway, but Windows 95 often needs you to close an application manually before it can shut down. Try to close the application normally, but if that fails, use the Task Manager to shut it down. If you click End Task and nothing happens, try again. I sometimes have to "End" Microsoft Word three or four times before it obeys.

Sound File

If the Windows Shutdown sound file corrupts, the system will not shut down. Use the Sound applet in the Control Panel to turn off the shutdown sound.

Beyond A+

Tweak UI

Tweak UI (short for Tweak the User Interface) is an handy little program written—but not officially supported—by Microsoft. It's actually part of a set of productivity tools developed by Microsoft that it calls PowerToys, all designed to do helpful 'extra' things to your system. Tweak UI enables you to adjust the Windows user interface in a variety of ways, some available elsewhere in Windows, some unique to Tweak UI. It enables you to access a variety of system settings that are not otherwise available to you in the default Windows user interface, including mouse settings, menu speed, Internet Explorer settings, window animation, taskbar settings, and a group of privacy settings that Microsoft's engineers cheekily labeled "Paranoia." Because changes made in Tweak UI change registry settings, Microsoft warns you that it's intended for "the advanced user" only. But luckily, since you're on your way to becoming a PC Tech, that's you!

Tweak UI v1.33 is the most recent pre-Windows XP version of this utility. It works with Windows 9*x*, Windows Me, and Windows NT/2000. It will also work with Windows XP, but if you're running Windows XP and have installed Service Pack 1 (you should have!) you can use version 2.10. Microsoft Windows 95 OSR2 is the absolute minimum version of Windows that can use this tool. The original Windows 98 version of Tweak UI was not updated for 98 SE or Me, and in fact won't work on Me. For that you need a more recent version.

Perhaps the most amusing tab in Tweak UI is the Paranoia tab. Its mission in life is basically to help you hide your tracks. You can order Windows to erase a variety of information each time you (or anyone else) logs on to the system, including your Document history, your Internet Explorer history, and records showing who last used the system, what programs they (or more importantly, you) ran, what files you searched for, and what network connections you made. See why it's called "Paranoia?"

> To find current information about Tweak UI in the Microsoft Knowledge Base, surf to www.microsoft.com/support and search for Tweak UI.

Chapter 15 Review

Chapter Summary

Maintain and Optimize a Healthy Windows 9x/Me System

- There are three different ways to update Windows: patches, service packs, and new versions. The Windows 98/Me Windows Update utility queries your system and provides a list of the updates you require. The best way to determine the patches currently loaded on your Windows 95 system is [illegible]
- To remove all the junk files Windows leaves on your system, you use a disk cleanup tool.
- The Windows Task Scheduler that comes with Windows 98 and Windows Me enables you to choose the program you wish to run, when and how often you want it to run, automating your disk maintenance chores.
- All versions of Windows use virtual memory—mapping a portion of the hard drive with memory addresses to mimic RAM. Windows creates a swap file that enables it to have more programs open on the screen than it could normally hold in real RAM. Windows 9*x*/Me sets the minimum swap file size to zero and the maximum to the size of the free space on the drive.
- A disk caching program such as *Vcache* (standard in Windows) grabs a small section of RAM and monitors CPU file requests. It stores a copy of frequently requested files in RAM, enabling it to respond to CPU requests for those files much faster than the hard drive could. Every version of Windows sets aside roughly one-fourth the total size of the RAM for a disk cache.
- On a Windows 9*x*/Me system, the System Resources percentage (Performance tab of System Properties) is the product of dividing current heap usage by heap usage at boot. Many systems can run down into the low 20s with absolutely no ill effect.
- Using the System Monitor you can track almost any process on your PC, including free physical memory, CPU usage, and network throughput.
- The Task Manager shows all running programs, including hidden ones.
- Part of proper system maintenance is to get your [illegible]

Install and Configure Devices on Windows 9x/Me Systems

- Most PnP install problems start due to lack of basic procedure knowledge about how to install a PnP device. Most hardware installation failures begin with the purchase of the wrong hardware.
- All versions of Windows 9*x*/Me can create a startup disk. A startup disk is a bootable floppy disk that contains just enough files to perform basic troubleshooting from an A:\ prompt.
- The most important backup task is to back up the Registry. When you install a new device, Windows changes the Registry to reflect that new device. You can use the REGEDIT program to make a backup of the Registry.
- Windows drivers manifest as special text files with the INF extension. The INF file will usually also come with any other files the hardware device needs, but the INF file is what Windows will look for when it prompts for a device driver.
- The Device Manager is the primary tool for dealing with devices and device drivers in Windows. It displays every device that Windows recognizes. If Windows detects a problem, it shows the device with a red "X" or a yellow exclamation point. The Device Manager organizes devices in special groups called *types*, grouped under type headings.

- Device-related applications break down into five groups: Built-in, Enhanced, Supplied Critical, Supplied Helpful, and Supplied Optional.
- Close attention to documentation and drivers will eliminate most PnP install issues. Failure to find a correct device driver is the most common PnP install issue.
- Always verify that your system has the latest BIOS. Name-brand PC makers list BIOS updates by system model. Check the motherboard maker's web site for BIOS updates for your motherboard. If your system is more than two years old, a BIOS update almost certainly exists.
- Windows often sees a PnP device and tries to install it, but for one reason or another fails to install the device properly. The vast majority of errors boil down to one of seven areas: failure to follow install procedures, corruption/incompatibility with drivers or an INF file, outdated support drivers, outdated BIOS, resource conflict, corrupted Registry, or a bad device.
- All PnP devices require a very careful series of steps to ensure proper installation, particularly when you're replacing one device with a different one. Some of the more common install procedures include the following: deleting the old driver first, running some SETUP program, checking for hardware incompatibilities, and verifying the version number of some Windows EXE, DLL, or driver.
- When a device shows an error, you can use the General tab under the device's properties in Device Manager to help locate the problem using its error code number.
- Corruption or incompatibility with drivers or an INF file can cause Device Manager errors to appear. File corruption is common, especially due to faulty execution of copy commands. The famous "Unknown Device" and "Unsupported Device" errors mean Windows isn't sure what is using its resources.
- The chipset, a controller, or other "middleman" device between the CPU and the device you install also needs a device driver.
- Even if your system has only PCI and AGP devices, as long as your system uses ISA slots, resource conflicts might arise. An ISA PnP device does not have access to every resource; the manufacturer specifies a range of resources in the INF file. Windows clearly reports resource conflicts in the error message, so you always know when they occur.
- PCI and AGP devices use IRQ channels (really just advanced, shareable IRQs) that eliminate the entire issue of IRQ conflicts. But ISA devices still need IRQs.
- IRQ steering is the more modern solution to keeping ISA devices from conflicting with PCI devices when interrupting.
- Memory is *not* RAM, memory is *not* ROM; memory is simply all of the permutations of ones and zeros that the CPU's address bus can generate. Even ultramodern PCI PnP devices often come with an onboard ROM chip, which needs a memory address. From the standpoint of Windows, a memory address is just another resource.
- When installing a legacy device in a PnP environment, you must still assess open resources (trivial using Device Manager), configure the device, and configure the device driver. Three critical legacy device installation questions are (1) What resources are available on the system?; (2) What resources can the legacy device use?; and (3) Do you have driver support for this device?
- Every CMOS will show at least one of the three main PnP settings: PNP OS Installed, Reset Configuration Data, and Resources Controlled By.

Troubleshoot Windows 9x/Me Problems Using Key Tools and Procedures

- Backup means to take a copy of a file and place it somewhere else so it can be retrieved in the event of a problem with the original. There are four different groups of files it may be advisable to back up (some of these overlap): personal data files; personal data used by applications, current system state files (the Registry), and in some cases, the complete contents of the hard drive.
- Backup programs use the archive bit to determine if a file has been changed since the last time it was backed up. Every time a file is accessed, Windows turns on the archive bit. Backup programs use this fact to reduce the amount of backup time.
- There are four types of backups: copy, full, incremental, and differential.
- The System Restore utility in Windows Me enables you to return your PC to a recent working configuration when something goes wrong.

- ConfigSafe is common third-party tool that does for Windows 98 what System Restore does for Windows Me. ConfigSafe can take a "snapshot" of your system, like the System Restore utility, and then restore your system from any snapshot you've previously made.
- Many pre-assembled PCs from the larger computer makers ship with a *Recovery Disc* CD-ROM that contains a snapshot of the system as it was when delivered, so you can restore your system to its original specifications. The problem with using one is that you will erase all the data off that PC.
- A virus is a program that has two functions: [illegible]
- Boot sector viruses change the code in the *master boot record* (MBR) of the hard drive. Executable viruses reside in executable files. Macro viruses are specially written application macros.
- Trojans are true, freestanding programs that do something other than what the person who runs the program thinks they will do. An example of a Trojan would be a program that a person thinks is a game but that is actually a CMOS eraser.
- A worm is a very special form of virus. Unlike all of the other viruses described, a worm does not infect other files on the computer. Instead, a worm replicates by making copies of itself on other systems on a network by taking advantage of security weaknesses in networking protocols.
- An antivirus program protects your PC in two ways. It can be both sword and shield, working in an active "seek and destroy" mode and in a passive "sentry" mode.
- Antivirus programs detect boot sector viruses simply by comparing the drive's boot sector to a standard boot sector.
- A polymorph virus attempts to change its signature to prevent detection by antivirus programs, usually by continually scrambling a bit of useless code.
- Most stealth virus programs are boot sector viruses that use various methods to hide from antivirus software. One popular stealth virus will hook on to a somewhat unknown, but often used, software interrupt, running only when that interrupt runs. Others make copies of innocent-looking files.
- Every PC gets slower and stodgier over time. The fix for a sluggish computer is to run the System Configuration Utility (actually a program called MSCONFIG), scan for viruses, and shut down all those unwanted programs, especially spyware.
- The error *No OS Found* points to a corrupted or missing IO.SYS or MSDOS.SYS. Insert the startup disk and use the SYS program to put back the missing file. From the A: prompt, type the [illegible]
- The error *Device Referenced in SYSTEM.INI Not Found* is exactly the same scenario as described for CONFIG.SYS, except this usually shows the device name in question.
- The error *HIMEM.SYS Not Loaded or MISSING or Corrupt HIMEM.SYS* tends to result from a hard drive that needs some serious ScanDisking. As a quick fix, boot off the startup disk and add this line to the CONFIG.SYS file using EDIT: **DEVICE= C:\HIMEM.SYS**. Then, copy the HIMEM.SYS file from the startup disk to the C: drive. Boot normally and check the hard drive.
- If a system fails to boot into the GUI, first blame a corrupted swap file. Boot into Safe mode and disable virtual memory. If the swap file was the culprit, the system will boot normally, although it may run rather slowly. Turn the swap file back on and reboot again. Second, try a step-by-step configuration from the boot menu. If necessary, restore a known good copy of the Registry. If you have Windows 98, boot to the startup disk and run the Windows Registry Checker tool. From the A: prompt, type **C:\WINDOWS\COMMAND\ SCANREG /fix**.
- Resource conflicts can sometimes prevent the GUI from booting. A quick boot to Safe mode and a check of the Device Manager should confirm this. A bad driver may cause problems. For this, use the

Automatic Skip Driver (ASD) tool in Safe mode. The ASD tool is in the Tools menu in the System Information tool, or you can click Start | Run and type **asd**.

- Sometimes some of the core Windows files get corrupted. If you have Windows 98/Me, you can run the System File Checker from a command prompt as follows: **sfc /scanboot /quiet**. SFC doesn't show much on the screen, but it will restore any corrupted core file from its own backups automatically. You must reboot after running SFC so that Windows can reload the core files.
- System lockups that take place immediately after you add a new program or device almost always point to resource conflicts or software version incompatibilities. "Lockups from nowhere" invariably point either to a virus attack or to a hardware problem, usually the power supply, RAM, or hard drive.
- Spontaneous reboots point to bad hardware or a virus. The power supply is the first item to check, followed by the CPU. Overheated CPUs love to reboot spontaneously. Make sure the fan works. Most CMOS setup utilities have a screen that enables you to set overheat alarms to monitor the CPU.
- General protection faults (GPFs) occur when one program tries to stomp on another program's memory area. If you get GPFs that always point to the same file as the culprit and the system has not been changed, the named file may be corrupt. Try reloading the file from the installation CD-ROM. Use the EXTRACT command to locate the file on the CD-ROM, and copy it to the same location as the potentially bad one. Use the search function to locate the bad file.
- Windows protection errors take place when a virtual device driver (VxD) fails to load or unload. VxDs support older Windows programs. This error usually occurs when a device's driver is present in both CONFIG.SYS and SYSTEM.INI or the Registry. Run SYSEDIT to edit CONFIG.SYS. Put semicolons in front of DEVICE= lines until the problem goes away. If that doesn't fix it, check for resource conflicts in the Device Manager and then restore the Registry.
- Fatal exception errors are caused by software or hardware that sends a particular type of error that Windows is not designed to contain. Uninstall any new program or device, and check the manufacturer's web site and the Microsoft Knowledge Base for known issues related to that software or device.
- The Dr. Watson utility generates a detailed report on the status of the system at the time of an error.
- Windows 98 normally "turns off" every device driver at shutdown. A tool called Fast Shutdown can change this setting, but gives some systems fits. Disable Fast Shutdown by clicking the Advanced button on the General tab in the System Configuration Utility, and unchecking the Disable Fast Save check box.
- Windows 95 often needs you to close an application manually before it can shut down. Try to close the application normally, but if that fails, click End Task in the Task Manager to shut it down.
- If the Windows Shutdown sound file corrupts, the system will not shut down. Use the Sound applet in the Control Panel to turn off the shutdown sound.

Key Terms

Automatic Skip Driver (ASD) *(581)*
Differential backup *(572)*
Disk cache *(544)*
General Protection Fault (GPF) *(582)*
Incremental backup *(572)*
INF file *(553)*
IRQ steering *(564)*
Legacy device *(565)*
MSCONFIG *(580)*
Restore points *(572)*
Service Pack *(538)*
Startup disk *(550)*
System Monitor *(545)*
System Restore *(572)*
Virtual device driver (VxD) *(583)*
Virtual memory *(542)*
Virus *(577)*
Worm *(578)*

Key Term Quiz

1. A portion of the hard drive mapped with memory addresses to mimic RAM is called __________.
2. A group of patches packaged together into a single EXE file that performs the patches simultaneously is called a(n) ____________.
3. Systems must have IRQ 9 or IRQ 11 available for ____________.
4. A(n) _______________ backs up only files and folders with the archive bit turned on, but does [illegible]
6. The System Configuration Utility is a program called __________.
7. A(n) _______________ occurs when one program tries to use another program's memory area.
8. A(n) _____________ is a bootable floppy disk that contains just enough files to perform basic troubleshooting.
9. Typical role of this computer and Read-ahead optimization are settings for changing the __________.

[illegible]

[illegible] Registry files?

   A. WIN.INI and SYSTEM.INI

   B. SYSTEM.DAT and USER.DAT

   C. BOOT.INI and CMOS

   D. COMMAND.COM and CONFIG.SYS

2. What Windows tool provides a graphic snapshot of system processes like CPU usage and allocated memory?

   A. Administrative Console

   B. Task Manager

   C. System Monitor

   D. System Resource Meter

3. What is the most common reason that a system would fail to boot into the GUI?

   A. A corrupted swap file

   B. A corrupted Registry

   C. Resource conflicts

   D. A bad driver

4. What type of file causes Windows protection errors?

   A. INF file

   B. Virtual device driver

   C. Batch file

   D. Registry key

[illegible] your Windows 95 system?

   A. MSCONFIG

   B. QFECHECK

   C. FDISK

   D. REGEDIT

6. What is the most common reason for changing the location of a system's swap file?

   A. To disable it

   B. To enable the Vcache utility

   C. To move it to a drive with more free space

   D. Trick question—you can't move it.

7. How do you access the Task Manager?

   A. Type TASKMAN at a command prompt.

   B. Select Start | Programs | System Tools | Task Manager.

   C. Double-click the Task Manager icon in your system tray.

   D. Press CTRL-ALT-DEL.

8. Which of the following is *not* a Registry root key in Windows 9*x*/Me?

   A. HKEY_CURRENT_MACHINE

   B. HKEY_CLASSES_ROOT

   C. HKEY_CURRENT_USER

   D. HKEY_LOCAL_MACHINE

9. Where can you find auto-starting programs in Windows 95?
   A. The root directory
   B. The \WINDOWS\START MENU\PROGRAMS\ STARTUP folder
   C. The \WINDOWS\SYSTEM\START folder
   D. The \PROGRAM FILES\SHARED\START MENU folder
10. What two files must you add to a Windows 95 startup disk to enable it to access CD-ROMs?
   A. CONFIG.SYS and MSCDROM.EXE
   B. AUTOEXEC.BAT and CDROM.INF
   C. OAKCDROM.SYS and MSCDEX.EXE
   D. CDROM.INI and DEVICEDR.COM
11. The Device Manager organizes devices in special groups called ________.
   A. Resource groups
   B. Types
   C. Device groups
   D. Tasks
12. What do you call an EXE file released by Microsoft to fix specific problems with its software?
   A. A DLL
   B. A Service Pack
   C. A Service Release
   D. A patch
13. What is the name of the swap file in Windows 9*x*/Me?
   A. WIN386.SWP
   B. PAGEFILE.SYS
   C. SWP386.SYS
   D. SWPFILE.SYS
14. What icon does the Windows Me Device Manager use to indicate a device that does not have optimal drivers installed?
   A. A yellow !
   B. A green !
   C. A yellow ?
   D. A green ?
15. Which of the following is *not* a type of virus?
   A. Boot sector
   B. Macro
   C. Executable
   D. Automatic

Essay Quiz

1. With the recent spate of viruses in the news, your boss is worried about viruses spreading to the company's computers. Write a memo describing three virus types and the best practices for preventing infection.
2. A client wants to get a new TV tuner card for his PC so he can watch CNN and surf at the same time. Write a memo explaining all the factors he needs to consider before he buys the card.
3. You work at the Help Desk at a university where professors often add new devices to their computer systems, so Plug and Play troubleshooting is a regular feature of your work. The boss has asked you to write an outline for new Help Desk employees to use when they get PnP calls. You should include all of the common PnP problems they may encounter, and how to deal with them. Be concise, but thorough.
4. Your company has decided to hand some routine maintenance tasks previously performed by tech support over to the users. Your boss asks you to explain three to five maintenance tasks that users should perform on a weekly/monthly basis.
5. A client has a group of PCs that are capable of running either Windows 98 or Windows Me. He can't decide which to choose. He's very concerned about losing his data if there's a system crash. Write a brief essay describing the differences in backing up the data, or the entire system profile, between Me and 98.

Lab Projects

• Lab Project 15.1

You know that Windows 98 lacks the System Restore feature of Windows Me, and so requires third-party system backup utilities such as ConfigSafe. Do an Internet search for this type of software and compare/contrast the claims of at least three competing programs. If you don't have Internet access, you can visit a computer store to see what's available and ask the salesperson how the different programs compare.

• Lab Project 15.2

This chapter talks about different ways to optimize by changing your cache size and look-ahead buffer,

Maintaining, Optimizing, and Troubleshooting Windows NT, 2000, and XP

"The more they overthink the plumbing, the easier it is to stop up the drain."

—Scotty, *Star Trek III: The Search for Spock*

In this chapter, you will learn how to

- **Select the proper tools for maintaining and optimizing Windows**
- **Maintain and optimize Windows NT/2000/XP**
- **Troubleshoot Windows NT/2000/XP**

Microsoft has used its 20-plus years of experience with OSs to optimize the latest versions of Windows, so that, out of the box, they are easy to maintain. They have also searched for ways to make the tasks of maintaining, optimizing and troubleshooting less onerous. A good place to start is by standardizing the "look and feel" of the software tools you use. For years techs have accepted as their lot in life the curse of using dozens of different graphical user interface (GUI) tools that simply did not behave in the same way. Microsoft addressed this issue in Windows 2000 and XP with the Microsoft Management Console (MMC). Before you encounter the actual tasks for maintaining, optimizing, and troubleshooting, take a look at the MMC info in the beginning of this chapter. In this section I'll also give you the cook's tour of just a few of the tools you'll work with. I'll show you the rest of the tools at work in the following sections, as we look at tasks for maintaining and optimizing Windows and my favorite troubleshooting tips.

■ Tools for Maintaining and Optimizing Windows

A few months ago a friend borrowed my favorite wood plane. Well, something happened to it (he never said exactly what), and what he returned to me wasn't my daddy's old wood plane with the wonderful veneer, but a brand new one. Probably the most expensive one he could find that was similar. Well, it works beautifully, actually better than my old one, but it just doesn't feel the same. I guess that's how I feel about Microsoft changing the look of my favorite GUI tools. They all work even better than the old ones, but they just don't feel the same.

Many techs and even more users show amazing reluctance to try a new operating system for the same reason that I miss my old wood plane. No

The Microsoft Management Console (MMC)

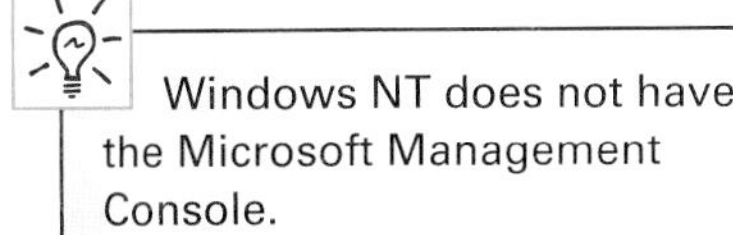

Windows NT does not have the Microsoft Management Console.

The **Microsoft Management Console** (MMC) is simply a shell program that holds individual utilities called **snap-ins**. You can start the MMC by opening the Run option and typing in **MMC** to get a blank MMC console. Blank MMC consoles aren't much to look at, as you can see in Figure 16.1. So I'll show you how to make it more useful, by adding a snap-in, which gives me a chance to show off **Device Manager**, one of my favorite all-time tools. Then I'll give you a short tour of the Event Viewer MMC console.

Device Manager

A blank console is made useful by adding snap-ins. Let's do that now. In Windows 2000, click Console; in Windows XP, click File. In either OS select Add/Remove Snap-in, and then click the Add button to see a list of available snap-ins (Figure 16.2).

Virtually every traditional Windows tool is available as a snap-in. Even good old Device Manager is a snap-in in Windows 2000 and XP. Let's add the Device Manager snap-in to our custom console. After you click Add, you need to choose the computer the snap-in will manage, so select Local computer and click Finish. After this, close the

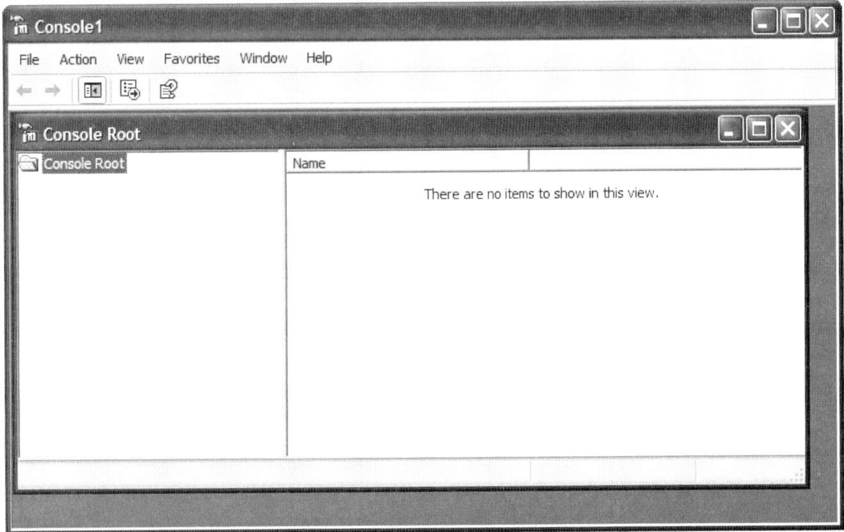

• **Figure 16.1** Blank MMC

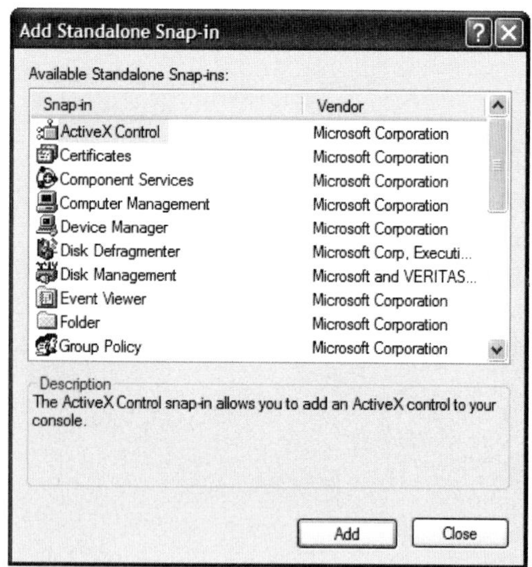

• **Figure 16.2** Available snap-ins

Add Standalone Snap-in box. The Device Manager will be listed in the Standalone page of the Add/Remove Snap-in box. Click OK to close it, and then click Device Manager under Console Root. The result should look like Figure 16.3.

You can add as many snap-ins as you'd like, and there are many to choose from. Many companies sell third-party utilities as MMC snap-ins. Once you've added the snap-ins you want, just save the console under any name you want, anywhere you want. I'll select File | Save As and save this console as DM (Device Manager) and drop it on my desktop. I'm now only a double-click away from the Device Manager! (Note that Windows NT doesn't have a Device Manager.)

If you want to, you can customize the MMC console. Select File (in XP) or Console (in 2000) | Options to change its icon, save it under a different name, or lock it up so it can't be changed. To lock it up you first need to change the console mode from the all-powerful Author mode to one of the other modes. Under any of these modes you simply select Do Not Save Changes To This Console. Once you check that box, and save and close the console, when it's reopened all the choices to modify or save the console are removed from the File (or Console) menu. This means that this console cannot be changed. Figure 16.4 shows the File menu when the console was "unlocked." Figure 16.5 shows this menu with the console "locked."

Microsoft also knows that some folks like things the old way so they created a bunch of pre-made, locked consoles for you and dropped them in the same places, or at least close

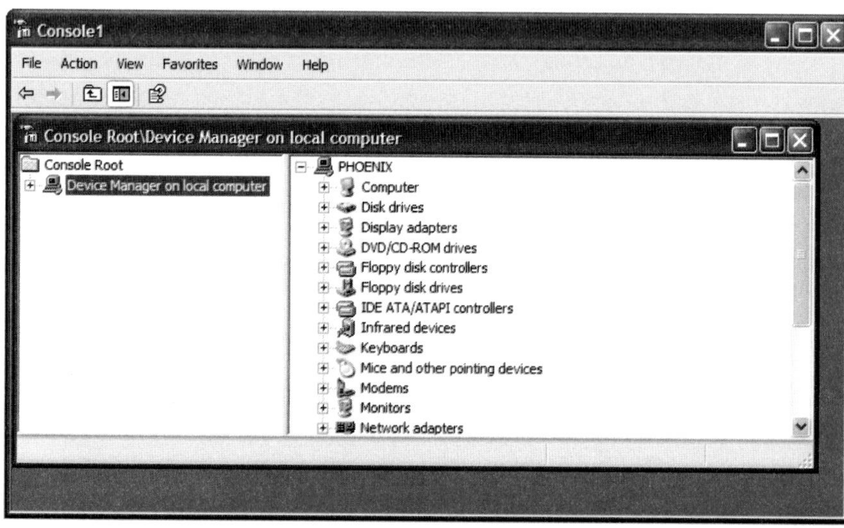

• **Figure 16.3** Device Manager as a snap-in

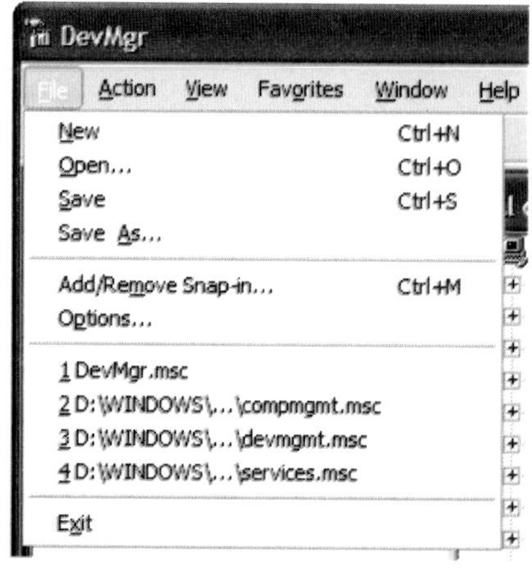

• **Figure 16.4** File menu on unlocked MMC console

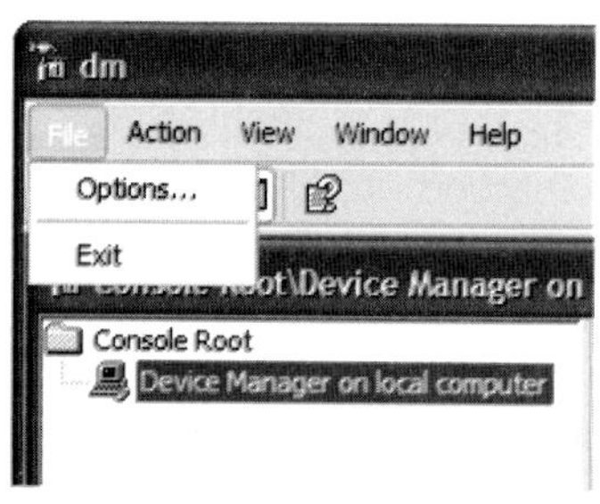

• **Figure 16.5** File menu on locked MMC console

to the same places, where you'd expect them to be (if you have previous experience with Windows 9*x*). You can open the System Information Utility in Windows 2000/XP, for example, by clicking Start | Programs | Accessories | System Tools | System Information. It's the good old System Information utility, but as you can see in Figure 16.6, it's an MMC snap-in. The snap-in versions of the old classics all look a tad different, but they still do the same job; in fact, they usually do it better!

Tech Tip

WinMSD

*Why mess around with five menu levels? Go to Start | Run and type **WINMSD** to open the System Information utility. It even works in Windows NT, although the tool is called Windows NT Diagnostics.*

Event Viewer

Event Viewer enables users of Windows NT, 2000, and XP to see what's happening behind the scenes with their OS. Work with the MMC snap-in Event Viewer for a while and you'll see that monitoring various log files reveals things about the health of the operating system through the behavior

Windows NT of course doesn't have the Event Viewer

Event Viewer icon. In Windows XP, open the Control Panel, double-click the Performance and Maintenance icon, then Administrative Tools, then Event Viewer. The Event Viewer will display events from three log files, Application, Security, and System. (More log files are available in server versions of Windows 2000.) Figure 16.7 shows the contents of a System event log in Event Viewer.

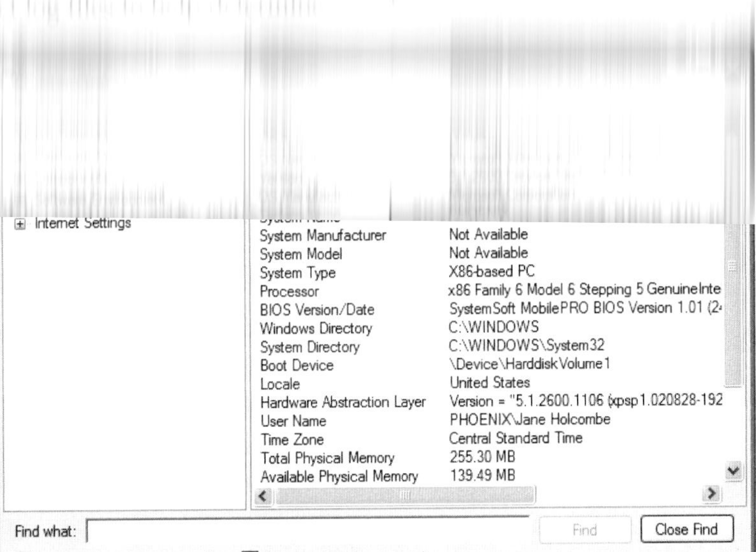

• **Figure 16.6** System Information as MMC

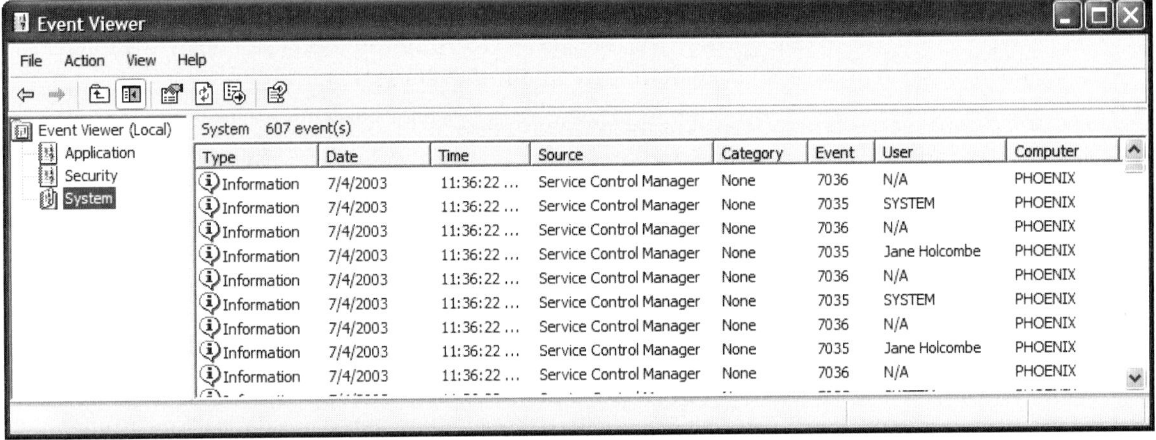

• **Figure 16.7** The System log in Event Viewer

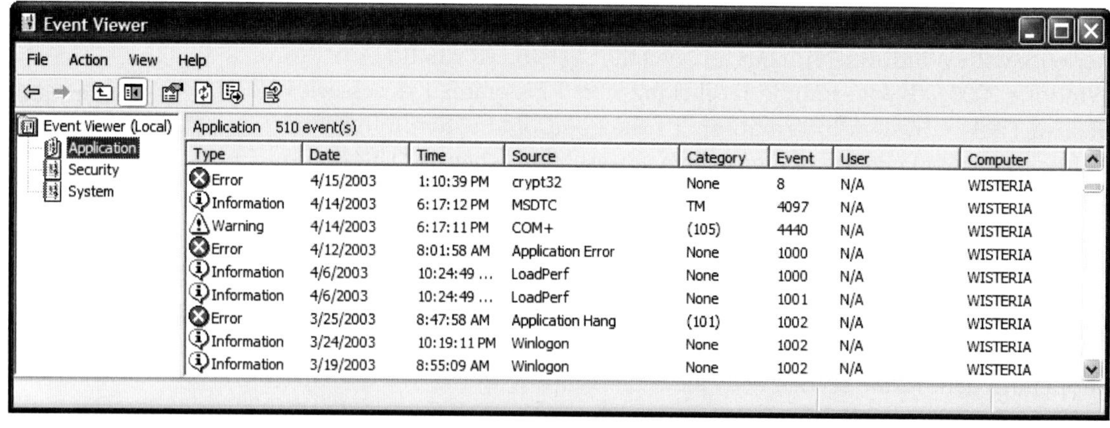

• **Figure 16.8** Application log showing three types of events

Tech Tip

Real techs don't waste time slogging through the menus for programs they use frequently. A quick way to start up Event Viewer is by selecting Start | Run and simply typing the name (the .MSC extension isn't necessary) of the saved console: EVENTVWR.

Types of Events Event Viewer displays five types of events. The System and Applications logs have Error, Warning, and Information events, while the Security log displays Success Audit and Failure Audit events. Figure 16.8 shows an Application log with three types of events displayed. An Error event is bad news—something's broken or data has been lost. In the Application log this can mean an entire application hung up or an operation failed. In the System log this can mean that a service failed. A service is a special program that provides specific functionality to the OS. A warning is something that isn't critical, but may mean there is trouble to come. For instance, if disk space is low, a Warning event is logged. An Information event is the only good news, because it means an application, driver, or service successfully completed an operation.

The success audit and failure audit events are only logged when auditing is turned on, and this is something that is usually only done on servers. It is rarely done on desktop computers.

Event Viewer Settings In Event Viewer, right-click on System and select Properties. In Properties look at the Log Size box, which defines the maximum size a log file may grow to, and what action should be taken when the log file reaches the maximum. The defaults are 512 KB and Overwrite Events Older Than 7 Days. I usually change this to 1024 KB and select Overwrite Events As Needed (see Figure 16.9), simply because I enjoy the longer log files. You can do this for all three event logs.

Try This!

Run Event Viewer

It's no fun just to read along and not play with the toys, so try this!

1. Select Start | Run.
2. In the Run box type **eventvwr** and press ENTER.
3. Select the Help menu and browse through the Event Viewer Help console.
4. When you're done, close Help.

Sometimes I get dizzy as I scroll through tons of events, but I can fix that with Filter settings. Now click on the Filter tab and I'll show you. Figure 16.10 shows the filter settings for what is displayed so that when you are viewing a large log file, you can filter out events based on type, source, category, ID, user, computer, and date. This only controls what Event Viewer displays; all events

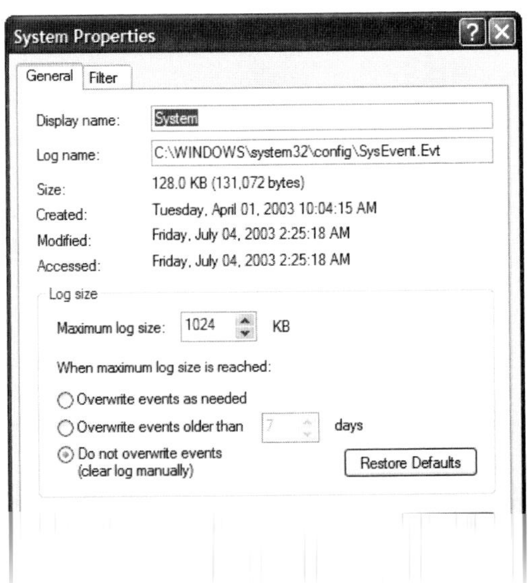

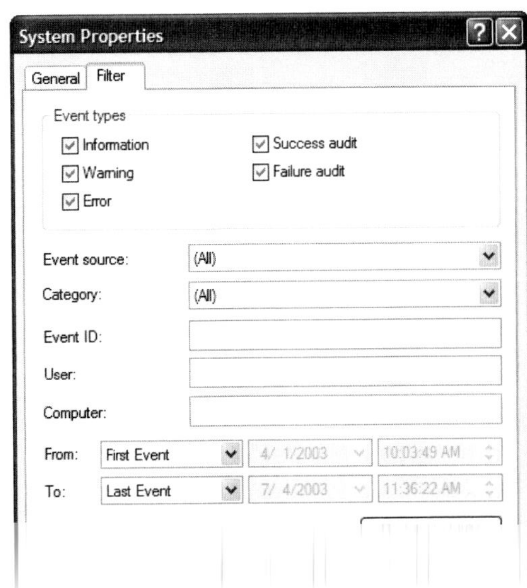

tings. Now click OK to close the Properties dialog box.

Clearing, Archiving and Opening a Log File Windows will tell you when it's time for spring cleaning by popping up the message, "Event log is full." You know it's time to open Event Viewer and clear the log! Clear the System Log by right-clicking System Log and selecting Clear all Events. You'll be prompted to save the System log. Click the Yes button.

You can archive a log file that you want to be able to view later by saving it to a different filename. I have a convention for naming log files: I begin with "sys" or "app" or "sec" to indicate the type of log, then I use the date. (I could depend on the file time stamp for the date, but I prefer this.) You can even save it to another location, like a network drive or removable disk.

To open the file you just saved, click on the Action menu, select Open Log File, select the file, then the log type (System, Application, or Security), and then click Open. Your saved log file will open. In Figure 16.11 notice how the open log archive appears in the left pane of Event Viewer.

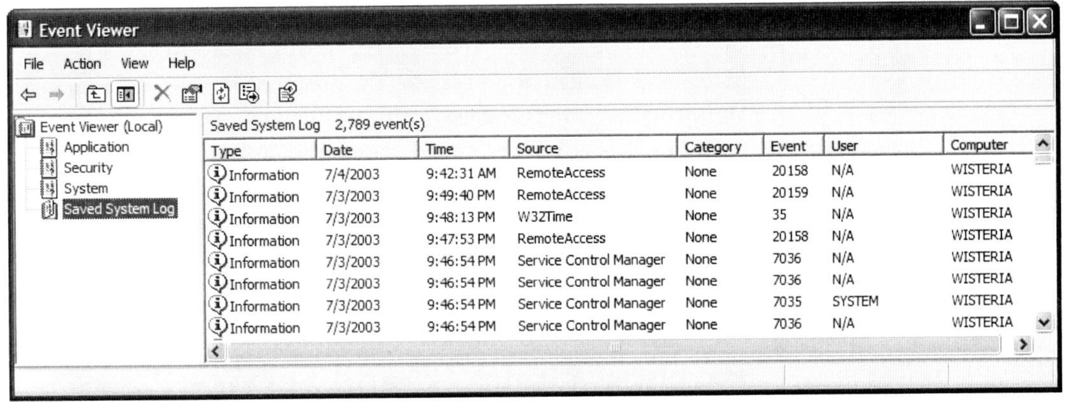

• **Figure 16.11** Viewing a saved log file

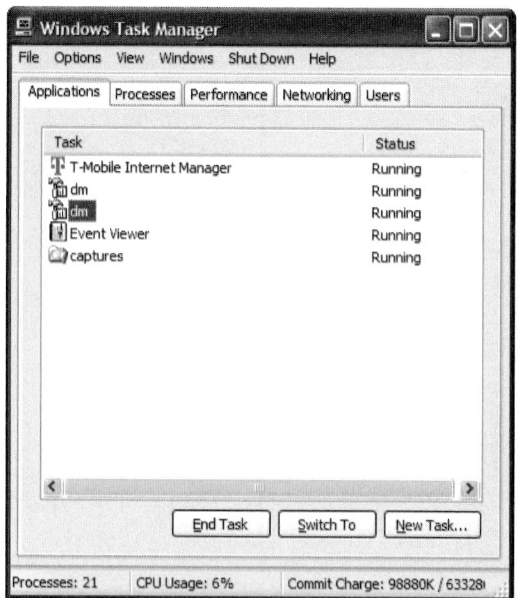

• **Figure 16.12** Applications tab

Task Manager

The **Task Manager** enables you to see applications and programs running on the PC and, in most cases, force them closed (Figure 16.12). Although not an MMC, the Task Manager is a primary tool in the tech's toolbox. To open Task Manager, press CTRL-SHIFT-ESC (NT/2000/XP) or CTRL-ALT-DEL *once* (9*x*/Me). By default the Task Manager window sits on top of all other open windows, even when you try to switch away. If you want to change that behavior, simply go to the Options menu and deselect (remove the check) from Always On Top.

Now you're ready to work with it. Task Manager shows you what applications and processes are running and how they're using your computer's resources. In particular, you can see how much memory and the percentage of the CPU an application is using. It is especially handy for ending a program that won't shut down normally. Figure 16.12 shows the application tab where you can select an application and click End Task to remove it or Switch to it with another button click. It also shows that I have two instances of an application open.

The Task Manager in Windows NT/2000/XP enables you to close down applications, but also goes one step further and enables you to shut off processes. The Processes tab (Figure 16.13) is your place of last resort for shutting down locked-up processes. Shutting down processes is a *very* dangerous thing to do. Don't bother memorizing all these processes because every version of Windows shows different ones; just make sure you know how to get to the Task Manager to shut down applications or processes! I'll come back to Task Manager later in this chapter when we look at performance tuning.

Alternate-click (right-click) an application in Task Manager to see other tasks you can perform.

Windows Task Manager

File Options View Shut Down Help

Applications | Processes | Performance | Networking | Users

Image Name	User Name	CPU	Mem Usage
msmsgs.exe	Jane Holme	00	3,176 K
explorer.exe	Jane Holme	01	6,708 K
mmc.exe	Jane Holme	00	15,788 K
mmc.exe	Jane Holme	00	1,144 K
atievxx.exe	SYSTEM	00	1,596 K
spoolsv.exe	SYSTEM	00	3,568 K
svchost.exe	LOCAL SERVICE	00	3,424 K
svchost.exe	NETWORK SERVICE	00	1,676 K
svchost.exe	SYSTEM	01	18,616 K
svchost.exe	SYSTEM	00	2,772 K
taskmgr.exe	Jane Holcombe	03	3,732 K
lsass.exe	SYSTEM	00	1,032 K
services.exe	SYSTEM	03	10,712 K
winlogon.exe	SYSTEM	00	2,032 K
csrss.exe	SYSTEM	00	3,472 K
smss.exe	SYSTEM	00	344 K
System	SYSTEM	01	216 K
System Idle Process	SYSTEM	91	20 K

Show processes from all users | End Process

Processes: 21 | CPU Usage: 9% | Commit Charge: 129764K / 6332

• **Figure 16.13** Processes tab

Maintaining and Optimizing Windows

Optimizing Windows means making sure that it runs as well as it can. Since many maintenance tasks contribute to the optimization of Windows, we'll lump these topics together here. Maintaining Windows NT/2000/XP requires you to do several things: keep the system patches up to date; keep it optimized to run smoothly using the typical tools—Disk Defragmenter, Check Disk (like Windows 9*x*/Me ScanDisk), and Disk Cleanup; and finally, prepare for possible (not quite inevitable as in the past) system crashes by maintaining good backups, current boot disks, and the Recovery Console. Maintenance of Windows also includes adding or removing Windows components, installing new applications, and installing and updating device drivers.

Patches, Updates, and Service Packs

Windows updates have been an important, but often neglected, task for computer users. Typically, Microsoft finds and corrects problems with its software in a timely fashion. Because earlier versions of Windows let users decide when, if ever, to update their computers, the net result could be disastrous. The Blaster worm hammered computers all over the world in the summer of 2003, causing thousands of computers to start rebooting spontaneously and even contributing to the massive power outage in the Northeast USA and parts of Canada. No small feat for a tiny piece of programming! Blaster exploited a flaw in Windows NT/2000/XP and spread like wildfire, but Microsoft had already corrected the flaw with a security update weeks earlier. If users had simply updated their computers, the virus-caused damage would not have been so widespread.

Windows NT has Check Disk, but not Disk Defragmenter or Disk Cleanup. You need third-party tools to defragment in NT.

To help avoid this problem in the future, Microsoft continues to improve their Windows Update web page, taking advantage of nearly universal Internet connectivity. They also have provided a Windows Update utility in Windows 2000/XP. If your computer is connected to the Internet, start the [illegible] patches and security updates. You can scroll through the list and review the

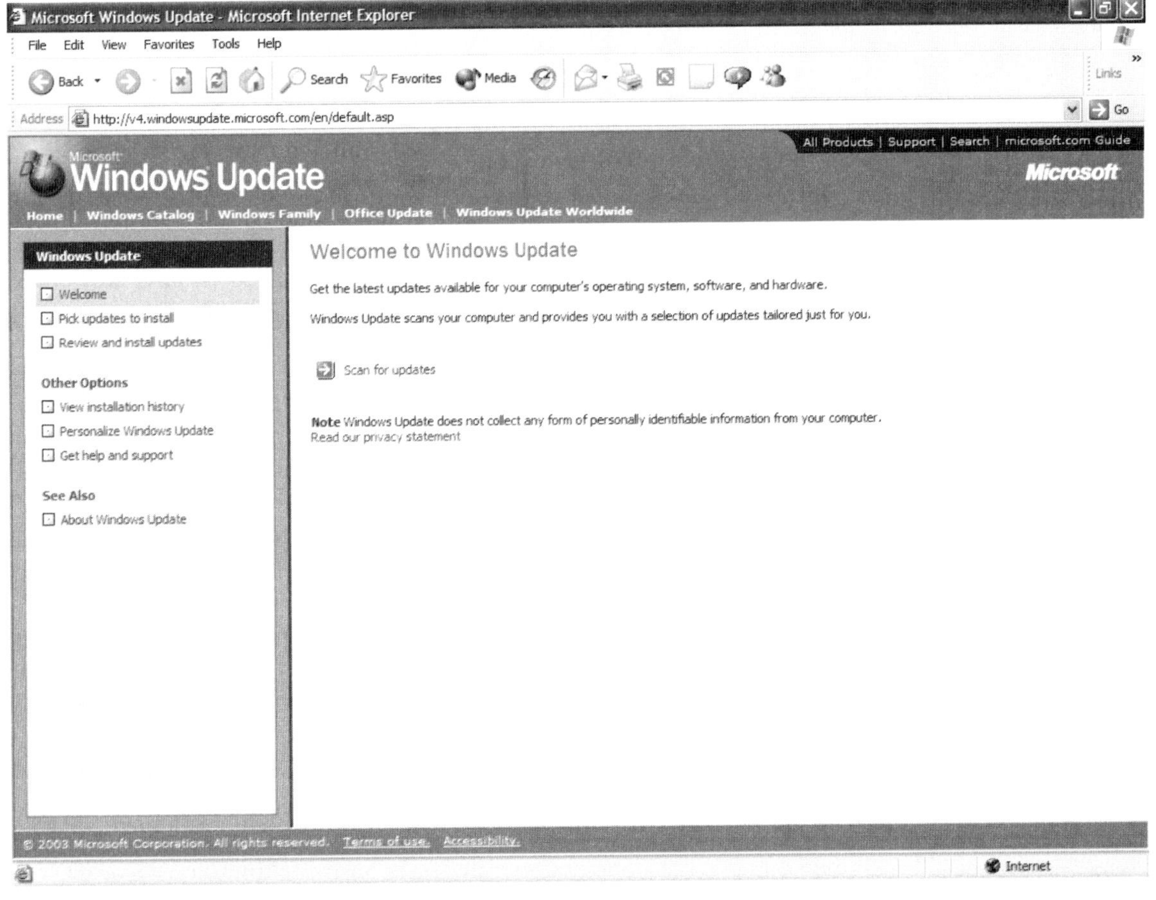

• **Figure 16.14** Microsoft Windows Update page

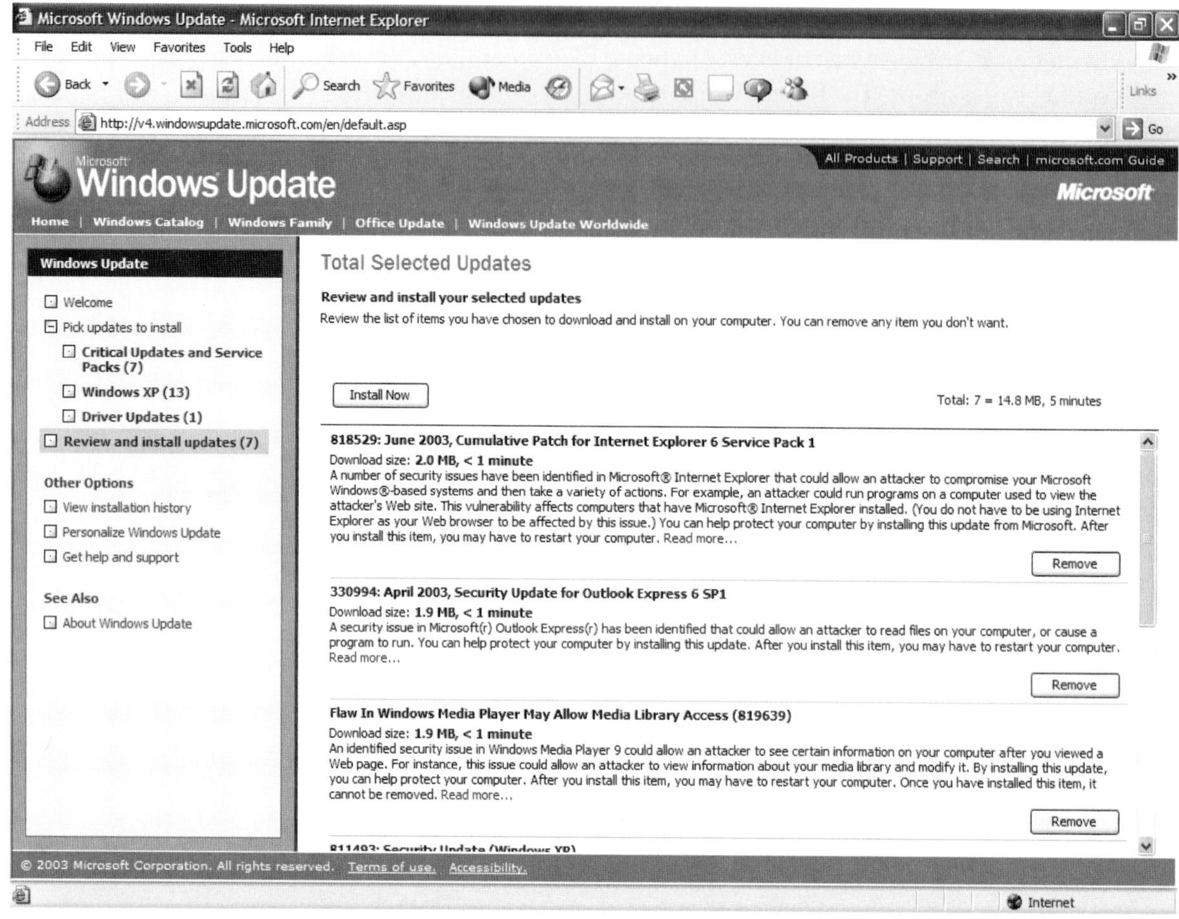

• **Figure 16.15** Choose updates to be installed.

description of each update. If you click the Remove button, that update will be removed from the list. When you click Install Now, all the updates remaining in the list are installed. This first involves copying all the files to the local hard disk drive, then installing the updates. A dialog box like that in Figure 16.16 appears during the copying and installing phases.

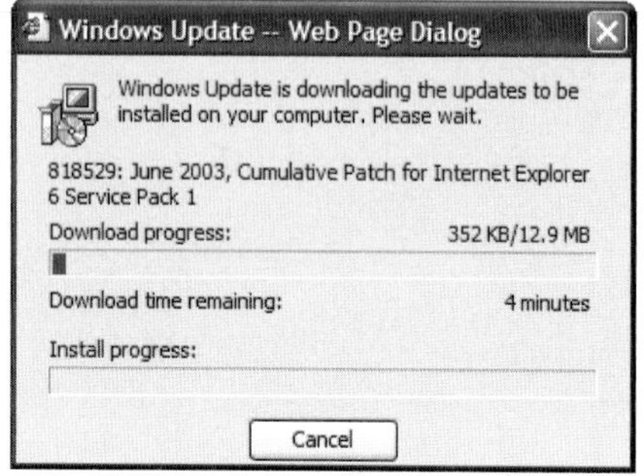

• **Figure 16.16** Windows Update download and install dialog box

Automatic Update

Because updates are so important Microsoft gives you the option to update Windows automatically. Actually, they nag you about it! Soon after installing XP (a day or two in my experience), a message balloon will pop up from the taskbar suggesting that you automate updates. If you click this taskbar, the Automatic Updates Setup Wizard will run, allowing you to configure the update program. You say you've never seen this message balloon, and would certainly like to automate the update process? No problem—simply right-click My Computer (on the Start menu), select Properties, then click the Automatic Updates tab and select Automatic Update options. Then, whenever your computer connects to the Web, it checks the Windows Update page. What happens next depends on the setting you choose. Your choices are listed here:

- Notify Me Before Downloading Any Updates And Notify Me Again Before Installing Them On My Computer
- Download The Updates Automatically And Notify Me When They Are Ready To Be Installed (This is the default setting when Automatic Updates is turned on.)
- Automatically Download The Updates, And Install Them On The Schedule That I Specify

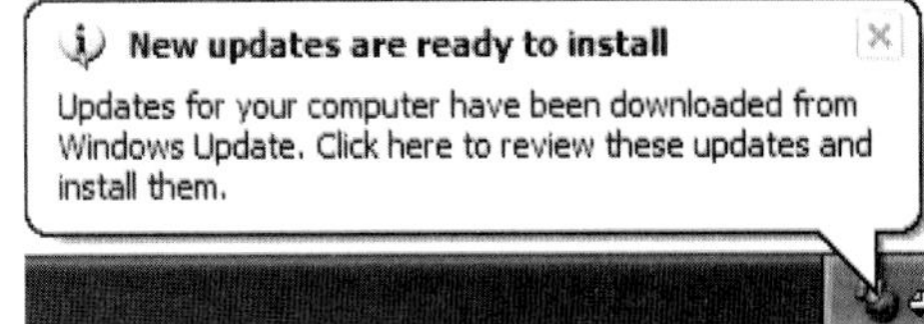

With the default setting, when a new patch is available it downloads the updates and a balloon message box pops up, as shown in Figure 16.17. If you click anywhere on the balloon (except on the Close button) it will display the list of updates available, and you can select those you wish to install. Then Windows Update installs it for you. [illegible]

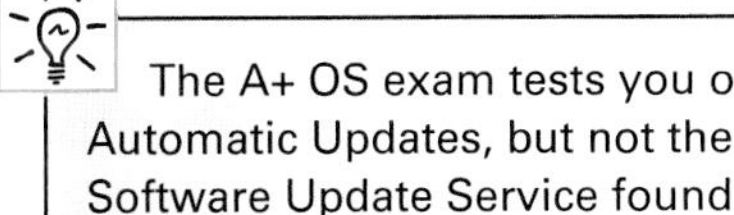

[illegible] works like to control the software added to each machine. They may want to test new updates in-house with their software and hardware configurations before releasing updates to the general population. Microsoft's answer to this situation is the Software Update Service (SUS), which software administrators can install on a Windows 2000 and higher network server. Once installed, the administrators can control the distribution of updates to the Windows desktops. This is not something you need to know for the A+ exam, but it's always nice to know what's going on around you.

The A+ OS exam tests you on Automatic Updates, but not the Software Update Service found in corporate offices.

Installing Software

Most application programs are distributed on CD-ROMs. Luckily, Windows supports Autorun, a feature that enables it to look for and read a special file called Autorun immediately after a CD-ROM is inserted and then run whatever program is listed in Autorun.inf. Most application programs distributed on CD have an Autorun file that calls up the installation program.

Sometimes, however, it is simply necessary to institute the installation sequence yourself. Perhaps the install CD lacks an Autorun installation program, or perhaps Windows is configured so that Autorun programs must be started manually. In some cases, a CD may contain more than one program, and you must choose which of them to install. Regardless of the reason, beginning the installation manually is a simple and straightforward process using the Add or Remove Programs (Add/Remove Programs in Windows 9*x*/Me/NT/2000) applet in the Control Panel. Click the Add New Programs button (Figure 16.18), follow the prompts and provide the disk or location of the files.

Typically, you will have to accept the terms of the software license before you are allowed to install the application. These steps are not optional since the installation simply won't proceed until you accept all terms the software manufacturer requires and enter the correct code. You may also be asked to make several decisions during the installation process. For example,

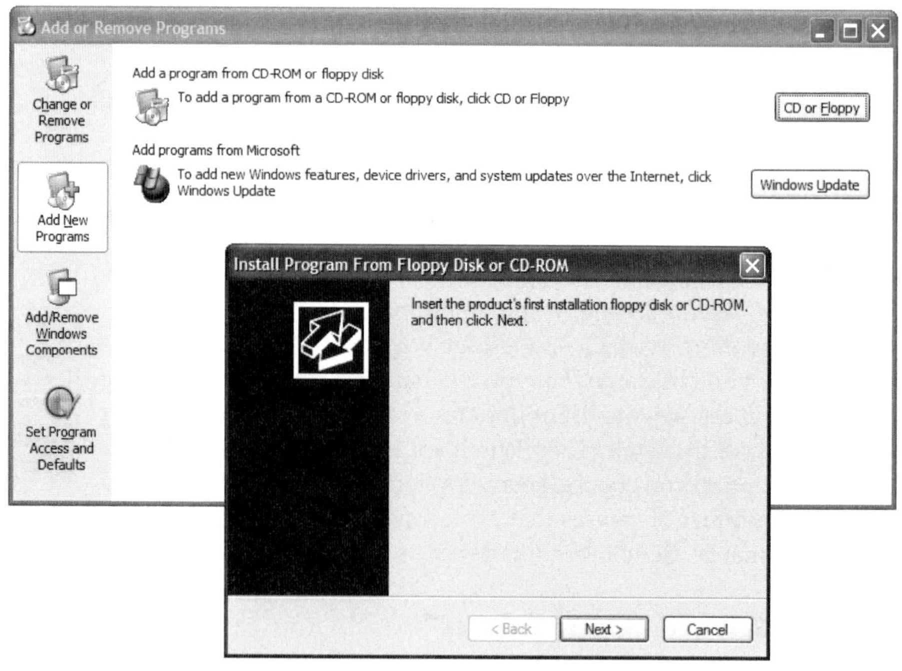

• **Figure 16.18** Install program from floppy disk or CD-ROM.

> Most application programs are licensed for use on a single computer. If you want to install the program on another computer, the license typically requires you to first remove it from the computer where it was installed.

you may be asked where you would like to install the program and if you would like certain optional components installed. Generally speaking, it is best to simply accept the suggested settings.

Removing Software

Each installed application program takes up space on your computer's hard disk, and programs that you no longer need or use simply waste space that could be used for other purposes, so removing them can be an important piece of housekeeping.

You remove a program from a Windows PC in much the same manner as you installed it. That is, you use the applications' own uninstall program, when possible. You will normally find the uninstall program listed under the application icon off the Start Menu, as shown in Figure 16.19.

If an uninstall program is not available, then use Windows' Add or Remove Programs applet from Control Panel. Figure 16.20 shows this applet. You select the program you want to remove and click the Change or Remove button. It does not all disappear in a flash. First you'll see a message warning you that the program will be permanently removed from your PC. If you're certain you want to continue, click Yes.

You may then see a message telling you that a shared file that

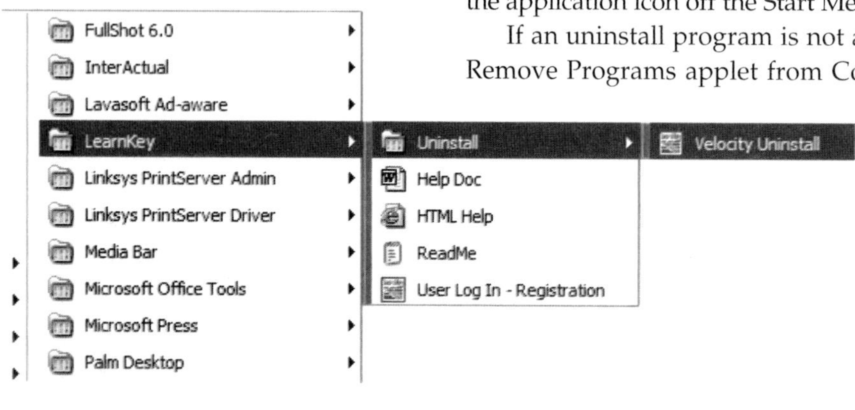

• **Figure 16.19** An application's uninstall program

appears to no longer be in use is about to be deleted, and asking your approval. Generally speaking, it's safe to delete such files. If you do not delete them, they will likely be orphaned and remain unused on your hard disk forever.

In some cases clicking the Change/Remove button will start the application's install program (the one you couldn't find before) so that you can modify the installed features

Figure 16.20 Confirm that you want to remove the program.

Adding or Removing Windows Components

When you installed Windows it tried to guess which optional Windows components you would need. It installed Notepad, modem support, and games on your computer. These Windows components can be removed from your system if you like, and other components can be added as well. If you're adding components, you'll need a copy of your Windows CD, or another location where the Windows source files are stored. This is a task that really hasn't changed from previous versions of Windows.

To add or remove a Windows component, open the Add or Remove Programs applet in Control Panel (Add/Remove Programs in Windows versions prior to XP) from Control Panel. From here select Add/Remove Windows Components, which opens the Windows Components Wizard (Figure 16.21). You can select an installed program; see how frequently it is used, how much disk space it uses, and (sometimes) the last time it was used.

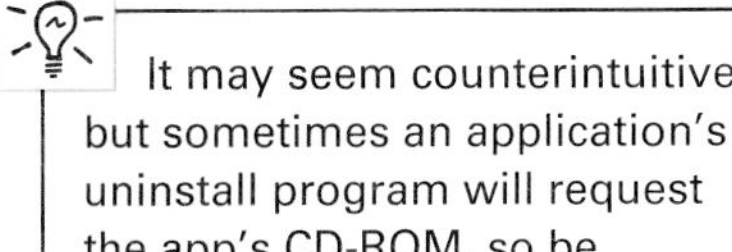

It may seem counterintuitive, but sometimes an application's uninstall program will request the app's CD-ROM, so be prepared.

Installing/Adding a Device

The processes for installing new hardware in Windows 2000 and Windows XP are absolutely identical to the procedures you use in Windows 9*x*/Me, even down to the troubleshooting and backup utilities. Just remember what you learned in Chapters 5 and 6: In the

Try This!

Remove an Application

Every tech needs to be comfortable removing an application, so try this!

1. Log onto your PC using an account with Administrator rights.
2. Open the Control Panel.
3. Open the Add/Remove Programs icon.
4. Examine the list of installed programs and remove one you no longer use.

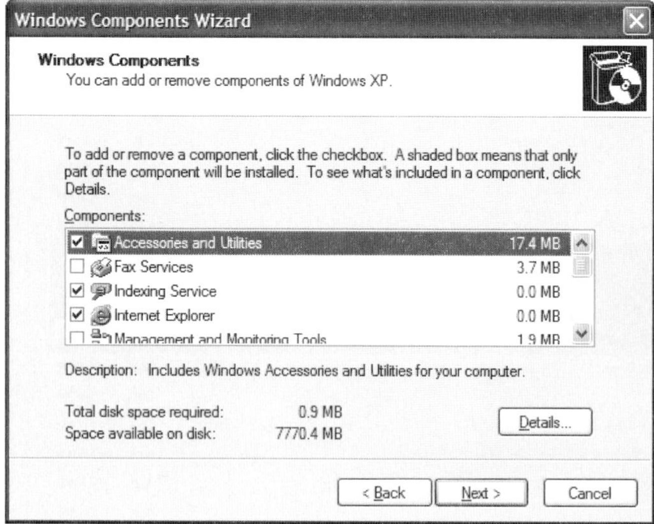

Figure 16.21 Windows Components Wizard

case of a resource conflict, you need to reserve the resource in CMOS! If you know how to install PnP and legacy devices in Windows 9*x*/Me, you know how to do it in Windows 2000 and Windows XP!

Drivers

One of the most wonderful things about personal computers is that you can turn a dumb machine into the exact tool or tools you desire by adding the hardware and software to build your dream machine. One reason this is possible is that Windows is very, very customizable. Windows can be made to control a hardware device that didn't even exist 6 months ago. How is this possible? The OS and the programs you run do not have to know the nitty-gritty details of every hardware device you use. They simply use generic commands for each type of hardware, like a printer, camera, mouse, or video adapter. Specialized driver software then takes these commands and translates them into the correct commands for the specific device. Some devices even require more than one driver.

In the DOS days a tech had to know the exact name of the driver file, had to copy it to the boot disk, and had to edit a configuration file to add the correct command. At bootup this configuration file was read by the OS and the device drivers were installed into the OS. In addition, the tech had to take the correct steps to configure the device, either at the hardware level or through software. Today with smarter hardware and software, a tech doesn't have to fiddle with directly editing configuration files, but you still may have to go looking for a correct device driver. Where do you find the driver? Look on the discs that come with each device, check Microsoft's web site and the web site of the device manufacturer.

> **Tech Tip**
>
> **Installing Devices in Windows NT**
>
> *Windows NT does not play well with a lot of devices out there, especially things like fancy video and sound cards, and as you know does not support Plug and Play. You've got to work at it if you want to install anything remotely modern in an NT machined!*
>
> *The process for installing devices in NT should follow a simple model. First, check the HCL for the device in question and if it's not there, plan for problems. Second, get the latest drivers specifically written for Windows NT. Don't bother with drivers written for 2000 or XP. Third, cross your fingers and install the device and driver. And don't say I didn't warn you!*
>
> *If you get in a bind and have to use a Plug and Play card, Microsoft offers a small ray of hope. You can add a driver that enables NT to detect and install some Plug and Play devices. Go to the Microsoft support site at http://support.microsoft.com and search for Knowledge Base article #156354.*

Driver Signing

Device drivers become part of the operating system and as such have the potential to cause lots of problems if they're written poorly. To protect Windows systems from bad device drivers, Microsoft introduced in Windows 2000 something called Driver Signing which means that the driver has a digital signature. Digital signatures are issued by Microsoft to drivers that have been tested at the Windows Hardware Quality Lab. Look on the packaging of a hardware device. If you see the Designed for Windows 2000 or the Designed for Windows XP logo, the driver packaged with the device is digitally signed. Any drivers included on the Windows CD-ROM or at the Windows Update web site are now required to be digitally signed. Once a **digitally signed driver** is installed, you can look at the Properties of the driver to see confirmation that it was digitally signed. Figure 16.22 shows a digitally signed network card driver.

However, many manufacturers issue drivers that are not digitally signed. I personally have installed many of them. When an unsigned driver is detected during hardware installation, you'll see the message in Figure 16.23 that offers the options to stop the installation or to continue it. So, you might

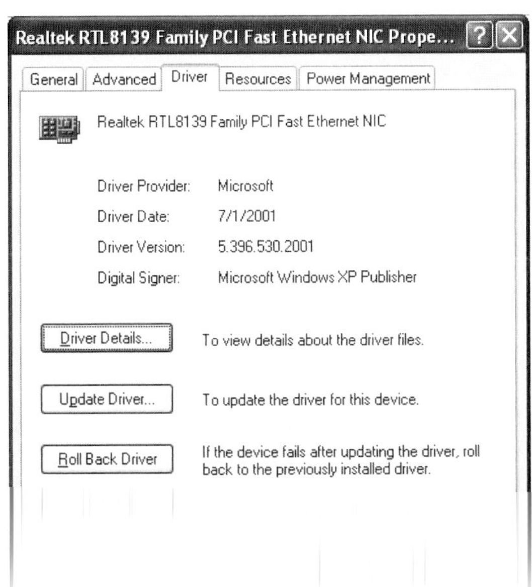

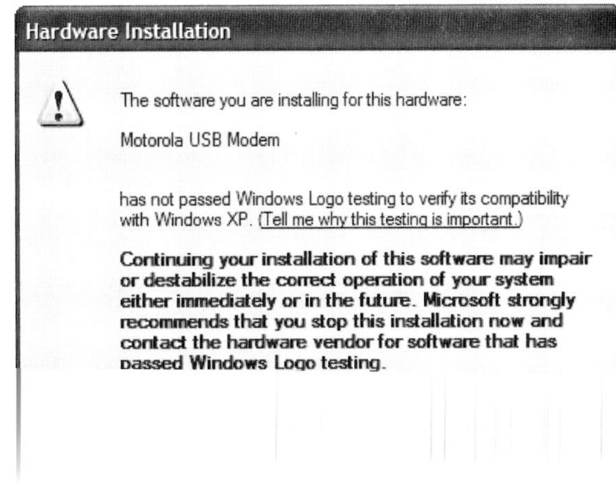

ask, "What's the point?" Well, I knew I was taking a chance with that driver, and, if a problem occurred after it was installed, I could use another new tool, System Restore, to restore my computer to the state it was in before I installed that driver.

You can control how Windows behaves when drivers are being installed. On the Hardware tab of the System Properties box click the Driver Signing button to display the Driver Signing Options page shown in Figure 16.24. If you select Ignore, Windows will install an unsigned driver without warning you. If you select Warn, you will be prompted when Windows detects an unsigned driver during driver installation, and you will be given the opportunity to either cancel the installation or continue. Choosing Block will simply not install unsigned drivers.

The default Driver Signing setting is Warn. This also is the default setting during installation, so you will always be warned when Windows detects an unsigned driver during Windows installation. This is no problem for an installation like the one we described in Chapter 14, where you are sitting at the computer, responding to all prompts—but it is a problem for automated, unattended installations. So now you have another reason to check out all your device drivers before installing Windows.

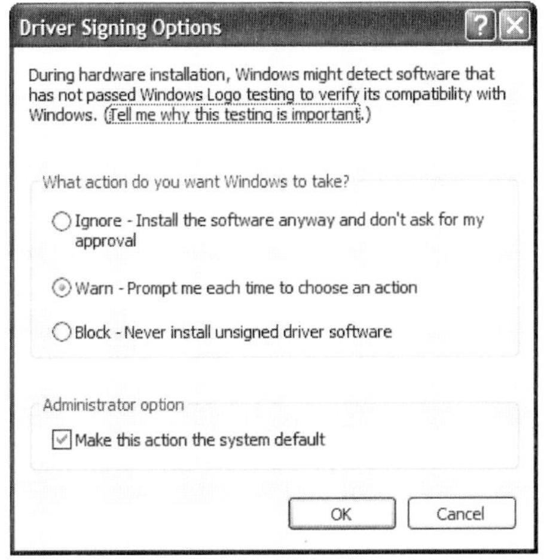

Figure 16.24 Driver Signing options

Device Manager

Device Manager is the software equivalent to my multipurpose pocket tool! Because it's so versatile it's been a favorite of techs since it first appeared in Windows 95. But like most multi-purpose tools, you can only have one tool out at a time. The user interface has progressively improved through Windows 98, Me, 2000, and XP (and still doesn't exist

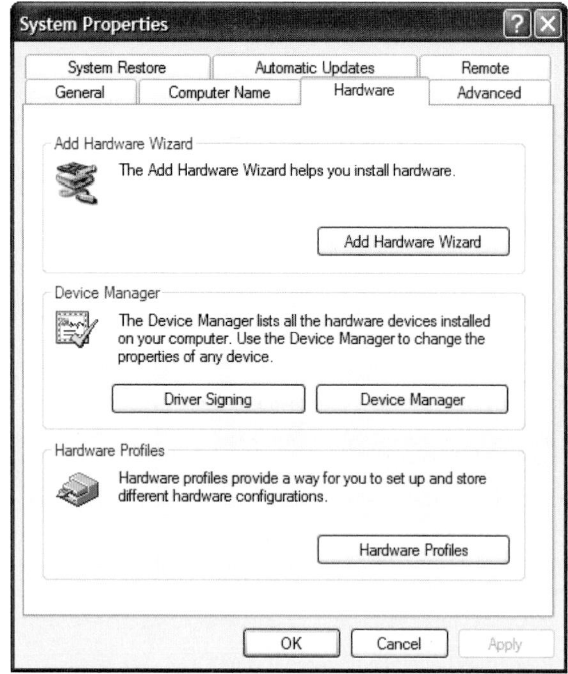

• **Figure 16.25** Hardware tab

for NT); and driver rollback in Windows XP may reduce the number of grey hairs earned by computer techs.

Earlier in this chapter I showed you how to make a custom console containing the Device Manager snap-in, but I didn't show you where you find it in Windows if you don't want to make your own console. If you worked with Device Manager in Windows 9*x*, try opening it in Windows 2000 or Windows XP the same old way. Open the properties for My Computer to display the System Properties. Hey, wait a minute! New choices are available! Of all those tabs, guess which one you need to click now to see the Device Manager? That's right, Hardware (Figure 16.25).

Hey! Where's the Device Manager? See the Device Manager button right in the middle? There you go!

Once you get Device Manager open you'll see the device tree, the list of active devices. At the root level is the computer itself (named Wisteria in Figure 16.26). The level below that contains device nodes. Each device node in turn contains one or more devices. I expanded some of the nodes in Figure 16.26 to show devices.

A right-click on one of the devices displays the context menu. From here you can choose to update or uninstall the driver, disable the device, scan for hardware changes, or display the Properties box. When you open the Properties box, there are buttons labeled Driver Details, Update Driver, Roll Back Driver, and Uninstall. Driver Details lists the driver files and locations on disk; Update Driver opens the Hardware Update Wizard; Roll Back Driver allows you to remove an updated driver, thus rolling back to the previous driver version; and Uninstall removes the driver.

An *active device* means exactly that—the device is connected and turned on. If it is inactive it will not be listed. For instance, when I unplug the Motorola USB modem, it disappears from the device tree.

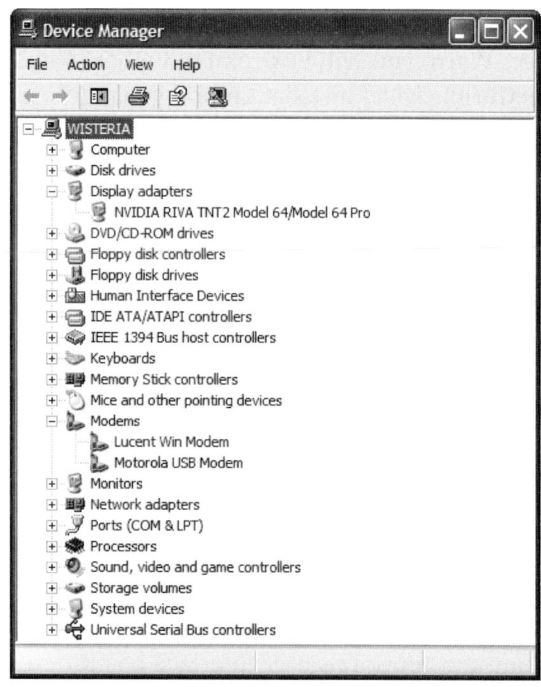

• **Figure 16.26** Device Manager with nodes expanded

Adding a Plug and Play Device

In theory, and almost always in practice, it is simple to install a new Plug and Play device to a Windows 2000/XP computer. You simply plug it in and Windows will detect it and install the driver. Of course, to be on the safe side, always read the documentation for the new device, just in case there is a new twist, like having to install the driver first.

If Windows does not detect

Try This!

Techs need to know the Device Manager inside and out because of its central importance as a tool for checking hardware, drivers, and resources. If you've not taken the time yet to master Device Manager yet, try this!

1. From the Start menu, right-click My Computer and select Properties.
2. In System Properties select the Hardware tab, and then click the Device Manager button.
3. Expand several device nodes.
4. Double-click a device icon to open the Properties dialog box.

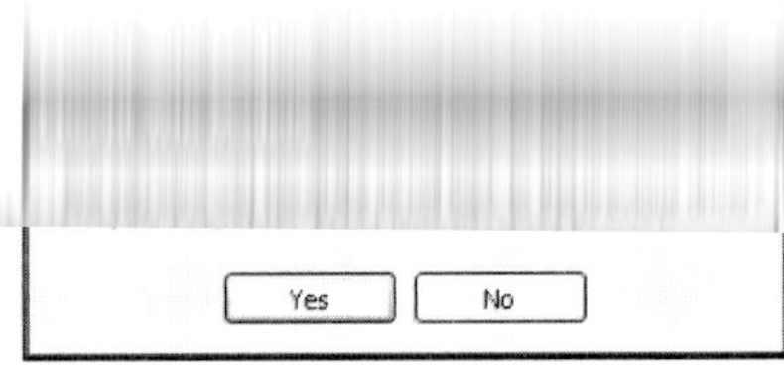

Figure 16.27 Driver rollback warning

Adding a Non-Plug and Play Device

As cool as this Plug and Play stuff is, a tech still has to know how to install non-Plug and Play devices, also called legacy devices. Windows even comes with drivers for non-Plug and Play devices and there are also many available from manufacturers. Some devices have Windows 2000 drivers, which might work in Windows XP if you're really lucky. Round up the driver beforehand, read any documentation you can find on the device, and then install the hardware. If you found a setup program with the driver, run that now.

If there is no setup program, then call on the Add Hardware Wizard. Click Next on the Welcome screen, and it will search for hardware that has

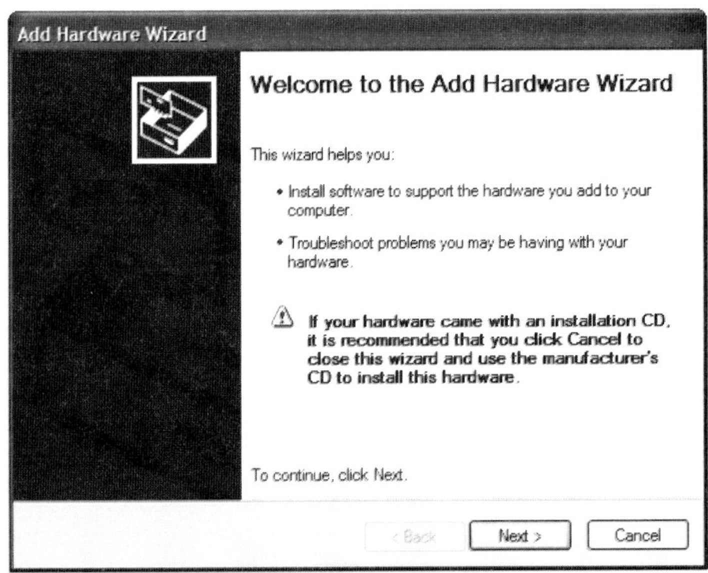

Figure 16.28 Add Hardware Wizard

The "plug" in Plug and Play really only applies to USB, IEEE 1394, and SCSI devices, which can simply be plugged in while the computer is running. When installing a PCI or ISA plug and play card, you've got to power down, install the card, and power up again before Windows will recognize the device and install the drivers.

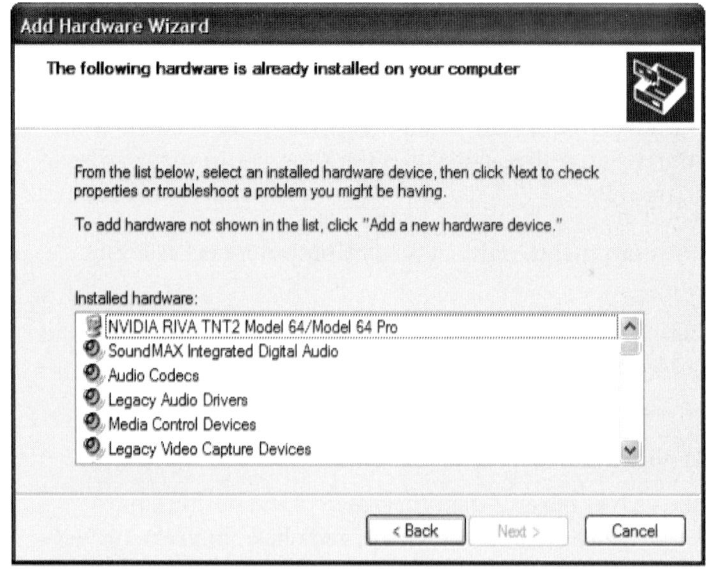

• **Figure 16.29** Installed hardware

been connected but does not yet have a driver installed. If it detects it, select the device and the wizard will install the driver. You may have to point to the source location for the driver files. If it does not detect the device, which is very likely, it will ask you if the hardware is connected. When you answer yes and click Next, it will give you a list of installed hardware, similar to that shown in Figure 16.29.

If the device is in the list, select it and click Next. If not, scroll to the bottom and select Add a New Hardware Device, and then click Next. If the device is a printer, network card, or modem, select Search For And Install The Hardware Automatically and click Next. In which case, once it detects the device and installs the driver, you're done. But if it is not one of these devices, your best hope is to select Install The Hardware That I Manually Select From A List. In the following screens select the appropriate device category, then select the device manufacturer and the correct model and respond to the prompts from the Add Hardware Wizard to complete the installation.

Adding a Printer in NT

Adding a printer in Windows NT 4.0 is similar to adding one in Windows 2000 or Windows XP, with screens that lead you through the process. The Windows NT screens don't look the same, but they offer almost the same features. The biggest difference, as you can well imagine, is that none of the screens offer Plug and Play settings! Note also that NT has a problem with most modern printers because NT does not support USB devices.

Adding a Printer

In spite of optimistic predictions heard many times over the years, the paperless office is still pretty much a pipe dream. Most computer users still need printers, so we'll look at the process of installing a printer in Windows 2000/XP (which you can do only if you are a member of the Administrators group). Adding a printer in Windows is really simply adding a printer driver, which you need to do whether the printer is directly connected to your computer or connected elsewhere on the network. When you install a local printer and then share it so that others on your network can use it, your computer plays the role of a print server. Remember that a printer directly connected to your computer (local) is still local even if you intend to share it on the network.

Always read the manufacturer's instructions before connecting and installing a new printer (or any device). The following are the most likely printer installation scenarios for installing a driver for a locally connected printer.

If you are installing a Plug and Play printer using a USB cable, run the printer's installation program. Then with Windows running and the printer powered on, plug in the cable. If all goes well, this is a non-event. You might notice a quick flicker in the tray area of the task bar, but otherwise you will have to open the Printers and Faxes console to confirm that the printer was installed.

If you are installing a Plug and Play printer connected via the parallel port, connect the printer, turn it on, and run the printer installation program. Respond to any prompts, and you're done. If the drivers come with Windows, or if you found drivers, but no special installation program, then open the Printers and Faxes folder or console. In Windows 2000 click the Add Printer icon to start the Add Printer wizard. In Windows XP select File | Add Printer to start the wizard. At the Welcome screen, click Next to continue.

On the Local or Network Printer page, choose Local Printer. Since the printer is Plug and Play, leave the check in the Automatically Detect And Install My Plug And Play Printer box (see Figure 16.30) and click Next. The printer should be detected and the drivers installed. The most you should have to do is provide the location for drivers not provided with Windows.

For a non-Plug and Play printer follow the instruction above, but when you get to the Local or Network Printer page clear the check box next to Automatically Detect And Install My Plug And Play Printer and then click Next. On the Select the

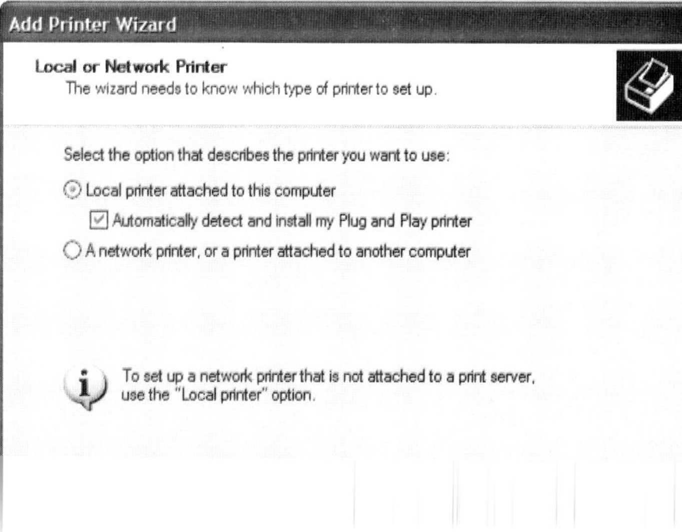

friendlier than the model name. This is not mandatory—the default is the model name—but you may want to do this to identify how the printer is being used: for example, Brochure Printer or Accounting Printer.

On the Printer Sharing page, if you plan to share the printer on a network, select Share As and give the printer yet another name—this time a share name by which it will be known on the network. Leave the default, or enter a short, friendly name; then click Next. On the Location and Comment page, enter a location for the printer and add a description in the Comment box. Then click Next.

When the Add Printer Wizard offers to print a test page, you should accept the offer and make sure the printer works. To close the wizard, click Finish.

Managing User Accounts and Groups

The most basic element of Windows security is the **user account**. Each user must present a valid username and the password of a local or domain user account in order to log on to an NT, 2000, or XP computer. Each user is also a member of one or more groups of users. Groups enable the system administrator to easily assign the same rights and permissions to all members of the group without the need to set those rights and permissions individually.

Windows NT, 2000, and XP have several built-in groups, and two user accounts created during installation—Administrator and Guest—

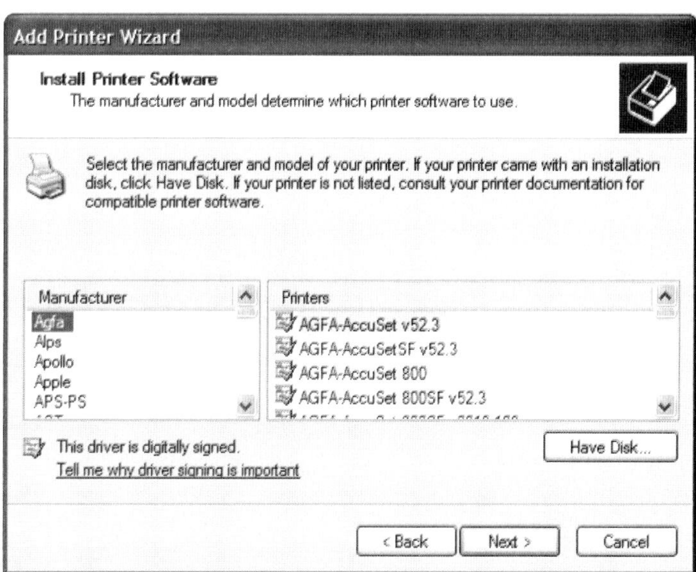

Figure 16.31 Install Printer Software page

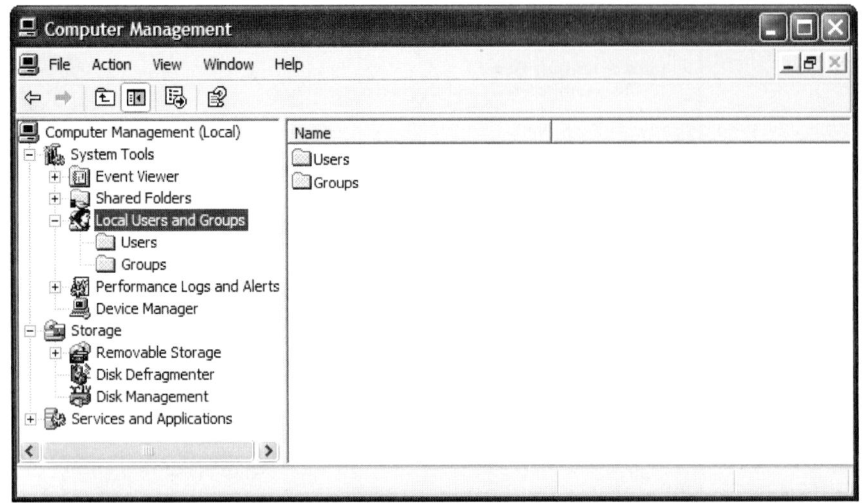

• **Figure 16.32** Local Users and Groups

with only the **Administrator account** enabled by default. When you install Windows you supply the password for the Administrator account. This is the only usable account you have to log on to the computer, unless you joined the computer to a domain (a Chapter 23 topic) or until you create a new local account. I'll assume that your computer doesn't belong to a domain and show you how to create local accounts on your Windows 2000 and Windows XP computer.

Network administrators will manage users and groups for either OS using the Local Users and Groups node in the Computer Management console. You can open this by right-clicking on My Computer and selecting Manage. (See Figure 16.32 and I'll show you more in Chapter 23.) Local Users and Groups can also be used on standalone computers, but Microsoft includes simpler GUI tools for that purpose in Windows 2000 and Windows XP. In Windows XP Microsoft made significant changes in the GUI tools for managing users and groups, so I'll break up this discussion between these two OSs.

> Managing users and groups in Windows NT almost precisely mirrors how you do it in Windows 2000, except the Administrative Tool is called User Manager.

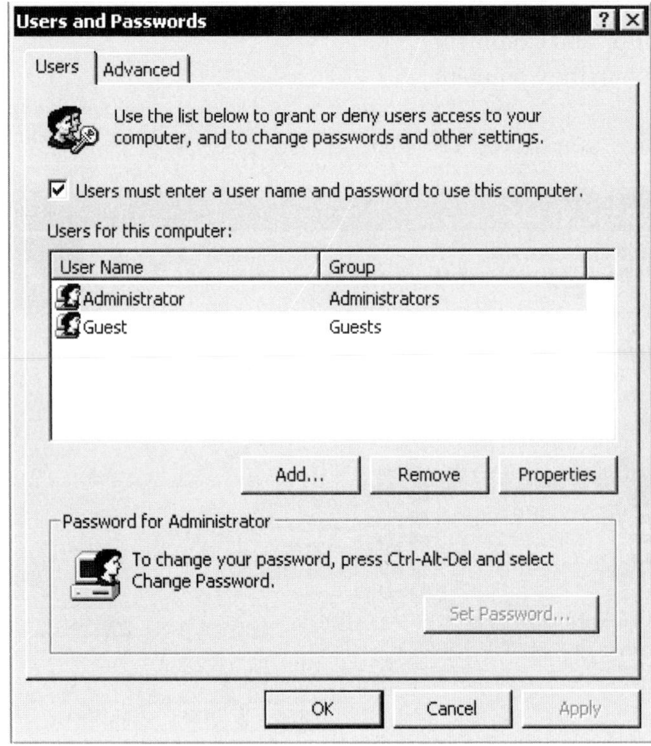

• **Figure 16.33** Security begins with turning on Users Must Enter A User Name And Password To Use This Computer.

Using the Users and Passwords Applet in Windows 2000

When you installed Windows 2000 Professional, if your computer was not made a member of a domain, you could choose to let the OS assume that you were the only user of the computer and did not want to see the logon dialog box. You can check this setting after installation (and refresh your memory) by opening the Users and Passwords applet in Control Panel to see the setting for Users Must Enter A User Name And Password To Use This Computer. Figure 16.33 shows this choice selected, which means that you will see a logon box every time you restart your computer. Also notice that the only user is Administrator. That's the account you're using to log on!

Using the Administrator account is just fine when you're doing administrative tasks, such as installing updates, adding printers, adding and removing programs and Windows components, and creating users and groups. However, even on your own computer, you should never log on with such a powerful account when you're doing ordinary tasks, such as writing and printing reports, browsing the Internet, and playing games (certainly not!). It is the administrator's job to create additional accounts.

Try This!

Turning on Logon Requirements and Secure Boot Settings

Security is all the rage in today's world, so it makes little sense to have a computer with wonderful built-in security features sitting there with those features disabled, so try this! Turn on the option to require a logon.

To complete this, you will need a computer running Windows 2000 Professional.

1. Open Control Panel and open Users and Passwords.
2. If it is unchecked, click to check the box by Users Must Enter A User Name And Password To Use This Computer.
3. Click the Advanced Tab and place a check (if needed) in the box

If the user name and password requirement is turned off, anyone with physical access to your computer can turn it on and use it without entering a user name and password. It is very important to enable this security setting.

Boot Settings. If checked, as shown in Figure 16.34, it requires users to press CTRL-ALT-DEL before logging on. This setting is a defense against certain viruses that try to capture your username and password, sometimes by presenting a fake logon prompt. Pressing CTRL-ALT-DEL will remove a program like that from memory, and allow the actual logon dialog box to appear.

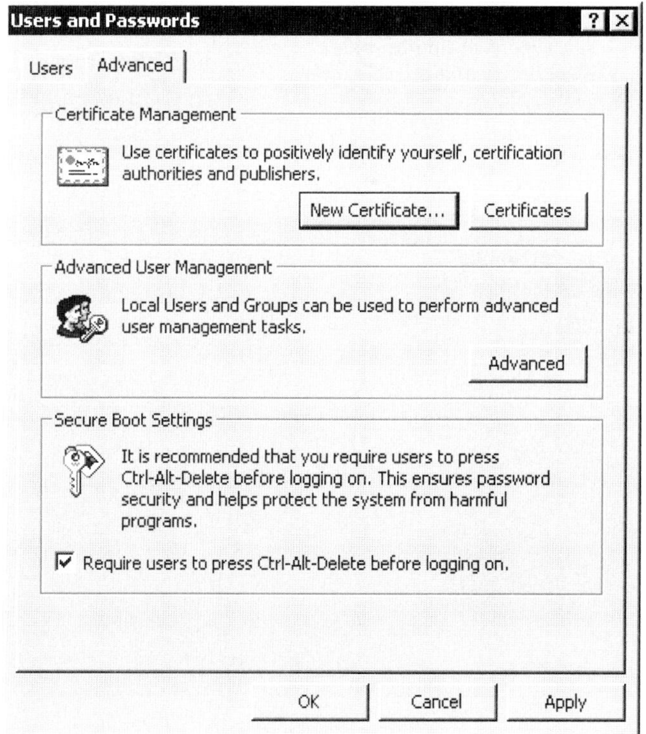

Figure 16.34 Make your computer more secure by enabling Secure Boot Settings.

Creating a New User

Creating a new user account enables that user to log in with a user name and password. This allows an administrator to set the rights and permissions for the user as well as to audit their access to certain network resources. If a Windows 2000 Professional computer is a member of a Windows NT or Active Directory domain, management of users and groups is mainly done at the domain level. But if a computer is a standalone computer or a member of a workgroup, (as you will often see in very small organizations), users and groups will have to be managed on each computer. For that reason it is good practice to create users on a desktop computer. You are also working with the same concepts on a small scale that an administrator must work with in a domain.

If you're logged on as the Administrator or a member of the local Administrators group, open the Users and Passwords applet from Control Panel, and click the Add button. This opens the Add New User Wizard. Enter the user name that the user will use to log on. Enter the user's first and last names in the Full

To create and manage users, you must be logged on as the Administrator or a member of the local Administrators group. Be sure to assign a password to the Administrator account so that only authorized users can access this all-powerful account.

name box, and, if you wish, enter something that describes this person in the Description box. If this is at work, enter a job description in this box. These last two fields are optional.

After entering the user information, click the Next button to continue. On the password page (Figure 16.35) you will then enter and confirm the initial password for this new user. Click the Next button to continue.

Now you get to decide what groups the new user should belong to. Select one of the two suggested options—Standard User or Restricted User—or select the Other option button and choose a group from the drop-down list. Select Standard user, which on a Windows 2000 Professional desktop makes this person a member of the local Power Users Group, as well as the local Users group. Click the Finish button to close the dialog box. You should see your new user listed in the Users and Password dialog box. While you're there, let's see how easy it is for an administrator to change a user's password. Simply select a user from the list, and then click on the Set Password button. Enter and confirm the new password in the Set Password box. Figure 16.36 shows the Set Password box with the Users and Password box in the background.

Now let's say you want or need to change your password. Select the new user in the Users For This Computer list on the Users page. Then click the set Password button on the Users page. Enter and confirm the new password and then click the OK button to apply the changes.

Blank passwords or those that are easily visible on a sticky note provide *no* security. Always insist on non-blank passwords that are not sitting out in the open.

A Word About Passwords

Passwords are a very important part of any security system. Most experts recommend using passwords that are at least eight characters long and that contain a mixture of numbers, letters (both upper- and lower-case), and non-alphanumeric characters. Passwords that use common words—such as the name of a pet—are easily guessed and therefore offer little in the way of real security.

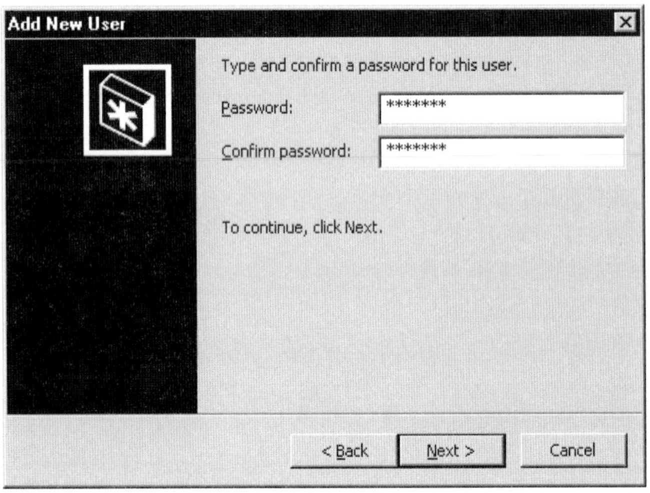

Add New User

Type and confirm a password for this user.

Password: ********

Confirm password: ********

To continue, click Next.

< Back | Next > | Cancel

• **Figure 16.35** Create user password page

Managing Users in Windows XP

Although Windows XP has essentially the same type of accounts database as Windows 2000, the User Accounts Control Panel applet replaces the former Users and Passwords applet and further simplifies user management tasks.

User Accounts—A Simple Tool In Windows XP, the User Accounts applet hides the complete list of users, using a simplistic reference to account types that is actually a reference to its group membership. An account that is a member of the local Administrators group is said to be a Computer administrator, while an account that only belongs to the Local Users group is said to be a **Limited account**. The users it shows depends on the currently logged-on user (see

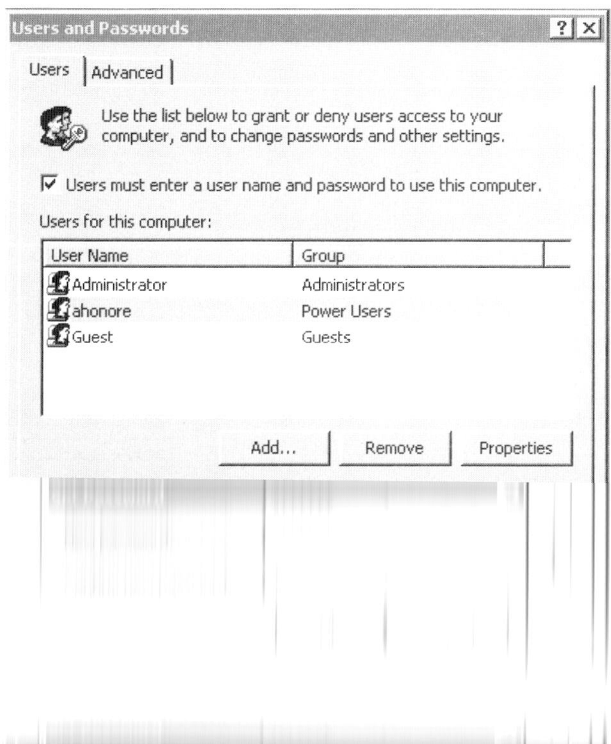

• **Figure 16.36** Set Password box

When creating new user accounts on a computer for a newbie, create both a Computer Administrator account and a Limited account for the user. If you instruct him to use the administrator account only whenever he needs to install new software or make changes to the computer, but use the Limited account for day-to-day work, you might protect his computer from newbie mistakes.

Figure 16.37). When an Administrator is logged on she will see both types of accounts and the Guest account. A Limited user only sees his or her own account in User Accounts.

Now create a new user in Windows XP. Open the User Accounts applet from Control Panel and click Create A New Account. On the Pick an Account Type page the option for Limited is grayed out (unavailable) if this is the first account you have created since installation. This first new account can only be a Computer Administrator (remember the need for redundancy). If you haven't created this account, create it now, following the prompts on the screen.

Once you have this second Computer Administrator account, the Pick an Account Type page looks like Figure 16.38, and you can create either type of account. Once again, you simply follow the prompts on the screen.

After you have created your local accounts you'll see them listed

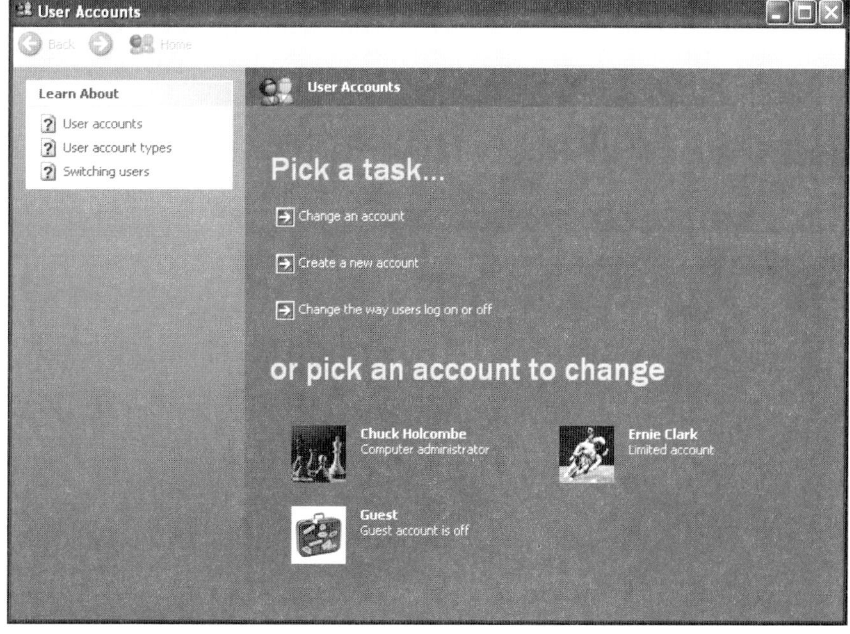

• **Figure 16.37** User Accounts showing a Computer Administrator, a Limited account, and the Guest account

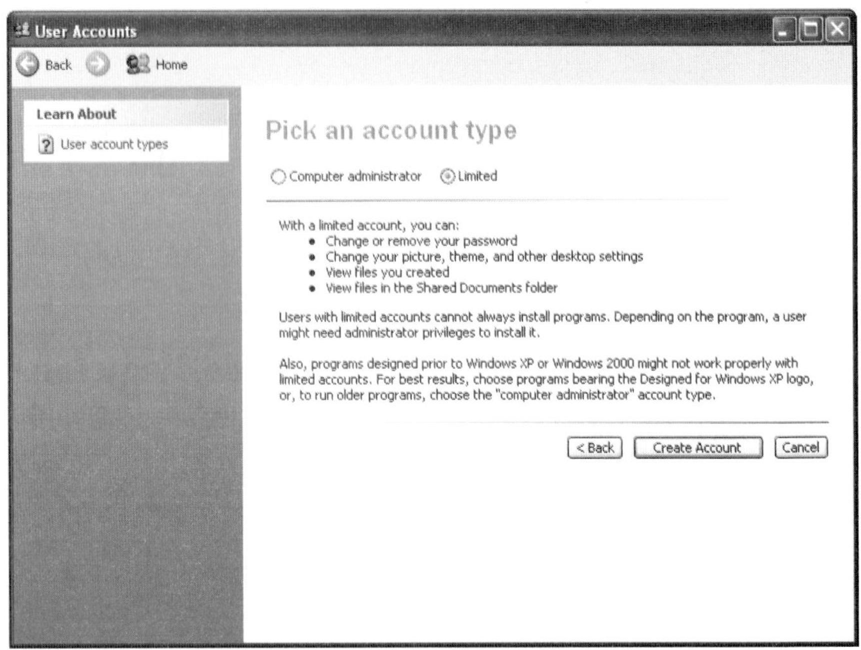

• **Figure 16.38** Pick an Account Type page

when you open the User Accounts applet, and it will look something like Figure 16.39.

More About Windows XP Accounts Creating users is a straightforward process. You need to provide a user name and an initial password. The user can change the password later. You also need to know the type of account to create: Computer Administrator or Limited.

Remember that if a computer is a member of a domain, users will log on using domain accounts. Therefore, creating local user accounts is mostly done on a standalone computer or a networked computer that is only a member of a workgroup. Then you should create one Limited account per user of the computer and an account that is a member of the local Administrators group (in addition to the one created during installation).

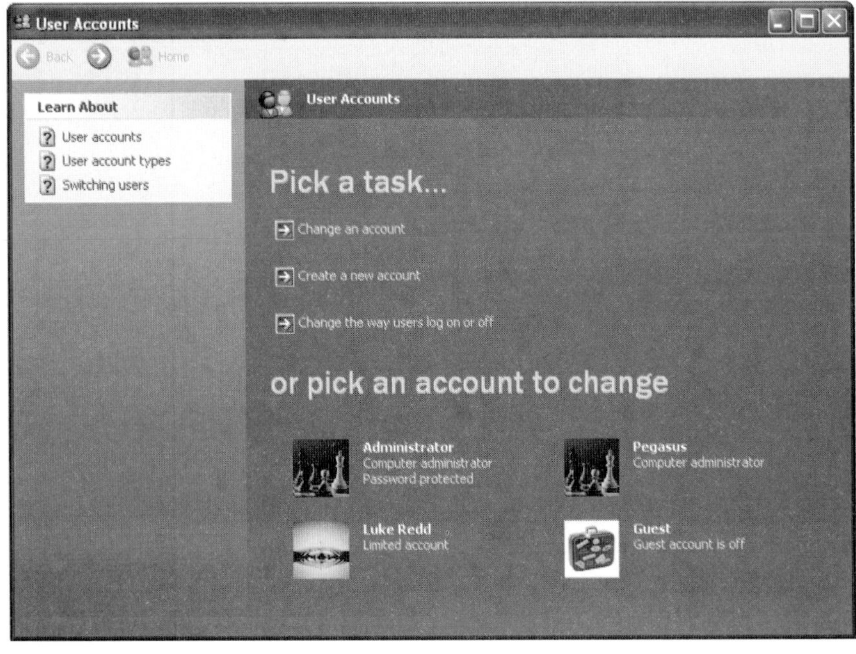

• **Figure 16.39** The User Accounts page

The reason for having two administrator accounts is so that if one administrator is not available or is not able to log on to the computer, another one can—simple redundancy. Windows XP actually reminds you to do this; the first time you try to create a local account after installing Windows XP it will only allow you to create a Computer Administrator account. After that, it will allow you to create limited accounts.

If you upgrade from Windows NT or Windows 2000 or from a Windows 9*x* installation in which user profiles were enabled, Setup will migrate the existing accounts to Windows XP.

Optimizing Windows 2000/XP

Windows 2000 and Windows XP come well optimized out of the box. In fact, these newer versions of Windows have few optimization features. For example, there's no obvious way to manipulate the disk cache (I could show you, but I'd have to rename the book, *A+ and Windows 2000 Professional and Windows XP Professional Exams*). Almost every optimization task that techs can perform in these newer versions of Windows follows basically the same [illegible]

[illegible] vanced tab, and select Performance Options (Windows 2000) or Performance Settings (Windows XP).

Visual Effects The Windows XP Performance Options dialog box has two tab sheets: Visual Effects and Advanced (Figure 16.40). The Visual Effects tab lets you adjust visual effects that impact performance. Try clicking on the top three buttons in turn, and watch the list of settings. Notice the tiny difference between the first two choices. The third choice, Adjust For Best Performance, turns off all visual effects, and the fourth option is an invitation to make your own adjustments.

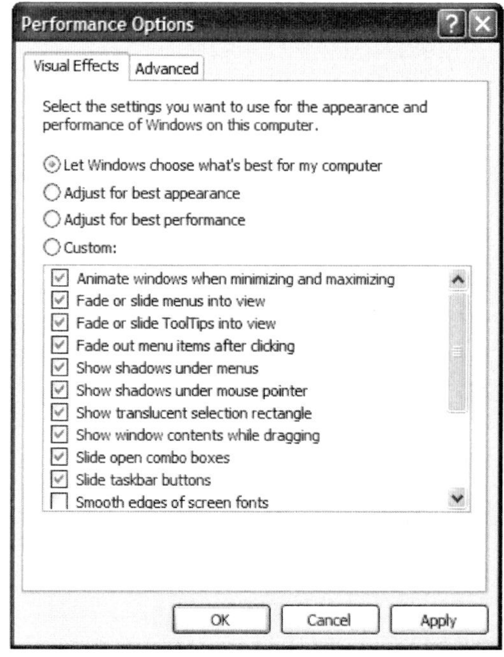

• **Figure 16.40** Performance Options Visual Effects

Applications and Background Services In Windows 2000 the Performance Options dialog box shows a pair of radio buttons called Applications and Background Services. These radio buttons set how processor time is divided between the foreground application and all other background tasks. Set this to Applications if you run applications that need more processor time. Set it to Background Services to give all running programs the same processor usage. You can also adjust the size of the swap file—now called a *paging file*—in this dialog box, but I don't mess with these settings and instead leave control of the paging to Windows.

In Windows XP the Advanced tab, shown in Figure 16.41, has the settings for processor scheduling, memory usage, and virtual memory. The previous choices of Applications and Background Services for processor scheduling are now called Programs and Background services. They work as they did in Windows 2000. The Memory usage settings let you allocate a greater share of memory to either programs or the system cache. Finally, the Virtual Memory section of this page lets you modify the size of the paging file on disk. I *still* don't recommend changing this!

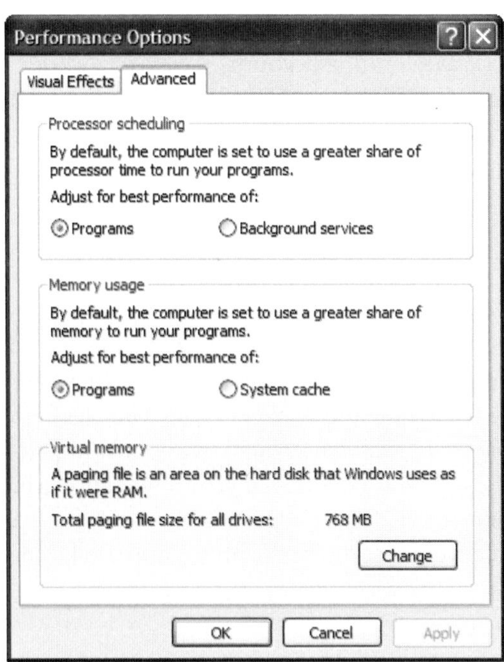

• **Figure 16.41** Advanced Performance Options

Resource Tracking

Resource tracking is very important for solving performance problems. Let's say your Windows 2000/XP computer seems to be running slower than previously. Task Manager and the Performance console are tools you can use to figure out what (if anything) has become a bottleneck. I'll show you how to use them.

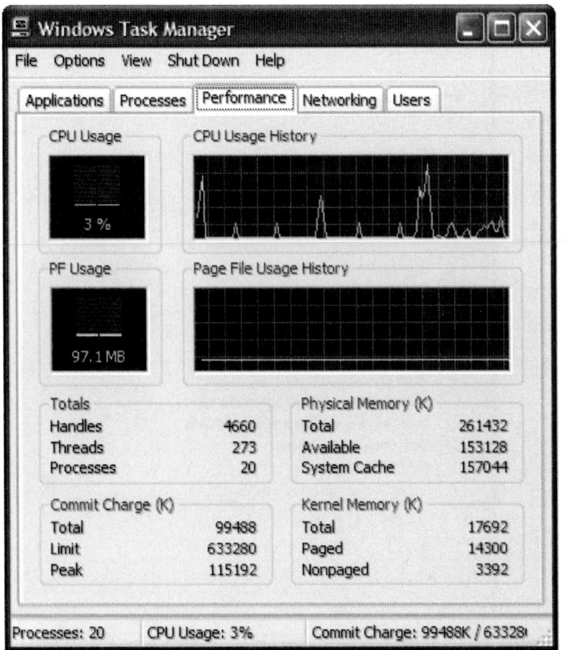

• **Figure 16.42** Performance tab

Task Manager

If you ever used System Monitor in Windows 9*x*/Me you'll remember that it gave you some quick, basic information on the system's performance. Well, Windows NT/2000/XP has something like this, but in a rather strange place: the Task Manager! Press CTRL-SHIFT-ESC to bring up the Task Manager and click the Performance tab (Figure 16.42).

This handy screen provides us with the most commonly used information: CPU usage, available physical memory, the size of the disk cache, commit charge (memory for programs), and kernel memory (memory used by Windows).

Performance Console

Windows NT had this great tool for measuring system performance called Performance Monitor, or "Perfmon" to its friends and followers. In Windows 2000/XP this tool has been improved upon and morphed into a MMC console called Performance. I guess it will always be Perfmon to me, and that's OK, because that helps me to remember its MMC console file name, PERFMON.MSC so that I can call it up from Start | Run rather than through the Performance icon in Administrative Tools. Use either method to open Performance and look at the Performance Console (Figure 16.43). As you can see, there are two nodes, System Monitor and Performance Logs and Alerts.

The information on Handles, Threads, and Processes (look for the Totals section below the graphical displays) offer a "gee whiz" factor to the Performance tab, giving you a quick snapshot of what's happening behind the scenes with your programs. You can't do much with the information, but it's there for you anyway. Here's what they mean:

Handles Opening one program usually involves opening other program or data files. Handles shows all interlinks between these programs

tions and services, as well as kernel-based programs.

Objects and Counters To begin working with the Performance console you need to understand two terms: object and counter. An **object** is a system component that is given a set of characteristics and can be managed by the operating system as a single entity. A **counter** is something that tracks specific information about an object. For example, the Processor object has a counter, %Processor Time, which tracks the percentage of elapsed time the processor uses to execute a non-idle thread. There can be many counters

has a shortcut key combination. If you want to add counters click the Add

You need to have a Computer Administrator account to perform some Performance tasks.

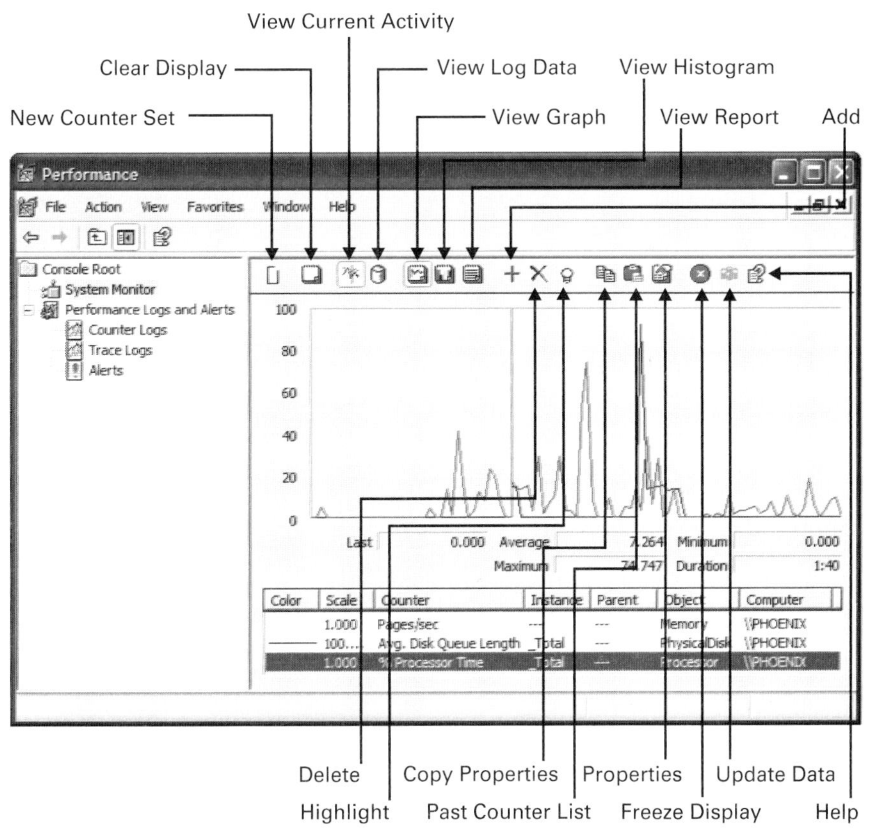

• **Figure 16.43** Performance Console

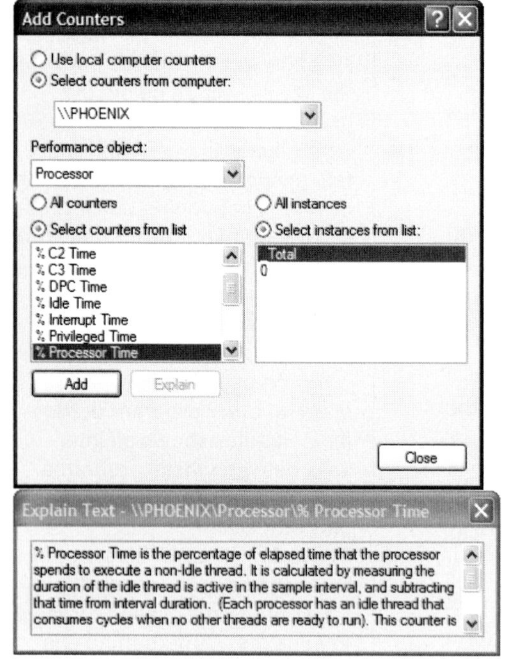

• **Figure 16.44** The Add Counters box with Explain Text

button (the one that looks like a plus sign) or press CTRL-I to open the Add Counters dialog box. Open the Performance object list and see the long list of objects you can monitor. Reselect Processor so the box will close and now look at the list under the list of counters below. The nice thing about the Add Counters dialog box is that you can select a counter and click the Explain button to learn about the counter, just like Figure 16.44. Try that now.

Even with just three counters selected, the graph can get a little busy. That's where one of my favorite System Monitor features shines. If I want the line of charted data from just one counter to stand out, I select the counter in the list below the graph and then press CTRL-H. See how this trick makes the %Processor Time line stand out in Figure 16.45? Imagine how useful that is when you are monitoring a dozen counters.

Performance Logs and Alerts The Performance Logs and Alerts snap-in enables Windows 2000/XP to create a written record of just about anything that happens on your system. Do you want to know if someone is trying to log onto your system when you're not around? The following procedure is written for Windows XP, but the steps are nearly identical in Windows 2000.

To create the new event log, alternate-click Counter Logs and select New Log Settings. Give the new log a name—in this example, "Unauthorized Access." Click OK and a properties box for the new log will open similar to that in Figure 16.46.

Select counters for the log. Click Add Counters, and then select the Use Local Computer Counter Objects radio button. Select Server from the Performance Object pull-down menu, highlight Errors Logon from the list of counters, and click Add, then Close.

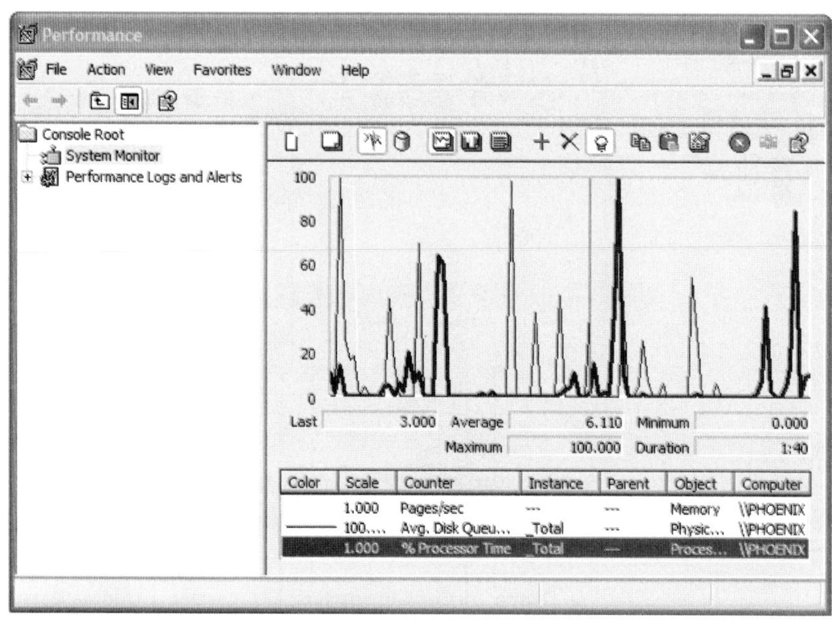

• **Figure 16.45** Highlight a single data line.

Back in the properties box, Click the Schedule tab and set up when you want this thing to start running—probably at the end of the work day today. Then select when it should stop logging—probably tomorrow morning when you start work. Click the Log Files tab to see where the log file will be saved—probably C:\PerfLogs and make a note of the filename. The filename will consist of the name you gave the log and a number. In the example I named the new performance log "Unauthorized Accesses" so the file name is Unauthorized Accesses_000001.blg.

When you come back in the morning, open the Performance console and select Performance Logs and Alerts, and then select Counter Logs. Your log should be listed in the right. The icon by the log name will be red if the log is still running, and green if it has stopped. If it has not stopped, select it, and then click the stop

Run the Disk Defragmenter and Check Disk (called Error-checking in the GUI) for system upkeep. There are several ways to access these tools; one way is to select the properties of the drive you wish to work with (Figure 16.48). For the experienced tech, Disk Defragmenter is just good old Defrag, although with a much prettier front end. Run Defragmenter on a regular basis to ensure that your system isn't slowing down due to having to write files into scattered locations on disk.

Temporary File Management with Disk Cleanup

Don't forget the occasional disk cleanup. Even though you can reach this tool the Windows 9*x*/Me way through the menus, you can also select properties for a drive and click the Disk Cleanup button from the General tab. Disk Cleanup calculates the space you will be able to free up, and then displays the Disk Cleanup dialog box (Figure 16.49). Near the top it tells you how much disk space (maximum) it could free up. But look! The list of Files to delete only

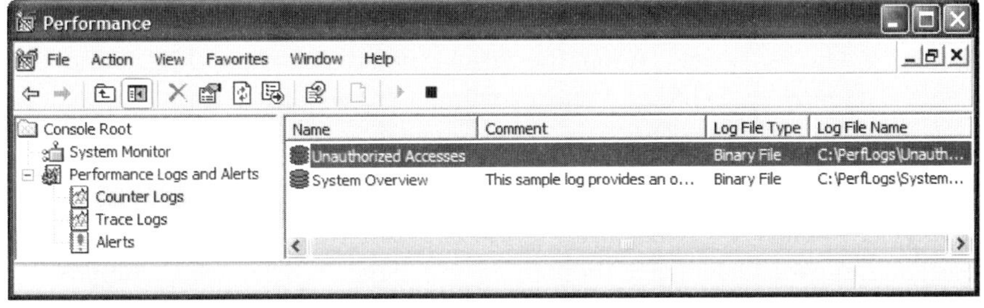

Figure 16.47 Counter logs

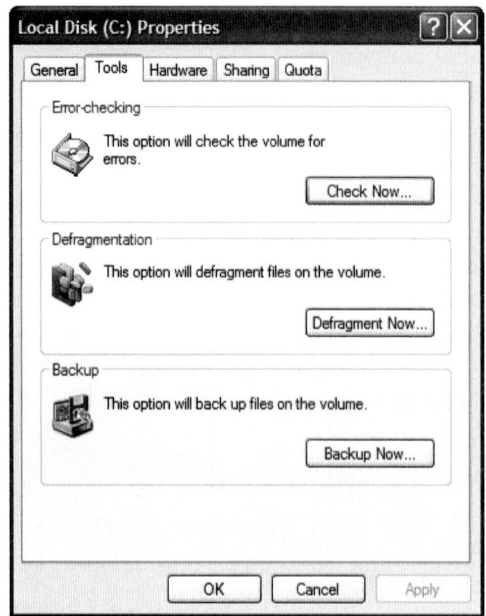

• **Figure 16.48** Essential tools for system optimization

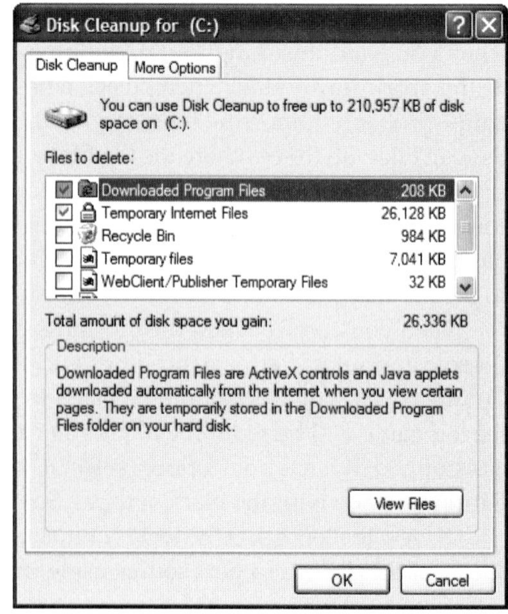

• **Figure 16.49** Disk Cleanup

has a few categories checked and the actual amount of disk space you will gain if you only allow Disk Cleanup to delete these files is much smaller than the estimate. As you select and deselect choices, watch the value for this total change. If you scroll down through the list you will see a choice to compress old files. What do you know? Disk Cleanup does more than just delete files? In fact, this file compression trick is where Disk Cleanup really, uh, cleans up. This is one of the few choices where you will gain the most space. The other big heavyweight category is temporary Internet files, which it will delete. Try Disk Cleanup on a computer that gets hours of use every day and you'll be pleased with the results.

Preparing for Problems

Just as with Windows 9*x*/Me, the secret to troubleshooting Windows NT, 2000, and XP is preparation. You need to have critical system files and data backed up on PCs you work with, and tools in place for the inevitable glitches. The various versions of Windows based on the NT core offer five different tools for the job, although none offer them all: **System Restore**, the **Backup and Restore Wizard** (called Backup in Windows NT and 2000), **Automated System Recovery** (ASR), the **Emergency Repair Disk** (ERD), and the **Recovery Console**. Table 16.1 shows which OS gets which tool.

System Restore

Every technician has war stories about the user who likes to add the latest gadget and cool software to their computer. Then he's amazed when things go very, very wrong: the system locks up, or refuses to boot, or simply acts

Table 16.1 Tools in Versions of Windows

	System Restore	Backup and Restore Wizard	Automated System Recovery	Emergency Repair Disk	Recovery Console
Windows NT 4.0	No	Yes, but called "Backup"	No	Yes	No
Windows 2000 Professional	No	Yes, but called "Backup"	No	Yes	Yes
Windows XP Home	Yes	No	No	No	No
Windows XP Professional	Yes	Yes	Yes	No	Yes

restore the system.

To create a restore point, go to Start | All Programs | Accessories | System Tools | System Restore. When the tool opens, select Create a Restore Point, and then click Next (Figure 16.50). Type in a description on the next screen (Figure 16.51). There's no need to include the date and time because the System Restore adds them automatically. Click Create and you're done (Figure 16.52).

The System Restore tool creates some of the restore points in time automatically. For instance, by default, every time you install new software, XP creates a restore point. Thus, if installation of a program causes your computer to malfunction, simply restore the system to a time point prior to that installation, and the computer should work again.

During the restore process, only settings and programs are changed. No data is lost. Your computer will include all programs and settings as of the restore date. This feature is absolutely invaluable for overworked techs. A simple restore will fix many user-generated problems.

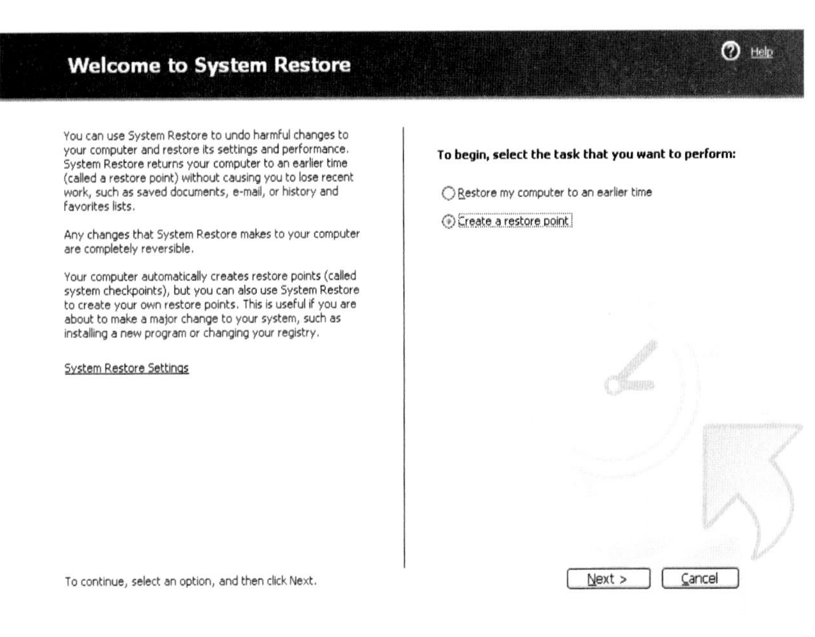

• **Figure 16.50** System Restore in action

Backup and Restore Wizard (Backup)

Windows 2000/XP Backup provides almost all the tools we need. It has come a long way from its origins in

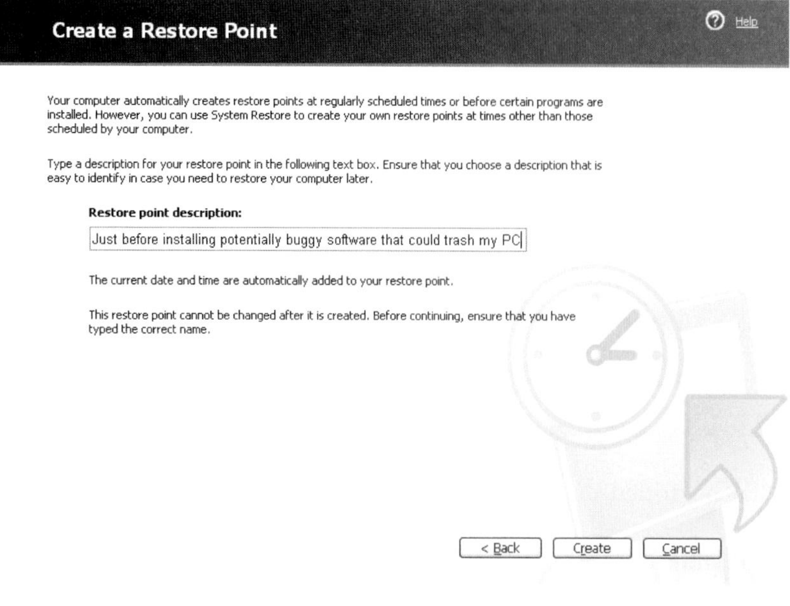

• **Figure 16.51** Adding a descriptive name

Windows NT. It supports a greater variety of devices, allowing you to network drives, logical drives, tape and removable disks (but not CD-R, CD-RW, or DVD-R). Most folks, however, still turn to third-party utilities to create system, e-mail, browser, and personal data backups.

You can start Backup by navigating the Start menu all the way to Accessories | System Tools, or by clicking the "Backup Now" button on the Tools page of the local disk properties box, but I prefer to start it from Start | Run with the command NTBACKUP. This technique works in both Windows 2000 and Windows XP and has the added advantage of bringing the XP version up in Advanced Mode (Figure 16.53), rather than Wizard mode. Windows 2000 Backup normally started in Advanced Mode (not called that at the time). In Windows XP experiment and see which mode you prefer.

Both versions of Backup have three choices on this page: Backup, Restore, and a third choice that is different in each version. The third option for Windows 2000 is the Emergency Repair Disk. As you can see in Figure 16.53, the third option in Windows XP is the Automated System Recovery Wizard—a new recovery feature in Windows XP.

Windows 2000 Emergency Repair Disk (ERD) Let's first consider the Windows 2000 Emergency Repair Disk (ERD). This disk saves critical boot

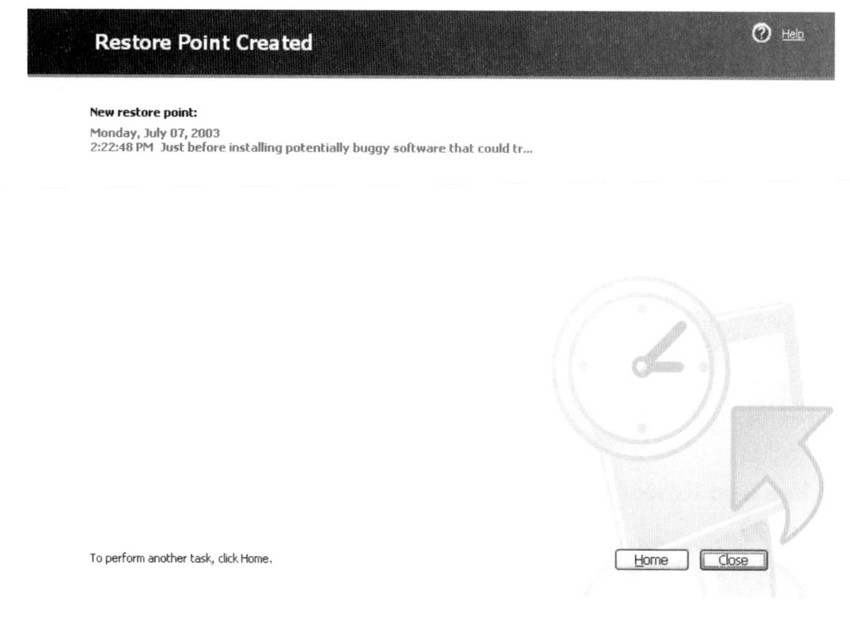

• **Figure 16.52** Restore point created!

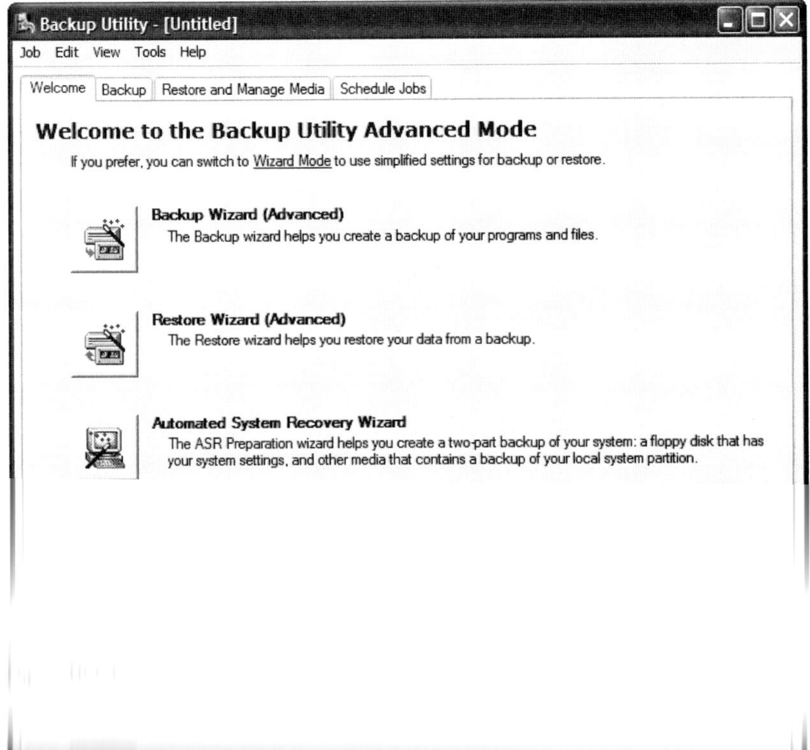

files and partition information and is our main tool for fixing boot problems. It is not a bootable disk, nor does it store very much information; the ERD does not replace a good system backup! It works with a special folder called \WINNT\REPAIR to store a copy of your Registry. It's not perfect, but it gets you out of most startup problems. I always make a new ERD before I install a new device or program. Then the ERD is ready if I need it.

Windows NT has a perfectly functional and often needed version of the ERD, but you create it from the Run dialog box. Go to Start | Run and type **RDISK**. Click OK to run the Repair Disk Utility and make an ERD.

Windows XP Automated System Recovery (ASR) The Automated System Recovery (ASR) Wizard lets you create a backup of your system. This backup includes a floppy disk and backup media (can you say "tape") containing the system partition and disks containing operating system components.

This is not a trivial, easy solution to a system failure, but something you do after first trying Safe Mode Boot and Last Known Good Configuration options.

The restore side of ASR involves a complete reinstall of the operating system, preferably on a new partition. You see, this is something you do when all is lost. You run setup, and press F2 when prompted during the text-mode portion of Setup. Follow the prompts on the screen, which will first ask for the floppy disk, then for the backup media.

Backup Wizard But we're not quite done with Backup. Data files are not backed up by the ERD nor by the ASR. Therefore, you have to backup data files. Go back to the Welcome screen and select Backup Wizard. When the wizard starts, click Next to see Figure 16.54.

You have three options here. The first two are fairly self-explanatory: You can back up everything or just system-critical files. The third option needs some explanation. The Only Back Up The System State Data radio button enables you to save "other" system-critical files, but with Windows 2000/XP, it's not much more than making an ERD with the Registry backup.

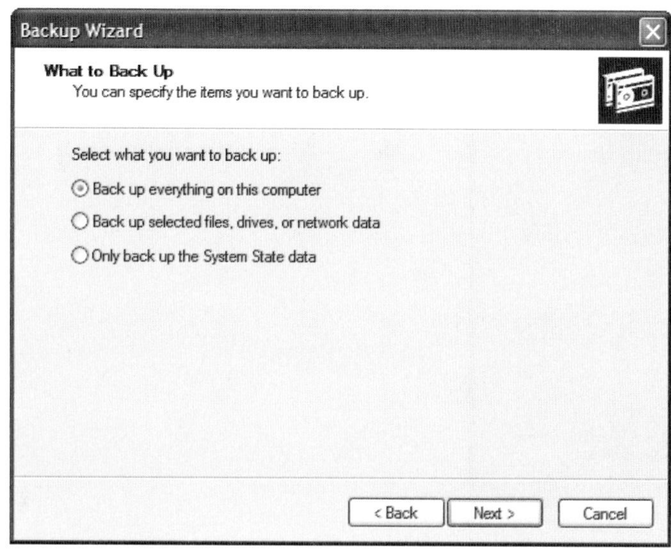

Figure 16.54 Backup Wizard

This option really makes sense for Windows 2000 Server systems because it saves Active Directory information (which your Windows 2000 Professional system does not store) as well as other critical, server-specific functions. (More on these topics in Chapter 23.) But the A+ Certification exams may still expect you to know about it!

Creating an MS-DOS Startup Disk

I still need to keep MS-DOS startup disks on hand for such tasks as repartitioning a hard disk, or booting up a new computer, connecting to a network share, and initiating an installation of an OS from the network share. It has been a long time since I actually had an MS-DOS machine around, so I used Windows 95, and then Windows 98 to create startup disks (preferably 98). I was happily surprised to find it there one day when I was formatting a diskette. Create An MS-DOS Startup Disk is an option when you format a diskette (see Figure 16.55). Windows NT and 2000 don't have the option of creating a MS-DOS boot diskette, but the feature reappears in Windows XP.

Installing Recovery Console

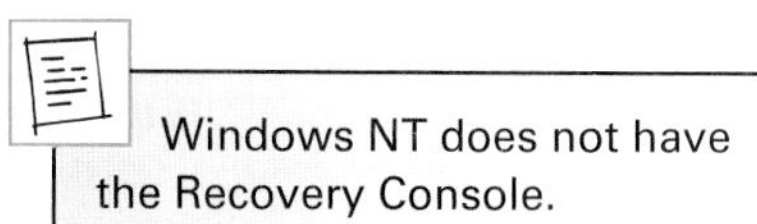

Windows NT does not have the Recovery Console.

Even though you can't really get Windows 2000/XP to boot to an MS-DOS environment, you can use something called the Recovery Console. The Recovery Console is as close as Windows now gets to the Windows 9*x* Safe Mode Command Prompt Only feature (as opposed to the new Safe Mode Command Prompt Only). You may even consider it better, because it works on an NTFS partition and pays attention to NTFS permissions.

If you have the Windows 2000/XP CD, you can start the Recovery Console by running Setup and selecting Repair, then selecting Recovery Console. However, if you like to be proactive you can install the Recovery Console on your hard drive so that it is one of your startup options and does not require the Windows 2000 or XP CD to run. The steps to do this in Windows 2000 and Windows XP are very nearly identical.

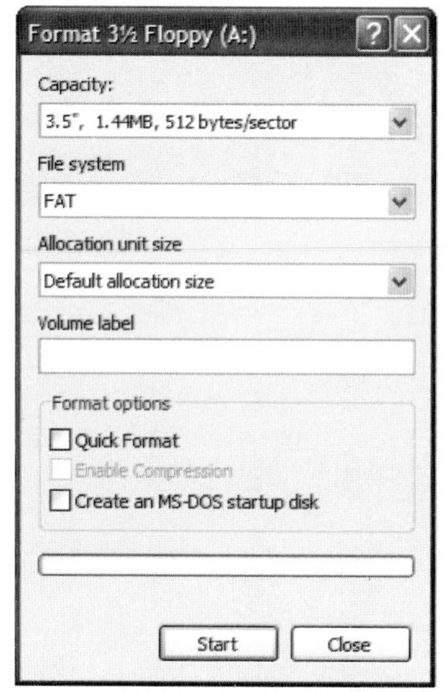

Figure 16.55 Create an MS-DOS Startup Disk option

First, you need to log into the system with the Administrator account. Grab your Windows 2000 or XP install CD-ROM and drop it in your system. If the Autorun function kicks in, just click the No button. To install the Recovery Console and make it a part of your startup options, click on the Start button, then select Run, and type the following:

```
d:\i386\winnt32 /cmdcons
```

If your CD-ROM drive uses a different drive letter, substitute it for the d: drive. Then just follow the instructions on the screen. If you are connected to the Internet, allow the Setup program to download updated files. From now on, every time the system boots, the OS selection menu will show your

Windows OS (Windows 2000 Professional or Windows XP) and the Microsoft Windows Recovery Console. It may also show other choices if yours is a multi-boot computer.

Cross Check

Windows 2000 vs. Windows XP

Windows 2000 and Windows XP handle many maintenance and optimization tasks in the same or very similar ways, but there are differences between these two versions of Windows. Do you know what they are? Which tools are located in different places? Which tasks use different tools? Which tools work in different ways?

Troubleshooting Windows

When it comes to troubleshooting tools, Windows 2000 and Windows XP have inherited the best of both Windows families. That is, they have such vintage Windows NT tools as the **Last Known Good Configuration** startup

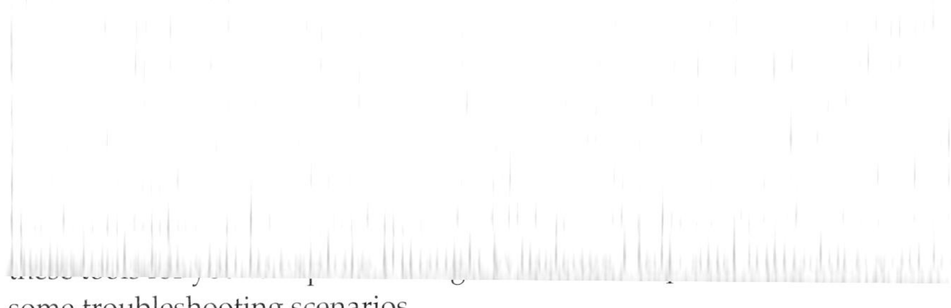

some troubleshooting scenarios.

Troubleshooting Windows 2000/XP with the Recovery Console

If you followed the instructions earlier in the lesson, then you've installed the Recovery Console onto your system and have it as an option when you boot the system. If not, start it as described earlier using the Windows 2000 or XP installation CD-ROM. When you select the Recovery Console, you will see a message about NTDETECT, another one that the Recovery console is starting up, and then you will be greeted with the following message and command prompt:

```
Microsoft Windows XP<TM> Recovery Console.
The Recovery Console provides system repair and recovery functionality.
Type Exit to quit the Recovery Console and restart the computer.

1: C:\WINDOWS
Which Windows XP installation would you like to log onto
<To cancel, press ENTER>?
```

The cursor is a small white rectangle sitting to the right of the question mark on the last line. If you are not accustomed to working at the command prompt, this may be disorienting. If there is only one installation of Windows XP on your computer, type the number 1 at the prompt, and press the ENTER key. If you press ENTER before typing in a valid selection, the Recovery Console will cancel and the computer will reboot. The only choice we can make in this example is 1. Having made that choice, the only change to the screen above is a new line:

```
Type the Administrator password:
```

This is also followed by the cursor. Enter the Administrator password for that computer and press ENTER. The password will not display on the screen, only asterisks in place of the password. The screen still shows everything that has happened so far, unless something has happened to cause an error message. It now looks like this:

```
Microsoft Windows XP<TM> Recovery Console.
The Recovery Console provides system repair and recovery functionality.
Type Exit to quit the Recovery Console and restart the computer.

1: C:\WINDOWS
Which Windows XP installation would you like to log onto
<To cancel, press ENTER>? 1
Type the Administrator password: ********
C:\Windows>
```

By now, you've caught on and know that there is a rectangular prompt immediately after the last line. Now what do you do? Use the Recovery Console commands, of course. Recovery Console uses many of the commands that worked in DOS as well as some uniquely its own. Here's a table listing the common Recovery Console commands:

Command	Description
attrib	Changes attributes of selected file or folder
cd (or chdir)	Displays current directory or changes directories
chkdsk	Runs CheckDisk utility
cls	Clears screen
copy	Copies from removable media to system folders on hard disk. No wildcards
del (or delete)	Deletes service or folder
dir	Lists contents of selected directory on system partition only
disable	Disables service or driver
diskpart	Replaces FDISK—creates/deletes partitions
enable	Enables service or driver
extract	Extracts components from .CAB files
fixboot	Writes new partition boot sector on system partition
fixmbr	Writes new Master Boot Record for partition boot sector
format	Formats selected disk
listsvc	Lists all services on system
logon	Lets you choose which W2K installation to logon to if you have more than one
map	Displays current drive letter mappings
md (or mkdir)	Creates a directory
more (or type)	Displays contents of text file
rd (or rmdir)	Removes a directory
ren (or rename)	Renames a single file
systemroot	Makes current directory system root of drive you're logged into
type	Displays a text file

The files that make up the Recovery Console reside on the system partition (in a folder called CMDCONS), making the Recovery Console useless for system partition crashes. The Recovery Console shines in the business of manually restoring registries, stopping problem services, rebuilding partitions (other than the system partition), or using the EXPAND program to extract copies of corrupted files from a CD-ROM or floppy disk.

You can reconfigure a service so that it starts with different settings, format drives on the hard disk, read and write on local FAT or NTFS volumes, and copy replacement files from a floppy or CD. The recovery console allows you to access the file system, and is still constrained by the file and folder security of NTFS, which makes it a more secure tool to use than some of the third-party solutions.

face date has at least one restore point. These points are created after you add or remove software or install Windows updates and during the normal shutdown of your computer. Select a date on the calendar, then select a restore point from the list on the right and click Next.

The last screen before the system is restored shows a warning. It advises you to close all open programs and reminds you that Windows will shut down during the restore process. It also states that the restore operation is

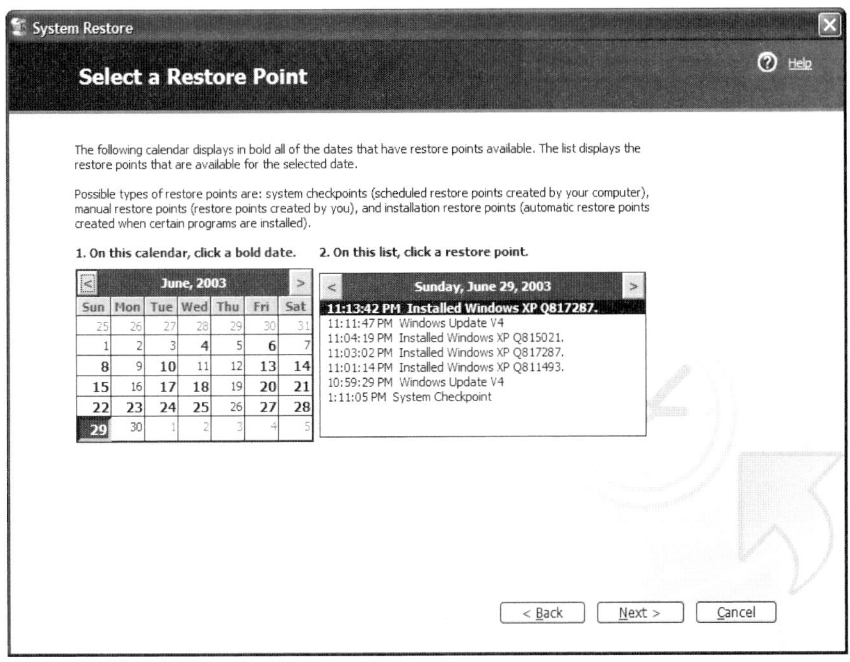

• **Figure 16.56** Select a restore point

completely reversible. Thus, if you go too far back in time, you can restore to a more recent date.

You don't have to count on the automatic creation of restore points. You can open System Restore at any time and simply select Create A Restore Point. This is something to consider doing before making changes that might not trigger an automatic restore point, such as directly editing the Registry.

System Restore is turned on by default and uses some of your disk space to save information on restore points. To turn System Restore off or change the disk space usage, open the System Properties applet in Control Panel and select the System Restore tab where you will find these settings (Figure 16.57).

Troubleshooting Startup Failures with Advanced Startup Options

When Windows fails to startup, consider using the Windows **Advanced Startup Options menu** to discover the cause. This Windows 2000/XP menu is an improvement on the trusty Microsoft Windows 9*x* Startup menu. To get to this menu, restart the computer and press F8 after the POST messages, but before the Windows logo screen appears. Windows 2000 and Windows XP have similar menus. Central to these advanced options are Safe Mode and Last Known Good. In all cases, you will have to log on with the local Administrator account, so be sure you know the password.

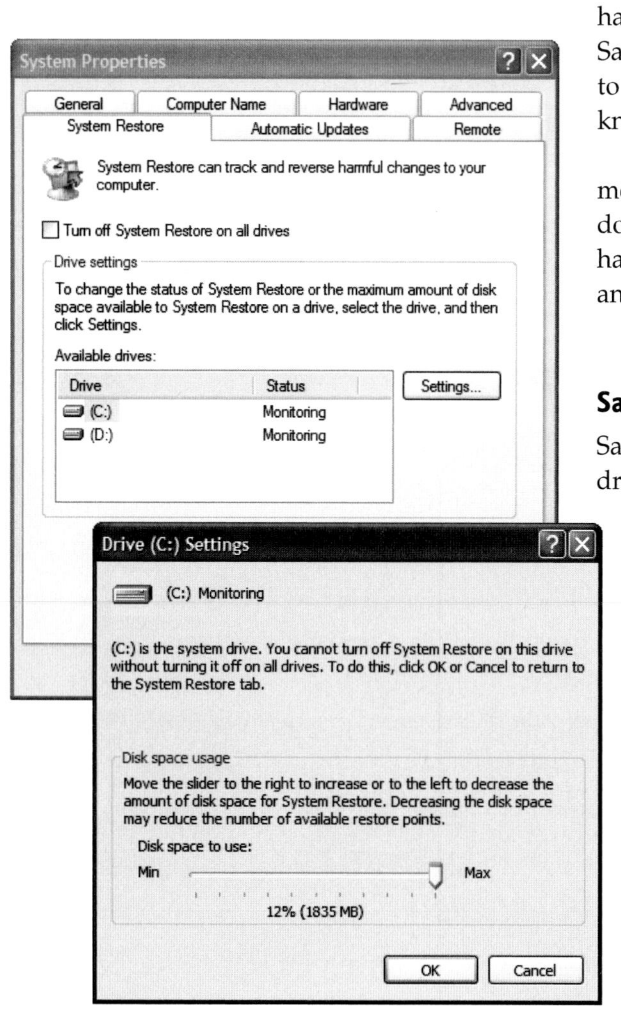

• **Figure 16.57** System Restore settings

There are three differences between the two OSs in this menu: the Windows 2000 option Boot Normally is "Start Windows Normally" in Windows XP. In addition, Windows XP has two other options not available in Windows 2000: Reboot and Return to OS Choices Menu.

Here's a rundown of the Menu Options.

Safe Mode

Safe Mode (Figure 16.58) starts up without using some drivers and components that would normally be started, including network support. It loads only very basic, non-vendor-specific drivers for mouse, VGA monitor, keyboard, mass storage, and system services. Some devices, like your USB mouse, may not work!

Then you can use tools like Device Manager to locate and correct the source of the problem. When you use Device Manager in Safe Mode you can access the properties for all the devices, even those that are not working in Safe Mode. The status displayed for the device is the status for a normal startup. Even the network card will show as enabled. You can disable any suspect device or perform other tasks, such as removing or updating drivers. If a problem with a device driver is preventing the operating system from starting normally, you can look here for yellow question mark warning icons that indicate an unknown device or yellow exclamation mark icons that indicate conflicts with existing devices.

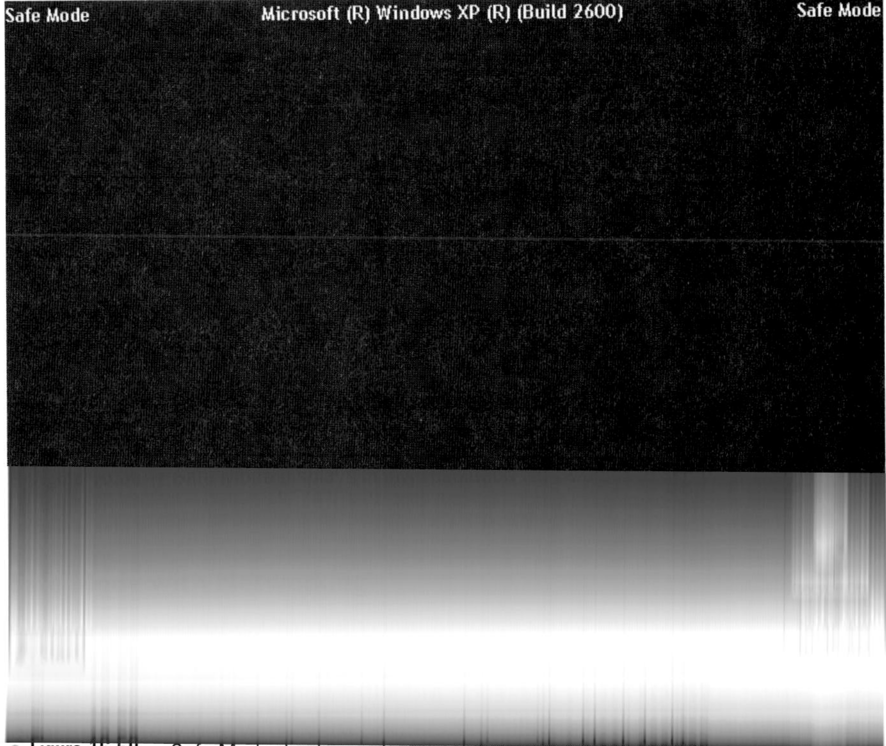

Figure 16.58 Safe Mode displays in low resolution with a black desktop.

Safe Mode with Networking

This mode is identical to plain Safe Mode, except that you have network support. I use these two modes to test for a problem with network drivers. If Windows won't start up normally, but does start up in Safe Mode, I then reboot into Safe Mode with Networking. If it fails to start up with Networking, then the problem is a network driver. I reboot back to Safe Mode, open Device Manager, and look at network components, beginning with the network adapter.

Safe Mode with Command Prompt

When you start Windows in this mode, after you log on, rather than loading the GUI desktop, it loads the command prompt (CMD.EXE) as the shell to the operating system, as seen in Figure 16.59. This is a handy option to remember if the desktop does not display at all, which, after you have eliminated video drivers, can be caused by the corruption of the EXPLORER.EXE program. From within the command prompt you can delete the corrupted version of EXPLORER.EXE and copy in an undamaged version. This requires knowing the command-line commands for navigating the directory structure, as well as knowing the location of the file that you are replacing. Although Explorer is not loaded, you can load other GUI tools that don't depend on Explorer. All you have to do is enter the correct command. For instance, to load Event Viewer type **eventvwr.msc** at the command line and press ENTER.

Typing **Help** at the command line will give you a list of the commands, and typing a command name followed by **/?** will give you the syntax for that command. Have fun!

Enable Boot Logging

This option starts Windows normally and creates a log file of the drivers as they load into memory. The file is named Ntbtlog.txt and saved in the

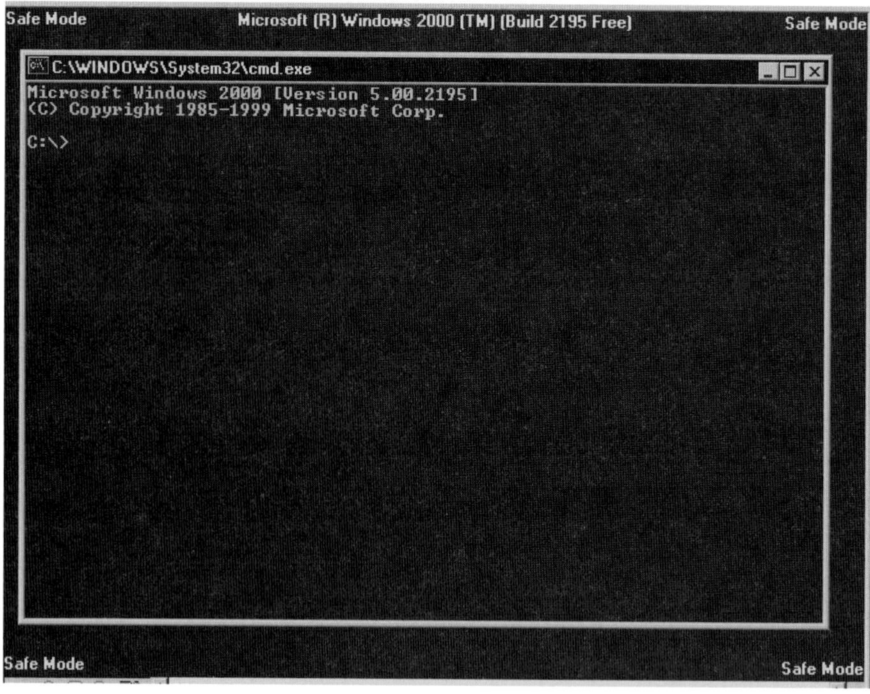

• **Figure 16.59** Windows 2000 Safe Mode with Command Prompt

%SystemRoot% folder. If the startup failed because of a bad driver, the last entry in this file may be the driver the OS was initializing when it failed.

Enable VGA Mode

If this mode works, it means that you are using the correct video driver, but it is configured incorrectly (perhaps with the wrong refresh rate and/or resolution). After successfully starting in this mode, open the Display Properties and change the settings. While Safe Mode loads a generic VGA driver, this mode loads the driver Windows is configured to use, but starts it up in standard VGA mode rather than using the settings for which it is configured.

> Last Known Good can only fix configuration problems if you use it before a successful reboot and logon after the change. Last Known Good cannot correct problems that are not related to configuration changes in the operating system. This includes problems caused by hardware failure, and corrupted files not related to a recent configuration change.

Last Known Good Configuration

When Windows fails immediately after installing a new driver, but before you have logged on again, you may want to try the Last Known Good option available from the Advanced Options menu. However, we have found this to be a rather fickle and limited tool. Also, it is not available on a computer with more than one hardware profile. Therefore, you will more often find yourself using a familiar, but improved Windows 9*x*-type Safe Mode option.

Directory Services Restore Mode (Does Not Apply to Professional)

The title says it all here—this option only applies to Active Directory domain controllers, and Windows 2000 Professional and Windows XP can never be domain controllers (see Chapter 23).

Debugging Mode

If you select this choice, Windows 2000/XP starts in kernel debug mode. It's a super-techie thing to do, and I doubt that even Ubertechs do debug mode anymore. To do this you have to connect the computer you are debugging to another computer via a serial connection, and as Windows starts up, a debug of the kernel is sent to the second computer, which must also be running a debugger program. I remember running debug for an early version of Windows NT. My co-workers and I did it back then simply because we were studying for the then-brand-new MCSE exams and expected to be tested on it! We all decided that it was an experience that didn't need to be repeated!

Start Windows Normally

This choice will simply start Windows normally, without rebooting. You al-

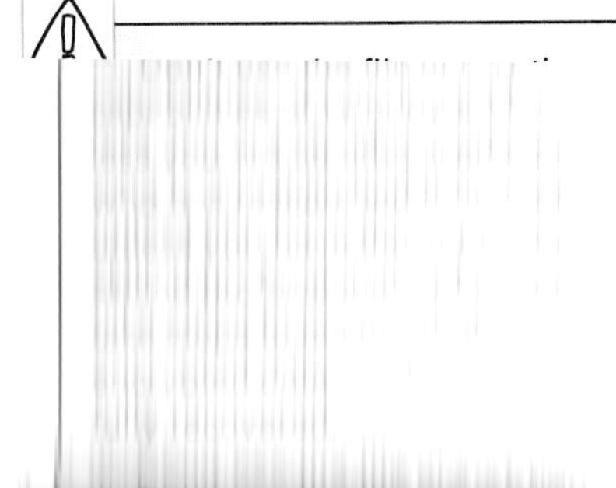

This choice will return you to the OS Choices menu from which you can select the operating system to load.

Resetting Forgotten Passwords in Windows XP

Windows XP allows the currently logged-on user to create a **Password Reset Disk** that can be used in case of a forgotten password. This is very important to have, because if you forget your password, and an administrator resets the password using User Accounts or Local Users and Groups, then when you log on using the new password, you will find that you will lose access to some items, including files that you encrypted when logged on with the forgotten password. When you reset a password with a Password Reset Disk, you can log on using the new password, and still have access to previously encrypted files.

Best of all, with the Password Reset Disk, users have the power to fix their own passwords. Encourage your users to create this disk soon, because you only have this power if you remember to create a Password Reset Disk before you forget the password!

If you need to create a Password Reset Disk for a computer on a network (domain), search the

Try This!

Password Reset Disk

Let's create a Password Reset Disk. First, you need to have a blank, formatted floppy disk.

1. Now open User Accounts and on the Pick a Task page select the account that you are currently logged on as.
2. On the next page select Prevent A Forgotten Password from the list of Related Tasks (on the left). Read the Welcome page of the Forgotten Password Wizard (Figure 16.60), and then click Next. Now insert the disk in drive A: and click Next.
3. On the Create User Account Password page enter the current user account password and click Next. The Creating Password Reset Disk page will show a progress bar while creating the disk.
4. When it is completed, click Next, and then click Finish to close the wizard.
5. Make sure the disk is properly labeled, including the account name and computer, and store it in a very safe place. Oh, and remember where you stored it!

• **Figure 16.60** Forgotten Password Wizard

Help system for *Password Reset Disk* and follow the instructions for Password Reset Disks for a computer on a domain.

> The Windows NT ERD is very different from the Windows 2000 ERD in that it does not contain boot information. Rather, it contains a copy of the backed-up registry information stored in the \WINNT\REPAIR folder. You can only successfully create a Windows NT ERD if all the registry files will fit on a floppy disk. With NT, when you run the Emergency Repair option from Setup and select repair registry, it requests the ERD. If one is not available, it attempts to find and use the backed-up registry information in the Repair folder.

Troubleshooting Using the Emergency Repair Disk

So, we've got this great Emergency Repair Disk that'll take care of all of our system repair problems, we just pop it in the floppy drive and go, right?

Not just yet. It may interest you to know that the ERD itself is not a bootable disk. To use the ERD, you must first boot the system using either the set of boot diskettes or the installation CD-ROM.

The ERD contains the following files:

File Name	Description
SETUP.LOG	Copied from the %SystemRoot%\REPAIR folder.
AUTOEXEC.NT	Copied from the %SystemRoot%\SYSTEM32 folder.
CONFIG.NT	Copied from the %SystemRoot%\SYSTEM32 folder.

The SETUP.LOG file changes any time you apply a Service Pack, install or remove Windows components, update drivers, or the system state changes. You should create an updated ERD any time you perform one of these actions.

Follow these steps to repair a system using the ERD:

1. Boot the system using either your set of boot diskettes or installation CD-ROM.
2. In the Welcome to Setup dialog box, press the R key to select the option to repair a Windows 2000 installation.

3. The Windows 2000 Repair Options menu appears. You have the option of either entering the Recovery Console or using the Emergency Repair Disk.
4. Press the R key to select the option to repair Windows 2000 using the emergency repair process.
5. The next screen offers the choice of Manual or Fast repair:
   - Manual repair option lets you select the following repair options; inspect the startup environment, verify the system files, and inspect the boot sector.
   - Fast repair doesn't ask for any further input.
6. Follow the on-screen instructions, and insert the ERD when prompted.

Now that you've learned how to maintain, optimize and troubleshoot Windows NT, 2000, and XP, go back and review Chapter 15 on Windows 9*x*/Me. The differences among the versions of Windows are pretty significant, and you should know what they are. What tools did the newer OSs inherit from Windows 9*x*? What new features and tools are available in 2000 and XP that 9*x* didn't have?

Chapter 16 Review

Chapter Summary

After reading this chapter and completing the exercises, you should understand the following about maintaining, optimizing, and troubleshooting Windows NT/2000/XP.

Select the Proper Tools for Maintaining and Optimizing Windows

- Numerous new tools for maintaining and optimizing Windows are included with current Microsoft Operating Systems.
- The Microsoft Management Console (MMC) is a shell program that holds individual utilities called snap-ins and provides a consistent graphical interface. Starting as a blank console, you can easily add snap-ins including all the traditional Windows tools and some new ones as well. While XP requires you to designate the computer that the snap-in will manage, the installation process is otherwise similar for both operating systems. In addition to Device Manager and other utilities from Microsoft, you can also add third-party utilities as MMC snap-ins. You can name the custom console and even place it on your desktop for easy access. It can also be locked so that it cannot be modified.
- By using the familiar Start | Programs | Accessories | System Tools, you can access utilities or pre-made, locked consoles such as System Information. These are actually snap-in versions of classic tools that usually work even better than the old utilities.
- The Event Viewer, another snap-in, creates three log files: Application, Security, and System. These files contain information about five types of events. The System and Application logs contain Error, Warning, and Information events, while the Security log displays Success Audit and Failure Audit events. An Error event indicates a failed operation or service or an application that hung up. A Warning event indicates a potential problem that may cause possible future difficulty. An Information event indicates successful completion of an operation. Commonly used on servers, the Security logs Success Audit and Failure Audit events. You can define the maximum size of the event log files and determine what action should be taken when they reach the maximum size. Using the Filter tab, you can control what the Event Viewer displays, although all events are still logged to the file. You can also clear the logs or archive them for later review.
- Although not an MMC, the Task Manager is the tech's primary tool. Accessed by pressing CTRL-SHIFT-ESC, it displays the applications and processes that are running and the computer resources they are using. If an application hangs, use the Task Manager to end the program. It can also be used to switch between applications or to shut down the computer. The Task Manager can also shut down locked-up processes, although this action may be dangerous.

Maintain and Optimize Windows NT/2000/XP

- Many maintenance tasks contribute to the optimization of Windows. These include installing up-to-date system patches; using tools such as the Disk Defragmenter, Check Disk, and Disk Cleanup; maintaining good backups, current boot disks, and the Recovery Console. It also includes adding or removing Windows components, installing applications, and updating device drivers.
- When Microsoft finds problems with its software, it issues updates that correct the flaws. Many Windows users don't update their systems, opening them for virus attacks. Windows 2000 and XP include a Windows Update utility that uses an Internet connection to scan for updates and patches. Windows can automatically download and install updates or provide a list of updates that the user can decide either to remove from the list or to install. Keeping Windows updates current should reduce virus attacks and optimize performance.
- Most application programs have an Autorun file on the CD that calls up the installation program if Windows is configured for Autorun. If the CD does not have an Autorun file, you can begin the

installation process manually by using the Add/Remove Programs applet. After accepting the terms of the software license, you may be asked to make decisions about which components to install. Usually, it is best to accept the suggested settings.

- Removing applications that are no longer needed is an important piece of housekeeping. When possible, use the uninstall program that came with the application. Be prepared to provide the application CD-ROM if prompted for it. If an uninstall program did not come with the application, use the Add or Remove Program applet from the Windows Control Panel. If [illegible]

[illegible] applet, simply select Add/Remove Windows Components. You should have your Windows CD handy. You will be prompted for it when you add a component. When you select a program that is already installed, the wizard will show you how much disk space it occupies and how often it is used.

- Windows 2000 and XP use the same process to install new hardware as Windows 9*x*/Me. As you learned in Chapters 5 and 6, you may need to reserve a resource in CMOS to avoid a conflict. Installing the proper driver for the hardware device is essential, especially for new devices. Although Windows includes generic device drivers, it is best to use the specialized driver software designed for a specific device. You can find the driver on the discs that come with the device, at Microsoft's web site or the site of the device manufacturer.

- Starting with Windows 2000, Microsoft issues digital signatures to drivers that have been tested at the Windows Hardware Quality Lab. These devices bear a logo indicating they were Designed for Windows 2000 or Designed for Windows XP. When installed, the Properties of the driver will also confirm that it was digitally signed. If the installation process detects a driver that has not been digitally signed, it issues a warning that allows you either to continue the installation or to stop it. Often unsigned drivers work fine. If not, you can use the System Restore tool to restore the computer to its previous state. You can also configure the Driver Signing Options for Windows to install an unsigned driver without warning you or to block all unsigned drivers.

- The interface for the versatile Device Manager tool has progressively improved with each new version of Windows and still remains one of the most important tools for checking hardware, drivers, and resources. Open the properties for My Computer and select the Hardware tab to find the Device Manager button. At the root of the device [illegible] updated driver and roll back to a previous version.

- Adding a Plug and Play device to Windows 2000/XP is simple, but you should always read the documentation for the device first. You might have to install the driver before you install the device itself. If Windows does not detect the new device, use the Add Hardware Wizard from the Hardware tab of the Systems Properties box. For non-Plug and Play or legacy devices, Windows may provide drivers or you can get them from the hardware manufacturer. Be sure you have read the documentation and have the appropriate driver before you run the setup program. If no setup program exists, see if the Add Hardware Wizard detects the device and installs the driver. If not, you may select the device from a list of installed hardware or choose Add A New Hardware Device.

- Adding a printer in Windows merely involves adding a printer driver. You may add a local printer and share it on the network or you may add a printer connected elsewhere on the network. For a USB printer, run the printer's installation program and then plug in the USB cable attached to the powered-on printer. For a parallel Plug and Play printer, connect the printer first and turn it on before you run the printer installation program. If you do not have an installation program, use the Add Printer feature to start the wizard. For a non-Plug and Play printer, after you disable the automatic detect and install feature, select the port to which the printer is attached and then select the manufacturer and model or click the Have Disk button. To share the printer on a network, on the Printer Sharing page, select Share As and give the printer a share name. It is a good idea to print a test page to make sure the printer works.

- Since Windows NT, 2000, and XP require a user name and password to log on, the user account is the most basic element of Windows security. Each user will be a member or one or more groups. Groups allow the administrator to assign the same rights and permissions to all group members. During installation, Windows NT, 2000, and XP create several groups and two user accounts: the Administrator and Guest. After supplying a password, the Administrator account is initially the only usable account for a computer that does not belong to a domain. Use the Local Users and Groups node in the Computer Management console to create and manage users and groups. While you will use the Administrator account for updates, adding programs or components, or creating users and groups, you should create additional accounts for everyday computer activities. Be sure the Secure Boot Settings in Windows 2000 are enabled so that a user must enter a user name and password. Requiring users to press CTRL-ALT-DEL before logging on protects your computer against certain viruses.
- To create a user or a group, you must be logged on as Administrator or a member of the local Administrators group. Open the Users and Passwords applet and click the Add button. A wizard guides you through the process. You will also decide what groups the new user will join. The Standard user selection includes the user in the local Power Users Group and the local Users group. After a user account has been set up, the user will be listed in the Users and Password dialog box. From here, you can easily change the user's password. Passwords should be at least eight characters long with a mixture of letters, numbers, and non-alphabetical characters.
- With Windows XP, the User Accounts Control Panel applet simplifies user management tasks. This applet displays account types rather than a complete list of users. While the administrator will see Computer Administrator, Guest, and Local Users or Limited accounts, a regular user will see only his own account. To create a new user with XP, select Create A New Account from the User Accounts applet and then select the account type. The first new account must be a Computer Administrator, used for redundancy. Additional new users may have either Computer Administrator or Limited accounts. If you upgrade to XP from NT, 2000, or 9*x*, setup will migrate existing accounts.
- Windows NT, 2000, and XP come well optimized and use basically the same optimization processes as Windows 9*x*/Me except for Performance Options and Task Manager. Performance Options for Windows 2000 or Performance Settings for Windows XP has two tabs: Visual Effects and Advanced. The Performance Options contains two radio buttons called Applications and Background Services that set how processor time is divided. From this location you can also adjust the size of the swap file or paging file, but it is best to let Windows control this feature.
- Resource tracking can help solve performance problems. The Task Manager and Performance tools help identify bottlenecks. To access the Task Manager, press CTRL-SHIFT-ESC and then click the Performance tab. Similar to the System Monitor in Windows 9*x*, this program tracks CPU usage, available memory, size of disk cache, and other resources or operations such as handles, threads, and processes.
- The Performance Monitor from NT has changed to the Performance MMC console. It includes the System Monitor node and the Performance Logs and Alerts node. You must understand the terms *object* (a system component with a set of characteristics that is managed as a single entity by the OS) and *counter* (something that tracks specific information about an object). An object may have many different counters. System Monitor gathers real-time data about objects and displays them in a graph, histogram, or report. You can add additional counters. The Performance Logs and Alerts counters track a variety of things happening on your system. You can determine when the tool will monitor performance and what the log file will be named.
- System upkeep also involves running the Disk Defragmenter and Check Disk (called Error-checking in the GUI) and Disk Cleanup. The Disk Cleanup tool not only deletes files such as

temporary Internet files, thus freeing up disk space, but it also compresses old files to gain space.

Troubleshoot Windows NT, 2000, and XP

- Preparation is the key to troubleshooting Windows NT, 2000, and XP. Five different tools prepare for possible problems: System Restore, Backup and Restore (or Backup), Automated System Recovery, Emergency Repair Disk, and Recovery Console.
- First introduced with Windows Me, System Restore enables you to create a restore point or configuration at a specific time. If the computer crashes or becomes corrupted, you can restore the [illegible] disks. Both 2000 and XP offer choices of Backup and Restore. With Windows 2000 the third choice is Emergency Repair Disk (ERD) while Windows XP offers the Automated System Recovery Wizard. The ERD saves critical boot files and partition information. While not a bootable disk, it works with the \WINNT\REPAIR folder to store a copy of the Registry. You should create a new ERD before you install a new device or program. Windows XP uses the Automated System Recovery Wizard (ASR) to create a backup of the system. It uses a floppy disk and a backup medium such as tape. The restore capability of ASR involves a complete reinstall of the operating system, preferably on a new partition. Neither the ERD nor the ASR backs up data files. You should use the Backup Wizard to back up everything or just system-critical files. A third option involves System State data that involves little more than an ERD with a Registry backup.
- You may want to create an MS-DOS Startup Disk for repartitioning or booting a new computer. Windows 9*x* and Windows 2000 offer the option of creating a MS-DOS boot disk when you use this format. This feature does not appear with Windows NT or 2000.
- The Windows 2000/XP Recovery Console is similar to the Windows 9*x* Safe Mode Prompt Only feature. To start this utility, run Setup and select Repair. If you wish you can install the Recovery Console on the hard drive as one of the startup options.
- Windows 2000 and XP have the best troubleshooting tools from both Windows families. From NT, it has Last Known Good Configuration, the Task Manager. From Windows 9*x*, it inherited the Device Manager and Safe Mode. Both also have the new Recovery Console and an improved Help facility. Windows XP also has System Restore.
- The Recovery Console works as a command-line utility. Many of its commands are those familiar to [illegible] and read and write on local FAT or NTFS volumes.
- With Windows XP, use the System Restore Wizard to restore the computer to an earlier restore point. You must first close all open programs. If you select the wrong restore point, you can reverse the process and restore to a different date. You can use the automatic restore points or you can create a restore point whenever you wish, such as before editing the Registry.
- If Windows will not start, use the Advanced Startup Options menu that is available when you press F8 after POST and before the Windows logo screen appears. You must log on as Administrator and enter your password. Both OSs offer similar menus but may use different terminology such as "Boot Normally" with Windows 2000 and "Start Windows Normally" with Windows XP. XP also includes two new options: Reboot and Return To OS Choices Menu. The two most commonly used options are Safe Mode and Last Known Good.
- Safe Mode starts with only basic, non-vendor-specific drivers. You can then use the Device Manager to locate the source of the problem. Look for yellow question mark warning icons indicating an unknown device or yellow exclamation mark icons indicating conflicts with existing devices. If you have a problem with a network driver, use the Safe Mode With Networking option. If the desktop

does not display, you can use Safe Mode With Command Prompt option. Then check video drivers and a corrupted EXPLORER.EXE program. You can still use other GUI troubleshooting utilities that don't depend on Explorer if you know the correct command. If you type **Help** at the command line, it displays a list of commands. You will see the syntax of a command if you type a command name followed by /?.

- Another option is Enable Boot Logging that creates a log file of drivers as they load into memory. If startup fails, the last entry in the file may be a bad driver. If the Enable VGA Mode works, you were using the wrong video driver or had it configured for the wrong refresh rate or resolution.
- The Last Known Good Configuration option may be useful if Windows fails after installing a new driver but before you have logged on again. This option is not available if the computer has more than one hardware profile.
- Debugging Mode starts Windows 2000/XP in kernel debug mode and requires a serial connection with another computer that is running a debugger program. This is an Ubertechie thing you'll probably never do.
- Without rebooting, you can also choose Start Windows Normally. Other alternatives include Reboot and Return To OS Choices Menu.
- Windows XP allows a currently logged-on user to create a Password Reset Disk that can be used to recover forgotten passwords. If the administrator resets the password instead, you may lose access to some items, including files encrypted with the forgotten password.
- The Emergency Repair Disk is not bootable. Before you can access it, you must first boot the system with a set of boot diskettes or the installation CD-ROM. The ERD contains three files: SETUP.LOG, AUTOEXEC.NT, and CONFIG.NT. The setup log changes whenever you install or remove components, update drivers or change the system state. Be sure to create a new ERD after these actions. To repair a disk using the ERD, press R for the Repair Options menu and R again for the ERD. You may then choose a Manual or Fast repair.

Key Terms

Administrator account *(610)*
Advanced Startup Options menu *(628)*
Automated System Recovery (ASR) *(620)*
Backup and Restore Wizard *(620)*
Counter *(617)*
Device Manager *(593)*
Digitally signed driver *(604)*
Emergency Repair Disk (ERD) *(620)*
Event Viewer *(595)*
Guest account *(613)*
Last Known Good Configuration *(625)*
Limited account *(612)*
Microsoft Management Console (MMC) *(593)*
Object *(617)*
Password Reset Disk *(631)*
Recovery Console *(620)*
Restore point *(621)*
Snap-ins *(593)*
System Restore *(620)*
Task Manager *(598)*
User account *(609)*

Key Term Quiz

Use the Key Terms list to complete the sentences that follow. Not all the terms will be used.

1. The Microsoft Management Console (MMC) is a shell program that holds individual utilities called __________.
2. If Microsoft has tested it at their Windows Hardware Quality Lab, a device bears a logo indicating it was designed for Windows 2000 or for XP. This seal indicates a ____________.
3. A(n) _________ is a system component with a set of characteristics that is managed by the OS as a single entity.
4. If Windows fails but you have *not* logged on, you can select _____________ to restore the computer to the way it was the last time a user logged on.
5. If the administrator resets the password, you may lose access to some items but if you use a __________, you will still have access to everything.

6. Windows XP uses the ____________ to create a backup of the system using both a floppy diskette and a backup medium such as tape, but restore involves completely reinstalling the operating system.
7. Although not bootable, the ____________ works with the \WINNT\REPAIR folder to store a copy of the Windows 20000 Registry.
8. System Monitor gathers real-time data about objects and places them in a(n) ________ that may be a graph, histogram, or report.
9. With Windows XP, an account that belongs only to the Local Users group is said to be a(n) _______.
10. Although not a MMC, the __________, accessed by pressing CTRL-ALT-DEL once, allows you to see all applications or programs currently running or to close an application that has stopped working.

Multiple-Choice Quiz

A. chkdsk
B. fdisk
C. fixmbr
D. fixboot

2. Your Windows 2000 Professional system fails to start normally. You have not added or changed any system components. What should your first action be to troubleshoot this problem?
   A. Attempt to start the system in Safe Mode.
   B. Boot the system using the set of boot disks, and use the ERD.
   C. Boot the system using the set of boot disks, and use the Recovery Console to restore the system state.
   D. Attempt to start the system in Last Known Good Configuration.
3. Which of the following commands would you use to install the Recovery Console?
   A. Start | Run, then type **d:\i386\winnt32 /cmdcons**.
   B. Start | Run, then type **d:\i386\winnt32 /rc**.
   C. Start | Run, then type **d:\i386\winnt32 /cmd:command_line**.
   D. Start | Run, then type **d:\i386\winnt32 /copydir:recovery_console**.

D. Recovery Console

5. Phil tried to install a printer on his Windows XP Professional machine, but found he didn't have permission. What could be the problem?
   A. Phil is logged on with a Limited account.
   B. Phil is logged on as a Local User.
   C. Phil is logged on as a Local Administrator.
   D. Phil does not have a user account.
6. Sendra wants to get a quick snapshot of her system resources on a Windows XP Home machine. How does she get to the appropriate tool?
   A. Start | Run | Perfmon
   B. Start | Control Panel | Administrative Tools | Performance
   C. Start | All Programs | Accessories | System Resources
   D. Press CTRL-ALT-DEL once and click the Performance tab.
7. What tool should Bill use to track who logs on and off of the busy library terminal for which he is responsible?
   A. Event Viewer
   B. Performance console
   C. System Resource Meter
   D. Task Manager

8. Sven loaded a new video card on his system, but now everything looks very bad. What should he do first?
   - A. Go to Event Viewer and check the log.
   - B. Go to Device Manager.
   - C. Go to the printed manual.
   - D. Call tech support.
9. Tariq got hit by a virus that causes coffee ad pop-ups to appear every fourth keyboard stroke. A tech friend suggested that it was a little program that monitored his keystrokes and told him to turn it off, but Tariq sees nothing running on the task bar or in Task Manager, Applications tab. What should he check next?
   - A. Processes tab in Task Manager
   - B. Services console in Administrative Tools
   - C. Component Services in Administrative Tools
   - D. Device Manager
10. James sets up a new Windows XP Professional PC for his client in an insecure, networked environment. What's his first step for making the data safe?
    - A. Make sure the user shuts the machine off every night.
    - B. Require the user to login with a password.
    - C. Require the user to login with a password composed of alpha-numeric characters.
    - D. Nothing. Anybody with a floppy disk can access the data on the PC.
11. The Event Viewer creates all the following log files EXCEPT __________.
    - A. System
    - B. Security
    - C. Audits
    - D. Application
12. Which of the following should be your first choice to remove an application that you no longer need?
    - A. Delete the program files.
    - B. Use the uninstall program that came with the application.
    - C. Use the Add or Remove Programs applet.
    - D. Use the Registry Editor to remove references to the application.
13. Which of the following is a command line utility?
    - A. Event Viewer
    - B. Microsoft Management Console
    - C. Task Manager
    - D. Recovery Console
14. Which of the following passwords will probably be the most secure one?
    - A. MaryEllen
    - B. MEO2144
    - C. M-21e44
    - D. MikeM
15. Which of the following statements best describes Windows XP user accounts?
    - A. Windows automatically creates the Administrator and the Guest user accounts and you can then create any other user accounts you want.
    - B. Windows automatically creates the Administrator and the Power User accounts and you must then create the Guest account before you can create other user accounts.
    - C. Windows automatically creates the Administrator account, the Computer Administrator account and the Guest account. The Administrator or the Computer Administrator may create only Limited accounts.
    - D. Windows automatically creates the Administrator and Guest accounts, but the first new user account that can be created must be a Computer Administrator.

Essay Quiz

1. A colleague of yours is about to set up the PCs for a new office in Lubbock, Texas. The office will have 16 computer stations for the 32 employees to share and all the PCs will run Windows XP Professional in the same Workgroup. What advice would you give your colleague about setting up the user accounts?

2. Your boss wants you to write a brief essay on how your users should back up their data for protection against accidental loss. Half the users have Windows 2000 PCs; the other half is running Windows XP Professional. Keep in mind that your target audience is users, not trained technicians, so you should go for the user-level tools.
3. You've been tasked with organizing the standard maintenance routines for the Lubbock office of 16 Windows XP Professional PCs. Write a couple of paragraphs describing the tools available and how often each should be run.
4. A fellow tech sends a message crying for help. He's afraid to try to boot the machine up until he hears back from you. He found a copy of the OS disc and a hand-labeled diskette called Emergency Repair Disk. What advice do you give him to try to get the system back up and running quickly?
5. Your friend Steve got a new Windows XP Home computer, but it's so loaded with trial-version software from the manufacturer that it confuses him. He wants to unload some of these useless programs, but he doesn't want to trash his new PC. Write a brief essay describing the tool(s) he needs to use to uninstall the programs and clean up afterward.

Lab Project 16.1

You learned that restore points are copies of your system's configuration at a specific point in time. You know that Windows automatically creates some restore points. But there may be situations when you would like to have a copy of the current system configuration. That's why Microsoft also allows users to create a restore point at any time. Review the process, decide on a description, and then create a restore point. Note that it automatically includes the date and time when you created it. If you are using Windows 2000, another prevention tool is the Emergency Repair Disk. Review the process for creating an ERD. Then create one and store it in a safe place in case of an emergency. (Note that Windows XP does not include the ERD option.)

Lab Project 16.2

After reading this chapter you know how critical it is to keep patches, updates, and service packs current to help the computer stay healthy and to protect it from viruses that may exploit flaws in the operating system. Now's a good time to make sure your operating system is current. Run the Windows Update utility and decide which updates to install. (Now, don't you feel better about your system?)

chapter 17

CD and DVD Media

"We decided on 75 minutes."

—Sony Chairman (and professional musician) Norio Ohga on the decision to make the CD format capable of holding Beethoven's Ninth Symphony in its entirety on one disc.

In this chapter, you will learn to

- **Identify variations of CD media technology**
- **Identify variants in DVD media technology**
- **Install CD and DVD media drives**
- **Troubleshoot CD and DVD media drives**

I like to use the phrase *CD and DVD media* as an umbrella phrase for all the nifty devices that use those shiny, 12-cm-wide discs that, if you're a slob like me, collect around your PC like pizza boxes in a fraternity house. CD stands for *compact disc*, a medium that was originally designed more than 20 years ago as a replacement for vinyl records. The CD now reigns as the primary method of long-term storage for sound and data. The DVD (Digital Versatile Disc) competes with VHS cassette tapes for the home movie market, but has also grown into a contender for backups and high-capacity storage. CD and DVD media include a number of technologies with names such as CD-ROM, CD-R, CD-RW, DVD, DVD+RW, and so on. Each of these technologies will be discussed in detail in this chapter—for now, appreciate the fact that although *CD and DVD media* describes a number of different, exciting formats, they all basically boil down to the same physical object: that little shiny disc.

The technology of high-capacity, tough, easy-to-make discs helped to move the computing world forward by breaking it free from relatively small, floppy-installed applications to the much larger scale applications available today. It is interesting to speculate on the path that application software might have taken if CDs hadn't come along when they did. Would we still be using 1.44-MB floppies? Would we need hundreds of floppies to install the software that CDs handle so beautifully with only one disc? At the very least, software complexity would not even approach its current levels without the cheap, large-capacity *compact disc read only memory* (**CD-ROM**) discs.

The best way to begin understanding the world of CDs is to sort out the many types of technologies available. You'll notice that we're skipping the Historical/Conceptual section—all you're about to read is relevant and fair game for the A+ Certification exams! Let's begin by looking at the original

■ CD Media

As you probably know, CDs didn't begin life in computers. Philips and Sony developed CDs in the late 1970s and unveiled the technology in 1980 as a replacement for vinyl records. This is the audio CD technology available in every music store—still the same today as it was more than 20 years ago. Audio CDs store up to 74 minutes of high-quality sound, and their high data density, random access capability (you can jump to any spot easily), small size, and great sound make them the most popular way to store music today. It didn't take computer folks long to figure out that the same technology that enabled you to listen to *The Best of the Monkees* could be used to store computer data as well. CD-ROM drives soon appeared on the PC.

How CD-ROMs Work

CD-ROMs store data using microscopic pits burned into a glass master CD-ROM with a powerful laser. Once the CD-ROM producer creates a master, expensive machines create plastic copies using a very high-tolerance injection molding process. The copies are coated with a reflective metallic coating, and then coated with lacquer for protection. CD-ROMs only store data on one side of the disc—we don't flip a CD-ROM as we used to flip vinyl records. The data on a CD-ROM is near the top of the CD-ROM, where the label is located (see Figure 17.1).

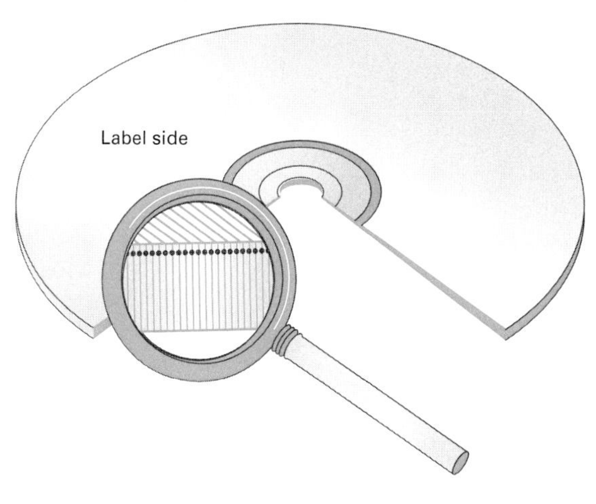

• **Figure 17.1** Location of the data

Many people believe that scratching a CD-ROM on the bottom makes it unreadable. This is untrue. If you scratch a CD-ROM on the bottom (the shiny side), just polish out the scratches—assuming that they aren't too deep—and reread

Try This!

Repairing a CD-ROM

To revive scratched CD-ROMs and other CD media in the comfort of your home or office, get a CD polishing kit and familiarize yourself with its operation. Try this:

1. Obtain a CD polishing kit from your local computer store, or find one online.
2. Take a CD-ROM *that you don't mind potentially ruining* and make light scratches on the bottom of the disc. Be sure not to scratch too heavily! Just try to replicate the everyday wear and tear that you've probably seen on CD-ROMs before. If you have a disc that's already lightly scratched, that's even better.
3. Use the CD polishing kit, following the provided instructions exactly.

the CD. A number of companies sell inexpensive CD-ROM polishing kits. It's the scratches on the *top* of the disc that wreak havoc on CD-ROMs. Avoid writing on the top with anything other than a soft pen, and certainly don't scratch the top! CD-ROM drives use a laser and mirrors to read the data off the CD-ROM. The metallic covering of the CD-ROM makes a highly reflective surface—the pits create interruptions in that surface, while the non-pitted spots, called *lands*, leave it intact. The laser picks up on the reflected pattern that the pits and lands create, and the CD-ROM drive converts this pattern into binary 1's and 0's. Because the pits are so densely packed on the CD-ROM, a vast amount of data can be stored: a CD-ROM can hold 5.2 billion bits, or 650 million bytes, of data.

CD-ROM Formats

CD-ROMs need defined formats for different jobs in the same way that hard drives need file formats like FAT16, FAT32, and NTFS. The first CD-ROMs, and all music CD-ROMs, organized the music in a special format called **CD-Digital Audio** (CD-DA), which we usually just call CD-Audio. CD-Audio divides the CD's data into variable length tracks; on music CDs, each song gets one track. CD-Audio is an excellent way to store music, but it lacks any error checking, making it a terrible way to store data! While your Rolling Stones CD can miss a few bits and you'd probably never even know it happened, you wouldn't want this to happen while you're copying an EXE file from a CD-ROM. A few missing bits would probably cause the system to lock up the moment you try to run that EXE file.

For this reason, The Powers That Be decided that storing data on a CD-ROM required error checking. This led to the next CD-ROM format: *ISO-9660*. This format is sometimes referred to as *High Sierra*, which is actually a slightly earlier standard; more often, it's referred to by a more generic term—the CD-ROM format. The vast majority of data CD-ROMs today use this format. If you go to the local software store to purchase a program, the CD in the box uses this format.

Most CD-ROM drives support a number of other formats besides plain CD-ROM and CD-Audio. You may never come across these formats, although you may see them listed among compatible formats on the packaging for a new drive: CD-I, CD-ROM/XA, and so forth. Don't let these oddball formats throw you—with few exceptions, they've pretty much fallen by the wayside. The one that you're most likely to see in real life is Kodak's **Photo-CD** format, a compressed format that stores many photos on one CD-ROM. Most CD-ROM drives can also read Photo-CDs, assuming that the system is loaded with the proper software. Photo-CD still enjoys a fairly good following, so you may encounter it—especially in the home computing arena. All but the earliest CD-ROM drives easily read all of the oddball formats, plus Photo-CD discs, making the issue of CD-ROM formats basically moot.

CD-ROM Speeds

The first CD-ROM drives processed data at roughly 150,000 bytes per second (150 KBps), copying the speed from the original CD-Audio format. Although this speed is excellent for listening to music, the CD-ROM industry quickly recognized that installing programs or transferring files from a CD-ROM at 150 KBps was the electronic equivalent of watching paint dry. So, since the day the first CD-ROM drives for PCs hit the market, there has been a desire to speed them up to increase their data throughput. Each in-

3x	450 KBps	16x	2,400 KBps	52x	7,800 KBps
4x	600 KBps	24x	3,600 KBps	60x	9,000 KBps
6x	900 KBps	32x	4,800 KBps	72x	10,800 KBps
8x	1,200 KBps	36x	5,400 KBps		

Keep in mind that these are maximum speeds that are rarely met in real-life operation. You can, however, count on a 32x drive reading data faster than an 8x drive. As multipliers continue to increase, so many other factors come into play that telling the difference between a 48x and a 52x drive, for example, becomes difficult. High-speed CD-ROM drives are so inexpensive, however, that most folks buy the fastest drive possible anyway—at least installations go faster!

CD-R

Because making CD-ROMs requires specialized, expensive equipment and substantial expertise, it's done by a relatively small number of CD-ROM production companies. Yet, since the day the first CD-ROMs came to market, demand has been terrific for a way that normal PC users could make their own CD-ROMs. The CD industry made a number of attempts to create a technology that would let users record, or *burn*, their own CD-ROMs. For years, a number of different **Write Once Read Many (WORM)** CD technologies appeared and then died, usually because of outrageously high equipment costs.

In the mid-1990s, the CD industry introduced the **CD Recordable (CD-R)** standard, which enables inexpensive CD-R drives, often referred to as *CD burners*, to add data to special CD-R discs. Any CD-ROM drive can then read the data stored on the CD-R, and all CD-R drives can read regular CD-ROMs. CD-R discs come in two varieties: a 74-minute disc that holds approximately 650 MB, and an 80-minute variety that holds approximately

• **Figure 17.2** A CD-R disc, with its capacity clearly labeled

700 MB (see Figure 17.2). A CD-R burner must be specifically designed to support the longer 80-minute CD-R format, but most drives you'll encounter can do this.

CD-R discs function similarly to regular CD-ROMs, although the chemicals used to make them produce a brightly colored recording side on almost all CD-R discs. CD-ROM discs, in contrast, have a silver recording side. CD-R drives record data using special organic dyes embedded into the disc. This dye is what gives the CD-R its distinctive bottom color. CD-R burners have a second burn laser, roughly ten times as powerful as the read laser, which heats the organic dye. This causes a change in the reflectivity of the surface, creating the functional equivalent of a CD-ROM's pits (see Figure 17.3).

Once the CD-R drive burns data onto a CD-R, the data cannot be erased or changed short of destroying the disc itself. Early CD-R drives required that the entire disc be burned in one burn session, wasting any unused part of the CD-R disc. These are called **single-session drives**. Almost all modern CD-R drives are **multisession drives** that enable you to go back and burn additional data onto the CD-R disc until the disc is full. Multisession drives also have the capability to "close" a partially filled CD-R so that no more data may be burned onto that disc.

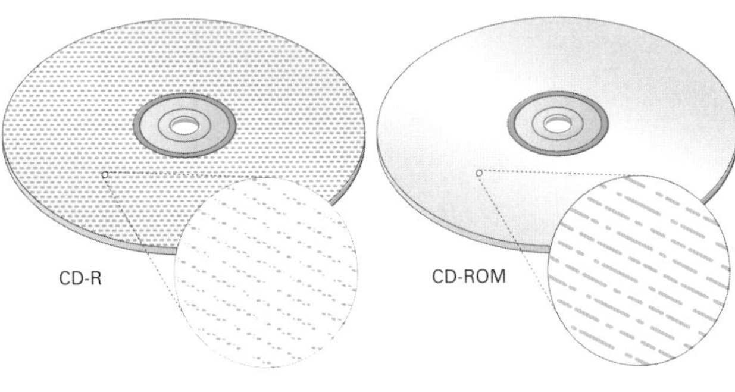

• **Figure 17.3** CD-R versus CD-ROM (reflectivity of the surface)

CD-R drives have two speeds that matter: the record speed and the read speed, both expressed as multiples of the 150-KBps speed of the original CD-ROM drives. The record speed, which is always listed first, is always equal to or slower than the read speed. So, for example, a CD-R drive with a specification of 8x/24x would burn at 8x and read at 24x.

A CD-R drive looks exactly like a regular CD-ROM drive in Windows. Windows displays a CD-R drive in My Computer with the typical CD-ROM icon, for example, and assigns it a drive letter like a CD-ROM drive. If you want to put data onto a CD-R disc, however, you need special *burner software* to get that data onto the disc. Almost every new CD-R drive comes with some type of burner software, so you rarely need to go out and buy your own unless you have a preference for a particular brand. Figure 17.4 shows the opening menu of one that I like, the popular Nero Express CD burning program.

CD-RW

For all their usefulness, CD-R drives have disappeared from the market. Notice that I didn't say CD-R *discs* have disappeared; more CD-R discs get burned now than ever before. Just as CD-R drives could both burn CD-R discs and read CD-ROMs, a newer type of drive called **CD-RW** (**CD ReWritable**) has taken over the burning market from CD-R drives, and although it has its own type of CD media, it can also burn to cheaper CD-R discs. The first CD-RWs required special software, but most CD-RW drives today use a function called *packet writing* under a special format called *Universal Data Format* (UDF), which gives true drag-and-drop capabilities to CD-RW drives.

CD-RW technology enables you not only to burn a disc, but to *burn over* existing data on a CD-RW disc. This is not something you'll want to do with every disc—for example, I create CD-R archives of my completed books to store the text and graphics for posterity—but it comes in handy in many situations. While I'm working on content for the CD that accompanies this book, for example, I may decide to delete an item—I couldn't do that with a CD-R. The CD-RW

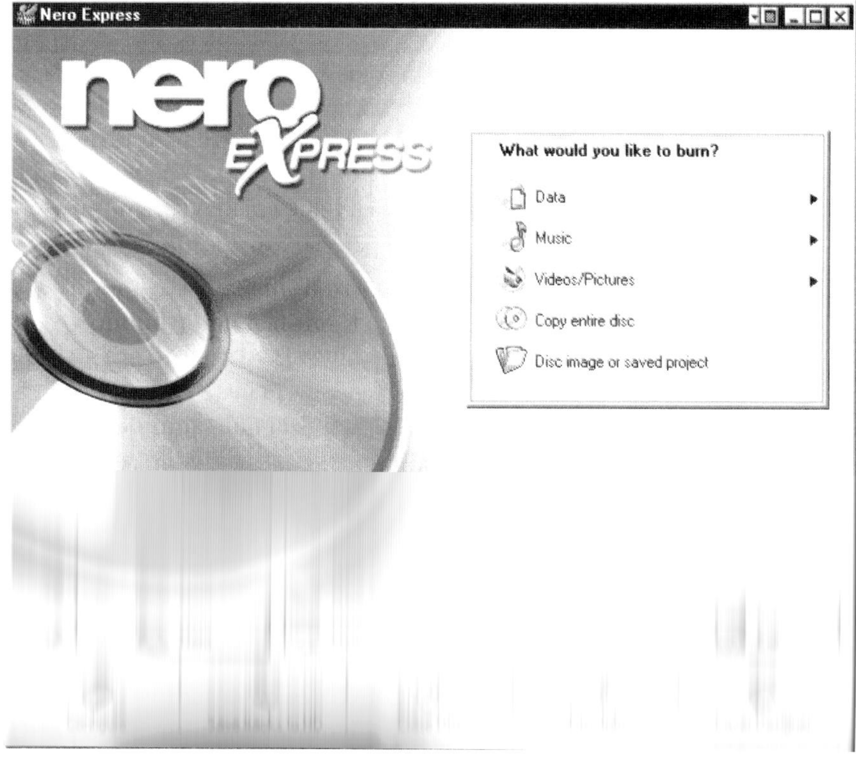

Figure 17.4 Ahead Software's Nero Express CD burning program

(non-crystalline) substance that, when cooled, slowly becomes crystalline. The crystalline areas are reflective, whereas the amorphous areas are not. The first CD-RW discs could not be read by regular CD-ROM drives, but the CD industry quickly introduced a method called MultiRead that enables CD-ROM drives to read CD-RW discs. All CD-ROM drives manufactured since around January 2000 have MultiRead capability. Because both CD-R and CD-RW drives require a powerful laser, it was a simple process to make a drive that could burn CD-Rs and CD-RWs, making plain CD-R drives disappear almost overnight. Why buy a CD-R drive when a comparably priced CD-RW drive could burn both CD-R and CD-RW discs?

CD-RW drive specs have three multiplier values. The first shows the CD-R write speed, the second shows the CD-RW rewrite speed, and the third shows the read speed. Write, rewrite, and read speeds vary tremendously among the various brands of CD-RW drives; here are just a few representative samples: 8 × 4 × 32, 12 × 10 × 32, and 48 × 24 × 48.

When I buy a new program on CD, the first thing I do is make a backup copy, then I stash the original under lock and key. If I break, melt, or otherwise destroy the backup, I quickly create a new one from the original. I can do this easily because even though CD-RW drives read CD-ROM discs, my system, like many, has both a regular CD-ROM and a CD-RW drive. I can place a CD in the CD-ROM drive and a CD-R or CD-RW disc in the CD-RW drive and run special software such as Adaptec's DiskCopy to create exact replicas of the CD. CD-RW drives work great for another, bigger type of backup—not the archival "put it on the disc and stash it in the closet" type backup, but rather the daily/weekly backups that most of us do (or should do!) on our systems. Using CD-R discs for these backups is wasteful; once a disc fills up, you throw it away at the next backup. But with CD-RW, you can use the same set of CD-RW discs time and again to perform backups.

Music CDs

• **Figure 17.5** CD recorder

Computers do not hold a monopoly on CD burning. Many companies offer consumer CD burners that work with your stereo system. These come in a wide variety of formats, but they're usually dual-deck player/recorder combinations (see Figure 17.5). These recorders do not use regular CD-R or CD-RW discs. Instead, under U.S. law, these home recorders must use a slightly different disc called a *Music CD-R*. Makers of Music CD-Rs pay a small royalty for each CD (and add it to your price). You can record *to* a Music CD-R, but you cannot record *from* one—the idea being to restrict duplication. If you decide to buy one of these burners, make sure to buy the special Music CD-Rs.

■ DVD Media

• **Figure 17.6** Sample laserdisc

For years, the video industry tried to create a CD media replacement for videotape. The 12-inch diameter *laserdisc* format originally introduced by Philips gained some ground in the 1980s and 1990s. But the high cost of both the discs and the players, plus various marketing factors, meant there was never a very large laserdisc market. You may still find one of them sitting around, however, or you may know someone who invested in a small collection during the laserdisc's heyday (see Figure 17.6).

The DVD was developed by a large consortium of electronics and entertainment firms during the early 1990s and released as digital *video* discs in 1995. The transformation of DVD to a data storage medium quickly required a name change, to digital *versatile* discs. You'll still hear both terms used.

With the exception of the DVD logo stamped on all commercial DVDs (see Figure 17.7), DVDs look exactly like CD media discs; but that's pretty much where the similarities end. DVD has become the fastest growing media format in history and will almost certainly replace the VHS tape within the next few years for video formats. It's already overtaken VHS in the video rental market. Additionally, one variant of DVD (the main DVD is called DVD-Video), DVD-RAM, has enjoyed some success as a mass storage medium.

• **Figure 17.7** Typical DVD

The single best word to describe DVD is *capacity*. All previous CD media stored a maximum of 700 MB of data or 80 minutes of video, whereas the lowest capacity DVD holds 4.37 GB of data, or two hours of video, and the highest capacity version DVDs store roughly 16 GB of data, or more than eight hours of video! DVD achieves these amazing capacities using a number of technologies, but three are most important. First, DVD uses smaller pits than CD media, and packs them much more densely. Second, DVD comes in both *single-sided* (SS) and *dual-sided* (DS) formats. As the name implies, a DS disc holds twice the data of an SS disc, but it also requires you to flip the disc to read the other side. Third, DVDs come in *single-layer* (SL) and *dual-layer* (DL) formats. DL formats use two pitted layers on each side, each with a slightly different reflectivity index. Table 17.1 shows the common DVD capacities.

Table 17.1 DVD Versions/Capacities	
DVD Version	**Capacity**
DVD-5 (12 cm, SS/SL)	4.37 GB, more than two hours of video
DVD-9 (12 cm, SS/DL)	7.95 GB, about four hours of video
DVD-10 (12 cm, DS/SL)	8.74 GB, about four and a half hours of video
DVD-18 (12 cm, DS/DL)	15.90 GB, more than eight hours of video

Tech Tip

MPEG Standards

Reproducing video and sound on the PC provides interesting challenges for developers. How do you take a motion picture from film, translate it into ones and zeroes that the CPU understands, process those bits, and then send high-quality video and sound to the monitor and speakers for the pleasure of the computer user? How much data do you think is

Moving Pictures Experts Group (MPEG) have released various coding standards, such as MPEG-1, MPEG-2, and MPEG-4. Each standard provides a different compression algorithm, which makes the files manageable. The standards also implement various technologies to handle movement and such, called motion compensation. The details of the standards matter a lot to the folks producing the movies and other video and audio content, but here's the short answer that should suffice for the purposes of a PC tech.

MPEG-1 is the standard upon which Video and MP3, among other technologies, are based. The most common implementations of this standard provide a resolution of 352 × 240 at 30 frames per second (fps). This video quality falls just below that of a conventional VHS video.

One very well-known subset of MPEG-1 is better known for audio than video. MPEG-1 Layer 3, better known as MP3 format, dominates the world of audio.

DVD-Video

The single greatest beauty of **DVD-Video** lies in its ability to store two hours of video on one side. You drop in a DVD-Video and get to watch an entire movie without flipping it over. DVD-Video supports TV-style 4:3 aspect ra-

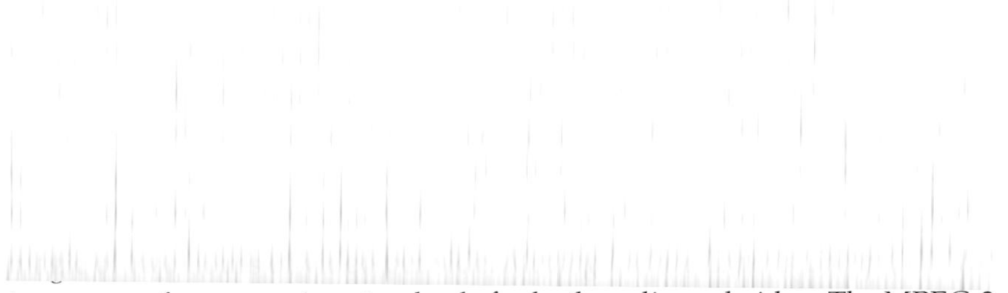

is a group of compression standards for both audio and video. The MPEG-2 standard offers resolutions of up to 1280 x 720 at 60 frames/sec, with full CD-quality audio. All this power creates the need for extra hardware to enjoy the full effect of DVD-Video.

Decoder

DVD-Videos must be able to uncompress MPEG data on the fly, using either hardware or software **decoders**. No two people seem to agree which to use. Personally, I think that software decoders are fine for someone who just wants to play DVDs on her laptop or home computer system, as long as that system packs a minimum of a 300 MHz processor with lots of extra RAM. Hardware decoders—usually just an extra PCI card with connections to your monitor and speakers—are a great choice for those who want to use high-quality speakers and reduce CPU overhead (see Figure 17.8).

Monitor

DVD-Video requires a monitor that can handle high-resolution output. An average computer displays DVD-Video quite well, but for watching movies, most folks want to use their television sets. To do this requires adding a video card that can output to the TV standard (NTSC in the United States, SECAM or PAL everywhere else in the world) used by the TV, and still the output will not even approach the true quality of DVD. To get the full benefit of DVD quality other than on your PC monitor, you need to purchase a *high-definition television* (HDTV) set, which is unfortunately still an expensive proposition!

Speakers

DVD-Video stores up to eight audio tracks. These tracks have many different uses. For example, a DVD producer may store four different languages

Tech Tip (continued)

MP3 takes an uncompressed audio file and compresses it dramatically, but the algorithm is so tight that the music that comes out of the speakers remains almost completely faithful to the original audio file. To paraphrase a catch phrase from the '80s—I want my MP3s!

MPEG-2 is the standard that supports such technologies as Digital TV set-top boxes and DVD. This standard provides resolutions of 720 × 480 and 1280 × 720 at 60 fps, plus CD-quality audio, making it adequate for all major TV standards, even HDTV. MPEG-2 is the standard that covers DVD-ROM technology—it can compress 2 hours of video into a file no larger than a few gigabytes. Although encoding video into MPEG-2 format requires a computer with some serious firepower, even a modest PC can decompress and play such a video.

The MPEG-4 standard is based on MPEG-1, MPEG-2, and Apple's QuickTime technology. MPEG-4 graphics and video files use what's known as wavelet compression to create files that are more compact than either JPEG or QuickTime files. This superior compression makes MPEG-4 popular for delivering video and images over the Web.

• **Figure 17.8** Typical hardware decoder

in stereo. The most common function available with these audio tracks is support for surround sound, which is covered in Chapter 20, "Sound."

DVD Players

Many companies sell DVD players for home theater systems. These systems *read* DVD-Video, but that's all they do; they are designed for easier connections to digital receiver systems that support surround sound speakers. All DVD players also include video outputs, which usually go to your television (see Figure 17.9).

DVD-ROM

DVD-ROM is the DVD equivalent of the standard CD-ROM data format, except that it's capable of storing up to almost 16 GB of data. Almost all DVD-ROM drives also fully support DVD-Video, as well as most CD-ROM formats. Most DVD drives sold with PCs are DVD-ROM drives.

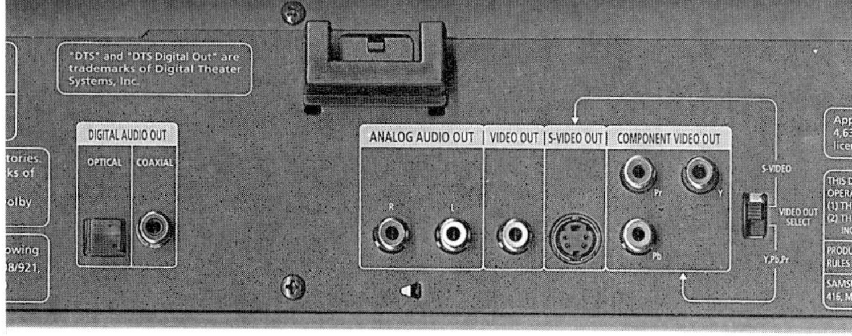

• **Figure 17.9** DVD player connections

Recordable DVD

The IT industry has no fewer than *six* distinct standards of recordable DVD media: DVD-R for general use, DVD-R for authoring, DVD-RW, DVD+R, DVD+RW, and DVD-RAM. Both DVD-R standard discs and DVD+R discs work like CD-Rs. You can write to them but not erase or alter what's written. **DVD-RW**,

DVD+RW , and DVD-RAM discs can be written and rewritten, just like CD-RW discs.

Although there is little if any difference in quality among the standards, the competition between corporations pushing their preferred standards has raged for years. Worse, no recordable DVD drive manufactured before 2003 could write any format except its own. You could plop down $250 USD on a brand-new DVD+RW drive, and still find yourself unable to edit a disc from your friend who used the DVD-RW format! Half of the time, the drive couldn't even *read* the competing format disc.

This competition initially meant very slow adoption for writeable or rewriteable DVD drives in the PC market, but the pace has picked up now. At present, no single standard has emerged the clear winner, but combination drives introduced in 2003 have made the standards war, if not quite a thing of the past, at least one without open hostilities.

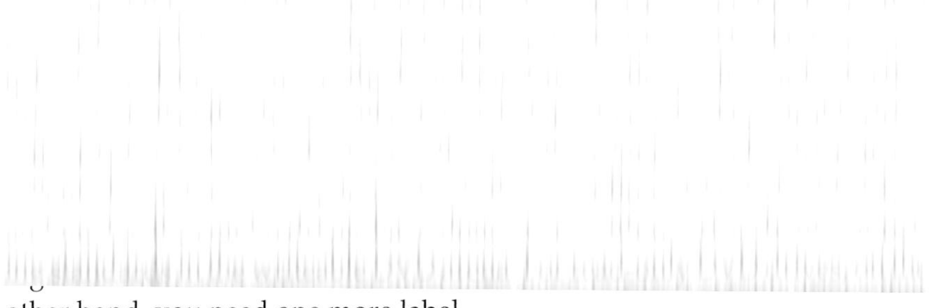

other hand, you need one more label.

confusing DVD muddle, look no further than Jim Taylor's excellent *DVD Demystified* book (McGraw-Hill/Osborne), or simply visit his web site, www.dvddemystified.com. Check out the FAQ!

DVD Multi

Drives that bear the rather silly moniker of DVD Multi can read discs of all six DVD formats. Plus they'll handle every CD media disc as well. You can safely and conveniently put any disc in the player and let it play, with a high degree of confidence in your success. Do your clients a favor and don't put a new DVD drive into a PC that doesn't bear the DVD Multi label!

Installing CD and DVD Media Drives

From ten feet away, CD-ROM, CD-R, CD-RW, DVD-RW, and DVD+RW drives look absolutely identical. Figure 17.10 shows CD-ROM, CD-R, and CD-RW drives. Can you tell them apart? In case you were wondering, the CD-R is on the top, the CD-ROM is in the center, and the CD-RW is on the bottom. If you look closely at a CD media drive, its function is normally either stamped on the front of the case or printed on a label somewhere less obvious (see Figure 17.11).

With the exception of some early CD-ROM drives, all CD and DVD media drives are either ATAPI or SCSI drives, making installation a snap. The following examples use CD-ROM drives, but the installation process applies to all CD and DVD media drives.

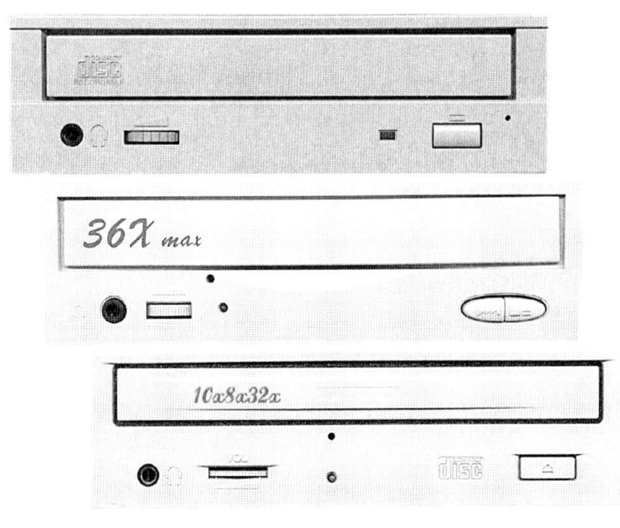

• **Figure 17.10** Hey! Which one is which?

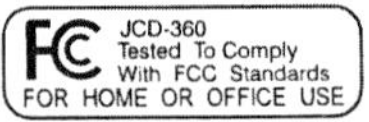

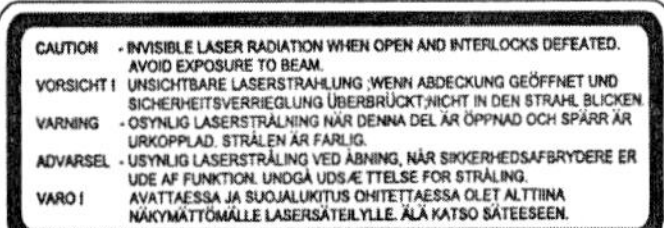
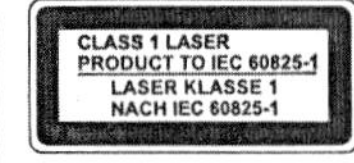

• **Figure 17.11** Label on CD media drive indicating its type and speeds

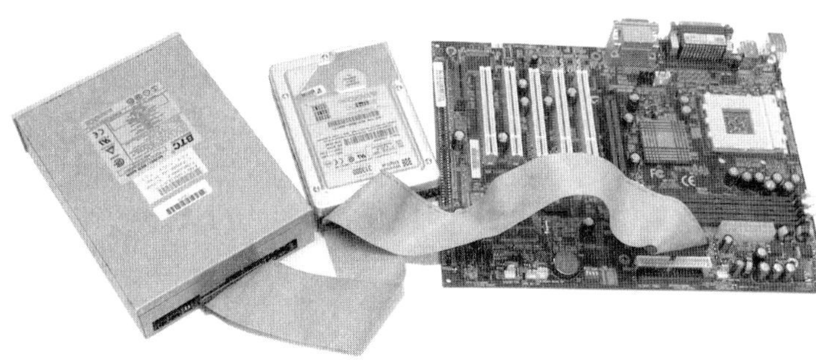

• **Figure 17.12** Typical installation

Connections

When the first CD-ROMs began to appear in the early 1990s, no standard connection existed to make them work in a PC, so the first CD-ROM makers had to provide their own controllers. The first generation of CD-ROM controllers could be broken down into three groups: Panasonic (also called Creative or MKE), Sony, and Mitsumi. Although these controllers operated acceptably well, the fact that they were proprietary—combined with the fact that they looked extremely similar—made them difficult to use and change. Proprietary controllers are long dead, so let's turn to the more typical connections, ATAPI and SCSI.

ATAPI

ATA Packet Interface (ATAPI) is an extension of the Enhanced Integrated Drive Electronics (EIDE) standard that enables mass storage devices other than just EIDE hard drives to use the PATA interface. The onset of the ATAPI standard made virtually all of the proprietary controllers obsolete overnight. Instead of having dedicated connectors and unique drivers, ATAPI treats a CD-ROM exactly as though it were an EIDE drive. ATAPI CD-ROMs have regular 40-pin IDE connectors and master/slave jumpers. You install them the same way you would install any EIDE hard drive. Like any EIDE drive, you must properly jumper an ATAPI CD-ROM for it to operate. These drives act either as master or slave and run on either the primary or secondary controller. Figure 17.12 shows a typical CD-ROM installation with the CD-ROM running as slave with a hard drive on a system's primary IDE controller.

Unlike EIDE drives, ATAPI drives require no CMOS changes as part of the install process. When the industry first introduced ATAPI drives, techs familiar with hard-drive installations swamped the CD-ROM makers' service departments asking how to set up the drives in CMOS. To reduce these calls, BIOS makers added a CD-ROM option in many CMOS setup utilities, just to give the techs something to do! You can find this option (see Figure 17.13) in many CMOS setup utilities dated between 1991 and 1996 (with exceptions). This setting actually didn't do anything at all; it just kept users from bothering the CD-ROM

Cross Check

Master/Slave Settings

You'll normally set up an ATAPI CD or DVD media drive as a slave to a hard drive master. You learned about master and slave settings for PATA drives in Chapter 10.

1. What are the various ways that you can determine which drive on an IDE controller acts as slave and which acts as master?
2. What factors should you consider when deciding where to install a CD drive, either as a master or as a slave? Any difference in your answer for a system with one hard drive vs. one with two hard drives?

makers with silly support calls. Modern motherboards will report the actual model number of the CD-ROM drive, giving a tech a degree of assurance that he or she configured and installed the drive correctly.

```
                         PhoenixBIOS Setup Utility
  Main    Advanced    Security   Power    Boot          Exit

                                                 Item Specific Help
 System Time:               [10:35:24]
 System Date:               [04/25/2001]

 Legacy Diskette A:         [1.44/1.25 MB 3½"]
 Legacy Diskette B:         [Disabled]

 ▸ Primary Master           [105MB]
 ▸ Primary Slave            [None]
 ▸ Secondary Master         [CD-ROM]
 ▸ Secondary Slave          [None]

 ▸ Keyboard Features

   System Memory:           640 KB
   Extended Memory:         15360 KB
   Language:                [English  (US)]

 F1  Help   ↑↓  Select Item   -/+    Change Values        F9   Setup Defaults
 Esc Exit   ←→  Select Menu   Enter  Select ▸ Sub-Menu    F10  Save and Exit
```

SCSI

Small Computer System Interface (SCSI) —you'll learn all about this in Chapter 19—predates ATAPI and, although not quite as com-

many CD-ROMs and load the requested one as needed (see Figure 17.14). SCSI CD-ROM drives are among the most common external SCSI devices.

Figure 17.14 CD-ROM carousel

Device Drivers

Once the CD-ROM drive is physically installed, and whatever jumpers the type of connection requires are set correctly, it's time to begin installation of device drivers and support software to make the drive work. The goal is to make the CD-ROM drive look like any other storage device—and that means that it needs a drive letter that can be accessed by the OS. The process of taking a CD-ROM and turning it into a device visible to the system, with its own drive letter, varies according to the type of CD-ROM connection and the computer's OS. Let's take a look at the device drivers and other programs used by Windows 9*x*/Me and by Windows NT/2000/XP to make a CD-ROM drive visible to the computer.

Working with Device Drivers from the Command Line

Although DOS is long gone, it's important that you understand how DOS installs device drivers. The big reason: Windows 9*x*/Me startup disks still use these tools. A startup disk must recognize the CD drive and provide it a drive letter so that you can load installation or repair CD-ROMs. Windows 98, 98 SE, and Me boot disks configure this automatically, whereas Windows 95 users have to set up their startup disk specifically to support the CD-ROM.

Microsoft developed a two-step process to install the CD-ROM in DOS. First, a hardware-specific device driver was installed via CONFIG.SYS to create an interface to the CD-ROM. Second, a higher-level, totally hardware-neutral program called MSCDEX was run from the AUTOEXEC.BAT to give the CD-ROM a drive letter. The CD-ROM manufacturer provides the

Tech Tip

External CD and DVD Media Drives

Almost all new PCs have one or both external expansion buses, USB and FireWire, and the makers of CD and DVD media drives have quickly taken this fact to heart. Many manufacturers have released external versions of CD and DVD drives, both readers and burners. Of the two expansion options, I prefer FireWire simply because it's the standard for most digital video cameras and the 400 Mbps sustained data transfer rate easily trumps the Hi-Speed USB 480 Mbps burst rate for transferring huge files.

The only benefit the USB versions have is that USB is still more common than FireWire, particularly on portable computers. In fact, quite a few super light laptops don't have a CD or DVD media drive built in and the only way to load an OS on them is through an external drive! (Note that some external drives for laptops connect via the IEEE1284 DB 25 parallel port.) If you can't decide on which expansion type to use, several manufacturers have taken pity on you. The Sony DVD±RW combo drive mentioned earlier, for example, offers both Hi-Speed USB and FireWire.

CD-ROM's device driver, while Microsoft provides a copy of MSCDEX with every version of Windows 9*x*/Me.

MSCDEX Once you load the device driver into the CONFIG.SYS file, you then need to place Microsoft's MSCDEX.EXE program into the AUTOEXEC.BAT file. **Microsoft CD-ROM Extensions (MSCDEX)** takes the device name set up in the CD-ROM's device driver line and assigns it a drive letter. Although MSCDEX has many options, the only required one is /D:, to match the /D: name set up in CONFIG.SYS. So, if a device driver line looked like this,

```
DEVICE=C:\DEV\HIT-IDE.SYS /D:CHIMCHIM
```

the MSCDEX line in AUTOEXEC.BAT looks like this:

```
MSCDEX /D:CHIMCHIM
```

Again, there is no significance to the /D: names as long as they match in the driver and MSCDEX. It would work equally well to set up CONFIG.SYS like this:

```
DEVICE=C:\DEV\HIT-IDE.SYS /D:MSCD001
```

And then set up the MSCDEX line in AUTOEXEC.BAT like this:

```
MSCDEX /D:MSCD001
```

Assuming you added the line to the AUTOEXEC.BAT file and remembered to copy the file, you should see what is shown in Figure 17.15.

Windows 9x/Me and Windows NT/2000/XP Device Drivers

Windows 9*x* eliminated the inefficiencies associated with CD-ROM usage in older operating systems. More specifically, Windows 95 replaced MSCDEX with the protected-mode *CD File System* (CDFS) driver. Not only was CDFS protected mode, it was also part of the Windows *Installable File System* (IFS) family of cooperative drivers for storage devices. The IFS drivers enabled tighter integration of different types of storage devices, resulting in more flexible caching, better cooperation with networked drives, and access to storage from other operating systems. Finally, CDFS, like all protected-mode drivers, didn't use conventional memory. Modern versions of Windows contain built-in basic drivers for all CD and DVD media drives. As long as you've properly installed the drive, Windows will automatically recognize it and assign a drive letter.

```
Preparing to start your computer.
This may take a few minutes. Please wait...

The diagnostic tools were successfully loaded to drive D.

MSCDEX Version 2.25
Copyright (C) Microsoft Corp.  1986-1995. All rights reserved.
     Drive E: = Driver MSCD001 unit 0

To get help, type HELP and press ENTER.


A:\>
```

• **Figure 17.15** Great drive letter!

Device Manager

When you install a new CD-ROM into an existing system, the first question to ask is, "Does Windows recognize my CD-ROM?" You can determine this by opening the My Computer icon and verifying that a

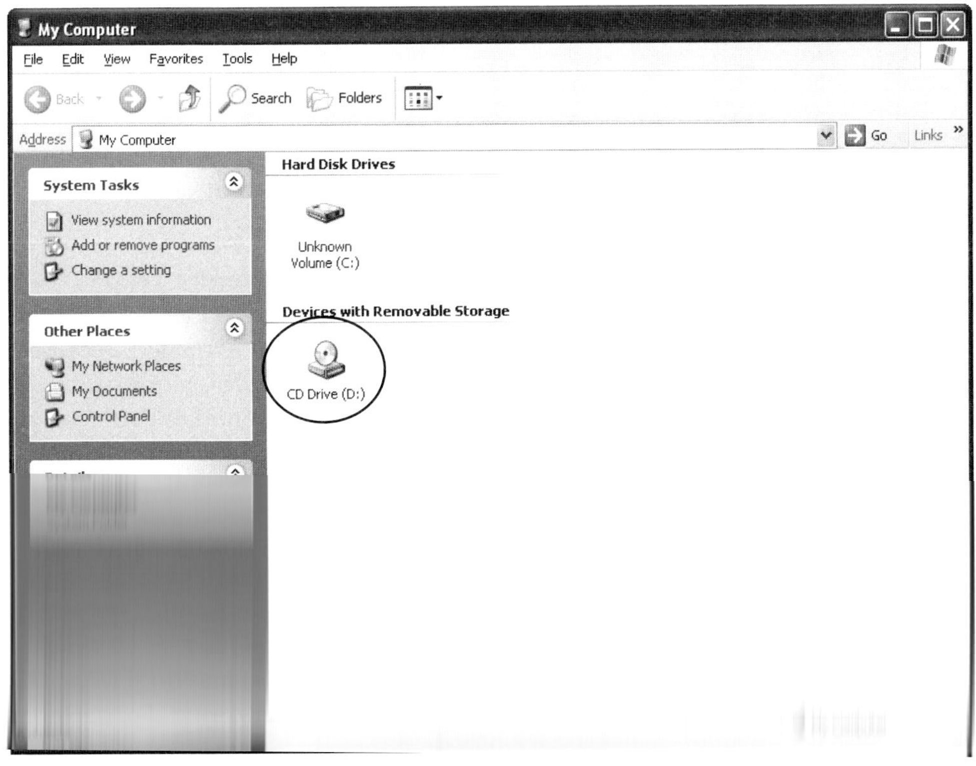

• **Figure 17.16** CD-ROM drive letter in My Computer

CD-ROM is present (see Figure 17.16). When you want to know more, go to Device Manager.

The Device Manager contains most of the information about the CD-ROM. The General tab tells you about the current status of the CD-ROM, basically saying whether the device is working properly or not—rather less useful than actually trying the device. Other tabs, such as the Driver tab shown in Figure 17.17, provide other pertinent information about the drive.

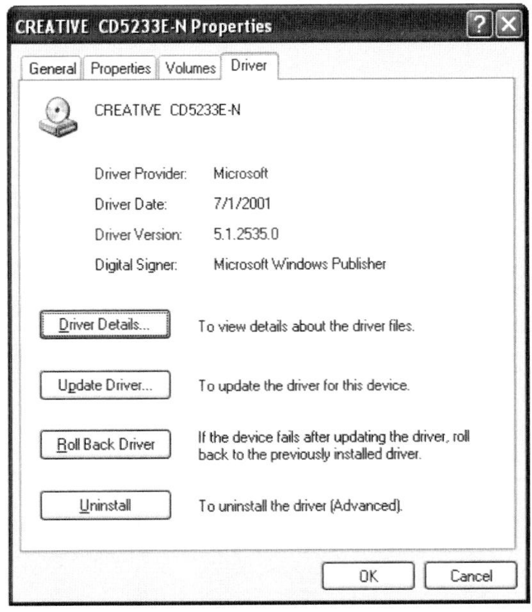

• **Figure 17.17** Driver tab in the Device Manager

Auto Insert Notification

Another setting of note is the Auto Insert Notification option, often referred to as *AutoRun* in Windows 9*x*/Me and *AutoPlay* in Windows 2000/XP. This setting enables Windows to detect automatically the presence of audio or data CD-ROMs when they are placed in the drive. If the CD is an audio disc, track 1 plays automatically. If the CD-ROM is a data disc, Windows searches the disc's root directory for a special text file called AUTORUN.INF.

Although handy, this option can sometimes be annoying and unproductive. In Windows 9*x*/Me, uncheck the Auto Insert Notification option and Windows will no longer automatically run CD-ROMs. Windows 2000 does not provide a simple method to turn off AutoPlay. The only way to turn it off is to edit the registry. You can use the REGEDT32

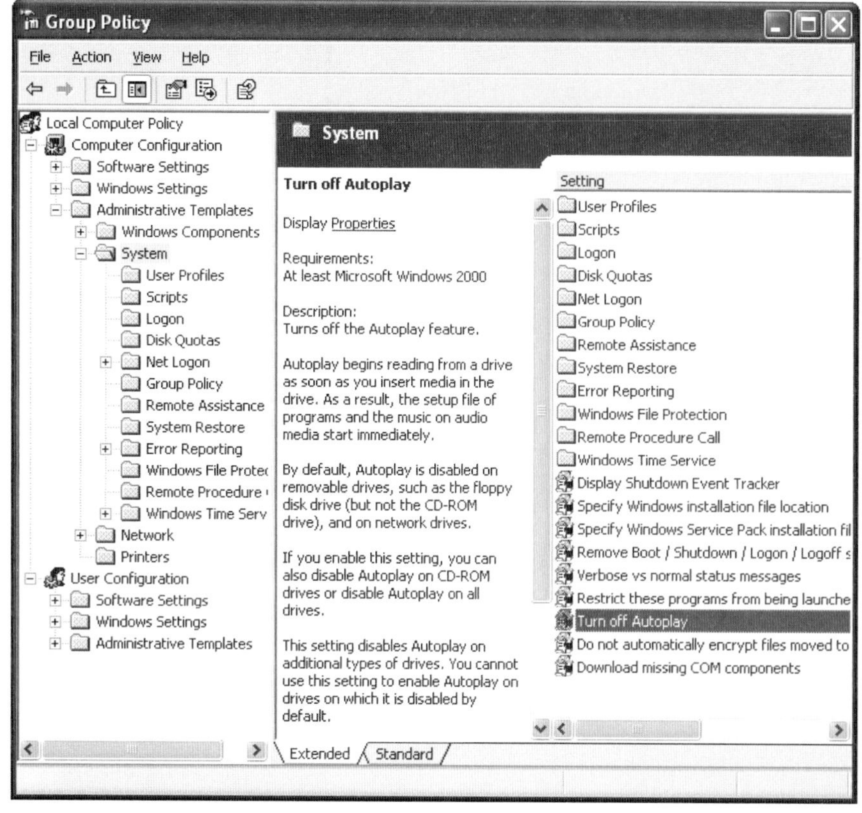

• **Figure 17.18** Group Policy MMC with Turn off Autoplay selected

version of the Registry Editor and do it directly. In REGEDT32, access this subkey:

HKEY_LOCAL_MACHINE\SYSTEM\CurrentControlSet\Services\Cdrom

Change Autorun 0 x 1 to 0 x 0.

Most techs will use Group Policy to make the change, because it gives you much more control in multiple CD and DVD drive situations. With Group Policy, you can turn off autoplay on your CD-RW drive, for example, but leave it enabled for your DVD drive. Group Policy is a very powerful tool that goes well beyond A+, so be careful with what you're about to do. To run Group Policy, go to Start | Run and type **gpedit.msc** in the Run dialog box. Click OK to open the MMC. To turn off AutoPlay, navigate down in the menu to the left as follows: Local Computer Policy | Computer Configuration | Administrative Templates. Select the System option and you'll see the Turn off Autoplay option in the Setting section on the right pane of the MMC (Figure 17.18).

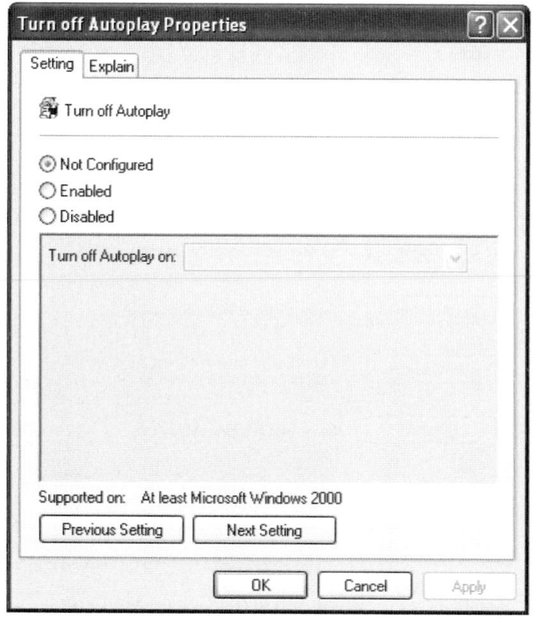

• **Figure 17.19** Turn off Autoplay Properties dialog box

Double-click or alternate-click Turn off Autoplay to open the Properties. Note in Figure 17.19 that the option is Not Configured by default, but that you can enable or disable it here. The words are messy here, so make sure you know what you're doing. Enabling Turn off Autoplay gives you the option to stop a CD or DVD media device from automatically playing a disc. *Disabling* Turn off Autoplay stops you or any other user from stopping any CD or DVD media device from automatically playing a disc. Got the distinction?

Windows XP provides a sophisticated and approach to AutoPlay on removable media devices. By default, when you insert a CD or DVD media disc that doesn't have an AUTORUN.INF file, XP usually asks you what you want to do (Figure 17.20). You can change the default behavior simply by accessing the properties for a particular drive in My Computer and accessing the AutoPlay tab. Figure 17.21 shows some of the options for a typical Windows XP machine.

As a final note, Windows 2000 and XP enable you change the drive letter for a CD or DVD media drive, just like you can change the letter of a hard drive. You'll find that option in the Disk Management snap-in (Figure 17.22).

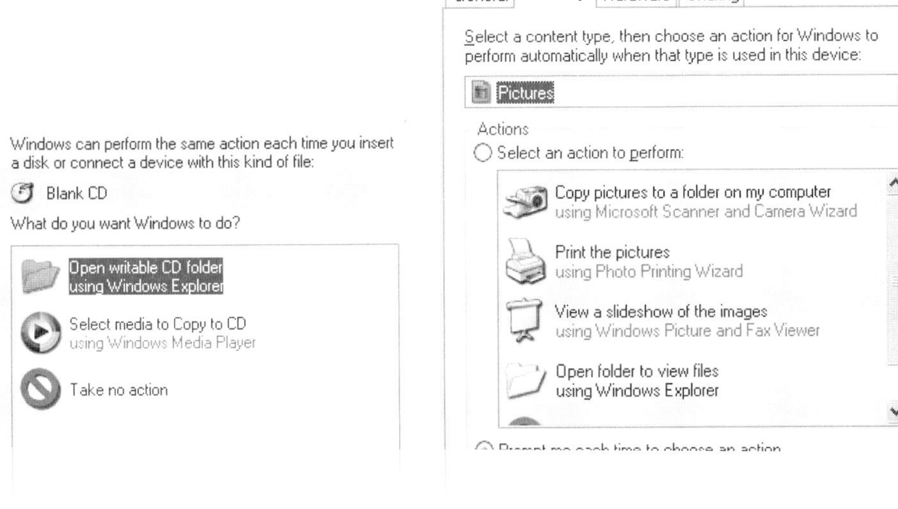

Applications

A regular CD-ROM drive installation involves no applications. You install it, Windows sees it, and you're done. CD-R and CD-RW drives, in contrast, require applications to enable their burning features; and DVD media

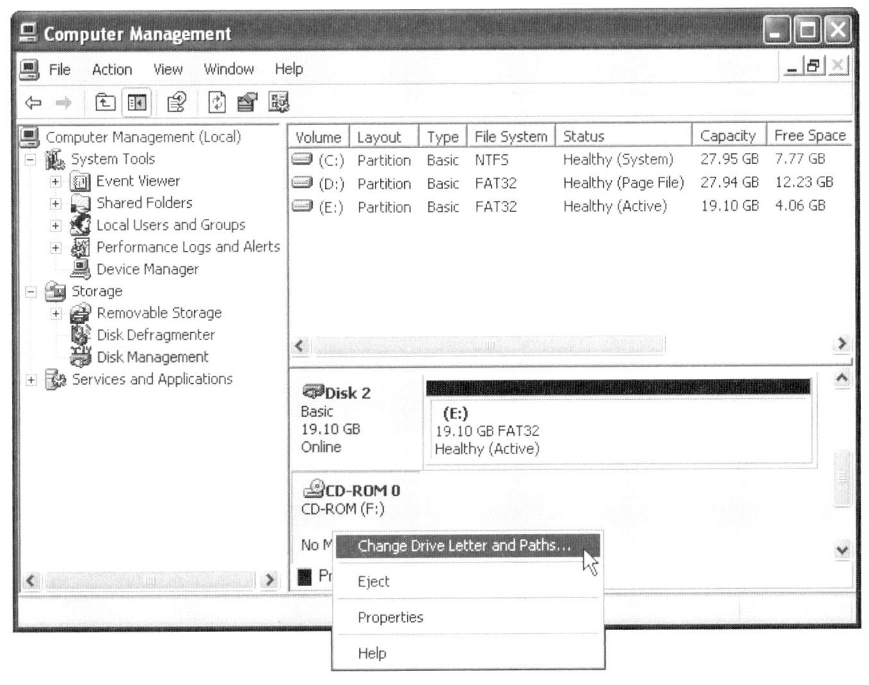

• **Figure 17.22** Change CD drive letter option in Disk Management

> Personally, I like the AutoRun/AutoPlay feature. It's nice to drop in my favorite audio CD and immediately enjoy the music, or to drop in an installation CD and have the install program start without having to search the CD for a setup program. On those rare occasions where I prefer the AutoRun not to start for a certain CD, I just press and hold SHIFT as I insert the CD.

Try This!

Burning Digital Music Files to a CD

Almost all computers and many portable CD players now have the ability to play recordable CDs loaded with MP3 files. That's a great feature—but where do digital audio files come from and how do you put them on a CD?

You can create MP3s from your favorite CDs by using a *ripper*. A ripper is a piece of software that takes standard CD-Audio files and compresses them, using specialized algorithms, into much smaller files while maintaining most of the audio qualities of the original file. One legal note, however—you should only make MP3s from CDs that you have purchased. Borrowing a CD from a friend and ripping MP3s from it is illegal! Likewise, downloading MP3s from unauthorized sources on the Internet is also illegal. You don't want to go to jail because you just had to listen to the latest, greatest single from your favorite artist, right?

After you've gathered your collection of MP3s, you've got to put them onto a CD-R disc. (Audio-only devices stand a much better chance of playing a CD-R successfully rather than a CD-RW). For this, you need two things—a recordable/rewriteable CD drive and some CD authoring software. Oh, and I almost forget, you'll also need a blank piece of CD media. You have a CD without a disc!

1. Confirm that you have a CD-R/RW drive installed in your computer. You don't have to have a drive like this in order to rip audio files from a CD but you have to one in order to burn digital audio to a CD-R.
2. Launch your favorite CD authoring software. Popular titles in this category include Nero Burning ROM from Ahead Software and Easy CD Creator from Roxio.
3. Most CD authoring programs use a simple drag-and-drop interface, similar to the Windows Explorer interface. Browse to the location of the audio files and select them. Then drag them into the appropriate area—this is often called the *queue*.
4. After you've selected all the files you want to have on your CD, it's time to burn! The procedure for initiating the CD burning sequence is different for each program. You should always make sure to *close* the CD after you've burned it. Most standalone CD players (even ones that play MP3s) won't play CD-Rs that haven't been closed.

Once you get all the configuration information keyed in, just sit back and watch the fireworks. Always be sure to use CD media that is rated appropriately for your drive, for both speed and media type. In no time at all, you'll be listening to MP3s while jogging around the park!

drives need software to enable you to watch movies, burn DVDs, and so on. As of this writing, the popular Roxio (Roxio is a wholly owned subsidiary of Adaptec) Easy CD Creator suite of programs reigns as the most popular CD burning software. One program that comes with Easy CD Creator is DirectCD. DirectCD takes advantage of advanced packet-writing features to make the CD-R or CD-RW act as a drag-and-drop device. To use this tool, you must download the Roxio UDF reader and install it on any system that will need to read that disc. Windows XP contains almost all the CD burning capabilities you'll ever need built into the operating system. With XP, you can readily drag and drop files to your CD-R or CD-RW drive and move those files from PC to PC. Almost all CD and DVD media drives will read the discs burned in an XP system.

Microsoft's Media Player that comes free with Windows makes an excellent DVD-watching application, but for DVD burning you need to turn to a third-party tool. Ahead Software (www.aheadsoft.com) makes the excellent Nero Burning ROM software that will handle every DVD recordable standard (as well as CD-R and CD-RW) that your drive can use.

Booting to CD-ROMs

Many utilities, and virtually all modern operating systems, come with bootable CDs. To boot from a bootable CD, your CMOS must have some method of setting the boot order. Figure 17.23 shows a typical CMOS boot order setting option. After you boot to the CD-ROM, be sure to set your CMOS back to the normal setting of **A:**, **C:** or you'll get a surprise next time you reboot with a bootable CD-ROM disk in your CD-ROM drive!

```
CMOS Setup Utility - Copyright (C) 1984-1999 Award Software
                 Advanced BIOS Features

Virus Warning                 : Disabled   Report No FDD For WIN 95 : No
CPU Internal Cache            : Enabled    Video BIOS Shadow        : Enabled
External Cache                : Enabled
CPU L2 Cache ECC Checking     : Disabled
Quick Power on Self Test      : Enabled
CPU Update Data               : Enabled
Boot Sequence                 : CD-ROM,A,C
Swap Floppy Drive             : Disabled
VGA Boot From                 : AGP
Boot Up Floppy Seek           : Enabled
Boot Up Numlock Status        : On
Typematic Rate Settings       : Disabled
Typematic Rate (Chars/Sec)    : 6
Typematic Delay (Msec)        : 250
Security Option               : Setup      ESC : Quit ↑↓→←: Select Item
PCI/VGA Palette Snoop         : Disabled   F1  : Help    Pu/PD/+/- : Modify
Assign IRQ For VGA            : Enabled    F5  : Old Values  (Shift)F2 : Color
OS Select For DRAM > 64MB     : Non-OS2    F6  : Load BIOS  Defaults
HDD S.M.A.R.T. capability     : Disabled   F7  : LOAD PERFORMANCE DEFAULTS
```

CD and DVD media drives are extremely reliable and durable PC components. However, there are times when that reliable and durable device decides to turn into an unreliable, nondurable pile of plastic and metal frustration. This section covers a few of the more common problems with CD and DVD media drives—connectivity, dust and scratches, and user error—and how to fix them.

Installation Issues

The single biggest problem with CD and DVD media drives, especially in a new installation, is the connections. Your first guess should be that the drive has not been properly installed in some way. A few of the more common problems are forgetting to plug in a power connector, inserting a cable backward, and misconfiguring jumpers/switches. Although you need to know the type of drive (ATAPI or SCSI), the test for an improper physical connection is always the same: using BIOS or DOS-level device drivers to see whether the system can see the CD or DVD media drive.

The way in which a BIOS detects a CD or DVD media drive really depends on the system. Most of the CD and DVD media drives used today are the ATAPI type. Knowing this, most BIOS makers have created intelligent BIOS software that can see an installed CD media drive. Here's a modern Award Software, Inc., BIOS recognizing an ATAPI CD-ROM during startup:

```
Award Plug and Play BIOS Extension v1.0A
Copyright (C) 2001, Award Software, Inc.
Found CDROM : TOSHIBA CD-ROM XM-6702B
```

This text tends to move by rather quickly during bootup, so a good eye and/or a fast press of PAUSE may be necessary to see this operation. Note that not every BIOS can recognize a CD or DVD media drive, and not even the most advanced BIOS will see a SCSI CD or DVD media device, with one possible exception: if the system has a SCSI host adapter with onboard BIOS, it will usually display text at boot that says something like this:

```
Press Ctrl-A for SCSI BIOS Selection
```

This will then enable the user to access configuration options. The goal here is to make the host adapter scan the SCSI bus and return a list of devices on the bus. If the SCSI CD or DVD media drive doesn't appear, there is a problem with the hardware. Look for options similar to Scan SCSI Bus or Diagnostic. Different SCSI host adapter makers give the function different names, but in any case, the result is a screen that will look something like this:

```
SCSI ID 0   Seagate ST4302
SCSI ID 1   No Device Detected
SCSI ID 2   No Device Detected
SCSI ID 3   No Device Detected
SCSI ID 4   No Device Detected
SCSI ID 5   IOMEGA ZIP100
SCSI ID 6   HITACHI CD20032
SCSI ID 7   ADAPTEC 2940
```

The fact that a CD-ROM is visible (Hitachi CD20032) tells you that it has a valid SCSI ID, it is properly connected and powered, and that the SCSI chain is properly terminated.

If no type of BIOS support is present, the only option is to boot to a DOS-level device driver. This is where a startup disk really comes in handy. Just boot off the startup disk and watch for the CD-ROM device driver:

```
DEVICE=C:\DOS\TRICD.SYS /D:MSCD001
Triones ATAPI CD-ROM Device Driver, Version 3.6
Copyright (c) 1994-1997 Triones Technologies, Inc. All rights reserved.
Secondary/Master: MATSHITA CD-ROM CR-584, Multi-word DMA 1
ATAPI CD-ROM Device Driver installed.
```

Here's the same boot with the data cable intentionally inverted:

```
DEVICE=C:\DOS\TRICD.SYS /D:MSCD001
Triones ATAPI CD-ROM Device Driver, Version 3.6
Copyright (c) 1994-1997 Triones Technologies, Inc. All rights reserved.
Error: No CDROM detected.
```

Of course, you should be sure to have the correct DOS driver for the CD or DVD media drive that is being tested! If the device is detected, yet can't read a supported CD or DVD media disc, first try a commercial CD-ROM disc. CD-R and CD-RW discs sometimes have compatibility issues with CD-ROM drives and, as noted above, DVD drives have serious issues with media incompatibility. Also, no CD or DVD media drive will read badly scratched discs.

If the drive still does not see a disc, try cleaning the drive. Most modern CD and DVD media drives have built-in cleaning mechanisms, but from time to time, you need to use a commercial CD and DVD media drive cleaning kit (see Figure 17.24). CD and DVD media drives are not cleaned too often, but the discs are. Although a number of fine CD and DVD media disc cleaning kits are available, most discs can be cleaned quite well with nothing more than a damp soft cloth. Occasionally, a mild detergent can be added. Always wipe from the center of the CD or DVD disc to the edge—never clean a CD or DVD using a circular motion! A common old tech's tale about cleaning CD or DVD media discs is that they can be washed in a dishwasher! Although this may seem laughable, the tale has become so common that it requires a serious response. This is *not true* for two reasons: First, the water in most dishwashers is too hot and can cause the CD and DVD media discs to warp. Second, the water pushes the discs around, causing them to hit other objects and get scratched. Don't do it!

The final problem with CD and DVD media drives—stuck discs—comes from user error and is not actually the fault of the drives. I can't tell you the number of times I've pulled a CD-ROM drive out of a system to replace it, only to discover that I left an essential disc inside the now-powerless drive. Luckily, most CD and DVD media drives have a small hole in the

cleaning kit

extent, the recordable DVD industry—has led to a substantial number of incompatibility issues between discs and drives. Some of these incompatibilities trace back to serious IO—Ignorant Operator—problems; people try to make these discs do jobs they aren't designed to do. But even when people read the manuals and jump through the proper hoops, real problems do arise, many of which you can easily solve with a few checks.

Know What It Can Do

Most mistakes take place at the point of purchase, when someone buys a drive without completely understanding its capabilities. Don't just assume that the device will do everything! Before I purchase a CD-RW drive, for example, I make it a point to get my hands on every technical document provided by the maker to verify exactly what capabilities the drive possesses. I make sure that the drive has a good reputation—just use any search engine and type in **review** and the model number of the drive to get several people's opinions.

Media Issues

The CD-R and CD-RW Orange book standards committees refused to mandate the types of materials used in the construction of discs. As a result, you see substantial quality differences among CD-R and CD-RW discs of different brands and sources (they are made in several different countries). As mentioned earlier, CD-R discs use organic inks as part of the burning process. Fellow techs love to talk about which color to use or which color gives the best results. Ignore them—the color itself means nothing. Instead, try a few different brands of CD-R discs when you first get your drive to determine what works best for you. If you have a particular reason for burning CDs, such as music recording, you may want to ask for opinions and recommendations among folks in online communities with the same focus.

They're usually happy to share their hard-won knowledge about what works and what's good.

In general, two items can affect media quality: speed and inks. Most CD-R and CD-RW media makers certify their CDs to work up to a certain speed multiplier. A media maker often has two product lines: a quality line guaranteed to work at a certain speed, and a generic line where you take your chances. As a rule, I buy both. I primarily use cheap discs, but I always stash five to ten good quality discs in case I run into a problem. Again, this will in large part depend on what you want them for—you may want to pull out the cheapies for temporary backups, while sticking with the high-end discs for archiving musical performances.

All of the discussion above about CD-Rs and CD-RWs definitely holds true for recordable DVD discs and drives as well, plus you've got to factor in the incompatibility of standards and you're looking at a fine mess. Do your homework before you buy or advise a client to buy a DVD writeable or rewriteable drive. Even the combo drives that don't have all the standards issues differ in quality of burn.

Buffer Underrun

Every CD and DVD burner comes with onboard RAM, called *buffer RAM*—usually just called the buffer—that stores the incoming data from the recording source. **Buffer underrun**, the inability of the source device to keep the burner loaded with data, creates more *coasters*—that is, improperly burned and therefore useless CDs and DVDs—than any other single problem. Buffer underrun most often occurs when copying from CD-ROM to CD-R or CD-RW or from DVD-ROM to DVD-writeable of all stripes. Many factors contribute to buffer underrun, but two stand out as the most important. The first factor is buffer size. Make sure you purchase drives with large buffers, a minimum of 2 MB. Unlike with system RAM, you can't get a buffer upgrade. Second is multitasking. Most systems won't enable you to run any other programs while the burner is running. One trick to reducing underrun is using an image file. A CD or DVD **image file** is a bit-by-bit image of the data to be burned on the CD or DVD—from one file to an entire disc—stored as a single file on a hard drive. Image files are particularly handy when copying from CD to CD or DVD to DVD. These huge files take up a lot of drive space. Unlike some CD and DVD media drives, *any* hard drive can keep up with a CD or DVD burner, dramatically reducing your chance of a buffer underrun adding to your coaster collection.

Most current CD-RW and DVD burners include the BURN-Proof technology developed by Sanyo, which has eliminated the underrun issue. These drives can literally turn off the burning process if the buffer runs out of information and automatically restart as soon as the buffer refills. I love this feature, as I can now burn CDs in the background and run other programs without fear of underruns. If you're buying a new CD-RW drive, make sure you get one that uses the BURN-Proof technology.

Firmware Updates

Almost all CD media drives come with an upgradeable flash ROM chip. If your drive doesn't read a particular type of media, or if any other non-intermittent reading/writing problems develop, check the manufacturer's web site to see if it offers a firmware upgrade. Almost every CD media drive seems to get one or two firmware updates during its production cycle.

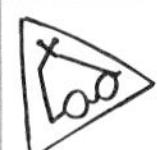

Tech Tip

CD Image Files

Disk images are something used quite often in the CD burning world. A CD image, more commonly known as an ISO image, is a complete CD stored as a single massive file on your hard drive. It is common practice to use your burning software to create an ISO image and then use that ISO image to make multiple copies of an audio or data CD. However, Windows XP currently does not

Beyond A+

Color Books

The term *color books* is often referred to in the world of CD media. Books are—well, books! In this case, they're the standards developed in the industry to describe various media. For example, the Red book describes the original audio CD format. If you have a lot of money—say U.S. $3000—you

Table 17.2 CD Media Book Colors

Application	Book	Subtypes
Audio CDs	Red book	N/A
Data CDs	Yellow book	Mode 1 Original Format Mode 2 Form 1 and Form 2
CD-I	Green book	N/A
Recordable CDs	Orange book	Part I CD-MO (Magneto-Optical) Part II CD-R, includes Photo-CD Part III CD-RW
Video CD	White book	N/A
CD Extra	Blue Book	N/A

Chapter 17 Review

Chapter Summary

After reading this chapter and completing the exercises, you should understand the following about CD media.

Identify Variations of CD Media Technology

- CDs are coated with a highly reflective metallic coating. A laser and mirror system in the CD drive reads data from the CD. The laser's light reflects off of the CD's pattern of pits and lands and translates them into a pattern of binary 1's and 0's that represent the CD's music or data content.
- A regular CD-ROM can hold about 650 MB of data that is actually stored near the top or the label side of the disc. Avoid writing on the top with anything other than a soft pen. Contrary to popular belief, scratching the bottom or shiny side of a CD-ROM usually does not make it unreadable. It is usually possible to polish out the scratches.
- CD-ROMs have different formats for different jobs. Music CDs use the CD-Digital Audio (CD-DA) format, which is also called simply CD-Audio. This format lacks any error checking capabilities, making it unusable for storing data. CD-ROM format, also called High Sierra, provides error checking for data CDs. Many other formats exist, but some are now obsolete. CD Interactive (CD-I) stores both sound and video and provides simultaneous playback. Kodak's Photo-CD format is able to store many photos on one CD-ROM by using compression.
- The Multimedia Personal Computer (MPC) standard defines a set of minimum specifications for multimedia systems, but it has no meaning now since it has not been updated for current hardware.
- CD speeds today are based on a multiplier of the speed of the original CD-ROM drives, which transferred data at 150 KBps; today's CD and DVD drives display their maximum speeds as a multiple of 150 KBps. For instance, a 60x drive would indicate 60 × 150 KBps, or 9000 KBps.
- Although the first CD drives were read-only, a number of different Write Once Read Many (WORM) CD technologies appeared and then died, primarily due to their high cost. Referred to as CD burners, CD recordable (CD-R) discs appeared in the mid-1990s and used two kinds of discs, a 74-minute disk holding about 650 MB and an 80-minute disk holding about 700 MB. Once data has been written to the disc with a CD-R drive, it cannot be changed or erased.
- Distinguished by their brightly colored recording side, CD-R discs used organic dyes to create a functional equivalent of a CD-ROM's pits. This technology used two lasers: a read laser and a burn laser. These early drives were single-session, requiring that the entire disc be written in one burn session. Today's CD-R drives are multisession, allowing data to be written to the same disc at later times. CD-R drives are rated by two speeds: the record speed first and then the read speed, each a multiple of the 150 KBps speed of the original CD-ROM drives.
- The CD Rewritable (CD-RW) drive can read, write, erase, and rewrite a disc using a laser to heat an amorphous (non-crystalline) substance so that it becomes a reflective crystalline area. When this technology first appeared, regular CD-ROM drives could not read CD-RW discs, but now all CD-ROM drives can, using a MultiRead capability. Modern CD-RW drives provide drag-and-drop capabilities through packet writing under the Universal Data Format (UDF). CD-RW drives advertise three speeds, in the following order: write, rewrite, and read.
- Stereo systems sometimes come with CD burners for creating music CDs. By U.S. law, the manufacturers of special Music CD-R discs must pay a small royalty for each CD. Also, while you can record to a Music CD-R, you cannot record from one, thus restricting duplication.

Identify Variants in DVD Media Technology

- Developed by a consortium of electronics and entertainment firms, DVD became the fastest growing media format in history and is likely to replace the VHS tape in the near future. DVD's main advantage is its large capacity, accomplished through three technologies. First, like CD media, DVD uses pits but packs them more densely.

Second, DVD comes in single-sided (SS) and dual-sided (DS) formats, but you must flip a DS disc to read the other side. Third, DVDs may have a single-layer (SL) or dual-layer (DL) format. DL uses two pitted layers, each with a different reflectivity index. Storage capacity for DVDs ranges from 4.37 GB (more than two hours of video) to 15.9 GB (more than eight hours of video).

- DVD-Video stores two hours of video in either TV's 4:3 aspect ratio or theater screens' 16:9 ratio. Extremely high quality, DVD-Video relies on the MPEG-2 standard for video and audio compression. Created by the Moving Picture Experts Group (MPEG), this compression standard offers [illegible] audio tracks, it is often used to create surround sound or to store various languages in stereo. You may set up a home theater system with a DVD player that supports a surround sound speaker system.
- PCs are increasingly including DVD-ROM drives that read DVD discs that contain up to 16 GB of data. Most are backward compatible, supporting most CD-ROM formats as well.
- Recordable DVD comes in six different and largely incompatible standards, DVD-R (G), DVD-R (A), DVD-RW, DVD+R, DVD+RW, and DVD-RAM. Combo drives that support multiple standards make modern purchasing options simpler, as does the DVD Multi label for reading all standard DVD formats.

Install CD and DVD Media Drives

- Except for early proprietary CD-ROM drives, all CD and DVD media drives are either the ATAPI or SCSI varieties, making them easy to install. ATA Packet Interface (ATAPI) is an extension of the EIDE standard that treats a CD or DVD drive as though it were an EIDE hard disk. These ATAPI drives use the regular 40-pin IDE connectors and master/slave jumpers, but are not configured through the CMOS setup utility.
- Although older than ATAPI, Small Computer System Interface (SCSI) technology allows many drives to be installed on a single machine. Although narrow SCSI CD and DVD media drives are most common, some newer drives use the wide SCSI format. Often used on networks for CD-ROM jukeboxes or carousels, SCSI CD and DVD media devices, while not as popular as ATAPI, are in many ways superior. These devices are also easy to install, requiring only a unique SCSI ID number and termination if they are placed on the end of a SCSI chain.
- After the CD or DVD media drive has been physically installed, it needs device drivers, [illegible] drivers, one for the host adapter and another for the DOS ASPI driver for the CD or DVD drive. ATAPI drives require only a single driver line in the CONFIG.SYS. Whether you are installing a SCSI drive or an ASPI drive, at the end of the line that loads the specific driver for the CD or DVD drive, you must add /D: followed by a name, such as CD001. The name assigned to the drive must match the name following the /D switch in the line in the AUTOEXEC.BAT that loads MSCDEX. Short for Microsoft CD-ROM Extensions, MSCDEX uses the device name in the device driver line and assigns it a drive letter.
- Instead of MSCDEX, Windows 95 uses the improved protected-mode CD File System (CDFS) driver that is part of the Windows Installable File System (IFS) family of drivers. CDFS provides more flexible caching, better cooperation with network drives, and access to storage from other operating systems. Windows includes built-in drivers for most common CD-ROM drives.
- After installing a CD or DVD media drive, check the Device Manager to confirm that the OS recognizes the drive and the device is working properly. You can use the Driver tab in Windows 9*x* to update the driver. The Settings tab allows you to select a range of reserved letters for the CD-ROM drive. If you set both ends of the range to a single letter, that letter will be assigned to the

drive. The Settings tab also includes the Auto Insert Notification option, called AutoRun in Windows 9*x* and AutoPlay in Windows 2000. When checked, this feature causes Windows to search the disc's root directory for the AUTORUN.INF file. While you can turn off this feature easily with Windows 9*x*, Windows 2000 requires that you edit the Registry to turn it off. However, if you hold down the SHIFT key when you insert a CD, it will prevent AutoRun from starting. Windows XP offers the AutoPlay tab on a CD or DVD media drive's Properties, enabling you to control what Windows does with particular files on discs.

- Writeable CD and DVD drives require application software to burn CDs. Windows XP has almost all you need built in, but good third party tools exist.
- Most of today's operating systems come on bootable CDs, but you must set the boot sequence option of the CMOS setup to boot from these discs.

Troubleshoot CD and DVD Media Drives

- If you have just installed a CD or DVD media drive that will not work, the problem is likely an incorrect installation. Check the power cable, the ribbon cable, and the jumpers/switches. If the BIOS or DOS-level device drivers can see the CD or DVD media drive, it is installed correctly. To check the installation of a SCSI drive, access the configuration options and select Scan SCSI Bus or Diagnostic. If the drive doesn't appear, check for a valid SCSI ID number, proper power and connections, and proper SCSI chain termination.
- If the computer recognizes the drive but you can't read a supported CD or DVD media disc, first try a commercial disc rather than a burned disc. If that doesn't work, try cleaning the drive, and check the disc for scratches. In place of a disc cleaning kit, you can use a soft damp cloth and a mild detergent. Wipe from the center to the edge of the disc, not in a circular motion. Never clean CD or DVD discs in the dishwasher!
- If you leave a disc in a drive when you turn off the computer, you can insert a wire (such as an opened paper clip) into the small hole in the front of the drive to eject the disk manually.
- Incompatibility problems between discs and drives may be avoided by researching to determine whether a drive has the features you need before you purchase it. Also, be sure to read the drive's user manual. Manufacturers of discs often offer two product lines: a quality line and a generic line. CD-RW and DVD ink colors mean nothing.
- CD and DVD burners come with onboard RAM that is used as a buffer to store incoming data from the recording source. Buffer underrun results if your drive does not have enough RAM to create a large enough buffer for your burner, resulting in useless CDs and DVDs. Be sure your drive has at least a 2 MB buffer because you can't upgrade it later. Many burners are unable to multitask while writing to a disc. To eliminate buffer underrun, create an image file on a hard drive first and then burn the disc from the file. Some newer CD-RWs and writeable DVD drives feature BURN-Proof technology that prevents buffer underruns by turning off the burning process if the buffer runs out of information.
- CD and DVD media drives have an upgradeable Flash ROM chip. Check the manufacturer's web site for a firmware upgrade if your drive has problems reading a particular kind of media or if it develops other non-intermittent reading/writing problems.

Key Terms

ATA Packet Interface (ATAPI) *(652)*
AUTORUN.INF *(655)*
Buffer underrun *(662)*
CD-Digital Audio (CD-DA) *(644)*
CD-Recordable (CD-R) *(645)*
CD-Rewritable (CD-RW) *(646)*
Compact Disc Read-Only Memory (CD-ROM) *(643)*
Decoder *(649)*
Digital Versatile Disc (DVD) *(642)*
DVD Multi *(651)*
DVD-ROM *(650)*
DVD-RW *(650)*
DVD+RW *(651)*
DVD-Video *(649)*
Image file *(662)*
Microsoft CD-ROM Extensions (MSCDEX) *(654)*
MultiRead *(647)*
Multisession drive *(646)*
Photo-CD *(644)*
Single-session drive *(646)*
Small Computer System Interface (SCSI) *(653)*
Write Once Read Many (WORM) *(645)*

Key Term Quiz

Use the Key Terms list to complete the sentences that follow. Not all the terms will be used.

1. To uncompress MPEG data, you must have a __________ that may be either hardware or software.
2. If you want to burn part of a disc and finish burning it at a later time, you need to select a __________.
3. Drives with BURN-Proof technology were designed to eliminate the problem of

6. Popular on networks for jukeboxes or carousels, __________ CD media devices are in many ways superior to ATAPI devices.
7. The first kind of CD disc was the __________ that is still used for music, but it is inappropriate for data since it lacks any error correction techniques.
8. While a CD-ROM disc holds about 650 MB of data, a __________ stores from 4.37 GB to 15.9 GB, depending on the number of sides and layers used.

Multiple-Choice Quiz

1. If a CD media drive experiences nonintermittent reading/writing problems or cannot read a particular kind of media, the problems may be solved by __________.
   - **A.** Updating the driver
   - **B.** Reinstalling the drive
   - **C.** Buying a new drive
   - **D.** Upgrading the flash ROM chip on the drive
2. Which of the following statements is true about the /D switch used with the driver line in the CONFIG.SYS and with the MSCDEX line in the AUTOEXEC.BAT.
   - **A.** It is optional.
   - **B.** It must include the brand name of the device.
   - **C.** It can be anything so long as it is the same in both the CONFIG.SYS and the AUTOEXEC.BAT.
   - **D.** It is followed by the letter that will be assigned to the drive.
3. All the following statements about a CD-ROM disc are true *except* __________.
   - **A.** It holds about 650 MB of data.
   - **B.** Data is stored near the top on the label side of the disk.
   - **C.** Scratching the bottom or shiny side makes it unreadable.
   - **D.** You can destroy the disc if you wash it in a dishwasher.
4. Both CD and DVD drive speeds are based on multiples of __________, the speed of the original CD-ROM drives.
   - **A.** 100 KBps
   - **B.** 150 KBps
   - **C.** 100 MBps
   - **D.** 150 MBps
5. A SCSI CD media device requires all of the following *except*__________.
   - **A.** Termination if placed on the end of a SCSI chain
   - **B.** Two device drivers
   - **C.** Correct configuration of the master/slave jumper
   - **D.** A unique SCSI ID number

6. If a CD-RW has a speed rating of 12 × 10 × 32, the three numbers refer, in order, to the ________, __________, and __________ speeds.

   A. Write, rewrite, read

   B. Read, write, rewrite

   C. Rewrite, read, write

   D. Write, read, rewrite

7. What settings in the CMOS setup must you change to install a CD media drive?

   A. Number of heads and cylinders the drive has

   B. Whether the drive is installed on the primary or secondary EIDE channel

   C. Whether the jumpers on the drive are set to master or slave

   D. None, because a CD media drive is not configured through the CMOS setup

8. For a DVD to store 15.9 GB of data or more than eight hours of video, the disc must be __________.

   A. Double-sided, single-layered

   B. Single-sided, single-layered

   C. Single-sided, double-layered

   D. Double-sided, double-layered

9. All the following statements about CD-R are true *except* __________.

   A. This technology is able to erase and rewrite by using a laser to heat an amorphous (noncrystalline) substance to turn it into a reflective crystalline area.

   B. CD-R discs use organic dyes to create the functional equivalent of pits.

   C. This technology uses two lasers: a read laser and a more powerful burn laser.

   D. CD-R drives have two speed ratings, the record speed and the read speed.

10. The high quality of DVD-Video is due to its use of ______________.

   A. Universal Data Format (UDF)

   B. The MPEG-2 standard for video and audio compression

   C. CD File System (CDFS)

   D. BURN-Proof technology

11. Most of the problems with using CD-RW discs in regular CD-ROM drives have been solved by a method called __________.

   A. MultiRead

   B. Multisession

   C. Packet writing

   D. Universal Data Format (UDF)

12. Which of the following kinds of discs is the best one to choose for performing regular backups?

   A. CD-ROM/XA

   B. CD-Interactive (CD-I)

   C. CD-R

   D. CD-RW

13. If you're using Windows 98, what tool can you use to prevent the drive letter of your CD-Media drive from shifting when you add a second hard drive?

   A. The Settings tab of the Device Manager

   B. The General tab of the Device Manager

   C. REGEDT32

   D. CONFIG.SYS

14. If you have the AutoRun or AutoPlay setting turned on, how do you prevent the disc you just inserted into your CD media drive from play automatically?

   A. Turn off the computer and then insert the CD before you reboot the system.

   B. Insert a wire, such as an opened paper clip, into the small hole in the front of the drive as you insert the CD.

   C. Hold down the SHIFT key as you insert the CD.

   D. Hold down the ALT key as you insert the CD.

15. With Windows 2000, you can use the Disk Management snap-in to change the ____________ on a CD or DVD media drive.

   A. Name

   B. Drive letter

   C. Supported media

   D. Master/slave setting

Essay Quiz

1. Your friend Jack's hard drive died last week, so he bought a new hard drive and installed it. Now he's trying to install Windows 2000, but his computer will not boot to the CD-ROM drive. He's called you for help. What does he need to do to get his computer to recognize and boot to the CD-ROM drive so he can install the OS?

2. Your department is getting ready to replace the old computers, and your boss Mr. Turner has asked you to investigate what kind of CD media devices the new computers should have. Write a

decided to buy an ATAPI CD-RW drive and does not know how to install it on her Windows 98 computer that currently has only a single EIDE hard drive. Guide her step-by-step through the installation process.

4. The problem of buffer underrun has resulted in many CD-RW drives producing discs that are unusable. Explain the buffer underrun problem and what can be done to lessen or eliminate it.

5. Assuming that your drive will work with the

Lab Projects

• Lab Project 17.1

You learned in this chapter that a wide variety of brands of discs exist from the generic to high quality. You also learned that it is important to buy discs that match the capabilities of your drive. Visit your local computer store or use the Internet to research different kinds of CD and DVD media. Compare brands and prices. Examine carefully the kinds of drives and the purposes for which each kind is recommended.

• Lab Project 17.2

Use the Internet to check these sites: www.compaq.com, www.dell.com, and www.gateway.com. What kinds of CD and DVD media devices do these companies offer with their new computers? Do any of the companies offer multiple CD and DVD media devices? If so, which ones and what devices? What upgrades for CD and DVD media devices do the companies offer and how expensive are the upgrades? If you were buying a new PC, which CD or DVD media device(s) would you want on your computer? Why?

• Lab Project 17.3

Adding a second CD or DVD media drive to a PC enables you to do some fun things, from making your own music CDs to watching movies. Assuming you want to install an ATAPI drive, you then need to face some issues. Which controller should you use, primary or secondary? Should both CD or DVD media drives be on the same controller or on different controllers? Why?

Most techs would install a burner as secondary master and put a read-only drive on the primary as slave, but different drives require different considerations. If you don't plan to copy CD to CD, there's no reason the read-only CD shouldn't be secondary slave. The key is you have to experiment.

Install a second CD or DVD media drive—preferably a burner—and run it through its paces. Copy files and burn discs to and from the CD/DVD and hard drive(s). Then change the configuration of your drives (such as having both CDs/DVDs on the same controller) and run through the testing process again. Any noticeable differences?

chapter 18

Video

"Quite exciting this video magic!"

—Viv Savage
in *This is Spinal Tap*
(1984)

In this chapter, you will learn how to

- **Explain how CRT monitors and LCD displays work**
- **Select the proper display adapter**
- **Install and configure video software**
- **Troubleshoot basic video problems**

The term *video* encompasses a complex interaction among numerous parts of the PC, all designed to put a picture on the screen. The monitor shows you what's going on with your programs and operating system. It's the primary output device for the PC. The video card or **display adapter** handles all of the communication between the CPU and the monitor (see Figure 18.1). The operating system needs to know how to handle communication between the CPU and the display adapter, which requires drivers specific for each card and proper setup within Windows. Finally, each application needs to be able to interact with the rest of the video system.

Let's look at monitors and video cards individually. I'll bring them back together as a team later in the chapter so that you can understand the many nuances that make video so challenging. We'll start with the monitor.

Test Specific

■ CRT and LCD Displays

To understand displays, you need a good grasp of each component and how they work together to make a beautiful (or not so beautiful) picture on the screen. Different types of displays use different methods and

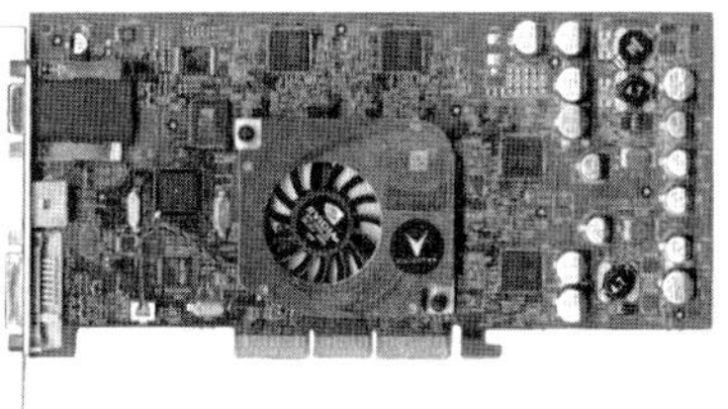

• **Figure 18.1** Typical video card and monitor

monitor contains a large cathode ray tube, a type of airtight vacuum tube. One end of this tube is a very slender cylinder that contains three electron guns. The other end of the tube, which is fatter and wider, is the display screen.

The inside of the display screen has a phosphor coating. When power is applied to one or more of the electron guns, a stream of electrons shoots towards the display end of the CRT (see Figure 18.2). Along the way, this stream is subjected to magnetic fields generated by a ring of electromagnets called a *yoke* that controls the electron beam's point of impact. When the phosphor coating is struck by the electron beam, it releases its energy as visible light.

When struck by a stream of electrons, a phosphor quickly releases a burst of energy. This happens far too quickly for the human eye and brain connection to register. Fortunately, the phosphors on the display screen have a quality called *persistence*, which means the phosphors continue to glow after being struck by the electron beam. Too much persistence and the image is smeary; too little and the image appears to flicker. The perfect combination of beam and persistence creates the illusion of a solid picture.

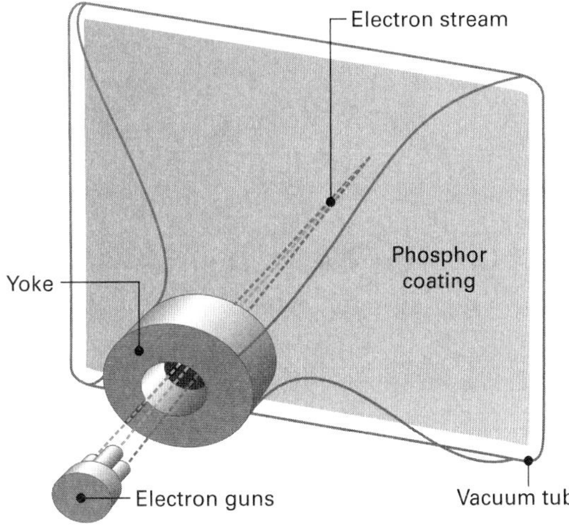

• **Figure 18.2** Electron stream in the CRT

Refresh Rate

The monitor displays video data as the electron guns

rior of a monitor might appear similar to the interior of a PC because of the printed circuit boards and related components, but that is where the similarity ends. No PC has voltages exceeding 15,000 to 30,000V, but most monitors do. So let's get one thing perfectly clear: Opening up a monitor can kill you! Even when the power is disconnected, certain components retain a substantial voltage for an extended period of time. You can inadvertently short one of the components and fry yourself—to death. Given this risk, certain aspects of monitor repair lie outside the necessary skill set for a normal PC support person and definitely outside the A+ Certification test domains! I will show you how to address the problems you can fix safely and make sure you understand the ones you need to hand over to a monitor shop.

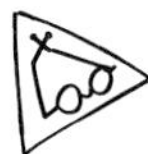

Tech Tip

Perfect Flat

Lots of manufacturers make CRT monitors, but only a handful of companies make the CRT—the tube inside the monitor—itself. All CRT tubes can be categorized into either of two types: traditional curved-screen CRTs and CRTs that are often referred to as perfect flat*—using a new kind of vacuum tube that has a completely flat screen and no bending around the edges. The perfect flat screens offer a wider viewing angle than standard CRT screens. About the only negative to the perfect flat screens is that they tend to lack true black, so pictures seem just shy of a natural richness of color and contrast.*

make a series of horizontal sweeps across the screen, energizing the appropriate areas of the phosphorous coating. The sweeps start at the upper-left corner of the monitor and move across and down to the lower-right corner. The screen is "painted" only in one direction, then the electron guns turn and retrace their path across the screen, to be ready for the next sweep. These sweeps are called *raster lines* (see Figure 18.3).

The speed at which the electron beam moves across the screen is known as the **horizontal refresh rate (HRR)**, as shown in Figure 18.4. The monitor draws a number of lines across the screen, eventually covering the screen with glowing phosphors. The number of lines is not fixed, unlike television screens, which have a set number of lines. After the guns reach the lower-right corner of the screen, they turn off and point back to the upper-left corner. The amount of time it takes to draw the entire screen and get the electron guns back to the upper-left corner is called the **vertical refresh rate (VRR)**, shown in Figure 18.5.

Monitors do not determine the HRR or VRR; video cards "push" the monitor at a certain VRR and then the monitor determines the HRR. If the video card is set to push at too low a VRR, the monitor produces a noticeable flicker, causing eyestrain and headaches for users. Pushing the monitor at too high of a VRR, however, causes a definite distortion of the screen image and will damage the circuitry of the monitor and eventually destroy it. The number one killer of monitors is improper VRR settings, and the number one reason your office is filled with crabby workers is due to the VRR being set too low. All good PC support techs understand this and take substantial time tweaking the VRR to insure that the video card pushes the monitor at the highest VRR without damaging the monitor—this is the Holy Grail of monitor support!

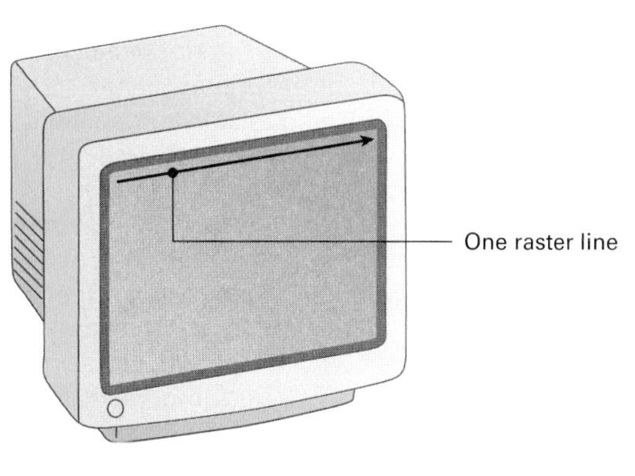

Figure 18.3 Electron guns sweep from left to right.

Phosphors and Shadow Mask

All CRT monitors contain dots of phosphorous or some other light-sensitive compound that glows *red*, *green*, or *blue* (RGB) when an electron gun sweeps over it. These phosphors are evenly distributed across the front of the monitor (see Figure 18.6).

A normal CRT has three electron guns: one for the red phosphors, one for the blue phosphors, and one for the green phosphors. It is important to understand that the electron guns do not fire colored light; they simply fire electrons at different intensities, which then make the phosphors glow. The higher the intensity of

Figure 18.4 Horizontal refresh rate

Figure 18.5 Vertical refresh rate

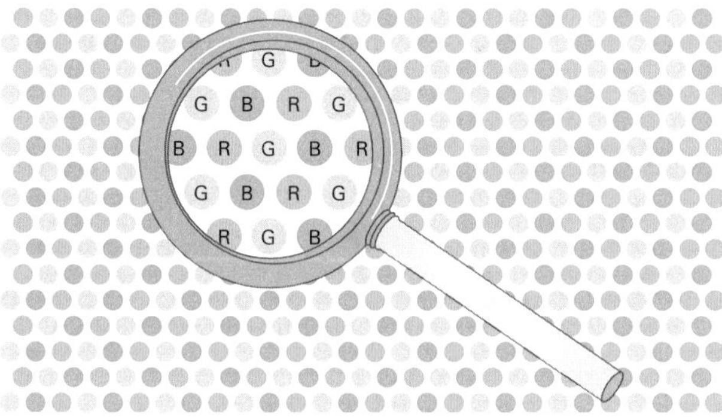

• **Figure 18.6** A monitor is a grid of red, green, and blue phosphors

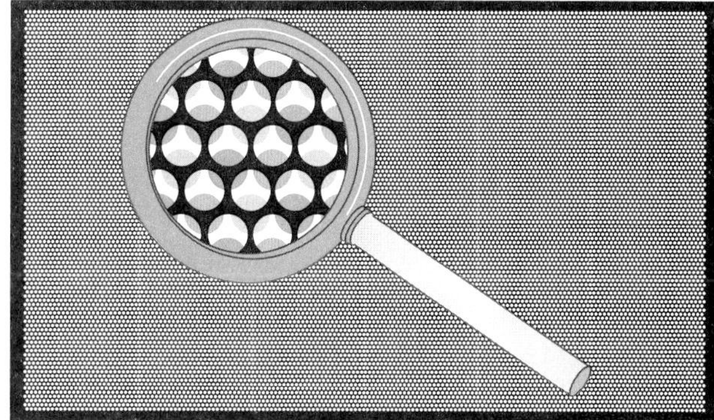

• **Figure 18.7** Shadow mask

that allows only the proper electron gun to light the proper phosphors (see Figure 18.7). This prevents, for example, the red electron beam from "bleeding over" and lighting neighboring blue and green dots.

so try this.

1. Most PCs have two places where you can discover the current refresh rate of the monitor. Many monitors offer a menu button for adjusting the display. Often it will show the refresh rate when pushed once.
2. Or, if that doesn't work, go to the Control Panel and open the Display applet. Select the Settings tab and then click the Advanced button. Select the Monitor tab in the Monitor Properties dialog box.
3. Write down your refresh rate. How does it compare with that of your classmates?

The electron guns sweep across the phosphors as a group, turning rapidly on and off as they move across the screen. When the group reaches the end of the screen, it moves to the next line. It is crucial to understand that turning the guns on and off, combined with moving the guns to new lines, creates a "mosaic" that is the image you see on the screen. The number of times the guns turn on and off, combined with the number of lines drawn on the screen, determines the number of mosaic pieces used to create the image. These individual "pieces" are called **pixels**, from the term *picture elements*. You can't hold a pixel in your hand; it's just the area of phosphors lit at one instant when the group of guns is turned on. The size of pixels can change, depending on the number of times the group of guns is turned on and off and the number of lines drawn.

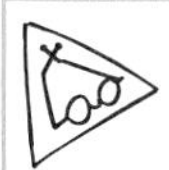

Tech Tip

Trinitron

Not all monitors use dots. The popular Sony Trinitron line of CRT monitors uses bars of red, green, and blue instead of dots. The holes in the shadow mask have a rectangular shape. Many people feel this makes the monitor's image much crisper and clearer. Somebody must agree with them since the Trinitron enjoys tremendous popularity. Even though the phosphors and shadow mask have a different shape, everything you learn here applies to Trinitrons also.

Resolution

Monitor **resolution** is always shown as the number of horizontal pixels times the number of vertical pixels. A resolution of 640 × 480, therefore, indicates a horizontal resolution of 640 pixels and a vertical resolution of 480 pixels. If you multiply the values together, you can see how many pixels are on each screen: 640 × 480 = 307,200 pixels per screen. An example of resolution affecting the pixel size is shown in Figure 18.8.

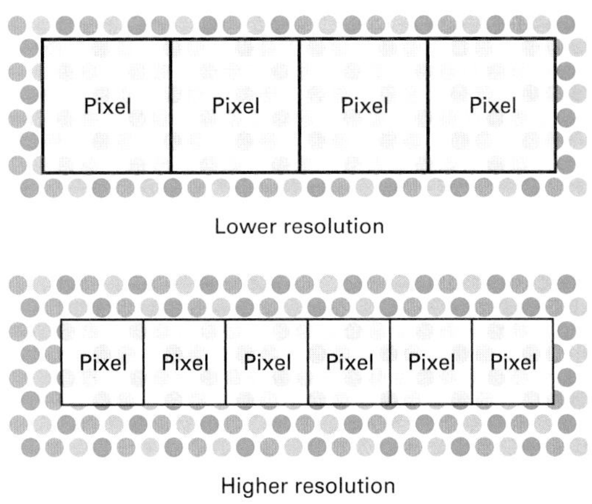

• **Figure 18.8** Resolution versus pixel size

Some common resolutions are 640 × 480, 800 × 600, 1024 × 768, 1280 × 1024, and 1600 × 1200. Notice that most of these resolutions match a 4:3 ratio. This is called the *aspect ratio*. Most monitors are shaped like television screens, with a 4:3 aspect ratio, so most resolutions are designed to match—or at least be close to—that shape.

The last important issue is to determine the maximum possible resolution for a monitor. In other words, how small can one pixel be? Well, the answer lies in the phosphors. A pixel must be made up of at least one red, one green, and one blue phosphor to make any color, so the smallest theoretical pixel would consist of one group of red, green, and blue phosphors: a **triad** (see Figure 18.9). Various limitations in screens, controlling electronics, and electron gun technology make the maximum resolution much bigger than one triad.

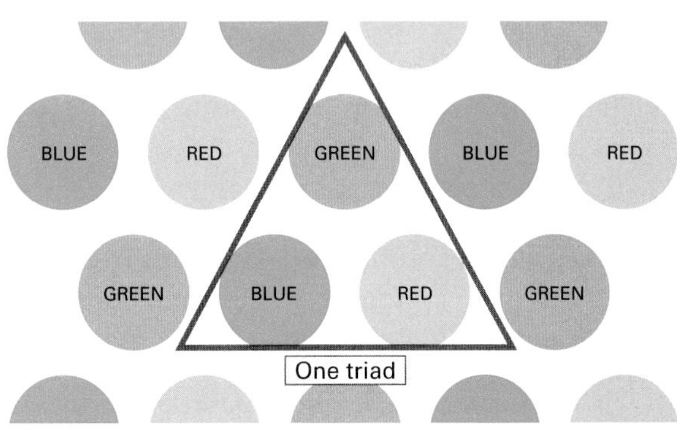

• **Figure 18.9** One triad

Dot Pitch

The resolution of a monitor is defined by the maximum amount of detail the monitor can render. The dot pitch of the monitor ultimately limits this resolution. The **dot pitch** defines the diagonal distance between phosphorous dots of the same color, and is measured in *millimeters* (mm). Because a lower dot pitch means more dots on the screen, it usually produces a sharper, more defined image (see Figure 18.10). Dot pitch works in tandem with the maximum number of lines the monitor can support in order to determine the greatest working resolution of the monitor. It might be possible to place an image at 1600 × 1200 on a 15-inch monitor with a dot pitch of .31 mm, but it would not be very readable.

The dot pitch can range from as high as .39 mm to as low as .18 mm. For most Windows-based applications on a 17-inch monitor, many people find that .28 mm is the maximum usable dot pitch that still produces a clear picture.

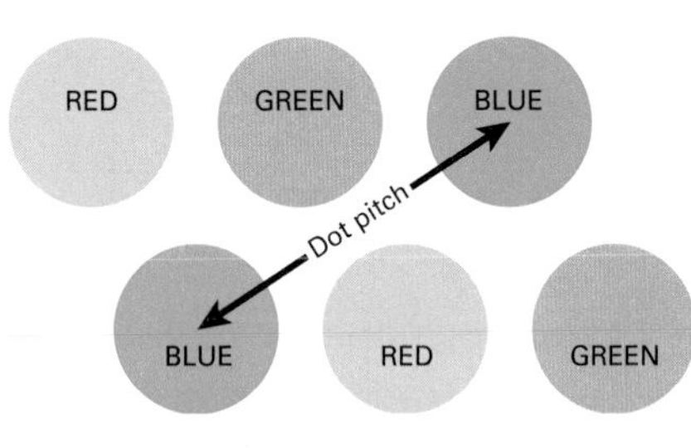

• **Figure 18.10** Measuring dot pitch

Bandwidth

Bandwidth defines the maximum number of times the electron gun can be turned on and off per second. Bandwidth is measured in *megahertz* (MHz). In essence, bandwidth tells us how fast the monitor can put an image on the screen. A typical value for a better-quality 17-inch color monitor would be around 150 MHz, which means that the electron beam can be turned on and off 150 million times per second. The value for a monitor's bandwidth determines the maximum VRR the video card should push the monitor for any given resolution. It reads as follows:

maximum VRR = bandwidth ÷ pixels per page

For example, what is the maximum VRR that a 17-inch monitor with a bandwidth of 100 MHz and a resolution of 1024 × 768 can support? The answer is

maximum VRR = 100,000,000 ÷ (1024 × 768) = 127 Hz

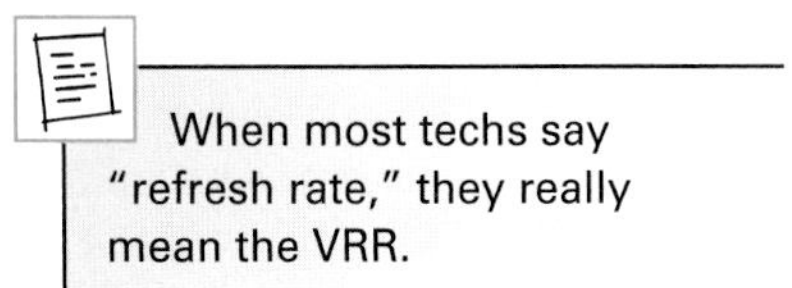

When most techs say "refresh rate," they really mean the VRR.

That's a pretty good monitor, as most video cards do not push beyond 120 Hz! At a resolution of 1200 × 1024, the vertical refresh would be

$$100{,}000{,}000 \div (1200 \times 1024) = 81 \text{ Hz}$$

So, we would make sure to set the video card's VRR to 80 Hz or less. If you had a monitor with a bandwidth of only 75 MHz, the maximum VRR at a 1200 × 1024 resolution would be only 61 Hz.

Most monitor makers know that people aren't going to take the time to do these calculations. Instead, they do the calculations

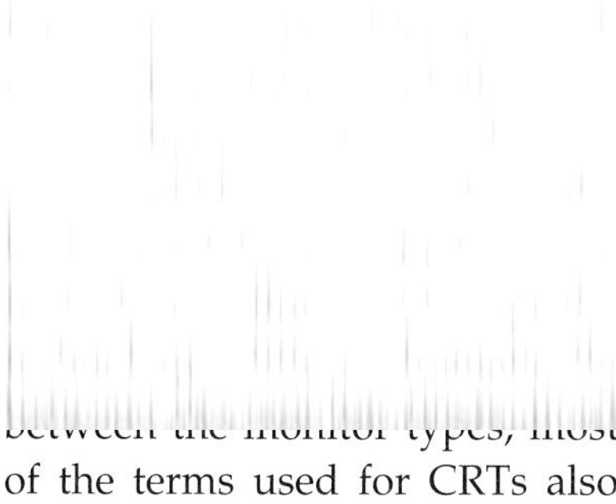

between the monitor types, most of the terms used for CRTs also apply to LCD functions.

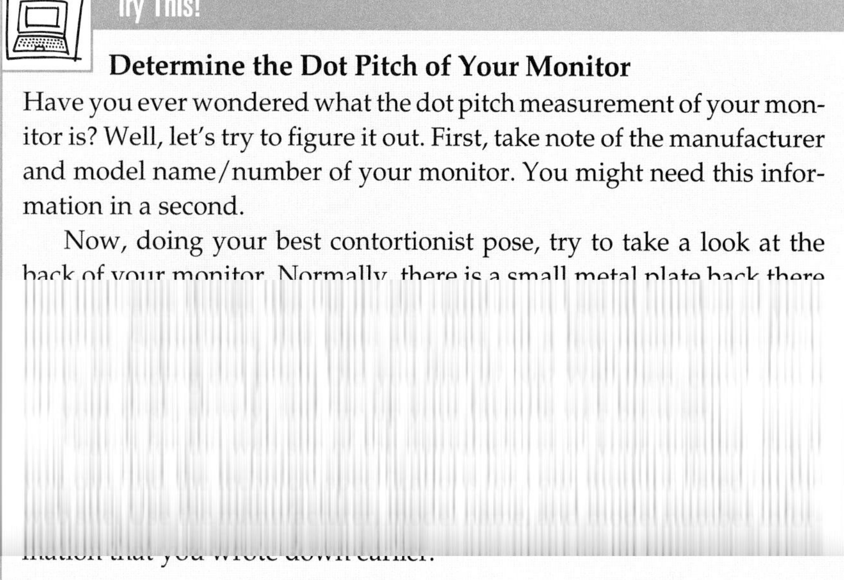

Try This!

Determine the Dot Pitch of Your Monitor

Have you ever wondered what the dot pitch measurement of your monitor is? Well, let's try to figure it out. First, take note of the manufacturer and model name/number of your monitor. You might need this information in a second.

Now, doing your best contortionist pose, try to take a look at the back of your monitor. Normally, there is a small metal plate back there

mation that you wrote down earlier.

LCD Displays

Once reserved only for laptops and people with way too much money, the ongoing price drops of **Liquid Crystal Displays (LCDs)** make them continue to appear on more and more desktops. LCD monitors have many advantages over CRTs: They are thinner and lighter, use much less power, are virtually flicker free, and don't emit potentially harmful radiation. LCDs come complete with their own family of abbreviations, jargon, and terms that you need to understand in order to install, maintain, and support LCDs.

How LCDs Work

The secret to understanding LCD panels is to understand the concept of the polarity of light. Anyone who played with a prism in sixth grade or looked at a rainbow knows that light travels in waves (no quantum mechanics here, please!) and the wavelength of the light determines the color. What you might not appreciate is the fact that light waves emanate from a light source in three dimensions. It's impossible to draw a clear diagram of three-dimensional waves, so instead, let's use an analogy. To visualize this, think of light emanating from a flashlight. Now think of the light emanating from that flashlight as though someone was shaking a jump rope. This is not a rhythmic shaking, back and forth or up and down; it's more as if a person went crazy and was shaking the jump rope all over the place—up, down, left, right—constantly changing the speed.

That's how light really acts. Well, I guess we could take the analogy one step further by saying the person has an infinite number of arms, each holding a jump rope shooting out in every direction to show the three-

> When comparing advertised prices, make a note of the monitor's dot pitch in the ad. Watch out for lower-priced monitors with an unacceptably high .39-mm dot pitch. By comparison, a mid-priced television has a dot pitch of approximately .35 mm. Also beware of monitor advertisements citing the *horizontal* dot pitch, which is a smaller number (often around .22 mm) instead of the standard vertical dot pitch.

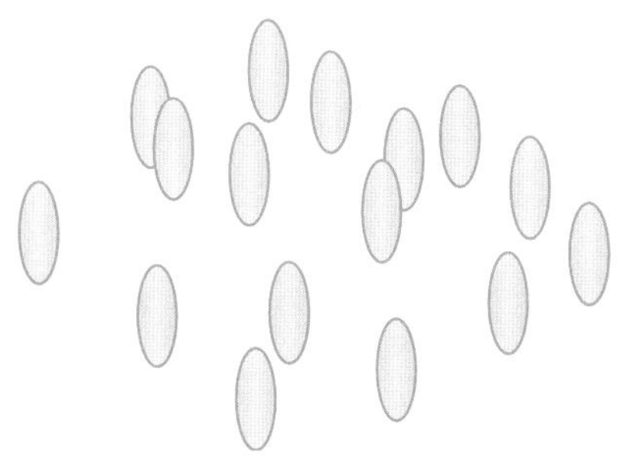

• **Figure 18.11** Liquid crystal molecules

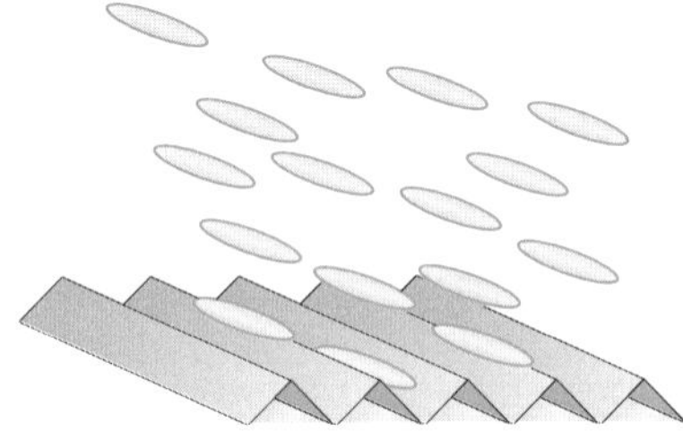

• **Figure 18.12** Liquid crystal molecules tend to line up together.

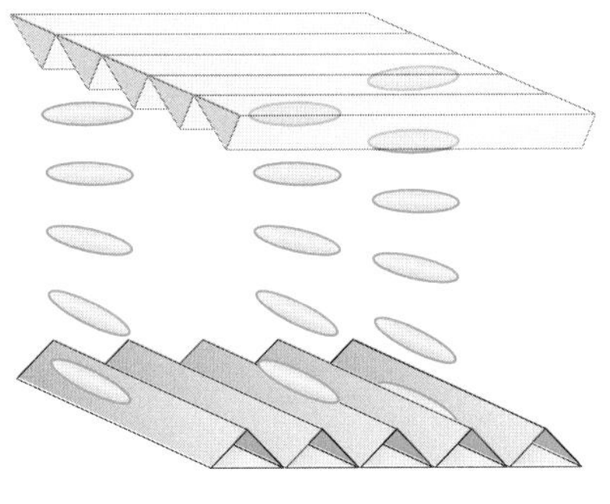

• **Figure 18.13** Liquid crystal molecules twisting

dimensionality of light waves, but (a) I can't draw that and (b) one jump rope will suffice to explain LCD panels. The different speeds create wavelengths, from very short to very long. When light comes into your eyes at many different wavelengths, you see white light. If the light came in only one wavelength, you would see only that color. Light flowing through a polarized filter (like sunglasses) is like putting a picket fence between you and the people shaking the ropes. You see all of the wavelengths, but only the waves of similar orientation. You would still see all of the colors, just fewer of them because you only see the waves of the same orientation, making the image darker. That's why many sunglasses use polarizing filters.

Now, what would happen if we added another picket fence but put the slats in a horizontal direction? This would effectively cancel out all of the waves. This is what happens when two polarizing filters are combined at a 90-degree angle—no light passes through.

Now, what would happen if a third fence was added between the two fences with the slats at a 45-degree angle? Well, it would sort of "twist" some of the shakes in the rope so that the waves could then get through. The same thing is true with the polarizing filters. The third filter twists some of the light so that it gets through. If you're really feeling scientific, go to any teacher's supply store and pick up three polarizing filters for about $3 U.S. each, and try it. It works.

Liquid crystals take advantage of the property of polarization. Liquid crystals are composed of a specially formulated liquid full of long, thin crystals that always want to orient themselves in the same direction, as shown in Figure 18.11. This substance acts exactly like a liquid polarized filter. If you poured a thin film of this stuff between two sheets of glass, you'd get a darn good pair of sunglasses.

Imagine cutting extremely fine grooves on one side of one of those sheets of glass. When you place this liquid in contact with a finely grooved surface, the molecules naturally line up with the grooves in the surface (see Figure 18.12).

If you place another finely grooved surface, with the grooves at a 90-degree orientation to the other surface, opposite of the first one, the molecules in contact with that side will attempt to line up with it. The molecules in between, in trying to line up with both sides, will immediately line up in a nice twist (see Figure 18.13).

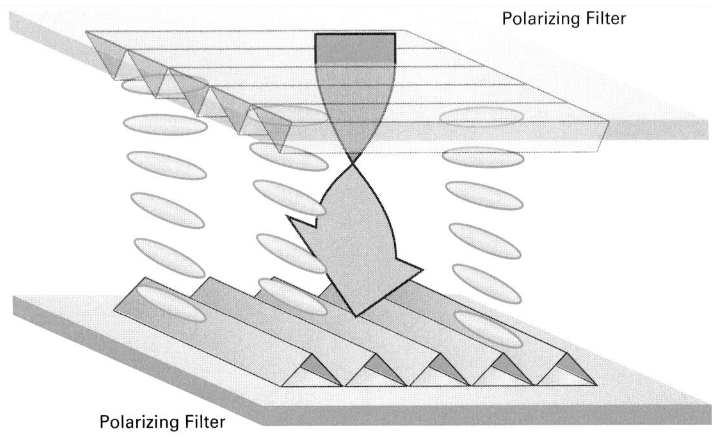

• **Figure 18.14** No charge, enabling light to pass

So, if two perpendicular polarizing filters are then placed on either side of the liquid crystal, the liquid crystal will twist the light and enable it to pass (see Figure 18.14).

But if you expose the liquid crystal to an electrical potential, the crystals will change their orientation to match the direction of the electrical field. The twist goes away and no light passes through (see Figure 18.15).

So, how do you charge the right spot? In the first LCDs, each viewable piece of the screen was filled with liquid crystal. To darken an area, it was charged. Figure 18.16 shows the number zero, a display made possible by charging six areas to make an ellipse of sorts. This process,

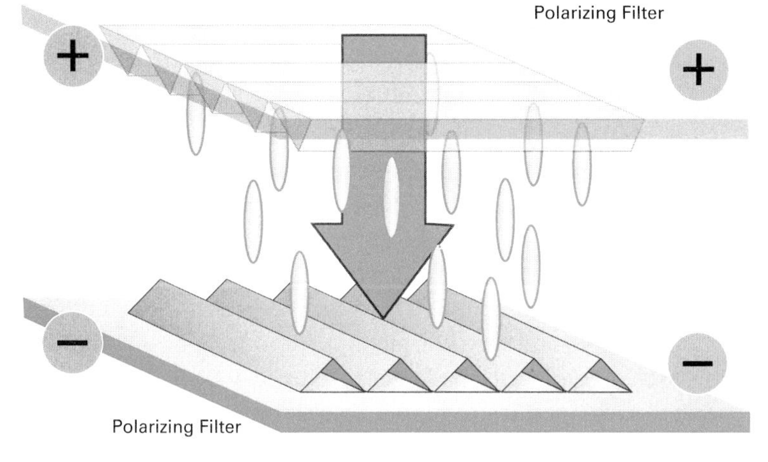

• **Figure 18.15** Electrical charge, enabling no light to pass

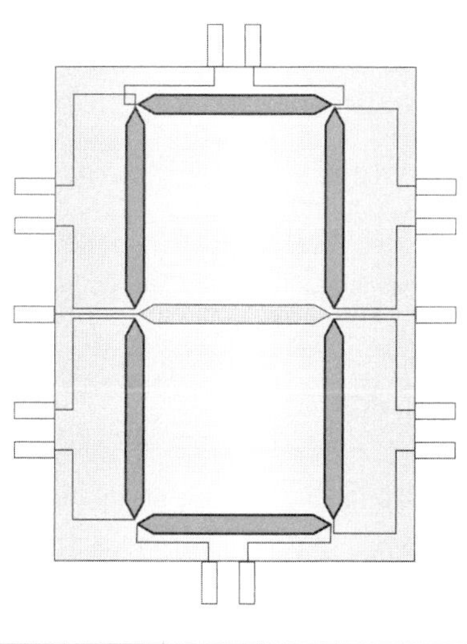

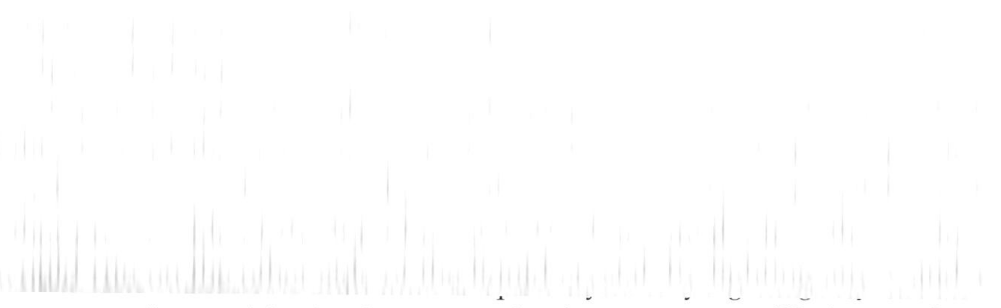

wire, a small part of the display received a charge, cutting off light transfer.

If you want color, you have three matrices. The three matrices intersect very close together. Above the intersections, the glass is covered with tiny red, green, and blue dots. The amount of voltage would enable different levels of red, green, and blue, creating colors (see Figure 18.18).

We call this usage of LCD technology *passive matrix*. All LCD displays on PCs used only passive matrix for many years. Unfortunately, passive matrix is slow and tends to create a little overlap between individual pixels. This gives a slightly blurred effect to the image displayed. Manufacturers eventually came up with a speedier method of display, called *dual-scan passive matrix*, where the screen refreshed two lines at a time. Although other LCD technologies have since appeared, dual-scan continues to show up on some lower-end LCD panels.

• **Figure 18.17** An LCD matrix of wires

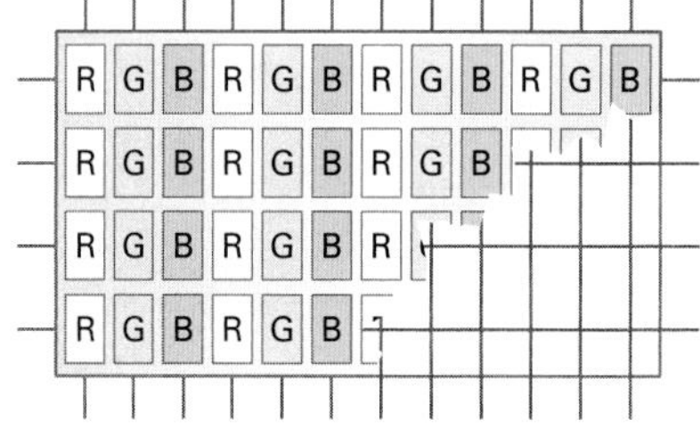

• **Figure 18.18** Color LCD matrix

Thin Film Transistor

A vast improvement over dual scan is called **active matrix** or **thin film transistor** (TFT). Instead of using X and Y wires, one or more tiny transistors control each color dot, providing faster picture display, crisp definition, and much tighter color control. TFT is the LCD of choice today, even though it is much more expensive than passive matrix (see Figure 18.19).

TFT displays have many advantages over passive displays. First, they are brighter with better contrast. Second, they can handle far more colors. Passive LCD's slow speed keeps it at a practical limit of no more than 256 colors (8-bit), whereas the latest TFT displays work at virtually unlimited color. Third, TFT displays have a much wider viewing area (see Figure 18.20). Passive matrix is rarely more than 45 degrees, whereas active is closer to 90–100 degrees.

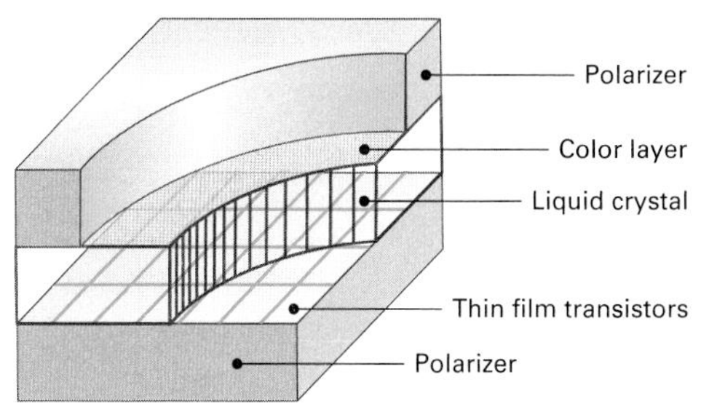

• **Figure 18.19** TFT cutaway

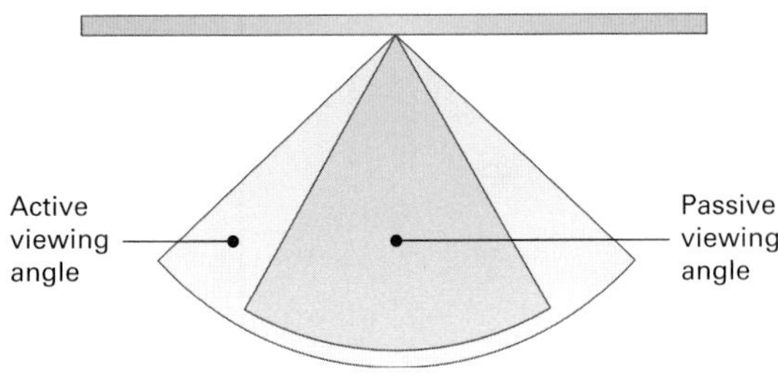

• **Figure 18.20** Viewing angles for active and passive matrix LCDs

LCD Resolution

All LCD monitors have a *native* resolution, such as 1024 × 768, that enables them to display the sharpest picture possible. The pixels are hard wired: one set of RGB dots equals one pixel. You simply cannot run an LCD at a resolution higher than the native one. Worse, because LCDs have no equivalent to a shadow mask, they can't run at a *lower* than native resolution without severely degrading image quality. Whereas a CRT can simply use more dots and the filtering and smoothing of the shadow mask to make a picture at a lower resolution look as good and crisp as the same picture at a higher resolution, an LCD cannot. The LCD has to use an edge-blurring technique called anti-aliasing to soften the jagged corners of the pixels when running at lower than native resolution, which simply does not look as good. Bottom line? Always set the LCD at native resolution!

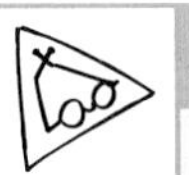

Tech Tip

Dealing with High Resolution LCDs

The hard-wired nature of LCD resolution creates a problem for techs and consumers when dealing with bigger, better quality monitors. A typical 15-inch LCD has a 1024 × 768 resolution, but a 17-inch usually has 1280 × 1024 or higher. These high resolutions make the menus and fonts on a monitor super tiny, a problem for people with less-than-stellar vision. Many folks throw in the towel and run these high-end LCDs at lower resolution and just live with the lower quality picture, but that's not the best way to resolve this problem.

With Windows XP (and to a lesser extent with the earlier versions of Windows), Microsoft allows incredible customizing of the interface. You can change the font size, shape, and color. You can resize the icons, toolbars, and more. You can even change the number of dots per inch (DPI) for the full screen, making everything bigger or smaller!

For basic customizing, start at the Control Panel, Display applet, Appearance tab. To change the DPI for the display, go to the Settings tab and click the Advanced button. Your clients will thank you!

Backlighting

LCD monitors usually have one or two cold fluorescent lights, called back lights, that provide the brightness for the monitor. The brightness is measured in **nits**, with 100 nits on the low end and 300 or more on the high end.

The potential problem with this technology arises from the nature of light shining through an object. What do you get when you look at a flashlight behind a piece of paper? A bright spot where the center of the beam hits the paper, and then increasing darkness out toward the edges. Light works in LCD monitors in the same way: many, if not most, are brighter in the center and darker along the edges.

Try This!

Test the Viewing Angle of LCDs

Take a trip to your local computer store to look at LCD displays. Don't get distracted looking at all the latest graphics cards, sounds cards, CPUs, motherboards, and RAM—actually, it's okay to look at those things. Just don't forget to look at LCDs!

Stand about two feet in front of an LCD display. Look directly at the image on the screen and develop a good sense for image quality, screen brightness, and color. Take a small step to your right. Compare the image you see now to the image you saw previously. Continue taking small steps to the right until you are no longer able to discern the image on the display. You've reached the edge of the viewing angle for that LCD.

Do this test with a few different monitors. Do smaller LCDs, like 15-inch displays, have smaller viewing angles? Do larger displays have better viewing angles? You might also want to test the vertical viewing angles of some monitors. Try to find an LCD that is on your eye level; then look at it from above and below—does it have a wide viewing range vertically?

Contrast Ratio

A big drawback of LCD monitors is that they don't have nearly the color saturation or richness of contrast that CRTs do. A good contrast ratio—the difference between the darkest and lightest spots that the monitor can display—is 450:1, but much lower levels (250:1 or 200:1) are common in LCDs.

Common Features

CRT or LCD, all monitors share a number of characteristics that you need to know for purchase, installation, maintenance, and troubleshooting.

> Not many people use the term *LCD monitor*. Instead, you'll often hear the terms flat-panel display or LCD panels. I prefer the term LCD monitor,

Size

You need to take care when buying CRT monitors. CRT monitors come in a

CRT monitor, for example, might have a 15.5-inch VIS.

LCD monitors dispense with the two values and simply express the VIS value. You must consider this issue when comparing LCDs to CRTs. A 15-inch LCD monitor will have about the same viewing area as a 17-inch CRT.

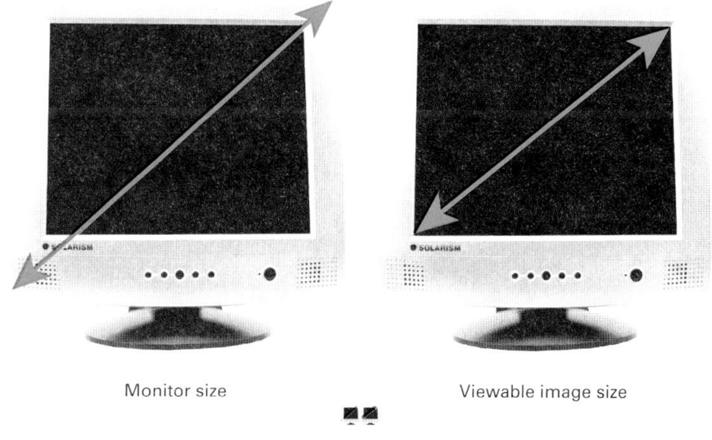

• Figure 18.21 Viewable image size of a CRT

Connections

CRT monitors for PCs all use the famous 15-pin, three-row, DB type connector (see Figure 18.22) and a power plug. Larger or multipurpose monitors may have a few other connectors, but as far as the CRT is concerned, these are the only two you need for video.

Unlike the analog **super video graphics array (SVGA)** CRTs, LCD monitors need a digital signal. This creates somewhat of an issue. The video information stored on a video card's RAM is clearly digital. All VGA and better video cards include a special chip (or function embedded into a chip that does several other jobs) called the **Random Access Memory Digital-to-Analog Converter (RAMDAC)**. As the name implies, RAMDAC takes the digital signal from the video card and turns it into an analog signal for the analog CRT (see Figure 18.23). The RAMDAC really defines the bandwidth that the video card outputs.

Well, RAMDACs certainly make sense for analog CRT monitors. However, if you want to plug your LCD monitor into a regular video card, you need circuitry on the LCD monitor to convert the signal from analog to digital (see Figure 18.24).

• Figure 18.22 A traditional CRT connection

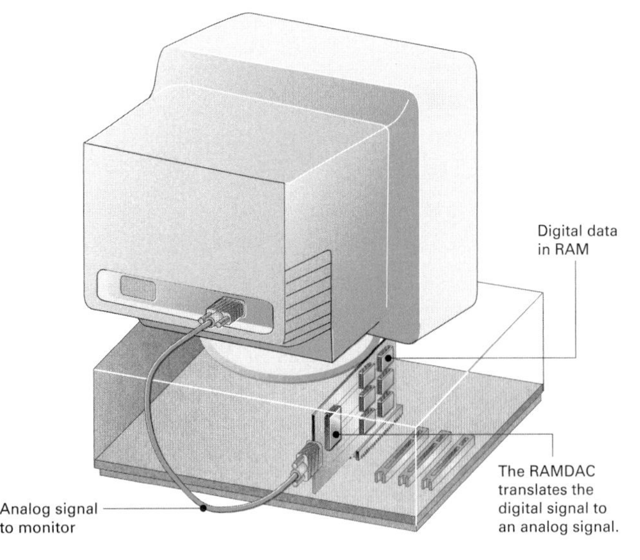

• **Figure 18.23** An analog signal sent to a CRT monitor

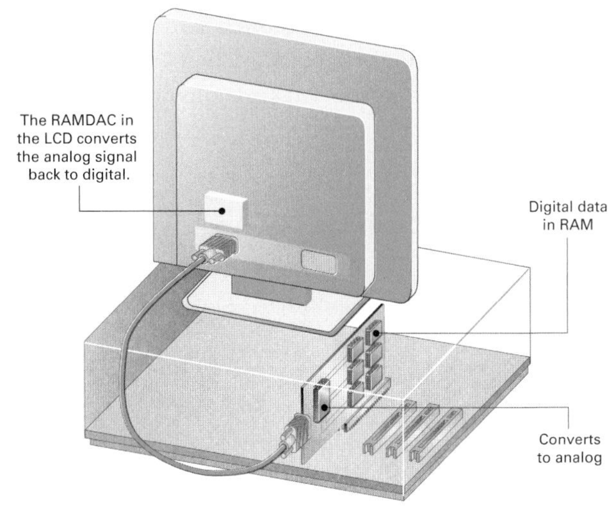

• **Figure 18.24** Converting analog back to digital on the LCD

Many LCD monitors use exactly this process. These are called *analog LCD monitors*. The monitor really isn't analog; it's digital, but it takes a standard SVGA input. These monitors have one advantage: You may use any standard SVGA video card. But these monitors require adjustment of the analog timing signal to the digital clock inside the monitor. This used to be a fairly painful process, but most analog LCD monitors now include intelligent circuitry to make this process either automatic or very easy.

But why convert the signal from digital to analog and then back to digital? Well, many monitor and video card people agree. We now see quite a few digital LCD monitors and digital video cards. They use a completely different connector than the old 15-pin DB connector used on analog video cards and monitors. After a few false starts with connection standards, under names like P&D and DFP, the digital LCD world, with a few holdouts, moved to the *Digital Video Interface* (DVI) standard. DVI is actually three different connectors that look very much alike: DVI-D is for digital, DVI-A is for analog (for backward compatibility if the monitor maker so desires), and the DVI-A/D or DVI-I (Interchangeable) accepts either a DVI-D or DVI-A (see Figure 18.25). DVI-D and DVI-A are keyed so that they will not connect. Just in case you were wondering—no, you cannot use an adapter to convert an analog LCD to use a digital video card or vice versa!

I'm convinced that, over time, digital will replace analog. Digital makes both the monitor and the video card cheaper, provides a clearer signal because no conversion is necessary, and makes installation trivial. Most digital LCD monitors come with a DVI-D connector, and all analog LCD monitors use the DB-15. Many LCD monitor makers hedge their bets by providing both types of connectors on their monitors. We need to call those monitors analog/digital! Just make sure that when you get an LCD (and you eventually will) that you either get an analog to use with your current video card or purchase a new digital video card if you decide on a digital monitor.

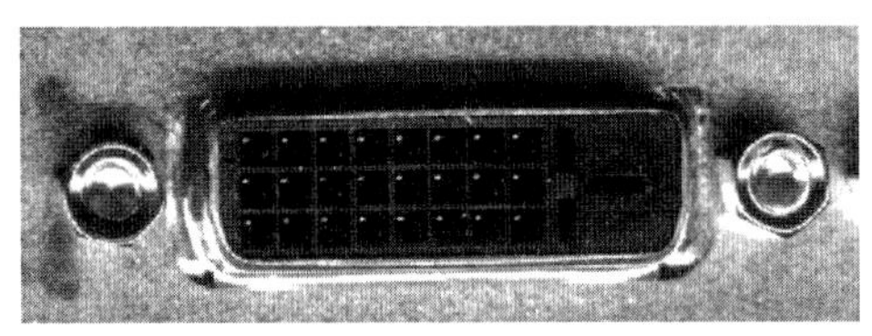

• **Figure 18.25** DVI-A connector

Adjustments

Most adjustments to the monitor take place at installation, but for now, let's just make sure you know what they are and where they are located. Clearly, all monitors have an On/Off button or switch. Also, see if you can locate the Brightness and Contrast buttons. Beyond that, most monitors (at least the only ones you should buy) have an onboard menu system, enabling a number of adjustments. Every monitor maker provides a different way to access these menus, but they all provide two main functions: physical screen adjustment (bigger, smaller, move to the left, right, up, down, and others) and color adjustment. The color adjustment lets you adjust the red, green, and blue guns to give you the best color tones. All these settings are a matter of personal taste. Make sure the person who

Contrast 50%
Brightness 78%
Horz. Size 58%
Vert. Size 23%
Horz. Center 25%
Vert. Center 54%
Pincushion 81%
Keystone 36%
Tilt 50%
▼ OR ▲ TO SELECT
- OR + TO ADJUST

Figure 18.26 Typical menu controls

reduce monitor power consumption by roughly 75 percent. This is accomplished by reducing or eliminating the signals sent by the video card to the monitor during idle periods. By eliminating these pulses, the monitor essentially takes catnaps. The advantage over simply shutting the monitor off is in the time it takes to restore the display. A typical CRT monitor consumes approximately 120 watts. During a catnap or power-down mode, the energy consumption is reduced to below 25 watts, while enabling the screen to return to use in less than ten seconds. Full shutoff is accomplished by eliminating all clocking pulses to the monitor. While this reduces power consumption to below 15 watts, it also requires anywhere from 15 to 30 seconds to restore a usable display.

DPMS works with Windows *Advanced Power Management* (APM) or *Advanced Configuration and Power Interface* (ACPI) software. We'll go into these specifications in detail in Chapter 21.

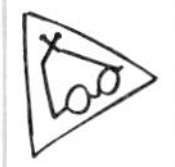

Tech Tip

Power Switch vs. DPMS

Turning off the monitor with the power switch is the most basic form of power management. The downside to this is the wear and tear on the CRT. The CRT is the most expensive component of a monitor, and one of the most damaging things to a CRT is to turn it on and off frequently. When using a non-DPMS monitor or video card, it is best to turn the monitor on once during the day, and then turn it off only when you are finished for the day. This on-off cycle must be balanced against the life of the CRT display phosphors. The typical monitor will lose about half its original brightness after roughly 10,000 to 15,000 hours of display time. Leaving the monitor on all the time will bring a noticeable decrease in brightness in just over a year (8766 hours). The only way around this is enabling the DPMS features of the monitor or taking care to turn the monitor off.

You Have the Basics

You've covered a big piece of ground in this section. Take some time to review the concepts of HRR, VRR, and bandwidth, and understand the differences in monitors. We can now move to the second part of the computer video duo: the video card.

■ The Video Card

The video card, or display adapter, handles the video chores within the PC, processing information from the CPU and sending it out to the monitor. The video card is composed of two major pieces: the video RAM and the video processor circuitry. The video RAM stores the video image. On the first video cards, this RAM was good old *Dynamic RAM* (DRAM), just like the

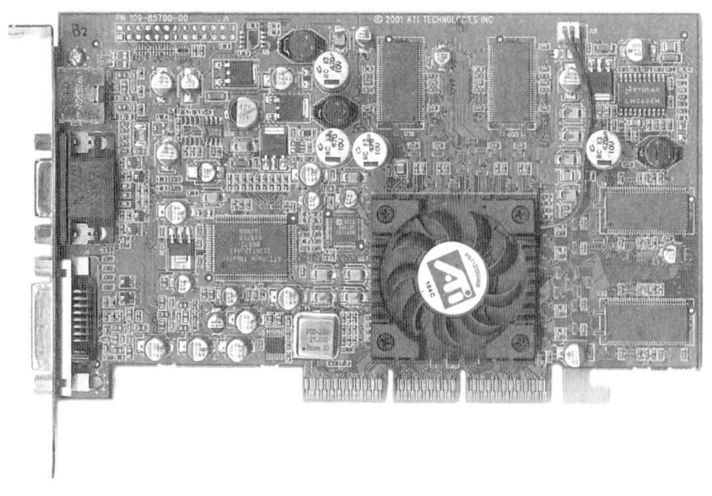

• **Figure 18.27** Video card with a cooling fan

RAM on the motherboard. Today's video cards often have better RAM than your system has! The video processing circuitry takes the information on the video RAM and shoots it out to the monitor. While early video processing circuitry was little more than an intermediary between the CPU and the video RAM, modern video processors are more powerful than Pentium II CPU! It's not at all uncommon to see video cards that need fans to cool their onboard processors (see Figure 18.27).

The trick to understanding video cards is to appreciate the beginnings and evolution of video. Video output to computers was around long before PCs were created. At the time PCs became popular, video was almost exclusively text-based, meaning that the only image the video card could place on the monitor was one of the 256 ASCII characters. These characters were made up of patterns of pixels that were stored in the system BIOS. When a program wanted to make a character, it talked to DOS or to the BIOS, which stored the image of that character in the video memory. The character then appeared on the screen.

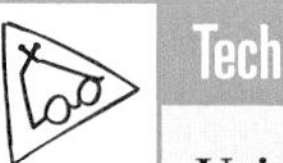

Tech Tip

Using DPMS to Your Advantage

Have you ever looked closely at the screen on an ATM? If so, you've likely seen the "burn-in" effects that happen when a monitor is left running 24 hours a day, 7 days a week. You should be able to faintly see the "Welcome to XXXXX Bank, please insert your card" message, even if that's not what text is displayed on the screen. If ATMs used DPMS, this could be avoided.

Of course, this is a worst-case scenario and it would take a long time for this type of damage to happen to your PC monitor. However, it's always a good idea to use the DPMS settings and have your monitor turn off after a designated period of inactivity. Personally, I like to have my monitor shut off after 30 minutes of non-use—that period of time is long enough to allow me to get up, make a sandwich, and return to my computer without my monitor taking a nap but short enough to prevent any damage from occurring.

The beauty of text video cards was that they were simple to use and cheap to make. The simplicity was based on the fact that only 256 characters existed, and no color choices were available—just monochrome text (see Figure 18.28).

You could, however, choose to make the character bright, dim, normal, underlined, or blinking. It was easy to position the characters, as space on the screen allowed for only 80 characters per row and 24 rows of characters.

Long ago, RAM was very expensive, so video-card makers were interested in using the absolute least amount of RAM possible. Making a monochrome text video card was a great way to keep down RAM costs. Let's consider this for a minute. First, the video RAM is where the contents of the screen are located. You need enough video RAM to hold all the necessary information for a completely full screen. Each ASCII character needs eight bits (by definition), so a monitor with 80 characters/row and 24 rows will need

80 characters × 24 rows = 1920 characters = 15,360 bits or 1920 bytes

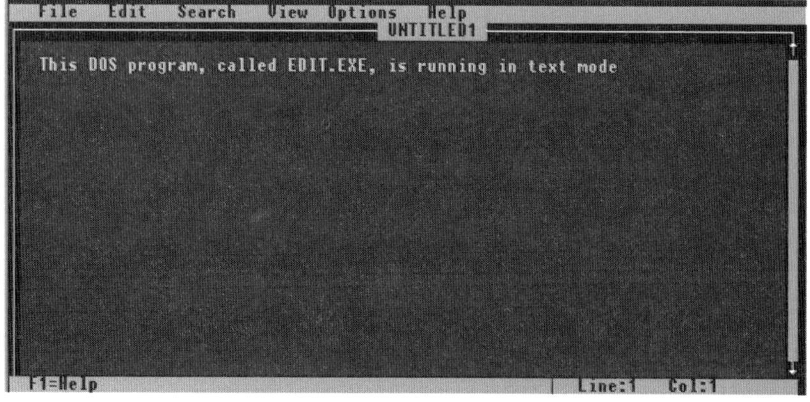

• **Figure 18.28** Text mode

The video card would need less than 2000 bytes of memory, which isn't much, not even in 1981 when the PC first came out. Now, be warned that I'm glossing over a few things—where you store the information about underlines, blinking, and so on. The bottom line is that the tiny amount of necessary RAM kept monochrome text video cards cheap.

Very early on in the life of PCs, a new type of video, called a *graphics video card*, was invented. It was quite similar to a text card. The text card, however, was limited to the 256 ASCII characters, whereas a graphics video card enabled programs to turn any pixel on the screen on or off. It was still monochrome, but programs could access any individual pixel, enabling much more creative control of the screen. Of course, it took more video RAM. The first graphics cards ran at 320 × 200 pixels. One bit was needed for each pixel (on or off), so

was how to store color information for each character (text cards) or pixel (graphics cards). This was easy—just set aside a few more bits for each pixel or character. So now the question becomes, "How many bits do you set aside?" Well, that depends on how many colors you want. Basically, the number of colors determines the number of bits. For example, if you wanted four colors, you need two bits (two bits per pixel). Then, you could do something like this

00 = black	01 = cyan (blue)
10 = magenta (reddish pink)	11 = white

So if you set aside two bits, you could get four colors. If you want 16 colors, set aside four bits, which would make 16 different combinations. Nobody ever invented a text mode that used more than 16 colors, so let's start thinking in terms of only graphics mode and bits per pixels. To get 256 colors, each pixel would have to be represented with eight bits. In PCs, the number of colors is always a power of 2: 4, 16, 256, 64 K, and so on. Note that as more colors are added, more video RAM is needed to store the information. Here are the most common color depths and the number of bits necessary to store the color information per pixel:

2 colors = 1 bit (mono)	4 colors = 2 bits	16 colors = 4 bits
256 colors = 8 bits	64 K colors = 16 bits	16.7 million+ colors = 24 bits

Most technicians won't say things like "I set my video card to show over 16 million colors." Instead, they'll say, "I set my color depth to 24 bits." Talk in terms of bits, not colors. It is assumed that you know the number of colors for any color depth.

up to 1024 × 768 with 16-bit color. While XGA enjoyed some success, the proliferation of SVGA standards (see the following section) quickly made XGA obsolete.

The last few years have seen a resurgence of the abbreviation "XGA" on some LCD panels, but this is merely to reflect their maximum of 1024 × 768 resolution. The terms XGA, SXGA, or one of the many other variants (XGA+ or UXGA) don't really have an official meaning as VESA provides equivalent SVGA standards for all these resolutions and color depths—but it sure makes for a good marketing angle for laptop makers. Why call your display SVGA when you can call it XGA!

Know your color depths both in terms of bits and numbers of colors!

Don't bother memorizing a bunch of modes' hex values. Do take some time to know the different types of video cards and appreciate how their modes compare to earlier/later video cards.

Modes

Based on what you know so far, it would seem as though four different types of video cards exist: monochrome text, color text, monochrome graphics, and color graphics. What if a PC wants to do more than one of these? Any PC might want to start with a text mode (at boot), and then switch into color graphics (like when Windows starts). So what are you going to do—keep two video cards in the PC, and then switch the cable? Of course not.

Instead, today's video cards support all of the previously defined video cards in one card. A modern video card displays text or graphics, monochrome or color, as needed. Each different level of operation is defined as a video mode. First IBM, and then the VESA defined specific, uniform video modes for video cards. These video modes are given a hexadecimal value. For example, video mode 06h is defined as monochrome graphics at 640 × 200 pixels.

VGA

With the introduction of the PS/2, IBM introduced the **video graphics array (VGA)** standard (see Table 18.1). This new standard offered 16 colors at a resolution of 640 × 480 pixels. VGA supported more colors by using an analog video signal instead of a digital one, as was the case prior to the VGA standard. A digital signal is either all on or all off. By using an analog signal, the VGA standard can provide 64 distinct levels for the three colors (RGB)—that is, 64^3 or 262,144 possible colors—although only 16 or 256 can be seen at a time. For most purposes, 640 × 480 and 16 colors defines VGA mode. This is typically the display resolution and color depth referred to on many software packages as a minimum display requirement. True VGA-only cards are very rare.

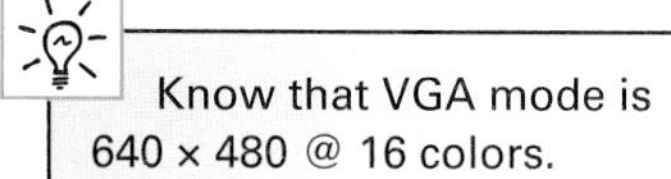

Know that VGA mode is 640 × 480 @ 16 colors.

SVGA

For years, SVGA was more of an opinion than an established standard. Any video-card maker who made a video card with a resolution greater than 640 × 480 and 16 colors called the card SVGA. For many years, the lack of an SVGA standard created serious confusion. The VESA established standards for SVGA resolutions, color depth, and video signal timings in the late 1980s. SVGA is an extensible standard, which is a cool way to say that VESA constantly adds to this list as higher resolutions and deeper color depths develop. The list of VESA SVGA modes would take many pages. Table 18.2 shows the more common ones.

Table 18.1 VGA Modes

Mode	Type	Colors	Resolution/ Characters
00h, 01h	Text	16	40 × 25
02h, 03h	Text	16	80 × 25
04h, 05h	Graphics	4	320 × 200
06h	Graphics	2	640 × 200
07h	Text	Mono	80 × 25
0Dh	Graphics	16	320 × 200
0Eh	Graphics	16	640 × 200
0Fh	Graphics	4	640 × 350
10h	Graphics	16	640 × 350
11h	Graphics	2	640 × 480
12h	Graphics	16	640 × 480
13h	Graphics	256	320 × 200

Resolution, Color Depth, and Memory Requirements

Different video modes require different amounts of RAM on the video card. To determine the amount of video memory required at a given resolution and color depth, multiply the resolution by the number of bytes of color depth. From the Chapter 4 on RAM, you know that memory on a PC is always in byte-sized units, and video memory is no exception. Because bits are used to refer to color depth, you need to convert the color depth bits into bytes. Suppose you have a video card with 1 MB of video memory and want to run your video at 800 × 600 with a 24-bit color depth. Does this card have enough memory to do this? Twenty-four bits (24/8) = three bytes, so you use the equation 800 × 600 × 3 for the memory requirement in bytes. To convert this to megabytes, divide the result by 1,048,576:

800 × 600 = 480,000 pixels per screen
480,000 × 3 = 1,440,000 bytes of memory per screen
1,440,000 ÷ 1,048,576 = 1.373 MB per screen

Table 18.2 Some Common VESA SVGA Modes

Mode	Type	Colors	Resolution/ Characters
101h	Graphics	256	640 × 480
102h	Graphics	16	800 × 600
103h	Graphics	256	800 × 600
104h	Graphics	16	1024 × 768
105h	Graphics	256	1024 × 768
106h	Graphics	16	1280 × 1024
107h	Graphics	256	1280 × 1024
110h	Graphics	32 K	640 × 480
111h	Graphics	64 K	640 × 480
118h	Graphics	16.7 M	1024 × 768
119h	Graphics	32 K	1280 × 1,024
11Ah	Graphics	64 K	1280 × 1,024
11Bh	Graphics	16.7 M	1280 × 1,024

Using more color depth slows down video functions. Data moving from the video card to the display has to go through the video card's memory chips and the expansion bus, and this can happen only so quickly. The standard PCI slots used in almost all systems are limited to 32-bit transfers at roughly 33 MHz, yielding a maximum bandwidth of 132 MBps. This sounds like a lot until you start using higher resolutions, high color depths, and higher refresh rates.

For example, take a typical display at 800 × 600 with a fairly low refresh of 70 Hz. The 70 Hz means the display screen is being redrawn 70 times per second. If you use a low color depth of 256 colors, which is 8 bits ($2^8 = 256$), you can multiply all the values together to see how much data per second has to be sent to the display:

800 × 600 × 1 byte × 70 = 33.6 MBps

If you use the same example at 16 million (24-bit) colors, the figure jumps to 100.8 MBps. You might say, "Well, if PCI runs at 132 MBps, it can handle that!" That statement would be true if the PCI bus had nothing else to do but tend to the video card, but almost every system has more than one PCI device, each requiring part of that throughput. The PCI bus simply cannot handle the needs of many current systems.

Table 18.3 RAM Requirements for Various Resolutions/Color Depths

Resolution	Number of Colors				
	16	256	64 K	16.7 M	4 G
640 × 480	0.15 MB	0.29 MB	0.59 MB	0.88 MB	1.17 MB
800 × 600	0.23 MB	0.46 MB	0.92 MB	1.37 MB	1.83 MB
1024 × 768	0.38 MB	0.75 MB	1.50 MB	2.25 MB	3.00 MB
1200 × 1024	0.63 MB	1.25 MB	2.50 MB	3.75 MB	4.69 MB
1600 × 1200	0.92 MB	1.83 MB	3.66 MB	5.49 MB	7.32 MB

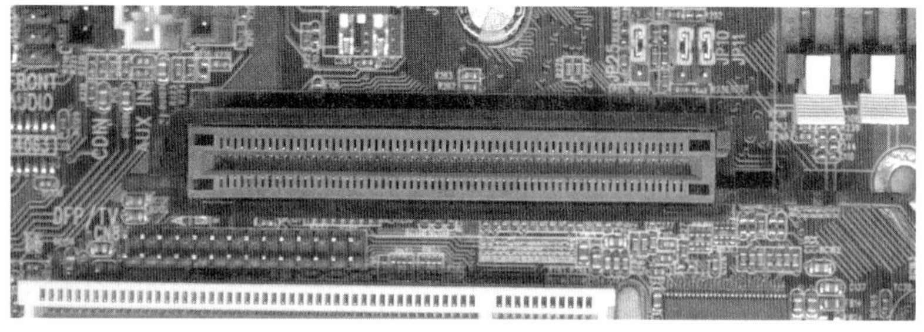

• **Figure 18.29** AGP

Intel answered the desire for video bandwidth even higher than PCI with the **Accelerated Graphics Port (AGP)**. AGP is a single, special port, similar to a PCI slot, which is dedicated to video. You will never see a motherboard with two AGP slots. Figure 18.29 shows an early generation AGP. AGP is derived from the 66-MHz, 32-bit PCI 2.1 specification, and is currently the fastest video available. AGP uses a function called *strobing* that increases the signals two-, four-, and eight-times for each clock cycle.

Simply leaving AGP as a faster PCI would seriously misrepresent the power of AGP. AGP has several technological advantages over PCI, including the bus, internal operations, and the capability to handle 3-D texturing.

• **Figure 18.30** An AGP bus

First, AGP currently resides alone on its own personal data bus, connected directly to the Northbridge (see Figure 18.30). This is very important because more advanced versions of AGP outperform every bus on the system except the frontside bus!

Second, AGP takes advantage of pipelining commands, similar to the way CPUs pipeline. Third, AGP has a feature called *sidebanding*—basically a second data bus that enables the video card to send more commands to the Northbridge while receiving other commands at the same time.

Many advanced 3-D video cards come with huge amounts of video RAM. It's very common to see cards with 32, 64, or even 128 MB of RAM! Why so much? Well, they do all kinds of neat stuff with this extra RAM; for example, many 3-D cards store copies of individual windows so that they can move around the screen very quickly. AGP provides a pathway so that the AGP card may "steal" chunks of the regular system memory to store video information, especially textures. This is called a *system memory access* and is quite popular.

AGP has gone through three sets of specifications (AGP1.0, AGP2.0, and AGP3.0), but the official names tend to be ignored. Most techs and consumers refer to the various cards by their strobe multiplier, such as AGP 1x, 2x, 4x, and 8x. The only problem with blurring the distinctions between the specifications comes from the fact that many new motherboards simply don't support the older AGP cards because the older cards require a different physical connection than the new ones. Table 18.4 shows the AGP specifications.

Cross Check

Multiple Actions per Clock Cycle

You've run into devices in the PC that can handle multiple actions during a single clock cycle, right? Refer back to Chapters 3 and 4 and cross check your memory. Which CPUs can clock double? What advantages does that bring to the PC? Which types of RAM run faster than the system clock? What chip or chips enables the PC to benefit from multi-action CPUs and RAM?

Table 18.4 AGP Types

	Bus Speed	Strobe	Width	Throughput	Side Band	Pipe	System Memory	Multiple Ports
AGP 1x	66 MHz	1x	32-bit	264 MBps	Yes	Yes	No	No
AGP 2x	66 MHz	2x	32-bit	528 MBps	Yes	Yes	Yes	No
AGP 4x	66 MHz	4x	32-bit	1 GBps	Yes	Yes	Yes	No
AGP 8x	66 MHz	8x	32-bit	2.1 GBps	Yes	Yes	Yes	Yes

Some motherboards support multiple types of AGP. Figure 18.31 shows an AGP slot that accommodates everything up to 8x, even the very rare AGP Pro cards. Note that the tab on the slot covers the extra pins required for AGP Pro [illegible] in the close connection tolerances required by the cards themselves. It's very common to snap in a new AGP card and power up just to get a no-video-card beep or a system that doesn't boot. Always take the time to ensure that an AGP card is snapped down securely and screwed in before starting the system.

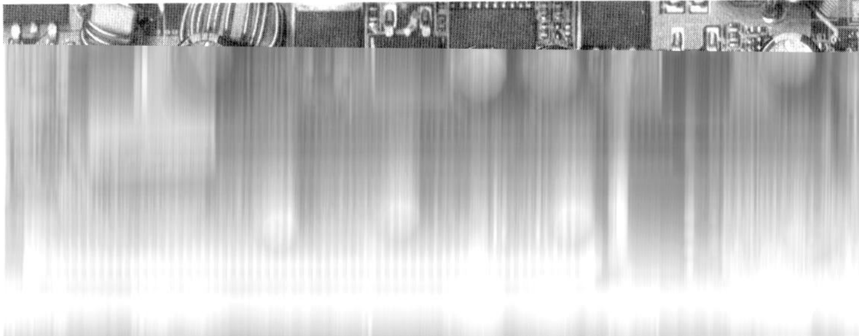

Figure 18.31 A universal AGP slot

Graphics Processor

The graphics processor handles the heavy lifting of taking commands from the CPU and translating them into coordinates and color information that the monitor understands and displays.

When we talk about video cards, we discuss their manufacturer, model number, graphic processor, and amount of video RAM. A typical video card might be called an ATI All-in-Wonder Radeon 9800 128 MB—ATI is the manufacturer, All-in-Wonder is the model, Radeon 9800 is the name of the graphics processor used on the card, and 128 MB is the amount of video RAM.

While there are many companies that make the hundreds of different video cards on the market, only three companies produce the vast majority of graphics processors found on video cards: NVIDIA, ATI, and Matrox. ATI and Matrox produce complete video cards as well as graphics processors; both ATI and NVIDIA sell their chips to third-party manufacturers, who then design, build, and sell video cards under their own branding. Figure 18.32 shows an NVIDIA GeForce4 Ti 4600 on a board made by VisionTek.

Your choice of graphics processor is your single most important decision in buying a video card. Low-end graphics processors will usually work fine for the run-of-the-mill user who wants to write letters or run a web browser. High-end graphics processors are designed to support the beautiful 3-D games that are so popular today.

• **Figure 18.32** An NVIDIA GeForce4 Ti 4600

A Word on Games

Your PC is capable of providing you with hours of incredible entertainment via a huge number of popular games that immerse you in 3-D environments full of light, shadows, explosions, and other amazing effects that create a fun and beautiful gaming experience. However, these 3-D games have special needs to do all this amazing stuff. One need is textures. A *texture* is a small picture that is tiled over and over again on walls, floors, and other surfaces to create the 3-D world. Take a look at the wall in Figure 18.33. It's made up of only three textures that are repeated over and over again on the surface.

Games also use hundreds of lighting effects such as transparency (water), shadows, reflection, and bump mapping—the process of laying multiple textures on the same spot to give a more textured (bumpy) look to the surface. These games are where the higher-quality graphics processors really shine.

The problem is deciding what graphics processor to choose, since the video industry is constantly coming out with new graphic processors. One of the best guides is price. The best (and newest) graphics cards usually cost around $400–500 US. The cheapest cards cost around $50. I usually split the difference and go for a card priced around $180 to $200—such a card will have most of the features you want without breaking your bank account.

If you use your computer only for 2-D programs (most office applications, such as word processors, e-mail, and web browsers, are 2-D), then almost all of the features of the more advanced graphics cards will do you little good. If you're not a gamer, think cheap; low-end video cards will more than meet your needs.

Video Memory

Video memory is crucial to the operation of a PC. It is probably the hardest-working set of electronics on the PC. Video RAM constantly updates to reflect every change that takes place on the screen. Memory produces two bottlenecks for data-access speed and data throughput. Typical low-cost video cards (usually $50 to $100) commonly use DRAM for data storage. A few aspects of DRAM slow it down, making it a less than optimal choice for video RAM. One is the need to refresh DRAM memory approximately 18.5 times per second. During these refresh periods, neither the CPU nor graphics processor can read the memory bits in the video RAM. Another slowdown is the access/response time of DRAM. Even the fastest commonly available DRAM (50 nanoseconds) is too slow to handle the higher resolutions and color depths found on larger monitors. The final bottleneck for DRAM is physical. Its data lines are used both for writing data to the video port and receiving data from the CPU.

Manufacturers have overcome these bottlenecks in two ways: upping the width of the bus between the video RAM and video processor and using specialized RAM that avoids the DRAM issues.

First, manufacturers reorganized the video display memory on cards from the typical 32-bit-wide structure to 64, 128, or even 256-bits wide. This would not be of much benefit—because the system bus is limited to 32 or 64 bits—if it weren't for the fact that most video display cards are really coprocessor boards. Most of the graphics rendering and processing is handled on the card by the video processor chip rather than by the CPU. The main system simply provides the input data to the processor on the video card. By making the memory bus on the video card as much as eight times wider than the standard 32-bit pathway (256 bits), data can be manipulated, and then sent to the monitor much more quickly.

Specialized types of video RAM have been developed for graphics cards [illegible] mands on any video card are high.

Once you've decided on features, price, and bus, you need to install the video card into your system. The only quirks to watch out for on the physical part of installation—aside from the tight tolerances in AGP slots, mentioned above—are long cards and proximity of the nearest PCI card. Some high end video cards simply won't fit in certain cases or they block access to needed motherboard connectors such as the IDE sockets. There's no clean fix for such a problem—you simply have to change at least one of the components (video card, motherboard, or case). Because high-end video cards run very hot, you don't want them sitting right next to a PCI card that has problems with minor overheating, such as a network card. A good practice is to leave the slot next to the AGP card empty to allow better air flow.

Once you've properly installed the video card and connected it to the monitor, you've conquered half the territory for making the video process work properly. You're ready to tackle the operating system and drivers, so let's go!

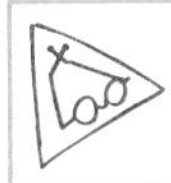

Tech Tip

When Enough Is Enough

Although I'm not overly concerned with the speed of my video RAM, I'm very interested in the amount *of video RAM. I'm not worried about having enough to handle my resolution and color depths because even the cheapest video cards come with approximately 8 MB of RAM. Because I do so much work (and play) with 3-D imagery, I need a video card that handles my high demands. Personally, I wouldn't even consider a video card with less than 32 MB of RAM. Now, don't try to tell me you don't need RAM for 3-D. I've built too many systems with cheap video cards just to see the customer come back two weeks later, wondering why their son/daughter/wife/brother can't play some cool game they just bought.*

Installing and Configuring Video Software

Once you've physically installed the video card, attached the monitor, and thrown a little electricity into the mix, you're ready to teach the system how to talk to that specific video card and optimize it in Windows. This is usually a two- step process. First you need to load drivers for the video card. Then you need to open the Control Panel and go to the Display applet to make your adjustments. Let's explore how to make the video card and monitor do Windows.

Try This!

Install a Video Card

You know how to install an expansion card from your reading in earlier chapters. Installing a video card is pretty much the same, so try this!

1. Refer to Chapter 6 for steps on installing a new card.
2. Plug the monitor cable into the video card port on the back of the PC and power up the system. If your PC seems dead after you install a video card, or if the screen is blank but you hear fans whirring and the internal speaker sounding off *long-short-short-short*, your video card likely did not get properly seated. Unplug the PC and try again.

Drivers

Just like any other piece of hardware, your video card needs a driver to function. Video card drivers install pretty much the same way as all of the other drivers we've discussed thus far: either the driver is already built into Windows or you must use the installation CD that comes with the video card.

Video card makers are constantly updating their drivers. Odds are good that any video card more than a few months old will have at least one driver update. If possible, check the manufacturer's website and use the driver located there if there is one. If the website doesn't offer a driver, then it's usually best to use the installation CD. Always avoid using the built-in Windows driver as it tends to be the most dated.

We'll explore driver issues in more detail after we discuss the Display applet. Like so many things about video, you can't really fully understand one topic without understanding at least one other!

Using the Display Applet

Especially useful to LCD monitor users, including folks with portable computers, is the Effects button on the Appearance tab of the Display Properties dialog box. The second option gives you a choice of font smoothing techniques, and many users exclaim joyously when they change the default from Standard to Clear Type.

With the driver installed, you're ready to configure your display settings. The Display applet on the Control Panel is your next stop. The Display applet provides a convenient, central location for all of your display settings, including resolution, refresh rate, driver information, and color depth.

The default Display applet in Windows XP (Figure 18.34) has five tabs: Themes, Desktop, Screen Saver, Appearance, and Settings. Earlier versions of Windows have a subset of these tabs. The first four tabs have options that enable you to change the look and feel of Windows and set up a screen saver; the fifth tab is where you make adjustments that relate directly to your monitor and video card. Let's take a close look at the Settings tab.

Settings Tab

The Settings tab (Figure 18.35) is the place to optimize monitors and video cards. At the bottom of the dialog box you'll see two options: Screen Resolution and Color Quality. By moving the Screen Resolution slider you can change—you guessed it!—the resolution of the screen. Resolution is measured in pixels. A system running with a resolution of 800 × 600 displays 800 pixels horizontally and 600 pixels vertically. The most common resolutions are 640 × 480, 800 × 600, 1,024 × 768, and 1,280 × 1,024. Keep in mind that these are only the most common resolutions—your system may have more or fewer resolution options.

Everyone has a favorite resolution, and higher isn't always better. Especially for those with trouble seeing small screen elements, higher resolutions can present a difficulty—those 20-pixel- square icons are *much* smaller at

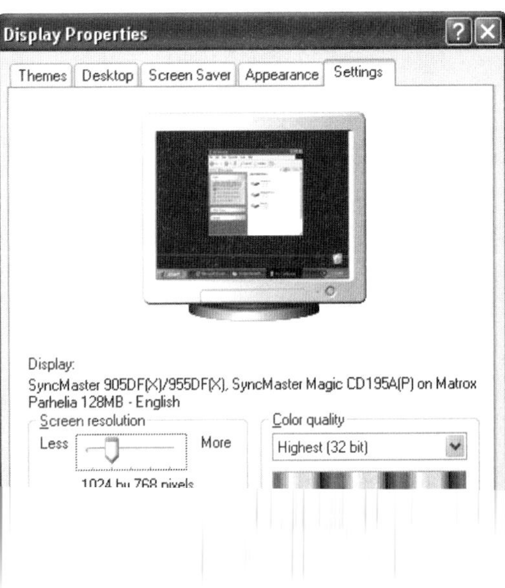

1,024 × 768 than at a basic VGA resolution of 640 × 480. Try all of the resolutions to see which you like.

The color quality is the number of colors displayed on the screen. Techs don't talk in terms of number of colors, but in terms of the **bit depth**. Use Table 18.5 to decode the correspondence between bit depth and number of colors. Not every computer will have the option of running all of these bit-depth options. In all but the last case, this is actually simple math: the number on the right is equal to 2 to the power of the bit-depth value; thus, 4-bit color produces $2^4 = 16$ colors. The 32-bit color doesn't use the extra 16 bits to add more colors, but rather to give the display additional abilities. You can change the screen resolution with a simple slider and adjust the color depth from 4-bit all the way up to 32-bit color.

Because even a young, healthy pair of human eyes has trouble distinguishing more than 16.7 million colors, running at 24-bit color is sufficient for many purposes. Running at 32-bit color gives a nice realistic tone to images, and many games insist on it. Up until about four years ago, many lower-end video cards required the system to run at lower bit depths, but

Table 18.5 Correspondence Between Bit Depth and Number of Colors

Bit Depth	Number of Colors
4-bit	16
8-bit	256
16-bit	65,536
24-bit	16.7 million
32-bit	16.7 million

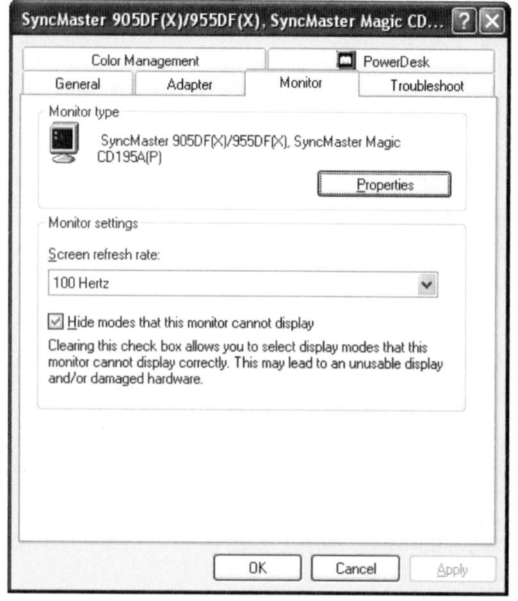

• **Figure 18.36** Monitor tab

unless you have an older video card or a significant video speed issue, you'll probably set your system for 32-bit color and never touch this setting again.

Clicking the Advanced button opens another dialog box with four or more tabs. Your monitor model serves as the title of the dialog box. Your video card driver determines which tabs show up here. You can ignore most of these tabs, but the Monitor tab is a handy place to adjust your refresh rate.

The Monitor tab gives you details about the currently installed monitor and enables you to make changes to the driver and the refresh rate. Click the Properties button to display the driver details for the monitor. In the Monitor Settings section of the Monitor tab, you can change the refresh rate using a drop-down dialog box (Figure 18.36).

Note the option, *Hide modes that this monitor cannot display*. If you have a video card that's substantially superior to your monitor, you could clear this check box to reveal a whole lot more refresh rates. You can toast a monitor by driving it too fast even in a relatively short length of time, however, so don't do this!

Working with Drivers

Now that you know the locations of the primary video tools within the operating system, it's time to learn about fine-tuning your video. You need to know how to work with video drivers from within the Display applet, including how to update them, roll back updates, and uninstall them.

Windows is very persnickety when it comes to video card drivers. You can crash Windows and force a reinstall simply by installing a new video card and not uninstalling the old card's drivers. This doesn't happen every time, but certainly can happen. As a basic rule, always uninstall the old card's drivers before you install drivers for a new card.

When you update the drivers for a card, you have a choice of uninstalling the outdated drivers and then installing new drivers—which makes the process the same as for installing a new card—or if you're running Windows XP, you can let it flex some digital muscle and install the new ones right over the older drivers.

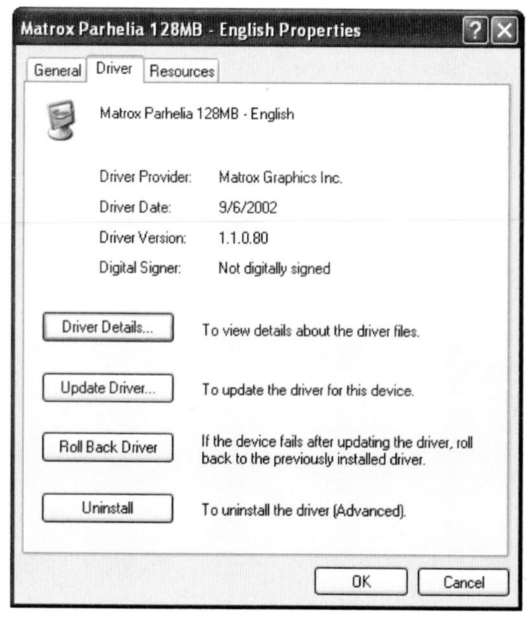

• **Figure 18.37** Adapter Properties dialog box

Updating

To update your drivers, go to the Control Panel and double-click the Display applet. In the Display Properties dialog box, select the Settings tab and click the Advanced button. In the Advanced button dialog box, click the Adapter tab and then click the Properties button. In the Properties dialog box for your adapter (Figure 18.37), select the Driver tab, and then click the Update Driver button to run the Hardware Update wizard.

3-D Graphics

No other area of the PC world reflects the amazing acceleration of technological improvements more than 3-D video—in particular,

3-D gaming. We are spectators to an amazing new world where software and hardware race to produce new levels of realism and complexity displayed on the computer screen. Powered by the wallets of tens of millions of PC gamers always demanding more and better, the video industry constantly introduces new video cards and new software titles that make today's games so incredibly realistic and fun. Although the gaming world certainly leads the PC industry in 3-D technologies, many other PC applications such as *Computer Aided Design* (CAD) programs quickly snatch up these technologies, making 3-D more useful in many ways other than just games. In this section, we'll add to the many bits and pieces of 3-D video encountered over previous chapters in the book and put together an understanding of the function and configuration of 3-D graphics.

Be careful updating video drivers! Every video card has a quirk of some form that you must address in order to install the new driver correctly. Many driver updates require you to delete the current video driver before you install the new one. Read the instructions carefully. I've had more than one situation where an otherwise simple video driver upgrade turned into a complete system rebuild!

Before the early 1990s, PCs did not mix well with 3-D graphics. Certainly, many 3-D applications existed, primarily 3-D design programs such

even the most powerful UNIX workstations of the early 1980s relegated almost all 3-D functions to CAD applications.

• **Figure 18.38** Wolfenstein 3D

The big change took place in 1992 when a small company called id Software created a new game called Wolfenstein 3D that launched an entirely new genre of games, now called *first-person shooters* (FPSs) (see Figure 18.38). In these games, the player looks out into a 3-D world, interacting with walls, doors, and items, and shoots whatever bad guys the game provides.

Wolfenstein 3D shook the PC gaming world to its foundations. An upstart little company suddenly appears with this new format, making Wolfenstein 3D and id Software overnight sensations. id Software knew that their 3-D game required substantial RAM and CPU strength for the time. They gambled that enough systems existed to handle the massive calculations required to keep track of the position of objects, keyboard inputs, and most importantly, the incredibly complex process of placing the 3-D world on the screen. The gamble paid off, making John Carmack and John Romero, the creators of id Software, the fathers of 3-D gaming.

• **Figure 18.39** Each figure has a limited number of sprites.

Early 3-D games used fixed 3-D images called *sprites* to create the 3-D world. A sprite is nothing more than a bitmapped graphic like a BMP file. These early first-person shooters would calculate the position of an object from the player's perspective and place a sprite to represent the object. Any single object would only have a fixed number of sprites—if you walked around an object, you noticed an obvious jerk as the game replaced the current sprite with a new one to represent the new position. Figure 18.39 shows different sprites for the same bad guy in Wolfenstein 3D. Sprites weren't pretty, but they worked without seriously taxing the 486s and early Pentiums of the time.

The second generation of 3-D began to replace sprites with true 3-D objects, which are drastically more complex than a sprite. A true 3-D object is composed of a group of points called *vertices*. Each vertex has a defined X, Y, and Z position in a 3-D world. Figure 18.40 shows the vertices for an airplane in a 3-D world.

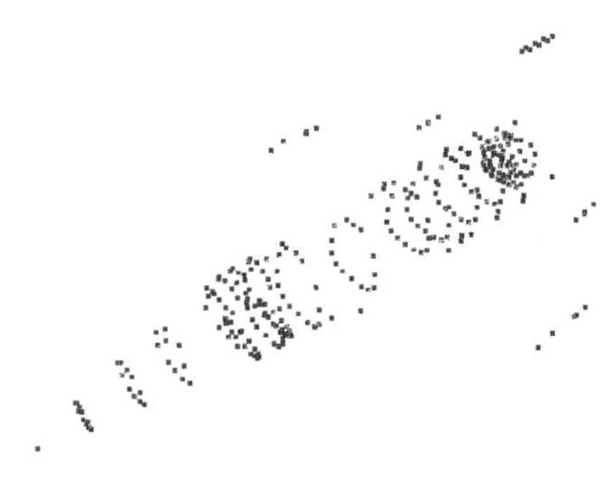

• **Figure 18.40** Vertices for a 3-D airplane

The computer must track all the vertices of all the objects in the 3-D world, including the ones you cannot currently see. Keep in mind that objects may be motionless in the 3-D world (like a wall), may have animation (like a door opening and closing), or may be moving (like bad monsters trying to spray you with evil alien goo). This calculation process is called *transformation* and, as you might imagine, is extremely taxing to most CPUs. Intel's SIMD and AMD's 3DNow! processor extensions were expressly designed to perform transformations.

Once the CPU has determined the positions of all vertices, the system then begins to fill in the 3-D object. The process begins by drawing lines (the 3-D term is *edges*) between vertices to build the 3-D object into many triangles. Why triangles? Well, mainly by consensus of game developers. Any shape works, but triangles make the most sense from a mathematical standpoint. I could go into more depth here, but that would require talking about trigonometry, and I'm gambling you'd rather not read that detailed of a description! All 3-D games use triangles to connect vertices. The 3-D process then groups triangles together into various shapes called *polygons*. Figure 18.41 shows the same model from Figure 18.40, now displaying all the connected vertices to create a large number of polygons.

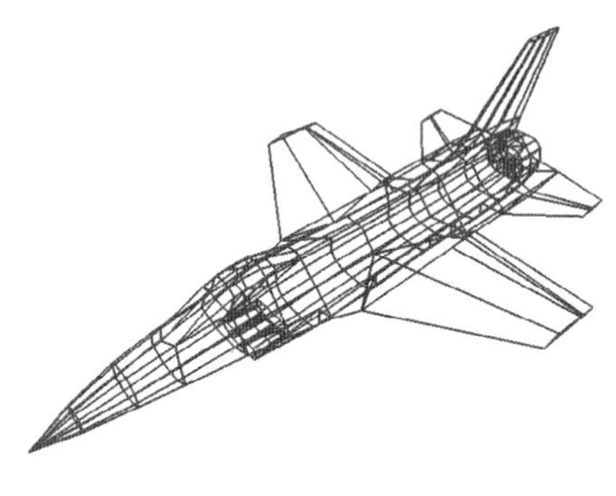

• **Figure 18.41** Connected vertices forming polygons on a 3-D airplane

Originally, the CPU handled these calculations to create triangles, but now special 3-D video cards do the job, greatly speeding up the process.

The last step in second-generation games was texturing. Every 3-D game stores a number of bitmaps called *textures*. The program wraps textures around the object to give it a surface. Textures work well as they provide dramatic detail without the need to use a lot of triangles. A single object may take one texture or many textures applied to single triangles or groups of triangles (polygons). Figure 18.42 shows the finished airplane.

• **Figure 18.42** 3-D airplane with textures added

These second-generation games made a much more realistic environment, but the heavy demands of true 3-D often forced game designers to use both 3-D and sprites in the same game. Figure 18.43 shows the famous game Doom. Note that the walls, floors, doors, and such were 3-D images, whereas the bad guys continued to manifest as sprites. Notice how pixilated the bad guy looks compared to the rest of the scene.

True 3-D, more often referred to as *rendered* objects, immediately created the need for massively powerful video cards and much wider data buses. Intel's primary motivation for creating AGP was to provide a big enough pipe for massive data pumping between the video card and the CPU. Intel gave AGP the ability to read system RAM to support textures. If it weren't for 3-D games, AGP would almost certainly not exist.

3-D Video Cards

No CPU of the mid-1990s could ever hope to handle the massive processes required to render 3-D worlds. Keep in mind that in order to create realistic movement, the 3-D world must refresh at least 24 times per second. That means that this entire process from transformation to texturing must repeat once every 1/24 of a second! Furthermore, while the game re-creates each screen, it must also

store textures, as well as powerful processors to deal with the creation of triangles and the placement of textures at incredibly high speeds.

But a problem exists with this setup: How do we talk to these cards? This is done by means of a device driver, of course, but wouldn't it be great if we could create standard commands to speed up the process? The best thing to do would be to create a standardized set of instructions that any 3-D program could send to a 3-D card to do all the basic work, such as "make a cone" or "lay texture 237 on the cone you just made."

The video card instructions standards manifested themselves into a series of **Application Programming Interfaces (APIs)**. In essence, an API is a translator—it takes the commands issued by the program currently using the video card and translates those instructions into a language that the device driver can understand. If you were to picture the graphics system of your computer as a layer cake, the top layer would be the program making a call to the graphics hardware. The next layer is the API. The device driver comes next and way down at the base of the cake is the actual graphics hardware—RAM, graphics processor, and RAMDAC.

Several different APIs have been developed over the years with no clear winner apparent among all of them. The OpenGL standard was developed for UNIX systems, but has since been *ported*, or made compatible with, a wide variety of computer systems, including Windows and Apple computers. As the demand for 3-D video became increasingly strong, Microsoft decided to throw its hat into the 3-D graphics ring with its own API, called DirectX. We look at DirectX in-depth in the next section.

Although they might accomplish the same task (for instance, translating instructions and passing them on to the video driver), every API handles things just a little bit differently. In some 3-D games, the OpenGL standard might produce more precise images with less CPU overhead than the DirectX standard. In general, however, you won't notice a large difference between the images produced using OpenGL and DirectX.

DirectX and Video Cards

In the old days, many applications communicated directly with much of the PC hardware and, as a result, could crash your computer if not written well enough. Microsoft tried to fix this problem by placing all hardware under the control of Windows, but programmers balked because Windows added too much work for the video process and slowed down everything. For the most demanding programs, such as games, only direct access of hardware would work.

This need to "get around Windows" motivated Microsoft to unveil a new set of protocols called *DirectX*. Programmers use DirectX to take control of certain pieces of hardware and to talk directly to that hardware; it provides the speed necessary to play the advanced games so popular today. The primary impetus for DirectX was to build a series of products to enable Windows to run 3-D games. That's not to say that you couldn't run 3-D games in Windows *before* DirectX; rather, it's just that Microsoft wasn't involved in the API rat race at the time and wanted to be. Microsoft's goal in developing DirectX was to create a 100-percent stable environment, with direct hardware access, for running 3-D applications and games within Windows.

DirectX is not only for video; it also supports sound, network connections, input devices, and other parts of your PC. Each of these subsets of DirectX has a name like DirectDraw, Direct3D, or DirectSound.

- **DirectDraw** Supports direct access to the hardware for 2-D graphics.
- **Direct3D** Supports direct access to the hardware for 3-D graphics—the most important part of DirectX.
- **DirectInput** Supports direct access to the hardware for joysticks and other game controllers.
- **DirectSound** Supports direct access to the hardware for waveforms.
- **DirectMusic** Supports direct access to the hardware for MIDI devices.
- **DirectPlay** Supports direct access to network devices for multiplayer games.
- **DirectShow** Supports direct access to video and presentation devices.

Microsoft constantly adds and tweaks this list. As almost all games need DirectX and all video cards have drivers to support DirectX, you need to verify that DirectX is installed and working properly on your system. To do this, use the DirectX diagnostic tool in the System Information program. After you open System Information (it usually lives in the Accessories | System Tools area of the Start menu), click the Tools menu and select DirectX Diagnostic Tool (see Figure 18.44).

The System tab gives the version of DirectX. The system pictured in Figure 18.44

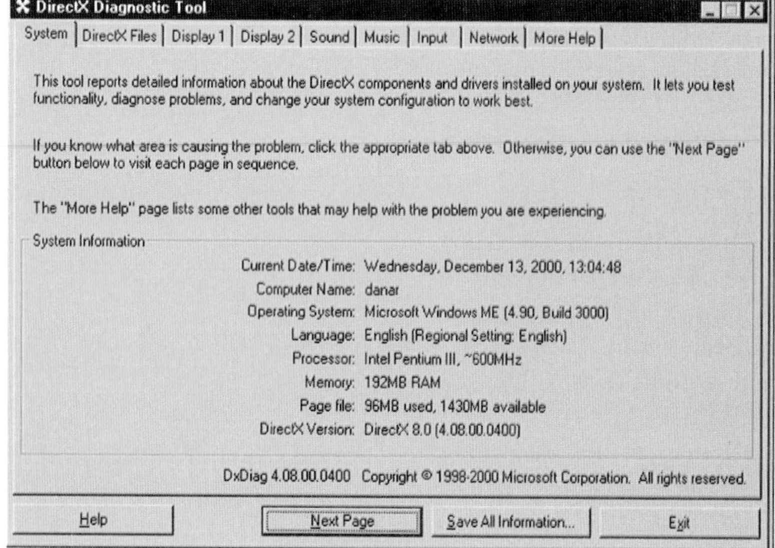

• **Figure 18.44** The DirectX Diagnostic Tool

runs DirectX 8.0. You may then test the separate DirectX functions by running through the other tabs and running the tests.

Try This!

Testing Your Video

You or your client needs to know right now whether his system will run the latest game, so turn to the DirectX diagnostic tool and give it a go. Although you can open the tool in System Information, you can also run it directly from the Start menu. Go to Start | Run, type **DXDIAG** and click OK.

1. Select the Display tab and click the Test DirectDraw button.
2. After the DirectDraw test runs, click the Test Direct3D button.
3. How did your system handle the test? If anything failed, you might think about replacing the card!

So, what does DirectX do for video cards? Well, video-card makers must find ways to make their video cards better than other video cards. To do this, the chip and card makers constantly add a number of interesting features, and then push Microsoft to add it to their DirectX tools. This has led to major upgrades of DirectX at a [illegible] tions! One good rule to help in a buying decision is to see what video chipset is hot at the moment. I make a point to check out these web sites whenever I'm getting ready to buy in order to see what everyone says is the best:

- www.arstechnica.com
- www.hardocp.com
- www.tomshardware.com
- www.sharkyextreme.com

Dual Monitors

Would you like to have a bigger monitor, but you don't have the cash to fork over to get some monster 21-inch monitor? Well, starting with Windows 98, your system now supports multiple monitors. If you have a video card that has dual outputs or if you just happen to have a few extra video cards lying around, you can turn any Windows 98, 98 SE, Me, 2000, or XP system into a multi-monitor beast with little effort.

The nicest part about multiple monitors is that it requires very little effort on your part. If you have two video cards installed (not all work together, but most do) and the drivers installed, you merely need to check out the Display Properties dialog box and activate the second monitor. You'll know if the dual monitor will work if you see two monitors in the Display Properties dialog box,

Cross Check

Keeping DirectX Updated

I always have the latest version of DirectX installed on my system. In my experience, each new version adds functionality and increases stability—both items are extremely important to me. Most versions of Windows have a tool for updating important system files, so flip back to Chapters 15 and 16 and run through the steps for updating. Which versions of Windows have the updating tool? What do you do if you *don't* have the tool?

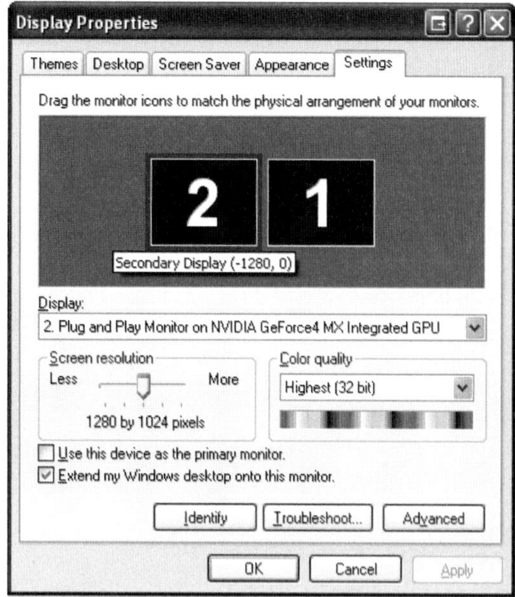

• **Figure 18.45** Dual monitor settings in Windows XP

as shown in Figure 18.45. The first installed monitor is called the primary monitor, and the other is called the secondary (you can have more than two monitors, but for the A+ think in terms of only two monitors).

Troubleshooting Video

Because of the inherent dangers of the high-frequency and high-voltage power required by monitors, and because proper adjustment requires specialized training, this section will concentrate on giving a support person the information necessary to decide whether a trouble call is warranted. Virtually no monitor manufacturers make schematics of their monitors available to the public because of liability issues regarding possible electrocution. To simplify troubleshooting, look at the process as two separate parts: external and internal adjustments.

External Adjustments

Monitor adjustments range from the simplest—brightness and contrast—to the more sophisticated—pincushioning and trapezoidal adjustments. The external controls provide users with the opportunity to fine-tune the monitor's image. Many monitors have controls for changing the tint and saturation of color, although plenty of monitors put those controls inside the monitor. Better monitors enable you to square up the visible portion of the screen with the monitor housing.

Finally, most monitors have the ability to **degauss** themselves with the push of a button. Over time, the shadow mask picks up a weak magnetic charge that interferes with the focus of the electron beams. This magnetic field makes the image look slightly fuzzy and streaked. Most monitors have a special built-in circuit called a *degaussing coil* to eliminate this magnetic buildup. When the degaussing circuit is used, an alternating current is sent through a coil of wire surrounding the CRT, and this current generates an alternating magnetic field that demagnetizes the shadow mask. The degaussing coil is activated using the Degauss button or menu selection on the monitor. Degaussing usually makes a rather nasty thunk sound and the screen goes crazy for a moment—don't worry, that's normal. Whenever a user calls me with a fuzzy monitor problem, I always have them degauss first.

Internal Adjustments

As shipped, most monitors do not produce an image out to the limits of the screen because of poor convergence at the outer display edges. **Convergence** defines how closely the three colors can meet at a single point on the display. At the point of convergence, the three colors will combine to form a single white dot. With misconvergence, a noticeable halo of one or more colors will appear around the outside of the white point. The farther away the colors are from the center of the screen, the more likely the chance for misconvergence. Low-end monitors are especially susceptible to this problem. Even though adjusting the convergence of a monitor is not difficult, it does require getting inside the monitor case and having a copy of the schematic, which shows the location of the variable resistors. For this reason, it is a good idea to leave this adjustment to a trained specialist.

I don't like opening a CRT monitor. I avoid doing this for two reasons: (1) I know very little about electronic circuits and (2) I once almost electrocuted myself. At any rate, the A+ exams expect you to have a passing understanding of adjustments you might need to perform inside a monitor. Before we go any further, let me remind you about a little issue with CRT monitors (see Figure 18.46).

• **Figure 18.46** Hey! That's 25,000 volts! *Be careful!*

The CRT monitor contains a wire called a **high-**

charge a CRT.

Discharging a CRT

There are 75,000 opinions on how to discharge a CRT properly. Although my procedure may not follow the steps outlined in someone's official handbook or electrical code, I know this works. Read the rules, and then look at Figure 18.47.

1. Make sure everything is unplugged.
2. If possible, let the monitor sit for a couple of hours. Most good monitors will discharge themselves in two to three hours, and many new monitors discharge in just a few moments.
3. Get a heavy, well-insulated, flat-bladed screwdriver.
4. Get a heavy gauge wire with alligator clips on each end.
5. Do not let yourself be grounded in any way. Wear rubber-soled shoes, and no rings or watches.
6. Wear safety goggles to protect yourself in the very rare case that the CRT implodes.
7. Remove the monitor's case. Remember where the screw went in.
8. Attach one alligator clip to an unpainted part of the metal frame of the monitor.
9. Clip the other end to the metal shaft of the screwdriver.
10. Slide the screwdriver blade under the suction cup. Make triple-sure that

Cross Check

Dangerous Toys

The CRT doesn't have a lock on being the only dangerous piece of high-voltage equipment inside the PC. Check out Chapter 8 on power supplies and answer these questions:

1. What other equipment should you avoid when working on a PC?
2. Should you ground yourself at all times?

neither you nor the screwdriver is in any incidental contact with anything metal.

11. Slide the blade under until you hear a loud pop—you'll also see a nice blue flash.
12. If anyone is in the building, they will hear the pop and come running. Tell them everything's okay.
13. Wait about 15 minutes and repeat.

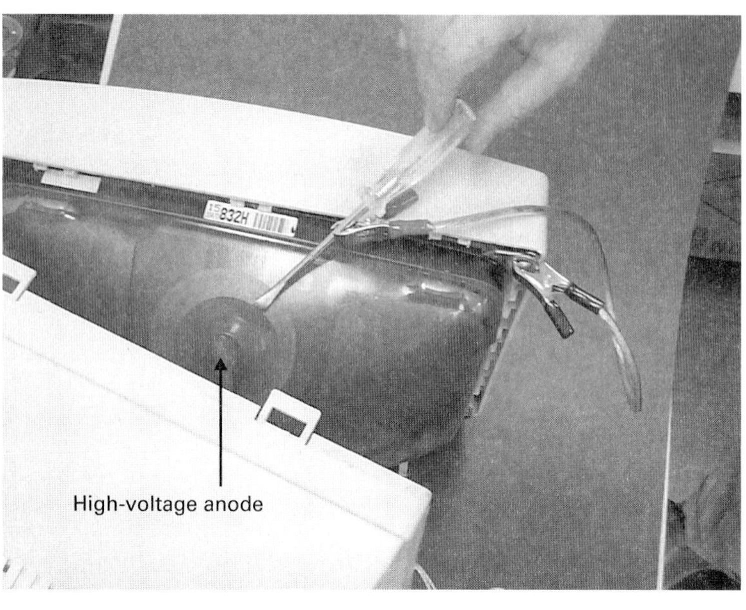

• **Figure 18.47** Discharging a CRT

The main controls that require you to remove the monitor case to make adjustments include those for convergence, gain for each of the color guns, and sometimes the focus control. A technician with either informal or formal training in component-level repair can usually figure out which controls do what. In some cases, you can also readily spot and repair bad solder connections inside the monitor case, and thus fix a dead or dying CRT. Still, balance the cost of repairing the monitor against the cost of death or serious injury—is it worth it? Finally, before making adjustments to the display image, especially with the internal controls, give the monitor at least 15 to 30 minutes of warm-up time. This is necessary for both the components on the printed circuit boards and for the CRT itself.

Cleaning Monitors

Cleaning monitors is easy. Always use antistatic monitor wipes or at least a general antistatic cloth. Some LCD monitors may require special cleaning equipment. Never use window cleaners or any liquid because the danger of liquid getting into the monitor may create a shocking experience! Many commercial cleaning solutions will also melt an LCD screen, which is never a good thing.

Common Monitor Problems

Although I'm not super comfortable diving into the guts of a CRT, you can fix a substantial percentage of monitor problems yourself. The following list describes the most common monitor problems and tells you what to do—even when that means sending it to someone else.

- Almost all CRT and LCD monitors have replaceable controls. If the Brightness knob or Degauss button stops working or seems loose, check with the manufacturer for replacement controls. They usually come as a complete package.
- For problems with ghosting, streaking, and/or fuzzy vertical edges, check the cable connections and the cable itself. These problems rarely apply to monitors; more commonly, they point to the video card.

- If one color is missing, check cables for breaks or bent pins. Check the front controls for that color. If the color adjustment is already maxed out, the monitor will require internal service.
- As monitors age, they lose brightness. If the brightness control is turned all the way up and the picture seems dim, the monitor will require internal adjustment. This is a good argument for power-management functions. Don't leave the monitor on with a picture on it, as this will reduce monitor life significantly. Do use the power-management options in Windows or use the power switch.
- If your LCD monitor cracks, it is not repairable.
- Almost everything else wrong with an LCD Panel *can* be fixed! Never pay to replace an LCD panel that is not broken. Search for a specialty LCD repair company. Hundreds of these companies exist [illegible]

[illegible] usually on the inside somewhere close to the flyback transformer. This is the transformer that provides power to the high-voltage anode.

- Hissing or sparking sounds are often indicative of an insulation rupture on the flyback transformer. This sound is usually accompanied by the smell of ozone. If your monitor has these symptoms, it definitely needs a qualified technician. Having replaced a flyback transformer once myself, I can say it is not worth the hassle and potential loss of life and limb.
- Big color blotches present on the display is an easy and cheap repair. Find the Degauss button and use it. If your monitor doesn't have a Degauss button, you can purchase a special tool called a degaussing coil at any electronics store.
- Bird-like chirping sounds occurring at regular intervals usually indicate a problem with the monitor power supply.
- Suppose you got a good deal on a used 17-inch monitor, but the display is kind of dark, even though you have the brightness turned up all the way. This points to a dying CRT. So, how about replacing the CRT? Forget it. Even if the monitor was free, it just isn't worth it, because a replacement tube runs into the hundreds of dollars. Nobody ever sold a monitor because it was too bright and too sharp. Save your money and buy a new monitor.
- The monitor displaying only a single horizontal or vertical line is probably a problem between the main circuit board and the yoke, or a blown yoke coil. This definitely requires a service call.
- A single white dot on an otherwise black screen means the high-voltage flyback transformer is most likely shot. Take it into the repair shop.

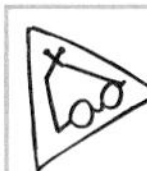

Tech Tip

The only time I'll open a monitor is to replace a control knob or switch, or to try and adjust the focus. These tips are great to know for the A+ Certification exams, but I'm just way too chicken to do most of these myself. Here is a list of a few last dos and don'ts that I abide by to keep my monitors happy:

- *Do keep the screen clean.*
- *Do keep the cables tightened.*

[illegible] *the manufacturer.*

- *Don't leave the monitor on all the time, even with a screen saver.*
- *Don't place magnetic objects such as unshielded speakers close to the monitor. (This can cause color problems at best and could permanently magnetize the shadow mask at worst.)*
- *Be careful when disposing of a dead monitor. Many local governments have laws regarding safe disposal of monitors. Be sure to check with your local waste disposal entity, or your company, to verify proper disposal methods.*

Beyond A+

Video and CMOS

I'm always impressed by the number of video options provided in CMOS, especially in some of the more advanced CMOS options. I'm equally impressed by the amount of disinformation provided on these settings. In this section, I'll touch on some of the most common CMOS settings that deal with video. You may notice that no power-management video options have been included.

Video

Every standard CMOS setup shows an option for video support. The default setting is invariably EGA/VGA. Many years ago, this setting told the BIOS what type of card was installed on the system, enabling it to know how to talk to that card. Today, this setting has no meaning. No matter what you put there, it will be ignored and the system will boot normally.

Init Display First

This CMOS setting usually resides in an advanced options or BIOS options screen. In multi-monitor systems, Init Display First enables you to decide between AGP and PCI as to which monitor initializes at boot. This will also determine the initial primary monitor for Windows 9*x* and Windows 2000.

Assign IRQ for VGA

Many video cards do not need an *interrupt request* (IRQ). This option gives you the ability to choose whether your video card gets an IRQ. In general, lower-end cards that do not provide input to the system do not need an IRQ. Most advanced cards will need one; try it both ways. If you need it, your system will freeze up without an IRQ assigned. If you don't need it, you get an extra IRQ.

VGA Palette Snoop

True-VGA devices only show 16 out of a possible 262,000 colors at a time. The 16 current colors are called the *palette*. VGA Palette Snoop opens a PCI video card's palette to other devices that may need to read or temporarily change the palette. I am unaware of any device made today that still needs this option.

Video Shadowing Enabled

As mentioned in previous chapters, this setting enables you to shadow the Video ROM. In most cases, this option is ignored as today's video cards perform their own automatic shadowing. A few cards require this setting to be off, so I generally leave it off now after years of leaving it on.

Chapter 18 Review

Chapter Summary

After reading this chapter and completing the exercises, you should be able to perform the following about Video:

Explain How CRT Monitors and LCD Displays Work

- The term *video* encompasses a complex interaction among numerous parts of the PC, all designed to put a picture on the screen. The monitor shows you [illegible] coated with phosphor at the wide end.
- The speed of the electron beam across the screen is the horizontal refresh rate (HRR), more commonly referred to as the refresh rate. The vertical refresh rate (VRR) is the time it takes to draw the entire screen and return the electron guns to the upper-left corner.
- Monitors do not determine the HRR or VRR. The video card "pushes" the monitor at a certain VRR that, in turn, determines the HRR.
- A monitor is a grid of red, green, and blue light-sensitive dots called phosphors.
- Dot pitch, measured in millimeters (mm) defines the diagonal distance between phosphorous dots of the same color.
- Although originally used for laptops, Liquid Crystal Displays (LCDs) are making their way into the desktop market. They offer many advantages over CRTs. An LCD monitor is thinner, lighter, uses less power, is virtually flicker free, and does not emit potentially harmful radiation.
- While dual-scan may still be found on some low-end LCD panels, most of today's LCD panels use active matrix or thin film transistor (TFT) technology.
- Measured from two opposite diagonal corners, size for CRT monitors is not usually the same as the viewable image size. A 17-inch CRT monitor might have only a 15.5-inch VIS. Because LCD monitors report only VIS, a 15-inch LCD monitor may have approximately the same viewing area as a 17-inch CRT.
- CRT monitors require two connectors, a 15-pin, 3-row DB connector and a power plug. Unlike the analog super video graphics array (SVGA) CRTs, [illegible] Standards Association (VESA) standard for power-management signaling (DPMS) specification can cut monitor power consumption by about 75 percent.

Select the Proper Display Adapter

- The video card has two major pieces, the video RAM and the video processing circuitry. Today's video cards support four different modes and can display text and graphics in both monochrome and color.
- To determine the amount of video memory required at a given resolution and color depth, multiply the resolution by the number of bytes of color depth.
- Video cards are identified by their manufacturer, model number, graphic processor, and amount of video RAM. While a number of companies produce video cards, the three major manufacturers of graphics processors are NVIDIA, ATI, and Matrox. The most important decision when buying a video card is the graphics processor, especially if you play 3-D games where texture and layering are important considerations.

Install and Configure Video Software

- Video card drivers install pretty much the same as all other drivers: either the driver is already built into Windows or you must use the installation CD that comes with the video card.

- The Display applet in the Control Panel provides a convenient, central location for adjusting all of your display settings, including resolution, refresh rate, driver information, and color depth.
- As a basic rule, always uninstall an old video card's drivers before you install drivers for a new card.
- Video cards use a series of Application Programming Interfaces (APIs) to translate instructions for the video device driver. If you were to picture the graphics system of your computer as a layer cake, the top layer would be the program making a call to the graphics hardware. The next layer is the API. The device driver comes next and way down at the base of the cake is the actual graphics hardware—RAM, graphics processor, and RAMDAC.
- Windows 98 and newer versions support multiple monitors with multiple video cards or a video card with dual outputs.

Troubleshoot Basic Video Problems

- Because monitors have high-voltage power that can harm or kill you, always leave it to the trained professional to work inside the monitor. Monitor troubleshooting falls into two categories: external and internal adjustments.
- Many monitors have a button to degauss themselves. When the shadow mask picks up a weak magnetic charge, it interferes with the focus of the electron beams, making the monitor appear fuzzy or streaked. A built-in circuit called a degaussing coil generates an alternating magnetic field that eliminates the magnetic buildup on the shadow mask.
- Convergence defines how closely the three colors meet at a single point on the display. With misconvergence, one or more of the colors will appear to have a halo outside the white point, with the problem more severe toward the outside of the screen.
- Clean CRT monitors with an antistatic monitor wipe. Never use window cleaners or other liquids. LCD monitors need special cleaning equipment.
- Common monitor problems are often related to cable breaks or bent pins. Monitors also lose brightness over time, especially if you are not using the power management functions.
- For best performance, keep the screen clean, the cables tightened, use power management, don't block the ventilation slots or place magnetic objects close to the monitor, and don't leave the monitor on all the time, even with a screensaver. If the monitor is dead, use proper disposal methods.
- In addition to the now meaningless video support setting of EGA/VGA, other CMOS settings relate to video. These include "Init Display First" for multi-monitor systems, "Assign IRQ for VGA," "VGA Palette Snoop," and "VGA Shadowing Enabled."

Key Terms

Accelerated Graphics Port (AGP) *(686)*
Active matrix *(677)*
Application Programming Interface (API) *(695)*
Bandwidth *(674)*
Bit depth *(691)*
Cathode ray tube (CRT) *(671)*
Convergence *(698)*
Degauss *(698)*
Display adapter *(670)*
Dot pitch *(674)*
High-voltage anode *(699)*
Horizontal refresh rate (HRR) *(672)*
Liquid Crystal Display (LCD) *(675)*
Nit *(678)*
Pixel *(673)*
Random Access Memory Digital-to-Analog Converter (RAMDAC) *(679)*
Resolution *(673)*
Super video graphics array (SVGA) *(679)*
Thin film transistor (TFT) *(677)*
Triad *(674)*
Vertical refresh rate (VRR) *(672)*
Video graphics array (VGA) *(684)*
Viewable image size (VIS) *(679)*

Key Term Quiz

Use the Key Terms list to complete the sentences that follow. Not all the terms will be used.

1. Perhaps the most important value of a monitor, ________ defines the maximum number of times the electron gun can turn on and off per second.
2. A(n) ________ consists of one red, one green, and one blue phosphor.

3. DirectX is one of a number of __________, programs that translate instructions for the video device driver.

4. Using an aspect ratio of 4:3, ____________ refers to the number of horizontal pixels times the number of vertical pixels.

5. The __________ bus, designed specifically for video cards, connects directly to the Northbridge.

6. If your monitor displays big color blotches, it indicates that you should __________ the monitor to eliminate the magnetic buildup on the shadow mask.

7. A(n) ____________ LCD panel has a transistor that controls each color dot.

8. The number of sweeps or raster lines that the electron guns make across the screen is called the __________, while the time it takes to draw the entire screen is called the ___________.

9. __________ defines how closely the red, green, and blue colors meet at a single point on the display.

10. Measured in millimeters, where the lower the number means the clearer the picture, __________ is the diagonal distance between phosphors of the same color.

A. The size of the screen

B. The pixel size

C. The amount of RAM on the video card

D. The number of lines on the screen

2. All of the following statements are true about pixels *except*:

A. A pixel has only one red, one green, and one blue phosphor.

B. The size of the pixel varies according to the resolution of the CRT monitor.

C. An LCD monitor has a set number of pixels.

D. Higher resolutions result in more pixels per row.

3. If one of the colors is missing on the monitor and you cannot fix the problem by adjusting the front controls, you should then check for ______________.

A. A refresh rate that is set higher than that recommended by the manufacturer

B. A corrupted video driver

C. A broken cable or bent pins

D. Misconvergence

4. All the following statements are true about LCD monitors *except*:

B. TFT LCDs are able to display far more colors than passive LCDs.

C. Active matrix LCDs provide faster refresh rates than passive matrix LCDs.

D. Passive matrix LCDs have about a 90-degree viewing area while active matrix LCDs are limited to about a 45-degree viewing area.

5. Which of the following resolutions will produce the best quality picture on the monitor?

A. 640 × 480

B. 800 × 600

C. 1024 × 768

D. 1280 × 1024

6. Which of the following problems would make it impossible to repair an LCD monitor?

A. A blown yoke coil

B. A broken LCD panel

C. A bad flyback transformer

D. Misconvergence

7. AGP offers all the following features *except*:

A. It uses strobing (or multiple signals) for each clock cycle.

B. Its data bus connects directly to the fast Northbridge.

C. It is capable of accessing system memory to store video information.

D. It offers greater color depth than PCI.

8. CRT monitors attach to the video card using a ________________ connector.

A. 9-pin, 2-row, DB

B. 36-pin Centronics

C. 15-pin, 3-row, DB

D. 25-pin, 2-row, DB

9. Which of these dot pitch numbers indicates a better quality monitor?

A. .39

B. .31

C. .28

D. .23

10. Today's video cards usually contain __________ memory chips.

A. WRAM or VRAM

B. DRAM or SRAM

C. SDRAM or DDR SDRAM

D. SRAM or SDRAM

11. Which of the following statements best describes the electron guns in a CRT monitor?

A. A single gun shoots electrons at the phosphors on the screen.

B. Three electron guns, one each for red, green, and blue phosphors, paint the screen.

C. The electron guns stay on all the time to shoot electrons that produce the solid image on the screen.

D. One electron gun shoots red phosphors, another shoots green phosphors, and the third shoots blue phosphors at the screen.

12. All of the following statements are true *except*:

A. The DVI-I adapter converts an analog LCD to use a digital video card or vice versa.

B. The Digital Video Interface (DVI) standard defines three different connectors for LCD monitors.

C. Since both the PC and the newer LCDs are digital, no conversion is necessary if you have a digital video card.

D. VGA and newer video cards include a RAMDAC chip that converts digital signals from the video card into an analog signal for the analog CRT.

13. If the monitor displays only a single horizontal or vertical line, the problem is likely to be caused by a _______.

A. Bad flyback transformer

B. Blown yoke coil

C. Bad monitor power supply

D. Bad electron gun

14. Among the advantages of LCD monitors over CRT monitors are all of the following *except*:

A. LCD monitors are thinner and lighter.

B. LCD monitors use less power.

C. LCD monitors allow you to adjust the resolution while CRT monitors have a set number of pixels.

D. LCD monitors do not emit potentially harmful radiation.

15. Only specially trained technicians should work inside a monitor because the ____________ produces over 25,000V that may harm or kill a person.

A. Flyback transformer

B. Yoke

C. Anode

D. Electron gun

Essay Quiz

1. Your company is getting ready to replace all their computers and monitors. You would like to see all the new PCs come with LCD monitors. Write a memo to your boss that shows the advantages of LCD monitors over CRT monitors.

2. The editor of your company's newsletter has asked you to prepare a short article for next month's edition that explains how to care for monitors to extend their lifespan. Explain at least four things that the average user can do.

3. Dave and Shannon disagree about whether the monitor should stay on all the time or not. Dave says that it's okay to leave the monitor on as long as you have a screensaver. Shannon disagrees, saying the monitor will become dim and burn out sooner if you leave it on. Dave thinks that leaving it on actually extends its life because turning the monitor on and off is bad for it. They've called you to save their monitor and their marriage. What will you tell them?

4. Brad is very upset because Eli, his four-year old, held a magnet up to the screen and now his new CRT monitor looks terrible. It's got some big spots on the corner and looks fuzzy. Explain to him what happened and what he can do to solve his problem.

5. Your company just hired two new technicians. You've been tapped to teach them what they can and cannot do to troubleshoot and repair a CRT monitor. What will you tell them?

new video system for your computer, what would you select? Go to the local computer store or to web sites such as www.newegg.com and pick out the best combination of monitor and video card that you

also received a $200 birthday gift and have decided to purchase an even better graphics card and monitor. Which ones will you select now that you have $700 to spend?

• Lab Project 18.2

Monitors are not the only output device for the computer. Research one of the following devices and prepare a short essay for the class about how the device works, its features, cost, and connections.

- Projectors
- Plasma monitors
- Touch screens

Chapter 19 SCSI

"All right, we don't understand the R2D2 crap. We're going to use the Star Trek system. One blink for yes, two blinks for no."

—JOHN CRICHTON, *FARSCAPE* (1999)

In this chapter, you will learn how to

- **Create a functional SCSI chain**
- **Describe the different flavors of SCSI**
- **Troubleshoot problems with SCSI installations**
- **Describe the benefits of using SCSI**

You've read a lot in this book about common hardware—the stuff that you can find in nearly every PC out there. Most systems have a PATA hard drive and a CD-ROM drive, for example, happily plugged into the primary IDE port on the motherboard. Mastering such information is vital for a tech, because it applies to the bread-and-butter work that you'll most often face on the job. But an A+ Certified technician must go beyond the common, everyday technology to tackle the more unusual stuff as well. To pass the Core Hardware exam and become an ace PC tech, you'll need to know how to handle nearly any hardware situation that comes your way.

Many specialized server machines and enthusiasts' systems use the small computer system interface (SCSI) technologies for various pieces of core hardware and peripherals, from hard drives to printers to high-end tape backup machines. Believe it or not, some of these systems don't have PATA or SATA drives at all! A competent A+ Certified tech, of course, can walk into a situation with machines using SCSI devices and troubleshoot and repair them without batting an eye. Let's dive into SCSI now, and see what this technology has to offer.

Historical/Conceptual

Shugart systems introduced SCSI in 1979 as a system-independent means of mass storage. SCSI can be best described as a miniature network *inside* your PC. Any type of peripheral can be built as a SCSI device. Common SCSI devices include the following:

- Hard drives
- Tape backup units
- Removable hard drives
- Scanners

name or number. Using Wide SCSI-2 as a basis, this chapter addresses the basic issues involved in implementing SCSI in a PC. Once you have a solid understanding of Wide SCSI-2, the most common standard today, the chapter explains the other types of SCSI so you can understand the differences among the many variations of SCSI.

Test Specific

SCSI Chains

SCSI manifests itself through a **SCSI chain**, a series of SCSI devices working together through a host adapter. The **host adapter** provides the interface between the SCSI chain and the PC. Figure 19.1 shows a typical PCI host adapter. Many techs refer to the host adapter as the *SCSI controller*, so be comfortable with both terms.

Note that the card has two connectors. The first connector, at the top of the figure, is for inside (internal) SCSI connections. The second connector (on the left) is for devices on the outside (external) of the PC. All SCSI chains connect to the PC through the host adapter. The host adapter in Figure 19.1 is PCI, but you can get SCSI host adapters for just about any expansion bus type. Figure 19.2 shows a 16-bit ISA SCSI host adapter. A lot of higher end motherboards and server motherboards have a built in SCSI controller.

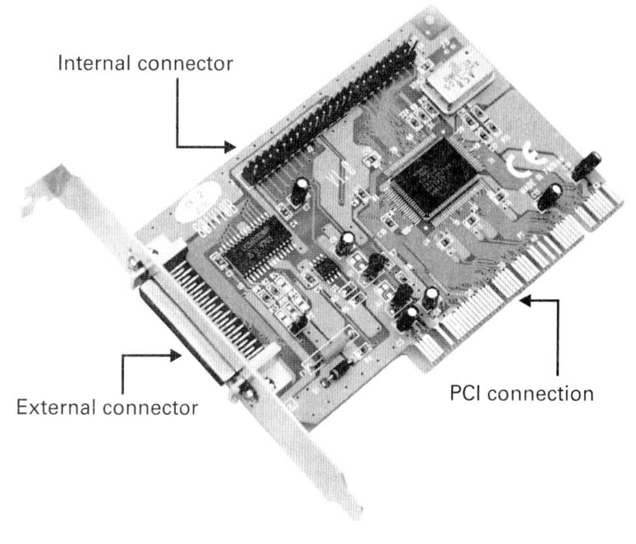

• **Figure 19.1** SCSI host adapter

All SCSI devices can be divided into two groups: internal and external. Internal SCSI devices obviously go inside the PC and connect to the host adapter through the latter's internal connector. Figure 19.3 shows an internal SCSI device, in this case a CD-ROM drive. External devices hook to the external connector of the host adapter. Figure 19.4 is an example of an external SCSI device.

Internal SCSI devices connect to the host adapter with a **68-pin ribbon cable** (Figure 19.5). This flat, flexible cable functions precisely like the more common 40-pin and 80-wire PATA cables that you know from Chapter 10, "Hard Drive Technologies," connecting the device and the SCSI controller. Many external devices connect to the host adapter with a **50-pin high density (HD) connector**. Figure 19.6 shows a host adapter external port. Higher-end SCSI devices use a **68-pin high density (HD) connector**. See the section, "SCSI Cables and Connectors."

You install internal SCSI devices similarly to how you install IDE devices. SCSI devices need power, of course, and most use a Molex connector. The ribbon cable runs between the controller and the device, with the red stripe on the cable oriented to pin 1 on both devices. But SCSI and IDE installations differ in at least one important respect. If you plug IDE devices in incorrectly, they just don't work. If you plug a SCSI device in incorrectly (such as with the cable backward), you can destroy both the device and the SCSI controller! Be careful to install SCSI devices properly the first time.

Multiple internal devices can be connected together simply by using a cable with enough connectors. The cable in Figure 19.5, for example, shows a cable that can take up to four SCSI devices, including the host adapter. Figure 19.7 illustrates two internal devices on a SCSI chain.

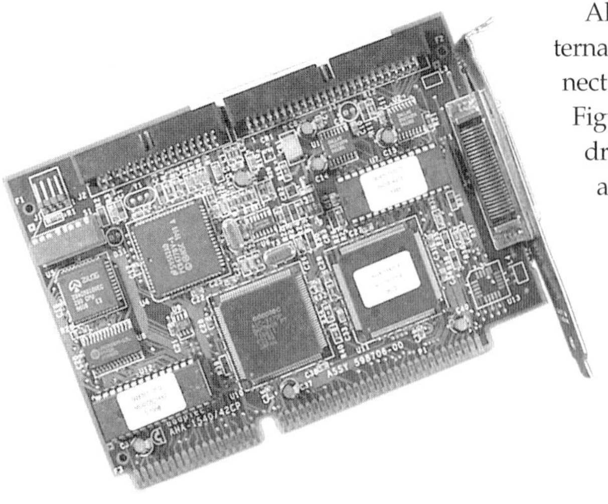

• **Figure 19.2** ISA SCSI host adapter

• **Figure 19.3** Internal SCSI CD-ROM

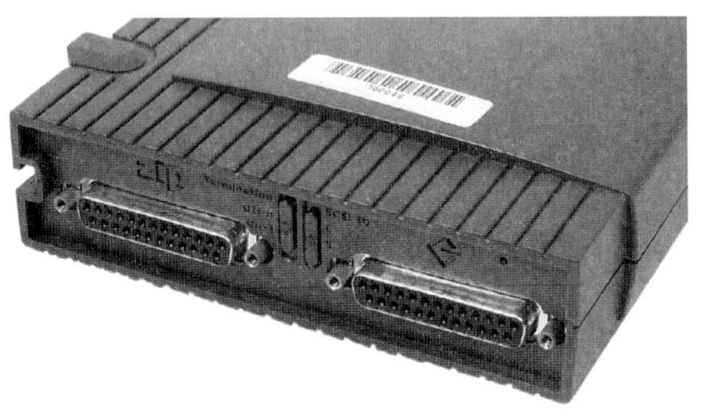

• **Figure 19.4** Back of external SCSI device

• **Figure 19.5** Typical 68-pin ribbon cable

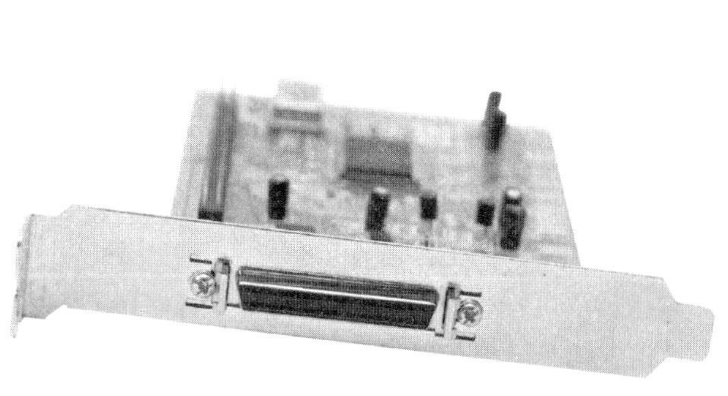

• Figure 19.6 50-pin HD port on SCSI host adapter

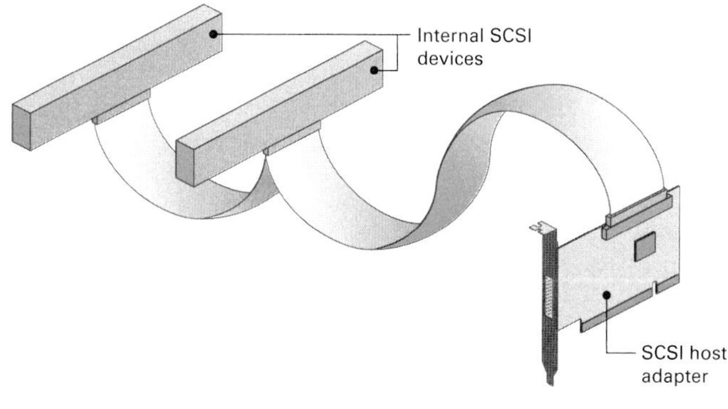

• Figure 19.7 Internal SCSI chain with two devices

• Figure 19.8 SCSI chain with two external devices

and a second for another SCSI device to plug into. The process of connecting device directly to device is called **daisy-chaining**.

Figure 19.8 shows a SCSI chain with two external devices. You can daisy-chain up to 15 devices to one host adapter in a typical Wide SCSI-2 setup, assuming you don't have any internal devices. SCSI chains can be internal, external, or both (see Figure 19.9). The maximum number of devices you can have on a Wide SCSI-2 chain, including the host adapter, is 16.

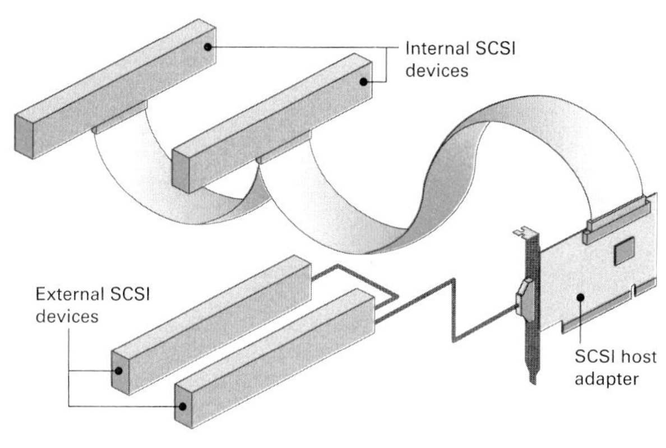

• Figure 19.9 Internal and external devices on one SCSI chain

SCSI IDs

If you're going to connect a number of devices on the same SCSI chain, you must provide some way for the host adapter to tell one device from another. To differentiate devices, SCSI uses a unique identifier called the **SCSI ID**. The SCSI ID number can range from 0 to 15. SCSI IDs are similar to many other PC hardware settings in that a SCSI device can theoretically have any SCSI ID, as long as that ID is not already taken by another device connected to the same host adapter.

Some conventions should be followed when setting SCSI IDs. Typically, most people set the host adapter to 7 or 15, but you can change this setting. Note that there is no order for the use of SCSI IDs. It does not matter which device gets which number and you can skip numbers. Restrictions on IDs only apply within a single chain. Two devices can have the same ID, in other words, as long as they are on different chains (Figure 19.10).

Every SCSI device has some method of setting its SCSI ID. The trick is to figure out how as you're holding the device in your hand. A SCSI device may use jumpers, dip switches, or even tiny dials; every new SCSI device is a new adventure as you try to determine how to set its SCSI ID.

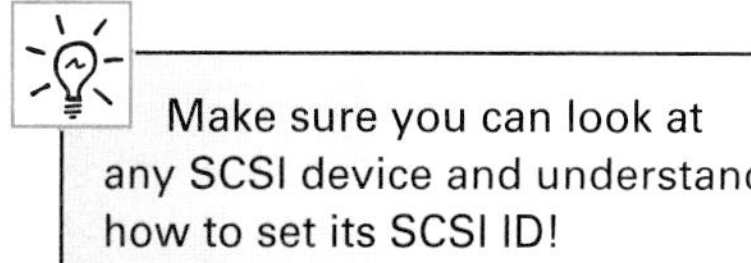

Make sure you can look at any SCSI device and understand how to set its SCSI ID!

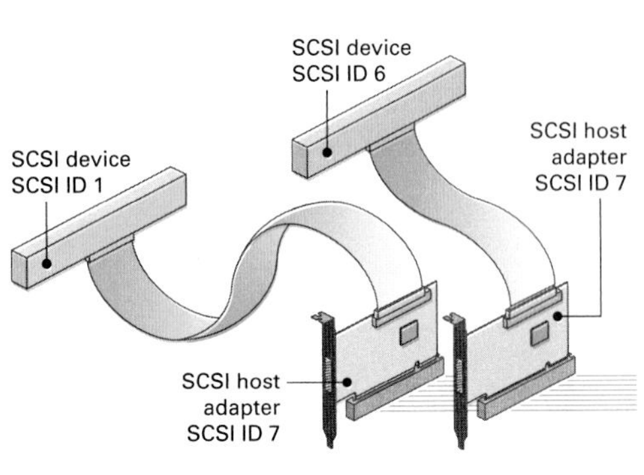

• **Figure 19.10** IDs don't conflict between separate SCSI chains.

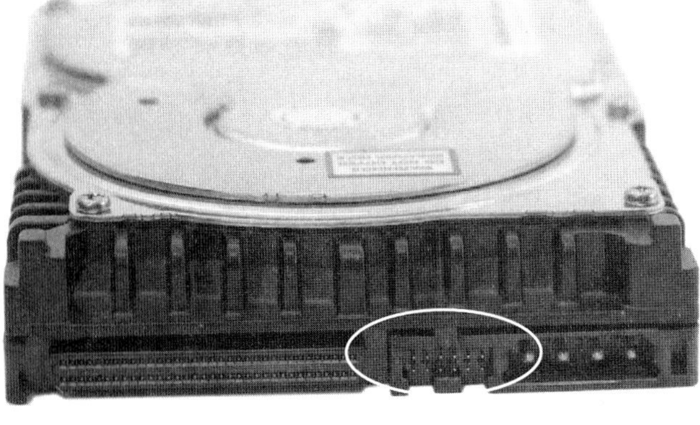

• **Figure 19.11** SCSI hard drive jumpers

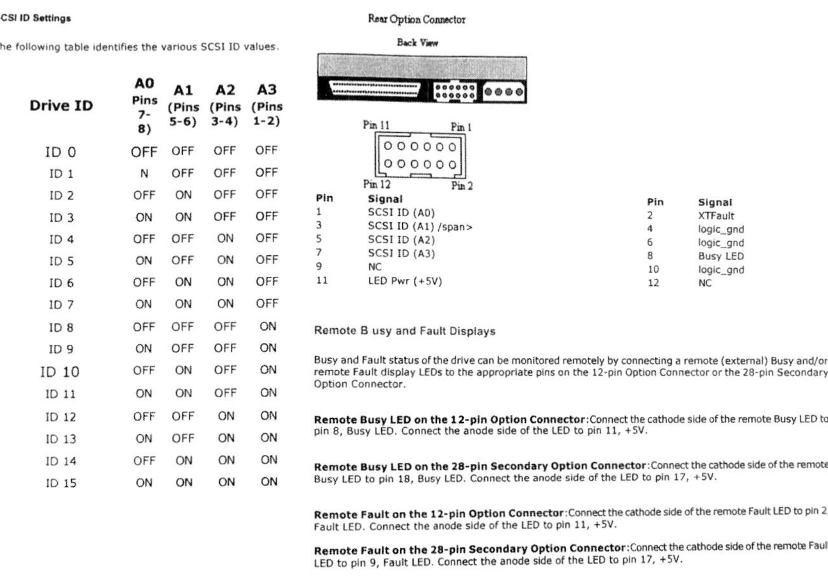

SCSI ID Settings

The following table identifies the various SCSI ID values.

Drive ID	A0 Pins 7-8)	A1 (Pins 5-6)	A2 (Pins 3-4)	A3 (Pins 1-2)
ID 0	OFF	OFF	OFF	OFF
ID 1	N	OFF	OFF	OFF
ID 2	OFF	ON	OFF	OFF
ID 3	ON	ON	OFF	OFF
ID 4	OFF	OFF	ON	OFF
ID 5	ON	OFF	ON	OFF
ID 6	OFF	ON	ON	OFF
ID 7	ON	ON	ON	OFF
ID 8	OFF	OFF	OFF	ON
ID 9	ON	OFF	OFF	ON
ID 10	OFF	ON	OFF	ON
ID 11	ON	ON	OFF	ON
ID 12	OFF	OFF	ON	ON
ID 13	ON	OFF	ON	ON
ID 14	OFF	ON	ON	ON
ID 15	ON	ON	ON	ON

Rear Option Connector

Back View

Pin 11 Pin 1

Pin 12 Pin 2

Pin	Signal
1	SCSI ID (A0)
3	SCSI ID (A1) /span>
5	SCSI ID (A2)
7	SCSI ID (A3)
9	NC
11	LED Pwr (+5V)

Pin	Signal
2	XTFault
4	logic_gnd
6	logic_gnd
8	Busy LED
10	logic_gnd
12	NC

Remote B usy and Fault Displays

Busy and Fault status of the drive can be monitored remotely by connecting a remote (external) Busy and/or remote Fault display LEDs to the appropriate pins on the 12-pin Option Connector or the 28-pin Secondary Option Connector.

Remote Busy LED on the 12-pin Option Connector:Connect the cathode side of the remote Busy LED to pin 8, Busy LED. Connect the anode side of the LED to pin 11, +5V.

Remote Busy LED on the 28-pin Secondary Option Connector:Connect the cathode side of the remote Busy LED to pin 18, Busy LED. Connect the anode side of the LED to pin 17, +5V.

Remote Fault on the 12-pin Option Connector:Connect the cathode side of the remote Fault LED to pin 2, Fault LED. Connect the anode side of the LED to pin 11, +5V.

Remote Fault on the 28-pin Secondary Option Connector:Connect the cathode side of the remote Fault LED to pin 9, Fault LED. Connect the anode side of the LED to pin 17, +5V.

• **Figure 19.12** SCSI hard drive documentation

Most internal SCSI devices use four jumpers to set the SCSI ID. Unfortunately, these jumpers work in different ways depending on who made the device, and—lucky you!—you get to figure out the method in each case. Figure 19.11 shows typical SCSI hard drive ID jumper pins. To determine how to set jumpers, check the documentation that came with the device or get the documentation from the manufacturer (Figure 19.12). In many cases, a device will have a label on one side that clearly shows which jumpers to short for various SCSI IDs.

All SCSI drives use simple binary to set the ID. The jumper in Figure 19.12 labeled A0 has a *value* of 1; the jumper labeled A1 has a *value* of 2; the jumper labeled A2 has a *value* of 4, and the jumper labeled A3 has a value of 8. To set SCSI ID 1, you would put a shunt over jumper A0. To get ID 3, you would jumper A0 and A1. To get ID 12, you would put shunts over jumpers A2 and A3. Add the value of each jumper and this will make sense (4 + 8 = 12).

Other devices use more or less obvious jumper labeling, so don't get tripped up if a drive has three jumpers labeled 0, 1, 2, 3; 1, 2, 3, 4; 1, 2, 4, 8; or A, B, C, D. In all jumper instances when setting SCSI IDs, use the *value* of the jumpers in binary: the first jumper has a value of 1, the second has a value of 2, the third has a value of 4, and the fourth has a value of 8.

Cross Check

Jumpering Drives

You've had experience with jumpering drives to set them up properly. It's time to check your memory and compare IDE to SCSI. Refer to Chapter 10, "Hard Drive Technologies," and answer these questions. Why do you need to jumper IDE hard drives? What jumper settings do you get on most drives? How does the jumpering process differ between IDE and SCSI?

If you want a SCSI drive to be C: (which is required if you want to boot Windows 9*x*/Me off the drive), you must set that drive to the ID specified by the host adapter as the "bootable" SCSI ID. Most manufacturers of host adapters use SCSI ID 0 as the default for bootable drives, but you can readily change that ID. Read the host adapter information or guess; you will not break anything if you are wrong. You also should change your CMOS set-

set only to SCSI ID 5 or 6. Work around it.

Try This!

Setting SCSI IDs

If you have a SCSI hard disk drive lying around, grab it and try to set it to the following SCSI IDs:

1. 4
2. 9
3. 14

If you get hung up, just remember that the jumpers represent the binary values of 1, 2, 4, and 8.

• **Figure 19.13** Changing ID on external device

Termination

Whenever you send a signal down a wire, some of that signal reflects back up the wire, creating an echo and causing electronic chaos. SCSI chains use termination to prevent this problem. **Termination** simply means putting something on the ends of the wire to prevent this echo. Terminators are usually pull-down resistors and can manifest themselves in many different ways. Most of the devices within a PC have the appropriate termination built in. On other devices, including SCSI chains and some network cables, you have to set termination during installation.

The rule with SCSI is that you *must* terminate *only* the ends of the SCSI chain. You have to terminate the ends of the cable, which usually means that you need to terminate the two devices at the ends of the cable. Do *not* terminate devices that are not on the ends of the cable. Figure 19.15 shows some examples of where to terminate SCSI devices.

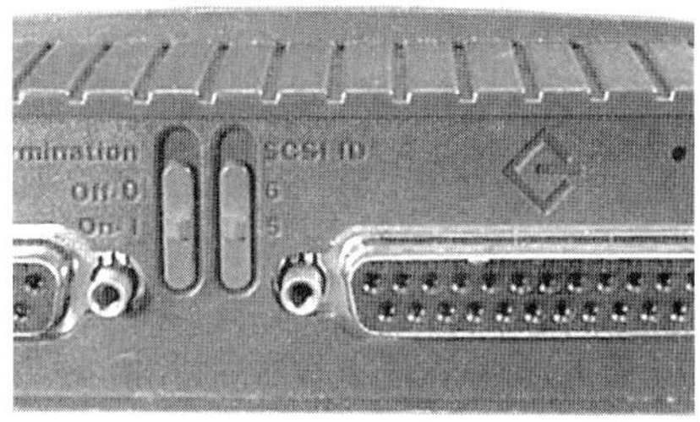

• **Figure 19.14** SCSI Zip drive

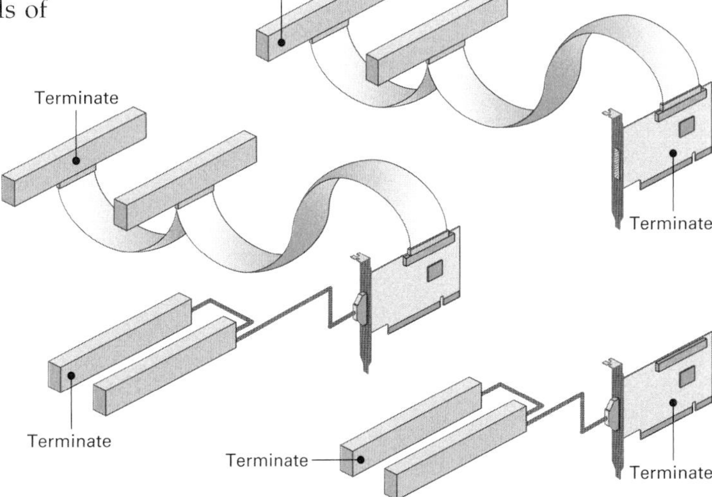

• **Figure 19.15** Location of the terminated devices

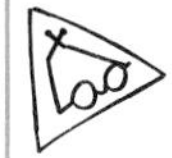

Tech Tip

Logical Unit Numbers

SCSI supports more than one device per ID if you use Logical Unit Numbers (LUNs) to provide a unique identifier for up to seven sub-units per ID number. These are used primarily in hard drive arrays, which create one large logical drive out of several smaller physical drives. LUNs are in the realm of network servers running NetWare, Windows NT/2000, and UNIX that require highly specialized software. With the previous exceptions, you can safely ignore LUNs.

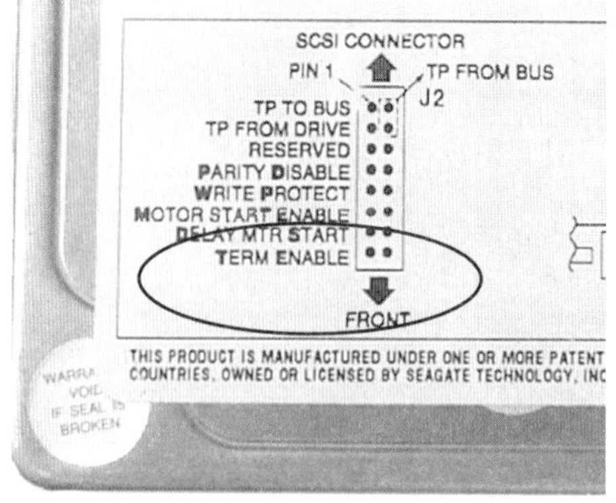

• **Figure 19.16** Setting termination

Because any SCSI device might be on the end of a chain, most manufacturers build SCSI devices that can self-terminate. Some devices will detect that they are on the end of the SCSI chain and will automatically terminate themselves. Most devices, however, require you to set a jumper or switch to enable termination.

The termination can be set in a number of different ways. Figure 19.16 shows a hard drive that is terminated with a jumper setting. The hard drive in Figure 19.17 has terminating resistors inserted. You must remove them to put the drive anywhere but on the end of the SCSI chain. Some host adapters have termination set through software. Figure 19.18 shows a typical host adapter configuration program.

• **Figure 19.17** Hard drive with removable terminating resistors

The ancient hard drive in Figure 19.19 is not capable of terminating itself. It needs a separate terminator piece. You can set it up properly by connecting the drive to a connector in the middle of the cable and then adding a terminating resistor to the end of the cable.

Be careful when you are terminating, because improper termination can cause damage to SCSI hard drives! Unlike setting SCSI IDs, termination can be a little tricky. But before we discuss the various types of termination options, you must understand the many flavors of SCSI.

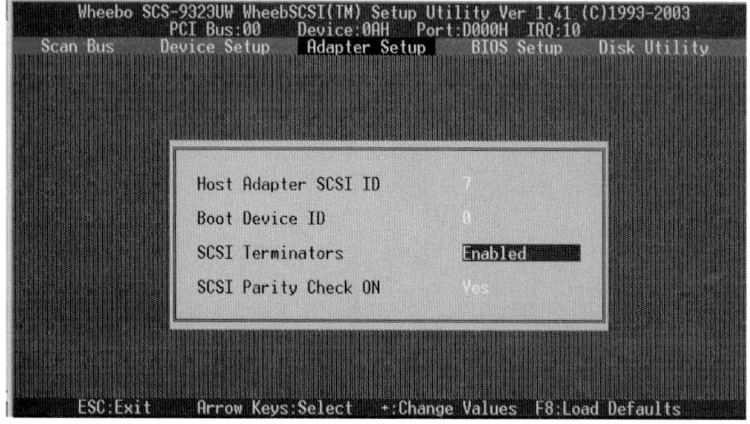

• **Figure 19.18** Software termination setting

SCSI Flavors

Any technology that survives more than 20 years must constantly improve or risk being replaced by newer technologies. SCSI has avoided extinction by evolving dramatically since its inception in 1979. SCSI was invented by a company called Shugart Associates, as mentioned earlier, but was given over to the IEEE in the early 1980s. Before that time, there was no single standard of SCSI, so devices made by various manufacturers were rarely, if ever, compatible with one another. This incompatibility came to an end with the first official standard for SCSI, called SCSI-1.

SCSI-1

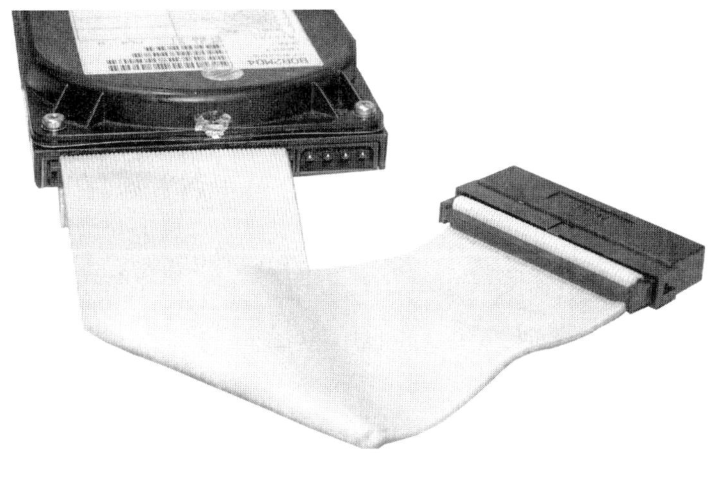

The **SCSI-1** standard defined an 8-bit, 5-MHz bus capable of supporting up to eight SCSI devices, but it was very fuzzy in describing many aspects of SCSI. As a result, many manufacturers of SCSI devices had different opinions as to how to implement those standards. So, SCSI-1 was really more of an opinion than a standard. Figure 19.20 shows an early SCSI-1 adapter.

In 1986, SCSI began to appear on IBM-compatible PC machines, and everyone seemed to have a proprietary SCSI device. The key word here is "proprietary" (meaning that *only* the SCSI device had its own command set, and no two command sets were the same. Trying to get one vendor's SCSI hard drive to work with another vendor's SCSI adapter card was often impossible.

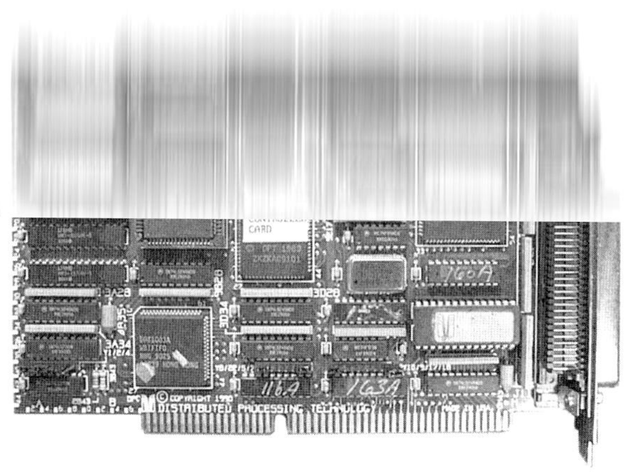

• **Figure 19.20** Early SCSI-1 adapter

SCSI-1 devices transferred data only through an 8-bit parallel path and supported up to seven devices on the chain (eight if you include the host adapter). For most PCs using SCSI-1 devices, the 8-bit pathway was not much of a bottleneck. Although the devices themselves were not capable of high-speed data transfers, neither were the 80286-based machines of the time. SCSI-1 devices seemed fast in comparison. Plus, the only common hard drive interface competition was the ST-506 controller, and 8-bit SCSI was far faster!

SCSI-2

The **SCSI-2** standard, finalized in 1990 but not officially adopted until 1994, was the first SCSI standard to address every aspect of SCSI in detail. Up until this time, the chances of getting two SCSI devices from different manufacturers to work together was challenging and often impossible; this was due not to physical problems, but to the way devices communicated. The SCSI-2 standard solved this problem by defining very carefully exactly what a device could or could not "say" on the SCSI chain.

One of the more important parts of the SCSI-2 standard was the definition of 18 commands that had to be supported by any device labeled *SCSI-2 compliant*. This set of commands, called the **common command set** (CCS), made hooking up devices from various manufacturers less of a nightmare. The CCS also introduced commands to address devices other than hard drives, including CD-ROM drives, tape drives, and scanners. Part of the

> Even though the SCSI-2 standard wasn't adopted until 1994, SCSI manufacturers were already using the entire SCSI-2 standard by 1991. Official SCSI standards always lag far behind the actual adoption of the technologies.

CCS included a new feature called *command queuing* that enabled a SCSI device to store multiple incoming commands.

SCSI-2 also defined the types of connectors to be used. Before SCSI-2, no true standard for SCSI connectors existed, although a few types became *de facto* standards. The new SCSI-2 connectors ensured that any two SCSI-2 compliant devices could be physically connected. SCSI-2 also more closely defined terminations.

The one area that creates the most confusion with SCSI-2 is the width of the data bus and the speeds. SCSI-2 defined two optional 16-bit and 32-bit buses called *Wide SCSI*, and a new, optional 10-MHz speed called *Fast SCSI*. SCSI-2 devices could be 8-bit (narrow), 16-bit (wide), or 32-bit (also called wide), or they could be 5 MHz (slow, the standard) or 10 MHz (fast). This means six "subflavors" of SCSI-2 are available (we'll add SCSI-1 for comparison). See Table 19.1.

Even though SCSI-2 defined a 32-bit SCSI bus, it was almost completely ignored by the industry due to its high cost and a lack of demand. In reality, Wide SCSI means 16-bit wide.

Fast SCSI-2 transfers data in fast synchronous mode, meaning the SCSI device being talked to (the target) does not have to acknowledge (ack) every individual request (req) for data from the host adapter (initiator). This allows for a doubling of transfer speed, from approximately 5 to 10 MBps. However, experience has shown that external Fast SCSI devices will rarely provide "fast" performance unless the cable provides proper shielding and electrical impedance, or load. Cables that do provide proper shielding and load are generally more expensive but are required to achieve true "fast" performance.

SE, HVD, and LVD SCSI

SCSI-1 devices used one wire for each bit of information, which meant that only eight wires on the data cable carried the data. This is called a **single-ended (SE)** system. The individual data wires were measured or referenced against the common ground provided by the metal chassis and in turn by the power supply of the system. Noise is usually spread through either the electrical power cables or the data cable and is called *common-mode noise*. An SE SCSI device is vulnerable to common-mode noise because it has no way of telling the difference between valid data and noise. When noise invades the data stream, the devices must resend the data. The amount of noise generated grows dramatically over the length of a SCSI cable, limiting the total length of an SE SCSI chain only to about six meters, depending on the type of SCSI.

Table 19.1 Standard SCSI vs. Fast SCSI

SCSI Type/Bit Width	5 MHz (Standard)	10 MHz (Fast)
SCSI-1: 8-bit	5 MBps	N/A
SCSI-2: 8-bit	5 MBps	10 MBps
SCSI-2: 16-bit (wide)	10 MBps	20 MBps
SCSI-2: 32-bit (wide)	20 MBps	40 MBps

To achieve much longer SCSI chains, SCSI-2 offered an optional solution with **High Voltage Differential (HVD)** SCSI (or what used to be called simply *differential SCSI*). HVD devices employ two wires per bit of data: one wire for data and one for the inverse of this data. The inverse signal takes the place of the ground wire in the SE cable. By taking the difference of the two signals, the device can reject the common-mode noise in the data stream. This allows for much longer SCSI chains—up to 25 meters.

No obvious difference exists between SE and HVD SCSI devices. The connectors and cabling seem to be identical. This is a bit of a problem, because under no circumstances should you try to connect SE and HVD devices on the same SCSI chain. At the very least, you will probably fry the SE device; if the HVD device lacks a security circuit to detect your mistake, you will probably smoke it as well.

Don't panic! Although HVD SCSI devices exist, they are rare and usu-

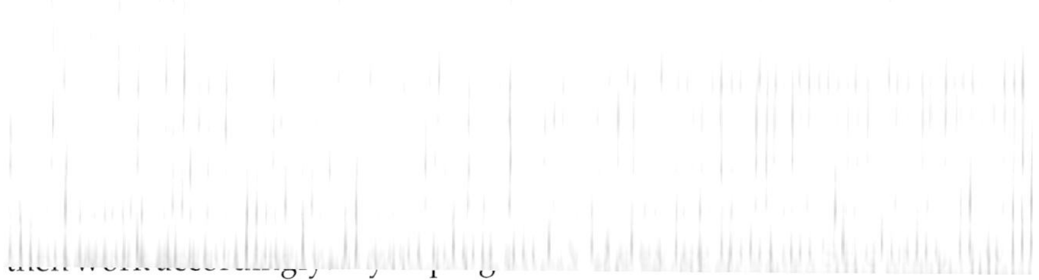

act as an SE device. If you plug an LVD device into LVD, it will run as LVD. LVD SCSI chains can be up to 12 meters in length. The safety, ease of use, and low cost of LVD has made it quite popular in higher-end PCs and servers.

SCSI-3

SCSI technology did not stand still with the adoption of SCSI-2. Manufacturers have developed significant improvements in SCSI-2, particularly in increased speeds and easier configuration. The T-10 SCSI committee collected these improvements and created a working set of standards collectively called **SCSI-3**. SCSI-3 devices have many names and technologies, such as Ultra2 or Wide Ultra. Let's take a minute to look at these.

Most manufacturers use the terms Ultra, Ultra2, and Ultra3 to define high-speed SCSI-3 buses—20, 40, and 80 MHz, respectively. You might still run into the older Adaptec-specific terms for the same buses—Fast-20, Fast-40, and Fast-80. The three buses also come in both narrow and wide varieties. Look at the differences in data transfer rates among the buses, listed in Table 19.2.

The SCSI-3 standard also includes optional hot swap capabilities. To *hot swap* means to be able to unplug a drive from the SCSI chain without

Table 19.2 Narrow SCSI-3 vs. Wide SCSI-3

SCSI Type	Bus Speed	8-Bit (Narrow)	16-Bit (Wide)
Ultra SCSI (Fast-20)	20 MHz	20 MBps	40 MBps
Ultra2 SCSI (Fast-40)	40 MHz	40 MBps	80 MBps
Ultra3 SCSI (Fast-80)	80 MHz	80 MBps	160 MBps

Cross Check

Hot Swapping Technologies

You've seen at least three hot swapping interfaces thus far in the book—USB, FireWire, and Serial ATA. Refer to Chapters 2 and 10 and check your knowledge. What advantages do you see with one technology over the other? Can you compare the two external buses with the internal SATA connections? What about SATA versus hot swapping SCSI? What gives you the better data transfer rate? Why would you or would you not pick SATA over SCSI-3?

rebooting or resetting the chain. Hot swapping is extremely helpful in laptops and servers, and has been popular for high-end SCSI drives for a long time.

With the development of SCSI-3 standards and devices, you might guess that older SCSI-2 devices would go away, but this has not been the case. Manufacturers continue to produce SCSI-2 devices and controllers and put them into the marketplace right alongside the higher end SCSI-3 devices and controllers. Even worse, they still make both SE and LVD flavors! The SCSI picture as far as techs are concerned is therefore somewhat complex. Table 19.3 shows the current SCSI picture, including the latest and greatest Ultra320 standard and the cabling length considerations for the many flavors.

Last Notes on Termination

Termination can be one of four flavors, depending on the type of SCSI chain: passive, active, forced perfect, and LVD termination.

Table 19.3 Current Parallel SCSI Picture (Courtesy of the SCSI Trade Association—//www.scsita.org)

			Maximum Bus Lengths, Meters[1]			
SCSI Trade Association Terms	**Bus Speed (MBps)**	**Bus Width (bits)**	**SE**	**LVD[3]**	**HVD[5]**	**Maximum Device Support**
SCSI-1[2]	5	8	6	[3]	25	8
Fast SCSI[2]	10	8	3	[3]	25	8
Fast Wide SCSI	20	16	3	[3]	25	16
Ultra SCSI[2]	20	8	1.5	[3]	25	8
Ultra SCSI[2]	20	8	3	–	–	4
Wide Ultra SCSI	40	16	–	[3]	25	16
Wide Ultra SCSI	40	16	1.5	–	–	8
Wide Ultra SCSI	40	16	3	–	–	4
Ultra2 SCSI[2,4]	40	8	[4]	12	25	8
Wide Ultra2 SCSI[4]	80	16	[4]	12	25	16
Ultra3 SCSI or Ultra160[6]	160	16	[4]	12	5	16
Ultra320[6]	320	16	[4]	12	5	16

[1] The listed maximum bus lengths may be exceeded in Point-to-Point and engineered applications.
[2] Use of the word "narrow" preceding SCSI, Ultra SCSI, or Ultra2 SCSI is optional.
[3] LVD was not defined in the original SCSI standards for this speed. If all devices on the bus support LVD, 12-meter operation is possible at this speed. However, if any device on the bus is single-ended only, the entire bus switches to single-ended mode and the distances in the single-ended column apply.
[4] Single-ended is not defined for speeds beyond Ultra.
[5] HVD (Differential) is not defined for speeds beyond Ultra2.
[6] After Ultra2 all new speeds are wide only.

Passive termination is a holdover from the dinosaur days of the ST-506. The termination is nothing more than a network of resistors, which are usually small, black, and shiny, resembling skinny black caterpillars. This type of termination is typically found only on plain old, 8-bit SCSI devices.

For the quicker fast/wide SCSI, you have to maintain a tighter tolerance on the voltage and impedance of the SCSI chain. To do this, you must use **active termination**, which uses voltage regulators instead of resistors.

Forced perfect termination (FPT) also maintains the correct voltage level on the bus, but it does so to a finer tolerance by using *diodes*. These diodes function like a resistor in the passive termination, with one exception: a diode has a lower resistance in one direction, or orientation, than it does in the other. This is called *polarity*. The higher resistance in one direction helps to block current flow backward along the data cable much better than a plain resistor.

In such a SCSI bus-mastering situation, the host adapter remains in the circuit only long enough to arbitrate the connection between the hard drive and the tape drive. Once establishing the data transfer, the host adapter drops off and lets the hard drive and tape unit communicate directly with each other while the backup runs. Once the backup is finished, or if the user interrupts the operation, the drives re-establish their presence on the SCSI chain. The great beauty of this lies in the lack of CPU and expansion bus usage. Once the connection is made, the two devices are, for all intents and purposes, no longer on the PC and not consuming any system resources.

SCSI Cables and Connectors

Although no official SCSI-1, SCSI-2, or Ultra SCSI cables or connectors exist, manufacturers generally follow similar guidelines today. Cable is based on whether the device is internal or external, what types of connectors are available, and the type of SCSI you use.

Internal Connectors

SCSI type A ribbon cables have 50 wires and are used for 8-bit data transfers in both the SCSI-1 and SCSI-2 standards. They are also used for 8-bit Fast SCSI-2 (see Figure 19.21).

Try This!

Identifying the Various Flavors of SCSI

Jump in the car or train or bike and take a trip down to your local computer superstore. If this isn't an option, surf the Web over to your favorite online hardware retailer. You're going hunting for SCSI devices!

1. Take a look around and determine how many SCSI hard disk drives are available for purchase. How does this number compare to the number of EIDE hard disk drives that are available?
2. Head over to the accessories area of the store and check out the SCSI cables and connectors. Try holding a SCSI ribbon cable next to a IDE ribbon cable. Can you see the differences?
3. See if the store has any SCSI devices other than hard disk drives—CD-ROMs, Zip drives, external hard disk drive enclosures. How do the prices on those items compare to their IDE counterparts (for internal drives) or to their USB/FireWire counterparts (for external drives)?

• **Figure 19.21** SCSI "A" cable

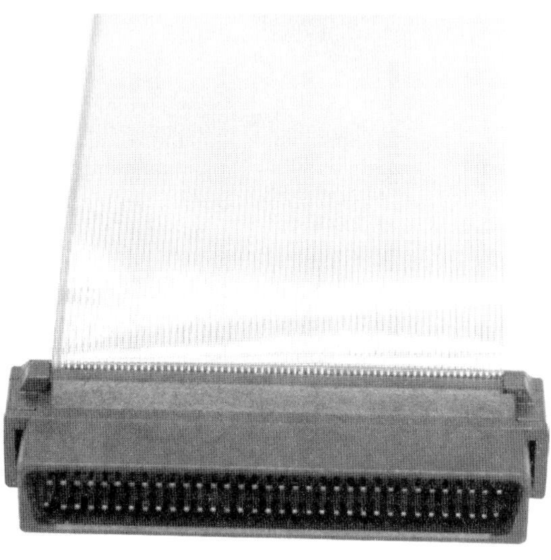

• **Figure 19.22** SCSI "P" cable

In the earliest days of SCSI-2, 16-bit data transfers required another cable: type B. It had 68 wires and was used in parallel with the 50-wire A cable. Because the industry was so underwhelmed at the dual-cable concept, the B cable quietly and quickly disappeared, to be replaced by the P cable. Like its predecessor, this cable also had 68 wires; unlike the B cable, the P cable can be used alone (see Figure 19.22).

Some of the higher-end SCSI-3 host adapters and drives use an 80-pin connector called an SCA 80. The 80-wire cables are called *D type* cables. The extra wires enable you to hot swap the drives, but that's about it. The drives will work fine with 68-pin cables and an adapter, or with their own 80-pin cable.

Types of External Connectors

All external connectors are female on the devices. The types of external connectors are as follows:

- 50-pin Centronics, an obsolete SCSI-1 connector
- 50-pin HD DB, used for SCSI-2
- 68-pin HD DB, used for wide SCSI-2 and SCSI-3
- 25-pin standard D-type (looks identical to parallel), SCSI-2, most commonly used on Macintoshes and Zip drives

SCSI Performance

Which can move more cars more quickly—a ten-lane freeway or a four-lane city street? That sums up the effect of the expansion bus on SCSI performance. SCSI is a bus-mastering device; that is, it takes control of the expansion bus to transfer data from one device into memory, or from one device to another device not on the SCSI host adapter. This is marvelous because it frees up the CPU to do more important things.

Unfortunately, if you plug a SCSI host adapter into an ISA slot, the best transfer speed you can obtain is approximately 5 MBps. Such a transfer rate cannot keep up with modern drives, although slower devices, such as Zip drives or tape backup units, should do fine.

If you really want to see things fly, you need a PCI SCSI host adapter. These buses can support transfers up to 132 MBps, the current sustained transfer rates for the fastest hard drives.

Compatibility Among Flavors of SCSI

Most flavors of SCSI devices can connect without a problem to any flavor of SCSI controller, as long as you provide the proper cabling for either end. You can plug a 50-pin SCSI-2 hard drive and a 68-pin SCSI-3 hard drive into a 68-pin SCSI-3 controller (as long as you have a cable with a 50-pin connector on one end and a 68-pin connector on the other for the SCSI-2 drive). Each device communicates at the maximum speed supported by that device. Mixing LVD and SE devices, however, provides the biggest exception to this rule. If you add one SE device to an LVD chain, the whole chain slows down to accommodate the slower device.

Compatibility with IDE

Contrary to a persistent tech myth, you *can* mix IDE and SCSI hard drives and devices in a single system and the system will work fine. If you have an IDE drive present on your system, it will most probably be the boot drive. Unless the

Try This!

Testing the Performance of SCSI

If you've got a pair of SCSI hard drives and a SCSI host adapter lying around, go ahead and install them in your PC.

1. Create a large, multi-megabyte file (somewhere around 50 MB). Try moving this file back and forth between the two SCSI hard drives. Keep an eye on the level of CPU usage while you do this task—use the Task Manager in Windows XP to monitor the levels.
2. Now, try moving the same file back and forth between two IDE hard drives. What does the CPU usage level look like when you're using the IDE drives? Higher or lower? Note that you

drive letters after the IDE. Last, if the BIOS allows, you can let the SCSI drive(s) boot first. This last method is system-specific. Most motherboards enable you to swap SCSI and IDE, so the former drives get drive letters before the latter drives. If you want to make a SCSI drive the boot drive, you simply make a quick switch in CMOS. Some older motherboards had a "SCSI-first BIOS" that enabled the first SCSI drive to boot as C:, but they then assigned drive letters to all IDE drives before getting the rest of the SCSI drives. This could lead to some wacky drive-lettering issues. You might have to play around with a system to get the drive lettering the way you want it.

Troubleshooting SCSI

Some folks who are just starting to work with SCSI seem to think that these devices are somehow special just because they're SCSI devices. This is just plain wrong! If you install a SCSI hard drive, you will still need to partition and format it to use it. If you have a SCSI CD-ROM drive, it will automatically appear in My Computer just as an ATAPI CD-ROM drive appears. If you have a SCSI tape backup device, it will appear in the Windows Backup program just like any other tape drive.

SCSI-specific problems almost always occur at installation. After the device is installed correctly, then you should look at device-specific issues. A SCSI hard drive that worked just fine for three months but now suddenly has bad clusters indicates a hard drive issue, not a SCSI issue *per se*. You'd run ScanDisk or Check Disk rather than any SCSI-specific utility. Let's look at SCSI troubleshooting issues.

Power and Connectivity

In any PC repair scenario, you should confirm connectivity and power before going any further. Nothing will work if the devices do not have power and if they cannot access the external data bus and address bus. Fortunately, most SCSI host adapters provide an excellent utility for determining whether or not devices are properly powered and connected: SCSI scan. As the host adapter initializes (provided that the host adapter's BIOS is active), a list of all the devices detected by the host adapter will be displayed on the screen. If one or more of your devices fails to appear, power or connectivity are the most likely problems. If the devices are not properly hooked up, they will not respond to the "identify yourself" commands sent out by the host adapter.

Power

What kinds of power problems could prevent a device from showing up? It's usually nothing more exotic than forgetting to plug it in. Make sure that both internal and external devices have power. Most SCSI devices, especially external ones, require power to provide termination, and all of them require power for operation.

Connectivity

Make sure that the devices are properly installed. Is the termination set properly (one terminator at each end of the chain and none in between)? Does each device have its own unique SCSI ID? Are the cables seated correctly and firmly? You'll probably need documentation to double-check settings for termination and SCSI IDs.

Boot Firmware

If you do not see a SCSI scan during the boot process before you see "Starting Windows 9x" or "Starting Windows XP," check to make sure that the ROM BIOS on the host adapter has not been disabled. In addition, other CMOS and SCSI ROM BIOS settings can cause problems. Is the ROM chip on the SCSI host adapter enabled or disabled? What IRQ, DMA, and I/O address is the card using? If you see an "HDD controller failure" or "HDD failure" message, is the CMOS set up to look for an IDE drive that is not present in the system?

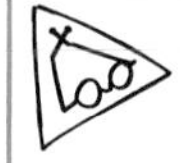

Tech Tip

Troubleshooting SCSI and IDE

If you're having a problem with your newly installed SCSI device, the first things you should check are connectivity and power. Follow the same procedure you would use if you were dealing with an IDE device. Despite the differences in cabling, connectors, and communication, SCSI devices are identical to IDE devices when it comes to troubleshooting!

Memory Chips

Problems with memory chips will usually cause problems with all the devices in a PC, not just the SCSI devices. Diagnose problems carefully. Does the symptom, whatever it happens to be, crop up only when using SCSI devices, or does it happen consistently with every device?

Storage

SCSI hard drives can have the same types of problems as any other hard drive. The partitions and file system—FAT or NTFS—are no different than with IDE drives. In fact, except for the SCSI interface itself, IDE and SCSI drives are virtually identical. For the most part, the same repair and maintenance techniques apply. At a bare minimum, use ScanDisk (Windows 9x/Me) or Check Disk (Windows NT/2000/XP) and Defrag on a regular basis. For any error that ends in "Abort, retry, fail" or "Abort, retry, fail, ignore," use a program such as Norton's Disk Doctor or its equivalent. Use the Sys command and the Fdisk /mbr command for boot problems. Treat SCSI hard drive errors the same way you treat IDE hard drive errors.

I/O

Certain legacy SCSI host adapters may have resource conflicts with other legacy cards and even a few *Plug and Play* (PnP) cards, although Windows 9*x*/Me and Windows 2000/XP do a good job of avoiding such problems. [illegible]

This problem is not limited to legacy host adapters! Some PnP SCSI host adapters also store information on an onboard chip. My brand new, ultra wide SCSI host adapter, for example, needs its termination set via its onboard settings. A recent power surge erased all my onboard data, and I had to rerun the setup just to reset the termination.

Device Drivers

If you have SCSI devices other than hard drives, they will require a device driver. Remember that some device drivers do not work well together, especially if you have a mix of legacy and PnP cards in a system. How do you determine whether you have a conflict between two device drivers? Device Manager is the important first place to look, but you knew that!

Try loading only the device drivers for the SCSI devices. Does the symptom still occur? If not, another device driver is causing the problem. Use the F8 key to determine which one. Once you know which device drivers are incompatible, you have several options. Look in the manuals or readme files of both devices. Your problem might be a known one with a solution. Go to the manufacturer's web site and seek an updated driver.

If the device driver is an executable, try running it with the `/?` option, which will usually show you a variety of command-line switches (for example, `MOUSE.EXE /?`). Try a variety of switches and see if any of them solve the problem. If not, attempt to find an updated driver for one or both of the devices. If none of those solutions fix the problem, you might be forced to choose between the devices or go to a multiple-boot configuration.

■ Costs and Benefits of SCSI

Although new SCSI implementations are definitely down, you might be called upon in certain circumstances to justify purchasing a SCSI setup over a non-SCSI setup. The owner of a small company might want to add a server system to handle volume of traffic or a new database for inventory. Will you put SCSI drives or SATA drives in the machine? You need to be prepared to give a knowledgeable recommendation! Here's a quickie guide to the costs and benefits of SCSI. SCSI is great for the following:

- File servers
- Workstations (both graphical and audio)
- Multitasking systems
- Any system moving large amounts of data among peripheral devices
- Any system with a large number of peripherals
- Any system requiring fault tolerance (mostly file servers)

Because the initial cost of SCSI is higher and the devices themselves are also more expensive, you must answer some questions to determine the need for SCSI:

- Is this a graphics/CAD workstation?
- Is this a network file server?
- Is this a stand-alone machine frequently running multitasking applications?

If the answer to any of these questions is "yes," it will probably be worth the money to invest in SCSI for two reasons. First, a data-intensive application, such as CAD/CAM design software, will benefit by the increased data throughput available with SCSI devices, especially hard drives and scanners. Second, SCSI is a bus-mastering device. In a multitasking environment, this leaves the CPU free to handle more important things, such as updating an Excel spreadsheet.

SCSI vs. IDE

SCSI no longer has as large an advantage over IDE for typical systems as it once did. For many years, SCSI hard drives were the only large hard drives available. Now PATA drives are pushing into the sizes that once belonged exclusively to SCSI drives. Data throughput for PATA drives has increased to as fast as 133 MBps, and fresh out of the gate, SATA drives are at 150 MBps. Although SCSI-3 might support a transfer rate of 360 MBps or more, remember that except for the chipset on the disk controller card, IDE and SCSI hard drives are made the same. So the limitation in data transfer speeds comes from the hard drive assembly, not necessarily the data bus.

Although SCSI's advantages in some areas are not as pronounced as they once were, it still possesses a number of advantages that justify its higher cost. The bus-mastering capability makes SCSI ideal for data-intensive operations. In addition, for external devices that are not hard drives, SCSI remains the high-performance interface of choice. Finally, higher-end parallel SCSI supports up to 15 devices on a single controller, and serial SCSI standards support dramatically more. For servers that need huge data storage capacity, SCSI is the only way to go. For personal systems, in contrast, you can easily and inexpensively add an ATA/133 controller card and attach up to four more hard drives.

Beyond A+

If you want a peek at some of the upcoming SCSI standards or want to go deeper into issues of high-end SCSI, you can check out the web sites of the SCSI Trade Association (www.scsita.org) and the T-10 (SCSI standards um-

Serial-Attached SCSI

Serial-Attached SCSI (SAS) is the industry's response to Serial ATA. SAS was actually developed in cooperation with the SATA II working group to leverage the technological advancements that brought us SATA.

Like current IDE devices, SCSI devices communicate in parallel. SAS is, as you've probably guessed, a serial version of SCSI. Like SATA, SAS is a point-to-point interface that uses a reduced-size data cable and has reduced power consumption demands. SAS isn't expected to compete with either parallel SCSI or SATA, but rather it complements both of those technologies as an enterprise-level storage solution. For the time being, details about SAS speeds and other specifications are hard to come by, as the standard is still being finalized, but available data suggests that SAS will achieve throughput speeds of 1.5 GBps!

Chapter 19 Review

Chapter Summary

After reading this chapter and completing the exercises, you should understand the following about SCSI.

Create a Functional SCSI Chain

- Introduced more than 20 years ago for system-independent mass storage, Small Computer System Interface (SCSI) works like a "miniature network" inside your PC. The variety of SCSI devices includes hard drives, scanners, and tape backup units.
- A SCSI chain is a series of SCSI devices working together through a host adapter. Available in a number of expansion bus types, a SCSI host adapter card can have connections for both internal and external devices. SCSI also uses a number of connectors, but a 68-pin cable is the most common type for internal Wide SCSI devices. If you do not plug in the cable correctly (with pin 1 to pin 1), you can damage the SCSI device. External SCSI devices can have two connectors, with one external device daisy-chaining to the next to form a SCSI chain. From the host adapter, you can create internal or external chains or combine both kinds. For a Wide SCSI chain, you may attach up to 16 devices, counting the host adapter itself.
- Each SCSI device, including the host adapter, must have a unique SCSI ID number. Devices may be numbered 0 through 15 in no particular sequence. You can even skip numbers. Typically, devices have jumpers or switches that set the SCSI IDs. The host adapter may specify the ID for the bootable device.
- Each end of the SCSI chain must be terminated to prevent the signal from reflecting back up the wire. Do not terminate devices in the middle of the cable. This would include the host adapter if the SCSI chain contains both internal and external devices. Some devices can self-terminate while others require you to set a jumper or switch or software setting to enable termination. Improper termination can damage SCSI devices.

Describe the Different Flavors of SCSI

- Defined as an 8-bit, 5-MHz bus able to support up to eight SCSI devices, SCSI-1 suffered from device incompatibility since many vendors still included proprietary technology. This was a more severe problem if users tried to use devices from different vendors.
- The SCSI-2 standard includes a common command set (CCS) consisting of 18 commands that any SCSI-2 compliant device must support. This CCS included support for devices other than hard drives. SCSI-2 defined the types of connectors to be used. It also offered three data bus widths and speeds of either 5 MHz or 10 MHz for six "subflavors." Widths included 8-bit (narrow), 16-bit (wide) and 32-bit (wide). When using properly shielded cables, SCSI-2 achieved 10-MBps speed by transferring data in fast synchronous mode without the sending device having to wait for an acknowledgment (ack).
- Since they use only one wire to communicate a single bit of information, SCSI-1 devices are single-ended (SE). An SE SCSI device is vulnerable to common-mode noise that increases dramatically with longer SCSI cable lengths. To control common-mode noise, an SE SCSI chain should be no longer than 6 meters.
- To achieve chains up to 25 meters, SCSI-2 introduced High Voltage Differential (HVD) SCSI, which cut down on common-mode noise by using two wires per bit of data, one for data and one for the inverse of the data. While the devices, connectors, and cabling appear identical, you cannot connect both SE and HVD devices on the same SCSI chain without frying the SE devices and possibly destroying the HVD devices as well.
- An improved differential SCSI known as Low-Voltage Differential (LVD) uses less power than HVD and allows SE controllers and devices on the same chain. The LVD device senses the kind of cable, making it backward compatible with SE, but it will act as an SE device. Because of lower cost, safety, and chains up to 12 meters, LVD-SCSI became popular for servers and higher-end PCs.

- With speeds of 20 (called Ultra), 40 (Ultra2), and 80 MHz (Ultra3), the SCSI-3 bus may be either narrow or wide. The latest versions include the speed in MBps in their names. For example, Ultra320 transfers data at 320 MBps. Contrary to what one might expect, SCSI-3 did not make SCSI-2 devices obsolete.
- Not only can you choose the type of SCSI chain, you can also select four types of termination: passive, active, forced perfect, and LVD termination. The old 8-bit SCSI devices used passive termination, which was nothing more than resistors. Fast/wide SCSI requires active termination, which includes voltage regulators

more efficient performance with less waiting.

- Used with both SCSI-1 and SCSI-2, type A ribbon cable has 50 wires and performs 8-bit data transfers. A 68-pin type B ribbon cable was introduced with SCSI-2 and used briefly along with the type A cable before it was replaced with 68-pin type P cable. An 80-wire type D cable contains extra wires to allow hot-swapping capabilities for SCSI-3 drives.
- On the external side, the vast majority of SCSI devices use either a 50-pin HD DB (narrow SCSI-2) or 68-pin HD DB (Wide SCSI-2 and SCSI-3). Macintoshes and Zip drives may use a 25-pin standard D-type cable. All external device connectors are female.
- You can mix IDE and SCSI devices with no problems. IDE drives get drive letters before the SCSI drives by default, but you can switch this in a modern CMOS.

Troubleshoot Problems with SCSI Installations

- SCSI problems fall into broad categories, some of which overlap. First, make sure the devices have power and are properly connected to the SCSI chain. Fortunately, when the host adapter initializes, it displays a list of all SCSI devices it detects. Suspect a connectivity problem if the device is not listed. The solution may be as simple as plugging in the power. Other connectivity problems may involve improper termination. Terminate each end of the chain with no termination in between. Finally, make sure each device has a unique SCSI ID number and that all cables are correctly seated.
- The SCSI host adapter includes a ROM BIOS that initializes the card and scans the SCSI bus. Make sure that the ROM BIOS is not disabled. Be sure you

you find an incompatibility, check the manuals or Readme files for a solution, or go to the manufacturer's web site for an updated driver.

Describe the Benefits of Using SCSI

- Although SCSI is great for servers, high-end workstations, multitasking systems, systems with a large number of peripherals, or systems requiring fault tolerance, both the initial cost of SCSI and the price of SCSI devices are higher than EIDE. Examine how the computer will be used to determine whether the increased throughput and bus-mastering capabilities of SCSI are worth the cost.
- While SCSI once had a distinct advantage over IDE in terms of both in drive size and transfer speed, with the improvements to EIDE drives, these advantages are quickly disappearing. Other advantages, though not as pronounced as they once were, may still justify the higher cost of SCSI for certain situations. These advantages include bus mastering, external devices other than hard drives, and support for up to 15 devices on a single controller.

Key Terms

50-pin high density connector (710)
68-pin high density connector ()
68-pin ribbon cable (710)
active termination (719)
common command set (CCS) (715)
daisy-chaining (711)
forced perfect termination (FPT) (719)

High Voltage Differential (HVD) *(717)*
host adapter *(709)*
Logical Unit Numbers (LUNs) *(714)*
Low Voltage Differential (LVD) *(717)*
Serial-Attached SCSI *(725)*
SCSI chain *(709)*
SCSI ID *()*
SCSI-1 *()*
SCSI-2 *()*
SCSI-3 *(717)*
single-ended (SE) *(716)*
termination *(713)*

Key Term Quiz

Use the Key Terms list to complete the sentences that follow. Not all the terms will be used.

1. In addition to being limited to no more than 6 meters, __________ chains frequently had incompatible devices, especially if they were purchased from different vendors.
2. The most commonly used internal cable for Wide SCSI-2 is the _______________.
3. ___________ prevents the signal from reflecting back up the wire.
4. Mark needs to use a _______________ to connect his narrow SCSI-2 printer to his host adapter.
5. A __________ consists of the SCSI host adapter and all internal and/or external devices.
6. __________ uses diodes and polarity to block backward current flow more effectively than resistors.
7. Each SCSI device, including the host adapter, must have a unique __________.
8. The terms Ultra, Ultra2, and Ultra3, operating at 20, 40, and 80 MHz, respectively, are used to define high-speed ____________ buses.
9. ___________ describes the action of attaching one external SCSI device to another directly.
10. John should use a _______________ to connect his SCSI-3 scanner to his host adapter.

Multiple-Choice Quiz

1. The default SCSI ID for a bootable SCSI drive is __________.
   - **A.** 0
   - **B.** 2
   - **C.** 7
   - **D.** 15
2. All the following describe correctly terminated SCSI chains *except* _______________.
   - **A.** With both internal and external devices, terminate the host adapter, the last internal device, and the last external device.
   - **B.** With only internal devices, terminate the host adapter and the last internal device.
   - **C.** With only external devices, terminate the host adapter and the last external device.
   - **D.** With both internal and external devices, terminate the last internal device and the last external device.
3. If you attach the ribbon cable backward so that pin 1 on the cable does not align with pin 1 on the SCSI device, what is likely to be the result?
   - **A.** The hard drive LED stays on, but it does no harm.
   - **B.** The device will not work and will probably be destroyed.
   - **C.** The device will work, but only as an IDE device.
   - **D.** SCSI devices do not have to match pin 1 to pin 1; the device will work perfectly.
4. All the following statements are true about the SCSI-2 standard *except* __________.
   - **A.** It was designed to eliminate incompatibilities among devices from different vendors.
   - **B.** It includes a common command set that supports devices other than hard drives.
   - **C.** With its three data bus widths and two speeds, it comes in six "subflavors."
   - **D.** Fast SCSI is serial, whereas normal SCSI is parallel.

5. The maximum length of a SCSI-2 chain composed of HVD devices is __________ meters, while LVD chains are limited to __________ meters.

   A. 25, 12

   B. 12, 6

   C. 6, 3

   D. 3, 1.5

6. If you just installed a SCSI device and the host adapter does not list the device when it initializes, which of the following could be the problem?

   [illegible]

7. By using __________, [illegible] seven devices under a single SCSI ID.

   A. LVDs

   B. HVDs

   C. LUNs

   D. Daisy-chaining

8. All the following statements correctly identify SCSI cables *except* __________.

   A. Type P has 68 wires.

   B. Type B is a 40-wire cable that is rarely used.

   C. Type A has 50 wires and is used for 8-bit data transfers in both SCSI-1 and SCSI-2 standards.

   D. Type D has 80 wires and allows you to hot swap the drives.

9. Which of the following statements is true about mixing IDE and SCSI devices on the same computer?

   A. The IDE drives will get a drive letter before the SCSI drives unless you configure the BIOS to boot to SCSI before IDE.

   B. The SCSI devices will be assigned drive letters before the IDE drives.

   C. The primary master SCSI device will be assigned drive C: while the secondary master IDE drive will become drive D:.

   D. You can't mix IDE and SCSI devices on the same computer.

10. All the following are advantages of using SCSI rather than EIDE devices *except* __________.

   A. While EIDE devices are limited to no more than four, you can have seven or more SCSI devices.

   B. SCSI devices provide faster data throughput than EIDE devices.

   C. SCSI devices are less expensive than EIDE devices.

   D. You can use both internal and external devices with SCSI, while EIDE supports only [illegible]

[illegible]

   D. USB

12. Which of the following statements is true?

   A. Various flavors of SCSI devices attached to the same host adapter communicate at the speed of the host adapter.

   B. Various flavors of SCSI devices attached to the same host adapter communicate at the maximum speed supported by each device.

   C. If your SCSI chain mixes LVD and SE devices attached to the same host adapter, the whole chain runs at the speed of the fastest device.

   D. You cannot mix LVD and SE devices on the same chain without destroying the SE devices and probably damaging the LVD devices.

13. If the jumper block on the SCSI device contains four jumpers identified as 1, 2, 3, and 4, what SCSI ID would the device get if you covered jumper 2 and jumper 3 but left jumpers 1 and 4 open?

   A. 1

   B. 5

   C. 6

   D. 7

14. Which of the following statements best describes bus mastering with SCSI devices?

    A. If SCSI devices are on the same SCSI host adapter, they can communicate directly with each other without the assistance of the CPU or the use of the expansion bus.
    B. The SCSI host adapter controls bus mastering transfers between devices attached to it.
    C. The CPU controls bus mastering transfers between all devices.
    D. Bus mastering uses the expansion bus to transfer data from one SCSI device to another, but the devices work independently of the CPU.

15. After a SCSI hard drive has been installed correctly, how do the steps that prepare it to hold data differ from those used with EIDE hard drives?

    A. You do not have to partition a SCSI drive, but you must format it before it can store data.
    B. You do not have to partition or format a SCSI drive since it comes from the factory ready to use.
    C. You partition and format a SCSI drive exactly the same way that you do an EIDE drive.
    D. You must use the software that comes with the SCSI host adapter to partition and format a SCSI drive.

Essay Quiz

1. SCSI hard drives are usually the choice for network servers with RAID. Why do you think SCSI drives are better for RAID than EIDE drives? What flavor of SCSI would you purchase if you were setting up RAID? Why did you choose that flavor?
2. Barbara is confused. Her new computer has a SCSI hard drive that is working perfectly, but when she looked at the hard drive settings in the CMOS setup program, it did not indicate that she had a hard drive at all. Investigate this situation and explain it to Barbara. While you're at it, explain any other CMOS settings that might affect SCSI drives.
3. The engineering firm where you work has a small network and uses CAD applications. The firm currently has EIDE hard drives, but it is planning to order new computers soon, both for the workstations and for the servers. Write a justification for purchasing SCSI hard drives rather than EIDE. Include at least three advantages of SCSI over EIDE. In addition to hard drives, what other SCSI devices might the firm need to purchase, and why?
4. Prepare a poster that can be placed on the bulletin board in your classroom illustrating what devices should be terminated for these three situations: (1) An internal SCSI chain with three devices plus the host adapter; (2) An external only SCSI chain with two devices plus the host adapter; (3) A SCSI chain composed of three internal and two external devices plus the host adapter. Be sure to include SCSI ID numbers on your illustration.
5. A client of yours—a medium-sized non-profit company—just received a donation of two dozen SCSI hard drives, ten SCSI controller cards (PCI), and five SCSI scanners. None of the company's in-house techs has dealt with SCSI, so your boss has tasked you to write a memo detailing the steps in installing SCSI.

Lab Projects

• Lab Project 19.1

Work has begun on a new SCSI standard called SPI-5 or Ultra5 SCSI (Ultra640). Use the Internet to research this emerging standard. Write a half-page report on its current status and its features.

• Lab Project 19.2

This chapter states that EIDE technology is taking away most of the advantages that SCSI formerly had. Does SCSI still offer larger faster hard drives than EIDE? Use the Internet to compare the speed, capacity, and cost of similar size IDE and SCSI hard drives.

chapter

20 Sound

"I can't hear too well. Do you suppose you could turn the music down just a little?"

—PETER SELLERS IN *DR. STRANGELOVE OR: HOW I LEARNED TO STOP WORRYING AND LOVE THE BOMB*

In this chapter, you will learn how to

- **Describe how sound works in a PC**
- **Select the appropriate sound card for a given scenario**
- **Install a sound card in a Windows system**
- **Troubleshoot problems that might arise with sound cards and speakers**

Racing down the virtual track, pixels flying across the screen, hearing the engine roar as you take another turn and press down the accelerator—or surfing the Web for lovely scenic nature photos with the sweet, mellifluous sounds of Mozart filling the room: sound has become an integral component of the computing experience, and setting up and optimizing sound for the personal computer has become an integral skill for all computer techs.

Correctly setting up sound for a PC requires you to know about quite a few things, because the sound process has many components. You need a properly installed sound card with the correct drivers loaded, reasonably high-quality speakers, support software such as the right API for a particular game and the correct settings in Windows applied, and your application set up to use the features of the sound card properly. And every great tech needs to know troubleshooting to handle both routine and uncommon problems with sound.

Historical/Conceptual

How Sound Works in a PC

Like the ripples that roll across a pond when you drop a rock in the center, sound flows from a source in invisible but measurable waves that cause the membranes in your ears to vibrate in certain ways. The sophistication of the human ear enables most people to differentiate the melodious from the raucous, the loud from the soft. Computers aren't nearly as sophisticated as the human ear and brain, so we need clear standards for converting music into a format that a PC can use to record and play sound. Computer folks use the

capturing the state or quality of a particular sound wave a set number of times each second. The sampling rate is measured in units of thousands of cycles per second, or **kilohertz** (KHz). The more often a sound is sampled, the better the reproduction of that sound. Most sounds in the PC world are recorded with a sampling rate of from 11 KHz (very low quality, like a telephone) to 128 KHz (ultra-high quality, better then the human ear).

The most famous of all sound cards is Creative Labs' popular SoundBlaster series.

Sounds vary according to their loudness (amplitude), how high or low their tone (frequency), and the qualities that differentiate the same note played on different instruments (timbre). All the characteristics of a particular sound wave—amplitude, frequency, timbre—need to be recorded and translated into 1's and 0's to reproduce that sound accurately within the computer and thus out your speakers.

The number of characteristics of a particular sound captured during sampling is measured by the **bit depth** of the sample, the number of bits used to describe the characteristics of a sound. The greater the bit depth used to capture a sample, the more characteristics of that sound can be stored and thus re-created. An 8-bit sample of a Jimi Hendrix guitar solo, for example, captures $2^8 = 256$ characteristics of that sound per sample. It would sound like a cheap recording of a recording, perhaps a little flat and thin. A 16-bit sample, in contrast, captures $2^{16} = 65{,}536$ different characteristics of that same sound and reproduces all the fuzzy overtones and feedback that gave Hendrix his unique sound.

The last aspect of sound capture is the number of different tracks of sound we capture. Most commonly, we capture either a single track (monaural) or two tracks (stereo). More advanced captures record many more sound tracks, but that's a topic for a more advanced sound capture discussion.

The combination of sampling frequency and bit depth determines how faithfully a digital version of a sound captures what your ear would hear. A

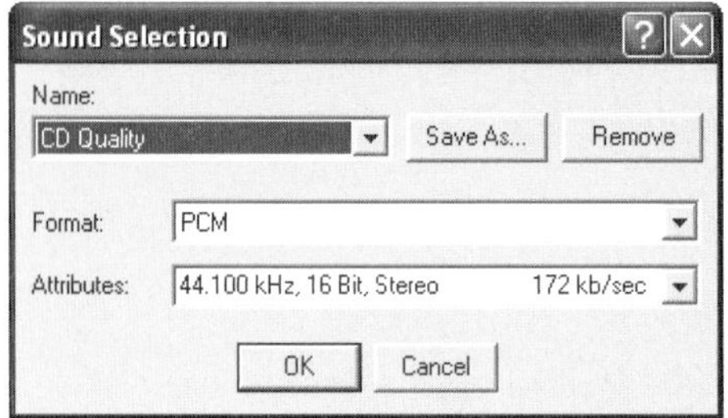

• **Figure 20.1** Sound Recorder settings

sound capture is considered **CD quality** when recorded at 44 KHz, with 16-bit depth, and in stereo.

Most recording programs let you set these values before you begin recording. Figure 20.1 shows the configuration settings for the popular Windows Sound Recorder.

Hey, wait a minute! Did you notice the Format setting in Figure 20.1? What's that? You can save those sampled sounds in lots of different ways—and that's where the term *format* comes into play.

Recorded Sound Formats

The granddaddy of all sound formats is *pulse code modulation* (PCM). PCM was developed in the 1960s to carry telephone calls over the first digital lines. With just a few minor changes to allow for use in PCs, the PCM format is still alive and well, although it's better known as the WAV format so common in the PC world. WAV files are great for storing faithfully recorded sounds and music, but they do so at a price. WAV files can be huge, especially when sampled at high frequency and depth. A four-minute song at 44 KHz and 16-bit stereo, for example, weighs in at a whopping 40-plus MB!

> WAV and MP3 are only two among a large number of file formats for sound. Not all sound players can play all of these formats; however, many sound formats are nothing more than some type of compressed WAV file, so with the right codec loaded, you can play most sound formats.

What's interesting about sound quality is that the human ear cannot perceive anywhere near the subtle variations of sound recorded at 44 KHz and 16-bit stereo. Clever programmers have written algorithms to store full-quality WAV files as compressed files, discarding unnecessary audio qualities of that file. These algorithms—really nothing more than a series of instructions in code—are called compressor/decompressor programs, or more simply just **codecs**. The most famous of the codecs is the Fraunhoffer MPEG-1 Layer 3 codec, more often called by its file extension, **MP3**.

Playing Sounds

A large number of programs can play sounds on a typical Windows computer. First, virtually every windows computer comes with Windows Media Player, possibly the most popular of all sound players (see Figure 20.2). However, many other players are available. This is good, because not all sound players can play all sounds.

• **Figure 20.2** Windows Media Player

MIDI

Every sound card can produce sounds, in addition to playing prerecorded sound files. Every sound card comes with a second processor designed to interpret standardized **musical instrument digital interface** (MIDI) files. It's important to note that a MIDI file is not an independent music file, unlike a WAV file, which will sound more or less the same on many different PCs; rather, a MIDI file is a text file that takes advantage of the sound processing hardware to enable the PC to produce sound.

Programmers use these small text files to tell the sound card what notes to play, how long, how loud, on which instruments, and so forth. Think of a MIDI file as a piece of electronic sheet music, with the instruments built into your sound card.

The beauty of MIDI files is that they're tiny in comparison to equivalent WAV files. The first movement of Beethoven's Fifth Symphony, for example, weighs in at a whopping 78 MB as a high-quality WAV file. The same seven-minute song as a MIDI file, in contrast, slips in at a svelte 60 KB.

MIDI is hardware dependent, meaning the abilities and quality of the individual sound card makes all the difference in the world on the sound produced. Sound cards play MIDI files using one of two technologies: FM synthesis or wave table synthesis.

FM Synthesis

the scale you go from that prime note.

Wave Table Synthesis

To address the odd techno-sound of early sound processors, manufacturers began embedding recordings of actual instruments or other sounds in the sound card. Many modern sound cards use these recorded sounds to reproduce an instrument much more faithfully than with FM synthesis. When asked to play a C on a piano or on a viola, for example, the sound processor grabs a prerecorded WAV file from its memory and adjusts it to match the specific sound and timing requested. This technique is called **wave table synthesis**. The number of instruments stored in a sound card is called the polyphony of that card. Decent sound cards have 64 instruments stored, and better cards have 256, 320, or more—a veritable symphony orchestra on a chip!

Other File Formats

The WAV, MP3, and MIDI formats may account for the majority of sound files, but plenty of other less common formats are out there. Here are the extensions of some other sound file formats you may run into in the PC world:

- **ASX** Microsoft created the ASX format to facilitate streaming audio over the Internet through Windows Media Player. It's more than just a format, though; it acts like a super play list and enables you to play other sound file types as well. The full name of the format is Microsoft Advanced Streaming Redirector.
- **ASM, WMA** Assembly Language Source (ASM) and Windows Media Audio (WMA) files are compressed sound formats often seen on the Internet and used in streaming sound.

Tech Tip

Compressing WAV Files to MP3 Format

Using MP3 compression, it is possible to shrink a WAV file by a factor of 12 without losing much sound quality. When you compress a WAV file into an MP3 file, the key decision is the bit rate. The bit rate is the amount of information (number of bits) transferred from the compressed file to the MP3 decoder in one second. The higher the bit rate of

A CD-quality MP3 bit rate is 128 Kbps.

MIDI files have the file extension .MID in the PC world.

MIDI files are much less popular than recorded formats on PCs. However, every Windows computer and every sound card still fully supports MIDI.

- **RM** RealMedia (RM) files play either just audio or audio and video. They are proprietary to RealMedia, a popular player often used on the Internet. You must have a RealMedia Player to play these files.
- **AIFF** Audio Interchange File Format (AIFF) files are a popular sound format used on Macintosh computers. These files are often seen at web sites, and you can use the well-known QuickTime player to play these files.
- **MOD, VOC** Two obsolete file formats promoted by Creative Labs in the early 1990s. They are rarely seen today; however, most sound players will still play these types of files. Neither extension is short for anything. Creative Labs must have simply liked the sound of them.
- **AU** Another popular format that is often seen in the Windows world. Many different players can play these files, including players on non-Windows systems, such as Sun, Next, Unix, and Macintosh.

This list scratches the surface 100+ sound file formats floating around out there, but it represents the ones that you're most likely to encounter.

Video

Recorded audio files and MIDI files aren't the only files that play sounds on your computer. Video files also have sound built into them. However, to play the sound that accompanies the video, the video player program must support the particular video file format. The most common video formats in the PC world are Audio Video Interleaves (AVI), Moving Pictures Experts Group (MPEG), QuickTime (MOV), Advanced Streaming Format (ASF), and RM.

Applications

Many applications, especially games, play sounds, too. In the not-too-distant past, a game or an application sometimes had its own sound format, but most applications and games today use standard WAV, MP3, or MIDI files.

Streaming Media

Streaming media is incredibly popular on the Internet. Streaming media is a broadcast of data that is played on your computer and immediately discarded. Streaming media has spawned an entire industry of Internet radio stations. The two most popular streaming media players are Windows Media Player and Winamp. ASF and RM are compressed audio/video file formats that were specially created to stream over the Internet.

Cross Check

MPEG Standards

You first ran into the MPEG standards in Chapter 17, "CD and DVD Media." Refer back to that chapter and cross check your memory. What standard(s) support DVD-ROM? What about streaming video over the Internet?

Getting the Right Sound Card

Sound cards have many capabilities built in, including two separate sound processors (one for all of the recorded formats such as WAV and another for MIDI), support chips for joysticks and other pointing devices that plug into the game port, recording capabilities, support for MIDI instruments, and more. All sound cards, from the cheapest to the most expensive, can play music and drive a pair of speakers, so techs need to delve a little deeper to understand the crucial differences among low-, mid-, and high-end sound

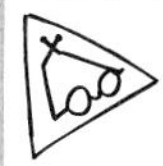

Tech Tip

Sound Cards

The hardware portion of sound-processing equipment in the PC either comes as a chip built into the motherboard or on an expansion card. Techs call both forms sound cards, *even though technically the first type is not a card at all. Still, the generic term has stuck for the time being.*

Processor Capabilities

Sound processor capabilities differ dramatically from the low end to the high end, even though the prices don't reflect the great divide. The sound processor handles the communication among the application, operating system, and CPU and translates commands into sounds coming out of the speakers. Low-end sound processors do little more than translate, which means that the CPU has to do the heavy lifting on the processing front.

Better sound processors, in contrast, shoulder much of the processing burden and bring a series of extra features to the table. By handling a lot of the processing on board, these better sound processors free up the CPU for other duties and, in effect and in name, *accelerate* the sound process. These decent sound processors also provide excellent sound reproduction, so your MP3s sound as awesome on your PC as they do on your stereo.

Play Sounds in Windows

The typical Windows PC comes with a number of applications for playing sound files. Take a tour of a typical Windows system to see the applications available for playing sound files. This exercise uses Windows XP, but almost any version of Windows (95 or later) will also work. For this exercise, you will need a Windows XP system with a functioning sound card, microphone, and speakers.

1. Using the file search feature in Windows, locate all of the files on your computer that have the extension .wav—all versions of Windows come with a number of WAV files. Double-click one of the files to play it. What program is associated with WAV files?
2. Repeat step 1, but this time look for files with the extension .mid. Not all versions of Windows have MIDI files. Double-click one of the files to play it. What program is associated with MIDI files?
3. From the Start button, search for any sound programs that may be on your system. You'll almost certainly run into Windows Media Player and Sound Recorder, but also see whether any third-party programs are installed.
4. If possible, install the popular sound player, Winamp, on your system. You can get a copy of this free program at www.winamp.com. Check Winamp's help file to see what types of file formats Winamp supports—it supports a lot of formats!
5. If you have an Internet connection, try running some streaming audio. If you have Windows Media Player version 7 or later, go to the Radio Tuner. If you have Winamp, try going to www.shoutcast.com.

Most mid-range and all high-end sound processors offer support for various surround sound standards, enabling equally equipped games and other applications to provide positional audio effects and detailed sound modeling—features that make PC gaming take on a whole new dimension. You'll learn about the various standards in detail in the "Speakers" section of this chapter, but for now let an example suffice. With properly implemented positional audio, when you're sneaking down the hall, ready to steal the Pasha's treasure, you will hear behind you the sounds of the guards marching up to capture you. Such added realism has many potential benefits beyond games, but games are currently the primary beneficiary of this technology.

Speaker Support

Every sound card supports two speakers or a pair of headphones, but many better sound cards support five or more speakers in discrete channels. These multiple speakers provide surround sound—popular not only for games but also for those who enjoy playing DVDs on their PCs. The card in Figure 20.3, for example, has inputs for front speakers (Out 1) and rear speakers (Out 2).

Another popular speaker addition is a **subwoofer**. Subwoofers provide the amazing low-frequency sounds that give all of your sounds, from the surround sound of a game to the music of a simple stereo MP3 file, an extra dimension. Better sound cards support both surround sound and a subwoofer and advertise this with a nomenclature such as Dolby Digital, DTS, or **5.1**. The *5* denotes the number of speakers: two in front, two in back, and one in the center. The *.1* denotes the subwoofer. Figure 20.4 shows one type of surround speaker system. You'll learn more about surround sound in the upcoming "Speakers" section.

• **Figure 20.3** A sound card with multiple speaker connections

• **Figure 20.4** Surround speakers

Recording Quality

Almost every sound card has an input for a powered microphone, but the high-end cards record with substantially lower amounts of noise or other audible artifacts. The measure that describes the relative quality of an input port is signal-to-noise ratio and is expressed in decibels. The smaller the number, the worse the card is for recording because the more likely you'll get noise. Most sound cards at the low end and in mid range have a signal-to-noise ratio of 30 to 50 decibels, which makes them unacceptable for recording. High-end cards offer a 96 to 100 signal-to-noise ratio, a level near what professional musicians use. Check the documentation (see Figure 20.5) before you buy or recommend a sound card for recording purposes.

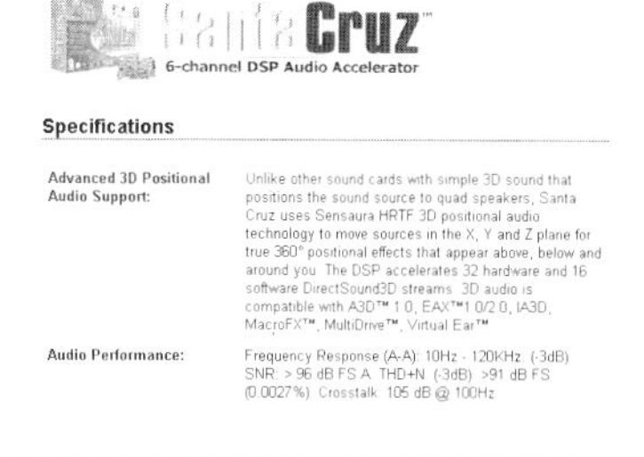

Santa Cruz™
6-channel DSP Audio Accelerator

Specifications

Advanced 3D Positional Audio Support:	Unlike other sound cards with simple 3D sound that positions the sound source to quad speakers, Santa Cruz uses Sensaura HRTF 3D positional audio technology to move sources in the X, Y and Z plane for true 360° positional effects that appear above, below and around you. The DSP accelerates 32 hardware and 16 software DirectSound3D streams. 3D audio is compatible with A3D™ 1.0, EAX™1.0/2.0, IA3D, MacroFX™, MultiDrive™, Virtual Ear™
Audio Performance:	Frequency Response (A-A): 10Hz - 120KHz (-3dB) SNR: > 96 dB FS A. THD+N (-3dB): >91 dB FS (0.0027%) Crosstalk: 105 dB @ 100Hz

Figure 20.5 The Turtle Beach Santa Cruz advertises its excellent 96+-decibel signal-to-noise ratio for recording.

Jacks

Virtually every sound card comes with at least three connections: one for a stereo speaker system, one for a microphone, and one for a secondary output called line out. If you look at the back of a motherboard with a built-in sound card, you'll invariably see these three connections (Figure 20.6). On most systems, the main stereo speaker connector is blue, the line-out connector is green, and the microphone connector is pink.

However, you'll often find plenty of other connectors (see Figure 20.7). Let's see what these connectors do for your sound card.

rear speakers for surround audio output.

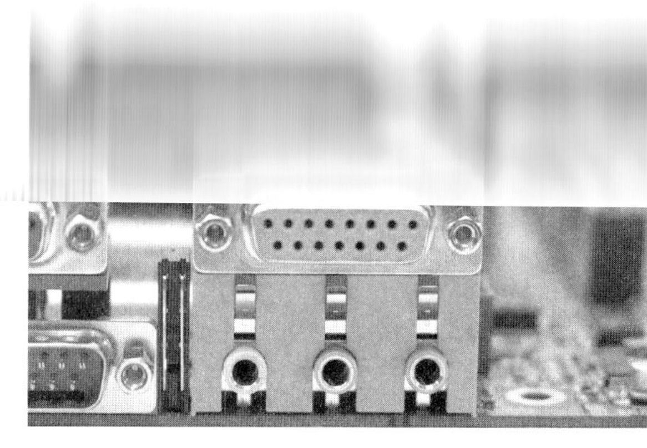

Figure 20.6 Typical audio connections on a motherboard sound card

- **Analog/Digital Out** The multifunction analog/digital out connection acts as a special digital connection to external digital devices or digital speaker systems, and it also acts as the analog connection to center and subwoofer channels. (See the "Speakers" section later in this chapter for a discussion of surround sound.)
- **Microphone** The microphone port connects to an external microphone for voice input.
- **Joystick** The joystick port connects a joystick or a MIDI device to the sound card. The joystick port is a two-row DB15 female connection, but as more and more peripherals go USB, more motherboard and sound card makers are dropping this venerable port from their models.

Figure 20.7 Lots of connections on a high-end sound card

Extra Features

With more motherboards coming with built-in sound, expansion sound card makers have responded by adding a host of extra goodies and abilities to their cards that, for some folks, prove irresistibly tempting. These include a digital output to integrate the PC with a home entertainment unit, allowing users to add a DVD receiver and surround sound speakers; a breakout box that adds recording and output ports in a 5.25-inch bay; and a FireWire connection for direct gaming, file sharing, and immediate MP3 playing from a portable MP3 device. Figure 20.8 shows a version of the Creative

• **Figure 20.8** Breakout box for a SoundBlaster Live! Platinum sound card

Labs' popular SoundBlaster breakout box. These features aren't for everyone, but they are compelling to many consumers.

Audio Cables

If you want to play audio CDs through your sound card, you need a special cable that runs from your CD media drive to the sound card. These cables have been around for a while, but the connectors were not standardized—for years, you had to use the cable that came with your sound card and hope that it would connect to your CD drive.

Today, a connector called *MPC2* is quite standard, and cables usually come with CD media drives, not sound cards. To accommodate the many other types of connections that are still out there, a special cable called a *universal audio cable* is also available (Figure 20.9). Universal audio cables have a set of connectors to enable a CD-ROM drive to connect to any sort of audio card. Universal audio cables were important when CD-ROM audio connections were not standardized.

The early SoundBlaster line of audio cards from Creative Labs came with a small, proprietary connection for CD-ROM drives. Because SoundBlaster dominated the field of sound cards for many years, you'll still run into audio cables with an MPC2 connector on one end and a SoundBlaster connector on the other end. These days, SoundBlaster cards use standard cables. You'll most commonly see MPC2 connections on sound cards, and MPC2/MPC2 audio cables (Figure 20.10) included with any new CD-ROM drive.

• **Figure 20.9** Universal audio cable

Speakers

It always blows me away when I walk into someone's study and hear tinny music whining from a $10 pair of speakers connected to a $2000 computer. If you listen to music or play games on your computer, a decent set of speakers can significantly improve the experience! Speakers come in a wide variety of sizes, shapes, technologies, and quality and can stump the uninformed tech who can't easily tell that the $50 set on the right sounds 100 times better than the $25 pair on the left (Figure 20.11).

Speaker Standards

The advent of surround sound in the computing world has created a number of speaker standards. You should know these standards so that you can choose the speakers that work best for you.

Stereo Stereo is the oldest speaker technology that you'll see in the PC world. Stereo speakers are just what you might imagine: two speakers, a left

and a right (Figure 20.12). The two speakers share a single jack that connects to the sound card. Most cheap speakers are stereo speakers.

Figure 20.12 Stereo speakers

2.1 Systems A 2.1 speaker system consists of a pair of standard stereo speakers—called *satellites*—combined with a subwoofer (Figure 20.13). The average 2.1 speaker system has a single jack that connects to the sound card and runs into the subwoofer. Another wire runs from the subwoofer to the two stereo speakers. If you want to enjoy great music and don't feel you need surround sound, this will be your speaker standard of choice.

Surround Speaker Standards Going beyond standard two-channel (stereo) sound has been a goal in the sound world since the 1970s. However, it wasn't until the advent of Dolby Laboratory's Dolby Digital sound standard in the early 1990s that surround sound began to take off. The Dolby Digital sound standard is designed to support five channels of sound: front-left, front-right, front-center, rear-left, and rear-right. Dolby Digital also supports a subwoofer—thus, the term *5.1*. Another company, Digital Theatre Systems (DTS) created a competing standard that also supported a 5.1 speaker system. When DVDs were introduced, they included both Dolby Digital and DTS 5.1 standards, making 5.1 speakers an overnight requirement for home theater. If you want to enjoy your DVDs in full surround sound on your PC, you must purchase a full 5.1 speaker system. A number of 5.1 speaker systems are available for PCs. The choice you make is usually determined by what sounds best to you.Many higher end sound cards come with a special Sony/Philips digital interface (SPDIF) connector that enables you to connect your sound card directly to a 5.1 speaker system or receiver (Figure 20.14). Using a single SPDIF instead of a tangle of separate wires for each speaker greatly simplifies your sound setup.

Only a few 5.1 PC speaker systems come with SPDIF. In most cases, you'll have to use the regular audio outputs on the sound card.

• **Figure 20.13** Typical 2.1 speakers

Games can also take advantage of 5.1 speakers, but they use a totally different standard: **DirectX**. Microsoft introduced the DirectX standard in Windows 95. DirectX offers numerous commands, also known as APIs, that issue instructions such as "make a sound on the right speaker" or "play music in both the right and left channels." DirectX simplifies the programming needed to create sound and video: rather than having to program sounds in different ways for each sound card option, games can talk DirectX; the hardware manufacturers simply have to ensure that their sound cards are DirectX compatible.

DirectX version 3 introduced **DirectSound3D** (DS3D), which offered a range of commands to place a sound anywhere in 3D space. This is known as positional audio, and it fundamentally changed the way most PC games are played. DS3D could not handle all sound information, but it supported extensions to its instructions for more advanced sound features. This challenged the sound card designers to develop more fully the concept of positional audio. Creative Labs responded by rolling out EAX. EAX (Figure 20.15) gives developers the ability to create a convincing sense of environment in entertainment titles and a realistic sense of distance between the player and audio events.

• **Figure 20.14** SPDIF connector

In late 2000, a number of EAX effects were incorporated into the DirectX audio component of DirectX 8.0. This signaled the acceptance of EAX as the standard for audio effects in gaming. Shortly afterward, Creative Labs started releasing audio cards that are Dolby 5.1 compatible out of the box. Now you can plug a 5.1 speaker system directly into your sound card. The sound card automatically applies the Dolby/DTS standards when you play a DVD and the EAX standards when you play a game.

Tech Tip

Speaker Systems

***Environmental Audio Extensions* (EAX) supports both 4.1 and 5.1 speaker systems. A 4.1 system lacks the center channel, and these systems are now starting to disappear. If you're going for surround sound, don't settle for 4.1 speakers—spend a few extra dollars and get a 5.1 speaker system.**

Many speaker systems and sound cards support more advanced speaker setups with such names as 4.2, 6.1, and 7.1. Little support is available for these, and unless you're a serious audiophile or in the music business, in most cases these are a waste of money.

Speaker Features

Speakers also come with a few other features that you should consider when choosing a set for yourself or your clients. Speakers offer different power sources, control locations and ease of use, and headphone jacks.

Power Many cheaper speakers use batteries. I hate batteries—they always seem to run out when I need them. Try to get speakers that use AC power.

Controls All speakers have volume controls as well as an on/off switch. Get a system that provides easy access to those controls by placing them on an easy-to-reach speaker or on a special control box.

Headphone Jack The problem with headphones is that you need to plug them into the back of the sound card and then tell Windows to output to them from the Sound applet on the Control Panel. Save yourself a lot of hassle and get a speaker system that has a handy microphone jack on one of the speakers or on a control box.

■ Installing a Sound Card in a Windows System

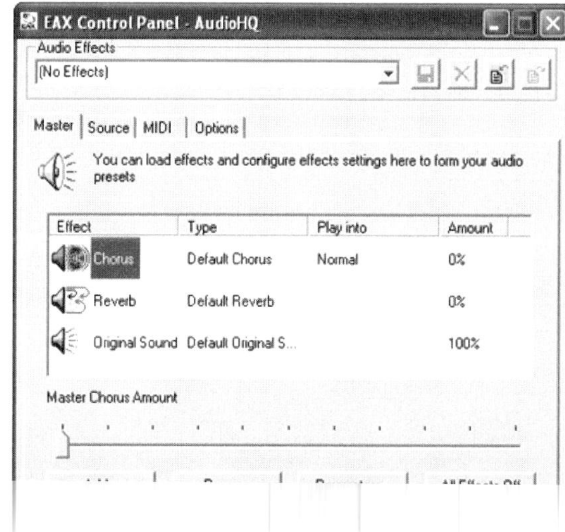

The installation process for a sound card is basically the same as the installation process for any other card. You snap the card into a slot, plug some speakers into the card, load a driver—and for the most part, you're done. Because so many disparate components are bundled into a single card, however, the sound card is one of the most complex expansion cards in a computer. Sound cards used to be the bane of hardware techs, but with Plug and Play, they're much easier to set up. Like most of the devices discussed in this book, sound card installation consists

cards so common today feature a variety of jacks so you will probably want to refer to your sound card documentation for details, but here are a few guidelines:

- The typical stereo or 2.1 speaker system will use only a single jack. Look for the jack labeled Speaker or Speaker 1.
- Surround speakers either use a single digital (SPDIF) connection, which in most cases runs from the sound card to the subwoofer, or need three separate cables: one for the front two speakers that runs to the Speaker 1 connector, one for the back two speakers that runs to the Speaker 2 connector, and a third cable for the center channel and subwoofer that runs to the Digital/Audio Out or Speaker 3 connector.

• **Figure 20.16** Typical sound card

Let's take a quick look at sound card installation. As with any PCI card, you'll need a Phillips-head screwdriver to install a sound card, as well as your electrostatic discharge (ESD) prevention equipment. Of course, you'll also need the sound card itself, a set of speakers, an audio cable, and a microphone if you want to be able to record sounds.

To begin, shut down your computer, unplug it, and open the case. Find an open

You cannot damage your speakers or sound card by inserting the wrong jacks into any of the connections on the back of the sound card, so don't be afraid to experiment when you're not positive where omething plugs in.

PCI slot and snap in the sound card. Remember to handle the card with tender loving care—especially if you're installing an expensive, high-end card! Make sure that the card is securely seated, and secure it to the chassis with a hex screw. Now connect the CD audio cable to the back of your CD or DVD media drive, and plug the other end into the CD Audio port on your sound card. Be sure to use the correct connector—many sound cards have multiple audio connectors. The one shown in Figure 20.17, for example, has separate connectors to use for a CD drive, DVD drive, or modem.

Now that the sound card is installed, test it out before you put the cover back on! Get your speakers and plug them into the speaker jack on the back of the sound card. Make sure that you plug the speakers in, turn on their power switch if applicable, and turn the volume to a moderate level. Plug the system unit back in and boot the PC, and then find a sound file and attempt to play it. Do you hear sound coming from the speakers? If so, go ahead and put the cover back on the PC. If you aren't getting any sound, try a different file, or start looking for the source of the problem—I'll cover troubleshooting later in this chapter.

• **Figure 20.17** Sound card with multiple audio connectors

Installing Drivers

Once the sound card is installed, start the system and let Windows Plug and Play install the sound card's drivers. As you might expect by now, you'll probably have a choice between the built-in Windows drivers and the driver that comes on a CD with your sound card. Just as with other cards, it's always best to use the driver that comes with the card. Most sound cards have easy-to-use autoplay-enabled installation CDs that step you through the process (Figure 20.18).

Sound card drivers are updated occasionally. Take a moment to check the manufacturer's web site to see whether your sound card has any driver updates.

After your driver is installed, make a quick trip to the Device Manager to make sure that the driver was installed correctly, and you're two-thirds of the way there. Installing the driver is never the last step for a sound card. Your final step is to configure the sound card using configuration programs and to test the sound card using an application. Most sound cards come with both special configuration programs and a few sound applications on the same CD that supplies the drivers. Let's look at these extra bits of software that we'll simply call sound programs.

Cross Check

Checking System Resources

In Chapter 5, you learned about system resources. Sound cards are almost always on the PCI bus, and like other PCI cards, they have resources assigned and can occasionally create conflicts. What steps should you take to install a sound card successfully? How do you check for resource conflicts?

Installing Sound Programs

You've already seen that you need a program to play sounds: Windows Media Player, Winamp, or something similar. But two other classes of sound programs also reside on your computer: programs for the configuration of your sound card and special applications that may or may not come with your sound card.

Configuration Applications

Every Windows computer comes with at least one important sound configuration program built right into the operating system: the Control Panel applet called **Sounds and Audio Devices** in Windows XP or Sounds and Multimedia in Windows 2000 and Windows Me, or the two applets called Sounds and Multimedia in Windows NT and Windows 9*x*. Whatever the name, this applet (or applets)

Audio, Voice, and Hardware. The most interesting is the Volume tab. This tab adjusts the volume for the speakers, and it also allows you to set up the type of speaker system you have, as shown in Figure 20.19.

The Sounds tab allows you to add customized sounds to Windows events, such as the startup of a program or Windows shutdown. The Audio tab (Figure 20.20) and Voice tab do roughly the same thing: they allow you to specify the device used for input and output of general sounds (Audio

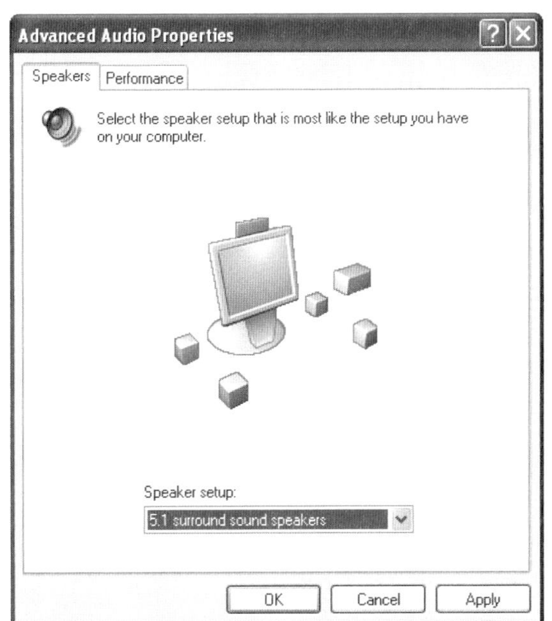

• **Figure 20.19** Advanced Audio Properties dialog box

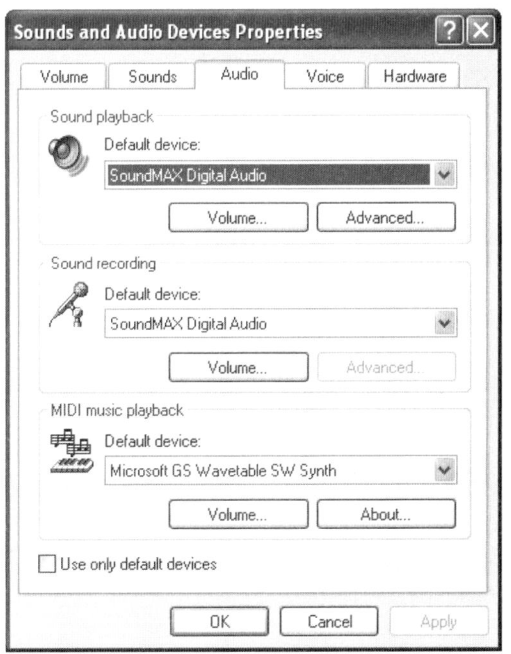

• **Figure 20.20** Audio tab (note the MIDI Music Playback option)

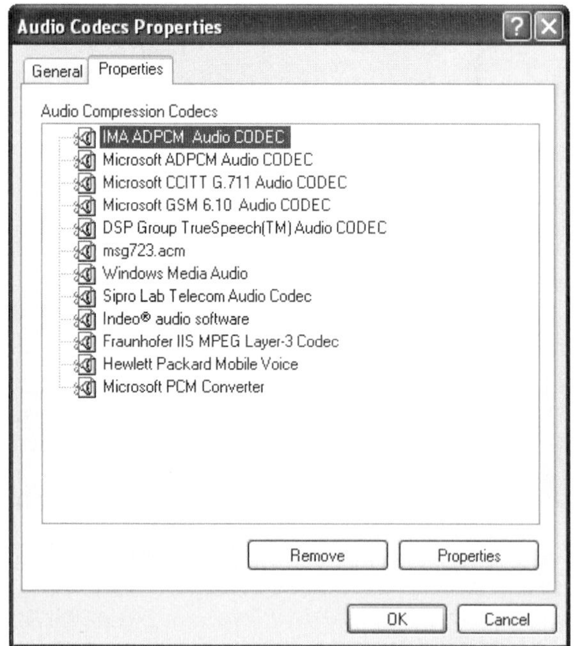

• **Figure 20.21** Audio codecs

tab) and voice (Voice tab). These settings are handy for folks like me who have a regular microphone and speakers but also use a headset with microphone for voice recognition or Internet telephone software. By telling Windows to use the microphone for normal sounds and to use the headset for voice recognition, I don't have to make any manual changes when I switch from listening to an MP3 to listening to my brother when he calls me over the Internet.

The Hardware tab isn't used very often, but it does have one interesting feature: it shows you all of the audio and video codecs installed in your system (Figure 20.21). Not long ago, you had to install codecs manually in your system to play certain compressed file formats. Today, most audio players automatically detect whether a file is using an unrecognized codec and will download the proper codec for you.

Proprietary Configuration Applications

Many sound cards install proprietary software to support configuration features not provided by Windows. Figure 20.22 shows one such application. This is a special configuration application that comes with Creative Labs' sound cards to add a few tweaks to the speaker setup that the Sounds and Audio Devices Control Panel applet doesn't support.

Most sound cards come with some form of configuration program. Take some time to experiment with them—this is a great way to learn about some of the features of your sound card that you might otherwise not even know are there.

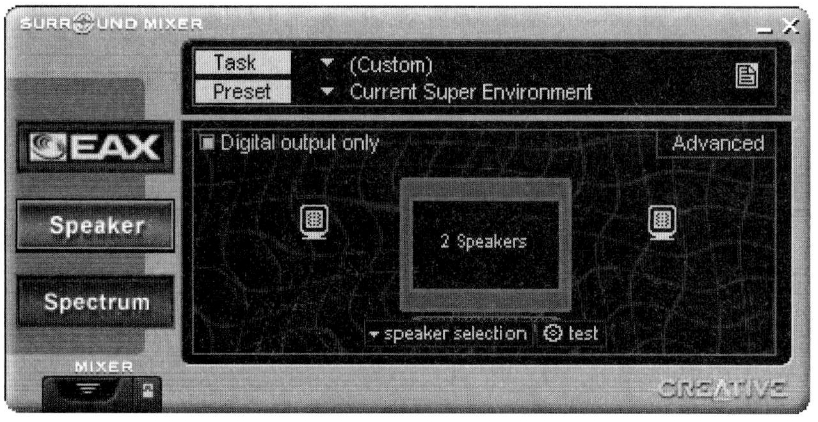

• **Figure 20.22** Creative Labs' Remote Center

Installing Applications

Some sound cards—Creative Labs' sound cards are by far the most infamous for this—install one or more applications, ostensibly to improve your sound experience. Whether you'll agree with this or not is a matter of opinion. Personally, I'm not a big fan of, for example, an electronic keyboard program—but then you might be just the type of person who loves it (Figure 20.23). Either way, be sure to install at least the applications that come with your card. If you don't like them, you can easily uninstall them.

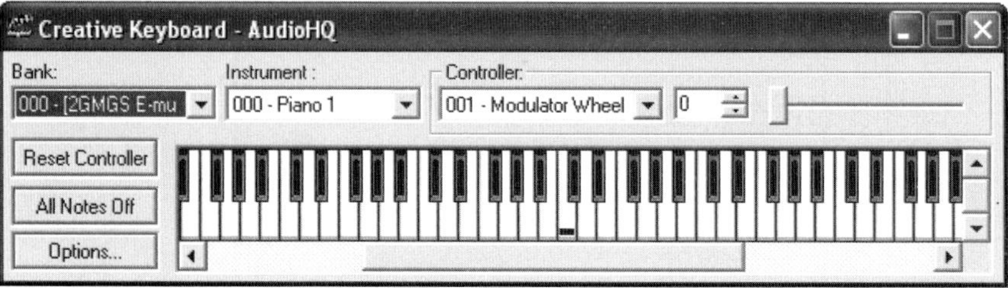

• **Figure 20.23** Creative Labs' keyboard program

Troubleshooting Sound

The problems that you'll run into with sound seem to fall into one of two camps: those that are embarrassingly simple to repair, and those that defy any possible logic and are seemingly impossible to fix. This section divides sound problems into three groups—hardware, configuration, and application problems—and gives you some ideas on how to fix these problems.

Hardware Problems

Hardware problems are by far the most common sound problems, especially if your sound card has worked for some amount of time already. Properly installed and configured sound cards almost never suddenly stop

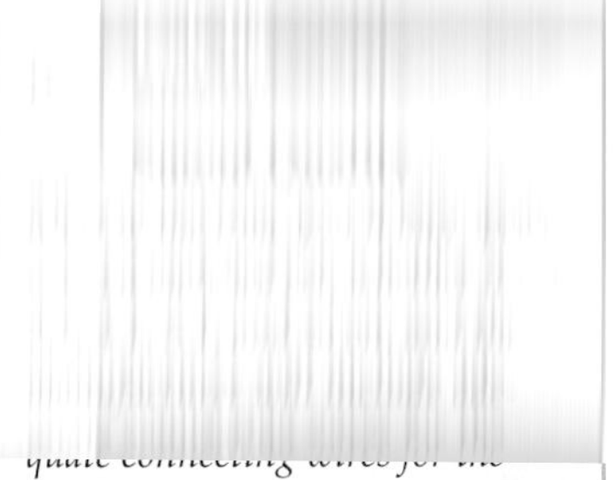

20.24) by clicking the little speaker icon on the taskbar, and make sure that both the master volume and the volume of the other controls are turned up.

Speakers

Your second place to look for sound problems is the speakers. Make sure that the speakers are turned on and are getting good power. Then make sure the speakers are plugged into the proper connection on the back of the sound card. If this all checks out, try playing a sound. If the sound *looks* like it is playing—maybe the application has an equalizer that is moving or a status marker that shows that the application is playing the sound—you may have blown speakers. Try another pair and see if the sound returns.

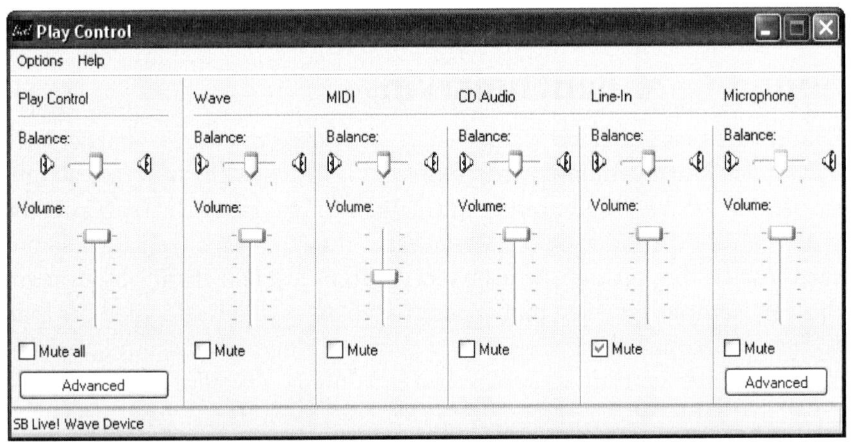

• **Figure 20.24** Volume controls in Windows

whole set. On occasion you might run into a system where the user has connected pairs of speakers from different sets or rigged a surround sound system by replacing the stock wires with much longer ones. Either option can create a perfectly functional surround sound system that works for a specific room, but you have to make sure that you use speakers that match in wattage required and that you use high-quality wire to connect them.

If you troubleshoot a system where two of the speakers are very quiet and two very loud, chances are that the wattages are different between the two pairs. A simple check of the labels should suffice to troubleshoot, or you can swap out one pair for a different pair and see if that affects the volume issues. Cheap wire, on the other hand, simply degrades the sound quality. If the speakers sounded good before getting strung on long wires but now have a lot of low grade noise, check the wire.

Technically speaking, turning down the volume in the volume control program is a configuration problem, but it's just something I always check at the same time I check the volume on the speakers.

Configuration Problems

Configuration errors occur when the sound card is physically good but some setting hasn't been properly configured. I also include drive problems in this category. These errors happen almost exclusively at installation, but they can appear on a working system, too.

The first place to check is the Device Manager. If the driver has a problem, you'll see it right there. Try reinstalling the driver. If the driver doesn't show any problems, again try playing a sound and see if the player acts as though the sound is playing. If that's the case, you need to start touring the Sounds and Audio Devices applet to see if you've made a configuration error—perhaps you have the system configured for 5.1 when you have a stereo setup, or maybe you set the default sound output device to some other device. Take your time and look—configuration errors always show themselves.

Application Problems

Application problems are always the hardest to fix and are the ones that do tend to occur on a system that was previously playing sounds without trouble.

First, look for an error message (Figure 20.25). If an error code appears, write it down *exactly* as you see it and head to the program's support site. Odds are very good that if you have the error text, you'll get the fix right away from the support site. Of course, you can always hope the built-in help has some support, but help systems tend to be a little light in providing real fixes.

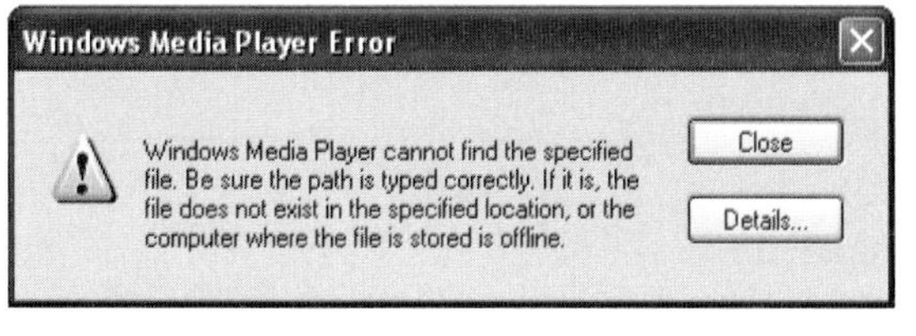

• **Figure 20.25** Sample error message

Don't always blame the sound application—don't forget that any sound file might be corrupted. Most sound players will display a clear error message, but not always. Try playing the sound file in another application.

Last, a good approach almost always is to reinstall the application.

Beyond A+

Sound Card Benchmarking

Sound cards can demand a huge share of system resources—particularly CPU time—during intense work (like gaming). Most techs who find an otherwise serviceable PC stuttering during games will immediately blame the video card or the video card drivers. What they don't realize is that sound cards can be the cause of the problem. A recent test of a client's built-in audio, for example, revealed that at peak usage the sound card took more than 30 percent of the CPU cycles. Thirty percent? Holy smokes! And he wondered why his Pentium III system bogged down on yesterday's games! He could just forget about playing Half-Life 2 or Doom III.

eTesting Labs makes an excellent sound card benchmarking utility that helps you analyze the particulars of any sound card, called Audio WinBench (Figure 20.26). (It was produced for *PC Magazine*, a Ziff Davis publication; hence the Ziff Davis branding.) It'll run a system through fairly

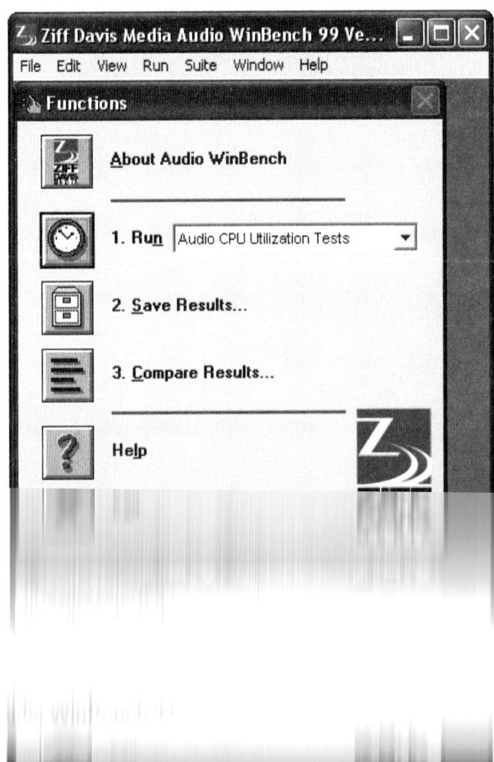

serious tests, from regular sound to 3-D positional audio, and will reveal whether or not the sound processor—built-in or expansion card—is causing a problem with resource use. You can find the utility at www.veritest.com/benchmarks/winbench/winbench.asp.

Chapter 20 Review

Chapter Summary

After reading this chapter and completing the exercises, you should understand the following aspects of sound.

Describe How Sound Works in a PC

- The process by which sounds are stored in electronic format on your PC is called sampling. Sounds are sampled thousands of times per second. The amount of information stored at each sampling is called the bit depth.
- The cornerstone of all file formats is pulse code modulation (PCM). The popular WAV file format as well as most other recorded sound formats are based on PCM. Compression is a popular way to reduce the file size of recorded sounds. The most popular compressed file type is MP3.
- To play sounds, you must have some form of player software.
- MIDI files are not recordings like WAV files. They are specialized text files that store notes that your sound card can play. Sound cards use one of two methods to store notes for MIDI: FM synthesis or wave table synthesis. A large number of other sound file formats is available. Not all players play all sound formats. Some file formats require their own proprietary players. Sounds can also be found in video formats, applications, and streaming media.

Select the Appropriate Sound Card for a Given Scenario

- The five major criteria for choosing a sound card are processor capability, speaker support, recording quality, jacks, and extra features.
- Surround sound is popular for games and DVD. A number of surround sound standards exist, but the most common are Dolby Digital and DTS. The Dolby Digital and DTS standards both require five speakers and a subwoofer. These speaker setups use the nomenclature 5.1.

Install a Sound Card in a Windows System

- Sound card installation can be divided into three major steps: physical installation, device driver installation, and configuration.
- While the physical installation of a sound card is straightforward, knowing where to plug in multiple speakers can be a bit of a challenge.
- It is preferable to use the driver that comes with the sound card as opposed to the Windows built-in drivers.
- Look for configuration programs in two places: in the Control Panel Sounds and Audio Devices applet and in any proprietary applications that are installed with the sound card.

Perform Basic Sound Card Troubleshooting

- You can divide sound problems into three groups: hardware, configuration, and application problems.
- The two first places to check when you suspect a hardware problem are the volume controls and speaker connectivity.
- Configuration errors almost always take place at installation of the sound card.
- Application problems are often the most challenging of all sound problems. Your best hope is an error message; you can then check the programs' web site for help.

Key Terms

2.1 *(741)*
5.1 *(738)*
bit depth *(733)*
CD quality *(734)*
codec *(734)*
Digital Theatre Systems (DTS) *(741)*
DirectSound3D (DS3D) *(742)*
DirectX *(742)*
Dolby Digital *(741)*
Environmental Audio Extensions (EAX) *(742)*
FM synthesis *(735)*
kilohertz (KHz) *(733)*
MP3 *(734)*

musical instrument digital interface (MIDI) *(734)*
sampling *(733)*
Sony/Philips digital interface (SPDIF) *(741)*
Sounds and Audio Devices *(745)*
subwoofer *(738)*
wave table synthesis *(735)*

Key Term Quiz

Use the Key Terms list to complete the sentences that follow. Not all terms will be used.

1. A sound's sampling rate is measured in thousands of cycles per second, called __________.
2. _______________ allows a sound card to simulate a number of different instruments.

____

6. __________ is the process of capturing the state or quality of a particular sound wave a set number of times each second.
7. The most common compressed audio format is ______________.
8. A(n) _______________ is a series of instructions telling a computer how to read a

Multiple-Choice Quiz

1. The number of characteristics of a particular sound captured when sampling is called the _______?
   A. Sample rate
   B. Kilohertz
   C. Bit depth
   D. Quality rating
2. CD-quality sound samples are recorded at 44 KHz, with 16-bit depth and what else?
   A. Monaural
   B. Stereo
   C. 5.1
   D. 2.1
3. All recorded sound formats used in PC today are derived from the _______ format.
   A. WAV
   B. Fraunhoffer
   C. MP3
   D. PCM
4. The most common compressed sound format is _______.
   A. MP3
   B. WAV
   C. VOC
   D. TXT
5. Almost all sound cards use the _______ expansion bus.
   A. ISA
   B. AGP
   C. Internal
   D. PCI
6. Which sound format contains no actual sound recording, but only a series of commands stored in a text file for the sound card to interpret?
   A. WMA
   B. WAV
   C. MIDI
   D. MP3
7. Which audio/video compression format was created specifically to stream over the Internet?
   A. MP3
   B. MIDI

C. WAV

D. ASF

8. How many speakers are in a Dolby Digital 5.1 setup?

A. Five speakers plus a subwoofer

B. Six speakers plus a subwoofer

C. Seven speakers plus a subwoofer

D. Eight speakers plus a subwoofer

9. Which component of DirectX offered only a range of commands to place a sound anywhere in 3D space?

A. DirectSound

B. DirectSound3D

C. EAX

D. A3D

10. What is the name of the extensions to the DirectSound3D standard developed by Creative Labs?

A. EAX

B. MP3

C. Positional audio

D. Reverberation

11. What is the name of the direct competitor to Dolby Digital?

A. DirectSound

B. DirectSound3D

C. DTS

D. Surround Sound

12. The *.1* in 5.1 or 2.1 refers to the ________?

A. Volumetric sound positioning

B. Subwoofer

C. Subchannels

D. Reverb positional matrices

13. What is the name of the standard digital connection that replaces many analog connections on some sound cards?

A. CD Audio connector

B. AUX connector

C. TAD connector

D. SPIDF connector

14. Which version of DirectX introduced DirectSound3D?

A. Version 8.0

B. Version 3

C. Version 2

D. Version 1

15. Jane's sound card is suddenly not making any sound. She suspects that the volume is turned down. She checks the speaker volume and sees that it is turned up. What should she check next?

A. The volume control program

B. The application

C. The speaker power

D. The Device Manager

Essay Quiz

1. Detail in your own words how you think sound aided the evolution of the computer. What aspects of sound are necessary to computers? Why is sound needed?

2. Outline how you could use the connections provided on a modern sound card to create a multimedia home theater with your computer. Be sure to include hardware discussed in previous chapters, such as DVD-ROM drives.

3. Write an essay on the kind of sound card you would need for your computer. Detail what you personally would like to accomplish with your computer and how a sound card would help you.

4. Your clients have been having trouble with getting sound working on a number of systems recently purchased. Write a memo describing the user-level things that everyone should check before calling for a technician.

5. Your boss has decided that all systems in the office need new speakers, because the company that games together has more cohesion and happiness. Write a few paragraphs describing the speaker choices available and why one is better than the others.

Lab Projects

• Lab Project 20.1

Take a tour of the web site for Creative Labs: www.creative.com. What sound-related products are currently featured there? Check out the specs for Creative's various SoundBlaster cards. Do you see sound cards that use an interface other than PCI? Which features are available only on high-end cards? Which model would you choose to upgrade your current system? Which would you choose if you were building a new system?

• Lab Project 20.2

Uninstall and reinstall the audio drivers on your

find. Do any problems crop up during the process?

chapter

21 Portable PCs

"The great thing about a computer notebook is that no matter how much you stuff into it, it doesn't get bigger or heavier."

—BILL GATES, *BUSINESS @ THE SPEED OF THOUGHT*

In this chapter, you will learn how to

- **Describe the many types of portable computing devices available**
- **Enhance and upgrade portable PCs**
- **Troubleshoot portable PCs**

There are times when the walls close in, when you need a change of scenery to get that elusive spark that inspires greatness... or sometimes you just need to get away from your co-workers for a few hours because they're driving you nuts! For many occupations, that's difficult to do. You've got to have access to your documents and spreadsheets; you can't function without e-mail or the Internet. In short, you need a computer to get your job done.

Portable computing devices combine mobility with accessibility to bring you the best of both worlds; put more simply, portables let you take some or even all of your computing abilities with you when you go. Some portable PCs feature Windows XP systems with all the bells and whistles and all your Microsoft Office apps for a seamless transition from desk to café table. Even the smallest portable devices enable you to check your appointments and address book, or play Solitaire during the endless wait at the doctor's office. This chapter takes an in-depth looks at portables, first going through the major variations you'll run into and then hitting the tech-specific topics of enhancing, upgrading, managing, and maintaining portable PCs. Let's get started!

Historical/Conceptual

Portable Computing Devices

All portable devices share certain features. For output, they have LCD screens, although these vary from 17-inch behemoths to microscopic 2-inch screens. Portable devices employ sound of varying quality, from simple beeps to fairly nice music reproductions. All of them run on DC electricity stored in batteries, although several different technologies offer a range of battery life, lifespan, and cost. Other than screen, sound, and battery, portable computing devices come in an amazing variety of shapes, sizes, and

even replacing the desktop. The one in Figure 21.1, for example, has all of the features you expect the PC to have, such as a fast CPU, lots of RAM, a high-capacity hard drive, CD-RW and DVD drives, an excellent sound system, and a functioning copy of Windows XP. Attach it to a network and you can browse the Internet and send e-mail. Considering it weighs almost as much as a mini-tower PC (or at least it feels like it does when I'm lugging it through the airport!), such a portable can be considered a **desktop replacement**, because it does everything that most people want to do with a desktop PC.

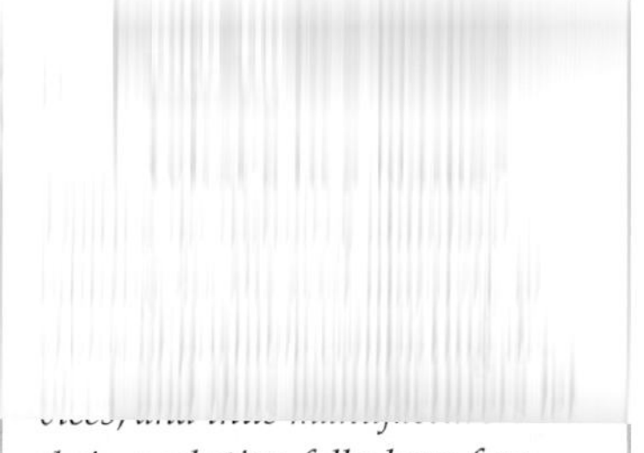

their marketing folks have fun with naming. What's the difference between a portable, a laptop, and a notebook? Nothing. One manufacturer might call its 12-inch LCD, four-pound portable a notebook, while another manufacturer might call its much larger desktop replacement portable a notebook as well. A laptop refers in general to the clamshell, keyboard-on-the-bottom and LCD-screen-at-the-top design that is considered the shape of mobile PCs. Most notebooks are laptops in the 8½ × 11-inch range.

For input devices, desktop replacements (and other portables) used trackballs in the early days, often plugged in like a mouse and clipped to the side of the case. Other models with trackballs placed them in front of the keyboard at the edge of the case nearest the user, or behind the keyboard at the edge nearest the screen.

The next wave to hit the laptop market was IBM's TrackPoint device, a pencil eraser-sized joystick situated in the center of the keyboard. The TrackPoint enables you to move the pointer around without taking your fingers away from the "home" typing position. You use a forefinger to push the joystick around, and click or alternate-click using two buttons below the spacebar. This type of pointing device has since been licensed for use by other manufacturers, and it continues to appear on laptops today.

Cross Check

LCD Monitors

Stretching back to the early days of mobile computing, almost every make and model of portable device has used an LCD monitor of some shape or size. You know all about LCD monitors from Chapter 18, "Video." Everything that applies to desktop LCDs applies to screens designed for portable devices as well, so turn to Chapter 18 and cross check your knowledge. What are the three variations of LCD screen you'll find today? Which technology offers the best picture? What connectors do you find with LCDs? Are there any special rules about cleaning LCD monitors? (Talk about a leading question!)

• **Figure 21.1** A notebook PC

But by far the most common laptop pointing device found today is the **touchpad** (Figure 21.2)—a flat, touch-sensitive pad just in front of the keyboard. To operate a touchpad, you simply glide your finger across its surface to move the pointer, and tap the surface once or twice to single- or double-click. You can also click using buttons just below the pad. Most people get the hang of this technique after just a few minutes of practice. The main advantage of the touchpad over previous laptop pointing devices is that it uses no moving parts—a fact that can really extend the life of a hard-working laptop. Some modern laptops actually provide both a TrackPoint-type device and a touchpad, to give the user a choice.

Desktop Extenders

Manufacturers offer **desktop extenders**, portable devices that don't replace the desktop, but rather extend it by giving you a subset of features of the typical desktop that you can take away from the desk. Figure 21.3 shows a portable with a good but small 12-inch screen. The system has 256 MB of RAM, a ~1-GHz processor, a 40-GB hard drive, and a battery that enables you to do work on it for more than five hours while disconnected from the wall socket. Even though it plays music and has a couple of decent, tiny speakers, you can't game on this computer (Solitaire, perhaps, but definitely not Half-Life 2!). But it weighs only four pounds., less than one-half the weight of the typical desktop replacement portable.

• **Figure 21.2** Touchpad on a laptop

Desktop extenders enable you to go mobile. When I'm on a roll writing, for example, I don't want to stop. But sometimes I do want to take a break from the office and stroll over to my favorite café for a latte or a pint of fine ale. At moments like those, I don't need a fully featured laptop with a monster 15-inch or 17-inch screen, but just a good word processing system—and perhaps the ability to surf the Internet on the café's wireless network so I can ~~goof off~~ research other important topics once I finish my project for the day. A lightweight laptop with a 12–13-inch screen, a reasonably fast processor, and gobs of RAM would do nicely.

PDAs

Finally, having a few computing essentials on hand at all times eases the day and makes planning and scheduling much more likely to succeed. Several companies, such as Palm, Sony, Toshiba, Hewlett-Packard, and Microsoft manufacture tiny hand-held portable computing devices that hold data such as your address book, personal notes, appointment schedules, and more. Such machines are called **Personal Digital Assistants (PDAs)**. All modern PDAs have many applications, such as word processors for jotting

ure 21.4 shows a Palm Zire 71 PDA.

PDAs don't run Windows XP or even 98, but rather require specialized OSs such as Windows CE, PocketPC, PalmOS, and Linux. All of these OSs provide a GUI that enables you to interact with the device by touching the screen directly. Many of today's PDAs use handwriting recognition combined with modified mouse functions, usually in the form of a pen-like stylus to make a type of input called *pen-based computing*. To make an application load, for example, you would slide the stylus out of its holder in the PDA case and touch the appropriate icon with the stylus tip.

Tech Tip

Ultralights

Ultralight portables are computers that normally weigh less than three pounds and are less than an inch in thickness. These machines usually have smaller displays, lower-capacity hard drives, and CPUs that operate at lower speeds than their more full-sized brethren. This class of portable computers is designed for the busy traveler who wants a nearly full-featured laptop in a small, easily transported package. Often, these laptops are much more expensive than larger, faster machines—think of it as paying more to get less! You'll hear the term subnotebooks *used to describe ultralight portables; the terms aren't quite synonymous, but the marketing waters for all portable computing devices are pretty muddy.*

HotSync

PDAs make excellent pocket companions because you can quickly add a client's address or telephone number, check the day's schedule before going to your next meeting, and modify your calendar entries when something unexpected arises. Best of all, you can then update all the equivalent features on your desktop PC automatically! PDAs synchronize with your primary PC so you have the same essential data on both machines. Many PDAs come with a cradle, a place to rest your PDA and recharge its battery. The cradle connects to the PC most often through a USB port. You can run special software to synchronize the data between the PDA and the main PC. Setting up the Zire 71 featured above, for example, requires you to install a portion of the Palm desktop for Windows. This software handles all the synchronization chores. You simply place the PDA in the properly-connected cradle and click the button to synchronize. Figure 21.5 shows a PDA in the

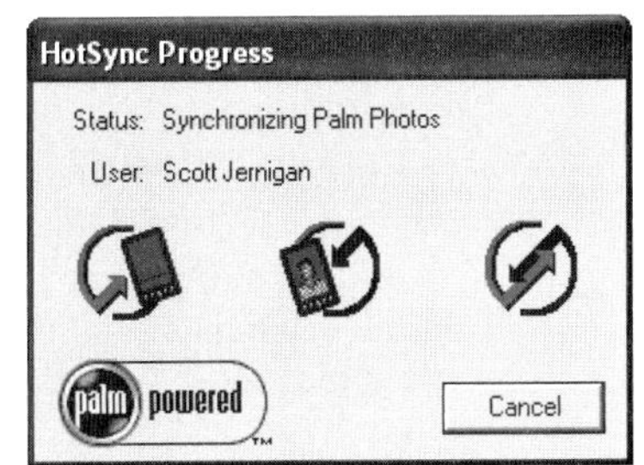

Figure 21.5 HotSync in progress

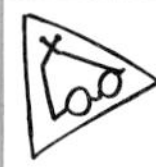

Tech Tip

Tablet PC

Looking and feeling like a cross between a traditional laptop PC and a PDA, Tablet PCs have been marked as the next great thing in portables for a while now. They feature ~1 GHz processors, a good amount of RAM, 20-40 GB hard drives, and integrated wireless networking. They run a version of Windows called Windows XP Tablet Edition and use a pen-based interface for the most part, although some models also include a keyboard. Tablet PCs currently have caught on in certain industries, such as medicine, but have not captured the fancy of the general public. Everything you learn about portable computing devices in this chapter applies to Tablet PCs.

• **Figure 21.6** CF (l) and SD cards

middle of a **HotSync** operation, PalmOS's term for the process of synchronizing.

PDA Memory

Almost every PDA has both internal Flash ROM memory of 1 MB or more, and some sort of removable and upgradeable storage medium. Compact Flash (CF) technology has the strongest market share among the many competing standards, but you'll find a bunch of different memory card types out there. CF cards are about an inch and a half square and fit in a special CF slot. Other popular media include the much smaller Secure Digital (SD) cards and Sony's proprietary Memory Stick. You'll find capacities for all the standards ranging from 8 MB up to 512 MB—on a card the size of a postage stamp! Figure 21.6 shows some typical memory cards.

Sorting out all the variations of portable computing devices out there would take entirely too much ink (and go well beyond A+). Table 21.1 lists

Table 21.1 Portable Computing Devices

	Screen Size	Weight	Features	Uses
Desktop Replacements	14–17-inch+	8–12+ lbs.	Everything on a desktop	Mobile multimedia editing, presentations, mobile gaming
Desktop Extenders	10–14-inch	4–7 lbs	Almost everything you'll find on a desktop. Better battery life than desktop replacements	Presentations, note-taking in class or meetings, traveling companion for business folks
Ultralights	6–12-inch	2–3 lbs	Ultimate mobility without sacrificing full PC status. Excellent battery life. Few have internal CD or DVD media drives	Long term traveling companion; in the purse or pack for writing or doing e-mail on the road; coolness factor
Tablet PCs	10–12-inch	4 lbs	Pen-based interface enables you to use them like a paper notepad; no CD or DVD media drives, but integrated wireless networking	Niche market for people who need hand-written notes that have to be transcribed to the PC
PDAs	3–4-inch	1 lb	Light, multi-function devices that carry address book, scheduler; many offer other features, such as MP3 and video playback	Helps busy people stay organized; helps get people organized; fun; can carry many electronic books (e-books) so you're never caught waiting in line and being bored

Table 21.1	Portable Computing Devices *(continued)*			
	Screen Size	**Weight**	**Features**	**Uses**
PDA-Phones[1]	2–inch	< 1 lb	Tiny PDA built into a cell phone; some offer e-mail and other Internet connectivity	Reduces the number of gadgets some folks carry

[1] PDA-phones are not covered in the text or the A+ exams. As of this writing, they haven't been available long enough for the market to assess their usefulness.

the six most common styles of portable computing devices, some of their key features, and the intended use or audience for the product. This table is in no way conclusive, but lists the highlights.

Tech Tip

Memory Cards

Memory cards of all stripes made the leap in 2003 from the exclu-

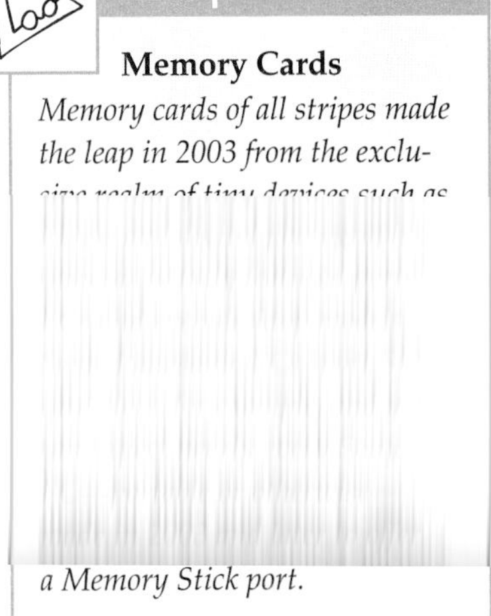

a Memory Stick port.

In the dark ages of mobile computing, you had to shell out top dollar for any device that would unplug, and what you purchased was what you got. Upgrade a laptop? Add functions to your desktop replacement? You had few if any options, so you simply paid for a device that would be way behind the technology curve within a year and functionally obsolete within two.

Portable PCs today offer many ways to enhance their abilities. Internal and external expansion buses enable you to add completely new functions to portables, such as attaching a scanner or mobile printer or both! You can take advantage of the latest wireless technology breakthrough simply by slipping a card into the appropriate slot on the laptop. Further, modern portables offer a modular interior. You can add or change RAM, for example—the first upgrade that almost every laptop owner wants to make. You can increase the hard drive storage space and, at least with some models, swap out the CPU, video card, sound card, and more. Gone forever are the days of buying guaranteed obsolescence! Let's look at four specific areas of technology that laptops use to enhance functions and upgrade

Try This!

Variations

Portables come in such a dizzying variety of sizes, styles, features, and shapes that a simple table in a book cannot do justice to the ingenuity and engineering of the manufacturers of these devices. Only a hands-on field trip can bring home the point for you, so try this!

1. Visit your local computer or electronics store and tour the portable computing devices.
2. How many variations of laptops are there? Do any offer funky features, such as a swivel screen or a portrait to landscape mode?
3. How many variations of PDA are displayed? What OSs do they run?
4. What other devices do you find? What about TabletPCs?
5. If you want to wander into the realm of extremes, check out www.dynamism.com. They specialize in bringing Japanese-only products to the English-speaking market. You'll find the hottest desktop replacement laptops and the sleekest sub-notebooks at the site, with all the details beautifully converted from native Japanese to English.

components: PC Cards, single and multiple function expansion ports, and modular components.

PC Cards

PC Cards are roughly credit-card sized devices that enhance and extend the functions of a portable PC. Still commonly known by their older name, **Personal Computer Memory Card International Association (PCMCIA) cards**, PC Cards are as standard on today's mobile computers as the hard drive. PC Cards are easy to use, inexpensive, and convenient. Figure 21.7 shows a typical PC Card.

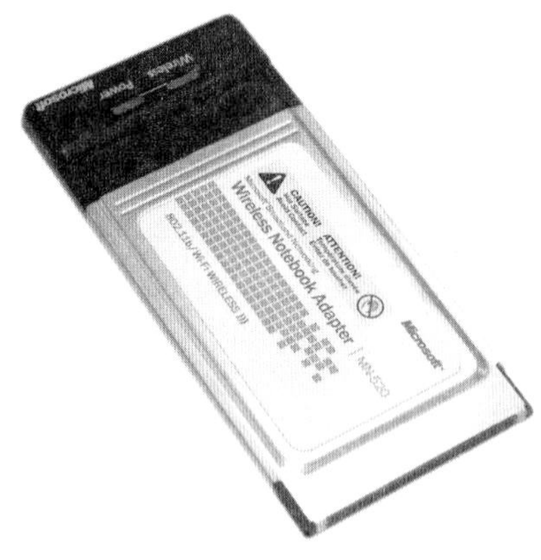

• **Figure 21.7** PC Card

Almost every portable PC has one or two PC Card slots, into which you insert a PC Card. Each card can have at least one function, but many have two, three, or more! You can buy a PC Card that offers connections for removable media, for example, such as combination SD and CF card readers. You can also find PC Cards that enable you to plug into multiple types of networks. All PC Cards are hot swappable, meaning you can plug them in without powering down the PC.

> Many manufacturers use the term *hot-pluggable* rather than hot-swappable to describe the ability to plug in and replace PC Cards on the fly. Look for either term on the exams.

> For CardBus to operate, the laptop must be running Windows 95 OSR2 or later. Windows NT and 95A or earlier cannot use CardBus sockets.

PC Cards come in two flavors, regular and **CardBus**, and each flavor comes in three different physical sizes, called Type I, Type II, and Type III. Regular PC Cards are 16-bit, 5-V cards that can have up to two distinct functions or devices, such as a modem/network card combination. CardBus PC Cards are 32-bit, 3.3-V cards that can have up to eight (!) different functions on a single card. Regular PC Cards will fit into and work in CardBus slots, but the reverse is not true. CardBus totally dominates the current PC Card landscape, but you might still run into older regular PC Cards.

Type I, II, and III cards differ only in the thickness of the card (Type I being the thinnest, and Type III the thickest). All PC Cards share the same 68-pin interface, so any PC Card will work in any slot that's high enough to accept that card type. Type II cards are by far the most common of PC Cards. Therefore, most laptops will have two Type II slots, one above the other, to enable the computer to accept two Type I or II cards or one Type III card (Figure 21.8).

Although PCMCIA doesn't require that certain sizes perform certain functions, most PC Cards follow their recommendations. Table 21.2 lists the sizes and typical uses of each type of PC Card.

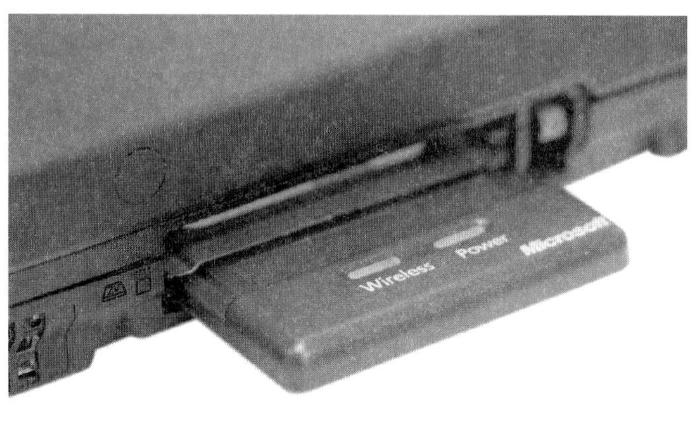

• **Figure 21.8** PC Card slots

The PCMCIA standard defines two levels of software drivers to support PC Cards. The first, lower level is known as **socket services**. Socket services are device drivers that support the PC Card socket, enabling the system to detect when a PC Card has been inserted or removed, and providing the necessary I/O to the device. The second, higher level is known as **card services**. The card services level recognizes the function of a particular PC Card and provides the specialized drivers necessary to make the card work.

In today's laptops, the socket services are standardized and are handled by the system BIOS. Windows itself handles all card services and has a large preinstalled base of PC Card device drivers, although most PC Cards come with their own drivers.

Table 21.2	PC Card Types and Their Typical Uses			
Type	**Length**	**Width**	**Thickness**	**Typical Use**
Type I	85.6 mm	54.0 mm	3.3 mm	Flash memory
Type II	85.6 mm	54.0 mm	5.0 mm	I/O (Modem, NIC, etc.)
Type III	85.6 mm	54.0 mm	10.5 mm	Hard drives

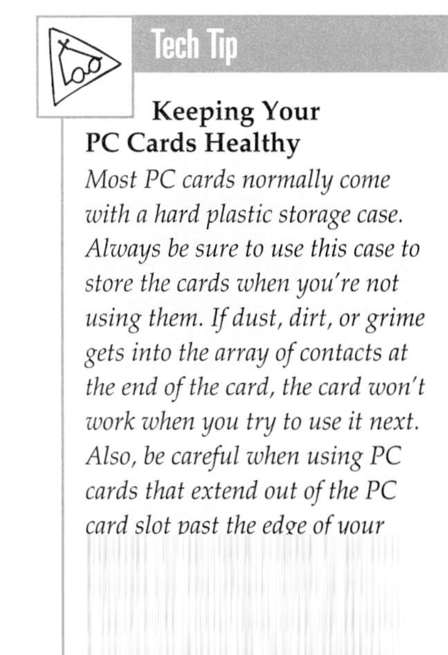

Tech Tip

Keeping Your PC Cards Healthy

Most PC cards normally come with a hard plastic storage case. Always be sure to use this case to store the cards when you're not using them. If dust, dirt, or grime gets into the array of contacts at the end of the card, the card won't work when you try to use it next. Also, be careful when using PC cards that extend out of the PC card slot past the edge of your

wasn't damaged, but the card was toast!

Microsoft introduced support for CardBus with Windows 95 OSR2, so every version of Windows beyond that supports it.

Limited-Function Ports

most current portable PCs come with built-in NICs or modems for networking support.

All limited-function ports work the same way on portable PCs as they do on desktop models. You plug in a device to a particular port and, as long as Windows has the proper drivers, you will have a functioning device when you boot. The only port that requires any extra effort is the video port.

Most laptops support a second monitor via an analog VGA port or a digital DVI port in the back of the box. With a second monitor attached, you can display Windows on only the laptop LCD, only the external monitor, or both simultaneously. Not all portables can do all variations, but they're more common than not. Most portables have a special Function key on the keyboard that, when pressed, adds a third option to certain keys on the keyboard. Figure 21.9 shows a close-up of a typical keyboard with the Function key and third options circled. To engage the second monitor or to cycle through the modes, hold the Function key and press the key with the oval as the third option.

• **Figure 21.9** Laptop keyboard with Function key and third key options highlighted

General-Purpose Ports

Most portable PCs have one or more general-purpose expansion ports that enable you to plug in many different types of devices. Older portables sport RS-232 serial and IEEE

Although many laptops use the Function key method to cycle the monitor selections, that's not always the case. You might have to pop into the Display applet in the Control Panel to click a check box. Just be assured that if the laptop has a VGA or DVI port, you can cycle through monitor choices!

1284 parallel ports for mice, modems, printers, scanners, external CD-media drives, and more.

Universal Serial Bus (USB) and **FireWire** (or more properly, **IEEE 1394**) are two technologies that have their roots in desktop computer technology, but have also found widespread use in portable PCs. Both types of connections feature an easy-to-use connector and gives the user the ability to insert a device into a system while the PC is running—you won't have to reboot a system in order to install a new peripheral. With USB and FireWire, just plug the device in and go! Because portable PCs don't have multiple internal expansion capabilities like desktops, USB and FireWire are two of the more popular methods for attaching peripherals to laptops.

USB

You should be familiar with the concept of USB, USB connectors, and USB hubs from the discussion of those concepts in Chapter 2. Let's take a little more in-depth look at USB as it applies to portable PCs.

When discussing USB, it is extremely important to use the right nomenclature. When you're speaking about a port that operates at 12 Mbps, just say "USB." If you're talking about a 480-Mbps port, then it's "Hi-Speed USB." For more information on each of the USB standards, check out www.usb.org.

There are two flavors of USB in use today—USB and Hi-Speed USB. Until 2003, the industry referred to these two types of USB as USB 1.1 and USB 2.0 respectively, and you'll still see that on marketing briefs. The first type of USB is the interface that most people are familiar with, operating at a slow 12 Mbps compared to 480 Mbps for Hi-Speed USB. In addition to a much faster transfer rate, Hi-Speed USB is fully backward compatible with devices that operate under the much slower USB standard. Those old devices won't run any faster than they used to—to see true increases in speed, you must connect Hi-Speed USB devices to Hi-Speed USB ports using Hi-Speed USB cables! Hi-Speed USB devices will also function when plugged into USB ports, albeit at 12 Mbps (and what's the fun in that?).

Watch out for questions on the A+ exams that haven't kept up with the times. You might see 12 Mbps USB referred to as USB 1.1.

In theory, the USB interface can support up to 127 devices on a single USB port. In reality, USB ports also supply power to connected devices, but too many devices on a single USB chain will overtax its power capabilities. Often, USB ports on portable computers cannot provide enough voltage and current to power certain items. Powering a device from the USB port on a portable is often not a good idea—by connecting the device, you are pulling energy from the battery. For this reason, only small, low-power devices should be powered by the USB ports on a portable computer—mice, keyboards, and network adapters are three good examples. All other devices, like USB hard disk drives and CD-ROMs, should be used with an external power supply providing power to the drive.

Watch the cable lengths with both versions of USB. USB specifications allow for a maximum cable length of 5 meters, although you may add a powered USB hub every 5 meters to extend this distance. Although most USB devices never get near this maximum, many devices such as digital cameras try to use very long (5-meter) cables. Pushing USB to these maximum lengths might cause problems. Because USB is a two-way (bi-directional) connection, as the cable grows longer, even a standard, well-shielded, 20-gauge, twisted-pair USB cable begins to suffer from electrical interference. I stick to around 2 meters maximum.

USB Configuration Improper USB CMOS and driver configuration will make your USB installations nightmarish. Always make sure to follow these steps:

1. Be sure that the CMOS provides an IRQ for the USB ports. Look for a setting similar to Figure 21.10.
2. Ensure that your operating system supports USB. This is a no-brainer in Windows because USB is supported by every version, with the exception of Windows 95A and Windows NT. If you have Windows 95A, just download the USB

```
CMOS Setup Utility - Copyright (C) 1984-1999 Award Software
                  PnP/PCI Configurations

  PNP OS Installed            No              |        Item Help
  Reset Configuration Data    Disabled        |
                                              |
  Resources Controlled By     Auto(ESCD)      | Menu Level  ▶
x IRQ Resources               Press Enter     |
x DMA Resources               Press Enter     | Select Yes if you are
                                              | using Plug and Play
  PCI/VGA Palette Snoop       Disabled        | capable operating
  Assign IRQ For USB          Enabled         | system Select No if
  INT Pin 1 Assignment        Auto            | you need the BIOS to
  INT Pin 2 Assignment        Auto            | configure non-boot
  INT Pin 3 Assignment        Auto            | devices
  INT Pin 4 Assignment        Auto            |
```

Windows 2000 and XP have a large number of built-in drivers for USB devices. You can count on Windows 2000 and Windows XP to recognize keyboards, mice, and other basic devices with its built-in drivers. Just be aware that if your new mouse or keyboard has some extras, the default USB drivers will probably not support them. I always install the driver that comes with the device or an updated one downloaded from the manufacturer's web site.

Port Replicators USB lives up to its *universal* moniker with **port replicators**, devices that plug into a USB port and offer common PC ports, such as serial, parallel, USB, network, and PS/2. By plugging your notebook computer into the port replicator, you can instantly connect it to non-portable components such as a printer, scanner, monitor, or a full-sized keyboard. Port replicators are typically used at home or in the office with the non-portable equipment already connected. Figure 21.11 shows a Dell portable computer connected to a port replicator.

Once connected to the port replicator, the computer is able to access any devices attached to it; there's no need to connect each individual device to the PC. As a side bonus, port replicators enable you to attach legacy devices, such as parallel printers, to a new laptop that only has modern multi-function ports such as USB and FireWire, and not parallel or serial ports.

• Figure 21.11 Port replicator for a Dell portable computer

Docking Stations **Docking stations** resemble port replicators in many ways, offering legacy and modern single- and multi-function ports. The typical docking station uses a proprietary connection, but has extra features built in, such as a DVD drive or PC Card slots for extra

Although portable PCs most often connect to port replicators via USB ports, some manufacturers have propriety connections for proprietary port replicators. As long as such a portable PC has a USB port, you can use either the proprietary hardware or the more flexible USB devices.

enhancements. You can find docking stations for most laptop models, but you'll find them used most frequently with the desktop extender and ultralight models. Most ultralights have no internal CD or DVD media drive (because the drives weigh too much), and so must rely on external drives for full PC functionality. Docking stations make an excellent companion to such portables.

FireWire

Although USB dominates the modern general-purpose, hot-swappable technologies on laptops, FireWire is quickly making inroads into this sector. As the CPU speed of laptops has increased, tasks that were once relegated to only the most powerful desktop computers can now be accomplished on a simple laptop. One such task is editing digital video, and this is an area where FireWire shines. Most modern digital video cameras use the IEEE 1394 interface for transferring video from camera to PC for editing. The high transfer speed of FireWire makes transferring large video files quick and easy. FireWire has two distinct types of connectors, both of which are commonly found on laptops. The first is a 6-pin *powered* connector. Like USB, a FireWire port is capable of providing power to a device. Once again, the same considerations must be made about powering high-power devices through the FireWire port. The other type of connector is a 4-pin *unpowered* connector. This type of connector does not provide power to a device, so you will need to find another method of powering the external device.

The Modular Laptop

For years, portable PC makers required completely proprietary components for each system model they developed. For the most part, this proprietary attitude still prevails, but we're starting to see some modularity in today's portable PCs, enabling us to make basic replacements and upgrades without going back to the manufacturer for expensive, proprietary components. You need to surf the Web for companies that sell the components, because very few storefronts stock them. Following are the most common ones.

RAM

Stock factory portable PCs almost always come with a minimal amount of RAM, so one of the first laptop upgrades you'll be called on to do is to add more RAM. Laptops running Windows XP Home routinely sit on store shelves and go home to consumers with 128 MB of RAM, an amount guaranteed to limit the use and performance of the laptop. The OS alone will consume more than half of the RAM! Luckily, every decent laptop has upgradeable RAM slots. Laptops use one of four types of RAM. Most older laptops use either 72-pin or 144-pin SO-DIMMs with SDRAM technology (Figure 21.12). DDR SDRAM systems primarily use 200-pin SO-DIMMs, although you'll also find 172-pin micro-DIMMs.

Cross Check

USB and FireWire

You've explored the general purpose or multi-function expansion ports before and should know quite a few details about them. Revisit Chapter 2, "The Visible PC," and cross check your knowledge. What kind of connectors do USB and FireWire use? What cable length limitations are there? What about number of devices on each controller?

How to Add/Replace RAM Upgrading the RAM in a portable PC requires a couple of steps. First, you need to get the correct RAM. Many portable PC makers use proprietary RAM solutions, which means you need to order directly from Dell, HP, or Sony and pay exorbitant prices for the precious extra megabytes. Other manufacturers take pity on consumers and the techs who take care of them, and use standard SO-DIMMs or micro-DIMMs. Refer to the manufacturer's web site or to the manual (if any) that came with the portable for the specific RAM needed.

Second, every portable PC offers a unique challenge to the tech who wants to upgrade the RAM because there's no standard for RAM placement in portables. More often than not, you need to unscrew or pop open a panel on the underside of the portable (Figure 21.13). Then you press out on the restraining clips and the RAM stick will pop up (Figure 21.14). Gently remove the old stick of RAM and insert the new one by reversing

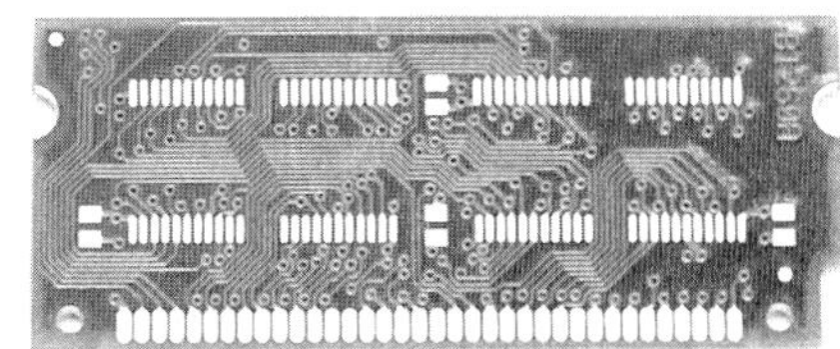

Figure 21.12 72-pin SO-DIMM stick (front

drives have suffered, however, from diminished storage capacity compared to their 3.5-inch brothers. Currently, large 2.5-inch hard drives hold less than 80 GB, while the 3.5-inch hard drives can hold more than 200 GB of data! Some manufacturers may require you to set the drive to use a cable select setting as opposed to master or slave, so check with the laptop maker for any special issues. Otherwise, no difference exists between 2.5-inch drives and their larger 3.5-inch brethren (Figure 21.15).

Figure 21.13 Removing a RAM panel

Modular CPUs

Both Intel and AMD have long sold specialized, modular CPUs for laptops, yet only now are folks realizing that they can easily upgrade many systems by removing the old module and replacing it with a new one. Be very careful to follow manufacturer's specifications! You should keep in mind, however, that replacing the CPU in a laptop often requires that you disassemble the entire machine. This can be a daunting task, even for professionals. If you want to upgrade the CPU in your laptop, it's often best to let the professionals take care of it.

Cross Check

How Much RAM Is Enough?

The amount of RAM needed to run a PC—portable or otherwise—smoothly and stably depends on both the type of applications that it will run and the needs of the OS. When making a recommendation to a client about upgrading a laptop's memory, you should ask the basic questions, such as what he or she plans to do on the laptop. If the laptop will be used for e-mail, word processing, and web surfing, in contrast, a medium level of RAM, such as 32-64 MB, should do fine. If the user travels, uses a high-end digital camera, and wants to use Photoshop to edit huge images, you'll need to augment the RAM accordingly. Then you need to add the needs of the OS to give a good recommendation. Turn to Chapter 12, "Understanding Windows," and cross check your knowledge about specific OS RAM needs. What's a good minimum for Windows 98 SE? What about Windows Me? And Windows XP Professional?

• Figure 21.14 Releasing the RAM

• Figure 21.15 The 2.5-inch and 3.5-inch drives are mostly the same.

Video Cards

Video card makers have rushed to join the modular laptop component arena. Although no single standard works in all systems, a quick phone call to the tech support department of the laptop maker often reveals upgrade options. Modular video cards are the least standardized of all modular components, but as manufacturers adopt more industry-wide standards, we'll be able to replace video cards in laptops more readily.

Modular Drives

In order to add functionality to laptops, manufacturers have started to include "modular drives" with their machines. CD-ROMs, DVD-ROMS, CD-R/RWs, and floppy disk drives are the most common modular drives that are included with portables, although combination CD-RW/DVD-ROM drives grace many higher-end laptops. The beauty of modular drives is that you can swap easily back and forth between different types of drives. Need that floppy disk drive? Just pull out the CD or DVD media drive and stick in the floppy disk drive. Need more storage space? Pull out the floppy disk drive and put in another hard drive. Many laptops enable you to replace a drive with a second battery, which obviously can extend the time you can go before you have to plug the laptop into an AC outlet.

I have a laptop that allows me to swap out my CD-ROM drive for a floppy disk drive. If I don't need either drive, I just take out the drive that's currently installed and put a blank faceplate into the empty slot—this is great to do when I'm traveling and I know that I won't be needing the CD-ROM. Removing the CD-ROM makes my hefty laptop weigh a little bit less, and every little bit helps!

Managing and Maintaining Portables

Most portable PCs come from the factory solidly built and configured. Manufacturers know that few techs outside their factories know enough to work on them, so they don't cut corners. From a tech's standpoint, your most common work on managing and maintaining portables involves taking care of the batteries and extending the battery life through proper power management, keeping the machine clean, and avoiding excessive heat.

Everything you normally do to maintain a PC applies to portable PCs. You need to keep current on Windows patches and Service Packs, and use stable, recent drivers. Run Check Disk or ScanDisk with some frequency, and definitely defragment the hard drive. Disk Cleanup is a must if the lap-

clear understanding of the quirks, you can *usually* spot and fix battery problems. The three types of batteries commonly used in mobile PCs are **Nickel-Cadmium (Ni-Cd)**, **Nickel-Metal Hydride (Ni-MH)**, and **Lithium-Ion (Li-Ion)** batteries. Manufacturers have also started working with fuel cell batteries, although most of that work is experimental at this writing.

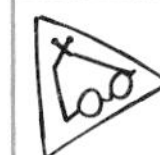

Tech Tip

Going Inside

To reach most modular components on a laptop, you need to do more than remove an exterior panel. You need to go inside to get access to devices directly connected to the motherboard. Many laptops have an easily removable keyboard that, once removed, gives you access to a metal heat spreader (just a plate that sits over the motherboard) and a

keyboard will be attached to a small cable that can easily disconnect if you pull hard. Don't forget to check this connection before you reinsert the keyboard at the end of the procedure! Avoid ESD like you would with any other PC, and definitely unplug the laptop from the wall and remove the battery *before you do any work inside!*

Nickel-Cadmium

Ni-Cds were the first batteries commonly used in mobile PCs, which means the technology was full of little problems. Probably most irritating was a little thing called *battery memory*, or the tendency of a Ni-Cd battery to lose a significant amount of its rechargeability if it was charged repeatedly without being totally discharged. A battery that originally kept a laptop running for two hours would eventually only keep that same laptop going for 30 minutes or less. Figure 21.16 shows a typical Ni-Cd battery.

To prevent memory problems, a Ni-Cd battery had to be discharged completely before each recharging. Recharging was tricky as well, because Ni-Cd batteries disliked being overcharged. Unfortunately, there was no way to verify when a battery was fully charged without an expensive charging machine, which none of us had. As a result, most Ni-Cd batteries lasted an extremely short time and had to be replaced. A quick fix was to purchase a **conditioning charger**. These chargers would first totally discharge the Ni-Cd battery, and then generate a special "reverse" current that, in a way, "cleaned" internal parts of the battery so that it could be recharged more often and would run longer on each

• **Figure 21.16** Ni-Cd battery

recharge. Ni-Cd batteries would, at best, last for 1,000 charges, and far fewer with poor treatment. Ni-Cds were extremely susceptible to heat and would self-discharge over time if not used. Leaving a Ni-Cd in the car in the summer was guaranteed to result in a fully discharged battery in next to no time!

But Ni-Cd batteries didn't stop causing trouble after they died. The highly toxic metals inside the battery made it unacceptable simply to throw them in the trash. Ni-Cd batteries should be disposed of via specialized disposal companies. This is very important! Even though Ni-Cd batteries aren't used in PCs very often anymore, many devices, such as cellular and cordless phones, still use Ni-Cd batteries. Don't trash the environment by tossing Ni-Cds in a landfill. Turn them in at the closest special disposal site; most recycling centers are glad to take them. Also, many battery manufacturers/distributors will take them. The environment you help preserve just might be yours—or your kids'!

You *must* use disposal companies or battery recycling services to dispose of the highly toxic Ni-Cd batteries.

Nickel Metal Hydride

Ni-MH batteries were the next generation of mobile PC batteries and are still quite common today. Basically, Ni-MH batteries are Ni-Cd batteries without most of the headaches. Ni-MH batteries are much less susceptible to memory problems, can better tolerate overcharging, can take more recharging, and last longer between rechargings. Like Ni-Cds, Ni-MH batteries are still susceptible to heat, but at least they are considered non-toxic to the environment. It's still a good idea to do a special disposal. Unlike a Ni-Cd, it's usually better to recharge a Ni-MH with shallow recharges as opposed to a complete discharge/recharge. Ni-MH is a popular replacement battery for Ni-Cd systems (Figure 21.17).

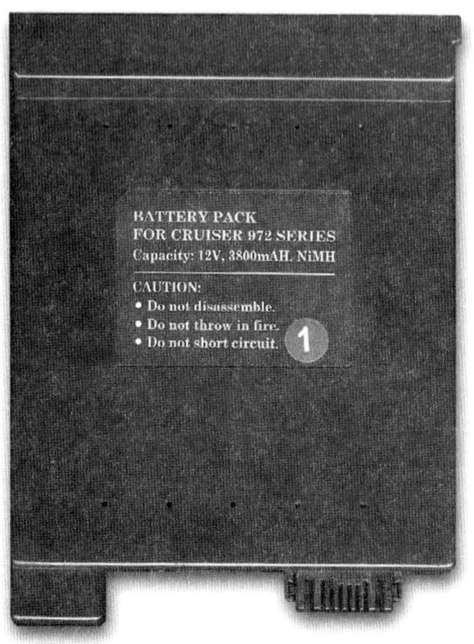

• **Figure 21.17** Ni-MH battery

Lithium Ion

The most common type battery used today is Li-Ion. Li-Ion batteries are very powerful, completely immune to memory problems, and last at least twice as long as comparable Ni-MH batteries on one charge. Sadly, they can't handle as many charges as Ni-MHs, but today's users are usually more than glad to give up total battery lifespan in return for longer periods between charges. Li-Ion batteries will explode if they are overcharged, so all Li-Ion batteries sold with PCs have built-in circuitry to prevent accidental overcharging. Lithium batteries can only be used on systems designed to use them. They can't be used as replacement batteries (Figure 21.18).

• **Figure 21.18** Li-Ion battery

Other Portable Power Sources

In an attempt to provide better maintenance for laptop batteries, manufacturers have developed a new type of battery called the **Smart Battery**. Smart Batteries tell the computer when they need to be charged, conditioned, or replaced.

Portable computer manufacturers are also looking at other potential power sources, especially ones that don't have the shortcomings of current batteries. The most promising of these new technologies are **fuel cells**. The technology behind fuel cells is very complex, but to summarize, fuel cells produce electrical power as a result of a chemical reaction between the hydrogen and oxygen contained in the fuel cell. It is estimated that a small fuel cell could power a laptop for up to 40 hours before it needs to be replaced or refilled. This technology is still a year or two from making it to the consumer market, but it's an exciting trend!

The Care and Feeding of Batteries

In general, keep in mind the following basics. First, always store batteries in a cool place. Although a freezer is in concept an excellent storage place, the moisture, metal racks, and food make it a bad idea. Second, condition

Power Management

Many different parts are included in the typical laptop, and each part uses power. The problem with early laptops was that every one of these parts used power continuously, whether or not the system needed that device at that time. For example, the hard drive would continue to spin whether or not it was being accessed, and the LCD panel would continue to display, even when the user walked away from the machine.

The optimal situation would be a system where the user could instruct the PC to shut down unused devices selectively, preferably by defining a maximum period of inactivity which, when reached, would trigger the PC to shut down the inactive device. Longer periods of inactivity would eventually enable the entire system to shut itself down, leaving critical information loaded in RAM, ready to restart if a wake-up event (such as moving the mouse or pressing a key) would tell the system to restart. The system would have to be sensitive to potential hazards, such as shutting down in the middle of writing to a drive, and so on. Also, this feature could not add significantly to the cost of the PC. Clearly, a machine that could perform these functions would need specialized hardware, BIOS, and operating system to operate properly. This process of cooperation among the hardware, the BIOS, and the OS to reduce power use is known generically as *power management*.

Try This!

Recycling Old Portable PC Batteries

Got an old portable PC battery lying around? Well, you've got to get rid of it, and since there are some pretty nasty chemicals in that battery, you can't just throw it in the trash. Sooner or later, you'll probably need to do this, so try this:

1. Do an online search to find the battery recycling center nearest to you.
2. Sometimes, you can take old laptop batteries to an auto parts store that disposes of old car batteries—I know it sounds odd, but it's true! See if you can find one in your area that will do this.
3. Many cities offer a hazardous materials disposal or recycling service. Check to see if and how your local government will help you dispose of your old batteries.

System Management Mode (SMM)

Intel began the process of power management with a series of new features built into the 386SX CPU. These new features enabled the CPU to slow down or stop its clock without erasing the register information, as well as enabling power saving in peripherals. These features were collectively called **System Management Mode (SMM)**. All modern CPUs have SMM. Although a power-saving CPU was okay, power management was relegated to special "sleep" or "doze" buttons that would stop the CPU and all of the peripherals on the laptop. To take real advantage of SMM, the system needed a specialized BIOS and OS to go with the SMM CPU. To this end, Intel put forward the **Advanced Power Management (APM)** specification in 1992 and the **Advanced Configuration and Power Interface (ACPI)** standard in 1996.

Requirements for APM/ACPI

APM and ACPI require a number of items in order to function fully. First is an SMM-capable CPU. As virtually all CPUs are SMM-capable, this is easy. Second is an APM-compliant BIOS, which enables the CPU to shut off the peripherals when desired. The third requirement is devices that will accept being shut off. These devices are usually called "Energy Star" devices, which signals their compliance with the EPA's Energy Star standard. To be an Energy Star device, a peripheral must have the ability to shut down without actually turning off and show that they use much less power than the non-Energy Star equivalent. Last, the system's OS must know how to request that a particular device be shut down, and the CPU's clock must be slowed down or stopped.

> Don't limit your perception of APM, ACPI, and Energy Star just to laptops! Virtually all desktop systems also use the power management functions.

ACPI goes beyond the APM standard by supplying support for hot-swappable devices—always a huge problem with APM. This feature aside, it is a challenge to tell the difference between an APM system and an ACPI system at first glance.

APM/ACPI Levels

APM defines four different power-usage operating levels for a system. These levels are intentionally fuzzy to give manufacturers considerable leeway in their use; the only real difference among them is the amount of time each takes to return to normal usage. These levels are as follows:

- **Full On** Everything in the system is running at full power. There is no power management.
- **APM Enabled** CPU and RAM are running at full power. Power management is enabled. An unused device may or may not be shut down.
- **APM Standby** CPU is stopped. RAM still stores all programs. All peripherals are shut down, although configuration options are still stored. (In other words, to get back to APM Enabled, you won't have to reinitialize the devices.)
- **APM Suspend** Everything in the PC is shut down or at its lowest power-consumption setting. Many systems use a special type of Suspend called **hibernation**, where critical configuration

information is written to the hard drive. Upon a wake-up event, the system is reinitialized, and the data is read from the drive to return the system to the APM Enabled mode. Clearly, the recovery time between Suspend and Enabled will be much longer than the time between Standby and Enabled.

ACPI handles all these levels plus a few more, such as "soft power on/off," which enables you to define the function of the power button.

Configuration of APM/ACPI

You configure APM/ACPI via CMOS settings or through Windows. Windows settings will override CMOS settings. Although the APM/ACPI standards permit a great deal of flexibility, which can create some confusion among different implementations, certain settings apply generally to CMOS [illegible] will present settings to determine wake-up events, such as directing the system to monitor a modem or a particular IRQ (Figure 21.19). A true ACPI-compliant CMOS provides an ACPI setup option. Figure 21.20 shows a typical modern BIOS that provides this setting.

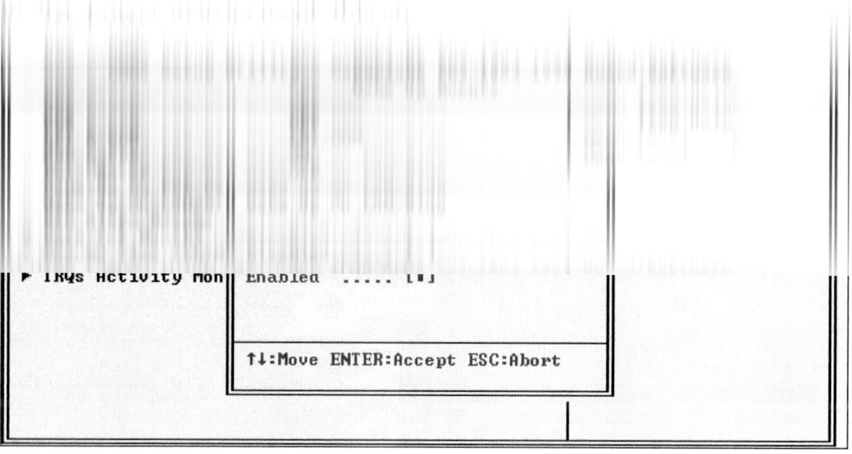

• **Figure 21.19** Setting a wake-up event in CMOS

APM/ACPI settings can be found in one of two areas in Windows. For Windows 9x/Me, the first place is the Display applet in the Control Panel. Because the monitor is one of the biggest power users on a computer, this is a great place to start the power management configuration process. From the Display applet, click on Settings, then Advanced, and select the Monitor tab (Figure 21.21).

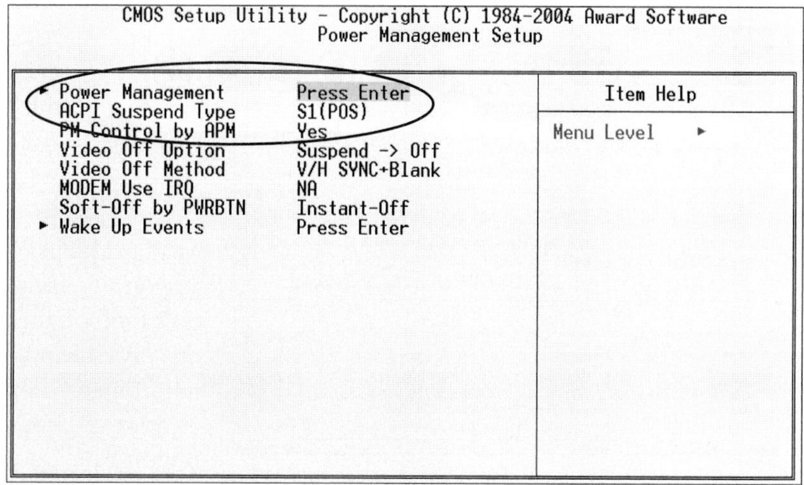

• **Figure 21.20** CMOS with ACPI setup option

Windows 9x/Me gives you limited control over individual components, but has several set overall *Power schemes* such as Home/Office and Portable that put the system into standby or suspend after a certain interval. You set these options in the Power Management Applet in the Control Panel. You can also require the system to go into standby after a set period of time or turn off the

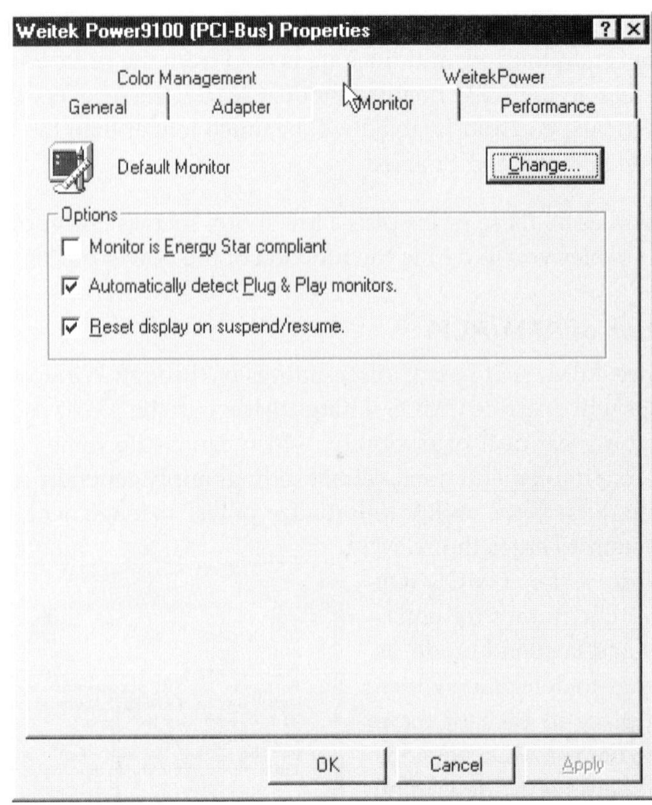

• **Figure 21.21** Monitor tab in Display applet—Windows 98

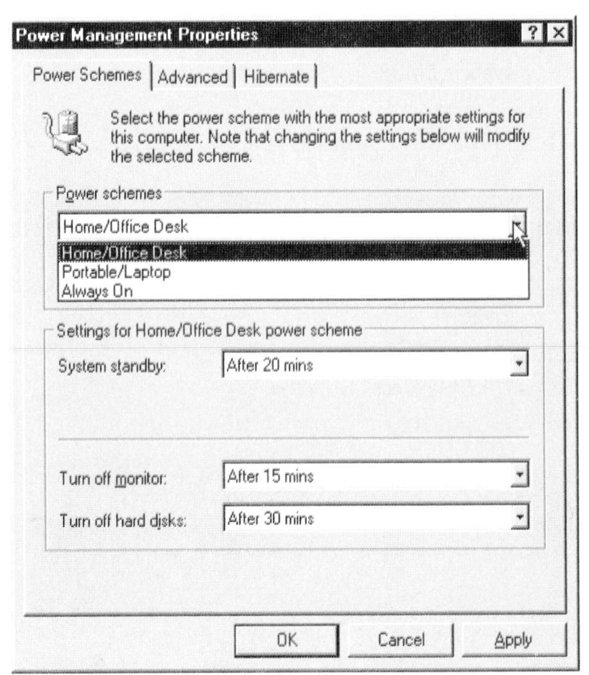

• **Figure 21.22** Power Management controls

monitor or hard drive after a time, thus creating your own custom power scheme (Figure 21.22).

Windows 2000/XP calls the applet Power Options and gives you a few configuration options in addition to those in Windows 9*x*. One feature, Hibernate mode, takes everything in active memory and stores it on the hard drive just before the system powers down. When the PC comes out of hibernation, Windows reloads all the files and applications into RAM. Figure 21.23 shows the Power Options Properties applet in Windows XP.

Cleaning

Most portable PCs take substantially more abuse than a corresponding desktop model. Constant handling, travel, airport food on the run, and so on can radically shorten the life of a portable if you don't take action. One of the most important things you should do is clean the laptop regularly. Use an appropriate screen cleaner (not a glass cleaner!) to remove fingerprints and dust from the fragile LCD panel. (Refer to Chapter 18 for specifics.) Compressed air works great for blowing out the dust and crumbs from the keyboard, and for

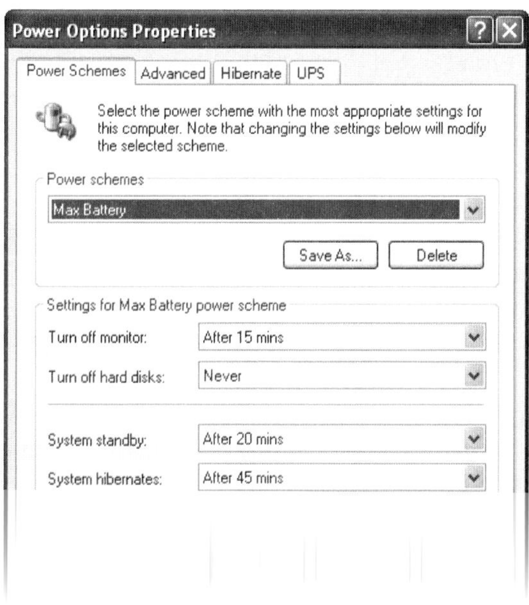

keeping PC Card sockets clear. Don't use water on your keyboard! Even a minor amount of moisture inside the portable can toast a component.

Heat

To manage and maintain a healthy portable PC, you need to deal with issues of heat. Every portable has a stack of electronic components crammed into a very small space. Unlike their desktop brethren, portables don't have lots of freely-moving air space that enables fans to cool everything down. Even with lots of low-power-consumption devices inside, portable PCs still crank out a good deal of heat. Excessive heat can cause system lockups and hardware failures, so you should handle the issue wisely. Try this as a starter guide.

- Use power management, even if you're plugged into the AC outlet. This is especially important if you're working in a warm (more than 80 degrees Fahrenheit) room.
- Keep air space between the bottom of the laptop and the surface on which it rests. Putting a laptop on a pillow on your lap, for example, creates a great heat retention system—not a good thing!
- Don't use a keyboard protector for extended amounts of time.

Adjusting Your System's Power Management

Go into the Power Options and take a look at the various settings. What is the current power scheme for your computer? If you're using a laptop, is your system still using the Home/Office Desk power scheme? If this is the case, go ahead and change the power scheme to Portable/Laptop.

Try changing the individual settings for each power scheme. For instance, set a new value for the System Standby setting—try making your computer go into standby after five minutes. Don't worry, you aren't going to hurt anything if you fiddle with these settings.

- Listen to your fan, assuming the laptop has one. If it's often running very fast—you can tell by the high-pitched whirring sound—examine your power management settings and your environment and change whatever is causing heat retention.

Beyond A+

Centrino Technology

As mentioned previously in this chapter, consumers have always, and will always, demand better performance, more features, and longer battery life from their portable PCs. Recently, Intel announced a new technology called Centrino that addresses these concerns. Intel's Centrino technology consists of two items—extremely low-power, yet speedy, CPUs and integrated wireless networking technology. (This will be discussed in Chapter 23.) These two ideas, when combined, produce portable PCs that not only are exceptionally powerful, but also boast an extremely long battery life!

ExpressCard

The PC Card has had a remarkably long life in portable PCs, but 2004 brings a much needed upgrade in the form of the ExpressCard. The ExpressCard, shown in Figure 21.24, comes in two widths: 54 mm and 34 mm. Figure 25 shows a 34 mm ExpressCard. Both cards are 75 mm long and 5 mm thick, which makes them shorter than all previous PC Cards and the same width as a Type II PC Card. ExpressCard technology is built on the PCI Express architecture and the USB 2.0 interface, which makes ExpressCards simpler to design and manufacture. Theoretically, that'll make them less expensive than standard or CardBus PC Cards, which would be a great development!

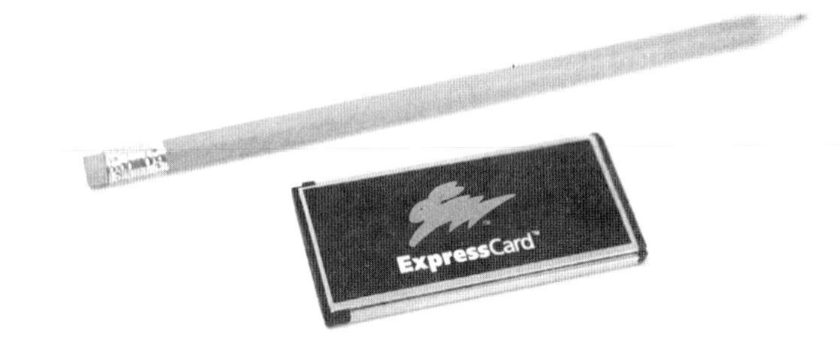

Figure 21.24 34 mm ExpressCard *(Photo courtesy of PCMCIA)*

Chapter 21 Review

Chapter Summary

After reading this chapter and completing the exercises, you should understand the following about portables.

Describe the Types of Portable Computing Devices

- All portable devices share certain features: video output using LCD screens, some kind of PC sound, and DC battery power. There's no industry [illegible] input device, and functions as a fully standalone PC. A portable PC can be considered a desktop replacement if it does everything that most people want to do with a desktop PC. Desktop extender portable devices don't replace the desktop, but rather extend it by giving you a subset of features of the typical desktop that you can take away from the desk. They are usually smaller and lighter than desktop replacement portables. Ultralight portables (sometimes called subnotebooks, though the terms aren't necessarily synonymous) normally weigh less than three pounds and are less than an inch in thickness. These machines usually have smaller displays, lower-capacity hard drives, and CPUs that operate at lower speeds than their more full-sized brethren.
- Personal digital assistants (PDAs) are tiny handheld portable computing devices that hold data such as your address book and appointment schedules. Small enough to fit into a pocket, today's PDAs are pen-based computers, using a pen-like stylus and handwriting recognition. PDAs require specialized OSs such as Windows CE, PocketPC, PalmOS, and Linux. All of these OSs provide a GUI that enables you to interact with the device by touching the screen directly. PDAs synchronize with your primary PC, most often using a cradle and USB port, so you have the same essential data on both machines.
- PDAs use USB, serial, or wireless connections to pass data to and from desktop systems. PDAs can synchronize (HotSync is the common term for it) with your primary PC so you have the same essential data on both machines. Almost every PDA has both internal Flash ROM memory of [illegible] pointing device found today, the touchpad, a flat, touch-sensitive pad that you slide your finger across to move the cursor or pointer around the screen, and tap on to perform 'mouse clicks'.

Enhance and Upgrade the Portable PC

- PC Cards are roughly credit-card-sized devices that enhance and extend the functions of a portable PC. Still commonly known by their older name, Personal Computer Memory Card International Association (PCMCIA) cards, PC Cards are as standard on today's mobile computers as the hard drive. Almost every portable PC has one or two PC Card slots. All PC Cards are hot-swappable.
- PC Cards come in two flavors, regular and CardBus, and each flavor comes in three different physical sizes, called Type I, Type II, and Type III. Type I, II, and III cards differ only in the thickness of the card (Type I being the thinnest, and Type III the thickest). Type II cards are by far the most common. All PC Cards share the same 68-pin interface. Regular PC Cards are 16-bit, 5-V cards that can have up to two distinct functions or devices, such as a modem/network card combination. CardBus PC Cards are 32-bit, 3.3-V cards that can have up to eight different functions on a single card. Regular PC Cards will fit into and work in CardBus slots, but the reverse is not true.

- The PCMCIA standard defines two levels of software drivers to support PC Cards. The first, lower level is known as socket services. Socket services are device drivers that support the PC Card socket, enabling the system to detect when a PC Card has been inserted or removed, and providing the necessary I/O to the device. The second, higher level is known as card services. The card services level recognizes the function of a particular PC Card and provides the specialized drivers necessary to make the card work. In today's laptops, the socket services are standardized and are handled by the system BIOS. Windows itself handles all card services and has a large preinstalled base of PC Card device drivers, although most PC Cards come with their own drivers.
- Every portable PC and many PDAs come with one or more single function ports, such as an analog VGA connection for hooking up an external monitor and a PS/2 port for a keyboard or mouse. The single PS/2 port on most laptops supports both keyboards and pointing devices. Most portable computing devices have a speaker port, and some have line-in and microphone jacks as well. Most current portable PCs come with built-in NICs or modems for networking support. Simply plug in a device to a particular port and, as long as Windows has the proper drivers, you will have a functioning device when you boot. The only port that requires any extra effort is the video port.
- Most portable PCs have one or more general-purpose expansion ports that enable you to plug in many different types of devices. Older portables sport RS-232 serial and IEEE 1284 parallel ports for mice, modems, printers, scanners, external CD-media drives, and more. Universal Serial Bus (USB) and FireWire (IEEE 1394) are popular and widespread methods for attaching peripherals to laptops. Both have easy-to-use connectors, and can be hot-swapped.
- There are two flavors of USB in use today—USB (previously called USB 1.1) and Hi-Speed USB (previously called USB 2.0). USB operates at 12 Mbps; Hi-Speed USB operates at 480 Mbps, but is backward compatible with regular USB. If a connection includes either a USB 1.1 plug or a USB 1.1 port, it will operate at the slower 12-Mbps speed.
- In theory, the USB interface can support up to 127 devices on a single USB port; in reality, too many devices on a single USB chain will overtax its power capabilities. USB specifications allow for a maximum cable length of 5 meters, although you may add a powered USB hub every 5 meters to extend this distance. Because USB is a two-way (bi-directional) connection, as the cable grows longer, even a standard, well-shielded, 20-gauge, twisted-pair USB cable begins to suffer from electrical interference. To be safe, stick to around 2 meters maximum.
- Configuration of USB involves an IRQ configured from CMOS along with a driver. Your operating system must also support USB. USB is supported by every version of Windows, with the exception of Windows 95A and Windows NT. If you have Windows 95A, just download the USB supplement from the Microsoft web site. Windows 2000 and XP have a large number of built-in drivers for USB devices, but they may not support special features. Always install the device driver for a new USB device *before* you plug it in.
- Port replicators are devices that plug into a USB port and offer common PC ports, such as serial, parallel, USB, network, and PS/2. Docking stations resemble port replicators in many ways, offering legacy and modern single- and multi-function ports, but have extra features built in, such as DVD drives or PC Card slots.
- The high transfer speed of FireWire makes transferring large video files quick and easy. Most modern digital video cameras use the IEEE 1394 interface for transferring video from camera to PC for editing. FireWire has two distinct types of connectors, both of which are commonly found on laptops: a 6-pin powered connector and a 4-pin unpowered connector.
- Although portable PCs used proprietary components, we're starting to see some modularity in today's portable PCs, making it possible to do basic replacements and upgrades without buying expensive proprietary components from the manufacturer. These replaceable components include RAM, hard drives, video cards, floppy drives, and CD-media devices. Modular video cards are the least standardized of all modular components, but manufacturers are beginning to adopt industry-wide standards. Many manufacturers use modular floppy disk drives and CD media devices, even allowing users to swap easily between different types of drives.

- Laptops use one of four types of RAM. Most older laptops use either 72-pin or 144-pin SO DIMMs with SDRAM technology. DDR SDRAM systems primarily use 200-pin SO DIMMs, although you'll also find 172-pin micro-DIMMs. Every decent laptop has upgradeable RAM slots. Get the correct RAM; many portable PC makers use proprietary RAM solutions. No standard exists for RAM placement in portables. More often than not, you need to unscrew or pop open a panel on the underside of the portable and press out on the restraining clips to make the RAM stick pop up so that you can remove and replace it.
- [illegible]

Troubleshoot Portables

- Portable computers use three different types of batteries: Nickel-Cadmium (Ni-Cd), Nickel-Metal Hydride (Ni-MH), and Lithium-Ion (Li-Ion).
- The first batteries used in mobile PCs were Nickel-Cadmium (Ni-Cd). If a Ni-Cd battery was not completely discharged before each recharge, it would lose a significant amount of its rechargeability. At best, Ni-Cd batteries would last for 1,000 charges, but they were very susceptible to heat. Because of the toxic metals inside these batteries, they had to be disposed of via specialty disposal companies. Although no longer used in PCs, Ni-Cd batteries are still found in cellular and cordless phones.
- The second generation of mobile PC batteries, the Nickel-Metal Hydride (Ni-MH) batteries are less susceptible to memory problems, tolerate overcharging better, take more recharging, and last longer between rechargings, but they are still susceptible to heat.
- Although some portable PCs still use Ni-MH batteries, Lithium-Ion (Li-Ion) is more common today. This third-generation battery takes fewer charges than Ni-MH, but it lasts longer between charges. Since Li-Ion batteries can explode if they are overcharged, PCs that use them have circuitry to prevent overcharging.
- A new type battery called the Smart Battery tells the computer when it needs to be charged, conditioned, or replaced.
- Research continues on other power sources, with the most promising technology being fuel cells that produce electrical power as a result of a chemical reaction between hydrogen and oxygen. Although a few years away, a small fuel cell may be able to power a laptop for up to 40 hours before it needs to be replaced or refilled.
- Batteries should be stored in a cool place, but not in [illegible]
- [illegible] the BIOS, and the OS to reduce power use is known generically as power management. Early laptops used power continuously, regardless of whether the system was using the device at the time or not. With power management features, today's laptops can automatically turn off unused devices or can shut down the entire system, leaving the information in RAM ready for a restart. To perform these power management functions requires specialized hardware, BIOS, and an operating system that supports power management.
- Starting with the 386SX, Intel introduced System Management Mode (SMM), a power management system that would make the CPU and all peripherals go to "sleep." In 1992, Intel introduced the improved Advanced Power Management (APM) specification, followed by the Advanced Configuration and Power Interface (ACPI) standard in 1996.
- To use APM or ACPI, the computer must have an SMM-capable CPU, an APM-compliant BIOS, and devices that can be shut off. Referred to as "Energy Star" devices, these peripherals can shut down without actually turning off. The OS must also know how to request that a particular device be shut down. ACPI extends power-saving to include hot-swappable devices.

- Virtually all laptops and desktops use power management functions. APM defines five power-usage levels, including Full On, APM Enabled, APM Standby, APM Suspend, and hibernation. Hibernation writes information from RAM to the hard drive and, upon waking up, must return the data to memory. ACPI also includes "soft power on/off."
- Configure APM/ACPI through CMOS or through Windows, with Windows settings overriding CMOS settings. Many CMOS versions allow configuration of wake-up events, such as having the system monitor a modem or particular IRQ. In Windows, APM/ACPI settings are found either in the Display applet or in the Power Management (Windows 9*x*/Me) or Power Options (Windows 2000/XP) applet of the Control Panel.

Key Terms

Advanced Configuration and Power Interface (ACPI) *(770)*
Advanced Power Management (APM) *(770)*
Card services *(760)*
CardBus *(760)*
Conditioning charger *(767)*
Desktop replacements *(755)*
Desktop extenders *(756)*
Docking Stations *(763)*
FireWire (IEEE 1394) *(762)*
Fuel cells *(769)*
HotSync (Synchronization) *(758)*
Hibernation *(770)*
Lithium-Ion (Li-Ion) *(767)*
Nickel-Cadmium (Ni-Cd) *(767)*
Nickel-Metal Hydride (Ni-MH) *(767)*
PC Card (PCMCIA) *(760)*
Personal Digital Assistant (PDA) *(756)*
Port replicator *(763)*
Smart Battery *(768)*
Socket services *(760)*
System Management Mode (SMM) *(770)*
Touchpad *(756)*
Universal Serial Bus (USB) *(762)*

Key Term Quiz

Use the Key Terms list to complete the sentences that follow. Not all the terms will be used.

1. PC cards require two levels of software drivers: __________ to allow the laptop to detect when a PC Card has been inserted or removed and __________ to provide drivers to make the card work.
2. Although ________ were the first batteries for mobile PCs, they are limited now to cellular and cordless phones because of their problems with battery memory.
3. The new _____________ tells the computer when it needs to be charged, conditioned, or replaced.
4. __________ provides the best bus for digital video editing.
5. John read an ad recently for a ___________ portable PC that had everything he could possibly want on a PC, desktop or portable!
6. Small, reduced-function portable computing devices, called __________, use cut-down operating systems such as Windows CE or Palm OS.
7. The 32-bit _______ uses 3.3-volt power while a regular 16-bit ________ uses 5-volt power.
8. Using a chemical reaction between hydrogen and oxygen, _________ may in a few years be able to provide laptops with electrical power for up to 40 hours.
9. A _________ is theoretically capable of supporting up to 127 devices.
10. With the 386SX, Intel introduced _____________, the first power management system with the ability to make the CPU and all peripherals go to sleep.

Multiple-Choice Quiz

1. All of the following are advantages of the CardBus over the standard PC Card *except* __________.
   A. The CardBus is hot-swappable, while the PC Card is not.
   B. The CardBus handles bus mastering, while the PC Card does not.
   C. The CardBus handles up to eight functions on a single card, while the PC Card is limited to only two functions.
   D. The CardBus slot can use a PC Card, while a

[illegible]

   D. An SEE-capable BIOS

3. Which of the following statements best describes hard drives typically found in laptops?
   A. They are 2.5-inch ATA drives, but they do not hold as much data as the 3.5-inch hard drives found in desktop PCs.
   B. They are 3.5-inch ATA drives just like those found in desktop PCs, but they usually require "cable select" settings rather than master or slave.
   C. They are 3.5-inch ATA drives that hold more data than the 2.5-inch hard drives found in desktop PCs.
   D. They are 2.5-inch PCMCIA drives while desktops usually have 3.5-inch SCSI drives.

4. All of the following statements about portable computer batteries are true *except* _________.
   A. If a Li-Ion battery is overcharged, it can explode.
   B. The Ni-MH battery is the most commonly used type of battery for today's portable PCs.
   C. If you charged a Ni-Cd or Ni-MH battery before it was completely discharged, it would last a shorter time on each recharge.
   D. The alkaline battery is unacceptable for portable computers because voltage drops as it loses power.

5. If your laptop has two Type II slots, you can simultaneously use all of the following combinations of PC Cards *except* _____________
   A. Two Type I cards
   B. Two Type II cards
   C. A Type I and a Type II
   D. A Type II and a Type III

[illegible]

   D. Hibernation

7. Which of the following operating systems do not include support for USB?
   A. Windows 95 and Windows 98
   B. Windows 95A and OSR2
   C. Windows 98 and Windows Me
   D. Windows 95A and Windows NT

8. All of the following statements are true about battery care *except* _______________.
   A. Clean battery contacts with alcohol or a dry cloth.
   B. Recycle old batteries rather than disposing of them in the trash.
   C. Do not touch a ruptured battery since it contains dangerous chemicals.
   D. Since batteries should be stored in a cool place, it is a good idea to keep them in the freezer.

9. Portable PCs typically use which of the following kinds of upgradeable RAM?
   A. 68-pin and 72-pin RIMMs
   B. 30-pin and 72-pin SIMMs
   C. 72-pin and 144-pin SO-DIMMs
   D. 30-pin and 72-pin SO-RIMMs

10. Where do you configure APM/ACPI in Windows XP? (Select all that apply.)
    A. Power Options applet in the Control Panel
    B. The Display applet in the Control Panel
    C. The Power Management applet in the Control Panel
    D. The Power and Devices applet in the Control Panel
11. FireWire uses which of the following kinds of connectors?
    A. A 6-pin mini-DIN and a 9-pin DB
    B. A 6-pin "powered" connector and a 4-pin "unpowered" connector
    C. A 5-pin mini-DIN and a 6-pin "powered" connector
    D. A PS/2 connector and a 4-pin "powered" connector
12. All of the following statements are true about USB devices *except* __________.
    A. You do not have to turn off the computer to install a USB device since USB is hot-swappable.
    B. The maximum cable length for USB is 5 meters.
    C. You should plug in a new USB device before you install the device driver.
    D. If you use a USB 2.0 device in a USB 1.1 port, it will work but will not exceed 12 Mbps.
13. Which of the following kinds of PC Cards is the most commonly used, especially for I/O functions?
    A. Type I
    B. Type II
    C. Type III
    D. Type IV
14. A(n) __________ is a list of devices that Windows automatically enables or disables in the Device Manager.
    A. EnergyStar
    B. APM
    C. Hardware profile
    D. Port replicator
15. Which of the following input devices will you most likely find on a portable PC?
    A. TrackPoint
    B. Touchpad
    C. Trackball
    D. Mouse

Essay Quiz

1. At the upcoming training seminar for new techs, your boss wants to make sure they understand and use power management settings. You've been asked to prepare a short presentation showing the range of power management settings available in Windows 2000 and XP and demonstrating how to set them. What will you include in your presentation?
2. Congratulations! A few weeks ago you wrote an article for the company's newsletter that was received so well that the editor has asked you to write another one. This time he wants you to explain PC Cards and how they work. Your article should include the differences in the three types of PC cards and what functions each type typically includes. Conclude your article with information about the new CardBus cards and how this technology differs from PC Cards.
3. Dylan is excited because he just got a new USB digital camera. He tried to install it on his laptop, but the computer doesn't recognize it. He's called you for help. What will you tell him?
4. Norm wants to upgrade his laptop's hard drive, CPU, and RAM. Since he's upgraded all of these components on his desktop, he doesn't think that he'll run into much trouble. What advice will you give him about selecting the components and upgrading the laptop?
5. Monica just received her aunt's old laptop. It uses a Ni-Cd battery, but no matter how long she charges it, it only runs her PC for about 30 minutes before it dies. She can't understand why

the battery runs out so fast, but she figures she needs a new battery. The local computer store has two kinds of batteries, Ni-MH and Li-Ion, both of which will physically fit into her computer. She's not sure which of these to buy or whether either of them will work with her PC. She's asked you whether her old battery is indeed bad and to help her select a new battery. What will you tell her?

Lab Projects

• Lab Project 21.1

• Lab Project 21.2

A local company just donated 10 laptops to your school library. They are IBM ThinkPad 600x PIII 500-Mhz laptops with 128 MB of RAM and two Type II PC slots. The school would like to let needy distance education students check out these computers, but the laptops do not have modems. Your hardware class has been asked to select PC Card modems for these laptops. What features will you look for in selecting the right modem? Either go to the local computer store or search the Internet to find the modem cards you will recommend.

chapter

22 Printers

"People believe almost anything they see in print."

—Charlotte the spider in *Charlotte's Web* by E. B. White

In this chapter, you will learn how to

- **Describe current printer technologies**
- **Explain the laser printing process**
- **Install a printer on a Windows PC**
- **Troubleshoot basic printer problems**

Despite all of the talk about the "paperless office," printers continue to be a vital part of the typical office. In many cases, PCs are used exclusively for the purpose of producing paper documents. Many people simply prefer dealing with a hard copy. Programmers cater to this preference by using metaphors such as page, workbook, and binder in their applications. The A+ Certification strongly stresses the area of printing and expects a high degree of technical knowledge of the function, components, maintenance, and repair of all types of printers.

Test Specific

Printer Technologies

No other piece of your computer system is available in a wider range of styles, configurations, and feature sets than a printer, or at such a wide price variation. What a printer can and can't do is largely determined by the type of printer technology it uses—that is, how it gets the image onto the paper. Modern printers break down into several broad types, including laser printers, impact printers, inkjet printers, thermal printers, and dye-sublimation printers.

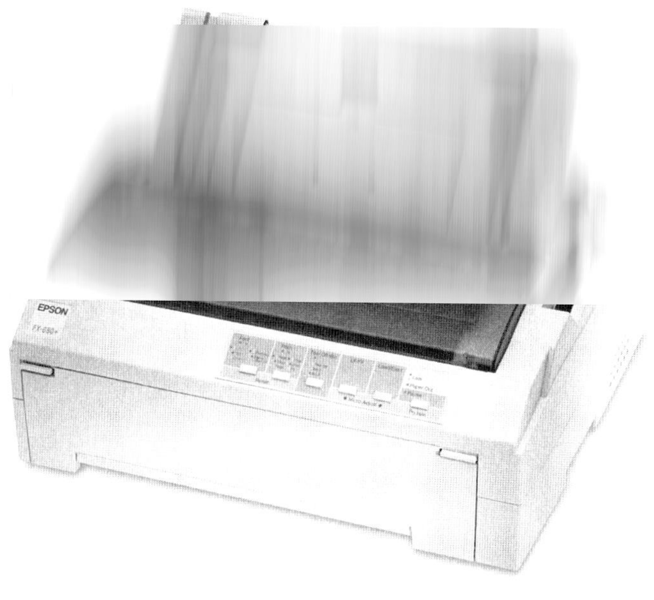

• **Figure 22.1** An Epson FX-880+ dot-matrix printer *(image courtesy of Epson America, Inc.)*

offices. While dot-matrix printers don't deliver what most home users want—high-quality and flexibility at a low cost—they're still widely found in businesses. There are two reasons for this: dot-matrix printers have a large installed base in businesses, and they can be used for multipart forms because they actually strike the paper. Impact printers tend to be relatively slow and noisy, but when speed, flexibility, and print quality are not critical, they provide acceptable results. PCs used for printing multipart forms (such as *Point of Sale* [POS] machines that need to print receipts in duplicate, triplicate, or more) represent the major market for new impact printers, although many older dot-matrix printers remain in use.

Dot-matrix printers (Figure 22.1) use a grid, or matrix, of tiny pins, also known as *printwires*, to strike an inked printer ribbon and produce images on paper. The case that holds the printwires is called a *printhead*. Using either 9 or 24 pins, dot-matrix printers treat each page as a picture broken up into a dot-based raster image. Nine-pin dot-matrix printers are generically called *draft quality*, while 24-pin printers are known as *letter quality* or *near-letter quality*. The BIOS for the printer (either built into the printer or a printer driver) interprets the raster image in the same way that a monitor does, "painting" the image as individual dots. Naturally, the more pins, the higher the resolution. Figure 22.2 illustrates the components common to dot-matrix printers.

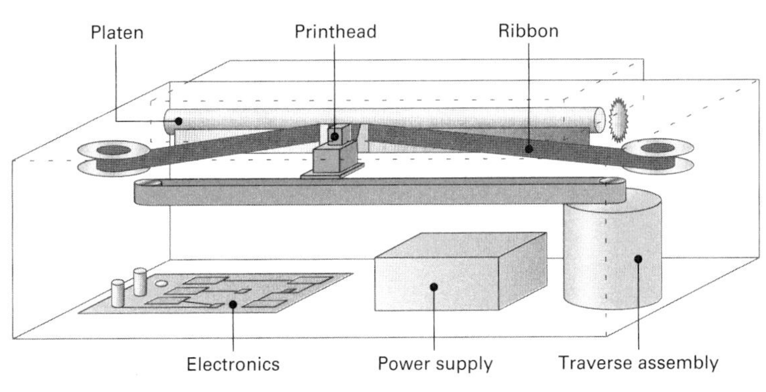

• **Figure 22.2** Inside a dot-matrix printer

Inkjet Printers

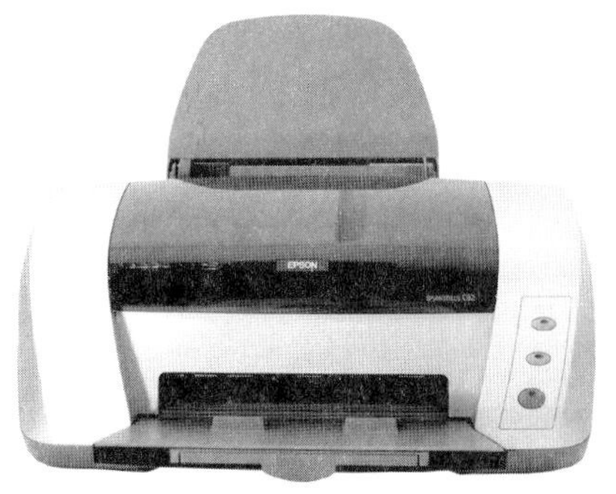

• **Figure 22.3** Typical inkjet printer

Inkjet printers are relatively simple devices, consisting of the printhead mechanism, support electronics, a transfer mechanism to move the printheads back and forth, and a paper feed component to drag, move, and eject paper (Figures 22.3 and 22.4). They work by ejecting ink through tiny tubes. Inkjet printers use heat or a mechanical method to move the ink. The heat-method printers use tiny resistors at the end of each tube to boil the ink, creating a tiny air bubble that ejects a droplet of ink. The mechanical method printers achieve the same result by forcing ink through the printhead (Figure 22-5).

The ink is stored in special small containers called *ink cartridges*; in most modern inkjet printers, there are four separate cartridges (Figure 22.6): one for each of the three colored inks (cyan, magenta, and yellow), and one for the black ink (often a larger cartridge than the other three, because even color printers use more black ink than colored ink). Some inkjet printers, however, use one combined color cartridge.

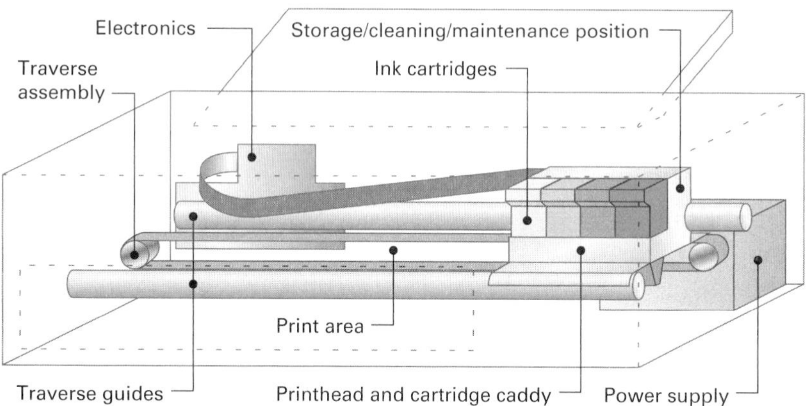

• **Figure 22.4** Inside an inkjet printer

The two key features of an inkjet printer are the **print resolution**—that is, the density of ink, which affects print quality—and the print speed. Resolution is measured in **dots per inch (dpi)**; higher numbers mean that the ink dots on the page are closer together, so your printed documents will look better. Resolution is most important when you're printing complex images such as full-color photos, or when you're printing for duplication and you care that your printouts look good. Print speed is measured in **pages per minute (ppm)** and it's normally indicated right on the printer's box. Normally a printer will have one (faster) speed for black and white printing and another for full-color.

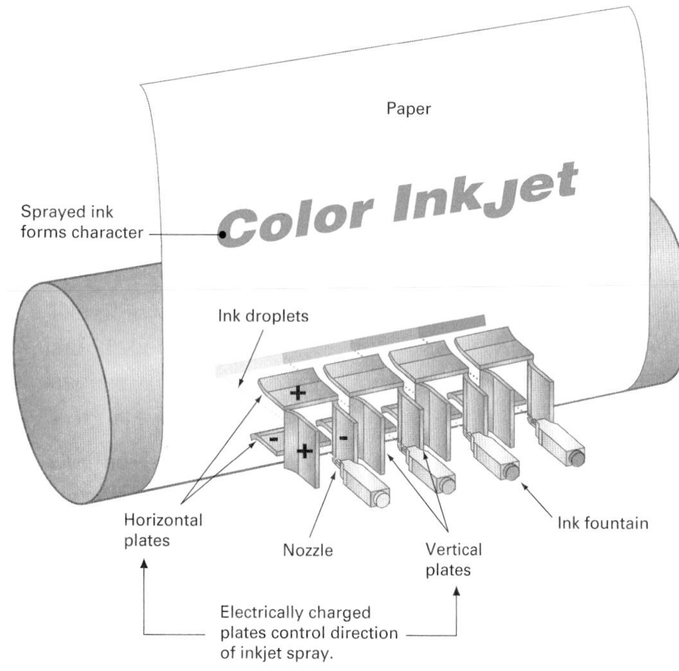

• **Figure 22.5** Detail of the inkjet printhead

Dye-Sublimation Printers

The term *sublimation* means to cause something to change from a solid form into a vapor and then back into a solid. This is exactly the process behind dye-sublimation printing, sometimes called *thermal dye transfer* printing. Dye-sublimation printers are used mainly for photo printing, high-end desktop publishing, medical and scientific imaging, or other applications where fine detail and rich color is more important than cost and speed. Smaller, specialized printers called *snapshot* printers use dye-sublimation specifically for printing photos at a reduced cost compared to their full-sized counterparts.

The dye-sublimation printing technique is an example of the so-called CMYK (**c**yan, **m**agenta, **y**ellow, blac**k**) method of color printing. It uses a roll of heat-sensitive plastic film embedded with page-sized sections of cyan (blue), magenta (red), and yellow dye; many also have a section of black dye. A print head containing thousands of heating elements, capable of precise temperature control, moves across the film, vaporizing the dyes

nologies' *dithered* images, which use closely packed, single-color dots to simulate blended colors. Dye-sublimation printers produce high-quality color output that rivals professional photo lab processing.

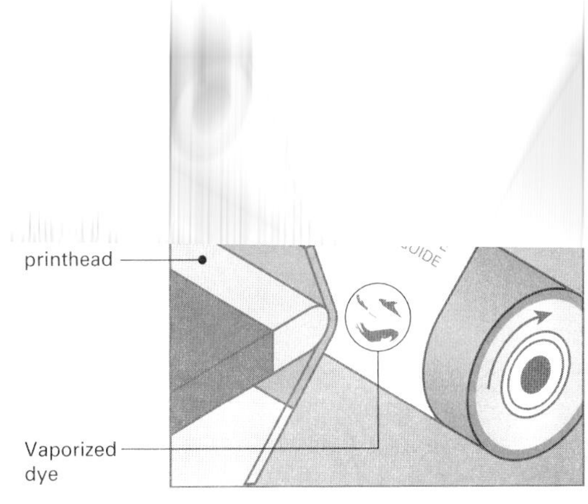

• **Figure 22.7** Dye-sublimation printing process

Thermal Printers

There are two kinds of thermal printers that you'll see in use. The first is the *direct thermal* printer, and the other is the *thermal wax transfer* printer. Direct thermal printers use a heated print head to burn dots into the surface of special heat-sensitive paper. If you remember the first generation of fax machines, you're already familiar with this type of printer. This type of printer is still used as a receipt printer in many retail businesses. Thermal wax printers work similarly to dye-sublimation printers, except that instead of using rolls of dye-embedded film, the film is coated with colored wax. The thermal print head passes over the film ribbon and melts the wax onto the paper. Thermal wax printers don't require special papers like dye-sublimation printers, so they're more flexible and somewhat cheaper to use, but their output isn't quite as good because they use color dithering.

Try This!

Pages per Minute Versus Price

Printer speed is a key determinant of a printer's price, and this is an easy assertion to prove. Try this:

1. Fire up your browser and head over to the web site for Hewlett-Packard (www.hp.com), Canon (www.usa.canon.com), Epson (www.epson.com), or Lexmark (www.lexmark.com). These four companies make most of the printers on the market today.
2. Pick a particular printer technology and check the price, from the cheapest to the most expensive. Then look for printers that have the same resolution but different ppm rates.
3. Check the prices and see how the ppm rate affects the price of two otherwise identical printers.

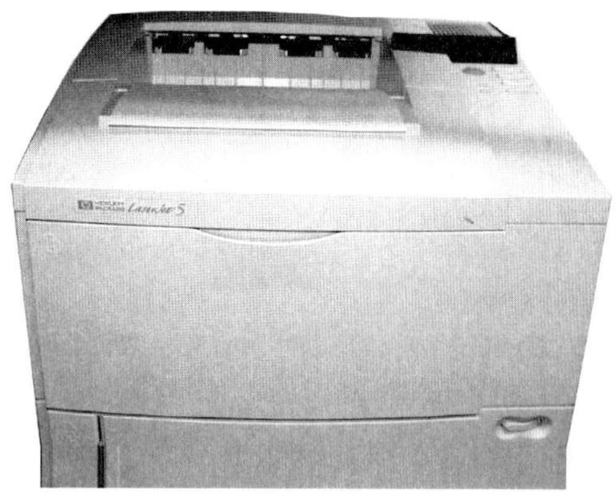

• **Figure 22.8** Typical laser printer

Laser Printers

Using a process called *electro-photographic imaging*, **laser printers** produce high-quality and high-speed output of both text and graphics. Figure 22.8 shows a typical laser printer. Laser printers rely on the photoconductive properties of certain organic compounds. *Photoconductive* means that particles of these compounds, when exposed to light (that's the "photo" part), will *conduct* electricity. Laser printers use lasers as a light source because of their precision.

Critical Components of the Laser Printer

Let's take a look at the many components of a laser printer and their functions (Figure 22.9).

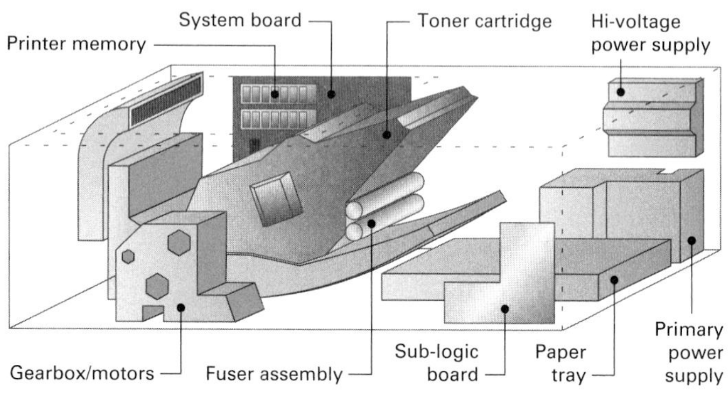

• **Figure 22.9** Components inside a laser printer

The Toner Cartridge

The **toner cartridge** in a laser printer (Figure 22.10) is so named because of its most obvious activity—supplying the toner that creates the image on the page. In order to reduce maintenance costs, however, many other laser printer parts, especially those that suffer the most wear and tear, have been incorporated into the toner cartridge. Although this makes replacement of individual parts nearly impossible, it greatly reduces the need for replacement; those parts that are most likely to break are replaced every time you replace the toner cartridge.

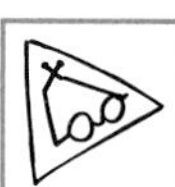

Tech Tip

Hidden Costs

Some printers use consumables at a much faster rate than others, prompting the industry to rank printers in terms of their cost per page. An inexpensive printer (laser or inkjet) costs around 4 cents per page, while an expensive printer can cost more than 20 cents per page—a huge difference if you do any volume of printing. This hidden cost is particularly pernicious in the sub-$100 inkjet printers on the market. Their low prices often entice buyers, who then discover that the cost of consumables is outrageous—these days, a single *set of color and black inkjet cartridges can cost as much as the printer itself, if not more!*

The Photosensitive Drum

The **photosensitive drum** is an aluminum cylinder coated with particles of photosensitive compounds. The drum itself is grounded to the power supply, but the coating is not. When light hits these particles, whatever electrical charge they may have had drains out through the grounded cylinder.

Erase Lamp

The erase lamp exposes the entire surface of the photosensitive drum to light, making the photosensitive coating conductive. Any electrical charge present in the particles bleeds away into the grounded drum, leaving the surface particles electrically neutral.

Primary Corona

The **primary corona** wire, located close to the photosensitive drum, never touches the drum. When the primary corona is charged with an extremely high voltage, an electric field (or corona) forms, enabling voltage to pass to the drum and charge the photosensitive particles on its surface. The *primary grid* regulates the transfer of voltage, ensuring that the surface of the drum receives a uniform negative voltage of between ~600 and ~1,000 volts.

Laser

The laser acts as the writing mechanism of the printer. Any particle on the drum struck by the laser becomes conductive, enabling its charge to be drained away into the grounded core of the drum. The entire surface of the drum has a uniform negative charge of between ~600 and ~1,000 volts following its charging by the primary corona wire. When particles are struck by the laser, they are discharged and left with a ~100 volt negative charge. Using the laser, we can "write" an image onto the drum. Note that the laser writes a

[illegible]

laser (~100 volts), particles of toner are attracted to the areas of the photosensitive drum that have been hit by the laser (that is, areas that have a *relatively* positive charge with reference to the toner particles).

Transfer Corona

To transfer the image from the photosensitive drum to the paper, the paper must be given a charge that will attract the toner particles off of the drum and onto the paper. The **transfer corona** is a thin wire, usually protected by other thin wires, that applies a positive charge to the paper, drawing the negatively charged toner particles to the paper.

In most laser printers, the transfer corona is outside the toner cartridge, especially in large commercial grade machines. The transfer corona is prone to a build-up of dirt, toner and debris through electrostatic attraction, and it must be cleaned. It is also quite fragile—usually finer than a human hair. Most printers with an exposed transfer corona will provide a special tool to clean it, but you can also—very delicately—use a cotton swab soaked in 90% denatured alcohol (don't use rubbing alcohol because it contains emollients). As always, never service any printer without turning it off and unplugging it from its power source.

Fuser Assembly

The **fuser assembly** is almost always separate from the toner cartridge. It is usually quite easy to locate as it will be close to the bottom of the toner cartridge and will usually have two rollers to fuse the toner. Sometimes the fuser is somewhat enclosed and difficult to recognize, because the rollers are hidden from view. To help you determine the location of the fuser, think about the path of the paper and the fact that fusing is the final step of printing.

Before fusing, the toner that's on the paper stays in place solely by the grace of gravity and static electricity. The toner must be permanently attached to the paper to make the image permanent. Two rollers, a pressure roller and a heated roller, are used to fuse the toner to the paper. The pressure roller presses against the bottom of the page while the heated roller presses down on the top of the page, melting the toner into the paper. The heated roller has a nonstick coating such as Teflon to prevent the toner from sticking to the heated roller.

Power Supplies

All laser printers have at least two separate power supplies. The first power supply is called the "primary power supply" or sometimes just the "power supply." This power supply, which may actually be more than one power supply, provides power to the motors that move the paper, the system electronics, the laser, and the transfer corona. The high-voltage power supply usually only provides power to the primary corona. The extremely high voltage of the high-voltage power supply makes it one of the most dangerous devices in the world of PCs! When inserting a new toner cartridge, it is imperative that you *always turn off* a laser printer before you open it up!

Turning Gears

A laser printer has many mechanical functions. First, the paper must be picked up, printed upon, and kicked out of the printer. Next, the photosensitive roller must be turned and the laser, or a mirror, must be moved from left to right. Finally, the toner must be evenly distributed, and the fuser assembly must squish the toner into the paper. All these functions are served by complex gear systems. In most laser printers, these gear systems are packed together in discrete units generically called *gear packs* or *gearboxes*. Most laser printers will have two or three gearboxes that a tech can remove relatively easily in the rare case when one of them fails. Most gearboxes will also have their own motor or solenoid to move the gears.

System Board

Every laser printer will contain at least one electronic board. On this board is the main processor, the printer's ROM, and RAM used to store the image before it is printed. Many printers will divide these functions among two or three boards dispersed around the printer. An older printer may also have an extra ROM chip and/or a special slot where you can install an extra ROM chip, usually for special functions such as PostScript.

Of particular importance is the printer's RAM. When the printer doesn't have enough RAM to store the image before it prints,

Cross Check

High Voltage—Keep Away!

The power supply inside a laser printer is not the only dangerous high-voltage toy in the world of PC equipment. You've learned about two other potentially hazardous electrical components that you should approach with caution.

1. What are they?
2. Which of these three items is potentially the most deadly?

To refresh your memory, check out Chapters 8 and 18.

you get a memory overflow problem. Also, some printers will store other information in the RAM, including fonts or special commands. Adding RAM is usually a very simple job—just snapping in a SIMM stick or two—but getting the *right* RAM is important. Call or check the printer manufacturer's web site to see what type of RAM you need. Although most printer companies will happily sell you their expensive RAM, most printers can use generic DRAM like the kind you use in your PC.

Ozone Filter

The coronas inside laser printers generate ozone (O3). Although not harmful to humans in small amounts, even tiny concentrations of ozone will cause damage to printer components. To counter this problem, most laser printers have a special ozone filter that needs to be vacuumed or replaced

they can become dirty or broken, sending a false signal to the printer. Simple inspection is usually sufficient to determine if a problem is real or just the result of a faulty sensor/switch.

Printer Languages

How do you tell a printer to make a letter "A" or to print a picture of your pet iguana? Printers are designed to accept predefined printer languages that handle both characters and graphics. Your software must use the proper language when communicating with your printer, so that your printer can output your documents onto a piece of paper. Let's look at the more common printer languages.

American Standard Code for Information Interchange (ASCII)

We usually think of ASCII as nothing more than a standard set of characters, the basic alphabet in upper and lower case with a few strange symbols thrown in. ASCII actually contains a variety of control codes for transferring data, some of which can be used to control printers. For example, ASCII code 10 (or 0A in hex) means "Line Feed," and ASCII code 12 (0C) means "Form Feed." These commands have been standard since before the creation of IBM PCs, and all printers respond to them. If they did not, the PRINT SCREEN key would not work with every printer. Being highly standardized has advantages, but the control codes are extremely limited. Utilizing high-end graphics and a wide variety of fonts requires more advanced languages.

PostScript

Adobe Systems developed the **PostScript** Page Description Language in the early 1980s as a device-independent printer language capable of high-resolution graphics and scalable fonts. PostScript interpreters are embedded in the printing device. Because PostScript is understood by printers at a hardware level, the majority of the image processing is done by the printer and not the PC's CPU, so PostScript printers print faster. PostScript defines the page as a single raster image; this makes PostScript files extremely portable—they can be created on one machine or platform and reliably printed out on another machine or platform (including, for example, high-end typesetters).

Hewlett-Packard Printer Control Language (PCL)

Hewlett-Packard developed its **Printer Control Language (PCL)** as a more advanced printer language to supercede simple ASCII codes. PCL features a set of printer commands greatly expanded from ASCII. Hewlett-Packard designed PCL with text-based output in mind; it does not support advanced graphical functions. The most recent version of PCL, PCL6, does feature scalable fonts and additional line drawing commands. Unlike PostScript, however, PCL is not a true page description language; it uses a series of commands to define the characters on the page. Those commands must be supported by each individual printer model, making PCL files less portable than PostScript files.

Windows GDI

Windows 9*x* and Windows 2000/XP use the **Graphical Device Interface (GDI)** component of the operating system to handle print functions. Although you *can* use an external printer language such as PostScript, most users simply install printer drivers and let Windows do all the work. The GDI uses the CPU rather than the printer to process a print job and then sends the completed job to the printer. When you print a letter with a TrueType font in Windows, for example, the GDI processes the print job and then sends bitmapped images of each page to the printer. The printer sees a page of TrueType text, therefore, as a picture, not as text. As long as the printer has a capable enough RIP and plenty of RAM, you don't need to worry about the printer language at all in most situations. We'll revisit printing in Windows in more detail later in this chapter.

Printer Connectivity

Most printers connect to one of two ports on the PC: a DB25 parallel port or a USB port. The parallel connection is the classic way to plug in a printer, and although most new printers use USB today, you'll still find parallel ports on most new motherboards, since printers often live long and prolific lives. You'll need to know how to support the more obscure parallel ports, cables, and connections as well as the plug-and-play USB connections.

Parallel Communication and Ports

The **parallel port** was included in the original IBM PC as a faster alternative to serial communication. The IBM engineers considered serial communication, limited to one bit at a time, to be too slow for the "high-speed" devices of the day (for example, dot-matrix printers). The standard parallel port has been kept around for backward compatibility despite several obvious weaknesses.

Parallel ports may be far faster than serial ports, but they are slow by modern standards. The maximum data transfer rate of a standard parallel port is still only approximately 150 *kilobytes per second* (Kbps). Standard parallel communication on the PC also relies heavily on software, eating up a considerable amount of CPU time that could be better used.

Parallel ports are hindered by their lack of true bidirectional capability. [illegible] communication was acceptable for simple line printers and

Although the phrase "Centronics standard" was commonly used in the heyday of parallel ports, there actually was no such animal. Prior to the development of IEEE 1284, there [illegible]

[illegible] *cal and Electronics Engineers* (IEEE) that a committee be formed to propose a standard for a backward-compatible, high-speed, bidirectional parallel port for the PC. The committee was the IEEE 1284 committee (hence the name of the standard).

Many techs confuse the concept of "duplex" printing—a process that requires special printers capable of printing on both sides of a sheet of paper—with bidirectional printing. They have nothing to do with each other!

The **IEEE 1284** standard requires the following:

- Support for all five modes of operation (compatibility, nibble mode, byte mode, EPP, and ECP)
- A standard method of negotiation for determining which modes are supported both by the host PC and by the peripheral device
- A standard physical interface (that is, the cables and connectors)
- A standard electrical interface (that is, termination, impedance, and so on)

Because there is only one set of data wires, all data transfer modes included in the IEEE 1284 standard are half-duplex: Data is transferred in only one direction at a time.

Compatibility Mode/Centronics Mode The standard parallel port in the original IBM PC is often referred to as a *Centronics* port. A 25-pin female **DB25 connector** on the PC connects to a corresponding male DB25 connector on one end of the printer cable; the other end of the printer cable has a 36-pin **Centronics connector** that plugs into the printer. Eight wires are used as grounds, four for control

Cross Check

LPT Port Resources

In Chapter 6, you learned about LPT ports, which come into play when you need to connect a printer to a parallel port.

1. Do you remember the chart of LPT and COM port system resources?
2. Can you name the IRQ and I/O address assignments for LPT1 and LPT2?

signals, five for status signals, and only eight wires are used for passing data, which travels in only one direction: from the PC to the peripheral device. All the IEEE 1284 transfer modes use this 25-pin cable for backward compatibility reasons, although other types of connections are included in the standard.

The advantage to Centronics mode is backward compatibility, but its disadvantages are clear. Data passes in only one direction, from the PC to the peripheral device (a.k.a., "forward" direction only). In addition, the CPU must constantly poll the status wires for error messages and handshaking signals, using up significant numbers of CPU clock cycles. Standard/Centronics mode transfers are limited to approximately 150 Kbps.

Some manufacturers support an enhanced form of Centronics mode that is not a part of the IEEE 1284 standard, referred to as "Fast Centronics" or "Parallel Port FIFO Mode." By having a hard-wired *First In First Out* (FIFO) buffer emulate the handshaking normally done by the software, Fast Centronics mode can achieve data transfer rates of up to 500 Kbps.

Nibble Mode Nibble mode will work on any PC parallel port, and when used in concert with compatibility/Centronics mode, it provides a very limited form of bidirectional communication. Nibble mode doesn't require special hardware or an IEEE 1284 parallel port. All parallel ports have five status wires that are designed to send signals from the peripheral to the PC. Using four of these wires at a time, we can transfer a byte (8 bits) of data in two pieces, one nibble (4 bits) at a time. Nibble mode is even more software intensive than compatibility/Centronics mode, eating up many CPU clock cycles. Nibble mode transfers data at a maximum of about 50 Kbps.

Byte Mode/Enhanced Bidirectional Port Although a combination of compatible/Centronics and nibble mode transfers can produce two-way communications, the resulting speed is not very satisfactory. Byte mode enables reverse direction (peripheral to PC) parallel communication using all eight data wires. Byte mode in conjunction with Centronics mode provides two-way eight-bit communication at speeds approaching 150 Kbps. Parallel ports capable of byte mode transfers are sometimes referred to as enhanced bidirectional ports.

Enhanced Parallel Port (EPP) For peripherals that require constant two-way communication with the PC, the Enhanced Parallel Port (EPP) protocol offers high-speed, two-way data transfers with relatively little software overhead. Hardware handles the handshaking and synchronization between the peripheral device and the PC. By removing the CPU from the handshaking process, an EPP port enables the CPU to transfer data to and from the port with a single command, saving a significant number of clock cycles. Data transfers using the EPP protocol can approach the speed of an ISA bus, transferring between 500 Kbps and 2 Mbps.

> The EPP protocol was developed before IEEE 1284, and early versions are slightly different from IEEE 1284. Because of this, IEEE 1284 EPP parallel ports can fail to recognize that a pre-IEEE 1284 device is not ready to receive or send data. IEEE 1284 peripherals, however, work just fine with the pre-IEEE 1284 parallel ports.

Extended Capability Port (ECP) The *Extended Capability Port* (ECP) protocol is considered the fastest of all the parallel standards. ECP data transfers are "loosely coupled," meaning that once the data transfer has begun, the software that initiated the transfer (for example, a printer driver) can't monitor the progress of the transfer—it must wait for a signal that the transfer has been completed. This reduces the number of clock cycles used by the transfer to a bare minimum. ECP is designed for operations that involve moving large chunks of data that don't require much monitoring, like a print job going out to a printer or an image coming in from a scanner.

ECP ports use a data compression method called *Run Length Encoding* (RLE). With RLE, data can be compressed by a ratio of up to 64:1. This enhances performance significantly, because printers and scanners deal with raster images, which tend to compress well. For RLE to work, both the device and the parallel port must support it. Note that RLE compres-

```
                    ROM PCI/ISA BIOS (2A69KS21)
                      INTEGRATED PERIPHERALS
                        AWARD SOFTWARE, INC.

 IDE HDD Block Mode            : Enabled   | Onboard Parallel Port : 378/IRQ7
 IDE Primary Master P10        : Auto      | Parallel Port Mode    :  EPP
 IDE Primary Slave  P10        : Auto      |
 IDE Secondary Master P10      : Auto      |
 IDE Secondary Slave  P10      : Auto      |
 IDE Primary Master UDMA       : Auto      |
 IDE Primary Slave  UDMA       : Auto      |
 IDE Secondary Master UDMA     : Auto      |
 IDE Secondary Slave  UDMA     : Auto      |
 On-Chip Primary    PCI IDE    : Enabled   |
 On-Chip Secondary PCI IDE     : Enabled   |
 USB Keyboard Support          : Disabled  |
 Init Display First            : PCI Slot  |
                                           |
 Onboard FDC Controller        : Enabled   | ESC : Quit   ↑↓ →← : Select Item
 Onboard Serial Port 1         : Disabled  | F1  : Help      PU/PD/+/-  :Modify
 Onboard Serial Port 2         : 2F8/IRQ3  | F5  : Old Values (Shift)F2:Color
 UR2 Mode                      : Standard  | F7  : Load Setup Defaults
```

ports, especially *Direct Memory Access* (DMA) channels.

use proper IEEE 1284-compliant cabling. The transfer speed drops with the longer cables, but it works and sometimes the trade-off between speed and distance is worth it.

Support for the Standard Because Centronics mode and nibble mode are controlled through software, any parallel port ever made for an IBM PC can do both. However, control for byte mode, ECP, and EPP resides in the hardware. Without the appropriate hardware support, devices capable of higher-speed communication must slow down to the speed of the parallel port. Check the parallel port settings in CMOS to verify that the port is set to the appropriate mode (Figure 22.11).

In almost all cases, you must install drivers before you plug a USB printer into your computer. You'll learn about installing printer drivers later in this chapter.

Connections, Cabling, and Electricity

Although no true standard exists, "standard parallel cable" usually refers to a printer cable with the previously-mentioned male DB25 connector on one end and Centronics connector on the other (Figure 22.12). The shielding (or lack thereof) of the internal wiring and other electrical characteristics of a standard printer cable are largely undefined except by custom. In practice, these standard cables are acceptable for transferring data at 150 Kbps, and for distances under six feet, but would be dangerously unreliable for ECP or EPP operations.

USB Printers

Most new printers now use USB connections. USB printers plug into any USB port on your computer. Unlike parallel printers, USB printers usually come with a USB cable, usually with the standard USB type A connector on one end and the smaller USB type B connector on the other end, although some use two type A connectors. Whichever configuration your USB printer has, just plug in the USB cable—it's literally that easy!

Figure 22.12 Standard parallel cable with 36-pin Centronics connector on one end and DB25 connector on the other

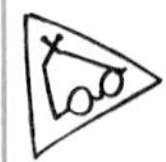

Tech Tip

No Cheap Cables!

Some parallel cables are cheaper than the IEEE 1284 cables, but these may—or may not—work. Don't set yourself up for unnecessary hassles—just get an IEEE 1284 cable! Installing a parallel cable is a snap. Just insert the DB-25 pin connector into the parallel port on the back of the PC and insert the Centronics connector into the printer's Centronics port, and you're ready to go to press!

Some printers come with both USB and parallel connections, but this is becoming increasingly rare, so if you need a parallel printer for a system, be sure to confirm that the particular model you want will work!

Be sure that you know the order of a laser printer's printing process!

The Laser Printing Process

The Physical Side

Most laser printers perform the printing process in a series of six steps. Keep in mind that some brands of laser printers may depart somewhat from this process, although most work in exactly this order:

1. Clean
2. Charge
3. Write
4. Develop
5. Transfer
6. Fuse

Clean the Drum

The printing process begins with the physical and electrical cleaning of the photosensitive drum (Figure 22.13). Before printing each new page, the drum must be returned to a clean, fresh condition. All residual toner left over from printing the previous page must be removed, usually by scraping the surface of the drum with a rubber cleaning blade. If residual particles remain on the drum, they will appear as random black spots and streaks on the next page. The physical cleaning mechanism either deposits the residual toner in a debris cavity or recycles it by returning it to the toner supply in the toner cartridge. The physical cleaning must be done carefully. Damage to the drum will cause a permanent mark to be printed on every page.

The printer must also be electrically cleaned. One or more erase lamps bombard the surface of the drum with the appropriate wavelengths of light, causing the surface particles to completely discharge into the grounded drum. After the cleaning process, the drum should be completely free of toner and have a neutral charge.

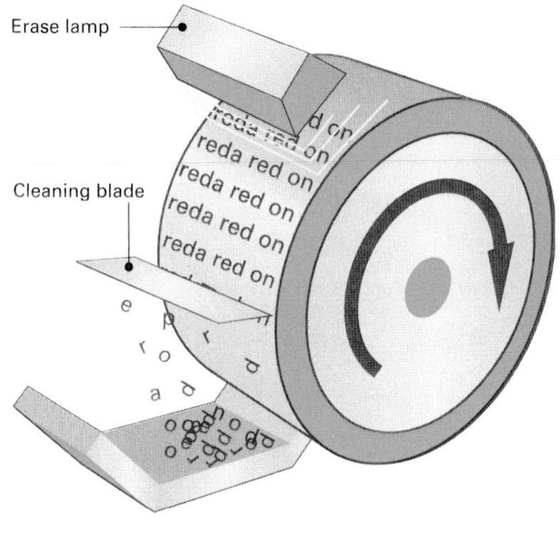

• **Figure 22.13** Cleaning and erasing the drum

Charge the Drum

To make the drum receptive to new images, it must be charged (Figure 22.14). Using the primary corona wire, a uniform negative charge is applied to the entire surface of the drum (usually between ~600 and ~1,000 volts).

Write and Develop the Image

A laser is used to write a positive image on the surface of the drum. Every particle on the drum hit by the laser will release most of its negative charge into the drum. Those particles with a lesser negative charge will be positively charged relative to the toner particles and will attract them, creating a developed image (Figure 22.15).

Transfer the Image

The printer must transfer the image from the drum onto the paper. Using the transfer corona, we charge the paper with a positive charge. Once the paper has a positive charge, the negatively charged toner particles leap from the drum to the paper. At this point the particles are merely resting on the paper. They must still be permanently affixed to the paper.

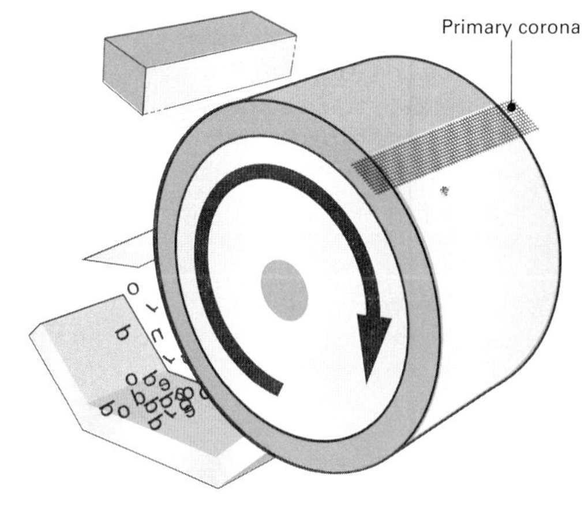

Fuse the Image

The particles must be fused to the paper. They have been attracted to the paper because of the positive charge given to the paper by the transfer corona, but if the process stopped there, the toner particles would fall off the page as soon as the page was lifted. The toner

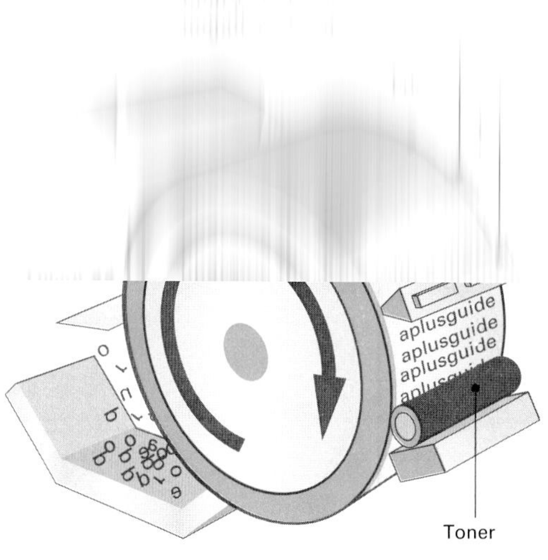

Figure 22.15 Writing the image and applying the toner

The Electronic Side of the Process

Now that we have looked at the many parts of a laser printer and discussed their basic functions, let's delve into some of the electronic functions of laser printing.

Raster Images

Impact printers transfer data to the printer one character or one line at a time, whereas laser printers transfer entire pages at a time to the printer. Laser printers generate a raster image of the page representing what the final product should look like. A raster image is merely a pattern of dots. Laser printers use a device (the laser) to "paint" a raster image on the photosensitive drum. Because laser printers have to paint the entire surface of the photosensitive drum before they can begin to transfer the image to paper, they have to process the image one page at a time.

Laser printers use a chip called the *Raster Image Processor* (RIP) to translate the raster image sent to the printer into commands to the laser. The RIP needs memory (RAM) in order to store the data that it must process. A laser printer must have enough memory to process an entire page. Some images that require high resolutions require more memory. Insufficient memory to process the image will usually be indicated by a memory overflow ("MEM OVERFLOW") error. If you get a memory overflow error, try reducing the resolution, printing smaller graphics, or turning off RET (see the following section for the last option). Of course, the best solution to a memory overflow error is simply to add more RAM to the laser printer.

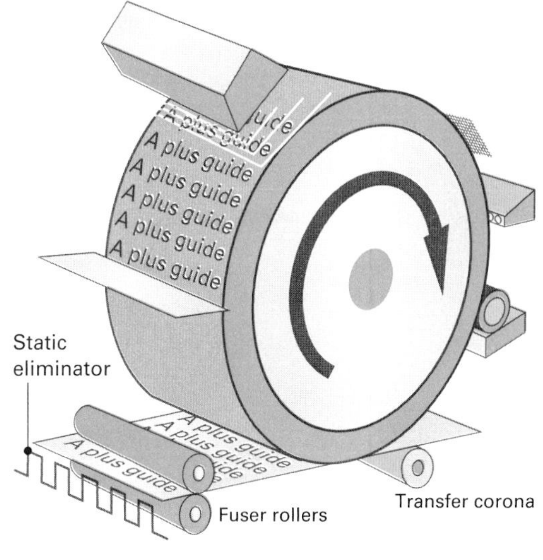

Figure 22.16 Transferring the image to the paper and fusing the final image

> The heated roller produces enough heat to melt some types of plastic media, particularly overhead transparency materials. This could damage your laser printer (and void your warranty), so make sure you're printing on transparencies designed for laser printers!

Do not assume that every error with the word "memory" in it can be fixed by simply adding more RAM to the printer. Just as adding more RAM chips will not solve every conventional PC memory problem, adding more RAM will not solve every laser printer memory problem. The message "21 ERROR" on an HP LaserJet, for example, indicates that "the printer is unable to process very complex data fast enough for the print engine." This means that the data is simply too complex for the RIP to handle. Adding more memory would *not* solve this problem; it would only make your wallet lighter. The only answer in that case is to reduce the complexity of the page image (that is, fewer fonts, less formatting, reduced graphics resolution, and so on).

Resolution

Laser printers can print at different resolutions, just as monitors can display different resolutions. The maximum resolution that a laser printer can handle is determined by its physical characteristics. Laser printer resolution is expressed in dots per inch (dpi). Common resolutions are 600 dpi × 600 dpi or 1200 dpi × 1200 dpi. The first number, the horizontal resolution, is determined by how fine a focus can be achieved by the laser. The second number is determined by the smallest increment by which the drum can be turned. Higher resolutions produce higher-quality output, but keep in mind that higher resolutions also require more memory. In some instances, complex images can only be printed at lower resolutions because of their high-memory demands. Even printing at 300 dpi, laser printers produce far better quality than dot-matrix printers because of *Resolution Enhancement Technology* (RET).

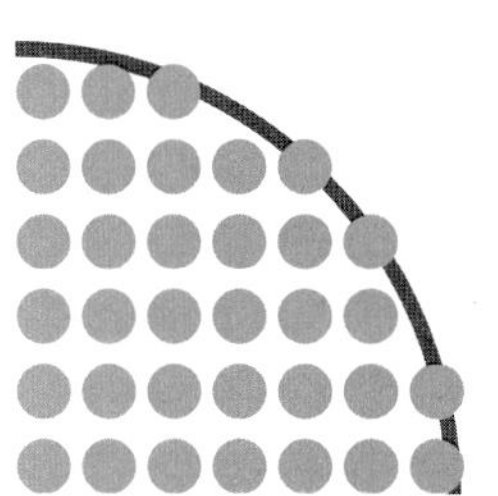

• **Figure 22.17** RET fills in gaps with smaller dots in order to smooth out jagged characters.

RET enables the printer to insert smaller dots among the characters, smoothing out the jagged curves that are typical of printers that do not use RET (Figure 22.17). Using RET enables laser printers to output high-quality print jobs, but also requires a portion of the printer's RAM. If you get a MEM OVERFLOW error, sometimes disabling RET will free up enough memory to complete the print job.

■ Installing a Printer in Windows

Although printing looks the same in Windows 9*x*/Me and Windows NT/2000/XP, various operating systems use very different printing methodologies. Let's take a moment to understand how Windows 9*x*/Me and Windows NT/2000/XP handle printing, and then see how to install, configure, and troubleshoot printers in each OS.

Windows 9*x* systems take a fairly simple approach to printing. The print mechanism is divided into three distinct parts: the printer, the print driver, and the print spooler (Figure 22.18). When you send out a print job (that is, when you click Print), the application sends the print job to the print spooler. The print spooler, working with the print driver, formats the print job in a language that the printer can understand and stores it as a temporary file on

• **Figure 22.18** Windows 9*x*: printer, print driver, and print spooler the hard drive. Once the print job has been "spooled" to the hard drive, the print job is then sent to the printer (to speed things up, you can also have the computer send the beginning of the print job to the printer *before* the entire print job has spooled).

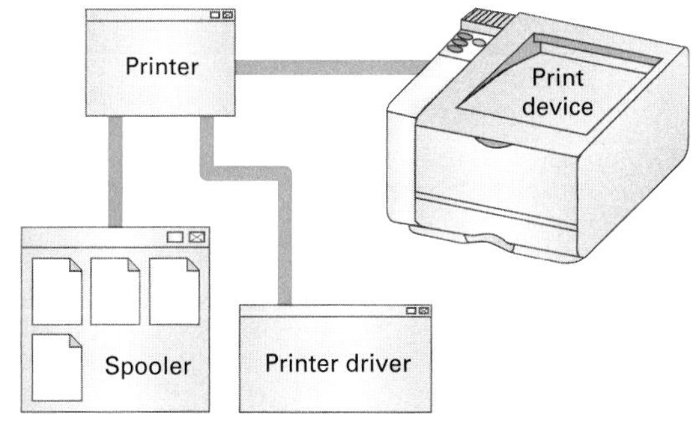

• **Figure 22.19** Windows NT/2000/XP: print driver and spooler

Windows NT, 2000, and XP use a dramatically more complex method. First, to Windows NT/2000/XP, a "printer" is not a physical device; it is a *program* that controls one or more physical printers. The *physical* printer is called a "print device." Print drivers and a spooler are still present, but in NT/2000/XP they are integrated into the "printer" itself (Figure 22.19). This arrangement gives Windows NT/2000/XP amazing flexibility. For example, one printer can support multiple print devices, enabling a system to act as a print server. If one print device goes down, the printer automatically redirects the output to a

matter of plugging it into a parallel port and following the Add Printer Wizard to set up drivers. Just make sure you have Windows NT drivers, and the print device will work fine.

Setting Up Printers

Setting up a printer is so easy that it's almost scary. Most printers are Plug and Play, so installing a printer is reduced to simply plugging it in and loading the driver if needed. If the system does not detect the printer or if the printer is not PnP, select Start | Printers and Faxes in Windows XP to open the Printers applet; in Windows 9*x*/Me and NT/2000, select Start | Settings | Printers. The icon for this applet can also be found in the Control Panel.

As you might guess, you install a new printer by clicking the Add Printer icon (somehow Microsoft managed to leave the name of this applet unchanged through all versions since 95). This starts the Add Printer Wizard. After a pleasant intro screen, you must choose to install a printer plugged directly into your system or a network printer. Windows XP displays the screen shown in Figure 22.20. In Windows 2000/XP, you also have the "Automatically detect and install My Plug and Play printer" option—a nice extra touch.

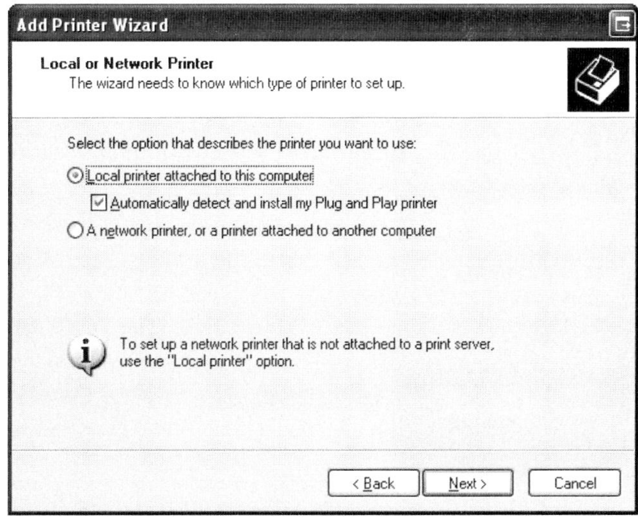

• **Figure 22.20** Choosing local or network printer in Windows XP

If you choose a local printer (see Chapter 23 for a discussion of networked printers)—let's use Windows 2000 in this example—the applet next asks you to select a port; pick the one where you installed the new printer. Figure 22.21 shows the relevant Windows XP screen. Once you select the port, Windows asks you to specify the type of printer, either by selecting the type from the list or using the Have Disk option, just as you would for any other device. Figure 22.22 shows this screen in Windows XP—note the handy Windows Update button you can use to get the latest printer driver from the Internet. Windows 9*x* reverses the port and

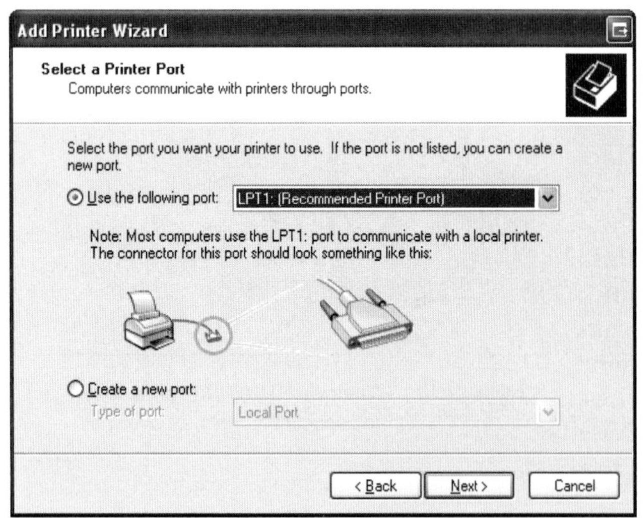

• Figure 22.21 Selecting a port in Windows XP

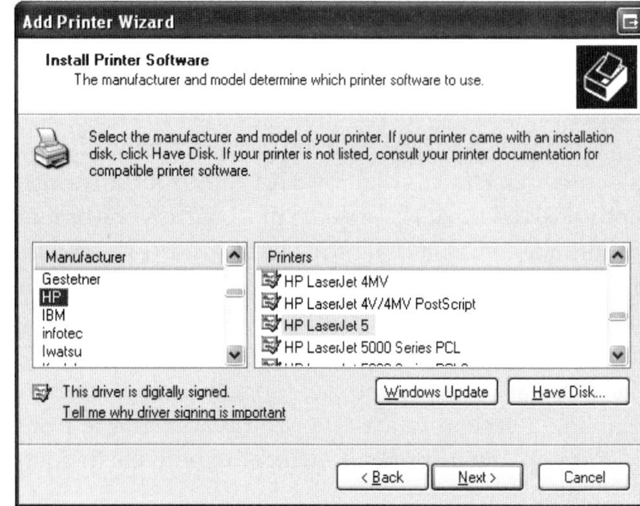

• Figure 22.22 Selecting a printer model/driver in Windows XP

printer type selection screens, but otherwise works the same way. Windows then installs the printer.

Figure 22.23 shows a typical Windows XP Printers and Faxes screen on a system with one printer installed. Note the small check mark in the corner; this shows that the device is the default printer. If you have multiple printers, you can change the default printer by selecting the printer's properties and checking Make Default Printer.

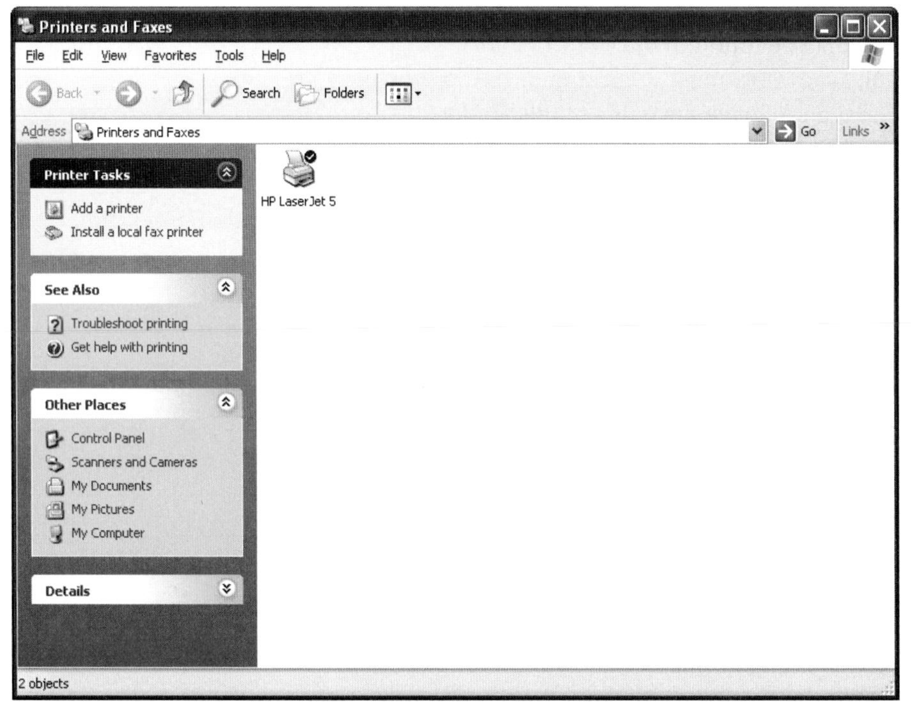

• Figure 22.23 Installed default printer in Windows XP Printers and Faxes applet

In addition to the regular driver installation outlined previously, some installations use printer emulation. *Printer emulation* simply means to use a substitute printer driver for a printer, as opposed to one made exclusively for that printer. You'll run into printer emulation in two circumstances. First, some new printers do not come with their own drivers. They instead emulate a well-known printer (such as an HP LaserJet 4) and run perfectly well on that printer driver. Second, you may see emulation in the "I don't have the right driver!" scenario. I keep about three different HP LaserJet and Epson inkjet printers installed on my PC as I know that with these printer drivers, I can print to almost any printer. Some printers may require you to set them into an *emulation mode* to handle a driver other than their native one.

Tech Tip

Readme Files

You've seen how to get your system to recognize a printer, but what do you do when you get a brand-new printer? Like most peripherals, you'll have an installation CD that contains various useful files. One of the most important, but least used, tools on this CD is the Readme file. This file, generally in TXT format, contains the absolute latest infor-

here is read first to avoid a headache later!

■ Troubleshooting Printers

As easy as printers are to set up, they are equally robust at running, assuming that you install the proper drivers and keep the printer well maintained. But printer errors do occasionally develop. Let's look at the most common print problems having to do with Windows 9*x*/Me and NT/2000/XP, as well as problems that crop up with laser printers.

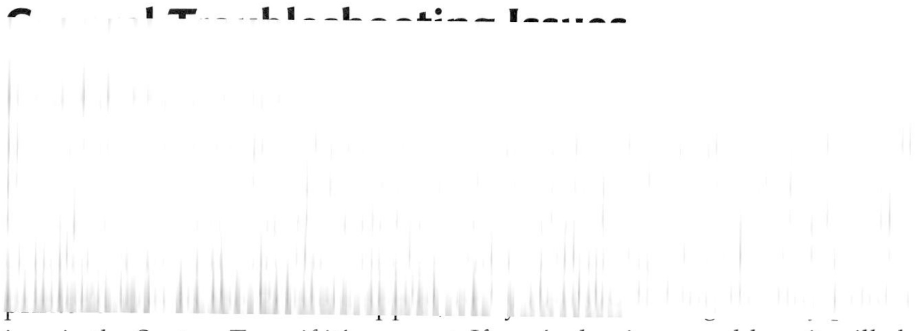

icon in the System Tray, if it's present. If you're having a problem, it will almost always be there (Figure 22.24).

Print spoolers can easily overflow or become corrupt due to a lack of disk space, too many print jobs, or one of a thousand other factors. This window shows all of the pending print jobs and enables you to delete, start, or pause print jobs. I usually just delete the print jobs and try again.

Print spoolers are awfully handy. If the printer goes out, you can just leave the print jobs in the spooler until the printer comes back online. Some versions of Windows require you to select Resume Printing manually, but others will automatically continue the print job(s). If you have a printer that isn't coming on anytime soon, the spooler window enables you simply to delete the print job and try another printer!

Strange Sizes

A print job that comes out a strange size usually points to a user mistake in setting up the print job. All applications have a Print command and a Page Setup. The Page Setup enables you to define a number of print options, which vary from application to application. Figure 22.25 shows the Page Setup options for Microsoft Word. Make sure the user is setting up the page properly.

If you know the page is set up correctly, recheck the printer drivers. If necessary, uninstall and reinstall the printer

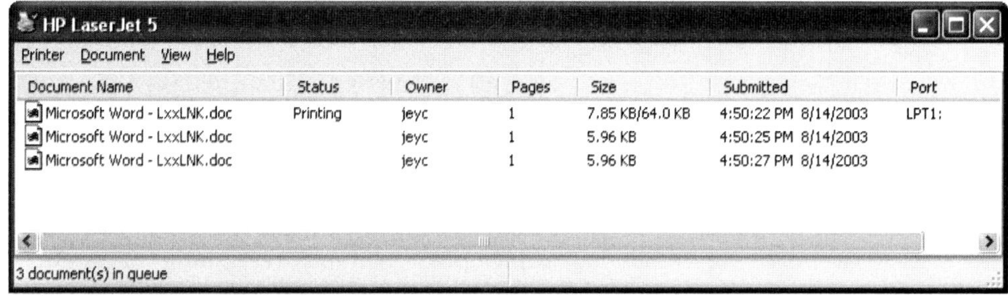

• **Figure 22.24** Print spooler status

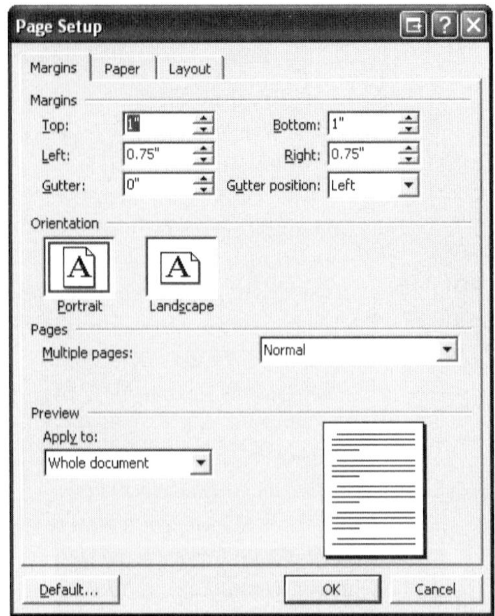

• **Figure 22.25** Page Setup options for Microsoft Word

Tech Tip

Check the MSDS

When in doubt about what to do with a component, check with the manufacturer for a Material Safety Data Sheet *(MSDS). These standardized forms provide detailed information about the potential environmental hazards associated with different components and proper disposal methods. For example, surf to www.hp.com/hpinfo/globalcitizenship/environment/productdata/index.html to find the latest MSDS for all Hewlett Packard products. This isn't just a printer issue—you can find an MSDS for most PC components. When in doubt about how to get rid of any PC component, check with the manufacturer for an MSDS.*

drivers. If the problem persists, you may have a serious problem with the printer's print engine, but that only comes up as a likely answer when you continually get the same strangely sized printouts using a number of different applications.

Misaligned or Garbage Prints

Misaligned or garbage printouts invariably point to a corrupted or incorrect driver. Make sure you're using the right driver (it's hard to mess this up, but not impossible) and then uninstall and reinstall the printer driver. If the problem persists, you may be asking the printer to do something it cannot do. For example, you may be printing to a PostScript printer with a PCL driver. Check the printer type to verify that you haven't installed the wrong type of driver for that printer!

Dealing with Consumables

All printers tend to generate a lot of trash in the form of what we call *consumables*. Impact printers use paper and ribbons, inkjet printers use paper and ink cartridges, and laser printers use paper and toner cartridges. In today's environmentally sensitive world, many laws regulate the proper disposal of most printer components. Be sure to check with the local sanitation department or disposal services company before throwing away any component. Of course, you should never throw away toner cartridges—certain companies will *pay* for used cartridges!

Problems Sharing Multiple Printers

If you want to use multiple printers hooked into the same parallel port, you have to use a switch box. Laser printers should never be used with mechanical switch boxes. Mechanical switch boxes create power surges that can damage your printer. If you must use a switch box, use a box that switches between printers electronically and has built-in surge protection.

Crashes on Power Up

Both laser printers and PCs require more power during their initial power up (the POST on a PC and the warm-up on a laser printer) than once they are running. Hewlett-Packard recommends a *reverse power-up*. Turn on the laser printer first and allow it to finish its warm-up before turning on the PC. This avoids having two devices drawing their peak loads simultaneously.

Troubleshooting Dot-Matrix Printers

Impact printers require regular maintenance, but will run forever as long as you're diligent. Keep the platen (the roller or plate on which the pins impact) clean and the printhead clean with denatured alcohol. Be sure to lubricate gears and pulleys according to the manufacturer's specifications. Never lubricate the printhead, however, because the lubricant will smear and stain the paper.

Bad-Looking Text

White bars going through the text point to a dirty or damaged printhead. Try cleaning the printhead with a little denatured alcohol. If the problem persists, replace the printhead. Printheads for most printers are readily available from the manufacturer, or from companies that rebuild them. If the characters look chopped off at the top or bottom, the printhead probably needs to be adjusted. Refer to the manufacturer's instructions for proper adjustment.

Troubleshooting Inkjet Printers

Inkjet printers are very reliable devices that require very little maintenance as long as they are used within their design parameters (high-use machines will require more intensive maintenance). Because of the low price of these printers, manufacturers know that people don't want to spend a lot of money keeping them running. If you perform even the most basic maintenance tasks, they will soldier on for years without a whimper. Inkjets generally have built-in maintenance programs that you should run from time to time to keep your inkjet in good operating order. Let's take a quick look at inkjet printer maintenance, and then cover the few common issues you should know how to deal with.

Inkjet Printer Maintenance

Inkjet printers don't get nearly as dirty as laser printers, and most manufacturers do not recommend periodic cleaning. Unless your manufacturer explicitly tells you to do so, don't vacuum an inkjet. Inkjets generally do not have maintenance kits, but most inkjet printers come with extensive maintenance software (Figure 22.26). Usually, the hardest part of using this software is finding it in the first place. Look for an option in Printing Preferences, a selection on the Start menu, or an icon on your desktop. Don't worry—it's there!

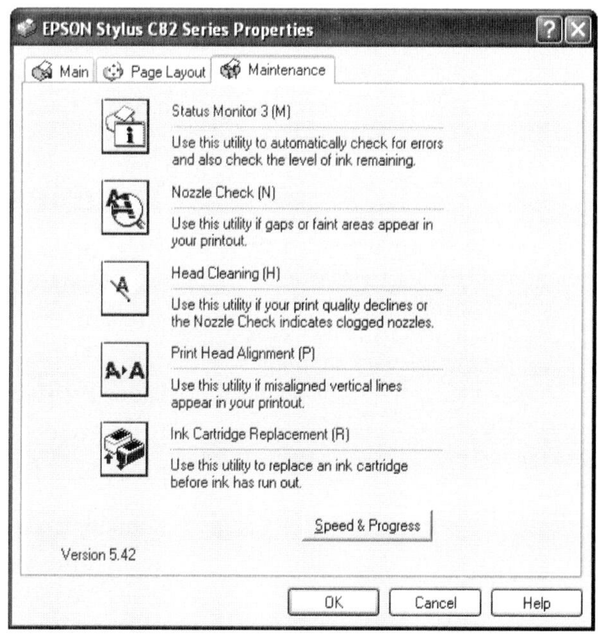

• **Figure 22.26** Inkjet printer maintenance screen

When you first set up an inkjet printer, it normally instructs you to perform a routine to properly align the printheads, wherein you print out a page and select from sets of numbered lines. If this isn't done, the print quality will show it, but the good news is that you can perform this procedure at any time. If a printer is moved or dropped or it's just been working away untended for a while, it's often worth running the alignment routine.

Inkjet Problems

All inkjet inks are water-based, and water works better than alcohol to clean them up.

Did I say that you never should clean an inkjet? Well, that may be true for the printer itself, but there is one part of your printer that will benefit from an occasional cleaning: the inkjet's printer head nozzles. The nozzles are the tiny pipes that squirt the ink onto the paper. A common problem with inkjet printers is the tendency for the ink inside the nozzles to dry out when not used even for a relatively short time, blocking any ink from exiting. If your printer is telling Windows that it's printing and it's feeding paper through, but either nothing is coming out (usually the case if you're just printing black text), or only certain colors are printing, the culprit is almost certainly dried ink clogging the nozzles.

Every inkjet has a different procedure for cleaning the printhead nozzles. On older inkjets, you usually have to press buttons on the printer to start a maintenance program. On more modern inkjets, you can access the head cleaning maintenance program from Windows.

Another problem that sometimes arises is the dreaded multi-sheet paper grab. This is often not actually your printer's fault—humidity can cause sheets of paper to cling to each other—but sometimes the culprit is an overheated printer, so if you've been cranking out a lot of documents without stopping, try giving the printer a bit of a coffee break. Also, make sure you give the paper a good fan before inserting it into the paper tray.

Finally, in the maintenance area where the printheads park, there is usually a small tank or tray to catch excess ink from the cleaning process. If the printer has one, check to see how full it is. If this tray overflows onto the main board or even the power supply, it will kill your printer. If you discover that it's about to overflow, you can remove excess ink by inserting a twisted paper towel into the tank to soak up some of the ink. It is advisable to wear latex or vinyl gloves while doing this. Clean up any spilled ink with a paper towel dampened with distilled water.

Troubleshooting Laser Printers

Before you service a laser printer, always, ALWAYS turn it off and unplug it! Don't expose yourself to the very dangerous high voltages found inside these machines.

There are quite a few possible problems that can arise with laser printers, but before we get into those details, let's review some recommended procedures for *avoiding* those problems.

Laser Printer Maintenance

Unlike with PCs, laser printer maintenance follows a fairly well established procedure. Follow these steps to insure a long, healthy life for your system.

Keeping It Clean Laser printers are quite robust as a rule. A good cleaning every time you replace the toner cartridge will help that printer last for many years. There are many examples of original HP LaserJet I printers continuing to run perfectly after a dozen or more years of operation. The secret is that they were kept immaculately clean.

There are generally only two ways to get your laser printer dirty. First is excess toner, which over time will slowly coat the entire printer. Second is paper dust, sometimes called *paper dander*. This tends to build up where the paper is bent around rollers or where pickup rollers grab paper. Unlike (black) toner, paper dust is easy to see and is usually a good indicator that a printer needs to be cleaned. Without being printer-specific, usually a thorough cleaning using a can of pressurized air to blow out the printer is the best cleaning you can do for that printer. It's best to do this outdoors or you may end up looking like one of those chimney sweeps from *Mary Poppins*! If you must clean a printer indoors, use a special low-static vacuum designed especially for electronic components (Figure 22.27).

Every laser printer has its own unique cleaning method, but one little area tends to be skipped in the cleaning instructions that come [illegible]

If you're ready to get specific, get the printer's service manual. Almost every printer manufacturer sells these; they are a key source for information on how to keep a printer clean and running. Sadly, not all printer manufacturers provide these, but most do. While you're at it, see if the manufacturer has a Quick Reference Guide; these can be very handy for most printer problems!

The photosensitive drum, usually contained in the toner cartridge, can be wiped clean if it becomes dirty, but be very careful if you do so! If the drum becomes scratched, the scratch will appear on every page printed from that point on. The only repair in the event of a scratch is to replace the toner cartridge.

Finally, be aware that Hewlett-Packard sells maintenance kits for most of their laser printers. These are sets of replacement parts for the parts most likely to wear out on each particular type of HP LaserJet. Although their use is not required to maintain warranty coverage, using these kits when prescribed by HP helps to assure the continuing reliability of your LaserJet.

Periodic Maintenance

Although keeping the printer clean is critical to its health and well being, every laser printer has certain components that will need to be replaced periodically. Your ultimate source for determining the parts that need to be replaced (and when to replace them) is the printer manufacturer. Following the manufacturer's maintenance guidelines will help to ensure years of trouble-free, dependable printing from your laser printer.

Some ozone filters may be cleaned with a vacuum and some can only be replaced—follow the manufacturer's recommendation. The fuser assembly may be cleaned with 90% or better denatured alcohol. Check the heat roller (the Teflon coated one with the light bulb inside) for pits and scratches. If there is surface damage on the rollers, replace the fuser unit. Most printers will give you an error code when the fuser is damaged or overheating and needs to be replaced; others will produce the error code at a preset copy count as a preventative maintenance measure. Again, follow the manufacturers recommendations. The transfer corona can be cleaned with 90% denatured alcohol on a cotton swab. If the wire is broken, you can replace it;

Failure of the thermal fuse (used to keep the fuser from overheating) can necessitate replacing the fuser assembly. Some machines contain more than one thermal fuse. As always, follow the manufacturer's recommendations.

Many manufacturers have kits that alert you to replace the fuser unit and key rollers and guides at predetermined page counts with an alarm code.

Always let the fuser assembly cool down before cleaning it, because they operate at 200 to 300 degrees Fahrenheit!

many just snap in, or are held in by a couple of screws. Paper guides can also be cleaned with alcohol on a fibrous towel.

Laser Printer Problems

Laser printers usually manifest problems by creating poor output. One of the most important tests you can do on any printer, not just a laser printer, is called a *diagnostic print page* or an *engine test page*. This is either done by holding down the On Line button as the printer is started or using the printer's maintenance software.

Blank Paper Blank sheets of paper usually mean the printer is out of toner. If the printer does have toner and nothing prints, print a diagnostic print page. If that is also blank, remove the toner cartridge and look at the imaging drum inside. If the image is still there, you know the transfer corona or the high-voltage power supply has failed. Check the printer's maintenance guide to see how to focus on the bad part and replace it.

Dirty Printouts If the fusing mechanism gets dirty in a laser printer, it will leave a light dusting of toner all over the paper, particularly on the back of the page. When you see toner speckles on your printouts, you should get the printer cleaned.

Ghosting Ghost images sometimes appear at regular intervals on the printed page. This can be caused either because the imaging drum has not fully discharged (and is picking up toner from a previous image) or because a previous image has used up so much toner that either the supply of charged toner is insufficient or the toner has not been adequately charged. Sometimes it can also be caused by a worn-out cleaning blade that isn't removing the toner from the drum.

Light Ghosting vs. Dark Ghosting A variety of problems can cause both light and dark ghosting, but the most common source of light ghosting is "developer starvation." If you ask a laser printer to print an extremely dark or complex image, it can use up so much toner that the toner cartridge will not be able to charge enough toner to print the next image. The proper solution is to use less toner. Ways you can fix ghosting problems include these:

- Lowering the resolution of the page (print at 300 dpi instead of 600 dpi)
- Using a different pattern
- Avoiding 50 percent grayscale and "dot-on/dot-off patterns"
- Changing the layout so that grayscale patterns do not follow black areas
- Making dark patterns lighter and light patterns darker
- Printing in landscape orientation
- Adjusting print density and RET settings
- Printing a completely blank page immediately prior to the page with the ghosting image, and as part of the same print job

In addition to these possibilities, low temperature and low humidity can aggravate ghosting problems. Check your users' manual for environmental recommendations. Dark ghosting can sometimes be caused by a damaged drum. It may be fixed by replacing the toner cartridge. Light ghosting would *not* be solved in this way. Switching other components will not usually affect ghosting problems because they are a side effect of the entire printing process.

Vertical White Lines Vertical white lines are usually due to clogged toner preventing the proper dispersion of toner on the drum. Try shaking the toner cartridge to dislodge the clog. If that doesn't work, replace the toner cartridge.

Blotchy Print This is most commonly due to uneven dispersion of toner, especially if the toner is low. Try shaking the toner from side to side and then try to print. Also be sure that the printer is level. Finally, make sure the paper is not wet in spots. If the blotches are in a regular order, check the fusing rollers and the photosensitive drum for any foreign objects.

Spotty Print If the spots appear at regular intervals, the drum may be

the photosensitive drum, you're going to have to use a new toner cartridge. An embossed effect can also be caused by the contrast control being set too high. The contrast control is actually a knob on the inside of the unit (sometimes accessible from the outside, on older models). Check your manual for the specific location.

Incomplete Characters Incompletely printed characters on laser-printed transparencies can sometimes be corrected by adjusting the print density. Be extremely careful to use only materials approved for use in laser printers.

Creased Pages Laser printers have up to four rollers. In addition to the heat and pressure rollers of the fusing assembly, other rollers move the paper from the source tray to the output tray. These rollers crease the paper in order to avoid curling that would cause paper jams in the printer. If the creases are noticeable, try using a different paper type. Cotton bond paper is usually more susceptible to noticeable creasing than other bonds. You might also try sending the output to the face up tray, which avoids one roller. There is no hardware solution to this problem. It is simply a side-effect of the process.

Paper Jams Every printer jams every now and then. If you get a jam, always first refer to the manufacturer's jam removal procedure. It is simply too easy to damage a printer by pulling on the jammed paper! If the printer reports a jam but there's no paper inside, you've almost certainly got a problem with one of the many jam sensors or paper feed sensors inside the printer, and you'll need to take it to a repair center.

Pulling Multiple Sheets If the printer grabs multiple sheets at a time, first try opening a new ream of paper and loading that in the printer. If that works, you've got a humidity problem. If the new paper angle doesn't work, check the separation pad on the printer. The separation pad is a small piece of cork or rubber that separates the sheets as they are pulled from the paper feed tray. A worn separation pad will look shiny and, well, *worn*! Most separation pads are easy to replace. Check out www.printerworks.com to see if you can replace yours.

Warped, Overprinted, or Poorly Formed Characters Poorly formed characters can indicate either a problem with the paper (or other media), or a problem with the hardware. Let's look at both.

Incorrect media causes a number of these types of problems. Avoid paper that is too rough or too smooth. Paper that is too rough interferes with the fusing of characters and their initial definition. If the paper is too smooth (like some coated papers, for example), it may feed improperly, causing distorted or overwritten characters. Even though you can purchase laser printer-specific paper, all laser printers will print acceptably on standard photocopy paper. Try to keep the paper from becoming too wet. Don't open a ream of paper until it is loaded into the printer. Always fan the paper before loading it into the printer, especially if the paper has been left out for more than just a few days.

The durability of a well-maintained laser printer makes hardware a much rarer source of character printing problems, but you should be aware of the possibility. Fortunately, it is fairly easy to check the hardware. Most laser printers have a self-test function—often combined with a diagnostic printout, but sometimes as a separate process. This self-test shows whether the laser printer can properly develop an image without having to actually send print commands from the PC. The self-test is quite handy to verify the question "Is it the printer or is it the computer?" Run the self-test to check for connectivity and configuration problems.

Possible solutions include replacing the toner cartridge, especially if you hear popping noises; checking the cabling; and replacing the data cable, especially if there are bends, crimps, or objects resting on the cable. If you have a Front Menu Panel, turn off Advanced Functions and High Speed Settings to determine if the advanced functions are either not working properly or not supported by your current software configuration (check your manuals for configuration information). If these solutions do not work, the problem may not be user serviceable. Contact an authorized service center.

Beyond A+

DOT4

The IEEE 1284.4 standard, commonly known as DOT4, was created for multifunction peripherals, or MFPs—those nifty gadgets that combine the functions of printer, fax, and scanner in one big piece of equipment. The DOT4 protocol enables the individual devices within the MFP to send and receive multiple data packets simultaneously across a single physical channel. All data exchanges are independent of one another, so you can cancel one—for example, a print job—without affecting the others. DOT4 is an enhancement of the IEEE 1284 protocol for parallel printing; look for products that use it the next time you find yourself in a computer superstore.

Chapter 22 Review

Chapter Summary

After reading this chapter and completing the exercises, you should understand the following aspects of printers.

Describe Current Printer Technologies

- Printers that create an image on paper by physically striking an ink ribbon against the paper's surface are known as impact printers. The most commonly used

9-pin (draft quality) and 24-pin (letter quality).

- The quality of a print image is called the print resolution. The resolution is measured in dots per inch (dpi), which has two values: horizontal and vertical. An example of a resolution is 600 × 600 dpi. Printing speed is measured in pages per minute (ppm).
- Inkjet printers include a printhead mechanism, support electronics, a transfer mechanism to move the printhead back and forth, and a paper feed component to drag, move, and eject paper. They eject ink (cyan, yellow, magenta, and black) through tiny tubes. The heat used to move the ink is created by tiny resistors or electroconductive plates at the end of each tube.
- Dye-sublimation printers are used to achieve excellent print quality, especially in color, but they're expensive. Documents printed through the dye-sublimation process display *continuous tone* images, meaning that each pixel dot is a blend of the different dye colors. This is in contrast to other print technologies' *dithered* images, which use closely packed, single-color dots to simulate blended colors.
- Two kinds of thermal printers create either quick one-color printouts (direct thermal), such as faxes or store receipts, or higher-quality (thermal wax transfer) color prints.
- Using a process called electro-photographic imaging, laser printers produce high-quality and high-speed output. Laser printers use lasers as a light source because of their precision. The toner cartridge in a laser printer supplies the toner that creates the image on the page; many other laser printer parts, especially those that suffer the most wear and tear, have been incorporated into the replaceable toner cartridge.

voltage, an electric field (or corona) forms, enabling voltage to pass to the drum and charge the photosensitive particles on its surface; the surface of the drum receives a uniform negative voltage of between ~600 and ~1,000 volts.

- The laser acts as the writing mechanism of the printer. When particles are struck by the laser, they are discharged and left with a ~100 volt negative charge. The toner in a laser printer is a fine powder made up of plastic particles bonded to iron particles. The toner cylinder charges the toner with a negative charge of between ~200 and ~500 volts. Because that charge falls between the original uniform negative charge of the photosensitive drum (~600 to ~1,000 volts) and the charge of the particles on the drum's surface hit by the laser (~100 volts), particles of toner are attracted to the areas of the photosensitive drum that have been hit by the laser. The transfer corona applies a positive charge to the paper, drawing the negatively charged toner particles on the drum to the paper. The toner remains in place on the statically-charged paper, which then proceeds through two rollers, a pressure roller and a heated roller. After the rollers fuse the toner to the page, a static eliminator removes the paper's charge.
- All laser printers have at least two separate power supplies. The primary power supply, which may actually be more than one power supply, provides

power to the motors that move the paper, the system electronics, the laser, and the transfer corona. The high-voltage power supply usually only provides power to the primary corona; it is one of the most dangerous devices in the world of PCs.

- A laser printer's mechanical functions are served by complex gear systems packed together in discrete units generically called gear packs or gearboxes. Most laser printers have two or three. Every laser printer has sensors that detect a broad range of conditions such as paper jams, empty paper trays, or low toner levels.
- Every laser printer contains at least one electronic system board (many have two or three) that contains the main processor, the printer's ROM, and RAM used to store the image before it is printed. When the printer doesn't have enough RAM to store the image before it prints, you get a memory overflow problem. Most printers can use generic DRAM like the kind you use in your PC, but check with the manufacturer to be sure.
- Because even tiny concentrations of ozone (O_3) will cause damage to printer components, most laser printers have a special ozone filter that needs to be vacuumed or replaced periodically.
- ASCII contains a variety of control codes for transferring data, some of which can be used to control printers; ASCII code 10 (or 0A in hex) means "Line Feed," and ASCII code 12 (0C) means "Form Feed." These commands have been standard since before the creation of IBM PCs, and all printers respond to them; however, the control codes are extremely limited. Utilizing high-end graphics and a wide variety of fonts requires more advanced languages.
- Adobe Systems' PostScript Page Description Language is a device-independent printer language capable of high-resolution graphics and scalable fonts. Because PostScript is understood by printers at a hardware level, the majority of the image processing is done by the printer and not the PC's CPU, so PostScript printers print faster. PostScript defines the page as a single raster image; this makes PostScript files extremely portable.
- Hewlett-Packard's Printer Control Language (PCL) features a set of printer commands greatly expanded from ASCII, but it does not support advanced graphical functions. PCL6 features scalable fonts and additional line drawing commands. PCL uses a series of commands to define the characters on the page, rather than defining the page as a single raster image like PostScript.
- Windows 9*x*/Me and NT/2000/XP use the Graphical Device Interface (GDI) component of the operating system to handle print functions. The GDI uses the CPU rather than the printer to process a print job and then sends the completed job to the printer. As long as the printer has a capable enough RIP and plenty of RAM, you don't need to worry about the printer language at all in most situations.
- Most printers connect to one of two ports on the PC: a DB25 parallel port or a USB port. The parallel connection is the classic way to plug in a printer, but most new printers use USB. The parallel port was included in the original IBM PC as a faster alternative to serial communication, and has been kept around for backward compatibility. Parallel ports are slow by modern standards, with a maximum data transfer rate of 150 Kbps. Parallel ports lack true bidirectional capability. A standard parallel connection normally manifests as a 25-pin female DB25 connector on the PC and a corresponding male connector on the printer cable. Eight wires are used as grounds, four for control signals, five for status signals, and eight for data signals going from the PC to the device. The parallel connector on the printer side is called a Centronics connector.
- IEEE 1284 was developed as a standard for a backward-compatible, high-speed, bidirectional parallel port for the PC. It requires support for compatibility, nibble mode, byte mode, EPP, and ECP; a standard method of negotiating compatible modes between printer and PC; standard cables and connectors; and a standard electrical interface.
- Using the non-standard Fast Centronics mode, some systems can achieve data transfer rates of up to 500 Kbps. Nibble mode used in concert with compatibility/Centronics mode provides a very limited form of bidirectional communication. Using four of the five status wires, it can transfer a byte (8 bits) of data in two pieces, one nibble (4 bits) at a time, from the peripheral to the PC. Nibble mode transfers data at a maximum of about 50 Kbps. Byte mode enables reverse direction (peripheral-to-PC) parallel communication using all eight data wires. Byte mode in conjunction with Centronics mode provides two-way

eight-bit communication at speeds approaching 150 Kbps. Parallel ports capable of byte mode transfers are sometimes referred to as enhanced bidirectional ports.

- The Enhanced Parallel Port (EPP) protocol offers high-speed, two-way data transfers with relatively little software overhead. By removing the CPU from the handshaking process, an EPP port enables the CPU to transfer data to and from the port with a single command. Data transfers using the EPP protocol can approach the speed of an ISA bus, transferring between 500 Kbps and 2 Mbps.
- The Extended Capability Port (ECP) protocol is [illegible] method called Run Length Encoding (RLE) that achieves a compression ratio of up to 64:1. Many manufacturers have added special capabilities to the ports, especially DMA channels.
- A standard parallel printer cable has a male DB25 connector on one end and a 36-pin Centronics connector on the other, and is acceptable for transferring data at 150 Kbps, and for distances under six feet. ECP and EPP devices can use IEEE 1284–compliant cables to reach distances up to 10 m, although data transfer speed drops significantly with very long cables. Unlike parallel printers, USB printers usually come with a USB cable, usually with the standard USB type A connector on one end and the smaller USB type B connector on the other end, although some use two type A connectors.

Explain The Laser Printing Process

- Laser printing is a six-step process: clean, charge, write, develop, transfer, and fuse.
- The printing process begins with the physical and electrical cleaning of the photosensitive drum. All residual toner left over from printing the previous page must be removed, usually by scraping the surface of the drum with a rubber cleaning blade. One or more erase lamps bombard the surface of the drum with the appropriate wavelengths of light, causing the surface particles to completely discharge into the grounded drum.
- Using the primary corona wire, a uniform negative charge is applied to the entire surface of the drum (usually between ~600 and ~1,000 volts) to make the drum receptive to new images. A laser is used to write a positive image relative to the toner particles on the surface of the drum, attracting them and creating a developed image. The transfer corona gives the paper a positive charge, making the negatively charged toner particles leap from the drum to the paper. The toner particles are mostly composed of plastic, so they can be melted to the page. Two rollers, a heated roller coated in a [illegible]
- Laser printers generate a pattern of dots, called a raster image, representing what each page should look like. Laser printers use the laser to "paint" the raster image on the photosensitive drum. Laser printers use a chip called the Raster Image Processor (RIP) to translate the raster image sent to the printer into commands to the laser.
- Laser printer resolution is expressed in dots per inch (dpi). Common resolutions are 600 dpi × 600 dpi or 1200 dpi × 1200 dpi. The first number, the horizontal resolution, is determined by how fine a focus can be achieved by the laser. The second number is determined by the smallest increment by which the drum can be turned. Higher resolutions produce higher-quality output, but also require more memory. Even printing at 300 dpi, laser printers produce far better quality than dot-matrix printers because Resolution Enhancement Technology (RET) enables the printer to insert smaller dots among the characters, smoothing out the jagged curves that are typical of printers that do not use RET.

Install a Printer in Windows

- Windows 9*x* systems take a fairly simple approach to printing. The print mechanism is divided into three distinct parts: the printer, the print driver, and the print spooler. When you send out a print job (that is, when you click Print), the application sends the print job to the print spooler. The print spooler, working with the print driver, formats the print job in a language that the printer can understand and stores it as a temporary file on the hard drive. Once the print job has been "spooled" to the hard drive, the print job is then sent to the printer.

- To Windows NT/2000/XP, a "printer" is not a physical device; it is a program that controls one or more physical printers. The physical printer is called a "print device." Print drivers and a spooler are still present, but in NT/2000/XP they are integrated into the "printer" itself.
- Select Start | Printers and Faxes in Windows XP to open the Printers applet; in Windows 9*x*/Me and 2000, select Start | Settings | Printers. The icon for this applet can also be found in the Control Panel. You install a new printer by clicking the Add Printer icon to start the Add Printer Wizard. You must choose to install a local or a network printer, and you must select a port for a local printer. You must specify the printer type from the Wizard's list, or using the Have Disk option. Windows XP's applet features a Windows Update button you can use to get the latest printer driver from the Internet.
- One printer will always be the default printer. If you have more than one printer installed, you can make any printer the default printer. The icon for the default printer will have a small check mark in the corner. If you have multiple printers, you can change the default printer by selecting the printer's properties and checking Make Default Printer.
- Printer emulation means using a substitute printer driver for a printer, as opposed to one made exclusively for that printer. Some printers are designed to emulate other, more widely supported models. If you don't have the specific driver for a printer, you can often use the driver from a similar model.

Troubleshoot Printers

- When troubleshooting a printer, first check all the obvious things. Is the printer on? Is it connected? Is it online? Does it have paper? Then check the spooler status, either by double-clicking the printer's icon in the Printers applet or by double-clicking the tiny printer icon in the System Tray, if it's present.
- A print job that comes out a strange size usually points to a user mistake in setting up the print job. Use the program's Page Setup feature to fix these problems. If you know the page is set up correctly, recheck the printer drivers. Misaligned or garbage printouts invariably point to a corrupted or incorrect driver.
- Printer manufacturers will supply a standardized form called a Material Safety Data Sheet (MSDS) for each of their products; these documents provide detailed information about the potential environmental hazards associated with different components and proper disposal methods. This isn't just a printer issue—you can find an MSDS for most PC components.
- If you want to use multiple printers hooked into the same parallel port, you have to use a switch box; use a box that switches between printers electronically and has built-in surge protection.
- Turn on the laser printer first and allow it to finish its warm-up before turning on the PC (a reverse power-up). This avoids having two devices drawing their peak loads simultaneously.
- With regular maintenance, impact printers will run forever. White bars going through the text point to a dirty or damaged printhead. Try cleaning the printhead with a little 90% or better denatured alcohol. If the characters look chopped off at the top or bottom, the printhead probably needs to be adjusted. If the page is covered with dots and small smudges—the "pepper look"—the platen is dirty. Clean the platen with denatured alcohol. If the image is faded, and you know the ribbon is good, try adjusting the printhead closer to the platen. If the image is okay on one side of the paper but fades as you move to the other, the platen is out of adjustment—take it to the manufacturer's local warranty/repair center.
- Inkjet printers generally have built-in maintenance programs that you should run from time to time to keep your inkjet in good operating order. Unless your manufacturer explicitly tells you to do so, don't vacuum an inkjet. A common problem with inkjet printers is the tendency for the ink inside the nozzles to dry out when not used even for a relatively short time, blocking any ink from exiting. If your printer is telling Windows that it's printing and it's feeding paper through, but either nothing is coming out (usually the case if you're just

printing black text), or only certain colors are printing, check for dried ink clogging the nozzles. To clean the nozzles on older inkjets, you usually have to press buttons on the printer to start a maintenance program. On more modern inkjets, you can access the head-cleaning maintenance program from Windows. All inkjet inks are water-based, and water works better than alcohol to clean them up.

- Laser printers usually manifest problems by creating poor output. One of the most important tests you can do on any printer, not just a laser printer, is called a diagnostic print page or an engine test page. This is done by either holding [illegible]

- Every laser printer has certain components that will need to be replaced periodically. Your ultimate source for determining the parts that need to be replaced (and when to replace them) is the printer manufacturer. A printer's service manual is a key source for information on how to keep it clean and running.

- Over time excess toner will slowly coat the interior of a laser printer. Paper dander will build up where the paper is bent around rollers or where pickup rollers grab paper. Use a small amount of 90% or better alcohol on a fibrous cleaning towel to remove the debris and any dead rubber. The fuser assembly and transfer corona can also be cleaned with alcohol. Follow the manufacturer's recommendations faithfully when servicing any of the internal components of a laser printer. Always let the fuser assembly cool down before cleaning it, as it operates at 200 to 300 degrees Fahrenheit.

- Blank sheets of paper usually mean the printer is out of toner. If the printer does have toner and nothing prints, print a diagnostic print page. If that is also blank, remove the toner cartridge and look at the imaging drum inside. If the image is still there, you know the transfer corona or the high-voltage power supply has failed. If the fusing mechanism gets dirty in a laser printer, it will leave a light dusting of toner all over the paper, particularly on the back of the page. Vertical white lines are usually due to clogged toner preventing the proper dispersion of toner on the drum. Try shaking the toner cartridge to dislodge the clog. Blotchy print is most commonly due to uneven dispersion of toner, especially if the toner is low; also check that the printer is level and the paper completely dry. If spots appear at regular intervals, the drum may be damaged or some toner may be stuck to the fuser rollers. An embossed effect almost certainly points to a foreign object on a roller.

- Ghost images can mean several things. It may be that the imaging drum has not fully discharged and is picking up toner from a previous image. It's also possible that a previous image has used up so [illegible] less toner. Low temperature and low humidity can also aggravate ghosting problems. Dark ghosting can sometimes be caused by a damaged drum, in which case it may be fixed by replacing the toner cartridge. Light ghosting would *not* be solved in this way.

- The rollers that move the paper from the source tray to the output tray crease the paper in order to avoid curling that would cause paper jams in the printer. If the creases are noticeable, try using a different paper type. Cotton bond paper is usually more susceptible to noticeable creasing than other bonds. If you get a paper jam, always first refer to the manufacturer's jam removal procedure. If the printer reports a jam but there's no paper inside, you've almost certainly got a problem with one of the many jam sensors or paper feed sensors. If the printer grabs multiple sheets at a time, it may be humidity, or a worn separation pad.

- Warped, overprinted, or poorly formed characters can indicate either a problem with the paper (or other media) or a problem with the hardware. Paper that is too rough interferes with the fusing of characters and their initial definition. Paper that is too smooth (like some coated papers, for example) may feed improperly, causing distorted or overwritten characters. All laser printers will print acceptably on standard photocopy paper.

- Hardware problems are a much rarer source of character printing problems. Most laser printers have a self-test function that shows whether the laser printer can properly develop an image without having to actually send print commands from the PC. Run the self-test to check for connectivity and configuration problems. Possible solutions include replacing the toner cartridge, especially if you hear popping noises; checking the cabling; and replacing the data cable, especially if there are bends, crimps, or objects resting on the cable.
- The IEEE 1284.4 standard, commonly known as DOT4, was created for multifunction peripherals (MFPs) that combine the functions of printer, fax, and scanner in one big piece of equipment. DOT4 is an enhancement of the IEEE 1284 protocol for parallel printing. The DOT4 protocol enables the individual devices within the MFP to send and receive multiple data packets simultaneously across a single physical channel.

Key Terms

DB25 connector *(791)*
Centronics connector *(791)*
Dot-matrix printer *(783)*
Dots per inch (dpi) *(784)*
IEEE 1284 *(791)*
Fuser assembly *(787)*
Graphical Device Interface (GDI) *(790)*
Impact printer *(783)*
Inkjet printer *(784)*
Laser printer *(786)*
Pages per minute (ppm) *(784)*
Parallel port *(791)*
Photosensitive drum *(786)*
PostScript *(790)*
Primary corona *(786)*
Print resolution *(784)*
Printer Control Language (PCL) *(790)*
Toner *(787)*
Toner cartridge *(786)*
Transfer corona *(787)*

Key Term Quiz

Use the Key Terms list to complete the sentences that follow. Not all terms will be used.

1. The __________ standard requires support for compatibility mode, nibble mode, byte mode, EPP, and ECP.
2. A standard parallel printer cable normally has a male __________ on one end and a 36-pin __________ on the other.
3. Printers that create an image on paper by physically striking an ink ribbon against the paper's surface are known as __________.
4. Laser printers use lasers to create the print image on the ______________.
5. The ____________ on a standard laser printer contains a pressure roller and a heated roller.
6. Adobe ___________ is a device-independent printer language capable of high-resolution graphics and scalable fonts.
7. Windows 9*x*/Me and NT/2000/XP use the ____________ component of the operating system to handle print functions.
8. The ___________ was included in the original IBM PC as a faster alternative to serial communication.
9. The resolution of a printer is measured in _________.
10. A printer's speed is rated in _________.

Multiple-Choice Quiz

1. Which part of a laser printer applies a positive charge to the paper that attracts the toner particles to it?

   A. Erase lamp

   B. Transfer corona

   C. Laser

   D. Primary corona

2. Dot-matrix printers come in 9-pin and ________-pin versions.

   A. 6

   B. ASCII

   C. Printer Control Language

   D. Graphical Device Interface

4. What is the approximate maximum data transfer rate of a standard parallel port?

   A. 50 Kbps

   B. 150 Kbps

   C. 500 Kbps

   D. 2 Mbps

5. The vast majority of printers use either a parallel or a _________ connection.

   A. USB

   B. PCI

   C. Serial

   D. VGA

6. Janet just bought a new Windows XP system. She wants to install her three-year-old inkjet printer on the new system but has lost the driver CD. She can't get on the Internet to download the latest drivers. What should she do for drivers?

   A. Install a driver for a similar printer.

   B. She's stuck until she can get on the Internet.

   C. She can use the Windows built-in drivers.

   D. She can install the printer without drivers.

7. If your computer has only a single parallel port, most likely it is preset to __________.

   A. COM1

   B. Primary

   C. USB

   D. LPT1

8. John just installed a second printer on his system. When he prints in Microsoft Word, the job goes to the wrong printer. What does he need to do to get print jobs always to go to one printer or the other?

   A. Select Start | Settings | Printers.

   B. Select Start | Printers and Faxes.

   C. Select Start | Printer Settings.

   D. Select Start | Printers | Settings.

10. Frank's color inkjet printer no longer prints the color yellow, though it prints all the other colors just fine. The printer worked fine last month, the last time he printed in color. Which of the following is the most likely problem?

    A. He turned off the yellow nozzle.

    B. He has run out of yellow ink.

    C. He has a corrupt printer driver.

    D. His printer is set to black-and-white mode.

11. Beth's laser printer is printing tiny specks on the paper. What should she do first?

    A. Wipe the paper with bleach.

    B. Run the printer maintenance program.

    C. Clean the nozzles.

    D. Vacuum the printer.

12. Ursula's laser printer has stopped working and is displaying this error message: "Error 81 – Service." What should she do first?

    A. Update the printer's firmware.

    B. Reinstall the printer driver.

C. Try to find the error in the user's guide or maintenance program or online.

D. Turn off the printer and call the manufacturer's help line.

13. Kevin's inkjet printer isn't printing blue (cyan). He checks the ink levels and sees that there's plenty of ink. What should he consider next?

A. A printhead is jammed.

B. A laser is blocked.

C. A nozzle is clogged.

D. An ink cartridge is missing.

14. The output from Diane's laser printer is fading evenly. What should she suspect first?

A. A laser is blocked.

B. The printer is out of toner.

C. A nozzle is clogged.

D. Her printer is dirty.

15. The dye-sublimation printing technique is an example of what method of color printing?

A. CMYK

B. Thermal wax transfer

C. RGB

D. Direct thermal

Essay Quiz

1. Your department needs a number of color inkjet printers. However, at your organization all purchases are handled through professional buyers. Sadly, they know nothing about color inkjet printers. You need to submit a Criteria for Purchase form to your buyers. This is the standard form that your organization gives to buyers so they know what to look for in the products they buy. What are the top three purchasing criteria that you think they need to consider? Write the criteria as simply and clearly as possible.

2. You support 25 laser printers for your department as part of your job description. The printers take so much of your time that you often need to work overtime to keep them running. You're often criticized for shutting down printers that people need when you clean them. You've just been given a promotion and have been asked by your old boss to write a memo on how your old job can be improved. Recommend to your boss that a professional laser printer company should handle laser printer maintenance for your organization. Give as many compelling reasons as you can think of.

3. Interview a person who uses a computer for work. Ask the person what he or she does and then write a short description of the type of printer that would most suit that person's needs. Explain why this printer would be the best choice.

4. Dot-matrix printers and multipart forms are an excellent match. Think of some businesses that could benefit from the ability of dot-matrix printers to handle multipart forms.

5. Describe the first printer you ever used. If you've never used a printer, ask another person about the first printer he or she used. Describe the printer, the technology, the size of paper it used, and the type of data that was printed. If possible, describe how the printer was maintained and serviced.

Lab Projects

• Lab Project 22.1

Laser printers often have rather complex maintenance procedures and schedules. Select a laser printer—preferably one that you actually have on hand—and answer the following questions.

1. Using the user's guide or online sources, determine the exact cleaning procedures for your laser printer. How often should it be vacuumed? Do any parts need to be removed for cleaning? Does the manufacturer [illegible]

2. [illegible] to include a vacuum. Locate sources for these products and determine the cost of the toolkit.

3. Determine the model number of the toner cartridge. Locate an online company that sells name-brand (such as Hewlett-Packard) toner cartridges. Locate an equivalent third-party toner cartridge. Assuming that the printer uses a toner cartridge every three months, what is your per-system annual cost savings using third-party toner cartridges?

4. All toner cartridges have a materials safety [illegible]

• Lab Project 22.2

Using the same laser printer you used in the first project, locate and compile, on paper, all of the following information about your printer:

- User's guide
- List of error codes
- Troubleshooting guides
- Location of the latest drivers for Windows XP

chapter

23 Networking

"Distributed computing is where someone tripping over a cable in another building can ruin your day."

—David K. Gifford (Professor of Computer Science, MIT)

In this chapter, you will learn how to

- **Explain network technologies**
- **Explain network operating systems**
- **Install and configure wired networks**
- **Install and configure wireless networks**
- **Troubleshoot networks**

Networks dominate the modern computing environment. A vast percentage of businesses have PCs connected in a small local area network (LAN), and big businesses simply can't survive with connecting their many offices into a single wide area network (WAN). Even the operating systems of today demand networks. Windows XP comes out of the box *assuming* you'll attach it to a network of some sort just to make it work past 30 days (Product Activation) and gets all indignant if you don't.

The A+ Certification exams have a rather mixed interpretation about what an A+ Certified technician should know about networking computers. The Core Hardware exam is fascinated by cables, connectors, and anything remotely, well, hardware. The OS Technologies exam tests you on configuring Windows for networks. Both tests are fine, but just giving you the test information won't prepare you for real life as a PC tech. Because networks are so common today, every good tech needs to know the basics of networking technology, operating systems, implementation, and troubleshooting. Accordingly, this chapter teaches you how to build and troubleshoot a basic network.

Historical Conceptual

Networking Technologies

When the first network designers sat down at a pub to figure out a way to enable two or more PCs to share data and peripherals, they had to write a lot of details on little white napkins to answer even the most basic questions. The first big question was: *How?* It's easy to say, "Well, just run a wire between them!" Although most networks do manifest themselves via some type of cable, this barely touches the thousands of questions that come into play here. Here are a few of the *big* questions:

- How can access to data and peripherals be controlled?

Clearly, making a modern PC network entails a lot more than just stringing up some cable! Most commonly, you have a *client* machine, a PC that requests information or services. It needs a **network interface card (NIC)** that defines or labels the client on the network; a NIC also helps break files into smaller data units, called *packets*, to send across the network, and helps reassemble the packets it receives into whole files. Second, you need some medium for delivering the packets between two or more PCs—most often this is a wire that can carry electrical pulses; sometimes it's radio waves or other wireless methods. Third, your PC's operating system has to be able to communicate with its own networking hardware, and with other machines on the network. Finally, modern PC networks often employ a *server* machine, one that gives out information or services. Figure 23.1 shows a typical network layout.

This section of the chapter looks at the inventive ways network engineers found to handle the first two of the four issues. After a brief look at core technology, the chapter dives into four specific types of networks. We'll turn to the software side of things later in the chapter.

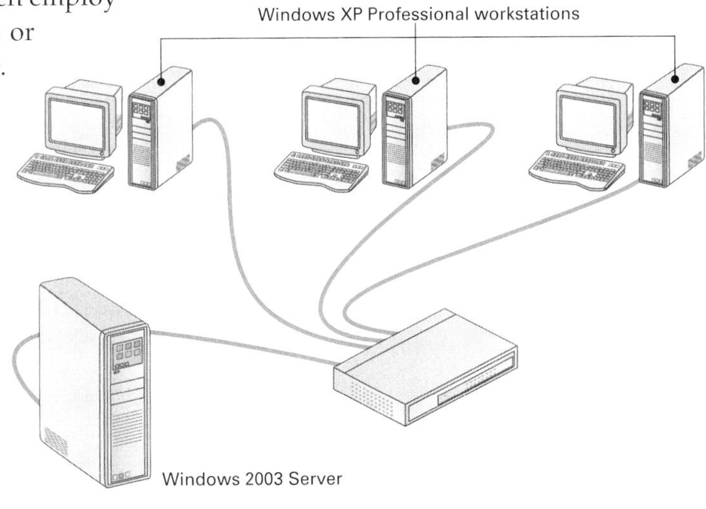

Figure 23.1 A typical network

Test Specific

Packets/Frames and NICs

Data is moved from one PC to another in discrete chunks called **packets** or *frames*. The terms *packet*

Even though MAC addresses are embedded into the NIC, some NICs will allow you to change the MAC address on the NIC. This is rarely done.

and *frame* are interchangeable. Every network interface card (NIC) in the world has a built-in identifier, a binary address unique to that single network card, called a **Media Access Control (MAC) address**. You read that right—every network card in the world has its own unique MAC address! The MAC address is 48 bits long, giving over 281 *trillion* MAC addresses, so there are plenty of MAC addresses to go around. MAC addresses may be binary, but we represent them using twelve hexadecimal characters. These MAC addresses are burned into every NIC and some NIC makers print the MAC address on the card as shown in the figure. Figure 23.2 shows the System Information utility description of a NIC, with the MAC address highlighted.

System Information

File Edit View Tools Help

Item	Value
Name	[00000001] Realtek RTL8139/810X Family F
Adapter Type	Ethernet 802.3
Product Type	Realtek RTL8139/810X Family Fast Ethernet
Installed	Yes
PNP Device ID	PCI\VEN_10EC&DEV_8139&SUBSYS_8139
Last Reset	8/21/2003 3:14 PM
Index	1
Service Name	RTL8139
IP Address	192.168.4.23
IP Subnet	255.255.255.0
Default IP Gateway	192.168.4.151
DHCP Enabled	Yes
DHCP Server	192.168.4.154
DHCP Lease Expires	8/29/2003 3:14 PM
DHCP Lease Obtained	8/21/2003 3:14 PM
MAC Address	00:20:18:8B:54:A3
I/O Port	0x0000A000-0x0000A0FF
Memory Address	0xDE001000-0xDE0010FF

Forced Hardware, I/O, IRQs, Memory, Components, Multimedia, CD-ROM, Sound Device, Display, Infrared, Input, Modem, Network, Adapter, Protocol, WinSock, Ports, Storage

Find what: Find Close Find

Search selected category only Search category names only

• **Figure 23.2** MAC address

Hey! I thought we were talking about packets? Well, we are but you need to understand MAC addresses in order to understand packets. All the many varieties of packets share certain common features (Figure 23.3). First, packets contain the MAC address of the network card to which the data is being sent. Second, they have the MAC address of the network card that sent the data. Third, is the data itself (at this point, we have no idea what the data is—certain software handles that question), which can vary in size depending on the type of frame. Finally, some type of data check (we call it a Cyclic Redundancy Check or CRC) is performed and information is stored in the packet to enable the receiving network card to verify if the data was received in good order.

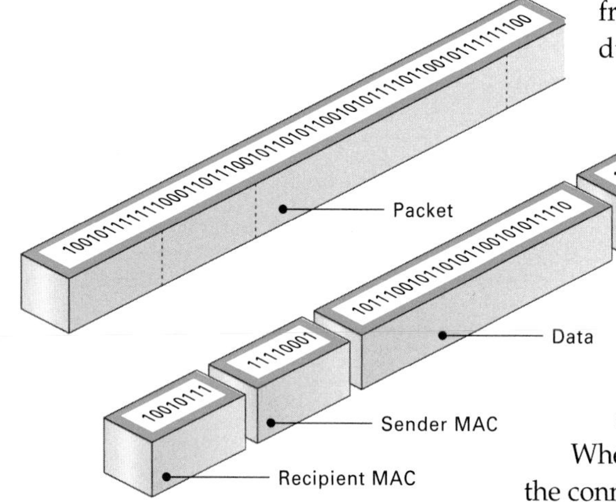

• **Figure 23.3** Generic packet/frame

This discussion of packets raises the question, how big is the packet? Or more specifically, how much data do you put into each packet? How do you ensure that the receiving PC understands the *way* that the data was broken down by the sending machine and can thus put the pieces back together? The problem in answering these questions is that they encompass so many items. When the first networks were created, *everything* from the frames to the connectors to the type of cable had to be invented from scratch.

To make a successful network, you need the sending and receiving PCs to use the same hardware protocol. A **hardware protocol** defines many aspects of a network, from the packet type to the cabling and connectors used. A hardware protocol defines everything necessary to get data from one computer to another. Two hardware protocols dominate the modern computing landscape, Ethernet and Token Ring.

A consortium of companies centered on Digital Equipment, Intel, and Xerox invented the first network in the mid-1970s. More than just creating a network, they wrote a series of standards that defined everything necessary to get data from one computer to another. This series of standards was called **Ethernet**, and it is the dominant standard for today's networks. Ethernet comes in three main flavors, defined by cabling type: coaxial, unshielded twisted pair, and fiber optic. Because all flavors of Ethernet use the same packet-type, you can have any combination of hardware devices and cabling systems on an Ethernet network and all the PCs will be able to communicate just fine.

IBM developed the *Token Ring* network standards, again defining all aspects of the network, but using radically different ideas of how networks should work. Token Ring is common in many government and large corporate networks, but is completely incompatible with Ethernet. Token Ring comes in many variations, but makes an easier tale to tell. This chapter lumps most discussion of Token Ring into a single section.

ence. The entire cable is then surrounded by a protective insulating cover.

RG-6. Watch out for questions on the exams dealing specifically with networking hardware protocols trying to trip you up with television-grade coaxial answers!

Thick Ethernet—10Base5

The original Xerox Ethernet specification that eventually became known as *10Base5* defined a very specific type of coaxial cabling for the first Ethernet networks, called *Thick Ethernet*. Thick Ethernet, also known as *Thicknet*, is a very thick (about half an inch in diameter) type of coaxial called *RG-8*. "RG" stands for Radio Grade, an industry standard for measuring coaxial cables. The "10" in 10Base5 refers to the fact that data can move through an RG-8 cable at up to 10 Mbps with this Ethernet standard.

Every PC in a 10Base5 network connects to a single cable, called a *segment* or *bus*. Thicknet supports attaching up to 100 devices to one segment. The maximum length of a Thicknet segment is 500 meters—that's what the "5" in 10Base5 means (Figure 23.4). Network engineers use the term *topology* to describe the physical layout of a network. Networks like 10Base5 are laid out in a bus topology.

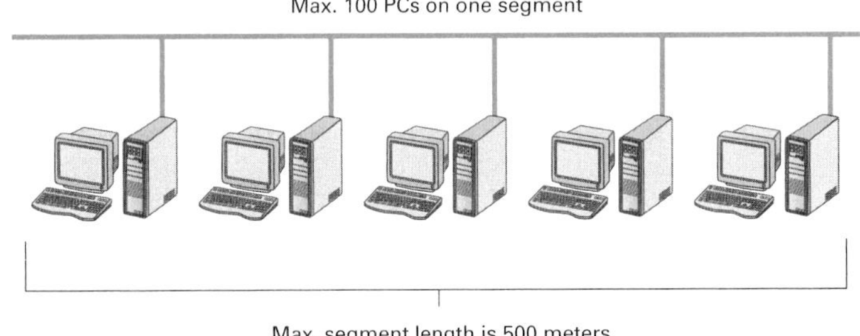

• **Figure 23.4** 10Base5

Bus Topology **Bus topology** works like a big telephone party line—before they can send a packet, devices on the bus must first determine that no other device is sending a packet on the cable (Figure 23.5). When a device sends its packet out over the bus, every other network card on the bus sees and reads the packet! This scheme of having devices communicate like they were in a chat room is called *Carrier Sense Multiple Access/Collision Detection* (CSMA/CD).

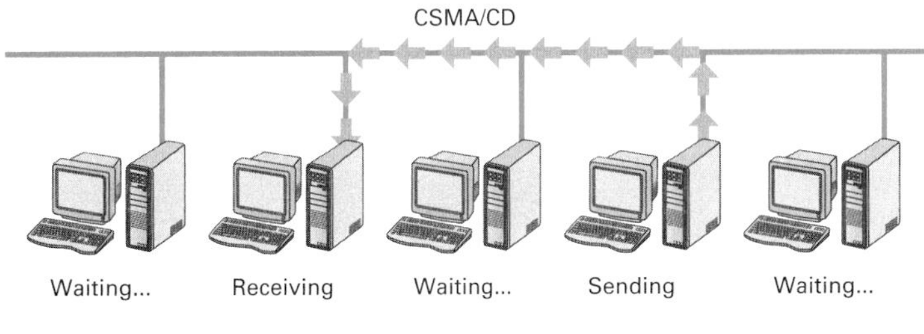

• **Figure 23.5** Devices can't send packets while others are talking.

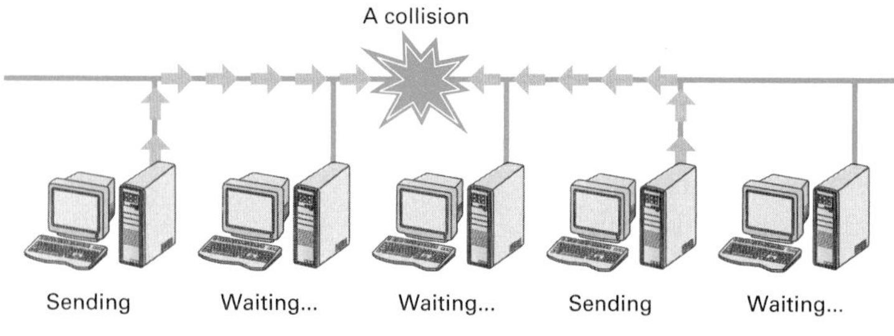

• **Figure 23.6** Collisions result when two devices send simultaneously.

Sometimes two cards talk (send packets) at the same time. This creates a collision, and the cards themselves arbitrate to decide which one will resend its packet first (Figure 23.6).

All PCs on a bus network share a common wire, which also means they share the data transfer capacity of that wire, or in tech terms, they share its *bandwidth*. This creates an interesting effect. Ten PCs chatting on a bus each get to use a much higher proportion of its total bandwidth than, for instance, 100 PCs on the same bus (in this case, one- tenth compared to one-hundredth). The more PCs on a bus, the more likely you'll have a communication traffic jam. This problem does not get solved until we get beyond coaxial Ethernet.

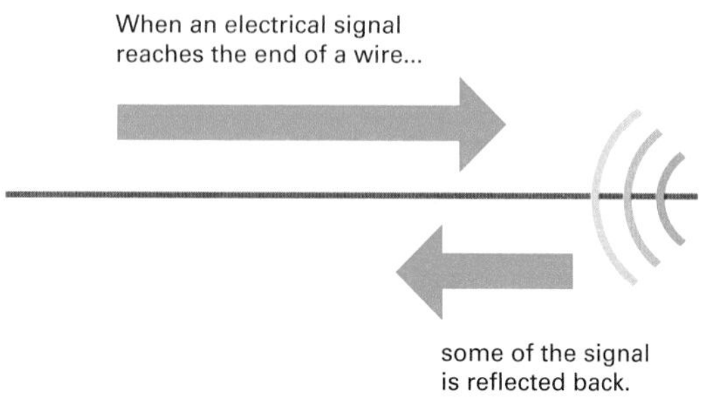

• **Figure 23.7** Reflection

Reflection and Termination The ends of the bus present a bit of a problem for the signal moving along the wire. Any time a device sends voltage along a wire, some voltage bounces back or *reflects* when it reaches the end of the wire (Figure 23.7). Network cables are no exception. As I've described bus topology thus far, the packets would uselessly reflect back and forth, while the NICs that want to send data wait for no reason. This situation is known as a *packet storm*. After a short while, the bus will get so full of reflecting packets that no other card can send data.

To prevent packets from being reflected, a device called a *terminator* must be plugged into the end of the bus cable. (Figure 23.8) A terminator is nothing more than a resistor that absorbs the signal, preventing reflection (Figure 23.9). This need for termination is a weak spot in bus topology. If the cable breaks anywhere, a packet storm is instantly created and no device can send data, even if the break is not between the devices exchanging data.

• **Figure 23.8** Terminator on back of PC

Connections Thicknet is clearly marked every 2.5 meters (Figure 23.10). These marks show where to connect devices to the cable. All devices on a Thicknet must be connected at these marks to ensure that all devices are some multiple of 2.5 meters apart.

Devices connect to Thicknet by means of a *vampire connector*. A vampire connector is so called because it actually pierces the cable to create the connection (Figure 23.11). A vampire connector is also a transceiver—a device that both receives and sends data. Transceivers enable connections between the networked devices and the common cable and detect when collisions take place. Actually, all networks use transceivers, but Thicknet uses an external transceiver—often referred to as an *Access Unit Interface* (AUI). The cable from the vampire connector/transceiver to the device must be no more than 50 meters in length.

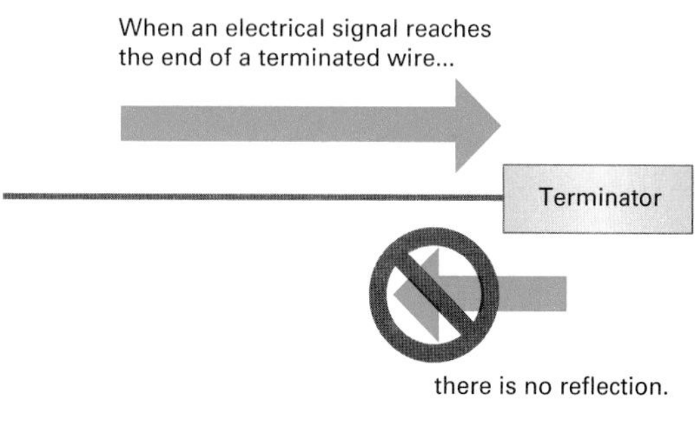

• **Figure 23.9** No reflection with a terminator

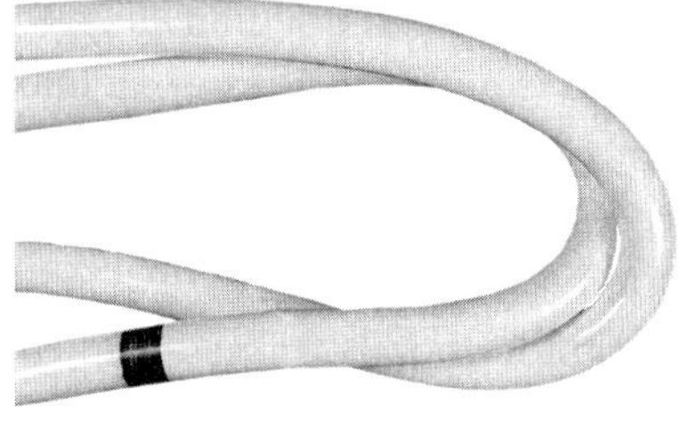

• **Figure 23.10** Connection mark

Thick Ethernet uses a bus topology so it needs terminators. A very specific

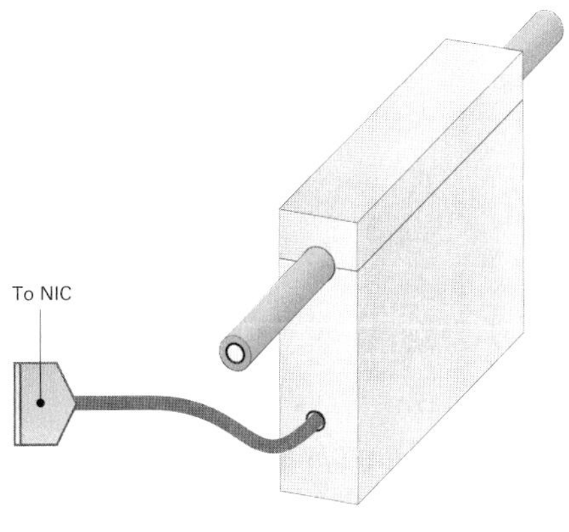

• Figure 23.11 10Base5 transceiver

• Figure 23.12 DIX or AUI port

terminators cost far more than those in any other network. Nevertheless, there is a massive installed base, and it is still actively used, especially where longer distances or heavy shielding is needed.

• Figure 23.13 RG-58 coaxial

Thin Ethernet—10Base2

Thin Ethernet, also known as *Thinnet* or *Cheapernet*, was invented as a cheap alternative to Thicknet. Thinnet uses a specific type of coax called RG-58 (Figure 23.13). This type of coax looks like a skinny version of the RG-59 or RG-6 coax used by your cable television, but don't be tempted to swap because it is quite different! The RG rating should be clearly marked on the cable. If it is not, it will say something like "Thinnet" or "802.3" to let you know you have the right cable (Figure 23.14).

• Figure 23.14 Cable markings

Although Thin Ethernet also runs at 10 Mbps, it has several big limitations compared to Thick Ethernet. Thin Ethernet supports only 30 devices per segment and each segment can be no more than 185 meters long (Figure 23.15). The "2" in 10Base2 originally meant 200 meters, but practical experience forced the standard down to 185 meters.

On the plus side, cabling with Thinnet is a snap compared with Thicknet. The cable is much thinner and more flexible than Thicknet. In addition, the transceiver is built into the Thinnet network card, so Thinnet does not require an external transceiver. Each Thinnet network card is simply connected to the bus cable with a T connector (Figure 23.16).

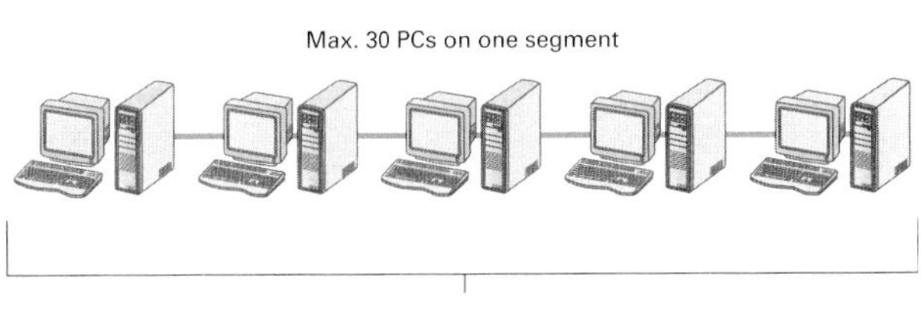

• Figure 23.15 10Base2

The Thinnet cable has twist-on connectors, called *BNC connectors* that attach to the T connector to form the network. Termination is handled by twisting small, specialized terminators onto the unused ends of the T connector on the machines at the ends of the chain. When installing Thinnet,

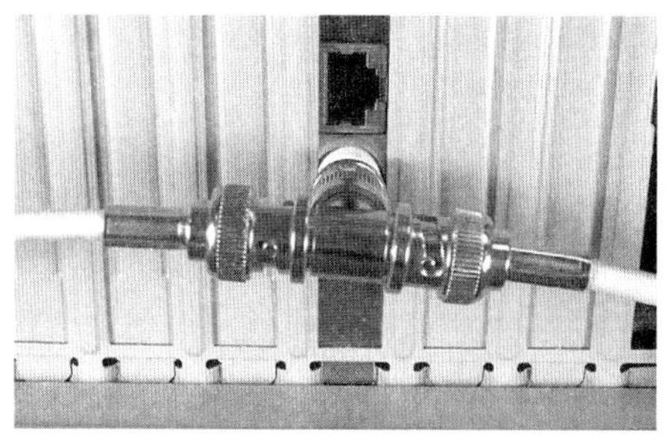

• **Figure 23.16** T connector

it is important that one of the terminators be grounded. Special terminators can be grounded to the case of the PC. Just be sure the PC is also grounded. You *must* use a T connector! To add another PC to a Thinnet network, simply remove the terminator from the last PC, add another piece of cable with another T connector, and add the terminator on the new end. It is also very easy to add a PC between two systems by unhooking one side of a T connector and inserting another PC and cable.

Thinnet, like its hefty-weight cousin, is on its way out. Very popular for a time in *small office/home office* (SOHO) networks, the fact that it uses a bus topology where any wire break means the whole network goes down makes 10Base2 unacceptable in a modern network.

UTP Ethernet (10^xBaseT)

Most modern Ethernet networks employ one of two technologies (and sometimes both), **10BaseT** or **100BaseT**. As the numbers in the names would suggest, 10BaseT networks run at 10 Mbps and 100BaseT networks run at 100 Mbps. Both standards are about to be eclipsed by Gigabit Ethernet, or 1000BaseT, which runs at 1 Gbps. Gigabit Ethernet is still very expensive, but the prices are dropping quickly in the face of competition from wireless networks (more on that later in this chapter!). All three technologies—collectively abbreviated as 10^xBaseT—use a *star bus* topology and connect via a type of cable called **unshielded twisted pair (UTP)**.

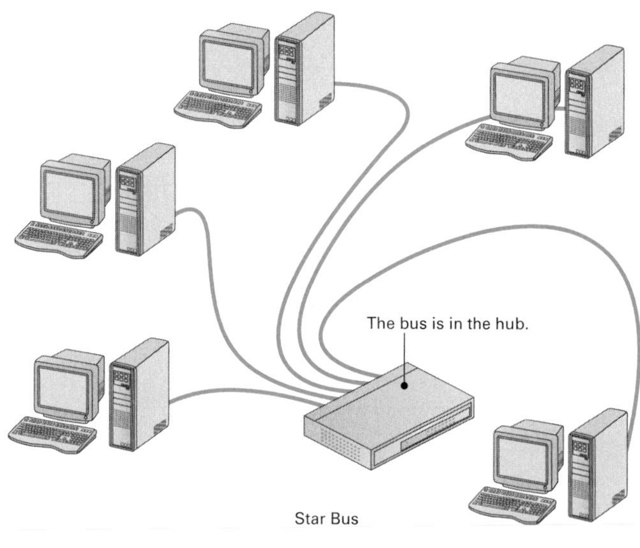

• **Figure 23.17** Star bus

Star Bus

Imagine if you took a bus network and shrunk the bus down so it would fit inside a box. Then, instead of attaching each PC directly to the wire, you attach them via cables to special ports on the box (Figure 23.17), and the box with the bus takes care of termination and all those other tedious details required by a bus network. The bus topology would sure look a lot like a star, wouldn't it?

The central box with the bus is called a hub or switch. The **hub** provides a common point for connection for network devices. Hubs can have a wide variety of ports. Most consumer-level hubs have four or eight ports, but business-level hubs can have 32 or more ports. Hub is the old style device, still in use in millions of networks. A switch is a newer, far superior version of a hub. Figure 23.18 shows a typical consumer-level switch.

• **Figure 23.18** A switch

A hub provides no cure for the bandwidth-sharing problem of Ethernet networks. If you put 32 PCs on a 32-port 100BaseT hub, you have 32 PCs sharing the 100 Mbps bandwidth. A switch does fix the problem by, in essence, making each port a separate Ethernet network. Each PC gets to use the full bandwidth available, because a switch stops all collisions. Bottom line? Swap out your old hubs for newer switches and you'll dramatically improve your network performance.

Cheap and centralized, a star bus network does not go down if a cable breaks. True, the network would go down if the hub itself failed, but that is very rare. Even if a hub fails, replacing a hub in a closet is much easier than tracing a bus running through walls and ceilings trying to find a break!

Unshielded Twisted Pair

UTP cabling is the defined cabling for 10^{x}BaseT and is the predominant cabling system used today. There are many different types of twisted pair cabling to choose from, depending on the needs of the network. Twisted pair cabling consists of AWG 22-26 gauge wire twisted together into color-coded pairs. These pairs are loosely encased in a common insulated jacket.

CAT Levels UTP cables come in categories that define the maximum speed at which data can be transferred (also called *bandwidth*). The major categories (CATs) are as follows:

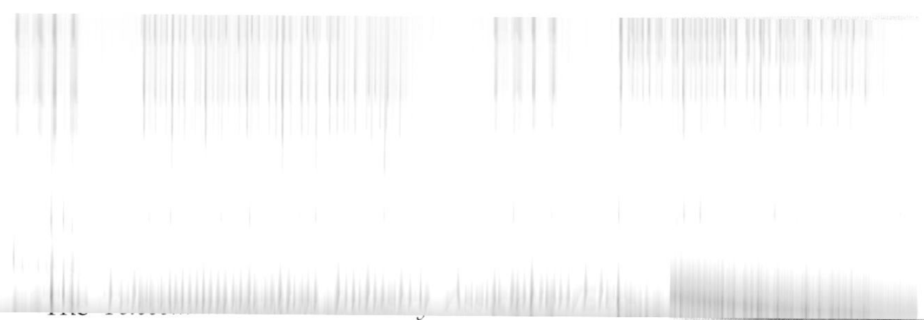

tronics Industries Alliance (TIA/EIA) establishes the UTP categories, which fall under the TIA/EIA 568 specification. Currently, most installers use CAT 5e or CAT 6 cable. Although many networks run at 10 Mbps, the industry standard has shifted to networks designed to run at 100 Mbps and faster. Because only CAT 5 or better handles these speeds, just about everyone is installing the higher rated cabling, even if they are running at speeds that CAT 3 or CAT 4 would do. Consequently, it is becoming harder to get anything but CAT 5, CAT 5e, or CAT 6 cables.

KRISTA UTP CAT.5 100MHZ 24AWGx4P

• **Figure 23.19** Cable markings for CAT level

Implementing 10^{x}BaseT

The 10^{x}BaseT cabling standards require two pairs of wires, a pair for sending and a pair for receiving. 10BaseT runs on CAT 3, CAT 4, or CAT 5 cable. 100BaseT requires at least CAT 5 to run, whereas 1000BaseT needs CAT 5e or CAT 6. These cables use a special connector called an **RJ-45** connector. The "RJ" designation was invented by Ma Bell (the phone company, for you youngsters) years ago and is still used today. Currently, only two types of RJ connectors are used for networking: RJ-11 and RJ-45 (Figure 23.20). RJ-11 is the connector that hooks your telephone to the telephone jack. It supports up to two pairs of wires, though most phone lines only use one pair. The other pair is used to support a second phone line. RJ-11 connectors are primarily used for dial-up networking (see Chapter 24) and not used in any common LAN installation, although a few weird (and out of business) "network in a box"-type companies used them. RJ-45 is the standard for UTP connectors. RJ-45 has connections for up to four pairs and is visibly much wider than RJ-11. Figure 23.21 shows the position of the #1 and #8 pins on an RJ-45 jack.

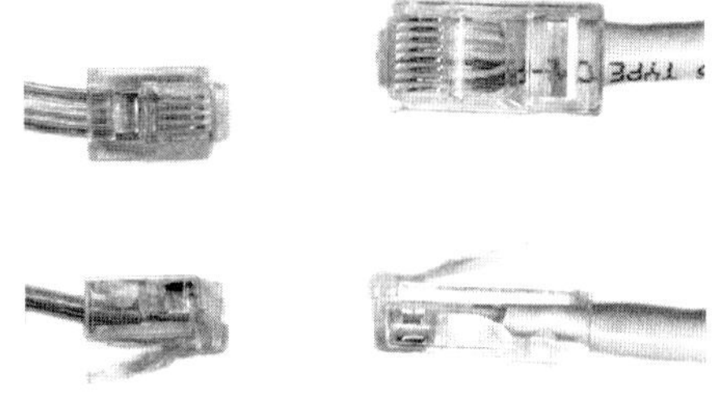

• **Figure 23.20** RJ-11 and RJ-45

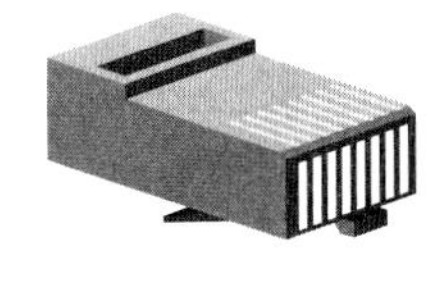

• **Figure 23.21** RJ-45 pin numbers

The TIA/EIA has two standards for connecting the RJ-45 connector to the UTP cable: the TIA/EIA 568A and the TIA/EIA 568B. Both are acceptable.

Tech Tip

Plenum vs. PVC

Most workplace installations of network cable go up above the ceiling and then drop down through the walls to present a nice port in the wall. The only potential problem with this cabling running through the walls and ceiling is that the protective sheathing for networking cables is made from plastic, and if you get any plastic hot enough, it will create smoke and noxious fumes.

To reduce the risk caused by burning buildings, all cables have fire ratings. The two most common fire ratings are PVC *and* Plenum. *PVC (Poly-Vinyl Chloride) has no significant fire protection. If you burn a PVC cable, it creates lots of smoke and noxious fumes. Burning Plenum cable creates much less smoke and fumes, but Plenum costs about three to five times as much as PVC. Most city ordinances require the use of Plenum-rated cable for network installations. Bottom line? Get Plenum!*

• **Figure 23.22** NIC built into motherboard

You do not have to follow any standard as long as you use the same pairings on each end of the cable; however, you will make your life simpler if you choose a standard. Make sure that all of your cabling uses the same standard and you will save a great deal of work in the end. Most importantly, *keep records*!

Like all wires, the wires in UTP are numbered. However, a number does not appear on each wire. Instead, each wire has a standardized color. Table 23.1 shows the official TIA/EIA Standard Color Chart for UTP.

Combo Cards All Ethernet networks share the same language, so you can easily have mixed or combined networks. All it takes is a network card capable of running at multiple speeds or even over multiple cables. Most NICs built into motherboards (Figure 23.22), for example, are 10/100 auto-sensing cards. If you plug into a 10BaseT network, they automatically run at 10 Mbps. If you log into a 100 Mbps network, they'll quickly ramp up and run at 100 Mbps. You can still find in use older cards that have both a RJ-45 port and a BNC connector for 10Base2. These sorts of cards can connect to either a 10BaseT or 10Base2 network (Figure 23.23).

Hubs and Switches In a 10^{X}BaseT network, each PC is connected to a 10^{X}BaseT hub or switch, as mentioned earlier. To add a device to the network, simply plug another cable into the hub or switch (Figure 23.24). Remember that 10^{X}BaseT uses the star bus topology. The hub holds the actual bus and allows access to the bus through the ports. Using a star bus topology creates a robust network; the failure of a single PC will not bring down the entire network.

In a 10^{X}BaseT network, the maximum distance from the hub to any device is 100 meters. No more than one PC can be attached to each segment, and the maximum number of PCs that can be attached to any one hub is 1,024—although you will be hard pressed to find a hub with that many connectors (Figure 23.25). Most hubs come with 4, 8, 16, or 24 ports. 10^{X}BaseT hubs act as repeaters, amplifying the signals between devices hooked into the network. They need power to provide this amplification, so make sure that the hubs are plugged into a good power source.

Duplex and Half-Duplex All modern NICs can run in full-*duplex* mode, meaning they can send and receive data at the same time. The vast majority of NICs and switches use a feature called *auto-sensing* to accommodate very old devices that might attach to the network and need to run in half-duplex mode. Half-duplex means that the device can send and receive but not at the same time. The walkie-talkies you played with as a kid that required you to press and hold the orange button to transmit—at which time you couldn't hear anything—are an obvious

Table 23.1 UTP Cabling Color Chart

Pin	568A	568B	Pin	568A	568B
1	White/Green	White/Orange	5	White/Blue	White/Blue
2	Green	Orange	6	Orange	Green
3	White/Orange	White/Green	7	White/Brown	White/Brown
4	Blue	Blue	8	Brown	Brown

• Figure 23.23 Ethernet 10Base2/10BaseT combo card

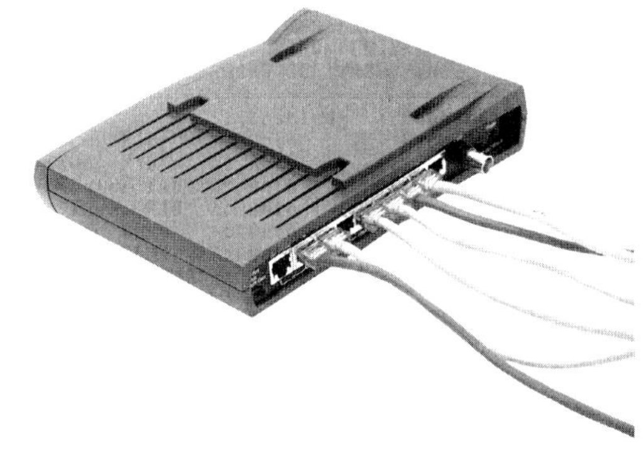

• Figure 23.24 Typical switch with several cables connected

or auto-sensing can sometimes enable these odd NICs to communicate.

Max. segment length is 100 meters.
Max. 1024 PCs per hub or switch.

• Figure 23.25 10^{X}BaseT

Fiber Optic Ethernet

Fiber optic cable is a very attractive way to transmit Ethernet network packets. First, because it uses light instead of electricity, fiber optic cable is immune to electrical problems like lightning, short circuits, and static. Second, fiber optic signals travel much farther, up to 2,000 meters (compared with 100 meters for 10^{X}BaseT) with some standards. Most fiber Ethernets use *62.5/125 multimode* fiber optic cable. All fiber Ethernets need two of these cables. Figure 23.26 shows the two most common connectors used in fiber optic networks. The square-shaped *SC* connector is on the right, and the round *ST* connector is on the left.

The two most common fiber optic standards are called 10BaseFL and 100BaseFX. As you can guess by the names, the major difference is the speed of the network (there are some important differences in the way hubs are interconnected, and so on). Unfortunately, fiber optic cabling is delicate, expensive, and difficult to use, so it is usually reserved for things like backbone (the main piece of Ethernet to which all other hubs are connected).

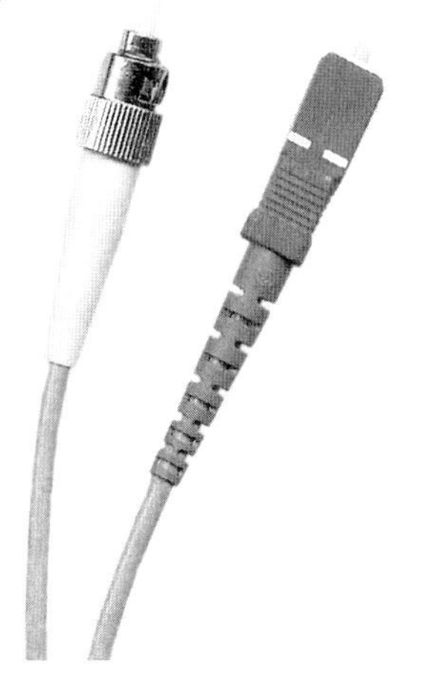

• Figure 23.26 Typical fiber optic cables with connectors

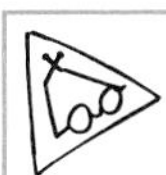

Tech Tip

Crossover Cables

You can actually hook two 10^{X}BaseT network cards together without a hub by using a special UTP cable called a crossover cable. *A crossover cable is a standard UTP cable but with one RJ-45 connector using the 568A standard and the other using the 568B. This reverses the signal between sending and receiving wires and thus does the job of a hub or switch. Crossover cables work great as a quick way to network two PCs. You can purchase a crossover cable at any computer store.*

Tech Tip

Multimode and Single Mode

Light can be sent down a fiber optic cable as regular light or as laser light. Each type of light requires totally different fiber optic cables. Most network technologies that use fiber optics use LED, or Light Emitting Diodes, to send light signals. These use multimode fiber *optic cabling. Multimode fiber transmits multiple light signals at the same time, each using a different reflection angle within the core of the cable. The multiple reflection angles tend to disperse over long distances, so multimode fiber optic cables are used for relatively short distances.*

Network technologies that use laser light use single-mode *fiber optic cabling. Using laser light and single-mode fiber optic cables allows for phenomenally high transfer rates and incredibly long distances. Single-mode is currently quite rare; if you see fiber optic cabling, you can be relatively sure that it is multimode.*

Token Ring

Token Ring is a set of network standards developed by IBM that define a complete network system. The Token Ring Standard is completely incompatible with Ethernet and is considered a competitor to Ethernet. Token Ring networks use a ring topology, most commonly today as a star ring.

Ring Topology

Ring topology connects all the PCs together on a single cable much like bus topology. As the name implies, however, this bus is shaped like a ring (Figure 23.27). Ring topologies use a transmission method called *token passing*. In token passing, a mini-packet called a *token* constantly passes from one NIC to the next in one direction around the ring (see Figure 23.28). A PC wanting to send a packet must wait until it gets the token. The PC's NIC then attaches data to the token and sends the packet back out to the ring. If another PC wants to send data, it must wait until a free token (one that doesn't have an attached packet) comes around.

Because ring topologies use token passing, the term *token ring* is often used when describing ring networks. There were cases where a ring topology used features other than token passing, but they were few and are long gone. All current ring networks use an IBM-trademarked version of token passing, appropriately called *Token Ring*. So if it's a ring topology these days, you can assume it's Token Ring.

Implementing Token Ring

The A+ Certification has a very old-school view of Token Ring networks, focusing on the traditional rather than the current iterations. As such, you'll find the exams test you only on the ancient 4 Mbps or 16 Mbps networks, which depended on the type of Token Ring network cards you bought. Token Ring was originally based around the IBM Type 1 cable. Type 1 cable is a two-pair, **shielded twisted pair (STP)** cable designed to handle speeds up

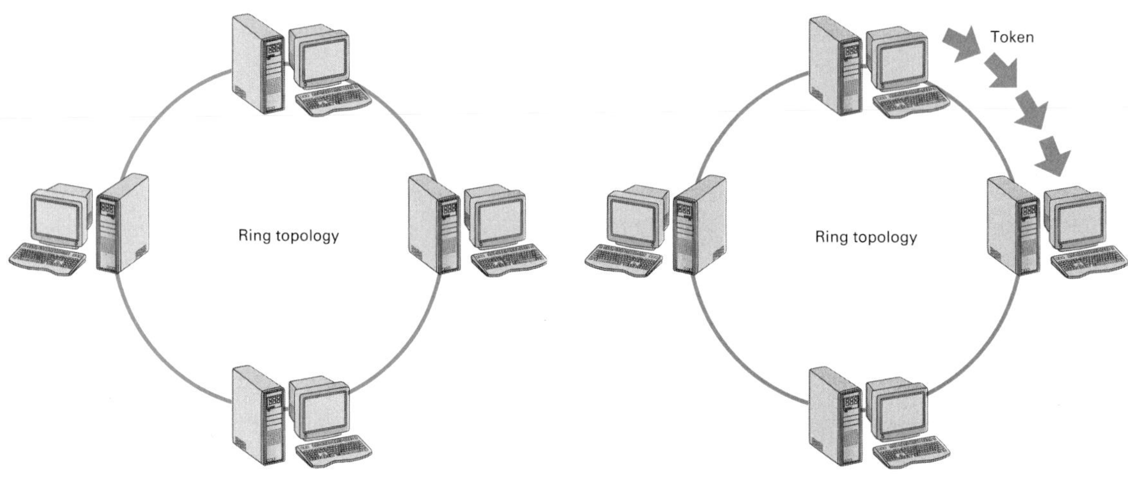

• **Figure 23.27** Ring topology

• **Figure 23.28** Token passing

to 20 Mbps (Figure 23.29). Today, Token Ring topologies can use either STP or UTP cables.

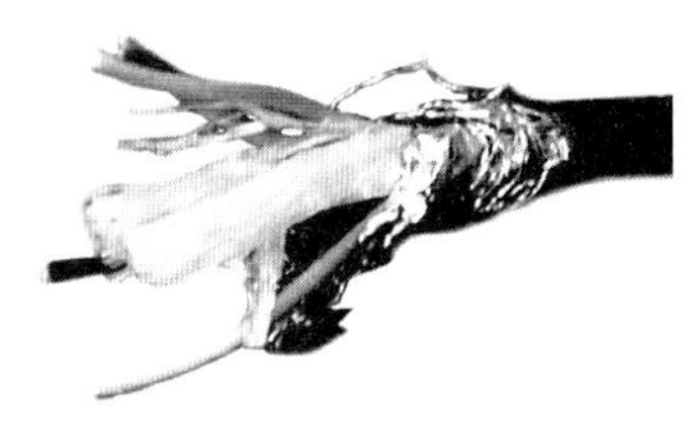

• Figure 23.29 Type 1 STP Token Ring cable

STP Types STP cables have certain categories. These are called types and are defined by IBM. The most common types are

- **Type 1** Standard STP with two pairs—the most common STP cable
- **Type 2** Standard STP plus two pairs of voice wires
- **Type 3** Standard STP with four pairs
- **Type 6** Patch cable—used for connecting hubs
- **Type 8** Flat STP for under carpets
- **Type 9** STP with 2 pairs—Plenum grade

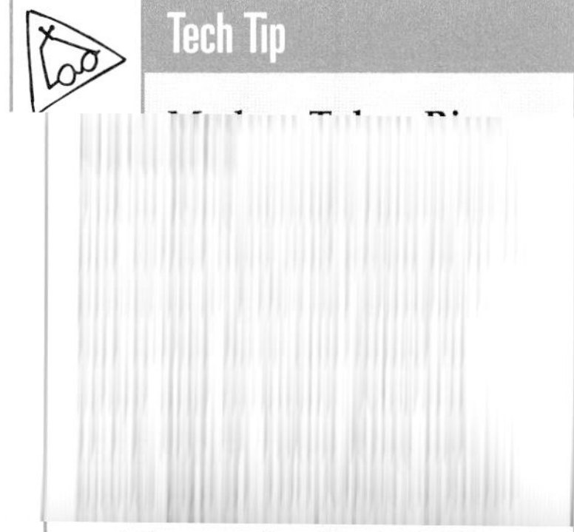

Tech Tip

and, because the ring technology does not suffer from the overhead of CSMA/CD, you get phenomenally faster performance from High Speed Token Ring (HSTR) networks than on comparably speedy Ethernet. Check them out here: www.token-ring.com.

bined with UTP, Token Ring uses an RJ-45 connector, so from a cabling standpoint, Token Ring UTP and Ethernet UTP look the same. Many Token Ring network cards are combo cards, which means they come with both a nine-pin connection for STP and an RJ-45 connection for UTP.

As discussed earlier, Token Ring uses a star ring topology; therefore, it also uses a hub. A Token Ring hub is *not* interchangeable with an Ethernet hub. IBM has a special name for its hubs. As mentioned, they are called either *multistation access units* (MSAU or MAU). Unfortunately, they are also sometimes just called hubs (usually by Ethernet people who do not know any better).

Token Ring can support up to 260 PCs using STP and up to 72 PCs using UTP. Using UTP, the maximum distance from any MAU to a PC is 45 meters. Using STP, the maximum distance from any MAU to a PC is 100 meters. (Figure 23.31). Token Ring also uses repeaters. Token Ring repeaters can only be used between MAUs. With a repeater, the functional distance between two MAUs increases to 360 meters (with UTP) and 720 meters (with STP).

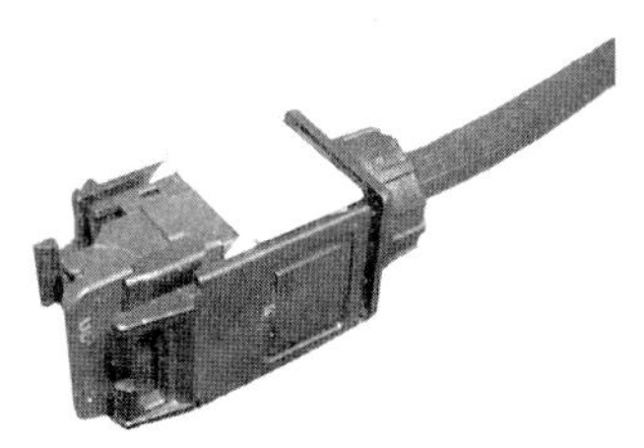

• Figure 23.30 IDC/UDC connector

Parallel/Serial

It would be unfair not to give at least a token nod to the possibility of making direct cable connections using the parallel or serial ports on a pair of PCs. All versions of Windows have complete support for allowing two, and no more than two, systems to network together using either parallel or serial cables. You need crossover versions of IEEE1284 cables for parallel and RS-232 cables for serial. These should only be considered as a last resort option, given the incredibly slow speeds of parallel and especially serial cable transmission compared to that of Ethernet and Token Ring. Direct cable connections should never be used unless there is no other viable alternative.

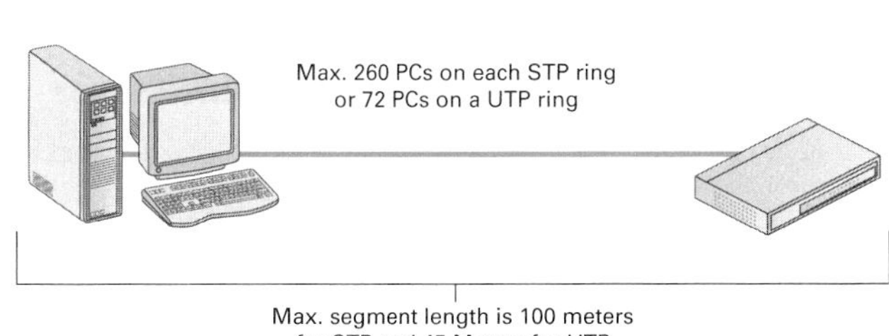

• Figure 23.31 Token Ring specifications

■ Network Operating Systems

At this point in the discussion of networking, you've covered two of the four main needs for making a network work. Through Ethernet or Token Ring hardware protocols, you have a NIC for the PC that handles splitting data into packets and putting the packets back together at the destination PC. You've got a cabling standard to connect the NIC to a hub/switch or MSAU, thus making that data transfer possible. Now it's time to dive into the third and fourth needs for a network. You need an operating system that can communicate with the hardware and with other networked PCs, and you need some sort of server machine to give out data or services. All of the third and fourth needs are handled by a network operating system.

In a classic sense, a **network operating system (NOS)** communicates with the PC hardware—of whichever hardware protocol—and makes the connections between multiple machines on a network. The NOS enables one or more PCs to act as a server machine and share data and services over a network—to share *resources*, in other words. You then need to run software on client computers to enable those computers to access the shared resources on the server machine.

Every Windows OS is an NOS and enables the PC to share resources and access shared resources. But it doesn't come out of the box ready to work on all networks! You need to configure Windows to handle all three tasks to make all this work: install a network protocol to communicate with hardware, enable server software to share resources, and install client software to enable the PC to access shared resources.

All NOSs are not alike, even among Windows. Before you can share resources across a network, you must answer a number of questions. How do you make that happen? Can everyone share his or her hard drives with everyone else? Should you place limits on sharing? If everyone needs access to a particular file, where will it be stored? What about security? Can anyone access the file? What if someone erases it accidentally? How are backups to be handled? Different NOSs answer these questions differently. Let's look at network organization and then turn to protocols, client software, and server software.

Network Organization

All NOSs can be broken into three basic organizational groups: client/server, peer-to-peer, and domain-based. All Windows PCs can function as network clients and servers, so this muddies the waters a bit. Let's take a look at traditional network organization.

Client/Server

The client/server solution to all the sharing resources questions is to take one machine and dedicate it as a resource to be shared over the network. This machine will have a dedicated NOS optimized for sharing files. This special OS includes powerful caching software that enables high-speed file access. It will have extremely high levels of protection and an organization that permits extensive control of the data. This machine is called a *dedicated* server. All of the other machines that use the data are called *clients* (because it's what they usually are) or *workstations*.

The client/server system dedicates one machine to act as a "server." Its only function is to serve up resources to the other machines on the network. These servers do not run Windows 9*x* or Windows XP. They use highly sophisticated and expensive NOSs that are optimized for the sharing and administration of network resources. Currently, only one NOS fits within the strictest definition of the client/server concept: the popular Novell NetWare.

A NetWare server is not used directly by anyone. That is, a NetWare server doesn't provide a user environment for running any applications except for tools and utilities. Novell NetWare just *serves* shared resources; it does not run programs like Excel or CorelDraw. Many network administrators will even remove the keyboard and monitor from a Novell NetWare server to keep people from trying to use it. NetWare has its own commands and requires substantial training to use, but in return, you get an amazingly powerful NOS!

The terms "client" and "server" are, to say the least, freely used in the Windows world. Keep in mind that a client generally refers to any process (or in this context, computer system) that can request a resource or service, and a server is any

works are much cheaper than client/server networks, because the software costs less and does not require you to purchase a high-end machine to be the dedicated server. The most popular peer-to-peer NOSs today are Windows 9*x*/Me and Windows 2000/XP.

The biggest limiting factor to peer-to-peer networking is that it's simply not designed for a large number of computers. Windows has a built-in limit to the number of users who can concurrently access a shared file or folder (10). Microsoft recommends that peer-to-peer workgroups not exceed 15 PCs. Beyond that, a domain makes more sense.

Security is the other big weakness of peer-to-peer networks. Each system on a peer-to-peer network maintains its own security. The Windows 9*x*/Me NOS has traditionally been weak in the area of network security. When a Windows 9*x*/Me system shares a resource like a folder or printer, it only has three levels of network permissions from which to choose: Read-Only, Full Access, and Depends on Password.

Windows NT Workstation, 2000 Professional, and XP Home Edition and Professional enable you to tighten security by setting NTFS permissions locally, but you are still required to place a local account on every system for any user that's going to access resources. So, even though you get better security in a Windows XP Professional peer-to-peer network, system administration entails a lot of running around to individual systems to create and delete local users every time someone joins or leaves the network. In a word: bleh.

Cross Check

NTFS Permissions

NTFS permissions enable strong data security, even when sharing files and folders across a network, so now is a good time to revisit Chapter 11 and refresh your memory on NTFS.

1. How do you access the permissions for a file or folder?
2. Which permission would stop someone from modifying a file on your server, but still enable him or her to read the contents of that file?
3. What's up with Windows XP Home and permissions, anyway?

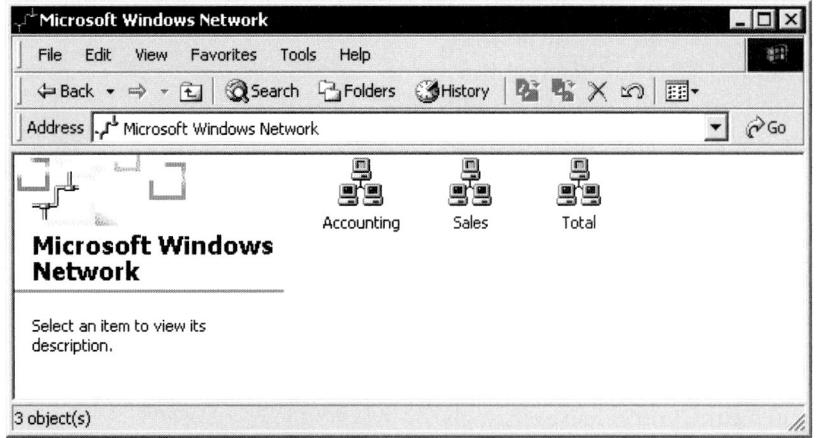

• **Figure 23.32** Multiple workgroups in a network

Peer-to-peer workgroups are little more than a pretty way to organize systems to make navigating through Network Neighborhood a little easier (Figure 23.32). In reality, workgroups have no security value. Still, if your networking needs are limited—such as a small home network—peer-to-peer networking is an easy and cheap solution.

Domain-Based

One of the similarities between the client/server network model and peer-to-peer networks is that each PC in the network maintains its own list of user accounts. If you want to access a server, you must log on. When only one server exists, the logon process takes only a second and works very well. The trouble comes when your network contains multiple servers. In that case, every time you access a different server, you must repeat the logon process (Figure 23.33). In larger networks containing many servers, this becomes a time-consuming nightmare not only for the user, but also for the network administrator.

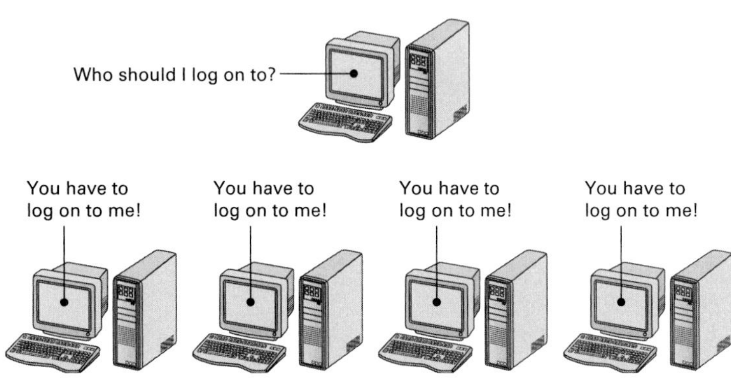

• **Figure 23.33** Multiple logins

A domain-based network provides an excellent solution for the problem of multiple logins. In a domain-based environment, one or more dedicated servers called *Domain Controllers* hold the security database for all systems. This database holds a list of all users and passwords in the domain. When you log on to your computer or to any computer, the logon request goes to an available Domain Controller, to verify the account and password (Figure 23.34).

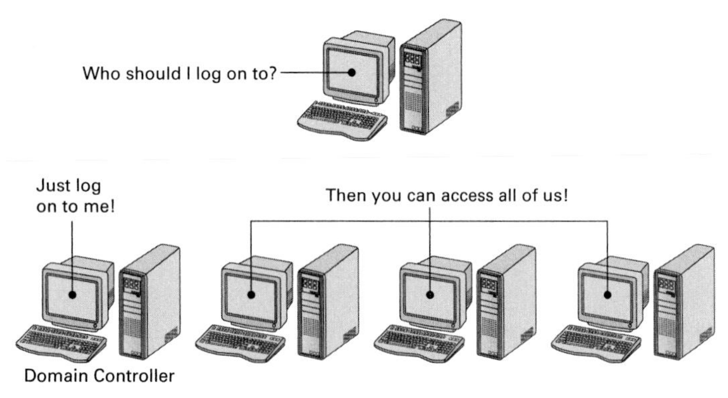

• **Figure 23.34** A domain controller eliminates the need for multiple logins.

Modern domain-based networks use what is called a *directory service* to store user and computer account information. Recent versions of Novell NetWare move from the strict client/server model described above to a directory service-based model implementing the appropriately-named *NetWare Directory Service* (NDS). Microsoft Windows 2000 and 2003 use the *Active Directory* (AD) directory service. Think of a directory service as a big, centralized index, similar to a telephone book, that each PC accesses to locate resources in the domain.

Server versions of Microsoft Windows look and act very similar to the workstation versions, but come with extra networking capabilities, services, and tools to enable them to take on the role of domain controller, file server,

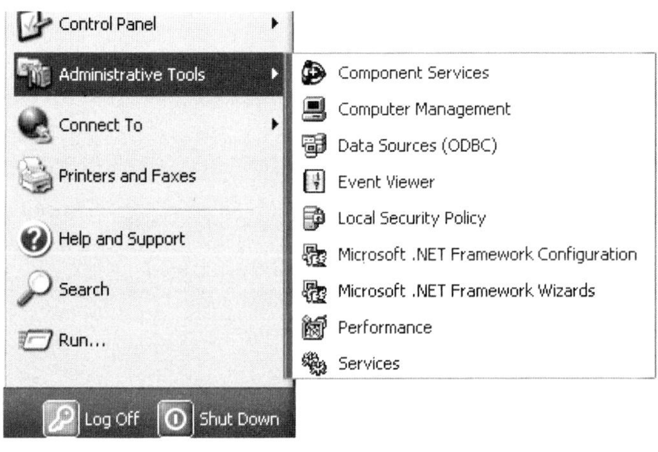

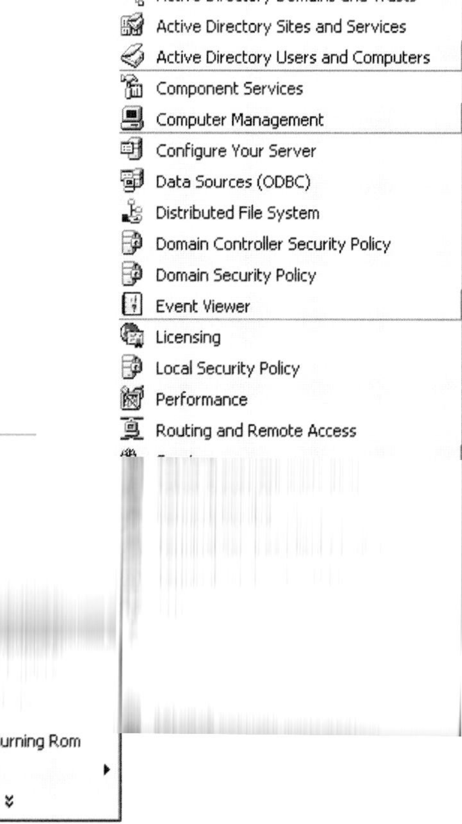

• **Figure 23.36** Administrative Tools in Windows 2000 Server

Tools options on a typical Windows XP workstation. These should be familiar to you. Figure 23.36 shows the many extra tools you need to work with Windows 2000 Server.

Every Windows NT system contains a very special account called the **Administrator account**. This one account has complete and absolute power over the entire system. When you install Windows NT, 2000 or XP, you must create a password for the Administrator account. Anyone who knows the Administrator password has the ability to read any file and run any program. As you might imagine, you should keep the Administrator password secret to all but the highest level of administrators. Equally important, losing the Administrator password usually requires completely reinstalling Windows NT or 2000—so don't lose it!

Any Windows 9*x*/Me system may also become a member of a domain, although Windows 9*x*/Me's use of non-NTFS file systems makes its sharing security much weaker than what you get with Windows NT, 2000, or XP systems. We usually add Windows 9*x*/Me systems to a domain simply as clients. To set up or change a Windows 9*x* system's workgroup membership, use the Identification tab in the Network Neighborhood properties (Figure 23.37).

Making or changing a domain membership takes a little more effort and each version of Windows does it differently. In Windows 9*x*, click the properties for Client for Microsoft Networks, check Log on

Cross Check

Administrative Tools

Windows NT, 2000, and XP come with a set of utilities called Administrative Tools, as you know from previous chapters. Refer to Chapter 12 and answer these questions.

1. How do you access Administrative Tools?
2. Which tool or tools might be useful for working with networks?
3. More specifically, which tool would help you analyze network performance?

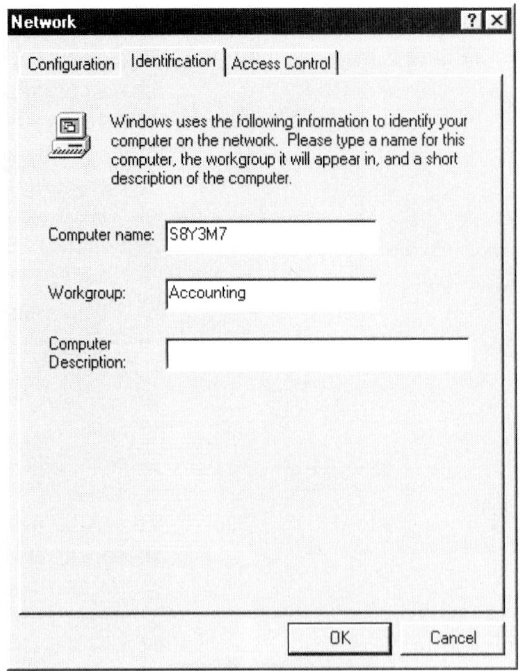

• **Figure 23.37** Changing the workgroup in Windows 98

• **Figure 23.38** Entering a domain name in Windows 98

to Windows NT Domain (even if this is a Windows 2000 domain), and then enter the domain name as shown in Figure 23.38. In Windows NT, open the properties for Network Neighborhood. You'll find the Identification tab here. Click the Change button to get to a screen that looks and functions similar to the screen in Windows 98.

Windows 2000, as usual, makes the process a little easier. Open the properties for My Computer, and select the Network Identification tab, as shown in Figure 23.39. This shows your current selection. Windows XP calls the tab Computer Name and renames a few of the buttons (Figure 23.40). Clicking the Network ID button opens the Network Identification Wizard, but most techs just use the Change button (Figure 23.41). They do the same thing as the Network ID button, but the wizard does a lot of explaining that you don't need if you know what you want to do. Make sure you have a good domain account or you won't be able to log into a domain.

At this point, you've prepared the OS to network in general, but now you need to talk to the specific hardware. For that, you need to load protocols.

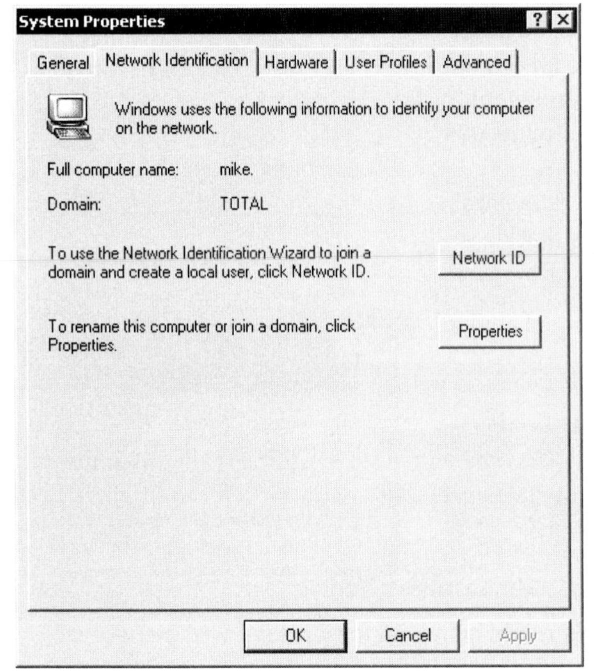

• **Figure 23.39** Network Identification tab in Windows 2000

Protocols

Simply moving data from one machine to another is hardly sufficient to make a complete network; many other functions need to be handled. For example, if a file is being copied from one machine to another, something must keep track of all the packets so that the file can be properly reassembled. If many

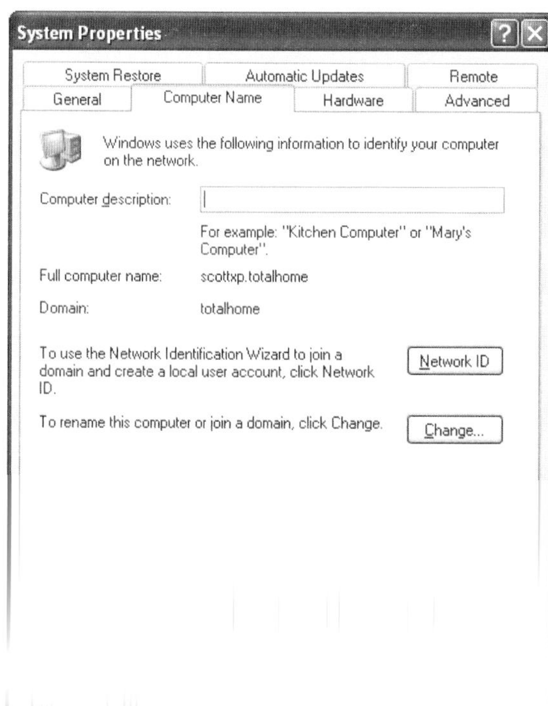

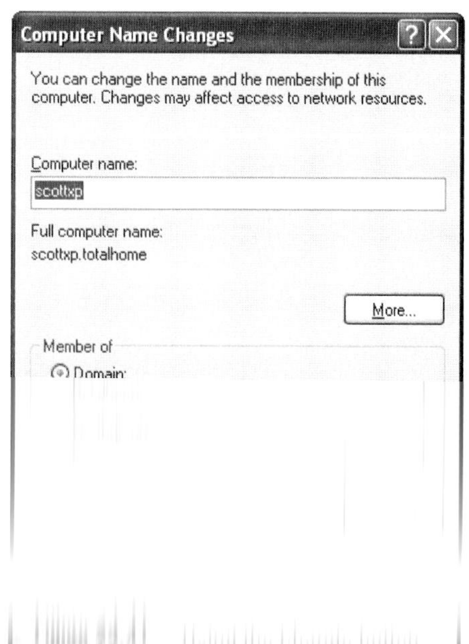

machines are talking to the same machine at once, that machine must somehow keep track of which packets it sends to or receives from each of the other PCs.

Another issue arises if one of the machines in the network has its network card replaced. Up to this point, the only way to distinguish one machine from another was by the MAC address on the network card. To solve this, each machine must have a name, an identifier for the network, which is "above" the MAC address. Each machine, or at least one of them, needs to keep a list of all the MAC addresses on the network, and the names of the machines, so that packets and names can be correlated. That way, if a PC's network card is replaced, the network, after some special queries, can update the list to associate the name of the PC with its new network card's MAC address.

Network protocol software takes the incoming data received by the network card, keeps it organized, sends it to the application that needs it, and then takes outgoing data from the application and hands it to the NIC to be sent out over the network. All networks use some protocol. Although many different protocols exist, the top three—NetBEUI from Microsoft, IPX/SPX from Novell, and TCP/IP from UNIX/Internet—hold a virtual lock on all networks.

A *node* is any device that has a network connection—usually this means a PC, but other devices can be nodes. For example, many printers now connect directly to a network and can therefore be termed nodes. I use the term *node* extensively in the rest of the chapter in place of *PC* or *networked computer*. This is especially true when I discuss wireless technologies, because that's the term the manufacturers use.

NetBEUI

During the 1980s, IBM developed *NetBIOS Extended User Interface* (NetBEUI), the default protocol for Windows for Workgroups, LANtastic, and Windows 95. NetBEUI offers small size and a relatively high speed, but it can't be used for routing. Its inability to handle routing limits NetBEUI to networks smaller than about 200 nodes.

Although IPX/SPX is strongly associated with Novell NetWare networks, versions of NetWare since version 5 have adopted TCP/IP as their default, native protocol.

IPX/SPX

Novell developed the *Internetwork Packet Exchange/Sequenced Packet Exchange* (IPX/SPX) protocol exclusively for their NetWare products. The IPX/SPX protocol is speedy, works well with routers, and takes up relatively little RAM when loaded. Microsoft implements a version of IPX/SPX called *NWLink.*

TCP/IP

Transmission Control Protocol/Internet Protocol (TCP/IP) was originally developed for the Internet's progenitor, the *Advanced Research Projects Agency Network* (ARPANET) of the U.S. Department of Defense. In 1983, TCP/IP became the built-in protocol for the popular BSD UNIX, and other flavors of UNIX quickly adopted it as well. TCP/IP is the best protocol for larger (>200 nodes) networks. The biggest network of all, the Internet, uses TCP/IP as its default protocol. Windows NT also uses TCP/IP as its default protocol. TCP/IP lacks speed and takes up a large amount of memory when loaded, but it is robust, well understood, and universally supported.

AppleTalk

AppleTalk is the proprietary Apple protocol. Similar to IPX, it is small and relatively fast. The only reason to use an AppleTalk protocol is to communicate with older Apple computers on a network. Apple's Macintosh OS X uses TCP/IP natively, so you won't need AppleTalk to plug a modern Mac into a Windows network.

Client Software

To access data or resources across a network, a Windows PC needs to have client software installed for every kind of server that you want to access. When you install a network card and drivers, Windows installs at least one set of client software, called Client for Microsoft Networks (Figure 23.42). This enables your machine to do the obvious: connect to a Microsoft network! To connect to a NetWare network, you'd need to add Client Service for NetWare. We'll go through the installation and configuration steps a little later in this chapter. For now, you need to know that Windows PCs don't just access shared data magically, but require client software to be installed.

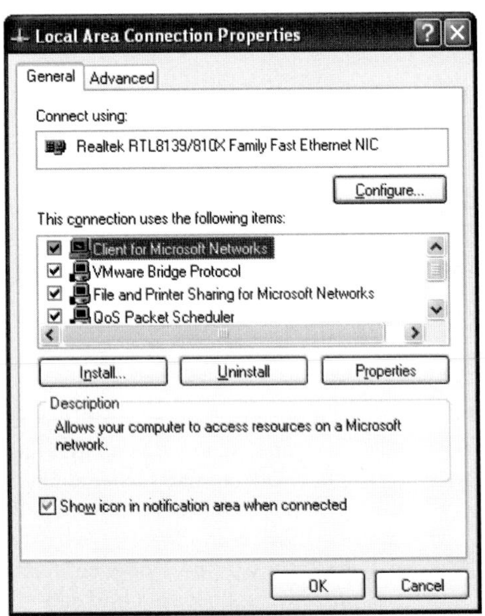

Figure 23.42 Local Area Connection Properties showing Client for Microsoft Networks installed (along with other network software)

Server Software

You can turn any Windows PC into a server, simply by enabling sharing of files, folders, and printers. Windows 2000 and XP have this installed but not activated by default, but activating it requires nothing more than a click on a check box, as you can see in Figure 23.42. On other versions of Windows you need to install the service and then enable it. It's pretty straightforward. Windows 9*x*/Me require a little more effort, but we'll go into that in the next section under installing and configuring.

Try This!

Discovering Protocols and Clients

If you have a network card loaded in your PC, chances are extremely high that you already have one or more protocols or clients installed. So try this!

1. Go to Network Neighborhood or My Network Places and get to the properties for your NIC. Windows 9*x*/Me users can simply alternate-click the Network Neighborhood icon and select Properties. Windows 2000/XP users need to do it twice: once on My Network Places and the second time on the Local Area Connection icon.

Almost halfway through the chapter and we're finally getting to the good stuff—installing and configuring a network! To have network connectivity, you need three things in place:

- **Network Interface Card** The physical hardware that connects the computer system to the network wire.
- **Protocol** The language that the computer systems use to communicate.
- **Network Client** The interface that allows the computer system to speak to the protocol. Strictly speaking, this component is optional, but is necessary for the majority of networks, so I'm including it here.

If you want to share resources on your PC with other network users, you also need to enable Microsoft's File and Print Sharing. This installs the services and software that turns a Windows PC into a server.

Plus, of course, you need to connect the PC to the network hub or switch via some sort of cable (preferably CAT 6 with Gigabit Ethernet cranking through the wires, but that's just me!). When you install a NIC, by default, Windows 2000 and XP Professional install the TCP/IP protocol (configured for Dynamic DHCP), the Client for Microsoft Networks, and File and Printer Service upon setup. Other versions of Windows require you to jump through a couple more hoops and install some or all of this stuff to get connectivity.

Installing a NIC

The NIC is your computer system's link to the network and installing one is the first step required to connect to a network. NICs are manufactured to operate on specific media and network types, such as 100BaseT Ethernet or

16 Mbps Token Ring. Follow the manufacturer's instructions for installation procedures. If your NIC is of recent vintage, it will be detected, installed, and configured automatically by Windows 2000 or Windows XP. Installing a NIC into any other Windows OS will require special drivers for that version of Windows from the manufacturer. You can usually download them from the Internet, but if you haven't connected to the Internet yet (because your NIC is sitting next to the PC), that won't help you here! The driver disc is therefore very important.

If you have the option, you should save yourself potential headaches and troubleshooting woes by acquiring new, name-brand NICs for your Windows installation.

Add/Remove Hardware Wizard The Add Hardware wizard automates installation of non-Plug and Play devices, or Plug and Play devices that were not detected correctly. Start the wizard by clicking Start | Settings | Control Panel, and double-clicking the icon for the Add Hardware applet. (Note that earlier versions of Windows call this the Add/Remove Hardware applet.) Click the Next button to select the hardware task you wish to perform, and follow the prompts to complete the wizard.

Configuring a Network Client

To establish network connectivity, you need a network client installed and configured properly. You need a client for every type of server NOS to which you plan to connect on the network. Let's look at the two most used for Microsoft and Novell networks.

Client for Microsoft Networks

Installed as part of the OS installation, the Client for Microsoft Networks rarely needs configuration, and, in fact, few configuration options are available. To start it in Windows XP, click Start, then alternate-click My Network Places and select Properties. In Windows 2000, select Start | Settings | Network and Dial-up Connections. In Windows 9*x*/Me, go to the Control Panel and double-click the Network applet, or alternate-click Network Neighborhood and double-click My Network Places.

In all versions of Windows, your next step is to double-click the Local Area Connection icon, click the Properties button, highlight Client for Microsoft Networks, and click the Properties button. Note that the Windows Locater service is specified as the Name Service Provider for the Remote Procedure Call (RPC) service by default. The only configuration option available is to click the Name Service Provider pull-down menu, and select DCE Cell Directory Services. If you do so, you will need to enter an address in the Network address field.

Do not change the Name Service Provider!

You don't need any special client software to connect to a Microsoft AD domain, assuming that you're using a modern version of Windows such as Windows 2000 or XP. Windows 95, 98, and NT 4.0 require the Active Directory Client Extensions software, available for download from Microsoft's web site.

Client Service for NetWare

Microsoft's Client Service for NetWare provides access to file and print resources on NetWare 3.*x* and 4.*x* servers. Client Service for NetWare supports some NetWare utilities and NetWare-aware applications. To connect

Microsoft client workstations to NetWare servers running NDS also requires the Microsoft Service for NetWare Directory Services (NDS). Once installed, Client Service for NetWare offers no configuration options.

Client Service for NetWare does not support the IP protocol used in NetWare 5.*x*.

Configuring Simple Protocols

Protocols come in many different flavors and perform differently on the network. Some, such as NetBEUI, lack elements that allow their signals to travel through routers, making them non-routable (essentially, this protocol is unsuitable for a large network that uses routers to re-transmit data). The network protocols supported by Windows include NetBEUI, NWLink (IPX/SPX), and TCP/IP. Windows XP drops support for NetBEUI. This section looks at installing and configuring the simple protocols used by Windows 9*x*/Me and NT/2000,

Windows except XP, follow these steps:

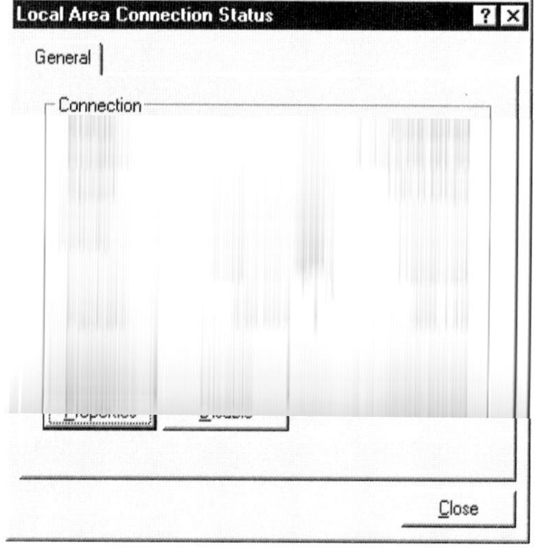

• **Figure 23.43** LAN Status dialog box in Windows 2000

1. In Windows 2000, select Start | Settings | Network and Dial-up Connections, double-click the Local Area Connection icon to bring up the Local Area Connection Status dialog box (Figure 23.43). In Windows 9*x*/Me, open the Control Panel and double-click the Network applet.
2. Click the Properties button to bring up the Local Area Connection Properties dialog box (Figure 23.44).
3. Click the Install button. In the Select Network Component Type dialog box, highlight Protocols and click the Add button (Figure 23.45).
4. In the Select Network Protocol dialog box, select NetBEUI protocol (Figure 23.46), and click the OK button. You will be prompted to reboot the system to make the changes take effect.

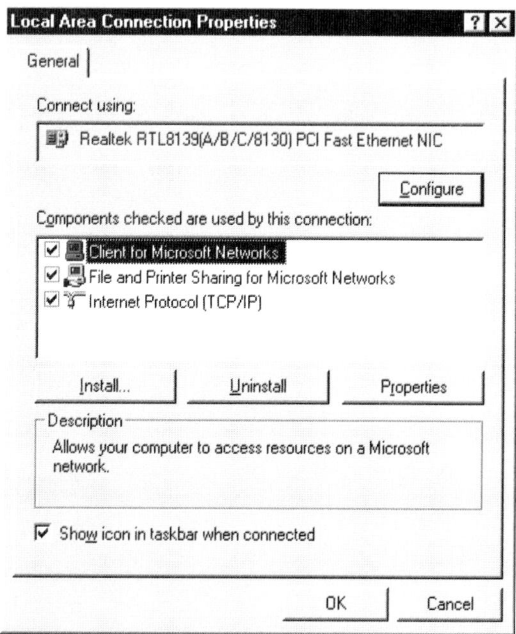

• **Figure 23.44** LAN Properties dialog box in Windows 2000

NWLink (IPX/SPX)

As mentioned earlier, NWLink is Microsoft's implementation of IPX/SPX protocol. The Microsoft version of NWLink provides the same level of functionality as the Novell protocol, and also includes an element for resolving NetBIOS names. NWLink packages data to be compatible with client/server services on NetWare networks, but does not provide access to NetWare File and Print Services. For this, you also need to install the Client Service for NetWare, as noted earlier.

Follow the same steps used to install NetBEUI to install NWLink, except choose NWLink rather than NetBEUI when you

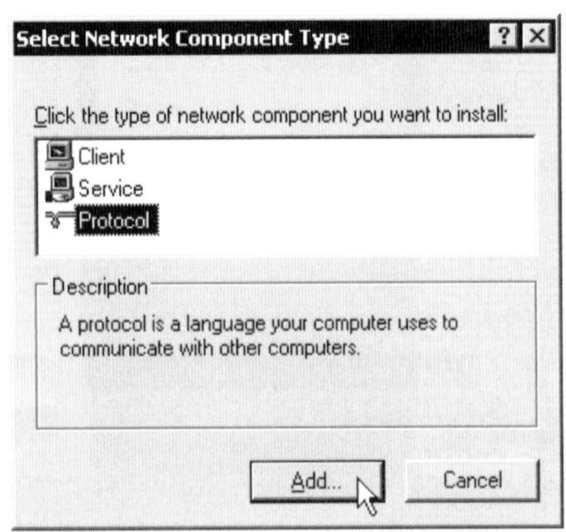

• **Figure 23.45** Adding a protocol

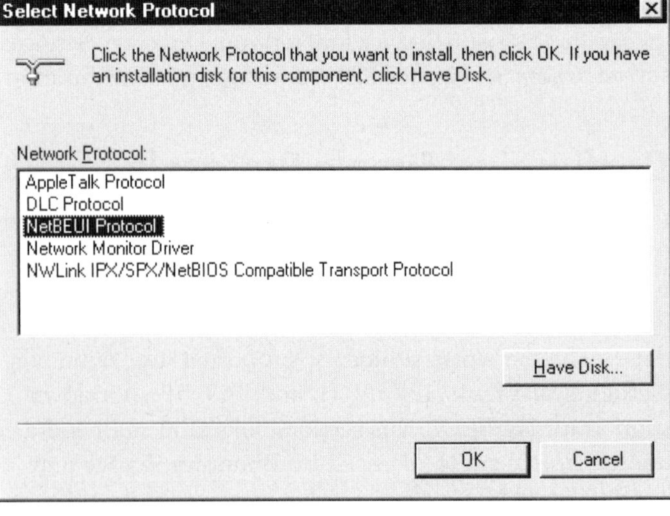

• **Figure 23.46** Selecting NetBEUI

When NWLink is set to Auto Detect the frame type, it will only detect one type, searching in the following order: (1) 802.2; (2) 802.3; (3) 802.5.

make your final selection. Note that Windows 9*x* calls the protocol IPX/SPX-compatible Protocol. You'll be prompted to reboot after adding the protocol.

NWLink is a relatively easy protocol to configure. Normally, the only settings you may need to specify are the internal network number and frame type (usually, however, the default values are sufficient). The internal network number is used to identify NetWare servers. The frame type specifies how the data is packaged for transport over the network. For computers to communicate by NWLink, they must have the same frame types. By default, the frame type is set to Auto Detect.

To configure NWLink properties manually, follow these steps:

1. In Windows XP, select Start | Control Panel and open the Network Connections applet. Double-click the Local Area Connection.
   In Windows 2000, select Start | Settings | Network and Dial-up Connections, and double-click the Local Area Connection icon.
   Finally, in Windows 9*x*/Me, go to the Control Panel and double-click the Network applet.
2. Click the Properties button, highlight NWLink IPX/SPX/NetBIOS Compatible transport Protocol, and click the Properties button.
3. In the NWLink IPX/SPX/NetBIOS Compatible Transport Protocol properties dialog box, set the internal network number and frame type (Figure 23.47).

Configuring TCP/IP

This final section on protocols covers TCP/IP, the primary protocol of the modern networks, including the Internet. For a PC to access the Internet, it must have the TCP/IP protocol loaded. TCP/IP has become so predominant that most network folks use it even on networks that do not connect to the Internet. Although TCP/IP is very powerful, it is also a bit of a challenge to set up. So whether you are installing a modem for a dial-up connection to the Internet or setting up 500 computers on their own private *intranet*, you must understand some TCP/IP basics. Let's go through the basic sections of the protocol and then look at specific steps to install and configure TCP/IP.

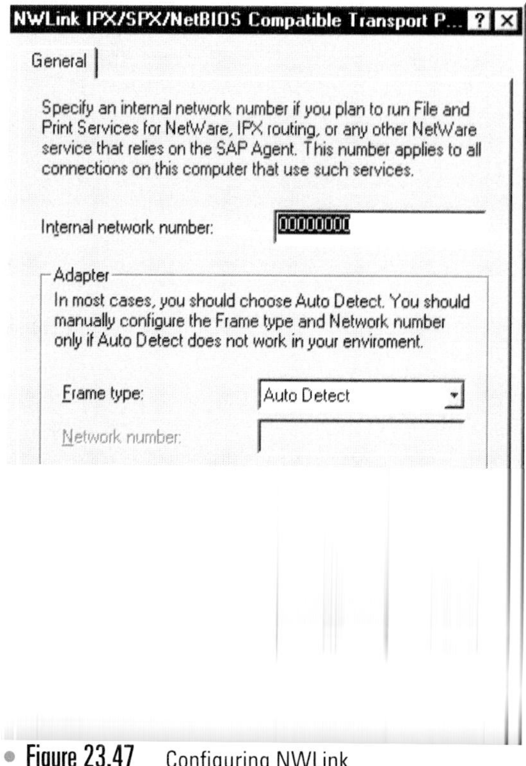

• **Figure 23.47** Configuring NWLink

Network Addressing

Any network address must provide two pieces of information. It must uniquely identify the machine and it must locate that machine within the larger network. In a TCP/IP network, the **IP address** identifies the PC and the **subnet mask** helps determine in which subnet within the network the machine resides.

IP Addresses In a TCP/IP network, the systems don't have names but rather use IP addresses. The IP address is the unique identification number for your system on the network. Part of the

Written in binary form, you'd get an address like

```
11110010.00000101.00000000.00001010
```

but the TCP/IP folks decided to write the decimal equivalents:

```
00000000 = 0
00000001 = 1
00000010 = 2
...
11111111 = 255
```

A traditional TCP/IP network divides IP addresses into classes, which correspond with the potential size of the network: Class A, Class B, and Class C. Class A addresses were intended for huge companies, such as major multinational corporations. Class C networks were targeted for LANs. The crushing need for more IP addresses for the Internet pretty much blew the class structure out the water, but here it is to satisfy your curiosity. Class A networks use the first octet to identify the network address, and the remaining three octets to identify the host. Class B networks use the first two octets to identify the network address, and the remaining two octets to identify the host. Class C networks use the first three octets to identify the network address, and the last octet to identify the host. Table 23.2 lists range (class) assignments.

Try This!

Adding a Simple Protocol

Knowing how to access and change protocols in a PC is an essential skill in today's wired world, and nothing beats doing something to reinforce what you learn, so try this!

1. Access the LAN Properties and, using the steps outlined above, add a simple protocol to your PC. If you have Windows XP, you're limited to NWLink, but earlier versions of Windows offer more choices.
2. If you're plugged into a network, what effect do you notice when you reboot and have a new protocol installed?

Table 23.2	Class A, B, and C addresses		
Network Class	**Address Range**	**Number of Network Addresses Available**	**Number of Host Nodes (Computers) Supported**
A	1–126	129	16,777,214
B	128–191	16,384	65,534
C	192–223	2,097,152	254

You'll note that the IP address ranges listed above skip from 126.x.x.x to 128.x.x.x. That's because the 127 address range (i.e., 127.0.0.1) is reserved for network testing (loopback) operations. That's not the only reserved range, either! Each network class has a specific IP address range reserved for *private* networks—traffic from these networks don't get routed to the Internet at large. Class A's private range goes from 10.0.0.1 to 10.255.255.254. Class B's private range is 172.16.0.1 up to 172.16.255.254. Class C has two private addresses ranges: 192.168.0.0 to 192.168.255.254 for manually-configured addresses, and 169.254.0.1 to 169.254.255.254 to accommodate the *Automatic Private IP Addressing* (APIPA) function.

Subnet Mask The subnet mask is a value that distinguishes which part of the IP address is the network address and which part of the address is the host address. The subnet mask blocks out (or "masks") the network portions (octets) of an IP address. Certain subnet masks are applied by default. The default subnet mask for Class A addresses is 255.0.0.0; for Class B, it's 255.255.0.0; and for Class C, 255.255.255.0. For example, in the Class B IP address 131.190.4.121 with a subnet mask of 255.255.0.0, the first two octets (131.190) make up the network address, and the last two (4.121) make up the host address.

The A+ Certification exams do not require you to configure IP addresses and subnet masks, but you should know what they are and how to find them on a PC.

TCP/IP Services

TCP/IP is a very different type of protocol. Although it supports File and Print Sharing, it adds a number of special sharing functions unique only to it, lumped together under the umbrella term of **TCP/IP services**. The most famous TCP/IP service is called *Hypertext Transfer Protocol* (HTTP), the language of the World Wide Web. If you want to surf the Web, you must have TCP/IP. But TCP/IP supplies many other services beyond just HTTP. Using a service called TELNET, you can access a remote system as though you were actually in front of that machine.

Another example is a handy utility called **Ping**. Ping enables one machine to check whether it can communicate with another machine. Figure 23.48 shows an example of Ping running on a Windows 2000 system. Isn't it interesting that many TCP/IP services run from a command prompt? Good

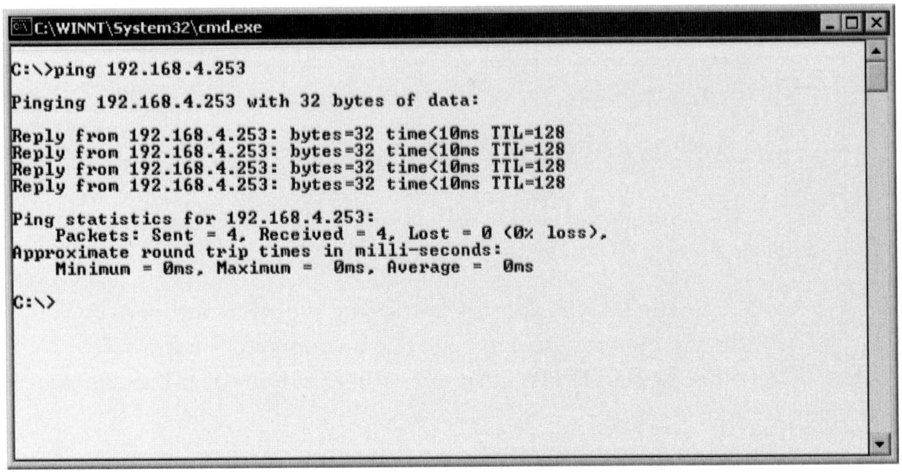

```
C:\WINNT\System32\cmd.exe

C:\>ping 192.168.4.253

Pinging 192.168.4.253 with 32 bytes of data:

Reply from 192.168.4.253: bytes=32 time<10ms TTL=128
Reply from 192.168.4.253: bytes=32 time<10ms TTL=128
Reply from 192.168.4.253: bytes=32 time<10ms TTL=128
Reply from 192.168.4.253: bytes=32 time<10ms TTL=128

Ping statistics for 192.168.4.253:
    Packets: Sent = 4, Received = 4, Lost = 0 (0% loss),
Approximate round trip times in milli-seconds:
    Minimum = 0ms, Maximum =  0ms, Average =  0ms

C:\>
```

• **Figure 23.48** Successful Ping in action

thing you know how to access one! There are plenty of other services that I'll show you in a moment.

The goal of TCP/IP is to link together multiple networks (which we'll call *local area networks* or LANs) to make an entire *wide area network* (WAN). LANs are usually linked together via some type of telephone service, ranging from basic dial-ups to dedicated, high-speed (and expensive) data lines (Figure 23.49). The goal is to make a WAN that uses the expensive links for as little traffic as possible. The machines that connect the phone lines to each LAN are specialized computers called *routers* (Figure 23.50). To reduce traffic, each router decides

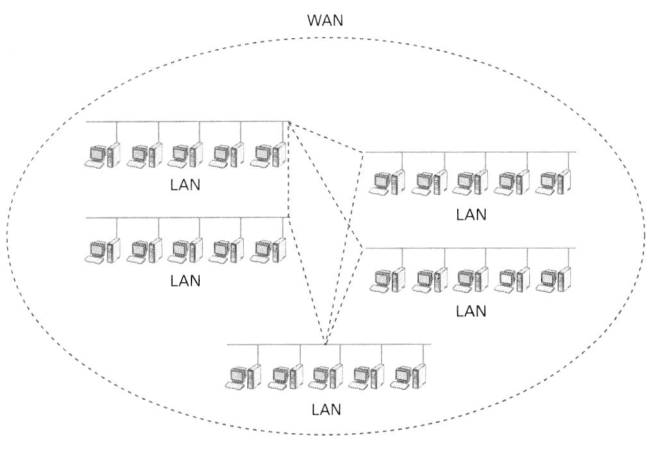

correctly to ensure proper network functioning. Unfortunately, these settings can be quite confusing, and there are quite a few of them. Not all settings are used for every type of TCP/IP network, and it's not always obvious where you go to set them. There are two primary locations for TCP/IP settings, one for dial-up connections (modems), and one for direct (NIC) connections. On Windows 9*x*/Me computers that use a modem to access the Internet, start in My Computer and click the Dial-up Networking icon. Alternate-click the connection whose TCP/IP properties you wish to set, and select Properties | Server Type | TCP/IP Settings (Figure 23.51). The place to configure TCP/IP settings for direct connections is the Control Panel. Select Networks | TCP/IP, and click the Properties button (Figure 23.52).

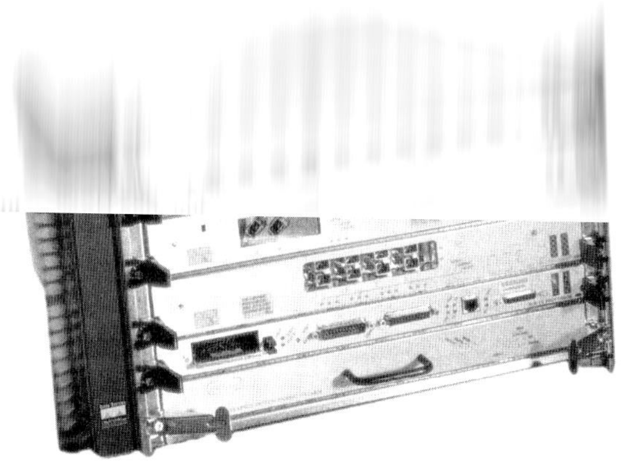

• **Figure 23.50** Typical router

Windows 2000/XP makes this a lot easier by letting you configure both dial-up and network connections using the My Network Places properties (Figure 23.53). Simply select the connection you wish to configure, and then set its TCP/IP properties.

The A+ Certification exams assume that someone else, such as a tech support person or some network guru, will tell you the correct TCP/IP settings for the network. Your only job is to understand roughly what they do and to know where to enter them so the system works. Let's discuss some of the most common TCP/IP settings.

Default Gateway A computer that wants to send data to another machine outside its LAN is not expected to know all the IP addresses of all the computers on the Internet. Instead, all IP machines know the name of one computer, to which they pass all the data they need to send outside the LAN. This machine is called the *default gateway*, and it is usually the local router (Figure 23.54).

TCP/IP Settings
Server assigned IP address
Specify an IP address
IP address: 0 . 0 . 0 . 0
Server assigned name server addresses
Specify name server addresses
Primary DNS: 208 . 194 . 194 . 9
Secondary DNS: 203 . 208 . 223 . 100
Primary WINS: 0 . 0 . 0 . 0
Secondary WINS: 0 . 0 . 0 . 0
Use IP header compression
Use default gateway on remote network
OK Cancel

• **Figure 23.51** TCP/IP Settings for Dial-Up Networking in Windows 95

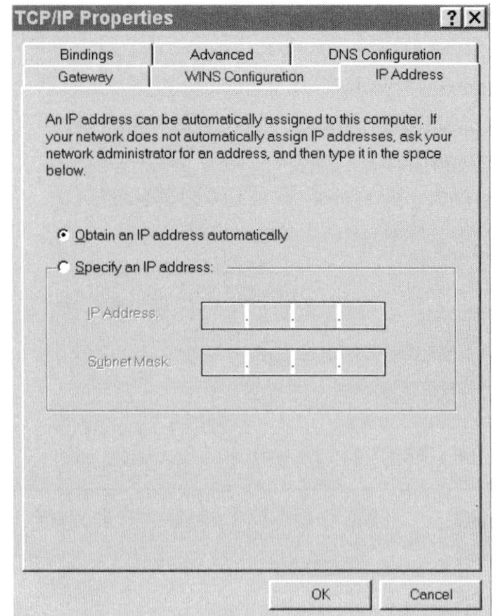

• **Figure 23.52** TCP/IP Properties in a Windows 95 system

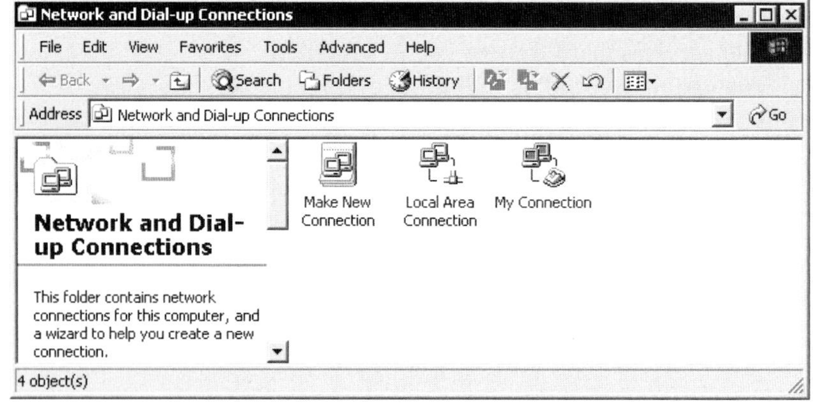

• **Figure 23.53** My Network Places showing a dial-up and a network connection

• **Figure 23.54** Setting a default gateway

Domain Name Service (DNS) Knowing that users were not going to be able to handle raw IP addresses, early Internet pioneers came up with a way to correlate those numbers with more human-friendly computer designations. Special computers, called *Domain Name Service* (DNS) servers, keep databases of IP addresses and their corresponding names. For example, a machine called TOTAL.SEMINAR1 will be listed in a DNS directory with a corresponding IP address, such as 209.34.45.163. So instead of accessing the \\209.34.45.163\FREDC directory to copy a file, you can ask to see \\TOTAL.SEMINAR1\FREDC. Your system will then query the DNS server to get TOTALSEMINAR1's IP address, and use that to find the right machine. Virtually all TCP/IP networks require you to set up DNS server names (Figure 23.55).

The Internet has very regulated domain names. If you want a domain name that others can access on the Internet, you must register your domain name and pay a small yearly fee. In most cases, your Internet service provider can handle this for you. Originally, DNS names all ended with one of the following seven domain name qualifiers, called *top level domains* (TLDs):

.com	General business	**.org**	Nonprofit organizations
.edu	Educational organizations	**.gov**	Government organizations
.mil	Military organizations	**.net**	Internet organizations
.int	International		

As more and more countries joined the Internet, an entire new level of domains was added to the original seven to indicate a DNS name in a particular country, like .uk for the United Kingdom. It's very common to see DNS names such as www.bbc.co.uk or www.louvre.fr. The *Internet Corporation for Assigned Names and Numbers* (ICANN) has announced the creation of several more new domains, including .name, .biz, .info, and others. Given

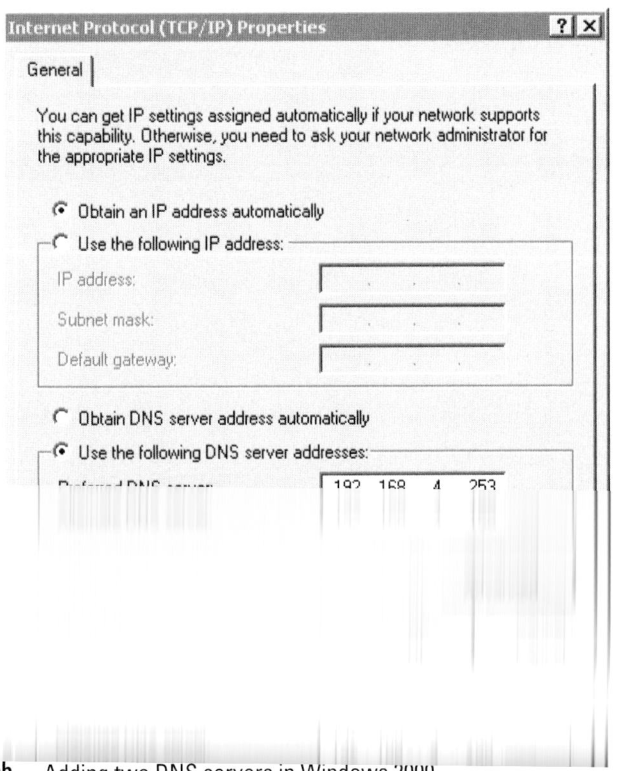

• **Figure 23.55** Adding two DNS servers in Windows 2000

The A+ Certification exams have a rather strange view of what you should know about networking. Take a lot of time practicing how to get to certain network configuration screens. Be ready for questions that ask, "Which of the following steps will enable you to change a particular value?"

the explosive growth of the Internet, these are unlikely to be the last ones! For the latest developments, check ICANN's web site at www.icann.org.

DHCP/WINS The last items that most TCP/IP networks require are *Dynamic Host Configuration Protocol* (DHCP) and *Windows Internet Name Service* (WINS). To understand DHCP, we must first remember that every machine must have an IP address. This can be added manually using the TCP/IP properties menu. A permanent IP address assigned to a machine is known as a *static* IP address (Figure 23.56).

DHCP enables you to create a pool of IP addresses that are given to machines when they need them and are taken away when they are no longer needed. DHCP is especially handy for networks that have a lot of dial-in systems. Why give a machine that is only on for a few minutes a day a static IP address? For that reason, DHCP is quite popular. If you add a NIC to a Windows system, the TCP/IP settings are set to use DHCP. When you accept those automatic settings, you're really telling the machine to use DHCP (Figure 23.57).

WINS enables Windows network names like SERVER1 to be correlated to IP addresses, like DNS does except we're talking about *Windows* network names, not Internet names. All you have to do to set up WINS is either type in the IP address for the WINS server, or let DHCP handle it for you (Figure 23.58). Windows 2000/XP don't use WINS; they use an improved "dynamic" DNS that supports both Internet names and Windows names.

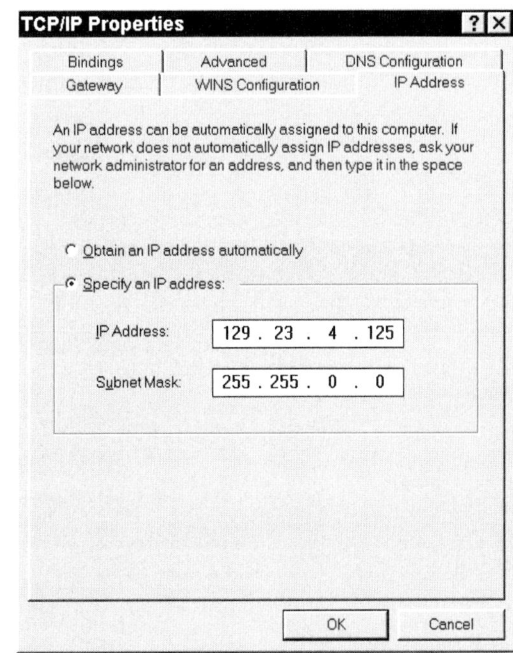

• **Figure 23.56** Setting a static IP address

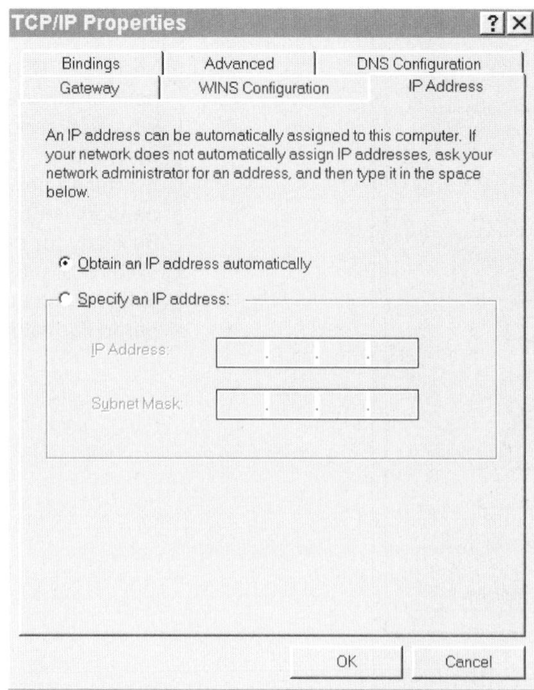

• **Figure 23.57** Automatically use IP address

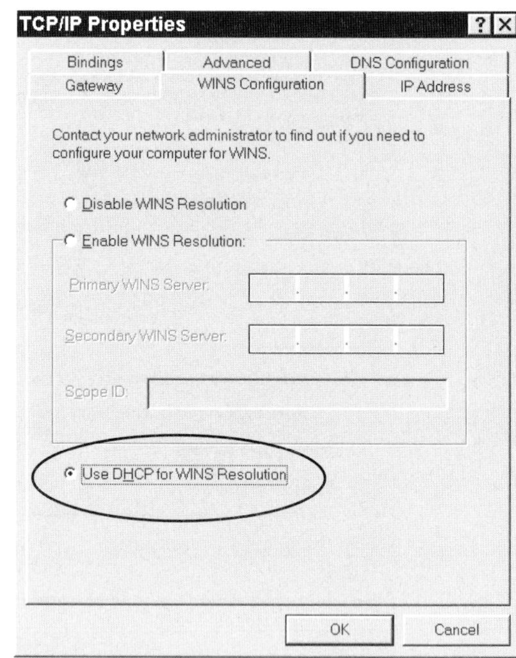

• **Figure 23.58** Setting up WINS to use DHCP

TCP/IP Tools

All versions of Windows come with handy tools to test TCP/IP. The ones you're most likely to use in the field are PING, WINIPCFG/IPCONFIG, NSLOOKUP, and TRACERT.

Ping You've already seen Ping, a really great way to see if you can talk to another system. Here's how it works. Get to a command prompt and type **ping** followed by an IP address or by a DNS name, such as **ping www.chivalry.com**. Press the ENTER key on your keyboard and away it goes! Figure 23.59 shows the common syntax for Ping.

```
C:\WINDOWS\System32\cmd.exe

C:\Documents and Settings\scottj>ping /?

Usage: ping [-t] [-a] [-n count] [-l size] [-f] [-i TTL] [-v TOS]
            [-r count] [-s count] [[-j host-list] | [-k host-list]]
            [-w timeout] target_name

Options:
    -t             Ping the specified host until stopped.
                   To see statistics and continue - type Control-Break;
                   To stop - type Control-C.
    -a             Resolve addresses to hostnames.
    -n count       Number of echo requests to send.
    -l size        Send buffer size.
    -f             Set Don't Fragment flag in packet.
    -i TTL         Time To Live.
    -v TOS         Type Of Service.
    -r count       Record route for count hops.
    -s count       Timestamp for count hops.
    -j host-list   Loose source route along host-list.
    -k host-list   Strict source route along host-list.
    -w timeout     Timeout in milliseconds to wait for each reply.

C:\Documents and Settings\scottj>_
```

• **Figure 23.59** Ping syntax

WINIPCFG/IPCONFIG Windows 9*x*/Me provides the handy WINIPCFG program. Type **winipcfg** from the Start | Run menu option to see Figure 23.60. Click the More Info button to see all your TCP/IP options (Figure 23.61). The Release and Renew buttons let you get new TCP/IP information from a DHCP server. Windows NT/2000/XP do not use WINIPCFG. Instead, you once again must go to a command prompt and run IPCONFIG. You can type **ipconfig /all** to see all of your TCP/IP settings (Figure 23.62).

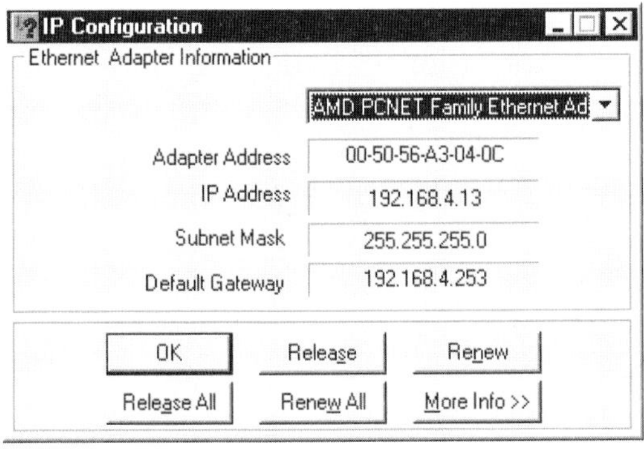

• **Figure 23.60** WINIPCFG in action on a Windows 98 system

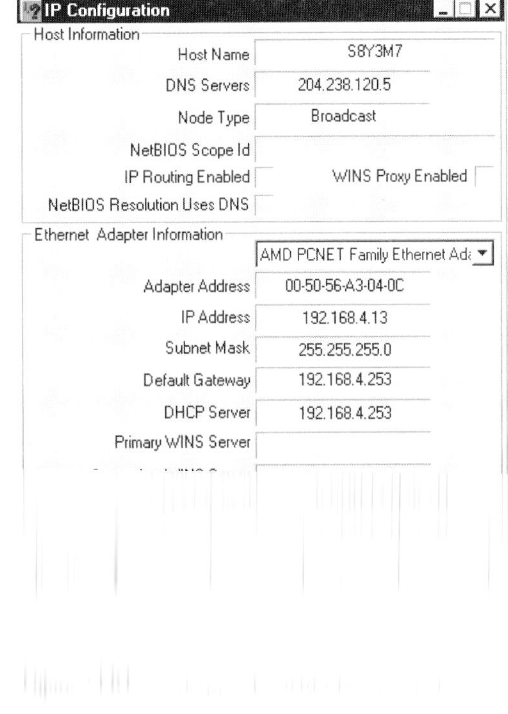

ton in WINIPCFG to renew the DHCP lease. If you get a DHCP server not available error, try Release All and then Renew All. If the error persists, you may have a problem with the DHCP server. IPCONFIG has the same release/renew capabilities. Just type **ipconfig /renew** or **ipconfig /release**.

Make sure you know that Windows 9*x*/Me use WINIPCFG and Windows NT/2000/XP use IPCONFIG.

NSLOOKUP NSLOOKUP is a powerful command line program that enables you to determine the name of a DNS server, among many other things. Every version of Windows makes NSLOOKUP available when you install TCP/IP. To run the program, type **nslookup** from the command line and press the ENTER key (Figure 23.63). Note that this gives you a little information. Note that the prompt has changed? That's because you're running the application. Type **exit** and press the ENTER key to return to the command prompt.

TRACERT The TRACERT utility shows the route that a packet takes to get to its destination. From a command line, just type **tracert** followed by a space and an IP address. The output describes the route from your machine to the destination machine, including all devices it passes through and how long each hop takes (Figure 23.64). TRACERT can come in handy when you have to troubleshoot bottlenecks.

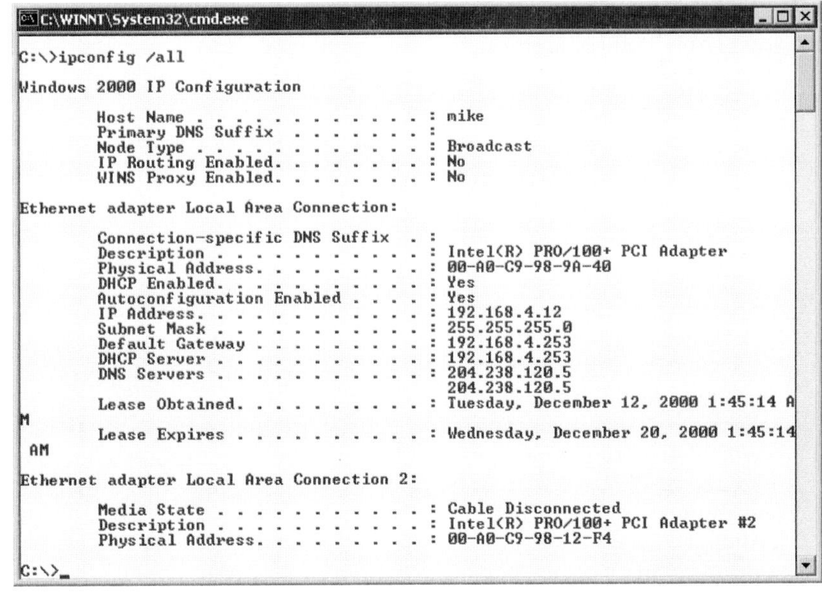

• **Figure 23.62** IPCONFIG /ALL on Windows 2000

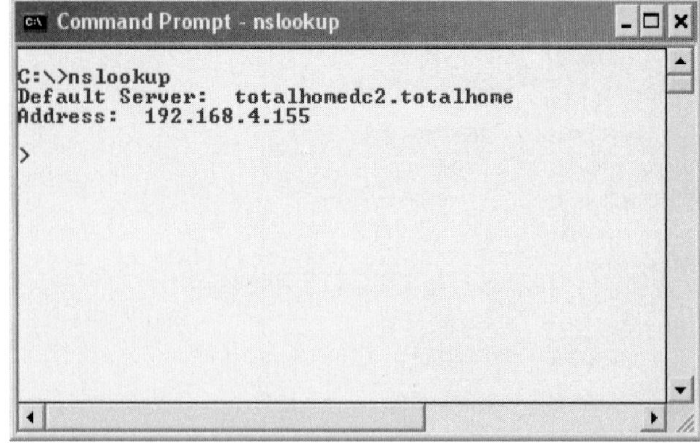

• **Figure 23.63** NSLOOKUP in action

When users complain that it's difficult to reach a particular destination using TCP/IP, you can run this utility to determine if the problem exists on a machine or connection over which you have control, or if it is a problem on another machine or router. Similarly, if a destination is completely unreachable, TRACERT can again determine if the problem is on a machine or router over which you have control.

Configuring TCP/IP

By default, the TCP/IP protocol is configured to receive an IP address automatically from a Dynamic Host Configuration Protocol (DHCP) server on the network (and automatically assign a corresponding subnet mask). As far as the A+ Certification exams are concerned, Network+ techs and administrators give you the IP address, subnet mask, and default gateway information and you plug them into the PC. That's about it, so here's how to do it manually.

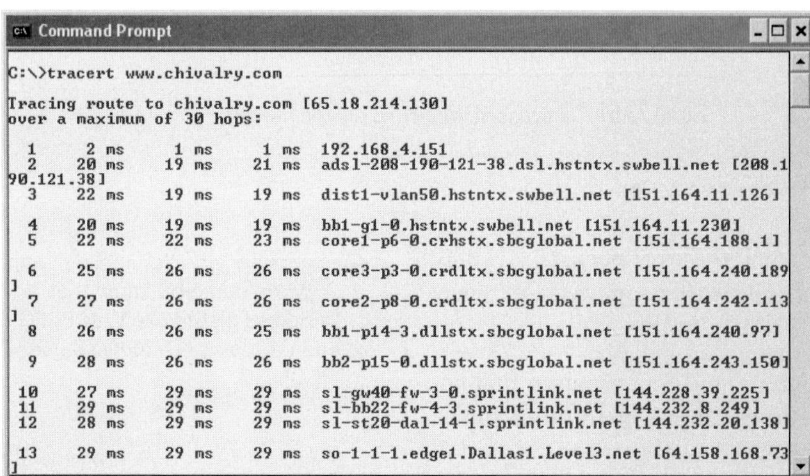

• **Figure 23.64** TRACERT in action

1. In Windows XP, open the Control Panel and double-click the Network Connections applet. Double-click the Local Area Connection icon. In Windows 2000, click Start | Settings | Network and Dial-up Connections, and double-click the Local Area Connection icon. In Windows 9*x*/Me/2000, alternate-click Network Neighborhood and double-click My Network Places to get to your network settings.
2. Click the Properties button, highlight Internet Protocol (TCP/IP), and click the Properties button.
3. In the dialog box, click the Use the Following IP Address Radio button.
4. Enter the IP address in the appropriate fields.
5. Press the TAB key to skip down to the Subnet Mask field. Note that the subnet mask is entered automatically (this can be over-typed, if you wish to enter a different subnet mask). See Figure 23.65.
6. Optionally, enter the IP address for a default gateway (router, or another computer system that will forward transmissions beyond your network).
7. Optionally, enter the IP address of a primary and secondary DNS server.
8. Click the OK button to close the dialog box.

You can do some cool stuff with NSLOOKUP and consequently some techs absolutely love the tool. It's way outside the scope of A+ Certification, but if you want to play with it some, type **help** at the NSLOOKUP prompt and press ENTER to see a list of common commands and syntax.

9. Click the Close button to exit the Local Area Connection Status dialog box.

10. Windows will alert you that you must restart the system for the changes to take effect.

Try This!

Running TRACERT

Ever wonder why your e-mail takes *years* to get to some people but others get it instantly? Or why some web sites are slower to load than others? Part of the blame could lie with how many hops away your connection is from the target server. You can use TRACERT to run a quick check of how many hops it takes to get to somewhere on a network, so try this!

1. Run TRACERT on some known source, such as www.microsoft.com or www.totalsem.com.

2. How many hops did it take? Did your TRACERT timeout or

Automatic Private IP Addressing

Windows 2000 and Windows XP support a feature called Automatic Private IP Addressing (APIPA) that automatically as-

If the computer system cannot contact a DHCP server, it generates an address in the form of 169.254.*x*.*y* (where *x*.*y* is the computer's identifier) and a 16-bit subnet mask (255.255.0.0) and broadcasts it on the network segment (subnet). If no other computer responds to the address, the system assigns this address to itself. When using the Auto Private IP, the system can only communicate with other computers on the same subnet that also use the 169.254.*x*.*y* range with a 16-bit mask. APIPA is enabled by default if your system is configured to obtain an IP address automatically.

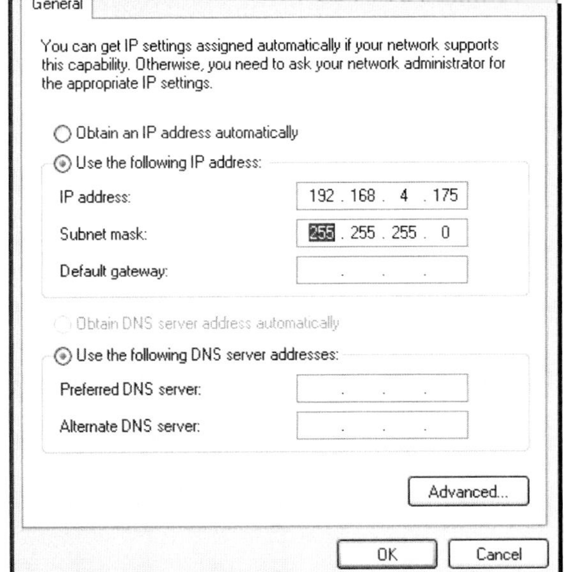

• **Figure 23.65** Setting up IP

Sharing and Security

Windows systems can share all kinds of resources: files, folders, entire drives, printers, faxes, Internet connections, and much more. Conveniently for you, the A+ Certification exams limit their interests to folders, printers, and Internet connections. Let's see how to share folders and printers now; we'll save Internet connection sharing for the TCP/IP section.

Sharing Drives and Folders

All versions of Windows share drives and folders in basically the same manner. Simply alternate-click any drive or folder and select Sharing. In Windows 98, the dialog box shown in Figure 23.66 appears. If you don't see the Sharing option, that means you have not enabled File sharing on the system.

By clicking the Shared As radio button, you can add a share name. This is the name that the other workstations will see when they are looking for resources to access. The trick here is to give the resource a name that clearly

A computer system on a network with an active DHCP server that has an IP address in this range usually indicates that there is a problem connecting to the DHCP server.

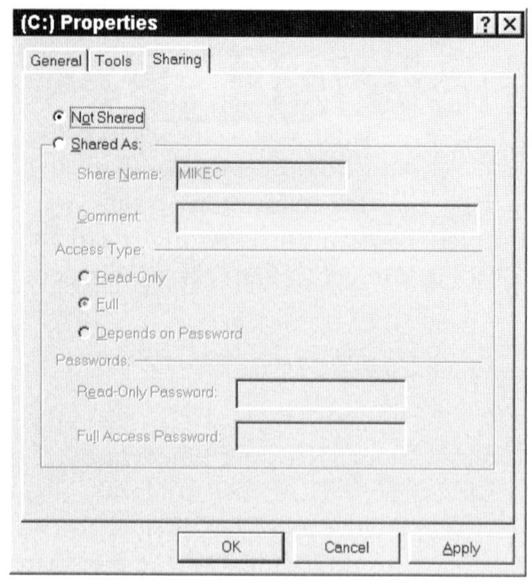

• **Figure 23.66** Sharing window

describes it. For example, if the goal is to share a particular C: drive, sharing that drive simply as "C:" could result in confusing this C: drive with other shared C: drives on the network. Instead, try a more detailed name like FREDC or SALES3C. As a rule, try to keep the name short and without spaces (Figure 23.67).

After establishing the share name for the resource, note that you can determine *how* it is to be shared. Under Windows 9*x*/Me, the options are simple: Full, Read-Only, and Depends On Password. This is one of the major limitations of Windows 9*x*/Me networks. We'll do Windows NT/2000/XP next to see some real sharing power! After you select the network name and the access level, click OK to see a little hand appear on the icon; this shows that the network resource is being shared (Figure 23.68).

Windows NT/2000/XP folder shares are created the same way, with a little added complexity due to Windows NT/2000/XP's use of NTFS. When you select the properties for a folder in Windows NT/2000/XP and select the Sharing tab, you see Figure 23.69. Select Share This Folder, add a Comment and a User Limit if you wish (they're not required), and click Permissions to see Figure 23.70.

Hey! Doesn't NTFS have all those wild permissions like Read, Execute, Take Ownership, and all that? Yes, it does, but NTFS permissions and network permissions are totally separate beasties. Microsoft wanted Windows 2000 and XP to support many different types of partitions (NTFS, FAT16, FAT32), old and new. Network permissions are Microsoft's way of enabling you to administer file sharing on any type of partition supported by Windows, no matter how ancient. Sure, your options will be pretty limited if you are working with an older partition type, but you *can* do it.

The beauty of Windows NT/2000/XP is that it gives you another tool—NTFS permissions—that can do much more. NTFS is where the power lies, but power always comes with a price: You have to configure two separate sets of permissions. If you are sharing a folder on an NTFS drive, as you

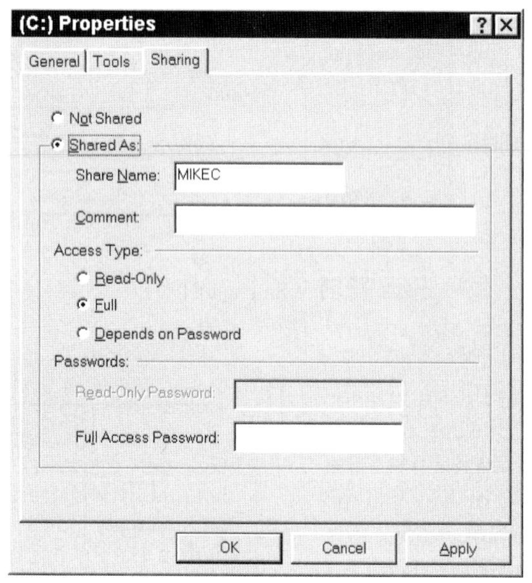

• **Figure 23.67** Sharing a drive

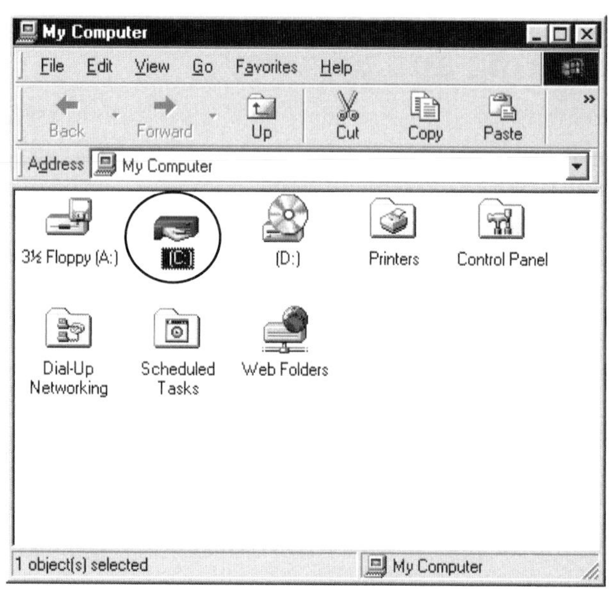

• **Figure 23.68** Shared drive

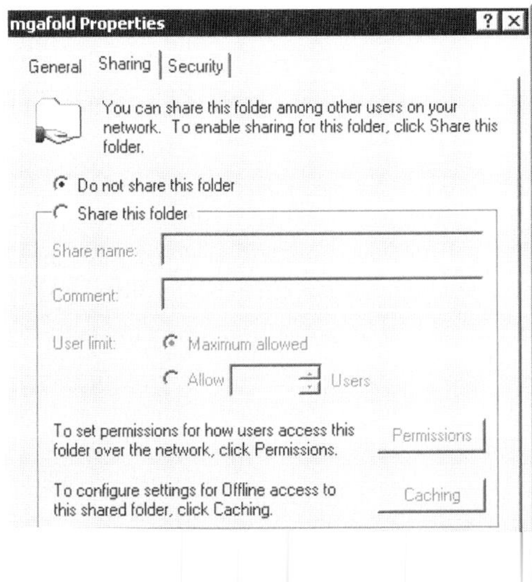

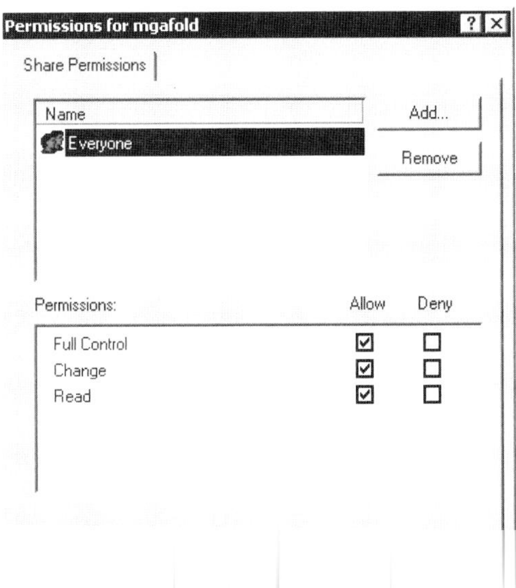

normally are these days, you must set *both* the network permissions and the NTFS permissions to let others access your shared resources. Some good news: This is actually no big deal! Just set the network permissions to give everyone full control, and then use the NTFS permissions to exercise more precise control over *who* accesses the shared resources and *how* they access them. Click the Security tab to set the NTFS permissions.

Windows NT/2000/XP has two types of sharing: Network permissions and NTFS permissions. Windows 9x/Me has only Network permissions.

Accessing Shared Drives/Directories

Once you have set up a drive or directory to be shared, the final step is to access that shared drive or directory from another machine. In Windows NT and 9*x*, you access the shared devices through the Network Neighborhood (Figure 23.71). Windows Me, 2000, and XP use My Network Places, although you'll need to do a little clicking to get to the shared resources (Figure 23.72).

Network resources can also be "mapped" to a local resource name. For example, the FREDC share can be mapped to be a local hard drive such as E: or F:. This can be done in Windows 9*x*/Me from Windows Explorer or by alternate-clicking a share in Network Neighborhood (My Network Places for Me) and selecting Map Network Drive. Mapping is usually done when you want a permanent connection, or to support older programs that might have trouble accessing a drive called FREDC.

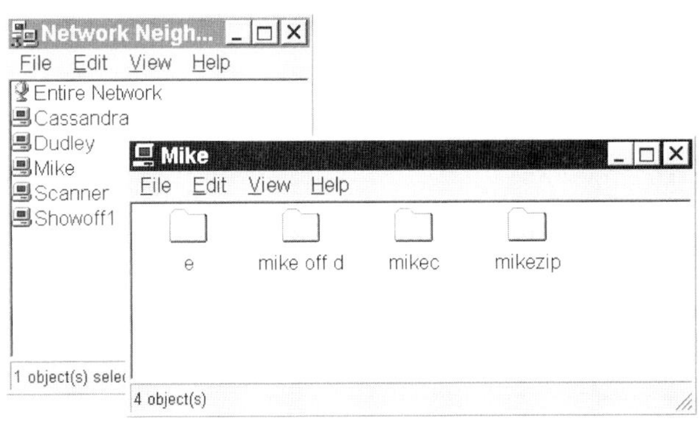

• **Figure 23.71** Shared resources in Network Neighborhood

Windows 2000 supports Map Network Drive, but adds a handy Add Network Place icon in My Network Places that lets you add network locations you frequently access without using up drive letters. Windows XP removes the icon, but adds the menu option in its context bar on the left. Here's my Windows 2000 system (Figure 23.73).

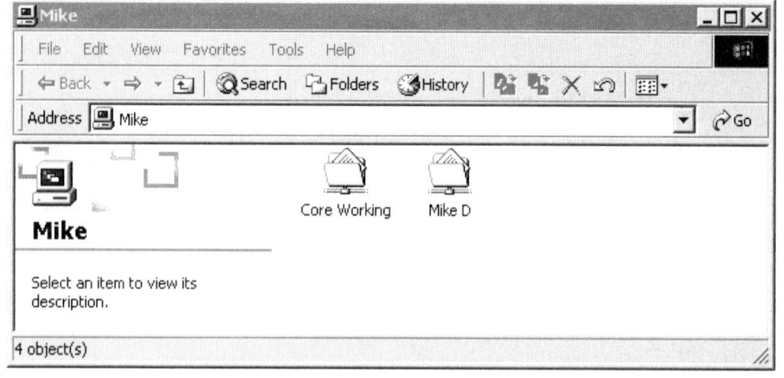

• **Figure 23.72** Shared resources in My Network Places

Mapping shared network drives is a very common practice as it makes a remote network share look like just another drive on the local system. The only downside to drive mapping stems from the fact that users tend to forget they are on a network. A classic example is the user who always accesses a particular folder or file on the network and then suddenly gets a "file not found" error when the workstation gets disconnected from the network. Instead of recognizing this as a network error, the user often imagines the problem as a missing or corrupted file.

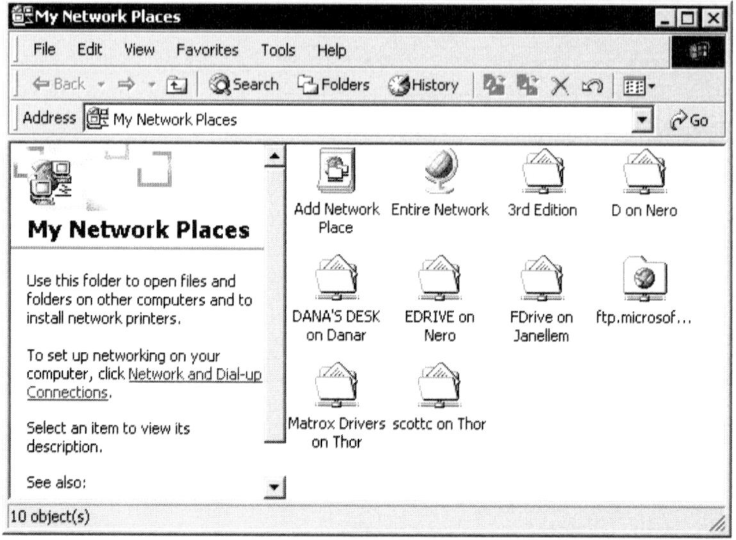

• **Figure 23.73** My Network Places

UNC

All computers that share must have a network name, and all of the resources they share must also have network names. Any resource on a network can be described by combining the names of the resource being shared and the system sharing. If a machine called SERVER1 is sharing its C: drive as FREDC, the complete name would be described like this:

```
\\SERVER1\FREDC
```

This is called the *Universal Naming Convention* (UNC). The UNC is distinguished by its use of double backslashes in front of the sharing system's name, and a single backslash in front of the shared resource's name.

Sharing Printers

Sharing printers in Windows is just as easy as sharing drives and directories. Assuming that the system has printer sharing services loaded, just go to the Printers folder in the Control Panel and alternate-click the printer you wish to share. Select properties, go to the Sharing tab, click Shared as, and give it a name (see Figure 23.74).

To access a shared printer in any version of Windows, simply click the Add Printer icon in the Printers folder. When asked if the printer is Local or Network, select Network; browse the network for the printer you wish to access, and Windows takes care of the rest! In almost all cases, Windows will copy the printer driver from the sharing machine. In the rare case where it doesn't, it will prompt you for drivers.

> All shared resources should show up in Network Neighborhood/My Network Places. If a shared resource fails to show up, make sure to check the basics first: Is File and Print Sharing activated? Is the device shared? Don't let silly errors fool you!

Before the advent of Windows 95, most network printing was done via the redirection of an LPT port. A printer would be installed and an unused LPT port, like LPT2 or LPT3, would then take all of the print information. This redirected LPT would then send the print job over the network to the proper network printer. Although this is unnecessary in most cases today, all versions of Windows still provide this option to support older applications (see Figure 23.75).

One of the most pleasant aspects of configuring a system for networking under all versions of Microsoft Windows is the amazing amount of the process that is automated. For example, if Windows detects a NIC in a system, it will automatically install the NIC driver, a network protocol (Windows 95 installed NetBEUI but later versions all install TCP/IP), and Client for Microsoft Networks (the NetBIOS part of the Microsoft networking software). So if you want to share a resource, everything you need is automatically installed. Note that while File and Print Sharing is also automatically installed, you still must activate it by clicking the check boxes.

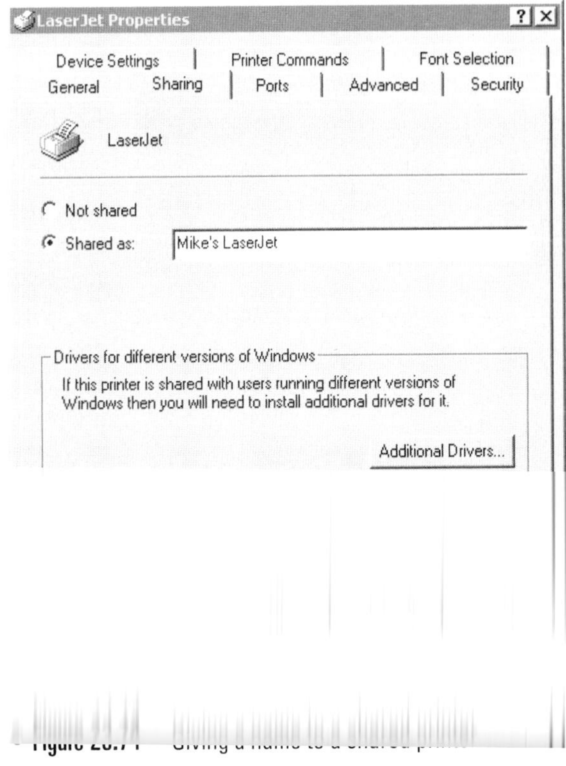

chance to get away from all the cables and mess and just *connect* has a phenomenal appeal. Because I see wireless as one of the most important areas of development in the PC, this section goes a good bit deeper into the technology than the A+ exams require. A highly skilled tech today should know this stuff, because that's what your customers will demand. To make it a little easier to study, I've included some exam tips in this section that you can skim before taking the Core Hardware and OS Technologies exams.

In most cases, the term "wireless network" is a bit of a misnomer. A term like "cable-less network" would probably be more accurate because the thing that you're eliminating is the Ethernet cabling that connects the PCs to each other. Instead of a physical set of wires running between network nodes, wireless networks use either radio waves or beams of infrared light to communicate with each other.

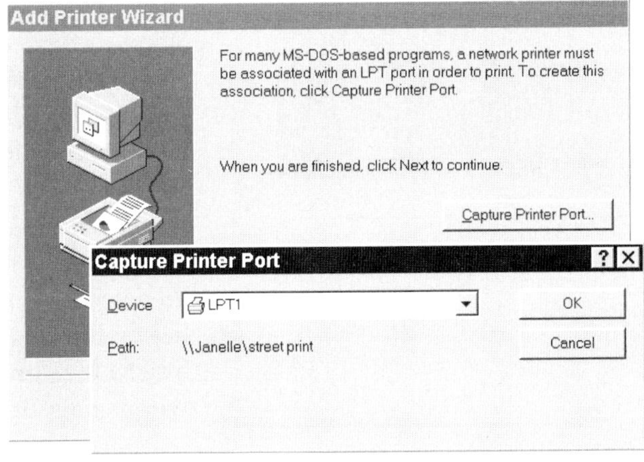

Figure 23.75 Capturing a printer port

Different kinds of wireless networking solutions have come and gone in the past. The types of wireless radio wave networks you'll find yourself supporting these days are those based on the IEEE 802.11 wireless Ethernet standard—*Home Radio Frequency* (HomeRF) and *Wireless Fidelity* (Wi-Fi)—and those based on the newer Bluetooth technology. Wireless networks using infrared light are limited to those that use the *Infrared Data Association* (IrDA) protocol.

Wireless Networking Components

Wireless networking capabilities of one form or another are built into many modern computing devices. Infrared *transceiver* ports have been standard

• **Figure 23.76** Infrared transceiver ports on a laptop and PDA

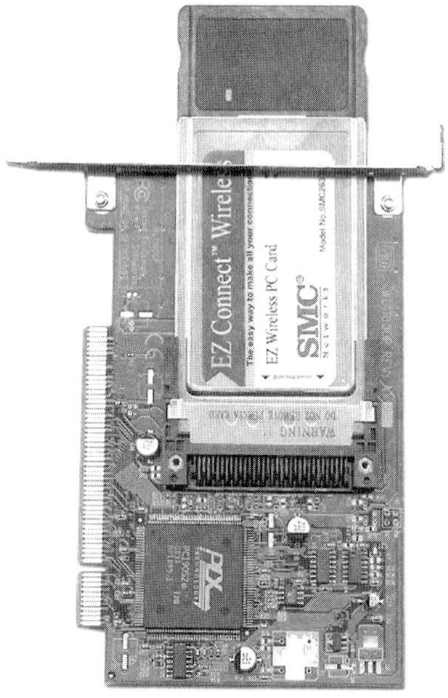

• **Figure 23.77** Wireless PCMCIA NIC inserted into PCI add-on card

The A+ Core Hardware Exam loves questions on cables and connectors, so look for questions on USB adapters and WAPs.

issue on portable computers, PDAs, and high-end printers for years, although they're curiously absent from many of the latest Tablet PCs. Figure 23.76 shows the infrared transceiver ports on a laptop computer and a PDA. Wireless Ethernet and Bluetooth capabilities are increasingly popular as integrated components, or can easily be added using PCI or PCMCIA add-on cards. Figure 23.77 shows a PCI card that accepts a wireless PCMCIA Ethernet card. You can also add wireless network capabilities using external USB wireless network adapters, as shown in Figure 23.78.

Wireless network adapters aren't limited to PCs. Many handheld computers and PDAs have wireless capabilities built-in or available as add-on options. Figure 23.79 shows a PDA accessing the Internet through a wireless network adapter card.

To extend the capabilities of a wireless Ethernet network, such as connecting to a wired network or share a high-speed Internet connection, you need a *wireless access point* (WAP). A WAP centrally connects wireless network nodes in the same way that a hub connects wired Ethernet PCs. Many WAPs also act as high-speed switches and Internet routers, such as the Linksys device shown in Figure 23.80.

Wireless communication via Bluetooth comes as a built-in option on newer PCs and peripheral devices, or you can add it to an older PC via an external USB Bluetooth adapter. Figure 23.81 shows a Bluetooth adapter with a Bluetooth-enabled mouse and keyboard.

Wireless Networking Software

Wireless devices use the same networking protocols and client that their wired counterparts use, and operate using the CSMA/CA networking scheme. The CA stands for collision *avoidance*, a slightly different standard than the collision *detection* standard used in wired Ethernet. Here's the difference. Wireless nodes listen in on the wireless medium to see if another node is currently broadcasting data. If so, then it waits a random amount of time before retrying. So far, this method is exactly the same as the method used by wired networks. Because wireless

• **Figure 23.78** External USB wireless NIC

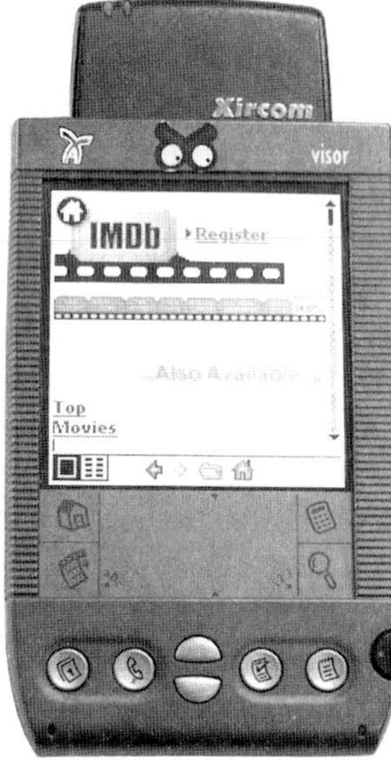

• **Figure 23.79** PDA with wireless capability

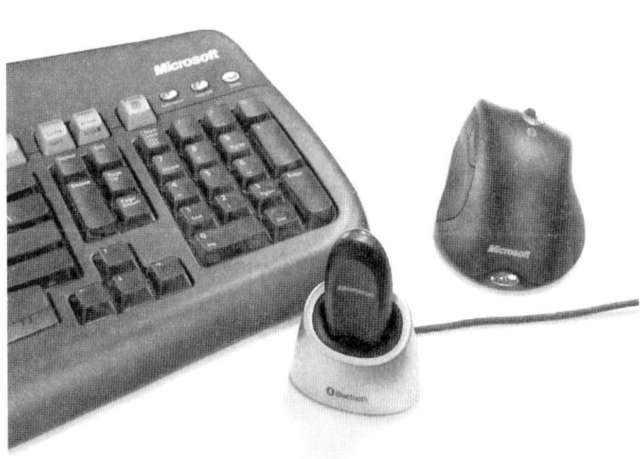

When enabled, a transmitting node that determines that the wireless medium is clear to use sends an RTS frame to the receiving node. The receiving node responds with a CTS frame, telling the sending node that it's okay to transmit. Then, once the data is sent, the transmitting node waits for an acknowledgement (ACK) from the receiving node before sending the next data packet. Very elegant, but keep in mind that using RTS/CTS introduces significant overhead to the process and can impede performance.

In terms of configuring wireless networking software, there's very little that you need to do. Wireless network adapters are Plug and Play, so any modern version of Windows will immediately recognize it when installed into a PCI or PCMCIA slot, or a USB port, prompting you to load any needed hardware drivers. You will, however, need a utility to set parameters such as your *Service Set Identifier* (SSID), also called a *network name*.

Windows XP has built-in tools for configuring these settings, but for previous versions of Windows, you need to rely on configuration tools provided by the wireless network adapter vendor. Figure 23.82 shows a typical wireless network adapter configuration utility. Using this utility, you can determine your link state and signal strength, configure your wireless networking *mode* (discussed next), set security encryption, power saving options, and so on.

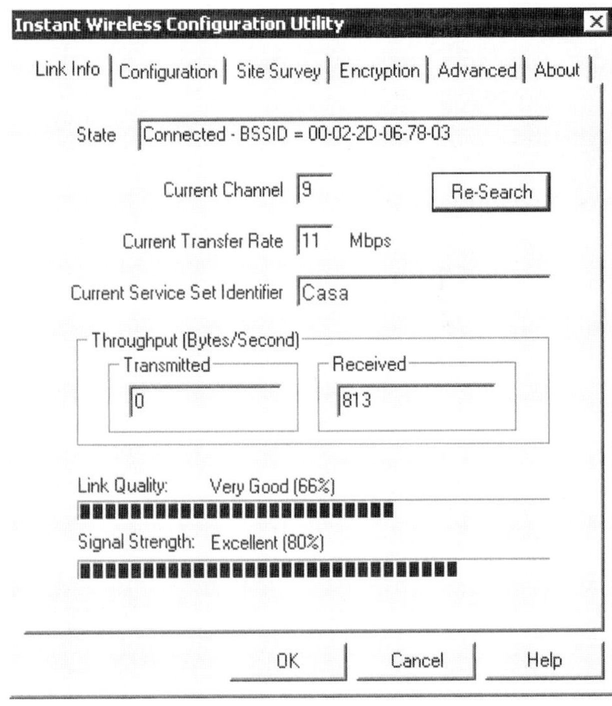

• **Figure 23.82** Wireless configuration utility

Wireless Network Modes

The simplest wireless network consists of two or more PCs communicating directly with each other *sans* cabling or any other intermediary hardware. More complicated wireless networks use a WAP to centralize wireless communication and bridge wireless network segments to wired network segments. These two different methods are called *ad hoc* mode and *infrastructure* mode.

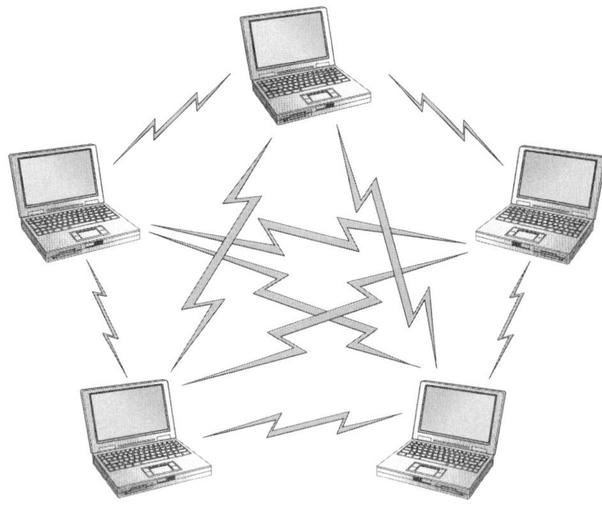

• **Figure 23.83** Wireless ad hoc–mode network

Ad hoc Mode

Ad-hoc mode is sometimes called peer-to-peer mode, with each wireless node in direct contact with each other node in a decentralized free-for-all, as shown in Figure 23.83. Two or more wireless nodes communicating in ad hoc mode form what's called an *Independent Basic Service Set* (IBSS). Ad hoc mode–networks are easier to configure than infrastructure mode networks, and are suited for small groups of computers (less than a dozen or so) that need to transfer files or share printers. Ad hoc networks are also good for temporary networks such as study groups or business meetings.

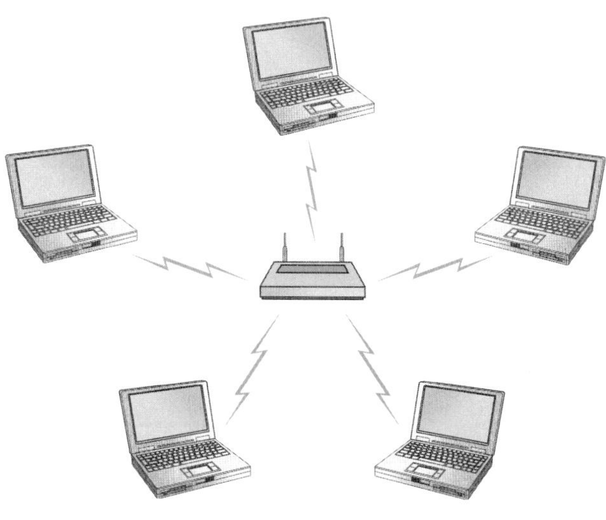

• **Figure 23.84** Wireless infrastructure mode network

Infrastructure Mode

Wireless networks running in infrastructure mode use one or more WAPs to connect the wireless network nodes to a wired network segment, as shown in Figure 23.84. A single WAP servicing a given area is called a *Basic Service Set* (BSS). This service area can be extended by adding more WAPs. This is called, appropriately, an *Extended Basic Service Set* (EBSS).

Wireless networks running in infrastructure mode require more planning and are more complicated to configure than ad hoc–mode networks, but they also give you finer control over how the network operates. Infrastructure mode is better suited to business networks or networks that need to share dedicated resources like Internet connections and centralized databases. If you plan on setting up a wireless network for a large number of PCs, or need to have centralized control over the wireless network, then infrastructure mode is what you need.

Wireless Networking Security

One of the major complaints against wireless networking is that it offers weak security. In many cases, the only thing you need to do to access a wireless network is walk into a WAP's coverage area and turn on your wireless device! Further, data packets are floating through the air instead of safely wrapped up inside network cabling. What's to stop an unscrupulous PC tech with the right equipment from grabbing those packets out of the air and reading that data himself?

Wireless networks use three methods to secure access to the network itself and secure the data that's being transferred. The SSID (network name) parameter ensures that only wireless network devices configured with the same SSID are permitted access to the network. You can tighten security even further by employing *MAC filtering*, a way of creating a list of machines that are permitted to access the network. Enabling wireless encryption through either *Wireless Equivalency Privacy* (WEP) or *Wi-Fi Protected Access* (WPA) ensures that the data packets themselves are secure while in transit.

SSID

One of the main security weaknesses with wireless networks is that, out of the box, there's *no* security configured at all! Wireless devices *want* to be heard, and WAPs are usually configured to broadcast their presence to their

network's coverage area. Data packets that lack the correct SSID name in the header are rejected.

MAC Filtering

Most WAPs also support MAC address filtering, a method that enables you to limit access to your wireless network based on the physical, hard-wired address of the units' wireless NIC. MAC filtering is a handy way of creating a type of "accepted users" list to limit access to your wireless network. A table stored in the WAP lists the MAC addresses that are permitted to participate in the wireless network. Any data packets that don't contain the MAC address of a node listed in the table are rejected.

WEP

The next step up in wireless security is enabling WEP encryption. Enabling WEP ensures that data is secured while in transit over the airwaves. WEP encryption uses a standard 40-bit encryption to scramble data packets. Many vendors also support 104-bit encryption. Note that some vendors advertise 128-bit encryption, but they actually use a 104-bit encryption key. WEP provides a level of authentication based on the wireless node's MAC address. Note that it doesn't perform user authentication at all.

One important note to consider is that WEP doesn't provide complete end-to-end encryption. WEP works on the two lowest OSI network layers, the Data Link and Physical layers. Encryption is stripped from the data packet as it travels "up" through the subsequent network layers. For true end-to-end encryption, you need to upgrade to WPA.

WPA

WPA addresses the weaknesses of WEP, and acts as a sort of security protocol upgrade to WEP-enabled devices. WPA offers security enhancements such as an encryption key integrity-checking feature and user authentication through the industry-standard *Extensible Authentication Protocol* (EAP). The use of EAP is a huge security improvement over WEP's MAC address authentication scheme. After all, MAC addresses are fairly easy to "sniff" out, since they're transmitted in unencrypted, clear-text format. User names and passwords are encrypted, and therefore much more secure. Even with these enhancements, WPA is only intended as an interim security solution until the IEEE 802.11i security standard is finalized and implemented.

Speed and Range Issues

Wireless networking data throughput speeds are dependent on several factors. Foremost is the standard that the wireless devices use. Depending on the standard used, wireless throughput speeds range from a measly 2 Mbps to a respectable 54 Mbps. One of the other factors affecting speed is the distance between wireless nodes (or between wireless nodes and centralized access points). Wireless devices dynamically negotiate the top speed at which they can communicate a without dropping too many data packets. Speed decreases as distance increases, so the maximum throughput speed is only achieved at extremely close range (less than 25 feet or so). At the outer reaches of a device's effective range, speed may decrease to around 1 Mbps before it drops out altogether.

Speed is also affected by interference from other wireless devices operating in the same frequency range—such as cordless phones or baby monitors—and by solid objects. So-called *dead spots* occur when something capable of blocking the radio signal comes between the wireless network nodes. Large electrical appliances such as refrigerators are *very* effective at blocking a wireless network signal! Other culprits include electrical fuse boxes, metal plumbing, air conditioning units, and so on.

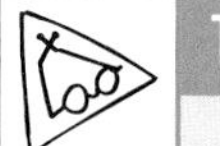

Tech Tip

Increasing Wireless Range

Range can be increased in a couple of ways. First, you can install multiple WAPs to permit "roaming" between one WAP's coverage area and another's—an EBSS, as described earlier in this chapter. Second, you can install a signal booster that increases a single WAP's signal strength, thus increasing its range.

Wireless networking range is hard to define, and you'll see most descriptions listed with qualifiers such as "*around* 150 feet" and "*about* 300 feet." This is simply because, like throughput speed, range is greatly affected by outside factors. Interference from other wireless devices affects range, as does interference from solid objects. The maximum ranges listed in the next section are those presented by wireless manufacturers as the theoretical maximum ranges. In the real world, you'll only see these ranges under the most ideal circumstances. True effective range is probably about half what you see listed.

Wireless Networking Standards

To gain a better understanding of wireless network technology, let's take a brief look at the standards that they use.

Look for basic troubleshooting questions on the A+ Certification exams dealing with factors that affect wireless connectivity, range, and speed.

IEEE 802.11-Based Wireless Networking

The IEEE 802.11 wireless Ethernet standard defines methods by which devices may communicate using *spread-spectrum* radio waves. Spread-spectrum broadcasts data in small, discrete chunks over the different frequencies available within a certain frequency range. All of the 802.11-based wireless technologies broadcast and receive at 2.4 GHz (with the exception of 802.11a, which uses 5 GHz). The original 802.11 standard has been extended to 802.11*a*, 802.11*b*, and 802.11*g* variations used in Wi-Fi wireless networks, and also *hybridized* (combined with another wireless communication technology) to form the *Shared Wireless Access Protocol* (SWAP) used in HomeRF networks.

Wireless devices can only communicate with other wireless devices that use the same standard. The exception to this is 802.11g, which is backwards-compatible with 802.11b devices (although at the lower speed of 802.11b). The following paragraphs describe the important specifications of each of the popular 802.11-based wireless networking standards.

While its theoretical range tops out at about 150 feet, in a typical office environment, its maximum range will be lower. Despite the superior speed of 802.11a, it isn't widely adopted in the PC world.

802.11b 802.11b is practically ubiquitous in wireless networking. The 802.11b standard supports data throughput of up to 11 Mbps (with actual throughput averaging 4 to 6 Mbps)—on par with older wired 10BaseT networks—and a maximum range of 300 feet under ideal conditions. In a typical office environment, its maximum range will be lower.

802.11b networks can be secured though the use of WEP and WPA encryption. The main downside to using 802.11b is, in fact, that it's the most widely used standard. The 2.4-GHz frequency is already a crowded place, so you're likely to run into interference from other wireless devices.

802.11g The latest-and-greatest version of 802.11, 802.11g offers data transfer speeds equivalent to 802.11a, up to 54 Mbps, with the wider 300-foot range of 802.11b. More importantly, 802.11g is backwards-compatible with 802.11b, meaning that the same 802.11g WAP can service both 802.11b and 802.11g wireless nodes.

Table 23.3 compares the important differences between the different versions of 802.11.

Table 23.3 Comparison of 802.11 Standards

Standard	802.11a	802.11b	802.11g
Max. Throughput	54 Mbps	11 Mbps	54 Mbps
Max. Range	150 feet	300 feet	300 feet
Frequency	5 GHz	2.4 GHz	2.4 GHz

Tech Tip

Spread-Spectrum Broadcasting

The 802.11 standard defines two different spread-spectrum broadcasting methods: direct-sequence spread-spectrum *(DSSS) and* frequency-hopping spread-spectrum *(FHSS). DSSS sends data out on different frequencies at the same time, while FHSS sends data on one frequency at a time, constantly shifting (or* hopping*) frequen-*

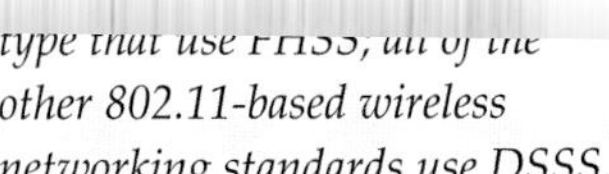

other 802.11-based wireless networking standards use DSSS.

Wi-Fi is by far the most widely adopted wireless networking type today. Not only do thousands of private businesses and homes have wireless networks, but many public places such as coffee shops and libraries also offer Internet access through wireless networks.

You need to know the differences between 802.11a, 802.11b, and 802.11g.

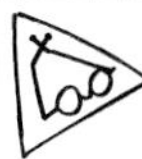

Tech Tip

Wi-Fi Certification

Technically, only wireless devices that conform to the extended versions of the 802.11 standard—802.11a, 802.11b, and 802.11g—are Wi-Fi certified. Wi-Fi certification comes from the Wi-Fi Alliance (formerly the Wireless Ethernet Compatibility Alliance, or WECA), a non-profit industry group made up of over 175 member companies who design and manufacturer wireless networking products. Wi-Fi certification ensures compatibility between wireless networking devices made by different vendors. First-generation devices that use the older 802.11 standard are not Wi-Fi certified, and so may or may not work well with devices made by different vendors.

Tech Tip

The 802.11 Standard

Devices that use the original 802.11 (with no letter) standard are a rarity these days. You're likeliest to find them in service on some brave early adopter's network. The original 802.11 standard was hampered by both slow speeds (2 Mbps maximum) and limited range (about 150 feet). However, 802.11 employed some of the same features that are in use in the current wireless standards. 802.11 uses the 2.4-GHz broadcast range, and security is provided by the use of industry-standard WEP and WPA encryption.

The A+ Certification exams focus on the 802.11 standards of wireless networking. You're unlikely to see questions on HomeRF.

Table 23.3 Comparison of 802.11 Standards *(continued)*

Standard	802.11a	802.11b	802.11g
Security	SSID, MAC filtering, Industry-standard WEP, WPA	SSID, MAC filtering, Industry-standard WEP, WPA	SSID, MAC filtering, Industry-standard WEP, WPA
Compatibility	802.11a	802.11b	802.11b, 802.11g
Spread-spectrum method	DSSS	DSSS	DSSS
Communication mode	Ad hoc or infrastructure	Ad hoc or infrastructure	Ad hoc or infrastructure
Description	Products that adhere to this standard are considered "Wi-Fi Certified." Eight available channels. Less prone to interference than 802.11b and 802.11g.	Products that adhere to this standard are considered "Wi-Fi Certified." Fourteen channels available in the 2.4-GHz band (only eleven of which can be used in the U.S. due to FCC regulations). Three non-overlapping channels.	Products that adhere to this standard are considered "Wi-Fi Certified." Improved security enhancements. Fourteen channels available in the 2.4-GHz band (only eleven of which can be used in the U.S. due to FCC regulations). Three non-overlapping channels.

Infrared Wireless Networking

Wireless networking using infrared technology is largely overlooked these days, probably due to the explosion of interest in the newer and faster wireless standards. This is a shame, because infrared provides an easy way to transfer data, often without the need to purchase or install any additional hardware or software on your PCs.

Infrared Data Association Standard Communication through infrared devices is enabled via the *Infrared Data Association* (IrDA) protocol. The IrDA protocol stack is a widely supported industry standard, and has been included in all versions of Windows since Windows 95.

Speed- and range-wise, infrared isn't very impressive. Infrared devices are capable of transferring data up to 4 Mbps. Not too shabby, but hardly stellar. The maximum distance between infrared devices is 1 meter. Infrared links are direct line-of-sight, and are susceptible to interference. An infrared link can be disrupted by anything that breaks the beam of light—a badly placed can of Mountain Dew, a co-worker passing between desks, or even bright sunlight hitting the infrared transceiver can cause interference.

Infrared is only designed to make a point-to-point connection between two devices in ad hoc mode. No infrastructure mode is available. You can, however, use an infrared access point device to enable Ethernet network communication using IrDA. Infrared devices operate at half-duplex, meaning that while one is talking, the other is listening—they can't talk and listen at the same time. IrDA has a mode that emulates full-duplex communication, but it's really half-duplex. Security-wise, the IrDA protocol offers exactly nothing in the way of encryption or authentication. Infrared's main security feature is the fact that you have to be literally within arm's reach to establish a link. Clearly, infrared is not the best solution for a dedicated network connection, but for a quick file transfer or print job without getting your hands dirty, it'll do in a pinch. Table 23.4 lists infrared's important specifications.

Configuring Wireless Networking

The mechanics of setting up a wireless network don't differ much from a wired network. Physically installing a wireless network adapter is the same as installing a wired NIC, whether it's an internal PCI card, a PCMCIA card, or an external USB device. Simply install the device and let Plug and Play handle detection and resource allocation. Install the device's supplied driver when prompted, and you're practically done. Unless you're using Windows XP, you also need to install the wireless network configuration utility supplied with your wireless network adapter so that you can set your

Wi-Fi and HomeRF wireless networks both support ad hoc and infrastructure operation modes. Which mode you choose depends on the number of wireless nodes you need to support, the type of data sharing they'll perform, and your management requirements.

Ad hoc Mode Ad hoc wireless networks don't need a WAP. The only requirements in an ad hoc–mode wireless network are that each wireless node be configured with the same network name (SSID), and that no two nodes use the same IP address. Figure 23.85 shows a wireless network configuration utility with Ad-hoc mode selected.

You may also have to select a common channel for all ad hoc nodes. The only other configuration steps to take are to make sure that no two nodes are using the same IP address (this step is usually unnecessary if all PCs are using DHCP), and to ensure that the File and Printer Sharing service is running on all nodes.

Table 23.4	Infrared
Standard	**Infrared (IrDA)**
Max. Throughput	Up to 4 Mbps
Max. Range	1 meter (39 inches)
Security	None
Compatibility	IrDA
Communication mode	Point-to-point ad hoc
Description	HomeRF is less prone to interference, and you can set up multiple HomeRF networks in the same area.

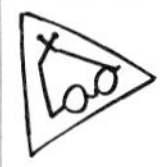

Tech Tip

HomeRF

HomeRF, as the name implies, is intended for home use, not for use in large business network environments. It is easy to set up and maintain but doesn't offer much in the way of range (about 150 feet, maximum). Early HomeRF devices were fairly slow, clocking in at a maximum of 2 Mbps, but the later version 2.0 operates at a respectable 10 Mbps, and also

Ethernet standard for data. HomeRF uses seven channels in the 2.4-GHz range, six of which are dedicated to voice communication with the remaining one used for data.

Because HomeRF devices use FHSS spread-spectrum broadcasting method, they are less prone to interference and somewhat more secure than Wi-Fi devices. HomeRF uses a proprietary 56-bit (128-bit in version 2.0) encryption algorithm instead of the industry-standard WEP and WPA that 802.11 uses. Also, instead of an SSID name, HomeRF uses what they call a Network ID (NWID)*, which is somewhat more secure.*

Apple computers also support IrDA, as do Linux PCs.

Tech Tip

Bluetooth Wireless

Bluetooth wireless technology (named for 9th-century Danish king Harald Bluetooth) is designed to create small wireless Personal Area Networks *(PANs) that link PCs to peripheral devices such as PDAs and printers, input devices like keyboards and mice, and even consumer electronics like cell phones, home stereos, televisions, home security systems, and so on. Bluetooth is* not *designed to be a full-function networking solution, nor is it meant to compete with either Wi-Fi or HomeRF. If anything, Bluetooth is poised to replace infrared as a means to connect PCs to peripherals.*

The IEEE organization has made Bluetooth the basis for its forthcoming 802.15 standard for wireless PANs. Bluetooth uses the FHSS spread-spectrum broadcasting method, switching among any of the 79 frequencies available in the 2.45-GHz range. Bluetooth hops frequencies some 1,600 times per second, making it highly resistant to interference. Bluetooth transfers data from 723 Kbps to 1, count 'em 1, Mbps, with a maximum range of 33 feet. Some high-powered Bluetooth devices have throughput speed of a whopping 2 Mbps and a maximum range of up to 300 feet, but these are uncommon.

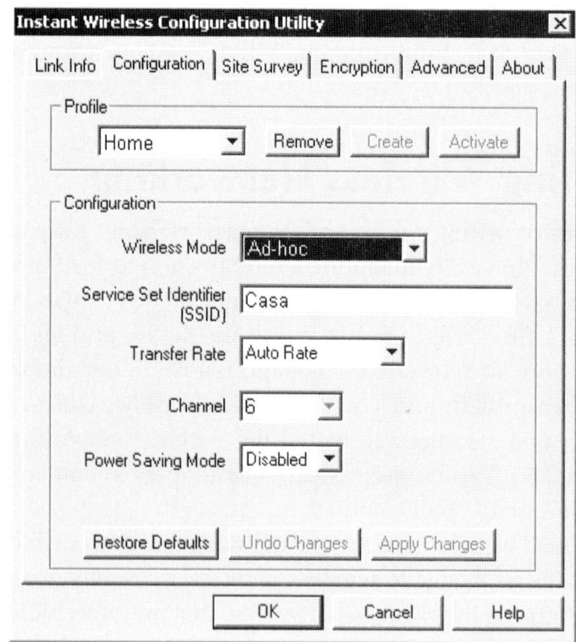

• **Figure 23.85** Selecting ad hoc mode in wireless configuration utility

Infrastructure Mode Typically, infrastructure mode wireless networks employ one or more WAPs connected to a wired network segment, a corporate intranet or the Internet, or both. As with ad hoc–mode wireless networks, infrastructure mode networks require that the same SSID be configured on all nodes and WAPs. Figure 23.86 shows a WAP

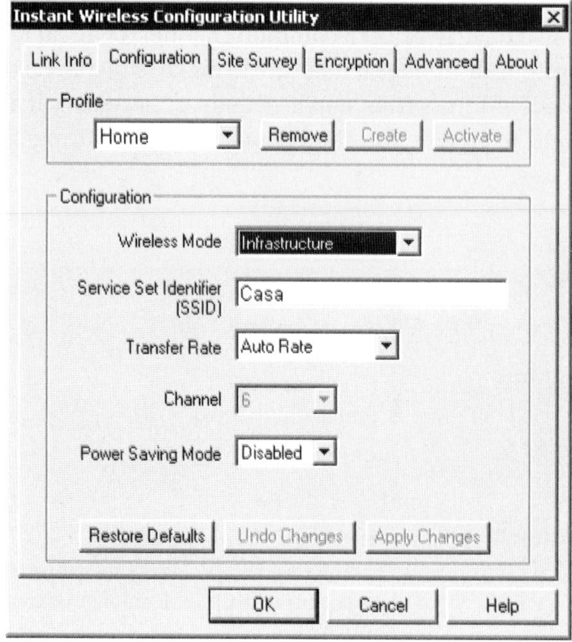

• **Figure 23.86** Selecting infrastructure mode in wireless configuration utility

configuration utility set to Infrastructure mode. Depending on the capabilities of your WAP, you may also configure DHCP options, filtering, and so on.

WAPs have an integrated web server and are configured through a browser-based setup utility. Typically, you fire up your web browser on one of your network client workstations and enter the WAP's default IP address, such as 192.168.1.1, to bring up the configuration page. You will need to supply an administrative password, included with your WAP's documentation, to log in (see Figure 23.87). Setup screens vary from vendor to vendor and from model to model. Figure 23.88 shows the initial setup screen for a popular Linksys WAP/router.

Configure the SSID option where indicated. Channel se-

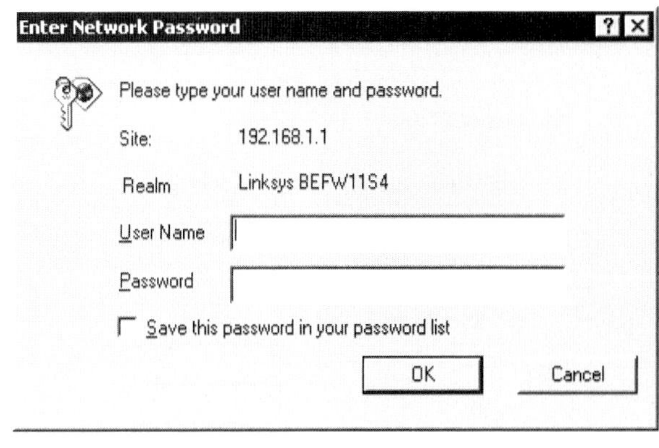

• Figure 23.87 Security login for Linksys WAP

To increase security even further, use MAC filtering. Figure 23.89 shows the MAC filtering configuration screen on a Linksys WAP. Simply enter the MAC address of a wireless node that you wish to allow (or deny) access to

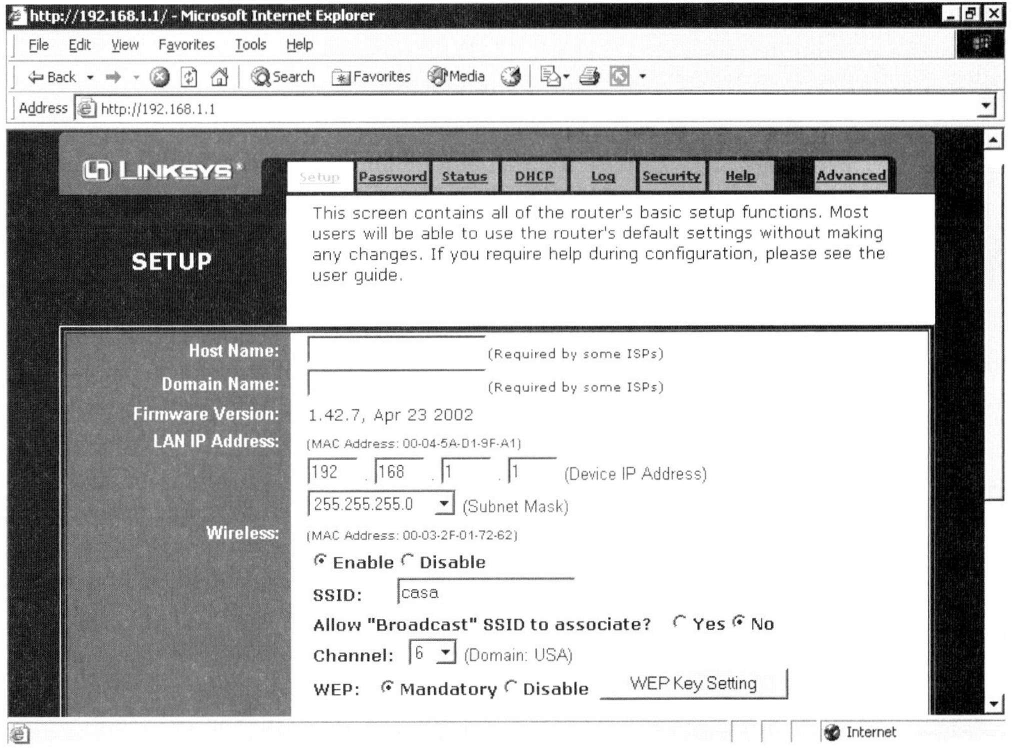

• Figure 23.88 Linksys WAP setup screen

Wireless Group MAC Table - Microsoft Internet Explorer

Wireless MAC Entry: 1~10

Station	MAC Address	Filter
1:	004756976f4a	☑
2:	0050da8cb777	☑
3:	0	☐
4:	0	☐
5:	0	☐
6:	0	☐
7:	0	☐
8:	0	☐
9:	0	☐
10:	0	☐

Apply Undo

• **Figure 23.89** MAC filtering configuration screen for a Linksys WAP

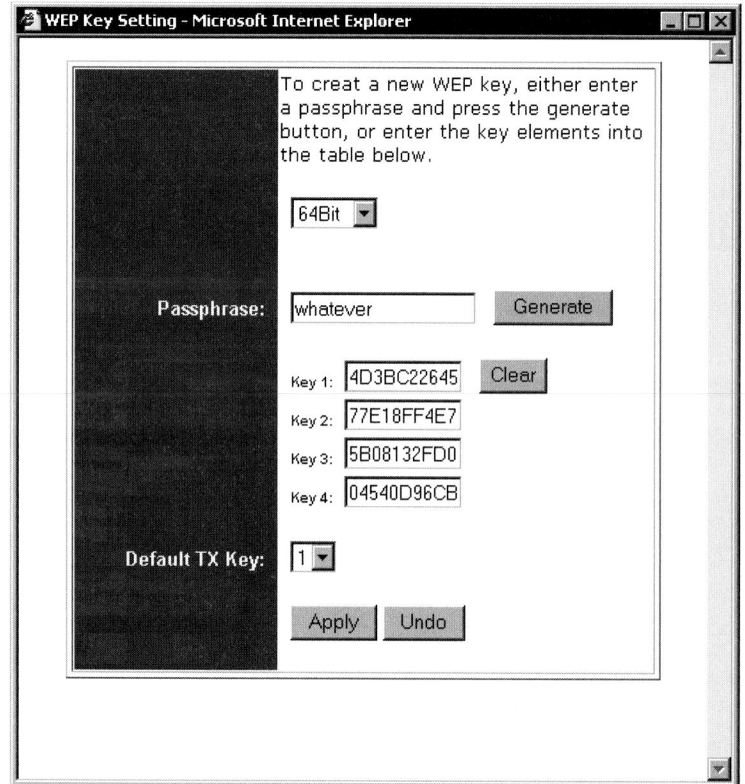

• **Figure 23.90** Encryption key configuration screen on Linksys WAP

your wireless network. Set up encryption by turning encryption on at the WAP and then generating a unique security key. Then configure all connected wireless nodes on the network with the same key information. Figure 23.90 shows the WEP key configuration dialog for a Linksys WAP.

You have the option of automatically generating a set of encryption keys or doing it manually—save yourself a headache and use the automatic method. Select an encryption level—the usual choices are either 64-bit or 128-bit—and then enter a unique passphrase and click the Generate button (or whatever the equivalent button is called on your WAP). Then select a default key and save the settings. The encryption level, key, and passphrase must match on the wireless client node or communication will fail. Many WAPs have the capability to export the encryption key data onto a floppy diskette for easy importing onto a client workstation, or you can manually configure encryption using the vendor-supplied configuration utility, as shown in Figure 23.91.

WPA encryption, if supported by your wireless equipment, is configured in much the same way. You may be required to input a valid user name and password to configure encryption using WPA.

Infrared

IrDA device support is very solid in the latest version of Windows—in fact, there's not much for us techs to configure. IrDA links are made between devices dynamically, without user interaction. Typically, there's nothing to configure on an infrared-equipped PC. Check your network settings to ensure that you've got the IrDA protocol installed and enabled, and you should be good to go (see Figure 23.92).

As far as networking goes with infrared, your choices are somewhat limited. Infrared is designed to connect only two systems together in ad hoc mode. This can be done simply to transfer files, or with a bit more configuration, you can configure the two PCs

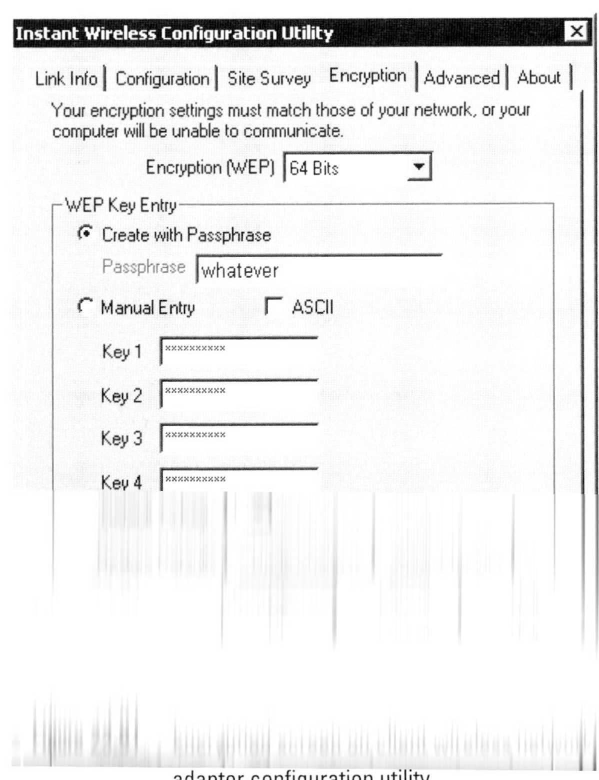

adapter configuration utility

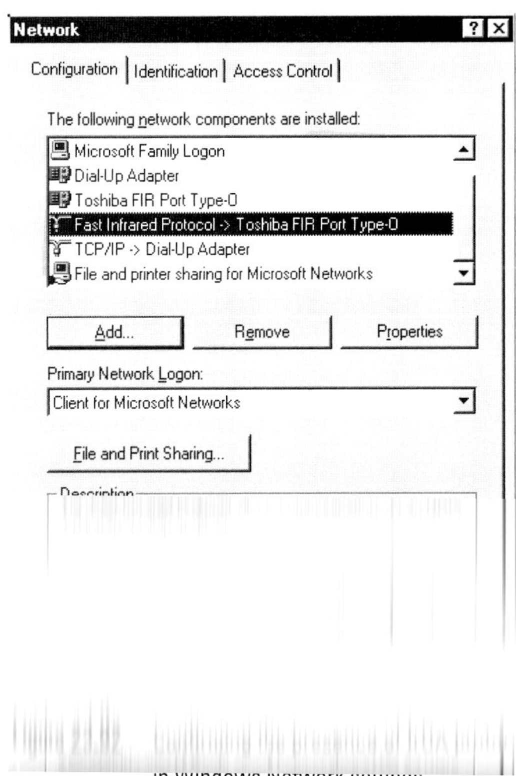

in Windows Network settings

to use IrDA in *direct-connection* mode. You can also use a special infrared access point to enable Ethernet LAN access via IrDA.

Transferring Files via Infrared File transfers via IrDA are as simple as can be. When two IrDA-enabled devices "see" each other, the sending (primary) device negotiates a connection to the receiving (secondary) device, and *voilà*. It's just "point and shoot"! Figure 23.93 shows Windows 2000's *Wireless Link* applet. Use this to configure file transfer options and the default location for received files. You can send a file over the infrared connection by specifying a location and one or more files using the Wireless Link dialog box; dragging and dropping files onto the Wireless Link icon; alternate-clicking the file(s) in Windows Explorer or My Computer and selecting Send To Infrared Recipient; or printing to a printer configured to use an infrared port.

Networking via Infrared Direct network connections between two PCs using infrared are similar to using a null-modem cable to connect two PCs together via a serial port. Modern versions of Windows make this type of connection extremely easy by employing wizards. Simply select Connect Directly to Another Computer and follow the prompts, choosing your infrared port as the connection device.

Try This!

Set Up a Wireless Network

Getting a wireless network up and running can be fun and it's certainly a useful skill to have, so try this!

1. Install wireless NICs in two or more PCs and then get them chatting in ad hoc mode. Don't forget to change the SSID!
2. Once you've got them talking in ad hoc mode, add a WAP and get them chatting in infrastructure mode.
3. If you don't have a lab, but do have access to an Internet cafe (or coffee shop offering wireless), go there and ask someone to show you how they connect. Don't be shy! People love showing off technology!

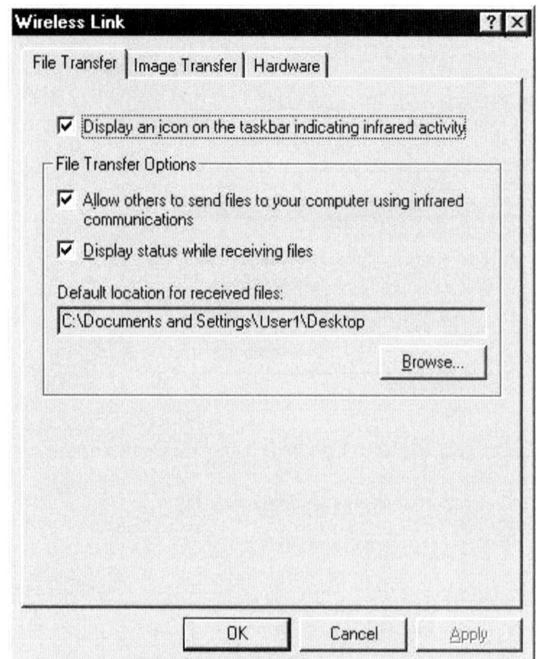

• **Figure 23.93** Windows 2000 Wireless Link applet

• **Figure 23.94** Laptop using infrared access point

An infrared access point combines an infrared transceiver with an Ethernet NIC and translates the IrDA protocol into an Ethernet signal, enabling you to log on to your network and access resources. Figure 23.94 shows a laptop accessing an Ethernet LAN through an infrared access point.

Troubleshooting Networks

Once you go beyond a single PC and enter the realm of networked computers, your troubleshooting skills need to take a giant leap up in quality. Think of the complexity added with networks. Suddenly you have multiple PCs with multiple users who could, at the drop of a hat, do all kinds of inadvertent damage to a properly functional PC. Networked PCs have a layer of networked hardware and resource sharing that adds a completely new dimension to a user's cry for help, "I can't print!"

Where can the problem lie in a *non-networked situation* if a person cannot print? Let's list out the obvious ones:

- Printer is not connected to the PC.
- Printer is out of ink.
- PC doesn't have the proper driver loaded.
- PC points by default to a printer other than the one to which the user thinks should print.

That's about it. Maybe the parallel port configuration is wrong in CMOS or the USB drivers aren't correct, but still... Now let's do the same thing with a *networked situation* where a user can't print. Here are the obvious *extra* issues, because all the local machine issues apply as well.

- Print server is down.
- Printer is locked by another user.
- The client PC doesn't have network connectivity.
- The NIC driver is bad or incorrect.
- The client PC doesn't have the proper printer drivers installed for the networked printer.
- The cable between the client PC's NIC and the nearest switch is bad.
- The port to which the cable connects is bad.
- The switch failed.
- Somebody in an office down the hall spilled coffee on the printer inside the mechanism and then didn't fess up to the accident.

Try This!

Working with Infrared Connections

If you have a couple of infrared-capable devices among your fellow students, check out the settings for infrared connectivity. With PDAs, as you'll recall from Chapter 21, the feature is called *beaming*. Try connecting to the other device or devices by sending a file.

That's a lot of variables, and it's just scratching the surface. We live in a networked world and it's time to elevate your troubleshooting skills and methodologies to the next level. This section gives you a series of steps to use when performing any type of PC or network troubleshooting. Let's look at ways to apply your tech skills and general communication skills to get to the bottom of a problem and get that problem fixed!

Verify the Symptom

The one thing that all PC problems have in common is a symptom. If there wasn't something happening (or not happening) to users as they tried to do whatever they need to do on their computer, you wouldn't have a problem at all, would you? Unfortunately, the vast majority of users out there aren't A+

[illegible]

Tom just started over in the Accounting department this week and has been a pain in the rear end to you. Ah, the things you might want to say to this person:

> **You:** "No. I only help non-pain-in-the-rear accountants."

> **You:** "Let me check my appointment schedule… Ah, yes. I can check on your problem in two weeks. Monday at 4:00 P.M. okay for you?"

But, of course, you had the audacity to choose the beloved profession of IT tech support, so you don't get to ask the questions you want to ask. Rather, you need to take a position of leadership and get to the bottom of the problem, and that means understanding the symptom. Take a deep breath, smile, and get to work. You have two issues to deal with at this point. First, if you're working with a user you must try to get the user to describe the symptom. Second, whether you're working on a system alone or if you're talking to a user on the telephone, you must verify that the symptom is legitimate.

Getting a user to describe a symptom is often a challenge. Users are not techs and as a result their perception of the PC is very different than yours. But on the same token most users know a bit about PCs—you want to take advantage of a user's skill and experience whenever you can. A personal example of verifying the symptom: once I got a call from a user telling me that his "screen was blank." I told him to restart his system. To which he responded, "Shouldn't I shut down the PC first?" I said: "I thought you just told me the screen was blank!" He replied: "That's right. There's nothing on the screen but my Desktop."

When Did It Happen?

Once you know the symptom, you need to try to inspect the problem yourself. This doesn't mean you need to go to the system, as many real problems are easily fixed by the user, under your supervision. But you must understand when the problem occurs in order to zero in on where to look for the solution. Does it happen at boot? It might be a CMOS/BIOS issue. Is it taking place as the OS loads? Then you need to start checking initialization files. Does it take place when the system runs untouched for a certain amount of time? Then maybe the power management could come into play.

What Has Changed?

Systems that run properly tend to continue to run properly. Systems that have a hardware or software change done to them have a much higher chance of not running properly than a system that has not had a change. If something has gone wrong, talk to the user to see if anything has happened since the system last worked properly. Has new software been installed? Did they add some new RAM? Have they changed the Windows Domain? Did they run a Windows Update? Did they drop the monitor on the floor? Not only do you need to consider those types of possible changes, you must then make sure that any unrelated changes don't send you down the wrong path. The fact that someone installed a new floppy drive yesterday probably doesn't have anything to do with the printer that isn't working today.

Last, consider side effects of changes that don't seem to have anything to do with the problem. I once had a customer's system that kept freezing up in Windows. I knew they had just added a second hard drive, but the system booted up just fine and ran normally—except it would freeze up after a few minutes. The hard drive wasn't the problem. The problem was that they unplugged the CPU fan in the process. When I discover a change has been made, I like to visualize the process of the change to consider how that change may have directly or indirectly contributed to a problem. In other words, if you run into a situation where a person added a NIC to a functioning PC that now won't boot, what part of the installation process could you foul up to cause a PC to stop working?

Check the Environment

I use the term *environment* in two totally different fashions. The first way is the most classic definition: the heat, humidity, dirt, and other outside factors that may affect the operation of the system. The other environment term is more technical and addresses the computing environment of the system and other surrounding systems: What type of system do they run? What OS? What is their network connection? What are the primary applications they use? What antivirus program do they run? Do other people use the system?

Answering these questions gives you an overview of what is affecting this system both internally and externally. A quick rundown of these issues can reveal possible problems that might not be otherwise recognized. I once got a call from a user complaining the CD-ROM would not eject a CD. After a few quick questions, I discovered this was a laptop in a cheese factory that was covered in a light dusting of dried whey! (For those of you who don't know, whey is the liquid part of the cheese that gets removed during the cheese making process.) Whey dries to the consistency of wood glue—it was amazing to me the laptop worked at all!

Reproducing the Problem

My official rule on problems with a PC is this: "If a problem happens only once, it is not a problem." PCs are notorious for occasionally locking up, popping errors, and all types of little things that a quick reboot fixes and they don't happen again. Why do these happen? I don't know, although I'm sure if someone wanted me to guess I could come up with a clever explanation. But the majority of PCs simply don't have redundancy built in, and it's okay for them to occasionally "hiccup."

A problem becomes interesting to me if it happens more than once. If it happens twice, then there's a much higher chance it will happen a third time. I want to see it happen that third time—under my supervision. I will direct the user to try to reproduce the problem while I am watching to see what triggers the failure. This is a huge clue to helping you localize the real

Isolating the Symptom

With so many bits and pieces to a PC, you must take the time to try to isolate the symptom to ensure your fix is going to the software or hardware that really needs it. In hardware, that usually means removing suspect parts until only one possible part remains. In software, that usually means removing background programs, booting into Safe Mode, or trying to create a situation where only the suspected program is running.

Isolation takes on a whole new meaning with networks. One of the greatest tools in networking is isolation—does this problem happen on other systems, on other workgroups, on other PCs running DHCP? Whenever a problem takes place in networking, isolation is the key to determining the problem!

Separating Hardware from Software

Many problems that occur on a PC are difficult to isolate given that it is very difficult to determine if the problem lies in the software or in the hardware. If you find yourself in this situation, there are a few steps you can do to help you zero in on which side of the PC to suspect.

Known Good Hardware

The absolute best way to know if a problem is hardware or software related is to replace the suspected piece of hardware with a known good part. If you can't tell whether a Windows page fault comes from bad RAM or a software incompatibility, quickly replacing the RAM with known good RAM should help you determine if the RAM or the software is to blame.

Uninstall/Reinstall

If you can do so easily, try uninstalling the suspected software and reinstalling. Many hardware/software problems magically disappear with a simple uninstall/reinstall.

Patching/Upgrading

Many hardware or software problems take place due to incompatibilities between the two suspect sides. Try upgrading drivers. Download patches or upgrades to software, especially if the hardware and the software are more than two years different in age. My new SoundBlaster Audigy has a very hard time running under Windows 95 without first properly patching Windows to the latest software drivers and support files!

Virus Check

Last, (maybe I should have put this first) always check for viruses! Today's viruses manifest so many different symptoms that failure to check for them is a study in time wasting. I recently got a new hard drive that started to make a nasty clicking noise—a sure sign of a failing hard drive. However, I ran an extensive virus check and guess what—it was a virus! Who would have thought! I checked with the hard drive maker's Web site, and my fears were confirmed. It just goes to show you—even the best of us can get caught by the simplest problems!

Research

Once you've got your mind wrapped around the problem, it's time to fix it. Unless the problem is either simple (network cable unplugged) or something you've seen before and know exactly how to fix, you'll almost certainly need to research the problem. The Internet makes this easy. One of my favorite tricks is when I get some bizarre error text—I just type the error into my search engine and most times get an automatic fix!

Make the Fix and Test

Once you have a good idea as to the problem and how to fix it, it's time to do the fix. Make sure you make backups—or at least warn the user of the risk to their system. If possible, try to remember how the system was before the fix so that you can go back to square one if the fix fails to work. After you perform the fix do whatever you need to do to make sure the system is now working properly. Have the user see the system is working properly so that they can "sign off" on your work.

Mike's Four-Layer Model

Network problems, by the very nature of the complexity of a network, usually make for more complex problems. Given that, I have a four-step process that I lovingly call "Mike's Four-Layer Model." These are the four things that go through my mind every time I have a problem. I think about four distinct "categories" to help me isolate the symptoms and make the right fix.

Hardware

Hardware is probably the most self-explanatory of the four categories. This covers the many different ways data can be moved from one PC to another. Does the system have a good connection—how's the cabling? This also covers network cards—are they installed properly and tested. Plus, the Hardware category hits on all of those interesting boxes, such as hubs, switches, and repeaters, among which all of the wires in the network run. If you can see it, it's under this category!

Protocols

This category covers the protocols like TCP/IP or NetBEUI. Is the protocol installed? Is it configured properly? Does any particular system's configuration prevent it from working with another system?

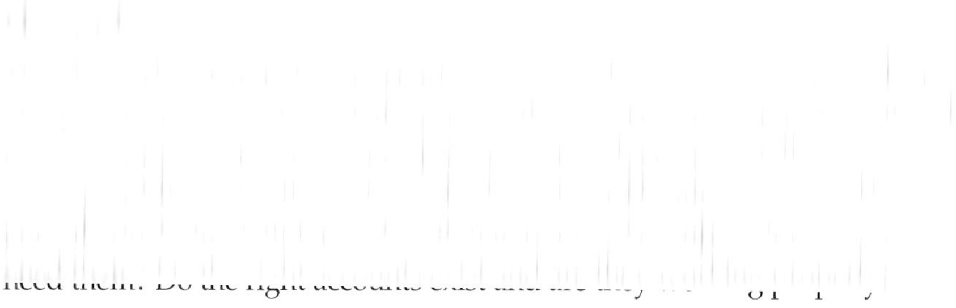

Shared Resources

Once all the systems, users, and groups are working properly, we need to identify the resources they will share. If a drive or folder is to be shared, the OS must provide a way to identify that drive or folder as available for sharing. The rules for naming shared resources are called *naming conventions*. A great example would be a system that offers its D:\FRED directory for sharing. This D:\FRED directory needs a network name such as SERVE_FRED. It is this network name that is displayed to all of the devices on the network.

Sharing a resource is only half the battle. Individual systems need to be able to access the shared resources. The network needs a process whereby a PC can look out on the network and see what is available. Having found those available resources, the PC then needs to make them look and act as though they were local resources. A network also needs to control access to resources. A laser printer, for example, might be available for sharing, but only for the accounting department, excluding other departments.

Beyond A+

Bluetooth

Bluetooth is *not* designed to be a full-fledged wireless networking solution. Bluetooth is made to replace the snake's nest of cables that currently connects most PCs to their various peripheral devices—keyboard, mouse, printer, speakers, scanner, and the like: but you won't be swapping out your 802.11-based networking devices with Bluetooth-based replacements anytime soon.

Having said that, there are areas where Bluetooth-enabled wireless networking is comparable to other wireless technologies:

- Like infrared, Bluetooth is acceptable for quick file transfers where a wired connection (or a faster wireless connection) is unavailable.
- Bluetooth's speed and range make it a good match for wireless print server solutions.
- Bluetooth is also more than acceptable for browsing the Internet via a PDA, handheld computer, cell phone, or laptop. Bluetooth's snail-like throughput speed of 1 to 2 Mbps is very compatible with the top speed of most cable or *x*DSL broadband Internet connections, and its 30-foot range is ideal for public Internet-enabled "hot spots" such as cafes, libraries, and airport lounges.

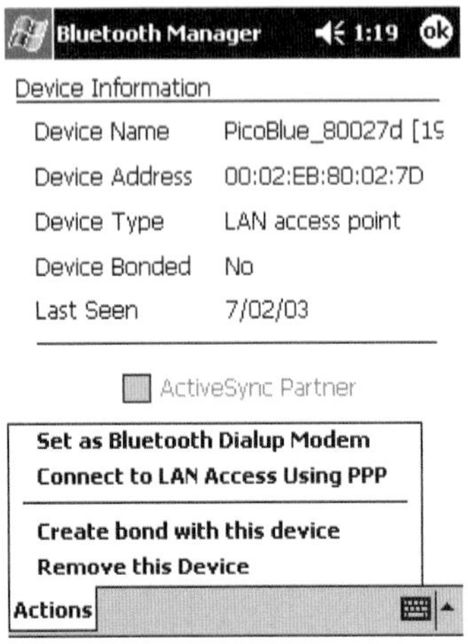

Figure 23.95 iPAQ Bluetooth Manager software connected to Bluetooth access point

Bluetooth Wireless Networking Hardware

Bluetooth hardware comes either integrated into many newer portable electronic gadgets like PDAs and cell phones or as an adapter added to an internal or external expansion bus. Bluetooth networking is enabled through ad hoc–styled PC-to-PC (or PDA, handheld computer, or cell phone-to-PC) connections, or in an infrastructure-like mode through Bluetooth access points. Bluetooth access points are very similar to 802.11-based access points, bridging wireless Bluetooth PAN segments to wired LAN segments.

Bluetooth Configuration

As with other wireless networking solutions, Bluetooth devices are completely Plug and Play. Just connect the adapter and follow the prompts to install the appropriate drivers and configuration utilities (these are supplied by your hardware vendor). Once installed, there's very little that you have to do: Bluetooth devices seek each other out and establish the master/slave relationship without any intervention on your part.

Connecting to a Bluetooth PAN is handled by specialized utility software provided by your portable device or Bluetooth device vendor. Figure 23.95 shows a Compaq iPAQ handheld computer running the Bluetooth Manager software to connect to a Bluetooth access point. Like their Wi-Fi counterparts, Bluetooth access points use a browser-based configuration utility. Figure 23.96 shows the main setup screen for a Belkin Bluetooth access point. Use this setup screen to check on the status of connected Bluetooth devices, configure encryption, MAC filtering, and other security settings, and use other utilities provided by the access point's vendor.

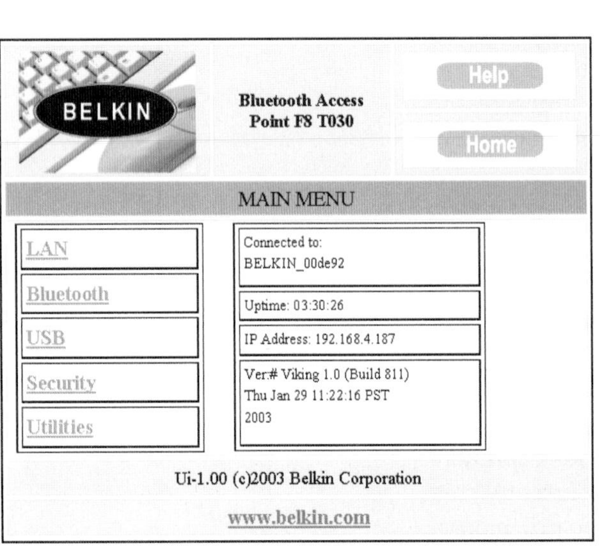

Figure 23.96 Belkin Bluetooth access point setup screen

Chapter 23 Review

Chapter Summary

After reading this chapter and completing the exercises, you should understand the following about networking.

Explain Network Technologies

- A PC connected to a network, called a client machine, must have a network interface card (NIC). Data is sent in discrete chunks called [illegible]
- The design of any network is based on one of several topologies, or physical layouts. 10Base5 is a bus topology, meaning that it sends data packets along one main cable, and every NIC on that cable reads every packet. Only one device can use the cable at a time, and collisions, which require devices to negotiate and re-send packets, are common. A cheaper alternative to Thicknet is Thin Ethernet, also called Thinnet or 10Base2. Most modern Ethernet networks use either 10BaseT or 100BaseT, both of which use unshielded twisted pair (UTP) cable.
- Modern NICs can run in full-duplex mode, meaning that they can both send and receive data at the same time.
- In a 10^{x}BaseT network, each PC connects to a hub via one of the hub's ports. The maximum distance from the hub to a connected device is 100 meters. Most hubs come with 4, 8, 16, or 24 ports, far fewer than the theoretical maximum of 1,024 ports per hub.
- Fiber optic Ethernet transmits light instead of electricity, achieving much greater maximum distances. Most fiber optic cables use one of two connectors: the square SC type and the round ST type.
- Token Ring networks are completely incompatible with Ethernet. They use a ring topology, most often a star ring. The ring topology uses a main bus cable that is a continuous ring. The connected NICs pass around a mini-packet called a token, and whichever NIC holds it has sole authority to send data.

Explain Network Operating Systems

- A network operating system (NOS) communicates with the PC hardware to make connections [illegible] called clients (because it's what they usually are) or workstations.
- A peer-to-peer network enables any or all of the machines on the network to act as a server. Every computer can perform both server and client functions.
- In a domain-based network environment, the security database for all systems is centralized on one or more servers called Domain Controllers. This database holds a single list of all users and passwords.
- Every Windows system based on the NT core kernel contains a very special account called Administrator that has complete and absolute power over the entire system. When you install Windows NT, 2000 or XP, you must create a password for the Administrator account.
- Any Windows 9*x*/Me system may become a member of a domain, although Windows 9*x*/Me's use of non-NTFS file systems makes its sharing security much weaker than later versions of Windows.
- Network protocol software takes the incoming data received by the network card, keeps it organized, sends it to the application that needs it, and then takes outgoing data from the application and

hands it to the NIC to be sent out over the network. All networks use some protocol.

- During the 1980s, IBM developed NetBIOS Extended User Interface (NetBEUI), the default protocol for Windows for Workgroups, LANtastic, and Windows 95. NetBEUI offers small size and a relatively high speed, but it can't be used for routing, limiting it to networks smaller than about 200 nodes.
- A node is any device that has a network connection—usually this means a PC, but other devices can be nodes.
- Novell invented the Internetwork Packet Exchange/Sequenced Packet Exchange (IPX/SPX) protocol and built all versions of its NetWare software around it. The IPX/SPX protocol is speedy, works well with routers, and takes up relatively little RAM when loaded.
- Transmission Control Protocol/Internet Protocol (TCP/IP) was originally developed for the Internet's DoD progenitor, ARPANET. TCP/IP is the best protocol for larger (>200 nodes) networks. The Internet uses TCP/IP as its default protocol. Windows NT also uses TCP/IP as its default protocol.
- To access data or resources across a network, a Windows PC needs to have client software installed for every kind of server that you want to access. When you install a network card and drivers, Windows installs at least one set of client software, called Client for Microsoft Networks, which enables your system to connect to a Microsoft network. To connect to a NetWare network, you need to add Client Service for NetWare.

Install and Configure Wired Networks

- To have network connectivity, you need a network interface card (the physical hardware that connects the computer system to the network wire), a protocol (the language that the computer systems use to communicate), a network client (the interface that allows the computer system to speak to the protocol), File and Print Sharing software that turns a Windows PC into a server, and the PC to the network hub or switch via some sort of cable.
- When you install a NIC, by default, Windows 2000 and XP Professional install the TCP/IP protocol (configured for Dynamic DHCP), the Client for Microsoft Networks, and File and Printer Service upon setup.
- Installing a NIC is the first step required to connect to a network. NICs are manufactured to operate on specific media and network types, such as 100BaseT Ethernet or 16-Mbps Token Ring. If your NIC is of recent vintage, it will be detected, installed, and configured automatically by Windows 2000 or Windows XP. Installing a NIC into any other Windows OS will require special drivers for that version of Windows from the manufacturer.
- To establish network connectivity, you need a network client installed and configured properly. The Client for Microsoft Networks is installed as part of the OS installation, and rarely needs configuration; in fact, few configuration options are available. To configure it in Windows XP, click Start, then alternate-click My Network Places and select Properties. In other versions of Windows, click Start | Settings | Network and Dial-up Connections. Double-click on the Local Area Connection icon. Click on the Properties button, highlight Client for Microsoft Networks, and click the Properties button.
- Client Service for NetWare provides access to file and print resources on NetWare servers. The NetWare server must be running Novell Directory Services (NDS) or bindery security (NetWare versions 3.*x* or 4.*x*). Client Service for NetWare supports some NetWare utilities and NetWare-aware applications. Once installed, Client Service for NetWare offers no configuration options. Client Service for NetWare does not support the IP protocol used in NetWare 5.*x*.
- Generally, all that is needed to establish a connection between computer systems using NetBEUI is a NetBIOS computer name.
- NWLink is Microsoft's implementation of IPX/SPX protocol, which includes an element for resolving NetBIOS names.
- Normally, the only settings you may need to specify to configure NWLink are the internal network number (used to identify NetWare servers) and frame type (which specifies how the data is packaged for transport over the network). Usually the default values are sufficient. By default, the frame type is set to Auto Detect.

- Systems in a TCP/IP network use IP addresses rather than names. IP addresses are four sets of eight binary numbers (octets) separated by a period (dotted-octet notation). The first part of the address identifies the network; the second part identifies the local computer (host) address. The subnet mask is a value that distinguishes which part of the IP address is the network address and which part is the host address. The subnet mask blocks out (or "masks") the network portions (octets) of an IP address.
- A traditional TCP/IP network divides IP addresses into classes, which correspond with the potential [illegible]
- A computer that wants to send data to another machine outside its LAN is not expected to know all the IP addresses of all the computers on the Internet. Instead, all IP machines know the name of one computer, called the default gateway, to which they pass all the data they need to send outside the LAN. This machine is usually the local router.
- IP addresses correlate with more human-friendly names. Special Domain Name Service (DNS) servers keep databases of IP addresses and their corresponding names.
- The last items that most TCP/IP networks require are Dynamic Host Configuration Protocol (DHCP) and Windows Internet Name Service (WINS). Every machine on a TCP/IP network must have an IP address. A permanent IP address assigned to a machine is known as a static IP address. DHCP enables you to create a pool of IP addresses that are given to machines when and only for as long as they need them. If you add a NIC to a Windows system, the TCP/IP settings are set to use DHCP.
- WINS enables Windows network names like SERVER1 to be correlated to IP addresses, like DNS does for Internet names. To set up WINS, either type in the IP address for the WINS server, or let DHCP handle it for you. Windows 2000 and XP use an improved "dynamic" DNS that supports both Internet names and Windows names.
- All versions of Windows come with handy tools to test TCP/IP. The ones you're most likely to use in the field are PING, WINIPCFG/IPCONFIG, NSLOOKUP, and TRACERT.
- All versions of Windows share drives and folders in basically the same manner. Simply alternate-click any drive or folder and select Sharing. Network resources can be mapped to a local resource name. This can be done in Windows 9*x*/Me from Windows Explorer or by alternate-clicking a share in Network Neighborhood (My Network Places for Windows Me) and selecting Map Network Drive.
- [illegible] standard—Home Radio Frequency (HomeRF) and Wireless Fidelity (Wi-Fi)—and those based on the newer Bluetooth technology. Wireless networks using infrared light are limited to those that use the Infrared Data Association protocol (IrDA).
- To extend the capabilities of a wireless Ethernet network, such as connecting to a wired network or sharing a high-speed Internet connection, you need a wireless access point (WAP).
- Wireless devices use the same networking protocols and client that their wired counterparts use, and operate using the CSMA/CA (Collision Avoidance) networking scheme, where nodes check before broadcasting. Wireless nodes also use the *Request to Send/Clear to Send* (RTS/CTS) protocol.
- The simplest wireless network consists of two or more PCs communicating directly with each other without cabling or any other intermediary hardware (ad hoc mode). More complicated wireless networks use a WAP to centralize wireless communication and bridge wireless network segments to wired network segments (infrastructure mode).
- Configuring a unique SSID name is the very least that you should do to secure a wireless network.
- Most WAPs also support MAC address filtering, a method that enables you to limit access to your

wireless network based on the physical, hard-wired address of the units' wireless network adapter.

- Enabling WEP encryption ensures that data is secured while in transit over the airwaves. WEP uses standard 40-bit encryption to scramble data packets. Many vendors also support 104-bit encryption. Although some vendors advertise 128-bit encryption, they actually use a 104-bit encryption key. WEP provides a level of authentication based on the wireless node's MAC address.
- WPA addresses the weaknesses of WEP, and acts as a sort of security protocol upgrade to WEP-enabled devices. WPA offers security enhancements such as an encryption key integrity-checking feature and user authentication through the industry-standard Extensible Authentication Protocol (EAP).
- Depending on the standard used, wireless throughput speeds range from a measly 2 Mbps to a respectable 54 Mbps.
- The IEEE 802.11 wireless Ethernet standard defines methods by which devices may communicate using spread-spectrum radio waves.
- Wi-Fi is by far the most widely adopted wireless networking type today. Technically, only wireless devices that conform to the 802.11a, 802.11b, and 802.11g standards are Wi-Fi certified, to ensure compatibility among different vendors. Only wireless devices that use the same standard can communicate, except that 802.11g is backward-compatible with 802.11b (although at the lower speed of 802.11b).
- Wireless networking using infrared (IR) technology is enabled via the Infrared Data Association—IrDA—protocol stack, a widely-supported industry standard, and has been included in all versions of Windows since Windows 95.
- Bluetooth wireless technology is designed to create small wireless Personal Area Networks (PANs) that link PCs to peripheral devices such as PDAs and printers, input devices like keyboards and mice, and even consumer electronics like cell phones, home stereos, televisions, home security systems, and so on. Bluetooth is not designed to be a full-function networking solution, nor is it meant to compete with either Wi-Fi or HomeRF.
- The mechanics of setting up a wireless network don't differ much from a wired network. Physically installing a wireless network adapter is the same as installing a wired NIC, whether it's an internal PCI card, a PCMCIA card, or an external USB device.
- Infrared is designed to connect two systems together in ad hoc mode to transfer files, or with a bit more configuration, in direct-connection mode (similar to using a null-modem cable to connect two PCs together via a serial port).

Troubleshoot Networks

- The one thing that all PC problems have in common is a symptom. If you're working with a user you must try to get the user to describe the symptom. Then you must verify that the symptom is legitimate. Try to inspect the problem yourself. Find out when it occurs in order to zero in on where to look for the solution.
- Systems are much more likely to have problems after a hardware or software change; check to see if that has happened since the system last worked properly.
- Check the environment to get an overview of what is affecting this system both internally and externally.
- If a problem happens twice, then there's a much higher chance it will happen a third time.
- Take the time to try to isolate the symptom to ensure your fix is going to the software or hardware that really needs it.
- Make backups—or at least warn the user of the risk—before you try a fix.
- Mike's Four-Layer Model is an approach to network troubleshooting. First, check the hardware, including connections, NICs, and hubs/switches/routers. Second, check that the protocols, like TCP/IP or NetBEUI, are installed and properly configured. Third, check the network setup, whether it includes a server or is peer-to-peer. Is the server set up as a server, with sharing enabled and a proper network name? Are appropriate users and groups defined, if needed, and appropriate accounts set up? Finally, check the shared resources. Have the appropriate resources been identified and made available for sharing to all relevant users? Are the individual systems set up to access the shared resources?

Key Terms

100BaseT *(822)*
10BaseT *(822)*
802.11b *(857)*
802.11g *(857)*
Administrator account *(831)*
Bus topology *(819)*
Coaxial cable *(819)*
Ethernet *(819)*
Hardware protocol *(818)*
Hub *(822)*
IP address *(839)*
Media Access Control (MAC) address *(818)*
Network interface card (NIC) *(817)*
Network operating system (NOS) *(828)*
Packets *(817)*
Ping *(840)*
RJ-45 *(823)*
Shielded twisted pair (STP) *(826)*
Subnet mask *(839)*
TCP/IP services *(840)*
Token Ring *(826)*
Unshielded twisted pair (UTP) *(822)*

Key Term Quiz

__________.

3. A(n) __________ enables a PC to act as a server and share data and services over a network.
4. The __________ is a value that distinguishes which part of an IP address is the network address and which part is the host address.
5. HTTP and TELNET are both examples of special sharing functions called __________.

surrounded by insulation and covered with a shield of braided cable.

9. The ________ connector is the standard connector used for UTP Ethernet installations.
10. A person logged into the __________ on a Windows NT system has the ability to read any file and run any program on the system.

Multiple-Choice Quiz

1. Everything worked fine on your 100BaseT network yesterday, but today no one can connect to the server. The server seems to be in good running order. Which of the following is the most likely problem?
   - **A.** Someone changed all the passwords for server access.
   - **B.** A malfunctioning hub.
   - **C.** Someone's T connector has come loose on the bus.
   - **D.** The server's cable is wired as TIA/EIA 568A and all the others are wired as TIA/EIA 568B.
2. Simon's Windows 2000 system can't contact a DHCP server to obtain an IP address automatically, but he can still communicate with other systems on his subnet. What feature of Windows 2000 makes this possible?
   - **A.** Subnet masking
   - **B.** Windows Internet Name Service
   - **C.** Automatic Private IP Addressing
   - **D.** Client for Microsoft Networks
3. Which of the following are true of NetBEUI? (Select all that apply.)
   - **A.** No logical addresses required
   - **B.** Supported only on Microsoft network systems
   - **C.** Supports routing
   - **D.** Supported by all versions of Windows through XP

4. Two wireless nodes that are communicating directly with each other, without any intermediary systems or hardware, are using what wireless mode?
   - **A.** Ad hoc
   - **B.** Bluetooth
   - **C.** Infrastructure
   - **D.** 802.11
5. James needs to connect his Windows XP system to a Windows 2000 network domain. Which of the following will get him to the screen he needs?
   - **A.** Control Panel | Client for Microsoft Networks | Log on to Windows NT domain
   - **B.** Alternate-click My Computer | Properties | Client for Microsoft Networks | Network ID
   - **C.** Control Panel | Network Connections | Network Identification | Log on to Windows NT domain
   - **D.** Alternate-click My Computer | Properties | Computer Name | Network ID
6. What is the maximum segment length of 10Base2 cable?
   - **A.** 20 meters
   - **B.** 54 meters
   - **C.** 185 meters
   - **D.** 240 meters
7. You need to change the TCP/IP settings on a Windows 9*x* computer that accesses the network directly through a NIC. How do you get to the proper screen to perform this task?
   - **A.** Control Panel | Networks | TCP/IP | Properties
   - **B.** My Computer | Networks | Server Type | TCP/IP Settings
   - **C.** My Computer | Networks | TCP/IP | Properties
   - **D.** Control Panel | Networks | Server Type | TCP/IP Settings
8. In a TCP/IP network, the two parts of a network address are the ________ and the _______.
   - **A.** Class, host
   - **B.** IP address, subnet mask
   - **C.** Client, server
   - **D.** TCP address, IP address
9. What is the meaning of the networking term *topology*?
   - **A.** The choice of network protocol
   - **B.** The cabling specification of a network
   - **C.** The physical layout of a network
   - **D.** A network that uses hubs
10. What device centrally connects wireless network nodes in the same way that a hub connects wired Ethernet PCs?
    - **A.** Bluetooth adapter
    - **B.** Wireless NIC
    - **C.** SSID
    - **D.** Wireless Access Point
11. What wireless security protocol supports user authentication through EAP?
    - **A.** WEP
    - **B.** WPA
    - **C.** MAC filtering
    - **D.** SSID
12. When two computers communicate across a network, the sender's MAC address, recipient's MAC address, data, and CRC are transmitted in a(n) _________.
    - **A.** Packet
    - **B.** IP unit
    - **C.** CSMA
    - **D.** Token
13. You need to check the status of the local area connection of a Windows XP machine on your Microsoft network. How do you get to the screen where you can perform this task? (Select all that apply.)
    - **A.** Start | alternate-click My Network Places | Properties | Local Area Connection
    - **B.** Start | Settings | Network and Dial-up Connections | Local Area Connection
    - **C.** Start | Control Panel | Network Connections | Local Area Connection
    - **D.** Alternate-click My Computer | Properties | Network Connections | Local Area Connection

14. What device must be plugged into the end of a bus cable to prevent packets from being reflected?

   A. A BNC connector

   B. A grounding plug

   C. A vampire connector

   D. A terminator

15. What is the defined cabling for 10BaseT networks?

   A. PVC

   B. UTP

   C. Plenum

   D. STP

Essay Quiz

1. Your office has recently received a box of networking equipment that's a mix of 10BaseT, [illegible]

[illegible] use. She inherited the building with some networking stuff in place, namely CAT5e strung through the walls and the ceiling to a central wiring area. All the offices have RJ-45 outlets for workstations. Write an essay detailing the technologies she could install using the existing equipment and why she might select one over the other(s). Include an explanation of the equipment she has already installed.

3. You get a late-night telephone call from a senior network tech with a crisis on her hands. "I need help getting 20 PCs networked within 24 hours, and your boss told me you might be able to assist [illegible]

[illegible] file server. Tag. You're it. Write a brief essay describing what you would need to know about your network and your boss to begin troubleshooting; describe the tool(s) you might use if your network uses TCP/IP.

5. Your company has decided to go wireless, but the department heads can't decide on a standard. Write an essay describing the differences between the three common 802.11 standards and any issues with security, and make a recommendation.

Lab Projects

Lab Project 23.1

This chapter described simple network protocols as almost interchangeable, that you could install NetBEUI on some networked PCs and it would enable them to communicate. Experiment with this idea. If you have a network of PCs that you can play with, install and enable just NetBEUI or IPX/SPX, but make sure TCP/IP is disabled. Try to share resources and access shared resources on other machines in the lab. Once you've tried that, install a different simple protocol and try it again.

• Lab Project 23.2

The PC is not the only device that can connect to an Ethernet network. Do an Internet search or a run to your local computer store and come back with a list of network devices. What did you find? How would they be used?

• Lab Project 23.3

Nearly every wireless hardware manufacturer wants to break the speed limits with wireless and have started debuting proprietary devices for running at over 100 Mbps. Do a search through the bigger companies' product lists and compare the devices. Companies include Linksys (www.linksys.com), Netgear (www.netgear.com), Microsoft (www.microsoft.com), and D-Link (www.d-link.com).

The Internet

chapter 24

"Let's see what's out there."

—Captain Jean-Luc Picard, *Star Trek: The Next Generation*, "Encounter at Farpoint"

In this chapter, you will learn how to

- **Explain how the Internet works**
- **Connect to the Internet**
- **Configure Internet software tools**

Imagine coming home from a long day at work building and fixing PCs, sitting down in front of your shiny new computer, double-clicking the single icon that sits dead center on your monitor... and suddenly you're enveloped in an otherworldly scene, where 200-foot trees slope smoothly into snow-white beaches and rich blue ocean. Overhead, pterodactyls soar through the air while you talk to a small chap with pointy ears and a long robe about heading up the mountain in search of a giant monster... TV show from the SciFi channel? Spielberg's latest film offering? How about an interactive game millions of people all over the planet play on a daily basis by connecting to the Internet? If you guessed the last one, you'd be right.

This chapter covers the skills you need as a PC tech to help people connect to the Internet. It starts with a brief section on how the Internet works along with the concepts of connectivity, and then goes into the specifics on hardware, protocols, and software that you use to make the Internet work for you. The "Beyond A+" section is beefier than other chapters because, although the A+ exams don't cover it, every tech needs to know how to assist clients with some of the *niceties* of the Internet. Let's get started!

■ Understanding the Internet

The Internet enables users to communicate with one another over vast distances, often in the blink of an eye. As a PC tech, you need to know how PCs communicate with the larger world for two reasons. First, knowing the process and pieces involved in the communication enables you to troubleshoot effectively when that communication goes away. Second, you need to be able to communicate knowledgeably with a network technician when he or she comes in to solve a more complex issue.

Root Servers and Backbones

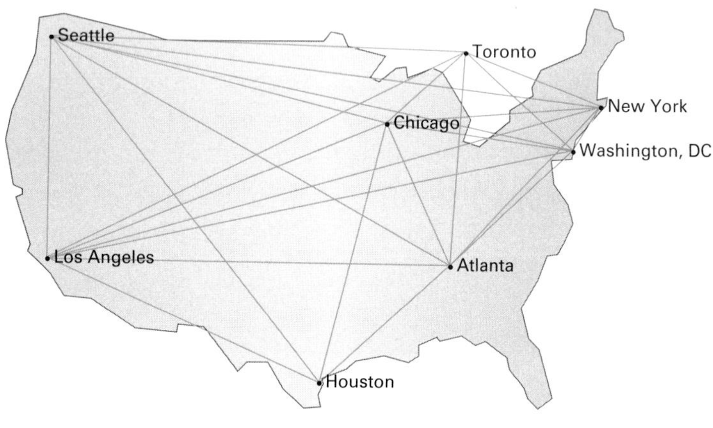

• **Figure 24.1** Internet root servers and backbones

The Internet consists of thousands of computers all over the world interwoven together through extremely fast networking connections called backbones. In the early days of the Internet, most of the computers were mainframe systems at universities around the United States. These eventually expanded to serve more and more of the world. Today, university mainframe and mini-computers still make up the majority of the *root servers* on the Internet, but major corporate and government computer centers provide much needed linkage and redundancy.

The Internet was designed to survive a catastrophic war or a devastating natural disaster by being extremely decentralized. All the root servers connect to more than one other root server, creating a big, interwoven framework for communication. Figure 24.1 illustrates the decentralized and interwoven nature of the Internet. The key reason for interweaving the backbones of the root Internet servers was to provide alternative pathways for data if one or more of the servers went down. If Jane in Houston sends a message to her friend Polly in New York City, for example, the shortest path between Jane and Polly in this hypothetical situation is this: Jane's message originates at Rice University in Houston, bounces to Emory University in Atlanta, flits through Virginia Commonwealth University in Richmond, and then zips into SUNY in New York City (Figure 24.2). Polly happily reads the message and life is great. The Internet functions as planned.

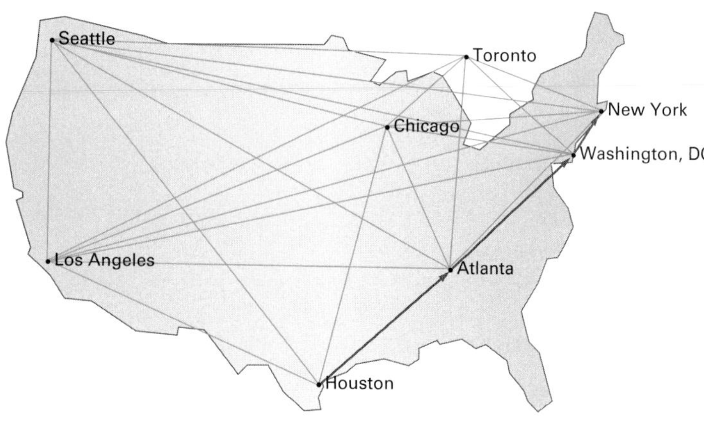

• **Figure 24.2** Message traveling from Houston to NYC

But what happens if the entire southeast USA experiences a huge power outage and every state from Virginia to Florida goes down? Jane's message would bounce back to Rice and the Rice computers. Being smart cookies, the computers would reroute the message to nodes that still functioned—say, Rice to University of Chicago, then University of Toronto, and then SUNY (Figure 24.3). All in a day's work for the highly redundant and adaptable Internet. At this point in the game (late 2003), the Internet simply cannot go down fully—barring, of course, a catastrophe of Biblical proportions.

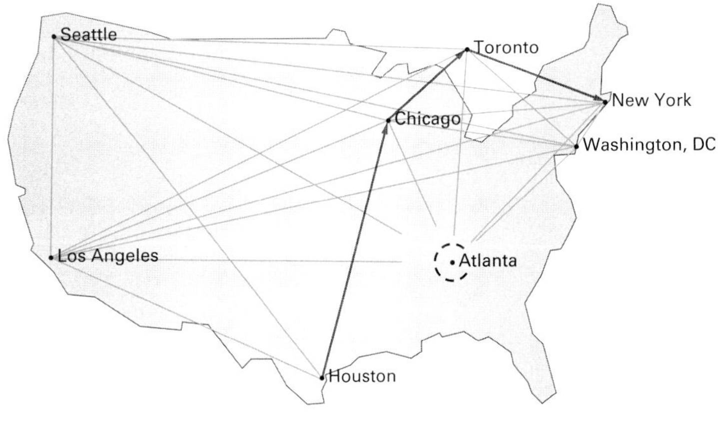

Figure 24.3 Rerouted message from Houston to NYC

provides the basic software structure for communication

You spent a good deal of Chapter 23 working with TCP/IP and you should have an appreciation for its adaptability and, perhaps more importantly, its extendibility. TCP/IP provides the naming scheme for computers that communicate on the Internet through IP addresses, such as 192.168.4.1 or 16.45.123.7. As a protocol, though, TCP/IP is much more than just a labeling system. TCP/IP provides the framework and common language for the Internet. And it offers a phenomenally wide-open structure for creative purposes. Programmers can write applications built to take advantage of the TCP/IP structure and features, creating what are called TPC/IP services. The cool thing about TCP/IP services is that they're limited only by the imagination of the programmers.

You'll learn much more about TCP/IP services in the software and "Beyond A+" sections of this chapter, but I must mention one service that you've most likely worked with yourself, whether you knew it by that term or not. The most famous service is **HyperText Transport Protocol (HTTP)**, the service that provides the structure for the **World Wide Web** ("the Web" for short), the graphical face of the Internet. Using your **Internet browser**—a program specifically designed to retrieve, interpret, and display web pages—an almost endless variety of information and entertainment is just click away. I can't tell you how many times I've started to look something up on the Web, and suddenly it's two hours later and I still haven't looked up what I started out wanting to know, but I don't actually care, because I've learned some amazing stuff! But then when I do go look it up, in just minutes I can find out information it used to take *days* to uncover. The Web can arguably claim the distinction of being both the biggest time-waster and the biggest time-saver since the invention of the book!

At this point, you have an enormous, beautifully functioning network. All the root servers connect together with fiber and thick copper cabling backbones, and TCP/IP enables communication and services for building applications for humans to interface across the distances. What's left? Oh, that's right: how do you tap into this great network and partake of its goodness?

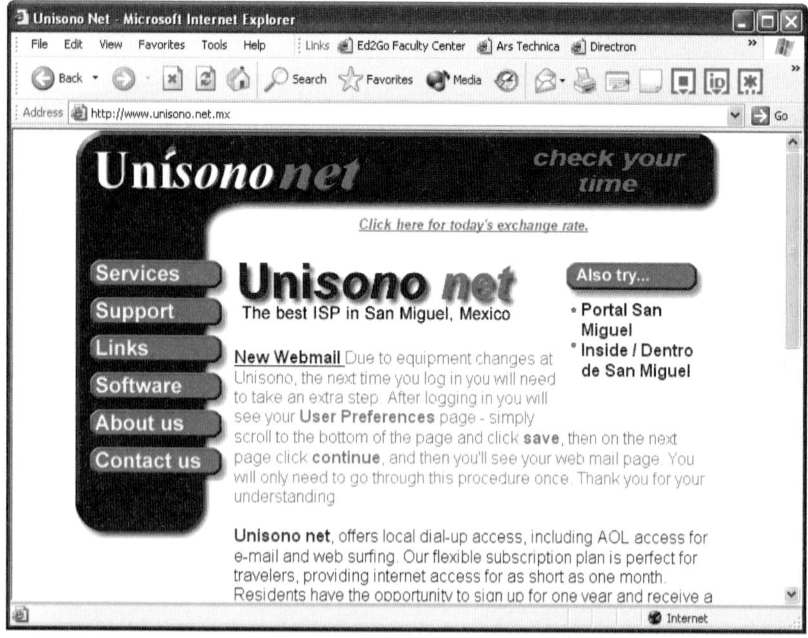

Figure 24.4 Unisono Net homepage

Internet Service Providers

Almost every backbone server leases connections to the Internet to companies called **Internet service providers (ISPs)**. ISPs essentially sit along the edges of the core Internet and tap into the flow. You can, in turn, lease some of the connections from the ISP and thus get on the Internet.

ISPs come in all sizes. America Online (AOL) has a huge pipe into the Internet, enabling its 26 million customers (in the U.S. alone) to connect from their local machines and surf the Web. Contrast AOL with Unisono Net, an ISP in San Miguel de Allende, Mexico (Figure 24.4). Billed as the Best ISP in San Miguel, it still only services a very small (but delightful) community and the busy tourist crowd. Functionally, though, Unisono Net does the same thing as AOL, just without all the bells, whistles, and mountains of free CD-ROM discs!

Microsoft calls the connections ISPs make to the Internet *access points*, which I think is a very bad name. You'd think we'd be able to come up with new terms for things! Instead, some folks in this industry continue re-branding things with the same phrases or catch words, only serving to confuse already bewildered consumers.

Connection Concepts

Connecting to an ISP requires two things to work perfectly together: hardware for connectivity, such as a modem and working telephone line; and software, such as protocols to govern the connections and the data flow (all configured in Windows), and applications to take advantage of the various TPC/IP services. Once you have a contract with an ISP to grant you access to the Internet, the ISP gives you TCP/IP configuration numbers and data so you can set up your software to connect directly to a router at the ISP that becomes your gateway to the Internet. The router you connect to at the ISP, by the way, is often referred to as the *default gateway*. Once you configure your software correctly, you can connect to the ISP and from there get to the greater Internet. Figure 24.5 shows a standard PC-to-ISP-to-Internet connection. Note that various protocols and other software manage the connectivity between your PC and the default gateway.

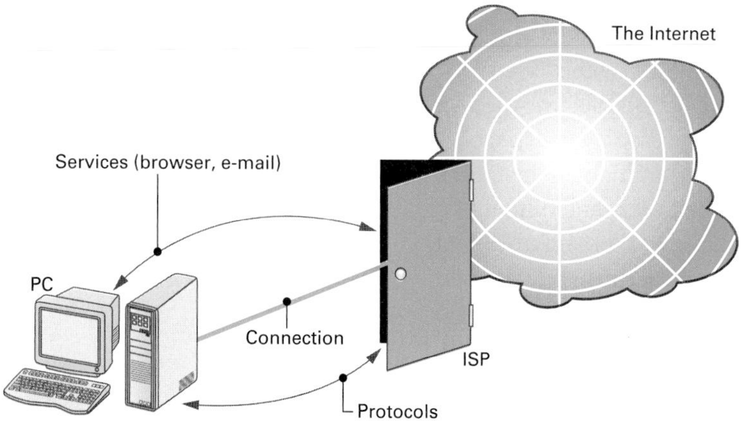

The Internet
Services (browser, e-mail)
PC
Connection
ISP
Protocols

Figure 24.5 Simplified Internet connectivity

Test Specific

Connecting to the Internet

PCs commonly connect to an ISP using one of seven technologies: dialup—both analog and ISDN; dedicated—such as DSL, cable, and LAN; wireless; and satellite. Analog dialup is the slowest of the bunch and requires a telephone line and a special networking device called a modem. ISDN uses digital dialup, so has much greater speed. All the others use a regular Ethernet NIC like you played with in Chapter 23. Satellite is the odd man out here; it may use either a modem or a NIC, depending on the particular configuration you have, although most folks will use a modem. Let's take a look at all

Let's look at the hardware first, then we'll explore software configuration.

Modems

At some point in the early days of computing, some bright guy or gal noticed a colleague talking on a telephone, then glanced down at a personal computer, and then put two and two together: why not use telephone lines for data communication? The basic problem with this idea is that traditional telephone lines use analog signals, while computers use digital signals (Figure 24.6). Creating a dial-up network required equipment that could turn digital data into an analog signal to send it over the telephone line, and then turn it back into digital data when it reached the other end of the connection. A device called a modem solved this dilemma.

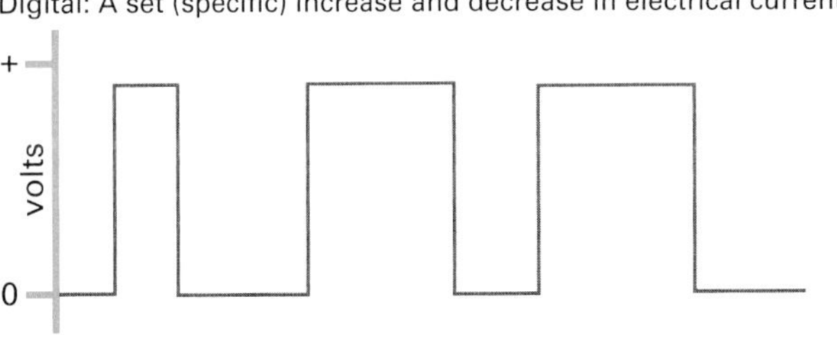

Figure 24.6 Analog signals used by a telephone line versus digital signals used by the computer

Modems enable computers to talk to each other via standard commercial telephone lines by converting analog signals to digital signals, and vice versa. The term "modem" is short for MOdulator/DEModulator, a description of transforming the signals. Telephone wires transfer data via analog signals, that is, continuously changing voltages on a wire. Computers hate analog signals. Instead, they need digital signals, voltages that are on or off, meaning the wire has voltage present or it does not. Computers, being binary by nature, use only two states of voltage: zero volts and positive volts. Modems take analog signals from telephone lines and turn them into digital signals that the PC can understand (Figure 24.7). Modems

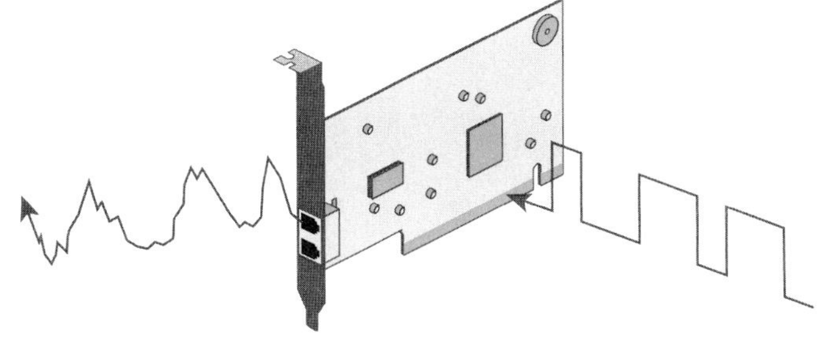

Figure 24.7 Modem converting analog signal to digital signal

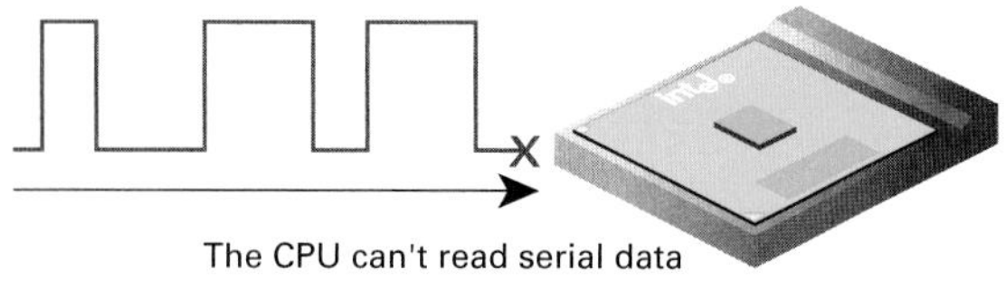

• **Figure 24.8** The CPU needs help communicating with the modem.

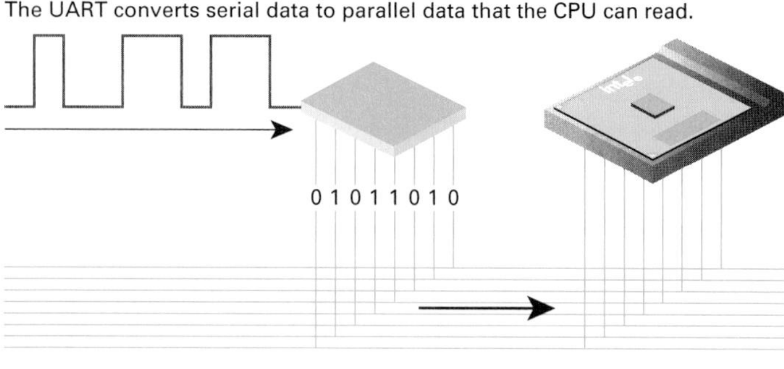

• **Figure 24.9** The function of the UART

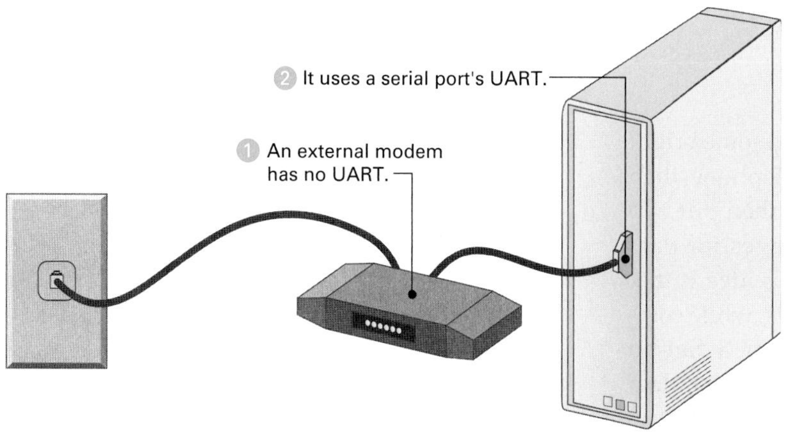

• **Figure 24.10** An external modem uses PC's serial port

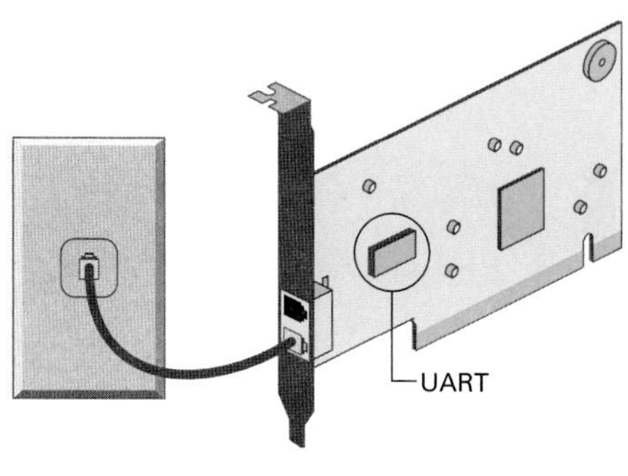

• **Figure 24.11** An internal modem has UART built in

also take digital signals from the PC and convert them into analog signals for the outgoing telephone line.

A modem does what's called *serial communication*: It transmits data as a series of individual 1's and 0's. The CPU can't process data this way (Figure 24.8). It needs parallel communication, transmitting and receiving data in discrete 8-bit chunks. The individual serial bits of data are converted into 8-bit parallel data that the PC can understand through the **Universal Asynchronous Receiver/Transmitter (UART)** chip (Figure 24.9).

There are many types of UARTs, each with different functions. All serial communication devices are really little more than UARTs. *External* modems can convert analog signals to digital ones and vice versa, but they must rely on the serial ports to which they're connected for the job of converting between serial and parallel data (Figure 24.10). Internal modems can handle both jobs because they have their own UART built in (Figure 24.11). Table 24.1 shows the UART chips that have been used in PCs.

Phone lines have a speed based on a unit called a **baud**, which is one cycle per second. The fastest rate that a phone line can achieve is 2,400 baud. Modems can pack multiple bits of data into each baud; a 33.6 kilobits per second (Kbps) modem, for example, packs 14 bits into every baud: 2400 × 14 = 33.6 Kbps. Thus it is technically incorrect to say, "I have a 56K baud modem." The correct statement is, "I have a 56 Kbps modem." But don't bother; people have used the term "baud" instead of **bps** so often for so long that the terms have become functionally synonymous.

Modern Modem Standards: V.90 vs. V.92

The fastest data transfer speed a modem can handle is based on its implementation of one of the international standards for modem technology: the **V standards**. Set by the International Telecommunication Union (ITU-T), the current top standards are V.90 and V.92. Both standards offer download speeds of just a hair under 56 Kbps, but differ in upload speeds: up to 33.6 Kbps for V.90, and up to 48 Kbps for V. 92 modems. To get anywhere near the top speeds of a V.90 or V.92 modem requires a comparable modem installed on the other line, and connecting telephone lines in excellent condition. In practice, you'll rarely get faster throughput than about 48 Kbps for downloads and 28 Kbps for uploads.

Table 24.1	UARTs
Chip	**Description**
8250	This is the original chip selected by IBM for use in the PC. It had several bugs in it, but IBM worked around them with built-in routines written in the PC and XT ROM BIOS.
8250A	This chip was developed to fix the bugs in the 8250, but the fix meant it did not work properly with the PC and XT BIOS, although it does work with the AT BIOS. This chip does not work adequately at speeds at or above 9600 bits per second (bps).
8250B	This chip was developed to fix the bugs in the previous chips, but still came with the interrupt enable bug contained in the 8250 chip. This made it compatible with the PC/XT BIOS, and possibly also with the AT BIOS. It retains the problems with bps rates above 9600.
16450	This chip was initially picked by IBM for their AT systems. It should be seen as the bare minimum for their OS/2 systems, otherwise the serial ports will not function properly. This chip has a higher throughput than the previous chips and has an added scratch register to aid in speed. The only drawback is that it cannot be used with the PC/XT BIOS due to the

Flow Control (Handshaking) Flow control, also known as *handshaking,* is the process by which two serial devices verify a conversation. Imagine people talking on a CB radio. When one finishes speaking, he will say "over." That way the person listening can be sure that the sender is finished speaking before he starts. Each side of the conversation is verified. During a file transfer, there are two distinct conversations taking place where flow control is required: local (between modem and COM port) and end-to-end (between modems).

The modems themselves handle end-to-end flow control. PCs can do local flow control between the modem and COM port in two ways: hardware and software. Hardware flow control employs extra wires in the serial connection between the modem and the COM port to let one device tell the other that it is ready to send or receive data. These extra wires are called *ready to send* (RTS) and *clear to send* (CTS), so hardware handshaking is often called RTS/CTS. Software flow control uses a special character called XON to signal that data flow is beginning, and another special character called XOFF to signal that data transmission is finished; therefore, software handshaking is often called XON/XOFF. Software handshaking is slower and not as dependable as hardware handshaking, so you rarely see it.

Bells and Whistles Although the core modem technology has changed little in the past few years, modem manufacturers have continued to innovate on many peripheral fronts—pardon the pun and the bad grammar. You can walk into a computer store nowadays, for example, and buy a V.92 modem that comes bundled with an excellent fax machine and a digital answering machine. You can even buy modems that you can call remotely that will wake up your PC (Figure 24.12). What will they think up next?

• **Figure 24.12** Some of the many features touted by the manufacturer of the SupraMax modem

Modem Connections: PCI and USB

Modems connect to the PC in two basic ways: internally or externally. Almost all internal modems connect to a PCI expansion bus slot inside the PC, although cost-conscious manufacturers may use smaller modems that fit in special expansion slots designed to support multiple communications features such as modems, NICs, and sound cards (Figure 24.13). On AMD's motherboards this is called an ACR (Advanced Communication Riser) slot, while Intel motherboards use the extremely similar CNR (Communication and Networking Riser) slot. Finally, and least expensive of all, many current motherboards dispense with expansion cards entirely and come with the modem integrated into the motherboard.

External modems connect to the PC through an available serial port (the old way) or USB port (Figure 24.14). Many PCs come with two 9-pin serial ports, whereas most external modems designed to connect to a serial port come with a 25-pin connector. That means you will probably need a 9-to-25-pin converter, available at any computer store. Virtually all computers today have two or more USB ports in addition to serial ports.

If you have the option, choose a USB modem, especially one with a volume control knob. The very low speeds of data communication over a modem make the physical type of the connection unimportant. Even the slowest interface—the aging serial

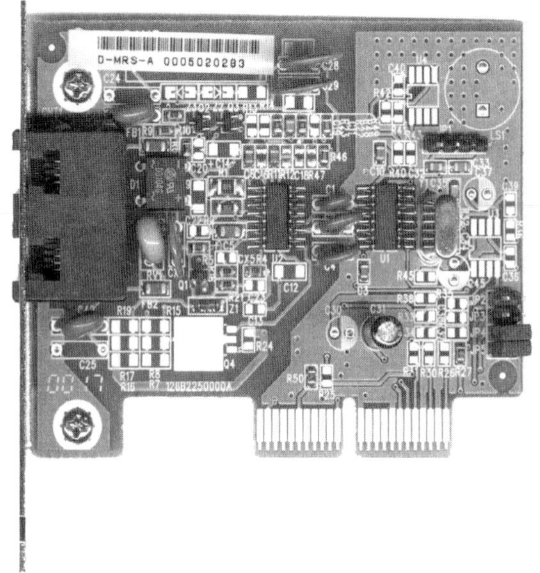

• **Figure 24.13** A CNR modem

• **Figure 24.14** A USB modem

interface—can more than adequately handle 56-Kbps data transfers. USB offers simple Plug and Play and easy portability between machines, plus such modems require no external electrical source, getting all the power they need from the USB connection.

Cross Check

Installing a PCI Modem

Installing a PCI modem card is pretty much the same process as installing any other PCI card. Refer to Chapter 6 and cross check your knowledge of the process.

1. What do you need to guard against when installing a PCI card?
2. Any issues involving drivers, Plug and Play, or other hardware topics?

Dial-up Networking

The software side of dial-up networks requires configuration within Windows to include information provided by your ISP. The ISP pro-

from the Pick a Category menu (Figure 24.15), then select *Set up or change your Internet connection* from the Pick a Task menu (Figure 24.16). The Internet Properties dialog box opens with the Connections tab displayed. All your work will proceed from here (Figure 24.17).

Windows 9x computers have

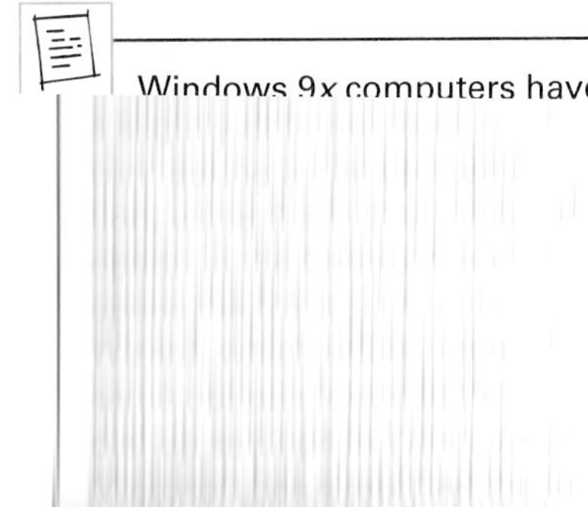

terface in its XP operating system. In Windows 2000, go to the Control Panel and open Network and Dial-up Connections. Choose Make new Connection and launch the wizard to set it up.

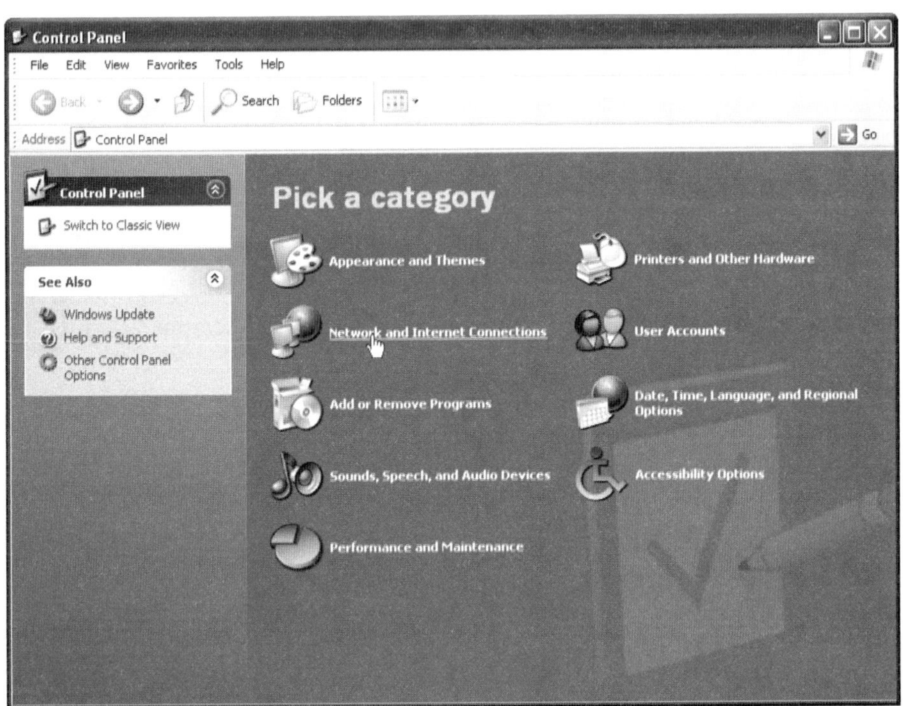

• **Figure 24.15** Opening the Network and Internet Connections applet

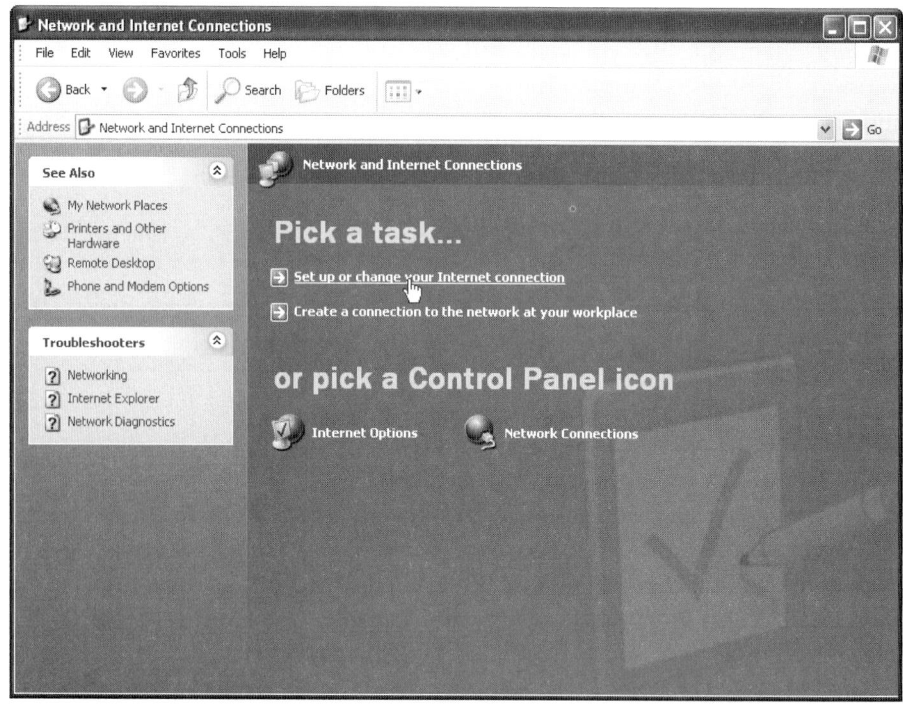

• **Figure 24.16** Picking a task...set up or change?

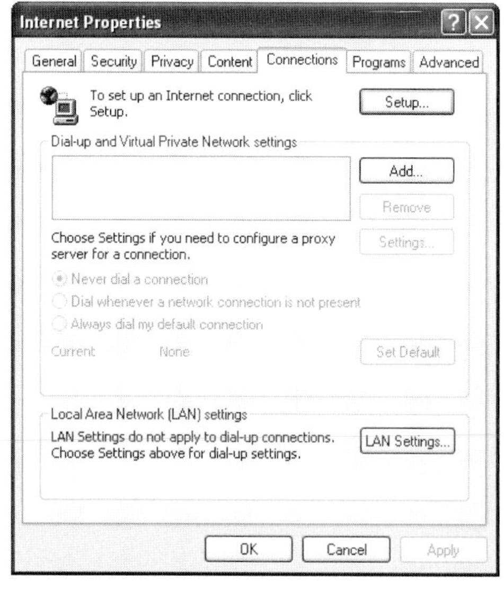

• **Figure 24.17** The Connections tab in the Internet Properties dialog box

Click the Setup button to run the New Connection Wizard and then work through the screens (Figure 24.18). At this point, you're going to need information provided by your ISP to configure your connection properly. When you finish the configuration, you'll see a new Connect To option on the Start menu. Figure 24.19 shows the option to connect to a fictitious ISP, Cool-Rides.com.

PPP Dial-up links to the Internet have their own special hardware protocol called **Point-to-Point Protocol (PPP)**. PPP is a streaming protocol developed especially for dial-up Internet access. To Windows, a

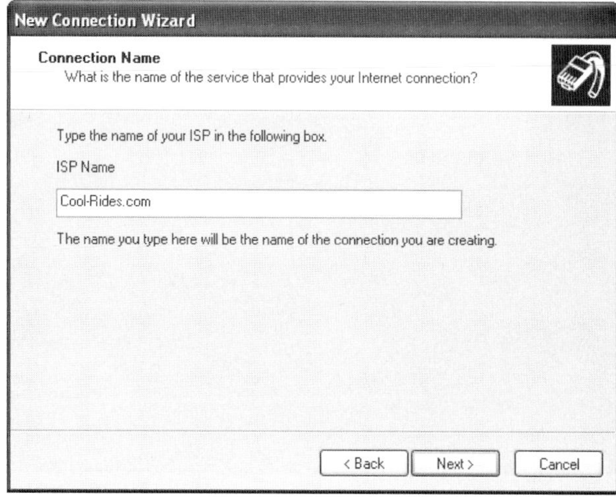

• **Figure 24.18** The New Connection Wizard

modem is nothing more than a special type of network adapter. Modems will have their own configuration entry in the Network Connections applet.

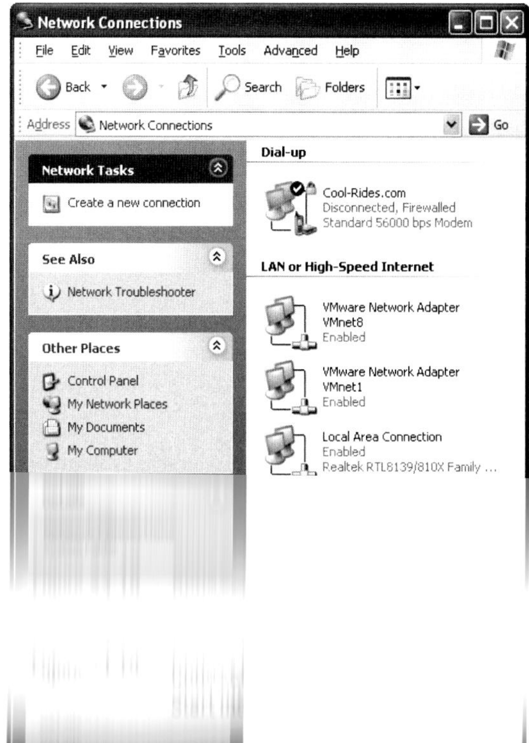

Modems also have a second set of settings in Dial-up Networking on Windows 9*x* systems. These properties are accessed from three windows: the main Properties window shown earlier, the Server Types window (Figure 24.20), and the TCP/IP Settings window (Figure 24.21). Notice that many of these settings seem redundant to the Network Settings window. The TCP/IP dial-up settings override the TCP/IP settings to enable multiple dial-up options—handy when traveling with a laptop!

Most dial-up "I can't connect to the Internet"-type problems are user errors. Your first area of investigation is the modem itself. Use the modem's properties to make sure the volume is [illegible] ured in the Dial-up Networking settings.

ISDN

There are many pieces to a standard telephone connection. First, there's the phone line that runs from your phone out to a Network Interface Box (the little box on the side of your house), and into a central switch belonging to the telephone company. (In some cases, there are intermediary steps.) Standard metropolitan areas have a large number of central offices, each with a central switch. Houston, Texas, for example, has nearly one hundred offices in the general metro area. These central switches connect to each other through high-capacity *trunk lines*. Before 1970, the entire phone system was analog;

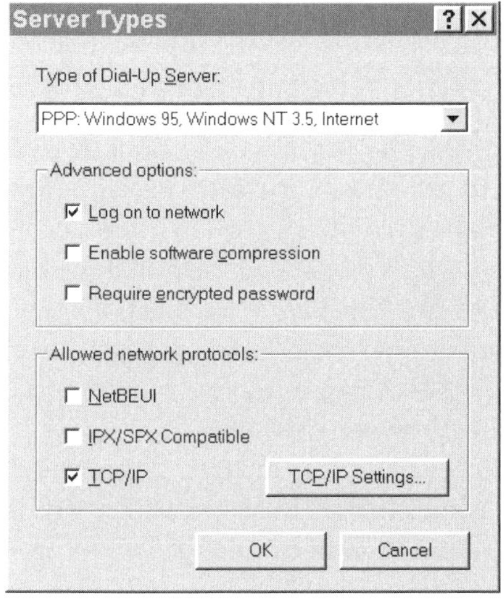

• **Figure 24.20** The Server Types window

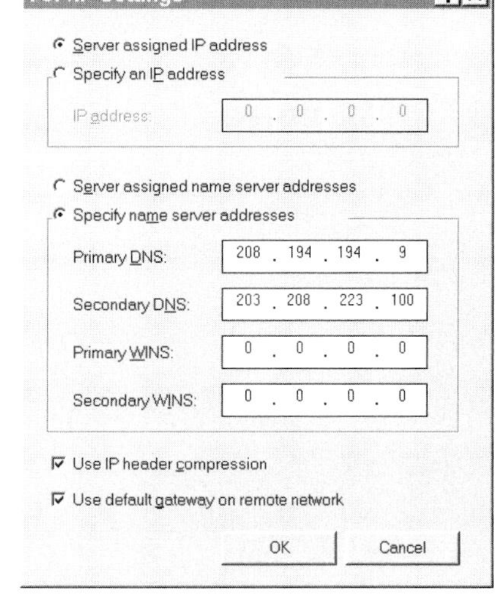

• **Figure 24.21** TCP/IP settings

over time, however, phone companies began to upgrade their trunk lines to digital systems. Today, the entire telephone system, with the exception of the line from your phone to the central office, is digital.

During this upgrade period, customers continued to demand higher throughput from their phone lines. The old telephone line was not expected to produce more than 28.8 Kbps (56K modems, which were a *big* surprise to the phone companies, didn't appear until 1995). Needless to say, the phone companies were very motivated to come up with a way to generate higher capacities. Their answer was actually fairly straightforward: make the entire phone system digital. By adding special equipment at the central office and the user's location, phone companies can now achieve a throughput of up to 64K per line (see the paragraphs following) over the same copper wires already used by telephone lines. This process of sending telephone transmission across fully digital lines end-to-end is called **Integrated Services Digital Network (ISDN)** service.

ISDN service consists of two types of channels: "Bearer" or "B" channels and "Delta" or "D" channels. B channels carry data and voice information at 64 Kbps. D channels carry setup and configuration information, and carry data at 16 Kbps. Most providers of ISDN allow the user to choose either one or two B channels. The more common setup is two B/one D, usually called a *Basic Rate Interface* (BRI) setup. A BRI setup uses only one physical line, but each B channel sends 64K, doubling the throughput total to 128K. ISDN also connects much faster than modems, eliminating that long, annoying, mating call you get with modems. The monthly cost per B channel is slightly more than a regular phone line, and there is usually a fairly steep initial cost for the installation and equipment. The big limitation is that you usually need to be within about 18,000 feet of a central office to use ISDN.

There is another type of ISDN, called PRI (Primary Rate Interface), composed of 23 64-Kbps B channels and 1 64-Kbps D channel, giving it a total throughput of 1.5 megabits per second. PRI ISDN lines are rarely used as dial-up connections—they are far more common on dedicated lines.

The physical connections for ISDN bear some similarity to analog modems. An ISDN wall socket is usually something that looks like a standard RJ-45 network jack. The most common interface for your computer is a device called a *terminal adapter* (TA). TAs look very much like regular modems, and like modems, come in external and internal variants. You can even get TAs that are also hubs, enabling your system to support a direct LAN connection.

• **Figure 24.22** A DSL receiver

Digital Subscriber Line (DSL)

Digital subscriber line (DSL) connections to ISPs use a standard telephone line but special equipment on each end to create always-on Internet connections at blindingly fast speeds, especially when compared with analog dial-up connections. Service levels vary around the U.S., but the typical upload speed is ~384 Kbps, while download speed comes in at a very sweet ~2 Mbps!

DSL requires very little setup from a user standpoint. A tech comes to the house to install a NIC in the Internet-bound PC and drop off a DSL receiver (often called a "DSL modem") (Figure 24.22). The receiver connects to the telephone line and the PC

(Figure 24.23). The tech (or the user, if knowledgeable) then configures the TCP/IP protocol options for the NIC to match the settings demanded by the DSL provider, and that's about it! Within moments, you're surfing at blazing speeds. You don't need a second telephone line. You don't need to wear a special propeller hat or anything. The only kicker is that your house has to be within a fairly short distance from a main phone service switching center, something like 18,000 feet. This pretty much stops everybody but inner city dwellers from having access to DSL service.

The two most common forms of DSL you'll find are *asynchronous* (ADSL) and *synchronous* (SDSL). ADSL lines differ between slow upload speed (such as 128, 256, or 384 Kbps) and faster download speed (usually 2 Mbps). SDSL has the same upload and download speeds, but telecom companies charge a lot more for the privilege. DSL encompasses many such variations, so you'll often see it referred to as *x*DSL.

Cable

Cable offers a different approach to high-speed Internet access, using regular cable TV cables to serve up lightning-fast speeds. It offers comparable [illegible]

PC via UTP Ethernet cable. Figure 24.24 shows a typical cable setup. One nice advantage of cable over DSL is that if you have a TV tuner card in your PC, you can use the same cable connection (with a splitter) to watch TV on your PC. One disadvantage is that unlike with DSL, where you're the lone occupant of your bandwidth in the local portion of the network, cable Internet keeps doors open for more users to join the party on your shared line, and the more sharing, the less bandwidth for you! Both DSL and cable modem Internet connections can be used by two or more computers if they are part of a LAN, including those in a home.

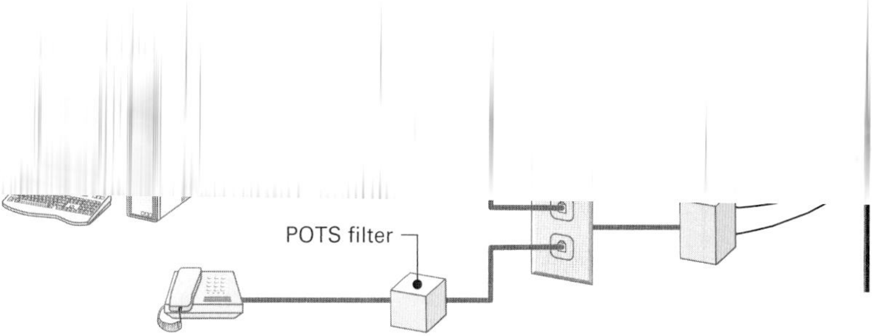

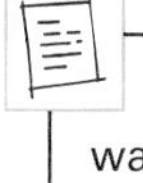

Figure 24.23 DSL connections

The term *modem* has been warped and changed beyond recognition in modern networking. Both DSL and cable fully digital Internet connections use the term modem to describe the box that takes the incoming signals from the Internet and translates it into something the PC can understand.

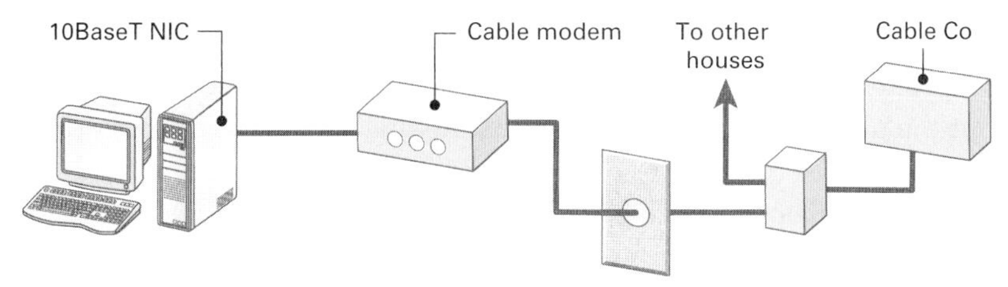

Figure 24.24 Cable connections

Figure 24.25 A wiring closet

There is a form of wireless communication that does not require local wires. *Wireless Broadband* relies on the ISP putting up a tower, and then any building within the line of sight (perhaps up to ten miles) can get a high-speed connection.

LAN

Most businesses connect their internal local area network (LAN) to an ISP via some hardware solution that Network+ techs deal with. Figure 24.25 shows a typical small-business wiring closet with routers that connect the LAN to the ISP. You learned all about wiring up a LAN in Chapter 23, so there's no need to go through any basics here. To complete a LAN connection to the Internet, you need to add a second NIC or a modem to one of the PCs and then configure that PC as the default connection. We'll revisit this idea in a moment with Internet Connection Sharing.

Wireless

Every once in a while a technology comes along that, once the kinks are smoothed out, works flawlessly, creating a magical computing experience. Unfortunately, the various wireless networking technologies out there today don't fulfill that dream yet. When they work, it's like magic. You walk into a coffee shop, sit down, and flip open your laptop computer. After firing up your Internet browser, suddenly you're quaffing lattes and surfing web sites—with no wires at all.

You spent a good deal of Chapter 23 working thorough wireless connectivity to a LAN, so I won't rehash any of that here. Suffice it to say that connecting to the Internet via wireless means that you must connect to a LAN that's wired to an ISP. The local Internet café purchases high-speed Internet service from the cable or telecom company, for example, and then connects a wireless access point (WAP) to its network. When you walk in with your portable PC with wireless NIC and open a web browser, the wireless NIC communicates with the *fully wired* DHCP server via the WAP and you're surfing on the Internet. It appears magically wireless, but the LAN to ISP connection uses wires. Barring satellite technology, that's your only common wireless option today.

Satellite

Satellite connections to the Internet get the data beamed to a satellite dish on your house or office; a receiver handles the flow of data, eventually sending it through an Ethernet cable to the NIC in your PC. I can already sense people's eyebrows raising. "Yeah, that's the download connection. But what about the upload connection?" Very astute, me hearties! The early days of satellite required you to connect via a modem. You would upload at the slow 26- to 48-Kbps modem speed, but then get superfast downloads from the dish. It worked, so why complain? Newer technology still requires the initial setup be done via modem, but the download and the upload go through the dish. You really can move to that shack on the side of the Himalayas to write the great Tibetan novel, and still have DSL-speed Internet connectivity. Sweet!

Satellite might be the most intriguing of all the technologies used to connect to the Internet today. As with satellite television, though, you need to have the satellite dish point at the satellites (toward the south if you live in the USA) and the signal will degrade in foul weather such as rain and snow.

Internet Connection Sharing

Windows 98 SE came out with a number of improvements over Windows 98, and one of the most popular was the inclusion of **Internet Connection Sharing (ICS)**. ICS enables one system to share its Internet connection with other systems on the network, providing a quick and easy method for multiple systems to use one Internet connection. Windows Me, 2000, and XP also provide this handy tool. Figure 24.26 shows a typical setup for ICS. Note the terminology here. The PC that connects to the Internet and then shares via ICS that connec-

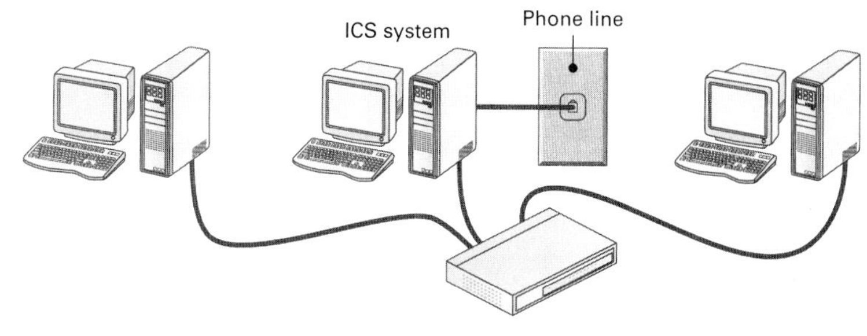

Figure 24.26 Typical ICS setup

bled to the DSL receiver, you'll need a second NIC in the ICS host machine to connect to the LAN and the client computers.

Second, in Windows 98 SE and Windows Me, you need to install ICS in the ICS host machine. Windows 98 SE and Me do not install ICS automatically. Most systems require you to install ICS via the Add/Remove Programs tab in Windows Setup. ICS is located under Internet Tools options.

Third, again only in Windows 98 SE and Windows Me, when you run ICS you get a simple client configuration floppy diskette that you need to run on all the client PCs. This configuration program does little more than tell the client machines to seek the IP address of the ICS host computer (which will be 192.168.0.1) when looking for Internet services of various types. ICS turns the sharing system into a mini-DHCP server, doling out IP addresses along the same numbering scheme, such as 192.168.0.10.

Setting up ICS in Windows 2000/XP is very simple. Open the properties dialog for My Network Places, and then access the properties of the connection you wish to share. Click the Sharing tab (Windows 2000) or the Advanced tab (Windows XP), and select Enable Internet Connection Sharing for this connection (Windows 2000) or Allow other network users to connect through this computer's Internet connection (Windows XP, Figure 24.27). Clients don't need

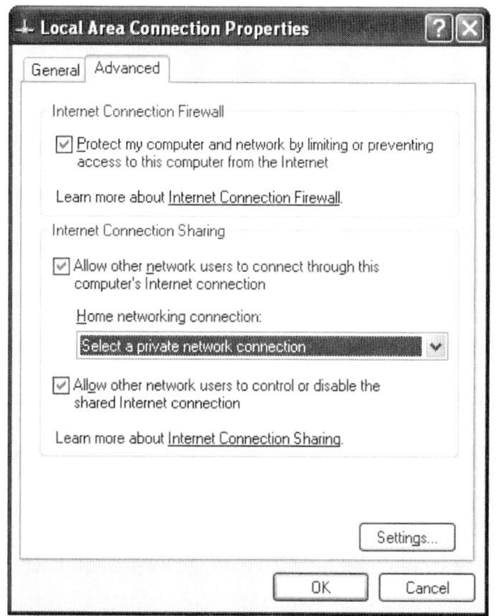

Figure 24.27 Enabling Internet Connection Sharing in Windows XP

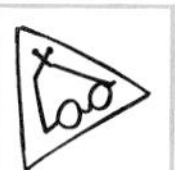

Tech Tip

Hardware Solutions for Connection Sharing

Several manufacturers offer robust, easy-to-configure hardware solutions that enable multiple computers to connect to a single Internet connection. These boxes require very little configuration and provide a level of firewall protection between the primary computer and the Internet. You'll find these boxes more commonly used with DSL and cable connections rather than any sort of dial-up. Linksys makes a great little DSL/Cable router, for example, that offers four 10/100 Ethernet ports for the LAN computers; plus you can configure it so that to the outside world the router is the PC. It therefore acts as a firewall, protecting your internal network from probing or malicious users from the outside.

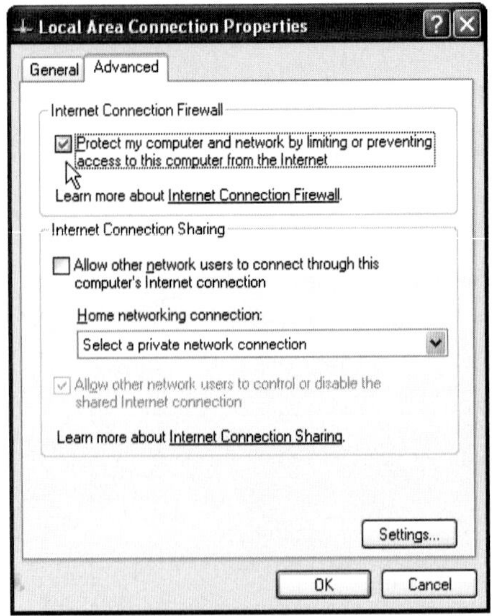

• **Figure 24.28** Implementing Internet Connection Firewall

ICF enables you to open up specific computers inside a LAN for specific tasks, such as running an FTP server.

any special configuration, but should simply be set to DHCP for their IP address and other configurations.

The Windows XP Internet Connection Firewall

Once you've established a connection to the Internet, you should start thinking about security. Windows 9*x*, Me, NT, and 2000 require you to use some third-party tool, such as a hardware firewall, but Windows XP offers the **Internet Connection Firewall (ICF)** built into the system. ICF basically stops all uninvited access from the Internet. ICF keeps track of when you initiate communication with a particular machine over your Internet connection and then allows communication back from that same machine. This works whether your connection is a single machine directly dialed into an ISP or a group of networked PCs connecting through an ICS host computer. ICF tracks the communication and blocks anything uninvited. You can implement ICF on the same screen as you would ICS (Figure 24.28).

When you're running a LAN, only implement ICF on the machine that directly connects to the Internet. If you enable ICF on other machines on the LAN, you can possibly create problems.

■ Internet Software Tools

Once you've established a connection between the PC and the ISP, you then still can do nothing on the Internet without applications designed to use one or more TCP/IP services, such as web browsing and e-mail. TCP/IP has the following commonly used services:

- The World Wide Web
- E-mail
- Newsgroups
- FTP
- Telnet

Each of these services (sometimes referred to by the overused term "TCP/IP protocols") requires a special application, and each of those applications has special settings. Let's look at all five services and see how to configure them.

The World Wide Web

The Web provides a graphical face for the Internet. Alongside, or in conjunction with, the Internet root servers are other servers running specialized software called web servers. These web servers in their simplest sense, provide web sites and web pages that you can access and thus get more or less useful information. Using web-browser software, such as Internet Explorer or Netscape Navigator, you can click a link on a web page and be instantly transported, not just to some web server in your home town, but anywhere in the world. Figure 24.29 shows Internet Explorer at the home

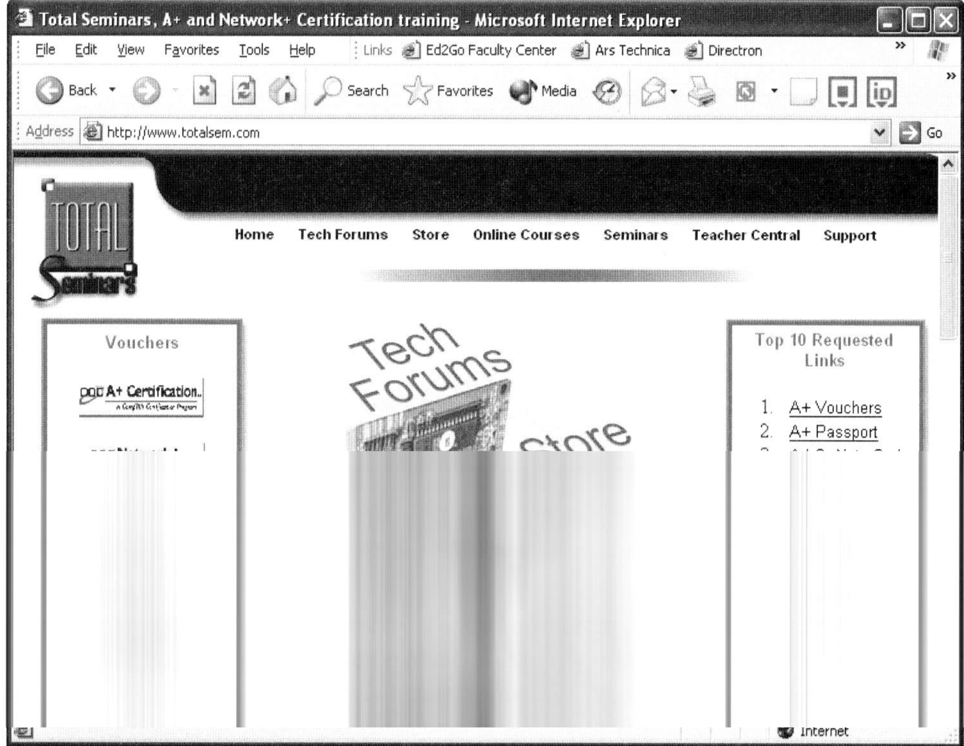

• **Figure 24.29** Internet Explorer showing a web page

page of my company's Web site, www.totalsem.com. Where is the server located? Does it matter? It could be in a closet in my office or on a huge clustered server in Canada. The great part about the Web is that you can get from here to there and access the information you need with a click or two of the mouse.

Although the Web is the most popular part of the Internet, setting up a web browser takes almost no effort. As long as the Internet connection is working, web browsers work automatically. This is not to say that there aren't plenty of settings, but the default browser settings work almost every time. If you type in a web address, such as the best search engine on the planet—www.google.com—and it doesn't work, check the line and your network settings and you'll figure out where the problem is!

Tech Tip

Ping

*The command-line tool Ping may be your best friend for diagnosing TCP/IP errors. Ping always works; you don't need to log on to a server or even log on to a system. Simply type in a DNS name or an IP address. To run Ping, get to a command prompt (Start | Run | type **CMD** | click OK) and type **ping** followed by a DNS name or IP address, like this:*

```
c:\>ping www.whitehouse.gov
```

Then press the ENTER key. If the web server is up, you'll get a reply to that effect.

*You can even ping yourself: just type **ping 127.0.0.1** (127.0.0.1 is known as the loopback address). If you get the famous "Request timed out" message, the device you are trying to ping is not available. Be aware, however, that "Request timed out" messages are fairly common when you use Ping on the Internet.*

Configuring the Browser

Web browsers are highly configurable. On most web browsers, you can set the default font size, whether it will display graphics or not and several other settings. Although all web browsers support these settings, where you go to make these changes varies dramatically. If you are using the popular Internet Explorer that comes with Windows, configuration tools are found in the Internet Options Control Panel applet or under the Tools menu.

Proxy Server If your Internet connection runs through a proxy server, you need to set your proxy settings within your browser (and any other Internet software you want to use). A *proxy server* is software that enables multiple connections to the Internet to go through one protected PC, much like how

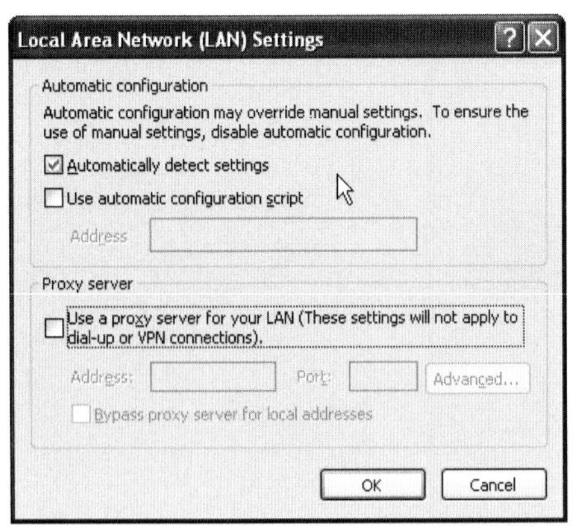

• **Figure 24.30** The LAN Settings dialog box

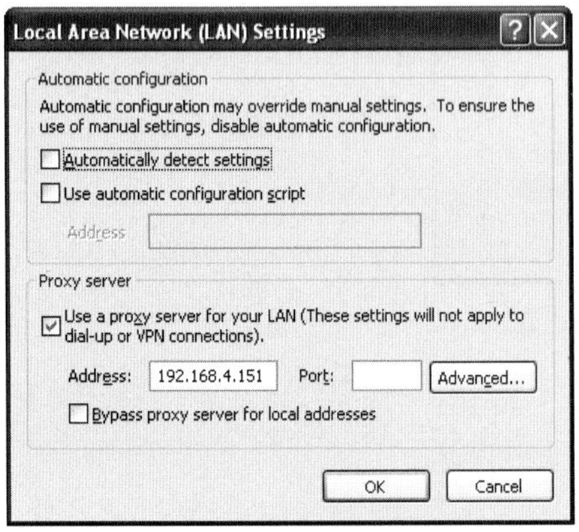

• **Figure 24.31** Specifying the proxy server address

ICS does at the LAN level. It's older technology, but it's still very much in use around the world. To configure proxy settings, go to the Tools menu and select the Connections tab. Then click the LAN Settings button to open the Local Area Network (LAN) Settings dialog box (Figure 24.30).

Note that you have three options here, with automatic detection of the proxy server being the default. You can specify an IP address for a proxy server by clicking the third radio button and simply typing it in (Figure 24.31). Your network administrator or a Network+ tech will give you information on proxy servers if you need it to configure a machine. Otherwise, you can safely leave the browser configured to search automatically for a proxy server.

Security and Scripts While we're on the subject of configuration, make sure you know how to adjust the security settings in your web browser. Many web sites come with programs that download to your system and run automatically. These programs are written in specialized languages and file formats with names like Java and Active Server Pages. They can make modern web sites very powerful and dynamic, but they can also act as a portal to evil programs. To help with security, all better web browsers let you determine whether you want these potentially risky programs to run. What you decide depends on personal factors. If your web browser refuses to run a Java program (you'll know because you'll get an warning message, like in Figure 24.32), check your security settings because your browser may simply be following orders! To get to the security configuration screen in Internet Explorer, go to Tool | Internet Options | Security tab (Figure 24.33).

Internet Explorer gives you the option to select preset security levels by clicking the Custom button on the Security tab and then optioning the pull-down menu (Figure 24.34). Changing from Medium to High security, for example, makes changes across the board, disabling everything from ActiveX to Java. You can also manually select which features to enable or disable in the scrolling menu, also visible in Figure 24.34.

Security doesn't stop with programs. Another big security concern relates to Internet commerce. People don't like

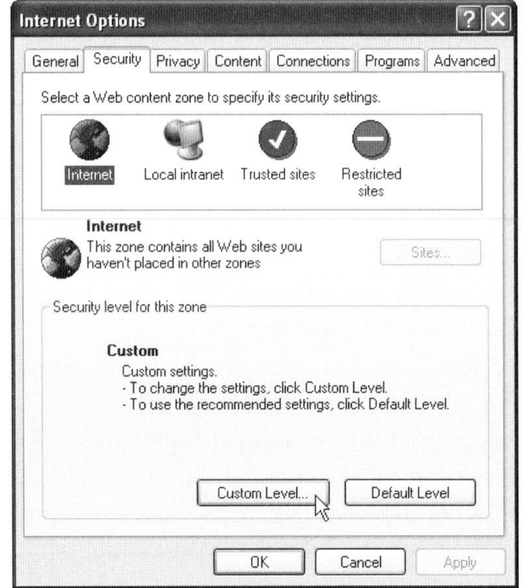

• **Figure 24.32** Warning message about running ActiveX

• **Figure 24.33** The Security tab in the Internet Options dialog box

to enter credit card information, home phone numbers, or other personal information for fear this information might be intercepted by hackers. Fortunately, there are methods of encrypting this information, the most common being **HTTP Secure (HTTPS)** web sites. It's easy to tell if your web site is using HTTPS because the web address will start with HTTPS—instead of just HTTP, as shown in Figure 24.35.

There's one security risk that no computer can completely defend against: you. In particular, be very careful when downloading programs from the Internet. The Internet makes it really easy to download programs that you can then install and run on your system. There's nothing intrinsically wrong with this unless the program you download has a virus, is corrupted, or is incompatible with your operating system. The watchword here is common sense. Only download programs from reli-

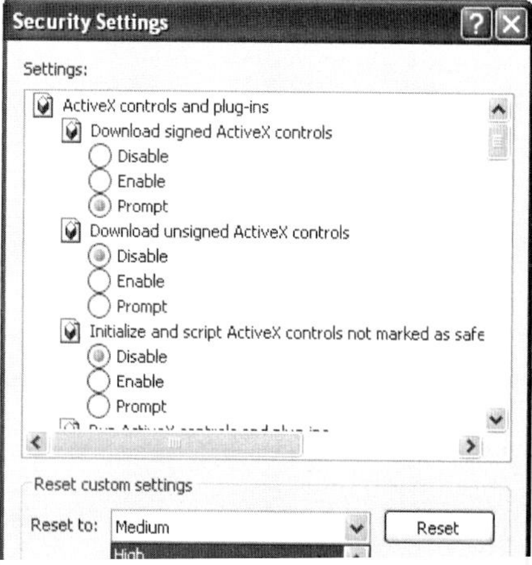

You need an e-mail program to access e-mail. The two most popular are Microsoft's Outlook Express and Netscape's Messenger. E-mail clients need a little more setup. First, you must provide your e-mail address and password. All e-mail addresses come in the now-famous accountname@Internet

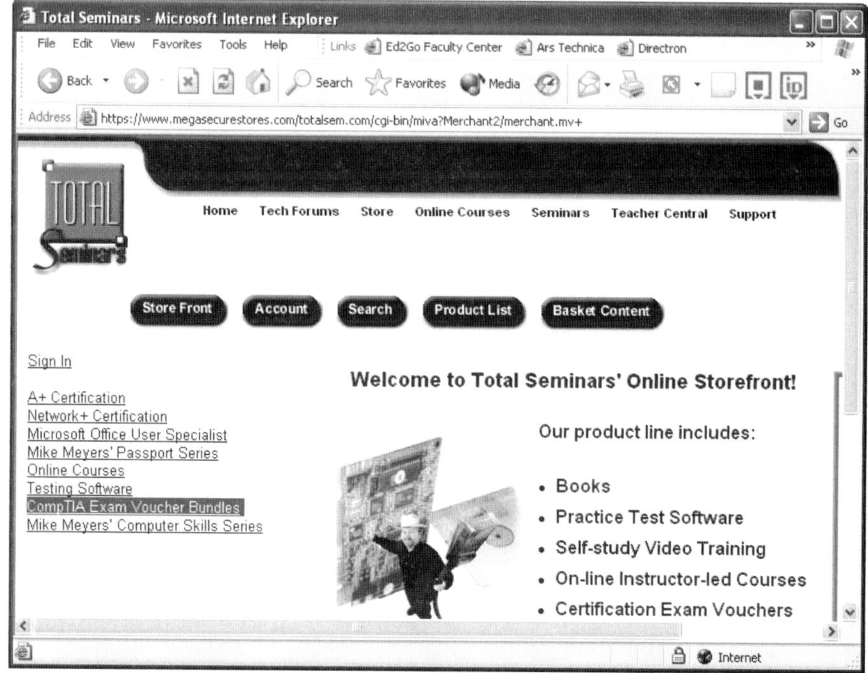

Figure 24.35 A secure web page (check out the little lock in the lower-right corner)

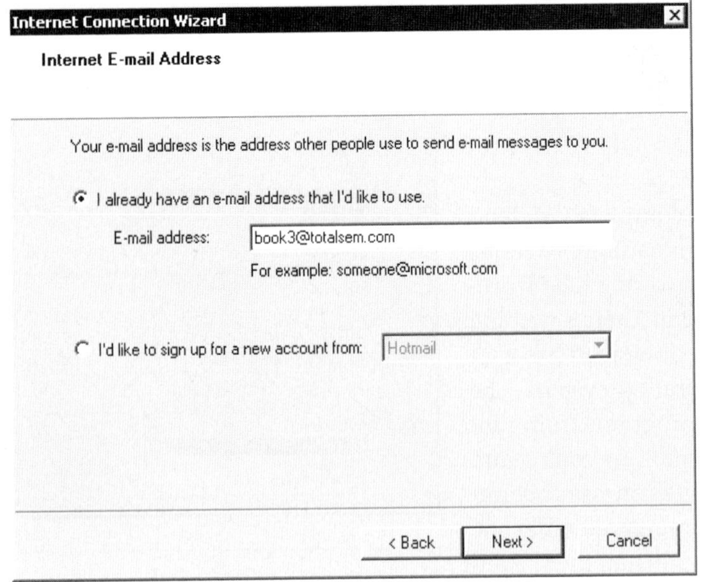

• **Figure 24.36** Adding an e-mail account to Outlook Express

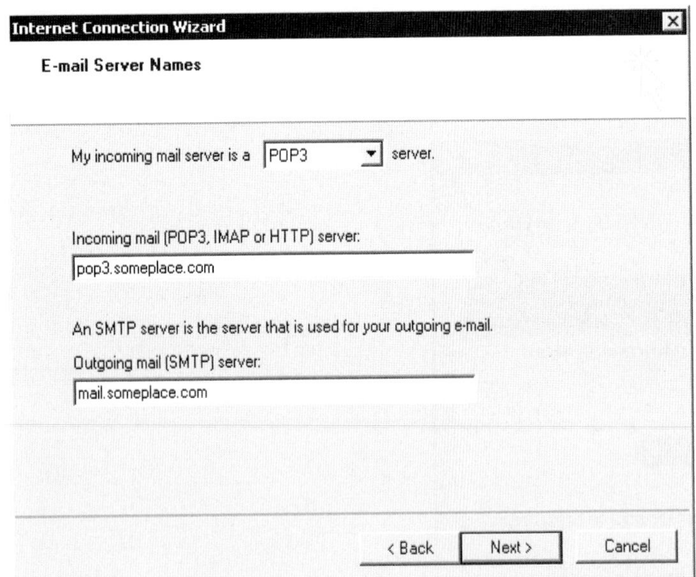

• **Figure 24.37** Adding POP3 and SMTP information in Outlook Express

domain format. Figure 24.36 shows e-mail information entered into the Outlook Express Internet Connection Wizard.

The second thing you must add are the names of the **PostOffice Protocol version 3 (POP3)** or **Internet Message Access Protocol** (IMAP) server and the **Simple Mail Transfer Protocol** (SMTP) server. The POP3 or IMAP server is the computer that handles incoming (to you) e-mail. POP3 is by far the most widely used standard, although the latest version of IMAP, *IMAP4,* supports some features POP3 doesn't. For example, IMAP4 enables you to search through messages on the mail server to find specific keywords, and select the messages you want to download onto your machine. Even with the advantages of IMAP4 over POP3, the vast majority of incoming mail servers use POP3.

The SMTP server handles your outgoing e-mail. These two systems may often have the same name, or close to the same name, as shown in Figure 24.37. All these settings should be provided to you by your ISP. If they are not, you should be comfortable knowing what to ask for. If one of these names is incorrect, you will either not get your e-mail or not be able to send e-mail. If an e-mail setup that has been working well for a while suddenly gives you errors, it is likely that either the POP3 or SMTP server is down, or that the DNS server has quit working.

When I'm given the name of a POP3 or SMTP server, I use Ping to determine the IP address for the device, as shown in Figure 24.38. I make a point to write this down. If I ever have a problem getting mail, I'll go into my SMTP or POP3 settings and type in the IP address (Figure 24.39). If my mail starts to work, I know the DNS server is not working.

Newsgroups

Newsgroups are one of the oldest services on the Internet. To access a newsgroup, you must use a newsreader program. A number of third-party newsreaders exist, such as the popular Forté Free Agent, but Microsoft's Outlook Express is the most common of all newsreaders (not surprising since it comes free with most versions of Windows). To access a newsgroup, you must know the name of a

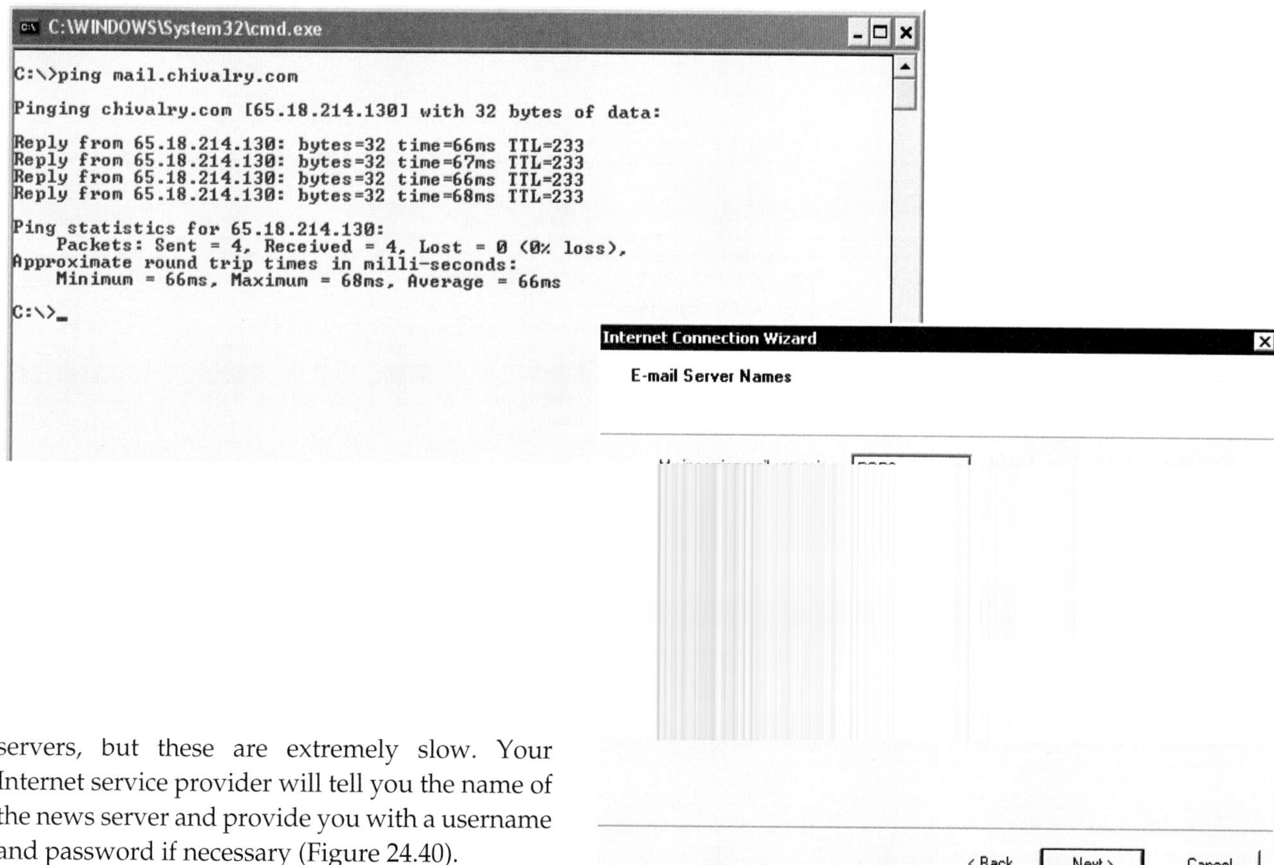

servers, but these are extremely slow. Your Internet service provider will tell you the name of the news server and provide you with a username and password if necessary (Figure 24.40).

Figure 24.39 Entering IP addresses into POP3 and SMTP settings

File Transfer Protocol (FTP)

File Transfer Protocol (FTP) can be used to access systems that you would otherwise not be able to access. FTP is also a great way to share files, but you need an FTP server. To access an FTP site, you must use an FTP client such as WS_FTP, although later versions of Internet Explorer and other web browsers provide support for FTP. Just type in the name of the FTP site. Figure 24.41 shows Internet Explorer accessing ftp.microsoft.com.

Even though you can use a web browser, all FTP sites require you to log on. Web browsers only know the most common method, using the username "anonymous" and then your e-mail address for a password. This is called an anonymous logon and works fine for most public FTP sites. However, if you need to access a site that requires a special username and password, third-party programs are preferable, because they store these settings. This enables you to access the FTP site more easily later. Figure 24.42 shows my personal favorite FTP application, WS_FTP.

Figure 24.40 Configuring Outlook Express for a news server

> The A+ Certification exams test your knowledge of a few networking tools, such as Telnet, but only enough to let you support a Network+ tech or network administrator. If you need to run Telnet, you will get the details from a network administrator. Implementation of Telnet falls well beyond A+.

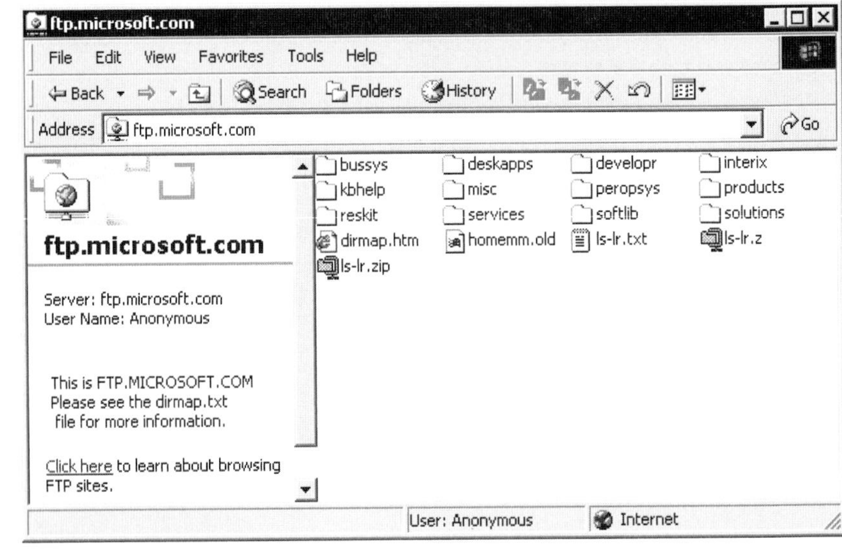

• **Figure 24.41** Accessing an FTP site in Internet Explorer

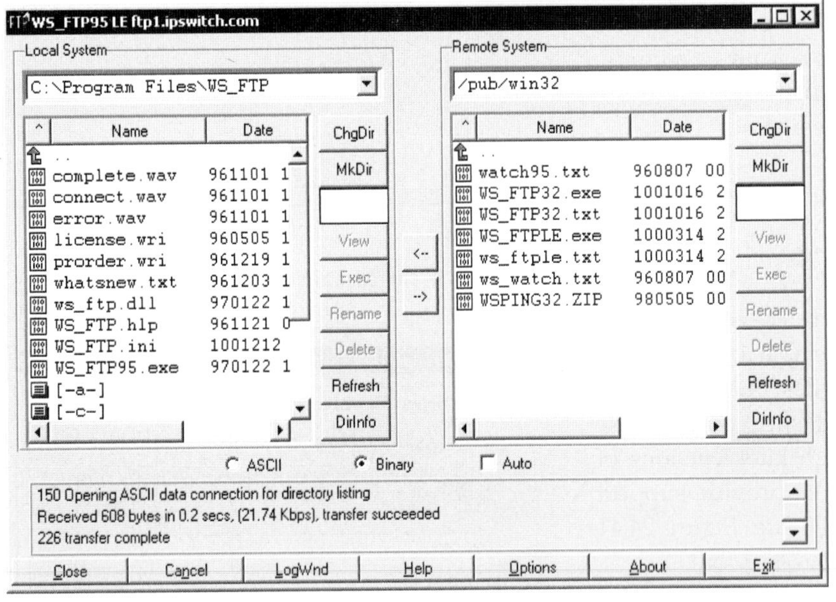

• **Figure 24.42** WS_FTP

Telnet

Telnet is a terminal emulation program for TCP/IP networks that enables you to connect to a server and run commands on that server as if you were sitting in right in front of it. This way, you can remotely administer a server and communicate with other servers on your network. As you can imagine, this is rather risky. If *you* can remotely control a computer, what's to stop others from doing the same? Of course, Telnet does not allow just *anyone* to log on and wreak havoc with your network. You must enter a special username and password in order to run Telnet.

Beyond A+

While the areas covered by the A+ Certification exams do a great job on the more common issues of dealing with the Internet, there are a few hot topics that, although beyond the scope of the A+ exams, are so common and important that you need to know them. Let's look at terminal emulation, browser hassles (such as pop-up ads and spyware), and online gaming.

Terminal Emulation

In Microsoft networking, we primarily share folders and printers. There are times when it would be convenient to be transported in front of another computer—to feel as if your hands were actually on its keyboard. This is called *terminal emulation*. Terminal emulation is old stuff—Telnet is one of the oldest TCP/IP applications, but the introduction of graphical user interfaces cost it much of its popularity. Today when we talk about terminal emulation we usually mean graphical terminal emulation programs.

Like so many other types of Windows applications, graphical terminal emulation originally came from third-party companies and then was eventually absorbed into the Windows operating system. While there are many third-party emulators, one of the most popular is the University of Cambridge's VNC. VNC is free and is totally cross-platform, allowing you to

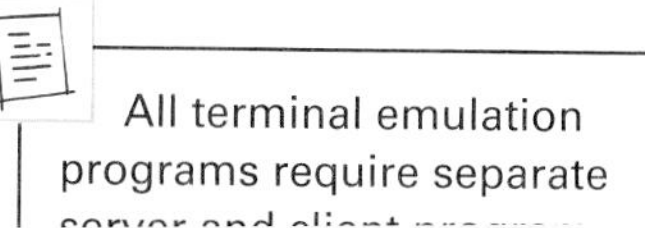

All terminal emulation programs require separate

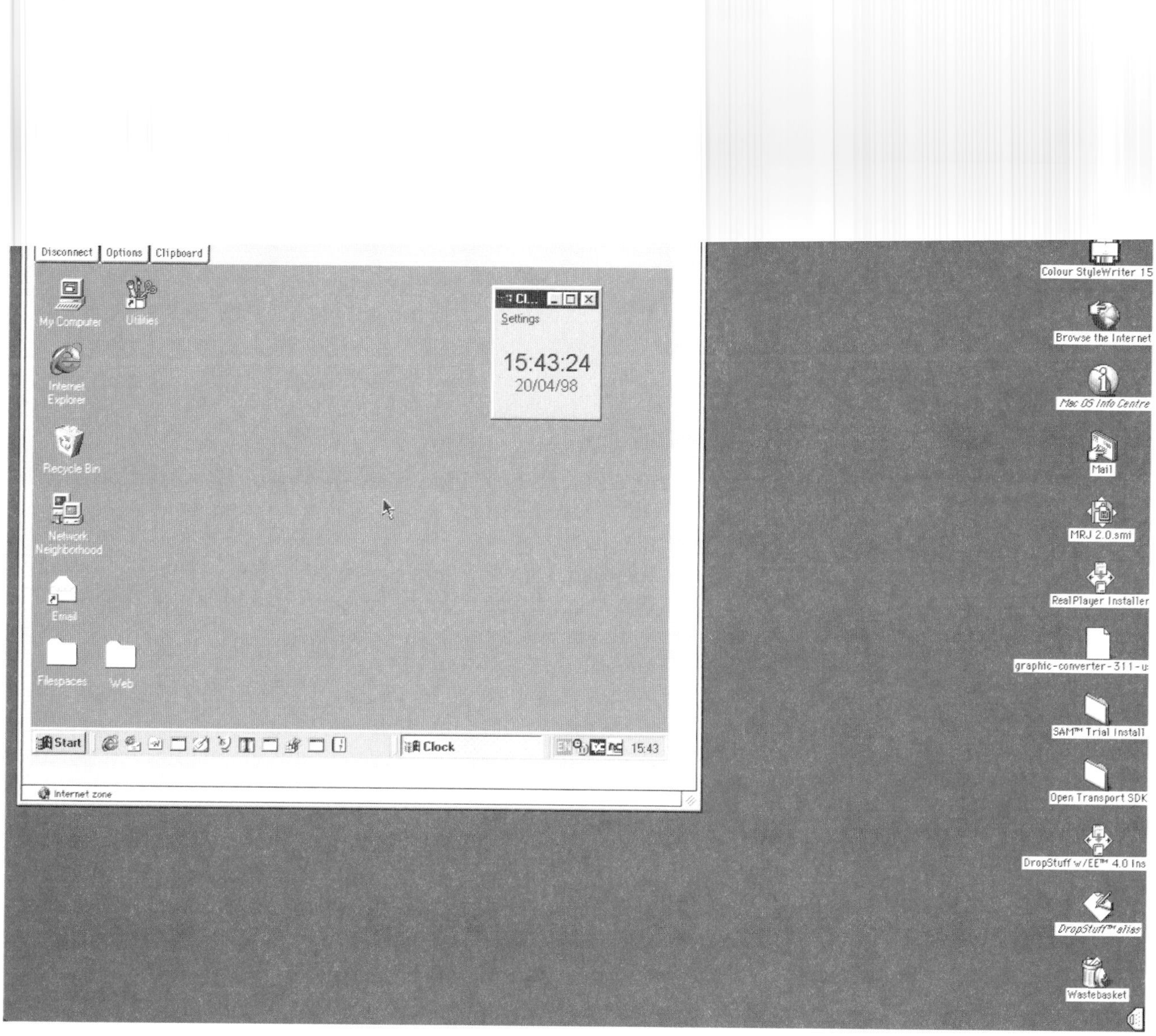

• **Figure 24.43** VNC

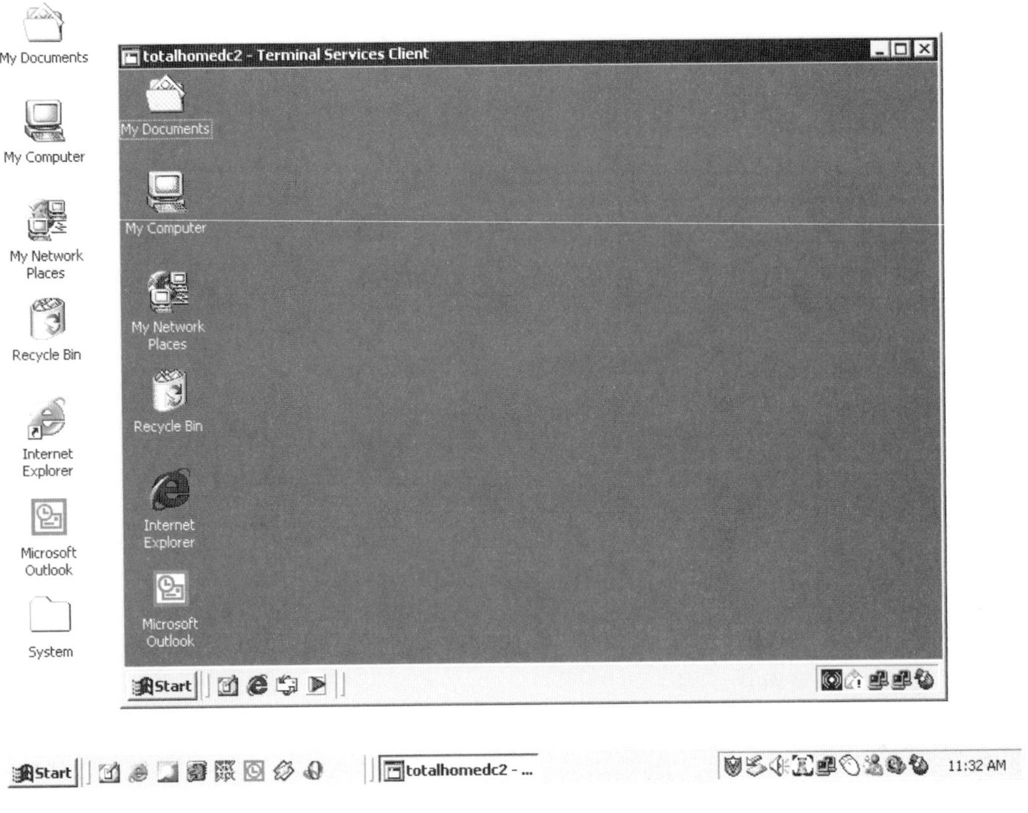

Figure 24.44 Terminal Services

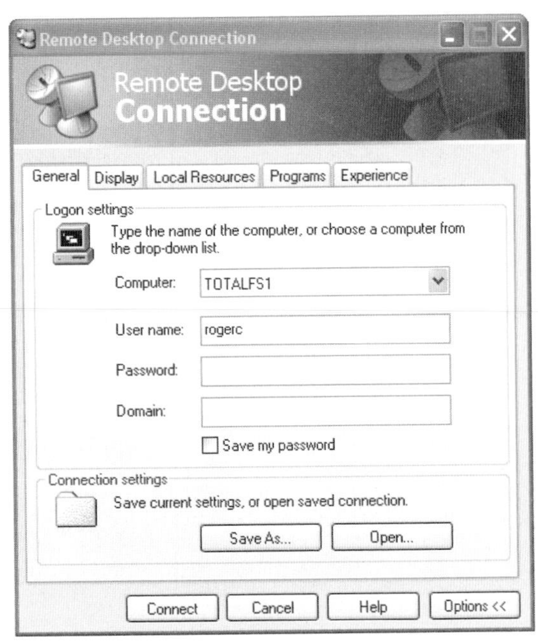

Figure 24.45 Windows XP Remote Desktop Connection dialog box

Windows 2000 Server (not Professional) was the first version of Windows to include a built-in terminal emulator called Windows Terminal Services. Terminal Services has a number of limitations: the server software only runs on Windows Server and the client software only runs on Windows—although the client works on *every* version of Windows and is free. Figure 24.44 shows Windows Terminal Services running on a Windows 2000 computer.

Windows XP offers a pair of online tools that make Telnet seem like a child's toy. Remote Desktop replaces Telnet control over a remote server with the fully graphical interface. Your desktop *becomes* the server desktop (Figure 24.45). It's quite incredible—although it's only for Windows XP.

Wouldn't it be cool if, when called about a technical support issue you could simply see what the client sees? I'm not talking voyeur cam here, but rather when the client says that something doesn't work, you could suddenly transfer yourself from your desk to your client's lap, and see precisely what he or she does. This would dramatically cut down on the miscommunication that can make a tech's life so very tedious. Windows XP's Remote Assistance does just that. Based on the "Shared Desktop" feature that used to come with the popular MSN Messenger program, Remote Assistance allows you to give anyone control of your desktop. If a user has a problem, he or she can request support directly from you. Upon receiving the support request e-mail, you can then log into his or her system and, with permission, take the driver's seat. Figure 24.46 shows Remote Assistance in action.

Remote Assistance enables you to do anything you would do from the actual desktop. You can troubleshoot some hardware configuration or driver problem. You can install drivers, roll back drivers, download new ones, and so forth. You're in command of the remote machine as long as the client allows you to be. The client sees everything you do, by the way, and can stop you cold if you got

The new graphical terminal emulators provide everything you need to access one system from another. They are very common, especially now that Microsoft provides free terminal emulators. Whatever type of emulator you use, remember that you will always need both a server and a client program. The server goes on the system to access the client and the client goes on the system you use to access the server. On many solutions, the server and the client software are integrated into a single product.

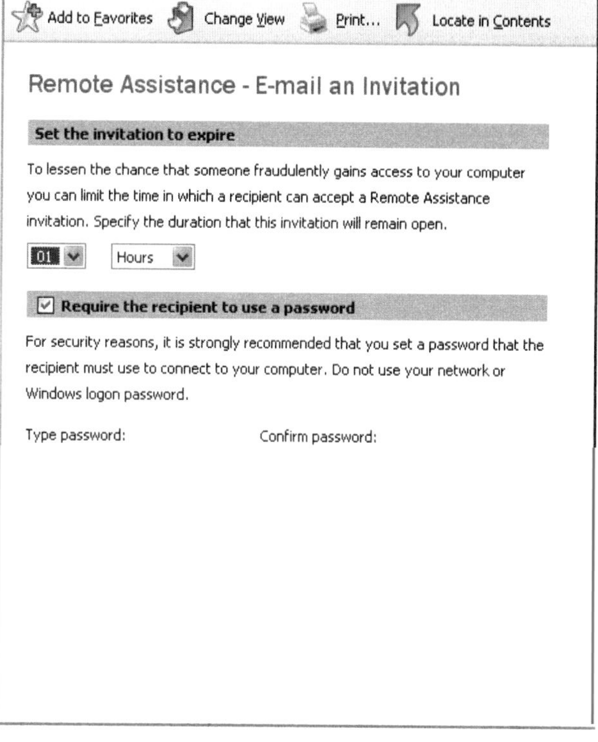

• **Figure 24.46** Remote Assistance

Browser Hassles: Pop-Ups and Spyware

On most systems, the Internet web browser client is the most often used piece of software. Over the years, web sites have come up with more and more ways to try to get you to see what they want you to see: their advertising. When the web first got underway, we were forced to look at an occasional banner ad. In the last few years, web site designers have become much more sophisticated, creating a number of intrusive and irritating ways to get you to part with your money in one form or another.

There are basically two irritating web browser problems: pop-ups and spyware. *Pop-ups* are those surprise browser windows that automatically appear when you visit a web site, proving themselves irritating and unwanted and nothing else. *Spyware,* meanwhile, defines a family of programs that run in the background on your PC, sending information to the company that installed it on your system about your browsing habits. Of the two, spyware is much less noticeable but far more nefarious. At its worst, spyware can fire up pop-up windows of competing products on the web site you're currently viewing. For example, you might be perusing a bookseller's web site only to have a pop-up from a competitor's site appear.

Pop-Ups

Getting rid of pop-ups is actually rather tricky. You've probably noticed that most of these pop-up browser windows don't look like browser windows at all. There's no menu bar, button bar, or address window, yet they are each separate browser windows. HTML coding permits web site and advertising designers to remove the usual navigation aids from a browser window so that all you're left with is the content. In fact, as I'll describe in a minute, some pop-up browser windows are deliberately designed to mimic similar pop-up alerts from the Windows OS. They may even have buttons similar to Windows' own exit buttons, but you may find that when you click them, you instead wind up with more pop-up windows! What to do?

The first thing you need to know when dealing with pop-ups is how to close them without actually having to risk clicking them. As I said, most pop-ups have removed all navigation aids, and many are also configured to appear on your monitor screen in a position that places the browser window's exit button—the little X button in the upper right-hand corner—outside of your visible screen area. Some even pop up behind the active browser window and sit there in the background. Most annoying! To remedy this, use alternate means to close the pop-up browser window. For instance, you can alternate-click the browser window's Taskbar icon to generate a pop-up menu of your own. Select Close, and the window should go away. You can also bring the browser window in question to the forefront by pressing ALT-TAB until it becomes visible, then press ALT-F4 to close it.

Software such as Tooto Technologies' Zero Popup, Google's Toolbar, and xFX JumpStart's Popup Killer are available to prevent pop-up ads in the first place, but I've found that these types of applications are sometimes *too* thorough. That is, they tend to prevent *all* new browser windows from opening, even those you want to view. Still, they're free to try, so have a look to see if they suit your needs. Applications like AdSubtract control a variety of Internet annoyances, including pop-up windows, cookies, and Java applets, and are more configurable—you can specify that what you want to allow on any particular domain address—but the fully-functional versions usually cost at least something, and that much control is too confusing for most novice-level users.

Dealing with Spyware

Some types of spyware go considerably beyond this level of intrusion. They can use your computer's resources to run *distributed computing* applications, capture your keystrokes to steal passwords, reconfigure your dial-up settings to use a different phone number at a much higher connection charge, or even use your Internet connection and e-mail address list to propagate itself to other computers in a virus-like fashion! Are you concerned yet?

Setting aside the legal and ethical issues, and there are many, you should at least appreciate that spyware can seriously impact your PC's performance and cause problems with your Internet connection. The threat is real, so what practical steps can you take to protect yourself? Let's look at how to prevent spyware installation, and how to detect and remove any installed spyware.

Preventing Spyware Installation How does this spyware get into your system in the first place? Obviously, a sensible person doesn't download and install something that they know is going to compromise their computer. Makers of spyware know this, so they bundle their software with some other program or utility that purports to give you some benefit.

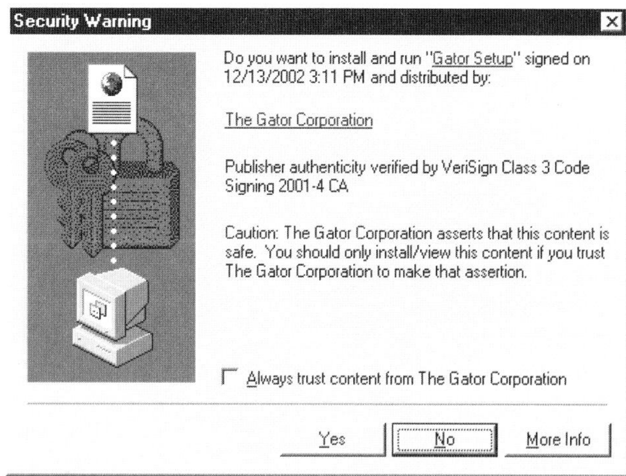

What kind of benefit? How about free access to MP3 music files? A popular program called Kazaa does that. How about a handy *e-wallet* utility that remembers your many screen names, passwords, and even your credit card numbers to make online purchases easier and faster? A program called Gator does that, and many other functions as well. How about browser enhancements, perfor-

software. Instead of offering you some sort of attractive utility, they instead use fear tactics and deception to try to trick you into installing their software. One popular method is to use pop-up browser windows crudely disguised as Windows' own system warnings (Figure 24.48). When clicked, these may trigger a flood of other browser windows, or may even start a file download.

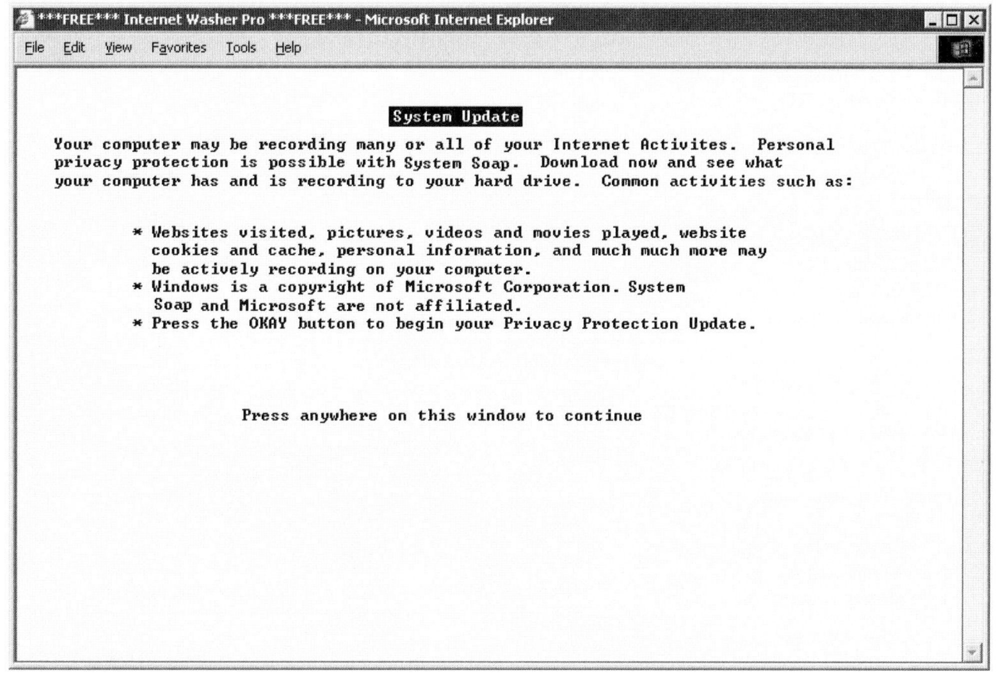

• **Figure 24.48** A spyware pop-up browser window, disguised as a Windows alert

The lesson here is simple—*don't install these programs!* Careful reading of the software's license agreement before you install a program is a good idea, but realistically, it does little to protect your PC. With that in mind, here are a couple of preventive measures you can take to keep parasitic software off of your system:

If you visit a web site and are prompted to install a third-party application or plug-in that you've never heard of, *don't install it.* Well-known and reputable plug-ins, such as Macromedia's *Shockwave* or *Flash*, are safe, but be suspicious of any others. Don't click *anywhere* inside of a pop-up browser window, even if it looks just like a Windows alert window or DOS command-line prompt—as I just mentioned, it's probably fake and the Close button is likely a hyperlink. Instead, use other means to close the window, such as pressing ALT-F4, or alternate-clicking the browser window's icon on the Taskbar and selecting Close.

You can also install spyware detection and removal software on your system and run it regularly. Let's look at how to do that.

Removing Spyware Some spyware makers are reputable enough to include a routine for uninstalling their software. Gator, for instance, makes it fairly easy to get rid of their programs—just use the Windows Add/Remove Programs applet in the Control Panel. Others, however, aren't quite so cooperative. In fact, because spyware is so—well, *sneaky*—it's entirely possible that your system already has some installed that you don't even know about. How do you find out?

Unfortunately, no version of Windows has a quick and easy way to determine this. It's possible, of course, to go into Task Manager and browse through the list of running applications, but this might not tell the whole story. The better solution is to install a dedicated spyware detection and removal program. There are several on the market, but two that I highly recommend are Lavasoft's Ad-aware (Figure 24.49) and PepiMK's Spybot Search & Destroy.

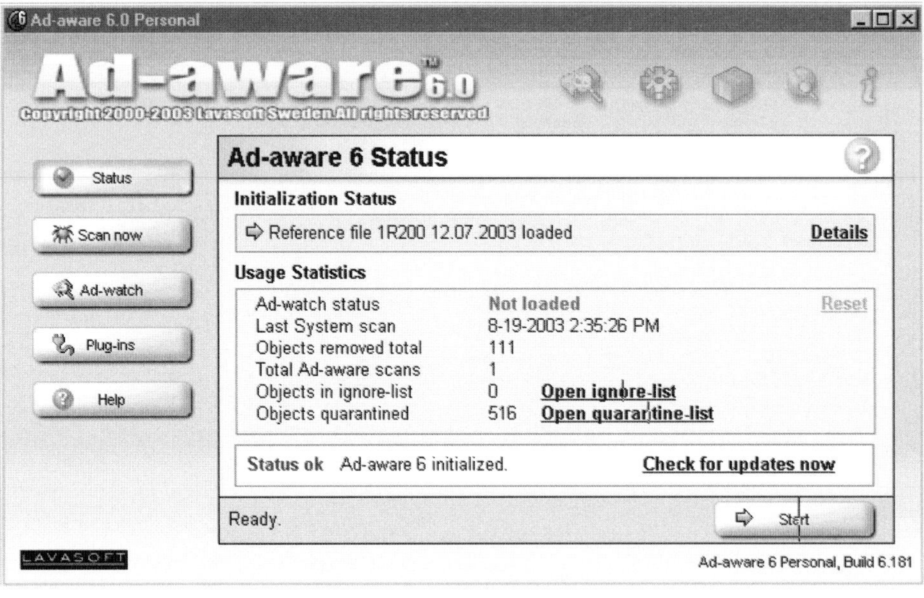

Figure 24.49 Lavasoft's Ad-aware

Both of these applications work exactly as advertised. They detect and delete spyware of all sorts—hidden files and folders, cookies, Registry keys and values, you name it. Ad-aware is free for personal use, while Spybot Search & Destroy is shareware. Many times I've used both at the same time, since one tends to catch what the other misses.

Beyond Browsing—The Power of the Internet

When we speak of the Internet, we tend to concentrate on just two applications: e-mail and the World Wide Web. Granted those two are the most popular, but in this chapter we've seen that there's more that just those two applications. However, TCP/IP and the Internet go even beyond the ap-

Playing computer games where the other person or people in the game are real makes for some amazing games. There are classics like Hearts and Backgammon that you can play against human players. Entire web sites are devoted to helping you find playing partners and thereby enjoy thousands of different games (Figure 24.50). Another popular genre of online gaming is the "first-person shooters" format These games place you in a small world with up to 32 other players. A great example is Id Software's Quake III or the aged but well loved Half-Life (Figure 24.51).

No discussion of online gaming is complete without talking about the most amazing game type of all—the Massively Multiplayer Online Role Playing Game (MMORPG). Imagine being an elfin wizard, joined by a band of friends, all going on adventures together in worlds so large that it would take a real 24-hour day to journey across! Imagine that in this same world there are 2000 to 3000 other players, as well as thousands of game-controlled characters! There are plenty of MMORPGs out there, but the oldest and most famous is Sony's EverQuest (Figure 24.52).

Figure 24.50 Folks playing games online

Figure 24.51 Half-Life, Mountain Hamlet map by Mats Wiberg

• **Figure 24.52** EverQuest

Each of these games employs good old TCP/IP to send information using special ports either reserved by the game itself or by DirectX. For instance, the Quake series of games uses port 26000, while DirectX uses ports 47624 and 2300–2400.

Chat

If there's one thing we human beings love to do, it's chat. The Internet provides you with a multitude of ways to do so, whether it be by typing or actual talking. Keep in mind that chatting occurs in real time. As fast as you can type or talk, the other person or persons hear or see what you have to say. In order to chat, however, you need some form of chat software. The oldest family of chat programs is based on the Internet Relay Chat protocol, and the single most common IRC chat program is probably mIRC. IRC protocols allow for a number of other little extras as well, such as the ability to share files.

Today, companies such as AOL, Yahoo, and Microsoft have made their own chat programs that not only provide text chat but also add features such as voice and video, turning your PC into a virtual replacement for your telephone! Figure 24.53 shows the very popular Microsoft Messenger software.

> There is actual technology that enables you to use the Internet like a telephone. It's referred to as Voice over IP, or VoIP, and it's the subject of much legislative and legal wrangling between the phone companies whose business it takes, and those that provide the service.

File Sharing

The last extra Internet function to discuss is also probably the most controversial: file sharing. File sharing basically consists of a whole bunch of computers with one program loaded, such as Napster or Kazaa. The file-sharing program enables each of the computers running that program to offer files to share, such as MP3 music files and MPEG movies. Once all the file sharing computers log into the Internet, any of them can download any file offered by any other in the group.

File sharing through such *distributed* sharing software becomes almost anonymous and free—and that's the problem. You can share *anything*, even copyright-protected music, movies, and more. The music industry in particular has come out swinging to try to stop file-sharing practices. As a result, the music industry is trying hard to come up with a way to shut down those persons who share lots of files. But software developers have countered, creating Internet protocols such as Gnutella to handle the distribution and make the file shar-

original concept of its designers, yet TCP/IP continues to show its power and flexibility. Pretty danged amazing!

Figure 24.53 Microsoft Messenger in action

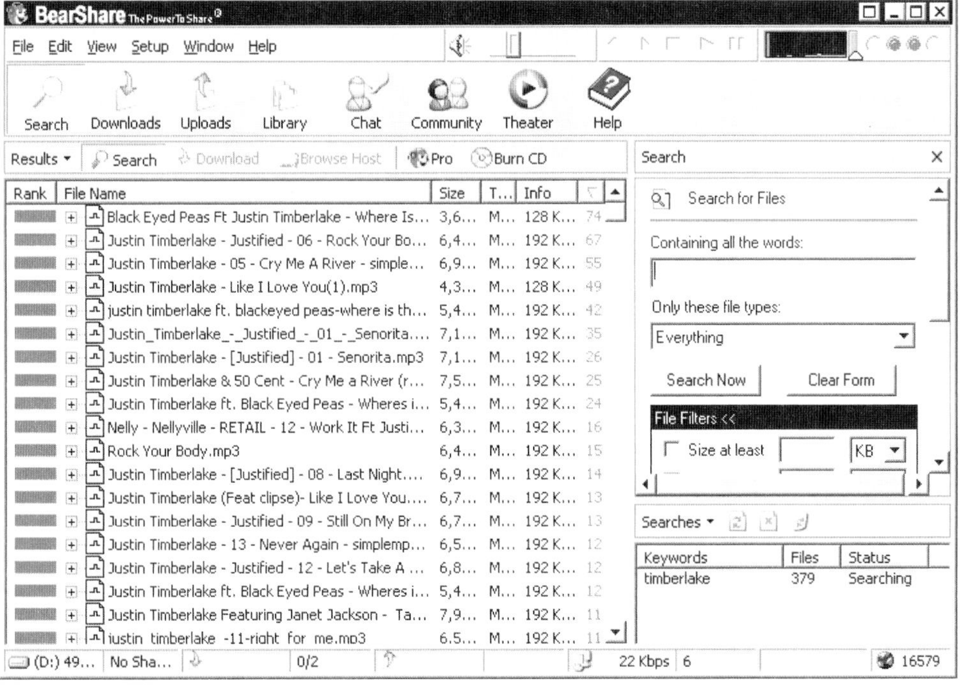

Figure 24.54 BearShare

Chapter 24 Review

Chapter Summary

After reading this chapter and completing the exercises, you should understand the following about the Internet:

Explain How the Internet Works

- A PC tech needs to know how PCs communicate with the world for two reasons: (1) to troubleshoot when a process or piece stops working, and (2) to communicate knowledgeably with a network technician when he or she comes in to solve a more complex issue.
- The Internet uses backbones or fast networking connections to connect computers all over the world. Designed originally to survive a catastrophic war or devastating natural disaster, the Internet still is a highly redundant and adaptable interwoven framework for communications, with all root servers connected to more than one other root server. The majority of the root servers on the Internet today are still university mainframe and mini-computers, but major corporate and government centers also provide linkage and redundancy.
- The TCP/IP protocol provides the basic software structure for Internet communications. It provides IP addresses and the naming scheme for computers on the Internet. This protocol suite also offers a variety of other services, including HyperText Transport Protocol (HTTP) that provides structure for the World Wide Web (or just Web for short).
- Internet service providers (ISPs) lease connections to the Internet from backbone servers. In turn, ISPs then lease connections to allow individuals and companies to get on the Internet. ISPs may serve customers nationwide, such as America Online (AOL), or they may be limited to only a small community of users.

Connect to the Internet

- To connect to an ISP, you must have connectivity hardware, such as a modem and telephone line, and software, including protocols and applications. When you get a TCP/IP configuration number from your ISP, you can set up your software to connect to a router at the ISP. That router then becomes your default gateway to the Internet.
- Seven technologies are commonly used to connect a PC to an ISP. These technologies fit into four categories: (1) dial-up (analog and ISDN), (2) dedicated (DSL, cable, and LAN), (3) wireless, and (4) satellite. An analog dial-up, the slowest connection, uses a telephone line and a modem. ISDN is a much faster digital dial-up method. With the exception of satellite that may use either a modem or a NIC, all the other technologies use an Ethernet NIC.
- A dial-up connection needs hardware, such as a modem or ISDN terminal adapter, and software such as Microsoft's Dial-up Networking (DUN).
- Named from MOdulator/DEModulator, a modem converts digital signals from the PC into analog signals that travel on telephone lines, and vice versa. An example of serial communication, the modem transmits data as a series of 1's and 0's. On the other hand, the computer processes data using parallel communication or data in discrete 8-bit chunks. A Universal Asynchronous Receiver/Transmitter (UART) chip converts serial to parallel, and vice-versa. An external modem uses the UART chip in the computer's serial port, while an internal modem has its own built-in UART. A number of different UART chips have been used over the years, but today's computer systems use the 16550A UART chip. This chip has 16-built-in first in, first out (FIFO) registers to receive and transmit at high speeds.
- Phone lines measure speed in bauds or cycles per second. However, the fastest baud rate a phone line can achieve is 2400 baud. Today's modems pack multiple bits of data into each baud. For example, a 33.6 kilobits per second (Kbps) modem packs 14 bits into every baud (or cycle). Although not technically correct, people use the term baud instead of bps so often that the terms have become synonymous.
- The International Telecommunication Union (ITU-T) sets V standards to define the fastest data transfer speed a modem can handle. Currently V.90 and V.92 are the highest standards, downloading data just a little under 56 Kbps. Upload speeds differ, with 33.6 Kbps being the fastest for V.90 and 48 Kbps proving the fastest for V.92 modems. Unless the telephone lines are in excellent

condition and both modems are comparable, you'll rarely get these speeds. In most instances, the download speed will be about 48 Kbps while the upload speed will be closer to 28 Kbps.

- Modems now include additional functions, such as a fax machine or digital answering machine.
- Modems may be internal or external. The less-expensive internal modems usually connect to a PCI expansion bus slot. Some motherboards include special expansion slots, used for multiple communications features such as modems, NICs, and sound cards. AMD calls such slots ACRs (Advanced Communication Risers) while Intel [illegible]

serial connector, you'll need a 9-to-25-pin converter. It is a good idea to choose a USB modem since you won't need an external electrical source and it'll likely include a volume control knob.

- Windows includes configuration options to set up dial-up networks. With XP, use the Network and Internet Connections applet, while Windows 9*x* has a Dial-up Networking option in the Control Panel and Windows Me and 2000 call this feature Network and Dial-up Connections. To configure dial-up networking, you'll need information from your ISP. Dial-up links to the Internet use a streaming hardware protocol called Point-to-Point Protocol (PPP).
- If you can't connect to the Internet, look at the modem's properties to make sure the volume is turned up. Listen, too, for a befuddled voice on the other end that would indicate your modem is dialing the wrong number. Other things to check: Be sure the line is plugged into a good phone jack, and make sure the number and password are correct. If you still can't connect to the Internet, call the network technicians to check that the dial-up networking settings are correct.
- A telephone connection has many pieces, including a Network Interface Box at your house, a central switch, and high-capacity trunk lines. With the exception of the line from your phone to the central office, the entire telephone system is now digital. By adding special equipment at the central office and the users location, the telephone company can produce an end-to-end digital line called an Integrated Services Digital Network (ISDN) service.
- An ISDN consists of two types of channels: "Bearer" or "B" channels that carry data and voice at 64 Kbps, and "Delta" or "D" channels that transmit setup and configuration information at 16 Kbps. Users can use one or two B channels, but the most common setup is the Basic Rate Interface (BRI) consisting of two B channels and one D to provide a throughput total of 128K. Except for the steep cost of installation and equipment, ISDN lines are only slightly more expensive than regular phone lines, but this service is limited to an area [illegible]
- A digital subscriber line (DSL) connects to an ISP using a standard telephone line and special connections on each end. Although service levels vary, typical upload speed is ~384 Kbps with a download speed of ~2 Mbps. A tech usually comes to the house to install a DSL receiver (often called a DSL modem) as well as a NIC in the PC. Using the same telephone line, you can talk on the phone and surf the Internet at the same time. However, DSL is usually limited to about 18,000 feet from a main phone service switching center.
- Cable TV companies offer high-speed Internet access, with an upload speed of about 384 K up and download transmission rates of 2 Mbps. With a TV tuner card, cable lets you watch TV on your PC.
- Many businesses connect their local area network (LAN) to an ISP. This configuration requires either a second NIC or a modem.
- Wireless Internet service requires connecting to a LAN that's wired to an ISP. The other wireless option is a satellite connection. Although early satellite technology required uploads through a slow modem (26–48 Kbps) and fast downloads through the dish, newer technology uses the modem only for the initial setup, sending both downloads and uploads through the dish.
- Windows 98 SE introduced Internet Connection Sharing (ICS), allowing multiple systems to use one Internet connection. Also included in Windows

Me, 2000, and XP, ICS uses an ICS host computer connected to the Internet that then shares the connection via a LAN with client computers. The ICS host computer must have a NIC or modem to connect to the Internet and a NIC that plugs into a hub. The other PCs then connect to the hub. With Windows 98 SE and Windows Me, ICS must be installed in the ICS host machine. You also need a client configuration floppy diskette for the client PCs. With Windows 2000/XP, setting up ICS is much simpler since clients can be set to DHCP for their IP address and other configurations. Some manufacturers, such as Linksys, offer hardware solutions for connection sharing with a bonus of providing firewall protection between the primary computer and the Internet.

- If you have a connection to the Internet, you should also have some kind of security. Windows 2000 and all earlier versions require you to use a third-party tool such as a hardware firewall. Windows XP, however, has a built-in Internet Connection Firewall (ICF) to stop uninvited access from the Internet. ICF lets you communicate only with machines that are responding to your initial communication. Be sure that ICF is enabled only on machines that connect directly to the Internet.

Configure Internet Software Tools

- Applications provide TCP/IP services, including World Wide Web, e-mail, newsgroups, FTP, and Telnet. Using web browser software, such as Internet Explorer or Netscape Navigator, you can access web sites and web pages from web servers throughout the world. If you are unsuccessful in connecting to a site, use the command-line tool ping to check if the server is up. Simply type **ping** followed by either the DNS name or the IP address. You can use the loopback address (127.0.0.1) to ping yourself. If the device you are trying to ping is not available, you'll get "Request timed out" messages.
- A proxy server is software that enables multiple connections to the Internet to go through one protected PC. Configure proxy settings through the Local Area Network Settings dialog box. Although automatic detection of the proxy server is the default setting, you can also specify an IP address for a proxy server.
- You should also know how to adjust security settings in your web browser. In IE, use the Security tab under the Internet Options of the Tools menu. You can set different security levels or manually select the features you want to enable or disable.
- Security also includes encrypting information such as credit card numbers, home phone numbers, or other personal information. The most common method of encrypting this information is HTTPS (HTTP Secure) web sites. You'll identify these sites by the HTTPS: at the beginning of the web address and the little lock icon located in the lower-right corner of a secure page.
- You, the user, may be a security risk. Use common sense. Download programs only from reliable sources. Read online documentation to make sure you are downloading a version of a program that works on your OS. Always have a good antivirus program that checks incoming programs for viruses before you install them.
- You need an e-mail program such as Microsoft's Outlook Express or Netscape's Messenger to receive e-mail. To set up an e-mail client, provide your e-mail address and password. E-mail addresses use the accountname@Internet domain format. You must also add the names of the Post Office Protocol version 3 (POP3) or Internet Message Access Protocol (IMAP) server and the Simple Mail Transfer Protocol (SMTP) server. POP3 and IMAP handle incoming mail while SMTP handles outgoing mail. Although POP3 is more widely used, IMAP4 offers more features, such as letting you search messages for specific keywords or select messages you want to download to your PC. Your ISP should provide you with information to set up POP3 and SMTP. If you use ping to determine the IP address of the POP3 or SMTP server, you can get and send mail, even if the DNS server is not working.
- You'll need a newsreader to access a newsgroup. Microsoft's Outlook Express is the most common one. News servers run Network News Transfer Protocol (NNTP). Check with your ISP to get the name of the news server, along with a username and password if necessary.
- File Transfer Protocol (FTP) allows you to send and receive files. You may use an FTP client such as WS_FTP, although later versions of IE and other web browsers provide support for FTP. You'll have to log on to an FTP site, although most public FTP sites allow anonymous logon. If you access a site that requires a special username and password, it is best to use third-party programs

such as WS-FTP because they store these settings for easier access later.

- Telnet is a terminal emulation program for TCP/IP networks. It lets you connect to a server and run commands as if you were sitting in front of the server. Telnet requires a special username and password.
- Today, terminal emulation usually means graphical terminal emulation programs from third-party companies or in the Windows operating system. Terminal emulation programs require separate server and client programs. Windows 2000 Server was the first Windows

Useful for giving a tech control of a computer to troubleshoot a hardware configuration or driver problem, Remote Assistance can also be used to install drivers or teach someone how to use a particular application.

- Pop-ups and spyware are two irritating web browser problems. Used for advertising, pop-up windows may bombard your computer when you visit a web site. Though irritating, they are not dangerous. Spyware, on the other hand, runs in the background on your PC, sending information to a company about your browsing habits. Spyware can fire up pop-up windows of competing products on the web site you're currently viewing. Pop-ups may be difficult to eliminate since they often have no menu bar, button bar, or address window. Some even look similar to pop-up alerts from the Windows OS, right down to the Exit button. However, when you click this Exit button, you may get more pop-up windows. You can close the pop-ups without clicking them by choosing the Taskbar and selecting Close or by pressing ALT-F4 to close the window in the forefront. Although software applications are available to prevent pop-up ads, many of them prevent all new browser windows from opening.
- Spyware can use your computer's resources to run distributed computing applications, capture your keystrokes to steal passwords, reconfigure dial-up settings, or even use your Internet connection and

plug-ins other than Macromedia's Shockwave or Flash. Don't click anywhere inside pop-up browser windows since the Close button is likely a hyperlink. It's a good idea to install a dedicated spyware detection and removal program such as Lavasoft's Ad-aware or PepiMK's Spybot Search & Destroy. These applications detect and delete spyware of all sorts.

- Internet gaming is growing in popularity. Entire web sites allow you to find human players and enjoy thousands of different games. Online games include card games, first-person shooters such as Quake or Doom3, or even Massively Multiplayer Online Role Playing Games (MMORPGs) such as Sony's EverQuest.

Key Terms

Baud *(884)*

Browser *(881)*

Bits per second (bps) *(884)*

Digital subscriber line (DSL) *(890)*

File Transfer Protocol (FTP) *(899)*

HTTP Secure (HTTPS) *(897)*

HyperText Transport Protocol (HTTP) *(881)*

Integrated Services Digital Network (ISDN) *(890)*

Internet Connection Firewall (ICF) *(894)*

Internet Connection Sharing (ICS) *(893)*

Internet Message Access Protocol IMAP *(898)*

Internet service provider (ISP) *(882)*

Modem *(883)*

Point-to-Point Protocol (PPP) *(888)*

PostOffice Protocol version 3 (POP3) *(898)*

Proxy server *(895)*

Simple Mail Transfer Protocol (SMTP) *(898)*

Telnet *(900)*

Universal Asynchronous Receiver/Transmitter (UART) *(884)*

V standards *(884)*

World Wide Web *(881)*

Key Term Quiz

Use the Key Terms list to complete the sentences that follow. Not all the terms will be used.

1. Today's computers use the 16550A ____________ chip.
2. Internet Explorer is a(n) ____________.
3. ____________ is the most common method used to encrypt information, such as credit card numbers, on the Internet.
4. A(n) ____________ is software that allows multiple connections to go to the Internet through one protected PC.
5. Although some people use the term to refer to modem speed, ____________ actually means the number of cycles per second, while ____________ is a more accurate measurement of actual data throughput.
6. By using an anonymous logon, ____________ allows you to send and receive files from a public site.
7. Set by the International Telecommunications Union (ITU-T), ____________ define(s) the fastest transfer speed a modem can handle.
8. ____________ is the service that provides the structure for the World Wide Web, allowing documents to be sent across the Web.
9. Dial-up links to the Internet use a streaming hardware protocol called ____________.
10. Windows XP has built-in ____________ that allows incoming communication only from machines with whom you have recently communicated.

Multiple-Choice Quiz

1. All of the following *except* ________ are dedicated technologies that allow you to connect your PC to an ISP.
   - **A.** LAN
   - **B.** ISDN
   - **C.** DSL
   - **D.** Cable
2. All of the following are true statements about Integrated Services Digital Network (ISDN) service *except* ____________.
   - **A.** An ISDN connection uses either an internal or an external terminal adapter (TA).
   - **B.** BRI has two B channels and one D channel for a throughput total of 128 Kbps.
   - **C.** PRI has 23 B channels and 1 D channel for a total throughput of 1.5 Mbps.
   - **D.** ISDN consists of end-to-end high-speed analog lines.
3. Remote Assistance can be used for all of the following *except* to ____________.
   - **A.** Install a driver.
   - **B.** Demonstrate how to configure an application.
   - **C.** Wake up a computer that is hibernating.
   - **D.** Troubleshoot a hardware configuration.
4. The router that your PC uses to connect to your Internet service provider is referred to as the ____________.
   - **A.** Loopback address
   - **B.** Backbone
   - **C.** IP address
   - **D.** Default gateway
5. To configure dial-up networks with Windows XP, use the ____________ applet.
   - **A.** Network and Internet Connections
   - **B.** Network Neighborhood
   - **C.** Internet Connection Sharing
   - **D.** Remote Assistance
6. All of the following statements are true *except*:
   - **A.** An external modem uses the UART chip in the computer's serial port.
   - **B.** An internal modem uses the UART chip in the computer's serial port.
   - **C.** An internal modem has a built-in UART chip.
   - **D.** A UART chip converts serial data to parallel data and vice-versa.

7. To check to see if the web server you are trying to reach is available or is down, you can use the command-line utility called __________.

   A. ping

   B. ICS

   C. Telnet

   D. NNTP

8. Which of the following Internet connection methods will allow you to watch television on your computer if you have a TV tuner card?

   A. DSL

   B. All lines on the Internet are busy.

   C. You dialed the wrong number.

   D. The modem is bad.

10. Modems may connect through all of the following expansion slots *except* ________.

   A. AGP

   B. PCI

   C. ACR

   D. CNR

11. A ___________ is either hardware or software that protects your computer or network from probing or malicious users.

   A. Router

   B. Firewall

   C. Protocol

   D. Spyware

12. Which of the following technologies will allow you to use the same line to talk on the phone and surf the Internet?

   A. DUN

   B. ISDN

   C. DSL

   D. Cable

13. Liz can receive her e-mail, but she cannot send

14. The extremely fast networking connections through which Internet transmissions take place are called ____________.

   A. Gateways

   B. Root servers

   C. Backbones

   D. ISPs

15. To connect to the Internet via wireless means, you must use ___________.

   A. Satellite technology

   B. A LAN that's wired to an ISP

   C. Both A and B

   D. None of the above

Essay Quiz

1. With the rash of worms and viruses that attack computers connected to the Internet, how can you protect your computer?

2. Andrew's wife, Talena, collects Hull pottery. Andrew found a shop on the Internet that has a piece she's been wanting. He'd love to get it for her birthday next week, but the only way it can arrive by then is if he pays for it with his credit card. He's a bit apprehensive about giving his credit card number over the Internet. He wants you to tell him whether you think the site is safe or not. How can you evaluate the site to determine if it uses encryption for credit card numbers?

3. Sean is planning to take some distance education courses next term. He currently uses a regular phone line and a modem to connect to the Internet. He's consulted you to figure out what

his options are for a faster connection. Review his options, giving him the advantages and disadvantages, along with any restrictions that may prevent his receiving the service.

- ISDN has a high initial cost for equipment and installation and is limited to an 18,000-foot radius of a central office. It will provide throughput up to 128K.
- DSL is also limited to about an 18,000-foot radius of a main phone-service switching center. It provides an upload speed of about 384 Kbps and a download speed as fast as 2 Mbps. From a single phone line, he will be able to use voice and data simultaneously.
- If he has cable TV, he will likely be able to get cable Internet service. Its cost and speed are similar to those of DSL.
- If he is so far out in the country that he can't get the other choices, he will be limited to satellite Internet service. Its speed is comparable to DSL and cable, but the initial cost may be greater since he'll have to purchase a satellite dish.

4. With a child in high school and another at a local college, it's always a struggle in Tom's house about who gets to use the computer to do Internet research. It's not feasible for Tom to install another line, but he does have a second computer. What solution can you offer to solve his problem?
5. By now, you've become a regular columnist for your company's monthly newsletter. Everybody in the company uses e-mail and browses the Web, but you're convinced that the company would benefit if employees knew how to use some of the other Internet services. You've decided that this month's article will highlight three other Internet services. Which three will you discuss and what will you include about each?

Lab Projects

• Lab Project 24.1

In this chapter, you learned how dangerous spyware can be. You may already have spyware on your computer and be unaware of it. Download the spyware detection and removal programs you learned about in this chapter: Lavasoft's Ad-aware and PepiMK's Spybot Search & Destroy. You'll rest better tonight after you run these applications to detect and delete any spyware that may be hiding on your computer!

• Lab Project 24.2

Have you heard of WebDAV? Web Distributed Authoring and Versioning is a set of extensions added to HyperText Transfer Protocol to support collaborative authoring on the Web. While HTTP is a reading protocol, WebDAV is a writing protocol created by a working group of the Internet Engineering Task Force (IETF). DAV offers a faster, more secure method of file transfer than FTP, and some predict that it may make FTP obsolete. It's already incorporated into most current operating systems and applications. Some authors say that WebDAV will change the way we use the Web. Use the Internet to learn more about WebDAV and its features. Apple calls it "a whole new reason to love the Net." After learning about WebDAV, see if you agree.

Numerals

1.44 MB The storage capacity of a typical 3.5-inch floppy disk.

10`BaseT Umbrella term for three Ethernet standards that use UTP: 10BaseT, 100BaseT, and 1000BaseT.

10Base2 Also called **Thinnet** or **Thin Ethernet**. An Ethernet LAN designed to run on common coax RG-58 cabling, almost ex- [illegible]

[illegible] standard spelling exists, so sometimes written 10BASE-5 or 10Base-5.

10BaseT An Ethernet LAN designed to run on UTP cabling. 10BaseT runs at 10 megabits per second. The maximum length for the cabling between the NIC and the hub (or switch, repeater, etc.) is 100 meters. It uses baseband signaling. No industry standard spelling exists, so sometimes written 10BASE-T or 10Base-T.

100BaseT A generic term for any Ethernet cabling system that is designed to run at 100 megabits per second on UTP cabling. It uses baseband signaling. No industry standard spelling exists, so it's sometimes written 100BASE-T or 100Base-T.

1000BaseT Gigabit Ethernet.

16450, 16550, 16550A, 16550AF, 16550AFN These are incremental improvements in UARTs. The 16550AFN is considered the most sophisticated UART available today. Note: the 16450 should not be used with any modem faster than a 14.4 Kbps modem.

16-bit Able to process 16 bits of data at a time.

16-bit ISA bus A new bus technology introduced with the first AT computers; provided backward compatibility for older 8-bit cards. Also known as the AT bus.

2.1 Speaker setup consisting of two stereo speakers combined with a subwoofer.

24-bit color Referred to as 24-bit or true color, using 3 bytes per pixel to represent a color image in a PC. The 24 bits enable up to 16,777,216 colors to be stored and displayed.

286 Also called **80286**. Intel's second-generation processor. The 286 has a 16-bit external data bus and a 24-bit address bus. It was the first Intel processor to achieve 286 protected mode.

3.5-inch floppy drive format All modern floppy disk drives are of this size; the format was introduced 1986 and is one of the longest surviving pieces of computer hardware.

30-pin SIMM An obsolete memory package that utilized 30 contacts to connect to the motherboard and required a whole bank to be filled before the memory was recognized.

34-pin ribbon cable This type of cable is used by floppy disk [illegible]

3-D sound A generic term for making sounds emanate from all directions—i.e., *surround sound*—and for making sounds realistic. Popular in 3-D games and home theaters.

4.1 Four speakers and a subwoofer.

40-pin ribbon cable This type of cable is used to attached EIDE devices (such as hard disk drives) or ATAPI devices (such as CD-ROMs) to a system.

486DX Intel's fourth generation CPU. Essentially an 80386DX with a built-in cache and math co-processor.

486DX/2, 486DX/3, 486DX/4 486 CPUs that operate externally at one speed and internally at a speed that is two, three, or four times faster. Although the internal speed can be more than two times as fast as the external speed, these CPUs are known collectively as "clock doublers."

486SX A 486DX without the built-in math coprocessor.

5.1 Five speakers and a subwoofer.

5.25-inch floppy drive format The predecessor to the modern 3.5-inch floppy drive format; very rarely used currently.

50-pin high density HD cable External cable for SCSI-2 devices.

50-pin ribbon cable Also called a **Type A cable**. A type of ribbon cable used for connecting internal SCSI-1 and SCSI-2 devices.

586 An unofficial, generic term that describes the Intel Pentium processor or Pentium family of CPUs.

686 An unofficial, generic term that describes the Intel Pentium II processor or equivalent CPUs.

68-pin high density HD cable External cable for wide SCSI-2 and SCSI-3 devices.

68-pin ribbon cable A type of cable that connects internal SCSI devices. There are two types of 68-pin ribbon cables: an obsolete Type B used in conjunction with a 50-pin Type A cable to connect early SCSI-2 devices, and a P type that can be used singularly.

72-pin SIMM An obsolete memory package that utilized 72 contacts to connect to the motherboard, replacing 30-pin SIMMs and eliminating some of the issues with banking.

8.3 naming system A file naming convention that specified a maximum of eight characters for a filename, followed by a 3-character file extension. Has been replaced by LFN (Long Filename) support.

80-wire cable Also called an **SCA 80 cable**. Special type of cable used with some SCSI-3 internal devices that allows for devices to be hot-swapped.

80-wire ribbon cable Cable used to connect internal UDMA hard drives. Required to achieve transfer speeds above 33 Mbps; pin-compatible with traditional 40-pin ribbon cable connections.

802.11b A wireless networking standard that operates in 2.4-GHz band with a theoretical maximum throughput of 11 Mbps.

8086 Mode *See* Real mode.

8086/8088 The first generation of Intel processor used in IBM PCs. The 8086 and 8088 were identical with the exception of the external data bus—the 8086 had a 16-bit bus while the 8088 had an 8-bit bus.

8237 The part number for the original DMA controller. Although long obsolete, the name is still often used in reference to DMA.

8259 The part number for the original IRQ controller. Although long obsolete, the name is still often used in reference to IRQ usage.

A

Access speed The amount of time needed for the DRAM to supply the Northbridge with any requested data.

ACPI (Advanced Configuration and Power Interface) A power management specification that far surpasses its predecessor, APM, by providing support for hot-swappable devices and better control of power modes.

Active directory A form of directory service used in networks with Windows 2000 Servers.

Active Matrix Also called **TFT (Thin Film Transistor)**. A type of liquid crystal display that replaced the passive matrix technology used in most portable computer displays.

Active partition One of the four primary partitions on a hard drive can be designated as the *active* partition, meaning the partition the master boot record scans for a boot sector and operating system files.

Active termination A method for terminating fast/wide SCSI that uses voltage regulators in lieu of resistors.

Address bus The wires leading from the CPU to the memory controller chip (chipset) that enable the CPU to address RAM. Also used by the CPU for I/O addressing. An internal electronic channel from the microprocessor to Random Access Memory, along which the addresses of memory storage locations are transmitted. Like a post office box, each memory location has a distinct number or address; the address bus provides the means by which the microprocessor can access every location in memory.

Address space The total amount of memory addresses that an address bus can contain.

Administrative tools A group of Control Panel applets, including Computer Management, Event Viewer, and Performance.

Administrator account A user account, created when the OS is first installed, that is allowed complete, unfettered access to the system without restriction. Think of this account as the "god" account.

ADSL (Asymmetric Digital Subscriber Line) A fully digital, dedicated connection to the telephone system that provides download speeds up to 9 Mbps and upload speeds of up to 1 Mbps.

Advanced Startup Options menu A menu that can be reached during the boot process that offers advanced OS startup options, such as boot in Safe Mode or boot into Last Known Good Configuration.

AGP (Accelerated Graphics Port) A 32/64-bit expansion slot designed by Intel specifically for video that runs at 66 MHz and yields a throughput of 254 Mbps, at least. Later versions (2X, 4X, 8X) give substantially higher throughput.

AIX (Advanced Interactive Executive) IBM's version of UNIX, which runs on 386 or better PCs.

Algorithm A set of rules for solving a problem in a given number of steps.

Alternating current (AC) A type of electricity where the flow of electrons alternates direction, back and forth, in a circuit.

ALU (Arithmetic Logic Unit) The circuit that performs CPU math calculations and logic operations.

AMD (Advanced Micro Devices) CPU and chipset manufacturer that competes with Intel. Produces the popular Athlon and Duron processors.

AMI (American Megatrends, Inc) Major producer of BIOS software for motherboards, as well as many other computer-related components and software.

Amperes (amps or A) The unit of measure for amperage, or electrical current.

Amplifier A device that strengthens electrical signals, enabling them to travel farther.

Analog An analog device uses a physical quantity, such as length or voltage, to represent the value of a number. By contrast, digital storage relies on a coding system of numeric units.

Analog video Picture signals represented by a number of smooth transitions between video levels. Television signals are analog, as opposed to digital video signals, which assign a finite set of levels. Because computer signals are digital, analog video must be converted into a digital form before it can be shown on a computer screen.

ANSI (American National Standards Institute) Body responsible for standards like ASCII.

ANSI character set The ANSI-standard character set, which defines 256 characters. The first 128 are ASCII, and the second group of 128 contain math and language symbols.

Anti-aliasing In computer imaging, a blending effect that smoothes sharp contrasts between two regions—e.g., jagged lines or different colors. This reduces the jagged edges of text or objects. In voice signal processing, it refers to the process of removing or smoothing out spurious frequencies from waveforms produced by converting digital signals back to analog.

Archive attribute An attribute of a file that shows whether the file has been backed up since the last change. Each time a file is opened, changed, or saved, the archive bit is turned on. Some types of backups will turn off this archive bit to indicate that a good backup of the file exists on tape.

ARP (Address Resolution Protocol) A protocol in the TCP/IP suite used with the command-line utility of the same name to determine the MAC address that corresponds to a particular IP address.

ASCII (American Standard Code for Information Interchange) The industry-standard 8-bit characters used to define text characters, consisting of 96 upper and lowercase letters, plus 32 non-printing control characters, each of which is numbered. These numbers were designed to achieve uniformity among different computer devices for printing and the exchange of simple text documents.

Aspect ratio The ratio of width to height of an object. Standard television has a 4:3 aspect ratio.

Asynchronous Communication whereby the receiving devices must send an acknowledgment or "ACK" to the sending unit to verify a piece of data has been sent.

AT (Advanced Technology) The model name of the second-generation, 80286-based IBM computer. Many aspects of the AT, such as the BIOS, CMOS, and expansion bus, have become *de facto* standards in the PC industry. The physical organization of the components on the motherboard is called the *AT form factor*.

ATA (AT Attachment) A type of hard drive and controller. ATA was designed to replace the earlier ST506 and ESDI drives without requiring replacement of the AT BIOS—hence, AT attachment. These drives are more popularly known as IDE drives. (*See* ST506, ESDI, and IDE.) The **ATA/33** standard has drive transfer speeds up to 33 Mbps; the **ATA/66** up to 66 Mbps; the **ATA/100** up to 100 Mbps; and the **ATA/133** up to 133 Mbps. (*See* Ultra DMA.)

ATA/133 *See* ATA (AT Attachment).

ATA/ATAPI-6 Data transfer standard for parallel drives; ATA-6 hard drives and controllers can handle transfer speeds up to 100 Mbps as long as an 80-wire cable is used.

ATAPI (ATA Packet Interface) A series of standards that enable mass storage devices other than hard drives to use the IDE/ATA controllers. Extremely popular with CD-ROM drives and removable media drives like the Iomega ZIP drive. (*See* EIDE.)

Athlon Popular CPU manufactured by AMD.

ATTRIB.EXE A command used to view the specific properties of a file; can also be used to modify or remove file properties,

matically recognized by the BIOS.

AUTOEXEC.BAT A batch file that DOS executes when you start or restart the system. AUTOEXEC.BAT is not necessary, but when you're running a computer to which you've attached several devices and several different software applications, the file is essential for efficient operation. AUTOEXEC.BAT files commonly include PATH statements that tell DOS where to find application programs, and commands to install a mouse or operate your printer.

Automated System Recovery (ASR) A utility, included with Windows XP, which allows a user to create a complete system backup.

Automatic Skip Driver (ASD) A utility for preventing "bad" drivers from running the next time you boot your computer. This utility examines startup log files and removes problematic drivers from boot process.

AUTORUN.INF A file included on some CD-ROMs that automatically launches a program or installation routine when the CD-ROM is inserted into a CD-ROM drive.

Award Software Major producer of BIOS software for motherboards.

B

Baby AT A derivative of the AT form factor with a much smaller footprint. *See also* AT (Advanced Technology).

Back up To save important data in a secondary location as a safety against loss of the primary data.

Backside bus The set of wires that connect the CPU to Level 2 cache. First appearing in the Pentium Pro, most modern CPUs have a special backside bus. Some buses, such as that in the later

Celeron processors (300A and beyond), run at the full speed of the CPU, whereas others run at a fraction. Earlier Pentium IIs, for example, had backside buses running at half the speed of the processor. *See also* Frontside bus and External data bus.

Backup and Restore Wizard A utility contained within Windows that allows a user to create system backups and set system restore points.

Bandwidth A piece of the spectrum occupied by some form of signal, such as television, voice, fax data, etc. Signals require a certain size and location of bandwidth in order to be transmitted. The higher the bandwidth, the faster the signal transmission, allowing for a more complex signal such as audio or video. Because bandwidth is a limited space, when one user is occupying it, others must wait their turn. Bandwidth is also the capacity of a network to transmit a given amount of data during a given period.

Bank The total number of SIMMs that can be accessed simultaneously by the chipset. The "width" of the external data bus divided by the "width" of the SIMM sticks.

Base I/O address The base I/O address refers to the first address in a device's I/O address set. Techs commonly refer to the full set of addresses by using only the base address and drop the leading zeros. A sound card that used the I/O address range of 0330 to 033F, for example, would be said to use I/O 330.

Baseband Digital signaling that has only one signal (a single signal) on the cable at a time. The signals are only ever in three states: one, zero, and idle.

Baseline Static image of a system's (or network's) performance when all elements are known to be working properly.

BASIC (Beginners All-purpose Symbolic Instruction Code) A commonly used personal-computer language first developed at Dartmouth during the 1960s and popularized by Microsoft.

Basic disks A hard disk drive partitioned in the "classic" way with a master boot record (MBR) and partition table. *See also* Dynamic disk.

Baud One analog cycle on a telephone line. In the early days of telephone data transmission, the baud rate was often analogous to bits-per-second. Due to advanced modulation of baud cycles as well as data compression, this is no longer true.

BBS (Bulletin Board System) A term for dial-up online systems from which users can download software and graphics, send and receive e-mail, and exchange information. Usually run by individuals from their homes. Although once very popular, BBS sites are rapidly diminishing due to the popularity of the Internet.

Beep codes A series of audible tones produced by a motherboard during the POST. These tones identify whether the POST has completed successfully or whether some piece of system hardware is not working properly. Consult the manual for your particular motherboard for a specific list of beep codes.

Binary numbers A number system with a base of 2, unlike the number systems most of us use which have bases of 10 (decimal numbers), 12 (measurement in feet and inches), and 60 (time). Binary numbers are preferred for computers for precision and economy. An electronic circuit that can detect the difference between two states (on-off, 0-1) is easier and more inexpensive to build than one that could detect the differences among ten states (0–9).

BIOS (Basic Input/Output Services) Classically, the software routines burned onto the System ROM of a PC. More commonly seen as any software that directly controls a particular piece of hardware. A set of programs encoded in Read-Only Memory (ROM) on computers. These programs handle startup operations and low-level control of hardware such as disk drives, the keyboard, and monitor.

Bit (binary digit) A bit is a single binary digit. Any device that can be in an on or off state.

Bit depth The number of colors a video card is capable of producing. Common bit depths are 16-bit and 32-bit, representing 65,536 colors and 16.7 million colors respectively.

BNC connector A connector used for 10Base2 coaxial cable. All BNC connectors have to be locked into place by turning the locking ring 90 degrees.

Boot To initiate an automatic routine that clears the memory, loads the operating system, and prepares the computer for use. The term is derived from "pull yourself up by your bootstraps." PCs must do that because RAM doesn't retain program instructions when power is turned off. A *cold boot* occurs when the PC is physically switched on. A *warm boot* loads a fresh OS without turning off the computer, lessening the strain on the electronic circuitry. To do a *warm* boot, press the CTRL-ALT-DELETE keys at the same time twice in rapid succession (the three-fingered salute).

Boot sector The first sector on an IBM-PC hard drive or floppy disk, track 0. The boot-up software in ROM tells the computer to load whatever program is found there. If a system disk is read, the program in the boot record directs the computer to the root directory to load the operating system.

Bootable disk A disk that contains a functional operating system; can also be a floppy disk or CD-ROM.

BOOT.INI A text file used during the boot process that provides a list of all OSs currently installed and available for NTLDR. Also tells where each OS is located on the system.

BOOTLOG.TXT A text file where information concerning the boot process is logged; useful when troubleshooting system boot errors and problems.

Bootstrap loader Lines of code in a system's BIOS that scan for an operating system; looks specifically for a valid boot sector and when one is found, control is handed over to boot sector and bootstrap loader removes itself from memory.

BPS (bits per second) Measurement of how fast data is moved from one place to another. A 56K modem can move 56,000 bits per second.

Bridge A device that connects two networks and passes traffic between them based only on the node address, so that traffic between nodes on one network does not appear on the other network. For example, an Ethernet bridge only looks at the Ethernet address. Bridges filter and forward packets based on MAC addresses and operate at Level 2 (Data Link layer) of the OSI seven-layer model.

Broadband A type of signaling that sends multiple signals (channels) over the cable at the same time. The best example of broadband signaling is cable television. The zero, one, and idle states (*see* Baseband) exist on multiple channels on the same cable.

Broadcast A broadcast is a packet addressed to all machines. In TCP/IP, the general broadcast address is 255.255.255.255.

Browser A program specifically designed to retrieve, interpret, and display web pages.

Buffer Electronic storage, usually DRAM, which holds data

Bug A programming error that causes a program or a computer system to perform erratically, produce incorrect results, or crash. The term was coined when a real bug was found in one of the circuits of one of the first ENIAC computers.

Bus A series of wires connecting two or more separate electronic devices that enable those devices to communicate.

Bus topology A configuration wherein all computers connect to the network via a central bus cable.

Byte Eight contiguous bits, the fundamental data unit of personal computers. Storing the equivalent of one character, the byte is also the basic unit of measurement for computer storage. Bytes are counted in powers of two.

C

CAB files Short for "cabinet files." These files are compressed and most commonly used during OS installation to store many smaller files, such as device drivers.

Cable modem A network device that enables a PC to connect to the Internet using RG-6 coaxial cabling (i.e., the same coax used for cable television). Capable of download speeds up to 1.5 megabits per second.

Cable tester Device that tests the continuity of cables. Some testers also test for electrical shorts, crossed wires, or other electrical characteristics.

Cache A special area of RAM that stores the data most frequently accessed from the hard drive. Cache memory can optimize the use of your systems.

Cache memory A special section of fast memory chips set aside to store the information most frequently accessed from RAM.

Caching The act of holding data in cache memory for faster access and use.

Card Generic term for anything that you can snap into an expansion slot.

Card services The uppermost level of PCMCIA services. The card services level recognizes the function of a particular PC Card and provides the specialized drivers necessary to make the card work.

CardBus 32-bit PC cards that can support up to eight (8) devices on each card. Electrically incompatible with earlier PC cards (3.3V versus 5V).

CAT3 Category 3 wire; an EIA/TIA standard for UTP wiring that can operate up to 20 megabits per second.

images. Also a shorthand way to describe a monitor that uses CRT rather than LCD technology.

CD quality CD quality audio has a sample rate of 44.4 KHz and a bit rate of 128-bits.

CD-DA (CD-Digital Audio) A special format used for early CD-ROMs and all audio CDs; divides data into variable length tracks. A good format to use for audio tracks but terrible for data due to lack of error checking.

CD-I CD Interactive "green disk" format by Philips; designed to play compressed movies.

CD-R (Compact Disk Recordable) A type of CD technology that accepts a single "burn" but cannot be erased after that one burn.

CD-ROM (Compact Disk Read-Only Memory) A read-only compact storage disk for audio or video data. Recordable devices, such as CD-Rs, are updated versions of the older CD-ROM players. CD-ROMs are read using *CD-ROM drives.*

CD-RW (Compact Disk Read/Write) A type of CD technology that accepts multiple reads/writes like a hard drive.

Celeron A lower-cost CPU based on Intel's Pentium II or Pentium III CPUs.

Centronics connector A type of connector commonly used with printers and SCSI-1 devices, distinguished by a central contact board rather than pins, and secured in place by clips.

Chipset Electronic chips that handle all of the low-level functions of a PC, which in the original PC were handled by close to 30 different chips. Chipsets usually consist of one, two, or three separate chips embedded into a motherboard to handle all of these functions.

CHS (Cylinder/Heads/Sectors per Track) The initials for the combination of the three critical geometries used to determine the size of a hard drive—Cylinders, Heads, and Sectors per Track.

CISC (Complex Instruction-Set Computing) CISC is a CPU design that enables the processor to handle more complex instructions from the software at the expense of speed. All Intel processors for PCs are CISC processors.

Clean installation An operating system installed on a fresh drive, following a reformat of that drive. A clean install is often the only way to correct a problem with a system when many of the crucial operating system files have become corrupted.

Cleaning kit A set of tools used to clean a device or piece of media.

Client A computer program that uses the services of another computer program. Software that extracts information from a server; your auto-dial phone is a client, and the phone company is its server. Also a machine that accesses shared resources on a server.

Client/server A relationship in which client software obtains services from a server on behalf of a user.

Client/server application An application that performs some or all of its processing on an application server rather than on the client. The client usually only receives the result of the processing.

Client/server network A network that has dedicated server machines and client machines.

Clock An electronic circuit utilizing a quartz crystal that generates evenly spaced pulses at speeds of millions of cycles per second. The pulses are used to synchronize the flow of information through the computer's internal communication channels. Some computers also contain a circuit that tracks hours, minutes, and seconds.

Clock cycle A single charge to the clock wire of a CPU.

Clock multiplying CPU A CPU that takes the incoming clock signal and multiples it inside the CPU to let the internal circuitry of the CPU run faster.

Clock speed The speed at which a CPU executes instructions, measured in MHz or GHz. In modern CPUs, the internal speed is general a multiple of the external speed. *See also* Clock multiplying CPU.

Cluster The basic unit of storage on a floppy or hard disk. Two or more sectors are contained in a cluster. When DOS/Windows 9*x* stores a file on disk, it writes those files into dozens or even hundreds of contiguous clusters. If there aren't enough contiguous open clusters available, the operating system finds the next open cluster and writes there, continuing this process until the entire file is saved. The FAT tracks how the files are distributed among the clusters on the disk.

CMOS (Complimentary Metal-Oxide Semiconductor) Originally, the type of non-volatile RAM that held information about the most basic parts of your PC such as hard drives, floppies, and amount of DRAM. Today, actual CMOS chips have been replaced by Flash-type non-volatile RAM. The information is the same, however, and is still called CMOS—even though it is now almost always stored on Flash RAM.

Coaxial cable Cabling in which an internal conductor is surrounded by another, outer conductor, thus sharing the same axis.

Code A set of symbols representing characters (e.g., ASCII code) or instructions in a computer program (a programmer writes *source* code, which must be translated into *executable* or *machine* code for the computer to use). Used colloquially as a verb—*to code* is to write computer code—and as a noun, "He writes clean/sloppy/bad code."

Codec (Compressor/Decompressor) Software that compresses or decompresses media streams.

Collision The result of two nodes transmitting at the same time on a multiple access network such as Ethernet. Both packets may be lost or partial packets may result.

Collision domain A set of Ethernet segments that receive all traffic generated by any node within those segments. Repeaters, amplifiers, and hubs do not create separate collision domains, but bridges, routers, and switches do.

COM port(s) A system name that refers to the serial communications ports available on your computer. When used as a program extension, .COM indicates an executable program file limited to 64K.

Command A request, typed from a terminal or embedded in a file, to perform an operation or to execute a particular program.

Command line interface A user interface for an OS devoid of all graphical trappings; interfaces directly with the OS.

Command processor The part of the operating system that accepts input from the user and displays any messages, such as confirmation and error messages.

Command prompt A text prompt for entering commands.

COMMAND.COM In DOS, a file that contains the command processor. This must be present on the startup disk for DOS to run. COMMAND.COM is usually located in the root directory of your hard drive.

Common command set (CCS) A set of 18 commands introduced with SCSI-2 devices that made installing and configuring SCSI devices much easier.

Communications program A program that makes a computer act as a terminal to another computer. Communications programs usually provide for file transfer between microcomputers and mainframes.

Compiler A program that translates human-readable programs into a form the computer understands. The input (source code) to the compiler is a description of an algorithm in a problem-oriented language; its output (object code) is an equivalent description of the algorithm in a machine-oriented language.

Complimentary Metal Oxide Semiconductor (CMOS) The small bit of volatile memory used to store BIOS configuration data.

Component failure Occurs when a system device fails due to manufacturing or some other type of defect.

Compression The process of squeezing data to eliminate redundancies, allowing files to be stored or transmitted using less space.

Conditioning charger A battery charger that contains intelligent circuitry that prevents portable computer batteries from being overcharged and damaged.

CONFIG.SYS An ASCII text file in the root directory that contains configuration commands. CONFIG.SYS enables the system to be set up to configure high, expanded, and extended memories by the loading of HIMEM.SYS and EMM386.EXE drivers, as

is an example of a connection-oriented protocol.

Connectors Used to attach cables to a system. Common types of connectors include USB, PS/2, and DB-25.

Control panel A collection of Windows applets, or small programs, that can be used to configure various pieces of hardware and software in a system.

Controller card A card adapter that connects devices, like a disk drive, to the main computer bus/motherboard.

Conventional memory In any IBM PC-compatible computer, the first 640 K of the computer's RAM. This amount proved to be insufficient because of programs that demanded more memory and users who wanted to run more than one program at a time. Many DOS users equipped their systems with extended or expanded memory and the memory management programs needed to access that memory.

Convergence A measure of how sharply a single pixel appears on a CRT; a monitor with poor convergence would produce images that are not sharply defined.

Copy backup A type of backup similar to Normal or Full, in that all selected files on a system are backed up. This type of backup *does not* change the archive bit of the files being backed up.

Counter Used to track data about a particular object when using the Performance console.

CPU (Central Processing Unit) The "brain" of the computer. The microprocessor that handles the primary calculations for the computer. They are known by names such as Pentium 4 and Athlon.

CRC (Cyclical Redundancy Check) A very accurate mathematical method that is used to check for errors in long streams of transmitted data. Before data is sent, the main computer uses the data to calculate a CRC value from the data's contents. If the receiver calculates a different CRC value from the received data, the data was corrupted during transmission and is resent. Ethernet packets have a CRC code.

CRIMM (Continuity RIMM) A passive device added to populate unused banks in a system that uses RAMBUS RIMMs.

Cross-linked file In DOS, a file-storage error that occurs when the FAT indicates that two files claim the same disk cluster. This occurs when the system is abnormally halted. To repair, run SCANDISK or NORTON'S Disk Doctor.

Crossover cable Special UTP cable used to connect hubs or to

flow through the network ultimately to reach address locations.

Cylinder A single track on all the platters in a hard drive. Imagine a hard disk drive as a series of metal cans, nested one inside another; a single can would represent a cylinder.

Cyrix Company that made CPUs in direct competition with Intel. Bought by Via Technologies in 2000.

D

Daily backup Also called **daily copy backup**. A backup of all files that have been changed on that day without changing the archive bits of those files.

Daisy-chaining A method of connecting together several devices along a bus and managing the signals for each device.

DAT (Digital Audio Tape) Higher storage capacity tape recording system that uses digital recording methods. Used for digital audio and video as well as data backups.

Data structure A term that is used interchangeably with the term "file systems." *See also* File system.

DB connectors D-shaped connectors used for a variety of connections in the PC and networking world. Can be male (with prongs) or female (with holes) and have a varying number of pins or sockets.

DB-15 DB connector (female) used in 10Base5 networks. *See also* DIX and AUI.

DB-25 connector DB connector (female), commonly referred to as a parallel port connector.

Debug To detect, trace, and eliminate errors in computer programs.

Decoder A tool used to decode data that has been encoded; for instance, a DVD decoder breaks down the code used to encrypt the data on a piece of DVD Video media.

Dedicated circuit Circuit that runs from a breaker box to specific outlets.

Dedicated server A machine that is not used for any client functions, only server functions.

Dedicated telephone line A telephone line on a circuit that is always open, or connected. Dedicated telephone lines usually do not have numbers.

Default A software function or operation that occurs automatically unless the user specifies something else.

Default gateway In a TCP/IP network, the nearest router to a particular host. This router's IP address is part of the necessary TCP/IP configuration for communicating with multiple networks using IP.

Defragmentation (DEFRAG) A procedure in which all the files on a hard disk are rewritten on disk so that all parts of each file reside in contiguous clusters. The result is an improvement of up to 75 percent of the disk's speed during retrieval operations.

Degauss The procedure used to break up the electromagnetic fields that can build up on the cathode ray tube of a monitor; involves running a current through a wire loop. Most monitors feature a manual degaussing tool.

Desktop A user's primary interface to the Windows operating system.

Desktop extenders A type of portable computer that offers some of the features of a full-fledged desktop computer, but with a much smaller footprint and lower weight.

Desktop replacement A type of portable computer that offers the same performance of a full-fledged desktop computer; these systems are normally very heavy to carry and often cost much more than the desktop systems they replace.

Detlog.txt A log file created during the initial operating system installation that tracks the detection, query, and installation of all devices.

Device driver A subprogram to control communications between the computer and peripherals.

Device Manager A utility that allows techs to examine and configure all the hardware and drivers in a Windows PC.

DHCP (Dynamic Host Configuration Protocol) A protocol that enables a DHCP server to set TCP/IP settings automatically for a DHCP client.

Differential backup Similar to an incremental backup. Backs up the files that have been changed since the last backup. This type of backup does not change the state of the archive bit.

Digital Theatre Systems (DTS) A technology for sound reductions and channeling methods, similar to Dolby Digital.

Digitally signed driver All drivers designed specifically for Windows 2000 and Windows XP are digitally signed, meaning they are tested to work stably with these operating systems.

DIMM (Dual In-line Memory Module) A type of DRAM packaging, similar to SIMMs with the distinction that each side of each tab inserted into the system performs a separate function. Comes in a compact 72-pin SO DIMM format, and full-size 144- and 168-pin formats.

DIR command A command used in the command line interface that displays the entire contents of the current working directory.

Direct current (DC) A type of electricity where the flow of electrons is in a complete circle.

Directory Another name for a file or folder.

DirectSound3D (DS3D) Introduced with DirectX 3.0, DS3D is a command set used to create positional audio, or sounds that appear to come from in front, in back, or to the side of a user. *See also* DirectX.

DirectX A series of standards promulgated by Microsoft that enables applications running on Windows platforms to control hardware directly.

Disk cache A piece of DRAM, often integrated into a disk drive, that is used to store frequently accessed data in order to speed up access times.

Disk cleanup A series of utilities, built into Windows, that can help a user clean up their disks by removing temporary internet files, deleting unused program files, and more.

Disk Drive Controller The circuitry that controls the physical operations of the floppy disks and/or hard disks connected to a computer.

Disk management A snap-in available with the Microsoft Management Console that allows a user to configure the various disks installed in a system; available from the Administrative Tools area of the Control Panel.

Disk mirroring Process by which data is written simultaneously to two or more disk drives. Read and write speed is decreased but redundancy in case of catastrophe is increased.

Disk striping Process by which data is spread among multiple (at least two) drives. It increases speed for both reads and writes of data. Considered RAID level 0, because it does *not* provide fault tolerance.

Disk striping with parity Provides fault tolerance by writing data across multiple drives and then including an additional drive, called a *parity drive*, that stores information to rebuild the data contained on the other drives. Disk striping with parity requires at least three physical disks: two for the data and a third for the parity drive. It provides data redundancy at RAID levels 3–5 with different options.

Disk thrashing A term used to describe a hard disk drive that is constantly being accessed due to the lack of available system memory. When system memory runs low, a Windows system will utilize hard disk space as "virtual" memory, thus causing the unusual amount of hard disk drive access.

Display adapter *See* Video card.

Dithering A technique for smoothing out digitized images; using alternating colors in a pattern to produce perceived color detail.

DIX Connector (Digital, Intel, Xerox) Also called an **AUI Connector**. The DIX standard was the original implementation of Ethernet. The DIX connector is the standard connector used with 10Base5 Ethernet.

DMA (Direct Memory Access) A technique that some PC

ports and drives to which you attach a portable PC. Most docking stations use a proprietary connector. Often confused with a *port replicator*, a similar device that lacks extra drives.

Documentation A collection of organized documents or the information recorded in documents. In the computer world, instructional material specifying the inputs, operations, and outputs of a computer program or system; for example, a manual and Getting Started card.

Dolby Digital A technology for sound reductions and channeling methods.

Domain Term used to describe groupings of users, computers, or networks. In Microsoft networking, a domain is a group of computers and users that share a common account database, called a SAM, and a common security policy. On the Internet, a domain is a group of computers that share a common element in their hierarchical name. Other types of domains exist—e.g., collision domain, etc.

Domain controller A Microsoft Windows NT machine that stores the user and server account information for its domain in a database called a SAM (security accounts manager) database.

DOS (Disk Operating System) The set of programming that allows a program to interact with the computer. Examples of early disk operating systems include Microsoft's MS-DOS, IBM's PC-DOS and OS/2, and Apple's MacOS System 7. Microsoft's Windows 3.1 was not technically an operating system, since it still required MS-DOS to work, but it was often referred to as one. Windows 9*x*/Me and Windows NT/2000/XP are true disk operating systems.

DOS prompt A symbol, usually a letter representing the disk drive followed by the greater-than sign (>), which tells you that the operating system is ready to receive a command. Windows 9*x* and 2000 systems use the term *command prompt* rather than DOS prompt.

DOS Protected Mode Interface (DPMI) A DOS-like environment found in Windows 9*x*/Me consisting of three main files: IO.SYS, MSDOS.SYS, and COMMAND.COM. Unlike DOS, the DPMI has support for FAT32 and long filenames.

DOSKEY A DOS utility that enables you to type more than one command on a line, store and retrieve previously used DOS commands, create stored macros, and customize all DOS commands.

Dot-matrix printer A printer that creates each character from an array of dots. Pins striking a ribbon against the paper, one pin for each dot position, form the dots. The printer may be a serial printer (printing one character at a time) or a line printer.

Double-sided double density A type of floppy disk that is capable of holding 360 KB on a 5.25-inch disk and 720 KB of data of 3.5-inch disk. This format can be read in all modern floppy disk drives.

Double word A group of 32 binary digits. Four bytes.

DPI (dots per inch) A measure of printer resolution that counts the dots the device can produce per linear (horizontal) inch.

DRAM (Dynamic Random Access Memory or Dynamic RAM) The memory used to store data in most personal computers. DRAM stores each bit in a "cell" composed of a transistor and a capacitor. Because the capacitor in a DRAM cell can only hold a charge for a few milliseconds, DRAM must be continually refreshed, or rewritten, to retain its data.

Drive change signal A signal created by a floppy disk drive when a floppy disk is inserted into the drive; transmitted on the 34th wire in a floppy disk drive cable. When Windows first reads a floppy disk, the directory is stored in RAM until the drive change signal indicates that the disk has been removed or that data has been changed.

DSL (Digital Subscriber Line) A high-speed Internet connection technology that uses a regular telephone line for connectivity. DSL comes in several varieties, including Asynchronous (ADSL) and Synchronous (SDSL), and many speeds. Typical home-user DSL connections are ADSL with a download speed of up to 1.5 Mbps and an upload speed of 384 Kbps.

DSP (Digital Signal Processor) A specialized microprocessor-like device that processes digital signals at the expense of other abilities, much as the FPU is optimized for math functions. DSPs are used in such specialized hardware such as high-speed modems, multimedia sound cards, MIDI equipment, and real-time video capture and compression.

Dual Inline Memory Module (DIMM) A 64-bit memory module that is currently the standard memory package on modern computers. Examples of DIMMs include SDRAM, DDR SDRAM, and SO DIMMs.

Dual Inline Pin Package (DIPP) An early type of RAM package that featured two rows of exposed connecting pins; very fragile and difficult to install. DIPPs were replaced first with SIPPs and later with SIMMs and DIMMs.

Duplexing Also called **disk duplexing** or **drive duplexing.** Similar to mirroring in that data is written to and read from two physical drives, for fault tolerance. Separate controllers are used for each drive, both for additional fault tolerance and additional speed. Considered RAID level 1.

Duron A lower-cost version of AMD's Athlon series of CPUs.

DVD (Digital Versatile Disk) A CD media format that provides for 4–17 GB of video or data storage.

DVD Multi A description given to DVD drives that are capable of reading all six DVD formats.

DVD+RW A type of rewriteable DVD media.

DVD-ROM The DVD-ROM is the DVD equivalent of the standard CD-ROM.

DVD-RW A type of rewriteable DVD media.

DVD-Video A DVD format used exclusively to store digital video; capable of storing more than two hours of high-quality video on a single DVD.

Dynamic disk A special feature of Windows 2000 and Windows XP that allows a user to span a single volume across two or more drives. Dynamic disks do not have partitions; they have volumes. Dynamic disks can be striped, mirrored, and striped or mirrored with parity.

Dynamic link A method of linking data so that it's shared by two or more programs. When data is changed in one program, it's changed in the other.

Dynamic Routing Protocol A protocol that supports the building of automatic routing tables, such as OSPF (Open Shortest Path First) or RIP (Routing Information Protocol).

Dynamic routing Process by which routers in an internetwork automatically exchange information with all other routers, enabling them to build their own list of routes to various networks, called a *routing table*. Dynamic routing requires a dynamic routing protocol, such as OSPF or RIP.

E

E-mail, Email (electronic mail) Messages, usually text, sent from one person to another via computer. E-mail can also be sent automatically to a group of addresses (mailing list).

EAX 3-D sound technology developed by Creative Labs, but now supported by most soundcards.

EDB (external data bus) The primary data highway of all computers. Everything in your computer is tied either directly or indirectly to the external data bus. *See also* Frontside bus and Backside bus.

EDO (Enhanced Data Out) DRAM An improvement on FPM DRAM in that more data can be read before the RAM must be refreshed.

EEPROM (Electrically Erasable Programmable Read-Only Memory) A type of ROM chip that can be erased and reprogrammed electrically. EEPROMs were the most common storage device for BIOS before the advent of Flash ROM.

EIA/TIA (Electronics Industry Association, Telecommunications Industry Association) The standards body that defines most of the standards for computer network cabling. Most of these standards are defined under the EIA/TIA 568 standard.

EIDE (Enhanced IDE) A marketing concept of hard drive maker Western Digital, encompassing four improvements for IDE drives. These improvements included >528 MB drives, four devices, increase in drive throughput, and non-hard drive devices. (*See* ATAPI, PIO.)

EISA (Enhanced ISA) An improved expansion bus, based on the ISA bus, with a top speed of 8.33 MHz, a 32-bit data path, and a high degree of self-configuration. Backwardly compatible with legacy ISA cards.

Emergency Repair Disk (ERD) This disk saves critical boot files and partition information and is our main tool for fixing boot problems in Windows 2000.

EMI (Electro-Magnetic Interference) EMI is electrical interference from one device to another, resulting in poor performance of the device being interfered with. An example is having static on your TV while running a blow dryer, or placing two monitors too close together and getting a "shaky" screen.

EMM386.EXE An expanded memory emulator that enables DOS applications to use the extended memory as if it were expanded memory. EMM386.EXE also enables the user to load device drivers and programs into the upper memory area.

EMS (Expanded Memory Specification) A method of memory management developed by Intel, Lotus, and Microsoft that enabled MS-DOS computers to use memory exceeding the 640K limit imposed by MS-DOS. Memory that conforms to this standard is called *expanded memory*. Originally, this standard required that a special hardware device be added to the computer, but that was quickly supplanted by a less efficient but much cheaper software solution. Expanded memory has been made almost obsolete by the Windows environment, which isn't limited by the 640K barrier. EMS is now required almost solely by DOS-based games.

Encapsulation Refers here to the process of putting the packets from one protocol inside the packets of another protocol. An example of this is TCP/IP encapsulation in NetWare servers, where IPX/SPX packets are placed inside TCP/IP packets, enabling Novell NetWare to use TCP/IP for transport while still allowing the network operating system to get the data it needs from IPX/SPX.

Encrypting file system (EFS) The encryption tool found in NTFS5.

End User License Agreement (EULA) An agreement that accompanies a piece of software which the user must agree to in order to use the software. This agreement outlines the terms of use for software and also lists any actions on the part of the user that violate the agreement.

EPROM (Erasable Programmable Read-Only Memory) A special form of ROM that can be erased by high-intensity ultraviolet light and then rewritten (reprogrammed).

from one body to another. ESD is a real menace to PCs as it can cause permanent damage to semiconductors.

ESDI (Enhanced Small Device Interface) Second-generation hard drives, distinguished from their predecessors—ST506—by greater data density and lack of dependence on CMOS settings. Completely obsolete.

Ethernet Name coined by Xerox for the first standard of network cabling and protocols. Ethernet is based on a bus topology.

Event Viewer A utility made available as an MMC snap-in that allows a user to monitor various system events, including network bandwidth usage and CPU utilization.

EXPAND A CAB file utility program included with Windows 2000. Usage of EXPAND is similar to usage of EXTRACT. *See also* EXTRACT.

Expansion bus Set of wires going to the CPU, governed by the expansion bus crystal, directly connected to expansion slots of varying types (ISA, PCI, AGP, etc.). Depending on the type of slots, the expansion bus runs at a percentage of the main system speed (8.33–66 MHz).

Expansion bus crystal A crystal, originally designed by IBM, which controls the speed of the expansion bus.

Expansion slots 1. Connectors on a motherboard that allow a user to add optional components to a system. *See also* AGP (Accelerated Graphics Port) and PCI (Peripheral Component Interconnect). 2. A receptacle connected to the computer's expansion bus, designed to accept adapters.

Extended partition A type of hard disk partition. Extended partitions are not bootable and you may only have one extended partition per disk. The purpose of an extended partition is to divide a large disk into smaller partitions, each with a separate drive letter.

Extension The three letters that follow a filename; an extension identifies the type of file. Common file extensions are .ZIP, .EXE, and .DOC.

External data bus (EDB) The primary data highway of all computers. Everything in your computer is tied either directly or indirectly to the external data bus. *See also* Frontside bus and Backside bus.

EXTRACT A program native to Windows 9*x*/Me that can be used to extract data from compressed CAB files. *See also* EXPAND.

ond cluster for that file is the address for the third cluster, and so on until the final cluster, which gets a special "end of file" code. This table is the only way DOS knows where to access files. There are two FATs, mirror images of each other, in case one is destroyed or damaged.

FAT16 File allocation table that uses 16 bits for addressing clusters. Commonly used with DOS and Windows 95 systems.

FAT32 File allocation table that uses 32 bits for addressing clusters. Commonly used with Windows 98 and Windows ME systems. Some Windows 2000 Professional systems also use FAT32, although most use the more robust NTFS.

FDISK A disk partitioning utility included with Windows 9*x*/Me.

Fiber Optics A high-speed channel for transmitting data, made of high-purity glass sealed within an opaque tube. Much faster than conventional copper wire such as coaxial cable.

File A collection of any form of data that is stored beyond the time of execution of a single job. A file may contain program instructions or data, which may be numerical, textual, or graphical information.

File allocation unit Another term for cluster. *See also* cluster.

File format The way information is encoded in a file. Two primary types are binary (pictures) and ASCII (text), but within those there are many formats, such as BMP and GIF for pictures; commonly represented by a suffix at the end of the filename, for example, .txt for a text file, or .exe for an executable).

File fragmentation The allocation of a file in a non-contiguous sector on a disk. Fragmentation occurs because of multiple deletions and write operations.

File server A computer designated to store software, courseware, administrative tools, and other data on a local- or wide-area network. It "serves" this information to other computers via the network when users enter their personal access codes.

File system A scheme that directs how an OS stores and retrieves data on and off a drive; FAT32 and NTFS are both file systems.

Filename A name assigned to a file when the file is first written on a disk. Every file on a disk within the same folder must have a unique name. Since Windows 95, you may use up to 32 characters for filenames, and filenames can contain any character (including spaces), except the following: \ / : * ? " < > |.

Firewall A device that restricts traffic between a local network and the Internet.

FireWire (1394) An IEEE 1394 standard to send wide-band signals over a thin connector system that plugs into TVs, VCRs, TV cameras, PCs, etc. This serial bus developed by Apple and Texas Instruments enables connection of 60 devices at speeds ranging from 100 to 400 megabits per second.

Firmware Embedded programs or code that is stored on a ROM chip. Firmware is generally OS-independent, thus allowing devices to operate in a wide variety of circumstances without direct OS support.

Flash ROM A type of ROM technology that can be electrically reprogrammed while still in the PC. Flash is overwhelmingly the most common storage medium of BIOS in PCs today, as it can be upgraded without even having to open the computer on most systems.

FlexATX A motherboard form factor. Motherboards built in accordance with the FlexATX form factor are very small, much smaller than microATX motherboards.

Flexing Flexing is caused when components are installed on a motherboard after it has been installed into a computer case. Excessive flexing can cause damage to the motherboard itself.

Floppy disk A type of removable storage media that can hold between 720 KB and 1.44 MB of data.

Floppy drive A piece of system hardware that uses removable 3.5-inch disks as storage media.

FM synthesis A method for producing sound that used electronic emulation of various instruments to more or less produce music and other sound effects.

Forced perfect termination (FPT) A method for terminating SCSI devices that uses diodes instead of resistors.

Form factor A standard for the physical organization of motherboard components and motherboard size. The most common form factors are ATX, NLX, and AT.

Formatting The process of magnetically mapping a disk to provide a structure for storing data; can be done to any type of disk, including a floppy disk, hard disk, or other type of removable disk.

FPM (Fast Page Mode) DRAM that uses a "paging" function to increase access speed and to lower production costs. Virtually all DRAMS are FPM DRAM. The name FPM is also used to describe older style, non-EDO DRAM.

FPU (Floating Point Unit) A formal term for the math co-processor (also called a *numeric processor*). This is a specialized processor that handles certain calculations faster than the CPU. A math co-processor calculates using floating point math (which allows for decimals), whereas the CPU can only deal with integers. Intel's 486 and later processors and Motorola's PowerPC have an FPU built into the CPU chip, whereas earlier designs needed a separate chip (such as Intel's 80387).

Fragmentation Occurs when files and directories get jumbled on a fixed disks and are no longer contiguous. Fragmentation can significantly slow down hard disk drive access times and can be repaired by using the DEFRAG utility that is included with each version of Windows. *See also* Defragmentation (DEFRAG), File fragmentation.

Freeware Software that is distributed for free, with no license fee.

Frontside bus Name for the wires that connect the CPU to the main system RAM. Generally running at speeds of 66–133 MHz. Distinct from the Expansion bus and the Backside bus, though it shares wires with the former.

FRU (Field Replaceable Unit) Any part of a PC that is considered to be replaceable "in the field," i.e. a customer location. There is no official list of FRUs—it is usually a matter of policy by the repair center.

FTP (File Transfer Protocol) A set of rules that allows two computers to talk to one another as a file transfer is carried out. This is the protocol used when you transfer a file from one computer to another across the Internet.

Fuel cells A new type of power source that uses chemical reactions to produce electricity. Lightweight, compact, and stable, these devices are expected to replace batteries as the primary power source for portable PCs.

Full-duplex Describes any device that can send and receive data simultaneously.

Function key A keyboard key that gives an instruction to a computer, as opposed to keys that produce letters, numbers, marks of punctuation, etc.

Fuser assembly A mechanism, found in laser printers, that uses two rollers to fuse toner to paper during the print process.

G

Gateway The technical meaning is a hardware or software setup that translates between two dissimilar protocols. For example, Prodigy has a gateway that translates between its internal, proprietary e-mail format and Internet e-mail format. Another, less technical meaning of gateway is any mechanism for providing access to another system, e.g. AOL might be called a gateway to the Internet. *See* Default gateway.

General Protection Fault (GPF) A Windows error that often causes a PC to lock up. Most commonly caused by two programs accessing the same resources. Also, General Protection Fault is a great geek-oriented comic strip you can find online at www.gpf-comics.com.

Giga- The prefix for the quantity 1,073,741,824. One gigabyte would be 1,073,741,824 bytes. One gigahertz would be 1,073,741,824 hertz.

Gigabyte 1,024 megabytes.

Graphical device interface (GDI) The portion of the Windows OS that supports graphical elements such as scroll bars, menus, icons, and the like.

Green PC A computer system designed to operate in an en-

"gooey"), on the other hand, enables the user to interact with the computer graphically, by manipulating icons that represent programs or documents with a mouse or other pointing device.

H

Half-duplex Any device that at any given moment can either send or receive data, but not both. Most Ethernet transmissions are half-duplex.

Handshaking A procedure performed by modems, terminals, and computers to verify that communication has been correctly established.

Hang When a computer freezes so that it does not respond to keyboard commands, it is said to "hang" or to have "hung."

Hang time The amount of seconds a too-often-hung computer is airborne after you have thrown it out a second-story window.

Hard disk *See* Hard drive.

Hard drive A data-recording system using solid disks of magnetic material turning at high speeds to store and retrieve programs and data in a computer. Also called a *hard disk.*

Hardware Physical computer equipment such as electrical, electronic, magnetic, and mechanical devices. Anything in the computer world that you can hold in your hand. A floppy drive is hardware; Microsoft Word is not.

Hardware Abstraction Layer (HAL) A part of the Windows OS that separates system-specific device drivers from the rest of the NT system.

Hardware Compatibility List (HCL) A list that is maintained by Microsoft that lists all the hardware that is supported by an operating system. This list is helpful to use when upgrading a system; with a quick glance, you can make sure that support is available for all the devices in a system before you begin the upgrade.

Hardware profile A list of devices that Windows automatically enables or disables in the Device Manager, depending on what devices the system detects.

Hardware protocol A hardware protocol defines many aspects of a network, from the packet type to the cabling and connectors used.

Hayes Command Set A standardized set of instructions used to control modems.

Heap In Microsoft Windows, a special memory area used for critical resources when a program is executed. These heaps are limited to 64K in size, and when a program tries to use more, the

waking up, all information is retrieved from the hard disk drive and returned to RAM.

Hidden attribute A file attribute that, when used, does not allow a file to be seen when using the DIR command.

Hierarchical directory tree The method by which Windows organizes files into a series of folders, called directories, under the root directory. *See also* Root directory.

High-level formatting A type of format that sets up a file system on a drive.

High-voltage anode A component in a CRT monitor. The high voltage anode has very high voltages of electricity flowing through it.

High Voltage Differential (HVD) A rare type of SCSI device that uses two wires for each bit of information: one wire for data and one for the inverse of this data. The inverse signal takes the place of the ground wire in the single-ended cable. By taking the difference of the two signals, the device can reject the common-mode noise in the data stream.

HIMEM.SYS A DOS device driver that configures extended memory and high memory so that programs conforming to XMS can access it.

HMA (High Memory Area) The first 64K of memory above 1 megabyte is known as the HMA. Programs that conform to XMS can use HMA as a direct extension of conventional memory. Most of the portions of DOS that must be loaded into conventional memory can be loaded into the HMA.

Horizontal refresh rate (HRR) The amount of time it takes for a CRT to draw one horizontal line of pixels on a display.

Host A single device (usually a computer) on a TCP/IP network that has an IP address—any device that can be the source or destination of a data packet. Also, in the mainframe world, a computer that is made available for use by multiple people simultaneously.

Host adapter An expansion card that serves as a host to a particular device; for instance, you can install a SCSI host adapter into a system to allow for SCSI functionality even if SCSI hardware was not originally included with the machine.

Host ID The portion of an IP address that defines a specific machine.

HOSTS file A static text file that is used to resolve host names to IP addresses.

HotSync (Synchronization) A term used to describe the synchronizing of files between a PDA and a desktop computer. HotSync is the name of the synchronization program that is used by PalmOS-based PDAs.

HTML (HyperText Markup Language) An ASCII-based script-like language for creating hypertext documents like those on the World Wide Web.

HTTP (HyperText Transfer Protocol) Extremely fast protocol used for network file transfers in the WWW environment.

HTTP Secure (HTTPS) A secure form of HTTP, used commonly for Internet business transactions or any time where a secure connection is required. *See also* HTTP.

Hub An electronic device that sits at the center of a star topology network and provides a common point for the connection of network devices. In a 10BaseT Ethernet network, the hub contains the electronic equivalent of a properly terminated bus cable; in a Token Ring network, the hub contains the electronic equivalent of a ring.

I

I/O (input/output) A general term for reading and writing data to a computer. The term "input" includes data from a keyboard, pointing device (such as a mouse), or loading a file from a disk. "Output" includes writing information to a disk, viewing it on a CRT, or printing it to a printer.

I/O addressing The process of using the address bus to talk to system devices.

I/O Controller Hub (ICH5) The official name for the Southbridge chip found in Intel's 875P chipset for the Pentium 4.

Icon A small image or graphic, most commonly found on a system's desktop, which launches a program when selected.

IDE (Intelligent [or Integrated] Drive Electronics) A PC specification for small to medium sized hard drives in which the controlling electronics for the drive are part of the drive itself, speeding up transfer rates and leaving only a simple adapter (or "paddle"). IDE only supported two drives per system of no more than 504 megabytes each, and has been completely supplanted by Enhanced IDE. EIDE supports four drives of over 8 GB each and more than doubles the transfer rate. The more common name for ATA drives. (*See* ATA.)

IEEE (Institute of Electronic and Electrical Engineers) IEEE is the leading standards-setting group in the United States.

IEEE 1284 A standard governing parallel communication. *See also* IEEE.

IFCONFIG A command-line utility for Linux servers and workstations that displays the current TCP/IP configuration of the machine, similar to IPCONFIG and WINIPCFG.

Image file A bit-by-bit image of the data to be burned on the CD or DVD—from one file to an entire disc—stored as a single file on a hard drive. Image files are particularly handy when copying from CD to CD or DVD to DVD.

Image installation An operating system installation that uses a complete image of a hard disk drive as an installation media. This is a helpful technique to use when installing an operation system on a large number of identical PCs.

Impact printer A type of printer that uses pins and inked ribbons to print text or images on a piece of paper. These printers are noisy, slow, and have very low print quality.

Impedance The amount of resistance to an electrical signal on a wire. It is used as a relative measure of the amount of data a cable can handle.

Incremental Backup A type of backup that backs up all files that have their archive bits turned on, meaning that they have been changed since the last backup. This type of backup turns the archive bits off after the files have been backed up.

INF file A Windows driver file.

Inkjet printer A type of printer that uses liquid ink, sprayed through a series of tiny jets, to print text or images on a piece of paper.

Interlaced The TV/video systems in which the electron beam writes every other line; then retraces itself to make a second pass to complete the final framed image. Originally, this reduced magnetic line paring, but took twice as long to paint, which added some flicker in graphic images.

Internet Connection Firewall (ICF) A software firewall built into Windows XP that protects your system from unauthorized access from the Internet.

Internet Connection Sharing (ICS) A method for allowing a single network connection to be shared among several machines. ICS was first introduced with Windows 98.

InterNIC Organization run by Network Solutions, Inc. (NSI) and AT&T that provides several services to Internet users, the most prominent being the registration of domain names and assignment of IP addresses.

Interrupt A suspension of a process, such as the execution of a computer program, caused by an event external to the computer and performed in such a way that the process can be resumed. Events of this kind include sensors monitoring laboratory equipment or a user pressing an interrupt key.

Interrupt 13 (INT13) Extensions An improved type of BIOS that accepts EIDE drives up to 137 GB.

Interrupt request (IRQ) IRQs are hardware lines over which devices can send interrupt signals to the microprocessor. When you add a new device to a PC, you sometimes need to set its IRQ number. This specifies which interrupt line the device may use. IRQ conflicts used to be a common problem when adding expansion boards, but the Plug-and-Play specification has removed this headache in most cases.

Intranet A private network inside a company or organization that uses the same kinds of software that you find on the public

shorthand numeric values. The IP address can be broken down into a network ID and a host ID.

IPCONFIG A command-line utility for Windows NT servers and workstations that displays the current TCP/IP configuration of the machine, similar to WINIPCFG and IFCONFIG.

IPX/SPX (Internetwork Packet Exchange/Sequence Packet Exchange) Protocol suite developed by Novell, primarily for supporting Novell NetWare-based networks.

IRC (Internet Relay Chat) The Internet Relay Chat, or just Chat, is an online group discussion.

IRQ steering A technique used by the PCI bus to avoid conflict with legacy devices. The PCI bus appears to support classic IRQs for PCI cards, but uses dynamically assigned interrupt channels when the cards actually need to interrupt.

ISA (Industry Standard Architecture) The Industry Standard Architecture design is found in the original IBM PC for the slots on the motherboard that allowed additional hardware to be connected to the computer's motherboard. An 8-bit, 8.33 MHz expansion bus was designed by IBM for its AT computer and released to the public domain. An improved 16-bit bus was also released to the public domain. Various other designs such as IBM's MicroChannel and EISA bus tried to improve on the design without much popularity. ISA only supports 8- and 16-bit data paths, so 32-bit alternatives such as PCI and AGP have become popular. Although ISA slots linger on most motherboards, they are on the way out, replaced by the newer 32-bit slots.

ISDN (Integrated Services Digital Network) The CCITT (Comité Consutatif Internationale de Télégraphie et Téléphonie) standard that defines a digital method for communications to replace the current analog telephone system. ISDN is superior to telephone lines because it supports up to 128 Kbps transfer rate for sending information from computer to computer. It also allows data and voice to share a common phone line.

ISP (Internet service provider) A company that provides access to the Internet, usually for money.

J

Joystick A peripheral often used while playing computer games; originally intended as a multi-purpose input device.

Joule A unit of measurement of energy. Surge suppressors are rated in the number of joules they can handle during an electrical surge or spike.

extra confusion to the IT industry, K is often misspoken as "kilo," the metric value for 1,000. 10 KB, for example, spoken as "10 kilobytes," actually means 10,240 bytes rather than 10,000 bytes.

Kbps (kilobits per second) Data transfer rate.

Kermit A communications protocol that enables you to transfer files between your computer and online network systems. Kermit has built-in error correction and can handle binary (non-text) files.

Kernel The core portion of the program that resides in memory and performs the most essential operating system tasks.

Keyboard An input device. There are two common types of keyboards—those that use a mini-DIN (PS/2) connection and those that use a USB connection.

Kilohertz (KHz) A unit of measure that equals a frequency of one thousand cycles per second.

Knowledge Base A large collection of documents and FAQs that is maintained by Microsoft. Found on Microsoft's web site, the Knowledge Base is an excellent place to search for assistance on most operating system problems.

L

LAN (local area network) A group of PCs connected together via cabling, radio, or infrared that use this connectivity to share resources such as printers and mass storage.

Laser printer An electro-photographic printer in which a laser is used as the light source.

Last Known Good Configuration An option on the Advanced Startup Options menu that allows your system to revert to a previous configuration in order to troubleshoot and repair any major system problems.

Layer In the communications field, a grouping of related tasks involving the transfer of information. Also, a level of the OSI reference model used for networking computers. In graphics work, images can be created in layers, which can be manipulated separately and then flattened into a single image.

Layer 1 The **Physical layer** defines hardware connections and turns binary into physical pulses (electrical or light). Repeaters and hubs operate at the Physical layer.

Layer 2 The **Data Link layer** identifies devices on the Physical layer. MAC addresses are part of the Data Link layer. Bridges operate at the Data Link layer.

Layer 2 Switch Also called a **Bridge**. Filters and forwards data packets based on the MAC addresses of the sending and receiving machines.

Layer 3 The **Network layer** moves packets between computers on different networks. Routers operate at the Network layer. IP and IPX operate at the Network layer.

Layer 3 Switch Also called a **Router**. Filters and forwards data packets based on the network addresses of the sending and receiving machines.

Layer 4 The **Transport layer** breaks data down into manageable chunks. TCP, UDP, SPX, and NetBEUI operate at the Transport layer.

Layer 5 The **Session layer** manages connections between machines. NetBIOS and Sockets operate at the Session layer.

Layer 6 The **Presentation layer**, which can also manage data encryption, hides the differences between various types of computer systems.

Layer 7 The **Application layer** provides tools for programs to use to access the network (and the lower layers). HTTP, FTP, SMTP, and POP3 are all examples of protocols that operate at the Application layer.

LBA (Logical Block Addressing) A translation (algorithm) of IDE drives promoted by Western Digital as a standardized method for breaking the 504 MB limit in IDE drives. Subsequently universally adopted by the PC industry and is standard on all EIDE drives.

LCD (Liquid Crystal Display) A display technology that relies on polarized light passing through a liquid medium rather than on electron beams striking a phosphorescent surface.

LED (Light Emitting Diode) Solid state device that vibrates at luminous frequencies when current is applied.

Legacy device Any device that is not Plug-and-Play compatible.

Limited account A type of user account that has limited access to a system. Accounts of this type cannot alter system files, cannot install new programs, and cannot edit settings using the Control Panel.

Linux Open source UNIX-clone operating system.

Liquid Crystal Display (LCD) A type of display commonly used on portable PCs. LCDs are slowly replacing CRTs as the display of choice for most desktop computer users, however, due in large part to rapidly falling prices. LCDs use liquid crystals and electricity to produce images on the screen.

Lithium-Ion (Li-Ion) A type of battery commonly used in portable PCs. Li-Ion batteries don't suffer from the memory effects of NiCd batteries and provide much more power for a great length of time.

LMHOSTS file A static text file used to resolve NetBIOS names to IP addresses.

Local bus A high-speed data path that directly links the computer's CPU with one or more slots on the expansion bus. This direct link means signals from an adapter do not have to travel through the computer expansion bus, which is significantly slower.

Localhost An alias for the loopback address of 127.0.0.1, referring to the current machine.

Logical address An address that describes both a specific network and a specific machine on that network.

Logical drives Sections of a hard drive that are formatted and assigned a drive letter, each of which is presented to the user as if it were a separate drive.

Logical Unit Numbers (LUNs) A specialized SCSI configuration that allows for multiple devices to share a single SCSI ID. This type of arrangement is found most commonly in high-end servers that have large hard disk arrays.

Loopback Address A reserved IP address for internal testing: 127.0.0.1. *See also* Localhost.

Low-level format Defining the physical location of magnetic tracks and sectors on a disk.

Low Voltage Differential (LVD) A type of differential SCSI. LVD SCSI requires less power than HVD and is compatible with existing SE SCSI controllers and devices. LVD devices can sense the type of SCSI and then work accordingly. If you plug an LVD device into an SE chain, it will act as an SE device. If you plug an LVD device into LVD, it will run as LVD. LVD SCSI chains can be up to 12 meters in length.

LPT port LPT (for line port or line printer) ports refer specifically to system resources assigned to parallel ports. LPT1 is the combination of I/O address 370 and IRQ7, for example, whereas LPT2 is I/O 270 and IRQ5. Most users and technicians refer to the 25-pin female parallel port found on older PCs as an LPT port. Also commonly referred to as a printer port.

Luminescence The part of the video signal that controls the luminance/brightness of the picture. Also known as the "Y" portion of the component signal.

M

MAC (Media Access Control) address Unique 48-bit address assigned to each network card. IEEE assigns blocks of possible addresses to various NIC manufacturers to help ensure that the address is always unique. The Data Link layer of the OSI model uses MAC addresses for locating machines.

Machine language A programming language or instruction code that is immediately interpretable by the hardware of the machine concerned.

Mass storage Hard drives, CD-ROMs, removable media drives, etc.

Master Boot Record (MBR) A tiny bit of code that takes control of the boot process from the system BIOS.

MAU (Multistation Access Unit) Also called **MSAU**. A hub used in Token Ring networks.

MB (megabyte) 1,048,576 bytes.

MCA (MicroChannel) Expansion bus architecture developed by IBM as the (unsuccessful) successor to ISA. MCA had a full 32-bit design as well as being self-configuring.

MCC (Memory Controller Chip) The chip that handles memory requests from the CPU. Although once a special chip, it has been integrated into the chipset on all PCs today.

MCH (Memory Controller Hub) Intel's name for the Northbridge chip in some of their chipsets.

Mega- A prefix that usually stands for the binary quantity 1,048,576 (2^{20}). One megabyte is 1,048,576 bytes. One megahertz, however, is a million Hertz. Sometimes shortened to **Meg**, as in "a 286 has an address space of 16 Megs."

Memory A device or medium for temporary storage of programs and data during program execution. The term is synonymous with storage, although it is most frequently used for referring to the internal storage of a computer that can be directly addressed by operating instructions. A computer's temporary storage capacity is measured in kilobytes (KB) or megabytes (MB) of RAM (random-access memory). Long-term data storage on disks is also measured in kilobytes, megabytes, gigabytes, and terabytes.

Mesh Topology Network wiring scheme where each computer has a dedicated connection to every other computer in a network.

MHz (Megahertz) A unit of measure that equals a frequency of one million cycles per second.

MicroATX A variation of the ATX form factor. MicroATX motherboards are generally smaller than their ATX counterparts, but retain all the same functionality.

Microchannel Architecture (MCA) An outdated expansion bus technology introduced by IBM.

Microcomputer A computer system in which the central processing unit is built as a single tiny semiconductor chip or as a small number of chips.

Microprocessor Also called **CPU**. The "brain" of a computer. The primary computer chip that determines the relative speed and capabilities of the computer.

Microsoft CD-ROM Extensions (MSCDEX) This program takes the device name set up in the CD-ROM's device driver line

Microsoft Product Activation (MPA) Introduced by Microsoft with the release on Windows XP, Microsoft Product Activation is to prevent unauthorized use of Microsoft's software by requiring a user to "activate" the software.

MIDI (Musical Instrument Digital Interface) MIDI is a standard that describes the interface between a computer and a device for simulating musical instruments. Rather than sending large sound samples, a computer can simply send "instructions" to the instrument describing pitch, tone, and duration of a sound. MIDI files are therefore very efficient. Because a MIDI file is made up of a set of instructions rather than a copy of the sound, it is easy to modify each component of the file. Additionally, it is possible to program many channels, or "voices," of music to be played simultaneously, creating symphonic sound.

MIME (Multipurpose Internet Mail Extensions) MIME is a standard for attaching binary files (such as executables and images) to the Internet's text-based mail (24 Kbps-packet size). The first packet of information received contains information about the file.

Mini power connector A type of connector used to provide power to floppy disk drives.

MIPS (Millions of Instructions per Second) Used for processor benchmarks.

Mirrored volume A volume that is mirrored on another volume. *See also* Mirroring.

Mirroring Also called **Drive mirroring**. Reading and writing data at the same time to two drives for fault tolerance purposes. Considered RAID level 1.

MMU (Memory-Management Unit) A chip or circuit that translates virtual memory addresses into physical addresses and may implement memory protection.

Mobile CPU A CPU designed for use in portable computers that uses much less power than a normal, desktop CPU.

Modem (MOdulator/DEModulator) A device that converts a digital bit stream into an analog signal (modulation) and converts incoming analog signals back into digital signals (demodulation). The analog communications channel is typically a telephone line and the analog signals are typically sounds.

Molex connector A type of computer power connector. CD-ROM drives, hard disk drives, and case fans all use this type of connector. A Molex connector is keyed to prevent it from being inserted into a power port improperly.

Motherboard A flat piece of circuit board that resides inside your computer case. The motherboard has a number of connectors on it; you can use these connectors to attach a variety of devices to your system, including hard disk drives, CD-ROM drives, floppy disk drives, and sound cards.

Motherboard book A valuable resource when installing a new motherboard. The motherboard book normally lists all the specifications about a motherboard, including the type of memory and type of CPU that should be used with the motherboard.

Mouse An input device that allows a user to manipulate a cursor on the screen in order to select items.

Mount point A drive that functions like a folder mounted into another drive.

MP3 Short for MPEG, Layer 3. MP3 is a type of compression used specifically for turning high-quality digital audio files into much smaller, yet similar sounding, files.

MSAU (Multistation Access Unit) Also called **MAU**. A hub used in Token Ring networks.

MSCONFIG A utility found in Windows that allows a user to configure a system's boot files and critical system files.

MS-DOS (Microsoft Disk Operating System) The first operating system released by Microsoft.

MSDOS.SYS One of the major system files of MS-DOS.

Multiboot installation A type of OS installation where multiple operating systems are installed on a single machine.

Multimedia Extensions (MMX) A set of specific CPU instructions that allows a CPU to handle many multimedia functions, such as digital signal processing. Introduced with the Pentium CPU, these instructions are now used on all x86 CPUs.

Multimeter A device that is used to measure voltage, amperage, and resistance.

Multiplexer A device that merges information from multiple input channels to a single output channel.

MultiRead The ability of most modern CD-ROM drives to read a wide variety of discs is called MultiRead. Modern CD-ROMs can read CD-ROM, CD-R, and CD-RW discs.

Multisession drive A recordable CD drive that is capable of burning multiple sessions on to a single recordable disc. A multisession drive also has the ability to "close" a CD-R so that no further tracks can be written to it.

Multitasking The process of running multiple programs or tasks on the same computer at the same time.

My Computer An applet that allows a user to access a complete listing of all fixed and removable drives contained within a system. Each version of Windows adds more functions to My Computer. With Windows XP, for example, My Computer offers quick access to the Control Panel, Add/Remove Programs, the System Information utility, and more.

My Documents Introduced with Windows 98, the My Documents folder provides a convenient place for a user to store his or her documents, log files, and any other type of files. Windows NT/2000/XP systems provide a separate My Documents folder for each user while Windows 9*x*/Me systems do not.

N

NBTSTAT A command-line utility used to check the current NetBIOS name cache on a particular machine. The utility compares NetBIOS names to their corresponding IP addresses.

NDS (Novell Directory Services) The default security and directory system for Novell NetWare 4.*x* and 5.*x*. Organizes users, servers, and groups into a hierarchical tree.

NetBEUI (NetBIOS Extended User Interface) A protocol supplied with all Microsoft networking products that operates at the Transport layer. Also a protocol suite that includes NetBIOS. NetBEUI does not support routing.

NetBIOS (Network Basic Input/Output System) A protocol that operates at the Session layer of the OSI seven-layer model. This protocol creates and manages connections based on the names of the computers involved.

NetBIOS Name A computer name that identifies both the specific machine and the functions that machine performs. A NetBIOS name consists of 16 characters: 15 characters of a name, with a 16th character that is a special suffix that identifies the role the machine plays.

NETSTAT A command-line utility used to examine the sockets-based connections open on a given host.

Network A collection of two or more computers interconnected by telephone lines, coaxial cables, satellite links, radio, and/or some other communication technique. A computer "network" is a group of computers that are connected together and that communicate with one another for a common purpose.

Network ID A number that identifies the network on which a device or machine exists. This number exists in both IP and IPX protocol suites.

Network Operating System (NOS) An NOS is an operating system that provides basic file and supervisory services over a network. While each computer attached to the network will have its own OS, the NOS describes which actions are allowed by each user and coordinates distribution of networked files to the user who requests them.

Newsgroup The name for discussion groups on Usenet.

NIC (Network Interface Card) An expansion card that enables a PC to physically link to a network.

Nickel-Cadmium (Ni-Cd) A type of battery that was used in the first portable PCs. Heavy and inefficient, these batteries also suffered from a memory effect that could drastically shorten the overall life of the battery. *See also* Nickel-Metal Hydride (Ni-MH), Lithium-Ion (Li-Ion).

functional units interconnect transmission lines.

Noise Undesirable signals bearing no desired information and frequently capable of introducing errors into the communication process.

Non-system disk or disk error An error that occurs during the boot process. Common causes for this error are leaving a non-bootable floppy disk in the floppy disk drive while the computer is booting.

Non-volatile A type of memory that retains data even if power is removed.

Normal backup A full backup of every selected file on a system. This type of backup turns off the archive bit after the backup.

Northbridge The Northbridge is the chip or chips that connect a CPU to memory, the PCI bus, Level 2 cache and AGP activities. The Northbridge chips communicate with the CPU through the FSB.

Ns (Nanosecond) A billionth of a second. Light travels 11 inches in one nanosecond.

NT File System (NTFS) A file system for hard drives that enables object-level security, long filename support, compression, and encryption. NTFS 4.0 debuted with Windows NT 4.0. Windows 2000 comes with the updated NTFS 5.0.

NTFS Permissions A set of restrictions that determine the amount of access given to a particular user on a system using NTFS.

NTFS4 A robust and secure file system that was introduced by Microsoft with Windows NT 4. NTFS provides an amazing array of configuration options for user access and security. Users can be granted access to data on a file by file basis.

NTFS5 An improvement of NTFS that was released with Windows 2000. *See also* NTFS.

NTLDR A Windows NT/2000/XP boot file. Launched by the MBR or MFT, NTLDR looks at the BOOT.INI configuration file for any installed operating systems.

NVIDIA A company that is one of the foremost manufacturers of graphics cards and chipsets.

NWLink Also called **IPX/SPX-Compatible Protocol**. Microsoft's implementation of IPX/SPX. *See also* IPX/SPX.

O

Object A system component that is given a set of characteristics and can be managed by the operating system as a single entity.

hardware.

OSI (Open Systems Interconnect) An international standard suite of protocols defined by International Organization for Standardization (ISO) that implements the OSI reference model for network communications between computers.

OSI Seven-Layer Model An architecture model based on the OSI protocol suite that defines and standardizes the flow of data between computers.

Overclocking To run a CPU or video processor faster than its rated speed.

Overdrive Generic name given to processors designed as aftermarket upgrades to computer systems.

P

P1 connector A type of connector used to provide power to ATX motherboards.

P4 12V connector A type of connector used to provide additional 12v power to motherboards that support Pentium IV processors.

P8 and P9 connectors A type of connector used to provide power to AT-style motherboards.

Packet Basic component of communication over a network. A group of bits of fixed maximum size and well-defined format that is switched and transmitted as a complete whole through a network. It contains source and destination address, data and control information.

Packets Small data units sent across a network.

Pages per minute (ppm) A measure of the speed of a printer.

Parallel ATA (PATA) A disk drive implementation that integrates the controller on the disk drive itself. *See also* ATA (AT Attachment).

Parallel port A connection for the synchronous, high-speed flow of data along parallel lines to a device, usually a printer.

Parity A method of error detection where a small group of bits being transferred are compared to a single "parity" bit that is set to make the total bits odd or even. The receiving device reads the parity bit and determines if the data is valid based on the oddness or evenness of the parity bit.

Partial Response Maximum Likelihood (PRML) An extremely advanced method of RLL used commonly on today's hard disk drives.

Partition A section of the storage area of a hard disk. A partition is created during initial preparation of the hard disk, before the disk is formatted.

Partition table A table located in the boot sector of a hard drive that lists every partition on the disk that contains a valid operating system.

Password Reset Disk A special type of floppy disk that can allow a user to recover a lost password without losing access to any encrypted, or password-protected, data.

Patch A small piece of software released by a software manufacturer that is used to correct a flaw or problem with a particular piece of software.

Patch cables Short (2–5 foot) UTP cables that connect patch panels to hubs.

Patch panel A panel containing a row of female connectors (ports) that terminate the horizontal cabling in the equipment room. Patch panels facilitate cabling organization and provide protection to horizontal cabling.

Path The route the operating system must follow to find an executable program stored in a subdirectory.

PCI (Peripheral Component Interconnect) A design architecture for the sockets on the computer motherboard that enable system components to be added to the computer. PCI is a "local bus" standard, meaning that devices added to a computer through this port will use the processor at the motherboard's full speed (up to 33 MHz), rather than at the slower 8 MHz speed of the regular bus. In addition to moving data at a faster rate, PCI moves data 32 or 64 bits at a time, rather than the 8 or 16 bits that the older ISA buses supported.

PCMCIA (Personal Computer Memory Card International Association) Also called **PC Card**. A consortium of computer manufacturers who devised the standard for credit card-sized adapter cards that add functionality in many notebook computers, PDAs, and other computer devices. The simpler term "PC Card" has become more common in referring to these cards.

PDA (Personal Digital Assistant) A handheld computer that blurs the line between the calculator and computer. Earlier PDAs were calculators that enabled the user to program in such information as addresses and appointments. Newer machines, such as the Palm Pilot, are fully programmable computers. Most PDAs use a pen/stylus for input rather than a keyboard. A few of the larger PDAs have a tiny keyboard in addition to the stylus.

Peer-to-Peer Networks A network in which each machine can act as both a client and a server.

Pentium Name given to the fifth generation of Intel microprocessors—has a 32-bit address bus, 64-bit external data bus, and dual pipelining. Also used for subsequent generations of Intel processors—the Pentium Pro, Pentium II, Pentium III, and Pentium 4.

Peripheral Any device other than the motherboard components of the computer. The CPU is not a peripheral; the floppy drive is a peripheral.

Phoenix Technologies Major producer of BIOS software for motherboards.

Phosphor An electro-fluorescent material used to coat the inside face of a cathode ray tube (CRT). After being hit with an electron, it glows for a fraction of a second.

Photo-CD A compressed image format developed by Kodak that allows for many photos to be stored on a single CD-ROM.

Photosensitive drum An aluminum cylinder coated with particles of photosensitive compounds that is used in a laser printer. The photosensitive drum is usually contained within the toner cartridge.

Physical address Defines a specific machine without any reference to its location or network. A MAC address is an example of a physical address.

Pin 1 A designator used to ensure proper alignment of floppy disk drive and hard disk drive connectors.

Pin Grid Array (PGA) A popular CPU package where a CPU is packaged in a ceramic material and a large number of pins extend from the bottom of the package in a regular pattern or array.

Ping (Packet Internet Groper) Slang term for a small network message (ICMP ECHO) sent by a computer to check for the presence and aliveness of another. Also used to verify the presence of another system.

PIO (Programmable Input/Output) Using the address bus to send communication to a peripheral. The most common way for the CPU to communicate with peripherals.

PIO Mode A series of speed standards created by the Small Form Factor committee for the use of PIO by hard drives. The PIO modes range from PIO mode 0 to PIO mode 4.

Pipeline A processing methodology where multiple calculations take place simultaneously by being broken into a series of steps. Often used in CPUs and video processors.

Pixel (picture element) In computer graphics, the smallest element of a display space that can be independently assigned color or intensity.

Platen The cylinder that guides paper through an impact printer and provides a backing surface for the paper when images are impressed onto the page.

Platform Hardware environment that supports the running of a computer system.

Plug and Play Also called **PnP**. A combination of smart PCs, smart devices, and smart operating systems that automatically configure all the necessary system resources and ports when you install a new peripheral device.

POP3 (Post Office Protocol) Also called **Point Of Presence**.

Port number Number used to identify the requested service (such as SMTP or FTP) when connecting to a TCP/IP host. Some example port numbers include 80 (HTTP), 20 (FTP), 69 (TFTP), 25 (SMTP), and 110 (POP3).

Port replicator A device that plugs into a USB port or other specialized port that offers common PC ports, such as serial, parallel, USB, network, and PS/2. By plugging your notebook computer into the port replicator, you can instantly connect it to non-portable components such as a printer, scanner, monitor, or a full-sized keyboard. Port replicators are typically used at home or in the office with the non-portable equipment already connected.

Ports A receptacle used to attach a cable to a system. All computers have at least two ports—one for a monitor or display device, another for an input device.

POST cards A diagnostic tool used to identify problems that occur during the POST. These cards usually fit into a PCI slot and have a series of LED indicators to indicate any problems that occur during the POST. *See also* Power-On Self Test (POST).

PostScript A language defined by Adobe Systems, Inc. for describing how to create an image on a page. The description is independent of the resolution of the device that will actually create the image. It includes a technology for defining the shape of a font and creating a raster image at many different resolutions and sizes.

Power supply A device that provides the electrical power for a PC. A power supply converts the 110-volt AC power into usable types of DC electricity in a PC.

Power supply fan A small fan located in a system power supply that draws warm air from inside the power supply and exhausts it to the outside.

Power-On Self Test (POST) A basic diagnostic routine completed by a system at the beginning of the boot process. The POST checks to make sure that a display adapter is installed, that a system's memory is installed, and then searches for an operating system before handing over control of the machine to an operating system, if one is found.

PPP (Point-to-Point Protocol) A protocol that enables a computer to connect to the Internet through a dial-in connection and enjoy most of the benefits of a direct connection. PPP is considered to be superior to SLIP because of its error detection and data compression features, which SLIP lacks, and the ability to use dynamic IP addresses.

PPTP (Point to Point Tunneling Protocol) Protocol that works with PPP to provide a secure data link between computers using encryption.

Print resolution The quality of a print image.

Printer An output device that can print text or illustrations on paper.

Printer Control Language (PCL) Hewlett-Packard's proprietary command set for controlling print jobs on printers.

Promiscuous Mode A mode of operation for a network interface card where the NIC processes all packets that it sees on the cable.

Prompt A character or message provided by an operating system or program to indicate that it is ready to accept input.

Proprietary Technology unique to a particular vendor.

Protected mode The operating mode of a CPU allowing more than one program to be run while ensuring that no program can corrupt another program currently running.

Protocol An agreement that governs the procedures used to exchange information between cooperating entities; usually includes how much information is to be sent, how often it is sent, how to recover from transmission errors, and who is to receive the information.

Protocol stack The actual software that implements the protocol suite on a particular operating system.

Protocol suite A set of protocols that are commonly used together and operate at different levels of the OSI seven-layer model.

Proxy server A device that fetches Internet resources for a client without exposing that client directly to the Internet. Most proxy servers accept requests for HTTP, FTP, POP3, and SMTP resources. The proxy server will often cache, or store, a copy of the requested resource for later use. A common security feature in the corporate world.

PSTN (Public Switched Telephone Network) Also called **POTS (Plain Old Telephone Service)**. Most common type of phone connection that takes your sounds—translated into an analog waveform by the microphone—and transmits them to another phone.

Q

QIC (Quarter Inch Cassette or **Cartridge)** Tape backup cartridges that use quarter-inch tape.

Queue The area where objects wait their turn to be processed. Example: the printer queue, where print jobs wait until it is their turn to be printed.

Quick Launch menu A toolbar that used to launch commonly used programs with a single click.

R

Radial misalignment A term used to describe misaligned read/write heads in a floppy disk drive.

RAID (Redundant Array of Independent or **Inexpensive Devices** or **Disks)** A way of creating a fault-tolerant storage system. There are six levels. Level 0 uses byte-level striping and provides no fault tolerance. Level 1 uses mirroring or duplexing. Level 2 uses bit-level striping. Level 3 stores error-correcting information (such as parity) on a separate disk, and uses data striping on the remaining drives. Level 4 is level 3 with block-level striping. Level 5 uses block level and parity data striping.

RAID-5 volume A striped set with parity. *See also* RAID (Redundant Array of Independent or Inexpensive Devices or Disks).

RAM (Random Access Memory) Memory that can be accessed at random, that is, in which any memory address can be written to or read from without touching the preceding address. This term is often used to mean a computer's main memory.

Rambus DRAM (RDRAM) A patented RAM technology that uses accelerated clocks to provide very high-speed memory.

RAMDAC (Random Access Memory Digital-to-Analog Converter) Converts digital signals from the CPU and video processor into analog signals that the monitor can understand and thus draw the computer display properly. The RAMDAC speed is measured in MHz; higher speed can handle higher refresh rates.

Raster The horizontal pattern of lines that form an image on the monitor screen.

Read-only attribute A file attribute that does not allow a file to be altered or modified. This is helpful when protecting system files that should not be edited.

Real mode The original 64K segmented memory, single-tasking operating mode of the Intel 8086 and 8088 CPUs.

Real-time The processing of transactions as they occur rather than batching them. Pertains to an application in which response to input is fast enough to affect subsequent inputs and guide the process and in which records are updated immediately. The lag from input time to output time must be sufficiently small for acceptable timeliness. Timeliness is a function of the total system: missile guidance requires output within a few milliseconds of input, scheduling of steamships requires response time in days. Real-time systems are those that respond in milliseconds, interactive systems in seconds, and batch systems in hours or days.

Recovery console A DOS-like interface that can be used to repair a Windows 2000 or Windows XP system that is suffering from massive OS corruption or other problems.

Recycle Bin When files are "deleted" from a modern Windows system, they are moved to the Recycle Bin. To permanently remove files from a system, they must be removed from the Recycle Bin.

Refresh The process of repainting the CRT screen, causing the phosphors to remain lit (or change).

REGEDIT.EXE A program used to edit the Windows registry.

REGEDT32.EXE A program used to edit the Windows registry. REGEDT32.EXE is available in Windows 2000 and XP only.

Registers Tiny temporary storage areas inside the CPU, used by the microprocessor to process complex commands. Modern registers come in 64- and 128-bit sizes.

Registry A complex binary file used to store configuration data about a particular system. To edit the Registry, a user can use the applets found in the Control Panel or REGEDIT.EXE or REGEDT32.EXE.

Remote Access The ability to access a computer from outside building in which it is housed. Remote access requires communications hardware, software, and actual physical links.

Remote Installation Services (RIS) A tool introduced with Windows 2000 that can be used to initiate either a scripted installation or an installation of an image of an operating system on to a PC.

Repeater A device that takes all of the data packets it receives on one Ethernet segment and re-creates them on another Ethernet segment. This allows for longer cables or more computers on a segment. Repeaters operate at Level 1 (Physical) of the OSI seven-layer model.

Resolution A measurement for CRTs and printers expressed in horizontal and vertical dots or pixels. Higher resolutions provide sharper details and thus display better-looking images.

Restore point A system snapshot created by the System Restore utility that is used to restore a malfunctioning system. *See also* System Restore.

RG-58 Coaxial cabling used for 10Base2 networks.

RIMM (not an abbreviation) An individual stick of Rambus RAM.

Ring Topology Network wiring scheme where all the computers on a network attach to a central ring of cable.

RISC (Reduced Instruction-Set Computing) RISC is a CPU design that requires the processor to handle very simple instructions. This enables the processor to execute these instructions at a very high speed. Motorola's PowerPC processors, used on both Mac and PC platforms, use RISC design.

Riser card A special adapter card, usually inserted into a special slot on a motherboard, that changes the orientation of expansion cards relative to the motherboard. Riser cards are extensively in slimline computers in order to keep total depth and height of the system to a minimum.

RJ (Registered Jack) UTP cable connectors, used for both telephone and network connections. **RJ-11** is a connector for

moved, which makes it the perfect medium for storing BIOS data or information such as scientific constants.

Root directory The directory that contains all other directories.

Router A device connecting separate networks that forwards a packet from one network to another based on the network address for the protocol being used. For example, an IP router looks only at the IP network number. Routers operate at Layer 3 (Network) of the OSI seven-layer model.

Routing table List of paths to various networks required by routers. This can be built manually or automatically.

RS-232C A standard port recommended by the Electronics Industry Association for serial devices.

Run dialog box Accessed by clicking on the Start menu and selecting Run from the options, the Run dialog box enables you to type the name of programs that Windows will then load. The Run dialog box saves you from searching for the program icon, as long as you know the actual file name. Also useful for getting to a command prompt by typing **command** or **cmd** (Windows NT/2000/XP only) in the dialog box.

S

Sampling The process of capturing sound waves in electronic format.

SATA bridge In order to use a PATA hard disk drive with a SATA controller, you must use a SATA bridge—a device that plugs into the 40-pin connector on the drive and has its own separate power connector.

ScanDisk A utility included with Windows designed to detect and repair bad sectors on a hard disk.

SCSI (Small Computer System Interface) A powerful and flexible peripheral interface popularized on the Macintosh and used to connect hard drives, CD-ROM drives, tape drives, scanners, and other devices to PCs of all kinds. Because SCSI is less efficient at handling small drives than IDE, it did not become popular on IBM-compatible computers until price reductions made these large drives affordable. Normal SCSI enables up to seven devices to be connected through a single bus connection, whereas Wide SCSI can handle 15 devices attached to a single controller.

SCSI chain A series of SCSI devices working together through a host adapter.

SCSI ID A unique identifier used by SCSI devices. No two SCSI devices may have the same SCSI ID.

SDRAM (Synchronous DRAM) DRAM that is tied to the system clock and thus runs much faster than traditional FPM and EDO RAM.

Sector A segment of one of the concentric tracks encoded on the disk during a low-level format. Sectors hold 512 bytes on data.

Sector translation The translation of logical geometry into physical geometry by the onboard circuitry of a hard disk drive.

Segment The bus cable to which the computers on an Ethernet network connect.

Serial ATA (SATA) A hard drive technology that offers many advantages over PATA (Parallel ATA) technology, including thinner cabling, keyed connectors, and hot swapability.

Serial port A common connector on a PC, used connecting input devices (such as a mouse) or communications devices (such as a modem).

Server A computer that shares its resources, such as printers and files, with other computers on a network. An example of this is a Network File System Server that shares its disk space with a workstation that does not have a disk drive of its own.

Service pack A collection of software patches released at one time by a software manufacturer.

Setuplog.txt A log file that tracks the complete installation process, logging the success or failure of file copying, Registry updates, and reboots.

Share Level Security Security system in which each resource has a password assigned to it; access to the resource is based on knowing the password.

Shareware A program protected by copyright; holder allows (encourages!) you to make and distribute copies under the condition that those who adopt the software after preview pay a fee to the holder of the copyright. Derivative works are not allowed, although you may make an archival copy.

Shell A term that generally refers to the user interface of an operating system. A shell is the command processor that is the actual interface between the kernel and the user.

Shunt A tiny connector of metal enclosed in plastic that creates an electrical connection between two posts of a jumper.

Simple volume A type of volume created when setting up dynamic disks. A simple volume acts like a primary partition on a dynamic disk.

Single Edge Cartridge (SEC) A radical CPU package where the CPU was contained in a cartridge that snapped into a special slot on the motherboard called *Slot 1*.

Single Inline Memory Module (SIMM) A type of DRAM packaging distinguished by having a number of small tabs that install into a special connector. Each side of each tab is the same signal. SIMMs come in two common sizes: 30-pin and 72-pin.

Single Inline Pin Package (SIPP) An early memory package that was the first to have individual RAM chips soldered onto small boards which were inserted into sockets on a motherboard. SIPPs were delicate, however, due to the exposed pins that were inserted into the motherboard connectors.

Single-ended (SE) A term used to describe SCSI-1 devices that used only one wire to communicate a single bit of information. Single-ended SCSI devices are vulnerable to common-mode noise when used in conjunction with SCSI cables over 6 meters in length.

Single-session drive An early type of CD-R drive that required a disc to be burned in a single session. This type of drives has been replaced by multisession drives. *See also* Multisession drive.

SL Enhanced A CPU that has the ability to turn off selected peripherals as well as run on low (3.3v or less) power. *See also* SMM.

Slimline A motherboard form factor used to create PCs that were very thin. NLX and LPX were two examples of this form factor.

SLIP (Serial Line Interface Protocol) A protocol that enables a computer to connect to the Internet through a dial-in connection and enjoy most of the benefits of a direct connection. SLIP has been nearly completely replaced by PPP, which is considered superior to SLIP because of its error detection and data compression, features that SLIP lacks, and the ability to use dynamic IP addresses.

Slot covers Metal plates that cover up unused expansion slots on the back of a PC. These items are useful in maintaining proper airflow through a computer case.

Small Outline DIMM (SO DIMM) A type of memory used in portable PCs because of its small size. SO DIMMs commonly have 72-, 144-, or 200-pins.

Smart Battery A new type of portable PC battery that tells the computer when it needs to be charged, conditioned, or replaced.

SMM (System Management Mode) A special CPU mode that enables the CPU to reduce power consumption via the selective shutdown of peripherals.

SMTP (Simple Mail Transport Protocol) The main protocol used to send electronic mail on the Internet.

Snap-ins Small utilities that can be used with the Microsoft Management Console.

SNMP (Simple Network Management Protocol) A set of standards for communication with devices connected to a TCP/IP network. Examples of these devices include routers, hubs, and switches.

Socket A combination of a port number and an IP address that uniquely identifies a connection. Also a mounting area for an electronic chip.

Socket services Device drivers that support the PC Card socket, enabling the system to detect when a PC Card has been inserted or removed, and providing the necessary I/O to the device.

Soft-off by PWRBTN A value found in the BIOS of most ATX motherboards. This value controls the length of time that the power button must be depressed in order for an ATX computer to turn off. If the on/off switch is set for a four-second delay, you must hold down the switch for four seconds before the computer cuts off.

Soft power A characteristic of ATX motherboards. They can use software to turn the PC on and off. The physical manifestation of soft power is the power switch. Instead of the thick power cord used in AT systems, an ATX power switch is little more than a pair of small wires leading to the motherboard.

Sony/Philips digital interface (SPDIF) A digital audio connector found on many high-end sound cards. This connector allows a user to connect their computer directly to a 5.1 speaker system or receiver.

Sound card An expansion card that can produce audible tones when connected to a set of speakers.

Sounds and audio devices A Control Panel applet used to configure audio hardware and software in Windows XP.

Southbridge The Southbridge is part of a motherboard chipset. It handles all the inputs and outputs to the many devices in the PC.

Spanned volume A volume that uses space on multiple dynamic disks.

Spool A scheme that enables multiple devices to write output simultaneously to the same device, such as multiple computers printing to the same printer at the same time. The data is actually written to temporary files while a program called a *spooler* sends the files to the device one at a time.

SPS (Stand-by Power Supply or **System)** A device that supplies continuous clean power to a computer system immediately following a power failure. *See also* UPS.

SRAM (Static RAM) A type of RAM that uses a flip-flop type circuit rather than the typical transistor/capacitor of DRAM to hold a bit of information. SRAM does not need to be refreshed and is faster than regular DRAM. Used primarily for cache.

ST506 A model of hard drive developed by Seagate. This drive, as well as the WD1003 controller, developed by Western Digital, created the standard for the first generation of hard drives and controllers. As a result, any drives that copy the connections and BIOS commands of the ST506 are known as ST506 drives.

Standby power supply (SPS) A type of power supply that provides battery power to a PC when the AC electricity drops below

pology is fault tolerance.

Star Topology Network wiring scheme where computers on a network connect to a central wiring point.

Start menu A menu that can be accessed by clicking the Start button on the Windows taskbar. This menu enables you to see all programs loaded on the system and to start them.

Startup disk A bootable floppy disk that contains just enough files to perform basic troubleshooting from an A:\ prompt.

Stepper motor A technology used to control the read/write arms on early hard disk drives. This technology moved the arm in fixed increments or steps and was prone toward breakage or deterioration.

STP (Shielded Twisted Pair) A popular cabling for networks composed of pairs of wires twisted around each other at specific intervals. The twists serve to reduce interference (also called *crosstalk*). The more twists, the less interference. The cable has metallic shielding to protect the wires from external interference. Token Ring networks are the only common network technology that uses STP, although Token Ring more often now uses UTP.

Stripe set Two or more drives in a group that are used for a striped volume.

Subdirectories A directory that resides inside of another directory.

Subnet In a TCP/IP internetwork, each independent network is referred to as a subnet.

Subnet mask The value used in TCP/IP settings to divide the IP address of a host into its component parts: network ID and host ID.

Subwoofer A large, powerful speaker capable of producing extremely low frequency sounds.

Super I/O chip A chip found on modern motherboards that provides legacy support.

Super video graphics array (SVGA) Any display mode that goes beyond VGA (640 × 480 at 16 colors) in either resolution or color depth can be labeled as SVGA, or Super VGA.

Surge suppressor An inexpensive device that protects your computer from voltage spikes.

Swap file A name for the large file used by virtual memory.

Switch A device that filters and forwards traffic based on some criteria. A bridge and a router are both examples of switches.

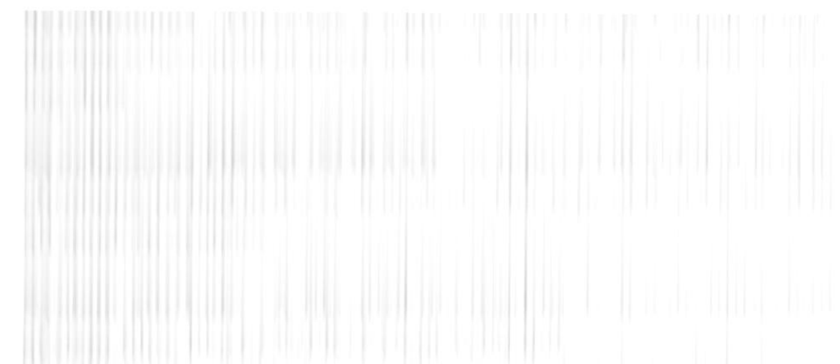

System BIOS The primary set of BIOS stored on an EPROM or Flash chip on the motherboard. Defines the BIOS for all the assumed hardware on the motherboard, such as keyboard controller, floppy drive, basic video, RAM, etc.

System monitor A utility that can be used to evaluate and monitor system resources, like CPU usage and memory usage.

System resources System resources are I/O addresses, IRQs, DMA channels, and memory addresses.

System Restore A utility in Windows Me that enables you to return your PC to a recent working configuration when something goes wrong. System Restore returns your computer's system settings to the way they were the last time you remember your system working correctly—all without affecting your personal files or e-mail.

System Tools menu A menu that can be accessed by selecting Start | Accessories | System Tools. In this menu, you can access tools like System Information and Disk Defragmenter.

System tray Located by default at the lower right edge of the Windows 98/Me/2000/XP taskbar, the system tray contains icons representing background processes and contains the system clock.

SYSTEM.INI An early Windows 3.*x* configuration file used to load device drivers. Windows 9*x*/Me systems require this file or they will not boot. Windows 2000 and XP systems do not require this file, but often have a copy in order to maintain backward compatibility with older Windows applications.

T

Task Manager The Task Manager shows all running programs, including hidden ones. You access the Task Manager by pressing CTRL-ALT-DEL. You can use it to shut down an unresponsive application that refuses to close normally.

Taskbar Located by default at the bottom of the Desktop, the Taskbar contains the Start button, the System Tray, the Quick Launch bar, and buttons for running applications.

TCP (Transmission Control Protocol) Part of the TCP/IP protocol suite, TCP operates at Layer 4 (the Transport layer) of the OSI seven-layer model. TCP is a connection-oriented protocol.

TCP/IP (Transmission Control Protocol/Internet Protocol) A set of communication protocols developed by the U.S. Department of Defense that enables dissimilar computers to share information over a network.

TCP/IP services A set of special sharing functions unique to TCP/IP. The most famous is Hypertext Transfer Protocol (HTTP), the language of the World Wide Web. Telnet and Ping are two other widely used TCP/IP services.

Telnet A program that enables users on the Internet to log in to remote systems from their own host system.

Tera- A prefix that usually stands for the binary number 1,099,511,627,776 (2^{40}). When used for mass storage, often shorthand usage for a trillion bytes.

Terabyte 1,099,551,627,776 bytes.

Terminal A "dumb" device connected to a mainframe or computer network that acts as a point for entry or retrieval of information.

Terminal emulation Software that enables a PC to communicate with another computer or network as if the PC were a specific type of hardware terminal.

Termination The use of terminating resistors to prevent packet reflection on a network cable.

Terminator A resistor that is plugged into the end of a bus cable to absorb the excess electrical signal, preventing it from bouncing back when it reaches the end of the wire. Terminators are used with coaxial cable and on the ends of SCSI chains. RG-58 coaxial cable requires resistors with a 50 Ohm impedance.

Text mode During a Windows installation, the period when the computer displays simple textual information on a plain background, before switching to full graphical screens. During this part of the installation, the system inspects the hardware, displays the EULA for you to accept, enables you to partition the hard drive, and copies files to the hard drive, including a base set of files for running the graphical portion of the OS.

Thin film transistor (TFT) A type of LCD screen. *See also* Active Matrix.

Token Ring A LAN and protocol in which nodes are connected together in a ring; a special packet called a *token* passed from node to node around the ring controls communication. A node can send data only when it receives the token and the token is not in use. This avoids the collision problems endemic to Ethernet networks.

Toner The toner in a laser printer is a fine powder made up of plastic particles bonded to iron particles, used to create the text and images during the printing process.

Toner cartridge The object used to store the toner in a laser printer. *See also* Laser printer, Toner.

Topology The pattern of interconnections in a communications system between devices, nodes, and associated input and output stations. Also describes how computers connect to each other without regard to how they actually communicate.

TRACERT Also called **TRACEROUTE**. A command-line utility used to follow the path a packet takes between two hosts.

Traces Small electrical connections embedded in a circuit board.

Transfer corona A thin wire, usually protected by other thin wires, which applies a positive charge to the paper during the laser printing process, drawing the negatively charged toner particles off of the drum and onto the paper.

Triad A group of three phosphors—red, green, blue—in a CRT.

TSR (Terminate and Stay Resident) A DOS program that closes immediately after starting up, but leaves a tiny piece of itself in memory. TSRs are used to handle a broad cross-section of DOS-l evel system needs, such as running hardware (MOUSE.COM) or applying higher-level functionality to hardware already under the control of device drivers. MSCDEX.EXE, for example, assigns a drive letter to a CD-ROM drive after the CD-ROM driver has loaded in CONFIG.SYS.

TWAIN (Technology Without an Interesting Name) A programming interface that enables a graphics application, such as a desktop publishing program, to activate a scanner, frame grabber, or other image-capturing device.

U

UART (Universal Asynchronous Receiver/Transmitter) A UART is a device that turns serial data into parallel data. The cornerstone of serial ports and modems.

UDP (User Datagram Protocol) Part of the TCP/IP protocol suite, UDP is an alternative to TCP. UDP is a connectionless protocol.

Ultra DMA A hard drive technology that enables drives to use direct memory addressing. Ultra DMA mode 3 drives—called ATA/33—have data transfer speeds up to 33 Mbps. Mode 4 and 5 drives—called ATA/66 and ATA/100, respectively—transfer data at up to 66 Mbps for mode 4 and 100 Mbps for mode 5. Both modes 4 and 5 require an 80-pin cable and a compatible controller in order to achieve these data transfer rates.

UMA (Upper Memory Area) The memory area between the first 640K and 1024K reserved for system use and device drivers.

UMB (Upper Memory Block) The open areas of the Reserved Memory (the 384K block above Conventional Memory) loading Adapter ROM and device drivers.

UNIX A popular computer software operating system developed by and for programmers at Bell Labs in the early 1970s, used on many Internet host systems because of its portability across different platforms.

Upgrade Advisor The Upgrade Advisor is the first process that runs on the XP installation CD. It examines your hardware and installed software (in the case of an upgrade) and provides a list of devices and software that are known to have issues with XP. It can also be run separately from the Windows XP installation, from the Windows XP CD.

Upgrade installation An installation of Windows on top of an

cation of a resource on the Internet. URLs are used most often in conjunction with HTML and the World Wide Web.

USB (universal serial bus) A 12 Mbps serial interconnect for keyboards, printers, joysticks, and many other devices. Enables hot-swapping and daisy chaining devices.

Usenet The network of UNIX users, generally perceived as informal and made up of loosely coupled nodes, that exchanges mail and messages. Started by Duke University and UNC-Chapel Hill. An information cooperative linking around 16,000 computer sites and millions of people. Usenet provides a series of "news groups" analogous to online conferences.

User Account A container that identifies a user to an application, operating system, or network, including name, password, user name, groups to which the user belongs, and other information based on the user and the OS or NOS being used. Usually defines the rights and roles a user plays on a system.

User interface A visual representation of the computer on the monitor that makes sense to the people using the computer, through which the user can interact with the computer.

User Level Security A security system in which each user has an account and access to resources is based on user identity.

User profiles A collection of settings that correspond to a specific user account and may follow the user regardless of the computer at which he or she logs on. These settings enable the user to have customized environment and security settings.

UTP (Unshielded Twisted Pair) A popular type of cabling for telephone and networks, composed of pairs of wires twisted around each other at specific intervals. The twists serve to reduce interference (also called *crosstalk*). The more twists, the less interference. The cable has *no* metallic shielding to protect the wires from external interference, unlike its cousin, STP. 10BaseT uses UTP, as do many other networking technologies. UTP is available in a variety of grades, called *categories*, as defined here:

Category 1 UTP Regular analog phone lines—not used for data communications.

Category 2 UTP Supports speeds up to 4 megabits per second.

Category 3 UTP Supports speeds up to 16 megabits per second.

Category 4 UTP Supports speeds up to 20 megabits per second.

Category 5 UTP Supports speeds up to 100 megabits per second.

ern CRTs have a VRR of 60 Hz or better.

VESA (Video Electronics Standards Association) A consortium of computer manufacturers that standardized improvements to common IBM PC components. VESA is responsible for the Super VGA video standard and the VLB bus architecture.

VGA (Video Graphics Array) The standard for the video graphics adapter that was built into IBM's PS/2 computer. It supports 16 colors in a 640 × 480 pixel video display, and quickly replaced the older CGA (Color Graphics Adapter) and EGA (Extended Graphics Adapter) standards.

VIA Technologies Major manufacturer of chipsets for motherboards. Also produces Socket 370 CPUs through its subsidiary Cyrix that compete directly with Intel.

Video card An expansion card that works with the CPU to produce the images that are displayed on your computer's display.

Viewable image size (VIS) A measurement of the viewable image that is displayed by a CRT rather than a measurement of the CRT itself.

Virtual Pertaining to a device or facility that does not physically exist, yet behaves as if it does. For example, a system with 4 MB of virtual memory may have only 1 MB of physical memory plus additional (slower and cheaper) auxiliary memory. Yet programs written as if 4 MB of physical memory were available will run correctly.

Virtual Device Driver (VxD) A special type of driver file used to support older Windows programs. Windows protection errors take place when VxDs fail to load or unload. This usually occurs when a device somehow gets a device driver in both CONFIG.SYS and SYSTEM.INI or the Registry.

Virtual memory A section of a system's hard drive that is set aside to be used when physical memory is unavailable or completely in use.

Virus A program that can make a copy of itself without you necessarily being aware of it; some viruses can destroy or damage files, and generally the best protection is always to maintain backups of your files.

Virus Definition These files are also called signature files depending on the virus protection software in use. These files enable the virus protection software to recognize the viruses on your system and clean them. These files should be updated often.

VLB (VESA Local Bus) VESA Local Bus is a design architecture for the sockets on the computer motherboard that enable system components to be added to the computer. VLB was the first "local bus" standard, meaning that devices added to a computer through this port would use the processor at its full speed, rather than at the slower 8 MHz speed of the regular bus. In addition to moving data at a faster rate, VLB moves data 32 bits at a time, rather than the 8 or 16 bits that the older ISA buses supported. Although common on machines using Intel's 486 CPU, modern computers now use PCI buses instead.

Voice coil motor A type of motor used to spin hard disk drive platters.

Volatile Memory that must have constant electricity in order to retain data. Alternatively, any programmer six hours before deadline after a non-stop 48-hour coding session, running on nothing but caffeine and sugar.

Volts (V) The pressure of the electrons passing through a wire is called voltage and is measured in units called volts (V).

Volume A physical unit of a storage medium, such as tape reel or disk pack that is capable of having data recorded on it and subsequently read. Also refers to a contiguous collection of cylinders or blocks on a disk that is treated as a separate unit.

Volume boot sector The first sector of the first cylinder of each partition also has a boot sector called the volume boot sector, which stores information important to its partition, such as the location of the operating system boot files.

VRAM (Video Ram) A type of memory in a video display adapter that's used to create the image appearing on the CRT screen. VRAM uses dual-ported memory, which enables simultaneous reads and writes, making it much quicker than DRAM.

W

WAN (Wide Area Network) A geographically dispersed network created by linking various computers and local-area networks over long distances, generally using leased phone lines. There is no firm dividing line between a WAN and a LAN.

Warm Boot A system restart performed after the system has been powered and operating. This clears and resets the memory, but does not stop and start the hard drive.

Wattage (watts or W) The amount of amps and volts needed by a particular device to function is expressed as how much wattage (watts or W) that device needs.

WAV (Windows Audio Format) The default sound format for Windows.

Wave table synthesis A technique that supplanted FM synthesis, wherein recordings of actual instruments or other sounds are embedded in the sound card as WAV files. When a particular note from a particular instrument or voice is requested, the sound processor grabs the appropriate prerecorded WAV file from its memory and adjusts it to match the specific sound and timing requested.

WB (Write Back) Defines a certain type of SRAM cache where instructions from the CPU to write changes are held in the cache until there is time available to write the changes to main memory.

Wildcard A character used during a search to represent search criteria. For instance, searching for "*.doc" will return a list of all files with a .doc extension, regardless of the filename. "*" is the wildcard in that search.

Windows Catalog Microsoft provides a list of applications and hardware compatible with Windows called the Windows Catalog. Theoretically, the Windows Catalog is for all versions of Windows, but it primarily applies to Windows XP. You can access the Windows Catalog directly at www.microsoft.com/windows/catalog.

WINIPCFG A command-line utility for Windows 9*x* machines that displays the current TCP/IP configuration of the machine; similar to IPCONFIG and IFCONFIG.

WINS (Windows Internet Name Service) A name resolution service that resolves NetBIOS names to IP addresses.

Winsock (WINdows SOCKets) Microsoft Windows implementation of the TCP/IP Sockets interface.

Word A group of 16 binary digits or two bytes.

Worm A worm is a very special form of virus. Unlike other viruses, a worm does not infect other files on the computer. Instead, it replicates by making copies of itself on other systems on a network by taking advantage of security weaknesses in networking protocols.

Write Once Read Many (WORM) Early CD technologies that allowed users to burn their own CD-ROMs, doomed by high equipment costs. Supplanted by CD-R technology.

WS (Wait State) A microprocessor clock cycle in which nothing happens.

WT (Write Through) Defines a certain type of SRAM cache where instructions from the CPU to write changes are pushed through the cache immediately, writing to the cache and the main memory at the same time.

WWW (World Wide Web) A system of Internet servers that support documents formatted in HTML and related protocols. The Web can be accessed using Gopher, FTP, HTTP, telnet, Usenet, WAIS, and other tools.

X

Xeon A line of Intel CPUs designed for servers by adding large L2 caches.

XGA (Extended Graphics Array) IBM video display to bring 1,024 × 768 resolution to monitors. Can display 65,536 colors at low resolution, and 256 at high resolution.

Xmodem A file transfer protocol (FTP) that provides error-free asynchronous communications through telephone lines.

Y

Ymodem A file transfer protocol (FTP) that is more robust than Xmodem; it features a time and date stamp transfer, as well as batch file transfers.

Z

ZIF (Zero Insertion Force) Socket A socket for CPUs that enables insertion of a chip without much pressure. Intel promoted the ZIF socket with its overdrive upgrades. The chip is dropped into the socket's holes and a small lever is flipped to lock them in. Somewhat replaced in modern motherboards by Slot 1 and Slot A architecture, but still in style in Super Socket 7, Socket A, and Socket 370 motherboards.

Zmodem Streaming synchronous file transfer protocol (FTP)

Numbers

A

B

C

D

F

G

H

I

J

K

L

M

N

O

Q

R

S

T